Jackson, Samuel Macauley; Schaff, Philip

The new Schaff-Herzog encyclopedia of religious knowledge

Vol. 2

Jackson, Samuel Macauley; Schaff, Philip

The new Schaff-Herzog encyclopedia of religious knowledge

Vol. 2

Inktank publishing, 2018

www.inktank-publishing.com

ISBN/EAN: 9783747768334

THE NEW SCHAFF-HERZOG ENCYCLOPEDIA OF RELIGIOUS KNOWLEDGE

EDITED BY

SAMUEL MACAULEY JACKSON, D.D., LL.D.
(*Editor-in-Chief*)

WITH THE ASSISTANCE OF

CHARLES COLEBROOK SHERMAN

AND

GEORGE WILLIAM GILMORE, M.A.
(*Associate Editors*)

AND THE FOLLOWING DEPARTMENT EDITORS

CLARENCE AUGUSTINE BECKWITH, D.D.
(*Department of Systematic Theology*)

HENRY KING CARROLL, LL.D.
(*Department of Minor Denominations*)

JAMES FRANCIS DRISCOLL, D.D.
(*Department of Liturgics and Religious Orders*)

JAMES FREDERIC McCURDY, PH.D., LL.D.
(*Department of the Old Testament*)

HENRY SYLVESTER NASH, D.D.
(*Department of the New Testament*)

ALBERT HENRY NEWMAN, D.D., LL.D.
(*Department of Church History*)

FRANK HORACE VIZETELLY, F.S.A.
(*Department of Pronunciation and Typography*)

VOLUME II
BASILICA — CHAMBERS

FUNK AND WAGNALLS COMPANY
NEW YORK AND LONDON

EDITORS

SAMUEL MACAULEY JACKSON, D.D., LL.D.
(EDITOR-IN-CHIEF.)
Professor of Church History, New York University.

ASSOCIATE EDITORS

CHARLES COLEBROOK SHERMAN
Editor in Biblical Criticism and Theology on "The New International Encyclopedia," New York.

GEORGE WILLIAM GILMORE, M.A.
New York, Formerly Professor of Biblical History and Lecturer on Comparative Religion, Bangor Theological Seminary.

DEPARTMENT EDITORS, VOLUME II.

CLARENCE AUGUSTINE BECKWITH, D.D.
(*Department of Systematic Theology.*)
Professor of Systematic Theology, Chicago Theological Seminary.

HENRY KING CARROLL, LL.D.
(*Department of Minor Denominations.*)
One of the Corresponding Secretaries of the Board of Foreign Missions of the Methodist Episcopal Church, New York.

JAMES FRANCIS DRISCOLL, D.D.
(*Department of Liturgics and Religious Orders.*)
President of St. Joseph's Seminary, Yonkers, N. Y.

HUBERT EVANS, Ph.D.
(*Office Editor.*)
Formerly of the Editorial Staff of the "Encyclopædia Britannica" Company, New York City.

JAMES FREDERICK McCURDY, Ph.D., LL.D.
(*Department of the Old Testament.*)
Professor of Oriental Languages, University College, Toronto.

HENRY SYLVESTER NASH, D.D.
(*Department of the New Testament.*)
Professor of the Literature and Interpretation of the New Testament, Episcopal Theological School, Cambridge, Mass.

ALBERT HENRY NEWMAN, D.D., LL.D.
(*Department of Church History.*)
Professor of Church History, Baylor Theological Seminary (Baylor University), Waco, Tex.

FRANK HORACE VIZETELLY, F.S.A.
(*Department of Pronunciation and Typography.*)
Associate Editor of the STANDARD DICTIONARY, etc., New York City.

CONTRIBUTORS AND COLLABORATORS, VOLUME II.

ERNST CHRISTIAN ACHELIS, Th.D.,
Professor of Practical Theology, University of Marburg.

SAMUEL JAMES ANDREWS (†), D.D.,
Late Pastor of the Catholic Apostolic Church, Hartford, Conn.

CARL FRANKLIN ARNOLD, Ph.D., Th.D.,
Professor of Church History, Evangelical Theological Faculty, University of Breslau.

FERENCZ BALOGH,
Professor of Church History, Reformed Theological Academy, Debreczin, Hungary.

EDUARD BARDE (†),
Late Professor of New Testament Exegesis, School of Theology, Geneva.

HERMANN BARGE, Ph.D.,
Gymnasial Professor in Leipsic.

SAMUEL JUNE BARROWS, D.D.,
Corresponding Secretary of the Prison Association of New York.

JOHANNES BELSHEIM,
Pastor Emeritus in Christiania, Norway.

KARL BENRATH, Ph.D., Th.D.,
Professor of Church History, University of Königsberg.

IMMANUEL GUSTAF ADOLF BENZINGER, Ph.D., Th.Lic.,
Formerly Privat-docent in Old Testament Theology, University of Berlin, Member of the Executive Committee of the German Society for the Exploration of Palestine, Jerusalem.

SAMUEL BERGER (†), D.D.,
Late Librarian to the Faculty of Protestant Theology, Paris.

CARL ALBRECHT BERNOULLI, Th.Lic.,
Professor in Berlin.

CARL BERTHEAU, Th.D.,
President of the Society for Innere Mission, and Pastor of St. Michael's Church, Hamburg.

WILLIBALD BEYSCHLAG (†), Th.D.,
Late Professor of Theology, University of Halle.

AMY GASTON BONET-MAURY, D.D., LL.D.,
Professor of Church History, Independent School of Divinity, Paris.

GOTTLIEB NATHANAEL BONWETSCH, Th.D.,
Professor of Church History, University of Göttingen.

FRIEDRICH BOSSE, Ph.D., Th.Lic.,
Extraordinary Professor of Theology, University of Greifswald.

GUSTAF BOSSERT, Ph.D., Th.D.,
Pastor Emeritus, Stuttgart.

JOHANNES FRIEDRICH THEODOR BRIEGER, Ph.D., Th.D.,
Professor of Church History, University of Leipsic.

CHARLES AUGUSTUS BRIGGS, D.D., Litt.D.,
Professor of Theological Encyclopedia and Symbolics, Union Theological Seminary, New York.

FRANTS PEDER WILLIAM BUHL, Ph.D., Th.D.,
Professor of Oriental Languages, University of Copenhagen.

KARL BURGER (†), Th.D.,
Late Supreme Consistorial Councilor, Munich.

WALTER CASPARI, Ph.D., Th.Lic.,
Professor of Practical Theology, Pedagogics, and Didactics, and University Preacher, University of Erlangen.

JACQUES EUGÈNE CHOISY, Th.D.,
Pastor in Geneva, Switzerland.

FERDINAND COHRS, Th.Lic.,
Consistorial Councilor, Ilfeld, Hanover.

ALEXIS IRÉNÉE DU PONT COLEMAN, M.A.,
Instructor in English, College of the City of New York.

GUSTAF HERMAN DALMAN, Ph.D., Th.D.,
Professor of Old Testament Exegesis, University of Leipsic, and President of the German Evangelical Archeological Institute, Jerusalem.

SAMUEL MARTIN DEUTSCH, Th.D.,
Professor of Church History, University of Berlin.

FRANZ WILHELM DIBELIUS, Ph.D., Th.D.,
Supreme Consistorial Councilor, City Superintendent, and Pastor of the Kreuzkirche, Dresden.

JAMES FRANCIS DRISCOLL, D.D.,
President of St. Joseph's Seminary, Yonkers, N. Y.

HENRY OTIS DWIGHT, LL.D.,
Recording Secretary of the American Bible Society, Coeditor of the "Encyclopedia of Missions," New York.

EMIL EGLI, Th.D.,
Professor of Church History, University of Zurich.

DAVID ERDMANN (†), Th.D.,
Late Professor of Church History, Evangelical Theological Faculty, University of Breslau.

ALFRED ERICHSON (†), Ph.D., Th.D.,
Late Professor of Theology, University of Strasburg.

CARL FEY, Ph.D.,
Pastor at Cösseln, near Halle.

JOHN FOX, D.D.,
Corresponding Secretary of the American Bible Society, New York.

EMIL ALBERT FRIEDBERG, Dr.Jur.,
Professor of Ecclesiastical, Public, and German Law, University of Leipsic.

THEODOR GEROLD, Th.D.,
President of the Consistory, Strasburg.

GEORGE WILLIAM GILMORE, M.A.,
Formerly Lecturer on Comparative Religion, Bangor Theological Seminary, Associate Editor of the SCHAFF-HERZOG ENCYCLOPEDIA.

WILHELM GLAMANN,
Pastor at Siebeneichen, near Löwenberg, Prussia.

WILHELM GOETZ, Ph.D.,
Honorary Professor of Geography, Technische Hochschule, and Professor, Military Academy, Munich.

CASPAR RENÉ GREGORY, Ph.D., Dr.Jur., Th.D., D.D., LL.D.,
Professor of New Testament Exegesis, University of Leipsic.

PAUL GRUENBERG, Th.Lic.,
Pastor in Strasburg.

GEORG GRUETZMACHER, Ph.D., Th.Lic.,
Extraordinary Professor of Church History and of the New Testament, University of Heidelberg.

REINHOLD GRUNDEMANN, Ph.D., Th.D.,
Pastor at Mörz, near Belzig, Prussia.

HERMANN GUTHE, Th.D.,
Professor of Old Testament Exegesis, University of Leipsic.

ADOLF HARNACK, M.D., Ph.D., Th.D.,
Professor of Church History, University of Berlin, and General Director of the Royal Library, Berlin.

ALBERT HAUCK, Ph.D., Dr.Jur., Th.D.,
Professor of Church History, University of Leipsic, Editor-in-Chief of the HAUCK-HERZOG REALENCYKLOPÄDIE.

HERMAN HAUPT, Ph.D.,
Professor and Director of the University Library, Giessen.

JOHANNES HAUSSLEITER, Ph.D., Th.D.,
Professor of the New Testament, University of Greifswald.

CARL FRIEDRICH GEORG HEINRICI, Ph.D., Th.D.,
Professor of New Testament Exegesis, University of Leipsic.

EDGAR HENNECKE, Th.Lic.,
Pastor at Betheln, Hanover.

HERMANN HERING, Th.D.,
Professor of Practical Theology, University of Halle.

MAX HEROLD, Th.D.,
Dean, Neustadt-an-der-Aisch, Bavaria, Editor of *Siona*.

JOHANN JAKOB HERZOG (†), Ph.D., Th.D.,
Late Professor of Reformed Theology, University of Erlangen, Founder of the HAUCK-HERZOG REALENCYKLOPÄDIE.

ALFRED HEGLER (†), Ph.D., Th.D.,
Late Professor of Church History, University of Tübingen.

JOHANNES HESSE,
Former Editor of the *Evangelisches Missions-Magazin* and President of the Publishing Society at Calw, Württemberg.

PAUL HINSCHIUS (†), LL.D.,
Late Professor of Ecclesiastical Law, University of Berlin.

HERMANN WILHELM HEINRICH HOELSCHER, Th.D.,
Pastor of the Nikolaikirche, Leipsic, Editor of the *Allgemeine Evangelisch-Lutherische Kirchenzeitung* and of the *Theologisches Literaturblatt*.

KARL HOLL, Ph.D., Th.D.,
Professor of Church History, University of Berlin.

ALFRED JEREMIAS, Ph.D., Th.Lic.,
Pastor of the Lutherkirche, Leipsic.

MARTIN KAEHLER, Th.D.,
Professor of Dogmatics and New Testament Exegesis, University of Halle.

ADOLF KAMPHAUSEN, Th.D.,
Professor of Old Testament Exegesis, University of Bonn.

PETER GUSTAF KAWERAU, Th.D.,
Consistorial Councilor, Professor of Practical Theology, and University Preacher, University of Breslau.

RUDOLF KITTEL, Ph.D.,
Professor of Old Testament Exegesis, University of Leipsic.

FRIEDRICH HERMANN THEODOR KOLDE, Ph.D., Th.D.,
Professor of Church History, University of Erlangen.

HERMANN GUSTAF EDUARD KRUEGER, Ph.D., Th.D.,
Professor of Church History, University of Giessen.

JOHANNES WILHELM KUNZE, Ph.D.,
Professor of Systematic and Practical Theology, University of Greifswald.

L. A. VAN LANGERAAD, Ph.D.,
Lekkerkerk, Holland.

LUDWIG LEMME, Th.D.,
Professor of Systematic Theology, University of Heidelberg.

EDUARD LEMPP, Ph.D.,
Superintendent of the Royal Orphan Asylum, Stuttgart.

AUGUST LESKIEN, Ph.D.,
Professor of Slavonic Languages, University of Leipsic.

FRIEDRICH ARMIN LOOFS, Ph.D., Th.D.,
Professor of Church History, University of Halle.

ANDERS HERMAN LUNDSTRÖM, Th.D.,
Professor of Church History, Royal University of Upsala, Sweden.

JAMES FREDERICK McCURDY, Ph.D., LL.D.,
Professor of Oriental Languages, University College, Toronto.

PHILIPP MEYER, Th.D.,
Supreme Consistorial Councilor and Member of the Royal Consistory, Hanover.

CARL THEODOR MIRBT, Th.D.,
Professor of Church History, University of Marburg.

ERNST FRIEDRICH KARL MUELLER, Th.D.,
Professor of Reformed Theology, University of Erlangen.

GEORG MUELLER, Ph.D., Th.D.,
Councilor for Schools, Leipsic.

JOSEF MUELLER, Th.D.,
Pastor in Ebersdorf, Reuss.

NIKOLAUS MUELLER, Ph.D., Th.D.,
Extraordinary Professor of Christian Archeology, University of Berlin.

CHRISTOF EBERHARD NESTLE, Ph.D., Th.D.,
Professor in the Theological Seminary at Maulbronn, Württemberg.

KARL JOHANNES NEUMANN, Ph.D.,
Professor of the History of Art, University of Kiel.

ALBERT HENRY NEWMAN, D.D., LL.D.,
Professor of Church History, Baylor Theological Seminary (Baylor University), Waco, Tex.

JULIUS NEY, Th.D.,
Supreme Consistorial Councilor in Speyer, Bavaria.

FREDERIK CHRISTIAN NIELSEN (†), Th.D.,
Late Bishop of Aalborg, Denmark.

FRIEDRICH AUGUST NITZSCH (†), Ph.D.,
Late Professor of Theology, University of Kiel.

HANS CONRAD VON ORELLI, Ph.D., Th.D.,
Professor of Old Testament Exegesis and History of Religion, University of Basel.

MARGARET BLOODGOOD PEEKE,
Inspectress-General of the Martinist Order for America.

CHARLES PFENDER,
Pastor of the Evangelical Lutheran Church, Paris.

BERNHARD PICK, Ph.D., D.D.,
Pastor of the First German Evangelical Lutheran Church, Newark, N. J.

FREDERICK DUNGLISON POWER, LL.D.,
Pastor of the Garfield Memorial Church, Washington, D. C.

WILLIAM PRICE,
Formerly Instructor in French, Yale College and Sheffield Scientific School, New Haven, Conn.

FRANZ PRAETORIUS, Ph.D.,
Professor of Oriental Languages, University of Halle.

GEORG CHRISTIAN RIETSCHEL, Th.D.,
Professor of Practical Theology and University Preacher, University of Leipsic.

SIEGFRIED RIETSCHEL, Dr.Jur.,
Professor of German Law, University of Tübingen.

HENDRIK CORNELIUS ROGGE (†), Th.D.,
Late Professor of History, University of Amsterdam.

EUGEN SACHSSE, Th.D.,
University Preacher and Professor of Practical Theology in the Evangelical Theological Faculty, University of Bonn.

DAVID SCHLEY SCHAFF, D.D.,
Professor of Church History, Western Theological Seminary, Allegheny, Pa.

PHILIP SCHAFF (†), D.D., LL.D.,
Late Professor of Church History, Union Theological Seminary, New York, Founder of the SCHAFF-HERZOG ENCYCLOPEDIA.

REINHOLD SCHMID, Th.Lic.,
Pastor at Oberholzheim, Württemberg.

RICHARD KARL BERNHARD SCHMIDT, Dr.Jur.,
Professor of Jurisprudence and Civil and Criminal Procedure, University of Freiburg.

JOHANN SCHNEIDER,
Pastor at Neckar-Steinach, Hesse

THEODOR SCHOTT (†), Ph.D., Th.D.,
Late Librarian and Professor of Theology, University of Stuttgart.

JOHANN FRIEDRICH RITTER VON SCHULTE, Dr.Jur.,
Professor of German Ecclesiastical Law and of the History of Law, University of Bonn.

VICTOR SCHULTZE, Th.D.,
Professor of Church History and Christian Archeology, University of Greifswald.

HANS SCHULZ, Ph.D.,
Gymnasial Professor at Steglitz, near Berlin.

LUDWIG SCHULZE, Ph.D., Th.D.,
Professor of Systematic Theology, University of Rostock.

OTTO SEEBASS, Ph.D.,
Educator in Leipsic, Germany.

REINHOLD SEEBERG, Th.D.,
Professor of Systematic Theology, University of Berlin.

EMIL SEHLING, Dr.Jur.,
Professor of Ecclesiastical and Commercial Law, University of Erlangen.

FRIEDRICH ANTON EMIL SIEFFERT, Ph.D., Th.D.,
Professor of Dogmatics and New Testament Exegesis, University of Bonn.

EMIL ELIAS STEINMEYER, Ph.D.,
Professor of German Language and Literature, University of Erlangen.

GEORG EDUARD STEITZ (†), Th.D.,
Late Pastor in Frankfort-on-the-Main.

ALFRED STOECKIUS, Ph.D.,
Astor Library, New York.

HERMANN LEBERECHT STRACK, Ph.D., Th.D.,
Extraordinary Professor of Old Testament Exegesis and Semitic Languages, University of Berlin.

PAUL TSCHACKERT, Ph.D., Th.D.,
Professor of Church History, University of Göttingen.

JOHANN GERHARD UHLHORN (†), Th.D.,
Late Consistorial Councilor, Hanover.

MARVIN RICHARDSON VINCENT, D.D.,
Professor of New Testament Exegesis and Criticism, Union Theological Seminary, New York.

WILHELM VOGT (†), Ph.D., Th.D.,
Late Professor of Old Testament Exegesis, University of Rostock.

STACY REUBEN WARBURTON,
Assistant Editor of *The Baptist Missionary Magazine*, Boston.

BENJAMIN BRECKINRIDGE WARFIELD, D.D., LL.D.,
Professor of Didactic and Polemical Theology, Princeton Theological Seminary.

AUGUST WILHELM WERNER, Th.D.,
Pastor Primarius, Guben, Prussia.

FRANCIS METHERALL WHITLOCK,
Pastor of the Bethlehem Congregational Church, Cleveland, O.

RICHARD PAUL WUELKER, Ph.D.,
Professor of English, University of Leipsic.

AUGUST WUENSCHE, Ph.D., Th.D.,
Titular Professor in Dresden.

THEODOR ZAHN, Th.D., Litt.D.,
Professor of New Testament Exegesis and Introduction, University of Erlangen.

HEINRICH ZIMMER, Ph.D.,
Professor of Celtic Philology, University of Berlin.

OTTO ZOECKLER (†), Ph.D., Th.D.,
Late Professor of Church History, University of Greifswald.

BIBLIOGRAPHICAL APPENDIX—VOLS. I AND II

The following list of books is supplementary to the bibliographies given at the end of the articles contained in volumes I and II, and brings the literature down to November, 1908. In this list each title entry is printed in capital letters.

ABRAHAM: F. Wilke, *War Abraham eine historische Persönlichkeit?* Leipsic, 1907.

ABULFARAJ: Bar Hebraeus, *Buch der Strahlen. Die grössere Grammatik des Barhebraeus. Uebersetzung nach einem kritisch berichtigen Texte mit textkritischem Apparat und einem Anhang: Zur Terminologie*, by A. Moberg. *Einleitung* and vol. ii., Leipsic, 1907 (the first part has not yet appeared).

AFRICA: J. D. Mullens, *The Wonderful Story of Uganda*, London, 1908.
A. H. Baynes, *South Africa*, London, 1908.
R. H. Milligan, *The Jungle Folk of Africa*, New York, 1908.

AGNOSTICISM: H. C. Sheldon, *Unbelief in the Nineteenth Century*, New York, 1907.

AGRAPHA: C. R. Gregory, *Das Freer-Logion*, Leipsic, 1908 (on the Logia-fragments possessed by C. L. Freer, of Detroit).
B. Pick, *Paralipomena: Remains of Gospels and Sayings of Christ*, Chicago, 1908.

ALEXANDER IV.: F Tenckhoff, *Papst Alexander IV.*, Paderborn, 1907

ALEXANDER OF HALES: K. Heim, *Das Wesen der Gnade und ihr Verhältnis zu den natürlichen Funktionen des Menschen bei Alexander Halesius*, Leipsic, 1907

ALTAR: R. Kittel, *Studien zur hebräischen Archäologie*, i.118–158, Leipsic, 1908.

AMBROSE, SAINT, OF MILAN: J. E. Niederhuber, *Die Eschatologie des heiligen Ambrosius*, Paderborn, 1907.
P. de Labriolle, *S. Ambroise*, Paris, 1908.

ANGELS: R. W. Britton, *Angels, their Nature and Service*, London, 1908.

APOCRYPHA: L. Couard, *Die religiösen und sittlichen Anschauungen der alttestamentlichen Apokryphen und Pseudepigraphen*, Gütersloh, 1907.
A. Fuchs, *Textkritische Untersuchungen zum hebräischen Ekklesiastikus*, Freiburg, 1907.
R. Smend, *Griechisch-syrisch-hebräischer Index zur Weisheit des Jesus Sirach*, Berlin, 1907
F. Steinmetzer, *Neue Untersuchungen über die Geschichtlichkeit der Juditherzählung*, Leipsic, 1907.
J. Müller, *Beiträge zur Erklärung und Kritik des Buches Tobit*, Giessen, 1908.

APOLOGETICS: W H. Turton, *The Truth of Christianity: a Manual of Christian Evidences*, London, 1908.
E. F. Scott, *The Apologetic of the New Testament*, New York, 1908.
H. Egerton, *The Liberal Theology and the Ground of Faith; being Essays towards a conservative Restatement of Apologetic*, London, 1908.

APOSTOLIC CONSTITUTIONS: F. X. Funk, *Didascalia et constitutiones apostolorum I.-II.*, Paderborn, 1906.

ARABIA: R. Dussiaud, *Les Arabes en Syrie avant l'Islam*, Paris, 1907.

ARCHEOLOGY, BIBLICAL: I. Benzinger, *Hebräische Archäologie*, Tübingen, 1907.

ARCHITECTURE: A. K. Porter, *Medieval Architecture*, New York, 1908.

ARIANISM: S. Rogala, *Die Anfänge des arianischen Streites*, Paderborn, 1907.

ART: S. F. H. Robinson, *Celtic Illuminative Art in the Gospel Books of Durrow, Lindisfarne and Kells*, London, 1908.
J. R. Allen, *Celtic Art in Pagan and Christian Times*, Philadelphia, 1908.
Margaret E. Tabor, *The Saints in Art*, New York, 1908.

ASCETICISM: *Bibliotheca Franciscana ascetica medii aevi*, vol. iv., Quarrachi, 1907

ASHERAH: F. Lundgreen, *Die Benützung der Pflanzenwelt in der alttestamentlichen Religion*, Giessen, 1908.

ASIA MINOR: F. Stähelin, *Geschichte der kleinasiatischen Galater*, 2d ed., Leipsic, 1907.

ASSYRIA: A. T. Olmstead, *Western Asia in the Days of Sargon of Assyria, B.C. 722–705*, New York, 1908.

AUGSBURG, BISHOPRIC OF: A. Steichele, *Das Bistum Augsburg, historisch und statistisch beschrieben*, vol. vii., Augsburg, 1906 sqq.

AUGSBURG CONFESSION AND ITS APOLOGY: *Acta comiciorum Augustae ex litteris Philippi Jonae et aliorum ad M. Luther*, ed. G. Berbig, Leipsic, 1907.

AUGUSTINE, SAINT, OF HIPPO: B. Dombart, *Zur Textgeschichte der Civitas Dei Augustins seit dem Entstehen der ersten Drucke*, Leipsic, 1907.
O. Blank, *Die Lehre des heiligen Augustinus vom Sakramente der Eucharistie*, Paderborn, 1906.
F. X. Eggersdorfer, *Der heilige Augustinus als Pädagoge und seine Bedeutung für die Geschichte der Bildung*, Freiburg, 1907
P. Friedrich, *Die Mariologie des heiligen Augustinus*, Cologne, 1907
O. Zänker, *Der Primat des Willens vor dem Intellect bei Augustin*, Gütersloh, 1907
Scripta contra Donatistas, part i., ed. Petschenig, Leipsic, 1908.
Saint Augustine of Hippo, with Introduction by the Bishop of Southampton (The Library of the Soul), London, 1908.
H. Becker, *Augustin. Studien zu seiner geistigen Entwickelung*, Leipsic, 1908.

AUGUSTINIANS: *Codex diplomaticus Ord. E. S. Augustini*, vol. iii., Papiae (Rome), 1907

BABYLONIA: M. Jastrow, *Die Religion Babyloniens und Assyriens*, Giessen, 1907.
Early Sumerian Psalms; Texts in Transliteration with Transl., Critical Commentary and Introduction, Leipsic, 1908.
O. A. Toffteen, *Researches in Assyrian and Babylonian Geography*, part 1, Chicago, 1908.
H. Radau, *Bel, the Christ of Ancient Times*, Chicago, 1908.

BACH, J. S.: H. Perry, *Life of Johann Sebastian Bach*, New York, 1908.

BAMBERG, BISHOPRIC OF: H. T. von Kohlhagen, *Das Domkapitel des alten Bisthums Bamberg und seine Canoniker*, Bamberg, 1907.
J. Körber, *Lose Blätter aus meines Bruders Leben und Skripten. Ein Stück Bamberger Geschichte als Scherflein zum 9. Bisthumscentenar*, Bamberg, 1907
J. Looshorn, *Die Geschichte des Bisthums Bamberg. Nach den Quellen bearbeitet*, vol. vii., *Das Bisthum Bamberg 1729–1808*, Bamberg, 1907 sqq.

BANKS, L. A.: *Sermons which have Won Souls*, New York, 1908.

BAPTISM: J. T. Christian, *The Form of Baptism in Sculpture and Art*, Louisville, Ky., 1907.
J. M. Lupton, *De baptismo*, Cambridge, 1908.

BAPTISTS: J. S. Flory, *Literary Activity of the German Baptist Brethren in the Eighteenth Century*, Elgin, Ill., 1908.
E. Y. Mullens, *The Axioms of Religion; a New Interpretation of the Baptist Faith*, Philadelphia, 1908.

BARLAAM AND JOSOPHAT: *Gui von Cambrai und Josophas, nach dem Handschriften von Paris und Monte Cassino*, ed. Carl Appel, Halle, 1907

BARNABAS: "Epistle," ed. Jos. Vizzini, Rome, 1907.

BEECHER, H. W.: S. M. Griswold, *Sixty Years with Plymouth Church*, New York, 1907.

BEECHER, W. J.: *The Dated Events of the Old Testament: being a Presentation of Old Testament Chronology*, Philadelphia, 1908.

BEET, J. A.: *The Church, the Churches, and the Sacraments*, London, 1907
A Shorter Manual of Theology, London, 1908.

BEHAISM: *Les Leçons de Saint-Jean-d'Acre d'Ad-Oul-Béha, recueilliés par Laura Clifford Barney, traduit du persan par Hippolyte Dreyfus*, Paris, 1908.
Abdu'l Baha. Some answered Questions: Collected and Translated from the Persian by Laura Clifford, Philadelphia, 1908.

BENEDICT OF NURSIA: L. Delisle, *Le Livre de Jean de Stavelot sur S. Benoît*, Paris, 1908.
Studien und Mitteilungen aus dem Benedictiner- und dem Cistercienser-Orden, 28 *Jahrgang*, Raigen, 1907
Die Regel des heiligen Benedictus erklärt in ihrem geschichtlichen Zusammenhang und mit besonderer Rücksicht auf das geistliche Leben, Freiburg, 1907.
G. Meier, *Der heilige Benedikt und sein Orden*, Regensburg, 1907.

BENEDICTION: W. H. Dolbeer, *The Benediction*, Philadelphia, 1908.

BENNETT, W. H.: *The Religion of the Post-Exilic Prophets*, Edinburgh, 1907.
The Life of Christ according to St. Mark, London, 1907.

BENTLEY, RICHARD: A. T. Bartholomew, *Richard Bentley, a Bibliography of his Works*, London, 1908.

BERKELEY, G.: *The Principle of Human Knowledge*, new ed., London, 1907.
The Querist; containing Several Queries proposed to the Consideration of the Public, parts 1–3, Dublin, 1735–37, reprinted Baltimore, 1908.

BERNARD, SAINT, OF CLAIRVAUX: *On Consideration*. Translated by George Lewis, London, 1908.

BESANT, A.: *London Lectures of 1907*, London, 1907.

BEZA, T.: *A Tragedie of Abraham's Sacrifice*, transl. by Arthur Golding, ed. M. W. Wallace, Toronto, 1906.

BIBLE SOCIETIES: J. Fox, *Round the World for the American Bible Society*, New York, 1908.

BIBLE VERSIONS, A, III.: F C. Burkitt, *Early Eastern Christianity*, lect. 2, New York, 1904.
The Four Gospels from the Codex Corbeiensis London, 1908.

BIBLE VERSIONS, B, IV.: A. F Gasquet, *The Old English Bible, and Other Essays*, New York, 1908.
M. B. Riddle, *The Story of the Revised New Testament*, Philadelphia, 1908.
J. I. Mombert, *Handbook*, 2d ed. London, 1907.
M. W. Jacobus, ed., *Roman Catholic and Protestant Bibles Compared: the Gould Prize Essays*, 2d ed., New York, 1908.
F. Vigouroux, *Dictionnaire de la Bible*, fasc. xxviii. cols. 1549–51, Paris, 1906.

BIBLICAL CRITICISM: J. R. Cohn, *The Old Testament in the Light of Modern Research*, London, 1908.

BIBLICAL INTRODUCTION: A. Schulz, *Biblische Studien*, ed. O. Bardenhewer, vol. xii., part 1, *Doppelberichte im Pentateuch. Ein Beitrag zur Einleitung in das Alte Testament*, Freiburg, 1908.
C. Rösch, *Die heiligen Schriften des Alten Testaments; ausführliche Inhaltsübersicht mit kurzgefasster spezieller Einleitung*, Münster, 1908.
F. Barth, *Einleitung in das Neue Testament*, Gütersloh, 1908.
C. F G. Heinrici, *Der litterarische Charakter der neutestamentlichen Schriften*, Leipsic, 1908.

BIBLICAL THEOLOGY: R. S. Franks, *The New Testament Doctrines of Man, Sin, and Salvation*, London, 1908.

BLACK, H.: *Christ's Service of Love* [Communion sermons and meditations], New York, 1907.

BLAVATSKY, H. V.: F. S. Hoffman, *The Sphere of Religion*, New York, 1908.

BLISS, E. M.: *The Missionary Enterprise*, New York, 1908.

BOEHME, J.: *The Supersensual Life, or the Life which is above Sense*, Eng. transl. by W. Law, new ed., London, 1907.

BOETHIUS: *In Isagogen Porphyrii commenta*, ed. S. Brandt, Vienna and Leipsic, 1906.

BONET-MAURY, G.: *France, christianisme et civilization*, Paris, 1907.

BOOTH, W.: *The Seven Spirits: or, What I teach my Officers*, London, 1907.

BORROMEO, C.: *Die Nuntiatur von Giovanni Francesco Bonhomini 1579–1581. Documente* vol. i., *Die Nuntiaturberichte Bonhominis und seine Correspondenz mit Carlo Borromeo aus dem Jahre 1579*, Solothurn, 1906.

BOSTON, T.: *A General Account of my Life*, ed. G. D. Low, London, 1908.

BOUSSET, W.: *What is Religion?* London, 1907.

BOYD, A. K. H.: *Sermons and Stray Papers. With Biographical Sketch by Rev. W W Tulloch*, London, 1907

BRAHMANISM: J. C. Oman, *The Brahmins, Theists, and Muslims of India*, London, 1907.

L. D. Barnett, *Brahma-Knowledge, an Outline of the Philosophy of the Vedanta, set forth by the Upanishads and by Sankara*, London, 1907.

M. Bloomfield, *The Religion of the Veda, the Ancient Religion of India*, New York, 1908.

BRENT, C. H.: *Leadership: The William Belden Noble Lectures at Harvard*, New York, 1908.

BRESLAU, BISHOPRIC OF: *Geschichte des Breslauer Domes und Seine Wiederherstellung*, Breslau, 1907

Veröffentlichungen aus dem fürstbischoflichen Diözesan-Archiv zu Breslau, Breslau, 1905 sqq.

BREVIARY: A. Schulte, *Die Psalmen des Breviers nebst den Cantica zum praktischen Gebrauche*, Paderborn, 1907.

BRIDGET, SAINT, OF KILDARE: J. A. Knowles, *St. Brigid, Patroness of Ireland*, London, 1907.

BRIDGET, SAINT, OF SWEDEN: K. Krogh-Tonning, *Die heilige Birgitta in Schweden*, Kempten, 1907.

BROOKE, S. A.: *The Sea Charm of Venice*, London, 1907

Studies in Poetry, London, 1907.

BROWN, A. J.: *The Foreign Missionary, An Incarnation of a World Movement*, New York, 1907.

BROWNE, R.: C. Burrage, *The "Retractation" of Robert Browne, Father of Congregationalism*, London, 1907.

BROWNE, SIR THOMAS: *Works*, ed. C. Sayle, 3 vols., Edinburgh, 1907

BUDDHISM: *Jataka*, by E. B. Cowell, vol. vi., New York, 1907

P. L. Narasu, *The Essence of Buddhism*, London, 1907.

D. T. Suzuki, *Outlines of Mahayana Buddhism*, London, 1907 (Japanese).

Soyen Shaku, *Sermons of a Buddhist Abbot*, London, 1907.

Taba Kanai, *The Praises of Amida. Seven Buddhist Sermons.* Translated from the Japanese by Rev. A. Lloyd, London, 1907

H. F Hall, *The Inward Light*, 2d impression, London, 1908 (Buddhism in Burmah).

K. von Hase, *New Testament Parallels in Buddhistic Literature*, New York, 1908.

BULLINGER, H.: *Bullingers Korrespondenz mit den Graubündern*, part iii., Oct., 1566–June, 1575, ed. T. Schiess, Basel, 1906.

BURNET, G.: T. E. S. Clarke and (Miss) H. C. Foxcroft, *Life of Gilbert Burnet, Bishop of Salisbury; with Bibliographical Appendixes; and an Introduction by C. H. Firth*, London and New York, 1908.

CABALA: *Kabbala denudata. The Kabbalah Unveiled: containing the following books from the Zohar: the Book of Concealed Mystery, the Greater Holy Assembly, the Lesser Holy Assembly, translated into English*, New York, 1908 (republication of edition of 1887).

CAJETAN, T.: P Kalkoff, *Cardinal Cajetan auf dem Augsburger Reichstage von 1518*, Rome, 1907

CALVIN, J.: A. Dide, *Michel Servet et Calvin*, Paris, 1907.

CAMBRIDGE PLATONISTS: E. A. George, *The Seventeenth Century Men of Latitude; the Forerunners of the New Theology*, London, 1908.

CAMPBELL, R. J.: *Christianity and the Social Order*, London, 1908.

Thursday Mornings at the City Temple, London, 1908.

CANON OF SCRIPTURE: J. Leipoldt, *Geschichte des neutestamentlichen Kanons*, 2 parts, Leipsic, 1907–08.

CANONESSES: K. H. Schäfer, *Die Kanonissenstifter im deutschen Mittelalter. Ihre Entwicklung und innere Einrichtung im Zusammenhang mit dem altchristl. Sanktimonialentum*, Stuttgart, 1907.

CAPITO, W.: P. Kalkoff, *W Capito im Dienste Erzbischof Albrechts von Mainz*, Berlin, 1907

CAPUCHINS: *Veröffentlichungen aus dem Archiv der rhein-westfälischen Kapuzinerordensprovinz*, Mainz, 1907.

CARLSTADT, A. R. B. VON: K. Müller, *Luther und Karlstadt. Stücke aus ihrem gegenseitigen Verhältnis untersucht*, Tübingen, 1907.

CARMELITES: *Monumenta historica Carmelitana*, vol. i., Lirin, 1905 07

CARTHAGE, SYNODS OF: A. Alcais, *Figures et récits de Carthage chrétienne*, Paris, 1907

CATECHISMS: F. Cohrs, *Die evangelischen Katechismusversuche vor Luthers Enchiridion*, Berlin, 1907.

CATHARINE OF SIENNA: *The Dialogue*, transl. by Algar Thorold, new and abridged ed., London, 1907.

LIST OF ABBREVIATIONS

[Abbreviations in common use or self-evident are not included here. For additional information concerning the works listed, see vol. i., pp. viii.-xx., and the appropriate articles in the body of the work.]

ADB	*Allgemeine deutsche Biographie*, Leipsic, 1875 sqq., vol. 53, 1907
Adv	*adversus*, "against"
AJP	*American Journal of Philology*, Baltimore, 1880 sqq.
AJT	*American Journal of Theology*, Chicago, 1897 sqq.
AKR	*Archiv für katholisches Kirchenrecht*, Innsbruck, 1857-61, Mainz, 1872 sqq.
ALKG	*Archiv für Litteratur- und Kirchengeschichte des Mittelalters*, Freiburg, 1885 sqq.
Am	American
AMA	*Abhandlungen der Münchener Akademie*, Munich, 1763 sqq.
ANF	*Ante-Nicene Fathers*, American edition by A. Cleveland Coxe, 8 vols. and index, Buffalo, 1887; vol. ix., ed. Allan Menzies, New York, 1897
Apoc	Apocrypha, apocryphal
Apol	*Apologia*, *Apology*
Arab	Arabic
Aram	Aramaic
art	article
Art. Schmal	Schmalkald Articles
ASB	*Acta sanctorum*, ed. J. Bolland and others, Antwerp, 1643 sqq.
ASM	*Acta sanctorum ordinis S. Benedicti*, ed. J. Mabillon, 9 vols., Paris, 1668-1701
Assyr	Assyrian
A. T.	*Altes Testament*, "Old Testament"
Augs. Con	Augsburg Confession
A. V.	Authorized Version (of the English Bible)
AZ	*Allgemeine Zeitung*, Augsburg, Tübingen, Stuttgart, and Tübingen, 1798 sqq.
Baldwin, *Dictionary*	J. M. Baldwin, *Dictionary of Philosophy and Psychology*, 3 vols. in 4, New York, 1901-05
Benzinger, *Archäologie*	I. Benzinger, *Hebräische Archäologie*, 2d ed., Freiburg, 1907
Bertholdt, *Einleitung*	L. Bertholdt, *Historisch-Kritische Einleitung . des Alten und Neuen Testaments*, 6 vols., Erlangen, 1812-19
BFBS	British and Foreign Bible Society
Bingham, *Origines*	J. Bingham, *Origines ecclesiasticæ*, 10 vols., London, 1708-22; new ed., Oxford, 1855
Bouquet, *Recueil*	M. Bouquet, *Recueil des historiens des Gaules et de la France*, continued by various hands, 23 vols., Paris, 1738-76
Bower, *Popes*	Archibald Bower, *History of the Popes . to 1758, continued by S. H. Cox*, 3 vols., Philadelphia, 1845-47
BQR	*Baptist Quarterly Review*, Philadelphia, 1867 sqq.
BRG	See Jaffé
Cant	Canticles, Song of Solomon
cap	*caput*, "chapter"
Ceillier, *Auteurs sacrés*	R. Ceillier, *Histoire des auteurs sacrés et ecclésiastiques*, 16 vols. in 17, Paris, 1858-69
Chron	*Chronicon*, "Chronicle"
I Chron	I Chronicles
II Chron	II Chronicles
CIG	*Corpus inscriptionum Græcarum*, Berlin, 1825 sqq.
CIL	*Corpus inscriptionum Latinarum*, Berlin, 1863 sqq.
CIS	*Corpus inscriptionum Semiticarum*, Paris, 1881 sqq.
cod	codex
cod. D	*codex Bezæ*
cod. Theod	*codex Theodosianus*
Col	Epistle to the Colossians
col., cols	column, columns
Conf	*Confessiones*, "Confessions"
I Cor	First Epistle to the Corinthians
II Cor	Second Epistle to the Corinthians
COT	See Schrader
CQR	*The Church Quarterly Review*, London, 1875 sqq.
CR	*Corpus reformatorum*, begun at Halle, 1834, vol. lxxxix., Berlin and Leipsic, 1905 sqq.
Creighton, *Papacy*	M. Creighton, *A History of the Papacy from the Great Schism to the Sack of Rome*, new ed., 6 vols., New York and London, 1897
CSEL	*Corpus scriptorum ecclesiasticorum Latinorum*, Vienna, 1867 sqq.
CSHB	*Corpus scriptorum historiæ Byzantinæ*, 49 vols., Bonn, 1828-78
Currier, *Religious Orders*	C. W. Currier, *History of Religious Orders*, New York, 1896
D	Deuteronomist
DACL	F. Cabrol, *Dictionnaire d'archéologie chrétienne et de liturgie*, Paris, 1903 sqq.
Dan	Daniel
DB	J. Hastings, *Dictionary of the Bible*, 4 vols. and extra vol., Edinburgh and New York, 1898-1904
DCA	W. Smith and S. Cheetham, *Dictionary of Christian Antiquities*, 2 vols., London, 1875-80
DCB	W. Smith and H. Wace, *Dictionary of Christian Biography*, 4 vols., Boston, 1877-87
DCG	J. Hastings, J. A. Selbie, and J. C. Lambert, *A Dictionary of Christ and the Gospels*, Edinburgh and New York, 1906 sqq.
Deut	Deuteronomy
De vir. ill	*De viris illustribus*
De Wette-Schrader, *Einleitung*	W. M. L. de Wette, *Lehrbuch der historisch-kritischen Einleitung in die Bibel*, ed. E. Schrader, Berlin, 1869
DGQ	See Wattenbach
DNB	L. Stephen and S. Lee, *Dictionary of National Biography*, 63 vols. and supplement 3 vols., London, 1885-1901
Driver, *Introduction*	S. R. Driver, *Introduction to the Literature of the Old Testament*, 5th ed., New York, 1894
E	Elohist
EB	T. K. Cheyne and J. S. Black, *Encyclopædia Biblica*, 4 vols., London and New York, 1899-1903
Eccl	*Ecclesia*, "Church"; *ecclesiasticus*, "ecclesiastical"
Eccles	Ecclesiastes
Ecclus	Ecclesiasticus
ed	edition; *edidit*, "edited by"
Eph	Epistle to the Ephesians
Epist	*Epistola, Epistolæ*, "Epistle," "Epistles"
Ersch and Gruber, *Encyklopädie*	J. S. Ersch and J. G. Gruber, *Allgemeine Encyklopädie der Wissenschaften und Künste*, Leipsic, 1818 sqq.
E.V.	English versions (of the Bible)
Ex	Exodus
Ezek	Ezekiel
fasc	*fasciculus*
Friedrich, *KD*	J. Friedrich, *Kirchengeschichte Deutschlands*, 2 vols., Bamberg, 1867-69
Fritzsche, *Exegetisches Handbuch*	O. F. Fritzsche and C. L. W. Grimm, *Kurzgefasstes exegetisches Handbuch zu den Apocryphen des Alten Testaments*, 6 parts, Zurich, 1851-60
Gal	Epistle to the Galatians
Gee and Hardy, *Documents*	H. Gee and W. J. Hardy, *Documents Illustrative of English Church History*, London, 1896
Gen	Genesis
Germ	German
GGA	*Göttingische gelehrte Anzeigen*, Göttingen, 1824 sqq.

Gibbon, *Decline and Fall*. . . . E. Gibbon, *History of the Decline and Fall of the Roman Empire*, ed. J. B. Bury, 7 vols., London, 1896–1900

Gk. . . . . Greek, Grecized

Gregory, *Textkritik*. . . . C. R. Gregory, *Textkritik des Neuen Testaments*, 2 vols., Leipsic, 1901–02

Gross, *Sources*. . . C. Gross, *The Sources and Literature of English History . . . to 1485*, London, 1900

Hab. . . . . Habakkuk

Haddan and Stubbs, *Councils*. . . . . . A. W. Haddan and W. Stubbs, *Councils and Ecclesiastical Documents Relating to Great Britain and Ireland*, 3 vols., Oxford, 1869–78

Hær. . . . . Refers to patristic works on heresies or heretics, Tertullian's *De præscriptione*, the *Pros haireseis* of Irenæus, the *Panarion* of Epiphanius, etc.

Hag. . . . . Haggai

Harduin, *Concilia*. . . . . . J. Harduin, *Conciliorum collectio regia maxima*, 12 vols., Paris, 1715

Harnack, *Dogma* A. Harnack, *History of Dogma from the 3d German edition*, 7 vols., Boston, 1895–1900

Harnack, *Litteratur*. . . . A. Harnack, *Geschichte der altchristlichen Litteratur bis Eusebius*, 2 vols. in 3, Leipsic, 1893–1904

Hauck, *KD*. . . A. Hauck, *Kirchengeschichte Deutschlands*, vol. i., Leipsic, 1904; vol. ii., 1900; vol. iii., 1906; vol. iv., 1903

Hauck-Herzog, *RE*. . . *Realencyklopädie für protestantische Theologie und Kirche*, founded by J. J. Herzog, 3d ed. by A. Hauck, Leipsic, 1896 sqq.

Heb. . . . . Epistle to the Hebrews

Hebr. . . . . Hebrew

Hefele, *Conciliengeschichte*. . . C. J. von Hefele, *Conciliengeschichte*, continued by J. Hergenröther, 9 vols., Freiburg, 1883–93

Heimbucher, *Orden und Kongregationen*. . . . M. Heimbucher, *Die Orden und Kongregationen der katholischen Kirche*, 2 vols., Paderborn, 1896–97

Helyot, *Ordres monastiques*. . . P. Helyot, *Histoire des ordres monastiques, religieux et militaires*, 8 vols., Paris, 1714–19; new ed., 1839–42

Henderson, *Documents*. . . . E. F. Henderson, *Select Historical Documents of the Middle Ages*, London, 1892

Hist. . . . . History, *histoire, historia*

Hist. eccl.. . . . . *Historia ecclesiastica, ecclesiæ*, "Church History"

Hom. . . . . *Homilia, homiliai*, "homily, homilies"

Hos. . . . . Hosea

Isa. . . . . Isaiah

Ital. . . . . Italian

J. . . . . Jahvist (Yahwist)

JA. . . . . *Journal Asiatique*, Paris, 1822 sqq.

Jaffé, *BRG*. . . . . P. Jaffé, *Bibliotheca rerum Germanicarum*, 6 vols., Berlin, 1864–73

Jaffé, *Regesta*. . . P. Jaffé, *Regesta pontificum Romanorum . . . ad annum 1198*, Berlin, 1851; 2d ed., Leipsic, 1881–88

JAOS. . . . . . . *Journal of the American Oriental Society*, New Haven, 1849 sqq.

JBL. . . . . *Journal of Biblical Literature and Exegesis*, first appeared as *Journal of the Society of Biblical Literature and Exegesis*, Middletown, 1882–88, then Boston, 1890 sqq.

JE. . . . . *The Jewish Encyclopedia*, 12 vols., New York, 1901–06

JE. . . . . The combined narrative of the Jahvist (Yahwist) and Elohist

Jer. . . . . Jeremiah

Josephus, *Ant*. . . Flavius Josephus, "Antiquities of the Jews"

Josephus, *Apion*. . . Flavius Josephus, "Against Apion"

Josephus, *Life*. . . . Life of Flavius Josephus

Josephus, *War*. . . . Flavius Josephus, "The Jewish War"

Josh. . . . . Joshua

JPT. . . . . *Jahrbücher für protestantische Theologie*, Leipsic, 1875 sqq.

JQR. . . . . *The Jewish Quarterly Review*, London, 1888 sqq.

JTS. . . . . *Journal of Theological Studies*, London, 1899 sqq.

Julian, *Hymnology*. . . . . . J. Julian, *A Dictionary of Hymnology*, revised edition, London, 1907

JWT . . . . *Jaarboeken voor Wetenschappelijke Theologie*, Utrecht, 1845 sqq.

KAT. . . . . See Schrader

KB. . . . . See Schrader

KD. . . . . See Friedrich, Hauck, Rettberg

KL. . . . . Wetzer und Welte's *Kirchenlexikon*, 2d ed., by J. Hergenröther and F. Kaulen, 12 vols., Freiburg, 1882–1903

Krüger, *History* G. Krüger, *History of Early Christian Literature in the First Three Centuries*, New York, 1897

Krumbacher, *Geschichte*. . . . K. Krumbacher, *Geschichte der byzantinischen Litteratur*, 2d ed., Munich, 1897

Labbe, *Concilia* P. Labbe, *Sacrorum conciliorum nova et amplissima collectio*, 31 vols., Florence and Venice, 1759–98

Lam. . . . . Lamentations

Lanigan, *Eccl. Hist*. . . . . . . J. Lanigan, *Ecclesiastical History of Ireland to the 13th Century*, 4 vols., Dublin, 1829

Lat. . . . . Latin, Latinized

Leg. . . . . *Leges, Legum*

Lev. . . . . Leviticus

Lichtenberger, *ESR* . . . . F. Lichtenberger, *Encyclopédie des sciences religieuses*, 13 vols., Paris, 1877–1882

Lorenz, *DGQ* . . O. Lorenz, *Deutschlands Geschichtsquellen im Mittelalter*, 3d. ed., Berlin, 1887

LXX. . . . . The Septuagint

I Macc. . . . . I Maccabees

II Macc. . . . . . . II Maccabees

Mai, *Nova collectio*. . . . . . A. Mai, *Scriptorum veterum nova collectio*, 10 vols., Rome, 1825–38

Mal. . . . . Malachi

Mann, *Popes*. . R. C. Mann, *Lives of the Popes in the Early Middle Ages*, London, 1902 sqq.

Mansi, *Concilia*. . G. D. Mansi, *Sanctorum conciliorum collectio nova*, 31 vols., Florence and Venice, 1728

Matt. . . . . Matthew

McClintock and Strong, *Cyclopædia*. . . . . J. McClintock and J. Strong, *Cyclopædia of Biblical, Theological, and Ecclesiastical Literature*, 10 vols. and supplement 2 vols., New York, 1869–87

MGH. . . . . *Monumenta Germaniæ historica*, ed. G. H. Pertz and others, Hanover and Berlin, 1826 sqq. The following abbreviations are used for the sections and subsections of this work: *Ant.*, *Antiquitates*, "Antiquities"; *Auct. ant.*, *Auctores antiquissimi*, "Oldest Writers"; *Chron. min.*, *Chronica minora*, "Lesser Chronicles"; *Dip.*, *Diplomata*, "Diplomas, Documents"; *Epist.*, *Epistolæ*, "Letters"; *Gest. pont. Rom.*, *Gesta pontificum Romanorum*, "Deeds of the Popes of Rome"; *Leg.*, *Leges*, "Laws"; *Lib. de lite*, *Libelli de lite inter regnum et sacerdotium sæculorum xi et xii conscripti*, "Books concerning the Strife between the Civil and Ecclesiastical Authorities in the Eleventh and Twelfth Centuries"; *Nec.*, *Necrologia Germaniæ*, "Necrology of Germany"; *Poet. Lat. ævi Car.*, *Poetæ Latini ævi Carolini*, "Latin Poets of the Caroline Time"; *Poet. Lat. med. ævi*, *Poetæ Latini medii ævi*, "Latin Poets of the Middle Ages"; *Script.*, *Scriptores*, "Writers"; *Script. rer. Germ.*, *Scriptores rerum Germanicarum*, "Writers on German Subjects"; *Script. rer. Langob.*, *Scriptores rerum Langobardicarum et Italicarum*, "Writers on Lombard and Italian Subjects"; *Script. rer. Merov.*, *Scriptores rerum Merovingicarum*, "Writers on Merovingian Subjects"

Mic. . . . . Micah

Milman, *Latin Christianity*. . . H. H. Milman, *History of Latin Christianity, Including that of the Popes to . . . Nicholas V.*, 8 vols., London, 1860–61

Mirbt, *Quellen*. . . C. Mirbt, *Quellen zur Geschichte des Papsttums und des römischen Katholicismus*, Tübingen, 1901

Moeller, *Christian Church*. . . W. Moeller, *History of the Christian Church*, 3 vols., London, 1892–1900

MPG. . . . . J. P. Migne, *Patrologiæ cursus completus, series Græca*, 162 vols., Paris, 1857–66

MPL. . . . . J. P. Migne, *Patrologiæ cursus completus, series Latina*, 221 vols., Paris, 1844–64

MS., MSS. . . . . . Manuscript, Manuscripts

Muratori, *Scriptores*. . . . . . L. A. Muratori, *Rerum Italicarum scriptores*, 28 vols., 1723–51

NA. . . . . *Neues Archiv der Gesellschaft für ältere deutsche Geschichtskunde*, Hanover, 1876 sqq.

Nah. . . . . Nahum

n.d. . . . . no date of publication

Neander, *Christian Church*. . A. Neander, *General History of the Christian Religion and Church*, 6 vols. and index, Boston, 1872–81

Neh. . . . . Nehemiah

Niceron, *Mémoires*. . . . . . R. P. Niceron, *Mémoires pour servir à l'histoire des hommes illustres . . .*, 43 vols., Paris, 1729–45

NKZ. . . . . *Neue kirchliche Zeitschrift*, Leipsic, 1890 sqq.

Nowack, *Archäologie*	W. Nowack, *Lehrbuch der hebräischen Archäologie*, 2 vols., Freiburg, 1894
n.p.	no place of publication
NPNF	*The Nicene and Post-Nicene Fathers*, 1st series, 14 vols., New York, 1887–92; 2d series, 14 vols., New York, 1890–1900
N. T.	New Testament, *Novum Testamentum*, *Nouveau Testament*, *Neues Testament*
Num.	Numbers
Ob.	Obadiah
OLBT	J. Wordsworth, H. J. White, and others, *Old-Latin Biblical Texts*, Oxford, 1883 sqq.
O. S. B.	*Ordo sancti Benedicti*, "Order of St. Benedict"
O. T.	Old Testament
OTJC	See Smith
P	Priestly document
Pastor, *Popes*	L. Pastor, *The History of the Popes from the Close of the Middle Ages*, 6 vols., London, 1891–1902
PEA	*Patres ecclesiæ Anglicanæ*, ed. J. A. Giles, 34 vols., London, 1838–46
PEF	Palestine Exploration Fund
I Pet.	First Epistle of Peter
II Pet.	Second Epistle of Peter
Pliny, *Hist. nat.*	Pliny, *Historia naturalis*
Potthast, *Wegweiser*	A. Potthast, *Bibliotheca historica medii ævi. Wegweiser durch die Geschichtswerke*, Berlin, 1896
Prov.	Proverbs
Ps.	Psalms
PSBA	*Proceedings of the Society of Biblical Archeology*, London, 1880 sqq.
q.v., qq.v.	quod (quæ) vide, "which see"
R	Redactor
Ranke, *Popes*	L. von Ranke, *History of the Popes*, 3 vols., London, 1896
RDM	*Revue des deux mondes*, Paris, 1831 sqq.
RE	See Hauck-Herzog
Reich, *Documents*	E. Reich *Select Documents Illustrating Mediæval and Modern History*, London, 1905
REJ	*Revue des études Juives*, Paris, 1880 sqq.
Rettberg, *KD*	F. W. Rettberg, *Kirchengeschichte Deutschlands*, 2 vols., Göttingen, 1846–48
Rev	Book of Revelation
RHR	*Revue de l'histoire des religions*, Paris, 1880 sqq.
Richter, *Kirchenrecht*	A. L. Richter, *Lehrbuch des katholischen und evangelischen Kirchenrechts*, 8th ed., by W. Kahl, Leipsic, 1886
Robinson, *Researches*, and *Later Researches*	E. Robinson, *Biblical Researches in Palestine*, Boston, 1841, and *Later Biblical Researches in Palestine*, 3d ed. of the whole, 3 vols., 1867
Robinson, *European History*	J. H. Robinson, *Readings in European History*, 2 vols., Boston, 1904–06
Rom.	Epistle to the Romans
RSE	*Revue des sciences ecclésiastiques*, Arras, 1860–74, Amiens, 1875 sqq.
RTP	*Revue de théologie et de philosophie*, Lausanne, 1873
R. V.	Revised Version (of the English Bible)
sæc.	*sæculum*, "century"
I Sam.	I Samuel
II Sam.	II Samuel
SBA	*Sitzungsberichte der Berliner Akademie*, Berlin, 1882 sqq.
SBE	F. Max Müller and others, *The Sacred Books of the East*, Oxford, 1879 sqq., vol. xlviii., 1904
SBOT	*Sacred Books of the Old Testament* ("Rainbow Bible"), Leipsic, London, and Baltimore, 1894 sqq.
Schaff, *Christian Church*	P. Schaff, *History of the Christian Church*, vols. i.–iv., vi., vii., New York, 1882–92, vol. v., part 1, by D. S. Schaff, 1907
Schaff, *Creeds*	P. Schaff, *The Creeds of Christendom*, 3 vols, New York, 1877–84
Schrader, *COT*	E. Schrader, *Cuneiform Inscriptions and the Old Testament*, 2 vols., London, 1885–88
Schrader, *KAT*	E. Schrader, *Die Keilinschriften und das Alte Testament*, 2 vols., Berlin, 1902–03
Schrader, *KB*	E. Schrader, *Keilinschriftliche Bibliothek*, 6 vols., Berlin, 1889–1901
Schürer, *Geschichte*	E. Schürer, *Geschichte des jüdischen Volkes im Zeitalter Jesu Christi*, 3 vols., Leipsic, 1898–1901; Eng. transl., 5 vols., New York, 1891
Script.	*Scriptores*, "writers"
Scrivener, *Introduction*	F. H. A. Scrivener, *Introduction to New Testament Criticism*, 4th ed., London, 1894
Sent.	*Sententiæ*, "Sentences"
S. J.	*Societas Jesu*, "Society of Jesus"
SK	*Theologische Studien und Kritiken*, Hamburg, 1826 sqq.
SMA	*Sitzungsberichte der Münchener Akademie*, Munich, 1860 sqq.
Smith, *Kinship*	W. R. Smith, *Kinship and Marriage in Early Arabia*, London, 1903
Smith, *OTJC*	W. R. Smith, *The Old Testament in the Jewish Church*, London, 1892
Smith, *Prophets*	W. R. Smith, *Prophets of Israel . . . to the Eighth Century*, London, 1895
Smith, *Rel. of Sem.*	W. R. Smith, *Religion of the Semites*, London, 1894
S. P. C. K.	Society for the Promotion of Christian Knowledge
S. P. G.	Society for the Propagation of the Gospel in Foreign Parts
sq., sqq.	and following
Strom.	*Stromata*, "Miscellanies"
s.v.	sub voce, or sub verbo
Swete, *Introduction*	H. B. Swete, *Introduction to the Old Testament in Greek*, London, 1900
Syr.	Syriac
TBS	Trinitarian Bible Society
Thatcher and McNeal, *Source Book*	O. J. Thatcher and E. H. McNeal, *A Source Book for Mediæval History*, New York, 1905
I Thess.	First Epistle to the Thessalonians
II Thess.	Second Epistle to the Thessalonians
ThT	*Theologische Tijdschrift*, Amsterdam and Leyden, 1867 sqq.
Tillemont, *Mémoires*	L. S. le Nain de Tillemont, *Mémoires . . . ecclésiastiques des six premiers siècles*, 16 vols., Paris, 1693–1712
I Tim.	First Epistle to Timothy
II Tim.	Second Epistle to Timothy
TJB	*Theologischer Jahresbericht*, Leipsic, 1882–1887, Freiburg, 1888, Brunswick, 1889–1897, Berlin, 1898 sqq.
TLB	*Theologisches Litteraturblatt*, Bonn, 1866 sqq.
TLZ	*Theologische Litteraturzeitung*, Leipsic, 1876 sqq.
Tob.	Tobit
TQ	*Theologische Quartalschrift*, Tübingen, 1819 sqq.
TS	J. A. Robinson, *Texts and Studies*, Cambridge, 1891 sqq.
TSBA	*Transactions of the Society of Biblical Archæology*, London, 1872 sqq.
TSK	*Theologische Studien und Kritiken*, Hamburg, 1826 sqq.
TU	*Texte und Untersuchungen zur Geschichte der altchristlichen Litteratur*, ed. O. von Gebhardt and A. Harnack, Leipsic, 1882 sqq.
TZT	*Tübinger Zeitschrift für Theologie*, Tübingen, 1838–40
Ugolini, *Thesaurus*	B. Ugolinus, *Thesaurus antiquitatum sacrarum*, 34 vols., Venice, 1744–69
V T	*Vetus Testamentum*, *Vieux Testament*, "Old Testament"
Wattenbach, *DGQ*	W. Wattenbach, *Deutschlands Geschichtsquellen*, 5th ed., 2 vols., Berlin, 1885; 6th ed., 1893–94
Wellhausen, *Heidentum*	J. Wellhausen, *Reste arabischen Heidentums*, Berlin, 1887
Wellhausen, *Prolegomena*	J. Wellhausen, *Prolegomena zur Geschichte Israels*, 6th ed., Berlin, 1905, Eng. transl., Edinburgh, 1885
ZA	*Zeitschrift für Assyriologie*, Leipsic, 1886–88, Berlin, 1889 sqq.
Zahn, *Einleitung*	T. Zahn, *Einleitung in das Neue Testament*, 3d ed., Leipsic, 1907
Zahn, *Kanon*	T. Zahn, *Geschichte des neutestamentlichen Kanons*, 2 vols., Leipsic, 1888–92
ZATW	*Zeitschrift für die alttestamentliche Wissenschaft*, Giessen, 1881 sqq.
ZDAL	*Zeitschrift für deutsches Alterthum und deutsche Litteratur*, Berlin, 1876 sqq.
ZDMG	*Zeitschrift der deutschen morgenländischen Gesellschaft*, Leipsic, 1847 sqq.
ZDP	*Zeitschrift für deutsche Philologie*, Halle, 1869 sqq.
ZDPV	*Zeitschrift des deutschen Palästina-Vereins*, Leipsic, 1878 sqq.
Zech.	Zechariah
Zeph.	Zephaniah
ZHT	*Zeitschrift für die historische Theologie*, published successively at Leipsic, Hamburg, and Gotha, 1832–75
ZKG	*Zeitschrift für Kirchengeschichte*, Gotha, 1876 sqq.
ZKR	*Zeitschrift für Kirchenrecht*, Berlin, Tübingen, Freiburg, 1861 sqq.
ZKT	*Zeitschrift für katholische Theologie*, Innsbruck, 1877 sqq.
ZKW	*Zeitschrift für kirchliche Wissenschaft und kirchliches Leben*, Leipsic, 1880–89
ZPK	*Zeitschrift für Protestantismus und Kirche*, Erlangen, 1838–76
ZWT	*Zeitschrift für wissenschaftliche Theologie*, Jena, 1858–60, Halle, 1861–67, Leipsic, 1868 sqq.

SYSTEM OF TRANSLITERATION

The following system of transliteration has been used for Hebrew:

א = ʼ or omitted at the beginning of a word.	ז = z	ע = ʻ
בּ = b	ח = ḥ	פּ = p
ב = bh or b	ט = ṭ	פ = ph or p
גּ = g	י = y	צ = ẓ
ג = gh or g	כּ = k	ק = ḳ
דּ = d	כ = kh or k	ר = r
ד = dh or d	ל = l	שׂ = s
ה = h	מ = m	שׁ = sh
ו = w	נ = n	תּ = t
	ס = s	ת = th or t

The vowels are transcribed by a, e, i, o, u, without attempt to indicate quantity or quality. Arabic and other Semitic languages are transliterated according to the same system as Hebrew. Greek is written with Roman characters, the common equivalents being used.

KEY TO PRONUNCIATION

When the pronunciation is self-evident the titles are not respelled; when by mere division and accentuation it can be shown sufficiently clearly the titles have been divided into syllables, and the accented syllables indicated.

ɑ as in sof*a*	ɵ as in n*o*t	iu as in d*u*ration
ā " " *a*rm	ɵ̄ " " n*o*r	c = k " " cat
a " " *a*t	u " " f*u*ll[2]	ch " " *ch*urch
â " " f*a*re	ū " " r*u*le	cw = qu as in *qu*een
e " " p*e*n[1]	ʋ " " b*u*t	dh (*th*) " " *th*e
ê " " f*a*te	ʋ̄ " " b*u*rn	f " " *f*ancy
i " " t*i*n	ai " " p*i*ne	g (hard) " " *g*o
î " " mach*i*ne	au " " *ou*t	H " " lo*ch* (Scotch)
o " " *o*bey	oi " " *oi*l	hw (*wh*) " " *wh*y
ō " " n*o*	iū " " f*ew*	j " " *j*aw

[1] In accented syllables only; in unaccented syllables it approximates the sound of e in over. The letter ṇ, with a dot beneath it, indicates the sound of n as in ink. Nasal n (as in French words) is rendered n.
[2] In German and French names ü approximates the sound of u in dune.

THE NEW SCHAFF-HERZOG

ENCYCLOPEDIA OF RELIGIOUS KNOWLEDGE

BASILICA: 1. Legal codes. Since the great codification of the Roman law by Justinian, the *Corpus juris civilis*, was written in Latin, it could not meet the needs of the East, and required Greek translations. To do away with the uncertainty which had arisen from such versions, in 878 the emperor Basil the Macedonian had a handbook put together, covering forty titles, and put out a revision in 885. A further revision and codification of the older laws, edited once more under Leo the Wise (886), bears the Greek name of *ta basilika*. It is in sixty books, based on Justinian's compilation from the older versions and commentaries, with extracts from his later constitutions known as the *Novellæ*, and from Basil's handbook mentioned above. (E. Friedberg.)

2. Early form of Christian churches. See Architecture, Ecclesiastical.

Bibliography: C. E. Zacharia, *Historiæ juris Græco-Romani delineatio*, pp. 35–36, Heidelberg, 1839; Mortreuil, *Histoire du droit Byzantin*, part ii, pp. 1 sqq., part iii, pp. 230 sqq., Paris, 1843–46; Krumbacher, *Geschichte*, pp. 171, 257–258, 606, 607, 609, 610, 977.

BASILIDES, bas-i-lai'diz, **AND THE BASILIDIANS:** Basilides, a famous Gnostic, was a pupil of an alleged interpreter of St. Peter, Glaucias by name, and taught at Alexandria during the reign of Hadrian (117–138). He may have been previously a disciple of Menander at Antioch, together with Saturnilus. The *Acta Archelai* state that for a time he taught among the Persians. He composed twenty-four books on the Gospel, which, according to Clement of Alexandria (*Stromata*, iv, 12), were entitled "Exegetics." Fragments of xiii and xxiii, preserved by Clement and in the *Acta Archelai*, supplement the knowledge of Basilides furnished by his opponents. Origen is certainly wrong in ascribing to him a Gospel. The oldest

Basilides.

refutation of the teachings of Basilides, by Agrippa Castor (q.v.), is lost, and we are dependent upon the later accounts of Irenæus, Clement of Alexandria, and Hippolytus. The latter, in his *Philosophumena*, gives a presentation entirely different from the other sources. It either rests on corrupt accounts, or, more probably, on those of a later, post-Basilidian phase of the system. Hippolytus describes a monistic system, in which Hellenic, or rather Stoic, conceptions stand in the foreground, whereas the genuine Basilides is an Oriental through and through, who stands in closer relationship to Zoroaster than to Aristotle.

The fundamental theme of the Basilidian speculation is the question concerning the origin of evil and how to overcome it. The answer is given entirely in the forms of Oriental gnosis, evidently influenced by Parseeism. There are two principles, uncreated and self-existent, light and darkness, originally separated and without knowledge of each other. At the head of the "kingdom of light" stands "the uncreated, unnamable

His System.

God." From him divine life unfolds in successive steps. Seven such revelations form the first ogdoad, from which issued the rest of the spirit-world, till three hundred and sixty-five spirit-realms had originated. These are comprised under the mystic name Abrasax (q.v.), whose numerical value answers to the number of the heavens and days. Being seized with a longing for light, darkness now interferes. A struggle of the principles commences, in which originated our system of the world as copy of the last stage of the spirit-world, having an archon and angel at its head. The earthly life is only a moment of the general purification-process which now takes place to deliver the world of light from darkness. Hence everything which is bad and evil in this system of the world becomes intelligible when regarded in its proper relations. Gradually the rays of light find their way through the mineral kingdom, vegetable kingdom, and animal kingdom. Man has two souls in his breast, of which the rational soul tries to master the material or animal. For the consummation of the process an intervention from above is necessary, however. The Christian idea of the manifestation of God in Jesus Christ is the historical fact which Basilides subjects to his general thoughts. God's "mind" (Gk. *nous*) descended upon Jesus as dove at the Jordan, and he proclaimed salvation to the Jews, the chosen people of the archon. The suffering of Jesus, Basilides admitted as a historical fact, but he did not understand how to utilize it religiously. The Spirit of God is the redeemer, not the crucified one. Jesus suffered as man, whose light-nature was also contaminated through the matter of evil. But the belief in the redemption which came from above lifts man beyond himself to a higher degree of existence. How far the individual can attain it depends on the degree of pure entanglement in former degrees of the spirit-world. In the perfected spirit-world the place will be assigned to each which belongs to him according to the degree of his faith.

The Basilidians. Among the Basilidians, Basilides' son, Isidore, occupies a prominent place. Of his writings ("On the Excrescent Soul," "Exegetics," "Ethics") some fragments are extant. The sect does not seem to have spread beyond Lower Egypt. In opposition to the rigid ethics of their master, the Basilidians seem often to have advocated libertinism. According to Clement of Alexandria they celebrated the sixth or the tenth of January as the day of the baptism of Jesus. On the importance of this fact for the origin of the ecclesiastical festival of the Epiphany, cf. H. Usener, *Religionsgeschichtliche Untersuchungen*, i (Bonn, 1889).

G. KRÜGER.

BIBLIOGRAPHY: The fragments of Basilides are collected in J. E. Grabe, *Spicilegium SS. Patrum*, ii, 35–43, Oxford, 1699; in A. Stieren's edition of Irenæus, i. 901–903, 907–909, Leipsic, 1853; and in A. Hilgenfeld, *Ketzergeschichte des Urchristentums*, pp. 207–217, Leipsic, 1884. The sources are Irenæus (*Hær.*, I, xxiv, 1: cf. ii, 16 et passim), Clement of Alexandria (*Strom.*, ii, 8; iii, 1; iv, 12, 24, 26; v, 1), Origen (Hom. i on Luke; com. on Romans, v), Eusebius (*Chron.*, an. 133; *Hist. eccl.*, IV, vii, 7), the *Acta Archelai* (lv), Epiphanius (*Hær.*, xxiii, 1; xxiv; xxxii, 3), and Hippolytus (*Philosophumena*, vii, 2–15). Consult A. Neander, *Genetische Entwicklung der vornehmsten gnostischen Systeme*, Berlin, 1818 (the most exhaustive treatment); F. C. Baur, *Die christliche Gnosis*, Tübingen, 1835; J. L. Jacobi, *Basilidis philosophi gnostici sententias ex Hippolyti libri*, Berlin, 1852 (valuable); G. Uhlhorn, *Das basilidianische System*, Göttingen, 1855; H. L. Mansel, *Gnostic Heresies*, London, 1875 (has able lecture on Basilides); Hort, in *DCB*, i, 268–281 (very thorough); A. Hilgenfeld, in *ZWT*, xxi (1878), 228–250; idem, *Die Ketzergeschichte des Urchristentums*, pp. 207–218, Leipsic, 1884; G. Salmon, *The Cross-references in the Philosophoumena*, in *Hermathena*, xi (1885), 389–402; H. Stähelin, *Die gnostischen Quellen Hippolyts*, in *TU*, vi, 3, Leipsic, 1890; Schaff, *Christian Church*, ii, 466–472; Harnack, *Litteratur*, i, 157–161; ii, 1, 289–297; Krüger, *History*, pp. 70–71; Moeller, *Christian Church*, i, 141–144; J. Kennedy, in the *Journal of the Royal Asiatic Society*, 1902, pp. 377–415.

BASNAGE, bā″nāzh′: The name of a family of Normandy which has produced several men prominent in the history of French Protestantism.

1. Benjamin Basnage was for fifty-one years pastor at Sainte-Mère-Église, near Carentan (27 m. s.e. of Cherbourg), where he was born in 1580 and died in 1652. During the religious wars he was repeatedly chosen by his coreligionists, on account of the constancy of his character and his great learning, to represent them in political and ecclesiastical assemblies. He was president of the general synod at Alençon in 1637, and as deputy at Charenton in 1644 he did much to defend the rights of the Protestants and to reconcile the theologians. In the year of his death he was ennobled by the government of Louis XIV. Of the many polemical tractates which he wrote, the best known is *De l'état visible et invisible de l'Église et de la parfaite satisfaction de Jésus Christ, contre la fable du purgatoire* (La Rochelle, 1612).

2. Henri Basnage, younger son of Benjamin, was born at Sainte-Mère-Église Oct. 16, 1615; d. at Rouen Oct. 20, 1695. He was one of the most eloquent advocates in the parliament of Rouen and one of the most famous jurists of his time. He defended the cause of the Reformed Church courageously, and his reputation was such that after the revocation of the Edict of Nantes he was almost the only Protestant who could follow the profession of law in Rouen.

3. Samuel Basnage, son of Antoine, younger son of Benjamin, was born at Bayeux 1638; d. at Zütphen 1721. He was first pastor at Vauxcelles, then at Bayeux till 1685. He went with his father to the Netherlands and became pastor there of the Walloon congregation at Zütphen. Of his theological writings the most important are: *Morale théologique et politique sur les vertus et les vices des hommes* (2 vols., Amsterdam, 1703); and *Annales politico-ecclesiastici* (3 vols., Rotterdam, 1706).

4. Jacques Basnage (de Beauval), son of Henri, was born at Rouen Aug. 8, 1653; d. at The Hague Dec. 22, 1723. He first studied the classical languages at Saumur under Tanneguy, father of the famous Mme. Dacier, afterward theology at Geneva under Turretin and Tronchin, finally at Sédan under Jurieu. In 1676 he was chosen pastor at Rouen; after the suppression of the church at Rouen in 1685, Louis XIV granted him permission to retire to Holland. In 1691 he was made pastor of the Walloon congregation at Rotterdam, and in 1709 of the French congregation at The Hague. The prime minister Heinsius respected him highly and employed him in different diplomatic missions. The fame of his diplomatic ability reached the court at Versailles, and when, in 1716, the Abbé Dubois was sent to The Hague by the Duke of Orléans, then regent, in behalf of the triple alliance, he was instructed to associate with Basnage. When an insurrection of the Camisards in the Cévennes was feared, the regent applied to Basnage. He supported energetically the zealous Antoine Court, then twenty years old, in restoring the Protestant Church in Southern France, but, partial to the principles of passive obedience, as preached by Calvin, he severely condemned the insurrection of the Camisards and even blamed the first preachers in the Desert. About this time the States General of the Netherlands appointed him historiographer. His numerous works are partly dogmatic or polemic, partly historical. The former include especially his writings against Bossuet: *Examen des méthodes proposées par Messieurs de l'assemblée du clergé de France, en 1682, pour la réunion des Protestants à l'Église romaine* (Cologne, 1682); *Réponse à M. l'évêque de Meaux sur la lettre pastorale* (1686). His historical works are: *Histoire de la religion des Églises réformées* (2 vols., Rotterdam, 1690; 1725); *Histoire de l'Église depuis Jésus Christ jusqu'à présent* (1699); *Histoires du Vieux et du Nouveau Testament, représentées par des figures gravées en taille-douce par R. de Hooge* (Amsterdam, 1704); *Histoire des Juifs depuis Jésus Christ jusqu'à présent* (1706).

G. BONET-MAURY.

BIBLIOGRAPHY: J. Aymon, *Tous les synodes nationaux des églises réformées*, The Hague, 1710; P. Bayle, *Dictionnaire historique et critique*, Amsterdam, 1740; D. Houard, *Dictionnaire de la coutume de Normandie*, Rouen, 1780; Lamory, *Éloge de Basnage*, in *Bulletin d'histoire du protes tantisme français*, vol. x, p. 42; xiii, pp. 41–48; E. and É. Haag, *La France protestante*, 2d ed. by M. Bordier, 5 vols., Paris, 1877–86; F. Puaux, *Les Précurseurs français de la tolérance*, ib. 1881; J. Bianquis, *La Révocation de l'édit de Nantes*, Rouen, 1885.

BASSERMANN, HEINRICH GUSTAV: German Lutheran; b. at Frankfort-on-the-Main July 12, 1849. He was educated at the universities of Jena, Zurich, and Heidelberg in 1868–73, but served in the campaign of 1870–71 in the First Baden Dragoons. He was assistant pastor at Arolsen, Waldeck, from 1873 to 1876, when he became privat-docent of New Testament exegesis at the University of Jena. In the same year he was appointed associate professor of practical theology at Heidelberg, and full professor and university preacher in 1880. He wrote: *Dreissig christliche Predigten* (Leipsic, 1875); *De loco Matthæi v, 17–20* (Jena, 1876); *Handbuch der geistlichen Beredsamkeit* (Stuttgart, 1885); *Akademische Predigten* (1886); *System der Liturgik* (1888); *Geschichte der badischen Gottesdienstordnung* (1891); *Sine ira et studio* (Tübingen, 1894); *Der badische Katechismus erklärt* (1896–97); *Richard Rothe als praktischer Theolog* (1899); *Zur Frage des Unionskatechismus* (1901); *Ueber Reform des Abendmahls* (1904); *Wie studiert man evangelische Theologie?* (Stuttgart, 1905); and *Gott: Fünf Predigten* (Göttingen, 1905). From 1879 he edited the *Zeitschrift für praktische Theologie* in collaboration with Rudolf Ehlers. Died in Samaden (70 m. s.s.e. of St. Gall), Switzerland, Aug. 30, 1909.

BASTHOLM, CHRISTIAN: Danish court preacher, and an influential representative of the prevalent rationalism of his time; b. at Copenhagen Nov. 2, 1740; d. there Jan. 25, 1819. He had a varied education, and was specially attracted to philosophy and natural science, but was persuaded by his father to embrace a clerical career without any real love for Christian doctrine or the Church. He was preacher to the German congregation at Smyrna from 1768 to 1771. His renown as a great orator won him in 1778 the position of court preacher, to which other court offices were subsequently added. Full of the ideas of the "Enlightenment," he felt called upon to be a missionary in their cause to his countrymen, and published a number of works in popular religious philosophy and history which have long since fallen into oblivion. His greatest success was his text-book of sacred oratory (1775), which so impressed Joseph II that he introduced it into all the higher educational institutions of the empire, though its recommendations seem laughable to-day. He published a history of the Jews (1777–82), attempting to "rationalize" it after Michaelis, and a translation of the New Testament with notes (1780). A small treatise on improvements in the liturgy (1785) aroused a storm of controversy; his idea was to make the service "interesting and diversified," after the model of balls and concerts; to exclude from hymnody not only everything dogmatic but all that was not joyous; and to eliminate from the sacramental rites whatever was contrary to sound reason. In the days of the French Revolution, he offered so many concessions to the antireligious spirit that he made himself ridiculous even in the eyes of freethinkers; and his book on "Wisdom and Happiness" (1794) taught a Stoicism only colored by Christianity. In 1795 he lost his library by fire, and with the new century withdrew from public life and authorship to live quietly with his son, a pastor at Slagelse, absorbed in the study of philosophy and science. (F. Nielsen.)

BATES, WILLIAM: English Presbyterian; b. at London Nov., 1625; d. at Hackney July 14, 1699. He was graduated at Cambridge 1647, and was vicar of St. Dunstan's-in-the-West, London, until 1662, when he lost the benefice for non-conformity; he was one of the commissioners to the Savoy Conference (q.v.) in 1661 and represented the nonconformists on other occasions in negotiations with the Churchmen; was chaplain to Charles II and had influence in high places both under Charles and his successors. He is said to have been a polished preacher and a sound scholar. Perhaps the best known of his works is *The Harmony of the Divine Attributes in the Contrivance and Accomplishment of Man's Redemption* (2d ed., London, 1675). A collected edition of his works, with memoir by W Farmer, was published in four volumes at London in 1815.

BATHING: The bath in the East, because of the heat and the dust, is constantly necessary for the preservation of health, and to prevent skin-diseases. The bathing of the newly born is mentioned in Ezek. xvi, 4; bathing as part of the toilet in Ruth iii, 3; II Sam. xii, 20; Ezek. xxiii, 40, and elsewhere. As the Law attached great religious value to the purity of the body, it prescribed bathing and ablutions for cases in which it was apparently impaired (see Defilement and Purification, Ceremonial). Ablution was required when one approached the deity (cf. Gen. xxxv, 2; Exod. xix, 10; Lev. xvi, 4, for the high priest on the Day of Atonement). Bathing in "living" (i.e., running) water was regarded as most effective in every respect (Exod. ii, 5; II Kings v, 10; Lev. xv, 13). More accessible and convenient were the baths arranged in the houses. To a well-furnished house belonged a courtyard, in which was a bath—according to II Sam. xi, 2, an open basin. Susannah (verses 15 sqq.) bathes in a hedged garden and uses oil and some kind of soap; the Hebrew women used bran in the bath, or to dry themselves (*Mishnah Pesaḥim* ii, 7). The feet, being protected by sandals only, were exposed to dust and dirt, and no attentive host omitted to give to his guests water for their feet before he entertained them (Gen. xviii, 4; xix, 2; I Sam. xxv, 41; cf. Luke vii, 44; John xiii, 1–10). The washing of hands before meals was customary for obvious reasons; but it is not expressly attested before New Testament time, and then as a religious enactment which the Pharisees rigidly observed (Matt. xv, 2; Luke xi, 38); so in general with reference to washings and bathings the punctilious were at that time more exacting. The efficacy of warm springs was recognized at a very early period (cf. Gen. xxxvi, 24, R. V., and the name Hammath, Josh. xix, 35; xxi, 32). They were found near Tiberias (Josephus, *War*, II, xxi, 6; *Ant.*,

XVIII, ii, 3; *Life*, xvi; Pliny, v, 15), Gadara, the capital of Peræa, and Callirrhoë, east of the Dead Sea (Josephus, *War*, I, xxxiii, 5; Pliny, v, 16). Public baths are mentioned in Josephus, *Ant.*, XIX, vii, 5, but their existence in Palestine can not be proved before the Greco-Roman time.

C. VON ORELLI.

Abuses connected with the public baths in early Christian times called forth protests from many of the heathen and led some of the emperors to attempt restrictive precautions. The Church Fathers also raised their voices, but it is noteworthy that though there was public censure (e.g., of women, particularly of virgins who were immodest in the bath), there was no formal, ecclesiastical prohibition of the public baths. The use of the bath was remitted during public calamities, penance, Lent, and for the first week after baptism. From the time of Constantine it was usual to build baths near the basilicas, partly for the use of the clergy, and partly for other ecclesiastical purposes.

BIBLIOGRAPHY: For Hebr. custom consult *DB*, i, 257–258. On the Christian, *DCA*, i, 182–183; the article "Baden" in *KL*, i, 1843–46, covers both subjects.

BATH KOL: Literally "daughter of the voice," an expression which signifies in itself nothing more than a call or echo, for which it is also used. When the term is applied to a divine manifestation, it implies that it was audible to the human hearing without a personal theophany. In the Old Testament the notion is found in Dan. iv, 28 (A. V 31), "a voice fell from heaven." In the New Testament similar ideas are the heavenly voice at the baptism of Jesus (Matt. iii, 17; Mark i, 11; Luke iii, 22), at his transfiguration (Matt. xvii, 5; Mark ix, 7; Luke ix, 35), before his passion (John xii, 28), and the voices from heaven heard by Paul and Peter (Acts ix, 4; cf. xxii, 7 and xxvi, 14; x, 13, 15). A voice from the sanctuary is mentioned by Josephus (*Ant.*, XIII, x, 3; cf. *Bab. Soṭah* 33a; *Jerus. Soṭah* 24b), and was called *bath kol* by the rabbis, who were of opinion that such heavenly voices were heard during all the time of Israel's history, even in their own time. According to *Bab. Soṭah* 48b; *Yomah* 9a, this "voice" was the only divine means of revelation after the extinction of prophecy. They narrate legendary stories of such divine voices which settled religious difficulties. Different from the *bath kol* proper is the idea that natural sounds or words heard by accident are significant heavenly voices. This superstition was not uncommon, as *Jerus. Shabbat* 8c shows. Rabbi Joshua was of the opinion that such things must not influence any legal decision (*Bab. Paba Meẓi'a* 59b; *Berakot* 51b). Rabbi Johanan lays down as general rule that that which was heard in the city must be the voice of a man, in the desert that of a woman, and that either a twofold "Yea" or twofold "Nay" is heard (*Bab. Megillah* 32a).

(G. DALMAN.)

BIBLIOGRAPHY: F. Weber, *System der altsynagogalen palästinischen Theologie*, pp. 187, 194, Leipsic, 1880; W. Bacher, *Agada der Tannaiten*, i, 88, note 3, Strasburg, 1884; idem, *Agada der palästinischen Amoräer*, i, 351, note 3, ii, 26, ib. 1892–96; S. Louis, *Ancient Traditions of Supernatural Voices: Bath Kol*, in *TSBA*, ix, 18; *JE*, ii, 588–592.

BATIFFOL, PIERRE HENRI: French Roman Catholic; b. at Toulouse Jan. 27, 1861. He was educated at the Seminary of St. Sulpice, Paris (1878–82), and the University of Paris (1882–86; Docteur ès lettres, 1892), and since 1898 has been rector of the Institut Catholique at Toulouse. He was created a domestic prelate to the Pope in 1899, and in theology is an orthodox Roman Catholic, inclining toward the critical school in matters of history. Since 1896 he has been the editor of the *Bibliothèque de l'enseignement de l'histoire ecclésiastique*, founded by him in that year, and since 1899 has also edited the monthly *Bulletin de littérature ecclésiastique*. He has written *L'Abbaye de Rossano, contribution à l'histoire de la Vaticane* (Paris, 1892); *Histoire du brévière romain* (1893); *Six leçons sur les Évangiles* (1897); *Tractatus Origenis in libros sanctarum scripturarum* (1900); *Études d'histoire et de théologie positive* (1902); and *L'Enseignement de Jésus* (1905).

BATTEN, LORING WOART: Protestant Episcopalian; b. in Gloucester County, N. J., Nov. 12, 1859. He was educated at Harvard University, the Philadelphia Divinity School, and the University of Pennsylvania. He was ordered deacon in 1886 and ordained priest in the following year, and was instructor and professor of the Old Testament in the Philadelphia Divinity School from 1888 to 1899, when he became rector of St. Mark's, New York City. He is also lecturer on the Old Testament in the General Theological Seminary, New York City. In addition to numerous briefer studies, he has written *The Old Testament from the Modern Point of View* (New York, 1889) and *The Hebrew Prophet* (London, 1905).

BATTERSON, HERMON GRISWOLD: Protestant Episcopalian; b. at Marbledale, Conn., May 27, 1827; d. in New York City Mar. 9, 1903. He was educated privately, was rector at San Antonio, Texas, 1860–61, and at Wabasha, Minn., 1862–66. In 1866 he removed to Philadelphia and was rector of St. Clement's Church there 1869–1872, of the Church of the Annunciation 1880–89; became rector of the Church of the Redeemer, New York, 1891, but soon retired. He published *The Missionary Tune Book* (Philadelphia, 1867); *The Churchman's Hymn Book* (1870); *A Sketch Book of the American Episcopate* (1878; 3d ed., enlarged, 1891); *Christmas Carols and Other Verses* (1877); *Gregorian Music, a manual of plain song for the offices of the American Church* (New York, 1884; 7th ed., 1890); *Vesper Bells and Other Verses* (1895).

BAUDISSIN, WOLF WILHELM, GRAF VON: German Protestant; b. at Sophienhof, near Kiel, Germany, Sept. 26, 1847 He was educated at the universities of Erlangen, Berlin, Leipsic (Ph.D., 1870), and Kiel from 1866 to 1872, and was privat-docent at Leipsic in 1874–76, when he accepted a call to the University of Strasburg as associate professor of theology. Four years later he was promoted to full professor, but in the following year went to Marburg as professor of Old Testament exegesis. He remained at Marburg, where he was rector in 1893-94, until 1900, when he went to Berlin as professor of Old Testament exegesis, a chair which he still holds. In theology he is an adherent of the historical school of investigation, and seeks to elucidate the religion of the Old Testament by other Semitic faiths. He has written: *Translationis antiquæ arabicæ libri Jobi quæ supersunt nunc primum edita* (Leipsic, 1870); *Eulogius und Alvar, ein Abschnitt spanischer Kirchengeschichte aus der Zeit der Maurenherrschaft* (1872); *Jahve et Moloch, sive de ratione inter deum Israelitarum et Molochum intercedente* (1874); *Studien zur semitischen Religionsgeschichte* (2 vols., 1876-1878); *Die Geschichte des alttestamentlichen Priesterthums untersucht* (1889); *August Dillmann* (1895); *Einleitung in die Bücher des Alten Testaments* (1901); and *Esmun-Asklepios* (Giessen, 1906).

BAU'ER, BRUNO: A modern Biblical critic, of the most extreme radicalism; b. at Eisenberg (35 m. s. of Halle), in the duchy of Altenburg, Sept. 6, 1809; d. at Rixdorf, near Berlin, Apr. 15, 1882. He was educated in Berlin precisely in Hegel's most brilliant period. He took his place at first in the conservative wing of the Hegelian school, of which his teacher Marheineke was the leader, and reviewed the *Leben Jesu* of David Friedrich Strauss, who had been his fellow student, unfavorably, accusing Strauss of "entire ignorance of what criticism means." He undertook also to defend Marheineke's position by issuing (1836–38) the *Zeitschrift für spekulative Theologie*. In 1838 he published the *Kritik der Geschichte der Offenbarung* (2 vols., Berlin). A year later Altenstein, minister of public worship and instruction, appointed him to a position in the University of Bonn, and his prospects seemed promising. But he was already in a fair way to break with his past, as shortly appeared in his *Kritik der evangelischen Geschichte des Johannes* (Bremen, 1840) and *Kritik der evangelischen Geschichte der Synoptiker* (3 vols., Leipsic, 1841), which went beyond Strauss, and, adopting the theory of Wilke that Mark is the original gospel, derived the whole story, not, with Strauss, from the imagination of the primitive Christian community, but from that of a single mind. This extreme carrying out of Hegelian principles naturally aroused wide-spread excitement. Eichhorn, who had succeeded Altenstein as minister, put the question to the Prussian universities whether the holder of such views could be allowed to teach. The answers were not unanimous; but Bauer injured his own cause by a still more amazing and reckless onslaught on traditional theology (*Theologische Schamlosigkeiten*, in the *Hallische Jahrbücher für deutsche Wissenschaft*, Nov., 1841), and was deprived of his academic post in March, 1842. His literary activity continued incessant. Living on his small estate at Rixdorf, he poured forth a succession of volumes on the history of the eighteenth and nineteenth centuries between 1843 and 1849. In 1850 he came back to his old field, and in the next three years had renewed his attack on the gospels and included the Acts and the Pauline epistles, considering even the four admitted by the Tübingen school as second-century Western products. In the place of Christ and Paul, to him Philo, Seneca, and the Gnostics appeared the real creative forces in the evolution of Christian conceptions. He continued his attempts to prove the connection between Greco-Roman philosophy and Christianity in *Christus und die Cäsaren* (Berlin, 1877). Here he places the genesis of the Christian religion practically as late as the reign of Marcus Aurelius, and the original gospel in that of Hadrian, after which "clever men" were busy for some forty years in the composition of the Pauline epistles. Only the framework of the new religion was Jewish; its spirit came from further west; Christianity is really "Stoicism becoming dominant in a Jewish metamorphosis." Bauer left practically no followers in Germany for such remarkable theories. His fantastic hypercriticism found a home for a time in Holland with Allard Pierson, Naber, and Loman; and still later it made some attempts to gain a foothold in Switzerland with Steck's assault upon Galatians. (J. HAUSSLEITER.)

BIBLIOGRAPHY: Holtzmann, in *Protestantische Kirchenzeitung*, 1882, pp. 540–545; F. C. Baur, *Kirchengeschichte des neunzehnten Jahrhunderts*, Leipsic, 1862; O. Pfleiderer, *Die Entwicklung der protestantischen Theologie in Deutschland seit Kant*, pp. 295–297, Freiburg, 1891. On the teaching of Bauer and the opposition it aroused consult E. Bauer, *Bruno Bauer und seine Gegner*, Berlin, 1842; O. F. Gruppe, *Bruno Bauer und die akademische Lehrfreiheit*, ib. 1842.

BAUER, WALTER FELIX: German Protestant; b. at Königsberg Aug. 8, 1877. From 1895 to 1900 he studied at the universities of Marburg, Berlin, and Strasburg, and since 1903 has been privat-docent for church history at the University of Marburg. He has written *Mündige und Unmündige bei dem Apostel Paulus* (Marburg, 1902) and *Der Apostolos der Syrer in der Zeit von der Mitte des vierten Jahrhunderts bis zur Spaltung der syrischen Kirche* (Giessen, 1903).

BAUM, baum, **HENRY MASON:** Protestant Episcopalian; b. at East Schuyler, N. Y., Feb. 24, 1848. He was educated at the Hudson River Institute, Claverack, N. Y., but did not attend a college. He received his theological training at De Lancey Divinity School, Geneva, N. Y., and was ordained to the priesthood in 1870. He was successively rector of St. Peter's Church, East Bloomfield, N. Y. (1870–71), missionary to Allen's Hill, Victor, Lima, and Honeoye Falls, N. Y. (1871–1872), rector of St. Matthew's Church, Laramie City, Wyo. (1872–73), in charge of St. James's Church, Paulsborough, N. J. (1873–74), rector of St. Matthew's Church, Lambertville, N. J. (1875–76), and rector of Trinity Church, Easton, Pa. (1876–80). From 1880 to 1892 he was editor of *The Church Review*, and in 1901 founded the *Records of the Past*, which he edited until 1905. He has taken a keen interest in the preservation of the antiquities of the United States, and was the author of the act passed by the Senate in 1904 for the protection of these archeological remains. In that year he also founded the Institute of Historical Research at Washington, and has since been its president. In theology he is a firm believer in the historical accuracy of the Bible. He has written *Rights and Duties of Rectors, Church Wardens, and Vestrymen in* *the American Church* (Philadelphia, 1879) and *The Law of the Church in the United States* (New York, 1886).

BAUM, JOHANN WILHELM: Protestant German theologian; b. at Flonheim (17 m. s.s.w. of Mainz) Dec. 7, 1809; d. at Strasburg Nov. 28, 1878. When he was thirteen years of age, he was sent to Strasburg to the house of his uncle, where he prepared himself for the ministry. Having completed his studies, he was made teacher at the theological seminary at Strasburg in 1835. This position he resigned in 1844 and accepted the position of vicar of St. Thomas's in that city, whose first preacher he became in 1847. At the close of the Franco-Prussian war, the German government appointed him professor in the University of Strasburg. He belonged to the liberal Protestant party of his country, and made himself known by his writings on the history of the Reformation, as well as that of his own time, including *Franz Lambert von Avignon* (Strasburg and Paris, 1840); *Theodor Beza nach handschriftlichen Quellen dargestellt* (2 vols., Leipsic, 1843–45); *Johann Georg Stuber, der Vorgänger Oberlins im Steinthale und Vorkämpfer einer neuen Zeit in Strassburg* (Strasburg, 1846); *Die Memoiren d'Aubigné's des Hugenotten von altem Schrott und Korn* (Leipsic, 1854); *Capito und Butzer, Strassburgs Reformatoren* (Elberfeld, 1860), being the third part of *Leben und ausgewählte Schriften der Väter und Begründer der reformirten Kirche.* Besides these works written in German, he published in French *Les Églises réformées de France sous la croix* (Strasburg, 1869); *Les Mémoires de P. Carrière dit Corteis* (Strasburg, 1871); *Le Procès de Baudichon de la Maison-Neuve* (Geneva, 1873). For a number of years Baum assisted his colleagues Reuss and Cunitz in the edition of Calvin's works published in the *Corpus reformatorum.*

Bibliography: *Zur Erinnerung an J. W. Baum, Reden,* Strasburg, 1878; M. Baum, *J. W. Baum, ein protestantisches Charakterbild aus dem Elsass,* Bremen, 1880.

BAUMGARTEN, MICHAEL: German theologian and active promoter of free church life; b. at Haseldorf, near Hamburg, Mar. 25, 1812; d. at Rostock July 21, 1889. He was educated at Altona, Kiel, and Berlin, becoming in the last-named place an outspoken adherent of Hengstenberg. But the study of Dorner during a period of seven years (1839–46) spent at Kiel as a teacher convinced him that the traditional orthodox view of the person of Christ was inadequate to explain the mystery of redemption; he passed from Hengstenberg to Schleiermacher, with his principle that Christianity is not a doctrine but a life, and then to Hofmann, in whose *Weissagung und Erfüllung* he saw a theology that could lead him further on his road. In his treatise *Liturgie und Predigt* (Kiel, 1843) he lays down his programme, to which as an old man he was still proud of having adhered. Here he classes as stumbling-blocks in the Church's way a variety of ancient institutions, laws, and customs, viz.: the misleading notion of a "Christian State"; the use of compulsion in the Church (as in the case of baptism); the power of civil rulers within the Church, in allowing which the Reformers had brought back a Byzantine system; the diversity of teaching among Protestants; and the failure to recognize the menace of the Roman errors. About the same time (1843–44) appeared his commentary on the Pentateuch, to which Delitzsch appealed when in 1850 he recommended his friend to succeed him in the Rostock professorship, but which none the less he sharply criticized in some points. In the eventful years 1846–50 he was pastor of St. Michael's church at Sleswick, and was one of the leaders of the clergy of Sleswick-Holstein in their struggle for the German right to the duchies. After the battle of Idstedt, he was obliged to escape from Sleswick with his family to Holstein, where his call to Rostock found him. Here he was expected to take part in the upbuilding of the Church of the duchy, which was under Kliefoth's leadership; but two men more diametrically opposed in their whole way of looking at things could scarcely have been found. Baumgarten frankly expressed his own view of the earliest history of the Church in his *Apostelgeschichte* (2 vols., Halle, 1852), and of its modern needs in his *Nachtgesichte Sacharjas* (Brunswick, 1854). It was not difficult to make a collection of heretical propositions from the writings of a man who cared so little to express himself in time-honored formulas, and who was wrestling with such modern problems; and the attempt was soon made. The Grand Duke dismissed him from the theological commission in 1856; the consistory examined his works, it must be admitted without strict adherence to constitutional rules or to the principles of fairness, found a whole series of departures from the received doctrine, and deprived him of his position. He declined an invitation to go to India as a missionary, preferring to remain and carry on the struggle for a complete reconstruction of the Evangelical Church in Germany. With this aim he was for thirteen years a zealous member of the Protestant Union from 1863 to 1876, but left it when it showed intolerance in the Heidelberg case. His life grew more and more lonely, though he could always count on a few faithful friends, like Studt, Ziegler, and Pestalozzi. He was a member of the Reichstag from 1874 to 1881, in which he showed himself a determined opponent of Stöcker and of the Jesuits, and stood for his principles of religious liberty and complete separation of Church and State. He was a man of great natural endowment, fitted for useful constructive work in theology, if the unfortunate circumstances in his career had not forced him to expend his energy in the combat to which most of his numerous later writings have reference.

(J. Haussleiter.)

Bibliography: His autobiography was edited and published posthumously by K. H. Studt, 2 vols., Kiel, 1891.

BAUMGARTEN, OTTO: German Protestant; b. at Munich Jan. 29, 1858. He was educated at the universities of Strasburg, Göttingen, Zurich, and Heidelberg, and from 1882 to 1887 was pastor at Baden-Baden and Waldkirch, while from 1888 to 1890 he was chaplain to the orphan asylum at Berlin-Rummelsburg. In 1890 he became privat-docent at the University of Berlin, and in the same year was called to Jena as associate professor of practical theology, where he remained until 1894, when he went to Kiel as full professor of the same subject. He is also university preacher and chaplain of the academic sanitarium at the same institution of learning. He has written: *Volksschule und Kirche* (Leipsic, 1890); *Der Seelsorger unserer Tage* (1891); *Predigten aus der Gegenwart* (Tübingen (1902); *Neue Bahnen : Der Religions-Unterricht vom Standpunkte der modernen Theologie aus* (1903); *Predigt-Probleme, Hauptfragen der modernen Evangeliums-Verkündigungen* (1903); and *Die Voraussetzungslosigkeit der protestantischen Theologie* (Kiel, 1903).

BAUMGARTEN, SIEGMUND JAKOB: German theologian; b. at Wollmirstädt (8 m. n. of Magdeburg), Saxony, Mar. 14, 1706; d. at Halle July 4, 1757 He studied at the Halle Orphan Asylum, of which his father had been first inspector, and at the University of Halle. He became inspector of the Halle Latin School in 1726, assistant preacher to the younger G. A. Franke in 1728, associate on the theological faculty in 1730, and ordinary professor in 1743. He was a good teacher and his lectures were usually attended by from 300 to 400 hearers. His learning was vast and he was an industrious writer, publishing voluminous works on exegesis, hermeneutics, morals, dogmatics, and history, such as *Auszug der Kirchengeschichte* (4 vols., Halle, 1743–62); *Evangelische Glaubenslehre* (3 vols., 1759–60); *Geschichte der Religionsparteien* (1760); *Nachricht von merkwürdigen Büchern* (12 vols., 1752–57); and the first sixteen volumes in the *Allgemeine Welthistorie* (1744 sqq.). By adopting the formal scheme of the philosophy of Wolff and applying it to the theological ideas in which he was educated, Baumgarten came to form a transition from the Pietism of Spener and Francke to the modern rationalism. His enthusiastic disciple, J. S. Semler, who was called from Altdorf to Halle on his recommendation, edited many of his works and wrote his biography (Halle, 1758). (F Bosse.)

BAUMGARTEN-CRUSIUS, LUDWIG FRIEDRICH OTTO: German theologian; b. at Merseburg (56 m. s.s.e. of Magdeburg), Prussian Saxony, July 31, 1788; d. at Jena May 31, 1843. He studied theology and philology at Leipsic and became university preacher there in 1810; in 1812 extraordinary professor of theology at Jena, ordinary professor, 1817. He gave lectures on all branches of so-called theoretic theology except church history, especially New Testament exegesis, Biblical theology, dogmatics, ethics, and history of doctrine. Gentle and sympathetic, and shrinking from theological strife, he was misunderstood in his time. His exegesis was painstaking, free from prejudice, and acute; as historian of dogma he understood the origin and development of religious ideas and doctrines as few others have done; and as systematic theologian he was profound and truly evangelical. His principal works were: *Einleitung in das Studium der Dogmatik* (Leipsic, 1820); *Lehrbuch der christlichen Dogmengeschichte* (Jena, 1832); *Compendium der christlichen Dogmengeschichte* (Leipsic, 1840), completed by K. A. Hase (1846); *Theologische Auslegung der johanneischen Schriften* (2 vols., Jena, 1843–45). (F. Bosse.)

Bibliography: H. C. A. Eichstädt, *Memoria L. F. O. Baumgartenii-Crusii*, Jena, 1843; K. A. Hase's preface to his completion of the *Kompendium der Dogmengeschichte*, Leipsic, 1846; *ADB*, ii, 161 sqq.

BAUR, FERDINAND CHRISTIAN, AND THE LATER TÜBINGEN SCHOOL.

The treatment of both Ferdinand Christian Baur and the Later Tübingen School in the same article is justified by the fact that the period of distinctive theological and philosophical views which characterized the school in its palmy days really ceased with the death of its founder, or at least lost the former local identification. Considering the Tübingen School in this strictly limited sense, its history, together with that of Baur himself, may be divided into three periods—that of preparation, or of the history of dogma, before 1835; that of prosperity, or of Biblical criticism, 1835–1848; and that of disintegration, or of church history, after the latter date.

I. The Period of the History of Dogma: Baur was born at Schmiden, near Cannstatt (4 m. n.e. of Stuttgart), June 21, 1792; he died at Tübingen Dec. 2, 1860. He was the son of a Württemberg pastor and was educated first at Blaubeuren and then (1809–14) at Tübingen. Here, besides following the usual thorough course in philology, he was strongly attracted by the study of philosophy. Fichte and Schelling were then at the height of their influence; but that it did not draw the young student away from the standpoint of the older Tübingen School (q.v.), in which he had been brought up, may be seen from his first published writing, a review of Kaiser's *Biblische Theologie* in 1817, which condemned rationalistic caprice in the treatment of the Old Testament. After a short employment as tutor in the Tübingen seminary during the same year, he was named professor in the lower seminary which had grown out of his old school at Blaubeuren. The nine years of his stay here were active and happy ones. Though his work was mainly philological and historical, he showed his interest in the philosophical and theological movements of the time. The doctrines of Schleiermacher received his attention, and found an echo in his three-volume work *Symbolik und Mythologie* (Stuttgart, 1824–25). In this book, remarkable for its time, he indicated his future course in the phrase,

1. Baur's Early Life and Activity.

"Without philosophy, history seems to me dumb and dead." The attention it attracted won Baur a place in the theological faculty of Tübingen on its reorganization (1826) after the death of his old teacher Bengel. His impressive and inspiring personality at once drew the young men to him, and his influence in the faculty was contested only by Dr. Steudel, the sole survivor of the old school body.

2. Baur's Relation to Schleiermacher and Hegel.

The fact that in the course of his further intellectual development Baur gradually came into conflict with the theology of Schleiermacher may be partly explained by the difference in the mental constitutions of the two men. There was no trace in Baur's method of the fusion of sentiment and reason which characterized the other; only the intellectual side was allowed to be heard. His strong point was his faculty of conceiving historical phenomena objectively, amid the surroundings and from the standpoint of their age. His relation to the philosophy of Hegel is somewhat difficult to determine exactly; but it may be safely asserted that his fundamental views on the essence of religion and the course of history were taken from the Hegelian system. The transition from Schleiermacher to Hegel was a gradual process which took place between 1826 and 1835, in the nine years which have been called the period of preparation. It is probable that at first Baur was unconscious of its extent, and it was not until he applied the Hegelian principles to the canon that they brought him into sharp conflict with traditional orthodoxy. His *Symbolik* was logically followed by his works on Manicheanism and Gnosticism (Tübingen, 1831 and 1832)—phenomena lying on the border between theology and philosophy, between Christianity and paganism. In his tractate on the opposition between Roman Catholicism and Protestantism, in answer to Möhler (Tübingen, 1834), Hegelian terminology begins to appear distinctly, though the foundation still rests on Schleiermacher. The influence of the Hegelian system on Baur was a very fructifying one. No department of history had suffered more from the leveling tendency of rationalism than the history of dogma. Since Hegel had taught the application of the iron rule of development to the phenomena of the intellectual life as well as to other phenomena, he pointed the way to a profounder understanding of the beliefs which appeared frequently so haphazard and so arbitrary, to a knowledge of laws which prevailed over individual will. Thus, when Baur went on from the philosophy of religion to Christian dogma, and in that to the most important parts (the Atonement, Tübingen, 1838, the Trinity and the Incarnation, 1841–43), he became a pioneer of the history of dogma in the modern sense. Even though the Hegelian categories proved a bed of Procrustes for Christian dogmas, and though the understanding of these suffered from the defects of the Hegelian conception of religion, the impulse had none the less been given to a profounder study. More recent historians of dogma have felt themselves entitled to correct Baur's views, as set forth in the above-mentioned works, in almost every point; but these views had won him, by the end of this first period, a prominent place in the ranks of those who were trying to strike out new lines in the study of Christian history; and when Schleiermacher's chair at Berlin was vacant in 1834, the Prussian minister Altenstein thought for a time of appointing Baur to it.

II. The Period of Biblical Criticism: The second period, however, is the one which comes to mind when the Tübingen School is mentioned. Though certain books already named are of later date, the period may be properly begun with 1835, in which year Strauss's *Leben Jesu* drew general attention to the questions to which Baur was already inclined to turn. The application to the canon of Scripture of the Hegelian laws of historical development was peculiarly appropriate to the place in which Baur carried on his work, since the distinguishing mark of the older Tübingen School had been a Biblical supernaturalism, for which dogma was nothing more than the teachings of Scripture, arrived at by means of exegesis. He felt himself driven to a consideration of this question by the need of a settlement with the school from which he had sprung and with his own past; by his studies in the history of dogma, since the source of dogma, in the last resort, unless it is a mere collection of irresponsible opinions, is the Bible; and by his investigation of Gnosticism, which could not fail to raise the question of the canon.

In 1835 appeared (at Stuttgart and Tübingen) Baur's work on the Pastoral Epistles. According to his own account of this and of his article on the Corinthian parties (*TZT*, 1831), it was his lectures on the Epistle to the Corinthians which first opened up the vista of more far-reaching historico-critical investigation into the controversies of the apostolic age, and led him to follow out, by means of New Testament and patristic studies, his independent conception of the clash of heterogeneous elements in the apostolic and subapostolic days, their parties and tendencies, their conflicts and compromises—to demonstrate the growth of a catholic Church as nothing but the result of a previous historical process.

1. Historico-Critical Study of the New Testament.

Dealing with Schleiermacher's treatment of I Timothy, he considered the three pastoral epistles from the same historical standpoint, and defined the task of New Testament criticism by asserting that the origin of such writings (as to the authenticity of which more evidence was needed than the accepted name of an author on their face and a vague, uncertain, and late tradition) could only be explained by a complete view of the whole range of historical circumstances in which, according to definite data, they were to be placed. With this character of historic objectivity, the new criticism, which naturally could not but seem merely negative and destructive in contrast with the unfounded assumptions that it controverted, intended to meet the arbitrary subjectivity of the hypotheses which had, up to that time, played so large a part in New Testament criticism. The above statement, substantially in Baur's own words, expresses fully the guiding principle of the Tübingen School. In the name of fidelity to fact, Baur was conducting a regular siege of the fortifications which had been thrown up by his own predecessors around the Christian doctrines, when Strauss's assault upon the central bastion attracted general attention. It was not without value to him as a diversion, under cover of which he was able to pursue undisturbed for a while longer his critical work. During the next decade the Tübingen School acquired an importance which seemed to threaten the foundations of dogma from a new quarter, relentlessly contrasting the accepted image of Christ, as drawn according to the subjective Christian mind by Schleiermacher, with the results of objective historical criticism. The main part of the task seemed to be left to Baur himself; he was not so fortunate as the leaders of the old Tübingen School, who had their allies in the other theological chairs. On the other hand, he had with him a large number of young and enthusiastic disciples, such as the talented Eduard Zeller, later his son-in-law, the still bolder and braver Schwegler, Köstlin and Planck, Ritschl and Hilgenfeld, the last two the most prominent allies who came from outside of Württemberg.

Baur had begun his critical work with Paul, and the same apostle engaged the attention of the school in its later publications. Searching investigations of the Epistle to the Romans appeared in the *TZT* in 1836, and aroused alarm and opposition.

2. Applied to the Writings of Paul.

These, together with considerable material which he had published in the *Theologische Jahrbücher*, begun in 1842 by Zeller and edited from 1847 to 1857 by himself and Zeller jointly, which became the organ of the new school, he put together in 1845 (Stuttgart) into a monograph on Paul. The result reached by this part of his work was the denial of the authenticity of all the letters passing under the apostle's name, except Galatians, I and II Corinthians, and Romans, of which last also the two concluding chapters were questioned. Finally, in agreement with Schneckenburger but still more radically, the postapostolic origin of the Acts was asserted. It was not difficult to conjecture what would happen to the Gospels when they were thrown into the same crucible.

3. The Fundamental Assumption of the School.

The theory of the "objective criticism," as it developed, was that the older apostles, with their original body of disciples, were differentiated from the other Jews only by their belief that the crucified Jesus was the Messiah. All the elements of a new religion contained in his life and teaching were forgotten, or lay undeveloped in the apostles' memory, though a Stephen attempted to enforce them and sealed his testimony by his death. When Paul, by a wonderful divination, by a train of reasoning from the cross and the resurrection, rediscovered these elements of universality and freedom, the Church stood suspiciously aloof. The older apostles, indeed, with a liberality difficult to understand in the premises, accepted Paul as an equal fellow laborer and admitted his right to the mission to the Gentiles. But a section of the Church remained obstinately hostile. Paul appears, therefore, constantly prepared for combat, and when an epistle presents him in any other mood, it is *ipso facto* unauthentic. In view of these facts, it became all the more necessary for the next age to emphasize the unity of the Church; when, accordingly, there is perceived a conciliatory tone in an epistle, when it speaks much of the Church and its unity of belief, no further mark of a postapostolic origin is needed. The school believed itself able to prove from the Apocalypse, considered as a product not merely of Judaic narrowness but of positive opposition to Paulinism, and still more from the pseudo-Clementine homilies, that no accommodation took place in the apostles' lifetime.

These views, for all their possible usefulness as against an exaggerated notion in the opposite direction, still left one question unanswered—what really was the Christianity of Christ? This led inevitably to the question, burning since Strauss, of the status of the Gospels; but it was nearly ten years before Baur brought his disciples to that. In the *Jahrbuch* for 1844 he attempted to use his critical principles to disprove the authenticity of the Gospel of John. This treatment he supplemented by further investigations on the canonical gospels, and published the whole result in substantive form in 1847 (Tübingen).

4. Applied to the Gospels.

In a certain sense it was favorable to the traditional view. The order of the canon was approximately that of their composition. Matthew, in whom the Judaic tendency is strongest, would then be nearest to the source; Mark would show a tendency to accommodation and minimizing of differences; and this would show all the more clearly the Pauline tendency of Luke. The fourth Gospel, finally, was supposed to display in every feature the tendency to sink these differences in a higher unity, and to take a stand for the conflicts of the second century, Gnosticism, Montanism, and the nascent Trinitarian controversy. This work of Baur's marks the close of the great period of the school. His disciples were now ready to come to his aid. Schwegler's book on Montanism (Tübingen, 1841), Ritschl's on Luke and the Gospel of Marcion (Tübingen, 1846) and on the origin of the primitive catholic Church (Bonn, 1850), Köstlin's on the Johannine system (Berlin, 1843), were all important; but the most significant was Schwegler's on the subapostolic age (Tübingen, 1846), which attempted constructive reasoning, using the writings which had been declared unauthentic as memorials of the development of Judaism and Paulinism into what came later.

5. Developed by Schwegler.

According to Schwegler, Judaism had no need of further development; the impulse came from Paulinism, in such a way that the Judaic party decided, in order to preserve the unity of the Church (Gk. *monarchia*), to make some concessions, requiring things of similar import with those demanded by the *pseudadelphoi* of the New Testament, but more easily fulfilled by the Gentiles. If circumcision had to be abandoned, so much the more weight was laid upon baptism as the Christian equivalent; if the works of the Law were dropped, works were still required; Israel's primacy vanished, but a general aristocratic tendency could be maintained in the episcopate; Paul could not be cast out, but he could be subordinated to Peter. Schwegler then watches this development and compromise in two places, Rome and Asia Minor. In Rome he traces the succession of writings of Judaistic origin thus: first the *Shepherd* of Hermas and Hegesippus; then Justin, the Clementine Homilies, and the Apostolic Constitutions; then James, the Second Epistle of Clement, Mark, the Clementine Recognitions, and II Peter. On the Pauline side he finds the conciliatory writings to begin under Trajan with I Peter; then follow Luke and Acts; then the Pastoral Epistles and the letters of Ignatius. Montanism being in his view only an offshoot of Judaism, the Pauline victory falls in the pontificate of Victor (189-199), under whom Montanism was condemned at Rome. The Pauline party, indeed, had already made no slight concessions, in order to ward off Gnosticism—though the Gnostics and especially the Marcionites ultimately were of great service to Paulinism in securing the universality of Christianity.

He sees the process as somewhat different in Asia Minor, where the opponents of Paul rallied, not as in Rome around Peter, but around John; here the solution was the formation of a body of Christian dogma, while in Rome it had been a unity of organization with a Roman primacy. While at Rome the supposed Ebionite works are more numerous than the Pauline, it is the contrary in Asia Minor; the Apocalypse is here the single Ebionite memorial, while on the other side Galatians, Colossians, Ephesians, and the Johannine Gospel form an imposing series of steps in the development. Bold, however, and fascinating as are the combinations set forth in this work, and brilliant as is its execution, it may be pointed out (though space does not permit of illustration) that there is scarcely a theologian to-day who is disposed to accept this train of reasoning as even an approximately satisfactory solution of the problems suggested. And even in those days, the starting-point of the whole process of development still remained to be discussed. It was already obvious that without tracing it back to the person and teaching of Christ, the question of how the primitive catholic Church came into existence was insoluble. Attempts in the direction of establishing the entire critical position by showing a genetic development of the earliest organization and dogma out of the gospel of Christ himself marked a third period in the history of the Tübingen School.

III. The Period of Church History: The political upheaval of 1848 had its influence on the future of the school. The attempts made here and there to introduce its conclusions, under cover of the political movements of the time, into the general life of the Church could not fail to bring up the question whether ecclesiastical activity was possible for adherents of the school. It was answered in the negative not only by opponents; some of Baur's own disciples felt that they must either modify the scientific conclusions they had learned from him, or seek a secular calling, as Märklin, whose life was written by Strauss, had done in 1840.

1. Political Complications. It was not surprising, then, that the German governments thought twice before appointing to academic positions men whose influence was so disturbing, and that the younger generation hesitated to follow Baur further, after his most important disciple, Zeller, was obliged in 1849 to exchange a theological chair for that of philosophy at Marburg. Baur felt the isolation in which he thus began to find himself; but his temperament allowed him to hold fast longer than others to the illusion of the identity of church teaching and Hegelian speculation. He relaxed nothing of his zeal for the solution of the important problem which still remained, the establishment on a critical foundation of a positive story of the development of Christianity from its origin down through the centuries.

In 1852 Baur published a book (Leipsic) on the epochs of church history as a preliminary, containing brilliant and frequently sharp criticism of earlier historians. His own efforts in this direction began with the work *Das Christenthum und die christliche Kirche der drei ersten Jahrhunderte* (Leipsic, 1853), and was continued in *Die christliche Kirche vom Anfang des 4. bis Ausgang des 6. Jahrhunderts* (Leipsic, 1859).

2. Baur's Works on Church History. After his death appeared (Leipsic, 1861) the third part, completed by himself, *Die christliche Kirche des Mittelalters in den Hauptmomenten ihrer Entwicklung;* and two further volumes were published from his carefully prepared lecture-notes—*Kirchengeschichte des 19. Jahrhunderts*, edited by Zeller (Leipsic, 1862), and *Kirchengeschichte der neueren Zeit von der Reformation bis zum Ende des 18. Jahrhunderts*, edited by his son Ferdinand (Leipsic, 1863), thus completing the entire survey.

If there is sought in these books an answer to the question as to the real primitive Christianity which lay back of Paul and back of Ebionitism, as to the person of Christ himself, it may be put, once more substantially in Baur's own words (from the important controversial pamphlet against Uhlhorn, *Die Tübinger Schule und ihre Stellung zur Gegenwart*, Leipsic, 1859), as follows: The real inwardness of Christianity, its essential center point, may be found in what belongs to the strictly ethical content of the teaching of Jesus, in the Sermon on the Mount, the parables, and similar utterances; in his doctrine of the Kingdom of God and the conditions of membership in it, designed to place men in the right ethical relation to God.

3. His Theories and Conclusions. This is the really divine, the universally human element in it, the part of its content which is eternal and absolute. What raises Christianity above all other religions is nothing but the purely ethical character of its acts, teachings, and requirements. If this is the essential content of the consciousness of Jesus, it is one of the two factors which compose his personality; it must have a corresponding form, in order to enter, in the way of historical development, into the general consciousness of humanity; and this form is the Jewish conception of the Messiah, the point of contact between the mind of Jesus and the world that was to believe in him, the basis on which alone a religious community destined to broaden into a Church could be built. We can, therefore, have no clear and definite conception of the personality of Jesus if we do not distinguish these two sides of it and consider them, so to speak, under the aspect of an antinomy, of a process which develops itself gradually.

If we try to get at the heart of Baur's whole view of the subject, stripping his presentation of its somewhat pathetic enthusiasm, it will appear not so very different from Kant's expression, that the faith of pure reason came in with Christ, indeed, but was so overlaid in the subsequent history that if the question were asked which was the best period in the entire course of church history, it might be unhesitatingly answered by the choice of the present, in which a nearer approach than ever before is made to pure religious doctrine. As long as Baur had gone no further into the really primitive essential import of Christianity than to consider the Pauline dogmatics as representing it, the development of the Church could perfectly well seem to him to have proceeded in a wholly rational manner. The dogmatic and ecclesiastical decisions of the early ages could, in their context, appear "reasonable," and Baur himself, in contrast with a writer like Gottfried Arnold or with the unhistoric rationalism, almost an orthodox historian, always in harmony with the course of events as it proceeded. Not only Athanasius and Augustine, but Gregory VII and Innocent III had full justice at his hands. But this involved an equally tolerant acknowledgment of the claims of the nineteenth century. If the humanitarianism of Goethe and Schiller seemed better adapted to the needs of educated men in this age than the Church in its older form, here also the living must take precedence; and suddenly the place of the old Church was taken by a broad "communion" in which all the heroes of the intellect, even the most modern, took their place as saints. But when the question came to be asked what this prevalent humanism had in common with ancient Christianity, it became apparent that the whole long process of development was really a totally unnecessary *détour*, whose purpose it was difficult to discover. It could scarcely be denied that a historical method which saw the essence of Christianity in ethics exclusively, which knew nothing of the need of redemption, and which was unable to give any positive account of the person of Christ, was one in which the Hegelian conception of development practically disappeared. Yet the distinguishing mark of the school of Baur had been the application of this very conception to Christian history, especially that of the primitive age—the attempt to show the course of history as rational and necessary; and thus, in the person of its head, the Tübingen School deserted the fundamental principle which in its palmy days it had sought to enforce. It was, then, not surprising that uncertainty showed itself among the members of the school on the question of the Gospels. The less a definite tendency could be proved in the synoptics, the more they were shown to offer at least a substratum of purely historical matter, so much the more pressing became the question how the school's view of history could be reconciled with the actual course of events. When the attempt to construct the latter *a priori* failed, an advantage was given to the "literary-historical" method with which Hilgenfeld undertook to replace the criticism of tendency. In his *Historisch-kritische Einleitung in das neue Testament* (Leipsic, 1875) the Tübingen views were modified in a large number of points. Thus the results supposed to have been attained by the "objective criticism" of Baur were called in question by his own fellow workers; and when he died, it is hardly too much to say that his school, at least in the narrower sense, died with him.

4. Their Weakness and Decline.

(J. HAUSSLEITER.)

BIBLIOGRAPHY: Two of Ferdinand Christian Baur's books are accessible in English translation: *Paul, the Apostle of Jesus Christ*, 2 vols., London, 1873–75; *The Church History of the First Three Centuries*, 2 vols., ib. 1878–79. Consult: A. B. Bruce, *F. C. Baur and his Theory of the Origin of Christianity*, New York, 1886; *Worte der Erinnerung an Ferdinand Christian Baur*, Tübingen, 1861; H. Beckh, *Die Tübinger historische Schule, kritisch beleuchtet*, in *ZPK*, xlviii (1864), 1–57, 69–95; C. Weizsäcker, *Ferdinand Christian von Baur. Rede zur akademischen Feier seines 100. Geburtstages*, Stuttgart, 1892; O. Pfleiderer, *Zu F. C. Baur's Gedächtniss*, in *Protestantische Kirchenzeitung*, 1892, No. 25; R. W. Mackay, *The Tübingen School, and its Antecedents*, London, 1863; S. Berger, *F. C. Baur, Les Origines de l'école de Tubingue et ses principes*, Strasburg, 1867; C. H. Toy, *The Tübingen Historical School*, in *BQR*, iii (1869), 210 sqq. Works on N. T. Introduction usually discuss the Tübingen School, as do those on the church history of the nineteenth century.

BAUR, GUSTAV ADOLF LUDWIG: Lutheran; b. at Hammelbach (17 m. n.e. of Heidelberg), in the Odenwald, June 14, 1816; d. at Leipsic May 22, 1889. He studied at Giessen, where he became docent in 1841, professor extraordinary, 1847, ordinary, 1849; he became pastor at Hamburg, 1861, and professor of practical theology at Leipsic, 1870. He was a member of the commission for revising Luther's translation of the Bible. Besides numerous sermons he issued *Erklärung des Propheten Amos* (Giessen, 1847); *Grundzüge der Homiletik* (1848); *Geschichte der alttestamentlichen Weissagung* (first part, 1861); *Boëtius und Dante* (Leipsic, 1874); *Grundzüge der Erziehungslehre* (4th ed., Giessen, 1887); he wrote the greater part of the first volume of Schmid's *Geschichte der Erziehung* (Stuttgart, 1884), and *Die christliche Erziehung in ihrem Verhältnisse zum Judenthum und zur antiken Welt* (2 vols., 1892).

BIBLIOGRAPHY: G. A. Baur, *Trauerfeier bei dem Begräbniss G. A. L. Baurs*, Leipsic, 1889.

BAUSLIN, DAVID HENRY: Lutheran; b. at Winchester, Va., Jan. 21, 1854. He studied at Wittenberg College (B.A., 1876) and Theological Seminary, Springfield, O. (1878), and held pastorates at Tippecanoe City, O. (1878–81), Bucyrus, O. (1881–88), Second Lutheran Church, Springfield, O. (1888–93), and Trinity Church, Canton, O. (1893–96). In 1896 he was appointed professor of historical and practical theology in the Wittenberg Theological Seminary. He has been for several years a member of the "common service" committee for the General Synod of the Lutheran Church, and was president of the General Synod of the Evangelical Lutheran Church in the United States 1905–07. He has written *Is the Ministry an Attractive Vocation?* (Philadelphia, 1901), and has been editor of *The Lutheran World* since 1901.

BAUSMAN, BENJAMIN: Reformed (German); b. at Lancaster, Pa., Jan. 28, 1824. He was educated at Marshall College (B.A., 1851) and the Theological Seminary, Mercersburg, Pa. (1852). He was ordained to the Reformed ministry in 1853, and held successive pastorates at Lewisburg, Pa. (1853–61), Chambersburg, Pa. (1861–63), First Reformed Church, Reading, Pa. (1863–73), and St. Paul's Reformed Church, Reading, which he founded in 1873. He was president of the General Synod of the Reformed Church at Baltimore in 1884. He was editor of *The Reformed Messenger* in 1858 and of *The Guardian* from 1867 to 1882. In the year 1867 he founded *Der reformierte Hausfreund*, of which he is still the editor. He has written *Sinai and Zion* (Philadelphia, 1860); *Wayside Gleanings in Europe* (Reading, 1878); *Bible Characters* (1893); and *Precept and Practice* (Philadelphia, 1901); in addition to editing Harbaugh's *Harfe*, a collection of poems in Pennsylvania Dutch (Reading, 1870).

BAUSSET, bō″sê′, **LOUIS FRANÇOIS DE:** Cardinal; b. at Pondicherry Dec. 14, 1748; d. at Paris June 21, 1824. He studied in the Seminary of St. Sulpice; was appointed Bishop of Alais, 1784; emigrated in 1791, but returned in 1792 to Paris, and supported himself, after a short imprisonment, by literary labor. In 1806 he was made canon of St. Denys, and in 1815, after the second return of Louis XVIII, director of the council of the University of Paris, peer of France, and cardinal 1817 He wrote the *Histoire de Fénelon* (3 vols., Paris, 1808) and *Histoire de Bossuet* (4 vols., Versailles, 1814).

BAUTAIN, bō″tan′, **LOUIS EUGÈNE MARIE:** French philosopher; b. at Paris Feb. 17, 1796; d. at Viroflay, near Versailles, Oct. 15, 1867. He became professor of philosophy at Strasburg in 1819. He was a pupil of Cousin and a student of German philosophy, and, his teaching not being acceptable to the church authorities, he was suspended in 1822. He modified his views and took holy orders in 1828, and resumed teaching. In 1834 he again fell into difficulty with the Bishop of Strasburg because of his teachings concerning the relation of reason and faith; in 1838 he went to Rome and sought in vain to have his views approved there. In 1840 he submitted, became vicar-general of Paris in 1849, and professor at the Sorbonne in 1853. He held that the human reason can not prove such facts as the existence of God and the immortality of the soul, and that the truths of religion are communicated purely by divine revelation. His most important works were: *Philosophie du Christianisme* (2 vols., Strasburg, 1835); *Psychologie expérimentale* (2 vols., 1839; new ed., with title *Esprit humain et ses facultés*, Paris, 1859); *Philosophie morale* (2 vols., Paris, 1842); *La morale de l'Évangile comparée aux divers systèmes de morale* (1855). He had much repute as an orator and published an *Étude sur l'art de parler en public* (1856; Eng. transl., *The Art of Extempore Speaking*, London, 1858).

Bibliography: E. de Régny, *L'Abbé Bautain*, Paris, 1884.

BAUTZ, JOSEF: Roman Catholic; b. at Keeken (near Cleves) Nov. 11, 1843. He was educated at Münster, where he became privat-docent of apologetics and dogmatics in 1877, being promoted to the rank of associate professor in 1892. He has written *Die Lehre vom Auferstehungsleibe* (Paderborn, 1877); *Der Himmel, spekulativ dargestellt* (Mainz, 1881); *Die Hölle, im Anschluss an die Scholastik* (1882); *Das Fegfeuer Im Anschluss an die Scholastik* (1883); *Weltgericht und Weltende. Im Anschluss an die Scholastik* (1886); *Grundzüge der christlichen Apologetik* (1887); and *Grundzüge der katholischen Dogmatik* (4 vols., 1888–93).

BAVARIA: A kingdom in the southern part of the German Empire, and, next to Prussia, the largest of the states of the Empire; area, 29,282 square miles; population (1900), 6,176,057, of whom 4,357,133 (70.5 per cent.) are Roman Catholics; 1,749,206 (28.3 per cent.) Protestants; 5,430 Old Catholics; 3,170 Mennonites; 54,928 (.9 per cent.) Jews; and 4,142 of various faiths.

The division of the chief confessions is based in great part on the historic conditions prevailing in 1624 and 1648, although the development of the cities has been the cause of many changes, the proportion of Protestants having increased in Munich and that of the Roman Catholics in Nuremberg. The old Bavarian circles of Upper and Lower Bavaria, as well as the Upper Palatinate, have always been essentially Roman Catholic. Upper Bavaria received its first Protestant citizens in the early part of the nineteenth century, but in consequence of the rapid growth of Munich in recent years the Protestants of that city alone numbered 78,000 in 1900. Six pastorates and six immovable vicariates are also contained in the district, and seven small churches have been built in market-towns and villages. Since the sixteenth century Lower Bavaria has possessed the Protestant enclave of Ortenburg with certain neighboring places, while more recently communities have been established in the larger cities, especially Passau. The Upper Palatinate was not completely converted to Roman Catholicism in 1622–28, since the duchy of Sulzbach and the imperial city of Regensburg retained congregations of both confessions, who used the same churches; but with the increase in population the proportion of Protestants steadily declined. The district now has four deaneries with forty-eight pastorates. In the three old Bavarian districts provision is made for the Protestant Diaspora by itinerant preachers, four of whom work in Upper Bavaria

Protestantism in Bavaria.

and two in Lower Bavaria and the Upper Palatinate combined. Since 1805 Swabia has belonged in great part to Bavaria. It consisted originally of a group of territories belonging to free cities, the clergy, and knights of the empire. Only the first category was predominantly Protestant, and even here Roman Catholicism has gained steadily. Swabia contains the following Protestant deaneries: Augsburg, Ebermergen, Kempten (including Lindau and Kaufbeuren), Leipheim, Memmingen, Nördlingen, and Oettingen.

Frankish North Bavaria is composed, on the one hand, of the episcopal territories of the bishoprics of Eichstätt, Bamberg, Würzburg, and a portion of the electorate of Mainz, and, on the other, of the Protestant principalities of Ansbach and Baireuth, Nuremberg, Rothenburg, and other free cities, and enclaves of the orders. This entire region is strongly Roman Catholic, although Lower Franconia has a considerable number of Protestant communities (116 pastorates, exclusive of Würzburg, Schweinfurt, and Aschaffenburg). In the larger section of Bavaria the historical divisions between Protestant and Roman Catholic, at least in the smaller towns, are still maintained, but in the minor portion, the Rhine Palatinate, there are few political communities which do not have a considerable minority of adherents of one or the other creed. In Speyer the proportions are almost equal, Roman Catholics numbering about 9,000 and the Protestants 8,000.

The legal position of the Protestant Church in Bavaria is regulated by an edict of Sept. 8, 1809, while its foreign relations are governed by the constitution of 1818. Both Protestantism and Roman Catholicism are officially recognized, and controversies seldom arise between the two, except in regard to the creed in which children shall be brought up, methods of conversion, particularly in the Evangelical Diaspora, and the use of burial-grounds in Roman Catholic communities. In 1824 the official designation of the Protestants was declared to be "Protestant Church."

The Reformed Church in the Palatinate first regained official recognition together with the Lutherans at the general consistory at Worms in 1815, and the Bavarian government created a consistory at Speyer on Dec. 15, 1818, for the "Protestant Churches of the Palatinate," a presbyterial and synodical constitution being introduced at the same time. In 1848 the Protestant Church of the Palatinate and the consistory of Speyer were placed directly under the jurisdiction of the ministry of state. The attempt to create a more definite confessional status led, in the sixth decade of the last century, to a victorious agitation on the part of the liberal element. Since 1879 the presbyteries have had the right to propose candidates for vacant pastorates. In Bavaria proper diocesan synods are held annually, and general synods every four years.

There are few Protestants in Bavaria, except those who belong to the Evangelical Lutheran Church, nor are the professed adherents of sects numerous. A distinct organization was granted the Reformed in Bavaria proper in 1853, although they are still under the control of the Supreme Consistory. The Greek Church was recognized in 1826, but the Anglican Church is officially ignored like the Mennonites. The last-named have six communities in the Palatinate and four in Bavaria proper. Until 1887 the Old Catholics were reckoned as Roman Catholics, but are now declared to be a separate body, though full recognition has not been granted them.

Roman Catholicism in Bavaria.

The Roman Catholic Church in Bavaria is highly organized and extremely active, while its wealth and political influence are constantly increasing. The kingdom is divided into two archdioceses with eight dioceses. The archdiocese of Munich-Freising comprises the suffragan dioceses of Augsburg, Passau, and Regensburg; and the archdiocese of Bamberg includes the dioceses of Eichstätt, Würzburg, and Speyer. The education of the clergy, in agreement with the concordat of 1817, is entrusted to the bishops. The development of orders has been very rapid, especially in the sisterhoods for the education and the care of the sick. The number of cloisters has also increased rapidly, with a corresponding gain in real estate, and this development is aided by the generous gifts and foundations of the Roman Catholic population, the property of the 8,600 institutions being valued at more than 150,000,000 marks; while that of the 1,800 Protestant institutions is worth only 19,600,000 marks. The Roman Catholic clergy in Bavaria number some 4,900, or a proportion of one to 816 of the laity, while the Protestants have but about 1,300 clergymen, or one to 1,200 laymen.

WILHELM GOETZ.

BIBLIOGRAPHY: V. A. Winter, *Geschichte der Schicksale der evangelischen Lehre in und durch Bayern*, 2 vols., Munich, 1809–10; E. F. H. Medicus, *Geschichte der evangelischen Kirche im Königreich Bayern*, Erlangen, 1863; J. M. Mayer, *Geschichte Bayerns*, Ratisbon, 1874; J. Hergenröther, *Handbuch der Kirchengeschichte*, 3 vols., Freiburg, 1876–80 (literature of the subject is given, iii, 183); S. Riezler, *Geschichte Bayerns*, 4 vols., Gotha, 1878–99; Wand, *Handbuch der Verfassung und Verwaltung der protestantisch-ev.-christlichen Kirche der Pfalz*, 1880; *Beiträge zur Statistik des Königreichs Bayern*, Munich, 1892; *Statistische Mitteilungen aus den deutschen evangelischen Landeskirchen*, Stuttgart, 1880–96.

BAVARIANS, CONVERSION OF THE: The origin of the race later known as the Bavarians is uncertain. The older hypothesis that they came of Celtic stock is now generally abandoned. For a time it was thought that they were a conglomerate of the remains of several tribes belonging to the Gothic family; but the view put forward by Zeuss (*Die Herkunft der Bayern*, Munich, 1857) that they are to be identified with the Marcomanni is now almost universally accepted, and has strong support in the facts.

The Marcomanni are first mentioned by Cæsar (*Bel. Gal.*, i, 51). In his time they lived on the upper Main. Tacitus knows of them as inhabiting what is now Bohemia (*Germ.*, xlii; cf. *Annal.*, ii, 26 sqq.). Here they maintained their position for centuries, and here they took the name of Baiowarii or Baioarii. During this period, Christianity found an entrance among them. Paulinus, in his life of Ambrose (xxxvi), tells of a queen of the Marcomanni named Fritigil who was converted by a wandering Italian Christian, and asked Ambrose for written instructions in the faith, which he gave *in modum catechismi*. The account goes on to say that she thereupon came to Milan, but found the bishop dead. As Ambrose died Apr. 4, 397, she must have crossed the Alps in the summer of that year. If the queen was a Christian, it is hardly likely that her religion would have been unknown to her people. That Arianism also reached the Marcomanni through Gothic influences is not improbable. However that may be, the bulk of the people were pagan when they settled in 488 on the strip of territory granted them by the Romans between the Lech and the Enns.

First Acquaintance with Christianity.

The name of Bavarians is first applied in the Frankish list of tribes belonging to the first quarter of the sixth century. The territory which they occupied was no desolate wilderness. In the valleys and around the lakes there was a thin agricultural population which held to the Latin tongue and doubtless also to the Christian faith. Not all the cities were destroyed; Juvavum and Lauriacum lay in ruins; but neither Castra Batava nor Castra Regina was without inhabitants, and here also Christianity undoubtedly held its own with the Romanic population. Christians and heathens thus living as neighbors, a starting-point was afforded for missionary efforts. The ecclesiastical organization had, it is true, been broken up; only in southern Bavaria a bishopric founded in Roman times maintained its existence at Seben, and the diocese of Augsburg stretched over a part of the Bavarian territory. Under these circumstances the fact was of decisive importance that the Bavarians no sooner occupied their new home than they came into a position of dependence on the Frankish kingdom. The first ducal family, that of the Agilulfings, was of Frankish origin and professed Christianity, and the first outsiders who labored for the spread of the faith in Bavaria came from the Frankish kingdom. Eustasius of Luxeuil (q.v.), the successor of Columban, worked there, and left missionaries trained by him when he returned to Burgundy. Later, Rupert, bishop of Worms, found a wide field here for his activity; Emmeram and Corbinian (qq.v.) were Franks. Side by side with them there seem to have been at a very early period some Scoto-Irish monks, but there is no record of their labors. The result of the combined operation of these imperfectly known factors was the acceptance of Christianity by the Bavarian race as a whole, which was completed in the course of the seventh century. It is a remarkable fact that it was not accompanied by the organization of a local episcopate; as far as can be told the direction of ecclesiastical affairs was in the hands of the dukes; it is Theodo who invites Rupert thither, and who treats with the pope in regard to church institutions. From this fact it would appear that the Christian profession of the dukes played a decisive part in the conversion of the people at large. The existence of the Church without diocesan bishops was made possible by the fact that the wandering monks and missionaries were frequently in episcopal orders, and could thus perform the strictly episcopal functions.

Labors of Missionaries.

The above-mentioned Duke Theodo, acting in concert with the pope, endeavored to introduce a more regular organization. With this end in view, he visited Rome in 716, and had an agreement with Pope Gregory II as to the measures to be taken. At least four dioceses were to be founded corresponding to the divisions of the secular jurisdiction. The bishop of the most important place was to be set as metropolitan at the head of the Bavarian Church, the pope reserving the right to consecrate him, and if necessary to name an Italian. Order was to be brought into the ecclesiastical affairs by a general visitation; the Roman use was to be taken as the model in liturgical matters. But these plans were never carried into execution, apparently by reason of the death of Theodo. The organization of the Bavarian bishoprics, involving the termination of the missionary period, was only accomplished by Boniface (q.v.), who paid a short visit to the country in 719, and returned in 735 or 736 to make a formal visitation by virtue of what was practically a metropolitan jurisdiction over the whole of Germany, for the purpose of acquiring full information as to the prevailing conditions. His definite organizing work is introduced by a brief (738 or 739) from Gregory III to the bishops of Bavaria and Alemannia, enjoining them to receive Boniface with fitting honors as his representative, and to attend a synod to be held by him. In 739 Boniface undertook the settlement of diocesan boundaries and institutions, and provided three of the four bishoprics of Bavaria with bishops consecrated by himself—Erembrecht, brother of Corbinian, at Freising, Gavibald at Regensburg, and John, a newcomer from England, at Salzburg—while Vivilo, who had been consecrated by the pope, remained at Passau. Gregory III confirmed these arrangements on Oct. 29, and the subordinate divisions of archdeaconries and parishes were soon organized. The decisions of the Synod of Reisbach (799) show the parochial system in full operation. (A. Hauck.)

Organization of Bishoprics.

Bibliography: Hauck, *KD*, vol. i; S. Riezler, *Geschichte Bayerns*, vol. i, Gotha, 1873; Rettberg, *KD*, 2 vols.; Friedrich, *KD*, 2 vols.

BAVINCK, HERMAN: Dutch Reformed; b. at Hoogeveen (35 m. s. of Groningen), Holland, Dec. 13, 1854. He was educated at the gymnasium of Zwolle, the theological seminary of the Reformed Church at Kampen, and the University of Leyden (D.D., 1880); he was then pastor at Franeker, Friesland (1881–82), and professor of dogmatic theology in the theological seminary at Kampen (1882–1903). Since 1903 he has been professor of dogmatics and apologetics at the Free University, Amsterdam. In theology he adheres to the principles of the Heidelberg Confession and the canons of the Synod of Dort. He has written *De Ethiek van H. Zwingli* (Kampen, 1880); *De*

Wetenschap der heilige Godgeleerdheid (1883); *De Theologie van Prof. Dr D. Chantepie de la Saussaye* (Leyden, 1884); *De Katholiciteit van Christendom en Kerk* (Kampen, 1888); *De algemeene Genade* (1894); *Gereformeerde Dogmatiek* (4 vols., 1895–1901); *Beginselen der Psychologie* (1897); *De Offerande des Lofs* (The Hague, 1901); *De Lebenheid des Geloofs* (Kampen, 1901); *Hedendaagsche Moraal* (1902); *Roeping en Wedergeboorte* (1902); *Godsdienst en Godgeleerdheid* (Wageningen, 1902); *Christelijke Wetenschap* (Kampen, 1904); *Christelijke Wereldbeschouwing* (1904); *Pædagogische Beginselen* (1904); and *Bilderdijk als Denker en Dichter* (1906).

BAXTER, RICHARD: One of the greatest of English theologians; b. at Rowton (42 m. n.e. of Shrewsbury), Shropshire, Nov. 12, 1615; d. in London Dec. 8, 1691. Though without a university education, and always sickly, he acquired great learning. In 1633 he had a brief experience of court life at Whitehall (London), but turned from the court in disgust and studied theology. In 1638 he was ordained by the bishop of Worcester and preached in various places till 1641, when he began his ministry at Kidderminster (18 m. s.w. of Birmingham), as "teacher." There he labored with wonderful success so that the place was utterly transformed. When the Civil War broke out (1642) he retired temporarily to Gloucester and then to Coventry because he sided with the parliament, while all in and about Kidderminster sided with the king. He was, however, no blind partizan and boldly spoke out for moderation and fairness. After acting as an army chaplain he separated from the army, partly on account of illness, and returned to Kidderminster.

Ministry at Kidderminster.

In the spring of 1660 he left Kidderminster and went to London. He preached before the House of Commons at St. Margaret's, Westminster, Apr. 30, 1660, and before the lord mayor and aldermen at St. Paul's, May 10, and was among those to give Charles II welcome to his kingdom. Charles made him one of his chaplains and offered him the bishopric of Hereford, which he declined. He was a leader on the Non-conformist side in the Savoy Conference (1661) and presented a revision of the Prayer-book which could be used by the Non-conformists. He also preached frequently in different pulpits. Seeing how things were going, he desired permission to return to Kidderminster as curate, but was refused. On May 16, 1662, three days before the Act of Uniformity was passed, he took formal farewell of the Church of England and retired to Acton, a west suburb of London. From this time on he had no regular charge and until the accession of William and Mary in 1688 he suffered, like other Non-conformist preachers, from repressive laws often rigorously and harshly enforced. On Sept. 10, 1662, he married Margaret, daughter of Francis Charlton, of Shropshire, twenty-four years his junior, who possessed wealth and social position, and made him a devoted helpmeet, cheerfully going with him into exile and prison and spending her money lavishly in the relief of their less fortunate fellow sufferers. She died June 14, 1681, and Baxter has perpetuated her memory in a singularly artless but engaging memoir (London, 1681).

In London.

During all these years on the verge of trouble because he persisted in preaching, he was actually imprisoned only twice, once for a short period, and again from Feb. 28, 1685, to Nov. 24, 1686. The judge who condemned him the second time was George Jeffreys, who treated him with characteristic brutality. The charge was that in his *Paraphrase of the New Testament* (1685) Baxter had libeled the Church of England. But insult, heavy and indeed ruinous fines, enforced wanderings, anxiety as to personal safety, and imprisonment had no power to daunt Baxter's spirit. He preached constantly to great multitudes, and addressed through his writings a still vaster throng. The Toleration Act of 1688 ended his sufferings and he died in peace.

Imprisonment.

Baxter was one of the most voluminous of English authors, and one of the best. But there is no complete edition of his 168 treatises, only of his practical works. A few of his works are in verse (*Poetical Fragments*, reprinted, London, 1821), though he has small claim to be called a poet, and one familiar hymn ("Lord, it belongs not to my care") has been manufactured out of a longer one of his. The after-world knows him by reputation as the author of *The Reformed Pastor* (1656), a treatise on pastoral theology still usable; *A Call to the Unconverted to turn and live and accept of mercy while mercy may be had, as even they would find mercy in the day of their extremity: from the Living God* (1657), uttered as a dying man to dying men and impressive to-day; but chiefly because of *The Saints' Everlasting Rest or a treatise of the blessed state of the Saints in their enjoyment of God in glory. Wherein is shewed its excellency and certainty; the misery of those that lose it, the way to attain it, and assurance of it; and how to live in the continual delightful foretaste of it, by the help of meditation. Written by the author for his own use, in the time of his languishing, when God took him off from all publike imployment; and afterwards preached in his weekly lecture* (1650). The "*Saints' Rest*" gained a reputation it has never lost, but the 648 pages of the original edition have proved too many for posterity and the work is read nowadays, if at all, only in an abridgment of an abridgment. The best brief characterization of this faithful, fearless, and gifted religious teacher is on his monument at Kidderminster, erected by Churchmen and Non-conformists, and unveiled July 28, 1875: "Between the years 1641 and 1660 this town was the scene of the labours of Richard Baxter, renowned equally for his Christian learning and his pastoral fidelity. In a stormy and divided age he advocated unity and comprehension, pointing the way to everlasting rest." In many respects Baxter was a modern man.

Writings.

Baxter's theology was set forth most elaborately in his Latin *Methodus theologiæ Christianæ* (London,

His Theology.

1681); the *Christian Directory* (1673) contains the practical part of his system; and *Catholic Theology* (1675) is an English exposition. His theology made Baxter very unpopular among his contemporaries and caused a split among the Dissenters of the eighteenth century. As summarized by Thomas W. Jenkyn, it differed from the Calvinism of Baxter's day on four points: (1) The atonement of Christ did not consist in his suffering the *identical* but the *equivalent* punishment (i.e., one which would have the same effect in moral government) as that deserved by mankind because of offended law. Christ died for sins, not persons. While the benefits of substitutionary atonement are accessible and available to all men for their salvation, they have in the divine appointment a special reference to the subjects of personal election. (2) The elect were a certain fixed number determined by the decree without any reference to their faith as the ground of their election; which decree contemplates no reprobation but rather the redemption of all who will accept Christ as their Savior. (3) What is imputed to the sinner in the work of justification is not the righteousness of Christ but the faith of the sinner himself in the righteousness of Christ. (4) Every sinner has a distinct agency of his own to exert in the process of his conversion. The Baxterian theory, with modifications, was adopted by many later Presbyterians and Congregationalists in England, Scotland, and America (Isaac Watts, Philip Doddridge, and many others).

BIBLIOGRAPHY: Baxter's *Practical Works* were collected by W Orme and published in 23 vols., London, 1830; vol. i contains Orme's *Life and Times of Richard Baxter*, published separately in 2 vols., the same year; a table of the contents of this edition of Baxter's works is found in Darling's *Cyclopædia Bibliographica*, pp. 205–208, London, 1854; the *Practical Works* appeared also in 4 vols., ib. 1847; and *Select Practical Writings*, ed. L. Bacon, 2 vols., New Haven, 1844. An *Annotated List of the Writings of R. Baxter* is appended to the ed. of *What Must we do to be Saved?* by A. B. Grosart, London, 1868. The chief source for a life is the autobiographical material left to M. Sylvester, who published it as *Reliquiæ Baxterianæ*, London, 1696, abridged by E. Calamy, 1702, this enlarged and republished in 2 vols., 1713. A notable paper on Baxter by Sir James Stephen, originally published in the *Edinburgh Review*, is to be found in his *Essays*, vol. ii, London, 1860. Among the biographies may be mentioned A. B. Grosart, *Representative Nonconformists, II, Richard Baxter*, ib. 1879; G. D. Boyle, *Men Worth Remembering, Richard Baxter*, ib. 1883; J. Stalker, *Richard Baxter*, Edinburgh, 1883; *DNB*, iii, 429–437; J. H. Davies, *Life of Richard Baxter*, London, 1887. The account of his trial is given by Macaulay in his *History of England*, vol. ii. Consult also Baxter's *Making Light of Christ, with an Essay on his Life, Ministry and Theology*, by T. W. Jenkyn, London, 1846.

BAYLE, bêl, **PIERRE**: French Protestant; b. at Carla (11 m. w. of Pamiers), department of Ariège, Nov. 18, 1647; d. at Rotterdam Dec. 28, 1706. He was the son of a Calvinist clergyman, and, in 1666, began his studies at the Protestant Academy at Puylaurens, whence he went to the University of Toulouse in 1669. Not satisfied with the objections of the Reformed against the dogma of a divinely appointed judge in matters of faith, he became a Roman Catholic. He spent eighteen months at the Jesuits' College in Toulouse, and then returned to Protestantism and went to Geneva (1670), where, living as a tutor in private families, he studied theology as well as the Cartesian philosophy. His friendship with Jacques Basnage and Minutoli began there. Later he accompanied pupils to Rouen and in 1675 to Paris. Then he spent several years as a lecturer on philosophy at Sédan; when that academy was closed by order of the king (1681), he accepted an appointment as lecturer on philosophy at the "École illustre" of Rotterdam. In this refuge of liberty, Bayle wrote most of his works. The revocation of the Edict of Nantes raised his indignation, and several of the best Protestant works called forth by that disgraceful piece of policy proceeded from the pen of Bayle. The conclusion at which he arrives by his close reasoning is: that matters of belief should be outside the sphere of the State as such—a dangerous principle for Catholicism, and the book was at once put on the Index. Even among Protestants Bayle had adversaries. Jurieu, his jealous and violent opponent at Rotterdam, considered toleration equal to indifference, and reproached Bayle with dangerous skepticism, which made his position very difficult. He tried for an appointment in Berlin. But the realization of this wish was prevented by the death of the great Elector Frederick William. Jurieu continued his attacks and even went so far as to represent Bayle as the head of a party working into the hands of Louis XIV by aiming at a split between the princes allied against France. William III gave credence to this and influenced the magistrate of Rotterdam to remove Bayle from his position (1693). From that time he lived for his literary work, chiefly bearing on philosophy and the history of literature. His *Dictionnaire historique et critique* [(2 vols. in three parts Rotterdam, 1697; 2d ed., 3 vols., 1702; 11th ed., 16 vols., Paris, 1820–24; Eng. transl., 5 vols., London, 1734–38)] was most favorably received by all the learned men of Europe, though it brought on him a revival of the reproach of skepticism, of want of respect for the Holy Scriptures, even of Manicheism. Called to justify himself before a commission appointed by the presbytery of Rotterdam, he was treated with great moderation, and consented to change some of the offensive articles, which appeared in their new form in the second edition of his *Dictionnaire*. Accusations against him came up again from time to time, and he tried to refute them in minor philosophical works. Besides the *Dictionnaire* his works include: *Lettres à M. L. D. A. C., docteur en Sorbonne, où il est prouvé que les comètes ne sont point le présage d'aucun malheur* (Cologne, 1682); *Critique générale de l'Histoire du Calvinisme de M. Maimbourg* (Amsterdam, 1682); *Recueil de quelques pièces concernant la philosophie de M. Descartes* (Amsterdam, 1684); *Nouvelles de la République des lettres* (1684–1687); *Ce que c'est que la France toute catholique sous le règne de Louis-le-Grand* (St. Omer, 1685); *Commentaire philosophique sur ces paroles de J. C.: "Contrains-les d'entrer"* (Amsterdam, 1686); *Réponse de l'auteur des Nouvelles de la République des lettres en faveur du P Malebranche sur les plaisirs des sens* (Rotterdam, 1686); *Avis important aux réfu-*

giés sur leur prochain retour en France (Amsterdam, 1690; 1709); *Lettres choisies avec des remarques* (Rotterdam, 1714); *Nouvelles lettres* (The Hague, 1739).

G. Bonet-Maury.

Bibliography: B. de la Monnoye (pseudonym for Du Revest), *Histoire du Mr. Bayle et ses ouvrages*, Amsterdam, 1716; P. des Maizeaux, *Vie de P. Bayle*, The Hague, 1730, reprinted from the 3d ed. of the *Dictionnaire*, Amsterdam, 1730, reproduced in the Eng. transl. of the "Dictionary," ut sup.; E. and É. Haag, *La France protestante*, ii, 60–63, 9 vols., Paris, 1846–59; L. Feuerbach, *P. Bayle, ein Beitrag zur Geschichte der Philosophie und der Menschheit*, Leipsic, 1848; J. P. Damiron, *Mémoire sur Bayle et ses doctrines*, Paris, 1850; C. A. St. Beuve, in *Lundis*, vol. ix, ib. 1852; F. Bouillier, *Histoire de la philosophie cartésienne*, ii, 476, ib. 1854; C. Lenient, *Étude sur Bayle*, ib. 1855; É. Jeanmaire, *Essai sur la critique religieuse de Bayle*, Strasburg, 1862; Voltaire, *Siècle de Louis XIV*, chap. 36; A. Deschamps, *La Genèse du scepticisme érudit chez Bayle*, Brussels, 1879; J. Denis, *Bayle et Jurieu*, Caen, 1886; P. Janet, *Histoire de la science politique dans ses rapports avec la morale*, Paris, 1887.

BAYLEY, JAMES ROOSEVELT: Roman Catholic archbishop of Baltimore; b. at Rye, N. Y., Aug. 23, 1814; d. in Newark, N. J., Oct. 3, 1877 He was a nephew of Elizabeth (Bayley) Seton (" Mother Seton "), founder of the order of Sisters of Charity in America; was graduated at Washington (Trinity) College, Hartford, Conn., 1835; rector of St. Peter's church, Harlem, New York, 1840–41; received into the Roman Catholic Church at Rome, 1842; studied in Paris and Rome, and was ordained priest in New York, 1843; was professor in St. John's College, Fordham, New York, and its acting president, 1845–46; became secretary to Bishop Hughes of New York, 1846, bishop of Newark, 1853, archbishop of Baltimore and primate of America, 1872. He published a volume of pastoral letters; *Sketch of the History of the Catholic Church on the Island of New York* (New York, 1853); *Memoirs of Simon Gabriel Bruté, First Bishop of Vincennes* (1861).

BAYLY, LEWIS: Anglican bishop; b. perhaps at Carmarthen, Wales, perhaps at Lamington (6 m. s.w. of Biggar), Scotland, year unknown; d. at Bangor, Wales, Oct. 26, 1631. He was educated at Oxford; became vicar of Evesham, Worcestershire, and in 1604, probably, rector of St. Matthew's, Friday street, London; was then chaplain to Henry Prince of Wales (d. 1612), later chaplain to King James I, who, in 1616, appointed him bishop of Bangor. He was an ardent Puritan. His fame rests on *The Practice of Piety, directing a Christian how to walk that he may please God* (date of first ed. unknown; 3d ed., London, 1613). It reached its 74th edition in 1821 and has been translated into French, German, Italian, Polish, Romansch, Welsh, and into the language of the Massachusetts Indians. It was one of the two books which John Bunyan's wife brought with her—the other one being Arthur Dent's *Plain Man's Pathway to Heaven*—and it was by reading it that Bunyan was first spiritually awakened.

Bibliography: A biographical preface by Grace Webster is prefixed to the *Practice of Piety*, London, 1842; consult also A. à Wood, *Athenæ Oxonienses*, ed. P. Bliss, ii, 525–531, 4 vols., ib. 1813–20.

BAY PSALM BOOK: A metrical translation of the Psalms, published by Stephen Daye at Cambridge, Mass., in 1640 and the first book printed in America. The work of translation was begun in 1636, the principal collaborators being Thomas Welde, Richard Mather, and John Eliot, the missionary to the Indians. The rendering, as the translators themselves recognized in their quaint preface to the book, was a crude specimen of English, and carrying to the extreme their belief in the inspiration of the Bible, they tortured their version into what they conceived to be fidelity to the original. The meter, moreover, is irregular, and the rimes are frequently ludicrous. The general spirit and form of the translation may be represented by the following rendering of Ps. xviii, 6–9:

6. " I in my streights, cal'd on the Lord,
and to my God cry'd: he did heare
from his temple my voyce, my crye,
before him came, unto his eare.

7. " Then th' earth shooke, & quak't, & moũtaines
roots mov'd, & were stird at his ire,

8. " Vp from his nostrils went a smoak,
and from his mouth devouring fire;
By it the coales inkindled were.

9. " Likewise the heavens he downe-bow'd,
And he descended, & there was
under his feet a gloomy cloud."

Of the first edition of the *Bay Psalm Book* only eleven copies are known to exist. In 1647 a second edition, better printed and with the spelling and punctuation corrected, was published either by Stephen Daye or possibly by Matthew Daye or even in England, and this edition long remained in general use among the Puritans of New England. A reprint of the first edition (71 copies) was issued privately at Cambridge in 1862.

Bibliography: R. F. Roden, *The Cambridge Press*, New York, 1906.

BDELLIUM, del'i-um (Hebr. *bedholaḥ*): One of the products of the land of Havilah, mentioned with gold and the *shoham*-stone (E. V. " onyx ") in Gen. ii, 11–12. In Num. xi, 7, manna is said to have resembled it. It was, therefore, something well known to the Hebrews, but the exact meaning is uncertain. Some have thought that it was a precious stone, perhaps the pearl; others identify it with myrrh or with musk. The most probable and generally accepted explanation is that it was the gum of a tree, much prized in antiquity and used in religious ceremonies. Pliny (*Hist. nat.*, xii, 35) describes it as transparent, waxy, fragrant, oily to the touch, and bitter; the tree was black, of the size of the olive, with leaves like the ilex, and fruit like the wild fig; he designates Bactria as its home, but states that it grew also in Arabia, India, Media, and Babylonia. It probably belonged to the balsamodendra and was allied to the myrrh.

I. Benzinger.

BEACH, HARLAN PAGE: Congregationalist; b. at South Orange, N. J., Apr. 4, 1854. He was educated at Yale College (B.A., 1878) and Andover Theological Seminary (1883). He was instructor in Phillips Andover Academy 1878-80, and was ordained in 1883. He was missionary in China for seven years, and from 1892 to 1895 was instructor and later superintendent of the School for Christian Workers, Springfield, Mass. He was appointed educational secretary of the Student Volunteer Movement for Foreign Missions in 1895, and held this position until 1906, when he was chosen professor of the theory and practise of missions in the Yale Divinity School. He has been a corporate member of the American Board of Commissioners for Foreign Missions since 1895 and of the cooperating committee of the same organization since 1906, as well as chairman of the exhibit committee and executive committee of the Ecumenical Conference in 1900, member of the Bureau of Missions Trustees since 1901, member of the executive committee of the Yale Foreign Missionary Society since 1903, member of the advisory board of Canton Christian College and trustee of the Hartford School of Religious Pedagogy since 1905. In theology he is a moderate conservative. He has written *The Cross in the Land of the Trident* (New York, 1895); *Knights of the Labarum* (1896); *New Testament Studies in Missions* (1898); *Dawn on the Hills of T'ang : or, Missions in China* (1898); *Protestant Missions in South America* (1900); *Geography and Atlas of Protestant Missions* (2 vols., 1901–03); *Two Hundred Years of Christian Activity in Yale* (New Haven, 1902); *Princely Men of the Heavenly Kingdom* (New York, 1903); and *India and Christian Opportunity* (1904).

BEARD, CHARLES: English Unitarian; b. at Higher Broughton, Manchester, July 27, 1827, son of John Relly Beard, also a well-known Unitarian minister and educator (b. 1800; d. 1876); d. at Liverpool Apr. 9, 1888. He studied at Manchester New College 1843–48, was graduated B.A. at London University 1847, and continued his studies at Berlin 1848–49; became assistant minister at Hyde Chapel, Gee Cross, Cheshire, 1850, minister 1854, minister at Renshaw Street Chapel, Liverpool, 1867 From 1864 to 1879 he edited *The Theological Review*. Besides sermons, addresses, etc., he published *Port Royal, a Contribution to the History of Religion and Literature in France* (2 vols., London, 1861); *The Reformation in its Relation to Modern Thought* (Hibbert lectures for 1883); and *Martin Luther and the Reformation in Germany until the Close of the Diet of Worms* (ed. J. F. Smith, 1889).

BEARD, RICHARD: Cumberland Presbyterian; b. in Sumner County, Tenn., Nov. 27, 1799; d. at Lebanon, Tenn., Nov. 6, 1880. He was licensed in 1820; graduated at Cumberland College, Princeton, Ky., 1832, and was professor of Greek and Latin there 1832–38, and in Sharon College, Sharon, Miss., 1838–43; president of Cumberland College 1843–54; professor of systematic theology in Cumberland University, Lebanon, Tenn., after 1854. He published the following books. *Why am I a Cumberland Presbyterian ?* (Nashville, 1872); *Lectures on Theology* (3 vols., 1873–75); *Brief Biographical Sketches of Some of the Early Ministers of the Cumberland Presbyterian Church* (1874).

BEARDSLEE, CLARK SMITH: Congregationalist; b. at Coventry, N. Y., Feb. 1, 1850. He was educated at Amherst College (B.A., 1876), Hartford Theological Seminary (1879), and the University of Berlin. He was instructor in Hebrew at Hartford Theological Seminary from 1878 to 1881, and then held successive pastorates at Le Mars, Ia. (1882–85), Prescott, Ariz. (1885–86), and West Springfield, Mass. (1886–88). In 1888 he was appointed associate professor of systematic theology at Hartford Theological Seminary, and four years later was made professor of Biblical dogmatics and ethics, a position which he still holds. In theology he is a Biblical Evangelical. He is the author of *Christ's Estimate of Himself* (Hartford, 1899); *Teacher-Training with the Master Teacher* (Philadelphia, 1903); and *Jesus the King of Truth* (Hartford, 1905).

BEATIFICATION: An intermediate stage in the process of canonization. It is in modern usage itself the result of a lengthy course of inquiry into the life of the person under consideration, and is solemnly declared in St. Peter's at Rome. By it the title of " Blessed " is attributed to the subject, and a limited and partial cultus of him permitted, as in a certain country or order. See CANONIZATION.

BEATIFIC VISION: The direct and unhindered vision of God, which is part of the reserved blessedness of the redeemed (I Cor. xiii, 12; I John iii, 2; Rev. xxii, 3, 4). The conception of its nature must necessarily be very vague, but belief in its existence is said to be founded upon Scripture and reason. The only question concerns its time. This has been much disputed. The Greek Church and many Protestants, especially Lutherans and Calvinists, put the vision after the judgment day (so Dr. Hodge, *Systematic Theology*, iii, 860). According to the view prevalent among Roman Catholic theologians, the vision, though essentially complete before the resurrection, is not integrally so until the soul is reunited to the glorified body (consult H. Hurter, *Theologiæ dogmaticæ compendium*, vol. iii, *De Deo consummatore*, chap. v, 10th ed., Innsbruck, 1900).

BEATON, bī'ton **(BETHUNE),** be-thūn' or be-tūn', **DAVID:** Cardinal-archbishop of St. Andrews; b. 1494; assassinated at St. Andrews May 29, 1546. He was the third son of John Beaton of Auchmuty, Fifeshire; studied at the universities of St. Andrews and Glasgow, and at the age of fifteen went to Paris and studied law; became abbot of Arbroath in 1523; bishop of Mirepoix in Languedoc 1537; cardinal Dec., 1538. He was made lord privy seal in 1528; succeeded his uncle, James Beaton, as archbishop of St. Andrews in 1539; was consecrated archbishop of Glasgow at Rome in 1552; became chancellor and prothonotary apostolic and legate *a latere* in 1543. He served his country in many important diplomatic missions

In the bitter political contests of the time between the French and English parties he sided with the former, and fought with energy and courage for the independence of Scotland against the plans of Henry VIII. In the religious contests between Romanists and Reformers he took as decidedly the part of the hierarchy and did not scruple to use intrigue and force when argument and persuasion failed. His memory has been darkened by his severity against heretics and his immoral life. The case of George Wishart (q.v.) is adduced as a particularly flagrant piece of religious persecution; but it must be remembered that he lived in a rude country in turbulent times, and the Reformers were implicated in political intrigues and treasonable plots. The execution of Wishart was the immediate cause of a conspiracy to put Beaton out of the way, and certain members of the Reform party murdered him in his bedchamber.

Bibliography: R. Chambers, *Lives of Illustrious Scotchmen*, ed. T. Thomson, 5 vols., Edinburgh, 1835; C. R. Rogers, *Life of George Wishart*, ib. 1876; *DNB*, iv, 17-18; J. Herkless, *Cardinal Beaton, Priest and Politician*, London, 1891.

BEATTIE, FRANCIS ROBERT: Presbyterian; b. at Guelph, Ont., Mar. 31, 1848; d. at Louisville, Ky., Sept. 4, 1906. He was educated at the University of Toronto (B.A., 1875), Knox Theological College, Toronto (1878), Illinois Wesleyan University (Ph.D., 1884), and Presbyterian Theological College, Montreal (D.D., 1887). He was tutor in Knox College in 1876–78, and held Canadian pastorates at Baltimore and Coldsprings (1878–82) and Brantford (1882–88), in addition to being examiner to Toronto University in 1884–1888. In the latter year he entered the Presbyterian Church, South, and was appointed professor of apologetics in Columbia Seminary, Columbia, S. C., remaining there until 1893, when he became professor of apologetics and systematic theology in the Presbyterian Theological Seminary of Kentucky at Louisville. He published *Utilitarian Theory of Morals* (Brantford, Ont., 1884); *Methods of Theism* (1887); *Radical Criticism* (Chicago, 1894); *Presbyterian Standards* (Richmond, Va., 1896); and *Apologetics* (vol. i, 1903). He also edited the *Memorial Volume of the Westminster Assembly Celebration at Charlotte, N. C.* (Richmond, Va., 1897), and was associate editor of the *Christian Observer* from 1893 and of *The Presbyterian Quarterly* from 1895.

BEATTIE, JAMES: Scotch poet; b. at Laurencekirk (70 m. n.n.e. of Edinburgh), Kincardineshire, Oct. 25, 1735; d. at Aberdeen Aug. 18, 1803. He studied at the Marischal College, Aberdeen (M.A., 1753), and, after seven years as a school-teacher, became professor of moral philosophy and logic at that institution in 1760. In reply to Hume he wrote *An Essay on the Nature and Immutability of Truth* (London, 1770), which was popular and successful, but has little value as a philosophical work. Other works of his were: *Dissertations, Moral and Critical* (1783); *Evidences of the Christian Religion* (2 vols., Edinburgh, 1786); and *Elements of Moral Science* (2 vols., 1790–93). His poems, of which the chief is *The Minstrel* (books i–ii, 1771–1774), are much better than his philosophical writings; and it is for them that he is remembered.

Bibliography: Sir William Forbes, *An Account of the Life and Writings of James Beattie*, Edinburgh, 1806; *DNB*, iv, 22-25.

BEAUSOBRE, bō″sō′br, **ISAAC DE:** One of the most distinguished preachers of the French Protestant Church; b. at Niort (220 m. s.w. of Paris), in the present department of Deux-Sèvres, Mar. 8, 1659; d. in Berlin June 5, 1738. He was descended from a Protestant family of Gascogne, whose head took refuge in Geneva in 1578. He began his theological studies at the celebrated academy of Saumur, was ordained at the last synod of Loudun, and was called to be minister of the church at Chatillon, department of Indre, 1683. During the religious persecution, he fled in Nov., 1685, to Rotterdam, where he was welcomed at the house of the princess of Orange and, through her, was appointed chaplain to her daughter, princess of Anhalt-Dessau. In 1694 he was appointed chaplain to the elector of Brandenburg, Frederick III, and was called to Berlin as minister of the French Church. He stayed there for thirty-six years, preaching with much success, and was loaded with favors by King Frederick II. Among other honorable missions, he was sent in 1704 to the Duke of Marlborough, and, in 1713, to the commissioners of the Treaty of Utrecht, to ask for the exchange of Huguenot galley-slaves for French prisoners. He was privy councilor of the king of Prussia, director of the French House and of the French schools, and superintendent of all the French churches in Berlin.

His works are: *Défense de la doctrine des Réformés sur la Providence, la prédestination, la grâce, et l'Eucharistie* (Magdeburg, 1693); *Les Psaumes de David mis en rime française* (Berlin, 1701); *Le Nouveau-Testament de J. C. traduit en français sur l'original grec, avec des notes littérales* (Amsterdam, 1718); *Histoire critique de Manichée et du Manichéisme* (1739); *Sermons* (4 vols., Lausanne, 1755); *Histoire de la Réformation ou origine et progrès du Luthéranisme dans l'Empire de 1517 à 1530* (4 vols., Berlin, 1785–86). G. Bonet-Maury.

Bibliography: A life is prefixed by A. B. de la Chapelle to Beausobre's *Remarques . . . sur le Nouveau Testament*, 2 vols., The Hague, 1742. Consult J. H. S. Formey, *Éloge des académiciens de Berlin*, 2 vols., Berlin, 1757; E. and É. Haag, *La France protestante*, ed. H. L. Bordier, ii, 127, Paris, 1877; C. J. G. Bartholmess, *Le Grand Beausobre*, in *Bulletin de la société d'histoire du protestantisme français*, ib. 1876.

BEBB, LLEWELLYN JOHN MONTFORT: Church of England; b. at Cape Town Feb. 16, 1862. He was educated at New College, Oxford (B.A., 1885), and was fellow (1885–98), tutor (1889–98), and librarian (1892–98) of Brasenose College. He was examining chaplain to the bishop of Salisbury from 1893 to 1898, and to the bishop of St. Asaph from 1898 to 1902, and was also curator of the botanical garden, Oxford, in 1896–98 and Grinfeld lecturer on the Septuagint in the University of Oxford in 1897–1901. From 1892 to 1896 he was vice-principal of Brasenose College, Oxford, and since 1898 has been principal of St. David's College, Lampeter, Wales. He was select preacher at Cambridge in 1904, and has written *Evidence of the Early Versions and Patristic Quotations on the Text of the New Testament*, in *Studia Biblica*, ii (Oxford, 1890), and has edited *Sermons Preached before the University of Oxford* (1901) and U. Z. Rule's *Graduated Lessons from the Old Testament* (1902).

BEBENBURG, LUPOLD VON: Bishop of Bamberg, best known for his writings on ecclesiastico-political subjects; d. 1363. He came of a knightly Frankish family, and studied canon law at Bologna. From 1338 to 1352 he was a member of the chapters of Würzburg and Mainz and dean of St. Severus at Erfurt. In 1353 he was made bishop of Bamberg, and remained there till his death. In the struggle between Louis the Bavarian and Popes John XXII, Benedict XII, and Clement VI, he was among the jurists who took the emperor's side. His treatise *De juribus regni et imperii Romanorum* (ed. J. Wimpfeling, Strasburg, 1508; S. Schard, in *De jurisdictione, auctoritate, et præeminentia imperiali ac potestate ecclesiastica variis auctoribus scripta*, Basel, 1566, and often), dedicated to Louis' supporter, the elector Baldwin of Treves, deals less with abstract ideas and Aristotelian politics than with historical considerations. Two minor works of his have also been preserved, one in praise of the devotion of the old German princes to the Church (in Schard, ut sup.), the other a lament over the condition of the Holy Roman Empire (ed. Peter, Würzburg, 1842).
(E. FRIEDBERG.)

BIBLIOGRAPHY: J. Looshorn, *Die Geschichte des Bisthums Bamberg*, iii, 246–306. *Bischof Lupold III von Bebenburg*, Munich, 1891: A. Ussermann, *Episcopatus Bambergensis*, pp. 178–180, San Blas, 1802: S. Riezler, *Die literarischen Widersacher der Päpste*, pp. 107–114, 180–192, Leipsic, 1874; F. Joel, *Lupold III von Bebenburg*, vol. i. *Sein Leben*, Halle, 1891 (the result of diligent research).

BEC, ABBEY OF: Benedictine abbey of Normandy, situated at the present village of Le Bec-Hellouin (7 m. s.w. of Rouen). It was founded about 1034 by Herluin, a noble Norman, who was first abbot. Mainly because of its great teachers, Lanfranc (who came to the abbey about 1042 and was prior 1045 or 1046–66) and Anselm (entered the abbey 1060; prior 1063–78; abbot 1078–93; see ANSELM, SAINT, OF CANTERBURY), it became a famous center of learning for Normandy and, after the Conquest, for England. Among those who studied there were: Anselm of Lucca, afterward Pope Alexander II; Anselm of Laon; Gilbert Crispin, abbot of Westminster, author of the life of Herluin; Milo Crispin, biographer of Lanfranc and certain of the early abbots; Arnulf and Gundulf, bishops of Rochester; Ivo of Chartres; Gutmund, archbishop of Aversa; and William, archbishop of Rouen. Its fifth abbot, Theobald, became archbishop of Canterbury (1139); and the seventh abbot was Vacarius, who about the middle of the twelfth century introduced the study of the Roman law into England. The abbey was destroyed during the French Revolution

BIBLIOGRAPHY: The *Chronicon Beccensis abbatiæ*, with the lives by the Crispins above referred to, are in D'Achéry's edition of the works of Lanfranc, Paris, 1648; reprinted in *MPL*, cl; and the *Gesta* of seven Abbots of Bec, by Peter the Monk, written 1150, are in *MPL*, clxxxi.

BECAN (VERBEECK, VAN DER BEECK), MARTIN: Jesuit; b. at Hilvarenbeeck (35 m. n.e. of Antwerp), in Brabant, Jan. 6, 1563; d. in Vienna Jan. 24, 1624. He joined the Jesuits in 1583; taught philosophy and theology at schools of the order in Cologne, Würzburg, Mainz, and Vienna; and became confessor to the emperor Ferdinand II. in 1620. He engaged in controversy with Lutherans, Calvinists and Anabaptists, and in particular attacked the Church of England. In his *Controversia Anglicana de potestate pontificis et regis* (Mainz, 1613) he defended the morality of assassinating a heretic king; and in *Quæstiones de fide hæreticis servanda* (1609) he declared that no promise or oath given to a heretic was binding. The former work was condemned at Rome. His collected works were published in two volumes at Mainz, 1630–31.

BECK, JOHANN TOBIAS: German theologian; b. at Balingen (40 m. s.s.w. of Stuttgart), Württemberg, Feb. 22, 1804; d. at Tübingen Dec. 2?, 1878. He studied at Tübingen 1822–26, was pastor at Waldthann and Mergentheim, went to Basel as extraordinary professor in 1836, and in 1843 to Tübingen, where he remained as professor and morning preacher till his death. He has been characterized as the most important representative of the strictly Biblical school of theology in the nineteenth century. He aimed to base all doctrine on the Bible, and allowed value to Church teachings only as interpretations of the Bible. He held an extreme view of revelation and inspiration, and hardly entered into critico-historical questions. His life was plain and simple, and his kind heart won general affection. He published, besides several collections of sermons, the following works: *Einleitung in das System der christlichen Lehre* (Stuttgart, 1838, 2d ed., 1870); *Die Geburt des christlichen Lebens, sein Wesen und sein Gesetz* (Basel, 1839); *Die christliche Lehrwissenschaft nach den biblischen Urkunden*, i, *Logik* (Stuttgart, 1841, 2d ed., 1875); *Die christliche Menschenliebe, das Wort und die Gemeinde Christi* (Basel, 1842); *Umriss der biblischen Seelenlehre* (Stuttgart, 1843, 3d ed., 1873; Eng. transl., *Biblical Psychology*, Edinburgh, 1877); *Leitfaden der christlichen Glaubenslehre für Kirche, Schule und Haus* (Stuttgart, 1862, 2d ed., 1869); *Gedanken aus und nach der Schrift für christliches Leben und geistliches Amt* (Frankfort, 1859; 2d ed., 1878). After his death were published commentaries on the epistles to Timothy (Gütersloh, 1879) and the Romans (2 vols., 1884), and on Rev. i–xii (1883); *Pastorallehren des Neuen Testaments* (1880; Eng. transl., *Pastoral Theology*, Edinburgh, 1882); *Vorlesungen über christliche Ethik* (3 vols., 1882–83); *Briefe und Kernworte* (1885); *Vorlesungen über christliche Glaubenslehre* (2 vols., 1886–87); *Vollendung des Reiches Gottes* (1887). (A. HAUCK.)

BIBLIOGRAPHY: For his life consult: *Worte der Erinnerung*, Tübingen, 1879 (the part by Weizsäcker is especially valuable); B. J. Riggenbach, *T. Beck, ein Schriftgelehrter zum Himmelreich*, Basel, 1888. On his theology consult: F. Liebetrut, *J. T. Beck und seine Stellung zur Kirche*.

Berlin, 1858; C. Sturhahn, *Die Rechtfertigungslehre nach Beck mit Berücksichtigung von Ebrard's Sola*, Leipsic, 1890. On his work as a preacher: A. Brömel, *Homiletische Charakterbilder*, 2 vols., ib. 1874; A. Nebe, *Geschichte der Predigt*, vol. iii, Wiesbaden, 1879.

BECKET, THOMAS (commonly called **Thomas à Becket**): Archbishop of Canterbury 1162–70, the most determined English champion of the rights and liberties of the Church in his day; b. in London between 1110 and 1120; assassinated at Canterbury Dec. 29, 1170. His parents were of the middle class. He received an excellent education, which he completed at the University of Paris. Returning to England, he attracted the notice of Theobald, archbishop of Canterbury, who entrusted him with several important missions to Rome, and finally made him archdeacon of Canterbury and provost of Beverley. He so distinguished himself by his zeal and efficiency that Theobald commended him to King Henry II when the important office of chancellor was vacant. Henry, like all the Norman kings, desired to be absolute master of his dominions, in both Church and State, and could well appeal to the traditions of his house when he planned to do away with the special privileges of the English clergy, which he regarded as so many fetters on his authority.

Life before his Consecration.

Becket struck him as an instrument well adapted for the accomplishment of his designs; the young man showed himself an accomplished courtier, a cheerful companion in the king's pleasures, and devoted to his master's interests with such a firm and yet diplomatic thoroughness that scarcely any one, unless perhaps it was John of Salisbury, could have doubted that he had gone over completely to the royal side. Archbishop Theobald died Apr. 18, 1161, and the chapter learned with some indignation that the king expected them to choose Thomas his successor. The election was, however, consummated in May, and Thomas was consecrated on June 3, 1162.

At once there took place before the eyes of the astonished king and country an unexpected transformation in the character of the new primate. Instead of a gay, pleasure-loving courtier, he stood forth an ascetic prelate in simple monastic garb, ready to contend to the uttermost for the cause of the hierarchy. In the schism which at that time divided the Church, he declared for Alexander III (q.v.), a man whose devotion to the same strict hierarchical principles appealed to him; and from Alexander he received the pallium at the Council of Tours. On his return to England, he proceeded at once to put into execution the project he had formed for the liberation of the Church of England from the very limitations which he had formerly helped to enforce. His aim was twofold: the complete exemption of the Church from all civil jurisdiction, with undivided control of the clergy, freedom of appeal, etc., and the acquisition and security of an independent fund of church property. The king was not slow to perceive the inevitable outcome of the archbishop's attitude, and called a meeting of the clergy at Westminster (Oct. 1, 1163) at which he demanded that they should renounce all claim to exemption from civil jurisdiction and acknowledge the equality of all subjects before the law. The others were inclined to yield, but the archbishop stood firm. Henry was not ready for an open breach, and offered to be content with a more general acknowledgment and recognition of the "customs of his ancestors." Thomas was willing to agree to this, with the significant reservation "saving the rights of the Church." But this involved the whole question at issue, and Henry left London in anger.

Archbishop, 1162.

Henry called another assembly at Clarendon for Jan. 30, 1164, at which he presented his demands in sixteen constitutions. What he asked involved the abandonment of the clergy's independence and of their direct connection with Rome; he employed all his arts to induce their consent, and was apparently successful with all but the primate. Finally even Becket expressed his willingness to agree to the constitutions; but when it came to the actual signature he definitely refused. This meant war between the two powers. Henry endeavored to rid himself of his antagonist by judicial process and summoned him to appear before a great council at Northampton on Oct. 8, 1164, to answer charges of contempt of royal authority and maladministration of the chancellor's office.

The Constitutions of Clarendon.

Becket denied the right of the assembly to judge him, appealed to the pope, and, feeling that his life was too valuable to the Church to be risked, went into voluntary exile on Nov. 2, embarking in a fishing-boat which landed him in France. He went to Sens, where Pope Alexander was, while envoys from the king hastened to work against him, requesting that a legate should be sent to England with plenary authority to settle the dispute. Alexander declined, and when, the next day, Becket arrived and gave him a full account of the proceedings, he was still more confirmed in his aversion to the king. Henry pursued the fugitive archbishop with a series of edicts, aimed at all his friends and supporters as well as himself; but Louis VII of France received him with respect and offered him protection. He spent nearly two years in the Cistercian abbey of Pontigny, until Henry's threats against the order obliged him to move to Sens again. He regarded himself as in full possession of all his prerogatives, and desired to see his position enforced by the weapons of excommunication and interdict. But Alexander, though sympathizing with him in theory, was for a milder and more diplomatic way of reaching his ends. Differences thus arose between pope and archbishop, which were all the more embittered when legates were sent in 1167 with authority to act as arbitrators. Disregarding this limitation of his jurisdiction, and steadfast in his principles, Thomas treated with the legates at great length, still conditioning his obedience to the king by the rights of his order. His firmness seemed about to meet with its reward when at last (1170) the pope was on the point of fulfilling his threats and excommunicating the king, and Henry, alarmed

Becket Leaves England.

by the prospect, held out hopes of an agreement which should allow Thomas to return to England and resume his place. But both parties were really still holding to their former ground, and the desire for a reconciliation was only apparent. Both, however, seem for the moment to have believed in its possibility; and the contrast was all the sharper when it became evident that the old irreconcilable opposition was still there. Henry, incited by his partizans, refused to restore the ecclesiastical property which he had seized, and Thomas prepared to issue the pope's sentence against the despoilers of the Church and the bishops who had abetted them. It had been already sent to England for promulgation when he himself landed at Sandwich on Dec. 3, 1170, and two days later entered Canterbury.

The tension was now too great to be endured, and the catastrophe which relieved it was not long in coming. A passionate word of the angry king was taken as authority by four knights, who immediately plotted the murder of the archbishop, and accomplished it in his own cathedral on Dec. 29. The crime brought its own revenge. Becket was revered by the faithful throughout Europe as a martyr, and canonized by Alexander in 1173; while on July 12 of the following year Henry humbled himself to do public penance at the tomb of his enemy, which remained one of the most popular places of pilgrimage in England until it was destroyed at the Reformation (see CANTERBURY).

Becket Assassinated.

(CARL MIRBT.)

BIBLIOGRAPHY: The sources for a life were collected by J. C. Robertson in *Materials for the Hist. of Thomas Becket*, 8 vols., in *Rolls Series*, London, 1875–85 (contains all the known contemporary lives, others of later date, the *Epistles*, and other material); cf. the *Vita, epistolæ et reliquiæ*, ed. J. A. Giles in *PEA*, 8 vols., Oxford, 1845–46, and J. A. Giles, *Life and Letters of Thomas à Becket*, 2 vols., London, 1846. For later discussions and lives consult: M. Cournier, *L'Archevêque de Cantorbéry*, 2 vols., Paris, 1845; J. C. Robertson, *Becket*, London, 1859; W F. Hook, *Lives of the Archbishops of Canterbury*, ii, 354–507, ib. 1862; E. A. Freeman, in *Historical Essays*, series 2, ib. 1880; idem, in *Contemporary Review*, Mar.–Apr., 1878; J. A. Froude, *Life and Times of Becket*, in *Short Studies*, vol. iv, ib. 1883; idem, in *Nineteenth Century*, ii (1877), 15–27, 217–229, 389–410, 669–691; C. P. Stanley, *Historical Memorials of Canterbury*, pp. 59 125, 189–302, London, 1883; W. H. Hutton, *St. Thomas of Canterbury*, ib. 1889 (from contemporary lives); J. Morris, *Life and Martyrdom of St. Thomas Becket*, ib. 1891 (Roman Catholic, deals with monasteries and churches associated with Becket); M. Schmitz, *Die politischen Ideen des Thomas Becket*, Crefeld, 1893; E. A. Abbott, *St. Thomas of Canterbury: his Death and Miracles*, 2 vols., London, 1898 (traverses the earlier accounts in a critical examination); *DNB*, lvi, 165–173.

BECKWITH, CHARLES MINNIGERODE: Protestant Episcopal bishop of Alabama; b. in Prince George Co., Va., June 3, 1851. He studied at the University of Georgia (B.A., 1873), was master of the Sewanee Grammar School, University of the South (Sewanee, Tenn.), 1875–79, and was graduated from Berkeley Divinity School, Middletown, Conn., in 1881. He was ordered deacon and advanced to the priesthood in the same year, and was rector of St. Luke's, Atlanta, Ga. (1881–86), Christ Church, Houston, Tex. (1886–92), and Trinity, Galveston, Tex. (1892–1902). In 1902 he was consecrated fourth bishop of Alabama. He has written *The Trinity Course of Church Instruction* (New York, 1898) and *The Teacher's Companion to the Trinity Course* (1901).

BECKWITH, CLARENCE AUGUSTINE: Congregationalist; b. at Charlemont, Mass., July 21, 1849. He studied at Olivet College, Olivet, Mich. (B.A., 1874), Yale Divinity School (1874–76), and Bangor Theological Seminary, from which he was graduated in 1877. He became pastor of the First Congregational Church, Brewer, Me., in 1877, of the South Evangelical Congregational Church, West Roxbury, Mass., in 1882, professor of Christian theology at Bangor Theological Seminary in 1892, and professor of systematic theology at Chicago Theological Seminary in 1905. He holds that "the realities of the Christian religion and the facts of Christian experience which we share with Christians of all ages are to be interpreted by us in terms of modern thought." He has written *Realities of Christian Theology* (New York, 1906).

BECKX, PIERRE JEAN: General of the Jesuits; b. at Sichem (33 m. s.e. of Antwerp) Feb. 8, 1795; d. at Rome Mar. 4, 1887 He entered the Society of Jesus at Hildesheim in 1819, and was professed in 1830. He was active as a pastor at Hamburg, Hildesheim, and Brunswick, and in 1826 was stationed at Köthen as the confessor of the newly converted duke and duchess of Anhalt-Köthen. From 1830 to 1848 he was in Vienna, where he exercised much influence, especially over Metternich, and was made procurator of the Society of Jesus in that country in 1847; when his Order was expelled from Austria in 1848, he was appointed rector of the University of Louvain. Four years later, however, the Jesuits were readmitted to Austria, largely through his unceasing activity, and in 1852 he returned to Vienna as provincial of the Society. In the following year he was elected general, and held this office until 1883, when, on account of his advancing years, the vicar-general Antoine M. Anderledy was appointed to assist him. In the following year Beckx resigned the generalship in favor of Anderledy. The successful fortunes of the Jesuits during the attacks upon them both in Austria and Germany were due in great part to his ability and tact, and in his administration the numbers of the Society were almost doubled. He was the founder and editor of the famous *Civiltà Cattolica*, and also wrote the anonymous *Der Monat Mariä* (Vienna, 1838; Eng. transl. by Mrs. Edward Hazeland, London, 1884).

BIBLIOGRAPHY: A. M. Verstraeten, *Leven van den hoogeerwaarden Pater Petrus Beckx*, Antwerp, 1889.

BEDE or **BÆDA** (called "the Venerable"): The first great English scholar; b. in Northumbria (according to tradition, at Monkton, Durham, 5 m. e. of Newcastle) 672 or 673; d. at the monastery of Jarrow (6 m. e. of Newcastle) May 25, 735. Almost all that is known of his life is contained in a notice added by himself to his *Historia ecclesiastica* (v, 24), which states that he was placed in the monastery at Wearmouth at the age of seven, that he became deacon in his nineteenth year, and priest in his thirtieth. He was trained by the abbots Benedict Biscop and Ceolfrid (qq.v.), and probably accompanied the latter to Jarrow in 682. There he spent his life, finding his chief pleasure in being always occupied in learning, teaching, or writing, and zealous in the performance of monastic duties. His works show that he had at his command all the learning of his time. He was proficient in patristic literature, and quotes from Pliny the Younger, Vergil, Lucretius, Ovid, Horace, and other classical writers, but with some disapproval. He knew Greek and a little Hebrew. His Latin is clear and without affectation, and he is a skilful story-teller. Like all men of his time he was devoted to the allegorical method of interpretation, and was credulous concerning the miraculous; but in most things his good sense is conspicuous, and his kindly and broad sympathies, his love of truth and fairness, his unfeigned piety, and his devotion to the service of others combine to make him an exceedingly attractive character. His works were so widely spread throughout Europe and so much esteemed that he won the name of " the teacher of the Middle Ages."

Bede's writings are classed as scientific, historical, and theological. The scientific include treatises on grammar (written for his pupils), a work on natural phenomena (*De rerum natura*), and two on chronology (*De temporibus* and *De temporum ratione*). The most important and best known of his works is the *Historia ecclesiastica gentis Anglorum*, giving in five books the history of England, ecclesiastical and political, from the time of Cæsar to the date of completion (731). The first twenty-one chapters, treating of the period before the mission of Augustine, are compiled from earlier writers such as Orosius, Gildas, Prosper of Aquitaine, and others, with the insertion of legend and tradition. After 596, documentary sources, which Bede took pains to obtain, are used, and oral testimony, which he employed not without critical consideration of its value. His other historical works were lives of the abbots of Wearmouth and Jarrow, and lives in verse and prose of St. Cuthbert. The most numerous of his writings are theological, and consist of commentaries on the books of the Old and New Testaments, homilies, and treatises on detached portions of Scripture. His last work, completed on his death-bed, was a translation into Anglo-Saxon of the Gospel of John.

Bibliography: The collected editions of Bede's works (such as by J. A. Giles, with Eng. transl. of the historical works and life, *Patres ecclesiæ Anglicanæ*, 12 vols., London, 1843–44; in *MPL*, xc–xcv) leave much to be desired. Good editions of the historical works, particularly of the *Historia ecclesiastica*, have been issued by J. Smith, Cambridge, 1722; J. Stevenson, *Hist. eccl.*, London, 1838, *Opera historica minora*, 1841; G. H. Moberly, Oxford, 1869; J. E. B. Mayor and J. R. Lumby, *Hist. eccl.*, books iii and iv, Cambridge, 1881; A. Holder, Freiburg, 1890; C. Plummer, 2 vols., Oxford, 1896; *Eccl. Hist.*, transl., introduction, life, and notes, by A. M. Sellar, London, 1907. The two works on chronology have been edited by T. Mommsen in *MGH, Chron. min.*, iii (1898). There are English versions of the *Ecclesiastical History* by Stevens, 1723, revised by J. A. Giles, London, 1840; J. Stevenson, ib. 1853; and L. Gridley, Oxford, 1870. The old Eng. version of the *Hist. eccl.*, with transl. and introduction, was ed. by T. Miller, in 4 parts, ib. 1870. For Bede's life consult the introductions and notes to the editions mentioned, particularly those of Stevenson and Plummer; G. F. Browne, *The Venerable Bede*, in *The Fathers for English Readers*, London, 1879, New York, 1891; K. Werner, *Beda der Ehrwürdige und seine Zeit*, Vienna, 1881; J. B. Lightfoot, in *Leaders of the Northern Church*, London, 1890 (biographical sermons); F. Phillips, in *Fathers of the English Church*, vol. i, London, 1891 (simple, scholarly, fair); W. Bright, *Early English Church History*, pp. 367–371 et passim, Oxford, 1897.

BEDELL, WILLIAM: Irish bishop; b. at Black Notley, near Braintree (50 m. n.e. of London), Essex, England, on or near Christmas day, 1571; d. at Drum Corr, near Kilmore, County Cavan, Ireland, Feb. 7, 1642. He studied at Emmanuel College, Cambridge (B.A., 1588; M.A., 1592; B.D., 1599), was ordained priest Jan. 10, 1597, and settled at Bury St. Edmunds, Suffolk, in 1602. In 1607 he went to Venice as chaplain to Sir Henry Wotton, British ambassador at that city, and there he made the acquaintance of a number of noteworthy men, including Marco Antonio de Dominis and Father Paolo Sarpi, author of the *History of the Council of Trent*, the last two books of which, as well as Sarpi's *History of the Venetian Interdict*, he afterward translated into Latin. He returned to Bury St. Edmunds in 1610, and removed to Horningsheath, a neighboring parish, in 1616. In 1627 he was appointed provost of Trinity College, Dublin; in 1629 he became bishop of the united dioceses of Kilmore and Ardagh (County Longford); in 1633 he resigned the latter see owing to conscientious objections to pluralities, and the belief that the proper administration of the diocese required a separate bishop. His position was difficult; the dioceses were in wretched condition, and his earnest efforts to effect improvement stirred up opposition. Nevertheless he reformed many abuses and enjoyed great esteem among the people. He wrote a short summary of Christian doctrine in English and Irish (published, Dublin, 1631), and a translation of the Old Testament into Irish was made under his supervision (published, London, 1685). When the rebellion of 1641 broke out, he refused to leave his diocese, and, after suffering many hardships, died of fever brought on by the privations which he had undergone. His *Life with the Letters between Waddesworth and Bedell* was published by Bishop Burnet (London, 1685), and has been rewritten several times. The best biography is one by his son (ed. for the Camden Society T. W Jones, London, 1872).

BEECHER, CHARLES: Congregationalist, fifth son of Lyman Beecher; b. at Litchfield, Conn., Oct. 7, 1815; d. at Georgetown, Mass., Apr. 21, 1900. He was graduated at Bowdoin College 1834 and at Lane Theological Seminary 1835; became pastor of the Second Presbyterian Church, Fort Wayne, Ind., 1844; of the First Congregational Church, Newark, N. J., 1851; of the First Church, Georgetown, Mass., 1857. He lived in Florida 1870–1877, and for two years was State superintendent of schools. He published: *The Incarnation* (New York, 1849); *A Review of the Spiritual Manifestations* (1853); *David and his Throne* (1855); *Redeemer* *and Redeemed* (Boston, 1864); and *Spiritual Manifestations* (1879). With John Zundel he edited the music for *The Plymouth Collection of Hymns and Tunes* (New York, 1855), and, alone, the *Autobiography, Correspondence, etc.* of his father (2 vols., 1865).

BEECHER, EDWARD: Congregationalist, second son of Lyman Beecher; b. at East Hampton, L. I., Aug. 27, 1803; d. in Brooklyn July 28, 1895. He was graduated at Yale 1822; began his theological studies at Andover and continued them while acting as tutor at Yale 1825–26; was pastor of the Park Street Church, Boston, 1826–30; president of Illinois College, Jacksonville, Ill., 1830–44; pastor of the Salem Street Church, Boston, 1844–55, and editor of *The Congregationalist* 1849–1853; pastor at Galesburg, Ill., 1855–71; after 1871 resided in Brooklyn. He was lecturer on church institutions at the Chicago Theological Seminary (Congregational) 1859–66. In 1837 he defended the freedom of the press in the case of Elijah P. Lovejoy, an antislavery agitator at Alton, Ill. When Lovejoy's presses were destroyed by the mob, Beecher helped to obtain and secrete a new one, and was with Lovejoy and his brother, Owen, the night before the former was killed (Nov 7, 1837). To resist the mob spirit he aided in founding the Illinois State Antislavery Society, drew up its constitution, and issued a *Statement of Antislavery Principles, and Address to the People of Illinois.* He published a *Narrative of Riots at Alton* (Cincinnati, 1838). His views as to the nature and cause of sin and on the atonement were set forth in two works, *The Conflict of Ages, or the Great Debate on the Moral Relations of God and Man* (Boston, 1853) and *The Concord of Ages, or the Individual and Organic Harmony of God and Man* (New York, 1860), in which he expressed the belief that the present life is a continuation of a preceding existence as well as a preparation for a future one; that the material system is adapted to regenerate men, who have made themselves sinful in the previous state; and that ultimately the conflict between good and evil will disappear, and harmony be established. The doctrine of divine suffering he held to present the character of God in its most affecting and powerful aspects, and to be essential to a true view of the atonement. He also published. *On the Kingdom of God* (Boston, 1827); *Baptism with Reference to its Import and Modes* (New York, 1849); *The Papal Conspiracy Exposed and Protestantism Defended in the Light of Reason, History, and Scripture* (New York, 1855); *History of Opinions on the Scriptural Doctrine of Retribution* (1878).

BEECHER, HENRY WARD: Congregationalist, fourth son of Lyman Beecher; b. at Litchfield, Conn., June 24, 1813; d. in Brooklyn Mar. 8, 1887 He was graduated at Amherst 1834, and at Lane Theological Seminary 1837; became pastor of the Presbyterian Church at Lawrenceburg, Ind., 1837, at Indianapolis 1839, and of Plymouth Church (Congregational), Brooklyn, 1847. The congregation was newly formed at that time, but soon became famed for its numbers and its influence, while Beecher attained to the position of the most popular and widely known preacher in America. As a public lecturer he was no less successful. In his sermons he disregarded conventionalities both in subject and manner. His wit and humor appeared in his preaching, which, nevertheless, was earnest and edifying, and revealed a great character, sincere and reverent; his public prayers in particular were truly devotional (cf. *Prayers from Plymouth Pulpit*, New York, 1867). No slight dramatic power, robust health and physical strength, and a striking personal appearance added to the effect of his eloquence. Personally he was a most estimable and attractive man, of generous instincts, of rare humanity, and catholic sympathies. He was active in the antislavery contest, but deprecated revolutionary measures. In 1863 he publicly advocated the Union cause in a series of addresses in the cities of England at a time when the sympathies of the people of England were strongly with the Southern Confederacy, and his success at this time before bitterly hostile audiences is one of the greatest feats of intellectual and oratorical achievement (these addresses were published as *The American Rebellion: Report of the Speeches delivered in Manchester, etc.*, Manchester, 1864, and are reprinted in *Patriotic Addresses from 1850 to 1885 by Henry Ward Beecher, edited, with a review of Mr. Beecher's personality and influence in public affairs*, by John R. Howard, New York, 1889).

In later life the development of Beecher's mind led him to desire a freedom which he thought could not be attained within strictly denominational lines, and, actuated also by the wish not to compromise his brethren by alleged heresies, in 1882, with his church, he withdrew from the Congregational Association to which he belonged. The chief points of his divergence from the orthodox position of the time related to the person of Christ, whom he considered to be the Divine Spirit under the limitations of time, space, and flesh; to miracles, which he considered divine uses of natural laws; and to future punishment, the endlessness of which he denied, inclining to a modification of the annihilation theory.

Beecher was a regular contributor to *The Independent* from its foundation in 1848 to 1870, and its editor for not quite two years (1861–63). He was editor of *The Christian Union* (since 1893 known as *The Outlook*), 1870–81, and made it the pioneer non-denominational religious paper. He also wrote much for *The New York Ledger*. His sermons were published weekly after 1859 (under the title *The Plymouth Pulpit*), and have appeared in book-form in numerous volumes. *Sermons selected from published and unpublished discourses and revised by their author*, edited by Lyman Abbott (2 vols., New York, 1868), is a representative collection. His addresses, lectures, and articles were also gathered into many books, such as *Lectures to Young Men* (Indianapolis, 1844; rev. eds., New York, Boston, 1850 and 1873); the *Star Papers, or experiences of art and nature* (selections from *The Independent*; so called from his signature, *; 2 vols., New York, 1855–58); *Eyes and Ears* (reprinted from *The New York Ledger*, Boston, 1862);

Lecture-Room Talks (New York, 1870); *A Summer Parish* (1875); *Evolution and Religion* (1885). His books of most permanent value were *The Life of Jesus the Christ* (i, New York, 1871; ii, left incomplete at his death and supplemented by extracts from his sermons, 1891), and the *Yale Lectures on Preaching* (Lyman Beecher lectures before the Yale Divinity School, 1872–74; 3 vols., also collected edition in one volume, New York, 1881). He compiled *The Plymouth Collection of Hymns and Tunes* (1855), and wrote *Norwood, or Village Life in New England*, a novel (1867).

Bibliography: Lyman Abbott and S. B. Halliday, *Henry Ward Beecher*, Hartford, 1887; the *Biography* by his son William C. Beecher and Samuel Scoville, assisted by his wife, 1888; John Henry Barrows, *Henry Ward Beecher, the Shakespeare of the Pulpit*, New York, 1893; the *Autobiographical Reminiscences* edited by T. J. Ellinwood, his private stenographer for thirty years, 1898; Lyman Abbott, *Henry Ward Beecher*, Boston, 1903; N. L. Thompson, *The History of Plymouth Church*, New York, 1873.

BEECHER, LYMAN: Presbyterian; b. at New Haven, Conn., Oct. 12, 1775; d. at Brooklyn Jan. 10, 1863. He was graduated at Yale 1797; studied theology under President Dwight the following year, and, after preaching on probation for a year at East Hampton, L. I., was ordained as pastor there, 1799; in 1810 he removed to Litchfield, Conn., and in 1826 to Boston, as pastor of the Hanover Street Church (Congregational). In 1832 he became president and professor of theology at the newly formed Lane Theological Seminary, Cincinnati, where for the first ten years he also served as pastor of the Second Presbyterian Church. In 1851 he returned to Boston, and after 1856 lived in Brooklyn. He was a profound student of theology, but eminently practical in his preaching, which was marked by an uncommon union of imagination, fervor, and logic. His convictions were strong, his courage great, and he acted with an impulsive energy which generally succeeded in accomplishing what he thought should be done. The death of Alexander Hamilton called forth a sermon on dueling (preached before the Presbytery of Long Island, Apr. 16, 1806; published in several editions) which did much to awaken the popular conscience on the subject. At Litchfield he took a decided stand in favor of a general reformation of public morals, and in particular against the convivial habits of the time. During his Boston pastorate he was a leader on the conservative side in the Unitarian controversy. In Cincinnati hard feelings evoked by the antislavery contest, and certain problems inevitable during the formative period of the seminary and in a new society, made his career a stormy one; but he worked with characteristic energy and retired with honor. During the earlier stages of the differences which led to the disruption of the Presbyterian Church in 1837 he was charged with holding heretical views on the atonement, and was tried and acquitted by both presbytery and synod in 1835; throughout the entire contest he was one of the New School leaders. His seven sons all became clergymen and his daughters, Catherine Esther Beecher, Harriet Beecher Stowe, and Isabella Beecher Hooker, became well known for literary and philanthropic work. During his second residence in Boston Lyman Beecher prepared a collected edition of his *Works* (i, *Lectures on Political Atheism and Kindred Subjects; Six Lectures on Intemperance*, Boston, 1852; ii, *Sermons*, 1852; iii, *Views of Theology as Developed in Three Sermons and on his Trials*, 1853).

Bibliography: His *Autobiography, Correspondence, etc.* was edited by his son Charles Beecher, rev. ed., 2 vols., New York, 1865; consult also D. H. Allen, *The Life and Services of Lyman Beecher, a Commemorative Discourse*, Cincinnati, 1863; J. C. White, *Personal Reminiscences of Lyman Beecher*, New York, 1882; E. F. Haywood, *Lyman Beecher*, Boston, 1904.

BEECHER, THOMAS KINNICUTT: Congregationalist, sixth son of Lyman Beecher; b. at Litchfield, Conn., Feb. 10, 1824; d. at Elmira, N. Y., Mar. 14, 1900. He was graduated at Illinois College, Jacksonville, Ill., 1843; became school principal at Philadelphia, 1846, at Hartford, Conn., 1848; pastor at Williamsburg (Brooklyn), L. I., 1852, of the Independent Church (afterward called the Park Church), Elmira, 1854, where he served a long pastorate and became widely known for his eccentricities, but still more esteemed for his charities and respected for the practical good sense of many of his plans and ideas. He developed one of the first "institutional" churches, and his Sunday-school was a model one. His chief publication was *Our Seven Churches* (New York, 1870), a volume of discourses upon the different denominations in Elmira. *In Time with the Stars*, a book of children's stories, appeared posthumously (1902).

BEECHER, WILLIS JUDSON: Presbyterian; b. at Hampden, O., Apr. 29, 1838. He studied at Hamilton College (B.A., 1858) and Auburn Theological Seminary (1864), and was ordained to the ministry in 1864. After a pastorate at Ovid, N. Y., 1864–65, he was appointed professor of moral science and belles-lettres in Knox College, Galesburg, Ill. In 1869 he became pastor of the First Church of Christ in the same city. Two years later he was appointed professor of the Hebrew language and literature in Auburn Theological Seminary. In 1902 he delivered the Stone Lectures at Princeton Theological Seminary. He was a member of the Assembly's Committee on the Revision of the Confession of Faith (1890–92), and in theology is a progressive conservative. Besides preparing the Old Testament Sunday-school lessons for the *Sunday School Times* since 1893, he has written *Farmer Tompkins and his Bibles* (Philadelphia, 1874); *General Catalogue of Auburn Theological Seminary* (Auburn, 1883); *Drill Lessons in Hebrew* (1883); *Index of Presbyterian Ministers, 1706–1881* (Philadelphia, 1883; in collaboration with his sister Mary A. Beecher); *The Prophets and the Promise* (New York, 1905); and *The Teaching of Jesus concerning the Future Life* (1906).

BEELZEBUB, be-el′ze-bub (properly, in all the New Testament passages—Matt. x, 25; xii, 24, 27; Mark iii, 22; Luke xi, 15, 18, 19—*Beelzeboul*): The name of the prince of the demons; i.e., of Satan. The reading *Beelzeboul* has also this in its favor that the Greek *oikodespotēs*, "master of the house" (Matt. x, 25), seems to play upon *be'el zebul* (*be'el* being the Aramaic form for the Hebrew *ba'al*). Nothing more than a play upon the word is to be sought in *oikodespotēs*, which is not a translation of the Aramaic; "master of the (Satanic) kingdom" would be a meaningless designation of the prince of hell. In spite of the correctness of the reading *Beelzeboul*, it is justifiable to trace this name to the much older name Baal-zebub, which is found in the Old Testament as that of an idol.

Baal-zebub was honored in Ekron, where he had a temple and an oracle, which was consulted by Ahaziah, king of Israel (II Kings i, 2, 3, 16). The name as it stands means "lord of flies"; the Septuagint calls the god directly "fly"; so also Josephus (*Ant.*, IX, ii, 1). In classical mythology, there was a god who protected from flies. It is related that Hercules banished the flies from Olympia by erecting a shrine to Zeus Apomuios ("averter of flies"); and the Romans called Hercules Apomuios. A similar deity is mentioned as acting and honored in different places, the excuse for such worship being the plague which flies cause in those warm countries. Both the sending of flies and the driving them away were referred to the same divinity. As may be inferred from the name Baal, the Baal-zebub of the Philistines was essentially identical with the principal god or gods of the Phenicians. He may have been lord of flies as sun-god, because flies are most numerous in midsummer, when the sun is hottest. And that he had an oracle is to be explained by a substitution of effect for cause. Flies come obedient to certain atmospheric conditions; hence the god was considered to have caused these conditions, and so at length his control was extended to other events, and accordingly he was consulted (see BAAL).

Beelzebul was early identified with Baal-zebub, and, as was so often the case, was turned into a bad demon, in accordance with later Jewish ideas. Since Lightfoot (*Horæ Heb.*, s.v.), it has been common to say that the name of the demon Beelzebul was purposely made out of Beel-zebub, in order to express contempt and horror; i.e., "lord of dung," instead of "lord of flies." But, inasmuch as such a name for Satan does not occur outside of the New Testament, it is better to seek its derivation in the old Ekronic worship, which might, in New Testament times, have still existed. Beelzebul may therefore be looked upon as the same name as Beel-zebub, and therefore as having the same meaning.

BIBLIOGRAPHY: E. C. A. Riehm, *Handwörterbuch des biblischen Alterthums*, s.v., Bielefeld, 1893–94 (revives the theory that the Syriac form may have meant simply "an enemy," cf. *KAT*, p. 461); J. Selden, *De dis Syris*, London, 1617; J. Lightfoot, *Horæ hebraicæ* on Matt. xii. 24, and Luke xi. 15, ib. 1675; F. C. Movers, *Die Phönizier* i. 260 261, Bonn, 1841; idem, in *JA*, 1878, pp. 220–225; P. Scholz, *Götzendienst und Zauberwesen bei den alten Hebräern*, pp. 170–173, Regensburg, 1877; Nowack, *Archäologie*, ii, 304–305; *EB.* i. 514–515; *JE*, ii, 629–630.

BEER, bēr, GEORG: German Lutheran; b. at Schweidnitz (31 m. s.w. of Breslau) Nov. 12, 1865. He studied in Berlin and Leipsic (Ph.D., 1887), taught in Erbach 1889–91, and became privat-docent at Breslau in 1892. Two years later he went in the same capacity to Halle, and in 1900 to Strasburg as associate professor of the Old Testament. Became ordinary professor of Old Testament at Heidelberg, 1909. He has written *Al-Gazzâli's Makâsid al-falâsifat, i, die Logik* (Leyden, 1888); *Individual- und Gemeinde-psalmen* (Marburg, 1894); and *Der Text des Buches Hiob untersucht* (1897); besides preparing the translation of the *Martyrdom of Isaiah* and of the *Book of Enoch* for E. Kautzsch's *Apokryphen und Pseudepigraphen des Alten Testaments* (Tübingen, 1900).

BEER, RUDOLF: German Protestant; b. at Bielitz (40 m. w.s.w. of Cracow) Dec. 5, 1863. He was educated at the universities of Vienna and Bonn, and since 1893 has been reader in Spanish at the latter university, as well as a custodian at the Imperial and Royal Library at Vienna since 1888. He is a collaborator on the Vienna *Corpus patrum ecclesiasticorum latinorum*. In theology he advocates "the scientific investigation of Christian revelation." Among his works special mention may be made of his *Die Anecdota Borderiana Augustineischer Sermonen* (Vienna, 1887); *Heilige Höhen der Griechen und Römer* (1891); *Die Quellen für den liber diurnus concilii Basiliensis des Petrus Bruneti* (1891); and *Urkundliche Beiträge zu Johannes de Segovia* (1896); in addition to editions of Wyclif's *De compositione hominis* (London, 1887); and *De ente prædicamentali quæstiones tredecim* (1891), and of the *Monumenta conciliorum generalium* (3 vols., Vienna, 1892–96).

BEET, bīt, JOSEPH AGAR: English Wesleyan; b. at Sheffield Sept. 27, 1840. He attended Wesley College, Sheffield (1851–56), and took up mining engineering, but afterward studied theology at the Wesleyan College, Richmond (1862–64). He was pastor 1864–85 and professor of systematic theology in Wesleyan College, Richmond, 1885–1905. He was also a member of the faculty of theology in the University of London 1901–05. He delivered the Fernley Lecture on *The Credentials of the Gospels* in 1889, and lectured in America in 1896. Though long recognized as one of the ablest theologians and exegetes of his denomination, his sympathy with the modern critical school of interpretation and particularly his views on eschatology have occasioned much criticism. In *The Last Things* (London, 1897; 2d ed., 1905) he opposed the belief that the essential and endless permanence of the soul is taught in the Bible and denied that eternal punishment necessarily means endless torment, holding that the sinner may suffer a relative annihilation of his mental and moral faculties and sink into a dehumanized state. He reiterated these views in *The Immortality of the Soul* (1901). Charges of heresy were brought against him at the Conference of 1902, but he was reelected to his professorship on condition that he refrain from expressing his opinions on immortality and future punishment. To regain liberty of speech in 1904 he gave notice that he would retire from his chair in twelve months. His other works are: *Commentary on Romans* (London, 1877); *Holiness as Understood by the Critics of the Bible* (1880); *Commentary on Corinthians* (1881); *Commentary on Galatians*

(1883); *Commentary on Ephesians, Philippians, Colossians, and Philemon* (1890); *Through Christ to God* (1892); *The Firm Foundation of the Christian Faith* (1892); *The New Life in Christ* (1895); *Nature and Christ* (New York, 1896); *Key to Unlock the Bible* (1901); *Transfiguration of Jesus* (1905); and *Manual of Theology* (1906).

BEETS, bêtz, **HENRY:** Christian Reformed; b. at Koedijk (a village near Alkmaar, 20 m. n.w. of Amsterdam), Holland, Jan. 5, 1869. He came to the United States at an early age, and studied at John Calvin College and Theological Seminary of the Christian Reformed Church, Grand Rapids, Mich. After graduation in 1895, he was pastor at Sioux Center, Ia., until 1899, and since the latter year has been pastor of the Lagrave Street Christian Reformed Church, Grand Rapids. He has been secretary of the Board of Heathen Missions of his Church since 1900, stated clerk of its synod since 1902, and a member of the joint committee of American and Canadian Churches for the revision of the Psalms in meter since 1902. In theology he is a firm Calvinist, adhering strictly to the creeds of the Synod of Dort and the Westminster Standards. He has been associate editor of *De Gereformeerde Amerikaan*, a monthly, since 1898 and editor-in-chief of *The Banner*, a weekly, since 1904. He has written *Het Leven van Pres. McKinley* (Holland, Mich., 1901); *Sacred History for Juniors* (Grand Rapids, Mich., 1901); *Sacred History for Seniors* (1902); *Compendium of the Christian Religion* (1903); *Primer of Bible Truths* (1903; in collaboration with M. J. Bosma); and *Kerkenorde der Christelijke Gereformeerde Kerk* (1905; in collaboration with W. Heyns and G. K. Hemkes).

BEGG, JAMES: Minister of the Free Church of Scotland; b. at New Monkland, near Airdrie (10 m. e. of Glasgow), Lanarkshire, Oct. 31, 1808; d. in Edinburgh Sept. 29, 1883. He studied at Glasgow and Edinburgh; was ordained minister at Maxwelltown, Dumfries, May, 1830; became colleague at Lady Glenorchy's Chapel, Edinburgh, Dec., 1830, minister in Paisley 1831, at Liberton, near Edinburgh, 1835, and, after the Disruption in 1843, at Newington, a suburb of Edinburgh. In 1865 he was moderator of the General Assembly of the Free Church. He began his career as an ardent supporter of evangelical views and a decided opponent of the "moderate" party in the Church. He was strongly opposed to lay patronage and to voluntaryism. He strenuously resisted the aggressions of the civil courts on the jurisdiction of the Church and was disposed to continue the fight within the Establishment; but in May, 1843, he left with his brethren. (See the section on the Free Church of Scotland in the article PRESBYTERIANS.) In the Free Church he became the leader of a minority opposed to all change and when he was charged with standing in the way of progress he gloried in his steadfast adherence to the ideas of his youth; his followers were most numerous in the Highlands. He was an advocate and supporter of popular education and was interested in a movement to secure better homes for the working classes. He wrote much for periodicals and edited several journals at different times (*The Bulwark*, for the maintenance of Protestantism; *The Watchword*, against the union with the United Presbyterians; *The Signal*, against instrumental music in worship). Among his larger publications were *A Handbook of Popery* (Edinburgh, 1852); *Happy Homes for Workingmen and How to Get Them* (London, 1866); *Free Church Principles* (Edinburgh, 1869), and *The Principles, Position, and Prospects of the Free Church of Scotland* (1875).

BIBLIOGRAPHY: T. Smith, *Memoirs of James Begg*, 2 vols., Edinburgh, 1885–88; *DNB*, iv, 127–128.

BEGHARDS, BEGUINES.

Beghards and Beguines are the names applied to certain religious communities which flourished especially in the Middle Ages. The Beguines were women and earlier in origin than the male associations, the Beghards (also called in France *Béguins*). As early as the thirteenth century the authentic tradition as to the origin of the Beguines had been lost, so that it was possible in the fifteenth for the belief to gain acceptance that they had been founded by Begga, the canonized daughter of Pepin of Landen and mother of Pepin of Heristal.

1. Origin. This belief was supported by several scholars in the early seventeenth century, and approved at Mechlin and at Rome. In 1630 Puteanus (van Putte), a Louvain professor, produced three documents supposed to date from 1065, 1129, and 1151, relating to a convent of Beguines at Vilvorde, near Brussels. The view as to the date of their origin which these documents supported was prevalent for two centuries, and is presupposed in the modern works of Mosheim and of Lea; but the researches of Hallmann proved finally in 1843 that Puteanus's documents were forgeries, probably belonging to the fourteenth and fifteenth centuries. The origin of these communities is now, accordingly, almost universally placed in the twelfth century, and attributed to a priest of Liége, Lambert le Bègue (q.v.).

The scarcity of information about the earliest period has caused the significance of the movement to be underestimated or misconceived. As a matter of fact, the career of Lambert has many points of affinity with those of his younger contemporaries Peter Waldo and Francis of Assisi. Like them, he renounced his property, to endow with it the hospital of St. Christopher at Liége and the new convent of Beguines there. He felt his special mission to be the preaching of repentance, which brought him into conflict with the ecclesiastical authorities when he attacked the vices of the clergy, but had an enduring influence especially on the women of Liége. By 1210 there is contemporary testimony to the existence there of "whole troops of holy maidens"; the ascetic spirit took hold also of the married women, who frequently made vows of continence. Religious excitement did not fail to produce pathological phenomena; stories are told of visions, prophecies, convulsions, incessant tears, loss of speech, and the like. Probably between 1170 and 1180 some of Lambert's followers, to whom his opponents gave the name of Beguines in mockery, had formed a sort of conventual association on a suburban estate belonging to him. By the analogy of the later Beguinages, they probably inhabited a number of small houses grouped about the church and hospital of St. Christopher, and shut off by a wall from the outer world. The first inmates were mostly women of position, who renounced their property and supported themselves by their own labors.

2. The Early Communities.

The religious impulse given by Lambert continued active after his death (probably 1187), and familiarized the people of the Netherlands with the idea of ascetic following of Christ long before the advent of the mendicant orders. Throughout the next century, the need of founding similar institutions for the large numbers of Beguines was felt, first in Flanders and then in the neighboring French and German districts. In France St. Louis showed them special favor, and erected a large Beguinage in Paris, modeled after the Flemish, in 1264; others sprang up, large or small, in all parts of France during the thirteenth and fourteenth centuries. The extension of the system in the other Latin countries was probably considerable, but exact data are wanting. In Germany only a few towns on the lower Rhine, such as Aix-la-Chapelle and Wesel, had Beguinages in the strict sense. Here the usual rule was for women who wished to renounce the world at first to live separately in their own houses or in solitary places; as time went on, they came together in larger or smaller houses put at their disposal by pious gifts, and formed communities of a monastic type. The growth of these convents was remarkable, and continued from the first third of the thirteenth century to the beginning of the fifteenth, by which time the majority of German towns had their convents of Beguines. The statutes varied much in the different houses; the number of inmates was between ten and twenty on an average. There was no uniform dress, but most of the members wore hoods and scapulars resembling a religious habit. Sometimes those who had property retained full control of it; in other cases a portion fell to the convent when they died or left. Celibacy was required as long as they stayed, but they were always free to leave and marry.

3. Extension during the Twelfth Century.

The name of "voluntary poor," which many convents bore, and the regulations of such houses, show the continuance of Lambert's influence in favor of desertion of the world and penitential asceticism; but the Franciscan ideas, very similar in their tendency, which were widely spread not long after, found here a fruitful soil. As early as the thirteenth century a large proportion of the Beghards or Beguines of France, Germany, and northern Italy were under the direction of Franciscans or Dominicans, and so closely related with the penitential confraternities attached to both these orders that the members of these (tertiaries) were commonly known in the Latin countries as *beguini* and *beguinæ*—a fact which has caused much confusion in the study of the history of the real Beguines. The disapproval of these latter by the papal authorities brought about, when it came, a still closer identification with the tertiaries; many joined these for protection, and in the fifteenth century numerous Beguinages were transferred to the Augustinian order. While the original Beguines abstained from begging, it became more common among them in France and Germany by the beginning of the thirteenth century. As in the Latin countries the Beguines are found among the extreme defenders of the Franciscan ideal of poverty, so we find frequently among those of Germany the belief that their strict poverty designated them as the true followers of Christ. In accordance with this view, they were apt to withdraw themselves from the teaching of the clergy and listen rather to the exciting exhortations of their "mistresses" or of wandering preachers in sympathy with their beliefs. They developed a system of extreme corporal austerity, and lost themselves in mystic speculations which increased their tendency to see visions and to condemn the ordinary means of grace; even the moral law seems at times to have been regarded as not binding upon them. The impulse of apocalyptic enthusiasm, given by Joachim of Fiore (q.v.) and spread by the "spiritual" Franciscans among the laity, as well as the quietistic mysticism of the Brethren of the Free Spirit (q.v.), found an entrance into their houses before the end of the thirteenth century. Early in the next century, the influx of women of high social position declined more and more, and the new foundations took on more of the modern character of benevolent institutions. By the end of the fifteenth century, in Germany at least, they had almost completely lost their first religious fervor and had forfeited much of the popular respect they had formerly enjoyed.

4. Relation to the Mendicant Orders.

As to the Beghards or male communities, the question whether the first associations known by this name can be directly connected with Lambert le Bègue, or sprang up after his death in imitation of the Flemish Beguinages, can not be decided with our present knowledge. They are first met with in Louvain (c. 1220) and Antwerp (1228). The names *beguin* and *begard* (Flemish usually *bogard;* Middle High German *begehart* and *biegger*) were given in mockery and are of Walloon origin; other names are Lollards (probably from the Middle Dutch *löllen,* to murmur; see LOLLARDS), "voluntary poor," *boni pueri, boni valeti,* etc. In the course of the thirteenth and fourteenth centuries they spread throughout Germany, into Poland and the Alpine districts, and even into the

5. The Male Communities.

Latin countries; but their numbers were much smaller than those of the Beguines. As early as the thirteenth century a number of their houses, too, connected themselves with the tertiaries of the two great mendicant orders. Like the Beguines, many of them were partizans of the views of the "spiritual" Franciscans and Fraticelli. They practised begging ostentatiously, frequently had no fixed abode, and wandered about in small groups, begging and winning adherents for their cause. They did not abandon this mode of life even after papal prohibitions were directed against them, but strengthened themselves by the adhesion of sympathizers who were expelled from the convents, and remained in close relations with the Beguines, by whom they were regarded as martyrs to the Franciscan ideal of poverty and channels of mystical revelations. In the Netherlands the fifteenth-century Beghards appear for the most part as regular Franciscan tertiaries, organized from 1443 as a separate *Congregatio Zepperensis beghardorum tertiæ regulæ S. Francisci*, with the convent of Zepperen, near Hasselt, as their mother house. Internal dissensions later split them into two branches. In the seventeenth century they were united with the Lombard congregation of regular tertiaries, and did not survive the Revolution. The internal organization of their houses corresponded generally to that of the Beguines. The earliest Dutch Beghards were mostly weavers, who continued to follow their trade; later they frequently copied and sold manuscripts. The German Beghards followed a variety of occupations; but at the end of the Middle Ages begging was their main source of revenue. A special inner group was that of the "Voluntary Poor" (also called Poor Brothers, Cellites, Alexians; in the Netherlands Lollards, *Matemans, Cellebroeders;* see ALEXIANS), who required the entire abandonment of property by their members and bound them by permanent vows. Their strict organization, their enthusiasm for poverty, their zealous devotion to charitable duties, all point to a tradition reaching back to the beginning of the Beghard system. They are further contrasted with the ordinary Beghards by the fact that they held aloof for the most part from the Franciscan affiliations which have been seen to be so common. In the fifteenth century they associated themselves with the Augustinians. Public opinion, by the end of the Middle Ages, was even more unfavorable to the Beghards than to the Beguines; popular satirists and preachers alike speak of them as hypocritical beggars with a tendency to deceit and immorality; and the Reformation swept away the last remnants of them, in Germany at least.

The persecution of Beghards and Beguines as a heretical sect began in the second half of the thirteenth century, probably as a consequence of their relation to the "spiritual" Franciscans (see FRANCIS, SAINT, OF ASSISI, AND THE FRANCISCAN ORDER). By 1300 the name *beguinus* was commonly used in the Latin countries as the accepted designation for the heretical "spiritual" party and Fraticelli, which naturally prejudiced the general opinion of the orthodox convents of Beghards and Beguines. Still more damaging was the fact that the German bishops, about the same time, assumed that the pantheistic heresy of the Brethren of the Free Spirit (q.v.) found its chief support in their houses. Though, as a matter of fact, this was probably true only of a small section, the name of Beghards was commonly adopted in Germany for the adherents of that heresy. During the fourteenth century the belief spread that in some convents of Beghards and Beguines there existed an inner circle of "the perfect" who were alien from the doctrines of the Church and the laws of morality, to which the younger members were admitted only after years of probation. Whether or not these accusations were true, which it is now next to impossible to determine, the bitter hostility shown against the Beghards and Beguines probably finds its simplest explanation in the conflicts which arose at the end of the thirteenth century between the episcopate and the secular clergy, on the one hand, and the mendicant orders, especially the Franciscans, on the other, since these latter gained their lay following largely through the numerous houses of Beghards and Beguines. Several German provincial councils (Cologne 1306, Mainz 1310, Treves 1310) passed strong measures against them, and the Council of Vienne (1311) struck at them even harder, undertaking to suppress them entirely on the charge of spreading heretical doctrines under a cloak of piety. The execution of these decrees of suppression, which took place under John XXII, caused great confusion in the Church of Germany, the mendicants and sometimes the magistrates attempting to defend the Beguines. Since their total suppression appeared impracticable, John XXII compromised by making a distinction and granting toleration to the orthodox Beguines. Persecution did not, however, cease; and with the powerful support of the Emperor Charles IV, it was taken up once more by Urban V and Gregory XI. Without regard to the varying senses of the names, all Beghards and Beguines alike were condemned as heretics, excommunicated, and outlawed. Their property was to serve for pious purposes, for the support of the inquisitors, or for repairing city walls and roads. Between 1366 and 1378 remorseless persecution raged against them throughout Germany; but even then they found advocates, especially among the secular magistrates, and Gregory XI was finally prevailed upon to repeat the distinction between orthodox and heretical Beguines and Beghards, and to tolerate the former. About 1400 another storm broke out, aroused by the attacks which the clergy of Basel, especially the Dominican Johannes Mulberg made upon the Beguines of that city. By 1410 the Beguines in the dioceses of Constance, Basel, and Strasburg were driven from their convents. At the time of the Council of Constance (1414-18), which showed itself well disposed toward them, they won a victory of some importance when they secured the condemnation as heretical of a treatise directed both against them and against the Brethren of the Common Life by the Dominican Matthæus Grabo. Attacks were still made upon them, none the less, and that a general feeling inspired such attacks is

6. Persecution as Heretics.

shown by the fact that the name "Beghard" continued through the fifteenth century to be applied to the most various heretics, until it adhered permanently to the Bohemian Brethren or Picards.

7. Surviving Beguinages in the Netherlands.

In what is now Belgium and Holland, the example of Lambert's first followers was widely followed, as has been seen; here the Beguines flourished most, and here they have maintained their existence to the present day. A long series of accounts of mystical visions, hysterico-ecstatic phenomena, and extreme austerities shows that the strong religious impulse of the beginning remained operative until after the Reformation. Heretical mysticism was not without its adherents: in 1310 Margareta Porete, a Beguine of Hainault and the author of a book of apparently pantheistic libertinism, was executed in Paris, and the mystic Hadewich Blommaerdine (q.v.) of Brussels (d. 1336) found adherents among the Beguines of Brabant and Zeeland. The bishops and princes, however, protected the communities in times of persecution. In the fourteenth century the contemplative life was largely given up in favor of diligent work for the sick and poor, and later for the education of girls. The French Revolution deprived these institutions of their religious character, which they regained in 1814. At present there are fifteen Beguinages in Belgium, only two of which are of any size, both at Ghent, numbering 869 inmates in 1896. The larger one, transferred in 1874 to St. Amandsberg just outside the city, is a complete model of a small town, with walls, gates, streets, and gardens. The total number of Beguines in Belgium was 1,790 in 1825, 1,480 in 1866, and about 1,230 in 1896. In Holland two houses have survived, one at Amsterdam with thirteen inmates and one at Breda with forty-six. (HERMAN HAUPT.)

BIBLIOGRAPHY: E. Hallmann, *Die Geschichte des Ursprungs der belgischen Beghinen*, Berlin, 1843 (perhaps the best book on the subject); J. L. von Mosheim, *De Beghardis et Beguinabus*, Leipsic, 1790; F. von Biedenfeld, *Ursprung . . . sämtlicher Mönchs- und Klosterfrauen-Orden*, Weimar, 1837; G. Uhlhorn, *Die christliche Liebesthätigkeit im Mittelalter*, Stuttgart, 1884; H. Haupt, *Beiträge zur Geschichte der Sekte von freiem Geiste und des Beghardentums*, in *Zeitschrift für Kirchengeschichte*, vii (1884), 503 sqq.; H. C. Lea, *History of the Inquisition*, ii, 350-517, Philadelphia, 1888; P. Frédéricq, *Les Documents de Glasgow concernant Lambert de Bègue*, in *Bulletins de l'académie de Belgique*, third series, xxix (1895), 148-165, 990-1006; Heimbucher, *Orden und Kongregationen*, i, 501, ii, 422-425; A. Neander, *Christian Church*, iv, passim, v, passim; W. Moeller, *Christian Church*, ii, 475-478.

BEGIN, bê″gan′, **LOUIS NAZAIRE**: Roman Catholic archbishop of Quebec; b. at Lévis, Quebec, Jan. 10, 1840. He was educated at the Seminary of Quebec (1857–62) and Laval University (B.A., 1863). He then began the study of theology at the Grand Seminary of Quebec, but was chosen to fill a chair in the newly established faculty of theology in the University of Laval, and was sent to Rome to study. He was ordained to the priesthood in 1865, and returned to Quebec in 1868, where he taught dogmatic theology and ecclesiastical history at Laval University until 1884, in addition to being prefect of the Little Seminary and having charge of the pupils of the University during the last few years of this period. In 1884 he accompanied the archbishop of Quebec to Rome to defend the rights of Laval University, and on his return was appointed principal of the Normal School, remaining there until 1888. In the latter year he was consecrated bishop of Chicoutimi, and three years later was appointed coadjutor, with the title of archbishop of Cyrene, to Cardinal Taschereau. On the death of the Cardinal in 1898, he became archbishop of Quebec. He has written *La Primauté et l'infaillibilité des souverains pontifes* (Quebec, 1873); *La Sainte Écriture et la règle de la foi* (1874; English translation by G. M. Ward, London, 1875); *Le Culte catholique* (1875); *Aide-mémoire, ou chronologie de l'histoire du Canada* (1886); and *Catéchisme de controverse* (1902).

BEHAISM: A development of Babism (q.v.). The Bab had taught that the greatest and last of all manifestations of divinity was to appear and, through his teachings, wipe out all distinctions of sects. In 1862, twelve years after the Bab's execution, Beha Ullah, a high-born Persian and Babite leader, claimed to be the fulfilment of this teaching. He was imprisoned and exiled and died in Acre, Syria, in 1892. His son, Abdul Beha Abbas, then became the leader and "Center of the Covenant." From his residence in Acre, where he lives under government surveillance, a far-reaching propaganda has gone forth and pilgrims find their way thither even from distant America.

Behaist missionaries are not allowed to accept money, though they may be entertained by converts or others interested. Their message consists in a recital of the history of their religion and the lives of the Bab and Beha Ullah. The Old and New Testament prophecies and the sacred books of ethnic religions are studied in the belief that they establish the Behaist doctrines. Their sacred writings are the works of Beha Ullah, of which the most remarkable is the *Book of Ighan*. They are mostly short sentences called "communes," consisting of prayers or truths for the guidance of life. The explanation of the *Book of Ighan* and the "Hidden Words" in Arabic and Persian is a part of the regular preaching. The beauty of service to the poor and suffering is a cardinal precept. Simplicity in food and dress is another, and herein Abdul Beha is an example to his followers. Polygamy is not allowed and all goods are held in common. It is believed that God has manifested himself at different times according to the needs of the race, the chief manifestations having been three in number; viz., Jesus—whose life and teachings are commended,—the Bab, and Beha Ullah, who is the greatest and last; after him there will be no other manifestation, and whosoever does not believe on him after having heard his words will not have another chance to enter the kingdom. Certain feasts are observed commemorating events in the life of Beha Ullah, and one which was instituted by the Bab consists in a simple repast such as fruits, nuts, and cool water, held at the home of a believer every nineteen days; a vacant seat is left at the head of the table for the absent master, and passages from the "Hidden Words" are read as the food is passed.

Behaist congregations are known as "assemblies." The first in America was established in Chicago by a Syrian, Ibrahim Kheirallah, in 1894. There are now thirty-five in America, each independent of the others and owning no authority but that of Abdul Beha. It is claimed that the mission of Behaism is to unify the world and bring all religions into one.[1]

MARGARET B. PEEKE.

BIBLIOGRAPHY: Consult the literature given under BABISM; E. D. Ross, *Babism*, in *Great Religions of the World*, London, 1901; Mirza Hussain Ali, *Le Livre de la certitude . . . traduit . . . par H. Dreyfus*, Paris, 1904; *Le Beyan arabe, le livre sacré du Babyeme*, transl. by A. Nicolas, Paris, 1905; Beha Ullah, *Les Préceptes du Béhaisme: les ornements — les paroles du paradis, les splendeurs, les révélations*, transl. by H. Dreyfus and U. Chirazi, Paris, 1906.

BEHMEN, JACOB. See BOEHME.

BEIRUT. See PHENICIA, I, § 6.

BEISSEL, JOHN CONRAD. See COMMUNISM, II, 5; DUNKERS, I, 2.

BEISSEL, STEPHAN: German Jesuit; b. at Aachen Apr. 21, 1841. He was educated at the universities of Bonn and Münster and at the seminary at Cologne. He was ordained to the priesthood in 1871 and lived two years in France, three in England, fifteen in Holland, and four in Luxemburg, passing the remainder of his time at Aachen and Cologne. He has written *Baugeschichte der Kirche des heiligen Viktor zu Xanten* (Freiburg, 1883); *Geldwert und Arbeitslohn im Mittelalter* (1884); *Verehrung der Heiligen in Deutschland bis zum Beginn des dreizehnten Jahrhunderts* (1885); *Bilder der Handschrift des Kaisers Otto im Münster zu Aachen* (Aachen, 1886); *Geschichte der Ausstattung der Kirche des heiligen Viktor zu Xanten* (Freiburg, 1887); *Geschichte der trierschen Kirchen und ihrer Reliquien* (2 parts, Treves, 1889); *Evangelienbuch des heiligen Bernward von Hildesheim* (Hildesheim, 1891); *Verehrung der Heiligen und ihrer Reliquien in Deutschland während der zweiten Hälfte des Mittelalters* (Freiburg, 1893); *Vatikanische Miniaturen* (1893); *Der heilige Bernward von Hildesheim als Künstler* (Hildesheim, 1895); *Fra Giovanni Angelico da Fiesole, sein Leben und seine Werke* (Freiburg, 1895); *Die Verehrung Unserer Lieben Frau in Deutschland während des Mittelalters* (1895); *Bilder aus der Geschichte der altchristlichen Kunst und Liturgie in Italien* (1899); *Das Leben Jesu Christi, geschildert auf den Flügeln des Hochaltars zu Kalkar* (in collaboration with J. Joest, Gladbach, 1900); *Das Evangelienbuch Heinrichs III und die Dome zu Goslar in der Bibliothek zu Upsala* (Düsseldorf, 1900); *Die Aachenfahrt* (1902); *Betrachtungspunkte für alle Tage des Kirchenjahres* (10 vols., 1904–05); and *Geschichte der Evangelienbücher in der ersten Hälfte des Mittelalters* (Freiburg, 1906); in addition to two volumes of the *Zur Kenntnis und Würdigung der mittelalterlichen Altäre Deutschlands* (Frankfort, 1895–1905) begun by E. F. A. Münzenberger.

[1] Requests for literature may be addressed to Mr. John Mason Remey, Corcoran Building, Washington, D. C.

BEKKER, BALTHASAR: Dutch precursor of rationalism; b. at Metslawier (4 m. n.e. of Dokkum) Mar. 30, 1634; d. in Friesland June 11, 1698. He studied at Groningen under J. Alting and in Franeker, where he was rector of the Latin school, was made doctor of theology, and preacher in 1666. Being an enthusiastic follower of the Cartesian philosophy, he published at Wesel in 1668 an *Admonitio sincera et candida de philosophia Cartesiana*, and gave greater offense by his catechisms in 1668 and 1670. He was accused of Socinianism, although Alting and other theologians pronounced him to be orthodox. After many controversies, he accepted a call as preacher to Weesp, and, in 1679, to Amsterdam. The appearance of a large comet in 1680 induced him to issue a work against popular superstition, which stirred up more commotion; and, in 1691, in *De betoverde Wereld*, published at Leeuwarden, he denied the existence of sorcery, magic, possessions by the devil, and of the devil himself. The consistory of Amsterdam instituted a formal process against him, and he was deposed July 30, 1692. He went to Friesland, where he edited the last two books of his work.

H. C. ROGGE†.

BIBLIOGRAPHY: A complete list of Bekker's writings and of the opposing works called out is given in A. van der Linden, *B. Bekker, Bibliographie*, The Hague, 1869. For his life consult J. G. Walch, *Einleitung in die Religionsstreitigkeiten ausserhalb der lutherischen Kirche*, vol. iii, part 3, 499 sqq., Jena, 1734; M. Schwager, *Beitrag zur Geschichte der Intoleranz, oder Leben, . . . B. Bekkers, mit einer Vorrede Semlers*, Leipsic, 1780; J. M. Schröckh, *Kirchengeschichte seit der Reformation*, viii, 713–722, ib. 1808; D. Lorgion, *B. Bekker in Franeker*, The Hague, 1848; idem, *B. Bekker in Amsterdam*, 2 vols., Groningen, 1850; W. P. C. Knuttel, *Balthasar Bekker*, The Hague, 1906.

BEKKOS, JOHANNES. See JOHANNES (JOHN) BEKKOS.

BEL: A great Babylonian god, whose name, like the equivalent Hebrew *Ba'al*, originally and all through the history of the language was also used in the sense of "lord" or "owner" (see BAAL). The usage of the two words as names of deities also ran through parallel courses; for Bel at one time in Babylonia was a local deity like each of the Baals of the Canaanites. He was the patron deity of the city of Nippur in central Babylonia (the modern Nuffar), where his temple, of great antiquity, has been unearthed by the Pennsylvania expedition. The reason why there were not many Bels in Babylonia was that political union on a large scale was very early effected in that country, while it was always impossible among the Canaanites; and Nippur was the center of an extensive community in very remote times.

When, under priestly influence, Babylonian theology was systematized, to this great god Bel was assigned sovereignty of the earth, while Anu ruled in the highest heaven, and Ea over the deep. These formed the chief trinity with primary and universal dominion.

But it is not the Bel of Nippur whose name appears in the Bible and Apocrypha. On account of the rise and supremacy of the city of Babylon under Hammurabi (2250 B.C.), Marduk (Merodach), the god of that city, was invested with the prerogatives and even with the name of Bel, so that in the comparatively modern Old Testament times "Bel" stands for "Merodach" and for him only (so in Isa. xlvi, 1; Jer. li, 44; in Jer. l, 2 both names occur together, meaning practically "Bel-Merodach").

The Babylonian Bel was not only adopted by the Assyrians as one of their chief gods (of course lower than Asshur), but like Ishtar (see ASHTORETH), Sin, and Nebo, he seems to have obtained worshipers in the West-land. Such, at least, is an inference which has been drawn from the proper names Bildad ("Bel loves"), Ashbel ("man of Bel"), and *Balaam*. Moreover, "Bel" is found as an element in several Phenician and Palmyrene names. See BABYLONIA, VII. J. F. MCCURDY.

BIBLIOGRAPHY: A. H. Sayce, *Religion of the Ancient Babylonians*, London, 1887; idem, *Religion of Ancient Egypt and Babylonia*, Edinburgh, 1902; M. Jastrow, *Religion of Babylonia*, Boston, 1898; idem, in *DB*, extra vol., pp. 538-539, 545; Schrader, *KAT*, pp. 354-358.

BEL AND THE DRAGON. See APOCRYPHA, A, IV, 3.

BELGIC CONFESSION: A statement of belief written in French in 1561 by Guy de Brès (q.v.) aided by H. Saravia (professor of theology in Leyden, afterward in Cambridge, where he died 1613), H. Modetus (for some time chaplain of William of Orange), and G. Wingen. It was revised by Francis Junius of Bourges (1545–1602), a student of Calvin, pastor of a Walloon congregation at Antwerp, and afterward professor of theology at Leyden, who abridged the sixteenth article and sent a copy to Geneva and other churches for approval. It was probably printed in 1562, or at all events in 1566, and afterward translated into Dutch, German, and Latin. It was presented to Philip II in 1562, with the vain hope of securing toleration. It was formally adopted by synods at Antwerp (1566), Wesel (1568), Emden (1571), Dort (1574), Middleburg (1581), and again by the great Synod of Dort, April 29, 1619. Inasmuch as the Arminians had demanded partial changes, and the text had become corrupt, the Synod of Dort submitted the French, Latin, and Dutch texts to a careful revision. Since that time the Belgic Confession, together with the Heidelberg Catechism, has been the recognized symbol of the Reformed Churches in Holland and Belgium, and of the Reformed (Dutch) Church in America.

The Confession contains thirty-seven articles, and follows the order of the Gallican Confession, but is less polemical, full, and elaborate, especially on the Trinity, the Incarnation, the Church, and the Sacraments. It is, upon the whole, the best symbolical statement of the Calvinistic system of doctrine, with the exception of the Westminster Confession.

The French text must be considered as the original. Of the first edition of 1561 or 1562 no copies are known. The Synod of Antwerp, in September, 1580, ordered a precise parchment copy of the revised text of Junius to be made for its archives, which copy had to be signed by every new minister. This manuscript has always been regarded in the Belgic churches as the authentic document. The first Latin translation was made from Junius's text by Beza, or under his direction, for the *Harmonia Confessionum* (Geneva, 1581). The same passed into the first edition of the *Corpus et Syntagma Confessionum* (Geneva, 1612). A second Latin translation was prepared by Festus Hommius for the Synod of Dort, 1618, revised and approved 1619; and from it was made the English translation in use in the Reformed (Dutch) Church in America. It appeared in Greek 1623, 1653, and 1660, at Utrecht.

BIBLIOGRAPHY: An excellent description and short history is given by Schaff in *Creeds*, i, 502–508, with the text in iii, 383–436, where the literature is given.

BELGIUM: A kingdom of northwestern Europe; area, 11,373 square miles; population, 6,800,000. After a revolt from Holland in 1830, Belgium was recognized with its present boundaries by the Powers in 1839, when it was declared to be neutral territory. The population belongs to two nationalities, the northern portion, which is the larger, being Flemish (Low German), and the southern Walloon (French); the vernacular of forty-one per cent. is French. The boundary between these two components may be defined as running from Maestricht west to the French department Nord.

The prevailing religion is Roman Catholic, since the Dutch Protestants, who were numerous from 1815 to 1830 have, for the most part, emigrated. [The Protestants constitute less than one-half of one per cent. of the entire population.] The Evangelical confessions are represented in many cities, however, by immigrants from Germany in recent decades, as well as by Anglicans and Methodists and converts to Protestantism. The most numerous of these Protestant communions is the *Union des Églises Évangéliques Protestantes de la Belgique*, which was founded in 1839 and consists of French, Dutch, and German congregations, being represented in Liége, Verviers, Seraing, Brussels, Antwerp, Ghent, La Bouverie, Dour, Paturages, Jolimont, and Tournai.

Protestants.

The permanent bond of the Union is a board of directors, chosen at the annual synod of the congregations interested. Recognition by the State as a legal ecclesiastical body assures state aid to its clergy, the usual salary being 2,220 francs, although it occasionally runs as high as 4,000 and 6,000. An "evangelization committee" of the Union cares for scattered members, and especially for the religious education of children by "evangelists" where Protestant schools do not exist. The Union has between 16,000 and 18,000 members. The *Société Évangélique* or *Église Chrétienne Missionnaire Belge* is a free church consisting of converts from Roman Catholicism or their children. It is strongest in the Walloon districts and has numerous places of worship, united into three districts, whose representatives (*Conseils Sectionnaires*) meet four times annually. Over these three councils, to which each congregation sends a pastor and a layman, is the synod, of which the permanent executive body is the *Comité Administrateur*. The clergy are trained chiefly in Switzerland and are subordinate to the synod. This Church possesses few schools of its own, but in public schools of one class with twenty Protestant children and in those of several classes with forty children it is entitled to give religious instruction through its own clergy. It has now about 11,000 members. There are English churches at Antwerp, Bruges, Brussels, and Ostend, and at Antwerp and Brussels there are Presbyterian congregations; in the first-named city an agent of the American Seamen's Friend Society is also active. The Dutch Reformed and the Swedish Lutherans have small congregations in Brussels and Antwerp respectively.

Roman Catholic Church.

The Roman Catholic Church of Belgium was organized in 1561, when the authority of the foreign bishops was abrogated, and in 1839 the system was readjusted to harmonize with the new boundaries. The most of the clergy receive their training at the episcopal seminaries and a small proportion at the University of Louvain. The State has no control over the appointment of priests, who are subject only to their bishops. The Roman Catholic Church, however, receives from the State an annual stipend of more than 4,800,000 francs, although it does not enjoy any ecclesiastical prerogative. Its influence on the life of the people is exerted chiefly through the monasteries, of which there are more than 220 for monks, with some 5,000 members, and about 1,500 nunneries, with over 27,000 sisters. The members are employed in large numbers in the public schools, the right being given the communities by the law of 1884 to "adopt" private schools, or schools conducted by the religious organizations. A number of intermediate schools are also under ecclesiastical control, as well as the University of Louvain. Academic training is also provided for by the state universities of Ghent and Liége, and by the free university of Brussels.

Diocesan Organization.

In its hierarchic organization, Belgium constitutes the province of Mechlin, and its dioceses are divided according to the political boundaries of the country. The archdiocese of Mechlin on the Dyle was created by a papal enactment of 1559, which first came into full operation in 1561. It contains fifty-five parishes and over 600 chapels of ease in the provinces of Brabant and Antwerp. The suffragan bishoprics are those of Bruges, Ghent, Liége, Namur, and Tournai (Doornik). Bruges, founded in 1559, has forty parishes and 245 chapels of ease; Ghent, established in the same year, also has forty parishes and 310 chapels of ease; Liége, dating from the fourth century, has an equal number of parishes and 570 chapels of ease; Namur, created in 1559 (1561), has the same number of parishes and 700 chapels of ease; and Doornik, the seat of a bishop since 1146, controls thirty-three parishes and 445 chapels of ease, its see comprising the Hennegau, with the exception of five parishes belonging to the French diocese of Cambrai.

II.—3

The Jews of Belgium, who number about 5,000, are divided into twelve rabbinical districts.

WILHELM GOETZ.

BIBLIOGRAPHY: Balan, *Histoire contemporaine de la Belgique*, Lyons, 1891; *Archives Belges, revue critique d'historiographie nationale*, Lüttich, 1899 sqq.; *La Belgique et le Vatican. Documents et travaux législatifs*, 3 vols., Brussels, 1880–81; G. Verspeyen, *Le Parti catholique belge*, Ghent, 1893; J. Hoyois, *La Politique catholique en Belgique depuis 1814*, Louvain, 1895; O. Coppin, *L'Union sacerdotale, son histoire, son esprit et ses constitutions*, Namur, 1896; U. Berlière, *Monasticon belge*, vol. i, Paris, 1897; *La Belge ecclésiastique* (an annual).

BELIAL, bī'li-al ("worthlessness"): A word which occurs once in the New Testament (II Cor. vi, 15; better reading *Beliar*) as the name of Satan, hardly as that of Antichrist; the Peshito has "Satan." In the Old Testament *beliyya'al* is not used as a designation of Satan, or of a bad angel; it is an appellation, "worthlessness" or "wickedness" in an ethical sense, and is almost always found in connection with a word denoting the person or thing whose worthlessness or wickedness is spoken of; as, "man of Belial," "son of Belial," "daughter of Belial," "thoughts of Belial," etc. In a few instances *beliyya'al* denotes physical destruction; so probably Ps. xviii, 4 (II Sam. xxii, 5), "floods of destruction" (A. V "ungodly men"; R. V "ungodliness"). To understand this passage to refer to the prince of hell is against Old Testament usage. Occasionally the adjunct is omitted, as in II Sam. xxiii, 6; Job xxxiv, 18; Nahum i, 15, where the word means the "bad," the "destroyer," the "wicked." Although thus originally not a proper name, but an appellation, in the later Jewish and Christian literature it passed over into a name for Satan, not as the "worthless," but as the "destroyer." It is so used in II Cor. vi, 15, where Paul asks: "What harmony is there between Christ and Belial?" "Belial" stands for "Satan" also in Jewish epigrapha and apocalyptic writings, such as the Testaments of the Twelve Patriarchs, the Book of Jubilees, and the Jewish interpolations in the Sibylline Oracles.

BIBLIOGRAPHY: J. Hamburger, s.v., in *Real-Encyklopädie für Bibel und Talmud*, vol. i., Leipsic, 1891; W. Bousset, *Der Antichrist*, pp. 86–87, 99–101, Göttingen, 1895; T. K. Cheyne, in *Expositor*, 1895, pp. 435–439; F. Hommel, in *Expository Times*, viii. 472; *EB*, i. 525–527.

BELL, WILLIAM M'ILVIN: United Brethren; b. in Whitley Co., Ind., Nov. 12, 1860; entered the ministry 1879; elected bishop 1905.

BELLAMY, JOSEPH: Congregationalist; b. at New Cheshire, Conn., Feb. 20, 1719; d. at Bethlehem, Conn., Mar. 6, 1790. He was graduated at Yale, 1735, and was licensed to preach at the age of eighteen; was ordained pastor of the church at Bethlehem Apr. 2, 1740. During the Great Awakening he preached as an itinerating evangelist; later he established a divinity school in his house, where many prominent New England clergymen were trained. He was a disciple and personal friend of Jonathan Edwards, and the most gifted preacher among his followers, being thought by some to be equal to Whitefield. In his *True Religion Delineated* (Boston, 1750) he sets forth in spirited style the plan of salvation and of the Christian life after the Edwardean conception, and he explicitly advocates the doctrine of a general atonement. In the *Wisdom of God in the Permission of Sin* (1758) he argues that, while sin is a terrible evil, God permits it as a necessary means of the best good, and the universe is "more holy and happy than if sin and misery had never entered." God could have prevented sin without violating free will. On the whole his work was more general than specific, modifying the prevalent conceptions in the direction of greater simplicity and reasonableness. He sometimes approaches quite near subsequent forms of expression. A collected edition of his works appeared at New York (3 vols., 1811), and another (and better) at Boston, with memoir by Tryon Edwards (2 vols., 1850).

BELLARMINE, bel″lar-mîn′

In Louvain (§ 1). In Rome. The *Disputationes* (§ 2).
New Duties after 1589. Controversial Writings (§ 3).

Roberto Francesco Romolo Bellarmino, the famous Roman Catholic controversialist, was born at Montepulciano (26 m. s.w. of Arezzo), in Tuscany, Oct. 4, 1542; d. in Rome Sept. 17, 1621. He was a nephew of Pope Marcellus II, and came of a noble though impoverished family. His abilities showed themselves early; as a boy he knew Vergil by heart, and composed a number of poems in Italian and Latin; one of his hymns, on Mary Magdalene, is included in the Roman breviary. His father destined him for a political career, hoping that he might restore the fallen glories of the house; but his mother wished him to enter the Jesuit order, and her influence prevailed. He entered the Roman novitiate in 1560, remained in Rome three years, and then went to a Jesuit house at Mondovi in Piedmont. Here he learned Greek, and taught it as fast as he learned it. His systematic study of theology began at Padua in 1567 and 1568, where his teachers were Thomists, the Jesuits not yet having had time to develop a theology of their own.

1. In Louvain.

After a visit to Venice, where he increased his renown as a public speaker, Bellarmine was sent by the general, Francis Borgia, in 1569, to Louvain, then the most famous Roman Catholic university. He was ordained priest at Ghent on Palm Sunday, 1570, by the elder Jansenius. A strict Augustinian theology prevailed among the teachers at Louvain, represented by Bajus, the precursor of Jansenism (see BAJUS, MICHEL). Bellarmine had not enough deep knowledge of his own nature or Christian experience to be able to appreciate the Augustinian doctrines of the corruption of man and the necessity of divine grace to any good movement of the will. He contended accordingly against the propositions of Bajus, though his own views and expressions in the great controversy on grace were always a little uncertain. He was the first Jesuit to teach at the university, where the subject of his course was the *Summa* of St. Thomas; he also made extensive studies in the Fathers and medieval theologians, which gave him the material for his book *De scriptoribus ecclesiasticis* (Rome, 1613), which was later revised and enlarged by Sirmond, Labbeus, and Oudin. In the Netherlands he gained a knowledge of the great controversy with the Protestants which he could hardly have got in Italy, though he seems never to have come into personal contact with the evangelical leaders. Finally he learned Hebrew, and wrote his often reprinted grammar. His genius for teaching, clearness of thought, and adroitness in controversy were indisputable.

2. In Rome. The "Disputationes."

Bellarmine's residence in Louvain lasted seven years. His health was undermined by study and asceticism, and in 1576 he made a journey to Italy to restore it. Here he was detained by the commission given him by Gregory XIII to lecture on polemical theology in the new Roman College. He devoted eleven years to this work, out of whose activities grew his celebrated *Disputationes de controversiis christianæ fidei*, first published at Ingolstadt, 4 vols., 1581–93. It occupies in the field of dogmatics the same place as the *Annales* of Baronius in the field of history. Both were the fruits of the great revival in religion and learning which the Roman Catholic Church had witnessed since 1540. Both bear the stamp of their period; the effort for literary elegance, which was considered the principal thing at the beginning of the sixteenth century, had given place to a desire to pile up as much material as possible, to embrace the whole field of human knowledge, and incorporate it into theology. Bellarmine's exposition of the views and arguments of the Protestants is surprisingly full and accurate, so much so that the circulation of the book in Italy was for a time not encouraged. He fails, like most of his contemporaries, in understanding the principle of historical development, and his belief in authority, pressed to an extreme, injured his sense of truth and allowed him to handle both the Bible and history in an arbitrary manner. The first volume treats of the Word of God, of Christ, and of the pope; the second of the authority of councils, and of the Church, whether militant, expectant, or triumphant; the third of the sacraments; and the fourth of grace, free will, justification, and good works. The most important part of the work is contained in the five books on the Roman pontiff. In these, after a speculative introduction on forms of government in general, holding monarchy to be relatively the best, he says that a monarchical government is necessary for the Church, to preserve unity and order in it. Such power he considers to have been established by the commission of Christ to Peter. He then proceeds to demonstrate that this power has been transmitted to the successors of Peter, admitting that a heretical pope may be freely judged and deposed by the Church since by the very fact of his heresy he would cease to be pope, or even a member of the Church; this is almost like an echo of the great councils of the fifteenth century. The third section discusses Antichrist; Bellarmine gives in full the theory set forth by the Greek and Latin Fathers, of a personal Antichrist to come just before the end of the world and to be accepted by the Jews and enthroned in the temple at Jerusalem—thus endeavoring to dispose of the Protestant exposition which saw Antichrist in the pope. The fourth section sets forth the pope as the supreme judge in matters of faith and morals, though making the concessions (confirmed indeed by the Vatican Council) that the pope may err in questions of fact which may be known by ordinary human knowledge, and also when he speaks as a mere unofficial theologian, *doctor privatus*. His assertions are much more unbounded in the last part, which treats of the pope's power in secular matters. While he says that the pope has no direct jurisdiction in such things, he yet stoutly contends for the power of deposing kings, absolving subjects from their allegiance, and altering civil laws, when these actions are necessary for the good of the souls committed to the charge of the chief pastor.

3. New Duties after 1589. Controversial Writings.

Until 1589 Bellarmine was occupied altogether as professor of theology, but that date marked the beginning of a new epoch in his life and of new dignities. After the murder of Henry III of France Sixtus V sent Gaetano as legate to Paris to negotiate with the League, and chose Bellarmine to accompany him as theologian; he was in the city during its siege by Henry of Navarre. The next pope, Clement VIII (1591–1605), set great store by him. He wrote the preface to the new edition of the Vulgate, and was made rector of the Roman College in 1592, examiner of bishops in 1598, cardinal in 1599, and in 1602 archbishop of Capua. He had written strongly against pluralism and non-residence, and he set a good example himself by leaving within four days for his diocese, where he devoted himself zealously to his episcopal duties, and firmly executed the reforming decrees of the Council of Trent. Under Paul V (1605–21) arose the great conflict between Venice and the papacy, in which Fra Paolo Sarpi was the spokesman of the Republic, protesting against the papal interdict, reasserting the principles of Constance and Basel, and denying the pope's authority in matters secular. Bellarmine wrote three rejoinders to the Venetian theologians, and at the same time possibly saved Sarpi's life by giving him warning of an impending murderous attack. He soon had occasion to cross swords with a more prominent antagonist, James I of England, who prided himself on his theological attainments. Bellarmine had written a letter to the English archpriest Blackwell, reproaching him for having taken the oath of allegiance in apparent disregard of his duty to the pope. James attacked him in 1608 in a Latin treatise, which the scholarly cardinal answered at once, making merry with delicate humor over the defects of the royal Latinity. James replied with a second attack in more careful style, dedicated to the Emperor Rudolph II and all the monarchs of Christendom, in which he posed as the defender of primitive and truly Catholic Christianity. Bellarmine's answer to this covers more or less the whole controversy. In reply to a posthumous treatise of William Barclay, the celebrated Scottish jurist, he wrote another *Tractatus de potestate summi pontificis in rebus temporalibus*, which reiterated his strong assertions on the subject, and was therefore prohibited in France, where it agreed with the sentiments of neither the king nor the bishops. He was among the theologians consulted on the teaching of Galileo when it first made a stir at Rome. In his old age he was allowed to return to his old home, Montepulciano, as its bishop for four years, after which he retired to the Jesuit college of St. Andrew in Rome. He received some votes in the conclaves which elected Leo XI, Paul V, and Gregory XV, but only in the second case had he any prospect of election. Since his death the members of his order have more than once attempted to procure his canonization, but without success. The best of the older editions of his works is that in seven vols., Cologne, 1617; recent ones are those of Paris, 1870–74, and Naples, 1872. (A. HAUCK.)

BIBLIOGRAPHY: A list of the works of Bellarmine is given in H. Hurter, *Nomenclator literarius*, i, 273 sqq., Innsbruck, 1892. His autobiography, written in 1613, was issued in Lat. at Rome, 1675, at Louvain, 1753, and in Lat. and Germ., ed. J. J. I. von Döllinger and F. H. Reusch, Bonn, 1887; it was used in MS. by J. Fuligatti, *Vita del Cardinale R. Bellarmino*, Rome, 1624. The lives by D. Bartoli, Rome, 1677, N. Frison, Nantes, 1708, and F. Heuse, Paderborn, 1868, are mere eulogies and add nothing of value; indeed it is said that the autobiography and the works founded upon it have done much to prevent Bellarmine's canonization. Consult Niceron, *Mémoires*, xxxi, 1 sqq.; J. B. Coudere, *Le Vénérable Cardinal Bellarmin*, 2 vols., Paris, 1893.

BELLOWS, HENRY WHITNEY: American Unitarian; b. in Boston June 11, 1814; d. in New York Jan. 30, 1882. He was graduated at Harvard 1832, and at the Cambridge Divinity School 1837; was ordained pastor of the First Congregational Society (Unitarian), Chambers Street, New York, Jan. 2, 1838, and remained there till death; during his pastorate the church was twice moved, to Broadway between Spring and Prince Streets and the name changed to the Church of the Divine Unity, and again to 4th Avenue and 20th Street, where it took the name of All Souls' Church. Dr. Bellows was the organizer, president, and chief administrator of the United States Sanitary Commission (1862–78), and during the Civil War he superintended with rare efficiency the distribution of supplies valued at $15,000,000 and $5,000,000 in money; at a later period he was president of the first civil service reform association organized in the country. He was president of the National Unitarian Conference 1865–79. He wrote much for the periodicals of his denomination and was the chief originator of *The Christian Inquirer* (New York, 1846) and for five years its principal contributor. He also published a number of books, of merely personal and transient interest.

BELLS: The use of bells as adjuncts to Christian worship was not without precedent in pre-Christian times. Among the Jews the vestment of the high priest was adorned with little bells (Ex. xxviii, 33); and among the pagans the priests of Proserpine announced the beginning of the sacrifice by ringing bells. There is no evidence of early Christian use of them to summon people to prayer; this seems to have been done by word of mouth, even as late as Tertullian and Jerome.

In the Egyptian monasteries the Old Testament use of trumpets still survived, and the sound made by knocking pieces of wood together served the same purpose; this custom is still sometimes used in the Roman Catholic Church on the last three days of Holy Week, when the ringing of bells is forbidden [and survives in some places in the East]. **Early Use.** The first positive evidence of the use of bells in connection with Christian worship is found in Gregory of Tours (d. 595), who speaks of them as being rung at the beginning of the liturgy and the canonical hours. From the seventh century on, bells are often mentioned in the inventories of Western churches, and by 800 they were so common as to be found even in village churches. A capitulary of Charlemagne (801) prescribes that priests shall ring their bells at the accustomed hours of the day and night. In the ninth century some Eastern instances occur; thus Orso I, Doge of Venice, presented twelve bells to the Byzantine emperor, who placed them in a tower near St. Sophia. But outside of Russia they never attained the same importance as in the West. The Mohammedans usually removed them in the countries they conquered; and Zwingli attempted to abolish their use in Switzerland, though most of the Reformers only protested against superstition in the use of them, especially their consecration.

Walafrid Strabo distinguishes two classes of bells in his time, *vasa productilia* and *fusilia*, wrought and cast. Of the now rare examples of the former class the best known is the "Saufang" at Cologne, so called because the **Material and Form.** legend ran that it had been dug up by pigs about 613; it is made of three plates of iron fastened together with copper nails. Similar and perhaps older examples are in the Edinburgh Museum. For the casting of bells a mixture of copper and tin was employed in the Middle Ages; afterward lead, zinc, iron, and antimony were used with copper. At present the best bell-metal is supposed to be a mixture of 77 to 80 per cent. of good copper with 20 to 23 per cent. of pure tin. The earliest cast bells resemble cow-bells in form, though there are some shaped more like a beehive or a pear. Their dimensions are small.

As far as can be judged from the extant examples, the custom of putting inscriptions on bells does not go further back than the twelfth century, and is by no means general even then. On cast bells the inscriptions are rarely incised; where this occurs, it is a sign of antiquity. Later they are more commonly raised, and in either Roman or Gothic capitals down to the end of **Inscriptions.** the fourteenth century; then small letters were used until about 1550, and since then more modern types of letters have been usual, except in recent deliberate imitations of the old style. Until well into the fourteenth century Latin was the regular language; then the vernacular came into use. The earliest inscriptions were short; from the end of the sixteenth century much longer ones became usual, frequently almost filling the surface of the bell. They are mostly pious dedications or prayers, or declarations of the purpose of the bell, such as *Funera plango, fulgura frango, sabbata pango; excito lentos, dissipo ventos, paco cruentos.* Besides inscriptions, the sides of bells were adorned with pictures, coats of arms, seals, and various symbols, among the oldest being, besides the cross, the dove with the olive-branch, and the *Agnus Dei*.

As early as the Frankish sacramentaries and the Pontifical of Egbert special formulas for the benediction of bells are mentioned. This practise was connected in those days with superstitious notions, so that Charlemagne was obliged to regulate it in 789. But the formulas of benediction themselves attributed a quasimagical effect to **Benediction.** the bells thus consecrated. According to present Roman Catholic usage, the blessing of bells is an episcopal prerogative, though priests may exercise it in case of necessity with the pope's permission. The ceremonies somewhat resemble those of baptism, which has given rise to the practise of naming bells, and in the Middle Ages of appointing sponsors for them, from whom rich christening gifts were expected. The Schmalkald Articles declared bitterly against these practises as "popish jugglery" and "a mockery of holy baptism."

The main use of bells has always been to announce the time of public worship. It is also a common Roman Catholic practise to ring the church bell at the consecration in the mass, as in some Protestant localities at the Lord's Prayer after the sermon, that those who are absent may unite themselves in spirit with the congregation. During the mass, moreover, a small bell (called the "Sanctus" or "sacring" bell) is rung at **Present Use.** the specially solemn parts—the *Sanctus*, the beginning of the canon, the consecration, and the *Domine, non sum dignus*. Bells have been rung also at certain regular times to call to mind some mystery, as the passion and death or the incarnation of Christ (see ANGELUS), or to bid to prayer for sinners, for the faithful departed, or for peace. The ringing of joyous peals at marriages, and the announcement of a death by solemn tolling (originally intended to move the hearers to prayer for the soul, either before or after death) are ancient practises; the latter existed, at least in the monasteries, in the time of Bede. In some parts of England a special bell was tolled with a similar intention before the execution of a criminal. (NIKOLAUS MÜLLER.)

BIBLIOGRAPHY: Literature on the subject is given in H. T. Ellacombe, *Practical Remarks on Belfries and Ringers, with an Appendix on Chiming*, London, 1859–60; H. Otte, *Glockenkunde*, pp. 1–6, Leipsic, 1884, and F. W. Schubart, *Die Glocken im Herzogthum Anhalt*, pp. xiv–xvii, Dessau, 1896. H. T. Ellacombe has a series of works treating of English bells, among which are: *Sundry Words About Bells*, Exeter, 1864; *Church Bells of Devon*, ib. 1872; *Church Bells of Somerset*, 1875; *Church Bells of Gloucestershire*, 1881. Consult also: Joseph Anderson, *Scotland in Early Times*, 1st series, pp. 167–215, Edinburgh, 1881; F. W. Warren, *Liturgy and Ritual of the Celtic Church*, p. 92, Oxford, 1881; Margaret Stokes, *Early Christian Art in Ireland*, pp. 50 sqq., London, 1887; J. T. Fowler, *Adamnani Vita S. Columbæ*, pp. xliii–xliv, Oxford, 1894; K. H. Bergner, *Zur Glockenkunde Thuringens*, Jena, 1896; *Encyclopædia Britannica*, s.v., contains interesting material not easily found elsewhere; *DCA*, i, 184–186.

BELSHAM, THOMAS: English Unitarian; b. at Bedford Apr. 26, 1750; d. at Hampstead Nov. 11, 1829. He finished his studies at the Dissenting Academy of Daventry and in 1770 became teacher there; in 1778 he became minister of an independent chapel at Worcester, but returned to Daventry as teacher and preacher in 1781. Having adopted Unitarian views he resigned in 1789, and was professor of divinity at the college of Hackney until it ceased to exist in 1796. In 1794 he succeeded Dr. Priestley as minister of the Gravel Pit Unitarian Chapel at Hackney, and in 1805 became minister of the Essex Street Chapel, London. He published much, sermons, controversial writings, and general theological works, including *Elements of the Philosophy of the Mind and of Moral Philosophy* (London, 1801); *Letters to the Bishop of London in Vindication of Unitarians* (1815); *The Epistles of St. Paul Translated, with an Exposition and Notes* (2 vols., 1822); he was principal editor of *The New Testament in an Improved Version upon the Basis of Archbishop Newcome's New Translation; with a critical text and notes critical and explanatory* (1808). *American Unitarianism* (4th ed., Boston, 1815) is extracted from his *Memoirs of the Revd. T. Lindsey* (London, 1812).

BIBLIOGRAPHY: J. Williams, *Memoirs of Thomas Belsham*, London, 1833; *DNB*, iv, 202–203.

BELSHAZZAR. See BABYLONIA, VI, 7, § 3; PERSIA.

BELSHEIM, JOHANNES: Norwegian Protestant; b. at Valders (about 100 m. n.w. of Christiania) Jan. 21, 1829. He received only an elementary education in his early years, and from 1851 was a teacher in village schools until 1858, when he was enabled to enter the University of Christiania, and graduated three years later. He was tutor at a teachers' seminary in 1863–64, and was then appointed pastor of a small parish in Finmarken near the Russian frontier. Six years later he was called to a parish in Bjelland, in the extreme south of Norway, but resigned in 1875 and settled at Christiania, where he was enabled to continue his studies by his pension and a small additional stipend, while a government subvention later rendered it possible for him to visit foreign libraries. Died at Christiania July 15, 1909. His writings are *Om Bibelen, dens Opbevaring, Oversættelse, og Udbredelse* (3d ed., Christiania, 1884); *Til Forsvar for nogle omtvistede Steder i det Nye Testamente* (1876); *Veiledning i Bibelens Historie, med udförligere Oplysninger om det Nye Testamentes Böger* (Christiania, 1880); *Den evangeliske Histories Troværdighed og de Nytestamentlige Skrifters Oprindelse* (1891); *De Gammeltestamentlige Skrifters Troværdighed og Oprindelse* (1892); *Om Mosebögerne og nogle andre Gammeltestamentlige Skrifter: Et Indlæg imod den moderne Kritik* (1896). He likewise edited *Codex aureus, sive quatuor Evangelia ex codice purpureo aureoque in Bibliotheca Regia Holmensi asservata* (Christiania, 1879); *Die Apostelgeschichte und die Offenbarung Johannes aus dem Gigas Librorum auf der königlichen Bibliothek zu Stockholm* (1879); *Das Evangelium des Matthæus aus dem lateinischen Cod. ff 1 Corbiensis auf der kaiserlichen Bibliothek zu St. Petersburg, nebst dem Briefe Jacobi* (1881); *Der Brief des Jacobus in alter lateinischer Uebersetzung nach dem Cod. ff 1 Corbiensis in St. Petersburg* (1884); *Palimpsestus Vindobonensis: Antiquissima Veteris Testamenti fragmenta* (1885); *Epistulæ Paulinæ e Cod. Sangermaniense Petropolitano* (1885); *Evangelium des Marcus nach dem griechischen Codex Theodoræ purpureus Petropolitanus* (1885); *Codex Vindobonensis purpureus antiquissimus: Evangeliorum Lucæ et Marci translationis Latinæ fragmenta* (Leipsic, 1885); *Fragmenta Vindobonensia: Bruchstücke der Apostelgeschichte, des Briefes Jacobi und ersten Briefes Petri nach einem Palimpsest auf der kaiserlichen Hofbibliothek zu Wien* (Christiania, 1886); *Codex ff 2 Corbiensis, sive quatuor Evangelia . Latina translatio e codice in Bibliotheca Nationali Parisiensi asservata* (1887); *Appendix epistularum Paulinarum e codice Germanensi* (1887); *Codex Colbertinus Parisiensis: Quatuor Evangelia Latina translatio post editionem Petri Sabatarii cum isto codice collata* (1888); *Evangelium secundum Matthæum Latina translatio e codice olim Claramontano, nunc Vaticano* (1892); *Libri Tobit, Judit, Ester Latina translatione codice olim Freisingensi, nunc Monachensi* (Trondhjem, 1893); *Acta Apostolorum . Latina translatio e codice Latino-Græco Laudiano Oxoniensi* (Christiania, 1893); *Codex Vercellensis: Quatuor Evangelia ex reliquiis codicis Vercellensis et ex editione Juliana principi* (1894); *Evangelium Palatinum: Reliquiæ quatuor Evangeliorum cum Latina translatione e codice purpureo Vindobonensi et ex editione Tischendorfiana* (1896); *Fragmenta Novi Testamenti in translatione Latina ex libro qui vocatur Speculum* (1899); and *Codex Veronensis: Quatuor Evangelia e codice in bibliotheca episcopali Veronensi asservato et ex editione Blanchini* (Prague, 1904). Of these the first, second, fifth, sixth, seventh, ninth, tenth, eleventh, and fourteenth are *editiones principes*. Of his numerous translations, special mention may be made of versions of the catechism of Cyril (Christiania, 1882) and the *De Imitatione Christi* of Thomas à Kempis (1890).

BEMA: In classical literature a semicircular platform at the end of a basilica, which supported the official seat of the judge. When the basilican style was adapted to Christian use (see ARCHITECTURE, ECCLESIASTICAL), the apse, or similar semicircular termination of the building, was reserved for the seats of the bishop and clergy, and the same name was sometimes applied to it. In a more restricted sense it signifies any elevated place in the church, such as that from which the gospel was read, and is thus synonymous with ambo (q.v.).

BEMBO, PIETRO: Cardinal and humanist; b. in Venice May 20, 1470; d. in Rome Jan. 18, 1547. He was the son of a senator, and studied at Padua and Ferrara, in the latter place attracting the attention of Alfonso d'Este and his wife, Lucrezia Borgia. He spent six years at the court of Urbino, where he became acquainted with Raffael. He then went to Rome, where Leo X recognized his ability as a Latinist by making him his secretary. As he held this office to the death of the pope (1521), the sixteen books of Latin letters of Leo X are practically, as to their form, of Bembo's composition. Returning to Padua, Bembo made his house the meeting-place of humanist circles. In 1530 he was commissioned by the Venetian senate to complete the history of the republic begun by Marcantonio Sabellico. His part of the work, covering the years 1487–1513, has been justly criticized as to historic accuracy by Justus Lipsius (*Politica*, i, Leyden, 1589, 9, note). On the other hand, not only in the *Rime*, but also in his letters, there is a regrettable tendency to a loose frivolity strongly bordering on pagan morals. This tendency, shown also in his manner of life—he was the father of several illegitimate children—was no obstacle to his being made a cardinal (1539). From that time on (he was now sixty-nine), he is said to have changed his life. He held two bishoprics, Gubbio and Bergamo, but he lived in Rome till his death. His *Opera* were published in three vols. at Basel, 1567; Strasburg, 1611–52; four vols., Venice, 1729. His *Rime* (Venice, 1530) have often been reprinted; as has his *Gli Asolani* (1505), a dialogue on the nature of love. K. Benrath.

Bibliography: The first *Vita* was issued by Giovanni della Casa at Florence, 1567, a second is found in the Venice edition of his works, ut sup., while a third was published by L. Beccadelli in *Monumenti di varia letteratura*, vol. i, Bologna, 1799, and also by W. P. Greswell, *Memoirs of . . . Petrus Bembus*, Manchester, 1801. Consult also V Cian, *Un Decennio della vita di M. P. Bembo, 1521–31*, Turin, 1885; J. P. Niceron, *Mémoires*, xi, 358, xx, 32, 43 vols., Paris, 1729–45; W. W. Westcott, *Tabula Bembina; The Isiac Tablet of Cardinal Bembo, its History and Significance*, Bath, 1887.

BENAIAH ("whom Yahweh built"): The name of several Israelites. The most important of them is the valorous son of Jehoiada of Kabzeel, a city in the south of Judah (Josh. xv, 21). He is honorably mentioned (II Sam. xxiii, 20 ff.; cf. I Chron. xi, 22 ff.) among the mighty men of David, to whom he always faithfully adhered. Three heroic exploits of his are mentioned in justification of his rank: he slew the two sons of Ariel (according to the LXX), either a distinguished Moabite (so Josephus, *Ant.*, VII, xii, 4) or the king of Moab in the war with that people (II Sam. viii, 2); he killed a lion which had fallen into a pit in time of snow; and, finally, he overcame an Egyptian giant, who carried a spear so large that it seemed like a tree thrown across a ravine (according to an addition of the LXX), or like a weaver's beam (according to I Chron. xi, 23); Benaiah disarmed his opponent and killed him with his own weapon. Being prominent among David's "thirty heroes," Benaiah was set over the Cherethites and Pelethites, David's body-guard (II Sam. viii, 18; xx, 23). In the beginning of Solomon's reign, to whom he became devoted at once (I Kings i, 8), Benaiah still held this office and executed the judgment of the king upon Adonijah and Joab (I Kings ii, 25, 30, 34), and became Joab's successor as commander-in-chief (I Kings ii, 35). When, under David, the army was organized, besides his regular office he had command over one of the twelve divisions of 24,000 men (I Chron. xxvii, 5, 6, where his father, Jehoiada, strange to say, is called "the priest," which is no doubt a mistaken gloss founded upon I Chron. xii, 27). C. von Orelli.

BENDER, WILHELM (FRIEDRICH): German Protestant; b. at Münzenberg (10 m. s.e. of Giessen), Hesse, Jan. 15, 1845; d. at Bonn Apr. 8, 1901. He studied at Göttingen and Giessen, 1863–66, and at the theological seminary at Friedberg, 1866–67; became teacher of religion and assistant preacher at Worms, 1868; ordinary professor of theology at Bonn, 1876; was transferred to the philosophical faculty, 1888. He belonged to the extreme Ritschlian school, and published *Der Wunderbegriff des Neuen Testaments* (Frankfort, 1871); *Schleiermachers Theologie mit ihren philosophischen Grundlagen* (2 vols., Nördlingen, 1876–78); *Friedrich Schleiermacher und die Frage nach dem Wesen der Religion* (Bonn, 1877); *Johann Konrad Dippel. Der Freigeist aus dem Pietismus* (1882); *Reformation und Kirchenthum, eine akademische Festrede zur Feier des vierhundertjährigen Geburtstags Martin Luthers* (1883), which caused a great stir and many protests against Bender; *Das Wesen der Religion und die Grundgesetze der Kirchenbildung* (1886); *Der Kampf um die Seligkeit* (1888); *Mythologie und Metaphysik, Grundlinien einer Geschichte der Weltanschauungen* (Stuttgart, 1899).

BENEDICITE: The name given, from its first word in the Latin, to the canticle which stands in the Anglican Prayer-book as an alternative to the Te Deum, commonly used in Advent and Lent, and in the Roman breviary as a part of the priest's thanksgiving after celebrating mass. It is taken from the apocryphal fragment of the Song of the Three Holy Children (verses 35–65), which supplements the narrative of Dan. iii, and seems to have been used in public worship in the postexilic Jewish Church, and in the Christian at least from the fourth century.

BENEDICT: The name of fourteen popes and one antipope.

Benedict I: Pope 574–578. He was a Roman by birth, the son of Boniface, and succeeded John III, who died July 13, 573, but was unable to be consecrated before June 3, 574, because the Lombards had cut off communication with Constantinople and the imperial confirmation could not be obtained. Owing to the troubles of the barbarian invasion and a great famine, which occupied his mind, the *Liber pontificalis* (ed. Duchesne, i, Paris, 1886, 308) finds scarcely anything to say of his acts. He died July 30 or 31, 578, during the siege of Rome by the first Lombard Duke of Spoleto. (A. Hauck.)

Bibliography: Paulus Diaconus, *Historia Langobardorum*, ii, 10, iii, 11, in *MGH, Script. rer. Langob.*, pp. 12–187, ed. Waitz, Hanover, 1878; Jaffé, *Regesta*, i, 137; Bower, *Popes*, i, 380–382; F. Gregorovius, *Geschichte der Stadt Rom*, ii, 19–20, Stuttgart, 1876, Eng. transl., London, 1895; L. M. Hartmann, *Geschichte Italiens*, ii, 48, 165, Gotha, 1903.

Benedict II: Pope 683–685. He was elected after the death of Leo II, which took place on July 3, 683, though the imperial confirmation was delayed for almost a year. The *Liber pontificalis* (ed.

Duchesne, i, Paris, 1886, 363) asserts that the emperor Constantine Pogonatus conceded the right to proceed at once to consecration for the future; but this is very doubtful, as it would amount to a total renunciation of the right of confirmation, and it is certain that several successors of Benedict waited to obtain it either from the emperor himself or his representative, the Exarch of Ravenna. During the interval intervening before his consecration, Benedict signed himself with the designation *presbyter et in Dei nomine electus sanctæ sedis apostolicæ*. Like his predecessor, he had at heart the complete recognition by the Western Church of the sixth ecumenical council (Third Constantinople, 680). With this end in view, Leo II had sent the notary Peter to Spain, and immediately after his election Benedict wrote to Peter to carry out his commission. His wish was gratified by the condemnation of monothelitism in the fourteenth Council of Toledo (Nov., 684). Even before his consecration, which finally took place June 26, 684, he espoused the cause of Wilfrid of York (q.v.) and wrote in recognition of his innocence and his rights. Benedict died May 8, 685.

(A. HAUCK.)

BIBLIOGRAPHY: The *Vita* is in *ASB*, 7th May, ii, 197–198. Consult *Vita Wilfridi*, chap. xlii sqq., in T. Gale, *Historiæ Anglicanæ scriptores quinque*, i, 74 sqq., Oxford, 1691; Mann, *Popes*, vol. i, part 2, pp. 54–63, Lond., 1902; Jaffé, *Regesta*, i, 241; J. Langen, *Geschichte der römischen Kirche von Leo I bis Nikolaus I*, p. 579, Bonn, 1885; Hefele, *Conciliengeschichte*, iii, 322, Eng. transl., v, 215; Bower, *Popes*, i, 487–489; L. M. Hartmann, *Geschichte Italiens*, ii, 262–263, Gotha, 1903.

Benedict III: Pope 855–858. He was chosen immediately after the death of Leo IV by the clergy and people of Rome, but owing to the setting up of an antipope, Anastasius, by the emperor Lothair and his son Louis II, was not consecrated for more than two months (Sept. 29). Soon afterward the Saxon king, Ethelwulf, and his son Alfred, visited Rome and made liberal gifts to the Church. In his relations with secular powers and important prelates, Benedict displayed the same unbending principle which was carried out by his famous successor Nicholas I (q.v.), already a person of much influence. He confirmed the powerful Hincmar, archbishop of Reims, in his primacy, only on condition that the rights of the apostolic see should be safeguarded. In England he protested against the deposition of bishops by tyrannous lay nobles. The struggle with the Eastern Church in which Nicholas was involved had its origin in Benedict's pontificate, arising out of the case of the archbishop of Syracuse, who was deposed by the patriarch of Constantinople, Ignatius (q.v.), and appealed to Leo IV and after his death to Benedict. Before Ignatius was expelled by a faction and replaced by the famous Photius, Benedict died (Apr. 7, 858). (A. HAUCK.)

BIBLIOGRAPHY: *Liber pontificalis*, ed. Duchesne, ii, 140, Paris, 1892; *Epistolæ Nicolai I*, in Mansi, *Concilia*, vol. xv; Jaffé, *Regesta*, i, 339–340; J. Hergenröther, *Photius*, i, 358 sqq., Regensburg, 1867; R. Baxmann, *Die Politik der Päpste von Gregor I bis auf Gregor VII*, i, 355 sqq., Elberfeld, 1868; J. Langen, *Geschichte der römischen Kirche von Leo I bis Nikolaus I*, p. 884, Bonn, 1885; Hefele, *Conciliengeschichte*, iv, 201; Bower, *Popes*, ii, 227–229.

Benedict IV: Pope 900–903. Owing to the scantiness of the sources for the history of the papacy at this period, the chronology is very uncertain; the exact date of Benedict's elevation can not be determined, though it is probably May, not later than June, 900. Like his predecessor, John IX, he recognized Formosus (q.v.), by whom he was himself ordained priest, as a lawful pope at a Roman synod in August. When Louis of Burgundy (Louis III) made his victorious descent into Italy and wrested it from Berengar, Benedict crowned him as emperor in Feb., 901. He died in July or Aug., 903. (A. HAUCK.)

BIBLIOGRAPHY: *Liber pontificalis*, ed. Duchesne, ii, 233, Paris, 1892; Jaffé, *Regesta*, i, 443; Hefele, *Conciliengeschichte*, iv, 570–571; Bower, *Popes*, ii, 304–305.

Benedict V (called Grammaticus): Pope 964. At the end of 963, the emperor Otto I deposed the dissolute John XII in a synod at Rome and caused a prominent Roman layman to be put in his place as Leo VIII, taking an oath of the people that they would thenceforth choose no pope without his consent and that of his son. He had scarcely left the city when John XII returned and drove out and anathematized Leo. The emperor came back to chastise this rebellion, but before he arrived John XII died (May 14, 964). A deputation met Otto and begged him not to replace Leo, but to permit a new election. In spite of his refusal, the Romans chose the cardinal deacon Benedict, a man of blameless life and great learning who had been one of the opponents of John's unworthy rule. He had pledged fidelity both to Otto and to Leo, but the fear of imperial domination of the Church had brought him to support John on the latter's return. The people were firm in their intention to defend Benedict against the emperor; but the pressure of famine forced them to give him up (June 23, 964). He was brought to trial before a synod. After asking the pardon of Otto and of Leo, and surrendering the insignia of his office to the latter, he was deprived of his episcopal and priestly functions, though allowed to retain those of deacon. To avoid any possibility of his changing his mind, he was sent to Germany, where he remained practically a prisoner, in the charge of the archbishop of Hamburg, until his death, which occurred not earlier than July 4, 966. (A. HAUCK.)

BIBLIOGRAPHY: *Liber pontificalis*, ed. Duchesne, ii, 151, Paris, 1892; Jaffé, *Regesta*, i, 469; J. M. Watterich, *Romanorum pontificum . . vitæ*, i, 45, Leipsic, 1862; A. von Reumont, *Geschichte der Stadt Rom*, ii, 289, Berlin, 1868; W von Giesebrecht, *Geschichte der deutschen Kaiserzeit*, i, 468, Brunswick, 1873; F. Gregorovius, *Geschichte der Stadt Rom*, iii, 364, Stuttgart, 1876; Bower, *Popes*, ii, 320–321; Hefele, *Conciliengeschichte*, iv, 619, 626; Hauck, *KD*, iii, 235–238.

Benedict VI: Pope 972–974. He was elected immediately after the death of John XIII (Sept. 6, 972), but was not consecrated until the 19th of the following January, apparently waiting for the emperor Otto's confirmation. After the death of Otto I, the affairs of the empire fell into disorder. Crescentius, the son of Theodora, conspired with the deacon Boniface to overthrow Benedict, who was imprisoned and, after Boniface had assumed the papal authority, was strangled in July, 974. (A. HAUCK.)

BIBLIOGRAPHY: *Liber pontificalis*, ed. Duchesne, ii, 255, Paris, 1892; Jaffé, *Regesta*, i, 477; J. M. Watterich, *Pontificum Romanorum . . vitæ*, i, 65–66, Leipsic, 1862; Neander, *Christian Church*, iii, 330–331 (reference to a letter of Benedict, given Mansi, *Concilia*, xix, 53); Hefele, *Conciliengeschichte*, iv, 632; Bower, *Popes*, ii, 324.

Benedict VII: Pope 974–983. He was a Roman by birth, said to have been a kinsman of the powerful Roman prince and senator Alberic. He was bishop of Sutri when, on the flight of Boniface VII, he was called to the papal throne, and confirmed by the emperor Otto II. As far as we know, his first act was to condemn Boniface in a synod at Rome. He displayed a great desire to maintain friendly relations with the German prelates; Archbishop Willigis of Mainz was appointed papal legate for Germany and Gaul, with the right of crowning the German kings. Benedict showed his subserviency to the emperor by agreeing to the suppression of the bishopric of Merseburg in a synod at Rome (Sept. 10, 981), without regard to the arguments brought against such a proceeding. He was a devoted friend of monasticism, as is shown not only by the numerous privileges bestowed upon monasteries, but by the restoration of that of Saints Boniface and Alexius on the Aventine and the building of the monastic church of Subiaco. He supported the reforming movement, condemning simony at a synod in March, 981. That he upheld the claim of the papacy to universal jurisdiction may be inferred from the fact that he sought to establish relations with places as distant as Carthage and Damascus, giving an archbishop once more to the North African Church, and appointing the metropolitan of Damascus, who had been driven out by the Arabs, abbot of St. Boniface. He died in Oct., 983. (A. HAUCK.)

BIBLIOGRAPHY: *Liber pontificalis*, ed. Duchesne, ii, 258, Paris, 1892; Jaffé, *Regesta*, i, 479; J. M. Watterich, *Romanorum pontificum . . vitæ*, i, 66, 686, Leipsic, 1862; A. von Reumont, *Geschichte der Stadt Rom*, ii, 294, Berlin, 1868; F. Gregorovius, *Geschichte der Stadt Rom*, iii, 372, Stuttgart, 1876; Bower, *Popes*, ii, 325; Hefele, *Conciliengeschichte*, iv, 633; Hauck, *KD*, iii, passim.

Benedict VIII (Theophylact): Pope 1012–24. He was the son of Count Gregory of Tusculum, chosen by his brothers' influence, after they had defeated, by force of arms, the Crescentian party, who set up another Gregory as antipope (see GREGORY VI, antipope). Benedict was consecrated Apr. 20, 1012, and Gregory fled to the court of Henry II, who, however, recognized Benedict, and was rewarded by a promise of coronation in St. Peter's. He descended into Italy toward the end of 1013, and was crowned, with his wife Cunigunde, in the following February. Soon afterward a synod was held in his presence, at which, it is said at his suggestion, the Constantinopolitan Creed was made a part of the Roman liturgy; after this he left Pope Benedict to contend with his numerous enemies—the Crescentian faction, the Arabs, and the Greeks. The first he suppressed; the Mohammedan invaders, who threatened Italy from Sardinia, were defeated and driven out of the island in June, 1016, by the aid of the Pisans and Genoese; he supported those who were attempting to free southern Italy from the Byzantine rule, and gained them the help of a body of Norman knights, who conquered the Greeks, though only temporarily. He accepted Henry's invitation to meet him in 1020 at Bamberg, where the emperor renewed the "Ottonian privilege" to the Church, and gave up Bamberg to ecclesiastical rule. In the following year Henry crossed the Alps for the third time; Benedict met him at Benevento in 1022, and was present when he conquered the Greek fortress of Troja and broke the power of Pandulf IV of Capua, an ally of the Byzantines. These successes, again temporary, are less important than the synod held by the pope and emperor jointly at Pavia Aug. 1, 1022. Here Henry's reforming plans were extended to Italy. After a strong exhortation from the pope, the synod renewed the condemnation of clerical marriage and took measures to prevent the alienation of church property. Henry wished to carry his reforms into France also, and with this purpose met King Robert at Ivois in Aug., 1023. Another synod at Pavia was projected, but before it could be held both Benedict and Henry had died, the former Apr. 9, 1024. (A. HAUCK.)

BIBLIOGRAPHY: *Liber pontificalis*, ed. Duchesne, ii, 268, Paris, 1892; Jaffé, *Regesta*, i, 506; J. M. Watterich, *Romanorum pontificum . . vitæ*, i, 69, 700, Leipsic, 1862; A. von Reumont, *Geschichte der Stadt Rom*, ii, 329, Berlin, 1868; W. von Giesebrecht, *Geschichte der deutschen Kaiserzeit*, ii, 122 sqq., Brunswick, 1875; P. F. Sadee, *Die Stellung Heinrichs II zur Kirche*, Jena, 1877; Hefele, *Conciliengeschichte*, iv, 670; Bower, *Popes*, ii, 335–337; Hartmann, in *Mittheilungen des Instituts für österreichische Geschichte*, xv (1894), 482 sqq.; Hauck, *KD*, iii, 518 sqq.; P. G. Wappler, *Papst Benedikt VIII*, Leipsic, 1897.

Benedict IX (Theophylact): Pope 1033–48. He was the son of Count Alberic of Tusculum, and nephew of Benedict VIII and John XIX, the latter of whom he succeeded by his father's intrigues and violence, though he was only ten years old. His life was incredibly scandalous, and the strife of factions continued. A murderous assault upon him and his expulsion from Rome followed (the date can not be determined). He owed his restoration to the emperor Conrad II, who came into Italy in the winter of 1036. Benedict met him obsequiously at Cremona in the following June, taking no notice of the fact that he had broken the Church's laws by imprisoning Aribert, archbishop of Milan, and expelling the bishops of Piacenza, Cremona, and Vercelli from their sees; in fact, in Mar., 1038, he went so far as to excommunicate Aribert. By similar complaisances he won the favor of Conrad's successor, Henry III, for whom, in 1041, he obligingly excommunicated the Hungarian nobles, who had driven out their king, Peter. The Romans bore with these conditions until the end of 1044, when they rose and drove Benedict out, afterward electing John, bishop of Sabina, in his stead, under the title of Sylvester III. Benedict succeeded in sending John back to Sabina inside of two months; but, doubting his own ability to maintain his position, he decided to abdicate, adding one more shameless act of simony by selling the papacy (May 1, 1045) to the archpriest John Gratian (who called himself Gregory VI, q.v.) for the sum of a thousand pounds of silver and the continued enjoyment of the Peter's pence from England. Henry III came to Italy in the autumn of 1046, and decided to remove Gregory. He convened a synod at Sutri, which deposed Sylvester even from the priesthood and induced Gregory to resign his claims (Dec. 20, 1046); a few days later, another synod in Rome deposed Benedict also, and Suidger of Bamberg succeeded to an undisputed papacy as Clement II. When he died, however, nine months later, Benedict made an attempt to recover his see. He was soon put down by the imperial authority, and retired to Tusculum. When and where he died is not known.

(A. Hauck.)

Bibliography: Jaffé, *Regesta*, i, 519; J. M. Watterich, *Romanorum pontificum . . vitæ*, i, 71, 711, Leipsic, 1862; A. von Reumont, *Geschichte der Stadt Rom*, ii, 338, Berlin, 1868; O. Lorenz, *Papstwahl und Kaisertum*, p. 09, Berlin, 1874; F. Gregorovius, *Geschichte der Stadt Rom*, iv, 39, Stuttgart, 1877; Bower, *Popes*, ii, 340–343; Neander, *Christian Church*, iii, 375–377, 409, 445, 448; Hefele, *Conciliengeschichte*, iv, 706–707, 714; Hauck, *KD*, iii, 559, 569–571.

Benedict X (Johannes Mincius): Pope 1058–59. He was bishop of Velletri before, unwillingly, he was elected and enthroned in the night between Apr. 3 and 4, 1058, by the noble factions which had so long dominated the papacy and were soon to lose their power. Peter Damian and the other reforming cardinals fled; but before they left Rome they pronounced an anathema upon the new pope. Meantime Hildebrand was on his way back from Germany. At Florence he heard the news, and after conferring with the empress Agnes, regent for her son Henry IV, arranged for the election of a pope acceptable to the strict churchmen. At Sienna in December Gerard, bishop of Florence, was chosen and took the title of Nicholas II. In January he held a synod at Sutri which pronounced the deposition and excommunication of Benedict X. The latter was driven from Rome by the forces set in motion by Hildebrand, and finally found it expedient to abdicate, which he did formally at a synod in the Lateran, Apr., 1060. He is said to have lived twenty years longer as a prisoner in the monastery of St. Agnes. Gregory VII, in whose reign he died, permitted him to be buried with the obsequies of a rightful pope, as which, indeed, he was reckoned until the fourteenth century.

(A. Hauck.)

Bibliography: *Liber pontificalis*, ed. Duchesne, ii, 279, Paris, 1892; Jaffé, *Regesta*, i, 556; J. M. Watterich, *Romanorum pontificum . vitæ*, i, 203, 738, Leipsic, 1862; W. von Giesebrecht, *Geschichte der deutschen Kaiserzeit*, iii, 24, Brunswick, 1875; F. Gregorovius, *Geschichte der Stadt Rom*, iv, 107, Stuttgart, 1877; J. Langen, *Geschichte der römischen Kirche von Nikolaus I bis Gregor VII*, p. 500, Bonn, 1892; Bower, *Popes*, ii, 340–343; Neander, *Christian Church*, iii, 387; Hefele, *Conciliengeschichte*, iv, 798, 828; Hauck, *KD*, iii, 679–681.

Benedict XI (Niccolo Bocasini): Pope 1303–1304. He was born in 1240 at Treviso, entered the Dominican order in 1254, and spent fourteen years in diligent study, which enabled him to write several Biblical commentaries. He became prior of his house, provincial of Lombardy, and in 1296 general of the order. Boniface VIII made him a cardinal priest in 1298, and soon after cardinal bishop of Ostia and Velletri. In 1302 he went to Hungary as papal legate. He remained true to Boniface VIII, and on his death was elected (Oct. 22, 1303) to succeed him. He found himself at once in difficulties as the heir to the policy and the enemies of Boniface (see Boniface VIII), but by a conciliatory prudence he found his way out of them. First he won back the powerful Colonna family, restoring to them their dignities and possessions under certain limitations which marked his sense of their misconduct. Frederick of Sicily was brought to a sense of his feudal obligations toward the papacy, which he had thought to escape. To Tuscany, Benedict sent Nicholas of Prato, his successor as cardinal bishop of Ostia, to make peace between the Bianchi and Neri factions in Florence. This mission was not very successful, but Benedict had better fortune with the most difficult task left to him by his predecessor, the effecting of a reconciliation with France. Philip the Fair was ready for peace, but apparently made the condition that a general council should be called to pass a *post-mortem* condemnation on Boniface. Benedict met him half way, and on Mar. 25, 1304, released him from his excommunication; then he annulled a number of other measures of his predecessor which had been specially felt as grievances in France, and on May 13 withdrew the sentences passed against Philip and his counselors, even those who had taken part in the outrage of Anagni, with the exception of the ringleader William of Nogaret. He, together with all the Italians who had taken part in the violence offered to Boniface, was excommunicated on June 7, and summoned to appear before Benedict to receive sentence. A few weeks later, however (July 7), Benedict died in Perugia, whither he had retired on account of turbulence in Rome. The rumor immediately spread that he had been poisoned, at the instigation, it was variously asserted, of Philip the Fair, of the Colonna, of the Franciscans (who were jealous of the favor shown to the Dominicans), of the opposition cardinals, or of William of Nogaret, who had most to gain by a change, and who, in fact, received his absolution from Benedict's successor.

(A. Hauck.)

Bibliography: Ptolemæus of Lucca, *Vitæ pontificum Romanorum*, in Muratori, *Scriptores*, xi, 1224; B. Guidonis, *Vitæ pontificum Romanorum*, ib. iii, 672; W. Drumann, *Geschichte Bonifacius VIII*, ii, 147, Königsberg, 1852; L. Gautier, *Benoît XI, étude sur la papauté au commencement du xiv. siècle*, Paris, 1863; C. Grandjean, *Benoît XI*, Paris, 1863; idem, *Le Registre de Benoît XI, recueil de bulles*, Paris, 1884 85; P. Funke, *Papst Benedikt XI*, Münster, 1891; Bower, *Popes*, iii, 56–58; Neander, *Christian Church*, v, 19; Hefele, *Conciliengeschichte*, vi, 375–390.

Benedict XII (Jacques Fournier): Pope 1334–1342. He was a native of Languedoc, of humble origin, and as a boy entered the Cistercian monastery of Bolbonne in the diocese of Mirepoix, migrating later to that of Fontfroide in the diocese of Narbonne, of which his uncle was abbot. The latter sent him to the University of Paris. Pope John XXII gave him the bishopric of Pamiers and later of Mirepoix, and made him cardinal in 1327.

He was rather unexpectedly elected pope Dec. 20, 1334, and began his reign with reforming measures. The bishops and abbots who lingered at the court of Avignon were sent home, the system of petitions was regulated, and care was taken to select worthy men for vacant benefices. Benedict planned to restore the strict discipline of the Benedictines and Cistercians, as well as of the mendicant orders, and entirely avoided the reproach of nepotism. Soon after his elevation, the Romans begged him to return to them, and he promised to do so, but was prevented by the French majority in the Sacred College. Later he thought of removing to Bologna, but finally settled down in Avignon and began the building of a magnificent palace. His attitude toward theological and ecclesiastical controversies was a pacific one. He condemned the opinion so strongly held by his predecessor, that the souls of the just do not enjoy the Beatific Vision until after the last judgment. Negotiations took place with the Eastern Church looking toward reunion; in 1339 the emperor Andronicus sent ambassadors to Avignon, really with a view to gaining military aid against the Turks, but holding out prospects of ecclesiastical accommodation, which, however, came to little. He won a moral triumph in Spain by inducing Alfonso XI of Castile to break off his adulterous connection with Eleonora de Gusman, and rendered no slight service to the Christian cause in the peninsula by making peace between Castile and Portugal, and thus enabling the Christian forces to unite against the Mussulmans and to defeat them completely at Tarifa. The most difficult problem was the treatment of Louis of Bavaria. Benedict showed himself conciliatory, and Louis sent an embassy to Avignon (1335); but Philip VI, against whose interests this reconciliation would have been, prevented it then, and a second time in the autumn of the following year. This gave the alliance of Louis to Edward III of England against France. The electoral princes finally asserted their rights; on July 15, 1338, they swore to defend the customs and liberties of the empire and to prevent any infringement of their electoral prerogative; the next day they declared that the king of the Romans chosen by them stood in no need of papal confirmation, and notified Benedict of their attitude. At the diet held in Frankfort (Aug. 6, 1338), Louis went even further, denying any connection between the coronation by the pope and the right to bear the title of emperor, at the same time asserting the invalidity of all the censures pronounced against himself and the empire by John XXII. None the less, in the following year he reopened negotiations with Benedict; and when he had an opportunity of concluding peace with Philip VI, he deserted his English ally, hoping to gain Philip's support with the pope. He spoiled his own case, however, by his encroachments on the Church's law of marriage and its power in such matters. In order to marry his son, Louis, margrave of Brandenburg, to Margaret, heiress of the Tyrol, he declared her previous marriage with Prince John of Bohemia null and void (following an opinion of Occam's), and on Feb. 10, 1342, in spite of the impediment of consanguinity in the third degree between the couple, had the marriage performed. Benedict had no opportunity to pass judgment upon these acts, as he died on Apr. 25 of the same year. (A. HAUCK.)

BIBLIOGRAPHY: *Liber pontificalis*, ed. Duchesne, ii, 486, 527, Paris, 1892; eight accounts of his life are collected in É. Baluze, *Vitæ paparum Avenonensium*, i, 197–244, Paris, 1693; Muratori, *Scriptores*, iii, 527 sqq.; J. M. Watterich, *Romanorum pontificum vitæ*, i, 203–204, Leipsic, 1862; A. Pichler, *Geschichte der kirchlichen Trennung zwischen dem Orient und Occident*, i, 358, Munich, 1864; C. Müller, *Der Kampf Ludwigs . . . mit der römischen Curie*, vol. ii, Tübingen, 1880; A. Rohrmann, *Die Procuratorien Ludwigs des Baiern*, Göttingen, 1882; Bower, *Popes*, iii, 88–92; Pastor, *Popes*, i, 84–86; *Benoît XII, Lettres closes, patentes et curiales se rapportant à la France*, ed. G. Daumet, Paris, 1899; Hefele, *Conciliengeschichte*, vi, 636–653.

Benedict XIII: **1.** The title was first borne by Pedro de Luna from 1394 to 1417, in the Great Western Schism. He came of a noble family in Aragon, studied in France, taught canon law at the University of Montpellier, and was made cardinal by Gregory XI. When the schism broke out between the partizans of Urban VI and Clement VII, he took the latter's side, and went to Spain and Portugal as Clement's representative in 1379. In 1393, again, he appeared at a meeting of English and French dignitaries, in the hope of winning England away from the party of Boniface IX, the pope elected in Rome to succeed Urban VI. When the University of Paris in 1394 suggested three ways to end the schism—the resignation of both claimants, the submission of both to the decision of a tribunal agreed upon between them, or the calling of a general council—Clement sent him to Paris to prevent the choice of the first; but in fact he declared in favor of it, possibly with an eye to his own chances. Clement died the same autumn, and the cardinals of his party nearly all agreed that whichever of them might be chosen pope should do all in his power to end the schism, even by abdicating if necessary; and no voice was louder in this agreement than Pedro de Luna's. He was unanimously chosen on Sept. 28, consecrated and crowned Oct. 11. He reiterated his willingness to do anything for peace; but when the next year an embassy representing the king of France, a national synod, and the University of Paris approached him to urge the abdication of both popes, he declined, recommending rather a personal meeting of both to discuss the question. To this he adhered in spite of the opposite view of all his cardinals but one and of the personal entreaties of the dukes of Berry, Burgundy, and Orléans. Charles VI held a second national council at Paris (end of Aug., 1396), and tried to gain the support of the European sovereigns for his plan. In June, 1397, the ambassadors of France, England, and Castile pressed the necessity of abdication upon Benedict, who declined for himself while recommending it to Boniface IX. No more success attended a joint embassy (1398) from Charles and Wenceslaus, king of the Romans, headed by Pierre d'Ailly, bishop of Cambrai.

Sides with Clement VII in the Great Schism.

Charles held a third council in May, 1398, which decided that France should withdraw from Benedict's obedience. When this decision received the royal assent and was promulgated (July 27), all the cardinals but three forsook Benedict, and open warfare broke out. Benedict, practically a prisoner in his palace, yielded so far (Apr., 1399) as to sign a solemn undertaking to abdicate whenever his rival would do the same or should die or be expelled from Rome; but he secretly protested that his promise was null and void, as having been given under compulsion. France was now practically without a pope; and the longer this anomalous condition continued, the more uneasiness it caused.

Course of Events in France.

Leading churchmen, such as Gerson and Nicholas de Clémanges, began to write in favor of a return to Benedict XIII. Finally Charles called a meeting of bishops and nobles (May, 1403), to reconsider the question. Before they met Benedict had contrived to escape from Avignon, and the city had declared for him, once he was free. It is not surprising, therefore, that the assembled magnates declared for a restoration of France to his obedience, though on condition that he should renew his promise in regard to abdication, and undertake to submit the question how to end the schism to a general council within a year. This left things much as they had been in 1394 and 1395. Boniface IX died soon after (Oct. 1, 1404); but his successor, Innocent VII, showed just as little inclination to abandon his claims. Benedict, still attached to his own plan of a personal conference, undertook a journey to Genoa, without any result except to produce fresh irritation in France, whose clergy were taxed to pay the expenses of the experiment. Another national council (1406) declared in favor of withdrawing his right to present the bishoprics and benefices; but the Duke of Orléans stood out for complete obedience and hindered the execution of this decision. New hopes were aroused, on the death of Innocent VII, by the choice (Nov. 30, 1406) of Gregory XII, who at once declared himself willing to take any measures, even that of abdication, to end the schism. A meeting was planned between the rivals for the autumn of 1407, but it fell through. In November Benedict lost a powerful friend by the murder of the Duke of Orléans, and was so unwise in 1408 as to attempt to enforce the observance of the French obedience by threats of excommunication. In May Charles proclaimed France absolutely neutral in the contest. Benedict, fearing for his safety, fled to his native Aragon.

The cardinals of both factions deserted their respective popes and in June took counsel together with a view to calling a general council. This met in 1409 at Pisa, summoned both claimants before it, proceeded to hear testimony when they did not appear, and on June 5 declared both, as heretics, schismatics, and perjurers, not only deposed but excommunicated.

The Councils of Pisa and Constance.

Benedict still asserted his claims, and Spain, Portugal, and Scotland adhered to him. New negotiations with him were undertaken by the Council of Constance in 1414, but he stubbornly refused to yield, even to the persuasions of the emperor Sigismund. Finally the patience of his own supporters in Spain and Scotland was worn out, and they renounced him in the Concordat of Narbonne (Dec., 1415). He entrenched himself in the mountain fastness of Peñiscola, near Valencia, which belonged to his family, and proudly told the envoys of the council that the true Church was there only. On July 26, 1417, the Council of Constance once more deposed and excommunicated him; and he remained in his castle, with a court of but four cardinals, until his death at the age of nearly ninety in Nov., 1424. (A. Hauck.)

2. Benedict XIII was also the name borne by Pietro Francesco d'Orsini-Gravina, pope 1724–30. He was born Feb. 2, 1649, at Gravina in the kingdom of Naples, and in 1667, renouncing his rights of succession to the ducal estates, entered the Dominican order at Venice, taking the name of Vincenzo Maria. He studied theology at Venice and Bologna, philosophy at Naples. In 1672 he was made a cardinal by Clement X, and archbishop of Benevento in 1686. After administering his diocese admirably for thirty-eight years, and spending his leisure in the composition of theological works, he was almost unanimously elected pope (May 29, 1724), after the death of Innocent XIII. At first he took the name of Benedict XIV, but changed it to Benedict XIII in the conviction that Pedro de Luna was a schismatic and not a legitimate pope. His pontificate began with an attempt to restrain the pomp and luxury of the cardinals, which was as vain as his similar attempts to reform the rest of the clergy. Though the prescriptions of the Lateran council of 1725 in this direction were not much heeded, it is memorable because in it Benedict confirmed the constitution *Unigenitus*, and thus aided the Jesuits. He had the satisfaction of receiving in 1728 the unconditional submission of De Noailles, archbishop of Paris, the head of the Gallican opposition. Weakness was the principal characteristic of his dealings with the secular powers of Europe. He left such matters almost entirely in the hands of his favorite Cardinal Coscia, whose interest it was to keep on good terms with the powers. Thus the emperor Charles VI obtained the privileges which he claimed in Sicily as the successor of the older rulers, who had been *legati nati* of the Holy See. Thus also the king of Sardinia got the best of a long contest with Rome; and only one state found the curia stubborn. The king of Portugal, John V, requested the red hat for Bichi, the papal nuncio at Lisbon, and when it was refused showed great hostility to the pope, even threatening in 1728 to break off all relations between the Church of Portugal and Rome. Benedict was unpopular in Rome, owing to the misgovernment of Coscia, who, when the pope died (Feb. 21, 1730), was obliged to flee in disguise, and later was imprisoned for ten years by Clement XII. (A. Hauck.)

Bibliography: 1. Pedro de Luna: A *Vita* is found in É. Baluze, *Vitæ paparum Avenoniensium*, i, 561 568, Paris, 1693; the Eng. transl. of several original documents which are pertinent is given in Thatcher and McNeal, *Source Book*, pp. 325-329; Theodoric of Nieheim, *De Schismate*, ed. G. Erler, ii, 33 sqq., Leipsic, 1890: *Chartularium Universitatis Paris*, ed. H. Denifle, iii, 552 sqq., Paris, 1894; Kehrmann, *Frankreichs innere Kirchenpolitik*, Jena, 1890; Bower, *Popes*, iii, 145–149, 152, 162–163, 205; Neander, *Christian Church*, v, 56, 62–77, 84, 105–107; Hefele, *Conciliengeschichte*, vi, 827–1031; Pastor, *Popes*, i, 165–201; N. Valois, *La France et le grand schisme d'occident*, 2 vols., Paris, 1896; Creighton, *Papacy*, i, 146–315, 374. 2. Pietro Francesco: His works were issued in 3 vols., Ravenna, 1728, and the bulls are in the *Bullarium Romanum*, vol. xxii, Turin, 1871. For his life consult A. Borgia, *Benedicti XIII vita*, Rome, 1752; A. von Reumont, *Geschichte der Stadt Rom*, iii, 652–653, Berlin, 1868; Bower, *Popes*, iii, 339; J. Chantrel, *Le Pape Benoît XIII*, 1724–30, Paris, 1874; M. Brosch, *Geschichte des Kirchenstaats*, ii, 61 sqq., Gotha, 1882; Ranke, *Popes*, vol. iii, No. 158.

Benedict XIV (Prospero Lorenzo Lambertini): Pope 1740–58. He was born [Mar. 31] 1675 at Bologna; at thirteen he entered the *Collegium Clementinum* at Rome, and after studies in theology and philosophy, took up the law, practising as advocate of the consistory, and as *promotor fidei*, in which office he laid the foundations of his famous work on beatification and canonization. Clement XI and Innocent XIII gave him several Roman dignities; Benedict XIII made him archbishop of Ancona (1727) and cardinal (1728); in 1731 Clement XII transferred him to the more important see of Bologna, where he found time to write his works on the mass, on the festivals, and *Quæstiones canonicæ*. After the death of Clement XII the conclave was at a deadlock for six months between the French, Austrian, and Spanish factions, and finally agreed on Lambertini as a compromise candidate (Aug. 17, 1740).

Benedict was a man of great learning and piety, and did much for the welfare of the Pontifical States, by the promotion of agriculture, commerce, and manufactures and by a decrease in taxation. His expressed principle that in him "the pope must take precedence of the temporal ruler" was carried out both in the strenuous efforts which he made to raise the tone of the clergy and in his efforts to remove all the misunderstandings which had existed between the curia and the European powers, even at the cost of considerable concessions. He was not able entirely to remove the antagonism between the eighteenth-century spirit and religion, but he composed more than one difference temporarily.

Friendly Relations with Other Rulers.

Thus he appeased John V of Portugal by the privilege of enjoying the revenues of vacant bishoprics and abbeys in his kingdom, as well as by the title of *Rex fidelissimus*. In a concordat with Naples (1741) he went even beyond the concessions which Benedict XIII had made, and concluded another with the king of Sardinia which was still less favorable to the extreme claims of the Church. Still another was made with Spain in 1753, which went so far as to allow King Ferdinand VI the right of nomination to all the ecclesiastical benefices in his kingdom except fifty-two. Friendly relations were also maintained with the empire, and strict neutrality observed in the war of the Austrian Succession, although the contending armies not seldom crossed the boundaries of the Papal States. When Albert of Bavaria was elected emperor as Charles VII and applied to Benedict for confirmation, he gave him his hearty good wishes, but refused at first to recognize his successor, Francis I, who had neglected to observe this formality. He abandoned his opposition, however, and became an active ally of Austria in the contest with Venice over Aquileia. As a compromise measure, he finally divided the patriarchate into two dioceses, that of Görz, which was to be Austrian, and that of Udine, Venetian. Though he refused to confirm the guaranties which the landgrave of Hesse-Cassel, on becoming a Roman Catholic, was obliged to give for the preservation of the rights of his evangelical subjects, Benedict showed none of the temper of a persecutor, and had friendly personal relations with many Protestants. He was the first pope to concede the title of king of Prussia to the ruler whom the curia had previously styled margrave of Brandenburg; and he yielded to Frederick the Great's wishes so far as to allow the bishop of Breslau to decide all Catholic causes in Prussia, appeals to the pope being forbidden. In the Gallican controversy he took a wise and tolerant part, reversing a decision of De Beaumont, the archbishop of Paris, which made formal assent to the constitution *Unigenitus* a condition for receiving the sacraments; in an encyclical of Oct. 16, 1756, he laid down the rule that the ministrations of the Church should be refused only to those who had publicly contemned the bull.

Benedict's conciliatory temper made him little likely to sympathize with the Jesuits, with whom he dealt at the very beginning of his reign in a way that did not please them, deciding against them, in the controversy over the "Chinese rites," the question how far the principles of Christianity might be accommodated for the purpose of making more speedy conversions among the heathen, in two bulls—the *Ex quo singulari* of 1742, and the *Omnium sollicitudinum* of 1744 (see ACCOMMODATION, § 9).

The Jesuits.

Though he was no partizan of the Jesuits, it was not until shortly before his death that he undertook (1758) the long-planned reform of the order, at least in Portugal, entrusting its execution to Saldanha, the patriarch of Lisbon.

In 1750 Benedict celebrated a jubilee with great pomp, and invited the Protestants also to attend—naturally with no other result than to call out a number of polemical replies. To the end of his life he found his chief diversion in the company of learned men, of whom a circle assembled round him once a week. During his pontificate he composed his most important work, *De synodo diœcesana*. He had a catalogue of the Vatican library drawn up by the learned Assemani, founded societies for the study of Roman and Christian antiquities and of church history, and cooperated in the foundation of the archeological academy with Winckelmann, who came to Rome in 1755. He died as he had lived, with cheerful, good-humored words upon his lips, May 3, 1758.

(A. HAUCK.)

BIBLIOGRAPHY: His works were collected by Azevedo in 12 vols., Rome, 1747–51, more completely, 15 vols., Venice, 1767, and in 17 vols., Prato, 1839–46; vols. 15–17 of the Prato ed. contain the bulls; *Briefe Benedicts XIV an Pier*

Francesco Peggi à Bologna, 1729–58, ed. F. X. Kraus, Freiburg, 1888; *Opera inedita*, ed. F. Heiner, St. Louis, 1904. Consult: R. de Martinis, *Acta Benedicti XIV*, 2 vols., Naples, 1884–85; A. Borgia, *Vie de Benoît XIV*, Paris, 1783; H. Formby, *Life and Miracles of Benedict XIV*, London, 1858; A. von Arneth, *Geschichte Maria Theresias*, ii, 178, iv, 54 sqq., Vienna, 1864, 1870; M. Brosch, *Geschichte des Kirchenstaats*, ii, 68, Gotha, 1882; Ranke, *Popes*, ii, 433–443, iii, No. 164.

BENEDICT OF ANIANE: The reformer of the Benedictine order in the Frankish empire. He was born about 750 in his father's county of Maguelone in Languedoc; d. at Inden (13 m. n.e. of Aix-la-Chapelle) Feb. 11, 821. His youth was spent at the court of Pepin and of Charlemagne, where, as a page, he had opportunity to distinguish himself in feats of arms. During Charles's first Lombard campaign, Benedict rescued his brother from drowning at the risk of his own life, and the shock brought to a head the resolve which had been slowly forming in him, to renounce the world and give himself to the service of God in the monastic life. This he entered in 773 at Saint-Seine in the diocese of Langres. Returning home in 779, he built a small monastery on his own land near the little river Aniane (where the town of Aniane, 16 m. w.n.w. of Montpellier, later grew up), which was replaced by a larger one lower down when the number of his disciples increased, and by a third still larger about 792. This became the center of Benedict's efforts for the reformation of the monastic life in the south and southwest of France. King Louis of Aquitaine, who had favored him from the outset, entrusted him with the oversight of all the monasteries within his territory, and the greatest churchmen, such as Alcuin and Leidrad of Lyons, sought his counsel. He had a wide knowledge of patristic literature, and forwarded the cause of education with zeal. He stood out as a champion of the orthodox faith against Adoptionism (q.v.), and wrote two treatises against it, the first of which is specially interesting as showing how close was the practical connection between Adoptionism and Arianism. His influence became still wider with the accession of Louis the Pious, who first brought him up to the Alsatian abbey of Maurmünster, and then, to have him nearer at hand, founded another for him at Inden, giving him the general oversight of all the monasteries in the empire. He could now hope to accomplish his great purpose of restoring the primitive strictness of the monastic observance wherever it had been relaxed or exchanged for the less exacting canonical life. This purpose was clearly seen in the capitularies drawn up by an assembly of abbots and monks at Aix-la-Chapelle in 817, and enforced by Louis's order throughout the empire.

Benedict's chief works are compilations of the older ascetic literature. The first of them is called by his biographer, Ardo, *Liber ex regulis diversorum patrum collectus*; an enlarged edition of this was prepared by Lucas Holsten (published at Rome only after Holsten's death, in 1661, with the title *Codex regularum*). The other work, called *Concordia regularum* by Benedict himself, is based on the first; in it the sections of the Benedictine rule (except ix–xvi) are given in their order, with parallel passages from the other rules included in the *Liber regularum*, so as to show the agreement of principles and thus to enhance the respect due to the Benedictine. The *Concordia* was first published in 1638 by H. Menard of the Congregation of St. Maur, with valuable notes (reprinted in *MPL*, ciii). A third collection of homilies, to be read daily in the monasteries, has not been definitely identified. Benedict's place is in the second rank of the men who made the reigns of Charles and Louis glorious. He had not the breadth of view possessed by Charlemagne himself or by Adalhard, nor the lofty endeavor for a fusion of secular and spiritual learning of Paulus Diaconus and Alcuin. He was primarily an ecclesiastic, who zealously placed his not inconsiderable theological learning at the service of orthodoxy, but gave the best thing he had, the loving fervor of an upright Christian soul, to the cause of Benedictine monasticism.

(Otto Seebass.)

Bibliography: The *Vita* by Ardo Smaragdus, his successor as abbot, with preface by Henschen, is in *ASB*, 12 Feb., ii, 606–620, in *MPL*, ciii, and is edited by Waitz in *MGH, Script.*, xv, 198–220, Hanover, 1887. There is a Fr. transl., Montpellier, 1876. P. A. J. Paulinier, *St. Benoît d'Aniane et la fondation du monastère de ce nom*, Montpellier, 1871; P. J. Nicolai, *Der heilige Benedict, Gründer von Aniane*, Cologne, 1865; R. Foss, *Benedikt von Aniane*, Berlin, 1884; O. Seebass, in *ZKG*, xv (1895), 244–260; Hauck, *KD*, ii, 528–545.

BENEDICT BISCOP: First abbot of Wearmouth and Jarrow; b. of noble family about 628; d. at Wearmouth (on the north side of the Wear, opposite Sunderland, Durhamshire) Jan. 12, 689 or 690. Biscop was his Saxon name, his ecclesiastical name was Benedict, and he was also called Baducing as a patronymic. He was a thane and favorite of Oswy, king of Northumbria (q.v.), but in 653 decided to abandon the world and went to Rome. He became a monk at the monastery of Lerins about 665, and was appointed by Pope Vitalian to conduct Theodore of Tarsus (q.v.) to Canterbury in 668. In 674 he began to build the monastery of St. Peter at Wearmouth on land given by Egfrid, king of Northumbria. In 681 or 682 he founded the sister house, dedicated to St. Paul, at Jarrow (5 m. farther north, on the south bank of the Tyne). He made six visits to Rome, learned the Roman ecclesiastical usages and the rules of monastic life, and strove faithfully to introduce them in England; he also brought back a rich store of books, vestments, pictures, and the like. He induced John, the archchanter of St. Peter's at Rome, to accompany him to England and instruct his monks; and he brought skilled workmen from Gaul to build his monasteries, including the first glass-makers in England.

Bibliography: The source for a biography is the life by his great scholar Bede, *Vita beatorum abbatum*, chaps. 1–14, best and most accessible in the ed. of C. Plummer, i, 364–379, with notes, ii, 355–365, Oxford, 1896, Eng. transl. by P. Witcock, Sunderland, 1818; cf. also Bede, *Hist. eccl.*, iv, 18, v, 19; *Hom.*, xxv. Consult also C. F. Montalembert, *Les Moines de l'occident*, iv, 456–487, Paris, 1868; *DNB*, iv, 214–215.

BENEDICT OF NURSIA AND THE BENEDICTINE ORDER.

I. The Life of Benedict: The only early authority on the life of Benedict, since the *Vita Placidi* has been admitted to be untrustworthy ever since Mabillon, and the worthlessness of the *Vita sancti Mauri* has been recently demonstrated by Malnory, is practically the single biography written by Gregory the Great. But the expectations aroused by a life written only fifty years after Benedict's death by so distinguished an author are disappointed when he is found, in the spirit of his time, exalting the greatness of his hero by the number and importance of his miracles. This tendency has gone so far that Grützmacher is inclined to see nothing actually historical in all this mass of legendary details except the names of the places where Benedict lived and worked, and the names of his disciples. But this is going somewhat too far; Gregory expressly names four abbots, themselves among these disciples and one of them (Honoratus) still living at Subiaco, as witnesses to the truth of his story; and the tradition must have been still full and clear among the monks who had migrated from Monte Cassino to the Lateran when he wrote.

1. The Life of Benedict by Gregory the Great.

According, then, to what is left of Gregory's account after removal of the legendary halo around the saint's head, Benedict came of a considerable family in the "province of Nursia," in the Umbrian Apennines, and was born toward the end of the fifth century. He received at Rome the education of his day, which, however, did not mean much acquaintance with the Roman classical authors, and seems to have included no Greek. Shocked by the immorality around him, he left both the school and his father's house for a life of solitary mortification. His first permanent abode was a cave by the Anio, not far from Subiaco, where a monk, Romanus, provided him with the rough monastic garb and with scanty nourishment. Here Benedict spent three years of stubborn conflict with his lower nature, until the spreading of his fame by shepherds brought his solitude to an end. The monks of a neighboring monastery (perhaps at Vicovaro), whose head had just died, begged him to come and rule them. He accepted with reluctance, probably foreseeing what actually happened when he attempted strictly to enforce their rule. When their insubordination went as far as an attempt to poison him, he discovered the plot and gently rebuked them, then retired to his beloved cave. Here, as new disciples came around him, he established twelve small communities, each with twelve inmates and a "father" at their head. Gregory does not say how long Benedict remained in the neighborhood of Subiaco as director of these pious groups; but the tradition of Monte Cassino ascribes his migration thither to the opposition of a jealous cleric named Florentius, and places it in 529. The new place was about halfway between Rome and Naples, the *Castrum Casinum* of the Romans, who had had a military colony there. On the summit of the mountain (now Monte San Germano), which had been dedicated to the worship of Apollo by a population still largely pagan, Benedict built two chapels, under the invocation of St. John Baptist and St. Martin, and then laid the foundations of the monastery which was to have such a long and renowned history. Though Gregory does not say so definitely, the traditional view may be accepted that he soon drew up his rule, the mature outcome of his experience in guiding and governing aspirants to the monastic life of perfection. The disturbances of the time, the wars between the Goths and the Byzantine empire from 534, probably helped to increase the numbers of those who sought a peaceful shelter at Monte Cassino; and a daughter house was established at Terracina. In the summer of 542, Totila, king of the Goths, on his way through Campania, desired to see the famous abbot. Gregory relates that, to test his prophetic powers, the king sent one of his officers in royal array to Benedict, who perceived the deception instantly, and, when the young king knelt before him, told him that he should enter Rome, cross the seas, and reign nine years—which came to pass. Gregory mentions Benedict's sister, Scholastica, in connection with the last meeting between the two in a house near the monastery; she had been dedicated to the service of God from her earliest youth. The date of Benedict's death can not be determined from any of the authorities. His body was buried near Scholastica's in the chapel of St. John Baptist, and, according to Paulus Diaconus, was translated about a century later to the monastery of Fleury on the Loire.

2. Early Life.

3. Monte Cassino.

II. The Rule of Benedict: Especially since the celebration of the fourteen-hundredth anniversary of Benedict's birth in 1880, his rule has been made the subject of thoroughgoing studies, and it is everywhere recognized as a code which corresponded admirably to its purpose of regulating the common life of the western monks. In the concluding passage of the prologue, probably added later by Benedict, occur the words "*Constituenda est ergo a nobis dominici schola servitii.*" Under the later empire, the word *schola* was commonly employed to designate the body of guards in the imperial palace under the *magister officii;* thence the name passed to the garrisons of provincial towns, and was used sometimes for other bodies or associations existing in them. As these military organizations would have a definite code of regulations, so it was natural for Benedict (called "*magister*" in the first line of the prologue) to lay down a rule that should serve for all who were enlisted in the spiritual army ("*servitium dominicum*")—priests or laymen, rich or poor.

1. General Characteristics.

It separated the monks more absolutely from the world than Basil or Cassian had done. Besides the requirements of poverty, silence, and chastity, others appear for the first time; that of "stability" or a permanent residence in one monastery as opposed to the wandering life of the earlier monks, and a specially designated habit. The aim of this life is complete surrender to the will of God, accomplished through entire obedience to the abbot and the rule. The abbot thus appears as an absolute ruler, responsible to God alone. It is true that in weighty matters he is to seek the counsel of the brethren, but the ultimate decision rests with him. Benedict seems to have hesitated in placing a *præpositus* or prior next to him as assistant and, if need were, representative.

In laying down the system of daily prayer, Benedict departed somewhat from the earlier practise by instituting the office of compline as the seventh of the canonical hours. The longest and fullest of all the offices was the *nocturna vigilia* (matins), recited at two o'clock. The day hours were much shorter—lauds at daybreak, not long after matins; prime; terce, with which at least on Sundays and festivals the Eucharist was connected; sext; none; vespers; and compline. One of the principles on which the system of devotion was laid out was the weekly recitation of the entire Psalter. When this is compared with the requirement by Columban of the recitation of the whole 150 Psalms in the night office of Saturday and Sunday, a second principle is perceived which governed Benedict not merely in the arrangement of the devotional exercises but in all his rule—a wise moderation and gentleness.

2. Moderation.

It appears especially in the regulations for meals, of which he allows two daily, except at times of fasting; it comes out in the rules for labor, which show consideration for the weaker brethren, and also in the system of punishment. Small offenses, as unpunctuality at meals or office, are to be punished without harshness; more serious ones call for two private warnings and one in public, after which the offender is cut off from the society of the brethren at meals and prayers. If he is still obstinate, corporal punishment is the next step, and finally, if the prayers of the brethren have no effect, he is to be expelled from the monastery. Penitents may be twice taken back, but on a third lapse there is no further possibility of restoration.

The fact that, in his provision for the clothing of the monks, Benedict took account of the conditions of more than one province has been made a ground for disputing the authenticity of the rule; but the climatic difference between the hill-country of his first settlement and the Campanian plain on the banks of the Liris is sufficiently notable to find some reflection in the rule. Benedict had lived as an anchorite and as a cenobite, in convents of varying size and in different parts of Italy, at the head of a single small house and of a whole group of houses. When, therefore, with this manifold experience of what suited the monastic life of his time, he drew up a rule for every part of it, in such a definite legislative shape as none of his predecessors—Basil, Cassian, Pachomius, Jerome, Augustine—had given their prescriptions, we may well believe that he was acting to a certain extent with the consciousness that he was giving to Italian monasticism a new form, stronger and more consistent than had been known before.

3. Organization and Direction of the Monastic Life.

This is the special importance of Benedict's work, both for the Church and for the world at large. About the time when the Roman See, vindicating and even increasing its independence of Arian kings and Byzantine emperors, was preparing to erect its universal empire on the ruins of the old, the monk appeared who knew how to apply the old Roman talents of legislation and organization to the growing but as yet incoherent monasticism. Thus he became the founder of the great Benedictine Order which for centuries concentrated in itself the extraordinary spiritual force of the technically "religious" life, and contributed in so marked a degree to the extension of the Western Church. The striking influence of the order would, however, be inexplicable if it had not early become the guardian of learning and literature. The rule required the brothers, in addition to their manual labor, to devote one or two hours daily to reading; it provided for a convent library from which the monks were to take certain books for study at appointed times; each brother was to have his tablet and stylus; Benedict himself undertook the education of the children of prominent Romans; and in at least one passage of the rule those who can not read are spoken of as an inferior class. All these things speak of learned and literary interests as belonging to the original foundation. Cassiodorus even goes further than Benedict, in whose lifetime probably he founded the double convent of Squillace, providing expressly for the study of classical literature—though it is impossible to determine how far this influenced the Benedictine Order after the infusion with it of Cassiodorus's monasteries.

III. The Earlier History of the Benedictine Order: The history of the early extension of Benedict's society is only scantily told. According to the traditions of Monte Cassino, the third abbot, Simplicius, achieved great success in this work. Under the fifth, Bonitus, the mother house was destroyed in 589 by the Lombards, the monks fleeing to Rome (the universal refuge of those days), carrying with them the copy of the rule written by Benedict's own hand.

1. Period of Growth to the Time of Charlemagne.

There was probably already a monastery there which followed this rule—that of St. Andrew, founded by the future Pope Gregory the Great in 575; but Gregory's attachment to the order was presumably increased by the coming of the fugitives, who settled in a place given them at the Lateran by Pope Pelagius. The mission of Augustine to the Anglo-Saxons from the monastery of St. Andrew in 596 (see ANGLO-SAXONS, CONVERSION OF THE) opened a new field to the order. The Latin rules of the Spanish bishops Isidore of Seville (d. 636) and Fructuosus of Bragara show distinct traces of an acquaintance with that of Benedict. But more important was its introduction into the Frankish kingdom in the first half of the seventh century, since the attempt was there made to submit to it the entire monastic body. However it was introduced, it soon become predominant, and took the place of the rules of Columban and Cæsarius. At a Burgundian synod of 670 it was designated, with the canons, as the only standard for monasteries; and similarly in the synods held under the auspices of Carloman and Boniface in 742 and 743 it is called the norm for convents both of monks and of nuns. The language of the capitularies of 811, implying that only obscure traces of the prior existence of other rules remained, shows how completely it had occupied the field by the time of Charlemagne.

In spite, however, of this supremacy, and of the glory reflected on the order by such men as Aldhelm and Bede, Alcuin and Paulus Diaconus, an acute observer could already perceive traces of decay. In some places the abbots abused the power given them by the rule; in others laxity had begun to creep in. There was thus room for the reforming activity of Benedict of Aniane (q.v.), who attempted not only to restore the pristine strictness, but to supplement the rule by special ordinances for the purpose of securing uniformity in the daily life of the Frankish monasteries. His success, powerfully seconded as he was by the emperor Louis the Pious, was not lasting. The ninth century saw a considerable number of new foundations, especially in Saxony, and the literary activity promoted by Charlemagne continued; but there were many complaints not only of the giving of monasteries to laymen but of decay in morality and strict monastic discipline. In addition to these things, grievous havoc was wrought in many different quarters by the irruptions of the barbarians—in England by the Danes, in northern Germany and France by the Normans, in the south of Germany and the north of Italy by the Huns, and on the Mediterranean coast by the Saracens.

2. Period of Decline.

(OTTO SEEBASS.)

IV. The History of the Order since the Ninth Century: The palmy days of the order, from Benedict of Aniane to Innocent III (821–1200) may be designated as the time of ecumenical activity. The family of monks which proceeded from Monte Cassino controlled with its influence the civilization of the entire Christian West. The Basilian monasteries of South Italy and Sicily, as well as the monks and hermits of the Celtic Church in the British isles, were able only for a time to maintain the independence of their institutions. Patronized and at the same time monopolized by Rome, the Benedictine monastic character made itself the standard of monasticism throughout Latin Christendom. True, from the ninth century on there were marked departures from the founder's ideal, in consequence of which, even after the reform by Benedict of Aniane (q.v.), a number of similar efforts at reform became necessary; but the call to return to the original vigor of the rule ever proved its purifying power, and the total influence of the order was rather enhanced than decreased by the growing number of these reform congregations. The most important of them after the tenth century was the reform of Cluny (from 910), with which were gradually blended more or less the smaller reforms of a like tendency originating almost simultaneously in Flanders under Gerard of Brogne (d. 959), in Lorraine under John of Gorze (d. 974), in England under Dunstan of Glastonbury (d. 988), from the monastery of St. Benignus at Dijon (c. 990) under William of Volpiano (d. 1031) and in southern Italy by Alferius of Cava (d. 1050) (see CLUNY, ABBEY AND CONGREGATION OF; JOHN OF GORZE; GERARD, SAINT, 1; DUNSTAN). More independent of the Benedictine institutions, though proceeding from the order, were some reforming movements of the eleventh century. Among these were the famous congregation of Hirschau (q.v.), c. 1060, which was distinguished by the rigor of its discipline; that of Vallombrosa (see GUALBERTO, GIOVANNI), 1038, which, like Hirschau, developed with especial care the institution of lay brothers (*fratres conversi*), thus setting an important example for later orders (see MONASTICISM); those of Camaldoli, 1000; Grammont, 1076; Fontévraud, c. 1100; (see CAMALDOLITES; GRAMMONT, ORDER OF; FONTÉVRAUD, ORDER OF); and finally that of Cîteaux, 1098. The last of these reforms, the ripest and noblest fruit of the older Benedictine ideal, grew so rapidly, and, especially under the influence of St. Bernard, showed such power in the field of missionary and civilizing effort that it was obliged to leave the Benedictine family and form, not a new congregation but a new order, in spite of its adherence to the fundamental form of monastic discipline as delineated in the *Regula Benedicti* (see CISTERCIANS). By this separation of the youngest daughter from the mother, the latter ceased to be regarded as the only normal type for western monasticism. The ecumenical period of Benedictine history ends with the last decades of the twelfth century. It must thenceforth be traced as the history of one order among several in the life of western civilization.

1. 821–1200. Ecumenical Activity. New Congregations.

The period from Innocent III to the Council of Trent (1200–1563) is a time of increasing inner decay and of futile efforts at reform. The first attempt to restore discipline in the monasteries of the order, which had become very worldly, was made in 1215 by the Fourth Lateran Council under Innocent III. It ordered that every three years a general chapter should be held, and that the visitators prescribed by this chapter should be made by Cistercian abbots. Under this regulation the archbishops of Canterbury and York introduced the triennial

2. 1200–1563. Decay and Attempts at Reform.

visitations into the Benedictine monasteries of England, and enforced them in repeated provincial councils. For the monasteries of the Continent, special importance attached to the edict of Benedict XII, himself a Cistercian, who, after introducing a stricter discipline into his own order (1335), issued in the following year an edict concerning the Benedictines. This constitution, known as *Summa Magistri* or *Constitutio Benedictina,* decrees that in each monastery a general chapter is to be held annually. For each of the thirty-six provinces into which the order is divided by it, triennial provincial chapters are prescribed. But in spite of this measure, which had a temporarily beneficial effect, spirituality constantly declined. The reforms introduced afterward by the Council of Constance (1415), by a provincial chapter of the Mainz province of the order held at Petershausen (1417), by the congregation of Bursfelde (q.v.) organized for the North-German territories of the order, as well as by many Spanish congregations (e.g., the Observance of Valladolid under Ferdinand the Catholic, 1493), brought about merely a temporary improvement in the conditions.

3. 1563–1800. Tridentine Reform. New Congregations.

The Tridentine reforming period (1563–1800) was introduced by the decree *De regularibus et monialibus* passed in the twenty-fifth session of the Council of Trent (Dec. 3, 1563), which opposes the mischievous excess of exemptions (q.v.), puts the female members of the order without exception and the male members for the most part under the supervision of the bishops, and insists upon strict observance of the older regulations concerning the holding of general chapters, visitations, etc. Several new Benedictine congregations sprang up under the influence of the Tridentine decrees; in South Germany one for Swabia (1564), one at Strasburg (1601), one at Salzburg (1641), one for Bavaria (1684); in Flanders the congregation of St. Vedast near Arras, founded about 1590; in Lorraine that of St. Vanne and St. Hydulph, which Abbot Didier de la Cour founded in 1600 and Pope Clement VIII confirmed in 1604. An outgrowth of the latter was the congregation of St. Maur, founded in 1618 under the direction of the same Abbot Didier, which spread all over France, attaining the number of 180 monasteries, and raised the work of the order in the direction of learning to a prosperity which it never had before (see St. Maur, Congregation of). But after about 1780, first the forcible secularization under Joseph II, and then the storm of the Revolution in France and the neighboring countries to the south brought about the ruin of the order.

4. The Nineteenth Century.

The epoch of restoration, which coincides with the nineteenth century, has been able to save only about 500 houses (with about 4,300 monks), out of the 37,000 houses (abbeys or priories) which the order numbered before the catastrophes of the eighteenth century. Yet in some of the congregations there is at present a healthy and vigorous life as far as the morals and discipline are concerned and also as to achievements in theological learning and Christian art (painting, sculpture, etc.). In the latter respect the South-German congregation of Beuron is especially distinguished. The two other South-German congregations (the Bavarian and the Swabian) and those of northern France and Belgium (especially in the monasteries of Solesmes and Maredsous) have recently produced some able scholars and theologians. The Benedictines of the mother house of the order at Monte Cassino (q.v.) and the American congregations connected with it have also rendered considerable services in the same lines.

O. Zöckler†.

Bibliography: The somewhat voluminous early literature on Benedict in the shape of poems and lives may be found in part in *MGH, Poet. Lat. med. ævi,* i. 36–42, Berlin, 1881 (the *Carmina* of Paul the Deacon); *MGH, Script.,* vol. xv, part 1, pp. 480–482, 574, Hanover, 1887 (*Ex adventu corporis S. Benedicti in agrum Floriacensem*); four works on the Miracles are published in *MGH, Script.,* vol. xv, part 1, pp. 474–500, part 2 (1888), 863, 866, ix (1851), 374–376. The *Vitæ* by Gregory and other writers as well as the poems and relations of miracles may be found in *ASM,* sæc. i, pp. 28, 29–35, and sæc. ii, pp. 80, 353–358, 369–394; in *ASB,* Mar., iii, 276, 288–297, 302–357; and in *MPL,* lxxx, xcv, cxxiv, cxxvi, cxxxiii, cxxxiv, clx. Consult: P. K. Brandes, *Leben des heiligen Benedikt,* Einsiedeln, 1858; P. Lechner, *Leben des heiligen Benedict,* Regensburg, 1859; C. de Montalembert, *Les Moines d'Occident,* ii, 3–92 (on St. Benedict), 7 vols., Paris, 1860–77, Eng. transl., 7 vols., London, 1861–79, new ed., with introduction by Dom Gasquet on the *Rule,* 6 vols., 1896; P. Hügli, *Der heilige Benedikt,* in *Studien und Mittheilungen aus dem Benedict.-Orden,* year VI, vol. i (1885), 141–162; J. H. Newman, *Mission of St. Benedict,* in *Historical Sketches,* vol. ii, London, 1885; F. C. Doyle, *Teaching of St. Benedict,* London, 1887; G. Grützmacher, *Die Bedeutung Benedikts . . und seiner Regel,* Berlin, 1892; L. Tosti, *St. Benedict; Historical Discourse on his Life,* transl. from the Ital., London, 1896, cf. *St. Benedict and Grottaferra, Essays on Tosti's Life of St. Benedict,* ib. 1896.

On the order: *Bibliographie des Bénédictins de France,* Solesmes, 1889; the fundamental work is J. Mabillon, *Annales ordinis S. Benedicti,* 6 vols., Paris, 1703–39; Montalembert, ut sup.; Sir Jas. Stephens, *The French Benedictines,* in *Essays in Ecclesiastical Biography,* London, 1867; S. Brunner, *Ein Benediktinerbuch,* Würzburg, 1880; *Scriptores ordinis S. Benedicti in imperio Austriaco-Hungarico,* Vienna, 1881; B. Weldon, *Chronicle of English Benedictine Monks,* London, 1882 (covers the period from Mary to James II); H. C. Lea, *History of Sacerdotal Celibacy,* Philadelphia, 1884, and cf. his *History of the Inquisition,* new ed., New York, 1906; J. H. Newman, *Benedictine Schools,* in *Historical Sketches,* ut sup.; F. Æ. Ranbek, *Saints of the Order of St. Benedict,* London, 1890; E. L. Taunton, *English Black Monks of St. Benedict,* 2 vols., ib. 1897; Heimbucher, *Orden und Kongregationen,* i, 92–263. Of the *Rule* among old editions the best is by L. Holstenius, *Codex regularum monasticarum,* i, 111–135, Augsburg, 1759; another is by E. Martène in his *Commentarius in regulam S. Benedicti,* Paris, 1690. The best edition is by E. Woelfflin, *Benedicti regula monachorum,* Leipsic, 1895; serviceable are E. Schmidt, *Die Regel des heiligen Benedicts,* Regensburg, 1891, and P. K. Brandes, *Leben und Regel des . . Benedikt,* vols. ii, iii, Einsiedeln, 1858–63. The *Latin and Anglo-Saxon Interlinear Translation* was edited by H. Logeman, London, 1888. The *Rule* was published in Eng. transl., London, 1886, ib. 1896, in Thatcher and McNeal, *Source Book,* pp. 432–485, in Henderson, *Documents,* pp. 274–313; and by D. O. H. Blair, London, 1906. A bibliography of commentaries is in *KL,* ii, 324–325.

BENEDICTINES. See Benedict of Nursia.

BENEDICTION: In the Roman Catholic Church a part of every liturgical act, belonging to the class of sacramentals (q.v.)—i.e., things which were instituted, not by Christ but by the hierarchic Church with divine authority, and which are supposed, in their application to persons and things, to communicate *quasi ex opere operato* through ordained priests the grace of God consisting in purification, supernatural revivification, and sanctification. The higher the hierarchical position of him who bestows the blessing, the more powerful it is. Benediction and exorcism are always connected; the latter breaks demoniac influences and drives away the demons, while the former communicates divine powers, not only positively, but also negatively in the way of purification, by blotting out sins of omission and the temporal punishment of sins, and removing satanic influences, thus having itself a sort of exorcism though not explicit. Where exorcism alone takes place, it is in an imperative manner, whereas the benediction is precative, yet with an effective divine power *quasi ex opere operato* by means of the sign of the cross. The personal benediction effects either a lasting *habitus* (e.g., anointing at baptism), or a *forma gratiæ actualis* for a passing object and condition (e.g., benediction for travelers, and the sick); both kinds work either in the main negatively by the removal of satanic influences or positively in illumination and bestowal of supernatural strength in body and soul. Benedictions of things are always primarily negative, and positive only in the second place, that the use and enjoyment of the objects may conduce to the welfare of man's body and soul. The supernatural powers are attached to the things by means of the benediction, and in their effect they are independent of the conduct of man; either they make the things permanently *res sacræ*, affecting men in a purifying and sanctifying manner (baptismal water, holy water, rosaries, etc.), or they are of transient effect as conveying God's grace and protection. Sometimes they are also connected with indulgences. If anointing is applied, the benediction becomes a consecration, whereby the thing is dedicated to the service of God (e.g., monstrances, crosses, pictures, flags, organs, etc.).

As to the Evangelical conception of the benedictions, the words of Johann Gerhard give the proper point of view: "The priests [in the Old Testament] blessed by praying for good things; God blessed by bestowing the good things. Their blessing was votive, his effective. God promises to confirm this sacerdotal blessing on condition that it is given according to his word and will." Thus it is only God who effectively blesses; that is, communicates divine powers of his grace and his spirit; all human blessing is only intercession with God for his blessing. [According to the Roman Catholic view, the objective difference between liturgical and extraliturgical, ecclesiastical and private benediction is that in the former the efficacy emanates from the Church as a body by whose authority the rite was instituted and in whose name it is conferred and, in consequence, is supposed to be greater than in the latter where the effect depends on the intercession of an individual.] According to the Evangelical idea, there exists no objective difference between liturgical and extraliturgical, ecclesiastical and private benediction; it is only in a psychological way that the former may be more efficacious for the fulfilment of the subjective conditions of the hearing of prayer. Again, only persons, not things, can be blessed with God's spirit and grace. If things are nevertheless blessed, it means that they are set apart for ritual use; and so long as they are thus employed, they will be sacred, while they are desecrated when used lightly apart from ritual purposes. The benediction of things takes place only by metonymy; the things are mentioned, but the persons are meant who use them. Thus, e.g., a cemetery is dedicated to its special use and handed over to the reverential protection of the living; a church edifice is dedicated by its being used and offered to the living congregation as a valuable religious possession because of its use. But the Roman Catholic traditions still in many ways influence the ideas held even among Protestants on the subject of benediction.

E. C. ACHELIS.

BIBLIOGRAPHY: J. Gretser, *De benedictionibus*, Ingolstadt, 1615; J. Gerhard, *De benedictione ecclesiastica*, pp. 1252-1290, Jena, 1655; E. Martène, *De antiquis ecclesiæ ritibus*, vol. iii, Rouen, 1700; J. C. W. Augusti, *Denkwürdigkeiten aus der christlichen Archäologie*, iii, 392-393, x, 165 sqq., 12 vols., Leipsic, 1817-31; A. J. Binterim, *Segen und Fluch*, in *Denkwürdigkeiten*, vol. vii, part 2, Mainz, 1841; L. Coleman, *Apostolical and Primitive Church*, chap. xiv, London, 1844; V. Thalhofer, *Handbuch der katholischen Liturgik*, ii, 523-524, Freiburg, 1890; Bingham, *Origines*, XIV, iv, 16, XV, iii, 29; *DCA*, i, 193-200 (elaborate).

BENEFICE.

1. Meaning of the Term. Benefice (*beneficium ecclesiasticum*) is a term which includes two meanings: the spiritual, relating to the ecclesiastical duties attached to it; and the temporal, relating to the income and other worldly advantages of the office. The latter is more strictly the meaning of the word, though the connection of the two was early recognized in the phrase *beneficium datur propter officium*. Indeed, the term *beneficium* is not generally used where there is only the temporal side, with no corresponding duties. Such a case may be a *commenda*, whose holder has a right to the revenues of a church without any responsibilities; or a *præstimonium*, which is a charge for support on the revenues of the church; or a *pensio*, the use of a part of the revenues. These relations, however, when they are permanent fall under the general rules applicable to benefices. The benefice proper is ordinarily permanent, though sometimes founded for a specified time.

Historically in the primitive Church all the property of a diocese formed one whole, administered by the bishop; its purpose was primarily the support of the poor—bishop and clergy lived as belonging to that class, and were supposed, if they had no private means, to support themselves by their own labors. Those who had no other means of support received a monthly stipend from the general fund. With the recognition of the Church under Constantine, and the consequent accession of considerable property and state subventions, the system changed. But in law the episcopal church was still the unit in any consideration of diocesan property, and the bishop still its exclusive custodian. This remained the case when church property was divided into three or into four parts (see CHURCH BUILDING, TAXATION FOR) and one part destined for the support of the clergy. While, however, it was long before the theory changed, in practise there was a tendency to decentralization, and the individual parishes began to be recognized as separate units. This arose largely from donations and endowments destined by the donor for a particular church, whose clergy were to be supported out of their returns. After the fifth century it became customary for the bishops, instead of paying their clergy out of a central fund, to assign pieces of land for their support and that of the poor and of public worship. These assignments became gradually irrevocable, and thus finally the diocesan unity was dissolved, and the separate churches came into permanent possession of these properties.

2. Remuneration of Clergy.

The intimate connection between *officium* and *beneficium* is shown by a review of the provisions affecting benefices. They are divided into regular and secular, according as they are served by monastic or secular clergy; into *beneficia curata*, those to which the cure of souls is attached, and *non curata*, such as those of chaplains, canons of cathedrals, and the like. The Council of Trent forbade changing a *beneficium curatum* into a *non curatum* or *simplex*. The erection or constitution of a benefice, the permanent attachment of certain revenues to the performance of certain duties, was held to be reserved to the ecclesiastical authorities. The foundation of bishoprics was originally a function of provincial synods, but later came to the pope, who also had power alone to found collegiate churches. The bishop has power to found other benefices within his diocese, and his officials decide whether the endowment is sufficient and whether the proposed foundation will be useful and not injure any other party. The founder has certain rights of imposing conditions for the tenure of his benefice, which, once confirmed, are perpetual.

3. Provisions Affecting Benefices.

The appointment to a benefice (*provisio, institutio canonica*) includes the choice of the person (*designatio*) and the conferring of the benefice (*collatio, concessio, institutio* in the narrower sense). The designation to the greater benefices (bishoprics and the like) is sometimes by election, sometimes by nomination of the sovereign; to the lesser, by the choice of the bishop, frequently on the nomination of a patron. The collation is the act of ecclesiastical superiors—of the pope to bishoprics (*confirmatio*), of the bishop to the lesser benefices.

4. Appointment to a Benefice.

The conditions of a proper canonical appointment to a benefice are several: (1) A vacancy must exist, and that a real one, not such as would be caused by the forcible expulsion of the incumbent. Thus expectancies (q.v.) are forbidden; but the election of a coadjutor-bishop *cum jure successionis* is allowed. (2) The person appointed must be a *persona regularis* and *idonea*, i.e., properly qualified to hold the benefice. Under this head comes the possession of the qualifications necessary for ordination (q.v.), though, where it is required, a delay of a year or other specified time may be granted. Intellectual qualifications are included, to be determined, according to the Council of Trent, by examination; and the law has sometimes required native birth also, other things being equal. (3) The appointment must be made within the legal time, the rule being that no benefice shall remain vacant more than six months; otherwise the right of presentation is lost (see DEVOLUTION, LAW OF). (4) There must be no simony involved. (5) What are called subreption and obreption are also forbidden; this affects especially cases where a person obtains a benefice without letting it be known that he already holds another. The church law forbids plurality of benefices, except, for example, in cases where a *beneficium simplex* is held concurrently with a *beneficium curatum*, these being held to be compatible. This rule was often violated by papal dispensation, which caused great dissatisfaction. (6) The proper forms, both in the designation and in the collation, must be observed (see BISHOP; INVESTITURE; etc.).

5. Rights of a Benefice.

The rights and duties connected with a benefice are partly matters of universal law, partly special to the particular case. The incumbent has a right to the usufruct of any property belonging to the benefice, tithes, fees, oblations, etc. All this is his absolutely; but the view that he ought only to use so much of it as will suffice for his support, devoting the rest to ecclesiastical purposes and especially to the poor, influenced legislation very early, so that what came from the Church was supposed to revert to the Church, if it had not been used, at the cleric's death. This rule, which at one time was positive, has been very much relaxed, within certain limits. Of course the incumbent's power over church property is limited by the rights of his successor, and no arrangements can be made lasting beyond his lifetime, unless by the concurrence of the proper authorities.

6. Tenure.

A benefice is supposed to be conferred for life, and is normally vacated only by the death of the incumbent, but it may be vacated earlier by resignation, either express or tacit. Resignation can not be arbitrary with the incumbent, as he has by his acceptance of it incurred certain obligations from which he must be released—bishops by the pope, the lower clergy by their bishops. There must also be a valid ground for it. Tacit resignation may come about through any act which *ipso facto* dissolves the relationship: the taking monastic vows by the holder of a *beneficium sæculare*, the acceptance of a secular office, marriage (see CELIBACY), the acceptance of another incompatible benefice, change of faith, etc. Vacation as a penalty may occur through deprivation or remotion; this includes the transfer of a priest, as a disciplinary measure, to a smaller charge.

[The technical use of the word benefice in Protestant Churches is largely confined to the Church of England, where a great part of the prescriptions given above is still in force. In the statute law of England the term is practically restricted to a benefice with cure of souls, as distinct from cathedral preferment. In the State Churches of Germany also the distinction between *beneficium* and *officium* is still maintained, and the erection and alteration of benefices is a matter concerning jointly the ecclesiastical and secular authorities. Here the ordinary collator to a benefice is the consistory. The tendency of the most modern legislation is toward giving the congregation a voice in the selection of the pastor.

(E. FRIEDBERG.)

BIBLIOGRAPHY: Bingham, *Origines*, book v; L. Thomassin, *Vetus et nova ecclesiæ disciplina*, II, iii, 13, § 6, Paris, 1698; C. Gross, *Das Recht an der Pfründe*, Graz, 1887; Galante, *Il beneficio ecclesiastico*, Milan, 1895; U. Stutz, *Geschichte des kirchlichen Benefizialwesens von seinen Anfängen bis auf die Zeit Alexanders III*, Berlin, 1895.

BENEFICIUM COMPETENTIÆ: The privilege by which a condemned debtor is allowed to retain so much of his income as is absolutely necessary to his maintenance. Such a privilege exists in many places, in the interest of the public service, for officials and also for clerics. For the latter the custom is usually referred to the decree of Gregory IX (1271–76) *De solutionibus* (iii, 23). This passage, however, only establishes the principle that an unbeneficed clerical debtor can not be forced to pay by spiritual penalties, and that the creditors are to be content with sufficient security for payment when the debtor's circumstances improve. The glosses, and common practise following them, base the privilege upon the decree, and statute law has confirmed it, restricting any levy upon the salary or other income of such a cleric so that a certain sum is left to him as *congrua* (*sustentatio*). This privilege can not be pleaded in the case of debts arising from unlawful transactions or of public taxes. (E. FRIEDBERG.)

BENEFIT OF CLERGY: A privilege claimed by the medieval Church, as part of its general plea of immunity from secular interference. It allowed members of the clergy to have their trial for offenses with which they were charged, not before any secular tribunal, but in the bishop's court. In England this covered practically all cases of felony except treason against the king, and by the reign of Henry II it had given rise to great abuses. In many cases grossly criminal acts of clerics escaped unpunished, and other criminals eluded the penalty of their acts by declaring themselves clerics. The question was one of those on which the quarrel between the king and Becket reached its acute stage; and by the Constitutions of Clarendon (1164; see BECKET, THOMAS) Henry attempted to deal with it by decreeing that clerics accused of crime were to be first arraigned in the king's court, which might at its discretion send them to an ecclesiastical court. If convicted here and degraded (see DEGRADATION), the clerk was to lose his benefit of clergy and be amenable to lay justice. Edward III extended the privilege in 1330 to include all persons who could read (see CLERK); and it was not until the fifteenth century that any very definite regulation of this dangerous latitude was arrived at. Later statutes guarded against the evasion of their provisions by expressly declaring that their operation was "without benefit of clergy," and the privilege was finally abolished in 1827. There are a few early cases of its use in the American colonies, but Congress put an end to it here in 1790.

BENEZET, ben″e-zet′, **ANTHONY:** Quaker philanthropist; b. at St. Quentin, France, Jan. 31, 1714; d. at Philadelphia May 3, 1784. He belonged to a Huguenot family which settled in England in 1715, joined the Quakers there, and came to Philadelphia in 1731. He was a cooper by trade, but gave his life after coming to America to teaching and to philanthropic efforts, against slavery and war, in behalf of the American Indians, and the total abstinence cause. In 1742 he became English master in the Friends' School at Philadelphia and in 1755 established a girls' school there. In 1750 he undertook an evening school for slaves. Besides many tracts against the slave-trade, he published *A Short Account of the People Called Quakers* (Philadelphia, 1780); *The Plainness and Innocent Simplicity of the Christian Religion* (1782); *Some Observations on the Situation, Disposition, and Character of the Indian Natives of this Continent* (1784).

BIBLIOGRAPHY: R. Vaux, *Memoir of Anthony Benezet*, Philadelphia, 1817, revised by W. Armistead, London, 1859.

BENGEL, ERNST GOTTLIEB. See TUEBINGEN SCHOOL, THE OLDER.

BENGEL, JOHANN ALBRECHT: German Lutheran; b. at Winnenden (12 m. n.e. of Stuttgart), Württemberg, June 24, 1687; d. at Stuttgart Nov. 2, 1752. He studied at Tübingen, and devoted himself especially to the sacred text; he was also intent upon philosophy, paying particular attention to Spinoza. After a year in the ministry as vicar at Metzingen, he became theological repetent at Tübingen in 1708; and in 1713 was appointed professor at the cloister-school at Denkendorf, a seminary for the early training of candidates for the ministry. During this year he traveled through Germany, visiting the schools, including those of the Jesuits, to learn their methods. At Denkendorf he published in 1719 his first work, an edition of the *Epistolæ Ciceronis ad familiares*, with notes; then *Gregorii panegyricus græce et latine* (1722), and *Chrysostomi libri vi de sacerdotio* (1725), to which he added *Prodromus Novi Testamenti recte cauteque ordinandi*. His chief work, however, was upon the New Testament. While a student, he was much perplexed by the various readings in the text, and with characteristic energy and perseverance he immediately began to investigate the subject. He procured all the editions, manuscripts, and translations possible, and in 1734 published his text and an *Apparatus criticus*, which became the starting-point for modern text-criticism of the New Testament. His famous canon was: "The more difficult reading is to be preferred." This critical work was followed by an exegetical one, *Gnomon Novi Testamenti* (Tübingen, 1742), which has often been reprinted in Latin, and was translated into German by C. F. Werner (1853, 3d ed., 1876) and into English in Clark's Library (5 vols., Edinburgh, 1857–58) and in an improved edition by Lewis and Vincent (2 vols., Philadelphia, 1860–1861). As a brief and suggestive commentary on the New Testament, the *Gnomon* is still of use.

Bengel's chief principle of interpretation, briefly stated, is to read nothing into the Scriptures, but draw everything from them, and suffer nothing to remain hidden that is really in them. His *Gnomon* exerted considerable influence on exegesis in Germany, and John Wesley translated most of its notes and incorporated them into his *Annotatory Notes upon the New Testament* (London, 1755). In 1740 appeared Bengel's *Erklärte Offenbarung Johannis*, often reprinted (Eng. transl. by John Robertson, London, 1757); in 1741 his *Ordo temporum*, and in 1745 his *Cyclus sive de anno magno consideratio*. In these chronological works he endeavored to fix the "number of the beast" and the date of the "millennium," which he placed in the year 1836. In 1741 he was made prelate of Herbrechtingen; in 1749 member of consistory and prelate of Alpirspach, with residence at Stuttgart; and two years later Tübingen honored him with the doctorate.

(A. Hauck.)

Bibliography: The best life is by O. Wächter, *J. A. Bengel, Lebensabriss*, Stuttgart, 1865; cf. idem, *Bengel und Otinger*, Gütersloh, 1883; a life was written by his son and included in the *Introduction* to the *Gnomon*, where it is usually found; in more complete form by his great-grandson J. C. F. Burk, *J. A. Bengels Leben und Wirken*, Stuttgart, 1831, Eng. transl. by Walker, London, 1837; E. Nestle, *Bengel als Gelehrter*, Tübingen, 1893.

BENHAM, WILLIAM: Church of England; b. at Westmeon (16 m. n.e. of Southampton), Hants, Jan. 15, 1831. He was educated at St. Mark's College, Chelsea, and King's College, London (Theological Associate, 1857), and was a village schoolmaster from 1849 to 1852, and a private tutor from 1853 to 1856. He was ordered deacon in 1857 and ordained priest in the following year, and after acting as tutor in St. Mark's College from 1857 to 1864, was editorial secretary of the Society for the Promotion of Christian Knowledge from 1864 to 1867, and professor of modern history in Queen's College, London, from 1864 to 1871. He was successively curate of St. Lawrence, Jewry, London (1865–67), vicar of Addington (1867–73), St. John the Baptist, Margate (1873–80), and Marden, Kent (1880–82), as well as Six-Preacher of Canterbury Cathedral from 1872 to 1888, and Boyle Lecturer in 1897 From 1882 he was rector of St. Edmund's, Lombard Street, and was honorary canon of Canterbury from 1885. He was also rural dean of East City from 1903. In theology he was a Broad-church disciple of F. D. Maurice. Died at London July 30, 1910. His works are: *The Gospel of St. Matthew, with Notes and a Commentary* (London, 1862); *English Ballads, with Introduction and Notes* (1863); *The Epistles for the Christian Year, with Notes and Commentary* (1864); *The Church of the Patriarchs* (1867); *Companion to the Lectionary* (1872); *A New Translation of Thomas à Kempis' "Imitatio Christi"* (1874); *Readings on the Life of our Lord and His Apostles* (1880); *How to Teach the Old Testament* (1881); *Annals of the Diocese of Winchester* (1884); *A Short History of the Episcopal Church in America* (1884); *The Dictionary of Religion* (1887); and *Old St. Paul's Cathedral* (1902). He collaborated with R. P. Davidson and with C. Welsh in *Mediæval London* (1901); and edited the *Life of Archbishop Tait* (London, 1891); *The Writings of St. John*, in the *Temple Bible* (1902), and the *Ancient and Modern Library of Theological Literature*.

BENJAMIN OF TUDELA (a town of Navarre, on the Ebro, 160 miles n.e. of Madrid): Properly Benjamin ben Jonah, a Spanish rabbi, who in 1160 (or 1165; cf. Grätz, *Geschichte der Juden*, vi, note 10) left home and traveled through Catalonia, southern France, Italy, Greece, the islands of the Levant, Syria, Palestine, and Mesopotamia to Bagdad; thence he proceeded to Egypt by way of Khuzistan, the Indian Ocean, and Yemen; and finally returned to Spain in 1173. The information which he gathered with great diligence not only concerning the places visited, but also of adjoining lands, was written down in a Hebrew work (*Massa'oth shel rabbi Binyamin*, "Itinerary of the Rabbi Benjamin"), which is one of the most famous of early books of travel. Benjamin was credulous, perhaps deficient in general information, and interested primarily in things Jewish; his book abounds in errors and absurdities, but it does not justify the charge of deliberate falsification, and it contains much that is true and valuable not only concerning the numbers, status, and dispersion of the Jews of the twelfth century, but also concerning general history, political conditions, trade, descriptions of places, and the like.

Bibliography: The "Itinerary" was first published at Constantinople in 1543; then Ferrara, 1556; Freiburg, 1583; and many times subsequently. Arias Montanus and C. l'Empereur issued the text with a Latin translation, the former at Antwerp, 1575; the latter at Leyden, 1633. An English translation (from the Latin of Arias Montanus) was published in *Purchas's Pilgrims*, London, 1625, and is given in Bohn's *Early Travels in Palestine*, London, 1848. Others (with text) are by A. Asher, 2 vols., London, 1840–41, and M. N. Adler, London, 1907, the latter based on a British Museum MS. which differs considerably from other copies. A Germ. transl., with text, notes, etc., by L. Grünhut and M. N. Adler, was published at Frankfort, 2 vols., 1903–04. Consult also M. N. Adler, in the Palestine Exploration Fund *Quarterly Statement*, Oct., 1894.

BENNETT, JAMES: Congregationalist; b. in London May 22, 1774; d. there Dec. 4, 1862. He studied for the ministry at Gosport under the Rev. David Bogue; was ordained at Romsey, Hampshire, 1797, and was minister there till 1813, when he became theological tutor of the Rotherham Independent College, and minister of the church there; pastor of the church in Silver Street (afterward removed to Falcon Square), London, 1828–60. He was an associate of the Haldanes in some of their tours, was a secretary of the London Missionary

Society, was chairman of the Congregational Union 1840, and attracted much attention by his defense of Christianity against the unbelief of his time. His publications include *The History of Dissenters from the Revolution to 1808*, in collaboration with Dr. Bogue (4 vols., London, 1808–12; 2d ed., 2 vols., 1833), continued in *The History of Dissenters during the Last Thirty Years* (1839); *The Star of the West, being memoirs of R. Darracott* (1813); *Lectures on the History of Jesus Christ* (3 vols., 1825; 2d ed., 2 vols., 1828), supplemented by *Lectures on the Preaching of Christ* (1836); *Memoirs of the Life of David Bogue* (1827)· *An Antidote to Infidelity*, lectures delivered in 1831, and *A Second Antidote to Infidelity* (1831); *Justification as Revealed in Scripture in Opposition to the Council of Trent and Mr. Newman's Lectures* (1840); *The Theology of the Early Christian Church Exhibited in Quotations from the Writers of the First Three Centuries*, Congregational lecture, 1841; *Lectures on the Acts of the Apostles* (1846).

Bibliography: *Memorials of the Late James Bennett, D.D., including Sermons Preached on the Occasion of his Death*, London, 1863; *DNB*, iv, 242–243.

BENNETT, WILLIAM HENRY: English Congregationalist; b. at London May 22, 1855. He was educated at Lancashire Independent College (1873–82) and Owens College, Manchester, London University (B.A., 1875), and St. John's College, Cambridge (B.A., 1882), and was professor in Rotherham College from 1884 to 1888 and lecturer in Hebrew in Firth College, Sheffield, in 1887–88. He has been professor of Old Testament exegesis in Hackney College, London, since 1888 and in New College, London, since 1891. He was also first secretary to the Board of Theology in the University of London in 1901–03, and has been examiner in the Old Testament to the University of Wales since 1904, as well as a recognized teacher in the same institution since 1901. He has edited *Chronicles* and *Jeremiah* in *The Expositor's Bible* (London, 1894–95); *Joshua* in *The Sacred Books of the Old Testament* (1895) and in *The Polychrome Bible* (New York, 1899); *General Epistles* and *Genesis* in *The Century Bible* (London, 1901, 1903); and *Joshua* in *The Temple Bible* (1904). He has also written *Theology of the Old Testament* (London, 1896); *Primer of the Bible* (1897); and *Biblical Introduction* (1899; in collaboration with W F Adeney).

BENNO: Bishop of Meissen; b. at Hildesheim or Goslar 1010; d. at Meissen June 16, 1106, according to the traditional accounts. The first certain fact in his life is that he was a canon of Goslar. He was made bishop of Meissen in 1066, and appears as a supporter of the Saxon insurrection of 1073, though Lambert of Hersfeld and other contemporary authorities attribute little weight to his share in it. Henry IV imprisoned him, however, but released him in 1076 on his taking an oath of fidelity, which he did not keep. He appeared again in the ranks of the king's enemies, and was accordingly deprived of his bishopric by the Synod of Mainz in 1085. Benno betook himself to Guibert, the antipope supported by Henry as Clement III, and by a penitent acknowledgment of his offenses obtained from him both absolution and a letter of commendation to Henry, on the basis of which he was restored to his see. He promised, apparently, to use his influence for peace with the Saxons, but again failed to keep his promise, returning in 1097 to the papal party and recognizing Urban II as the rightful pope. With this he disappears from authentic history; there is no evidence to support the later stories of his missionary activity and zeal for church-building and for ecclesiastical music. His elevation to the fame of sainthood seems to have been due partly to the need of funds to complete the cathedral of Meissen, and partly to the wish to have a local or diocesan saint. He was officially canonized by Adrian VI in 1523, as a demonstration against the Lutheran movement, which Luther acknowledged by a fierce polemical treatise. His relics were solemnly dug up and venerated in 1524; but as the Reformation progressed they were no longer appreciated in Meissen, and Albert V of Bavaria obtained permission to remove them in 1576 to Munich, of which city Benno is considered the patron saint. (A. Hauck.)

Bibliography: Several early accounts in prose and verse of Benno's life and miracles were collected in *ASB*, June, iii, 148–231. Consult: O. Langer, *Bischof Benno von Meissen*, in *Mittheilungen des Vereins für Geschichte der Stadt Meissen*, i, 3 (1884), pp. 70–95, i, 5 (1886), pp. 1–38, ii, 2 (1888), pp. 99–144; E. Machatschek, *Geschichte der Bischöfe des Hochstiftes Meissen*, pp. 65–94, Dresden, 1884; R. Doebner, *Aktenstücke zur Geschichte der Vita Bennonis*, in *Neues Archiv für sächsische Geschichte*, vii, 131–144, Dresden, 1886; K. P. Will, *Sanct Benno, Bischof von Meissen*, Dresden, 1887.

BENOIST (BENOIT), be-nwā', ÉLIE: French Protestant; b. at Paris Jan. 20, 1640; d. at Delft Nov. 15, 1728. His parents were servants of the Protestant family La Tremoille. He early displayed fondness for the classics, studied at Montaigu College and at La Marche (Paris), and taught privately in divinity at Montauban. In 1664 he was ordained, and the following year was called to Alençon, where he served for twenty years as Protestant minister, with as much prudence as capacity. He met with much opposition from the Roman Catholics, especially from the Jesuit De la Rue, who attacked him and even incited a riot against him. After the revocation of the Edict of Nantes, Benoist went to Holland, and was called as minister to the church of Delft, near The Hague, where he stayed thirty years. He wrote *Lettre d'un pasteur banni de son pays à une Église qui n'a pas fait son devoir dans la dernière persécution* (Cologne, 1666); *Histoire et apologie de la retraite des pasteurs à cause de la persécution de France* (Frankfort, 1687); *Histoire de l'Édit de Nantes* (5 parts, Delft, 1693–95; Eng. transl., London, 1694). G. Bonet-Maury.

Bibliography: P. Pascal, *Élie Benoist et l'église réformée d'Alençon*, Paris, 1892; E. and É. Haag, *La France protestante*, ii, 269 sqq., 2d ed. by Bordier, Paris, 1877 sqq.; *Bulletin de la société d'histoire du protestantisme français*, 1876, p. 259, 1884, pp. 112, 162.

BENOIST (BENOIT), RENÉ: Roman Catholic theologian; b. at Savenières, near Angers, in 1521; d. at Paris Mar. 7, 1608. He accompanied Mary

Stuart to Scotland as her confessor in 1561; after his return to France was appointed pastor of the church of St. Eustache in Paris in 1569, and played a conspicuous part in the controversies of the *Ligue* as one of the leaders of the opposition to the Guises and the Ultramontanes. In 1566 he published a translation of the Bible, which, however, was little more than a reprint of the Geneva translation; it has been said that he knew little of either Hebrew or Greek. The translation was condemned by the theological faculty of the University of Paris in 1567 and by Pope Gregory XIII in 1575, and Benoist was expelled from the Sorbonne in 1572. He was reinstated by Henry IV and, to reenter the faculty, subscribed his own condemnation. He exasperated the Ultramontanes still more by maintaining that the king did not forfeit his right to the throne by professing the Protestant faith. He had influence in bringing about Henry's change of faith, and the latter made him his confessor and appointed him bishop of Troyes, but the pope refused confirmation, and in 1604 he had to renounce the office. He was a voluminous writer.

Bibliography: J. C. F. Hoefer, *Biographie générale*, v. 395, 46 vols., Paris, 1852–66; C. du Plessis d'Argentré, *Collectio judiciorum*, II. i, 392–393, 533–534, 3 vols., Paris, 1728–36.

BENRATH, KARL: German Protestant theologian; b. at Düren (22 m. s.w. of Cologne) Aug. 16, 1845. He was educated at the universities of Bonn, Berlin, and Heidelberg (1864–67), and taught in his native city until 1871. From 1871 to 1875 he studied in Italy, chiefly in Rome. In 1876 he became privat-docent at Bonn and associate professor in 1879. In 1890 he was called to Königsberg as professor of church history. He has written *Bernardino Ochino von Siena* (Leipsic, 1875); *Die Quellen der italienischen Reformationsgeschichte* (Bonn, 1876); *Geschichte der Reformation in Venedig* (Halle, 1887); and *Julia Gonzaga* (1900). He has also edited *Die Summa der heiligen Schrift, ein Zeugniss aus dem Zeitalter der Reformation* (Leipsic, 1880); *Luther's Schrift an den christlichen Adel deutscher Nation* (Halle, 1884); and K. R. Hagenbach's *Lehrbuch der Dogmengeschichte* (6th ed., Leipsic, 1889).

BENSLY, ROBERT LUBBOCK: Orientalist; b. at Eaton (2 m. s.w. of Norwich), Norfolk, England, Aug. 24, 1831; d. at Cambridge Apr. 23, 1893. He was educated at King's College, London, and Gonville and Caius College, Cambridge; studied in Germany; was appointed reader in Hebrew at Gonville and Caius College 1863; elected fellow 1876; became lecturer in Hebrew and Syriac in his college; was made professor of Arabic 1887; examiner in the Hebrew text of the Old Testament in the University of London; was a member of the Old Testament Revision Company; accompanied Mrs. Lewis and Mrs. Gibson on the trip to Sinai on which the palimpsest of the Syriac Gospels was discovered (see Bible Versions, A, III, 1, § 2). He has edited *The Missing Fragment of the Latin Translation of the Fourth Book of Ezra, discovered and edited with an Introduction and Notes* (Cambridge, 1875); contributed *The Harklean Version of Heb. xi, 28–xiii, 25* to the *Proceedings of the Congress of Orientalists* of 1889; assisted in the editing of the Sinaitic palimpsest; edited IV Maccabees (to which he devoted twenty-seven years of labor), published posthumously (Cambridge, 1895); wrote *Our Journey to Sinai, Visit to the Convent of St. Catarina, with a chapter on the Sinai Palimpsest* (London, 1896); edited *St. Clement's Epistles to the Corinthians in Syriac* (London, 1899).

Bibliography: H. T. Francis, *In Memoriam R. L. Bensly*, Cambridge, 1893; *DNB*: Supplement, vol. i, 171.

BENSON, EDWARD WHITE: Archbishop of Canterbury; b. at Birmingham July 14, 1820; d. at Hawarden (6 m. e. of Chester) Oct. 11, 1896. He studied at Trinity College, Cambridge (B.A., 1852); became master at Rugby 1852; was ordained priest 1857; in 1859 was appointed first head master of Wellington College (on the border of Windsor forest, near Wokingham, Berkshire); was appointed examining chaplain by the bishop of Lincoln (Christopher Wordsworth) in 1868, prebendary of Lincoln 1869, and chancellor and residentiary canon 1872, when he resigned his mastership and took up his residence at Lincoln. In 1877 he was consecrated first bishop of Truro (Cornwall); and was translated to Canterbury in 1883. He was a man of great energy, determined, and self-reliant. His industry was unremitting, and he found time for reading and study, the fruits of which appeared in the posthumous publications *Cyprian, his Life, his Times, his Work* (London, 1897) and *The Apocalypse* (1899). His administrative ability was shown in the development of Wellington College, which was practically his creation, and the thorough and efficient organization of the new diocese of Truro, where he formed a divinity school to train candidates for holy orders, began the erection of a cathedral, and founded and strengthened schools. He was the first bishop to appoint a canon missioner. As archbishop he strove for legislation effecting reforms in church patronage and discipline; opposed and prevented the disestablishment of the Church of Wales; created, in 1886, a body of laymen to act in an advisory capacity with the convocation of his province; cultivated cordial relations with the Nestorians and other Eastern Christians, but repelled what may have been intended as an advance to his own Church from Rome. He sat as judge in the trial of Bishop King of Lincoln, charged with certain ritual offenses (1889–90), and in the judgment which he delivered produced a masterly exposition of the law of the prayer-book, based upon the entire history of the English Church. Besides the works already mentioned, a volume of *Prayers, Public and Private* appeared posthumously (1899), and he published during his lifetime several volumes of sermons and addresses.

Bibliography: A. C. Benson, *Life of E. W. Benson*, 2 vols., London, 1899, abridged ed., 1901 (by his eldest son); J. H. Bernard, *Archbishop Benson in Ireland*, London, 1896; *DNB*, Supplement, vol. i, 174–179.

BENTLEY, RICHARD: English theologian and scholar; b. at Oulton, near Wakefield (25 m. s.w. of York), Yorkshire, Jan. 27, 1662; d. at Cambridge July 14, 1742. He was the son of a blacksmith, was grounded in Latin by his mother, studied at the grammar-school at Wakefield, and was admitted at the age of fourteen (the usual age of matriculation was seventeen or eighteen) to St. John's College, Cambridge. He took his first degree in 1680 with honor in logic, ethics, natural science, and mathematics, and became schoolmaster at Spalding in Lincolnshire. But Stillingfleet, the wealthy and learned dean of St. Paul's, soon called him to London to superintend his son's studies. He took his pupil in later years to Oxford and reveled there among the manuscripts in pursuance of his researches in profane and especially Biblical literature, entering on his life's work of treating and publishing texts. He had taken his M.A. at Cambridge in 1684 and received the same degree from Oxford probably in 1689. Before his twenty-fourth year he had started for himself a hexapla dictionary; in the first column stood every Hebrew word in the Bible and in the other five all the different translations of these words in Chaldee, Syriac, Latin, and Greek (both the Septuagint and Aquila). His Latin letter of ninety-eight pages to John Mill appeared in 1691 as an appendix to an edition of the chronicle of Malalas and presented a mass of critical research, including much drawn from manuscripts; he moved over the field of classical literature as if it were his library of which he knew every inch, and showed himself a master in criticizing the origin of books, in following up etymological rules, in explaining their use, and in dealing with meter. In this, his virgin effort, he gave explanations and corrections for some sixty Greek and Latin authors. He wrote like an authority, and in the happiest manner. He published *Callimachus* (1693), *Phalaris* (1699; the debate is still interesting), *Menander and Philemon* (1710), *Horace* (1711), *Terence* (1726), and *Manilius* (1739); his edition of Milton's *Paradise Lost* appeared in 1732.

Ordained 1690, probably at once Stillingfleet's house-chaplain, he became canon of Worcester in 1692, librarian to the king in 1694, chaplain in ordinary to the king in 1695, D.D. from Cambridge and Master of Trinity in 1699, vice-chancellor of the University 1700, archdeacon of Ely 1701. His intrigues secured his election as regius professor of theology in 1717. His apparent love of power led the academic senate, Oct. 17, 1718, to deprive him, illegally, of his academic degrees, which a decree of court restored to him in 1724. He was almost always in hot water either in literature, in his college, or in politics. Legally deprived of his mastership in 1734, he kept it, simply because the man who should oust him did not choose to move.

He delivered the first Boyle lectures (see BOYLE, ROBERT) in 1692, his intimate friend Isaac Newton helping him. He wrote against the freethinker Collins in 1713. Sterne quoted in *Tristram Shandy* his sermon on papistry, 1715. In 1691 he wrote to John Mill about the text of the New Testament, in 1713 he discussed the readings, and in 1720 he published his proposals for a new edition. At least from 1716 on, and apparently as late as 1732, he caused collations to be made in the libraries from London to Rome. But he did not publish an edition, probably because he found it impossible to give what he wished to give. His collations are in the library of Trinity College.

CASPAR RENÉ GREGORY.

BIBLIOGRAPHY: The best life is by R. C. Jebb, in *English Men of Letters*, London, 1887. Consult also J. H. Monk, *Life of Richard Bentley . . . with an Account of his Writings*, 2d corrected ed., ib. 1833; A. A. Ellis, *Bentleii critica sacra*, Cambridge, 1862; *DNB*, iv, 306–314.

BENTON, ANGELO AMES: Protestant Episcopalian; b. at Canea (Khania), on the island of Crete, July 3, 1837. He studied at Trinity College, Hartford, Conn. (B.A., 1856) and the General Theological Seminary, New York city (1860). He held various parishes in North Carolina from 1860 to 1883, when he was appointed professor of mathematics and modern languages at Delaware College, Newark, Delaware, being transferred to the chair of Greek and Latin two years later. In 1887 he accepted a call to the University of the South as professor of dogmatic theology, where he remained until 1894, being likewise rector of the Otey Memorial Church, Sewanee, from 1893 to 1895. He was then rector at Albion, Ill., in 1895–1904, this being interrupted by a temporary charge at Tarentum, Pa. Since 1905 he has held a temporary charge at Foxburg, Pa. His chief literary work has been the editing of the *Church Encyclopedia* (Philadelphia, 1884).

BENZINGER, IMMANUEL (GUSTAV ADOLF): German Orientalist; b. at Stuttgart Feb. 21, 1865. He was educated at the University of Tübingen (Ph.D., 1888; licentiate of theology, 1894), and after a pastorate at Neuenstadt, Württemberg, from 1894 to 1898, was privat-docent for Old Testament theology at the University of Berlin until 1901, when he retired, and has since resided in Palestine. In theology he belongs to the historico-critical school. He has been a member of the *Deutscher Palästinaverein* since 1888, editing its journal in 1897–1902, and has also been on the executive committee of the *Deutscher Verein zur Erforschung Palästinas* since 1897. He has written *Hebräische Archäologie* (Freiburg, 1894, 2d ed. 1907); *Commentar zu den Königsbüchern* (1899) and *Commentar zu der Chronik* (1901), both in the *Kurzer Hand-Kommentar zum Alten Testament;* and *Geschichte des Volkes Israels* (Leipsic, 1901). He likewise collaborated with R. J. Hartmann in *Palästina* (Stuttgart, 1899), and with Frohnmeyer in *Bilderatlas zur Bibelkunde* (1905), and has edited Baedeker's *Palästina und Syrien* since the third edition (1889).

BENZO: Bishop of Alba, a zealous partizan of Henry IV; b. about the beginning of the eleventh century; d. not earlier than 1085 or 1086. Little that is definitely attested can be related of his life; but it may be reasonably conjectured that he came originally from southern Italy, that he gained some sort of a position at the German Court, possibly as one of the chaplains of Henry III, and that before 1059 he was raised to the bishopric of Alba by Henry's influence. He was one of the most devoted upholders of the Italian claims of the

German kings, and a bitter opponent of the Hildebrandine party. His most prosperous days fell in the period of the schism between Honorius II and Alexander II, when he went to Rome (at the end of 1061) charged by the empress Agnes with the mission of supporting the former, the imperial candidate for the papacy, to whom he remained faithful even after Alexander's supremacy was assured. Later, he was a victim of the Patarene movement (see PATARENES), when in 1076 or 1077 popular disturbances drove him from his see. Ill luck followed him during the rest of his life. Though he may have taken part in Henry IV's first expedition to Rome, we never again find him in an important political position; and the latest indications to be gathered from his writings leave the picture of a man broken by poverty and illness, and still waiting for the emperor to reward him for long and faithful services. His *Libri vii ad Henricum IV* do not make up a single work, but are a collection of separate writings in both prose and verse which he put together into a sort of mosaic shortly before his death. Their special interest lies in the fact that they give an admirable insight into the views of the extreme imperialists, who were carried away by boundless hatred of Gregory VII. Benzo puts forth original views on the constitution of the State and on ecclesiastical politics from the standpoint of a convinced supporter of the empire. His *Panegyricus*, since the time and manner of the composition of its several books have been definitely determined, is now more highly regarded as an authority on the period of the schism. CARL MIRBT.

BIBLIOGRAPHY: Benzo's *Ad Henricum IV imperatorem libri septem*, ed. K. Pertz, is in *MGH*, *Script.*, xi, 591–681, Hanover, 1854. On his life and work consult: W. von Giesebrecht, *Annales Altahenses*, pp. 123, 213–227, Berlin, 1841; idem, *Geschichte der Kaiserzeit*, ii, 535, Brunswick, 1875 (in opposition to the work of K. J. Will, next mentioned); K. J. Will, *Benzos Panegyrikus*, Marburg, 1857; H. Lehmgrübner, *Benzo von Alba, . . sein Leben und "Panegyricus,"* Berlin, 1887; idem, *Benzo von Alba, . eine Quellenuntersuchung*, ib. 1886; T. Lindner, *Benzos Panegyricus auf Heinrich IV*, pp. 497–526, Göttingen, 1866; O. Delarc, in *Revue des questions historiques*, xliii (1888), 5–60; E. Steindorff, in *Göttinger Gelehrte Anzeiger*, No. 16, 1888, pp. 593 sqq.; Wattenbach, *DGQ*, ii (1886), 202, ii (1894), 328–329; C. Mirbt, *Die Publizistik im Zeitalter Gregors VII.*, Leipsic, 1894; Hauck, *KD*, vol. iii.

BERENGAR OF POITIERS: A younger contemporary and zealous adherent of Abelard (q.v.). Practically nothing is known of his life except what may be learned from his few brief writings. These, however, are not without interest, partly because (in spite of their being by no means completely trustworthy) they are among the authorities for the history of the Council of Sens in 1141, and partly for the light which they throw on the mental attitude and literary tone which prevailed among the disciples of Abelard and opponents of Bernard about the middle of the twelfth century. There are three of them extant: an *Apologeticus* against Bernard, an *Epistola contra Carthusienses*, and an *Epistola ad episcopum Mimatensem*, the bishop of Mende. The first was written not long after the Council of Sens, but not until the sentence of Innocent II against Abelard was known. Toward the end of it Berengar points out that other teachers, such as Jerome and Hilary of Poitiers, had made mistakes without being deposed; but a large part of the tractate is a personal attack on Bernard, accusing him of having made frivolous songs in his youth, taught the preexistence of the soul, and made up his commentary on the Canticles of a lot of heterogeneous material, partly borrowed from Ambrose. Especially bitter are his accusations of duplicity and unfairness in connection with the Council of Sens. The shorter but equally malicious letter against the Carthusians, who had taken a stand against Abelard, accuses them of breaking their vow of silence to speak calumny, and, while abstaining from the flesh of beasts, devouring their fellow men. The third letter is written in a different tone. Berengar's boldness had apparently stirred up so much hostility that he feared for his safety, left home, and sought an asylum in the Cévennes, whence he wrote to beg the bishop's protection, not exactly as a penitent, though he implies that he has approached more nearly to Bernard's standpoint. Whether he succeeded in setting himself right can not be told, as nothing is known of his later life. (F. NITZSCH†.)

BIBLIOGRAPHY: Berengar's works are usually printed among Abelard's, e.g., in Cousin's ed., ii, 771 sqq., 2 vols., Paris, 1849–59; also in *MPL*, clxxviii. Consult also *Histoire littéraire de la France*, xii, 254 sqq., Paris, 1763; Hefele, *Conciliengeschichte*, v, 427–428; S. M. Deutsch, *Die Synode von Sens, 1141, und die Verurteilung Abälards*, pp. 37–40, Berlin, 1880.

BERENGAR OF TOURS.

Berengar of Tours was born perhaps at Tours, probably in the early years of the eleventh century; d. in the neighboring island of St. Cosme Jan. 6, 1088. He laid the foundations of his education in the school of Bishop Fulbert of Chartres, who represented the traditional theology of the early Middle Ages, but did not succeed in imposing it upon his pupil. He was less attracted by pure theology than by secular learning, and brought away a knowledge of the Latin classics, dialectical cleverness, freedom of method, and a general culture surprising for his age. Later he paid more attention to the Bible and the Fathers, especially Gregory and Augustine; and it is significant that he came to formal theology after such preparation.

1. Early Life.

Returning to Tours, he became a canon of the cathedral and about 1040 head of its school, which he soon raised to a high point of efficiency, bringing students from far and near. The fame which he acquired sprang as much from his blameless and ascetic life as from the success of his teaching. So great was his reputation that a number of monks requested him to write a book that should kindle their zeal; and his letter to Joscelin, later archbishop of Bordeaux, who had asked him to decide a dispute between Bishop Isembert of Poitiers and his chapter, is evidence of the authority attributed to his judgment. He became archdeacon of Angers, and enjoyed the confidence of not a few bishops and of the powerful Count Geoffrey of Anjou.

Amid this chorus of laudation, however, a discordant voice began to be heard; it was asserted that Berengar held heretical views on the Eucharist. In fact, he was disposed to reject the teaching of Paschasius Radbertus, which dominated his contemporaries. The first to take formal notice of this was his former fellow student Adelmann

2. Controversy over the Eucharist.

(q.v.), then a teacher at Liége, who wrote to question him, and, receiving no answer, wrote again to beseech him to abandon his opposition to the Church's teaching. Probably in the early part of 1050, Berengar addressed a letter to Lanfranc, then prior of Bec, in which he expressed his regret that Lanfranc adhered to the eucharistic teaching of Paschasius and considered the treatise of Ratramnus (q.v.) on the subject (which Berengar supposed to have been written by Scotus Erigena) to be heretical. He declared his own agreement with the supposed Scotus, and believed himself to be supported by Ambrose, Jerome, Augustine, and other authorities. This letter found Lanfranc in Rome, after it had been read by several other people; and as Berengar was not well thought of there, Lanfranc feared his association with him might be prejudicial to his own interests, and laid the matter before the pope. The latter excommunicated Berengar at a synod after Easter, 1050, and summoned him to appear personally at another to be held at Vercelli in September. Though disputing the legality of his condemnation, he proposed to go, first passing through Paris to obtain permission from King Henry I, as nominal abbot of St. Martin at Tours. Instead of granting it, however, the king threw him into prison, where Berengar occupied himself with the study of the Gospel of John, with a view to confirming his views. The synod was held at Vercelli without him; two of his friends, who attempted to defend him, were shouted down and barely escaped personal violence; Ratramnus's book was destroyed; and Berengar was again condemned. He obtained his release from prison, probably by the influence of Geoffrey of Anjou; but the king still pursued him, and called a synod to meet in Paris Oct., 1051. Berengar, fearing that its purpose was his destruction, avoided appearing, and the king's threats after its session had no effect, since Berengar was sheltered by Geoffrey and by Bishop Eusebius Bruno of Angers, and found numerous partizans among less prominent people.

In 1054 Hildebrand came to France as papal legate. At first he showed himself friendly to Berengar, and talked of taking him back to Rome to get Pope Leo's authority with which to silence his foes. But when he found that the latter could

3. Berengar Submits at Rome.

do more to disturb the peace of the Church than Berengar's friends, he drew back. Under these circumstances Berengar decided to concede as much as he could, and the French bishops showed that they wished a speedy settlement of the controversy, when the Synod of Tours declared itself satisfied by Berengar's written declaration that the bread and wine after consecration were the Body and Blood of Christ. The same desire for peace and the death of Pope Leo were reasons why Hildebrand did not press for Berengar's going to Rome at once; later he did so, confident of the power of his influence there, and accordingly Berengar presented himself in Rome in 1059, fortified by a letter of commendation from Count Geoffrey to Hildebrand. At a council held in the Lateran, he could get no hearing, and a formula representing what seemed to him the most carnal view of the sacrament was offered for his acceptance. Overwhelmed by the forces against him, he took this document in his hand and threw himself on the ground in the silence of apparent submission.

Berengar returned to France full of remorse for this desertion of his faith and of bitterness against the pope and his opponents; his friends were growing fewer—Geoffrey was dead and his successor hostile. Eusebius Bruno was gradually

4. Reasserts his Views in France.

withdrawing from him. Rome, however, was disposed to give him a chance; Alexander II wrote him an encouraging letter, at the same time warning him to give no further offense. He was still firm in his convictions, and about 1069 published a treatise in which he gave vent to his resentment against Nicholas II and his antagonists in the Roman council. Lanfranc answered it, and Berengar rejoined. Bishop Raynard Hugo of Langres also wrote a treatise *De corpore et sanguine Christi* against Berengar. But the feeling against him in France was growing so hostile that it almost came to open violence at the Synod of Poitiers in 1076. Hildebrand as pope tried yet to save him; he summoned him once more to Rome (1078), and undertook to silence his enemies by getting him to assent to a vague formula, something like the one which he had signed at Tours. But his enemies were not satisfied, and three months later at another synod they forced on him a formula which could mean nothing but transubstantiation except by utterly indefensible sophistry. He was indiscreet enough to claim the sympathy of Gregory VII, who commanded him to acknowledge his errors and to pursue them no further. Berengar's courage failed him; he confessed that he had erred, and was sent home with a protecting letter from the pope, but with rage in his heart. Once back in France, he recovered his boldness and published his own account of the proceedings in Rome, retracting his recantation. The consequence was another trial before a synod at Bordeaux (1080), and another forced submission. After this he kept silence, retiring to the island of Saint-Cosme near Tours to live in ascetic solitude. Apparently his convictions were unchanged at his death, and he trusted in the mercy of God under what he considered the unjust persecutions to which he had been subjected.

Berengar's real significance for the development of medieval theology lies in the fact that he asserted the rights of dialectic in theology more definitely than most of his contemporaries. There are propositions in his writings which can be understood in a purely rationalistic sense. But it would be going quite too far to see in rationalism Berengar's main standpoint, to attribute to him the deliberate design of subverting all religious authority—Scripture, the Fathers, popes, and councils. This would be to ascribe to a man of the eleventh century views of which his age knew nothing, which it even had no terms to express. The contrast which he sets forth is not between reason and revelation, but between rational and irrational ways of understanding revelation. He did not recognize the right of the prevailing theology to claim his assent, because it made irrational assertions; the authorities to which he refused to submit were, in his judgment, only human authorities. He spoke bitterly and unjustly of popes and councils, unable to forgive them for making him untrue to himself; but this meant no rejection of the Catholic conception of the Church. His opposition was limited to the eucharistic doctrine of his time, and he controverted the theory of Paschasius not least because he believed it was contrary to Scripture and the Fathers, and destructive of the very nature of a sacrament. (A. Hauck.)

5. Berengar's Significance.

Bibliography: An edition of Berengar's works was begun by A. F. and F. T. Vischer, vol. i only was published containing his *De sacra cœna*, Berlin, 1834; cf. Mansi, *Collectio*, xix, 761 sqq.; the works are also in Bouquet, *Recueil*, xiv, 294-300. A collection of letters relating to him (one of his own) was published by E. Bishop in *Historisches Jahrbuch der Görres-Gesellschaft*, i, 272–280, Münster, 1880. For his life consult H. E. Lehmann, *Berengarii Turonensis vita ex fontibus haustæ*, part i, Rostock, 1870 (no more published); J. Schnitzer, *Berengar von Tours, sein Leben und seine Lehre*, Munich, 1890. Consult the works of Bernold of San Blas, in Labbe, *Concilia*, ix, 1050, in Bouquet, *Recueil*, xiv, 34–37, and in *MPL*, cxlviii; B. Hauréau, *Histoire de la philosophie scolastique*, i, 225 sqq., Paris, 1872; Hefele, *Conciliengeschichte*, vols. iv, v; *KL*, ii, 391–404; Neander, *Christian Church*, iii, 502–521, iv, 84, 86, 92, 335, 337, 355.

BERENGOZ: Abbot of St. Maximin's at Treves in the twelfth century; d. about 1125. In the records of the abbey he is first mentioned as abbot in 1107, and for the last time in 1125. The register of deaths contains his name against the date of Sept. 24, without naming the year; but as his successor, Gerhard, was installed in 1127, he must have died either in 1125 or 1126. He rendered considerable services to the monastery by procuring from Henry V the restitution of a number of alienated fiefs, and, besides five sermons for saints' days, wrote two larger works: three books *De laude et inventione sanctæ crucis*, and a series of discourses *De mysterio ligni dominici et de luce visibili et invisibili per quam antiqui patres olim meruerunt illustrari*. In the former he treats of the legend of the discovery of the cross of Christ by Helena, the mother of Constantine the Great, adducing a large number of Old Testament types of the cross. The latter deals with Christ under the aspect of the light of the world, shining from the beginning of its history. Whether the commentary on the Apocalypse which the Benedictines of St. Maur printed as an appendix to the second volume of their edition of St. Ambrose, ascribing it to a certain Berengaudus, is his or not must remain uncertain. (A. Hauck.)

Bibliography: Berengoz's works were edited by Christophorus, Cologne, 1555, and appear in M. de la Bigne, *Magna bibliotheca*, vol. vii, ib. 1618, also in *MPL*, clx. Consult J. Marx, *Geschichte des Erzstifts Trier*, ii, 95, Trier, 1860; H. V. Sauerland, *Trierer Geschichtsquellen*, Trier, 1889; Hauck, *KD*, iii, 971–972.

BERGEN FORMULA (*Das bergische Buch*). See Formula of Concord.

BERGER, DANIEL: One of the United Brethren in Christ; b. near Reading, Pa., Feb. 14, 1832. He studied privately at Springfield, O., taught school 1852–58, and served as pastor 1858–64. From 1864 till 1897 he was editor in the publishing house of the United Brethren in Christ at Dayton, O., having charge of the denominational Sunday-school literature 1869–93, and was a member of the International Sunday-School Lesson Committee from 1884 to 1896. In theology he is an Arminian. He wrote the *History of the Church of the United Brethren in Christ* for the *American Church History Series* (New York, 1894), and a larger work with the same title (Dayton, 1897), which is the official history of the denomination.

BERGER, bār''zhê', **SAMUEL:** French Lutheran; b. at Beaucourt (10 m. s.s.e. of Belfort), France, May 2, 1843; d. in Sèvres July 13, 1900. He studied at Strasburg and Tübingen; in 1867 became assistant preacher in the Lutheran Church in Paris; in 1877, librarian to the Paris faculty of Protestant theology. He was the author of *F. C. Baur, les origines de l'école de Tubingue et ses principes* (Paris, 1867); *La Bible au seizième siècle, étude sur les origines de la critique* (1879); *De glossariis et compendiis biblicis quibusdam medii ævi* (1879); *Du rôle de la dogmatique dans la prédication* (1881); *La Bible française au moyen âge* (1884); *De l'histoire de la Vulgate en France* (1887); *Le Palimpseste de Fleury* (1889); *Quam notitiam linguæ Hebraicæ habuerint Christiani medii ævi temporibus in Gallia* (1893); *L'Histoire de la Vulgate pendant les premiers siècles du moyen âge* (1893); *Notice sur quelques textes latins inédits de l'Ancien Testament* (1893); *Un Ancien Texte latin des Actes des Apôtres* (1895); *Une Bible copiée à Porrentruy* (*Études de Théologie et d'Histoire*, 1901, 213–219); and *Les Préfaces jointes aux livres de la Bible dans les manuscrits de la Vulgate, mémoire posthume* (1902).

BERGIER, bār''zhyê', **NICOLAS SYLVESTRE:** French Roman Catholic; b. at Darnay (18 m. s.e. of Mirecourt), Lorraine, Dec. 31, 1718; d. at Paris Apr. 19, 1790. He gained repute while a teacher at the college at Besançon by essays in philology and mythology; abandoned this line of study to devote himself to Christian apologetics, and polemics against the Encyclopedists. In 1765–68 he published at Paris *Le Déisme réfuté par lui-même* (2 vols.) and in 1768 the *Certitude des preuves du christianisme* (2 vols.), which achieved a great success and called forth replies from Voltaire and Anacharsis Cloots. In 1769 followed *Apologie de la religion chrétienne* (2 vols.) against Holbach, in 1771 *Examen du matérialisme* (2 vols.), and in 1780 *Traité historique et dogmatique de la vraie religion avec la réfutation des erreurs qui lui ont été opposées dans les différens siècles* (12 vols.). He also wrote a *Diction-*

naire théologique (3 vols., 1780), which formed part of the *Encyclopédie*, but has several times been separately edited (latest by Le Noir, 12 vols., 1876). As a reward for his services he was made canon of Notre Dame in Paris and confessor to the aunts of the king, with a pension of 2,000 livres.

BIBLIOGRAPHY: *Biographie nouvelle des contemporains*, ii, 378, Paris, 1821; *Biographie générale*, v, 14.

BERGIUS, JOHANNES: Reformed theologian; b. at Stettin Feb. 24, 1587; d. at Berlin Dec. 19, 1658. He studied at Heidelberg and Strasburg; in 1615 became professor at Frankfort-on-the-Oder, where the theological faculty represented the Reformed faith; 1623 court preacher at Berlin. He was present at the Colloquy of Leipsic (1631) and the Thorn Conference (1645), but declined to attend the Synod of Dort (1618), as he wished for union rather than the establishment of Calvinism. He was emphatically a mediator, and showed himself temperate and dignified in controversy. He published many sermons.

BIBLIOGRAPHY: D. H. Hering, *Beiträge zur Geschichte der evangelisch-reformirten Kirche in den preussisch-brandenburgischen Ländern*, i, 16 sqq., ii, 82, Breslau, 1784–85; H. Landwehr, *Die Kirchenpolitik Friedrich Wilhelms des Grossen Kurfürsten*, pp. 150 sqq., Berlin, 1894.

BERKELEY, GEORGE: Bishop of Cloyne (in County Cork, about 15 m. e.s.e. of the city of Cork); b. probably at Dysert Castle, near Thomastown (90 m. s.w. of Dublin), County Kilkenny, Ireland, Mar. 12, 1685; d. at Oxford Jan. 14, 1753. He studied at Trinity College, Dublin (B.A., 1704; M.A. and fellow, 1707; B.D. and D.D., 1721), and filled various college offices from tutor (1707) to junior dean (1710) and junior Greek lecturer (1712). He lived there in an atmosphere "charged with the elements of reaction against traditional scholasticism in physics and metaphysics." His *Common-Place Book* (first printed in the Oxford ed. of his works, 1871, iv, 419–502) shows how the stimulus worked upon a mind naturally inclined to independent investigation. Very early he adopted the idea that no existence is conceivable, and therefore none is possible, which is not either conscious spirit or the ideas (i.e., objects) of which such spirit is conscious. Locke had affirmed secondary and primary qualities of the material world; the secondary qualities, such as color and taste, do not exist apart from sensations; primary qualities exist irrespective of our knowledge. Berkeley denied this distinction, and held that external objects exist only as they are perceived by a subject. Thus the mind produces ideas, and these ideas are things. There are, however, two classes of ideas: the less regular and coherent, arising in the imagination; the more vivid and permanent, learned by experience, "imprinted on the senses by the Author of nature" which are the real things—a proof for the existence of God. According to Berkeley matter is not an objective reality but a composition of sensible qualities existing in the mind. "No object exists apart from the mind; mind is therefore the deepest reality; it is the *prius*, both in thought and existence, if for a moment we assume the popular distinction between the two." Berkeley appeared as an author with this theory already developed, and from it he never wavered. In 1709 he published an *Essay toward a New Theory of Vision*, an examination of visual consciousness to prove that it affords no ground for belief in the reality of the objects apparently seen. In 1710 appeared a *Treatise concerning the Principles of Human Knowledge*, in which his theory received complete exposition.

Berkeley's Philosophy.

Meanwhile Berkeley had taken orders, and, in 1713, he left Dublin, went to London, formed many desirable acquaintances, and gained an enviable reputation for learning, humility, and piety. The same year he published *Three Dialogues Between Hylas and Philonous* (ed. in *Religion of Science Library*, No. 29, Chicago, 1901), "the finest specimen in our language of the conduct of argument by dialogue." He visited the Continent in 1713–14 and again in 1716–20. In 1721 he returned to Ireland, again filled college offices at Dublin (divinity lecturer and senior lecturer, 1721; Hebrew lecturer, 1722; proctor, 1722), and was appointed dean of Dromore (1722) and dean of Derry, "the best preferment in Ireland" (1724).

Berkeley now became devoted to a plan of establishing a college in the Bermuda Islands, went to London to further the project in 1724, and in 1725 published *A Proposal for the Better Supplying of Churches in our Foreign Plantations, and for converting the savage Americans to Christianity by a college to be erected in the Summer Islands, otherwise called the Isles of Bermuda*. By his enthusiasm and persuasive powers he won many expressions of sympathy, and came to believe that the government would support the plan. In Sept., 1728, he sailed for America and landed at Newport, R. I., Jan., 1729. Three years of waiting convinced him that his hopes were futile, and in Feb., 1732, he returned to London. He published immediately *Alciphron or the Minute Philosopher*, the result of his studies in America and probably the most famous of his works. It is a powerful refutation of the freethinking then popular and fashionable. In 1734 he was made bishop of Cloyne, and there he lived, happy in his family and beloved for his goodness and benevolence, till 1752, when he went to Oxford to end his days with his son, a senior student at Christ Church. He kept up his studies after his appointment as bishop and published a number of books, including the curious *Philosophical Reflections, and Inquiries concerning the Virtues of Tar-water* (1744; three eds. the same year, the second called *Siris, a Chain of Philosophical Reflections, etc.*), in which he set forth a revision of his philosophy, and expressed his faith in tar-water as a universal medicine, good for man and beast; it was the most popular of his works.

Berkeley's American Scheme.

On first coming to America Berkeley bought a farm near Newport and built there a house, still standing, which he called "Whitehall" after the English palace. The shore is about a mile from the house, and a cleft in the rocks is still pointed out as a retreat whither he was wont to go and where he wrote much of *Alciphron*. This book is indeed a permanent record of his life at Newport, and not a little of its charm is due to this fact. He helped found a philosophical society at Newport and preached there in Trinity Church, a fine old wooden structure, which is still standing. He made at least one convert, the Rev. Samuel Johnson (q.v.), episcopal missionary at Stratford, Conn., and afterward first president of Columbia College, New York. Attempts to show that he directly influenced the early idealistic thought of Jonathan Edwards have not proved successful. His American plans and dreams inspired the poem, written at uncertain date, which ends with the stanza:

Westward the course of empire takes its way;
The four first acts already past,
A fifth shall close the drama with the day;
Time's noblest offspring is the last.

Bibliography: The standard edition of Berkeley's complete works is by A. C. Fraser, 4 vols., Oxford, 1871, reissued 1901, of which vol. iv includes his *Life and Letters* and *An Account of his Philosophy*. Prof. Fraser has also edited a volume of *Selections* from Berkeley, 5th ed., London, 1899, and contributed *Berkeley* to the *Philosophical Classics* series, Edinburgh, 1881. There is an edition of *The Works of George Berkeley*, by G. Sampson, with biographical introduction by A. J. Balfour, in Bohn's *Philosophical Library*, 3 vols., London, 1897–98. An American edition of the *Principles*, by C. P. Krauth, Philadelphia, 1874, presents a valuable epitome of opinions concerning Berkeley. The sources for a biography are a *Life* by Bishop Stock first published 1776, reprinted in the *Biographia Britannica*, vol. ii, 1780, and prefixed to the first edition of Berkeley's *Collected Works*, 1784, the details being obtained from Bishop Berkeley's brother, Dr. Robert Berkeley; S. A. Allibone gives interesting details of Berkeley's residence at Newport in *Critical Dictionary of English Literature*, i, 174–177, Philadelphia, 1891; *DNB*, iv, 348–356 adds a list of the works chronologically arranged. Consult further D. Stewart, *Philosophical Essays*, Edinburgh, 1810; vol. v of his *Collected Works*, 11 vols., ib. 1854–60 (on the idealism of Berkeley); S. Bailey, *A Review of Berkeley's Theory of Vision*, London, 1842 (adverse in its pronouncement); J. S. Mill, *Dissertations and Discussions*, ii, 162–197 and cf. vol. iv, Boston, 1865; F. Frederichs, *Der phenomenale Idealismus Berkeley's und Kant's*, Berlin, 1871; W. Graham, *Idealism, an Essay*, London, 1872 (connects Berkeley and Hegel); G. Spicker, *Kant, Hume und Berkeley*, Berlin, 1875; A. Penjon, *Étude sur la vie et sur les œuvres philosophiques de George Berkeley*, Paris, 1878; J. Janitsch, *Kant's Urtheile über Berkeley*, Strasburg, 1879; T. Loewy, *Der Idealismus Berkeley's, in den Grundlagen untersucht*, Vienna, 1891; T. H. Huxley, *Collected Essays*, vi, 241–319, New York, 1894; M. C. Tyler, *George Berkeley and his American Visit*, in *Three Men of Letters*, ib. 1895.

BERLEBURG BIBLE. See Bibles, Annotated, I, § 3.

BERN, DISPUTATION OF: The decisive point in the contest which definitely established the Reformation at Bern. At first the movement made slow progress there, as both the character of the people and their manner of life rendered them little susceptible to new ideas; even after a reforming party arose, for several years things continued in an undecided and vacillating condition. The somewhat violent and domineering manner in which the Roman Catholic authorities attempted to use their victory at the Conference of Baden (1526; see Baden, Conference of) brought on a crisis which, after the fashion of the time, it was attempted to meet by means of a disputation. Some of the Reformers invited to participate declined, having in mind the result at Baden, and the Roman Catholic dignitaries and celebrities generally refused to attend. But a great number of delegates and clergy appeared from Switzerland and the South German states, including Zwingli, Œcolampadius, Butzer, Capito, Ambrose Blaurer, and others. The opening session was held on Jan. 6, 1528, and the discussions lasted from the following day till Jan. 26. They were based on ten theses carefully prepared by Berthold Haller and Franz Kolb and revised by Zwingli. The outcome was that the ten theses were subscribed to by most of the clergy of Bern, the mass was done away with, the images were quietly removed from the churches, and on Feb. 7 the Reformation edict was issued, which gave the theses force of law, annulled the power of the bishops, and made the necessary regulations concerning the clergy, public worship, church property, etc. The majority of the country congregations soon gave in their adherence. The influence of the disputation was felt even in France, the Netherlands, and England.

Bibliography: The acts of the disputation were published at Zurich, 1528, and again in 1608 and 1701; the Ten Theses are given in English in Schaff, *Creeds*, i, 364–366, and *Christian Church*, vii, 104–105, in German and Latin, *Creeds*, iii, 208–210. Consult S. Fischer, *Geschichte der Disputation und Reformation in Bern*, Bern, 1828; S. M. Jackson, *Huldreich Zwingli*, pp. 280–283, New York, 1903.

BERN, SYNOD OF: The name given to the first Reformed synod at Bern (1532). The Reformation was established at Bern by the Disputation and the edict of Feb. 7, 1528 (see Bern, Disputation of), but much remained to be done in the way of consolidation and to finish the building of the new Church. This task was entrusted to a general synod, to which all the clergy of the land, 220 in number, were invited. It met on Jan. 9–14; Capito from Strasburg was the principal figure, and he collected the results of the discussion with much care and labor. They form a church directory and pastor's manual which is noteworthy, even among the monuments of the Reformation time, for its apostolic force and unction, its warmth and sincerity, its homely simplicity and practical wisdom.

Bibliography: The acts of the synod were officially printed at Basel, 1532, again in 1728 and 1778. Both the original and a modernized text were issued by Lauener, Basel, 1830. Consult M. Kirchhofer, *Berthold Haller*, pp. 169 sqq., Zurich, 1828; Billeter, in the *Berner Beiträge*, ed. F. Nippold, Bern, 1884 (especially useful); E. Bloesch, *Geschichte der schweizerisch-reformierten Kirchen*, i, 74–81, Bern, 1898.

BERNARD OF BOTONE: Canonist of the thirteenth century; b. in Parma c. 1200; d. at Bologna May, 1263. He studied law at Bologna, where he became professor and canon; then spent some time in Rome in an important official position at the papal court, but toward the end of his life returned to Bologna to lecture, especially on the decretals. He is best known as the author or compiler of the *Glossa ordinaria* (see Glosses and Glossators of Canon Law) on the decretals of Gregory IX., but wrote also *Casus longi* and a *Summa super titulis decretalium* (cf. J. F. von Schulte, *Die Geschichte der Quellen des kanonischen Rechts*, ii, Stuttgart, 1877, pp. 114 sqq.

(E. Friedberg.)

BERNARD OF CLAIRVAUX.

I. Life and Far-reaching Activity: St. Bernard of Clairvaux (*Bernardus Claraevallis*) is one of the most prominent personalities of the twelfth century, of the entire Middle Ages, and of church history in general. He gave a new impulse to monastic life, influenced ecclesiastical affairs outside of monasticism in the most effective manner, and contributed not a little toward awakening an inner piety in large circles.

1. Bernard's Importance.

As he knew how to inspire the masses by his powerful preaching, so also he understood how to lead individual souls by his quiet conversation, to ease the mind, and to dominate the will. It was said in his time that the Church had had no preacher like him since Gregory the Great; and that this was no exaggeration is proved by Bernard's orations, which in copiousness of thought and beauty of exposition have few equals. Revered by his contemporaries as saint and prophet, his writings, which belong to the noblest productions of ecclesiastical literature, have secured him also a far-reaching influence upon posterity. Praised by Luther and Calvin, Bernard's name has retained a good repute among Protestants, though he represented many things which the Reformation had to oppose.

Bernard was born at Fontaines (20 m. n.e. of Dijon), France, 1090; d. at Clairvaux (in the valley of the Aube, 120 m. s.e. of Paris) Aug. 20, 1153. He was the third son of the knight Tecelin and Aleth, a very pious lady, whose influence decided his future. While yet a boy he lost his mother, and, not being qualified for military service, he was destined for a learned career. He was educated at Chatillon and for a time seemed to be influenced by the world (cf. *MPL*, clxxxviii, 1857; *Vita*, I, iii, 6). But this period can not have been of long duration; the memory of his mother and the impressions of a solitary journey called him back, and he resolved quickly and firmly to break entirely with the world. He induced some of his brothers, relatives, and friends to follow him, and, after spending half a year together at Chatillon, they entered the "new monastery" at Citeaux (see CISTERCIANS).

2. Early Career. Abbot of Clairvaux.

In 1115 a daughter monastery was founded at Clairvaux and Bernard became abbot. He gave all his energies to the foundation of the monastery, and spent himself in ascetic practises, which the famous William of Champeaux, then bishop of Chalons, checked from time to time (*Vita*, I, vii, 31–32). Bernard soon became the spiritual adviser not only of his monks but of many who sought his advice and always left Clairvaux impressed by the spirit of solemnity and peace which seemed to be spread over the place (*Vita*, I, vii, 33–34). His sermons also began to exercise a powerful influence, which was increased by his reputation as prophet and worker of miracles (*Vita*, I, x, 46). According to the constitution which the new order adopted, Clairvaux became the mother monastery of one of the five principal divisions into which the Cistercian community was organized, and Bernard soon became the most influential and famous personality of the entire order. As early as the pontificate of Honorius II (1124–30) he was one of the most prominent men of the Church in France; he enjoyed the favor of the papal chancellor Haimeric (*Epist.*, xv), communicated with papal legates (*Epist.*, xvi–xix, xxi), and was consulted on important ecclesiastical matters. At the Synod of Troyes (1128), to which he was called by Cardinal Matthew of Albano, he spoke in favor of the Templars, secured their recognition, and is said to have outlined the first rule of the order (M. Bouquet, *Historiens des Gaules et de la France*, xiv, Paris, 1806, 232). In the controversy which originated in the same year with King Louis VI, who was not antagonistic to the Church but jealously guarded his own rights, Bernard and his friars defended the bishop before the king (*Epist.*, xlv), afterward also before the pope (*Epist.*, xlvi, cf. xlvii), though at first unsuccessfully.

With the schism of 1130 Bernard enters into the first rank of the influential men of his time by espousing from the very beginning the cause of Innocent II against Anacletus II. This partizanship of Bernard and others was no doubt induced by the fear that Anacletus would allow himself to be influenced by family interests. On this account they overlooked the illegal procedure in the election of Innocent, regarding it as a mere violation of formalities, defending it with reasons of doubtful value, and emphasizing the personal worth of that pope. At the conference which the king held at Étampes with spiritual and secular grandees concerning the affair, Bernard seems to have taken the part of reporter.

3. Activity for Innocent II and against Anacletus II.

He also worked for the pope by personal negotiations and by writing (*Epist.*, cxxiv, cxxv). When Innocent was unable to maintain his ground at Rome and went to France, Bernard was usually at his side. Later, probably in the beginning of 1132, he was in Aquitaine, endeavoring to counteract the influence of Gerhard of Angoulême upon Count William of Poitou, who sided with Anacletus (*Vita*, II, vi, 36). His success here was only temporary (*Epist.*, cxxvii, cxxviii), and not until 1135 did Bernard succeed, by resorting to stratagem, in changing the mind of the count (*Vita*, II, vi, 37–38). When in 1133 Lothair undertook his first campaign against Rome, Bernard accompanied the pope from his temporary residence in Pisa to Rome, and prevented the reopening of the proceedings concerning the rights of the opposing popes (*Epist.*, cxxvi, 8 sqq.). He had previously visited Genoa, animated the people by his addresses, and inclined them to an agreement with the Pisans, as the pope needed the support of both cities (cf. *Epist.*, cxxix, cxxx). It was also

Bernard who in the spring of 1135 induced Frederick of Staufen to submit to the emperor (*Vita*, IV, iii, 14; Otto of Freising, *Chron.*, vii, 19). He then went to Italy, where in the beginning of June the Council of Pisa was held; according to the *Vita* (II, ii, 8), everybody surrounded him here, so that it looked as if he were not *in parte sollicitudinis*, but *in plenitudine potestatis*. Nevertheless, resolutions were passed at that time regarding appeals to the papal see, which could hardly have been to the liking of Bernard. After the council he succeeded in inducing Milan and other cities of Upper Italy to submit to the pope and emperor (*Epist.*, cxxix–cxxxiii, cxxxvii, cxl). In Milan they attempted to elevate him almost with force to the see of St. Ambrose (*Vita*, II, ii–v). During the last campaign of Lothair against Rome, Bernard went to Italy for the third time, in 1137; he worked there successfully against Anacletus, and after the Pentecost of 1138 he finally brought about the submission of his successor to Innocent and thus ended the schism (*Epist.*, cccxvii). After this he left Rome. How great Bernard's influence in Rome was at this time may be seen from his successful opposition to Abelard (q.v.).

The ecclesiastico-political affairs of France soon made a new claim upon Bernard's attention. The young king, Louis VII, by making reckless use of his royal prerogatives, caused friction, as when he refused to invest Peter of Lachâtre, whom the chapter of Bourges had elected archbishop. The pope consecrated him, nevertheless, and thus provoked a conflict which was enhanced by the partizanship of Count Theobald of Champagne. After a while Bernard was asked to mediate; he faithfully performed this difficult task and enjoyed the confidence of the king to the end of his life (cf. *Epist.*, cceiv), whereas his relations to the pope appear to have been troubled toward the end (*Epist.*, ccxviii; ccxxxi, 3).

A very unexpected event was the election of Bernard, abbot of Aquæ Silviæ near Rome, formerly a monk in Clairvaux, as Pope Eugenius III (1145–53). Bernard writes a little later (*Epist.*, ccxxxix) that all who had a cause now came to him; they said that he, not Eugenius, was pope. And it is true that he exercised a remarkable influence in Rome especially at first, but Eugenius did not always follow his counsels and views; he had to consider the cardinals who were envious of Bernard. About this time Bernard, at the request of Cardinal Alberic of Ostia, undertook a journey to Languedoc, where heresy had advanced greatly and Henry of Lausanne (q.v.) had a large following. Bernard's presence there, especially at Toulouse, was not without effect, but to win permanent success continual preaching was required. A more important commission was given to him in the following year by the pope himself, to preach

4. The Second Crusade. the crusade. At Vezelay, where the king and queen of France took the cross, Mar. 21, 1146, Bernard's address was most effective. He then traversed the north of France and Flanders, and the officious doings of the monk Radulf induced him to go into the regions of the Rhine; he succeeded in checking the persecutions of the Jews at Mainz, which Radulf had occasioned. His journey along the Rhine was accompanied by numerous cures, of which the *Vita* (vi) contains notices in the form of a diary. But he regarded it as the wonder of wonders that he succeeded on Christmas day, 1146, in influencing King Conrad in favor of the crusade, in the face of all political considerations. During the crusade Eugenius sought a refuge in France. Bernard accompanied him, and was present at the great council in Reims, 1148; in the debates against Gilbert of Poitiers (see GILBERT DE LA PORRÉE) following the council, Bernard appeared as his main opponent; but the jealousy of the cardinals brought it about that Gilbert escaped unhurt (*Vita*, III, v, 15; Otto of Freising, *De gestis Frid.*, i, 55–57; *Hist. pont.*, viii, *MGH*, *Scrip.*, xx, 522 sqq.). About this time the first unfavorable news of the crusade became known, and tidings of its complete failure followed. No one felt the blow more keenly than Bernard, who with prophetical authority to speak had predicted a favorable issue (*De consid.*, ii, 1). In the last years of his life he had to experience many things which caused him sadness. Men with whom he had had a lifelong connection died; his relations with Eugenius III were sometimes troubled (*Epist.*, cccvi); the frailty and the pains of his body increased. But his mental vitality remained active; his last work, *De consideratione*, betrays freshness and unimpaired force of mind.

II. Ecclesiastical and Theological Significance: Bernard's entire life was dominated by the resolution he made while a youth. To work out the salvation of his soul, and—which meant the

1. Asceticism. same thing to him—to dedicate himself to the service of God, was thenceforth the sum of his life. To serve God demanded above all a struggle against nature, and in this struggle Bernard was in earnest. Sensual temptations he seems to have overcome early and completely (*Vita*, I, iii, 6) and an almost virginal purity distinguished him. To suppress sensuality in the wider sense of the word, he underwent the hardest castigations, but their excess, which undermined his health, he afterward checked in others (cf. *Vita*, I, xii, 60). He always remained devoted to a very strict asceticism (*Epist.*, cccxlv; *Cant.*, xxx, 10–12; *Vita*, I, xii, 60), but castigation was to him only a means of godliness not godliness itself, which demands of man still other things. The new life comes only from the grace of God, but it requires the most serious work of one's own nature. How much importance Bernard attached to this work, whose preliminary condition is a quiet collection of the mind, may be learned from the admonitions which he gives on that point to Eugenius. That he prefers the contemplative life to the active is nothing peculiar in him; and he doubtless had the desire to devote himself entirely to it. He may have believed that only duty and love impelled him to act. And yet, as he was eminently fitted for action, such work was probably also in harmony with his inclinations. From his own experience he received the strength to work, the thorough education of the personality, by which he exercised an almost fascinating power over others; on the other hand, his practical activity excited in him a stronger desire for contemplation and made it the more fruitful for him (*De diversis, sermo* iii, 3–5).

2. Study of the Bible.

Of Bernard's quiet hours, in spite of the many pressing claims on him, one part was devoted to study, and his favorite study was the Holy Scripture. His knowledge of the Bible was remarkable; not only does he often quote Bible-passages, but all his orations are impregnated with Biblical references, allusions, and phrases, to pay regard to which is often essential for the correct understanding. It is true that his exegesis did not go beyond the average of his time, yet he allows the great fundamental thoughts and vital forms of the Holy Scripture to influence him the more. As he was nourished by them he also knew in a masterly manner how to bring them near to others. All qualities of the great preacher were united in him; besides being vitally seized by the grace of God, he had a hearty desire to serve his hearers, an impressive knowledge of the human heart, and a wealth of thoughts and fascinating exposition, which was indeed not free from mannerism. What is missing in his sermons is reference to the variety of the relations of life, and this is intelligible, because he had monks as his hearers.

3. Grace and Works.

Religious geniality is the most distinguishing quality in the whole disposition of Bernard; his other rich gifts serve it, to it is due the impression which he made upon his time, and the importance which he obtained in the history of the Church. At the same time, Bernard is also a child of his time; above all, of the Church of his time, in which his religious life could develop without conflict. In this respect Bernard is related not to Luther, but to Augustine, and between Augustine and him stand Leo I, Nicholas I, and Gregory VII. Thus elements are found in Bernard which point to future developments combined with those which belong only to the ecclesiastical consciousness of the time. Bernard is most deeply permeated by the feeling of owing everything to the grace of God, that on the working of God rests the beginning and end of the state of salvation, and that we are to trust only in his grace, not in our works and merits. From the forgiveness of sin proceeds the Christian life (*De diversis, sermo* iii, 1). Faith is the means by which we lay hold of the grace of God (*In vigil. nativ. domini*, v, 5; *In Cant., sermo* xxii, 8; cf. also *In Cant.*, lxvii, 10; *In vigil. nat. dom., sermo* ii, 4). Man can never be sure of salvation by resting his hope upon his own righteousness, for all our works always remain imperfect. On the other hand, Bernard does not deny that man can and should have merits, but they are only possible through the preceding and continually working grace of God; they are gifts of God, which again have rewards in the world to come as their fruit, but without becoming a cause of self-glory. Before God there is no legal claim, but an acquisition for eternity through the work of the pious, made possible and directed by God's grace.

A characteristic contrast to these thoughts, which lead man again and again to humility, is the excessive glorification which Bernard devotes to the saints, above all to the Virgin Mary. Though he opposes (*Epist.*, clxxiv) the new doctrine of her immaculate conception, he nevertheless uses expressions concerning the mother of Jesus which go very far (e.g., *In nativ. Beat. Virg. Mariæ*, v, 7; *In assumpt. Beat. Virg. Mariæ*, i, 4; *In adv. dom.*, ii, 5). The same concerns also other saints (e.g., *In vigil. Petri et Pauli*, § § 2, 4, and at the end of the second oration *In transitu B. Malachiæ*). But the importance of such expression which a Protestant consciousness will never be able to adopt is restricted by this, that they are only used on special occasions, such as a feast of the saints. Otherwise the saints stand in the background, Christ alone stands in the foreground.

4. Bernard's Mysticism.

Bernard has always been regarded as a main representative of Christian mysticism, and his writings have been much used by later mystics and were the main source for the *Imitatio Christi*. But just here becomes evident how different the phenomena are which are comprised under the name of mysticism. With the Neoplatonic-Dionysian mysticism that of Bernard has some points of contact, but it differs from it as to its religious character. It is known how depreciatingly Luther speaks of the Areopagite, but this animadversion does not concern Bernard's mysticism. It is not man who soars to divine height, but the grace of God in Christ, which first pardons the sin and then lifts up to itself the pardoned sinner. On this account the whole mysticism of Bernard centers about Christ, the humbled and exalted one; it likes to dwell upon his earthly appearance, his suffering and death, for it is the " work of redemption " which more than anything else is fit to excite love in the redeemed (*In Cant.*, xx, 2; *De grad. hum.* in its first chapters). At the same time Bernard perceives that a sensual devotion, as it were, to the suffering of Christ is not the goal with which one must be satisfied; the thing necessary is rather to be filled with the spirit of Christ and through it to become like Christ. By Christ's work of redemption the Church has become his bride. To it, i.e., to the totality of the redeemed, belongs this name first and in a proper sense, to the individual soul only in so far as it is a part of the Church (*In Cant.*, xxvii, 6, 7; lxvii; lxviii, 4, 11). What it receives from him is in the first place mercy and forgiveness of sins, then grace and blessing. The climax of grace is the perfect union, but in the earthly life this is experienced by the pious at the utmost in single moments (*De consid.*, V, ii, 1; *De grad. hum.*, viii; *De dilig. Deo*, x). When Bernard speaks of becoming one with Christ and with God, his thought is clothed with Biblical expressions; but that Bernard in point of fact does not intend to go beyond the meaning of these words can be seen by reading the explanations (*In Cant.*, lxxi, 7 sqq.), where the union with God, to which the pious soul attains, is most keenly distinguished from a consubstantiality, as it exists between Father and Son in the Trinity. Bernard is entirely free from pantheistic thoughts, and that mysticism does not bring him in opposition to the Church his entire ecclesiastical attitude shows.

The Church as organized, with its hierarchy, at whose head stands the Roman bishop as successor of Peter and vicar of Christ, is to Bernard the exhibition of the kingdom of Christ on earth. On this account it must enjoy perfect autonomy, having a right of supervision over everything in Christendom, even over princes and states. It even has a right over the worldly sword (*De consid.*, IV, 7; cf. *Epist.*, cclvi, 1). Nevertheless Bernard is no blind adherent of the views of Gregory VII.

5. Doctrine of the Church.

In the first place Bernard demands a perfect separation between secular and spiritual affairs; the secular as such is to be left to the secular government, and only for spiritual purposes and in a spiritual sense is the pope to have supervision (*De consid.*, i, 6). But Bernard is also an opponent of the absolute papal power in the Church. As certainly as he recognizes the papal authority as the highest in the Church, so decidedly does he reprove the effort to make it the only one. Even the middle and lower ranks of the Church have their right before God. To withdraw the bishops from the authority of the archbishops, the abbots from the authority of the bishops, that all may become dependent on the curia, means to make the Church a monster (*De consid.*, iii, 8).

Notwithstanding Bernard's many-sided activity, he was and remained above all things a monk, and would not exchange his monachism either for the chair of St. Ambrose or for the primacy of Reims. Monachism is to him the ideal of Christianity. He acknowledges indeed that true Christianity is also possible while living in the world (*Apol.*, iii, 6; *In Cant.*, lxvi, 3; *De div.*, ix, 3), but such a life compared with monastic life seems to him a lower, and in spiritual relation,

6. Monasticism.

a dangerous position (*De div.*, xxvii, 2), a partition of the soul between the earthly and heavenly. Monasticism itself he regards in an ideal manner; it appeals to him also not so much from the point of view of merit as from that of the safest way to salvation. To this the whole order of the monastery is subservient, aside from this it is of no value. Besides, Bernard had relations with the different monasteries and monkish associations and was interested in them (cf. with regard to the Premonstratensians *Epist.*, viii, 4; lvi; and especially ccliii; concerning other regular canons, *Epist.*, iii; xxxix, 1; lxxxvii-xc; and elsewhere). In his many relations with the Cluniacensians, frictions were not wanting (cf. *Epist.*, i; clxiv; cclxxxiii; etc., and especially the *Apologia ad Guilelmum*), for the rise of the new order took place partly at the expense of the old. Nevertheless Bernard was highly esteemed by the Cluniacensians, and close friendship associated him with their head, the noble Peter the Venerable. That it was not interrupted is mainly due to Peter, who knew how to bear occasional lack of consideration by his great friend (cf. *Epist.*, clxvi, 1; clxviii, 1) without resentment (*Epist.*, ccxxix, 5). There existed a mutual true affection and admiration; the letters which they exchanged with each other are an honorable monument for both men, and without regard to differences of times and confessions modern readers can appreciate them.

III. Writings: The works of Bernard include a large collection of letters; a number of treatises, dogmatic and polemic, ascetic and mystical, on monasticism, and on church government; a biography of St. Malachy, the Irish archbishop; and sermons. Hymns are also ascribed to him (see below). The most important are the letters, which constitute one of the most valuable collections of church history; and the sermons, of which those on the Song of Songs furnish the chief source of knowledge of Bernard's mysticism. The first and fifth books of his *De consideratione* are also of a mystic character, whereas ii, iii, and iv contain a critique of church affairs of his time from Bernard's point of view and lay down a programme for papal conduct which a contemporary pope would have found it difficult to follow.

S. M. Deutsch.

IV. Hymns: Five hymns are ascribed to Bernard, viz.: (1) the so-called *Rhythmus de contemptu mundi*, "*O miranda vanitas! O divitiarum!*" (2) the *Rhythmica oratio ad unum quodlibet membrorum Christi patientis*, a series of *salves* addressed to the feet, knees, etc. of the Crucified; (3) the *Oratio devota ad Dominum Jesum et Beatam Mariam matrem ejus*, "*Summe summi tu patris unice*"; (4) a Christmas hymn, "*Lætabundus exultet fidelis chorus*"; (5) the *Jubilus rhythmicus de nomine Jesu*, "*Jesu dulcis memoria*," on the blessedness of the soul united with Christ. All these poetical productions, besides being beautiful in form and composition, are distinguished by a tender and living feeling and a mystic fervor and holy love. If they are really Bernard's, he deserves the title of *Doctor mellifluus devotusque*. An addition to the *Salve regina*, closing with the words, "*O clemens, O pia, O dulcis virgo, Maria*," is also ascribed to him. Mabillon denies Bernard's authorship of all these hymns in spite of the ancient and prevalent tradition. But one is inclined to accept the tradition, especially since the scholastic Berengar, in his *Apologia Abelardi contra S. Bernardum*, states that Bernard was devoted to poetry from his youth. German adaptations of the last section of (2) by Paul Gerhard (1659), "O Haupt voll Blut und Wunden," and of (5), "O Jesu süss, wer dein gedenkt," are in common use; there are several English versions—as by J. W. Alexander, "O Sacred Head, now wounded" and "Jesus, how sweet thy memory is," and Ray Palmer's "Jesus, the very thought of thee."

M. Herold.

Bibliography: A very accurate list of the literature (2,761 entries, arranged chronologically) is given by L. Janauschek, in *Bibliographia Bernardina*, Vienna, 1891. The best edition of the works of Bernard is by J. M. Horstius, revised and enlarged by J. Mabillon, Paris, 1667, corrected and enlarged 1690 and 1719, reprinted in *MPL*, clxxxii–clxxxv, of which the last vol. contains the old *Vitæ*, and some valuable additions not found in Mabillon. A new critical ed. of the *Sermones de tempore, de sanctis*, and *de diversis* has been published by B. Gsell and L. Janauschek in vol. i of *Xenia Bernardina*, Vienna, 1891. An Eng. transl. by S. J. Eales of the *Life and Works of St. Bernard of Clairvaux* from the ed. of Mabillon, 4 vols. only completed, London, 1888-97, contains the preface of Mabillon to his second edition of the *Opera*, a *Bernardine Chronology*. *List and Order of the Letters*, and transl. of the *Letters*, *Sermons*, and *Cantica Canticorum*. Of the early biographies the most important is the *Vita prima*, *MPL*, clxxxv, 225–466, the first book of which, by William of Thierry, was written during Bernard's lifetime, the second, by Ernald, abbot of Bona Vallis, the other books by Gaufrid of Clairvaux, cf. G. Hüffer, *Vorstudien zu . Bernhard von Clairvaux*, Munster, 1886. Of later literature note J. Pinio, *Commentarius de S. Bernardo*, in *ASB*, Aug., iv. 101 sqq., and in *MPL*, clxxxv, 643–944 (still very useful); and Mabillon's *Præfatio* (translated in Eales, ut sup.). Of modern lives the following deserve mention: A. Neander, *Der heilige Bernhard und sein Zeitalter*, Berlin, 1813, ed. S. M. Deutsch, in *Bibliothek theologischer Klassiker*, vols. xxii–xxiii, Gotha, 1889, Eng. transl. of 1st ed., *Life of St. Bernard*, London, 1843; J. C. Morrison, *Life and Times of St. Bernard*, London, 1877; F. Böhringer, *Bernhard von Clairvaux*, No. xiii, in *Die Kirche Christi und ihre Zeugen*, Leipsic, 1878; S. J. Eales, *St. Bernard*, in *The Fathers for English Readers*, London, 1890 (Roman Catholic); A. C. Benson and H. F. W Tatham, in *Men of Might*, ib. 1892; R. S. Storrs, *Bernard of Clairvaux, the Times, the Man, and his Work*, New York, 1892; W. J. Sparrow-Simpson, *Lectures on St. Bernard of Clairvaux*, London, 1895 (Roman Catholic); E. Vacandard, *Vie de Saint Bernard*, Paris, 1895 (displays knowledge of the subject and good taste and judgment so far as the ultramontane point of view of the author allows). Consult further: W. von Giesebrecht, *Geschichte der deutschen Kaiserzeit*, vol. iv, Brunswick, 1874; W. Bernhardi, *Jahrbücher des deutschen Reichs unter Lothair von Supplinberg*, Leipsic, 1879, and *unter Konrad III*, ib. 1883; B. Kugler, *Analekten zur Geschichte des zweiten Kreuzzuges*, Tübingen, 1879; idem, *Neue Analekten*, ib. 1883; K. F. Neumann, *Bernhard von Clairvaux und die Anfänge des zweiten Kreuzzuges*, Heidelberg, 1882; G. Hüffer, *Die Anfänge des zweiten Kreuzzuges*, in *Historisches Jahrbuch der Görres-Gesellschaft*, vol. viii, Bonn, 1887. On Bernard's relation to Abelard: S. M. Deutsch, *Die Synode zu Sens 1114 und die Verurteilung Abälards*, Berlin, 1880; E. Vacandard, *Abélard, sa lutte avec S. Bernard*, Paris, 1881. On Bernard as a preacher: A. Brömel, *Homiletische Charakterbilder*, pp. 53-96, Berlin, 1869; E. Vacandard, *S. Bernard, orateur*, Rouen, 1877; R. Rothe, *Geschichte der Predigt*, pp. 216 sqq., Bremen, 1881; A. Nebe, *Zur Geschichte der Predigt*, i, 250 sqq., Wiesbaden, 1879; E. C. Dargan, *Hist. of Preaching*, pp. 208 sqq., New York, 1905. On Bernard's teaching: A. Ritschl, *Die Christliche Lehre von der Rechtfertigung und Versöhnung*, i, § 17, Bonn, 1870; idem, *Lesefrüchte aus dem heiligen Bernhard*, in *TSK*, 1879, pp. 317–335; H. Reuter, in *ZKG*, vol. i, 1876; G. Thomasius, *Dogmengeschichte*, ed. Seeberg, ii, 129 sqq., Leipsic, 1889; A. Harnack, *Dogmengeschichte*, vol. iii, Freiburg, 1898. On Bernard as a hymnist: R. C. Trench, *Sacred Latin Poetry*, pp. 136–141, London, 1864; S. W. Duffield, *English Hymns*, pp. 299, 300, 317, 430, 600, New York, 1886; idem, *Latin Hymn-Writers*, passim, especially pp. 186–193, ib. 1889; Julian, *Hymnology*, pp. 136–137; P. Schaff, *Literature and Poetry*, ib. 1890. Discussions of St. Bernard from various points of view will be found in the Church Histories dealing with his period and also in works on the History of Philosophy.

For Bernard's hymns: H. A. Daniel, *Thesaurus hymnologicus*, 5 vols., Halle, 1841–56; C. J. Simrock, *Lauda Sion*, Cologne, 1850; J. F. H. Schlosser, *Die Kirche in ihren Liedern durch alle Jahrhunderte*, Freiburg, 1863; P. Schaff, *Christ in Song*, New York, 1868; J. Pauly, *Hymni breviarii Romani*, 3 vols., Aachen, 1868–70; F. A. March, *Latin Hymns with English Notes*, pp. 114–125, 276–279, New York, 1874; W. A. Merrill, *Latin Hymns Selected and Annotated*, Boston, 1904.

BERNARD OF CLUNY (*Bernardus Morlanensis*, often called Bernard of Morlaix, *Morlanensis* being improperly rendered Morlaix instead of Morlas): Monk of Cluny; b. probably at Morlas (5 m. n.e. of Pau, and then the capital of the province of Béarn); d. at Cluny probably about the middle of the twelfth century. Nothing more is known of him, except that he wrote a satirical poem of 2,991 lines, divided into three books, and entitled *De contemptu mundi*, dedicating it to Peter the Venerable. The theme is a monastic and ascetic commonplace, but its handling reveals vigor and satirical power. The meter is a medieval adaptation of the dactylic hexameter, so difficult that Bernard believed he had divine assistance in keeping it up for so many lines; each pair of lines rimes and the first third of each line rimes with the second, thus (lines 1–2):

> "Hora novissima, tempora pessima sunt, vigilemus.
> Ecce minaciter imminet arbiter ille supremus."

As to contents the poem is a satirical arraignment of the twelfth century for its vices in Church and society, sparing not even monks and nuns, but so exaggerated that it can not be accepted as history. The opening of the first book and the concluding part of the third are on spiritual themes of uncommon beauty. The poem exists in at least nine contemporary manuscripts and so must have been popular in its day. But it was forgotten until Matthias Flacius Illyricus discovered it and, with a view of showing that the evils of medieval Romanism of which the Protestants complained were already pilloried by Rome's faithful sons, printed a few lines from its third book in his *Catalogus testium veritatis qui ante nostram ætatem reclamarunt papæ* (Basel, 1556), and the next year the entire poem in the collection of similar poems which he entitled *Varia doctorum piorumque virorum de corrupto Ecclesiæ statu poemata ante nostram ætatem conscripta*. This collection was reprinted in 1754, probably at Frankfort. The first to bring Bernard's poem out separately was Nathan Chytræus (Bremen, 1597), and he was followed by Eilhard Lubin (Rostock, 1610), Petrus Lucius (Rinteln, 1626), and Johann and Heinrich Stern (Luneburg, 1640). Finally Thomas Wright reprinted it in his *Anglo-Latin Satirical Poets of the Twelfth Century* (London, 1872, Rolls Series, No. 59). The first complete translation, in prose, was published by Henry Preble (*AJT*, Jan.–July, 1906). In 1849 Trench published in his *Sacred Latin Poetry* (London) ninety-six lines from its first book, and these attracted the delighted attention of John Mason Neale, who translated them in his *Mediæval Hymns and Sequences* (London, 1851). His translation from Bernard leaped into wonderful popularity and was separately printed along with other lines not in Trench, as *The Rhythm of Bernard de Morlaix, Monk of Cluny, on the Celestial Country* (London, 1859; often reprinted). One of the hymns made by division out of this translation, "Jerusalem the golden," is found in all hymnbooks. Other pieces in prose and poetry are also attributed to Bernard.

Bibliography: S. M. Jackson, *The Source of "Jerusalem the Golden" and Other Pieces Attributed to Bernard of Cluny*, Chicago, 1909 (contains Preble's translation of the *De contemptu mundi*, and an elaborate introduction and bibliography).

BERNARD OF CONSTANCE: German teacher and author of the eleventh century; d. at Corvey 1088. He was a Saxon by birth, and about the middle of the century presided with notable success over the school at Constance, which he left to teach at Hildesheim. During his residence here he was asked by his teacher Adalbert and his pupil Bernold (q.v.) to write on the questions raised by the Roman synod of 1076, and answered in a lengthy treatise against the opponents of Gregory VII. His standpoint comes out even more clearly in his *Liber canonum contra Henricum IV*, which on its first publication (M. Sdralek, *Die Streitschriften Altmanns von Passau und Wezilos von Mainz*, Paderborn, 1890) was erroneously ascribed to Bishop Altmann of Passau. It was written after the Synod of Quedlinburg at Easter, 1085, when the Gregorian party was in great difficulties, and is an uncompromising declaration of fidelity to the papal cause. Bernard was, in short, as his pupil Bernold describes him, not only " a most learned man " but also " most fervent in the cause of St. Peter." CARL MIRBT.

BIBLIOGRAPHY: The two works mentioned above have been edited by F. Thaner in *MGH, Lib. de lite*, ii (1892), 29-47, and i (1891), 472-516 respectively. Consult C. Mirbt, *Die Publizistik im Zeitalter Gregors VII*, Leipsic, 1894; F. Thaner, *Zu zwei Streitschriften des 11. Jahrhunderts*, in *Neues Archiv für ältere deutsche Geschichte*, xvi (1889), 529-540; Hauck, *KD*, vol. iii.

BERNARD OF MENTHON: Founder of the hospices on the Great and Little St. Bernard. Little is known of his life, as modern criticism has hardly touched it, and the older biographies are untrustworthy and legendary. According to them he was born at Menthon, near Annecy (25 m. s. of Geneva), Savoy, in 923, and studied the liberal arts, law, and theology. To avoid a marriage planned by his parents, he fled to Aosta, where he was ordained and later became archdeacon. In addition to the most faithful performance of his priestly duties, he founded the two hospices and placed them in charge of canons regular, finally dying at Novara in 1007. A sequence preserved in the *Acta Sanctorum*, and dating probably from the end of the eleventh or beginning of the twelfth century, speaks of a meeting between him and Henry IV, which may possibly have occurred. It is known that in the ninth century there was a hospice under clerical auspices on the Mons Jovis, the present Great St. Bernard, which may later have fallen into decay. First in 1125, and often after that date, we find mention of the church of St. Nicholas on the Mons Jovis; in 1145 of the *hospitale*, which in 1177 is called *domus hospitalis SS. Nicolai et Bernardi Montis Jovis*. It is thus not improbable that Bernard restored the older foundation; but it is more likely that this took place at the beginning of the twelfth than at the end of the eleventh century. The date of 1081 for Bernard's death is no better attested than that of 1007. Innocent XI canonized him in 1681. The larger hospice, on which till 1752 the smaller depended, was reformed during the Council of Basel, receiving a very original constitution in 1438. Napoleon, pleased by his reception there, placed the hospice founded by him on the Simplon pass under the care of the same community, and endowed the foundation, which had lost a great part of the rich possessions formerly held by it in fourteen dioceses. It is now supported by voluntary offerings from all the Swiss cantons. A statue of Bernard was erected near the hospice in 1905. (A. HAUCK.)

BIBLIOGRAPHY: The old lives are in *ASB*, 15 June, ii, 1071-1089; Alban Butler, *Lives of the Fathers*, June 15, 2 vols., London, 1857-60; an old text *Le Mystère de St. Bernard de Menthon* was published by A. L. de la Marche, Paris, 1889. Consult L. Burgener, *Der heilige Bernhard von Menthon*, Lucerne, 1870; *Mémoires et documents publiés par la société d'histoire de la Suisse*, vol. xxix, Lausanne, 1875; A. Lütolf, *Ueber das wahre Zeitalter des heiligen Bernard von Menthon (996–1081)*, in *TQ*, lxi (1879), 179-207; J. A. Duc, in *Miscellanea di storia Italiana*, xxxi, 343-388, Turin, 1894; Wattenbach, *DGQ*, ii (1886), 214, ii (1894), 241.

BERNARD OF MORLAIX. See BERNARD OF CLUNY.

BERNARD OF TOLEDO: Archbishop of Toledo 1086-1125; b. at Agen (73 m. s.e. of Bordeaux), France, c. 1050; d. in Spain 1125. His significance in the history of Spain lies in the fact that from him dates the emergence of the Spanish Church from its isolation and its dependence on Rome. He became a monk in the monastery of Cluny, whence he was sent to Spain with others to assist the cause of the reforms of Gregory VII. Here he was made (1080) abbot of St. Facundus at Sahagun in the diocese of Leon, and finally named by Alfonso VI for the archbishopric of Toledo. Gregory's plans for Spain included (besides a general crusade against clerical marriage, simony, and lay investiture) the substitution of the Roman liturgy for the Mozarabic and the recognition of the obligations of tribute from the Spanish Church. The former point had been practically gained before his death, in spite of strenuous opposition. Urban II, by raising Bernard's see to primatial dignity, gave him the power necessary to prosecute the work of Romanizing. His cooperation made possible Urban's intervention at the Synod of Leon (1091) and ignoring of the royal right of investiture when Alfonso attempted to appoint a Spaniard to the see of St. Jago, apparently in order to counterbalance the influence of the French Benedictines with whom the primate was filling the episcopal sees. His care r was throughout that of a devoted adherent of the papacy. Some reminiscences of his youthful days as a knight appear in his forcible seizure of the Mohammedan mosque at Toledo in his first year as archbishop and in his plans for a crusade against the Saracens of the East, which both Urban II and Paschal II forbade, in view of the tasks which Spanish Christian chivalry had at home. Four of his sermons, on the *Salve Regina*, are included among those of the great Bernard. CARL MIRBT.

BIBLIOGRAPHY: J. Aschbach, *Geschichte Spaniens und Portugals zur Zeit der Herrschaft der Almoraviden und Almohaden*, i, 129 sqq., 339, 358 sqq., Frankfort, 1833; *Historia Compostellana: España sagrada*, ed. H. Florez, xx, 1-598, 615, Madrid, 1791; A. F. Gfrörer, *Papst Gregorius VII und sein Zeitalter*, iv, 484, 500-501, Schaffhausen, 1854; Hefele, *Conciliengeschichte*, v, 200, 251, 326-327; idem, *Der Kardinal Ximenes*, pp. 150 sqq., Arnheim, 1853.

BERNARD, CLAUDE: Called the "poor priest" and " Father Bernard "; b. in Dijon Dec. 23, 1588; d. at Paris Mar. 23, 1641. He was the son of a jurist, studied law himself, and for a time led a life of pleasure, but was converted by what he believed was a vision of his departed father. He became a priest and made Paris his residence, where he spent his time preaching and visiting the poor and sick, not shrinking from the most disgusting diseases. He gave away all that he had, including an inheritance of 400,000 francs.

BERNARD, JOHN HENRY: Church of Ireland, dean of St. Patrick's Cathedral, Dublin; b. at Raniganj, Bardwan (126 m. n.w. of Calcutta), India, July 27, 1860. He was educated at Trinity College, Dublin (B.A., 1880), where he was elected fellow and tutor in 1884, retaining his fellowship until 1902. In 1886 he was ordained to the priesthood, and was chaplain to the Lord Lieutenant of Ireland from 1887 to 1902. Since 1888 he has been Archbishop King's lecturer in divinity in the University of Ireland, and has been dean of St. Patrick's since 1902, where he had already been treasurer from 1897 to 1902. He was examining chaplain to the bishop of Down in 1889, and was select preacher to the University of Oxford in 1893 1895 and to the University of Cambridge in 1898, 1901, and 1904. He has repeatedly been examiner in mental and moral philosophy for the India Civil Service, and has been a member of the Council of the University of Dublin since 1892, as well as a commissioner of national education for Ireland from 1897 to 1903. He was likewise a member of the General Synod of the Church of Ireland in 1894, and of the Representative Church Body in 1897, while in 1902 he became a warden of Alexandra College, Dublin, a commissioner of charitable donations and bequests for Ireland in 1904, and a visitor of Queen's College, Galway, in 1905. He has written or edited the following works: Kant's *Critical Philosophy for English Readers* (2 vols., London, 1889; in collaboration with J. P Mahaffy); Kant's *Criticism of Judgment* (1892); *From Faith to Faith* (university sermons, 1895); *Archbishop Benson in Ireland* (1896); *Via Domini* (cathedral sermons, 1898); *The Irish Liber Hymnorum* (1898; in collaboration with R. Atkinson); *The Pastoral Epistles*, in *The Cambridge Bible*, (Cambridge, 1899); *The Works of Bishop Butler* (2 vols., London, 1900); *The Second Epistle to the Corinthians*, in *The Expositor's Bible* (1903); *St. Patrick's Cathedral* (1904); *The Prayer of the Kingdom* (1904): and has translated and edited *The Pilgrimage of St. Silvia* (1896) and other publications of The Palestine Pilgrims' Text Society

BERNARD, THOMAS DEHANY: Church of England; b. at Clifton (a suburb of Bristol), Gloucestershire, Nov. 11, 1815; d. at Wimborne (21 m. n.e. of Dorchester), Dorsetshire, Dec. 7, 1904. He was educated at Exeter College, Oxford (B.A., 1838), was ordered deacon in 1840 and priest in the following year, and was successively curate and vicar of Great Baddow, Essex (1840–46), vicar of Terling, Essex (1848), and rector of Walcot, Somerset (1863–86). He was prebendary of Haselbere and canon resident of Wells Cathedral from 1868 to 1901, and chancellor of the same cathedral after 1879, while from 1880 to 1895 he was proctor for the dean and chapter of Wells. He was also select preacher at Oxford in 1855, 1862, and 1882, and was Bampton Lecturer in 1864. He wrote *The Witness of God* (university sermons, London, 1862); *Progress of Doctrine in the New Testament* (Bampton lectures, 1864, 4th ed., 1878); *The Central Teaching of Jesus Christ* (1892); and *The Songs of the Holy Nativity* (1895).

BERNARDIN OF SIENNA: Franciscan; b. of noble parents at Massa (33 m. s.w. of Sienna) Sept. 8, 1380; d. at Aquila (58 m. n.e. of Rome) May 20, 1444. He entered the Franciscan order 1402; became its vicar-general 1437, and effected many reforms in discipline and government. He was the most famous preacher of his time and spoke to great crowds in all parts of Italy with wonderful effect. Three times he refused the offer of a bishopric. He was canonized by Nicholas V in 1450 and his day is May 20. His writings were first printed at Lyons (1501), afterward at Paris (4 vols., 1636; 5 vols., 1650) and at Venice (4 vols., 1745). The first volume contains his life by his scholar, St. John of Capistrano. Bernardin's writings are for the most part *tractatus seu sermones*, which are not so much sermons according to the modern view as formal treatises upon morals, asceticism, and mysticism.

Bibliography: The older accounts of his life are collected in *ASB*, 20 May, vi, 262–318. Consult: P. Thureau-Dangin, *Un Prédicateur populaire . St. Bernardin de Sienne (1380–1444)*, Paris, 1896, Eng. transl., London, 1906; Berthaumier, *Histoire de S. Bernardin de Sienne*, Paris, 1862; J. P. Toussaint, *Leben des heiligen Bernardin*, Regensburg, 1873; F. Apollinaire, *La vie et les œuvres de S. Bernardin*, Poitiers, 1882; E. C. Dargan, *Hist. of Preaching*, pp. 317 sqq., New York, 1905.

BERNARDINES. See Cistercians.

BERNICE, ber-nai'sê or ber'nis (for BERENICE): Eldest daughter of Herod Agrippa I. See Herod and his Family.

BERNO (BERN, BERNARD) OF REICHENAU: Abbot of Reichenau (Benedictine abbey on an island in the *Untersee* of Lake Constance, 4 m. w.n.w. of Constance) 1008 till his death, June 7, 1048. He was monk in a monastery at Prüm near Treves when appointed abbot; under his rule Reichenau regained its prosperity, which had been lost under his predecessor, the abbot Immo; the library was enriched, scholars were attracted to the school, and the church of St. Mark was rebuilt. He was renowned personally as scholar, as poet, and, above all, as musician; he accompanied the emperor, Henry II, to Rome in 1014 for his coronation and after his return introduced reforms in German church music. Besides lives of saints and theological and liturgical treatises he left a number of letters and works upon music, which are published in Gerbert, *Scriptores ecclesiastici de musica sacra*, ii (St. Blaise, 1784). His writings are in *MPL*, cxlii.

(A. Hauck.)

BERNOLD: German ecclesiastical author; b. probably in southern Swabia c. 1054; d. at Schaffhausen Sep. 16, 1100. He was educated at Constance under Bernard (q.v.), with whom he continued in close relations. He began writing early, and was present in Rome at the great synod of

1079 when Berengar was condemned. The next certain date is his ordination by the cardinal-legate Otto of Ostia at Constance in 1084. From 1086 to 1091 he was certainly an inmate of the monastery of St. Blaise in the Black Forest; in the latter year he migrated to Schaffhausen, where he remained (though not without interruption, as his presence at the battle of Pleichfeld shows) until his death. He was a versatile author. His *Chronicon* (ed. G. Waitz, in *MGH, Script.*, v, 1844, 385–467) is a valuable source for his own lifetime, though colored by his partizan support of Gregory VII. His treatise *De Berengarii hæresiarchæ damnatione multiplici* is interesting for the light which it throws on the attitude of German theology before the beginning of the strictly scholastic period. Most of his extant works, however, are of a practical nature, dealing with the vexed questions of the church life of his time. Though a zealous upholder of the reforming papacy, he was not a fanatic.

Carl Mirbt.

Bibliography: C. Mirbt, *Die Publizistik im Zeitalter Gregors VII*, Leipsic, 1894; A. Ussermann, *Germaniæ sacræ prodromus*, ii, 432–437, Freiburg, 1792; E. Strelau, *Leben und Werke des Mönches Bernold von St. Blasien*, Jena, 1889; G. Meyer von Knonau, *Jahrbücher des deutschen Reichs unter Heinrich IV und Heinrich V*, Leipsic, 1890–1904.

BERNWARD: Bishop of Hildesheim 993–1022. He came of a noble Saxon family, being the grandson of the count palatine Adalbero and the nephew of Bishop Folkmar of Utrecht. He was educated at the cathedral school of Hildesheim by Thangmar, later his biographer, and ordained by Willigis of Mainz. In 987 he became chaplain at the imperial court and tutor to the young Otto III. On Jan. 15, 993, he was consecrated bishop of Hildesheim. He protected his diocese vigorously from the attacks of the Normans, and only once took a wrong step as a temporal magnate—when, at the accession of Henry II, he took the side of Margrave Ekkehart, whose death, however, saved him from the consequences of his mistake. He rendered great services to literature and art. He died Nov. 20, 1022, a few weeks after the consecration of the magnificent church of St. Michael which he had built. Celestine III canonized him in 1193.

(A. Hauck.)

Bibliography: The *Vita* by Thangmar is in *MGH, Script.*, iv, 754–782, the *Miracula*, ib. pp. 782–786, Hanover, 1841; the continuation of the *Vita* by Wolfherius, ib. xi, 165–167, 1854. Consult: A. Schultz, *Der heilige Bernward und seine Verdienste*, Leipsic, 1879; W. A. Neumann, *Bernward von Hildesheim und seine Zeit*, in *Mittheilungen des kaiserlichen österreichischen Museums für Kunst*, v, 73–80, 97–104, 124–130, 141–152, 168–173, Vienna, 1890; B. Sievers, *Der heilige Bernward*, in *Studien und Mittheilungen aus dem Benedict- und dem Cisterz.-Orden*, xiv (1893), 398–420; Wattenbach, *DGQ*, i (1893), 318, 346–350, ii, 25, 360, 511; S. Beissel, *Der heilige Bernward von Hildesheim*, Hildesheim, 1895.

BERŒANS OR BARCLAYITES. See Barclay, John.

BERQUIN, bâr"kañ', LOUIS DE: French Reformer; b. at Passy-Paris June, 1490; d. at Paris Apr. 17, 1529. He belonged to a noble family of Artois and was lord of the estate of Berquin, near Abbeville. In 1512 he came to Paris to finish his studies, became acquainted with Lefèvre d'Étaples and the publisher Josse Badius, and was introduced to Marguerite of Valois, sister of Francis I, through whom he gained the king's favor. He belonged to that group of godly humanists who wished a reformation of the Church, but without a rupture with Rome. He hated equally the ignorance of the monks and the coarseness of Luther. Erasmus seemed to him the true Reformer; with him therefore he opened correspondence and translated several of his tracts, as well as Luther's *De votis monasticis*. The doctors of the Sorbonne denounced him as a heretic and on May 13, 1523, the trial was held before the Parliament. Seven of Berquin's writings and one of his translations from Luther and Melanchthon were condemned by the theological faculty and by the Parliament. On Aug. 1, he was made prisoner, but was set free by order of the king, Aug. 8. The Parliament had already burned his papers and books. The siege of Pavia and the captivity of the king (Feb., 1525) increased the Parliament's power, and the queen regent, Louise de Savoie, established (May 20) an extraordinary court to judge the heretics. On the same day three of Erasmus's treatises were censured. Berquin would have been permitted to retire and live on his estates if he had consented to keep silence. But he could not help speaking the truth and (Jan. 8, 1526), being denounced by the bishop of Amiens, he was again imprisoned. His books were again judged and forty of his propositions were declared heretical. He defended himself by saying that his propositions were taken from Erasmus and nobody adjudged the latter a heretic. His books were nevertheless condemned and he would have been burned with them if Marguerite of Valois had not invoked the clemency of her brother. Aug. 17 Francis sent a letter to the Parliament commanding them to take no definite steps without his advice. Although Erasmus advised silence, Berquin, confident of the king's favor, resumed the struggle and quoted from Noël Beda's writings against Erasmus, against the Sorbonne, and Lefèvre d'Étaples, twelve propositions as false and heretical, and asked the king to allow the Parliament to give judgment. From July, 1528, until March, 1529, Berquin lived in security. He was then again imprisoned and Parliament condemned him "to have his tongue branded with a red-hot iron and to remain a prisoner for the rest of his life." Apr. 16 Berquin appealed to the king, and the next day Parliament, taking advantage of the king's absence at Blois, ordered Berquin to be burned at the Place de Grève. He was the first Protestant martyr of France. Théodore Beza said of him: "If Francis had upheld him to the last, he would have been the Luther of France." Berquin's original works are all lost, only a few of his translations being left: *Enchiridion du chevalier chrestien* (Antwerp, 1529); *Le vray moyen de bien et catholiquement se confesser, par Érasme* (Lyons, 1542); *Paraphrases sur le Nouveau Testament*, and *Le symbole des apôtres* (both from Erasmus, n.p., n.d.).

G. Bonet-Maury.

Bibliography: Sources for a biography are in T. Beza, *Histoire ecclésiastique des églises réformées de France*, i. 7, Paris, 1882; A. L. Herminjard, *Correspondance des Réformateurs*, vol. ii and viii, especially vol. ii, containing letters by Erasmus to Berquin, ii. 155-157, 159 160, and the letter of Erasmus to C. Utenhovius, ii. 1893, 193, ib. 1878, 1893: a brief but lucid account of Berquin's life is contained in A. Chevillier, *L'Origine de l'imprimerie de Paris*, ib. 1694. Consult: *Histoire du protestantisme français*, xi, 129, ib. 1846; *Journal d'un bourgeois de Paris*, ed. L. Lalanne, ib. 1894; Hauréau, in *Revue des deux mondes*, Jan. 15, 1869; H. M. Baird, *Rise of the Huguenots*, i, 128-158, London, 1880.

BERRUYER, bār″rü″yê′, **JOSEPH ISAAC:** French Jesuit; b. at Rouen Nov. 7, 1681; d. at Paris Feb. 18, 1758. He served as teacher of his order for many years and won notoriety from an attempt to rewrite the Bible in French in the form of a romance fitted to the taste of his time; in carrying out the idea, however, he introduced much that was unfitting, heretical, and even blasphemous and obscene. He published the first part, *Histoire du peuple de Dieu depuis son origine jusqu'à la venue du Messie*, in seven volumes at Paris, 1728. It was put on the Index in 1734, but reissued in expurgated shape in 8 vols. 1733-34. The second part included the Gospels, 4 vols. 1753, also put on the Index in 1755. The third part included the Epistles, in 2 vols. 1757, but was condemned by the pope in 1758. The whole work has appeared in Italian, Spanish, Polish, and German transls., and was reissued (expurgated) in 1851 in 10 volumes.

Bibliography: E. H. Landon, *Ecclesiastical Dictionary*, ii. 204, London, 1853; A. de Backer, *Bibliothèque des écrivains de la compagnie de Jésus*, iv. 340, 7 vols., Paris, 1853-1861; F. H. Reusch, *Der Index der verbotenen Bücher*, ii. 804, Bonn, 1885.

BERRY, JOSEPH F.: Methodist Episcopal bishop; b. at Aylmer, Can., May 13, 1856; received his education at Milton Academy, Ontario; entered the ministry of his denomination, 1874; was associate editor of the Michigan *Christian Advocate*, 1884-90; editor of *Hepworth Herald*, 1890-1904; and was elected bishop 1904.

BERSIER, bār″syê′, **EUGÈNE ARTUR FRANÇOIS:** French Reformed; b. at Morges (7 m. w. of Lausanne), Switzerland, Feb. 5. 1831; d. at Paris Nov. 19, 1889. He came of Huguenot parentage, took elementary studies at Geneva and Paris; visited America, 1848-50; studied theology at Geneva, Göttingen, and Halle; became pastor in Paris 1855—in the Free Church until 1877 (until 1861 over the Faubourg St. Antoine Church; until 1874, assistant of Pressensé in the Taitbout Church; until 1877, over the Étoile Church), when he and his congregation joined the Reformed (established) Church of France. He was the author of several popular volumes of sermons, some of which have been translated into English: in the *Protestant Pulpit* series (2 vols., London, 1860); *Oneness of the Race in its Fall and its Future* (translated by Annie Harwood, London, 1871); *Sermons, with Sketch of the Author* (London, 1881; 2d series, 1885); *St. Paul's Vision* (translated by Marie Stewart, New York, 1881; new ed. 1890); *The Gospel in Paris; Sermons, with Personal Sketch of the Author* by Rev. Frederick Hastings (London, 1884). There are translations also into German, Danish, Swedish, and Russian. He wrote also *Solidarité* (Paris, 1869); *Histoire du Synode de 1872* (2 vols., 1872); *Liturgie* (now used in the Reformed Church of France, 1874); *Mes actes et mes principes* (1878); *L'Immutabilité de Jésus Christ* (1880); *Royauté de Jésus Christ* (1881); *Coligny avant les guerres de religion* (1884; 3d ed., 1885; Eng. transl., *Coligny: the Earlier Life of the Great Huguenot*, London, 1885); *La Révocation, discours sur l'édit de révocation* (1886); *Les Réfugiés français et leur industries* (1886); *Projet de révision de la liturgie des Églises Réformées en France* (1888); *Quelques pages d'histoire des Huguenots* (1890).

Bibliography: E. Stapfer, *La Prédication d'Eugène Bersier*, Paris, 1893; J. F. B. Tinling, *Bersier's Pulpit: Analysis of Public Sermons of Eugène Bersier*, London, 1900; W. C. Wilkinson, *Modern Masters of Pulpit Discourse*, pp. 251-281, New York, 1905 (highly laudatory).

BERTHEAU, bār″tō′, **CARL:** German Lutheran; b. at Hamburg July 6, 1836. He was educated at the universities of Göttingen (1855-57, 1858-59) and Halle (1857-58), and after teaching in the schools of his native city became pastor of St. Michael's Church there in 1867 Since 1897 he has been president of the Hamburg *Verein für innere Mission*. In theology he belongs to the positive evangelical school. He prepared the third volume of K. Hirsche's *Prolegomena zu Thomas à Kempis* (Berlin, 1894) and edited Luther's catechisms (Hamburg, 1896).

BERTHEAU, ERNST: German Lutheran; b. at Hamburg Nov. 23, 1812; d. at Göttingen May 17, 1888. He studied in Berlin and Göttingen (Ph.D., 1836) and became repetent at Göttingen 1836 extraordinary professor of Oriental languages and Old Testament exegesis 1842, ordinary professor 1843. From 1870 he was a member of the commission to revise Luther's Bible. His publications include: *Carminis Ephraemi Syri textus Syriacus secundum codicem bibliothecæ Angelicæ denuo editus ac versione et brevi annotatione instructus* (Göttingen, 1837); *Die sieben Gruppen mosaischer Gesetze in den drei mittleren Büchern des Pentateuchs* (1840); *Zur Geschichte der Israeliten, zwei Abhandlungen* (1842); an edition of the Syriac grammar of Bar Hebræus (1843); and commentaries upon Judges and Ruth (1845; 2d ed., 1883), Chronicles (1854; 2d ed., 1873), Ezra, Nehemiah, and Esther (1862), and Proverbs (1847; 2d ed., 1883), in the *Kurzgefasstes exegetisches Handbuch zum Alten Testament*. (Carl Bertheau.)

BERTHIER, bār″tyê′, **GUILLAUME FRANÇOIS:** French Jesuit; b. at Issoudun (130 m. s. of Paris), department of Indre, Apr. 7, 1704; d. at Bourges Dec. 15, 1782. He joined the Jesuits in 1722. He added six volumes (Paris, 1749) to the twelve already completed by Longueval, Fontenay, and Brumoy of the *Histoire de l'église gallicane*, bringing the narrative down to 1529; from 1745 to 1762 he edited the *Mémoires de Trévoux* and displayed much moderation as well as learning under attacks from the Encyclopedists and Voltaire. After the expulsion of his order from France in 1762 he was appointed tutor to the princes afterward Louis XVI and Louis XVIII, but had to leave the country in 1764; after an absence of ten years he returned to Bourges. He translated the Psalms (8 vols., 1785) and the Book of Isaiah (5 vols., 1788–89) into French with notes. His *Œuvres spirituelles* were published at Paris in five volumes in 1811.

Bibliography: A. de Backer, *Bibliothèque des écrivains de la compagnie de Jésus*, s.v., 7 vols., Paris, 1853–61.

BERTHOLD OF CHIEMSEE. See Pürstinger, Berthold.

BERTHOLD OF LIVONIA: Early missionary and second bishop among the Livonians. He was abbot of the Cistercian monastery in Lokkum, and was consecrated bishop to succeed Meinhard about 1196 by Hartwig II, bishop of Bremen. After he had failed to win the heathen by mild means with peril of his life, he went to Saxony and returned with a body-guard in 1198. The Livonians gathered and were defeated in battle, but the bishop was slain July 24, 1198. His successor was Albert of Riga (q.v.).

BERTHOLD OF REGENSBURG: Franciscan friar, the greatest popular preacher of the Middle Ages in Germany; b. at Regensburg probably earlier than the traditional date of 1220; d. there Dec. 14, 1272. He was a member of the Franciscan community founded at Regensburg in 1226. His novitiate was passed under the guidance of David of Augsburg; and by 1246 he is found in a position of responsibility. By 1250 at the latest, he had begun his career as an itinerant preacher, first in Bavaria, where he endeavored to bring Duke Otto II back to obedience to the Church; then he appears farther westward, at Speyer in 1254 and 1255, then passing through Alsace into Switzerland. In the following years the cantons of Aargau, Thurgau, Constance, and Grisons, with the upper Rhine country, were the principal scenes of his activity. In 1260 he went farther afield, traversing after that date Austria, Moravia, Hungary, Silesia, Thuringia, and possibly Bohemia, reaching his Slavonic audiences through an interpreter. Some of his journeys in the East were probably in the interest of the crusade, the preaching of which was specially entrusted to him by Pope Urban IV in 1263.

The German historians, from Berthold's contemporary, Abbot Hermann of Niedernaltaich, down to the middle of the sixteenth century, speak in the most glowing terms of the force of his personality and the effect of his preaching, which is said to have attracted almost incredible numbers, so that the churches could not hold them, and he was forced to speak from a platform or a tree in the open air. The gifts of prophecy and miracles were soon attributed to him, and his fame spread from Italy to England. He must have been a preacher of great talents and success. Although the manuscript reports of his sermons, which began to circulate very early, are by no means to be trusted as literal productions, we can still form from them a tolerably accurate idea of the matter and manner of his preaching. It was always of a missionary character, based formally on the Scriptures for the day, but soon departing from them to apply the special theme which Berthold wished to enforce. This generally finds its point in the insistent call to true sorrow for sin, sincere confession, and perfect penance; penance without contrition has no value in God's sight, and neither a crusade nor a pilgrimage has any good result unless there is a firm purpose to renounce sin. From this standpoint Berthold criticizes the new preachers of indulgences. The extremely mixed character of his audiences led him to make his appeal as wide and general as possible. He avoids subtle theological questions, and advises the laity not to pry into the divine mysteries, but to leave them to the clergy, and content themselves with the *credo*. The weighty political occurrences of the time are also left untouched. But everything that affects the average man—his joys and his sorrows, his superstitions and his prejudices—is handled with intimate knowledge and with a careful clearness of arrangement easy for the most ignorant to follow. While exhorting all to be content with their station in life, he denounces oppressive taxes, unjust judges, usury, and dishonest trade. Jews and heretics are to be abhorred, and players who draw people's minds away to worldly pleasure; dances and tournaments are also condemned, and he has a word of blame for the women's vanity and proneness to gossip. He is never dry, always vivid and graphic, mingling with his exhortations a variety of anecdotes, jests, and the wild etymologies of the Middle Ages, making extensive use of the allegorical interpretation of the Old Testament and of his strong feeling for nature.

(E. Steinmeyer.)

Bibliography: The sermons in German of Berthold were edited or given in abstract by C. F. Kling, Berlin, 1824, on which cf. J. Grimm in *Wiener Jahrbücher der Literatur*, xxxii (1825), 194–257, and the *Kleinere Schriften* by J. Grimm, Vienna, 1869. A complete edition of his *Predigten*, ed. F. Pfeiffer, appeared vol. i, Vienna, 1862 (cf. K. Schmidt in *TSK*, xxxvii, 1864, pp. 7–82), vol. ii, ed. J. Strobl, Vienna, 1880 (cf. A. Schönbach, in *Anzeiger für deutsches Altertum*, vii [1881], 337–385). On the Latin sermons consult H. Leyser, *Deutsche Predigten des 13. und 14. Jahrhunderts*, Leipsic, 1838; G. Jacob, *Die lateinischen Reden des seligen Berthold von Regensburg*, Regensburg, 1880; *Sermones ad religiosos viginti*, ed. P. de a. Hoetzel, Munich, 1882. On his life and work consult: K. Hoffmann, *Sitzungsberichte der Münchener Akademie*, ii (1867), 374 sqq., ii (1868), 101; L. Rockinger, *Berthold von Regensburg und Raimund von Peniafort*, in *Abhandlungen der Münchener Akademie, historische Classe*, xiii, 3 (1877), 165 sqq.; K. Unkel, *Berthold von Regensburg*, Cologne, 1882. For his preaching consult: W. Wackernagel, *Altdeutsche Predigten*, Basel, 1876; R. Cruel, *Geschichte der deutschen Predigt im Mittelalter*, pp. 306–322, Detmold, 1879; A. Linsenmayer, *Geschichte der Predigt in Deutschland*, pp. 333–354, Munich, 1886; E. C. Dargan, *A History of Preaching*, New York, 1905.

BERTHOLD OF RORBACH: Heretical mystic; d. 1356. He appears first in Würzburg, where he was tried on a charge of teaching heresy, but saved himself by recantation of the doctrines attributed to him. He was again brought to trial at Speyer in 1356, but this time refused to recant and was burned. The accounts of his teaching show him as an adherent of the quietistic mysticism of the

Brothers of the Free Spirit, sharing their disbelief in the meritoriousness of prayer and asceticism; those who are "enlightened by God," laymen as well as priests, may preach the Gospel and change bread and wine into the divine substance. The strange and shocking views attributed to him on the passion of Christ can scarcely be reconciled with his other teachings, and have probably come down in a distorted form. (HERMAN HAUPT.)

BIBLIOGRAPHY: A. Jundt, *Histoire du panthéisme populaire du moyen âge*, p. 105, Paris, 1875; H. Haupt, *Die religiösen Sekten in Franken*, p. 8, Würzburg, 1882.

BERTHOLD THE CARMELITE. See CARMELITES.

BERTHOLDT, LEONHARD: Professor at Erlangen; b. at Emskirchen (14 m. w.n.w. of Nuremberg), Bavaria, May 8, 1774; d. at Erlangen Mar 22, 1822. He studied at Erlangen and became professor extraordinary on the philosophical faculty 1805; full professor of theology 1810, in recognition of his work upon Daniel (2 vols., Erlangen, 1806–08). His principal work was the *Historisch-kritische Einleitung in die sämmtlichen kanonischen und apokryphischen Schriften des Alten und Neuen Testaments* (6 vols., 1812). Of less interest is his *Einleitung in die theologischen Wissenschaften* (2 vols., 1821–22); and of still less, his *Handbuch der Dogmengeschichte* (2 vols., 1822–23). As a teacher, however, and as editor of the *Kritisches Journal der neuesten theologischen Litteratur*, one of the principal organs of the rationalistic party, his activity was stimulating in many ways.

BERTHOLET, bār″tō″lé′, **ALFRED:** Swiss Protestant; b. at Basel Nov. 9, 1868. He was educated at the universities of his native city, Strasburg, and Berlin, and, after being Franco-German pastor at Leghorn, in 1892–93, became privat-docent for Old Testament exegesis in the university of his native city in 1896. In 1899 he was appointed associate professor of the same subject, and in 1905 was promoted to his present position of full professor. He was general secretary of the Second International Congress for the History of Religion held at Basel in 1904, and has prepared the commentaries on Leviticus, Deuteronomy, Ruth, Ezra, Nehemiah, and Ezekiel in K. Marti's *Kurzer Handkommentar zum Alten Testament* (5 vols., Freiburg and Tübingen, 1897–1902), and has written *Der Verfassungsgesetzentwurf des Hesekiel in seiner religionsgeschichtlichen Bedeutung* (Freiburg, 1896); *Die Stellung der Israeliten und der Juden zu den Fremden* (1896); *Zu Jesaja 53* (1899); *Die israelitischen Vorstellungen vom Zustand nach dem Tode* (Tübingen, 1899); *Buddhismus und Christentum* (1902); *Die Gefilde der Seligen* (1903); *Seelenwanderung* (Halle, 1904); *Der Buddhismus und seine Bedeutung für unser Geistesleben* (Tübingen, 1904); and the section on the Apocrypha and Pseudepigrapha in K. Budde's *Geschichte der althebräischen Literatur* (Leipsic, 1906).

BERTRAM: The name by which **Ratramnus** (q.v.) was formerly sometimes quoted.

BERTRAM, ROBERT AITKIN: English Congregationalist; b. at Hanley (147 m. n.w. of London), Staffordshire, Nov. 8, 1836; d. in London Nov. 14, 1886. He ended his studies at Owens College (Victoria University), Manchester, 1858; was pastor at Lymm, Cheshire, at Openshaw (Manchester), and at Barnstaple, Devonshire; edited *The Christian Age*, 1880–83. He compiled *The Cavendish Hymnal* (Manchester, 1864), and published *Parable or Divine Poesy, Illustrations in Theology and Morals Selected from Great Divines and Systematically Arranged* (London, 1866); *A Dictionary of Poetical Illustrations* (1877); *A Homiletical Encyclopedia of Illustrations in Theology and Morals, a Handbook of Practical Divinity and a Commentary on Holy Scripture* (1878); *A Homiletical Commentary on the Prophecies of Isaiah* (i, 1884; ii, jointly, with Alfred Tucker, 1888).

BÉRULLE, PIERRE DE. See NERI, PHILIP.

BERYLLUS OF BOSTRA. See MONARCHIANISM.

BESANT, bes′ant, **ANNIE (WOOD):** Theosophist; b. at London Oct. 1, 1847. She was educated by private tutors at Clearmouth, Dorsetshire, London, Bonn, and Paris, and later passed B.Sc. and M.B. at London University. Originally a member of the Church of England, she married Rev. Frank Besant, vicar of Sibsey, Lincolnshire, in 1867, but was divorced from him six years later and renounced Christianity altogether. She then joined the National Secular Society, and as a scientific materialist worked with Charles Bradlaugh, with whom she edited the *National Reformer*. She was also prominent in socialistic and labor movements, and was a member of the Fabian Society and the Social Democratic Federation. In 1887–90 she was a member of the London School Board for Tower Hamlets, but declined reelection. Meanwhile, her views had undergone further change as a result of psychological study, and in 1889 she joined the Theosophical Society, of which she has since been a distinguished member, and its president in 1907. She has made extensive journeys to all parts of the world in the interests of theosophy, but has of late years resided chiefly in India. In 1898 she founded the Central Hindu College, Benares, and is still the president of its council, while in 1904 she established the Central Hindu Girls' School in the same city. In addition to a large number of briefer articles and pamphlets, she has written *Natural Religion Versus Revealed Religion* (London, 1874); *History of the Great French Revolution* (1876); *The Law of Population: Its Consequences and its Bearing upon Human Conduct and Morals* (1877); *The Gospel of Christianity and the Gospel of Free Thought* (1877); *Heat, Light, and Sound* (1881); *Legends and Tales* (1885); *The Sins of the Church* (1886); *Reincarnation* (1892); *Seven Principles of Man* (1892); *Autobiography* (1893); *Death and After* (1893); *Building of the Cosmos* (1894); *In the Outer Court* (1895); *Karma* (1895); *The Self and its Sheaths* (1895); *The Path of Discipleship* (1896); *Man and his Bodies* (1896); *Four Great Religions* (1897); *The Ancient Wisdom* (1897); *Evolution of Life and Form* (1899); *Dharma* (1899); *Story of the Great War: Lessons from the Mahābhārata* (1899); *Avatāras* (1900); *Ancient Ideals in Modern*

Life (1901); *Esoteric Christianity* (1901); *Thought Power: Its Control and Cultivation* (1901); *The Religious Problem in India* (Madras, 1902); *The Pedigree of Man* (Benares, 1903); *Study in Consciousness* (London, 1904); and *Theosophy and New Psychology* (1904). She has also translated a number of free-thought works as well as the *Bhagavadgītā* (London, 1895), and has edited *Our Corner* (London, 1883–88), and, in collaboration with G. R. S. Mead, *The Theosophical Review*.

BESS, BERNHARD: German librarian and historian; b. at Nentershausen (near Cassel) May 19, 1863. He was educated at the universities of Marburg and Göttingen, and, after being privat-docent at the former university for several years, was appointed to his present position of librarian of the University of Halle in 1896. In 1902–1903 he was also entrusted with the organization of the library of the Prussian Historical Institute at Rome. He has written *Frankreichs Kirchenpolitik und der Prozess des Jean Petit* (Marburg, 1891), and *Luther und das landesherrliche Kirchenregiment* (1894). Since 1891 he has been the editor of the *Zeitschrift für Kirchengeschichte*.

BESSARION, bes-sé'ri-on, **JOHANNES or BASILIUS:** Cardinal; b. at Trebizond 1395; d. at Ravenna Nov. 19, 1472. He studied at Constantinople and at Misithra in the Peloponnesus under Gemistos Plethon; entered the Basilian order; became archbishop of Nicæa in 1437. As such he labored at Ferrara and Florence, 1438–39, for the union of the Greek and Roman Churches (see FERRARA-FLORENCE, COUNCIL OF). Having been made a cardinal, he remained in Italy, by voice and pen working for the union. His house at Rome became the center not only for his fugitive countrymen, but also for the cultivation of Greek literature in the West; and during his activity as legate in Bologna, 1451–55, he worked in the same interest at that ancient *gymnasium illustre*. At the papal election in 1455 he lacked only a few votes of being chosen pope, and his influence in the curia may be seen from the numerous diplomatic missions with which he was entrusted. While returning from a missionary tour to France, which he had undertaken for the sake of reconciling Louis XI and the duke of Burgundy, he died at Ravenna.

K. BENRATH.

BIBLIOGRAPHY: On the works of Bessarion consult: Fabricius-Harles, *Bibliotheca Græca*, x, 491, xi, 480, Hamburg, 1807–08; *MPG*, clxi. On his life and activities consult: Pastor, *Popes*, vol. iv, passim (well worth using); Creighton, *Papacy*, vols. ii–v, passim (gives an excellent treatment of the subject); G. Voigt, *Die Wiederbelebung des classischen Alterthums*, Berlin, 1859; J. Burckhardt, *Kultur der Renaissance in Italien*, Basel, 1860, Eng. transl., 2 vols., London, 1878; H. Vast, *Le Cardinal Bessarion*, Paris, 1878; R. Rocholl, *Bessarion*, Leipsic, 1904.

BESSEL, GOTTFRIED: Abbot of Göttweig, near Vienna; b. at Buchhain, near Mainz, Sept. 5, 1672; d. at Göttweig Jan. 20, 1749. He studied at Salzburg, entered the Benedictine order in 1693, was ordained priest 1696, and was employed in various diplomatic negotiations by the elector of Mainz. In 1707 he converted the princess Elizabeth Christine of Brunswick to the Roman Catholic faith, and, in 1710, her grandfather, the duke Anton Ulrich, at which time he published *Quinquaginta Romanocatholicam fidem omnibus aliis præferendi motiva* (Mainz, 1708). In 1714 he became abbot of Göttweig. He prepared a chronicle of the monastery, of which only the first part, *Prodromus*, has been published (2 vols., Tegernsee, 1732).

BESSER, WILHELM FRIEDRICH: German preacher and theological writer; b. at Warnstedt, in the Harz, Sept. 27, 1816; d. near Dresden Sept. 26, 1884. He studied at Halle under Gesenius and Tholuck (1837), then went to Berlin, where he was influenced by Neander and Twesten, but still more by Hengstenberg, Otto von Gerlach, and others. He returned to Halle in 1838 as secretary to Tholuck, but a year later went as private tutor to the house of Major von Schenkendorf at Wulkow near Puppin. This had a decisive influence on his life, through his intercourse there with a persecuted Lutheran pastor, a guest in the house, who had such an effect on him that, at his ordination in 1841 as pastor at Wulkow, he refused to sign the Union formula except with the reservation that the Union related to common ecclesiastical organization without prejudice to the authority of the Augsburg Confession. In 1845 he withdrew his subscription, and after long negotiations was deprived of his office in 1847. Connecting himself with the Lutheran Church of Prussia, he became pastor of Seefeld in Pomerania, and zealously supported the movement to obtain equal rights for the Lutherans with the Union. In 1853 he was called to assist Graul in the direction of the Evangelical Lutheran mission-house; but the strain of continuous teaching was not suited to his vivacious and impulsive nature, and sharp controversies broke out over the then burning question of the Indian castes, so that he returned willingly to pastoral life in 1857, becoming minister of Waldenburg in Silesia and also (1864) a member of the Lutheran superior council of Breslau. Failing health compelled him to resign his offices at Easter, 1884. His *Bibelstunden*, which he began to write in 1843 and continued at intervals till he had covered most of the New Testament, have had a salutary influence far beyond Germany. The list of his minor writings is a long one, and includes a number of controversial tractates against what he thought a hollow and deceiving compromise, popular biographies, devotional works, and sermons. (H. HÖLSCHER.)

BIBLIOGRAPHY: A sketch of Besser's life appears in his *Predigten und Predigtauszüge*, Breslau, 1885. His autobiography (uncompleted) was continued to the year 1850 by Greve, *Aus Bessers Leben*, in *Gotthold*, year 20, 1894–1895, and completion is promised; cf. *ALKG*, 1884, pp. 1036–39.

BESTMANN, best"män', **HUGO JOHANNES:** German Lutheran; b. at Delve, Holstein, Feb. 21, 1854. He studied in Leipsic, Tübingen, Kiel, Berlin, and Erlangen (lic. theol., 1877), and was privat-docent in theology at Erlangen 1877–83. He was then instructor in the gymnasium of the orphan asylum at Halle 1883–84 and at the Missionary Seminary in Leipsic 1884–86. Since the latter year he has been pastor in Mölln

(Lauenburg). He has been a member of the committee of the Mölln conference for theological studies since 1896, and has written *Qua ratione Augustinus notiones philosophiæ græcæ ad dogmata anthropologica describenda adhibuerit* (Erlangen, 1877); *Geschichte der christlichen Sitte* (2 vols., Nördlingen, 1880–85); *Die theologische Wissenschaft und die Ritschl'sche Schule* (1881); *Die Anfänge des katholischen Christentums und des Islams* (1884); *Der Protestantismus und die theologischen Fakultäten* (Kiel, 1891); and *Geschichte des Reichs Gottes im Alten und Neuen Bunde* (2 vols., Leipsic, 1896–1900). He edited also J. C. K. von Hofmann's *Theologische Encyclopädie* (Nördlingen, 1879) and *Der christliche Herold* (Hamburg and Mölln, 1898–1899).

BETH, KARL: German Protestant; b. at Förderstädt (15 m. s. of Magdeburg) Feb. 12, 1872. He studied in Tübingen and Berlin (Ph.D., 1898), and was privat-docent in Berlin 1901–06. Since 1906 he has been professor of systematic and symbolic theology at the University of Vienna. He has written *Die Grundanschauungen Schleiermachers in seinem ersten Entwurf der philosophischen Sittenlehre* (Berlin, 1898); *Die orientalische Kirche der Mittelmeerländer, Reisestudien zur Statistik und Symbolik der griechischen, armenischen und koptischen Kirche* (1902); *Das Wesen des Christentums und die moderne historische Denkweise* (1904); and *Die Wunder Jesu* (1905).

BETHLEHEM: A town in southern Palestine, in the territory of Judah, often called Bethlehem Judah (e.g., Judges xvii, 7, 8; cf. Matt. ii, 1, 5). Its significance for the Judah of Davidic times or earlier is as the home of Jesse (I Sam. xvi, 1), of Joab, Abishai, and Asahel (II Sam. ii, 32), of Elhanan (II Sam. xxi, 19), and as a place of sacrifice (I Sam. xvi, 3, 5). It was occupied by the Philistines in their war with David (II Sam. xxiii, 14).

Old Testament History.

Rehoboam made of it a city of defense (II Chron. xi, 6), as it commanded the roads south and west. Though in early times it was a place of importance because of its situation on caravan routes, it became overshadowed by the growth of the capital. After the exile it was reckoned to the Jewish community (Ezra ii, 21), and was inhabited by Calebites who were driven north by the Edomites pressing up from the south. This possession is explained by the Chronicler on genealogical grounds, regarding the town as founded by Salma, a son of Caleb. The district of Ephratah, which extended from Kirjath-jearim to Bethlehem, became a possession of the Calebites and gave occasion for the name Bethlehem Ephratah, used Micah v, 2. The inhabitants were engaged in agriculture, viticulture, and cattle-raising.

For the Hebrews its fame rests upon its being the home of David (Luke ii, 4, 11); to Christians everywhere its name is familiar as the birthplace of Jesus, according to the accounts in the Gospels of Matthew and Luke. It has retained its name unchanged to the present. *Bait-laḥm* lies five and a half miles south of Jerusalem, a little east of the central watershed, at a level above the sea of about 2,500 feet. The slopes above it have been terraced from early times, and their fertility rewards richly the labor of the inhabitants in producing olives, almonds, figs, and grapes.

Present Condition.

The numerous trees of the terraces give the place a refreshing appearance, especially to the traveler from the bare heights of Jerusalem. There is a spring some fifteen minutes eastward from the town, and water is taken from the aqueduct on the south leading into Jerusalem. For the rest of the water-supply, dependence is had upon cisterns. The population is about 8,000; 3,827 are Roman Catholics, 3,662 Greeks, 260 Mohammedans, 185 Armenians; the rest are Copts, Syrians, and Protestants. Two-thirds are engaged in various handicrafts, the rest in husbandry, and all are oppressed by burdensome taxes. Attempts have been made at various times to connect particular parts of the town with David, naming for him a house, a tower, and a well, but the traditions are insecurely founded. The "Well of David" is the name given since the fifteenth century to three large cisterns in the northeast.

More secure is the tradition about the birthplace of Jesus, covered by the celebrated Church of St. Mary, a basilica mentioned as early as 334 as built by Constantine's order. Eusebius ("Life of Constantine") confirms this report; Socrates and Sozomen ascribe its erection to the empress Helena; and Eutychius to Justinian. De Vogüé supports the first hypothesis on the ground of the unity of plan, conformity of extent of choir and grotto, and absence of architectural marks of the Justinian period.

The Church of St. Mary.

In this opinion he is supported by the architect T. Sandel, who made a new examination in 1880. This may well be the oldest church in the world. It was thoroughly restored by the emperor Manuel Comnenus, who adorned it with mosaics, of which work but little remains, though a description by F. Quaresmio (1616–26) with what is left suffices to give a good idea of the whole. In 1478 (or 1482) the roof was repaired by Philip of Burgundy and Edward IV of England, and renewed in 1672 by the Greek patriarch Dositheos. In the latter year the Greeks obtained possession, which the Latins had had since the crusades. In 1852 Napoleon brought it about that the Latins were given a share in holding it. The church, now in decay, can not be restored for fear of renewing outbreaks among Latins, Greeks, and Armenians.

From the southeast the church rises prominently like a fortress; the north, east, and south sides are less pleasing to one approaching from those directions because of the cells of the monks of the different communions. It has a nave and double aisles, and its floor space is about ninety-eight feet by eighty-seven between the cross aisles. The transept and apse are unfortunately concealed by a wall built by the Greeks in the seventeenth or eighteenth century. The entire length of the present church, including the entrance hall, is about 230 feet. Two flights of steps to the north and south lead from the choir to the chapel of the nativity, the walls of which are marble-lined and hung with tapestries. The place of birth is marked by a silver star in the floor of a niche. Opposite is the place, a marbled hollow, of the old "genuine" manger. A passage westward leads to the tomb and chapel of Jerome.

The Traditional Place of Jesus's Birth.

This subterranean room, according to tradition continuous since Constantine, is accepted as the place of Jesus's birth. A tradition can be traced back to Justin Martyr that Jesus was born in a cave, since Joseph could find no accommodation in the village. But it has been disproved that the present chapel is a [natural] cave, while it must be noted that as early as 728 it was reported that the form of the cave was changed and an oblong room hewn out. The use of caves as adjuncts to inns or "shelters" is in Palestine a peculiarity of the country.

Five minutes southeast from the church of St. Mary is the so-called "Milk Grotto" of the Latins, in which Joseph, Mary, and the child are said to have concealed themselves from Herod's fury before the flight into Egypt. The white of the limestone is attributed to the fall of a drop of milk from Mary's breast. Ten minutes northeast from Beth Sahur (itself fifteen minutes east from Bethlehem) is shown the "Grotto of the Shepherds," in which the angels are said to have announced to the shepherds the birth of the Holy Child. The underground chapel is reached by a passage between two ancient olive-trees.

One of the fruits of modern missions is the honoring of Jesus in his birthplace, not by sanctuaries in stone, but by provision for the education of the young. Since 1860 there have been a number of Protestant and Roman Catholic schools and establishments, the founding of which has spurred the Greeks and Armenians to accomplish something for the instruction of children belonging to their communities. (H. GUTHE.)

BIBLIOGRAPHY: Robinson, *Researches*, vol. ii; T. Tobler, *Bethlehem in Palästina*, Bern, 1849; V. Guérin, *Description de la Palestine, Judée*, i, 120 sqq., Paris, 1869; *Survey of Western Palestine, Memoirs*, vol. iii, sheet xvii, London, 1883; P. Palmer, *Das jetzige Bethlehem*, in *ZDPV*, xvii (1894), 89 sqq.; Baedeker, *Palestine and Syria*, pp. 119–127, New York, 1898; *DB*, i, 281; *EB*, i, 560–562. On the church consult M. de Vogüé, *Les Églises de la terre sainte*, Paris, 1860; Quaresmius, *Elucidatio terræ sanctæ*, ii, 643 sqq., Antwerp, 1639, reissued Venice, 1880–82; G. Ebers and H. Guthe, *Palästina in Bild und Wort*, 2 vols., Leipsic, 1883–84.

BETHLEHEMITES: The name of three religious orders. (1) An association of *Bethleemitæ*, known only from Matthew Paris (*Hist. maj.*, 839), who states that they existed at Cambridge, England, about 1257 and wore the Dominican habit, with a red star, referring to Matt. ii, 9–10. (2) The Knights and Hospitalers of the Blessed Mary of Bethlehem (*Religio militaris ac hospitalis beatæ Mariæ Bethlemitanæ*), founded by Pius II in 1459 to fight against the Turks. They wore a white habit with a red cross, were given the island of Lemnos as their seat, and did not survive the capture of the island by the Turks in the year of their foundation. (3) More important are the Bethlehem Brothers (*Fratres Bethlemitæ*; Spanish, *Orden de Belemitas*) of Guatemala (Central America), founded there about 1650 by Pierre de Bethencourt and after his death (1667) under the leadership of the brothers Rodrigo and Antonio de la Cruz. Originally entrusted only with the care of the hospital of Mary of Bethlehem in Guatemala, the order was confirmed by Innocent XI in 1687 and given a constitution and dress like that of the Capuchins. Clement XI in 1707 granted them the privileges of the mendicant orders. A society of Sisters of Bethlehem was founded in Guatemala by Anna Maria del Galdo in 1668, and both the male and female branches spread in Mexico, Peru, and elsewhere. A secularization-decree of the Spanish Cortes in 1820 suppressed both branches.

O. ZÖCKLER†.

BIBLIOGRAPHY: Heimbucher, *Orden und Kongregationen*, i, 497–498; G. Voigt, *Enea Silvio . als Papst Pius*, ii, 652, Berlin, 1863; Karl vom heiligen Aloys, *Die katholische Kirche in ihrer gegenwärtigen Ausbreitung*, pp. 510–511, Regensburg, 1855; Helyot, *Ordres monastiques*, iii, 347–357, viii, 365 sqq.; *KL*, ii, 540–544 (contains list of literature in Spanish).

BETHPHANY: A name sometimes given to the festival more commonly known as the Epiphany. It is a barbarous invention of the schoolmen, from the Hebrew *bēth*, "house," and the Greek *-phaneia*, "manifestation," which forms the latter part of the word Epiphany; and was intended to emphasize the miracle (in the house) at Cana in Galilee, which is the third event commemorated by the festival of the Epiphany (q.v.).

BETHSAIDA. See GAULANITIS.

BETHUNE, be-thūn′, **GEORGE WASHINGTON:** Reformed (Dutch) clergyman; b. in Greenwich, now a part of New York City, Mar. 18, 1805; d. at Florence, Italy, Apr. 27, 1862. He was graduated at Dickinson College, Carlisle, Pa., 1823; studied at Princeton Seminary 1823–25; served for a year as missionary among the negroes and sailors at Savannah, Ga.; was ordained Nov., 1827, and was pastor of Reformed (Dutch) churches at Rhinebeck (1827–30) and Utica (1830–34), N. Y., Philadelphia (First Church, 1834–37; Third Church, 1837–49), and Brooklyn (1851–59); was associate minister at the Twenty-first Street Church, New York, 1859–61. He was famed as a preacher and orator, as a poet, and as a wit. Of his numerous publications, perhaps that of most permanent value was his edition of Walton's *Complete Angler* (New York, 1847; new ed., 2 vols., 1880).

BIBLIOGRAPHY: A. R. Van Nest, *Memoirs of Rev. George W. Bethune*, 2 vols., New York, 1880.

BETHUNE-BAKER, JAMES FRANKLIN: Church of England; b. at Birmingham Aug. 23, 1861. He was educated at Pembroke College, Cambridge (B.A., 1884), and was head master's assistant at King Edward's School, Birmingham, and assistant curate of St. George's, Edgbaston, from 1888 to 1890. In the following year he was elected fellow and dean of Pembroke College, and since 1905 has also been examining chaplain to the bishop of Rochester. He has been the editor of the *Journal of Theological Studies* since 1903, and has written *The Influence of Christianity on War* (Cambridge, 1888); *The Sternness of Christ's Teaching* (1889); *The Meaning* *of Homoousios in the Constantinopolitan Creed* (1901); *An Introduction to the Early History of Christian Doctrine* (London, 1903); and *Christian Doctrines and their Ethical Significance* (1905).

BETKIUS, bêt'kî-ūs (**BETKE**), **JOACHIM**: Lutheran preacher and forerunner of the Pietistic movement; b. at Berlin Oct. 8, 1601; d. at Linum, near Fehrbellin (33 m. n.w. of Berlin), Dec. 12, 1663. After finishing his course at Wittenberg, he became associate rector at Ruppin, then was for more than thirty years pastor at Linum. He wrote several theological and devotional works, by the reading of which Spener said he had profited. They contain edifying exhortations against forgetting the need of sanctification in addition to justification, but are marred by intemperate fanaticism; Betkius holds the clergy responsible for all the anti-Christian phenomena of his time, and for the divine judgments of the Thirty Years' war.

(F. W DIBELIUS.)

BETRAYAL OF PILATE. See APOCRYPHA, NEW TESTAMENT, B, I, 7.

BEURLIN, boi''er-lîn, **JAKOB**: German Lutheran theologian; b. at Dornstetten (35 m. s.w. of Stuttgart) 1520; d. at Paris Oct. 28, 1561. In Nov., 1533, he entered the university of Tübingen. When the Reformation was introduced in 1534, he remained faithful to Catholicism, but diligently studied philosophy and the writings of the Church Fathers, so that his transition to the new doctrine took place quietly. In 1541 he was made governor of the Martinianum, and at the same time lectured on philosophy. In 1549 he accepted the pastorate of Derendingen near Tübingen, and in 1551 he was called as professor to Tübingen. On June 2, 1557, he examined and signed, together with other theologians, the *Confessio Wirtembergica*, which had been prepared for the Council of Trent, and in the month of August, together with Brenz's friend Johann Isenmann (q.v.), he went to Langensalza and afterward to Saxony to come to an understanding with the theologians and councilors of the elector Maurice concerning the Württemberg Confession as compared with the Saxon, which had also been prepared for the Council of Trent. In Nov., 1551, in company with Luther's former steward, Jodocus Neuheller, pastor at Entringen, he was sent as theological adviser of the Württemberg delegates to Trent, where they took notes of the disputations. On Jan. 13, 1552, both returned home, but on Mar. 7, Beurlin, Brenz, Heerbrand, and Vannius again started for Trent to oppose the erroneous decisions of the council, and to defend the *Confessio Wirtembergica* before it; but the council would not hear them in a public session, and they returned home. Beurlin now devoted all his time to his academic duties. He lectured on Melanchthon's *Loci*, the Gospel and First Epistle of John, and the Epistles to the Romans and Hebrews, and drilled the young theologians in admirably conducted disputations. In May, 1554, the duke sent him to Prussia to pacify those who had been stirred up by Osiander's teaching. He was unsuccessful, however, and, disgusted with the behavior of the factions, he declined the bishopric offered to him by Duke Albert, and returned home. In the interest of his academic office he now retired in favor of Jakob Andreä, who was a more willing interpreter of the theology and ecclesiastical policy of Brenz (q.v.). In Oct., 1557, Beurlin and his father-in-law, Matthæus Alber, went to the religious conference at Worms in place of the Thuringian theologians. At the Stuttgart synod Beurlin also remained in the background, but he assisted Brenz in the defense of the *Confessio Wirtembergica* against Peter a Soto, and his attack upon the central point of the Roman system is still worthy of consideration. Vice-chancellor of the university after 1557, Beurlin was the leader of the Swabians at the Erfurt Conference, Apr., 1561, and was still more prominent on his last journey made in the service of the Evangelical Church. King Antony of Navarre sought both at Stuttgart and Heidelberg for a theologian to advise him in the controversy which arose in Sept., 1557, at the religious conference in Poissy between the cardinal of Guise and Beza concerning the relation of the French Protestants to the Augsburg Confession. Duke Christopher sent three theologians, Jakob Beurlin, Jakob Andreä, and Balthazar Bidembach. Before leaving, Beurlin was made chancellor of the university and provost of the Collegiate Church (Sept. 29). The theologians left Oct. 3, and arrived at Paris Oct. 19. Meanwhile the conference at Poissy had been broken off, and the theologians had to wait till the king called them. On Oct. 24 Beurlin fell ill with the plague and died in Paris.

G. BOSSERT.

BIBLIOGRAPHY: The sources are: T. Schnepffius, *J. Beurlinus redivivus et immortalis*, Tübingen, 1613; J. V. Andreä, *Fama Andreana*, Strasburg, 1530. Consult G. C. F. Fischlin, *Memoria theologorum Villebergensium resuscitata*, i, 82–87, Ulm, 1710; C. F. Sattler, *Geschichte von Württemberg unter der Regierung der Herzoge*, Ulm, 1771; H. F. Eisenbach, *Beschreibung und Geschichte der Stadt und Universität Tübingen*, pp. 108–112, Tübingen, 1822; H. L. J. Heppe, *Geschichte des deutschen Protestantismus*, vol. i, Marburg, 1852–59; C. von Weizsäcker, *Lehrer und Unterricht an der evangelisch-theologischen Fakultät . Tübingen*, Tübingen, 1877; C. A. Hase, *Herzog Albrecht von Preussen und sein Hofprediger*, Leipsic, 1879; G. Bossert, *Die Reise der württembergischen Theologen nach Paris 1561*, in *Württembergische Vierteljahrshefte*, 1899, pp. 387–412.

BEVAN, bev'an, **ANTHONY ASHLEY**: Church of England layman; b. at Trent Park, Barnet (11 m. n.n.w. of London), Herts, May 19, 1859. He was educated at the Gymnase littéraire, Lausanne (1877–79) and the University of Strasburg (1881–1883), and in 1884 became a member of Trinity College, Cambridge, where he was elected fellow in 1890. Since 1893 he has been Lord Almoner's reader in Arabic in the University of Cambridge. In addition to minor studies, he has written *A Short Commentary on the Book of Daniel* (Cambridge, 1892) and the *Hymn of the Soul Contained in the Syriac Acts of St. Thomas, Reedited with an English Translation*, in *Cambridge Texts and Studies*, v (1897).

BEVAN, LLEWELYN DAVID: Congregationalist; b. at Llanelly (15 m. s.e. of Carmarthen), Carmarthenshire, Wales, Sept. 11, 1842. He studied at New College, London (B.A., University of London, 1861; LL.B., 1866), and after being assistant minister to Thomas Binney (q.v.) at the King's Weigh-House Chapel, London (1865–69), held pastorates at Tottenham-Court Road Chapel, London (1869–76), the Brick Presbyterian Church, New York City (1876–82), and Highbury Quadrant Church, London (1882–86). Since 1886 he has been pastor of the Collins Street Congregational Church, Melbourne, Victoria. While in England, he was associated with F. D. Maurice (q.v.) in the Workingmen's College, London, and was for several years a professor in New College.

BEVERIDGE, WILLIAM: Bishop of St. Asaph; b. at Barrow (8 m. n. of Leicester), and baptized there Feb. 21, 1637; d. in London Mar. 5, 1708. He was educated at Cambridge; was rector of Ealing, a west suburb of London, 1661–72; of St. Peter's, Cornhill, London, 1672–1704, when he became bishop. In his day he was styled "the great reviver and restorer of primitive piety" because in his much admired sermons and other writings he dwelt so affectionately upon the Church of the early centuries. His collected works (incomplete) are in the *Library of Anglo-Catholic Theology* in 12 vols. (Oxford, 1842–48) and embrace six volumes of sermons; *The Doctrine of the Church of England Consonant to Scripture, Reason, and the Fathers: A Complete System of Divinity* (2 vols.); *Codex canonum ecclesiæ primitivæ vindicatus ac illustratus*, with the appendices, I. *Prolegomena in Συνοδικὸν, sive pandectas canonum*; and II. *Præfatio ad annotationes in canones apostolicos* (2 vols.); and the still read *Private Thoughts on Religion*, and *Church Catechism Explained.* His *Institutionum chronologicarum libri duo, una cum totidem arithmetices chronologicæ libellis* (London, 1669) was once an admired treatise on chronology.

BIBLIOGRAPHY: T. H. Horne, *Memoir of the Life and Writings of W. Beveridge*, London, 1824, also prefixed to his works in the *Library of Anglo-Catholic Theology*, ut sup.; *DNB*, iv, 447–448.

BEYER, bai'er, **HARTMANN:** Reformation preacher of Frankfort, where he was born Sept. 30, 1516, and died Aug. 11, 1577. In 1534 he went to Wittenberg as student of philosophy and theology, and received the master's degree there in 1539 and became private teacher of mathematics. He returned to his native city as preacher in 1546. The Reformation, introduced in Frankfort in 1522 by Hartmann Ibach, had been carried on in the earlier years by compulsion and rash zeal on the part of its adherents, and in later time was marked by doctrinal controversies between the Lutheran and Reformed tendencies. Beyer came with the determination to win the victory for Lutheranism, and to his activity was it due that by 1554 a compact Lutheran congregation stood opposed to all insinuations of Calvinism, while the earlier democratic and radical tendencies had been suppressed. In the year named, three congregations of Protestants from the Netherlands, who had first taken refuge in England but fled that country after the accession of Mary, came to Frankfort under the lead of Velerandus Polanus and Johannes a Lasco (qq.v.), bringing with them a Reformed creed and Reformed practises. Beyer was the soul of an opposition which induced the city council to deprive them of the church they had used for worship in 1561. In 1596 even the right of holding services privately was forbidden.

The success of the emperor in the Schmalkald war and the promulgation of the Augsburg Interim (May, 1548) brought the Frankfort Reformers face to face with dangers which for the time quieted doctrinal disputes. The council accepted the interim cautiously, but its attempts to forbid preaching against the new law and against Roman teachings and practises, to reestablish church festivals, to prohibit the eating of meat on fast-days, and like measures met with determined and courageous resistance from Beyer and his colleagues. The former repeatedly expressed his conviction that church ordinances could be established only with the consent of the congregation. The struggle went on till 1577, but the preachers gained the victory.

Beyer issued two pseudonymous writings against the Roman Catholics in 1551 and while in Wittenberg prepared a treatise on mathematics. His sermons are preserved in forty-nine volumes in manuscript in Frankfort. They are marked by a beauty and force of language which make them powerful even to-day. (G. E. Steitz†.)

BIBLIOGRAPHY: G. E. Steitz, *Der lutherische Prädikant, Hartmann Beyer*, Frankfort, 1852.

BEYSCHLAG, bai'shlōH, **WILLIBALD:** German Protestant; b. at Frankfort Sept. 5, 1823; d. at Halle Nov. 26, 1900. He studied at Bonn and Berlin 1840–44; became vicar at Coblenz 1849; assistant pastor and religious teacher at Treves 1850; court preacher at Carlsruhe 1856; ordinary professor of theology at Halle 1860; and after 1876 editor of the *Deutsche Evangelische Blätter*, an organ of the so-called *Mittelpartei*, whose leader he was till the end of his life. To oppose the ultramontane aggressions in Germany, he founded in 1886 the *Evangelischer Bund* (see Bund, Evangelischer). Of his very numerous writings, besides sermons, the following are worthy of mention: *Die Christologie des Neuen Testaments* (Berlin, 1866); *Die paulinische Theodicee Röm. ix–xi* (Berlin, 1868, 2d ed., 1895); *Die christliche Gemeindeverfassung im Zeitalter des Neuen Testaments* (Haarlem, 1874); *Zur Johanneischen Frage* (Gotha, 1876); the biographies of his brother, F. W. T. Beyschlag (*Aus dem Leben eines Frühvollendeten*, 2 parts, Berlin, 1858–59, 6th ed., 1889), of Carl Ullmann (Gotha, 1867), of Carl Immanuel Nitzsch (Halle, 1872, 2d ed., 1882), and of Albrecht Wolters (1880); *Zur deutschchristlichen Bildung* (1880, 2d ed., 1899); *Das Leben Jesu* (2 vols., Halle, 1885–86, 4th ed., 1902); *Der Friedensschluss zwischen Deutschland und Rom* (Halle, 1887); *Reden in der Erfurter Vor-Conferenz des evangelischen Bundes* (1888); *Godofred, ein Märchen fürs deutsche Haus* (1888); *Luther's Hausstand in seiner reformatorischen Bedeutung* (Barmen, 1888); *Die Reformation in Italien* (1888); *Die römisch-katholischen Ansprüche an die preussische Volksschule* (1889); *Zur Verstän-*

digung über den christlichen Vorsehungsglauben (Halle, 1889); *Erkenntnisspfade zu Christo* (1889); *Die evangelische Kirche als Bundesgenossin wider die Socialdemokratie* (Berlin, 1890); *Neutestamentliche Theologie* (2 vols., 1891–92, 2d ed., 1896; Eng. transl., *New Testament Theology*, 2 vols., Edinburgh, 1895, 2d ed., 1896); *Christenlehre* (Halle, 3d ed., 1903).

BIBLIOGRAPHY: Consult his autobiography, *Aus meinem Leben*, 2 vols., Halle, 1896–98; K. H. Pahncke, *Willibald Beyschlag, ein Gedenkblatt*, Tübingen, 1905.

BEZA, bî'za, THEODORE.

Early Life (§ 1).
Teacher at Lausanne (§ 2).
Journeys in behalf of the Protestants (§ 3).
Settles in Geneva (§ 4).
Events of 1560–63 (§ 5).
Calvin's Successor (§ 6).
Course of Events after 1564 (§ 7).
The Colloquy of Mümpelgart (§ 8).
Last Days (§ 9).
Humanistic and Historical Writings (§ 10).
Theological Works (§ 11).
Beza's Greek New Testament (§ 12).

Theodore Beza (Théodore de Bèze or de Besze), Genevan Reformer, was born at Vézelay (8 m. w.s.w. of Avallon), in Burgundy, June 24, 1519; d. at Geneva Oct. 13, 1605. His father, Pierre de Bèze, royal governor of Vézelay, descended from a Burgundian family of distinction; his mother, Marie Bourdelot, was known for her generosity. Theodore's father had two brothers; one, Nicholas, was member of Parliament at Paris; the other, Claude, was abbot of the Cistercian monastery Froimont in the diocese of Beauvais. Nicholas, who was

1. Early Life.

unmarried, on a visit to Vézelay was so pleased with Theodore that, with the permission of the parents, he took him to Paris to educate him there. From Paris Theodore was sent to Orléans (Dec., 1528) to enjoy the instruction of the famous German teacher Melchior Wolmar. He was received into Wolmar's house, and the day on which this took place was afterward celebrated as a second birthday. Young Beza soon followed his teacher to Bourges, whither the latter was called by the duchess Margaret of Angoulême, sister of Francis I. Bourges was one of the places in France in which the heart of the Reformation beat the strongest. When, in 1534, Francis I issued his ediet against ecclesiastical innovations, Wolmar returned to Germany, and, in accordance with the wish of his father, Beza went back to Orléans to study law, and spent four years there (1535–39). This pursuit had little attraction for him; he enjoyed more the reading of the ancient classics, especially Ovid, Catullus, and Tibullus. He received the degree of licentiate in law Aug. 11, 1539, and, as his father desired, went to Paris, where he began practise. His relatives had obtained for him two benefices, the proceeds of which amounted to 700 golden crowns a year; and his uncle had promised to make him his successor.

Beza spent two happy years at Paris and soon gained a prominent position in literary circles. To escape the many temptations to which he was exposed, with the knowledge of two friends, he became engaged in the year 1544 to a young girl of humble descent, Claudine Denosse, promising to make this engagement public as soon as his circumstances would allow it. He published a collection of Latin poems, *Juvenilia*, which made him famous, and he was everywhere considered one of the best Latin poets of his time. But he fell ill and his distress of body revealed to him his spiritual needs Gradually he came to the knowledge of salvation in Christ, which he apprehended with a joyous faith He then resolved to sever his connections of the time, and went to Geneva, the French city of refuge for the Evangelicals, where he arrived with Claudine Oct. 23, 1548.

He was heartily received by Calvin, who had met him already in Wolmar's house, and was at once publicly and solemnly married in the church. Beza was at a loss for immediate occupation, so he went to Tübingen to see his former teacher Wolmar. On his way home he visited Viret at Lausanne, who at once detained

2. Teacher at Lausanne.

him and brought about his appointment as professor of Greek at the academy there (Nov., 1549). In spite of the arduous work which fell to his lot, Beza found time to write a Biblical drama, *Abraham Sacrifiant* (published at Geneva, 1550; Eng. transl. by Arthur Golding, London, 1577, ed., with introduction, notes, and the French text of the original, M. W. Wallace, Toronto, 1906), in which he contrasted Catholicism with Protestantism, and the work was well received. In June, 1551, he added a few psalms to the French version of the Psalms begun by Marot, which was also very successful. About the same time he published his *Passavantius*, a satire directed against Pierre Lizet of ill repute, formerly president of the Parliament of Paris, and principal originator of the "fiery chamber" (*chambre ardente*), who, being at the time (1551) abbot of St. Victor near Paris, was eager to acquire the fame of a subduer of heresy by publishing a number of polemical writings. Of a more serious character were two controversies in which Beza was involved at this time. The first concerned the doctrine of predestination and the controversy of Calvin with Bolsec (see CALVIN, JOHN; BOLSEC, JÉRÔME HERMÈS). The second referred to the burning of Michael Servetus (q.v.) at Geneva Oct. 27, 1553. In defense of Calvin and the Genevan magistrates, Beza published in 1554 the work *De hæreticis a civili magistratu puniendis* (translated into French in 1560).

In 1557 Beza took a special interest in the Waldensians of Piedmont, who were harassed by the French government, and in their behalf went with Farel to Bern, Zurich, Basel, Schaffhausen, thence to Strasburg, Mümpelgart, Baden, and Göppingen. In Baden and Göppingen, Beza and Farel had to declare themselves concerning their own

3. Journeys in behalf of the Protestants.

and the Waldensians' views on the sacrament, and on May 14, 1557, they presented a written declaration in which they clearly stated their position. This declaration was well received by the Lutheran theologians, but was strongly disapproved in Bern and Zurich. In the autumn of 1557 Beza undertook a second journey with Farel to Worms by way of Strasburg to bring about an intercession of the Evangelical princes of the empire in favor of the persecuted brethren at Paris. With Melanchthon and other theologians then assembled at Worms, Beza considered a union of all Protestant Christians, but this proposal was decidedly negatived by Zurich and Bern. False reports having reached the German princes that the hostilities against the Huguenots in France had ceased, no embassy was sent to the court of France, and Beza undertook another journey in the interest of the Huguenots, going with Farel, Johannes Buddæus, and Gaspard Carmel to Strasburg and Frankfort, where the sending of an embassy to Paris was resolved upon.

Upon his return to Lausanne, Beza was greatly disturbed. In union with many ministers and professors in city and country, Viret at last thought of establishing a consistory and of introducing a church discipline which should inflict excommunication especially at the celebration of the communion. But the Bernese would have no Calvinistic church government. This caused many difficulties, and Beza thought it best (1558) to settle at Geneva. Here he occupied at first the chair of Greek in the newly established academy, and after Calvin's death also that of theology; besides this he was obliged to preach. He completed the revision of Olivetan's translation of the New Testament, begun some years before. In 1559 he undertook another journey in the interest of the Huguenots, this time to Heidelberg; about the same time he had to defend Calvin against Joachim Westphal in Hamburg and Tileman Hesshusen (qq.v.). More important than this polemical activity was Beza's statement of his own confession. It was originally prepared for his father in justification of his course and published in revised form to promote Evangelical knowledge among Beza's countrymen. It was printed in Latin in 1560 with a dedication to Wolmar. An English translation was published at London 1563, 1572, and 1585. Translations into German, Dutch, and Italian were also issued.

4. Settles in Geneva.

In the mean time things took such shape in France that the happiest future for Protestantism seemed possible. King Antony of Navarre, yielding to the urgent requests of Evangelical noblemen, declared his willingness to listen to a prominent teacher of the Church. Beza, a French nobleman and head of the academy in the metropolis of French Protestantism, was invited to Castle Nérac, but he could not plant the seed of Evangelical faith in the heart of the king. In the year following (1561) Beza represented the Evangelicals at the Colloquy of Poissy (q.v.), and in an eloquent manner defended the principles of the Evangelical faith. The colloquy was without result, but Beza as the head and advocate of all Reformed congregations of France was revered and hated at the same time. The queen insisted upon another colloquy, which was opened at St. Germain Jan. 28, 1562, eleven days after the proclamation of the famous January edict which granted important privileges to those of the Reformed faith. But the colloquy was broken off when it became evident that the Catholic party was preparing (after the massacre of Vassy, Mar. 1) to overthrow Protestantism. Beza hastily issued a circular letter (Mar. 25) to all Reformed congregations of the empire, and with Condé and his troops went to Orléans. It was necessary to proceed quickly and energetically. But there were neither soldiers nor money. At the request of Condé, Beza visited all Huguenot cities to obtain both. He also wrote a manifesto in which he showed the justice of the Reformed cause. As one of the messengers to collect soldiers and money among his coreligionists, Beza was appointed to visit England, Germany, and Switzerland. He went to Strasburg and Basel, but met with failure. He then returned to Geneva, which he reached Sept. 4. He had hardly been there fourteen days when he was called once more to Orléans by D'Andelot. The campaign was becoming more successful; but the publication of the unfortunate edict of pacification which Condé accepted (Mar. 12, 1563) filled Beza and all Protestant France with horror.

5. Events of 1560–63.

For twenty-two months Beza had been absent from Geneva, and the interests of school and Church there and especially the condition of Calvin made it necessary for him to return. For there was no one to take the place of Calvin, who was sick and unable longer to bear the burden resting on him. Calvin and Beza arranged to perform their duties jointly in alternate weeks, but the death of Calvin occurred soon afterward (May 27, 1564). As a matter of course Beza was his successor. Until 1580 Beza was not only *modérateur de la compagnie des pasteurs*, but also the real soul of the great institution of learning at Geneva which Calvin had founded in 1559, consisting of a gymnasium and an academy. As long as he lived, Beza was interested in higher education. The Protestant youth for nearly forty years thronged his lecture-room to hear his theological lectures, in which he expounded the purest Calvinistic orthodoxy. As a counselor he was listened to by both magistrates and pastors. Geneva is indebted to him for the founding of a law school in which François Hotman, Jules Pacius, and Denys Godefroy, the most eminent jurists of the century, lectured in turn (cf. Charles Borgeaud, *L'Académie de Calvin*, Geneva, 1900).

6. Calvin's Successor.

As Calvin's successor, Beza was very successful, not only in carrying on his work but also in giving peace to the Church at Geneva. The magistrates had fully appropriated the ideas of Calvin, and the direction of spiritual affairs, the organs of which were the "ministers of the word" and "the consistory," was founded on a solid basis. No doctrinal controversy arose after 1564. The discussions concerned questions of a practical, social, or ecclesiastical nature, such as the supremacy of the magistrates over the pastors, freedom in preaching, and the obligation of the pastors to submit to the majority of the *compagnie des pasteurs*. Beza obtruded his will in no way upon his associates, and took no harsh measures against injudicious or hot-headed colleagues, though sometimes he took their cases in hand and acted as mediator; and yet he

7. Course of Events after 1564.

often experienced an opposition so extreme that he threatened to resign. Although he was inclined to take the part of the magistrates, he knew how to defend the rights and independence of the spiritual power when occasion arose, without, however, conceding to it such a preponderating influence as did Calvin. His activity was great. He mediated between the *compagnie* and the magistracy; the latter continually asked his advice even in political questions. He corresponded with all the leaders of the Reformed party in Europe. After the massacre of St. Bartholomew (1572), he used his influence to give to the refugees a hospitable reception at Geneva. About this time he wrote his *De jure magistratuum*, in which he emphatically protested against tyranny in religious matters, and affirmed that it is legitimate for a people to oppose an unworthy magistracy in a practical manner and if necessary to use weapons and depose them. To sum up: Without being a great dogmatician like his master, nor a creative genius in the ecclesiastical realm, Beza had qualities which made him famous as humanist, exegete, orator, and leader in religious and political affairs, and qualified him to be the guide of the Calvinists in all Europe. In the various controversies into which he was drawn, Beza often showed an excess of irritation and intolerance, from which Bernardino Ochino, pastor of the Italian congregation at Zurich (on account of a treatise which contained some objectionable points on polygamy), and Sebastian Castellio at Basel (on account of his Latin and French translations of the Bible) had especially to suffer. With Reformed France Beza continued to maintain the closest relations. He was the moderator of the general synod which met in April, 1571, at La Rochelle and decided not to abolish church discipline or to acknowledge the civil government as head of the Church, as the Paris minister Jean Morel and the philosopher Pierre Ramus demanded; it also decided to confirm anew the Calvinistic doctrine of the Lord's Supper (by the expression: "substance of the body of Christ") against Zwinglianism, which caused a very unpleasant discussion between Beza and Ramus and Bullinger. In the following year (May, 1572) he took an important part in the national synod at Nîmes. He was also interested in the controversies which concerned the Augsburg Confession in Germany, especially after 1564, on the doctrine of the person of Christ and the sacrament, and published several works against Westphal, Hesshusen, Selnecker, Johann Brenz, and Jakob Andreä. This made him, especially after 1571, hated by all those who adhered to Lutheranism in opposition to Melanchthon.

The last polemical conflict of importance Beza encountered from the exclusive Lutherans was at the Colloquy of Mümpelgart (q.v.), Mar. 14–27, 1586, to which he had been invited by the Lutheran Count Frederick of Württemberg at the wish of the French noblemen who had fled to Mümpelgart. As a matter of course the intended union which was the purpose of the colloquy was not brought about; nevertheless it called forth serious developments within the Reformed Church. When the edition of the acts of the colloquy, as prepared by J. Andreä, was published, Samuel Huber, of Burg near Bern, who belonged to the Lutheranizing faction of the Swiss clergy, took so great offense at the supralapsarian doctrine of predestination propounded at Mümpelgart by Beza and Musculus that he felt it to be his duty to denounce Musculus to the magistrates of Bern as an innovator in doctrine. To adjust the matter, the magistrates arranged a colloquy between Huber and Musculus (Sept. 2, 1587), in which the former represented the universalism, the latter the particularism, of grace. As the colloquy was resultless, a debate was arranged at Bern, Apr. 15–18, 1588, at which the defense of the accepted system of doctrine was at the start put into Beza's hands. The three delegates of the Helvetic cantons who presided at the debate declared in the end that Beza had substantiated the teaching propounded at Mümpelgart as the orthodox one, and Huber was dismissed from his office.

8. The Colloquy of Mümpelgart.

After that time Beza's activity was confined more and more to the affairs of his home. His faithful wife Claudine had died childless in 1588, a few days before he went to the Bern Disputation. Forty years they had lived happily together. He contracted, on the advice of his friends, a second marriage with Catharina del Piano, a Genoese widow, in order to have a helpmate in his declining years. Up to his sixty-fifth year he enjoyed excellent health, but after that a gradual sinking of his vitality became perceptible. He was active in teaching till Jan., 1597. The saddest experience in his old days was the conversion of King Henry IV to Roman Catholicism, in spite of his most earnest exhortations (1593). Strange to say, in 1596 the report was spread by the Jesuits in Germany, France, England, and Italy that Beza and the Church of Geneva had returned into the bosom of Rome, and Beza replied in a satire that revealed the possession still of his old fire of thought and vigor of expression. He was not buried, like Calvin, in the general cemetery, Plain-Palais (for the Savoyards had threatened to abduct his body to Rome), but at the direction of the magistrates, in the monastery of St. Pierre.

9. Last Days.

In Beza's literary activity as well as in his life, distinction must be made between the period of the humanist (which ended with the publication of his *Juvenilia*) and that of the ecclesiastic. But later productions like the humanistic, biting, satirical *Passavantius* and his *Complainte de Messire Pierre Lizet* prove that in later years he occasionally went back to his first love. In his old age he published his *Cato censorius* (1591), and revised his *Poemata*, from which he purged juvenile eccentricities. Of his historiographical works, aside from his *Icones* (1580), which have only an iconographical value, mention may be made of the famous *Histoire ecclésiastique des Églises réformées au Royaume de France* (1580), and his biography of Calvin, with which must be

10. Humanistic and Historical Writings.

named his edition of Calvin's *Epistolæ et responsa* (1575).

11. Theological Works.

But all these humanistic and historical studies are surpassed by his theological productions (contained in *Tractationes theologicæ*). In these Beza appears the perfect pupil or the *alter ego* of Calvin. His view of life is deterministic and the basis of his religious thinking is the predestinate recognition of the necessity of all temporal existence as an effect of the absolute, eternal, and immutable will of God, so that even the fall of the human race appears to him essential to the divine plan of the world. In most lucid manner Beza shows in tabular form the connection of the religious views which emanated from this fundamental supralapsarian mode of thought. This he added to his highly instructive treatise *Summa totius Christianismi*.

12. Beza's Greek New Testament.

Of no less importance are the contributions of Beza to Biblical science. In 1565 he issued an edition of the Greek New Testament, accompanied in parallel columns by the text of the Vulgate and a translation of his own (already published as early as 1556). Annotations were added, also previously published, but now he greatly enriched and enlarged them. In the preparation of this edition of the Greek text, but much more in the preparation of the second edition which he brought out in 1582, Beza may have availed himself of the help of two very valuable manuscripts. One is known as the *Codex Bezæ* or *Cantabrigensis*, and was later presented by Beza to the University of Cambridge; the second is the *Codex Claromontanus*, which Beza had found in Clermont (now in the National Library at Paris). It was not, however, to these sources that Beza was chiefly indebted, but rather to the previous edition of the eminent Robert Stephens (1550), itself based in great measure upon one of the later editions of Erasmus. Beza's labors in this direction were exceedingly helpful to those who came after. The same thing may be asserted with equal truth of his Latin version and of the copious notes with which it was accompanied. The former is said to have been published over a hundred times. It is to be regretted that the author's view of the doctrine of predestination exercised upon the interpretation of Scripture too preponderating an influence. However, there is no question that Beza added much to a clear understanding of the New Testament.

EUGÈNE CHOISY.

BIBLIOGRAPHY: J. W. Baum, *T. Beza nach handschriftlichen und anderen gleichzeitigen Quellen*, Leipsic, 1843-52 (masterly, but extends only to 1563); his life by Heppe is in vol. vi of *Leben und ausgewählte Schriften der Väter der reformierten Kirche*, Elberfeld, 1861 (complete and excellent, inferior only to Baum); A. de la Faye, *De vita et obitu T. Bezæ*, Geneva, 1606 (by a favorite pupil of Beza); Jérôme Bolsec, *Histoire de la vie, mœurs, doctrine et débordements de T. de Bèze*, Paris, 1582, republished Geneva, 1835 (Roman Catholic, a scurrilous and malignant libel); F. C. Schlosser, *Leben des Theodor Beza und des Peter Martyr Vermigli*, Heidelberg, 1809; E. and É. Haag, *La France protestante*, 2d ed. by Bordier, ii, 520–540, Paris, 1879; H. M. McCracken, *Lives of the Leaders of Our Church Universal*, from the Germ. of F. Piper, pp. 352–362, Philadelphia, 1879; Schaff, *Christian Church*, vol. vii, passim, especially chap. xix; Moeller, *Christian Church*, vol. iii, passim; C. v. Procadij, *T. Beza medearbeiter en opvolger van Calvijn*, Leyden, 1895; H. M. Baird, *Theodore Beza, the Counsellor of the French Reformation*, New York, 1899 (the one book in English, and a worthy treatment of the subject), cf. his *Rise of the Huguenots*, passim, ib. 1879; A. Bernus, *T. de Bèze à Lausanne*, Lausanne, 1900; E. Choisy, *L'État chrétien calviniste à Genève au temps de T. de Bèze*, Geneva, 1902; *Cambridge Modern History*, vol. ii, *The Reformation*, passim, vol. iii, London, 1904; *À Théodore de Bèze (1605–1905)*, Geneva, 1906.

BEZOLD, bê''zōld', CARL ERNST CHRISTIAN: German Orientalist; b. at Donauwörth (25 m. n.n.w. of Augsburg), Bavaria, May 18, 1859. He was educated at the universities of Munich (1876–79), Leipsic (1879–80; Ph.D., 1881), and Strasburg (1881), and became privat-docent at Munich in 1883. He continued his studies at Rome in the spring of 1884 and at London in the summer of 1882 and 1887, while from 1888 to 1894 he was employed in the British Museum. Since the latter year he has been professor of Oriental philology and director of the Oriental seminar at the University of Heidelberg. In 1884 he founded, at Leipsic, the *Zeitschrift für Keilschriftforschung*, which was continued in the following year as the *Zeitschrift für Assyriologie*, and which he has edited to the present time. He likewise edited the second edition of C. F. A. Dillmann's *Grammatik der äthiopischen Sprache* (Leipsic, 1899) and the *Orientalische Studien* in honor of the seventieth birthday of T. Nöldeke (2 vols., Giessen, 1906), and was the founder and editor of the *Semitistische Studien* (Berlin, 1894 sqq.). In 1904 he became one of the editors of the *Archiv für Religionswissenschaft*. He has also written *Die grosse Dariusinschrift am Felsen von Behistun* (Leipsic, 1881); *Die Achämenideninschriften* (1882); *Die Schatzhöhle, syrisch und deutsch* (2 vols., 1883–88); *The Ordinary Canon of the Mass according to the Use of the Coptic Church*, in C. A. Swainson's *Greek Liturgies* (London, 1884); *Kurzgefasster Ueberblick über die babylonisch-assyrische Literatur* (Leipsic, 1886); *Catalogue of the Cuneiform Tablets in the Kouyunjik Collection of the British Museum* (5 vols., London, 1889–99); *The Tell-el-Amarna Tablets in the British Museum* (1892); *Oriental Diplomacy* (1893); *Ninive und Babylon* (Bielefeld, 1903); *Die babylonisch-assyrischen Keilinschriften und ihre Bedeutung für das Alte Testament* (Tübingen, 1904); *Babylonisch-Assyrische Texte übersetzt : i. Die Schöpfungslegende* (Bonn, 1904); and *Kebra Nagast, die Herrlichkeit der Könige* (Ethiopic text and German translation, Munich, 1905).

BIANCHINI, bî''ān-kî'nî (BLANCHINUS), GIUSEPPE: Italian Biblical scholar; b. at Verona Sept. 9, 1704; d. after 1760. He was a member of the Congregation of the Oratory, and the author of two works bearing on the history of the Itala: *Psalterium duplex juxta antiquam italicam versionem* (Rome, 1740) and *Evangeliarium quadruplex Latinæ versionis antiquæ seu veteris Italicæ* (2 vols., 1749). The detailed statements in the first volume are valuable, but the text is inferior to Sabatier's *Bibliorum sacrorum Latinæ versionis antiquæ* (Reims, 1739 sqq.). The second, containing some older codices, supplements Sabatier.

K. BENRATH.

BIBLE.

The word "Bible" (from Gk. *biblia*, "books") or "Holy Scripture" is the customary term in Church and theology for the ecclesiastically acknowledged collection of the Old and the New Testament writings. As the writings of the Old Testament canon are indicated in the New Testament by the term "The Scriptures" or "The Scripture," so in the Middle Ages the whole was designated by "The Books." By a misunderstanding of the Greek form, the word was received into the modern languages as a singular of feminine gender.

The separation of these writings from all other literature as "the Book of Books" is derived from the practise of Jesus, who, with his contemporaries, acknowledged the authority of the Old Testament literature (M. Kaehler, *Jesus und das Alte Testament*, Leipsic, 1895). The Old Testament was conveyed, in the Greek translation of the Septuagint, as the Word of God, to the Gentile Christians by the followers of Jesus. At the latest in the beginning of the third century, the New Testament canon was added to the Old Testament, as is witnessed by the Syriac version (see CANON OF SCRIPTURE). And from that time the bipartite collection was always treated as a whole, although the uncertainty about some books (the so-called *Antilegomena*) was not forgotten during the Middle Ages, was recognized by Luther and other Reformers, and was treated from a dogmatic standpoint by Martin Chemnitz (*Examen concilii Tridentini*, Frankfort, 1596). The controversy about the Old Testament Apocrypha has never been settled. What esteem the Bible enjoyed in the ancient catholic Church is seen from its controlling position in divine service, in the reading of Scripture, and in the delivery of sermons founded on it, but especially from the labor spent in translating it (see BIBLE VERSIONS, A).

1. The Bible in the Early Church.

It must not be imagined that the Middle Ages did not rightly appreciate the Bible. It is necessary to take into account the great difficulties which confronted the Church at that time in forming an ecclesiastical language, and even a literary language, for the Germanic and Slavic nations. In the absence of modern philology the efforts made are worthy of acknowledgment. The hierarchical development of the Church tended to paralyze it by enforcing uniformity in use of the church-language at the expense of intelligibility, and in the interest of an easier management put the "heretical book" into the keeping of the ecclesiastical magistracy. But the Reformation introduced a new epoch of wide propagation and appreciation of the Bible. The efforts of the Reformers to make this book accessible to all Christians were taken up by Pietism under Spener; the founding of the Canstein Bible Institute (see BIBLE SOCIETIES, II, 1; CANSTEIN, KARL HILDEBRAND, BARON OF) and the sending out of the first missionaries opened the double way by which the Bible, especially in the nineteenth century, has obtained its commanding position in the world; knowledge of the Bible has been spread by the Bible Societies (q.v.) through hundreds of new translations (a work in which Englishmen and Scotchmen, well read in the Scriptures, have distinguished themselves). The Bible has become in the fullest sense the people's book in all Protestant countries of the Old World, and the same process is being repeated among the non-Christian nations, to which missionary cooperation gives the Bible and with it often also an alphabet and a literary language.

2. In the Middle Ages and Reformation Period.

This zeal for the propagation of the Bible has its root in the unique importance which the theology of the Reformation ascribes to it. In opposition to the ecclesiastical position of Rome, the Evangelicals developed their doctrine of the "normative or decisive authority of Scripture" on the basis of the uncontroverted character of the Scripture as revelation. This high regard has as its foundation the doctrine of "verbal inspiration" (see INSPIRATION), which ascribes to the Bible all requisite qualities, such as "perfection" in communicating the "knowledge necessary for salvation," "transparency," and the "power of interpreting itself by itself." Unobserved, the body of pure doctrine, by the help of which the renewal of evangelical activity had been accomplished, became transformed into a set of doctrines which were mechanically combined, regardless of their historical origin. In opposition to the adulterated tradition of Rome, Protestantism could happily refer to the bulwark of Scripture, in which Roman Catholics also acknowledged divine revelation. But evangelical theology first succumbed to the attack which the "Enlightenment" (*Aufklärung*), about the middle of the eighteenth century, made upon all history and tradition and especially upon historical revelation. In vain the effort was made to prove dogmatically the immediate divine origin of the Bible-letter, while proof was also given in an ever-cogent manner that the Bible is a production of human authorship and tradition. This crisis was gradually overcome by the victory gained for the "historico-critical" method of treating the Bible, but the right of historical revelation was established over against "natural morality and religion." As in earlier times historical development within the Bible was now and then perceived (e.g., by Coccejus and Bengel), so now students see in its writings documents of divine revelation which entered into the human world as historical facts (so the Erlangen School). Only one group of theologians of the nineteenth century (e.g., Hengstenberg and Rudelbach) went back again to the old doctrine of verbal inspiration; most investigators assumed a new attitude toward Scripture. Documents to have value must be shown to be ancient and to be derived from a time near the events they relate; there must be testimony to their genuineness and credibility. But such merely histor-

3. Modern Views and Criticism.

ical consideration of the Bible proved insufficient and dangerous in the next period. "Liberal theology, endowed with technical skill," showed error in Biblical tradition from a critical point of view, and in place of the Biblical evidences it substituted conjecturally the details of a natural history of religion, which it composed after the Hegelian formula to the effect that in the "historical revelation" there is to be seen the development of a religious idea, an act in the drama of the natural development of humanity (so F. C. Baur, E. Reuss, and Wellhausen). The results of this modern criticism were propagated among the people through the press and by pamphlets in a wild confusion along with the older, would-be enlightening defamations of the Bible (so by Reimarus, Venturini, and Bahrdt). Over against this sprang up a comprehensive literature which sought to gain those who were estranged from the Bible and to reassure disquieted readers. It was based on an acknowledgment of the part the revelation of God has played in the education of the race, and in a scientific manner discarded the unjustified conclusions of the so-called constructive criticism, at least as far as the New Testament is concerned. In this intellectual battle it became evident that the estimate of the Bible stands in an indissolubly reciprocal relation to the position taken toward positive Christianity in general.

It is therefore absolutely necessary (especially for the ministry and for ecclesiastical instruction) to have a clear insight into that which makes our Bible the unique "Book of Books." This is obtained by observing what it is that has given the Bible its historical position. Throughout the whole course of its working in the human race the Bible appears only in close connection with the Church, the essential activity of which, according to the Augsburg Confession (vii), is the preaching of "the Word." The common object of both is to convey the revelation of the living God. Whoever has become a believer in the Gospel and recalls his experience perceives also that the service of the Church by which he was led to it was inspired by the Bible, and further observation of life and history teaches that the efficacy of the work of the Church is dependent on the use it makes of the Bible. For only in the Scripture is found the unchangeable and therefore authoritative form of

4. Wherein the Bible is Unique.

preaching which first induced faith in Christ and continues so to do. On the other hand, the Christian also recognizes that his personal relation to the Bible is due to the "living voice of the Gospel" and that through the Church he comes into personal relation with the Bible. He understands also that the Bible is the book of the Church (so Luther), but not a text-book or devotional book which in all its parts is immediately useful to the individual Christian. In it are found productions which are far remote from one another in date, which originally were intended for entirely different circles with quite peculiar wants. On this account only the cooperation of different gifts and the diligence of generations working on a scientific basis can bring out its full content. Under the assumption of this service of the Church each living Christian has the possibility of coming thus through his Bible into immediate touch with the historical revelation of his God from the promise of the covenant to the beginning of the mission to the Gentiles. While historical inquiry establishes the historical continuation, and divides the whole Bible into single historical accounts and documents, the view of most Bible-readers is directed only to the Bible as a whole, and seeks in every fragment a word of God applicable to immediate questions and wants. These divergent interests must be united by observing that the individual parts, by being comprehended as "the Bible," receive a new worth, and that in this very form they obtain an imperishable, effective continuity, instead of being merely individual monuments of past times. The collection is not an accidental one, but transcribes in characteristic features the life of the human race as it developed under the influence of the history of revelation. To him therefore who sees in reliance on God the stay of human life, the Bible will also be the book of the human race. For Christian belief the Bible appears thus as the great fact in which God has inseparably interwoven the faith-awakening knowledge of his revelation with the history of the human race, and in it is discerned the clear testimony to the goal of the human race and the conquering offer of God's grace.

M. KAEHLER.

BIBLIOGRAPHY: M. Arnold, *Literature and Dogma*, latest ed., New York, 1902 (a rich book, but on rationalistic basis; it called forth many replies which were answered in *God and the Bible*, 1884); J. H. Crooker, *The New Bible and its New Uses* (Unitarian, ultrarationalistic); G. J. Metzger, *Der alte Bibelglaube und der moderne Vernunftglaube*, Stuttgart, 1893 (evangelical); J. T. Sunderland, *The Bible . . . its Place among the Sacred Books of the World*, New York, 1893 (Unitarian); J. Denney, *Studies in Theology*, London, 1895 (by a leader in English evangelical thought); A. M. Fairbairn, *Place of Christ in Modern Theology*, London, 1896 (moderate in its theological position); P. Müller, *Freisinn und Bibelglaube*, Hamburg, 1896; W. Sanday, *Inspiration*, London, 1896 (advanced in the O. T. part, conservative in treating the N. T.); R. L. Ottley, *Aspects of the Old Testament*, London, 1898; T. Zahn, *Die bleibende Bedeutung des neutestamentlichen Kanons für die Kirche*, Leipsic, 1898; S. Bernfeld, *Das Buch der Bücher*, Berlin, 1899; C. A. Briggs, *General Introduction to the Study of Holy Scripture*, New York, 1899 (comprehensive and scholarly); R. S. MacArthur, *Bible Difficulties and their Alleviative Interpretations*, Boston, 1898; idem, *The Old Book and the Old Faith*, ib. 1899 (decidedly conservative); L. W. Batten, *The Old Testament from the Modern Point of View*, New York, 1901; R. G. Moulton, *Short Introduction to the Literature of the Bible*, Boston, 1901; P. Gardner, *Historic View of the New Testament*, London, 1904 (from a scientific standpoint); F. Bettex, *Die Bibel Gottes Wort*, 3d ed., Stuttgart, 1903, Eng. transl., Cincinnati, 1904; J. E. Carpenter, *The Bible in the Nineteenth Century*, London, 1903 (scholarly and reverent, but on scientific basis); J. Haussleiter, *Die Autorität der Bibel*, Munich [1904], 1905; M. Dods, *The Bible, its Origin and Nature*, New York, 1905 (Dr. Dods is well known as a conservative critic); J. M. McMullen, *The Supremacy of the Bible*, ib. 1905; W Barry, *The Tradition of Scripture, its Origin, Authority, and Interpretation*, London, 1906; C. F. Kent, *Origin and Permanent Value of the O. T.*, New York, 1906; A. T. Pierson, *The Bible and Spiritual Criticism*, ib. 1906; G. F. Wright, *Scientific Confirmations of O. T History*, ib. 1906; W C. Selleck, *New Appreciation of the Bible*, Chicago, 1907; H. F. Waring, *Christianity and its Bible*, ib. 1907.

BIBLE CHRISTIANS. See METHODISTS, I., 8.

BIBLE CHRISTIANS (BRYANITES).

William O'Bryan (§ 1).
Early Organization and Growth (§ 2).
Dissension (§ 3).
Extension to America and Australia (§ 4).
Union with the Methodists in Canada (§ 5).
Union in Australia and England (§ 6).

Bible Christians or Bryanites are popular names of a body of Christians officially known as the Bible Christian Connection. The designation "Bryanites" is from their founder, William O'Bryan; that of "Bible Christians" was due to the persistent use of the Bible in private devotions and public services by a peasantry in general but scantily provided with the book, and to the consistent practise of its precepts by their early ministry. The sect has usually been classed with the Methodists and is now united with them.

1. William O'Bryan. William O'Bryan, the founder, was born in Gunwen (near Lostwithiel, 23 m. w. of Plymouth), Cornwall, England, Feb. 6, 1778. He was the son of a yeoman, was possessed of a vigorous mind and retentive memory, and, having a good elementary education, was, intellectually, considerably above his class. His home influences were devoutly religious and resulted in his conversion at eighteen, when he began at once to exhort. He was licensed shortly after as a "local preacher" with the hope of entering the Wesleyan itinerancy; meanwhile he engaged in business.

Serious illness (1804) reawakened in him a profound conviction of his call, which delay and opposition had weakened for a time. For five years more he was content to work on the Bodmin circuit as a local preacher of the Wesleyans, while still in business. His fine presence, courteous manner, great magnetism, and above all his fervent godliness gave him much popularity as a preacher. In his keen hunting for souls, he grew restive under restraint, overstepped the boundary of the circuit and plunged into the "wild wastes of Cornwall and North Devon," where the voice of Methodism had never been heard.

This in the mind of the Wesleyan authorities was a "dangerous irregularity" of method, against which Mr. O'Bryan had been cautioned, and, when he appeared at the district meeting as a candidate for the itinerancy, caused his "first" rejection; the financial responsibility which would be incurred by accepting a married man, as he now was, was named as the "second" cause for his "final" rejection. He at once entered unoccupied fields in a new campaign. His unquestioned moral uprightness, indefatigable labors, and unsparing self-sacrifice made his evangelical message remarkably successful; and the generosity which prompted him to urge all his converts to enter the Church that had rejected him from its highest office of ministry compels admiration. A tendency to despotic rule, to which by nature and force of circumstances he was inclined (see below, § 3), led to a separation in 1829 from the Connection which he had founded, and in 1835 to his emigration to the United States with residence in New York City. He revisited his spiritual children more than once and was heartily welcomed. A generous pension was provided for his support by the body. He died in Brooklyn, Jan. 8, 1868, and was buried in Greenwood Cemetery.

2. Early Organization and Growth. The germ of the Bible Christian denomination consisted of twenty-two persons, converts of Mr. O'Bryan, who were organized into a society on Oct. 9, 1815, in the house of John Thorne, Shebbear, Devonshire, England. Within a year this number became eighteen ministers and 1,500 members; and at the sixth year seventy-eight ministers and 6,200 members. To carry forward a work extending so rapidly, Mr. O'Bryan adopted John Wesley's plan and "chose and appointed" both men and women as itinerants. The proportion of women was large in the early history of the Church, and their work was eminently successful; yet their number steadily declined and ultimately none remained in the itinerancy. With this working force evangelism was extended into Devonshire and Cornwall, the Scilly and Channel Islands, and later by emigration (1820–30) to America.

Organization into societies and circuits required meeting-places and chapels—at first preaching was mostly in the field, the village green, in hired halls, and in houses—and all property acquired for such purpose was held in Mr. O'Bryan's name. He also presided over the conference, the first being held at Launceston (1819), and composed of ministers only.

3. Dissension. To all this absolutism, there was serious objection, and an effort to secure an amended deed by which all property should be held in trust for the Connection was begun in 1826. A crisis was reached at the eleventh conference (1829), when opposition to Mr. O'Bryan's expressed intention "that if all the conference were opposed to his views, his single vote was to determine every case," resulted in his adjourning the conference, and withdrawing with comparatively few sympathizers. The conference refused to recognize his authority, elected Andrew Cory president in his stead, and proceeded with business. It was resolved "that the conference be the organ of government; its membership, ministers and laymen; and its next place of meeting annually fixed." The conference thus declared against an episcopacy, as it also decided against ecclesiasticism by admitting laymen to church government in equal numbers with clerical members. Eight years later these separatists negotiated terms of reunion, but Mr. O'Bryan never again united.

4. Extension to America and Australia. Many members of the infant Church emigrated to the colonies and the United States. In 1831 the Missionary Society of the Bible Christians in England sent John Glass and Francis Metherall as missionaries to Canada West and Prince Edward Island respectively. They also organized missions (1846) in the States of Wisconsin, Ohio, and Michigan. In 1850 James Way and James Rowe were sent out to Australia, and later work was begun in New Zealand. For the next quarter of a century the Church enjoyed undisturbed prosperity, establishing three publishing houses, and a denominational college at Shebbear, Devonshire, England. In 1882, 300 ministers and 34,000 members were reported. This was the high-water mark numerically.

These years of extension had awakened, in a much divided Methodism, a sense of the advisability of "union," in both England and the colonies. The center of discussion was Canada, where five Methodist sects wasted their energy in vigorous, if not unseemly, rivalry. As early as 1866 the Bible Christians and Methodist New Connection approached the Methodist Protestants of the United States upon the question of union, but the overture ended in friendly expressions only. In 1870 the Methodist New Connection made overtures to the Bible Christians, and in 1874 the former were absorbed by the Wesleyan Methodists of Canada. The Bible Christians announced as their policy—a policy consistently held since organization—"That any basis of union to be acceptable to this Conference *must secure to the laity their full share of privileges* in the government of the Church." In 1882 a committee was appointed by the Bible Christians to meet with three other committees, representing the Wesleyan Methodists, the Primitive Methodists, and the Methodist Episcopal Church of Canada. This committee was explicitly instructed to reaffirm "That no union would be possible for their Church that did not provide for a representation of the laity in all church courts." A basis of union was provided acceptable to all parties, voted upon by every society, and in 1884 union was fully and legally perfected. The uniting churches chose as a name "The Methodist Church of Canada." The parent body graciously consented to the separation, which affected the work in Canada and the United States only.

5. Union with the Methodists in Canada.

The energy and resources of the English and Australian conferences were now devoted to an enlargement of home missions and the establishment of a foreign mission in China, which has been successful. A union of the Australian conference with other Methodist sects in that colony left but the parent body bearing the name; and in Aug., 1906, this Church voted unanimously to unite with the Methodist New Connection and the United Methodists, the union to be formally and legally consummated in 1907. The name of "United Methodist Church" was chosen for the new organization. At the time of approving the union the Bible Christians had 638 chapels, 202 ministers, and 30,000 members.

6. Union in Australia and England.

Francis Metherall Whitlock.

Bibliography: J. Thorne, *A Jubilee Memorial of the Rise and Progress of the Bible Christian Connexion*, London, 1866; J. G. Hayman, *A Hist. of the Methodist Revival of the Last Century in Relation to North Devon*, ib. 1885; [John Thorne], *James Thorne of Shebbear, a Memoir . . from his Diary and Letters, by his Son*, ib. 1873; F. W. Bourne, *The Centenary Life of James Thorne*, ib. 1895; *Brief Biographical Sketches of Bible Christians*, Jersey, 1905; *The Book of Discipline for the People Known as Bible Christians*, London, the Bible Christian Book Room.

BIBLE READING BY THE LAITY, RESTRICTIONS ON.

I. The Ancient Church: It is indisputable that in Apostolic times the Old Testament was commonly read (John v, 47; Acts viii, 28; xvii, 11; II Tim. iii, 15). Roman Catholics admit that this reading was not restricted in the first centuries, in spite of its abuse by Gnostics and other heretics. On the contrary, the reading of Scripture was urged (Justin Martyr, xliv, *ANF*, i, 177–178; Jerome, *Adv. libros Rufini*, i, 9, *NPNF*, 2d ser., iii, 487); and Pamphilus, the friend of Eusebius, kept copies of Scripture to furnish to those who desired them. Chrysostom attached considerable importance to the reading of Scripture on the part of the laity and denounced the error that it was to be permitted only to monks and priests (*De Lazaro concio*, iii, *MPG*, xlviii, 992; *Hom. ii in Matt.*, *MPG*, lvii, 30, *NPNF*, 2d ser., x, 13). He insisted upon access being given to the entire Bible, or at least to the New Testament (*Hom. ix in Col.*, *MPG*, lxii, 361, *NPNF*, xiii, 301). The women also, who were always at home, were diligently to read the Bible (*Hom. xxxv on Gen. xii*, *MPG*, liii, 323). Jerome recommended the reading and studying of Scripture on the part of the women (*Epist.*, cxxviii, 3, *MPL*, xxii, 1098, *NPNF*, 2d ser., vi, 259; *Epist.*, lxxix, 9, *MPG*, xxii, 730–731, *NPNF*, 2d ser., vi, 167). The translations of the Bible, Augustine considered a blessed means of propagating the Word of God among the nations (*De doctr. christ.*, ii, 5, *NPNF*, 1st ser., ii, 536); Gregory I recommended the reading of the Bible without placing any limitations on it (*Hom. iii in Ezek.*, *MPL*, lxxvi, 968).

II. The Middle Ages: Owing to lack of culture among the Germanic and Romanic peoples, there was for a long time no thought of restricting access to the Bible there. Translations of Biblical books into German began only in the Carolingian period and were not originally intended for the laity. Nevertheless the people were anxious to have the divine service and the Scripture lessons read in the vernacular. John VIII in 880 permitted, after the reading of the Latin gospel, a translation into Slavonic; but Gregory VII, in a letter to Duke Vratislav of Bohemia in 1080 characterized the custom as unwise, bold, and forbidden (*Epist.*, vii, 11; P. Jaffé, *BRG*, ii, 392 sqq.). This was a formal prohibition, not of Bible reading in general, but of divine service in the vernacular.

With the appearance, in the twelfth and thirteenth centuries, of the Albigenses and Waldenses, who appealed to the Bible in all their disputes with the Church, the hierarchy was furnished with a reason for shutting up the Word of God. The Synod of Toulouse in 1229 forbade the laity to have in their possession any copy of the books of the Old and the New Testament except the Psalter and such other portions as are contained in the Breviary or the Hours of the Blessed Mary. "We most strictly forbid these works in the vulgar tongue" (Harduin, *Concilia*, xii, 178; Mansi, *Concilia*, xxiii, 194). The Synod of Tarragona (1234) ordered all vernacular versions to be brought to the bishop to be burned. James I renewed this decision of the Tarragona synod in 1276. The synod held there in 1317 under Archbishop Ximenes prohibited to Beghards, Beguines, and tertiaries of the Franciscans the possession of theological books in the vernacular (Mansi, *Concilia*, xxv, 627). The order of James I was renewed by later kings and confirmed by Paul II (1464–71). Ferdinand and Isabella (1474–1516) prohibited the translation of the Bible into the vernacular or the possession of such translations (F. H. Reusch, *Index der verbotenen Bücher*, i, Bonn, 1883, 44).

In England Wyclif's Bible-translation caused the resolution passed by the third Synod of Oxford (1408): "No one shall henceforth of his own authority translate any text of Scripture into English; and no part of any such book or treatise composed in the time of John Wycliffe or later shall be read in public or private, under pain of excommunication" (Hefele, *Conciliengeschichte*, vi, 984). But Sir Thomas More states that he had himself seen old Bibles which were examined by the bishop and left in the hands of good Catholic laymen (Blunt, *Reformation of the Church of England*, 4th ed., London, 1878, i, 505). In Germany, Charles IV issued in 1369 an edict to four inquisitors against the translating and the reading of Scripture in the German language. This edict was caused by the operations of Beghards and Beguines. In 1485 and 1486, Berthold, archbishop of Mainz, issued an edict against the printing of religious books in German, giving among other reasons the singular one that the German language was unadapted to convey correctly religious ideas, and therefore they would be profaned. Berthold's edict had some influence, but could not prevent the dissemination and publication of new editions of the Bible. Leaders in the Church sometimes recommended to the laity the reading of the Bible, and the Church kept silence officially as long as these efforts were not abused.

III. The Roman Catholic Church since the Reformation: Luther's translation of the Bible and its propagation could not but influence the Roman Catholic Church. Humanism, through such men as Erasmus, advocated the reading of the Bible and the necessity of making it accessible by translations; but it was felt that Luther's translation must be offset by one prepared in the interest of the Church. Such editions were Emser's of 1527, and the Dietenberg Bible of 1534. The Church of Rome silently tolerated these translations.

1. Action by the Council of Trent.

At last the Council of Trent took the matter in hand, and in its fourth session (Apr. 18, 1546) adopted the *Decretum de editione et usu librorum sacrorum*, which enacted the following: "This synod ordains and decrees that henceforth sacred Scripture, and especially the aforesaid old and vulgate edition, be printed in the most correct manner possible; and that it shall not be lawful for any one to print, or cause to be printed, any books whatever on sacred matters without the name of the author; or in future to sell them, or even to possess them, unless they shall have been first examined and approved of by the ordinary." When the question of the translation of the Bible into the vernacular came up, Bishop Acqui of Piedmont and Cardinal Pacheco advocated its prohibition. This was strongly opposed by Cardinal Madruzzi, who claimed that "not the translations but the professors of Hebrew and Greek are the cause of the confusion in Germany; a prohibition would produce the worst impression in Germany." As no agreement could be had, the council appointed an index-commission to report to the pope, who was to give an authoritative decision.

2. Rules of Various Popes.

The first index published by a pope (Paul IV), in 1559, prohibited under the title of *Biblia prohibita* a number of Latin editions as well as the publication and possession of translations of the Bible in German, French, Spanish, Italian, English, or Dutch, without the permission of the sacred office of the Roman Inquisition (Reusch, ut sup., i, 264). In 1564 Pius IV published the index prepared by the commission mentioned above. Herein ten rules are laid down, of which the fourth reads thus: "Inasmuch as it is manifest from experience that if the Holy Bible, translated into the vulgar tongue, be indiscriminately allowed to every one, the rashness of men will cause more evil than good to arise from it, it is, on this point, referred to the judgment of the bishops or inquisitors, who may, by the advice of the priest or confessor, permit the reading of the Bible translated into the vulgar tongue by Catholic authors, to those persons whose faith and piety they apprehend will be augmented and not injured by it; and this permission must be had in writing. But if any shall have the presumption to read or possess it without such permission, he shall not receive absolution until he have first delivered up such Bible to the ordinary." Regulations for booksellers follow, and then: "Regulars shall neither read nor purchase such Bibles without special license from their superiors." Sixtus V substituted in 1590 twenty-two new rules for the ten of Pius IV Clement VIII abolished in 1596 the rules of Sixtus, but added a "remark" to the fourth rule given above, which particularly restores the enactment of Paul IV The right of the bishops, which the fourth rule implies, is abolished by the "remark," and the bishop may grant a dispensation only when especially authorized by the pope and the Inquisition (Reusch, ut sup., i, 333). Benedict XIV enlarged, in 1757, the fourth rule thus: "If such Bible-versions in the vernacular are approved by the apostolic see or are edited with annotations derived from the holy fathers of the Church or from learned and Catholic men, they are permitted." This modification of the fourth rule was abolished by Gregory XVI in pursuance of an admonition of the index-congregation, Jan. 7, 1836, "which calls attention to the fact that according to the decree of 1757 only such versions in the vernacular are to be permitted as have been approved by the apostolic see or are edited with annotations," but insistence is placed on all those particulars enjoined by the fourth rule of the index and afterward by Clement VIII (Reusch, ut sup., ii, 852).

In England the reading of the Bible was made by Henry VIII (1530) to depend upon the permission of the superiors. Tyndale's version, printed before 1535, was prohibited. In 1534 the Canterbury convocation passed a resolution asking the king to have the Bible translated and to permit its reading. A folio copy of Coverdale's translation was put into every church for the benefit of the faithful, and fastened with a chain. In Spain the Inquisitor-General de Valdes published in 1551 the index of Louvain of 1550, which prohibits "Bibles (New and Old Testaments) in the Spanish or other vernacular" (Reusch, ut sup., i, 133). This prohibition was abolished in 1778. The Lisbon index of 1624 in Portugal prohibited quoting in the vernacular in any book passages from the Bible. In Italy the members of the order of the Jesuits were in 1596 permitted to use a Catholic Italian translation of the Gospel-lessons. In France the Sorbonne declared, Aug. 26, 1525, that a French translation of the Bible or of single books must be regarded as dangerous under conditions then present; extant versions were better suppressed than tolerated. In the following year, 1526, it prohibited the translation of the entire Bible, but permitted the translation of single books with proper annotations. The indexes of the Sorbonne, which by royal edict were binding, after 1544 contained the statement: "How dangerous it is to allow the reading of the Bible in the vernacular to unlearned people and those not piously or humbly disposed (of whom there are many in our times) may be seen from the Waldensians, Albigenses, and Poor Men of Lyons, who have thereby lapsed into error and have led many into the same condition. Considering the nature of men, the translation of the Bible into the vernacular must in the present be regarded therefore as dangerous and pernicious" (Reusch, ut sup., i, 151). The rise of Jansenism in the seventeenth century, and especially the appearance, under its encouragement, of Quesnel's New Testament with moral reflections under each verse (*Le Nouveau Testament en françois avec des reflexions morales sur chaque vers*, Paris, 1699), which was expressly intended to popularize the reading of the Bible, caused the renewal, with increased stringency, of the rules already quoted. The Jesuits prevailed upon Clement XI to publish the famous bull *Unigenitus*, Sept. 8, 1713, in which he condemned seven propositions in Quesnel's work which advocated the reading of the Bible by the laity (cf. H. J. D. Denzinger, *Enchiridion*, Würzburg, 1854, 287). In the Netherlands, Neercassel, bishop of Emmerich, published in 1677 (in Latin) and 1680 (in French) a treatise in which he dealt with the fourth rule of the Tridentine index as obsolete, and urged the diligent reading of the Bible. In Belgium in 1570 the unlicensed sale of the Bible in the vernacular was strictly prohibited; but the use of the Antwerp Bible continued. In Poland the Bible was translated and often published. In Germany papal decrees could not very well be carried out and the reading of the Bible was not only not prohibited, but was approved and praised. Billuart about 1750, as quoted by Van Ess, states, "In France, Germany, and Holland the Bible is read by all without distinction." In the nineteenth century the clergy took great interest in the work of Bible Societies. Thus Leander van Ess (q.v.) acted as agent of the British and Foreign Bible Society for Catholic Germany, and the society published the New Testament of Van Ess, which was placed on the Index in 1821. The prince-bishop of Breslau, Sedlnitzki, who afterward joined the Evangelical Church, was also interested in circulating the Bible. As the Bible Societies generally circulated the translations of heretics, the popes—Leo XII (May 5, 1824); Pius VIII (May 25, 1829); Gregory XVI (Aug. 15, 1840; May 8, 1844); Pius IX (Nov. 9, 1846; Dec. 8, 1849)—issued encyclicals against the Bible Societies. In the syllabus of 1864 "socialism, communism, secret societies, and Bible Societies" are placed in the same category. As to the effect of the papal decrees there is a difference of opinion within the Catholic Church. In theory the admonition of Gregory XVI no doubt exists, but practise often ignores it.

3. Rules and Practise in the Different Countries.

IV. The Greek Church knows of no such restriction of use of the Bible as that of the Roman Church. Nevertheless the Synod of Jerusalem of 1672 answered the first of the four questions: "Whether the Holy Scripture can be read by all Christians," in the negative. Nicholas I of Russia abolished in 1826 the Bible Society founded by Alexander I for the propagation of the Bible in the Russian vernacular.

V. The Evangelical Churches: Luther strove to open the Bible to all, and his version served that purpose. The principle that every Evangelical Christian is at liberty to read the Bible remained uncontroverted, though Semler (*De antiquo ecclesiæ statu commentatio*, 37, 60, 68) makes the assertion that the sacred writings, especially the apostolic epistles, were not intended for the use of the people and the congregations; that in the ancient Church no universal use of the Bible existed, and that the catechumens especially were prohibited from using the Bible. Bible-compendiums for special purposes and separate circles also came into use in the Evangelical Church. Veit Dietrich published in 1541 his *Summarium* of the Old and the New Testament; Cromwell's soldiers had *The Soldier's Pocket Bible* of 1643 (facsimile edition, *Cromwell's Soldier's Bible*, London, 1895). The restriction upon Bible-reading in the Evangelical Church became of practical importance only in the schools. For didactic purposes Amos Comenius recommended compendiums and special manuals of Scripture, which the scholar was to use till he could read the Gospel in the original. The didactic needs were gradually satisfied by the introduction of text-books of "Biblical history," the Catechism, and collections of Bible sentences. From time to time the question has been agitated whether the whole Bible or so-called school Bibles should be used in the schools. The principal reason adduced in favor of the latter is that certain passages are objectionable because they deal with sexual relations. But these reasons are not well founded, since reading of the Bible has never been a cause of demoralization. The moral earnestness which without veiling calls things by their right names is to be preferred to a careful paraphrasing and veiling of the sense which only the more excite impure desires.

(GEORG RIETSCHEL.)

BIBLIOGRAPHY: T. G. Hegelmaier, *Geschichte des Bibelverbots*, Ulm, 1783; N. Le Maire, *Sanctuarium profanis occlusum sive de sanctorum bibliorum in lingua vulgari seu vernacula tractatus*, Würzburg, 1662 (from the Fr. of 1651), this was reproduced in substance in *Die Bibel kein Lesebuch für Jedermann*, Münster, 1845; A. Arnauld, *De la lecture de l'écriture sainte*, Paris (c. 1690); C. W. F. Walch, *Kritische Untersuchungen vom Gebrauch der heiligen Schrift unter den alten Christen in den ersten drei Jahrhunderten*, Leipsic, 1779; F. von Ess, *Der heilige Chrysostomus oder die Stimme der katholischen Kirche über das nützliche, heilsame und erbauliche Bibellesen*, Darmstadt, 1824; J. B. Malon, *La Lecture de la sainte Bible en langue vulgaire*, 2 vols., Louvain, 1846; *Vom Lesen der heiligen Schrift*, Mainz, 1846; F. H. Reusch, *Die Indices librorum prohibitorum des sechszehnten Jahrhunderts*, Tübingen, 1886; W. Walther, *Die deutsche Bibelübersetzung des Mittelalters*, Braunschweig, 1889; J. H. Kurtz, *Church History*, §§ 105, 3; 185, 1, New York, 1890; the text of the bull *Unigenitus* may be found in Reich, *Documents*, pp. 386–389, and the authoritative statement of the Greco-Russian Church in Schaff, *Creeds*, iii, 433–434.

BIBLE SOCIETIES.

Bible societies are benevolent associations formed to increase the circulation of the Bible and making special efforts to supply the Scriptures to those who from poverty or other causes are destitute of them. Printing the Bible or New Testament in suitable styles, translation into all important languages and even into the less important dialects, and some effective system of distribution in all accessible places are commonly regarded as essential features of the work of such societies. In some cases the books are given without price; but it is not usual to give away a large proportion. The cost of manufacture and of distribution, however, has to be provided by voluntary contributions.

The Society for the Promotion of Christian Knowledge (q.v.), founded in London in 1698, was the first to undertake to provide the common people with the Bible. It continues this beneficent work as one branch of its publication enterprise, and has been the means of providing fairly good translations of the Scriptures in many obscure languages of Asia, Africa, and the Pacific Islands. The Society for the Propagation of the Gospel (q.v.), founded in 1701, has also done and is still doing a good work in circulating the Scriptures in connection with its extensive missions. The Scottish Society for Propagating Christian Knowledge, founded in 1709, added the work of circulating the Bible to its missionary enterprises in Scotland and in America. The first society formed for the exclusive purpose of publishing the Bible at a low price seems to have been the Canstein Bible Institute, established in 1710 at Halle in Germany by Baron Canstein (see below, II, 1).

I. British Bible Societies.—1. Precursors of the British and Foreign Bible Society: In the last half of the eighteenth century several societies sprang up in Great Britain which had Bible distribution as part of their programme; such as the Book Society for Promoting Religious Knowledge among the Poor (1750), the Bible Society, later known as the Naval and Military Bible Society (1780), the Society for the Support and Encouragement of Sunday Schools (1785), the Association for Discountenancing Vice and Promoting the Knowledge and Practise of the Christian Religion (established in Dublin, 1792), the French Bible Society (established in London for printing the Bible in France, 1792), and the Religious Tract Society (London, 1799; see TRACT SOCIETIES).

2. The British and Foreign Bible Society: These enterprises, however, did not supply the need. The Rev. Thomas Charles (q.v.) of Bala in Wales became much impressed with the need of the common folk about him, who could not obtain the Bible except by persevering effort and much self-denial; the Bible was not only scarce but costly. Mr. Charles finally devoted himself to finding some effective means of supplying his people with the Scriptures. At a meeting of the Religious Tract Society in London in 1802, he aroused great interest by his vigorous presentation of the need of the people of Wales. The Rev. Joseph Hughes, secretary of the Religious Tract Society, exclaimed, "Surely a society might be formed to provide Bibles for Wales; and if for Wales, why not for the world?" This remark contained the germ from which grew the British and Foreign Bible Society.

1. Origin and Constitution.

The idea of a Bible Society for the world led to discussion and to study of the destitution of the people. The Rev. C. F. A. Steinkopf, pastor of the German Lutheran Church in London, gave effective information of the situation in European countries. Members of the Religious Tract Society, although they did not publicly appear, had much to do with the preparatory work. On Mar. 7, 1804, a public meeting was held at the London Tavern, on the call of Mr. Hughes. Three hundred persons attended the meeting. It was quickly evident that a society for increasing the circulation of the Bible presented common ground, upon which all sects and parties could stand. Dissenters met churchmen, and in their interest in the needs of the masses, they forgot for a time their divergent interpretations of the same book. The sole condition necessary to union of action was that a text accepted by all should be issued without note or comment.

At this meeting a hastily drawn up set of by-laws was adopted. An executive committee of thirty-six laymen was chosen, fifteen from the Church of England, fifteen from the Dissenting bodies, and six foreigners residing in London. The Rev. Joseph Hughes (Baptist) and the Rev. Josiah Pratt (Church of England) were elected secretaries. Seven hundred pounds were subscribed for the work of the society, and the Bishop of London, Dr. Porteus, was elected President.

The constitution of the society was soon afterward prepared; the Rev. John Owen, of the Church of England, was added to the staff of the society as a third secretary, and on nomination of Lord Teignmouth, a former governor-general in India, the Rev. C. F A. Steinkopf was appointed secretary for foreign lands. Besides the Bishop of London, the Bishops of Durham, Exeter, and St. Davids, and many other influential persons, among whom were William Wilberforce and Granville Sharp, long known as antislavery leaders, joined this movement.

As at present organized, the business of the society is directed by a committee made up as indicated above. Every subscriber of five guineas annually is a governor, and every subscriber of one guinea annually is a member of the society.

2. Present Organization.

Every governor, and every minister who is a member, has the privilege of attending and voting at all meetings of the committee. The president, the vice-presidents (numbering more than a hundred), and the treasurer are considered *ex officio* members of the committee. There are two secretaries and three superintendents charged with different departments of the work besides several assistant secretaries. To excite wider interest and to facilitate the distribution of the Bible, auxiliary and branch societies are formed, which pay their collections into a common fund and receive back a certain proportion of the sum collected in Bibles for distribution. There were in 1906 more than 5,800 of the auxiliary and branch societies and associations in England and Wales alone.

The society began its career by first meeting the wants of Wales. Twenty thousand Welsh Bibles and five thousand Testaments were printed. Providentially but a short time before this, the art of stereotyping had been invented. When in 1806 the first wagon-load of Bibles came into Wales, it was received like the ark of the covenant; and the people with shouts of joy dragged it into the city. The society also distributed the Bible in an improved Gaelic translation in the Highlands of Scotland, and turned its attention to the Irish; in short, it undertook to supply Great Britain and Ireland with Bibles.

But the society did not forget that it is a foreign as well as a British Bible Society. When it began operations Europe was convulsed with war and not so much was done as would otherwise have been accomplished in the way of supplying the destitute in European countries. Mr. Steinkopf and Robert Pinkerton made extensive tours through Germany, Switzerland, and Russia, and everywhere local

3. Foreign Work.

Bible societies sprang into existence in their wake. Many of these societies, formed in 1812 and later, have done good work, being aided with funds and with grants of Bibles by the British Society About the time of the formation of the British Society two Scotchmen, John Paterson and Ebenezer Henderson, went to Copenhagen, intending to go out as missionaries to India under the Danish-Halle mission at Tranquebar. Their plan fell through, but they met an Icelander, Thorkelin, in Copenhagen, who told them of the destitution of his countrymen. There were said to be only fifty Bibles in Iceland for a population of fifty thousand. The two Scotchmen laid the matter before the British and Foreign Bible Society, which promised to pay half of the expense of printing five thousand Testaments in Icelandic. The printing was stopped by the outbreak of war. But in 1812 Mr. Henderson received permission to remain in Copenhagen to complete the printing of the whole Bible in Icelandic, and, notwithstanding the war, to correspond with the Bible society in England regarding this work. The confidence thus shown in the motives of the society was certainly remarkable at that epoch; and it had much to do with the founding of the Danish Bible Society in 1814.

The British Society extended its work gradually to the British colonies, where it works through auxiliary societies. In Canada, the Canadian Bible Society, which has united a large number of local auxiliaries in one, is a society auxiliary to the British Society, and has a secretary appointed by the parent society in London. In Australia the society has fifty-two auxiliaries with nearly 500 branches. In India, with the exception of Burma, the society carries on its work through six strong auxiliary societies. In Cape Colony the South-African auxiliary has for its field the whole territory south of the Orange River. The whole number of auxiliaries and branch societies affiliated with the British Society outside of the United Kingdom exceeds 2,200. The whole number of these local societies, in Great Britain and abroad, which the British and Foreign Society aids and from which it receives donations, is over 8,160. Besides these auxiliary societies the parent society makes use of agencies, each in charge of a special agent, devoted to the increase of the circulation of the Bible in his own field. These agencies cover the continent of Europe, and Turkey, Siberia. China, Korea, and Japan in Asia. In the three last-named countries special arrangements with the American Bible Society and the National Bible Society of Scotland prevent clashing and secure combination for the translation of the Scriptures. Agencies of the British society also promote the distribution of the Bible in Egypt and North Africa and in nearly all of the colonies of East and West Africa. Where neither auxiliary nor agency has been established the society works through the missions which are in occupation of the ground in any part of the world.

This wide-spread work has not been brought to its present extension without hindrances and difficulties. The High-church party in the Church of England has at times opposed the Bible Society, preferring to work through the Society for the Promotion of Christian Knowledge, which takes care to have the Bible supplemented by the Book of Common Prayer. Others have insisted that the Bible is a dangerous book to put in the hands of ignorant men without note or comment, and for this reason have opposed the Bible Society. In 1825 dissension arose within the Bible Society, which continued during two years, over the question of the Apocrypha. It was formally resolved in 1827 that the fundamental law of the society forbids its circulating the Apocrypha, and that therefore no persons or societies that circulate the Apocrypha can receive aid from the society. This decision led to the separation of a considerable number of European societies from the British society which had founded them.

4. Dissensions. Seceding Societies.

The discussion also resulted in the secession of the Scottish societies which originated the agitation against the publication of the Apocrypha (see below, 3). In 1831 another agitation was raised against the presence of Unitarians on the Board of Managers. The society having refused to alter its constitution so as to exclude non-Trinitarians, a separate society called the Trinitarian Bible Society was formed (see below, 5). With the growth of foreign missions, a question as to translation of the words relating to baptism became acute; and the controversy finally led to the formation of the Bible Translation Society, which was supported by Baptists who preferred to translate "immerse" rather than to transfer the Greek word *baptizein* (see below, 6).

But there has been a continuous and remarkable growth of the society in spite of all obstacles and opposition. In 1904 the centenary of the society was celebrated in almost all countries of the Christian and non-Christian world. "Bible Day" in Mar., 1904, will long be remembered not only as a day of an immense popular declaration of faith in the Bible as the revelation of God's will to men, but as a time for expressing the warmest love and sympathy, and gratitude withal, to the society which then completed a hundred years of self-sacrificing service of the nations. Not only were special gifts sent into the treasury for the general work of the society, but a special centenary fund of $1,250,000 was raised in that and the following year to be used as a reserve for more firmly planting the outposts of the society. The total issues of the British and Foreign Bible Society, in the year ending Mar. 31, 1906, amounted to 5,416,569 copies of the Bible or its parts. The total issues of the society from its organization to Mar. 31, 1907, amount to 203,931,768 copies, of which more than 80,000,000 copies were in the English language. The president of the British and Foreign Bible Society is the Marquis of Northampton. Its headquarters are at 146 Queen Victoria St., London, E. C.; its periodicals are *The Bible in the World* and *The Bible Society Gleanings*.

3. The National Bible Society of Scotland: In 1809 the Edinburgh Bible Society was formed, in 1812 the Glasgow Bible Society, and in 1821 the Glasgow Auxiliary Bible Society. As mentioned above, these societies seceded from the British and Foreign Bible Society in consequence of the controversy about circulating editions of the Bible containing the Apocrypha. In 1859 the National Bible Society was formed, and in 1861 all these Scottish societies combined to form a new organization which was incorporated as the National Bible Society of Scotland. The fields of this society are in Europe and Asia. One-fifth of its issues in 1906-1907 were in Roman Catholic countries and about one-half in China. Its issues in the year ending Mar., 1907, amounted to 1,671,900 copies.

4. The Hibernian Bible Society: This society was organized in 1806 as an auxiliary to the British and Foreign Bible Society. It is now independent, and devotes its attention mainly to the needs of Ireland. In the year ending Mar., 1907, it circulated 37,258 copies, which were purchased by the society. The headquarters are in Dublin.

5. The Trinitarian Bible Society: Formed in 1831 as a protest against Unitarianism, this society issued in the year ending Dec. 31, 1907, 89,214 copies of the Bible or its parts. The headquarters of the society are at 7 Bury St., London, W. C.

6. The Bible Translation Society: This society was organized in 1843 to serve the special interests of the British Baptist missions. It is now a part of the Baptist Missionary Society, making no separate publication of its issues, and having its headquarters at the Mission House, 19 Furnival St., London.

II. Bible Societies on the Continent of Europe.—1. Germany: The first German Bible Society was the **Canstein Bible Institute,** founded in Halle in 1710 by Karl Hildebrand, Baron Canstein (q.v.), with the definite purpose of placing the Bible within reach of the poor. The Institute has issued up to the beginning of 1907, over 7,000,000 copies of the Bible and its parts. The issues for 1907 were 38,696 copies. The (first) **Nuremberg Bible Society** was formed in 1804, and received aid from the British and Foreign Bible Society. In 1806 it was removed to Basel in Switzerland and took the name of the **Basel Bible Society.** Its issues during the year 1906 amounted to 32,708 copies. The **Berlin Bible Society** was formed in 1806 as a result of the energy of Father Jänicke, a Moravian pastor, and was aided by the British and Foreign Bible Society in its early years. In 1814 it was converted into the **Prussian Bible Society.** It now has many branches and devotes its attention mainly to the circulation of the Bible in Germany. In the year 1906 its issues amounted to 212,911 Bibles and Testaments. The headquarters of the society are Klosterstrasse 71, Berlin C. The **Württemberg Bible Institute** was formed in 1813 under the influence of Messrs. Steinkopf and Pinkerton, of the British and Foreign Bible Society. Its issues reported in 1906 were 334,953 copies. The headquarters are at Christophstrasse 6, Stuttgart. The **Berg Bible Society** was formed at Elberfeld in the old Duchy of Berg in 1814. It furnishes Scriptures for use abroad in some small quantities. The total of its issues in 1906 was 151,558 copies, and the total of its issues in the 93 years of its existence are 2,228,353 copies. The headquarters of the society are at Marienstrasse 28, Elberfeld. The **Saxon Bible Society** was formed in the year 1814. It has forty-two branches, and besides its publications in German, it has published an edition of the New Testament in the Chagga language, spoken in the northern part of German East Africa. Its total issues in 1906 amounted to 48,065 copies. The headquarters are at Zinzendorfstrasse 17, Dresden. The **Bavarian Protestant Bible Society** was formed in 1823. It is also called the **Central Bible Society**. Its issues in 1906 were 12,930 copies. The headquarters of the society are at Nuremberg. There are also many local and state societies, of which those of Hamburg, Sleswick, and Strasburg print as well as distribute Bibles. A Roman Catholic Bible Society, the **Regensburg Bible Institute**, was organized in 1805 by G. M. Wittmann, head of the seminary at Regensburg, with the assistance of some bishops and many laymen. A translation of the New Testament was prepared and 60,000 copies were distributed in ten years, but in 1817 the Institute was suppressed by Pope Pius VII. In 1815 another Roman Catholic Bible Society was founded at Heiligenstadt, which connected itself with the Prussian society and organized auxiliaries. Leander van Ess (q.v.) at Marburg was especially interested and his translation of the New Testament was widely disseminated. He also founded the **Christian Brotherhood for Disseminating the Holy Scriptures** with the support of the British and Foreign Bible Society. The Heiligenstadt society flourished till 1830 and maintained an existence till 1864, but received its support chiefly from Protestants after the former date. The translation of the New Testament made by J. E. Gossner (q.v.) was also circulated by the English society.

2. France: The **French Bible Society** (London) referred to above began the Bible movement in France, but the outbreak of the Revolution prevented the circulation of French Bibles printed with English money. The **Protestant Bible Society of Paris** was formed in 1818, and received aid from the British and Foreign Bible Society for a time. The subsidy was withdrawn after a few years because the Paris Society included the Apocrypha in its Bibles. The issues of this society in 1906 were 8,061 copies. A sharp controversy among the French Protestants respecting the French version led in 1864 to the formation of the **Bible Society of France**. This society excluded the Apocrypha from its Bibles and held to the version of J. F. Osterwald (q.v.) of which it is now publishing a new revision. It has received aid from the American Bible Society, and it circulates the Bible in the French colonies in Asia and Africa. Its issues in 1906 were 34,556 copies.

3. The Netherlands: The **Netherlands Bible Society** was formed in 1814. Its issues in the year 1904 amounted to 93,977 copies, of which 57,573 copies were sent abroad to the Dutch East Indies, Dutch Guiana, and South Africa. The headquarters of the society are at Heerengracht 366, Amsterdam.

4. Scandinavia: The **Danish Bible Society** was organized in 1814. Its circulation in 1906 amounted to 45,289 copies. The **Norwegian Bible Society** was formed in 1816 under the influence of the British and Foreign Bible Society. Its issues in 1904 were 63,300 copies, of which 751 copies were sent to Denmark, and 11,041 copies to the United States of America. Its total issues in eighty-eight years ending Dec. 31, 1904, were 1,153,260 copies. The headquarters of the society are at Christiania. The **Swedish Bible Society** was organized in 1814. Its circulation in 1906 was 12,414 copies and its total circulation from the beginning, 1,242,515 copies, of which 666 were in the Lapp language.

5. Russia: The **Russian Bible Society with Imperial Sanction** was formed in 1863. It circulates the Bible in Russian and other languages under the supervision of the Holy Synod. Its reports show the contributions of the czar and czarina and the grand dukes, but do not specify clearly the circulation. It makes use of colporteurs and seems to do serious work. A Russian Bible Society formed in 1812 did an important work in Bible translation, but was suppressed by imperial ukase in 1826. The **Russian Evangelical Bible Society** was organized in 1831 for the purpose of circulating the Bible among Lutherans and in the German language. Its circulation in 1904 was 22,219 copies. The **Finnish Bible Society** was formed in 1812 and its issues in 1903 were about 30,000 copies.

6. Switzerland: The **Basel Bible Society**, transferred to Basel from Nuremberg, has been mentioned above (II, 1). Local Bible societies exist in many of the cantons of Switzerland. They seem, however, to be merely agents of distribution receiving Bibles from other societies, notably from the British and Foreign Bible Society. Their circulation is therefore included in that of the other societies. HENRY OTIS DWIGHT.

III. Bible Societies in America.—1. The American Bible Society: The Revolutionary War produced a great scarcity of Bibles in the United States. One year after the Declaration of Independence Congress was memorialized to authorize the printing of an edition of the Bible. This memorial was referred to a committee, who found the difficulties, especially of procuring proper material, type, and paper, to be so great that Congress ordered the importation at its own expense of 20,000 English Bibles from Holland, England, or elsewhere. The scarcity still continuing, in 1782 Congress recommended to the people of the United States an edition of the Bible printed by Thomas Aitken, of Philadelphia, "being satisfied of the care and accuracy of the execution of the work." It was not until 1808 that the first Bible Society was organized in Philadelphia. In 1809 societies were organized in Connecticut, Massachusetts, New York, and New Jersey in the order named and by 1816 there were 128 such societies.

The idea of uniting these societies in one organization was a natural one and was much discussed. The missionary travels of the Rev. Samuel J. Mills (q.v.) in the West and South, reported in religious periodicals, increased the desire for a national organization, which he strongly advocated. On Jan. 1, 1816, Elias Boudinot (q.v.), the president of the New Jersey Bible Society, made a public communication on the subject, and on Jan. 17 he issued a circular letter appointing Wednesday, May 8, 1816, as the time for holding a convention for this purpose in New York. Sixty delegates representing twenty-eight Bible societies (besides several other persons admitted to seats in the convention) met on the day named in the Garden Street Collegiate Reformed Dutch Church, representing the Presbyterian, Congregational, Methodist, Episcopal, Dutch Reformed, and Baptist Churches, and the Society of Friends. The convention was in session for two days, adopted a constitution and in accordance therewith elected managers, who met in the City Hall, May 11, and elected officers, Elias Boudinot being made president.

1. Organization.

Under this constitution "the sole object shall be to encourage a wider circulation of the Holy Scriptures without note or comment" (art. i). The board of managers is composed of thirty-six laymen, one-fourth of whom go out of office every year, but are eligible for reelection. Every clergyman who is a life member may meet and vote with the board of managers, provided he receives no salary or compensation for services from the society. The managers meet regularly every month, consider and act on all matters presented by ten standing committees besides other matters originating in the board itself and report all their proceedings to the annual meeting of the members of the society held on the second Thursday of May and usually in New York.

2. Constitution and Management.

The society was incorporated in 1841. The societies which already existed became for the most part auxiliary to the national organization and in addition many other auxiliary societies were organized under its direction, the number at one time reaching 2,200. Many of these, however, have ceased to exist, the number now being 541. The "Bible House," Astor Place, N. Y., the society's headquarters, was erected in 1852 and was paid for by funds contributed for the special purpose and not from current receipts for benevolent work.

3. Summary of Work.

The ninety-first annual report of the board of managers was presented May 9, 1907. The total cash receipts were $575,820.94. The total issues of that year were 1,910,853, of which 1,010,777 were issued from the Bible House in New York, and 900.076 from the society's agencies abroad, being printed on mission presses in China, Japan, Siam, Syria, and Turkey. The total issues of the society in Bibles, Testaments, and portions amount to 80,420,382 copies, distributed as follows: Bibles 20,293,636 Testaments and portions 58,215,889.

The efforts of the society were at first directed mainly to meeting the needs of the people of the United States, but from the very first it was in spirit and intention a foreign as well as a home mission society. Bibles at the very beginning were supplied to the North-American Indians. The third annual report shows that steps were already taken for sending Spanish Bibles to Buenos Ayres and the next year the society was reaching out to West Africa. In 1836 the first foreign agency was instituted in Constantinople, and in 1864 the agency for the La Plata region in South America.

4. Foreign Work.

During the past thirty years this work has largely increased and regular agencies have been established in Japan, China, Brazil, Mexico, Korea, Cuba, Siam and Laos, Central America, Porto Rico and the Philippines, besides Venezuela and Colombia, where the agencies have been temporarily discontinued. These agencies have distributed a total of 9,453,918 Bibles, Testaments, and portions in China alone. Besides this the society has continually cooperated with missions and missionaries in countries in all quarters of the globe. It has stimulated Bible translation, initiating it in some cases, cooperating with others more frequently and securing needed revisions under its patronage and partly or wholly at its expense. It has been thus interested in about 100 translations and revisions in all.

The labors of the society have been broken twice by serious differences among its friends and supporters. In 1835 missionaries in Burma published at the expense of the society a translation of the New Testament which rendered the Greek word *baptizein* and its cognate terms by the English "immerse" or an equivalent. After much discussion the managers resolved that they felt at liberty "to encourage only such versions as conform in the principle of their translation to the common English Version—at least so far as that all the religious denominations represented in this society can consistently use and circulate such versions in their several schools and communities," and missionary boards were requested in asking aid to state that the versions they proposed to circulate were in accordance with this resolution. The Baptists took offense and a controversy ensued, the consequence of which was the formation of the American and Foreign Bible Society (see below, 2).

5. Controversies.

In 1847 the committee on versions was instructed to undertake a careful collation of different editions of the English Bible with a view to perfecting its text in minutiæ. Their final report, made May 1, 1851, stated that in collating five standard copies of English and American imprint with the original edition of 1611 nearly 24,000 variations were found solely in the text and punctuation, not one of which marred the integrity of the text or affected any doctrine or precept of the Bible. A standard then determined upon with the unanimous approval of the board of managers was accepted generally by the public and for several years Bibles printed accordingly circulated without the slightest objection. But in 1856, and more decidedly in 1857, the right of the society to circulate such an edition was sharply challenged. Considerable public excitement followed; the matter was debated in religious and even secular journals as well as in ecclesiastical bodies, and the board of managers after long consideration, and debate finally took action, Jan. 28, 1858, as follows:

> Resolved, that this society's present standard English Bible be referred to the standing committee on versions for examination; and in all cases where the same differs in the text or its accessories from the Bibles previously published by the society, the committee are directed to correct the same by conforming it to previous editions printed by this society, or by the authorized British presses, reference being also had to the original edition of the translators printed in 1611; and to report such corrections to this board, to the end that a new edition, thus perfected, may be adopted as the standard edition of the society.

The committee reported in 1859 and 1860; and from this "standard edition" all the society's English Bibles are now printed.

The constitution of the society originally restricted it to circulating only "the version now in common use," in the English language. In 1904 at the annual meeting of the society on the recommendation of the board of managers the constitution was amended so as to permit the publication of the Revised Version of the English Bible, either in its British or American form, and under this permission some editions of the American Standard Revised Version are now published by the society under an arrangement with the publishers. JOHN FOX.

2. The American and Foreign Bible Society and the **American Bible Union:** The American and Foreign Bible Society was organized at Philadelphia in April, 1836, by Baptists who felt aggrieved at the action of the American Bible Society concerning the translation of the Greek *baptizein*, referred to above (see III, 1, § 5). Rev. S. H. Cone was made president. The society was declared to be "founded upon the principle that the originals in the Hebrew and Greek are the only authentic standards of the Sacred Scriptures, and that aid for the translating, printing, or distributing of them in foreign languages should be afforded to such versions only as are conformed as nearly as possible to the original text; it being understood that no words are to be *transferred* which are susceptible of being literally *translated*." The constitution adopted declared (art. ii) "that in the distribution of the Scriptures in the English language, the commonly received version shall be used until otherwise directed by the society." Dissatisfaction with this policy led to the secession of certain members and the formation in 1850 of the American Bible Union, which demanded that the principle of circulating "such versions only as are conformed as nearly as possible to the original text" should be applied to the English version, and avowed as its object "to procure and circulate the most faithful versions of the Sacred Scriptures in all languages throughout the world." The Union secured the services of a number of Baptist and other Biblical scholars, especially the Rev. Drs. H. B. Hackett, A. C. Kendrick, and T. J. Conant. The entire New Testament and portions of the Old were revised and published. Italian, Spanish, Chinese (Ningpo colloquial), Siamese, and Sgau-Karen New Testaments were also prepared. The Union ultimately reunited with the American and Foreign Bible Society, and in 1882 the latter passed over its work and good-will to the American Baptist Publication Society (Philadelphia), which since then has performed the duties of the Bible Society, and is carrying on the work of revision inaugurated by the earlier societies. The revision has now (1907) reached the Book of Ezra, and will be completed, it is hoped, by the end of 1908.

3. The Bible Association of Friends in America was organized in 1830. It has been, in the main, a distributing agency, circulating the Scriptures printed by others, but in 1905-06 printed an edition of 2,925 Testaments and Psalms. In 1906 it reported total receipts of $3,930.59 and payments of $2,412.06. Its distribution in that year was 6,534 volumes, of which 2,030 were Bibles. The headquarters are at 207 Walnut Place, Philadelphia, Pa.

BIBLIOGRAPHY: On the general question consult: *Abriss der Geschichte des Ursprunge und Wachsthums der Bibelgesellschaften*, Barmen, 1870; *Summary Notice concerning Bible Societies in General and Those of France in Particular*, from the Fr., Northampton, 1827; W. H. Wyckoff, *A Sketch of the Origin, History of Bible Societies*, New York 1848.

On the BFBS consult: W. Canton, *Hist. of the BFBS*, 2 vols., London, 1904; idem, *Story of the Bible Society*, ib. 1904; J. Owen, *Hist. of the Origin and First Ten Years of the BFBS*, 2 vols., ib. 1816; *Papers Occasioned by the Attempts to Form Auxiliary Bible Societies in Various Parts of the Kingdom*, ib. 1812; *Jubilee Memorial of the BFBS*, ib. 1854; G. Browne, *Hist. of the BFBS*, 2 vols., ib. 1859; *La Société biblique britannique et étrangère, 1804-89. Notice au point de vue historique, philosophique, et religieux*, Nantes, 1889; H. Morris, *Founders and Presidents of the Bible Society*, London, 1895; *Bible House Papers*, ib. 1899 sqq. (in progress); *Behold a Sower. Popular Report of BFBS for 1900-01*, ib. 1902; T. H. Darlow and H. F. Moule, *Catalogue of the Printed Editions of Holy Scripture in the Library of the BFBS*, 2 vols., ib. 1904; T. H. Darlow, *There is a River*, ib. 1906; *Bible Association Reports*. By Helen Plumptre, Worksop, 1843.

The organs of the society are the *Monthly Reporter of the BFBS*, London, 1858-88, succeeded by the *Bible Society Monthly Reporter*, 1889 sqq. The other British Societies issue various publications, such as *Annual Reports*, *Quarterly Records*, and *Occasional Papers*, in which their history may be traced.

For the foreign societies there are also available their reports, besides which the following may be consulted: C. F. Hezekiel, *Geschichte der Cansteinschen Bibel Anstalt*, ed. A. H. Niemeyer, Halle, 1827; O. Bertram, *Geschichte der Cansteinschen Bibelanstalt*, ib. 1863; W. Thilo, *Geschichte der preussischen Haupt-Bibelgesellschaft, 1814-64*, Berlin, 1864; E. Breest, *Die Entwickelung der preussischen Haupt-Bibelgesellschaft, 1864-91*, ib. 1891.

For the American Bible Society consult: *The American Bible Society's Manual, containing a Brief Sketch of the Society*, New York, 1865, revised ed., 1887; W. P. Strickland, *Hist. of the American Bible Society*, ib. 1849; *American Bible Society's Reports*, 1816-71, 4 vols., ib. n.d. (a reprint); *American Bible Society. Report of the Transference of the Library of the Society to the New York Public Library*, ib. 1897. The organ is the *Bible Society Record* (a monthly).

BIBLE TEXT.

I. The Old Testament.—1. The Premasoretic Period: The extant Hebrew text of the Old Testament text is commonly called the Masoretic, to distinguish it from the text of the ancient versions as well as from the Hebrew text of former ages. This Masoretic text does not present the original form but a text which within a certain period was fixed by Jewish scholars as the correct and only authoritative one. When and how this official Masoretic text was fixed was formerly a matter of controversy, especially during the seventeenth century. One party headed by the Buxtorfs (father and son), in the interest of the view of inspiration then prevalent, held to the absolute completeness and infallibility, and hence the exclusive value, of the Masoretic text. They attributed it to Ezra and the men of the Great Synagogue, who, under the inspiration of the Holy Spirit, were supposed to have purified the text from all accumulated error; added the vowel-points, the accents, and other punctuation-marks (thus settling the reading and pronunciation); fixed the canon; made the right division into verses, paragraphs, and books; and, finally, by the providence of God and the care of the Jews, the text thus made was believed to have been kept from all error, and to present the veritable Word of God. This view of the text prevailed especially when Protestant scholasticism was at its height, and may be designated as the orthodox Protestant position. It was opposed by another party headed by Jean Morin and Louis Cappel, who, in the interest of pure historicity or in Antiprotestant polemics, combated these opinions, maintained the later age of the Masoretic text, and sought to vindicate value and usefulness for the old versions and other critical helps. They fell into many errors in respect to the details of the history of the text and overrated the value of Extramasoretic critical helps; but their general view was supported by irresistible arguments and is now universally adopted. This view, instead of deriving the existing text from a gathering of inspired men in Ezra's time, assigns it to a much later date and quite different men, and, instead of absolute completeness, claims for it only a relative one with a higher value than other forms of the text. A glance at the history of the text will show how this agreement has been brought about.

1. The Masoretic Text.

Concerning the oldest history of the text of the Old Testament writings there exists almost no positive information. The books were written probably upon skins, perhaps also on linen; as paper was used from very early times in Egypt, it is possible that it was employed; parchment appears to have been used later. The roll seems to have been the usual form (Ps. xl, 8; Jer. xxxvi, 14 sqq.; Ezek. ii, 9; Zech. v, 1); the pen was a pointed reed (Jer. viii, 8; Ps. xlv, 1); the character was the Old Hebrew, which was almost identical with the Phenician and Moabitic (on the Moabite Stone, q.v.). Specimens of this writing are also preserved in the Siloam inscription (c. 700 B.C.), on gems (of the eighth or seventh century), on coins of the Hasmoneans and those belonging to the time of the Jewish-Roman war, and, in somewhat different form, in Samaritan writings. Like the Phenicians and Moabites, the Hebrews separated the words by a point or stroke, but these signs do not seem to have been used regularly, since the Septuagint often makes word-divisions different from those of the Masoretic text. Jewish tradition mentions several passages in which the separation of words was regarded as doubtful.

2. The Earlier Text.

The difference between ancient and modern texts consisted in this, that the former were written without vowels and accents. The Hebrew writing, like Semitic writing in general, was essentially consonantal; vowels were not written. While the language lived, this occasioned no difficulty to the speakers or readers. No details are at hand concerning the way in which the text was multiplied and preserved; but inasmuch as the writings did not then have in popular estimation the character they came later to possess, it is likely that they were less carefully handled, and that the same amount of pains was not taken in copying them. This statement rests upon the fact that those parts of the Old Testament which we possess in double forms vary in ways that indicate a corruption of the text reaching back to precanonical times when copies were neither made nor corrected so laboriously.

A new epoch commenced after the Exile, when the holy writings were raised to canonical dignity and as holy writings were venerated and handled with ever-increasing care and conscientiousness. This veneration was not accorded to all Biblical writings at once, but only to that part of the canon called the law. The epoch begins with Ezra, and extends to the close of the Talmud, c. 500 A.D. During this period not only were the form of writing and the text fixed, but also the pronunciation and division; in short, the major part of the present Masorah was collected in verbal form. A change of an external kind was the development of a sacred writing, under the influence of the Aramaic character, the so-called "square" or "Assyrian" character. Jewish tradition ascribes the introduction of the square character to Ezra, and calls it expressly an Aramaic writing that the Jews adopted in place of their Hebrew, which they left to the Samaritans. A study of Assyrian, Persian, and Cilician seals and coins, of the Aramaic monuments from the third to the first century B.C., and of the Palmyrene inscriptions from the first to the third century A.D. has permitted the tracing of the development of the present Hebrew alphabet through a thousand years, back to the eighth century. Ezra, therefore, may have influenced the use of the Aramaic alphabet, but the square character was not developed in his day, nor for centuries afterward; nor was the Aramaic alphabet then used outside of the narrow circle of the scribes. For not only did the Samaritans retain the ancient script for their Pentateuch, but among the Jews also it must have been used for a long time, since it is found on coins down to the time of Bar Kokba. Matt. v, 18 proves that the Aramaic writing had become popular by the time that Gospel was written, since in the ancient Hebrew the letter "*yodh*" was by no means the smallest. Taking all in all, it may be assumed with certainty that the use of the new alphabet in Bible-manuscripts of the last Prechristian centuries was general, a result which is also confirmed by a careful examination of the Septuagint with reference to the manuscripts used by the translators (especially must this have been the case with the Tetragrammaton retained in many copies of the Greek translation, which was no doubt written in the Aramaic script, since it was read erroneously by the Christians). Considering this development it may be assumed that the latest Old Testament writings were written, not in the ancient Hebrew but in Aramaic, by the authors themselves. After the Aramaic writing was once in use among the Jews, it soon took the form in which we now have it. The descriptions which Jerome and the Talmud give of the different letters fully harmonize with the form which is still found in manuscripts. The minute rules laid down by the Talmud as to calligraphy and orthography made further development of the square writing impossible, and therefore the writing of the manuscripts varies scarcely at all through centuries (excepting perhaps that the German and Polish Jews have the so-called *Tam* script, which is somewhat angular, whereas the Spanish Jews have the *Welsh* or more rounded script).

3. Change in Style of Writing.

The veneration shown for the canonical writings during this period naturally led to a greater care in treatment of them and above all to perception of the necessity of critically fixing the text. As soon as the ancient writings obtained canonical authority, were used in divine service, and became the standard of doctrine and life, the necessity of having one standard text naturally asserted itself. The preparation of such a text began with the law; the other two divisions (the prophets and the hagiographa) became authoritative only in the course of centuries (see CANON OF SCRIPTURE, I), and naturally their text did not receive attention in the earlier period. However, criticism during that period was of little value. There is no doubt that faithful and correct copies existed, especially of such books as were publicly read, but this could not prevent errors and mistakes from creeping into copies which were generally circulated. When Josephus (*Contra Apion*, I, viii) and Philo (cf. Eusebius, *Præparatio evangelica*, VIII, vi, 7) speak of the great care bestowed by the Jews upon their sacred writings, this can not be referred to earlier centuries, and concerns more the contents than the linguistic minutiæ of the text. In the oldest critical documents—the Samaritan Pentateuch and the Septuagint—there is evidence (about 500–100 B.C.) to show that the manuscripts most approved and most widely diffused contained many verbal differences. And these variations are not to be charged, as was formerly done, to carelessness or wilfulness on the part of the Hellenistic Jews and Samaritans, but are explained by the lesser importance attached to exact uniformity of text and to the existence of mistakes in the current copies. And when the Septuagint and the Samaritan Pentateuch agree in good readings, and still oftener in bad ones, against the Masoretic text, it may be concluded that these readings were spread by many copies current among the Palestinian Jews, and are therefore not to be regarded as offensive. But after the destruction of Jerusalem, when Judaism was subject to the authority of the rabbis, it became possible to prepare a uniform standard text, although this idea was not realized until many generations had worked upon it. The Greek versions of the second century had already fewer variations from the Masoretic text. Still nearer the latter text is the Hebrew text of Origen and Jerome. The Talmud itself bears witness, by the agreement of its Biblical quotations with the Masoretic text, that the consonantal text was practically finished before the Talmudic era closed. It is not possible to say upon what principles the text was treated; but the way in which the custodians presented the individuality of the several authors, books, and periods is remarkable, and proves that intentional and arbitrary changes of the text were not made by these critics. That they changed passages for dogmatic, especially for Antichristian, reasons, as has sometimes been asserted, has long ago been acknowledged to be a

4. Attempts to Fix the Text.

baseless accusation. Where they mention changes, they make clear that they followed the testimony of manuscripts, the number of which was probably not very great. The fact that in the first centuries after Christ the text approximates our present Masoretic reading shows that a certain recension became authoritative which was possible only after a certain manuscript had been taken as the norm. Of such a standard codex, copies could easily be made, or one could correct his own copies in accordance with it. Scholars like Olshausen and Lagarde speak therefore of some such archetype, which was slavishly followed in every respect. The critical apparatus of the time is concealed in dissociated fragments in the later Masorah, but can not be separated from the other matter. The Talmud and the older midrashim allow a little insight into the critical efforts of the time. Thus mention is made of the "corrections of the scribes," of the "removals of the scribes" (meaning that in five passages a falsely introduced "and" was removed), and of the points in the Hebrew text over certain words to show that these words were critically suspected, such as the inverted "*nun*," Num. x, 35, and the three kinds of reading (*keri*; see KERI AND KETHIBH), viz., "read but not written," "written but not read," and "read [one way] but written [another]." The three kinds of reading have, it is true, for the most part only exegetical value; e.g., they give the usual instead of the unusual grammatical forms, show where one must understand or omit a word, or where the reader should use a euphemistic expression for the coarse one in the text; they are therefore scholia upon the text. It is possible that these "readings" are also fragments of the critical apparatus. However this may be, it is evident that at that period the text was fixed and that the matter in question concerned only subordinate details of the text.

The development of the pronunciation or of the vocalization and the division of words, verses, and sections kept pace with the settlement of the text. That the ancient writing had no vowel-points has already been stated; but even during this entire period to the close of the Talmud the sacred text was without vowels and other points. The old versions, particularly the Greek, and Josephus depart so widely from the Masoretic text that they could not possibly have used the present pointed text. The expedient which charges the translators with these differences is of no avail, since it is not any one version which alone shows such differences; they all differ. Origen, too, published a Hebrew text in the Hexapla which differed from the Masoretic. Jerome knew nothing about vowel-points, not even the diacritical point making the difference between "s" and "sh." The Talmud and the modern ecclesiastical or ritual manuscripts of the Jews present an unpointed text. There is no doubt that, as Elias Levita stated, the Masoretic system of punctuation is of later origin, and that during this entire period the sacred text was without points. But this does not mean that during the same period the reading of the unvoweled text was still unsettled among the Jews; it must rather be assumed that with the official fixing of the text there was developed also a certain mode of understanding and reading it. Of course time was required to bring it into vogue; but before the end of the period it was so firmly established that Jerome's pronunciation differed very little from the Masoretic, and he was so sure of its correctness that he appeals to it against the text of the versions; and the Talmud gives it throughout correctly. Before the Masoretes the pronunciation was fixed, not yet written, but handed down by word of mouth, although some scholars may have used signs in their books to assist their memory.

5. The Pronunciation Fixed, but the Text Still Unvocalized.

Closely connected and mutually dependent were pronunciation and the division of words. The latter must have been finally settled at this period. The sign of division was the small space between words. The final letters, being limited in number, can not be regarded as word-separating signs. Jerome used a text with a division of words and knew the final letters; in the Talmud, *Menahot* 30a states how large must be the space between the words; the synagogue-scrolls, though still without vowels, have nevertheless the division by spaces, following the custom of the ancient manuscripts from Talmudic time; and the fact that a number of "readings" correct the traditional division of words speaks again in favor of the high antiquity of the division of words in the present texts.

6. Word-Division.

The division into verses is by no means contemporary in origin with the vocalization, but much earlier. The verse-division depends in poetry upon the parallelism, in prose upon the division of sentences and clauses. That the latter were not marked in oldest times is certain; in poetical texts the members may have been distinguished either by space or by breaks of the line. This mode of writing poetical texts was formerly general, and is found in the older Hebrew manuscripts; for the poetical texts, Ex. xv; Deut. xxxii; Judges v; and II Sam. xxii, it is even prescribed (*Shabbat* 103b; *Sopherim* xii), and is therefore still customary. With the introduction of the Masoretic accents, poetry was written close, like prose. This verse-division was taught in the schools; but no rules are given for its writing, nor did any punctuation-marks indicate it in this period.

7. Division into Verses.

Earlier than the division into verses is that into larger or smaller sections; these were more necessary for the understanding of the Scriptures and for their reading in divine worship. Perhaps some of them were in the original text. The sections of the law were at least Pretalmudic; for they are mentioned in the Mishnah and frequently in the Gemara; in the latter they are traced to Mosaic origin; in *Shabbat* 103b, *Menahot* 30 care is enjoined as to the sections in copying the law, and therefore they occur also in synagogue-rolls. They are indicated by spacing; the larger sections by leaving the remainder of the line at

8. Division into Sections.

their close unfilled, the next great section beginning with a new line, on which account they were called "open"; the smaller sections were separated from each other by only a small space, and were therefore called "closed" or "connected." Thus not only the law but also the other two parts of the canon were divided. For the division of the whole canon, and the arrangement of the books, see CANON OF SCRIPTURE, I.

From what has been said, it follows that the reading of the text, the vocalization, the division into words, verses, and sections depend upon the gradual settlement by the scribes; their reading can claim neither infallibility nor any absolutely binding power; and though their labor betrays a thorough and correct understanding of the text, the necessity may yet arise when the exegete must deviate from tradition. Extraordinary pains were taken to perpetuate in its purity the text thus divided and vocalized. Signs of this care, such as the rules for calligraphy and for writing the extraordinary points, have already been mentioned. The Posttalmudic treatises *Masseket sopherim* and *Masseket sepher torah* contain full details for copying. Nevertheless fluctuations are met with in the Masoretic period, and it must therefore be assumed that learned labor had not yet covered all details or made final settlement.

2. The Masoretic Period: The third period of the textual history is usually reckoned as extending from the sixth until the eleventh Christian century (when Jewish learning was transferred from the East to North Africa and Spain); it embraces the age of the Masoretes proper, and has for the Bible text in general the same importance as the Talmudic period had for the law. The efforts of the scholars to fix the reading and understanding of the sacred text were overshadowed somewhat by the study of the Talmud. After the close of the Talmud the work was resumed and cultivated in Babylonia and Palestine (at Tiberias).

1. The Masoretes.

In both schools the work of former generations was continued; but the Palestinians, who acted more independently than the more Talmudically inclined Babylonians, finally got the victory over the Babylonian school. In both schools they were no longer satisfied with a mere oral transmission of rules and regulations, but committed them to writing. There is no continuous history of the men of the Masorah and of the progress of their work preserved; but the marginal notes in ancient Bible-manuscripts and the fragments of other works show that the oldest Masoretes can be traced back to the eighth century. The main effort of this period (as the name *Masorah*, "tradition," indicates; see MASORAH) was to collect and to write down the exegetico-critical material of the former period, and this makes sufficiently clear the one part of their work. But the Masoretes also added some new matter. Anxiously following the footsteps of the older critics in their effort to fix and to guard the traditional text, they laid down more minute rules of a linguistic and grammatical character, and in this respect a great part of the contents of the Masorah is indeed new.

They took the consonantal *textus receptus* just as it stood, and finally settled it in the minutest details, as is seen from the variants which became a matter of controversy between the East and the West, the Babylonians and the Palestinians, which to the number of 216 Jacob ben Hayyim published for the first time in the second edition of the Bomberg Rabbinic Bible; these have reference mostly to the vowel-points. This list of variants, as is now known, is by no means complete. They also appended critical notes to the text, in part derived from the Talmudic period, in part new (especially the "grammatical conjectures"), showing that where, according to the grammar and the genius of the language, one should expect another reading, nevertheless the text must stand. Finally the great majority of the alternative "readings" date from the Masoretes.

2. Their Work.

The Masoretes fixed the reading of the text by the introduction of the vowel-signs, the accents, and the signs which affect the reading of the consonants (*daghesh, mappiḳ, raphe*, and the diacritical point to distinguish between the letters "*sin*" and "*shin*"). The pronunciation they thus brought about was no invention, but embodied the current tradition. Nevertheless, one can not accept every Masoretic reading as infallible and unchangeable, especially when one considers that the tradition no doubt often fluctuated and that with such fluctuation the less correct reading may often have come into the text. Besides the system found in the majority of manuscripts, there exists another which has only recently become known called the "superlinear" system, because the vowel-signs are placed above the letters; this is found in some Babylonian and South Arabian manuscripts. The same is also the case with the accents.

The division of the text into verses, introduced by the Masoretes, was neither Babylonian nor Palestinian, but one which the Masoretes themselves seem to have established. At the beginning of this period the end of the verses was marked by *soph pasuḳ*, and, when the accents were introduced, by *silluḳ* besides. The old sections were retained, though not recognized as entirely correct, and the old traditional sign for the section, the smaller spacing (the little ס in printed texts), was respected. The closed sections were marked in manuscripts and prints by a ס, the open ones by a פ in the empty space before the initial word. In addition there were introduced the Babylonian division into sections or *parashiyoth* (in the law) and *haphtaroth* (in the prophets), for Sabbath public reading. As these sections generally agree with the beginning and the end of an open or closed section, they were marked by a threefold פ [i.e., פ פ פ] or ס [ס ס ס] in the empty space before the beginning.

But even these efforts could not entirely remove variations. Hence, before the end of this period, the learned either attempted to find out by an elaborate comparison the correct punctuation and to fix it, or marked the important variations in the punctuation, or added a caution to each apparently strange and yet correct punctuation. The greater mass of notes which the Masoretes added to the text relate to these matters. Besides some

3. Codices. other Masoretic manuscripts of the Bible which are quoted in the Masoretic notes of the codices or in the writings of the rabbis as authoritative, such as the *codex Hilleli*, the Jericho-Pentateuch, and others, two codices were especially famous as model codices of the Old Testament, the codex of Naphtali (Moses ben David ben Naphtali) and the codex of Asher (Aaron ben Moses ben Asher), both from the first half of the tenth century (Aaron lived at Tiberias, Moses in Babylon; but the latter can not be regarded as a representative of the "Babylonian" text-tradition.) They were once much examined by scholars; many of their variants are noted in the Masoretic Bible-manuscripts; a list of 864 (better 867) variants, which refer almost exclusively to vowels and accents, has been published after Jacob ben Hayyim in Bomberg's and the other Rabbinic Bibles, as well as in the sixth volume of the London Polyglot; but these variants are neither correct nor complete. On the codex of Asher finally rests the whole Masoretic text of the Occidentals; of the variant readings comparatively few were received into it.

As the older scribes had already shown extraordinary solicitude for the preservation of the text and its correct reading by counting its sections, verses, words, letters, and by noting where and how often and when certain words, letters, or anomalies occur in the Bible, which verse is the longest and which the shortest, and like minutiæ, the Masoretes of course continued this work, wrote it down, and preserved it in manuscripts.

The punctuation of the text as developed by the Masoretes proved itself so useful and met so well an essential need of those later times that it soon went over into manuscripts and, with the exception of synagogue-manuscripts, almost none were written which did not contain either the pointed text alone or the pointed beside the unpointed. The other Masoretic material was written either beside and below the text of the Biblical books on the margins and at the close of the same, or in separate masorah-collections (see MASORAH).

3. The Postmasoretic Period: After the completion of the Masoretic textual work and the collection of the notes having reference to it, no essential change was made in the text; consequently this period is the time of the faithful preservation, multiplication, and circulation of the Masoretic text. An essential innovation was the introduction of the now customary division into

1. The Chapter-Division. chapters, which was invented by Stephen Langton at the beginning of the thirteenth century, and applied to the Vulgate. Isaac ben Nathan adopted it for his Hebrew concordance (1437-38, published 1523), on which occasion the verses of the chapters were also numbered. The chapter-division was first applied to the Hebrew in the second edition of Bomberg's Bible, 1521; the numbering of verses was first adopted for the Sabionetta Pentateuch, 1557, and that of the whole Bible in Athias's edition of 1661 (see below, III, §§ 1-2).

Another feature of this period is that a sufficient number of manuscripts is preserved to give an immediate knowledge of the text. The Hebrew Bible-manuscripts may be divided into two classes, the public or sacred and the private or common. The first were synagogue-rolls, and have been prepared so carefully

2. Old Testament Manuscripts. and watched so closely that the intrusion of variants and mistakes was hardly possible. But they contain only the Pentateuch or the Pentateuch with the five Megilloth or "Rolls" (i.e., Song of Solomon, Ruth, Lamentations, Ecclesiastes, Esther), and the haphtaroth (see above, 2, § 1) in the text of the Masoretes without their additions. These manuscripts are, for the most part, of recent origin, although antique in form, being written on leather or parchment. The private manuscripts are written on the same material, and also upon paper in book form, with the Masoretic additions more or less complete. It is often difficult, indeed impossible, to determine the date and country of these manuscripts. But none of those now known are really very old. The oldest authentic date is 916 A.D. for the codex containing the prophets with Babylonian punctuation, and 1009 A.D. for an entire Hebrew Bible, both of which belong to the Firkowitsch collection in the Imperial Library at St. Petersburg. According to the most recent investigation the MS. orient. 4445 in the British Museum (containing Gen. xxv, 20-Deut. i, 33) may be a little older. As a rule the oldest manuscripts are the more accurate. The number of errors that crept in, especially in private manuscripts, which were prepared without any official oversight, awakened solicitude and led to well-directed efforts to get a pure text by means of collating good Masorah-manuscripts (cf. B. Kennicott, *Dissertatio generalis*, Oxford, 1780, l-lvi; J. G. Eichhorn, *Einleitung*, Leipsic, 1803, 136b). In this line the labors of Meïr ha-Levi of Toledo (d. 1244) in his work on the Pentateuch called "The Masorah, the Hedge of the Law" (Florence, 1750; Berlin, 1761) are celebrated.

The art of printing opened a way of escape from copyists' errors, and it was taken very early. The Psalter was printed first, at Bologna in 1477 [on the earlier prints, cf. B. Pick, *History of the Printed Editions of the Old Testament*, in *Hebraica*, ix (1892-1893), 47-116], the first complete Bible at Soncino

3. The Printed Text. in 1488; Gerson's edition (the edition which Luther used for his translation) followed (Brescia, 1494). Substantially the same text is contained in the first edition of Bomberg's Rabbinic Bible (1517; see BIBLES, RABBINIC), also in the editions of Robert Stephens (1539 sqq.) and of Sebastian Münster. The second independent edition derived from manuscripts is that in the Complutensian Polyglot (1514-17; see BIBLES, POLYGLOT, I). The text has vowels but no accents. The third important recension is contained in the *Biblia Rabbinica Bombergiana, ed. II., cura R. Jacob ben Chajim* (Venice, 1525-26); it is edited according to the

Masorah, which the editor first revised, and contains the entire Masoretic and Rabbinic apparatus. It is more or less reproduced in prints published during the sixteenth and in the beginning of the seventeenth centuries. Besides these original recensions, editions were published having a mixed text; the Hebrew text of the Antwerp Polyglot (1569–72), which is followed by the small editions of Plantin, the Paris and London Polyglots, and the editions of Reineccius, is based upon that of the Complutensian and Bomberg. Another recension is represented in the editions of Elias Hutter (1587), Buxtorf, and Joseph Athias with preface by J. Leusden (1661 sqq.), for which some very ancient manuscripts were collated. Athias's edition became also the basis of later editions like that of Jablonski (1699), Van der Hooght (1705), Opitz (1709), J. H. Michaelis (1720), Hahn (1832), and Theile (1849).

None of these editions presents the Masoretic text in its original form. The large collections of variants by B. Kennicott, *Vetus Testamentum Hebraicum cum variis lectionibus* (2 vols., Oxford, 1776–80), more especially by De Rossi, *Variæ lectiones Veteris Testamenti* (4 vols., Parma, 1784–88) and *Supplementa ad varias sacri textus lectiones* (1798), are valuable for some Extramasoretic readings which they offer, but they are less valuable for critical purposes. More important for text-critical purposes are (besides the work of Meïr ha-Levi, ut sup.) the "Light of the Law" of Menahem de Lonzano (Venice, 1618) and particularly the critical commentary on the Old Testament by Solomon Minorzi (Mantua, 1742–44; Vienna, 1813), the works of Wolf ben Samson Heidenheim, and especially the thorough work on the Masorah by S. Frensdorff (*Massora magna*, part I, Hanover, 1876, and *Oklah we-Oklah*, 1864).

4. Critical Works and Commentaries.

Of great service were the publication of the works of the oldest Jewish grammarians and lexicographers and the discovery of fragments and publication of codices like that on the prophets of the year 916 (published by Strack, *Prophetarum posteriorum codex Babylonicus Petropolitanus*, St. Petersburg, 1876). The fruits of these preliminary works are contained in the correct editions of the Masoretic text by Baer and Ginsburg. Baer, who was assisted by Delitzsch, published the Old Testament with the exception of Exodus, Leviticus, Numbers, and Deuteronomy [both editors died without completing their work]. Ginsburg's edition is entitled *The New Massoretico-Critical Text of the Hebrew Bible* [2 vols., London, 1894. It should be studied with the same author's indispensable *Introduction to the Massoretico-critical Edition of the Hebrew Bible* (London, 1897)].

Valuable as such correct editions of the Masoretic text are, they represent only a single recension, whose source is the *textus receptus* mentioned above, which was fixed in the first Christian centuries. With this recension the text-critical and exegetical treatment of the Old Testament can not be satisfied. Before the received text was made canonical there existed different forms of the text, which in many cases stood nearer to the original than that sanctioned by the Jews. The main witness here is the Septuagint, a correct edition of which is an absolutely necessary though extremely difficult task. But Old Testament textual criticism can not be satisfied with a comparison even with this older form of the text. In many cases the corruption of the text is so old that only a criticism both cautious and bold can approximate to the genuine text. In modern times some very important contributions have been made, such as J. Olshausen, *Emendationen zum Alten Testament* (Kiel, 1826); idem, *Beiträge zur Kritik des überlieferten Textes im Buche Genesis* (1870); J. Wellhausen, *Text der Bücher Samuelis* (Göttingen, 1871); F. Baethgen, *Zu den Psalmen*, in *JPT* (1882); C. H. Cornill, *Das Buch des Propheten Ezechiel* (Leipsic, 1886); S. R. Driver, *Notes on the Hebrew Text of the Books of Samuel* (London, 1890); A. Klostermann, *Die Bücher Samuelis und der Könige* (Munich, 1887), idem, *Deutero-Jesaia* (Munich, 1893); G. Beer, *Der Text des Buches Hiob* (part i, Marburg, 1895); the *Sacred Books of the Old Testament* (the so-called Polychrome or Rainbow Bible), ed. P. Haupt (Baltimore, London, and Leipsic, 1894 sqq.); and Kettel's edition, Leipsic, 1905–06. (F. Buhl.)

Bibliography: Besides the introductions to the Old Testament (especially of J. G. Eichhorn, 4th ed., Göttingen, 1823–25; W. M. L. de Wette, 8th ed. by E. Schrader, pp. 111–156, Berlin, 1869; C. H. Cornill, §§ 49–53, Freiburg, 1905; F. E. König, §§ 3–30, 92, Bonn, 1893; C. H. H. Wright, London, 1891, and W. H. Bennett, ib. 1900) and the works mentioned in the text consult: J. Morinus, *Exercitationum biblicarum de Hebræi Græcique textus sinceritate libri duo*, Paris, 1669; L. Capellus, *Critica sacra*, Paris, 1650, new edition with notes by Vogel and Scharfenberg, Halle, 1775–86; H. Hody, *De bibliorum textibus originalibus*, Oxford, 1705; H. Hupfeld, in *TSK*, 1830, 1837; A. Geiger, *Urschrift und Uebersetzungen der Bibel*, Breslau, 1857; L. Loew, *Beiträge zur jüdischen Alterthumskunde*, Leipsic, 1870 (deals with materials and products of writing); H. L. Strack, *Prolegomena critica in Vetus Testamentum Hebraicum*, Leipsic, 1873 (very full upon extant and lost MSS., and on the testimony of the Talmud to the text); A. Kuenen, *Les Origines du texte masorétique* (from the Dutch), Paris, 1875; *Palæographical Society, Oriental Series, Facsimiles of MSS. and Inscriptions*, London, 1875–83 (deals with many important codices of the O. T.); A. Harkavy, *Neuaufgefundene hebräische Bibelhandschriften*, St. Petersburg, 1884 (characterizes fifty-one Hebrew MSS. and fragments); V. Ryssel, *Untersuchungen über die Textgestalt und die Echtheit des Buches Micha*, Leipsic, 1887 (198 pages concern the text); G. C. Workman, *The Text of Jeremiah, a Critical Investigation of the Greek and Hebrew*, Edinburgh, 1889; T. K. Abbott, *Essays chiefly on the Original Texts of the Old and New Testaments*, London, 1891 (on Masoretic and Premasoretic text); F. Buhl, *Kanon und Text des Alten Testaments*, Leipsic, 1891, Eng. transl., Edinburgh, 1892 (useful for beginners); A. Loisy, *Histoire critique du texte et des versions de la Bible*, 2 vols., Paris, 1892–95; F. G. Kenyon, *Our Bible and the Ancient MSS., Being a History of the Text and its Translations*, London, 1896; W. A. Copinger, *The Bible and its Transmission*, . *View of the Hebrew and Greek Texts*, London, 1897; E. Kautzsch, *Abriss der Geschichte des alttestamentlichen Schrifttums*, in appendix to his edition of *Die heilige Schrift*, Freiburg, 1896, Eng. transl. as a separate work, New York, 1899; T. H. Weir, *A Short History of the Hebrew Text of the Old Testament*, London, 1899; R. Kittel, *Ueber die Notwendigkeit und Möglichkeit einer neuen Ausgabe der hebräischen Bibel*, Leipsic, 1902; P. Kahle, *Der masoretische Text des alten Testaments nach der Ueberlieferung der babylonischen Juden*, Leipsic, 1902; T. K. Cheyne, *Critica biblica*, parts 1–5, London, 1903–1905; F. W. Mozley, *Psalter of the Church; Septuagint Psalms Compared with the Hebrew*, ib. 1905. On the ancient Hebrew and square writing consult: D. von Muralt, *Bei-*

träge zur hebräischen Paläographie und zur Geschichte der Punktuation, in *TSK*, 1874; S. R. Driver, *Notes on the Hebrew Text of the Books of Samuel*, pp. xi–xxxv, London, 1890; Vollers, in *ZATW*, 1883, pp. 229 sqq.; L. Blau, *Zur Einleitung in die heilige Schrift*, pp. 48–80, Strasburg, 1894; R. Butin, *The Ten Nequdoth of the Torah; or the Meaning and Purpose of the Extraordinary Points of the Pentateuch*, Baltimore, 1906 (an important and scientific discussion of textual critical value). On the Masoretic material in the Talmud and Midrash consult: H. L. Strack, *Prolegomena critica in Vetus Testamentum*, ut sup.; L. Blau, *Masoretische Untersuchungen*, Strasburg, 1891; idem, *Zur Einleitung in die heilige Schrift*, 100 sqq., ut sup. On the vowels and accents (especially on the superlinear system) cf. Strack's edition of the Babylonian codex of the prophets, p. vii, ut sup.; idem, *Zeitschrift für die gesammte lutherische Theologie und Kirche*, 1877, pp. 17–52; idem, in *Wissenschaftliche Jahresberichte über die morgenländischen Studien*, 1879, p. 124; J. Derenbourg, in *Revue critique*, 1879, pp. 453 sqq.; W. Wickes, *A Treatise on the Accentuation of the Three Poetical Books*, 1881; *A Treatise on the Accentuation of the twenty-one so-called Prose-Books*, pp. 142 sqq., London, 1887; G. F. Moore, in *Proceedings of the American Oriental Society*, 1888; D. S. Margoliouth, *The Superlinear Punctuation*, in *PSBA*, 1893, pp. 164–205; A. Büchler, *Untersuchungen zur Entstehung und Entwickelung der hebräischen Accente*, Vienna, 1892. On the division into sections, chapters, etc., cf. *REJ*. iii, 282 sqq., vi, 122 sqq., 250 sqq., vii, 146 sqq.; Theodor, in *Monatsschrift für Geschichte und Wissenschaft des Judenthums*, 1885, 1886, 1887; O. Schmid, *Ueber verschiedene Eintheilungen der heiligen Schrift*, Graz, 1891. The catalogues of Hebrew MSS. are mentioned in H. L. Strack, *Prolegomena*, pp. 29–33, 119–121, ut sup.; idem, in *Einleitung in das A. T.*, p. 182, Munich, 1898; and with special fulness in Ginsburg, *Introduction*, ut sup.

II. The New Testament.—1. History of the Written Text: The autographs of the New Testament very early disappeared, owing to the constant use of the perishable papyrus; for this appears to have been the material (II John 12). If they were really not in the handwriting of the apostles, but in that of their amanuenses, as Paul's Epistles generally were (Rom. xvi, 22; II Thess. iii, 17), it is easier to account for the phenomenon. The papyrus rolls preserved to the present day were never much used; indeed, the most of them have been found in sarcophagi, and so, of course, were never used at all.

1. The Autographs of the New Testament Books.

The ink was lampblack mixed with gum dissolved in water, copperas (sulphate of iron) being sometimes added. The pen was of reed (*calamus*). The writing was entirely in uncials (capitals), with no separation of the words (except rarely to indicate the beginning of a new paragraph), no breathings, accents, or distinction of initial letters, and few, if any, marks of punctuation. The evangelists may have denominated their compositions "Gospels," although Justin regularly speaks of the "Memoirs of the Apostles"; but all addition to the name is later, and presupposes a collection of the Gospels. In the case of the Epistles the brief address, e.g., "To the Romans," was probably added by the original sender, and other marks of genuineness given (cf. II Thess. iii, 17). The Muratorian Canon (second half of the second century; see MURATORIAN CANON) calls Acts and the Apocalypse by these names, and so proves the early use of these designations. The designation "Catholic (i.e., General) Epistle" is first met with at the close of the second century (Apollonius, in Eusebius, *Hist. eccl.*, V, xviii, 5, where the First Epistle of John is probably meant). The application and limiting of the term to the whole of the present collection is of later date; for even in the third and fourth century it was customary to give this term to epistles, like that of Barnabas or those of Dionysius of Corinth, which were not specially addressed.

The external history of the New Testament text for a thousand years prior to the invention of printing can be traced by means of manuscripts. Before the formal close of the canon (end of fourth century) there were probably few single manuscripts of the entire New Testament.

2. The Manuscripts.

Of the three thousand known manuscripts of the New Testament, only about thirty include all the books. Some of those of the fourth and fifth century now preserved contain not only the Greek Old Testament (א, A, B, C), but also writings which, though not canonical, were read in churches and studied by catechumens. Thus, attached to the *Codex Sinaiticus* (א) were the Epistle of Barnabas and the Shepherd of Hermas; to the *Codex Alexandrinus* (A), two "epistles" ascribed to Clement of Rome (q.v.) and the so-called *Psalterium Salomonis*. The four Gospels were most frequently copied, the Pauline Epistles oftener than the Catholic Epistles or the Acts, least often the Apocalypse. The Gospels were usually arranged in the present order, then came the Pauline Epistles, the Acts, and the Catholic Epistles; the Apocalypse always last. The arrangement of the Epistles differed; indeed, there was no model. (On the various arrangements cf. C. A. Credner, *Geschichte des neutestamentlichen Kanons*, ed. G. Volkmar, Berlin, 1860; C. R. Gregory, *Prolegomena*, Leipsic, 1884, pp. 131 sqq.; T. Zahn, *Geschichte des neutestamentlichen Kanons*, Erlangen, 1883, ii, 343 sqq.)

After papyrus had gone out of use, parchment or vellum came in and was used from the fourth to the eleventh century; then came in cotton paper, and afterward linen paper (cf. W Wattenbach, *Das Schriftwesen im Mittelalter*, Leipsic, 1896, pp. 139 sqq.). The growing scarcity of parchment led to the reuse of the old skins, the former writing being erased or washed off; and unfortunately it oftener happened that it was a Biblical manuscript which was thus turned into a patristic one than the reverse. Such manuscripts are termed *Codices palimpsesti* (palimpsests) or *rescripti*.

3. Their Material and Form.

By the use of chemicals the original text has often been recovered in modern times. The most famous New Testament palimpsest is the *Codex Ephraemi* (C), of the fifth century, rewritten upon in the twelfth. As papyrus disappeared from use, the book form was generally substituted for the rolls, in manuscripts written on parchment or paper. The books were mostly made up of quaternions, i.e., quires of four sheets, doubled so as to make sixteen pages, less frequently of five, though later quires of six sheets were common. The division of the page into columns was at first retained, two being the usual number (e.g., *Cod. Alex.*); but in many manuscripts (e.g., *Cod. Ephraemi*) the lines ran across the page. [Exceptionally, א has four columns, B three.] From the seventh and eighth centuries the present accents were more or less used, but very arbitrarily and irregularly. The uncials gradually changed their earlier simple round or square forms, and from the tenth century yielded to the cursives. The earliest punctuation was by means of a blank space and a simple point. Euthalius, a deacon in Alexandria, in the year 458 published an edition of the Epistles of Paul, and soon after of the Acts and Catholic Epistles, written stichometrically, i.e., in single lines containing only so many words as could be read, consistently with the sense, at a single inspiration. This mode of writing was used long before in copying the poetical books of the Old Testament. It involved, however, a great waste of parchment, so that, in manuscripts of the New Testament, it was superseded after a few centuries by punctuation-marks.

Divisions of the text were early made for various purposes. In the third century Ammonius of Alexandria (q.v.) prepared a Harmony of the Gospels, taking the text of Matthew as the basis.

4. The Ammonian Sections.

Eusebius of Cæsarea, in the early part of the fourth century, availing himself of the work of Ammonius, divided the text of each Gospel into sections, the length of which, varying greatly (in John xix, 6 there are three, and in twenty-four other instances two, in a single verse), was determined solely by their relation of parallelism or similarity to passages in one or more of the other Gospels, or by their having no parallel. These sections (often erroneously ascribed to Ammonius) were then numbered consecutively in the margin of the Gospel in black ink; Matthew having 355, Mark 233 (not 236), Luke 342, and John 232. They were distributed by Eusebius into ten tables or canons prefixed to the Gospels, and containing the sections corresponding in—

I. Matthew, Mark, Luke, John, 71.
II. Matthew, Mark, Luke, 111.
III. Matthew, Luke, John, 22.
IV. Matthew, Mark, John, 26.
V. Matthew, Luke, 82.
VI. Matthew, Mark, 47
VII. Matthew, John, 7.
VIII. Luke, Mark, 14.
IX. Luke, John, 21.
X. Sections peculiar to Matthew 62, Mark 21, Luke 71, John 97

Under the number of each section in the margin of the several Gospels was written in red ink the number of the canon or table to which it belonged. On turning to its place in this table, the number of the corresponding section or sections in the other Gospels stands with it, so that the parallel passages may readily be found. For example, the first verse of Matt. iv forms the fifteenth Eusebian section; the number two under this refers to the second canon or table, where it appears that section fifteen in Matthew corresponds to six in Mark, and fifteen in Luke; i.e., to Mark i, 12, and Luke iv, 1. In some manuscripts the parallel sections are indicated at the bottom of the page. They thus correspond to our marginal references. Cf. Eusebius, *Epist. ad Carpianum;* J. Burgon, *The Last Twelve Verses of S. Mark* (London, 1871), pp. 295 sqq.

Wholly different in character and purpose from the Eusebian sections, and probably older, is a division of the Gospels into sections called *titloi*, also *kephalaia majora* (in Latin manuscripts, *breves*), found in most manuscripts from the Alexandrine and the Ephraem (A, C) of the fifth century

5. Early Divisions of the Text.

onward. Of these sections Matthew contains 68, Mark 48, Luke 83, John 18. The numbers by which they are designated in the margin of manuscripts refer to the titles describing their contents at the top or bottom of the page, or in a list prefixed to each Gospel, or often in both places. A certain portion at the beginning of each Gospel is not numbered; for example, the first chapter in Matthew corresponds with our chap. ii, 1–15, and is entitled *peri tōn magōn*, "Concerning the Magi." There is a similar division in the Acts and Epistles, to which Euthalius (about 458 A.D.), though not its inventor, gave wide currency by his stichometric edition of these books. The Apocalypse was divided by Andrew, bishop of Cæsarea in Cappadocia (about 500 A.D.), into twenty-four *logoi*, or chapters, and each of these chapters into three *kephalaia*, or sections, the former number answering to the twenty-four elders spoken of in the book (Rev. iv, 4); the latter suggested by the threefold division of human nature into body, soul, and spirit (comp. I Thess. v, 23), as the author himself declares. In the Vatican manuscript (B), there is a division of the Gospels into much shorter chapters (Matt. 170, Mark 62, Luke 152, John 80), very judiciously made. This has been found in only one other manuscript, the *Codex Zacynthius* (Ξ). In the Acts and Epistles the Vatican manuscript has a twofold division into chapters,—one very ancient, the other later, but both different from the Euthalian. In the older division, the Pauline Epistles are treated as one book. (For further details see Tischendorf, *Novum Testamentum Vaticanum*, Leipsic, 1867, p. xxx; Scrivener, *Introduction*, i, London, 1894, pp. 56 sqq.) Other ancient divisions of the New Testament into chapters were more or less widely current, especially in Latin and Syriac manuscripts.

The superscriptions, "Epistle of Paul," "Catholic Epistles," etc., can not be earlier than the fourth century, since they imply a canonical collection. The subscriptions at the end of the Pauline Epistles in many manuscripts are generally ascribed to Euthalius. At least six of these are untrustworthy (I Cor., Gal., I and II Thess., I Tim., Tit.). For the modern divisions of the Bible into chapters and verses see III below.

An ancient division of the text is the lessons, or lections, from the Gospels on the one

6. Divisions for Liturgical Reading.

hand, and the Acts and Epistles on the other, read in the public services of the Church. The history of these is obscure, and they varied much at different periods and in different regions. The lessons for the Sundays and chief festivals of the year seem to have been the earliest; next were added lessons for the Saturdays, and finally for every day in the week, with special commemoration of saints and martyrs. Euthalius marked, in the Acts, 16 of these "lessons"; in the Catholic Epistles, 10; in the Pauline Epistles, 31; in all, 57 He was probably not, as many have supposed, their inventor. The system of lessons which ultimately prevailed in the Greek Church appears in our evangelistaries and lectionaries (more properly praxapostoli), containing the lessons from the Gospels and the Acts and Epistles respectively. The ordinary manuscripts of the Greek Testament were often adapted for church service by marking the beginning and end of each lesson, with a note in the margin of the time or occasion for reading it, and by prefixing to them a *Synaxarion*, or table of the lessons in their order; sometimes also a *Menologion*, or calendar of the immovable festivals and the saints' days, with their appropriate lessons.

Turning to the internal history of the New Testament text, it is evident that its original purity was early lost. The quotations of the latter half of the second century contain readings which agree with later texts, but are not apostolic. Irenæus alludes (*Hær.*, V, xxx, 1) to the difference between the copies; and Origen, early in the third century, expressly declares that matters were growing worse (*in Matt.*, xix, 19, vol. iii, p. 671, ed. De la Rue, Paris, 1733–59), as is proved by the quotations of the Fathers of the third and fourth centuries. From this time onward we have the manuscript text of each century, the writings of the Fathers, and the various Oriental and Occidental versions, all testifying to varieties of reading for almost every verse, which undoubtedly occasioned many more or less important departures from the sense of the original text. How came this? The early Church did not know anything of that anxious clinging to the letter which characterizes the scientific rigor and the piety of modern times, and therefore was not so bent upon preserving the exact words. Moreover, the first copies were made rather for private than for public use; copyists were careless, often wrote from dictation, and were liable to misunderstand. Attempted improvements of the text in grammar and style; proposed corrections in history and geography; efforts to harmonize the quotations in the New Testament with the Greek of the Septuagint, but especially to harmonize the Gospels; the writing out of abbreviations; incorporation of marginal notes in the text; the embellishing of the Gospel narratives with stories drawn from non-apostolic though trustworthy sources, e.g., John vii, 53 to viii, 11, and Mark xvi, 9 to end,—it is to these causes that we must attribute the very numerous "readings," or textual variations. It is true that the copyists were sometimes learned men; but their zeal in making corrections may have obscured the true text as much as the ignorance of the unlearned. The copies, indeed, came under the eye of an official reviser; but he may have sometimes exceeded his functions, and done more harm than good by his changes.

7. Early Corruption of the Text.

Attempts were made by learned Fathers to get the original text; and three men of the third century—Origen, the Egyptian Bishop Hesychius, and the Presbyter Lucian of Antioch—deserve mention for their devotion to this object. The last two undertook a sort of recension of the New Testament (cf. Jerome, *Epist. ad Damasum*); but it is not known exactly what they did, and their influence was small. In regard to Origen, while he did not make a formal recension of the New Testament text, his critical work was of the highest importance. Notwithstanding these diversities, there were, as early as the fourth and fifth centuries, affinities between manuscripts prepared in the same district, which seem to betray certain tendencies, as is proved by the Fathers, the versions, and the Greek manuscripts themselves. Thus critics are justified in speaking of an Oriental and Occidental, or, more correctly, an Alexandrian or Egyptian, and a Latin, as also of an Asiatic or Greek, and a Byzantine or Constantinopolitan text. According to this theory, the Alexandrian was used by those Jewish Christians of the East who already used the Septuagint; particularly was this text preserved and spread by the learned Alexandrian school. The Latin text characterizes not only the manuscripts prepared by Latins, but the Greek manuscripts they used. The Asiatic manuscripts were used chiefly by native Greeks in Greece, or in the Asiatic provinces having intercourse with Greece. The Byzantine manuscripts belonged to the Church of that empire. The latter alone had a certain official uniformity, and were, in the latter centuries, almost the only manuscripts circulated in the empire. This class of manuscripts is also the only one perfectly represented in existing documents, and is the result of the gradual mixture of older recensions under the predominance of the Asiatic or Greek. Each of these recensions is more or less altered and corrupted; so that it is often more difficult to assign a particular reading to its proper class than to find out the original. Finally, the differences and relationships are by far most strongly marked in the Gospels, least so in the Apocalypse, and again are more distinct in the Pauline Epistles and the Acts than in the Catholic Epistles. (Cf. C. Tischendorf, *Novum Testamentum Græce, editio academica viii*, Leipsic, 1875, pp. xxiv sqq.)

8. Varieties of Text Produced by Early Criticism.

The number of uncial manuscripts of the New Testament, ranging in date from the fourth to the tenth century, is 111. This does not include eight psalters containing the text of the hymns in Luke i, 46–55, 68–79, ii, 29–32, designated by Tischendorf O^{a-h}, nor the lectionaries, evangelistaries, and praxapostoli. About half of these 111 are mere fragments, containing but a few verses or at most a few chapters. They may be arranged as follows with reference to their probable date:

9. The Uncial Manuscripts.

Cent. IV, 2: ℵ with the whole New Testament; B, Gospels, Acts, Catholic, and Pauline Epistles (mutilated).

Cent. V, 15: A C $I^{1,2,3}$ I^b Q_1 Q_2 T^{pg} T^{wol} Ξ_2 ...

Cent. VI, 24: D, D_2 E_2 H_3 $I^{4,7}$ N_1 N_a O_3 C^b_2 P, R_1 T^{woh} Z Θ^{cdfg} Σ Φ ...

Cent. VII, 17: F^a G_2 $I^{5,6}$ R_2 T^{dlmpq} W^{ilmn} Θ^{ab} $ℸ^{12}$
Cent. VIII, 19: B_2 E_1 L_1 S_2 T^{inore} W^{abk} Y Θ^d Ξ Ψ Ω $ℸ^{6.8}$.
Cent. IX, 31: E_2 $F_{1.2}$ G_3 G^b H_2 $K_{1.2}$ L_2 $M_{1.2}$ N_2 O_1 P_2 T^{fk} V W^{c-ho} X^b Γ Δ Θ^h Λ Π $ℸ^9$.
Cent. X, 6: G_1 H_1 S_1 U X $ℶ_1$.

Of these only one, ℵ, has the New Testament entire, and only four others, ABCΨ, the greater part of it. The remainder are distributed, according to the principal divisions of the New Testament, as follows:

Gospels, 81: Complete or nearly so, 12: D E K L M S U V Γ Δ Π Ω; containing considerable portions, 14: F G H N P Q R X Z Λ Ξ Σ Φ ℶ; containing at most a few chapters or verses, 55: F^a $I^{1,3,4,7}$ I^b N^a O $T^{a-f,\ h-r}$ T^{wol} W^{a-0} X^b Θ^{a-h} $ℸ^{u-12}$.

Acts, 13: Complete or nearly so, 5: D E L P S; the rest with larger (H) or smaller portions (G G^b F^a $I^{2,5,6}$ ℶ).

Catholic Epistles, 5: Complete or nearly so, 4: K L P S, and the fragment ℶ.

Pauline Epistles, 20: Complete or nearly so, 7: D E F G K L P; containing larger or smaller fragments, 13: F^a H I^2 M N O O^b Q R S T^{g} $ℸ^{14}$

Apocalypse: besides ℵ A C, B_2 contains the complete text; P has some small gaps.

In reference to the character of their text, Tischendorf classifies the uncials as follows: in the Gospels the oldest form of the text, predominantly Alexandrine in its coloring, is found, though with many differences, in ℵ A B C D I I^b L P Q R T^{abe} X Z Δ Θ^{cg} Ξ; next to these stand F^a N O W^{abc} Y Θ^{abef}. A later form of the text, in which the Asiatic coloring prevails, is presented by E F G H K M S U V Γ Λ Π Θ^h, among which E K M Γ Λ Π Θ^h incline most toward the first class. For the Acts and Catholic Epistles, ℵ A B C give the oldest text, to which, in the Acts, D I approach, and, less closely, E G; also, in the Catholic Epistles (except I Pet.), P; while in the Acts, H L P, and, in the Catholic Epistles, K L, come nearest to the later form of the text. In the Pauline Epistles the oldest text is represented by ℵ A B C H I O Q, with the Greco-Latin manuscripts D F G; M P approach this; while K L N stand nearest to the more recent text. The text of the Apocalypse appears in its oldest form in ℵ A C, to which P comes nearer than B (cf. Gregory, *Prolegomena*, pp. 185 sqq.). Tregelles exhibits the "genealogy of the text" and affinities of the manuscripts in the Gospels in the following form:

Western	*Alexandrine*	*Byzantine*
	B ℵ Z	
D		
	C L Ξ 1.33	
	P Q T R I N	A
	X Δ 69	K M Π
		E F G S U, etc.

Westcott and Hort attach a superlative value to B, Tischendorf to ℵ. The same manuscript may differ in character in different parts of the New Testament: thus, A is not so excellent in the Gospels as elsewhere; Δ is especially good in the Gospel of Mark; ℵ and D agree most closely in the Gospel of John; the cursive 1 is remarkably valuable in the Gospels, but not so in the rest of the New Testament.

The following is a complete list of the 114 uncial manuscripts:

ℵ: Codex Sinaiticus, found by Tischendorf (1844 and 1859) in the Convent of St. Catharine at the foot of Mount Sinai, now preserved in St. Petersburg. Forty-three leaves of the Old Testament portion of the manuscript, known as the Codex Friderico-Augustanus, are in the library of Leipsic University. Besides twenty-six books of the Old Testament, of which five form the Codex Friderico-Augustanus, the manuscript contains the entire New Testament without the least break, the Epistle of Barnabas, and the first third of the Shepherd of Hermas. The Alexandrian copyist has frequently shown his imperfect knowledge of Greek, and his haste. The license in handling the text, common in the first three centuries, is greater than in B A C, though much less than in D. Nevertheless, the superiority of the Codex Sinaiticus to all other New Testament manuscripts, with the single exception of B, is fully proved by the numerous places in which its reading has the support of the oldest quotations or the most ancient versions. The text is in four columns, which is a unique arrangement. The Pauline Epistles, among which is Hebrews after II Thessalonians, come directly after the Gospels; the Acts and the Catholic Epistles, then the Apocalypse, follow. The date of the codex is the fourth century. It has a special value from the fact that, owing to the corrections it received in the sixth and seventh centuries and later, its pages represent, after a fashion, the history of the changes in the New Testament text. The codex was published (1862) in facsimile type from the Leipsic press, in four folio volumes, at the expense of the emperor of Russia, Alexander II. The edition was limited to three hundred copies. The New Testament part was published separately in a critical edition by Tischendorf, *Novum Testamentum Sinaiticum cum epistola Barnabæ et fragmentis Pastoris etc.*, Leipsic, 1863, and in a more popular form, *Novum Testamentum Græce ex Sinaitico codice omnium antiquissimo*, Leipsic, 1865 (cf. C. Tischendorf, *Die Sinaibibel. Ihre Entdeckung, Herausgabe, und Erwerbung*, Leipsic, 1871; C. R. Gregory, *Prolegomena*, pp. 16–17; F. H. A. Scrivener, *A Full Collation of the Codex Sinaiticus*, Cambridge, 1867).

A: Codex Alexandrinus, now in the British Museum, presented in 1628 by Cyril Lucar, patriarch of Constantinople, to Charles I. The New Testament begins with Matt. xxv, 6, and contains the whole except John vi, 50–viii, 52, and II Cor. iv, 13–xii, 6, with the First Epistle of Clement and part of the second. It was printed in facsimile by C. G. Woide, London, 1786, in ordinary type by B. H. Cowper, ib. 1860, who corrected some mistakes of Woide, and in photographic facsimile by the trustees of the British Museum, ed. E. M. Thompson (4 vols., London, 1879–83). Tischendorf places it about the middle of the fifth century; Scrivener at the end of the fourth or very little later.

B_1: Codex Vaticanus, no. 1209, in the Vatican Library. The manuscript contains, besides the Old Testament, the entire New Testament, with the exception of Heb. ix, 14 to end and II Timothy, Titus, Philemon, and Revelation. Juan Sepulveda, writing to Erasmus about 1533, mentions it. The first collation of the manuscript, made in 1669, by Bartolocci, then librarian of the Vatican, exists only in manuscript in the Paris library. Another was made by Birch, 1788–1801. The collation made for R. Bentley by an Italian named Mico was published by Ford, 1790. J. L. Hug wrote a learned *Commentatio de antiquitate codicis Vaticani* (Freiburg, 1810). The manuscript was then in Paris, but it was later restored to Rome, when it became practically inaccessible. An inaccurate and critically worthless edition of the whole manuscript was issued by Cardinal Mai (5 vols., Rome, 1828–38). C. Vercellone, J. Cozza, and G. Sergio published an edition of the entire codex in 6 vols. (New Testament is vol. v) in Rome, 1868–81, and a photographic reproduction was published by the Vatican (1889). The age of the manuscript is about the same as that of the Sinaitic, and possibly corrections are by the same first hand in both, and in the Vatican by a second hand contemporary with the first.

B_2: Codex Vaticanus 2066 (eighth century), formerly Basilian Codex 105, contains Revelation, was first imperfectly edited by Tischendorf in *Monumenta sacra inedita* (Leipsic, 1846), and more completely in *Appendix Novi Testamenti Vaticani* (ib. 1869). By Tregelles the manuscript was designated Q.

C: Codex Ephraemi (fifth century), now no. 9 in the National Library at Paris; its text was altered in the sixth century and again in the ninth. In the twelfth century the original writing was washed off to make room for the Greek text of several ascetic works of Ephraem Syrus (d. 373). Pierre Allix, at about the close of the seventeenth century, noticed the traces of the old writing under the later characters. Wetstein in 1716 collated the New Testament part so far as it was legible. In 1834 and 1835 the librarian Carl Hase revived the original writing by the application of the Giobertine tincture (prussiate of potash). Tischendorf, after great labor, brought out in 1843 an edition of the New Testament part of the manuscript, and in 1845, of the Old Testament fragments, representing the manuscript line for line, in facsimile. The codex contains portions of the Old Testament on sixty-four leaves, and five-eighths of the New Testament.

D_1: Codex Bezæ (about 550 A.D.), from the monastery of St. Irenæus in Lyons, now in the University Library at Cambridge, a present in 1581 from Theodore Beza. It contains, with few lacunæ, the Greek and Latin text of the Gospels and Acts and III John 11–15, stichometrically written, perhaps in Gaul. Edited by Kipling in 1793, but in a far better manner by Scrivener (*Bezæ Codex Cantabrigiensis*) in 1864. No known manuscript has so many and so remarkable interpolations. Much study has been given to it, e.g., J. R. Harris, *Codex Bezæ* (Cambridge, 1891).

D_2: Codex Claromontanus of the Pauline Epistles, including Hebrews (second half of sixth century). Beza found it in the Monastery of Clermont, hence the name; now in the Paris Library. Contains the Greek and Latin text written stichometrically. It was retouched at different times, and exhibits especially two periods of the text. The Latin text represents the oldest version,—that of the second century. It was collated by Tregelles in 1849 and 1850, and edited by Tischendorf in 1852 in facsimile.

E_1: Codex Basiliensis A. N. III, 12 (750 A.D.), in Basel, a nearly complete manuscript of the four Gospels, collated by Tregelles (1846), also by Tischendorf and J. C. Müller (1843).

E_2: Codex Laudianus (end of sixth century), in the Bodleian Library at Oxford, a present from Archbishop Laud in 1636; was brought to England in 668; Bede (d. 735) used it when writing his *Expositio retractata* of the Acts. It contains an almost complete Greco-Latin text of the Acts; edited in 1715 by Hearne, and in 1870 by Tischendorf in *Monumenta sacra inedita, nova collectio*, vol. ix.

E_3: Codex Sangermanensis, a Greco-Latin manuscript of the Pauline Epistles (end of ninth century), now in St. Petersburg, the Greek text being a clumsy copy of the Codex Claromontanus. Of no critical value except for the Latin text. Sabatier published it in the third part of his *Bibliorum sacrorum Latina versio* (1749).

F_1: Codex Boreeli (ninth century), now in Utrecht University, contains the four Gospels, but with many lacunæ. Full description is given in J. Heringa, *Disputatio de codice Boreeliano*, ed. H. E. Vinke (Utrecht, 1843).

F_2: Codex Augiensis (ninth century), contains Pauline Epistles in Greek and Latin, Hebrews only in Latin, and the Latin is not an exact translation of the Greek. Richard Bentley bought it at Heidelberg and his nephew presented it to Trinity College, Cambridge. It was collated by Tischendorf (1842), Tregelles (1845), and edited by Scrivener (1859).

F^a: Designates those passages from the Gospels, Acts, and Pauline Epistles written on the margin of the Coislin Octateuch in Paris early in the seventh century. It was edited by Tischendorf in *Monumenta sacra inedita* (1846).

G_1: Codex Harleianus (tenth century), contains the Gospels, defective, now in the British Museum, brought by A. Seidel from the East in the seventeenth century. It was collated by J. C. Wolf (1723), Griesbach, Tischendorf, and Tregelles.

G_2: A seventh century fragment of the Acts (ii, 45–iii, 7), brought by Tischendorf from the East in 1859 (see L_2).

G^b: Six leaves of a ninth century manuscript now in the Vatican, five leaves edited by Cozza in *Sacrorum bibliorum vetustissima fragmenta*, iii (Rome, 1877). The sixth leaf was discovered by C. R. Gregory in 1886.

G_3: Codex Boernerianus (ninth century), contains the Pauline Epistles, is now in the Dresden Royal Library, is in Greek and Latin. The Greek text agrees closely with that of F_2. It was edited by Matthæi in 1792, partly collated by Tregelles and others (see under Δ).

H_1: Codex Seidelii (tenth century), contains the Gospels, but defectively, now in the Hamburg Public Library, was collated by Tregelles.

H_2: Codex Mutinensis (ninth century), contains Acts except about seven chapters, now at Modena, collated by Tischendorf (1843) and Tregelles (1845).

H_3: Fragments of a sixth century manuscript of the Pauline Epistles in the edition of Euthalius, of which forty-one leaves have been found; twenty-two are in the National Library at Paris, eight in the Laura Monastery on Mt. Athos, two in the Synodal Library at Moscow, one in the Rumjanzew Museum there, three in the Imperial Library at St. Petersburg, three in the Ecclesiastical Academy at Kief, and two in the University Library at Turin. (Cf. H. Omont, *Notice sur un très ancien manuscrit grec*, Paris, 1889.)

I^{1-7}: Codex Tischendorfianus II, twenty-eight palimpsest leaves from the fifth, sixth, and seventh centuries, under the Georgian language, in a text related to that of ℵABC. Seven leaves contain parts of Matthew; two, parts of Mark; five, parts of Luke; eight, parts of John; four, of Acts; two, of Pauline letters. They were discovered by Tischendorf in the East, and by him published in the *Monumenta sacra inedita, nov. col.*, vol. i (1855).

I^b (formerly N^b): Four palimpsest leaves (early fifth century), containing sixteen verses from John xiii, xvi; now in the British Museum; deciphered by Tischendorf and Tregelles, published by the former in *Monumenta sacra inedita, nov. col.*, vol. ii (1857).

K_1: Codex Cyprius of the Gospels, complete (middle or end of ninth century); now in the National Library in Paris. Collated by Tischendorf (1842) and Tregelles (1849 and 1850).

K_2: Codex Mosquensis of the Catholic and Pauline Epistles (ninth century); brought from Mount Athos to Moscow. Lacks a part of Romans and I Corinthians. Collated by Matthæi.

L_1: Codex Regius of the Gospels (eighth century), now in the National Library in Paris, almost complete. Closely related to ℵ and B and the text of Origen. Published by Tischendorf in *Monumenta sacra inedita* (1846), in facsimile.

L_2: Codex Angelicus of the Acts and Catholic Epistles (formerly G), and of the Pauline (formerly I) (ninth century), now in the Angelica Library of the Augustinian monks at Rome. Contains Acts viii, 10, to Heb. xiii, 10. Collated by Tischendorf (1843) and Tregelles (1845).

M_1: Codex Campianus of the Gospels, complete (end of ninth century), now in the National Library in Paris. Copied and used by Tischendorf (1849).

M_2: Codex Ruber of the Pauline Epistles (ninth century). Two folio leaves at Hamburg (Heb. i, 1–iv, 3, xii, 20–xiii, 25), and two at London (I Cor. xv, 52–II Cor. i, 15; II Cor. x, 13–xii, 5). Written in red, hence its name. Edited by Tischendorf in *Anecdota sacra et profana* (1855, corrected, 1861).

N_1: Codex Purpureus (late sixth century), a manuscript of the Gospels on purple parchment in silver letters. Forty-five leaves were early known: thirty-three are in the Monastery of St. John at Patmos, six in the Vatican, four in the British Museum, two in the Imperial Library at Vienna. One hundred and eighty-four leaves more were discovered in a village near Cæsarea in Cappadocia and bought by M. Nelidow, Russian ambassador at Constantinople (cf. C. R. Gregory, in *TLZ*, 1896, pp. 393–394). The Vienna, London, and Vatican leaves were edited by Tischendorf in his *Monumenta sacra inedita* (1846), who used the leaves from Patmos (as collated by John Sakkelion) in his *Novum Testamentum, ed. viii, critica major*. These last were also edited by Duchesne in *Archives des missions scientifiques* (3 series, iii, 386 sqq.).

N^a: Two fragments of a manuscript very much like N_1, seen by Tischendorf in the collection of Bishop Porfiri of St. Petersburg; they contain a portion of Mark ix, and came from the library of the Alexandrian patriarch in Cairo.

N_2: Two leaves (ninth century), containing Gal. v, 12–vi, 4, and Heb. v, 8–vi, 10, brought by Tischendorf to St. Petersburg.

O_1: Eight leaves (ninth century) containing a part of John i and xx, with scholia. Now in Moscow (S. Syn. 29, formerly 120). Edited by Matthæi (1785), and, after him, by Tregelles, with Codex Zacinthius (see below, Ξ), Appendix (1861).

O_2: Two leaves (sixth century) containing II Cor. i, 20–ii, 12. Brought from the East to St. Petersburg by Tischendorf in 1859.

O^{a-h}: Fragments (sixth century to ninth) containing the hymns from Luke i, 46 sqq., 68 sqq., ii, 29 sqq., now (O^a) in Wolfenbüttel, (O^b) Oxford, (O^c) Verona, (O^d) Zurich, (O^e) St. Gall, (O^f) Moscow, (O^g) Turin, and (O^h) Paris. O^a was edited by Tischendorf in *Anecdota sacra et profana* (1855), and O^{d} in *Monumenta sacra inedita, nov. col.*, vol. iv (1869), and O^{bc} by Bianchini (1740).

O^{b}: Pauline Epistles, a single leaf (sixth century), contains part of Eph. iv, 1–18, collated by Tischendorf at Moscow in 1868.

P_1: Codex Guelpherbytanus I (sixth century), a palimpsest at Wolfenbüttel, contains a part of all of the Gospels, was edited by Tischendorf in *Monumenta sacra inedita, nov. col.*, vol. vi (1869).

P_2: Codex Porphyrianus (ninth century), a palimpsest, contains Acts, Catholic and Pauline Epistles, and Revelation, but with lacunæ; the text of the Apocalypse is especially good. It was brought to St. Petersburg by the Russian bishop Porfiri, and edited by Tischendorf in *Monumenta sacra inedita, nov. col.*, vols. v–vi (1865–69).

Q_1: Codex Guelpherbytanus II (fifth century), a palimpsest containing fragments of Luke and John, now at Wolfenbüttel; was edited by Tischendorf in *Monumenta sacra inedita*, vol. iii.

Q_2: Papyrus fragments (fifth century) of I Cor. i, vi, vii, in the collection of Bishop Porfiri, collated by Tischendorf in 1862.

R_1: Codex Nitriensis (sixth century), a palimpsest containing parts of Luke, came from a monastery in the Nitrian desert, now in the British Museum, collated by Cureton, then by Tregelles (1854) and Tischendorf (1855), and edited by the last in *Monumenta sacra inedita, nov. col.*, vol. ii (1857).

R_2: Codex Cryptoferratensis (late seventh century), a palimpsest fragment containing II Cor. xi, 9–19, published by Cozza in *Sacrorum bibliorum vetustissima fragmenta*, ii (Rome, 1867).

S_1: Codex Vaticanus 354 (949 A.D.), containing the Gospels complete, collated by Tischendorf for his *ed. viii*.

S_2: Codex Athous Lauræ (eighth or ninth century), containing Acts, Catholic Epistles, and Rom., I Cor. i, 1–v, 8, xiii, 8–xvi, 24, II Cor. i, 1–xi, 23, Eph. iv, 20–vi, 20, in the Laura Monastery on Mt. Athos, examined by Gregory in 1886.

T^{a}: Codex Borgianus I (fifth century), fragments containing Luke xxii, 20–xxiii, 20, and John vi, 28–67, vii, 6–viii, 31, now in the College of the Propaganda at Rome, the first collated by H. Alford (1866), the second by Tischendorf and published by Giorgi (1789).

T^{b}: Fragments (sixth century) of John (i, 25–42, ii, 9–iv, 14, 34–50), now at St. Petersburg.

T^{c}: Fragments, similar to T^{a}, containing Matt. xiv, 19–27, 31–34, xv, 2–8.

T^{d}: Fragments (seventh century) of a Greco-Coptic evangelistary (Matt. xvi, 13–20, Mark i, 3–8, xii, 35–37, John xix, 23–27, xx, 30–31) discovered by Tischendorf in the Borgian Library at Rome.

T^{e}: A fragment (sixth century) containing Matt. iii, 13–16, found in Upper Egypt, now in the University Library at Cambridge, England, used by Hort, and copied by Gregory in 1883.

T^{f}: Another fragment (ninth century), also from Upper Egypt, of a Greco-Coptic evangelistary, containing Matt. iv, 2–11, copied by Gregory in 1883, now in the Bodleian Library at Oxford.

T^{g}: Two fragments (fourth to sixth century) containing I Tim. iii, 15–16, and vi, 2, now in the Egyptian Museum of the Louvre; published by T. Zahn in *Forschungen*, iii, 277 sqq. (Leipsic, 1884).

T^{h}: Three leaves (sixth or seventh century) containing Matt. xx, 3–32, xxii, 4–16, found in Cairo by A. Papadopulos-Kerameus.

T^{i-r}: Fragments (seventh to tenth century) of six Greco-Coptic and three Greek manuscripts, containing parts of the Gospels, found in the Schnudi Monastery near Akhmim, Egypt, now in the National Library at Paris, published by E. Amélineau in *Notices et extraits*, vol. xxxiv, part ii (Paris, 1895), 363 sqq. The text is related to that of T^{a}.

T^{s}: Two leaves (eighth to tenth century), also from the Schnudi Monastery, containing I Cor. i, 22–29.

T^{woi}: Nine leaves (fifth century) with Greco-Coptic text of Luke xii, 15–xiii, 32, John viii, 33–42, formerly owned by Woide, now in the library of the Clarendon Press at Oxford, published by Ford, 1799.

U: Codex Nanianus (ninth or tenth century), contains the Gospels, now in the Library of St. Mark, Venice, collated by Tischendorf and Tregelles.

V: Codex Mosquensis (eighth or ninth century), contains the Gospels nearly complete to John vii, 49, written at Mt. Athos, collated by Matthæi (1785).

W^{a}: Two leaves (eighth century) containing parts of Luke ix–x, now in the National Library at Paris, edited by Tischendorf in *Monumenta sacra inedita* (1846).

W^{b}: A palimpsest, probably originally belonging with W^{a}, of fourteen leaves, containing fragments of Matt., Mark, and Luke, found by Tischendorf at Naples and by him deciphered in 1866.

W^{c}: Three fragments (ninth century) of a Greco-Latin manuscript of the Gospels from Mark ii and Luke i, now at St. Gall, edited by Tischendorf in *Monumenta sacra inedita, nov. col.*, vol. iii (1860).

W^{d}: Fragments of four leaves (ninth century) containing parts of Mark vii, viii, ix, now in the library of Trinity College, Cambridge, published by Scrivener, *Adversaria critica sacra* (Cambridge, 1893), pp. xi sqq.

W^{e}: Twelve leaves (ninth century) containing parts of John ii–iv, seven leaves in the monastery of St. Dionysius on Mt. Athos (collated by Pusey for Alford), three in the library of Christ Church College, Oxford (examined by Tischendorf), and two in the National Library at Athens (discovered by Gregory in 1886).

W^{f}: A palimpsest (ninth century) containing part of Mark v, in the library of Christ Church College at Oxford.

W^{g}: Thirty-six leaves of a palimpsest (ninth century) containing part of the four Gospels, now in the British Museum.

W^{h}: Two leaves of a palimpsest (ninth century) containing parts of Mark iii, discovered by Gregory in 1883.

W^{i}: Two leaves (seventh or eighth century) with parts of Luke iv, copied by Gregory in Paris in 1884.

W^{k}: Two leaves (eighth or ninth century) with parts of Luke xx and xxiii, also copied by Gregory in Paris, 1884.

W^{l}: Two leaves of a palimpsest (seventh century) containing Mark xiii, 34–xiv, 29, discovered by Gregory in the National Library at Paris, 1885.

W^{m}: Four leaves of a palimpsest (seventh or eighth century) containing parts of Mark, in the National Library at Paris, discovered by Gregory, 1885.

W^{n}: Four leaves (seventh century) containing John vi, 71–vii, 46, in Vienna.

W^{o}: Sixteen leaves of a palimpsest (ninth century) containing parts of the Synoptic Gospels, in the Ambrosian Library at Milan.

X: Codex Monacensis (ninth or tenth century) containing numerous fragments of the Gospels and a commentary, in the University Library at Munich. Collated by Scholz, Tischendorf, and Tregelles.

X^{b}: Fourteen leaves (ninth or tenth century) containing Luke i, 1–ii, 40, incomplete, in the Court and State Library at Munich.

Y: Codex Barberini 225 (eighth century), six leaves containing parts of John, published by Tischendorf in *Monumenta sacra inedita* (1846).

Z: Codex Dublinensis rescriptus (sixth century), an important palimpsest with numerous fragments of Matthew, in Trinity College, Dublin. Published in facsimile by Barrett (1801), accurately deciphered by Tregelles (1853), newly edited by T. K. Abbott (Dublin, 1880).

Γ: Codex Tischendorfianus IV (ninth century) contains large parts of Matthew and Mark, Luke and John are complete. It was found by Tischendorf in the East, part of it is in the Bodleian Library at Oxford, and the larger part at St. Petersburg. It strongly resembles K_1.

Δ: Codex Sangallensis (ninth century), a nearly complete copy of the Gospels (one leaf lacking) with interlinear Latin translation approximating the Vulgate text. It is in St. Gall, possibly copied there, and is possibly the same (for the Gospels) manuscript as G_3 (Pauline Epistles). (Cf. J. R. Harris, *Codex Sangallensis*, Cambridge, 1891.)

Θ^{a}: Codex Tischendorfianus I (seventh century), four leaves with parts of Matt. xii–xv, found by Tischendorf in the East in 1844 and 1853, now in the library of the University of Leipsic, edited by Tischendorf in *Monumenta sacra inedita, nov. col.*, vol. ii (1857).

Θ^{b}: Six leaves (seventh century) containing fragments of Matt. xxii–xxiii and Mark iv–v, brought by Tischendorf to St. Petersburg in 1859.

Θ^{c}: Two folio leaves (sixth century) containing Matt. xxi, 19–24 and John xviii, 29–35, brought by Tischendorf and Bishop Porfiri to St. Petersburg.

Θ^{d}: A fragment (eighth century) containing Luke xi, 37–45, brought by Tischendorf to St. Petersburg.

Θ^{e}: A fragment (sixth century) containing Matt. xxvi, 2–7, 9.

Θ^{f}: Four leaves (sixth century) containing parts of Matthew and Mark.

Θ^{e}: A fragment (sixth century) containing John vi, 13–24, similar to O_2.

Θ^{h}: Three fragments (ninth century) of a Greco-Arabic manuscript of the Gospels. Θ^{a-h} are all in the collection of Bishop Porfiri at St. Petersburg, and were collated by Tischendorf.

Λ: Codex Tischendorfianus III (ninth century) containing Luke and John complete, with occasional scholia in uncials on the margin, partly of a critical kind. Now in the Bodleian Library, Oxford; collated by Tischendorf (who brought it from the East) and Tregelles.

Ξ: Codex Zacynthius (eighth century), a palimpsest containing Luke i, 1–xi, 33, with some gaps; brought from the Island of Zante, and presented in 1821 to the British and Foreign Bible Society, London; deciphered and published by Tregelles in 1861. The text, which is very valuable, is surrounded by a commentary.

Π: Codex Petropolitanus (ninth century) of the Gospels complete, excepting seventy-seven verses. Brought to St. Petersburg by Tischendorf from Smyrna.

Σ: Codex Rossanensis (sixth century), containing Matt. i, 1–Mark xvi, 14, and belonging to the chapter of the Cathedral Church at Rossano, written on very fine purple vellum in silver letters, with the three first lines in both columns at the beginning of each Gospel in gold. It is adorned with eighteen remarkable pictures in water-colors, representing scenes in the Gospel history, with forty figures of the prophets of the Old Testament. Its miniatures bear a striking resemblance to those of the celebrated Vienna purple manuscript of Genesis. It numbers a hundred and eighty-eight leaves, some of which have been much injured by dampness. It originally contained the four Gospels. The text, as well as the writing, resembles that of Codex N_1 of the Gospels. It was discovered in the spring of 1879, at Rossano in Calabria (Southern Italy), by Dr. Gebhardt of Göttingen and Professor Harnack of Giessen, who have published a full description of it, with two facsimiles of the writing and outline sketches of the miniatures, in an elegant quarto entitled *Evangeliorum codex Græcus Purpureus Rossanensis* (Leipsic, 1880). The illuminations are reproduced in exact facsimile by Antonio Munoz (Rome, 1907). The text seems to hold a position about midway between that of the older uncials and those of the ninth and tenth centuries, agreeing most remarkably with N_1, often with AΔΠ, or with D and the Old Latin, against the mass of later manuscripts.

Φ: Codex Beratinus (probably sixth century), containing Matt. vi, 3–Mark xiv, 62, with some lacunæ, on purple vellum and in possession of the Church of St. George at Berat, Albania, made generally known by P. Batiffol in 1885.

Ψ: Codex Athous Lauræ (eighth or ninth century), containing the New Testament except Matthew, Mark i, 1–ix, 4, Heb. viii, 11–ix, 19, and Revelation, is in the Laura Monastery on Mt. Athos, was examined by Gregory in 1886.

Ω: Codex Athous Dionysii (eighth or ninth century), containing the four Gospels, is in the Monastery of St. Dionysius on Mt. Athos, was examined by Gregory in 1886.

ב: Codex Athous Andreæ (ninth or tenth century), containing the four Gospels but with lacunæ, is in the Monastery of St. Andrew on Mt. Athos, was examined by Gregory in 1886.

ג: Codex Patiriensis (fifth century), twenty-one palimpsest leaves containing fragments of Acts and of the Catholic and the Pauline Epistles, now in the Vatican Library, was described by Batiffol (1891), partly read by W. Sanday (1895).

ד: The sign attached by Gregory to a fragment of N_1 before he knew its relationship.

$ו^{6-12,14}$: Small fragments (fifth to ninth century) of the Synoptics and I Corinthians in the convent of St. Catharine on Mt. Sinai, discovered by J. R. Harris and published in *Biblical Fragments from Mt. Sinai* (London, 1890).

10. The Cursive Manuscripts, Evangelistaries, etc.

Besides the uncials, there are known for the Gospels over 1,200 cursives designated by Arabic numerals, over 950 evangelistaries of which about 100 are in uncial writing, varying in date from the tenth to the twelfth century. For the Acts and the Catholic Epistles there are over 400 cursives, for the Pauline Epistles about 500, and for the Apocalypse 180. Of lectionaries there are known over 260, only a very few of which antedate the tenth century. The following are noteworthy, either because of the value of their readings or for the influence they have had on the text:

1 Gospels, Acts, Catholic and Pauline Epistles: Codex Basiliensis (tenth or twelfth century), especially valuable for the text of the Gospels, contains the apparatus of Euthalius on the Acts and Epistles. Kindred to it in the Gospels are 209, 118, 131.

1 Apocalypse: Codex Reuchlini (twelfth century), used by Erasmus (1516), in the University Library at Basel.

13 Gospels: Codex Parisiensis (thirteenth century), has some lacunæ, was collated by Wetstein, Griesbach, and W. H. Ferrar, and is closely related to 69, 124, and 346, while 543, 788, and 826 belong to the same group.

13 Acts and Catholic Epistles, 17 Pauline Epistles, and 33 Gospels are all parts of the same manuscript (ninth, tenth, or eleventh century), and the text agrees often with that of the best uncials; collated by Griesbach, and Tregelles (1850).

14 Apocalypse, 31 Acts and Catholic Epistles, 37 Pauline Epistles and 69 Gospels are parts of the same manuscript (Leicester Codex, fourteenth or fifteenth century), collated by Tregelles, Scrivener, and Abbott (cf. 13 supra).

34 Acts and Catholic Epistles, 40 Pauline Epistles, 61 Gospels, and 92 Apocalypse are parts of the same manuscript (Codex Montfortianus, sixteenth century), at Trinity College, Dublin, collated by O. T. Dobbin (1854).

47 Pauline Epistles (eleventh or twelfth century), in the Bodleian Library, collated by Tregelles.

95 Apocalypse (Codex Parham, eleventh or twelfth century), belongs among the best witnesses to Revelation, collated by Scrivener.

565 Gospels (ninth or tenth century) in letters of gold on purple parchment, with especially ancient readings in Mark; designated 81 by Westcott and Hort, now in St. Petersburg.

2. History of the Printed Text: For more than half a century after the invention of printing, the original text of the New Testament remained unpublished. The credit of first printing it belongs to Cardinal Ximenes de Cisneros, archbishop of Toledo, who made it vol. v of his Polyglot Bible (see BIBLES, POLYGLOT, I). The manuscripts depended upon were comparatively modern and of inferior value. Though the volume is dated June 10, 1514, the New Testament was not published before 1521 or 1522, and thus was preceded by the Greco-Latin New Testament of 1516, published by Froben of Basel, and edited by Erasmus, who used as the basis of his text, in the Gospels, an inferior Basel manuscript of the fifteenth century (cod. 2), and one of the thirteenth or fourteenth century in the Acts and Epistles (cod. 2). With these he collated more or less carefully one more manuscript of the Gospels (cod. 1), two in the Acts and Catholic Epistles (codd. 1 and 4), and three in the Pauline Epistles (codd. 1, 4, 7). The oldest of these (cod. 1, tenth century) has a good text in the Gospels; but Erasmus made very little use of it; the others are comparatively modern, and poor. For the Apocalypse he had only a single manuscript of the twelfth century, wanting the last six verses, which he translated into Greek from the Latin Vulgate. In various other places in the Apocalypse he followed the readings of the Vulgate in opposition to the Greek, as he did in a few cases elsewhere. The first edition of Erasmus was sped through the press with headlong haste (*præcipitatum fuit verius quam editum*, as Erasmus himself says) in order that the publisher, Froben, might get the start of the Complutensian. It consequently swarms with errors.

1. Complutensian and Erasmian Editions.

A more correct edition was issued in 1519: Mill observed about four hundred changes in the text. For this and later editions, one additional manuscript (cod. 3) was used in the Gospels, Acts, and Epistles. In the third edition (1522) the changes were much fewer; but it is noted for the introduction of I John v, 7, from the Codex Montfortianus (sixteenth century). In the fourth edition (1527) the text was altered and improved in many places, particularly in Revelation, from the Complutensian Polyglot. That of the fifth (1535) and last (Erasmus died in 1536) hardly differs from the fourth.

2. Editions of Stephens and Beza.

The next editions which call for notice are those of the great printer and scholar Robert Stephens (Estienne, Stephanus; see STEPHENS), three published at Paris (1546, 1549, and 1550; the first two, in small 12mo, are known as the *O mirificam* editions, from the opening words of the preface, which is the same in both; the last, a magnificent folio, is called the *editio regia*), and one at Geneva (16mo, 1551), in which the present division into verses was first introduced into the Greek text (see below, III, § 3). The edition of 1550, notwithstanding its various readings in the margin from fifteen manuscripts and the Complutensian Polyglot, is mainly founded on the fourth or fifth edition of Erasmus. Scrivener has noted a hundred and nineteen places in which it differs from all of the manuscripts used. The text of the edition of 1551 varies but slightly from that of 1550. The four folio editions of Theodore Beza (Geneva, 1565, 1582, 1588 or 1589, and 1598), as well as his five 8vo editions (1565, 1567, 1580, 1590, 1604) follow, for the most part, Stephens's editions of 1550 or 1551, with changes here and there, many of which are not improvements. Stephens's edition of 1551 is commonly spoken of in England as the *textus receptus*; but on the Continent the first Elzevir edition, printed at Leyden in 1624, has generally received that designation. The expression is borrowed from the preface to the second Elzevir edition (1633), in which occur the words, *Textum ergo habes, nunc ab omnibus receptum*. The text of the seven Elzevir editions (1624, 1633, 1641, Leyden; 1656, 1662, 1670, 1678, Amsterdam), among which there are a few slight differences, is made up almost wholly from Beza's smaller editions of 1565 and 1580; its editor is unknown. The *textus receptus*, slavishly followed, with slight diversities, in hundreds of editions, and substantially represented in all the principal modern Protestant translations prior to the nineteenth century, thus resolves itself essentially into that of the last edition of Erasmus, framed from a few modern and inferior manuscripts and the Complutensian Polyglot, in the infancy of Biblical criticism. In more than twenty places its reading is supported by the authority of no known Greek manuscript.

3. Editions between 1657 and 1830.

The editions from 1657 to 1830, with the exception of that of Griesbach (see below, § 3), are important, as regards the text, mainly for their accumulation of critical materials. In Walton's Polyglot (London, 1657; see BIBLES, POLYGLOT, IV), Stephens's Greek text of 1550 was accompanied by the Vulgate, Peshito-Syriac, Ethiopic, Arabic, and, in parts of the New Testament, other ancient versions, with a critical apparatus including the readings of Codd. A, D_1, D_2, Stephens's margin, and eleven cursive manuscripts collated by or for Archbishop Ussher. In Bishop Fell's edition (Oxford, 1675), which reproduces substantially the Elzevir text, other authorities, including readings of the Coptic and Gothic versions, are given in the notes, though the title page (*ex plus 100 MSS. codicibus*), is very misleading. The edition of John Mill (Oxford, 1707, fol.; improved and enlarged by Ludolph Kuster, Amsterdam, Leipsic, and Rotterdam, 1710), the work of thirty years, marks an epoch in the history of textual criticism by its vast additions to the store of critical material through the collation of the new manuscripts, the collection of readings from the ancient versions, and especially from the quotations found in the writings of the Christian Fathers, and by its very learned and valuable prolegomena. Mill gave his judgment on many readings in his notes and prolegomena, but did not venture to form a text of his own, reprinting Stephens's text of 1550 without intentional variation. The projected edition of the Greek Testament and Latin Vulgate in parallel columns, by the illustrious critic Richard Bentley (q.v.) deserves a brief notice. Proposals for printing were issued in 1720, and a large amount of materials was collected at great expense, including a collation of cod. B (published by Ford in 1799); but the work was never completed. It was to have been founded on the oldest Greek and Latin manuscripts compared with the principal ancient versions and the quotations in the Fathers of the first five centuries. (Cf. A. A. Ellis, *Bentleii critica sacra*, Cambridge, 1862; R. C. Jebb, *Bentley*, London, 1882.) The edition of Johann Albrecht Bengel (q.v.; Tübingen, 1734, 4to), while it had the advantage of some new manuscripts, was specially valuable for its discussions and illustrations of the principles of criticism, and its classification of manuscripts; but, except in the Apocalypse, Bengel did not venture to introduce any reading, even though he believed it unquestionably genuine, which had not previously appeared in some printed edition. His judgment of the value of different readings was, however, given in the margin (cf. E. Nestle, *Bengel als Gelehrter*, Tübingen, 1893, pp. 39 sqq.). The magnificent edition of Johann Jakob Wetstein (q.v.; 2 vols. fol., Amsterdam, 1751–52), the work of forty years, greatly enlarged the store of critical material by extensive collation of manuscripts and researches into the quotations of the Fathers, and by his description of this material in very valuable and copious prolegomena (reprinted, with additions by Semler, Halle, 1764). He gives also the readings of the chief printed editions which preceded him, and describes them fully. He introduced the present method of denoting the uncial manuscripts by Roman capitals, and the cursives and lectionaries by Arabic figures. Besides the critical matter, Wetstein's edition is a thesaurus of quotations from Greek, Latin, and Rabbinical authors, illustrating the phraseology of the New Testament, or containing passages more or less parallel in sentiment. His publisher insisted on his reprinting the *textus receptus* (substantially that of the Elzevirs); but he gives his critical judgment in the margin and the notes. Other editions to be briefly mentioned are those of F. C. Alter (Vienna, 1786–87), giving the readings of twenty-two Vienna manuscripts and of four manuscripts of the Slavonic version; of Andrew Birch (*Quatuor Evangelia Græce*, Copenhagen, 1788, 4to, and *Variæ lectiones*, 1798, 1800, 1801), exhibiting the readings of many manuscripts collated in the libraries of Italy, Spain, and Germany, by himself and others; and of C. F. Matthæi (*Novum Testamentum Græce et Latine* [the Vulgate], 12 vols., 8vo, Riga, 1782–88; also *Novum Testamentum Græce*, 3 vols., 8vo, Wittenberg, etc., 1803–07), for which over a hundred manuscripts were used, mostly from the library of the Holy Synod at Moscow. Matthæi was a careful collator, but a very poor critic; and his manuscripts generally were of inferior quality.

4. Griesbach and his Followers.

The first edition of Johann Jacob Griesbach (q.v.) was published in 1774–75 (the first three Gospels in synopsis); but it was only in the second edition (2 vols., 8vo, Halle, 1796–1806) that he first made really good use of the materials gathered by his predecessors, and augmented by his own collections. A manual edition was issued at Leipsic in 1805, the text of which, differing somewhat from that of the larger edition, expresses his later critical judgment. Following in the track of Bengel and Semler, Griesbach sought to simplify the process of criticism by classifying his manuscripts and other authorities. He made three classes or recensions—the Alexandrian, the Western, and the Constantinopolitan or Byzantine—to the latter of which the mass of later and inferior manuscripts belongs. Though his system is not now accepted in its details, much truth lay at the bottom of it. His principles of criticism were sound; and in his application of them he displayed rare tact and skill. In 1827 a third edition of the first volume of his Greek Testament was published, with important additions, under the editorship of Dr. David Schulz. Griesbach's *Symbolæ criticæ* (Halle, 1785–93), and *Commentarius criticus* on Matthew and Mark, parts i, ii, with *Meletemata critica* prefixed to part ii, Jena, 1798, 1811, are still valuable. A number of manual editions founded on that of Griesbach, but inclining more to the *textus receptus*, as those of H. A. Schott (Leipsic, 1805, 1813, 1825, 1839), with a good Latin translation; G. C. Knapp (Halle, 1797, 1813, 1824, 1829, 1840), with a useful *Commentatio isagogica*, or introduction, and carefully punctuated and divided; J. A. H. Tittmann (ster., Leipsic, 1820, 1828, 16mo; 1824, 1831, 8vo); A. Hahn (Leipsic, 1840, 1841, revised ed. 1861; reprinted at New York, 1842, by Edward Robinson); K. G. W. Theile (ster., Leipsic, 1844, 11th ed. 1875, by O. von Gebhardt), with the variations of the chief modern editors, parallel passages, etc.; also S. T. Bloomfield's *Greek Testament with English Notes* (London, 1832, 9th ed., 1855, 2 vols., 8vo), mark no progress in criticism beyond Griesbach, but rather a retrograde movement. The same is true of the large edition of the Catholic scholar J. M. A. Scholz (2 vols., 4to, Leipsic, 1830–1836), whose extensive travels and researches in libraries enabled him to add a very large number of new manuscripts (according to Scrivener, 616) to the list of those previously known. But of these only thirteen were collated entire; a few others in the greater part; many in only a few chapters; many more simply inspected, or only enrolled in the list. Scholz was a poor critic, and as an editor and collator incredibly careless. He divided his manuscripts into two classes or recensions—the Alexandrian and the Constantinopolitan, giving the preference to the latter. But in applying his system, he was happily inconsistent, particularly in his second volume, and at a later period of his life (1845) abandoned it. His edition met with no favor from intelligent scholars; but in England, where Biblical criticism was at its lowest ebb, it was welcomed and praised by many, and its text reprinted.

5. Lachmann.

A new period in the history of textual criticism was inaugurated by the appearance (Berlin, 1831) of a small edition of the Greek Testament by the distinguished classical scholar Carl Lachmann (q.v.), followed by a larger edition, in which the authorities for the Greek text were supplied by Philipp Buttmann, with the Latin Vulgate in the lower margin, critically edited from codd. Fuldensis, Amiatinus, and other manuscripts (2 vols., 8vo, Berlin, 1842–50). Lachmann's aim in these editions was not to reproduce the original text according to his best judgment (for this he deemed conjectural criticism to be necessary in some cases), but to present as far as possible on purely documentary evidence the text current in the Eastern churches in the fourth century as a basis for criticism. He paid no attention to the *textus receptus*, and used no cursive manuscripts, but founded his text wholly on ancient authorities; viz., codd. A B C D P Q T Z of the Gospels, A B C D E in the Acts and Catholic Epistles, A B C D G in the Pauline Epistles, and A B C in the Apocalypse, with the Latin Vulgate, and codd. *a* (Vercellensis, fourth century), *b* (Veronensis, fifth century), and *c* (Colbertinus, eleventh century) of the Old Latin, for the Gospels, besides the Latin versions of the Greco-Latin manuscripts in the above list; of the Fathers he used Irenæus, Cyprian, Hilary of Poitiers, Lucifer of Cagliari, and, in the Apocalypse, Primasius. His attempted task was not fully accomplished, partly because the text of some of the most important manuscripts which he used (B C P Q, and the Latin Codex Amiatinus) had been but very imperfectly collated or edited, partly because the range of his authorities was too narrow, and partly because he was sometimes, apparently at least, inconsistent in the application of his principles. But he was the first to found a text wholly on ancient evidence (Griesbach disregarded what he deemed unimportant variations from the received text); and his editions, to which his eminent reputation as a critic gave wide currency, especially in Germany, did much toward breaking down the superstitious reverence for the *textus receptus* which had long prevailed.

6. Tischendorf.

Next to be noted are the editions of Tischendorf and Tregelles. Through their combined labors we have a solid basis for a completely critical edition of the Greek Testament in the accurate knowledge, not possessed before, of all manuscripts of the oldest class (not including lectionaries), comprising many newly discovered, among them the Sinaitic of the fourth century. Lobegott Friedrich Constantin Tischendorf (q.v.) spent about eight years of his life in travels in search of manuscripts (for which he visited the East three times—in 1844, 1853, and 1859), or in collating with extreme care or transcribing and preparing for publication the most important of those in the various libraries of Europe which were before known, but had not been published or thoroughly examined. The following uncial Greek manuscripts (see the list above) were discovered by Tischendorf: ℵ G_2 I N_2 O_2 $T^{b,d}$ Γ Θ^{a-d} Λ Π; first used by him: F^a I^b N_1 O^{b-f} O^b_2 P_2 Q_2 $R_{1,2}$ $T^{a,c}$ W^{b-e} Θ^{e-h}; published: ℵ $B_{1,2}$ C D_2 E_2 F^a I I^b L_1 M_2 N_1 O^a $P_{1,2}$ Q_1 R_1 $W^{a,c}$ Y Θ^a (cf. C. R. Gregory's *Prolegomena* to Tischendorf's *Novum Testamentum Græce, ed. viii*, i, Leipsic, 1884, p. 31). His editions of the texts of Biblical manuscripts (including some of the Septuagint) comprise no less than seventeen large quarto and five folio volumes, not including the *Anecdota sacra et profana* (1855, new ed. 1861), or the *Notitia editionis Codicis Sinaitici* (1860), two quarto volumes containing descriptions or collations of many new manuscripts; and many of his collations, or copies of manuscripts, remain unpublished.

The titles of Tischendorf's various writings, most of them relating to Biblical criticism, fill pages 7–22 of Gregory's *Prolegomena*. His first edition of the Greek Testament (Leipsic, 1841) was promising as a first essay, but of no special importance except for the refutation, in the prolegomena, of Scholz's theory of recensions. In the *Editio Lipsiana secunda* (1849) the critical apparatus was much enlarged, and the text settled on the basis of ancient authority, generally with good judgment. In 1859 appeared the *Editio septima critica maior* (2 vols.), in which very large additions were made to the critical apparatus, not only from manuscripts, Greek and Latin, but from the quotations in the writings of the Christian Fathers, and the evidence was for the first time fully stated, both for and against the readings adopted. In the first volume, Tischendorf, influenced perhaps by Scrivener, showed a tendency to allow greater weight to the later uncials and cursives than he had done in his edition of 1849; but he soon found that he was on the wrong track; and on the whole, if orthographical changes are included, his edition of 1859 differs more widely from the *textus receptus* than that of 1849. Its publication was immediately followed by Tischendorf's third journey to the East, and the discovery of the great Sinaitic manuscript, together with the acquisition of much other new critical material. After the publication of the Codex Sinaiticus in 1862, in a magnificent edition of four volumes folio, in facsimile type, with twenty-one plates of actual facsimiles, at the expense of the Russian Government, the edition being limited to three hundred copies, he issued in 1863, in 4to, his *Novum Testamentum Sinaiticum*, in ordinary type, but representing the manuscript line for line, with full prolegomena; and his *Novum Testamentum Græce ex Sinaitico Codice, Vaticana itemque Elzeviriana lectione notata*, in 1865, 8vo, with a supplement of additions and corrections in 1870. After some other publications, particularly the second edition of his *Synopsis evangelica* in 1864, in which the Sinaitic manuscript was first used, he undertook his last great critical edition of the Greek New Testament, *Novum Testamentum Græce, editio octava critica maior* (issued in eleven parts, i, Leipsic, Oct., 1864, xi, at the end of 1872; collected into two volumes, 8vo, 1869–72). This edition far surpassed all that had preceded it in the richness of its critical apparatus, and, as compared with that of 1859, rests much more on the authority of the oldest manuscripts, particularly the Sinaitic. The preparation of the prolegomena by Tischendorf himself was prevented by his sudden illness and subsequent death, and was entrusted to an American scholar residing in Leipsic, Caspar René Gregory (q.v.), who had also the valuable assistance of Ezra Abbot (q.v.). In the interest of the work Dr. Gregory made special journeys through Europe and into the Orient, and was thus enabled to give first-hand descriptions and collations of many manuscripts. It was published in three parts at Leipsic, 1884–94. Besides the works mentioned, the most important publications of Tischendorf pertaining to the textual criticism of the New Testament are: *Codex Ephraemi Syri rescriptus* (1843, 4to; Old Testament part, 1845); *Monumenta sacra inedita* (1846, 4to); *Evangelium ineditum* (1847, 4to); *Codex Amiatinus* (Vulgate; 1850, new ed. 1854); *Codex Claromontanus* (1852, 4to); *Monumenta sacra inedita, nova collectio*, vols. i–vi, ix (1855–70, 4to); *Novum Testamentum Vaticanum* and *Appendix Novi Testamenti Vaticani* (1867–69, 4to); cf. *Responsa ad columnias Romanas* (1870, 8vo), also *Appendix codicum celeberrimorum, Sinaitici, Vaticani, Alexandrini* (1867, 4to); *Die Sinaibibel, ihre Entdeckung, Herausgabe, und Erwerbung* (1871, large 8vo). His *Novum Testamentum triglottum, Græce, Latine, Germanice* (Leipsic, 1854, 2d ed., 1865) is a convenient book, the three parts of which were also issued separately, and in various combinations. The Greek is his own text, with the variations of the *textus receptus*; the Latin, the Vulgate critically revised from the oldest manuscripts, with the variations of the Clementine edition; the German the genuine text of Luther, though in modern orthography. Tischendorf also issued many manual editions of the Greek Testament, the three latest in his lifetime being published in 1875 by Tauchnitz, Brockhaus (to match his edition of the Septuagint), and Mendelssohn (*Editio academica septima*), respectively. His large editions of 1859 and 1869–72 were issued with the critical apparatus greatly abridged, but giving the chief authorities for all the important various readings, with the titles *Editio septima critica minor* (1859) and *Editio octava critica minor* (1872–77).

Samuel Prideaux Tregelles (q.v.) ranks next to Tischendorf in the importance of his critical labors, and in single-hearted devotion to his chosen task. In 1848 he issued a Prospectus for a critical edition of the Greek Testament, the text of which was to be founded solely on the authority of the oldest Greek manuscripts, the ancient versions to the seventh century, and the citations of early writers, including Eusebius. No account was made of the "received text," or of the great mass of cursive manuscripts. Completeness and accuracy in the exhibition of the evidence of the witnesses used were especially aimed at. Like Tischendorf, Tregelles visited (in 1845–46, 1849–50, and 1862) the principal libraries in Europe for the purpose of collating manuscripts the text of which had not before been published. These were the uncials B_2 D_2 E_1 F_2 G_1 $H_{1,2}$ I^b K_1 L_2 $M_{1,2}$ R_1 U X Z Γ Λ, the cursives 1, 13, 17, 31, 37, 47, 61, 69, and also Codex Zacynthius (Ξ). In many cases Tregelles compared his collations with those of Tischendorf, and settled the differences by a reexamination of the manuscript. In 1861 he edited the *Codex Zacynthius* (Ξ), republishing in an appendix the fragments of O. His edition of *The Greek New Testament, Edited from Ancient Authorities, with their Various Readings in Full, and the Latin Version of Jerome,* was issued in London in seven successive parts: i, Matthew, Mark, 1857; ii, Luke, John, 1861; iii, Acts and Catholic Epistles, 1865; iv, Romans to II Thessalonians (iii, 3), 1869; v, Hebrews (with II Thess. iii, 3-18) to Philemon, 1870; vi, Revelation, 1872. Part vii, *Prolegomena and Addenda and Corrigenda*, appeared in 1879, four years after his death, edited by Dr. Hort and A. W. Streane. Though Tregelles added far less than Tischendorf to our store of critical material, he did more to establish correct principles of criticism, and his various writings had a wide and most beneficial influence in England. He also published, in 1854, *An Account of the Printed Text of the Greek New Testament, with Remarks on its Revision upon Critical Principles*, and, in 1856, *Introduction to the Textual Criticism of the New Testament*, forming part of vol. iv of the tenth and later editions of Horne's *Introduction*. This volume was also issued separately, and in the eleventh edition of Horne's *Introduction* (1861) appeared with "Additions" and a "Postscript."

7. Tregelles.

In 1881 appeared *The New Testament in the Original Greek. The Text Revised by Brooke Foss Westcott and Fenton John Anthony Hort* (Cambridge and London). The American edition (New York) has a valuable introduction by Philip Schaff, with the cooperation of Ezra Abbot. Dr. Schaff also prepared a compact manual of New Testament criticism, *A Companion to the Greek Testament and the English Version* (New York, 1883), which embodies the substance of this introduction, thoroughly revised. The text of Westcott and Hort is accompanied by an *Introduction and Appendix* (1882) in which the authors discuss the need of criticism for the text of the New Testament, the methods of textual criticism, the application of its principles to the text, the nature and details of their edition, and add notes on select readings and orthography, with orthographical alternative readings, and quotations from the Old Testament. In 1895 the text appeared in larger form, and, in 1896, the *Introduction* in finally revised form. This edition is not accompanied with any critical apparatus; it rather was the object of the authors, by a careful study of the materials furnished by their predecessors, augmented somewhat, however, by their own researches, to trace the history of the text as far as possible to distinguish its different types, and determine their relations and their comparative value to investigate the special characteristics of the most important documents and groups of documents; and, finally, to apply the principles of criticism which result from these studies to the determination of the original text. Their view of the genealogical relations of the chief ancient texts excited strong opposition in certain quarters but their work was recognized as the most important contribution to the scientific criticism of the New Testament text which had yet been made. They distinguish four principal types of text: the Western, characterized by a tendency to paraphrase or to modify the form of expression, and also to interpolate from parallel passages or from extraneous sources, represented especially by D and the Old Latin versions, also in part by the Curetonian Syriac; the neutral, represented by B and largely by ℵ, preserving best the original form; the Alexandrian, much purer than the Western, but betraying a tendency to polish the language; and the Syrian, the latest form, a mixed text, borrowing from all, and aiming to be easy, smooth, and complete. They regard B as preeminent above all other manuscripts for the purity of its text; the readings of ℵ and B combined as generally deserving acceptance as genuine, their ancestries having "diverged from a point near the autographs"; and they attach great weight to every combination of B with another primary Greek manuscript, as L C T D Ξ A Z 33, and, in Mark, Δ. Westcott and Hort (see WESTCOTT, BROOKE FOSS, HORT, FENTON JOHN ANTHONY) began their work in 1853. Their method of cooperation was first independent study, then comparison. The *Introduction* is chiefly the work of Dr. Hort, whose name is one of the greatest in the history of text-criticism. He carried into the study of the text a large knowledge of church history and patristic theology, and it was this breadth of historical knowledge which made the *Introduction* the great work it is. The genealogical theory, suggested by Bengel and elaborated by later scholars, was here worked into a truly monumental form. A thorough acquaintance with this book is necessary to the student if he would have a clear insight of the deepest tendencies in the text studies of the eighteenth and nineteenth centuries or an understanding of the course taken by text-study in the

8. Westcott and Hort.

present. Conscious agreement with it or conscious disagreement and qualification mark all work in this field since 1881.

Of the many other scholars whose labors have aided in the establishment of the text of the Greek New Testament, the Anglican scholar Frederick Henry Ambrose Scrivener (q.v.) deserves mention especially for his editions and collation of manuscripts.

9. Other Critics of the Text.

His *Plain Introduction to the Criticism of the New Testament* (Cambridge, 1861; 4th ed., by E. Miller, 2 vols., London, 1894) is a standard work. Scrivener was an able defender of the later manuscripts as witnesses to the original text against Tischendorf, Tregelles, and Westcott and Hort. In this contention he had the doughty support of John William Burgon (q.v.) in *The Revision Revised* (London, 1883). Among Americans, Ezra Abbot and Joseph Henry Thayer; among Hollanders, W C. Van Manen, J. Cramer, and J. J. Prins; among Frenchmen, P Batiffol, J. P P. Martin, and E. Amélineau; among Italians, Angelo Mai, Carlo Vercellone, and J. Cozza; and among Germans, F. Blass, E. Nestle, B. Weiss, E. Riggenbach, and O. von Gebhardt have made important contributions to textual criticism.

When Westcott and Hort published their text in 1881 and when, in 1882, Hort's masterpiece on introduction followed, there was a disposition in some quarters to believe that New Testament scholarship had come somewhere near a critical *textus receptus*. The genealogical theory first broached by Bengel seemed, after a century and a half of toil, to have led the student into a definite path which would surely lead to a final goal. But significant changes, in feeling if not in opinion, are beginning to manifest themselves.

10. More Recent Tendencies.

Westcott and Hort mark a main epoch in text-study. More clearly than their predecessors, they showed that the study of the text was inseparable from the study of church history. But the hypothesis which Hort so powerfully worked out has to some extent wrought its own undoing. The lines of study that it suggested have brought to light so many new facts and so many serious problems that the tone of certitude at one time in fashion has passed away. To Scrivener's description of Westcott and Hort's text as a *splendidum peccatum* few will assent. Yet, beyond question, the situation has materially changed. The "Western Text" or, to call it by a safer name, the "Syro-Western Text," which Westcott and Hort took to be a fairly well delineated fact, has become an imperious problem. The genealogical theory has fulfilled the chief function of a good working hypothesis by introducing order into chaos and pointing to the promising lines of attack upon the vast body of data awaiting the student. But genealogical certitude has declined. With its decline has come a growing disposition to concede to exegesis a certain right against the overweening authority of any group of manuscripts, however imposing. The good text-critic should also be an accomplished exegete. In Bernhard Weiss the two qualities are in a measure blended. Hence, at a critical point like Rom. v, 1, the exegete in him goes against the authority of A B C D E K L, Vulgate, Peshito, etc., and adopts ἔχομεν instead of ἔχωμεν.

Monumental work is not at present the order of the day. The searching investigations of the versions, the detailed and comprehensive study of patristic quotations, larger and clearer knowledge of the mental conditions under which an entire group of texts are likely to have undergone perceptible, even if inconsiderable, changes—in a word, a vast amount of labor lies ahead. The doing of it will require a very considerable time. Meanwhile the confidence and finality of a quarter-century ago are to be replaced by a restrained skepticism.

3. Principles of Textual Criticism: It is impossible, within the limits here allowed, to state and illustrate the principles of criticism applicable to the text of the Greek Testament. A few hints may, however, be given. The object, of course, is to ascertain which, among two or more variations of the text presented by our manuscripts or other authorities, is the original. No kind of evidence, external or internal, is to be neglected.

1. The Basal Rule.

The problem is to be solved by a process of reasoning upon probabilities; and what has to be considered, in every case, is which hypothesis will best explain all the phenomena. This fact is sometimes partially stated under the form of the rule that *that reading is to be accepted as genuine which will best explain the origin of the other variations*. This is an important rule; but there must be taken into account not merely the nature of the variations, but the number, independence, and character of the witnesses that support them. The process of criticism is not a mechanical one. Authorities must be weighed, not counted. One good, very early manuscript may be worth more than a thousand copies derived from a late and corrupted archetype. Again, though the presumption is in favor of the oldest manuscripts, mere antiquity does not prove the excellence of a copy.

One of the essential prerequisites to intelligent criticism is a thorough study of the occasions of error in manuscripts. This involves a knowledge of paleography and of the history of pronunciation. The similarity of certain letters or abbreviations in their older forms gave occasion to errors which can be only thus explained; and in the corruption of the Greek language, vowels and diphthongs originally distinct in sound were pronounced alike (itacism).

2. Other Canons.

A study of the tendencies and habits of transcribers is also involved. Many manuscripts, in the alterations they have received from later hands, illustrate the manner in which the text was corrupted. Among the maxims resulting from such a study, in connection with the consideration of external testimony, are these: (1) *The more difficult reading is to be preferred* (Bengel's great rule). This applies to those variations which are to be ascribed to design.

Transcribers would not intentionally substitute a harsh, ungrammatical, unusual, Hebraistic expression, one that caused a difficulty of any kind, for an easier one. (2) *The shorter reading is to be preferred* (Porson's "surest canon of criticism"). The tendency of scribes was almost always to add, rather than to omit. They did not like to have their copies regarded as incomplete. It was common to insert in the margin of manuscripts, or between the lines, glosses, or explanations of unusual or difficult expressions, also words or clauses which served to supplement the language of one Gospel from the parallel or similar passages in another, or to complete abridged quotations of the Old Testament from the fuller text of the Septuagint. Words accidentally omitted were also placed in the margin, or between the lines. A transcriber might thus easily mistake these glosses, or supplements, of his predecessor for accidental omissions and transfer them to his text. This rule does not apply to cases where an omission can be satisfactorily explained by homœoteleuton; that is, cases where two successive sentences or parts of sentences have a like ending. The scribe copies the first of these, then his eye glances to the like ending of the second, and he thinks that that is what he has just copied, and omits unconsciously the intervening words. Another prerequisite to successful criticism is a careful study of the principal documents and groups or classes of documents, in connection with the history of the text, so far as it can be traced, in order to determine by a process of comparative criticism their peculiar characteristics, their weak points and their strong points, and the relative antiquity and value of their texts. This process includes the ancient versions and the quotations in the writings of the principal Christian Fathers. It can not be here detailed. Griesbach did good work in this direction, and it has been the special study of Westcott and Hort. It is thus possible to weigh the external evidence in particular cases with some approach to accuracy.

4. Results of the Textual Criticism of the New Testament: The host of "various readings" which an examination of ancient manuscripts, versions, and quotations, has brought to light, perhaps a hundred and fifty thousand in number, alarms some simple-minded people. Analysis at once dispels the alarm. It is seen that a very large proportion of these readings, say nineteen-twentieths, are of no authority, no one can suppose them to be genuine; and nineteen-twentieths of the remainder are of no importance as affecting the sense. Of how much, or rather, of how little, importance, for the most part, the remainder are, can readily be seen by comparing the Revised Version of the New Testament (with its marginal notes) with the text of the Authorized Version, or by an examination of the various readings of the chief modern editors in Scrivener's *Novum Testamentum textus Stephanici A.D. 1550 accedunt variæ lectiones* (8th ed., Cambridge, 1877). The great number of various readings is simply the result of the extraordinary richness of critical resources. Westcott and Hort remark, with entire truth, that "in the variety and fulness of the evidence on which it rests, the text of the New Testament stands absolutely and unapproachably alone among ancient prose-writings."

BIBLIOGRAPHY: On the paleography of the N. T.: S. P. Tregelles, *An Account of the Printed Text of the Greek New Testament; with Remarks on its Revision upon Critical Principles, together with a Collation of the Critical Texts of Griesbach, Scholz, Lachmann, and Tischendorf, with that in Common Use*, London, 1854; E. A. Bond and E. M. Thompson, *Facsimiles of Ancient MSS*, ib. 1873–82; W. Wattenbach, *Anleitung zur griechischen Palæographie*, Leipsic, 1877; idem, *Schrifttafeln zur Geschichte der griechischen Schrift*, 2 parts, Berlin, 1876–77; idem and F. A. von Welsen, *Exempla codicum Græcorum litteris minusculis scriptorum*, Heidelberg, 1878; idem, *Scripturæ Græcæ specimina*, Berlin, 1883; N. Gardthausen, *Griechische Palæographie*, Leipsic, 1879; J. R. Harris, *New Testament Autographs*, in supplement to *AJP*, no. 12, 1882; idem, *Stichometry*, New York, 1893; T. W. Allen, *Notes on Abbreviations in Greek MSS, with Facsimiles*, Oxford, 1889; F. Blass, *Palæographie*, in *Handbuch der klassischen Alterthumswissenschaft*, vol. i, Munich, 1892; W. A. Copinger, *The Bible and its Transmission*, London, 1897; F. G. Kenyon, *Our Bible and the Ancient MSS*, ib. 1897; idem, *Bible Manuscripts in the British Museum, Facsimiles*, ib. 1901; C. F. Sitterly, *Praxis in Greek MSS of the N. T. The mechanical and literary Processes involved in their Writing and Preservation*, New York, 1898; R. Proctor, *The Printing of Greek in the Fifteenth Century*, no. 8 of *Illustrated Monographs*, issued by the Bibliographical Society, London, 1900; *DB*, iv, 944–957.

For the old printers consult—on Christopher Plantin: M. Rooses, *Christopher Plantin, imprimeur Anversois*, Antwerp, 1884; idem, *Christopher Plantin, Correspondance*, Ghent, 1886; T. L. de Vinne, *Christopher Plantin and the Plantin-Moretus Museum at Antwerp*, New York, 1885; L. Degeorge, *La Maison Plantin à Anvers*, Paris, 1886. On the Stephens: G. A. Crapelet, *Robert Estienne, imprimeur royal*, Paris, 1839; A. A. Renouard, *Annales de l'imprimerie des Estienne*, ib. 1843; L. Feugère, *Essai sur la vie et les ouvrages de Henri Estienne*, ib. 1853. On the Elzevirs: C. Pieters, *Annales de l'imprimerie Elsévirienne*, Ghent, 1860; A. Willems, *Les Elzévier: histoire et annales typographiques*, Brussels, 1880.

Late critical editions are: C. Tischendorf, *Novum Testamentum Græce, ed. 8. critica major*, Leipsic, 1864–72; *Prolegomena*, by C. R. Gregory, ib. 1884–94, small ed. of text of 8. ed., with selections of readings, ib. 1878; F. H. A. Scrivener and E. Palmer, *The Greek Testament with the Readings adopted by the Revisers of the Authorized Version*, Oxford, 1882; B. F. Westcott and F. J. A. Hort, *N. T. in the Original Greek*, Am. ed. with introduction by P. Schaff, 3d ed., New York, 1883; W. Sanday, *Lloyd's ed. of Mill's Text with Parallel References, Eusebian Canons and three Appendices* (published separately, containing variants of Westcott and Hort, and a selection of important readings with authorities, together with readings from Oriental versions, Memphitic, Armenian, and Ethiopic), Oxford, 1889; O. von Gebhardt, *Novum Testamentum* (with variants of Tregelles and Westcott and Hort), 6th ed., Leipsic, 1894; B. Weiss, *Das Neue Testament, Textkritische Untersuchungen und Textherstellung*, ib. 1894–1900; F. Blass, *Acta Apostolorum sive Lucæ ad Theophilum liber alter secundum formam quæ videtur Romanam*, ib. 1896; idem, *Evangelium secundum Lucam sive Lucæ ad Theophilum liber prior secundum formam quæ videtur Romanam*, ib. 1897; E. Nestle, *Testamentum Novum Græce cum apparatu critico*, Stuttgart, 1898 (the use of editions with the MS. variants will still be required); *Novum Testamentum Græcum, editio Stutgardiana*, ib. 1898 (based on collation of Tischendorf, Westcott and Hort, Weymouth, and Weiss; contains for the Gospels and Acts a selection of MS. readings, chiefly from *Codex Bezæ*).

Treatises on various phases of the history of N. T. textual criticism are: F. H. A. Scrivener, *A Full and Exact Collation of about twenty Greek MSS of the Holy Gospels (hitherto unexamined) in the British Museum, the Archiepiscopal Library at Lambeth, with a critical Introduction*, Cambridge, 1853; idem, *A Plain Introduction to the Criticism of the New Testament*, 4th ed., by E. Miller, London, 1894 (conservative); O. T. Dobbin, *The Codex*

Montfortianno, ib. 1854; F. W. A. Bäthgen, *Der griechische Text des Cureton'schen Syrers*, Leipsic, 1885; J. R. Harris, *The Origin of the Leicester Codex of the N. T.*, London, 1887; U. J. M. Bebb, *Evidence of the Early Versions and Patristic Quotations on the Text of . the N. T.*, in *Studia Biblica*, ii, Oxford, 1890; H. C. Hoskier, *A Full Account and Collation of the Greek Cursive Codex Evang. 604*, London, 1890 (contains in Appendix C, *A full and exact comparison of the Elzevir Editions of 1624 and 1633*); G. H. Gwilliam, *The Material for the Criticism of the Peshitto N. T.*, in *Studia Biblica*, iii, 47-104, Oxford, 1891; F. H. Chase, *The Old Syriac Element in the Text of Codex Bezæ*, London, 1893; Mrs. A. S. Lewis, *The Four Gospels translated from the Syriac Palimpsest*, ib. 1894; R. C. Bensley, J. R. Harris, and F. C. Burkitt, *The Four Gospels in Syriac transcribed from the Syriac Palimpsest*, Cambridge, 1894; G. N. Bonwetsch and H. Achelis, *Die christlichen griechischen Schriftsteller vor Eusebius*, Berlin, 1897; E. Miller, *The Present State of the Textual Controversy respecting the Holy Gospels*, London, 1899 (conservative); idem, *The Textual Controversy and the Twentieth Century*, ib. 1901; G. Salmon, *Some Thoughts on the Textual Criticism of the N. T.*, ib. 1897; M. R. Vincent, *A Hist. of the Textual Criticism of the N. T.*, New York, 1899; K. Lake, *The Text of the N. T.*, London, 1900; F. G. Kenyon, *Handbook to Textual Criticism of the N. T.*, ib. 1901; idem, *Evidence of Greek Papyri with Regard to Textual Criticism*, ib. 1905. On the Revisers' text consult W. M. Sanday in *Expositor*, 1881.

The principles of textual criticism are discussed at length in Hort's *Introduction* to Westcott and Hort's Greek Testament, London, 1881, where also is found the most elaborate discussion of the Sinaitic and Vatican MSS. On the Sinaitic MS. consult also F. H. A. Scrivener, *Collation of the Codex Sinaiticus*, 3d ed., London, 1867; C. Tischendorf, *Die Anfechtungen der Sinaibibel*, Leipsic, 1863; idem, *Die Sinaibibel, ihre Entdeckung, Herausgabe und Erwerbung*, ib. 1871; idem, *Waffen der Finsterniss wider die Sinaibibel*, ib. 1863. Convenient manuals are: E. Nestle, *Einführung in das griechische Neue Testament*, Göttingen, 1897. A valuable collection of editions of the Greek Testament, mostly amassed by the late Dr. Isaac H. Hall, is in the library of Union Theological Seminary, New York.

During the last three years considerable discussion has been aroused on the subject of the text, to which the following are the most important contributions:

For 1902: J. M. Bebb, in *DB*, iv, 848-855, 860-864; F. Blass, *Evangelium secundum Johannem cum variæ lectionis delectu*, Leipsic; F. C. Burkitt, *The Date of Codex Bezæ*, in *JTS*, vol. iii; F. C. Conybeare, *Three Early Doctrinal Modifications of the Text of the Gospels*, in *Hibbert Journal*, i, 96-113; M. D. Gibson, *Four remarkable Sinai MSS*, in *Expository Times*, xiii, 509-511; S. K. Gifford, *Pauli epistolas qua forma legerit Joannes Chrysostomus*, Halle; E. J. Goodspeed, *The Haskell Gospels*, in *JBL*, xxi, 100-107; C. R. Gregory, *Textkritik des N. T.*, vol. ii, Leipsic; C. E. Hammond, *Outlines of Textual Criticism applied to the N. T.*, Oxford; J. R. Harris, *A curious Bezan reading vindicated*, in *Expositor*, pp. 189-195; idem, *On a Recent Emendation in the Text of St. Peter*, ib., pp. 317-320; idem, *The History of a Conjectural Emendation* (ib., pp. 378-390); A. Hjelt, *Die altsyrische Evangelienübersetzung und Tatians Diatessaron*, in T. Zahn's *Forschungen*, viii, 1, Leipsic; K. Lake, *Codex 1 of the Gospels and its Allies*, Cambridge; idem, *Texts from Mount Athos*, in *Studia Biblica*, vol. v, part 2, pp. 89-185, London; A. S. Lewis, *Studia Sinaitica XI. Apocrypha Syriaca*, London; G. R. S. Mead, *The Gospels and the Gospel. Study in most recent Results of lower and higher Criticism*, London; A. Merx, *Die vier kanonischen Evangelien nach ihrem ältesten bekannten Texte. Uebersetzung und Erläuterung der syrischen im Sinaikloster gefundenen Palimpsesthandschriften*, part 2: *Erläuterungen*, 1st half: *Matthäus*, Berlin; E. Nestle, *The Greek Testament, with Introduction and Appendix on irregular Verbs*, by R. E. Weidner, New York; idem, in *DB*, iv, 645-652, 732-741; H. von Soden, *Die Schriften des N. T. in ihrer ältesten erreichbaren Textgestalt*, vol. i, part 1, Berlin; B. Weiss, *Das Neue Testament*, 3 vols., Leipsic; H. J. White, in *DB*, iv, 873-890.

For 1903: L. Blau, *Ueber den Einfluss des althebräischen Buchwesens auf die Originale und auf die ältesten Handschriften der LXX, des N. T. und der Hexapla*, Berlin; F. C. Burkitt, *On Codex Claromontanus*, in *JTS*, iv, 587-588; idem, *The Syriac Interpretation of John xiii. 4*, in *JTS*, iv, 436-438; idem, in *EB*, iv, 4981-5012; idem, *Further Notes on Codex k*, in *JTS*, v, 100-107; W. E. Crum, *Coptic Ostraka from the Collection of the Egypt Exploration Fund, the Cairo Museum, and others*, London; M. D. Gibson, *Four Remarkable Sinai Manuscripts*, in *Expository Times*, xiii, 509-511; J. E. Gilmore, *Manuscript Portions of three Coptic Lectionaries*, in *PSBA*, xxiv, 186-191; G. H. Gwilliam, *The Age of the Bodleian Syriac Codex Dawkins 3*, in *JTS*, iii, 452 sq.; idem, *Place of the Peshitto Version in the Apparatus criticus of the Greek N. T.*, in *Studia Biblica*, v, 3, pp. 187-237; K. Lake, *Dr. Weiss' Text of the Gospels*, in *AJT*, vii, 249-258; A. Schmidtke, *Die Evangelien einer alten Unzialcodex*, Leipsic; W. B. Smith, *The Pauline Manuscripts F and G*, in *AJT*, vii, 452-485, 662-688; C. Taylor, *The Pericope of the Adulteress*, in *JTS*, iv, 129-130; B. Weiss, *Die Perikope von der Ehebrecherin*, in *ZWT*, xlvi, 141-158; A. Wright, *A Synopsis of the Gospels in Greek*, 2d ed., London; O. Zöckler, *The Textual Question in Acts*, transl. by A. Steimle, New Rochelle.

For 1904: F. Blass, *Ueber die Textkritik im N. T.*, Leipsic; F. C. Burkitt, *Evangelion Da-Mepharreshe. The Curetonian Version of the four Gospels, with the Readings of the Sinai Palimpsest and the early Syriac patristic Evidence*, 2 vols., Cambridge; *Codex Veronensis . denuo ed. J. Belsheim*, Prague; R. D'Onston, *The Patristic Gospels. An English Version of the Holy Gospels as they existed in the second Century*, London; J. T. Marshall, *Remarkable Readings in the Epistles found in the Palestinian Syriac Lectionary*, in *JTS*, v, 437-445; J. B. Mayor, *Notes on the Text of II Peter*, in *Expositor*, pp. 284-293; idem, *Notes on the Text of the Epistle of Jude*, ib., pp. 450-460; J. O. F. Murray, *Textual Criticism*, in *DB*, extra vol., pp. 208-236; W. Sanday, *The Present Greek Testaments of the Clarendon Press*, in *JTS*, v, 279-280; *A New Greek Testament, prepared by E. Nestle. Text with Critical Apparatus*, London; *Novum Testamentum Latine secundum editionem sancti Hieronymi . recensuit* J. Wordsworth—H. J. White, part. ii, fasc. 2, *Actus Apostolorum*, Oxford; C. H. Turner, *A Re-Collation of Codex k of the Old Latin Gospels*, in *JTS*, v, 88-100.

1905: R. F. Weymouth, *The Resultant Greek Text*, with readings of Stephens (1550), Lachmann, Tregelles, Lightfoot, and (for the Pauline Epistles) Ellicott, also of Alford and Weiss for Matthew, the Basel ed., Westcott and Hort and Revisers, London, 1892, 3d ed., 1905.

1906: F. H. A. Scrivener, *Novum Testamentum, Textus Stephanici, Variæ Lectiones of Beza, the Elzevirs, Lachmann, Tischendorf, Tregelles, Westcott and Hort, and the Revisers*, London, 1887, ed. E. Nestle, 1906; A. Deissmann, *The New Biblical Papyri at Heidelberg*, in *Expository Times*, pp. 248-254.

The literature of the work which is being done may be found year by year in the *Bibliographie der theologischen Literatur* and in *AJT*.

III. Chapter and Verse Divisions: The purpose of the present division into chapters and verses was to facilitate reference. These divisions sometimes, but not generally, ignore logical and natural divisions. Common opinion concerning chapter divisions attributes them to Cardinal Hugo of Saint Cher (q.v.) for use in his concordance to the Latin Vulgate (c. 1240, first printed, with modification, at Bologna, 1479). This opinion rests on the direct testimony of Gilbert Genebrard (d. 1597), that "the scholastics who with Cardinal Hugo were authors of the concordance" made the division. Quétif and Echard, a century and a half later than Genebrard, ascribe to Hugo only the subdivision of the chapters presently to be mentioned. The better opinion is, that Stephen Langton, archbishop of Canterbury (d. 1228), made the chapter division to facilitate citation. Before the invention of printing it had already passed from Latin manuscripts to those of other tongues, and after the

1. Chapter Divisions.

invention of printing it became general. It has undergone slight variations from the beginning to the present day. Many early printed Bibles, especially Greek Testaments, besides these chapters retain also the old *breves* or *titloi* noted in the margin (see above, II, 1, § 5). The chapters were at first subdivided into seven portions (not paragraphs), marked in the margin by the letters A, B, C, D, E, F, G, reference being made by the chapter-number and the letter under which the passage occurred. In the shorter Psalms, however, the division did not always extend to seven. In Ps. cxix it seems not to have been used at all. This division (except in the Psalms) was modified by Conrad of Halberstadt (c. 1290), who reduced the divisions of the shorter chapters from seven to four; so that the letters were always either A–G or A–D. This subdivision continued long after the introduction of the present verses, but in the seventeenth century was much modified, some chapters having more than four, and less than seven, subdivisions.

2. Verse Divisions, Old Testament.

The present verses differ in origin for the Old Testament, New Testament, and Apocrypha. In the canonical Testament they appear in the oldest known manuscripts (see above, I, 1, § 7, 2, § 2), though they were not used for citation by the Jews till the fifteenth century. The earlier printed Hebrew Bibles marked each fifth verse only with its Hebrew numeral. Arabic numerals were first added for the intervening verses by Joseph Athias, at Amsterdam, 1661, at the suggestion of Jan Leusden. The first portion of the Bible printed with the Masoretic verses numbered was the *Psalterium Quincuplex* of Faber Stapulensis, printed at Paris by Henry Stephens in 1509. In 1528 Sanctes Pagninus published at Lyons a new Latin version of the whole Bible with the Masoretic verses marked and numbered. He also divided the Apocrypha and New Testament into numbered verses; but these were three or four times as long as the present ones.

3. Verse Divisions, New Testament.

The present New Testament verses were introduced by Robert Stephens in his Greco-Latin Testament of 1551 (see above, II, 2, § 2). Stephens says in his preface that the division is made to follow the most ancient Greek and Latin copies. But it will be difficult, if not impossible, to find any Greek or Latin manuscripts whose divisions coincide very nearly with Stephens's verses. Doubtless he made this division with reference to his concordance to the Vulgate, then preparing, published in 1555. This Latin concordance, like former ones, contains references to the letters A, B, C, D, E, F, G, and also to the numbers of the verses of each chapter "after the Hebrew method" of division. This latter, the preface states, has special reference to an *operi pulcherrimo et præclarissimo* which he is now printing, which must mean his splendid Bible of 1556–57, 3 vols., containing the Vulgate, Pagninus, and the first edition of Beza's Latin New Testament. Meanwhile, for present convenience, he is issuing a more modest Bible (Vulgate), with the verses marked and numbered. This latter was his Vulgate of 1555 (Geneva)—the first whole Bible divided into the present verses, and the first in which they were introduced into the Apocrypha. The text is continuous, not having the verses in separate paragraphs, like the New Testament of 1551, but separated by a ¶ and the verse-number. The verse-division differs in only a very few places from that of 1551; and a comparison shows that the concordance agrees rather with the division of 1551 than with that of 1555. The statement so often made that the division was made "on horseback" while on a journey from Paris to Lyons must be qualified. His son asserts that the work was done while on the journey, but the inference most natural and best supported is that the task was accomplished while resting at the inns along the road.

In other languages the division appeared first as follows: French, New Testament, Geneva, 1552, Bible, Geneva, 1553 (both R. Stephens); Italian, New Testament, L. Paschale (Geneva?), 1555; Dutch, New Testament, Gellius Ctematius (Gillis van der Erven), Embden, 1556, Bible, Nikolaus Biestkens van Diest, Embden, 1560; English, Genevan New Testament, 1557, Genevan Bible, 1560; German, Luther's Bible, perhaps Heidelberg, 1568, but certainly Frankfort, 1582.

In Beza's editions of the Greek Testament (1565–1604) sundry variations were introduced, which were followed by later editors, notably the Elzevirs (1633, etc.); and many minor changes have been made, quite down to the present day.

A very convenient and illuminating "table of ancient and modern divisions of the New Testament," giving the divisions in the Vatican manuscript, the *titloi*, the Ammonian *kephalaia*, the *stichoi*, *rēmata*, and the modern chapters and verses, is given in Scrivener, *Introduction*, i, 68. The *titloi*, *kephalaia*, and tables of the Eusebian canons are available in such editions as Stephens's Greek Testament of 1550, and Mill's of 1707, 1710. The Greek Testament by Lloyd (Oxford, 1827) and by Mill (1859) give the Eusebian canons. For a synopsis of variations in manuscripts consult J. M. A. Scholz, *Novum Testamentum Græce*, i, Frankfort, 1830, pp. xxviii–xxix.

The Stephanic verses have met with bitter criticism because of the fact that they break the text into fragments, the division often coming in the middle of the sentence, instead of forming it into convenient and logical paragraphs, an arrangement which has seldom found favor. But their utility for reference outweighs their disadvantage. They should never be printed in separate paragraphs (as in the English Authorized Version), but the text should be continuous and the numbers inserted in the margin (as in the Revised Version).

Bibliography: C. R. Gregory, *Prolegomena*, i, 140–182, Leipsic, 1894; the *Introductions* of Tregelles and Scrivener, ut sup. under II; B. F. Westcott and F. J. A. Hort, *N. T., Introduction and Appendix*, pp. 318 sqq., of Am. edition, New York, 1882; I. H. Hall, in *Sunday School Times*, Apr. 2, 1881. Consult also W. Wright, in Kitto's *Cyclopedia of Biblical Literature*, "Verse," London, 1845 (the ed. of 1870 is not so good); *DCA*, ii, 953–967.

BIBLE VERSIONS.

A. Ancient Versions.[1]

B. Modern Versions.

Bible versions, or translations of the original Hebrew and Greek of the Old and New Testaments, may be treated in an encyclopedia from different points of view: (1) from the critical, as instruments with which to reconstruct the original text; (2) from the exegetical, as showing how the Bible was understood in different times and places; (3) from the historical, as documents for showing the extent of the Bible and of its propagation among the nations of the earth; (4) from a literary and philological standpoint, since the Bible versions are often the earliest monuments of the respective languages.

Versions are either primary and direct, as the Septuagint, or secondary and indirect, derived versions, as the Old Latin. [They now exist, either for the entire Bible or a part, in more than five hundred languages. During 1906 eleven new versions were added and translation or revision is in progress in over one hundred tongues. Scriptures for the blind are issued by the British and Foreign Bible Society in fifteen languages.] Manifestly only a selection of the more important versions can be treated here.

[1] The principle of arrangement adopted in this series of articles is that of age, not simply, however, on account of chronological precedence, but because necessarily the earliest versions are, generally speaking, the most important for text-critical purposes. Two main divisions are thus formed: A, Ancient Versions; and B, Modern Versions. The versions treated under A are arranged approximately in order of text-critical value; under B, alphabetically.

Of the complete Bible in the original languages there is as yet but one edition in existence: *Biblia Sacra tam Veteris quam Novi Testamenti cum Apocryphis secundum fontes Hebræos et Græcos*, ed. C. B. Michaelis (2 vols., Züllichau, 1740–41; cf. the correspondence on this point in the *Sunday School Times*, Sept. and Oct., 1899, raised by a statement in the *TLZ*, 1899, no. 14). E. Nestle.

Bibliography: Among older works the following are indispensable: J. H. Hottinger, *Dissertationum theologico-philologicarum fasciculus*, Heidelberg, 1660 (deals with Jewish and Christian translations); Richard Simon, *Histoire critique du Vieux Testament*, Amsterdam, 1680, Eng. transl., London, 1682; idem, *Histoire critique des versions du Nouveau Testament*, Rotterdam, 1690, Eng. transl., London, 1692; idem, *Histoire critique du texte du Nouveau Testament*, Rotterdam, 1689, Eng. transl., London, 1689; idem, *Nouvelles observations sur le texte et les versions du Nouveau Testament*, Paris, 1695 (on Simon consult H. Margival, in *Revue d'histoire et de littérature religieuses*, Jan., Feb., 1896).

Bibliographical information is to be sought in the following: J. Le Long, *Bibliotheca Sacra, emendata ab A. G. Masch*, 2 parts in 5 vols., Halle, 1778–90 (part 1 deals with editions of the original texts, part 2, in 4 vols., deals with versions); Article *Bibel* in J. S. Ersch and J. G. Gruber, *Allgemeine Encyklopädie*, reprinted as a separate volume, Leipsic, 1823; *The Bibles in the Caxton Exhibition*, London, 1878; *British Museum Catalogue*, entry "Bible," 4 parts, including *Appendix*, London, 1892–99 (the fullest list printed of editions of the Bible and of its parts); T. H. Darlow and F. H. Moule, *Historical Catalogue of the Printed Editions of Holy Scripture in the Library of the British and Foreign Bible Society*, vol. i, *English*, London, 1903, vol. ii not yet issued. Of specific interest are: L. Hain, *Repertorium bibliographicum*, 5 vols., Stuttgart, 1826–91, *Supplement* by W. A. Copinger, 3 vols., London.

1891–1902, *Appendices* by D. Reichling, Munich, 1905–06; W. T. Lowndes, *Bibliographer's Manual*, 4 vols., London, 1857–64; J. C. Brunet, *Manuel du Libraire*, 7 vols., Paris, 1860–78. Consult also the works of Loisy, Copinger, and Kenyon given under BIBLE TEXT, I; the table of *Bible Translations* in J. S. Dennis, *Centennial Survey of Foreign Missions*, New York, 1904; T. Häring, *Das Verständniss der Bibel in der Entwicklung der Menschheit*, Tübingen, 1905, and *DB*, iv, 848–855, extra volume, 236–271, 402–420.

A. Ancient Versions.

I. Greek Versions.—1. The Septuagint: The Bible version most important in every respect is the Alexandrian translation of the Old Testament, the so-called Septuagint. "Custom now holds to the version which is called the Septuagint," writes Augustine (*De civitate Dei*, xviii, 42). The term "Septuagint" is an abbreviation of *secundum septuaginta interpretes;* the subscription of Genesis in the *Codex Vaticanus* is "According

1. Origin.

to the Seventy"; Codex A has before Isaiah, "the Edition of the Seventy"; this is based on the story that King Ptolemy Philadelphus, by the advice of his librarian Demetrius Phalereus, asked from the high priest Eleazar of Jerusalem seventy-two scholars, who translated for him in seventy-two days the law, and, after a later form of the legend, in seventy-two (or thirty-six) cells, the seventy-two or thirty-six copies being found without any variation when brought together and compared. The story is first told in the so-called "Letter of Aristeas" (see ARISTEAS), who pretends to be one of the officers sent by Philadelphus to Jerusalem, and is wholly unhistorical.

As the date of the version ancient chronicles mention the 2d, 7th, 17th, 18th, 19th, or 20th year of Philadelphus, the year 1734, 35, 36, or 37 of Abraham; as its day the 8th of Tebeth, a day of darkness like that on which the golden calf was made (cf. Margoliouth, in the *Expositor*, Nov., 1900, 318–349). Philo relates, on the contrary, that the Jews of Alexandria kept in his time an annual festival "in commemoration of the time when the interpretation first shone out, and they praised God for his works in times new and old." He knows that the interpreters asked God's blessing on this undertaking; "for he answered their prayers that more and more the whole race of men might be assisted to correctness of life in thought and deed." This aspiration was fulfilled when the version became one of the chief instruments for the preparation and propagation of Christianity (on this aspect of the version cf. E. W Grinfield, *Apology for the Septuagint*, London, 1850; W. R. Churton, *The Influence of the Septuagint on the Progress of Christianity*, London, 1861; A. Deissmann, *Die Hellenisierung des semitischen Monotheismus*, Leipsic, 1903). It is not yet certain whether the translation is due, as the legend purports, to the literary interest of a king who was a bibliophile; or, as is the common view at present, to the religious wants of the Jewish community of Alexandria; or to the needs of an intended Jewish propaganda. For the latter view the prologue of Ecclesiasticus may be mentioned, which is, at the same time, the first witness to speak of all three parts of the Hebrew Bible as already extant in Greek; Aristeas, Philo, and Josephus speak only of the law. Of the several books of the Old Testament only Esther has a statement about the translation of the book, which is referred generally to Soter II (114 B.C.), but by H. Willrich (*Judaica*, Göttingen, 1900) to Ptolemy XIV (48 B.C.). At the end of Job is the strange notice: "This is interpreted from the Syrian book."

The first part of the Septuagint to be multiplied by the printing-press was the Psalms in the Greek and Latin Psalter of Bonacursius (Milan, Sept. 20, 1481; in Greek alone, Venice, 1486, and again by Aldus Manutius about 1497). The complete editions fall into four classes according as they are derived from one or another of four original editions,

2. Printed Editions.

of which the first (designated as *c*) is the Complutensian Polyglot of Cardinal Ximenes, printed 1514–17 but not published until 1521 (see BIBLES, POLYGLOT, I; cf. Franz Delitzsch, *Studien zur Entstehungsgeschichte der Polyglottenbibel des Cardinals Ximenes*, Leipsic, 1871, supplemented 1878 sq.; T. H. Darlow and F. H. Moule, *Historical Catalogue of the BFBS*, ii, London, 1908, 1 sqq.). Of the manuscripts used for the Greek Old Testament we know with certainty *Vat. Gr.* 330 and 346, and *Venet.* 5 (=Holmes-Parsons 108, 248, and 68). The second (*a*) is the Aldine Bible published by Andreas Asulanus, father-in-law of the elder Aldus (Venice, 1518). Among the manuscripts used were Holmes-Parsons 29, 68, 121, all of Venice. The third and most important is the *Editio Sixtina* (*b*), published by Pope Sixtus V (Rome, 1586 [1587]) on the basis of *Codex Vat. Gr.* 1209 (=B, in the article BIBLE TEXT, II, 1, § 9). Besides *c* and *a*, the manuscripts Holmes-Parsons 16, 19, 23, 51 seem to have been used, especially for the scholia, which were collected chiefly by Petrus Morinus and enlarged by Flaminius Nobilius in the Latin translation published 1588. The fourth edition (4 vols. folio and 8 vols. 8vo, Oxford, 1707–20) was begun by Johannes Ernst Grabe (q.v.), who published vols. i and iv (1707, 1709), and after his death (1711) was completed by Francis Lee (vol. ii, 1719) and George Wigan (vol. iii, 1720). It is based on the *Codex Alexandrinus* (A; see BIBLE TEXT, II, 1, § 9) with use of other sources, especially Origen's Hexapla, has useful prolegomena, and possesses a merit of its own.

These editions have been often reproduced—the Sixtine edition most frequently—with more or less of editorial labor (for list of reprints, etc.; also mention of the more important editions of single books of the Greek Old Testament, cf. the Hauck-Herzog *RE*, iii, 4–9 and Swete, *Introduction*, 171–194). But no existing edition of the Septuagint satisfies present wants, for none gives an exact reproduction of the manuscript or manuscripts which it follows, nor does any provide a full *apparatus criticus*. The first attempt to satisfy the latter want was made in the great work begun by Robert Holmes (q.v.) and completed after his death (1805) by James Parsons, *Vetus Testamentum Græcum cum variis lectionibus* (5 vols., Oxford, 1798–1827; cf. Swete, *Introduction*, 184–187; *Church*

Quarterly Review, Apr., 1899, 102 sqq., and the annual accounts published during the progress of the work from 1789 to 1805). The text is that of *b*. Not less than 164 volumes of manuscript collations prepared for this work are still in the Bodleian Library. All manuscripts, versions, and quotations were put under contribution. Despite some drawbacks in the plan and still more in the execution, the work deserves admiration; it is still indispensable to all who wish full information about the Old Testament in Greek. The advance made in the course of the nineteenth century is due, on the one hand, to the discovery of new materials (e.g. the *Codex Sinaiticus*; see BIBLE TEXT, II, 1, § 9); on the other, to greater exactness in handling witnesses. Both these advantages are evident in the work of C. Tischendorf, P. de Lagarde, and H. B. Swete. Tischendorf (*Vetus Testamentum Græce juxta LXX interpretes*, 2 vols., Leipsic, 1850; 7th ed., 1887) repeated the text of *b* and enriched it with variants from the *Codex Alexandrinus, Ephraemi Rescriptus*, and (after 1869) the *Sinaiticus*, adding rich prolegomena. Lagarde's work, though left incomplete, was monumental (for list of his publications, see LAGARDE, PAUL ANTON DE). Swete reproduced in his edition (*The Old Testament in Greek according to the Septuagint*, 3 vols., Cambridge, 1887–94; 2d ed., 1895–99; 3d ed., 1901–07) for the first time not the printed text of *b*, but the Vatican manuscript itself, in the first edition according to the facsimile impression of Fabiani-Cozza (Rome, 1869–81), which for the second has been revised (by E. Nestle) after the photographic reproduction. Where the manuscript is deficient the text has been taken from the oldest manuscript accessible in a trustworthy form, while under the text variants have been given from some of the oldest manuscripts, as *Sinaiticus, Alexandrinus*, and *Ambrosianus*. The merit of this edition is that it gives the materials with greatest accuracy; its defect, that it does not make any attempt to construct the text according to the principles of textual criticism, but follows the leading manuscript even in its most glaring faults. And in some books at least (e.g. in Ecclesiasticus), the oldest manuscripts are far from being the best. But this deficiency is fully explained by the fact that the edition is intended to be but the basis of a great critical edition now in course of preparation, of which the first part has already appeared, *The Old Testament in Greek, according to the Text of Codex Vaticanus Supplemented from Other Uncial Manuscripts, with a Critical Apparatus Containing the Variants of the Chief Ancient Authorities for the Text of the Septuagint*, ed. A. E. Brooke and N. McLean, *vol. i, The Octateuch, part i, Genesis* (Cambridge, 1906; cf. *JTS*, iii, 601–621, and E. Nestle, *Die grosse Cambridger Septuaginta*, in *Verhandlungen des XIII. Internationalen Orientalistenkongresses*, 1902; idem, *Septuagintastudien*, vol. v, 1907).

There are two English translations: ***The Septuagint Version of the Old Testament according to the Vatican Text, translated into English, with the principal various readings of the Alexandrine copy, and a table of comparative chronology***, by Sir Lancelot Charles Lee Brenton (2 vols., London, 1844; has also the Greek text); the other by Charles Thomson (Philadelphia, 1808; new ed., *The Old Covenant, commonly called the Old Testament*, by S. F. Pells, 2 vols., London, 1904).

That there is yet not a satisfactory edition of the Septuagint is not because of want of materials for its preparation—there is on the contrary an *embarras de richesse*—but of its complicated history.

3. Early Corruption of the Text. The history of a translation will always be more complicated than that of an original text, but in this case it is the more so as the Septuagint is a work of Jewish origin, taken over into the Christian Church. Of the pre-Christian period of its history next to nothing is known. There are some Hellenistic writers who used the Septuagint, as Demetrius, Eupolemus, Aristeas (the historian), Ezekiel, and Aristobulus; but the preserved fragments of their writings are too few and incomplete to establish more than the mere fact that they used the Septuagint. Philo made extensive use of the law, but his quotations from the rest of the Old Testament are very few, and from Ruth, Esther, Ecclesiastes, Canticles, Lamentations, Ezekiel, and Daniel he does not quote at all. Besides, his writings can be traced back only to the library of Origen, and have been transmitted to us probably exclusively through Christian copyists. For Josephus we must be content to know that for his description of the restoration he used what is now called I Esdras; but about his relation to the chief manuscripts there is uncertainty. Even the quotations in the New Testament do not justify very definite statements, except that they prove that already in those times the copies were not free from textual corruption (cf. Heb. iii, 9, xii, 5). A little later the situation is described by Origen—speaking, it is true, chiefly of the manuscripts of the New Testament, but what he says holds good also of those of the Old Testament: "Now it is clear that there has come a great difference in copies, either through the laziness of scribes or from the audacity of those who introduced corruptions as amendments, or of others who took away from or added to their new text such things as seemed good to them."

If the situation was already bad, since any copyist or reader who was acquainted with the original might change single passages on comparison with the Hebrew, it became worse when new translations appeared, especially those of Aquila, Symmachus, and Theodotion (see below, 2). At last a systematic comparison of the Septuagint with the Hebrew and these versions was carried out by Origen in the Hexapla (see ORIGEN), and what appeared to him a safeguard against the calamity that threatened the text turned out—not by his fault, but through later ignorance and carelessness—the worst aggravation of it. In continuation of the passage just quoted, he goes on to say that through the guidance of God he found a way to correct the dissonance in the copies. Using the Hebrew as a criterion, and adopting the text of the Septua-

4. The Hexapla of Origen.

gint which confirmed the Hebrew, he made the two the ground text, and marked changes by diacritical signs. It is pardonable that he took his Hebrew text—whence he got it is not known—as the original text; but it was contrary to sound criticism to take those readings of the Septuagint which agreed with the Hebrew for the true ones, instead of those which differed from it (cf. the third axiom of Lagarde for the restoration of the Septuagint, *Mittheilungen*, i, 21). Nevertheless we should be extremely thankful if the work of Origen had been preserved. Until 1896 it was known only from the descriptions of Eusebius, Jerome, Epiphanius, and some later writers, and by specimens preserved in scholia of Biblical manuscripts, a great part also by a literal Syriac translation (see below, § 6). In 1896 Giovanni Mercati discovered in a palimpsest of the Ambrosian Library of Milan the first continuous fragments of a copy of the Hexapla, and in 1900 another and much older piece was found by C. Taylor among the Greek palimpsests from the Cairo genizah in the Taylor and Schechter collection. These fragments show that Origen put generally only one Hebrew word, or at the most two, in one line; the extent of the work, therefore, must have been much greater than was previously supposed. The later fate of the original is unknown. Jerome saw and used it in the library at Cæsarea; it may have been destroyed there during the invasion of the Arabs.

Origen arranged his work in six columns, the first containing the Hebrew text in Hebrew letters, the second the same in a Greek transcription, the third the translation of Aquila, the fourth that of Symmachus, the fifth the Septuagint, the sixth the translation of Theodotion. For some books, especially the Psalms, Origen had a fifth, sixth, and even a seventh translation at his disposal (see below, 2, § 3). In the Septuagint column he used the system of diacritical marks which was in use with the Alexandrian critics of Homer, especially Aristarchus, marking with an obelus—under different forms, as ÷, called lemniscus, and ⸓, called hypolemniscus—those passages of the Septuagint which had nothing to correspond in Hebrew, and inserting, chiefly from Theodotion under an asterisk (*), those which were missing in the Septuagint; in both cases a metobelus (γ) marked the end of the notation. This column was copied afterward with additional excerpts from the other versions on the margins; and, if it had been copied with all its critical marks, it would have been well, but later copyists neglected these completely and produced what we may call kryptohexaplaric manuscripts, completely spoiling by this carelessness the value of the Septuagint for critical purposes. Such a copy, for instance, is, for Kings, the *Codex Alexandrinus*; and it is but a poor defense of these copyists that the same process has been repeated in the nineteenth century by the Moscow and Athens reprints of Grabe's edition of that codex.

After Origen, Eusebius and his friend Pamphilus were careful to continue or disseminate his exegetical labors. Copies of the Pentateuch are known which were compared with the Samaritan text (cf. S. Kohn, *Samareitikon und Septuaginta*, in *Monatsschrift für Wissenschaft des Judenthums*, new series, i, 1894, pp. 1–7, 49–67; *ZDMG*, 1893, p. 650). Jerome mentions besides Eusebius and

5. Lucian and Hesychius.

Pamphilus, Lucian and Hesychius, the text of the former being used from Constantinople to Antioch, that of the latter in Alexandria and Egypt, while the provinces between, especially Palestine, kept to the copies of Origen as published by Eusebius and Pamphilus (*Præfatio in paralipomena; Adv. Rufinum*, ii, 27). About neither the work nor the person of Hesychius (see HESYCHIUS, 1) is there complete certainty. He may have been the martyr bishop mentioned by Eusebius (*Hist. eccl.*, viii, 13) together with Phileas of Thmuis. The result of his labors is sought now for the Octateuch in the manuscripts 44, 74, 76, 84, 106, 134; for the prophets, especially Isaiah and the Twelve, in the *Codex Marchalianus* and its supporters 26, 106, 198, 306 (cf. N. McLean, in *JTS*, ii, 1901, p. 306, and A. Ceriani, *De Codice Marchaliano*, Rome, 1890, pp. 48 sqq., 105 sqq.). Lucian was a deacon of Antioch, who died a martyr at Nicomedia 312 (see LUCIAN THE MARTYR). He must have known a Hebrew text which showed many peculiarities, especially in the historical books, and perhaps used for his purposes the Syriac version. The first part of his work has been edited by Lagarde in *Librorum Veteris Testamenti canonicorum, pars prior, græce* (Göttingen, 1883; cf. his *Mittheilungen*, ii, 171). But this revision must not be confounded with the original Septuagint any more than the English Revised with the Authorized Version. Since the fourth century very little has been done in the Greek Church for its Bible. Emperors directed beautiful copies of it to be written—e.g., Constantine ordered fifty copies through Eusebius for the new churches of his capital, and for Constans Athanasius procured "copies of the divine writings," one of which is perhaps preserved in the famous *Codex Vaticanus*. Other royal persons wrote them with their own hands.

Latin was probably the first language into which the Septuagint was translated. (On the Latin version, or rather versions, of the Septuagint see below, II, 1. It is a pity that so little of these labors has been preserved, and that these few remnants are so difficult of access.) After the Latin versions came

6. Versions Made from the Septuagint.

the Egyptian (see VII). Here the difficulty of the language makes these helps for restoration of the Septuagint accessible to few. Similar is the case with the most neglected branch of the Semitic languages, the Ethiopic (see VIII). The Arabic versions (see B, I) are for a great part too late to have much weight for the critic of the Septuagint. The Gothic version (see X) is an outcome of the Lucianic recension, for which it would have great importance, both for age and literalness, but very little of the Old Testament is preserved in Gothic. The Lucianic recension is also the basis of a Slavonic version (see B, XVI) and through it of the Georgian (see IX).

The Armenian version (see VI) is again of great importance, also the so-called Syro-Hexaplar version made in the year 616–617 by Paul, bishop of Tella (Constantine in Mesopotamia), in a cloister near Alexandria with the utmost fidelity from manuscripts which went back by few intervening links to the very copies of the Hexapla and Tetrapla of Origen. The greater is the pity, therefore, that only fragments have been preserved, and that especially the codex which André du Maes (Masius, d. 1573) had in his hands, containing the historical books (including part of Deuteronomy and Tobit), has been lost, and that only a part of this Bible (poetical and prophetic books) is still preserved in the Ambrosian Library at Milan, hence called *Codex Syro-hexaplaris Ambrosianus* (published in a photolithographic facsimile edition by A. Ceriani as vol. vii of the *Monumenta sacra et profana*, Milan, 1874). The fragments of Genesis, Exodus, Numbers, Joshua, Judges, and I and II Kings have been most carefully edited in the last work of Paul de Lagarde, *Bibliothecæ Syriacæ a Paulo de Lagarde collectæ quæ ad philologiam sacram pertinent* (Göttingen, 1892). For earlier works on this version cf. E. Nestle, *Litteratura Syriaca* (reprinted from his *Syrische Grammatik*, Berlin, 1888), 29–30; cf. also T. S. Rordam, *Libri Judicum et Ruth* (Copenhagen, 1859–61), and F. Field, *Otium Norvicense*, i (Oxford, 1864), and his edition of the Hexapla (Oxford, 1875). There are also fragments in the special dialect called Syro-Palestinian, on which cf. Swete, *Introduction*, 114, and F. C. Burkitt, in *JTS*, ii, 174 sqq.

Up to the present day in several Churches these versions based on the Septuagint have been retained and even in those where they have been replaced by translations from the original, as in the Latin West through Jerome or in modern Europe through the Reformation, the influence of the Septuagint is still very marked; note, for instance, the names of the Biblical books in the latest of these revisions, the English Revised Version.

The versions just mentioned are one of the three sources which exist for the recovery of the true text of the Septuagint, the first class being, of course, the Greek manuscripts still in existence, the third the quotations of ancient writers. A list of the more ancient manuscripts of the Septuagint was given in the eighteenth century by Stroth in Eichhorn's *Repertorium* (Leipsic, 1777 sqq.), vols. v sqq.; the most complete list was formerly that in the prefaces of Holmes-Parsons; then in the prolegomena of Tischendorf and in Lagarde's *Genesis Græce*; but reference may now be made to Swete, *Introduction*, pp. 122–170. A few remarks on some of them may be offered.

7. Manuscripts.

The four great uncials, ℵ or S, A, B, and C, are the chief manuscripts also for the New Testament (see BIBLE TEXT, II, 1, § 9). For ℵ there is needed a photographic reproduction or a complete new collation. The notations from A in Swete's Septuagint need revision, at all events in the first volume. Of B a new photographic reproduction is in preparation; on the suggestion of Rahlfs that B is dependent on Athanasius, cf. E. Nestle, *Introduction to the Textual Criticism of the Greek New Testament* (London, 1901), 62, 181, where (note 1) read Constantius instead of Constans. Concerning the famous illuminated *Codex Cottonianus* (D), which was badly injured by fire in 1731, nothing new has come to light since Swete wrote; it is well to mention the name of Martin Folkes as editor, by whom were issued the facsimiles in the *Vetusta monumenta* of 1747. On the purple illuminated Genesis of Vienna (L), there is a dissertation by W Ludtke (Greifswald, 1897), who is inclined to ascribe this oldest Biblical history with illuminations to the second part of the fifth century. To the eighteen uncial manuscripts enumerated by Swete (*Introduction*, pp. 146–148) as not yet used for any edition of the Septuagint and remaining without a symbolical letter or number, may be added: fragments of Genesis at Vienna (cf. *Philologischer Anzeiger*, xiv, 1884, 415); a Hebrew-Greek palimpsest containing fragments of Ps. cxliii, cxliv; and parts of four leaves from a papyrus codex of Genesis, of the late second or early third century (Oxyrhynchus papyri no. 656). On the minuscules scarcely anything has been done lately, except that some will be used in the Cambridge edition mentioned above (§ 2). For facsimiles, cf. F. G. Kenyon, *Facsimiles of Biblical Manuscripts in the British Museum* (London, 1901).

The question, in which set of manuscripts the purest text is to be found, is not yet settled. It is the more complicated since the Old Testament is a collection of books which in one and the same manuscript may have had a very different pedigree; for whole Bibles (*pandectes*, such as manuscripts ℵ, A, and B) do not seem to have been produced much before the time of Eusebius or Origen.

2. Later Greek Translations: The rupture between Church and Synagogue led to new translations. The authors of at least three of them are known by name, Aquila, Symmachus, and Theodotion.

Of the Fathers of the Church, Irenæus is the first who mentions Aquila of Pontus as a translator of the Bible. Epiphanius calls him a "Greek" and a relation of Hadrian, and tells that he was placed by Trajan in charge of the rebuilding of Jerusalem, that he became a Christian but returned to the Jewish faith. Epiphanius places his translation in the twelfth year of Hadrian, 430 years, four months, less nine days after the Septuagint. Jewish sources mention a proselyte Aquila, a contemporary of Rabbis Eliezer, Joshua, and Akiba, who met Hadrian and is called his nephew, and is praised as translator of the Bible in the words of Ps. xlv, "thou art fairer than the children of men"; some passages of his translation are quoted.

1. Aquila.

It is not clear as yet, whether or how the dates of Epiphanius and the statements of the Pseudo-Clementine writings about Aquila, the disciple of Simon Magus, are to be combined. That Aquila the translator of the Bible is the well-known husband of Priscilla in the New Testament is a fancy of Hausdorff. His translation, the use of which was permitted in the synagogue by Justinian, is the most literal ever produced, and enough has been preserved to judge of its value and character. Up to 1897 all known of it went back to the Hexapla of Origen (cf. F. Field, *Origenis Hexaplorum quæ supersunt*, 2 vols., Oxford, 1867–75, and, on Field, J. H. Burn, *Expository Times*, Jan., 1897). In 1897 for the first time a continuous portion of his translation came to light in a palimpsest of the Cairo Synagogue, showing the tetragrammaton written in Old Hebrew letters. The statement of Jerome that Aquila made two versions, "a second edition, which the Hebrews call 'the accurate one,'" seems to be correct. Some new fragments to be added to Field are in J. B. Pitra, *Analecta sacra* (Paris, 1876); E. Klostermann, *Analekta zur Septuaginta* (Leipsic, 1895); Jerome, in *Anecdota Maredsolana*, iii, 1.

2. Symmachus. According to Epiphanius, Symmachus was a Samaritan, and lived not under Severus, but under "Verus" (i.e., Marcus Aurelius; cf. Lagarde, *Symmicta*, ii, Göttingen, 1880). Geiger identified the translator with Symmachus ben Joseph, disciple of Rabbi Meir (*Jüdische Zeitschrift für Wissenschaft und Leben*, i, 1862, pp. 62–64). Origen got the manuscript of his translation from a certain Juliana of Cæsarea, who had received it with other works of Symmachus from Symmachus himself. Whether the Cæsarea where she lived was that of Palestine or Cappadocia is in doubt. In the sixteenth century Symmachus's works were still in existence at Rodosto near Constantinople (cf. R. Förster, *De antiquitatibus et libris manuscriptis Constantinopolitanis*, Rostock, 1877; T. Zahn, *TLB*, 1893, p. 43). Symmachus wrote the most elegant Greek of all these translators. Jerome quotes in three passages a second translation.

3. Theodotion. Theodotion, according to Irenæus, was from Ephesus; according to Epiphanius, from Pontus; he went over from Gnosticism to Judaism. His work is a revision of the Septuagint and has therefore been placed by Origen in his Hexapla next to the column of the Septuagint. For the same reason Origen made use chiefly of Theodotion to supply such passages as were missing in the Septuagint (cf. I Sam. xvii, 12 sqq.; Jer. xxxiii, 14–26; xxxix, 4–13). For the Book of Daniel his version came into general use in the Church, while the older Greek version has been preserved only in the one codex (*Chisianus*) discovered 1772. Readings similar to those of Theodotion are found before his time (on this question cf. E. König, *Einleitung*, ii, 108; *TLB*, 1897, 51; Stärk, *ZWT*, 1895, 288). Howorth offers some unconventional views (*PSBA*, 1891–92) on the question whether Chronicles and Ezra-Nehemiah in our editions of the Septuagint are from Theodotion. That his name has the same meaning as that of the Targumist Jonathan seems accidental.

Besides these versions, which covered the whole Old Testament—note, however, that for Samuel we have no quotations from Aquila—Origen succeeded in finding, at least for certain parts, more translations: the one which he numbered five, in Nicopolis near Actium; the sixth with other Hebrew and Greek books in a clay jar near Jericho in the time of Antoninus, the son of Severus.

Deserving of brief mention is a Greek translation which is 1,000 years younger than the preceding, the *Græcus Venetus*, which first became known in 1740 through the catalogue of the library of San Marco. The complete and final edition is due to O. von Gebhardt (*Græcus Venetus, Pentateuchi, Proverbiorum, Ruth, Cantici, Ecclesiastæ, Threnorum, Danielis græca versio*, with preface by F. Delitzsch, Leipsic, 1875). Delitzsch is inclined to see in the translation the work of a Jew, Elisseus, who lived at the court of Murad I in Prusa and Adrianople; von Gebhardt, that of a proselyte. The rendering of "Yahweh" by *ontourgos, ousiōtēs* and the use of the Doric dialect for the Aramaic portions of Daniel are interesting. E. Nestle.

Bibliography: The following is only a selection out of the vast body of literature available. The critical Introductions and Commentaries on the Old Testament and on separate parts deal more or less fully with the subject. For the literature on Polyglots see Bibles, Polyglot; for that on Aristeas see Aristeas; and on printed editions of the Septuagint cf. H. B. Swete, *Introduction*, pp. 171–194, London, 1902. On the Septuagint in general consult besides the works mentioned in the text: J. H. Hottinger, *Exercitationes Anti-Morinianæ*, Zurich, 1644; idem, *Dissertationum fasciculus*, Heidelberg, 1660; A. Calovius, *Criticus sacer*, Leipsic, 1646; L. Cappellus, *Critica sacra*, Paris, 1650; J. Buxtorf, *Anticritica, seu vindiciæ veritatis Hebraicæ*, Basel, 1653; J. Ussher, *De Græca septuaginta interpretum versione syntagma*, London, 1655; J. Morinus, *Exercitationes ecclesiasticæ et biblicæ*, Paris, 1669; H. Hody, *De bibliorum textibus originalibus*, Oxford, 1705; J. E. Grabe, *Epistola ad J. Millium*, Oxford, 1705; idem, *De vitiis septuaginta interpretum*, ib. 1710; E. Leigh, *Critica sacra*, 5th ed., London, 1706; A. Trommius, *Concordantiæ Græcæ versionis*, Amsterdam, 1718; W. Whiston, *Essay toward Restoring the True Text of the Old Testament*, London, 1722, and *Supplement* (to the same), 1723; J. G. Carpzov, *Critica sacra*, Leipsic, 1728; W. Wall, *The Use of the Septuagint Translation*, in his *Brief Critical Notes*, London, 1730; C. F. Houbigant, *Prolegomena in scripturam sacram*, Paris, 1746; B. Kennicott, *The State of the Printed Hebrew Text of the Old Testament*, Oxford, 1753; idem, a second *Dissertation* on the same subject 1759; J. D. Michaelis, *Programma über die 70 Dollmätscher*, Göttingen, 1767; H. Owen, *Enquiry into the Present State of the Septuagint Version*, London, 1769; idem, *Critica sacra*, 1774; idem, *A Brief Account of the Septuagint Version*, 1787; J. C. Biel, *Novus thesaurus philologicus*, The Hague, 1779–80; J. F. Schleusner, *Lexici in interpretes græci Veteris Testamenti*, Leipsic, 1784–86; C. A. Wahl, *Clavis librorum Veteris Testamenti*, Leipsic, 1853; G. Bickell, *De indole ac ratione versionis Alexandrinæ Jobi*, Marburg, 1862; F. Delitzsch, *Studien . . der complutensischen Polyglotte*, Leipsic, 1886; A. Scholz, *Masorethischer Text und die LXX-Uebersetzung des . Jeremias*, Regensburg, 1875; idem, *Die alexandrinische Uebersetzung des Jesaias*, Würzburg, 1880; E. Flecker, *Scripture Onomatology . . Critical Notes on the Septuagint*, London, 1883; W. J. Deane, in *The Expositor*, 1884, pp. 139–157, 223–237; E. Nestle, *Septuagintastudien*, vols. i–v, Ulm, 1886–1907, Maulbronn, 1899–1903; J. G. Carleton, *The Bible of our Lord and his Apostles*, London, 1888; E. Hatch, *Essays in Biblical Greek*, London, 1889 (cf. criticism by Hort, in *The Expositor*, Feb., 1897); A. Schulte, *De restitutione . versionis Græcæ . . Judicum*, Leipsic, 1889; G. C. Workman, *Text of Jeremiah Greek and Hebrew*, Edinburgh, 1889; P. de Lagarde, *Stichometrie*, in *Mittheilungen*, iv, 205, Göttingen, 1891; F. C. Conybeare, on *Philo's Text* in *The Expositor*, Dec., 1891, pp. 456–466; H. B Swete, on *Grätz's Theory*, in *Expository Times*, June, 1891, J. Taylor, *Massoretic Text and . . Versions of . . . Micah*, London, 1891; *Transactions of the Congress of Orientalists in London*, London, 1894; E. Hatch and H. A. Redpath, *Concordance to the Septuagint*, London, 1892–1900; F. C. Conybeare, *Philonean Text*, in *JQR*, Jan., 1893, pp. 246–280, Oct., 1895, pp. 88–122; H. A. Redpath, in *The Academy*, Oct. 22, 1893; G. Morin, *Une revision du psautier*, in *Revue bénédictine*, 1893, part 5, pp. 193–197; H. H. Howorth, in *The Academy*, 1893, July 22, Sept. 16, Oct. 7, Dec. 16, 1894, Feb. 17, May 5, June 9 (cf. W. A. Wright, ib. 1894, Nov. 3, and T. K. Cheyne, 1894, Nov. 10); V. Nourisson, *La Bibliothèque des Ptolémées*, Alexandria, 1893; S. Silberstein, *Codex Alexandrinus und Vaticanus des dritten Königsbuches*, in *ZATW*, 1893–94; G. A. Deissmann, *Bibelstudien*, Marburg, 1895–96, Eng. transl., Edinburgh, 1901; H. A. Kennedy, *Sources of New Testament Greek*, Edinburgh, 1895; E. Klostermann, *Analecta zur Septuaginta*, Leipsic, 1895; Max Löhr, *Vorarbeiten zu Daniel*, in *ZATW*. xv (1895), 75–103, 193–225; E. Nestle, *Zum Codex Alexandrinus*, in *ZATW*. xv (1895), 261–262; idem, *Zur Hexapla des Origenes*, in *ZWT*, xxxviii, 231; H. E. Ryle, *Philo and Holy Scripture*, London, 1895; F. Johnson, *Quotations of the New Testament*, London, 1896; A. F. Kirkpatrick, *The Septuagint*, in *The Expositor*, April, 1896, 213–257; E. Klostermann, *Die Mailänder Fragmente*, in *ZATW*. 1896, pp. 334–337; J. Fürst, in *Semitic Studies in Memory of A. Kohut*, Berlin, 1897; E. Nestle, *Einführung in das griechische Neue Testament*, Göttingen, 1897, Eng. transl., London, 1901; J. H. Moulton, *A Grammar of New Testament Greek*, vol. i, *Prolegomena*, pp. 1–41, Edinburgh, 1906; A. Merx, *Der Werth der Septuaginta für die Textkritik des A. T.*, in *JPT*, ix, 65; A. Rahlfs, *Septuaginta-Studien*, parts i–ii, Göttingen, 1904–07.

On Aquila, Symmachus, and Theodotion, besides the references in Irenæus, Origen, Eusebius, Jerome, and Epiphanius, consult: C. A. Thieme, *Pro puritate Symmachi*, Leipsic, 1755; R. Anger, *De Onkelo Chaldaico*, ib. 1845; F. Field, *Origenis Hexaplorum quæ supersunt*, i, pp. xvi sqq., Oxford, 1867; G. Mercati, *L'Età di Simmaco interprete*, Modena, 1892; L. Hausdorff, *Zur Geschichte der Targumim nach talmudischen Quellen*, in *Monatsschrift für Geschichte und Wissenschaft des Judentums*, xxxviii (1893), 5–7; L. Blau, *Zur Einleitung in die heilige Schrift*, Budapest, 1894; M. Friedmann, *Onkelos und Akylas*, Vienna, 1896; S. Kraus-Budapest, in *Festschrift zum achtzigsten Geburtstage M. Steinschneiders*, Leipsic, 1896; F. C. Burkitt, *Fragments of the Books of Kings . . .*, Cambridge, 1897; *DCB*, i, 150–151, ii, 14–23 (valuable); *DB*, iv, 864–865; *EB*, iv, 5017–19.

II. Latin Versions: The origin of the earliest Latin versions is unknown. This fact is easily explained if the case was stated correctly by Augustine: "Those who translated the Scriptures from Hebrew into Greek can be enumerated; but the Latin translators by no means. For in the early days of the faith when any one received a Greek manuscript into his hands and seemed to have ever so little facility in language, he dared to translate it" (*De doctrina Christiana*, ii, 11). Again (ii, 14) he mentions "the abundance of interpreters." Augustine is probably right in the supposition that Latin versions did not exist in pre-Christian times. At all events there are no traces of Jewish undertakings in this direction. The history of the Latin versions is divided into two unequal parts by the work of Jerome and closes with an account of later versions independent of Jerome, particularly those made by Protestants.

1. The Latin Bible before Jerome: The statement of Augustine about the great variety of Latin translations is corroborated by the documents, manuscripts, and quotations preserved, for the New Testament of course much more than for the Old. But even for the latter one may cite, e.g. for Deut. xxxi, 17, at least eight variant readings; and in the New Testament for Luke xxiv, 4, 5, at least twenty-seven variant readings. In other words, as Jerome says, "as many readings as copies"; and these readings are not merely different renderings of an identical Greek text, but correspond to various Greek readings, a fact which seems to demonstrate the more clearly the existence of different translations. Nevertheless Jerome speaks frequently as if there was but one ancient translation, which he opposes as "the common edition" and an "old translation" to his own undertaking. Some variations at least arose in the way sketched by Jerome—"by stupid interpreters badly translated, by presumptuous but unskilled men perversely amended, by sleepy copyists either added to or changed about." Nevertheless it is impossible to reduce all these variations to consecutive stages of one original translation and therefore scholars use the term "Old Latin versions" (in the plural) and avoid especially the name formerly used; viz., "Itala." This designation went back to a single passage of Augustine (*De doctrina Christiana*, ii, 14, 15); after he had fixed the principle "that the uncorrected texts should give way to the corrected ones at least when they are copies of the same translation," he goes on to say: "Among translations themselves the Itala is to be preferred to the others, for it keeps closer to the words, without prejudice to clearness of expression." There can be no doubt that he puts here one translation, which he prefers, in opposition to several other translations; therefore it was not well done to comprehend all that is left of the Latin Bibles from the time before Jerome under this name Itala. Some have tried to change the text, but *Itala* is the correct reading. Augustine must mean a version used in or having come from Italy, probably the northern part of the peninsula. Isidore of Seville (*Etymologiæ*, vi, 4) in the seventh century clearly understood by "Itala" the work of Jerome. This view was restated in 1824 by C. A. Breyther, was considered possible by E. Reuss, and well-founded by F. C. Burkitt (*The Old Latin and the Itala*, in *TS*, iv, 3), with the limitation that Augustine had not yet in view the whole of Jerome's labor, but only its beginning—the revision of the Gospels. It is therefore advisable to avoid completely the name "Itala" and to use "Old Latin" for the Bible before Jerome. The home of this Bible is not to be sought in Rome, where Greek was the language of the infant Church and its literature, but most probably in Africa. It is true, many of the linguistic peculiarities ascribed to Africa are shared by the *lingua rustica* in other parts of the Latin world, and it has become customary to distinguish an African and a European branch of the Latin Bible; nevertheless the origin of this whole literature seems to have been in Africa. Translations of certain books which in early times were of almost canonical standing—such as the Epistle of Barnabas, the *Shepherd* of Hermas, and the First Epistle of Clement—are closely connected with these versions (cf. Harnack, *Litteratur*, i, 883; O. Bardenhewer, *Geschichte der altkirchlichen Litteratur*, i, Freiburg, 1902).

1. The Old Latin Bible. The Itala.

Because the Old Latin versions have been replaced in the use of the Church by the version of

Jerome, only a few manuscripts of the Old Latin have survived and these as fragments and palimpsests only, but of high antiquity. It is a great pity that they are not yet collected in such a way as to make their use easy, especially for the Old Testament, since they are all important for the criticism of the Septuagint. This was recognized by the Roman commission which prepared the *Editio Sixtina* of the Septuagint. They collected with great care the Biblical quotations from the Latin ecclesiastical writers. Petrus Morinus, Antonius Agellius, and Lælius Malwerda were the members of the commission to whom this part of the task was entrusted. Their labors were used in the scholia of the Greek edition of 1586 [1587], but still more freely in its Latin translation, published by Flaminius Nobilius (Rome, 1588: reprinted with the Greek text at Paris, 1624; without it, Venice, 1609, 1628; Antwerp, 1616). But the chief work is *Bibliorum Sacrorum Latinæ versiones antiquæ opera et studio Petri Sabatier, O. S. B., e congregatione S. Mauri* (3 vols., Reims, 1739–49, with new title, Paris, Didot, 1751). Before Sabatier, are to be mentioned J. M. Carus (Cardinal Tommasi), *Sacrorum Bibliorum iuxta editionem seu LXX Interpretum seu B. Hieronymi veteres tituli*, etc. (2 vols., Rome, 1688; 2d ed. in *Thomasii Opera*, ed. Vezzosi, i, Rome, 1747); and *Ecclesiastes ex versione Itala cum notis Bossueti* (Paris, 1693). For full list of manuscripts and editions, cf. the Hauck-Herzog *RE*, iii, 28–33. The manuscripts of the New Testament are enumerated also in Scrivener's *Introduction*, ii (London, 1894), 45–54 (revised by H. J. White); in Gregory's *Prolegomena* to Tischendorf's New Testament, iii, 952–971, and *Textkritik des Neuen Testaments* (Leipsic, 1900), 598–613; and in the prefaces of Jerome's New Testament edited by J. Wordsworth and H. J. White (*Novum Testamentum Domini nostri Jesu Christi Latine secundum editionem S. Hieronymi ad codicum manuscriptorum fidem recensuit Johannes Wordsworth. In operis societatem adsumpto Henrico Juliano White*, part i, the four Gospels, Oxford, 1889–98; part ii, section i, Acts, 1905). In the critical apparatus of the New Testament they are designated by the small letters of the Latin alphabet.

2. Manuscripts and Editions.

The following additions may be made to what is contained in the *RE* (ut sup.):

Old Testament: P. Sabatier, *Bibliorum Sacrorum Latinæ versiones antiquæ*, i (Reims, 1744), 904 (for a fragment of Job; cf. S. Berger, *Histoire de la Vulgate*, Paris, 1893, 86); G. M. Bianchini, *Vindiciæ canonicarum scripturarum* (Rome, 1740; Psalms from the *Codex Veronensis*); F. Mone, *Lateinische und Griechische Messen* (Frankfort, 1850), 40 (for fragments of Psalms from a palimpsest in Carlsruhe); P. de Lagarde, *Probe einer neuen Ausgabe der lateinischen Uebersetzung des Alten Testaments* (Göttingen, 1885; for Psalms); H. Ehrensberger, *Psalterium vetus* (Tauberbischofsheim, 1887); *Heptateuchi partis posterioris versio Latina antiquissima e codice Lugdunensi* (Lyons, 1890; cf. F. Vigouroux, in *Revue des questions historiques*, Jan.–Apr., 1902); P. de Lagarde, *Septuagintastudien*, ii (Göttingen, 1892; for III Esdras); J. Belsheim, *Libri Tobit, Judit, Ester . . . Latina translatio e codice . . . Monachensi* (Trondhjem, 1893); V. Schultze, *Die Quedlinburger Itala-Miniaturen in Berlin* (Munich, 1898; he refers them to the fourth century); P. Corssen, *Zwei neue Fragmente der Weingartener Prophetenhandschrift, nebst einer Untersuchung über das Verhältnis der Weingartener und Würzburger Prophetenhandschriften* (Berlin, 1899); P. Thielmann, *Bericht über das gesammelte handschriftliche Material zu einer kritischen Ausgabe der lateinischen Uebersetzungen biblischer Bücher des Alten Testaments*, in *Sitzungsberichte der königlichen Bayerischen Akademie der Wissenschaften*, 1899, ii, 2; G. Hoberg, *Die älteste lateinische Uebersetzung des Buches Baruch* (Freiburg, 1902); A. M. Amelli, *De libri Baruch vetustissima Latina versione . . . epistola* (Montecassino, 1902); W. O. E. Oesterley, *Old Latin Texts of the Minor Prophets*, in *JTS*, v (1904), 76, 242, 378, 570, vi, 67, 217. The Psalms from the Mozarabic Liturgy are in *MPL*, lxxxv.

New Testament: Gospels: The *Fragmenta Curiensia* (*a*) are edited in *OLBT*, ii (London, 1888); for *Codex Saretianus* (*j*), cf. G. Amelli, *Un antichissimo codice biblico latino purpureo* (Montecassino, 1893); Acts: *Codex Demidovianus* (*dem*), probably of the thirteenth century, now lost, a mixed text, was edited by C. F. Matthæi (*Novum Testamentum*, Riga, 1782); for the *Codex Laudianus* (*e*), see BIBLE TEXT, II, 1, § 9; it was revised by White for Wordsworth-White; on the *Codex Perpinianus* (*p*), thirteenth century, a mixed text, collated by White, cf. S. Berger, *Un Ancien Texte latin des Actes des Apôtres*, in *Notices et Extraits des manuscrits*, xxxv (Paris, 1895); cf. further *Liber comicus sive lectionarius missæ quo Toletana ecclesia ante annos MCC utebatur*, ed. G. Morin (*Anecdota Maredsolana*, i, Maredsous, 1893). Pauline Epistles: for the manuscripts *d, e, f, g*, cf. H. Rönsch, in *ZWT*, 1882, p. 83. Apocalypse: cf. H. Linke, *Studien zur Itala* (Breslau, 1889). The *Codex Corbeiensis* (ff_2), with fragments of the Catholic Epistles, Acts, and the Apocalypse from the Fleury palimpsest (Paris, 6400 G), have been lately edited by E. S. Buchanan (Oxford, 1907, in *OLBT*, v).

On the relation of the different texts, cf. for the New Testament Hort's *Introduction* (London, 1881) and Wordsworth-White; for the Old Testament Kennedy in *DB*, iii 49 sqq. On the language, cf. H. Rönsch, *Itala und Vulgata* (Marburg, 1869), on which work cf. J. N. Ott, in *Neue Jahrbücher für Philologie*, cix, 1874, pp. 778, 833.

Of the highest importance for the restoration of the Old Latin Bible are the quotations of the older Latin writers. Their countries are known and thus the home of the Biblical texts is located. Yet many questions are still unsettled; e.g., did Tertullian know and use a Latin translation or are his quotations taken by him from the Greek and translated into Latin? Heinrich Hoppe (*Syntax und Stil des Tertullian*, Leipsic, 1903) denies that Tertullian knew a Latin version of the Old Testament. T. Zahn makes the same assertion for the New Testament.

3. Quotations in Latin Writers.

Quotations from almost all books are found in the *Liber de divinis scripturis sive speculum* (designated as *m*), ascribed to Augustine, published by A. Mai in *Spicilegium Romanum*, ix, 2 (Rome, 1843), 1–88, and in *Nova patrum bibliotheca*, i, 2 (1852), 1–117; better by F. Weihrich, in *CSEL*, xii (cf. Weihrich's dissertation, *Die Bibel-Excerpte de divina scriptura*, Vienna, 1893). Several fragments are also in C. Vercellone, *Dissertationi accademiche* (Rome, 1864). On the quotations in general, cf. H. Rönsch, in *ZHT*, x, 1867, 606–634, 1869, 433–479, 1870, 91–150, 1871, 531, 1875, 86; L. J. Bebb, in *Studia Biblia*, ii (London, 1890), 195 sqq.; Scrivener's *Introduction* (London, 1894), 167–174; Gregory's *Prolegomena*, iii (Leipsic, 1894), 1131–1246; and Kennedy, in *DB*, 52–53.

The writers that are of primary importance are: Alcimus Avitus, archbishop of Vienne c. 450–517; Ambrose, bishop of Milan 374–397; Ambrosiaster, the name given to a most important commentator on the thirteen Epistles of St. Paul (cf. T. Zahn, in *NKZ*, xvi, pp. 419 sqq., and A. Souter, *TS*, vii, 4, Cambridge, 1905); Arnobius, presbyter in Africa, fourth century; *Exhortationes de pœnitentia*, ascribed to Cyprian; *Liber de aleatoribus* (according to Harnack as early as Cyprian); *Liber de pascha computus* (written in Africa c. 243); *Liber de promissionibus* (ascribed to Prosper of Aquitaine); *Liber collationis legum Mosaicarum et Romanarum* (ed. P. Krüger and T. Mommsen in *Collectio librorum juris antejustiniani*, iii, Berlin, 1891); Augustine, bishop of Hippo

354–430 (from this author alone Lagarde collected 13,276 quotations of the Old Testament and 29,540 of the New Testament); Capreolus, bishop of Carthage c. 431; Cassian, monk at Marseilles (d. about 435); Commodian (perhaps middle of third century); Cyprian, bishop of Carthage (d. 258; cf. Sanday, in *OLBT*, ii; Lagarde, *Symmicta*, i. 74; *Mittheilungen*. ii, 54; P. Corssen, *Der cyprianische Text der Acta Apostolorum*, Berlin, 1892); Teaching of the Twelve Apostles; Philastrius, bishop of Brescia (c. 380; ed. Marx, in *CSEL*, xxxviii); Fulgentius, bishop of Ruspe (c. 468–533); Gildas of Britain; Eucherius; Hilarius, bishop of Poitiers (d. 380; cf. Zingerle, in *Kleine philologische Abhandlungen*, Innsbruck, 1887); Ireneus, bishop of Lyons (c. 180, *Novum Testamentum Irenæi;* to be published in *OLBT* by Prof. Sanday); Jovinian (in the time of Jerome); Lactantius (in Africa c. 260–340); Lucifer, bishop of Cagliari (d. 371; cf. Dombart, in *Berliner Philologische Wochenschrift*, 1866, no. 8); Julius Firmicus Maternus (c. 345); Maximin (cf. *TLZ*, 1900, 17); Novatian (at Rome c. 252; cf. Harnack, in *TU*, xiii. 4); Origen (Latin translation; c. 251); Optatus, bishop of Mileve in Numidia, c. 368; Primasius, bishop of Adrumetum, sixth century (cf. Haussleiter, in Zahn, *Forschungen zur Geschichte des neutestamentlichen Kanons*, iv, Berlin, 1900, 1–224); Pelagius of Ireland; Priscillian, bishop of Avila in Spain, fourth century (cf. *CSEL*, xviii); Salvianus of Marseilles, c. 450 (cf. Ulrich, *De Salviani scripturæ sacræ versionibus*, Neustadt, 1893); Tertullian of Carthage, c. 150–240 (cf. Rönsch, *Das Neue Testament Tertullians*, Leipsic, 1871, and J. N. Ott, in *Neue Jahrbücher für Philologie*, 1874, p. 856); Tyconius, in Africa, c. 340 (cf. F. C. Burkitt, in *TS*, iii, 1, 1894); Verecundus (cf. Lagarde, *Septuagintastudien*, i); Victorinus, bishop of Pettau in Pannonia, c. 300 (cf. Haussleiter, in *ZWT*, vii, 239–257); Vigilius, bishop of Thapsus, c. 484.

Some parts of the Old Latin Bible are still in ecclesiastical use and even in the works of Luther Denifle has shown readings from this source. The same is the case with some of the translations in the vernacular dialects of medieval Europe, such as the Anglo-Saxon (cf. for instance R. Handke, *Ueber das Verhältnis der westsächsischen Evangelienübersetzung zum lateinischen Original*, Halle, 1896; A. S. Cook, *Biblical Quotations in Old English Prose Writers*, New York, 1898; Max Förster, in *Englische Studien*, Leipsic, 1900, p. 480).

2. The Bible of Jerome (the Vulgate): Toward the end of the fourth century the inconvenience from which the Western Church suffered because there was no single authorized Latin version of the Bible must have been seriously felt, and Damasus, bishop of Rome (d. 384), commissioned Jerome (q.v.) to prepare an authoritative revision, probably in the year 382.

1. Jerome's Work. The New Testament.

The letter with which Jerome dedicated the first part (the Gospels) to the pope gives the only authentic record of the work and its scope (cf. *NPNF*, 2d ser., vi, 487–488). Jerome accepts the task set him by Damasus, notes its extreme difficulty and the resulting peril to himself, anticipates the harshest criticism of himself and of the results of his labor, and states that his emendations have been as conservative as possible. Notwithstanding Jerome's modesty concerning his work, it has had an unparalleled history, inasmuch as it became the Bible of the whole Occident.

To estimate Jerome's work properly, it would be necessary (1) to know what were the Latin texts which he had to revise; (2) what were the Greek texts which he chose as standard; (3) to have his work in its original form. The last is now realized, at least for the first part of the New Testament, since the monumental edition of Wordsworth-White. The Greek manuscript or manuscripts used by Jerome must have been of the type of the *Codices Vaticanus* and *Sinaiticus;* there are, however, some readings not attested by any Greek manuscript (cf., for instance, John x, 16, *unum ovile;* xvi, 13, *docebit;* and on this question cf. the letter of Wordsworth and White in *The Academy*, Jan. 27, 1894; their *Epilogue*, 657–672; E. Mangenot, in *RSE*, Jan., 1900). About Jerome's Latin texts there is still less information. Wordsworth and White printed under Jerome's text that of the *Codex Brixianus* (*f*) as most nearly related to it; but according to Burkitt and Kaufmann it is rather a text of Jerome himself adapted to the Gothic version. Jerome's statement in his prefatory letter that he changed as little as possible is probably true; for the language indicates that the Gospels came from different translators. Identical expressions in Greek are quite differently rendered into Latin (cf. the history of the Passion in the different Gospels, and notice for instance *lagenam aquæ baiulans* = *amphoram aquæ portans*, or the rendering of "high priest" in Matthew by *princeps sacerdotum*, in Mark by *summus sacerdos*, in John by *pontifex*). It is, therefore, quite wrong to treat the Vulgate of the Gospels as a harmonious work, and it is clear that the value of it for textual criticism is greatly enhanced, since it preserves the text of the time when the Gospels were not yet united into one collection. Whether also in the second part of the New Testament such differences can be detected has not yet been investigated. It is not even quite certain how far Jerome revised the second part of the New Testament. Only the Gospels have his prefaces, and Augustine writes to him only of the Gospel: "We give no small thanks to God for your work in which you have interpreted the Gospel from the Greek." Jerome, however, answers: "If, as you say, you suspect me of emending the New Testament"; and in 398 he wrote to Lucinius Beticus, to whom he sent the first copy ready (*Epist.*, lxxi, 5, *NPNF*, 2d series, vi, 154): "The New Testament I have restored to the authoritative form of the Greek." In his *De vir. ill.* he says: "The New Testament I have restored to the true Greek form, the Old I have rendered from the Hebrew."

Jerome's work on the Old Testament was more thorough. First he revised the Psalter [from the Septuagint] in 383 in Rome. This revision was introduced by Damasus into the liturgy and is hence called the *Psalterium Romanum* in distinction from the *Psalterium vetus* or the unrevised Old Latin. It was in use in Italy till Pius V (1566–72), and it is still used in St. Peter's in Rome and in Milan, partly in the Roman Missal and in one place in the Breviary, in the hortatory Psalm xcv (xciv). About

2. The Old Testament.

four years later in Palestine Jerome revised the Psalms a second time, making use of the critical marks of Origen, the obelus and asterisk. This revision is known as the Gallican Psalter, as it was first used chiefly in Gaul (it seems through Gregory of Tours), but finally it became the current version in the Latin Church (through Pius V), of course without the critical marks. At last Jerome translated the Psalms from the Hebrew at the suggestion of Sophronius about 392 (not 405, as Lagarde has it); but this remained a private labor and is not found in many manuscripts. The best edition of this version is Lagarde's *Psalterium juxta Hebræos Hieronymi* (Leipsic, 1874).

About the same time with his second revision of the Psalter Jerome revised the translation of Job (preserved in a few manuscripts, especially at Oxford and St. Gall; edited by Lagarde, *Mittheilungen*, ii, 189 sqq.: cf. Caspari, in *Actes du huitième congrès des Orientalistes*, i, Leyden, 1893, 37–51) and most of the books of the Old Testament; but he lost the work "by the deceit of somebody." Therefore he undertook the greater labor of translating the Old Testament afresh direct from the Hebrew. He began in 390 with Samuel and Kings and published them with his *Prologus galeatus* (q.v.); then followed Job, the Prophets, and Psalms. About the chronological order of the rest absolute certainty is not reached.[1] He left Wisdom, Ecclesiasticus, Maccabees, and Baruch without revision. According to his own statement he translated the three Solomonic writings in three days, Tobit in one day, Judith in one night; for the latter two his Jewish teacher translated to him the Aramaic into Hebrew and he dictated the Latin to a copyist (cf. G. Grützmacher, *Hieronymus*, i, Leipsic, 1901, 73–77 On Jerome's method, cf. G. Hoberg, *De S. Hieronymi ratione interpretandi*, Bonn, 1886; M. Rahmer, *Die hebräischen Traditionen in den Werken des Hieronymus*, Breslau, 1861).

3. History to the Invention of Printing.

At first Jerome's work was not well received, especially because he had dared to part with the Septuagint, which even Augustine believed to be equally inspired with the original Hebrew. An African bishop on finding *hedera* ("ivy") in the Book of Jonah in the new version instead of the accustomed *cucurbita* ("gourd") raised a tumult in his Church. Jerome's former friend Rufinus wrote expressly against the new work. "So great is the force of established usage," says Jerome, "that even acknowledged corruptions [of text] please the greater part, for they prefer to have their copies pretty rather than correct." On the other hand he knows "that they attack it in public and read it in secret." At the time of his death (420) the attacks and criticism of his opponents had ceased.

We are not informed where and when complete Bibles of Jerome's version were first produced and introduced into the use of the Church. In Spain it seems to have been at a pretty early time. Cassiodorus (d. about 570) was one of the first, if not the very first, who took care to produce correct copies. From his copies are derived the introductory pieces in the *Codex Amiatinus* (cf. H. J. White, in *Studia Biblica*, ii, Oxford, 1890, 273; P. Corssen, *Die Bibeln des Cassiodorius*, *JPT*, 1883, 1891). Pope Gregory the Great wrote at the end of the sixth century: "I indeed circulate the new translation; but when the course of argument demands it, I use now the new and now the old by way of proof; and this because the Apostolic See, over which under God I preside, uses both and by the study of both my toil is lightened." By that time the name *Vulgata* ("common," "ordinary"), which before had meant the Septuagint and its Latin translation, had gone over to the work of Jerome. Roger Bacon says of it "that [version] which is diffused among the Latins is that which the Church receives in these days." But even in the printed editions of the fifteenth and sixteenth centuries this name is not yet as invariable as we are inclined to suppose; and despite the warning of Walafrid Strabo, "let none desire to amend one from the other," mixing in all degrees of the old and the new texts took place and survives up to the present not only in manuscripts, but even in the printed text, as when in II Kings i, 18, the first part is from the Old Latin, and the second from Jerome.

Charlemagne found several recensions in use in his dominions. In a capitulary of 789 he ordered that there should be "in each monastery and parish good copies of the catholic books, and the boys must not be permitted to deface them either in reading them or by writing on them; and if there be necessity for writing [copying] a Gospel, Psalter, or Missal, men of maturity are to do it, using all care." In 797 he committed to Alcuin (q.v.) the "emendation of the Old and the New Testament"; and the copy of the Biblical books, "bound together in the sanctity of one most glorious body," which Alcuin offered to him on Christmas 801, must have been the first copy of this revision, of which the *Codex Vallicellanus* at Rome is the best representative in existence. As Alcuin was himself of Northumbria, he probably had his text brought from there, and fortunately just there the purest text seems to have survived (cf. Berger's *Histoire* and Wordsworth-White). At the same time Bishop Theodulf of Orléans (787–821) worked at a revision, but on very different lines. Being a Visigoth, he took Spanish manuscripts as the basis, but incorporated in the margins various readings; fortunately his work found no large circulation. It is still represented by some fine manuscripts (cf. Berger, 145–184. and Delisle, in *Bibliothèque de l'École des Chartes*, vol. xl, Paris, 1879). About the labors of Lanfranc of Canterbury (q.v.) precise information is not obtainable; but the normal copy produced with the help of Jewish scholars by Stephen Harding, third abbot of Cîteaux, for the members of his order is still preserved at Dijon (cf. J. P Martin, in *RSE*, 1887). Later on, critical observations on the true readings of certain passages were collected in the so-called *Correctoria Biblica*. The principal *Correctoria* are (1) the *Correctorium Parisiense*, prepared about 1236, also called *Senonense*, sneered at by Roger Bacon, who in 1267 called the Parisian text, in a letter to Pope Clement IV, "horribly corrupt"; "the correctors," he says, are "corruptors, for any reader whatsoever in the lower orders corrects as he pleases, in like manner also the preachers, and similarly the students change as they like what they

[1] White gives the following table: 394 Esdras; 396 Chronicles; 398 Proverbs, Ecclesiastes, Song of Solomon; 401? Genesis, followed by Exodus, Leviticus, Numbers, Deuteronomy; 405 Joshua, Judges, Ruth, Esther, Tobit, Judith, and the apocryphal parts of Daniel and Esther.

do not understand"; (2) the *Correctorium Sorbonicum*, a sort of epitome of the larger *Correctoria;* (3) the *Correctorium* of the Dominicans, prepared under the auspices of Hugo of St. Cher, which sometimes went back of the Latin text to Greek and Hebrew manuscripts; **(4)** the *Correctorium Vaticanum*, the work of **the** Franciscans, perhaps especially of Willermus de Mara. (Cf. on the *Correctoria*, besides S. Berger, in *RTP*, xvi, 41, especially Denifle, in *Archiv für Litteratur- und Kirchengeschichte*, iv, Berlin, 1888, 263, 471.) By the influence of the University of Paris the text used there was the one which was most current in the Middle Ages and consequently that which found its way into the first printed editions, and gained thereby still more influence.

To enumerate even the more important of the manuscripts of the Vulgate is here impossible. There are lists in J. Le Long, *Bibliotheca sacra* (i, Paris, 1723, 234 sqq.), and in C. Vercellone, *Variæ lectiones vulgatæ Latinæ Bibliorum editionis* (i, Rome, 1860, lxxxii sqq., ii, 1864, xvii sqq.). Scrivener's *Introduction* (ii, London, 1894, 67–90) has a select list of 181 manuscripts, chiefly of the New Testament, by H. J. White; Berger's *Histoire* (Paris, 1893, 374–422) one of 253; Gregory's *Prolegomena* (iii, Leipsic, 1894, 983–1108) notes some 2,270, and his *Textkritik* (2 vols., Leipsic, 1900–02) 2,369, reserving some for an appendix. H. J. White (*DB*, iv, 886–889) classifies them under the following headings: (1) Early Italian texts; (2) Early Spanish texts; (3) Italian texts transcribed in Britain; (4) Continental manuscripts written by Irish or Saxon scribes and showing a mixture of the two types of text; (5) Type of text current in Languedoc; (6) Other French texts; (7) Swiss manuscripts, especially of St. Gall; (8) Alcuinian recension; (9) Theodulfian recension; (10) Medieval texts.

4. Earlier Printed Editions.

Naturally Bibles and parts of the Bible were among the earliest of printed books, and as a matter of course the text presented was the Vulgate. The Mazarin Bible, so called, because a copy in the library of Cardinal Mazarin first attracted the attention of bibliographers—i.e., the Bible in forty-two lines, not that in thirty-six—is now proved to be the first Bible printed by Gutenberg. His Psalter of 1457 is the first book with a printed date, while the Psalter of 1459 is one of the most costly of books. A Bible printed at Mainz 1462 is the first dated Bible. The first Bible printed at Rome is of 1471, by Sweinheim and Pannartz, printed in 250 copies. Of ninety-two editions of the fifteenth century which can be localized, thirty-six belong to Germany (to Nuremberg 13, Strasburg 8, Cologne 7, Mainz 3, Speyer 2, Bamberg 1, and Ulm 1, the latter of 1480 being the first Bible with summaries); twenty-nine belong to Italy, twenty-four of them to Venice. In England in the whole period none is known. The first quarto Bible is believed to have been printed at Piacenza 1475, and the first octavo at Basel 1491 (because of its small size called the first "poor man's Bible"). An undated Bible, probably of 1478, has for the first time the verses:

Fontibus ex græcis hebræorum quoque libris
Emendata satis et decorata simul
Biblia sum præsens, superos ego testor et astra.

Copinger mentions 124 editions of the Latin Bible prior to 1500, of the sixteenth century he knows 438 editions, of the seventeenth 262, of the eighteenth 192, of the nineteenth (till 1892) 133, in all 1,149. These figures show that, under the influence of the religious and intellectual awakening, the sixteenth century was the time of the Latin Bible.

The bad state of the text soon became evident and attempts were made to improve it from the original texts, as by the editors of the Complutensian Polyglot (see Bibles, Polyglot, I), and, among Protestants, first by Andreas Osiander (Nuremberg, 1522) and at Wittenberg, in an edition of the Pentateuch, Joshua–Kings, and the New Testament, ascribed to Luther and Melanchthon (1529), then by Lukas Osiander at Tübingen (9 vols., 1573–1586), with an "exposition." Of greater importance are the attempts to correct the text from the Latin manuscripts, to which Lorenzo della Valle had called attention in the fifteenth century. Erasmus published his *In Latinam Novi Testamenti interpretationem ex collatione græcorum exemplarium annotationes apprime utiles* at Paris in 1505. The French printer Robert Stephens (q.v.) in particular corrected the text from manuscripts and put variant readings on the margins (cf. Wordsworth, in *OLBT*, i, 1883, 47–54). For his edition of 1528 he used three good manuscripts, for the larger of 1540 not less than seventeen; his impression of 1555 is the first complete Bible with the modern verse division, and his text became the basis of the official Roman text through the mediation of the edition undertaken by the theological faculty of Louvain under the guidance of Johannes Hentenius after comparison of some thirty manuscripts (Louvain, 1547).

5. The Sixtine-Clementine Edition.

All these editions were private undertakings. In its fourth session (Apr. 8, 1546), the Council of Trent decreed that "of all Latin editions the old and vulgate (*vulgata*) edition be held as authoritative in public lectures, disputations, sermons, and expositions; and that no one is to dare or presume under any pretext to reject it." The council decreed at the same time that "this same old and vulgate edition be printed in as correct form as possible." It does not appear that steps were taken to entrust a special person or body with the latter task. The edition of Hentenius was used for a long time as the best available. At last several popes took the matter in hand, and after various attempts of Pius IV and Pius V, at last Sixtus V carried the work to completion through a committee, with Cardinal Antonio Caraffa at its head, and published the *Biblia Sacra Vulgatæ Editionis tribus tomis distincta. Romæ: ex Typographia Apostolica Vaticana M.D.XC* (on a second title-page: *Biblia Sacra Vulgatæ Editionis ad concilii Tridentini præscriptum emendata et a Sixto V P M recognita et approbata*). In the constitution *Æternus ille* (Mar. 1, 1589; not included in the *Bullarium Romanum;* printed in Thomas James, *Bellum papale*, London, 1600, and L. van Ess, *Geschichte der Vulgata*, Tübingen, 1821, 269) Sixtus had declared the edition "true, lawful, authentic, and not to be questioned in disputations, either public or private." No future edition was to be published without the express permission of the Holy See, and for the next ten years it was forbidden to reprint it in any place except the Vatican; all future editions were to be carefully collated with it, "that no smallest part be changed, added to, or taken away," and they were to be accompanied with the official attestation of the inquisitor of the province or of the bishop of the diocese, no variant readings, scholia, or glosses being allowed on the margins. In August of 1590 Sixtus V died, and was followed by several short-lived popes; in 1592 Clement VIII called in all copies of the edition which were within reach—copies are, therefore, of extreme rarity—and replaced it under the direction of Cardinal Bellarmine with a new *Biblia Sacra Vulgatæ Editionis. Romæ: Ex Typographia Apostolica Vaticana M.D.XCII* (on the second title-page: *Biblia Sacra Vulgatæ Editionis Sixti Quinti Pont. Max. Jussu recognita atque edita*). The accompanying bull decreed: "From the form of this copy let not even the least particle be changed, added to, or taken away, unless it happens that some fault is unmistakably due to typographical carelessness—let this be inviolably observed." The reasons for this whole proceeding are not quite clear. That the printing of the first edition was not correct enough is not true; as a matter of fact the Sixtine edition is typographically more correct than the Clementine, but the text of the Clementine is an improvement on that of the Sixtine. Sixtus was personally interested in the work and changed the text frequently to accord with that of Stephens, while the editors of the Clementine edition followed more often that of Hentenius. There are some 3,000 differences between the two editions. Nevertheless the names of both popes were placed on the title-pages of the later reprints, first, it seems, at Lyons, 1604, then at Mainz, 1609, the official title being now: *Sixti V et Clementis VIII. Pontt. Maxx. jussu recognita atque edita.* A quarto edition was issued in 1593 with "marginal references, explanations of Hebrew names, and an index of subjects," and a small quarto edition in 1598 with a *correctorium*. All four editions (1590, 1592, 1593, 1598) are compared by Leander van Ess in his edition of the Vulgate (3 parts, Tübingen, 1822–24). Of editions by other editors, those of C. Vercellone (Rome, 1861) and particularly M. Hetzenauer (Innsbruck, 1906) may be mentioned; the latter has useful appendices.

Since the edition of 1592 scarcely any attempt has been made in the Roman Church to apply to its Bible the most necessary emendation.

6. Later Work. Problems. D. Vallarsi printed an emended text (Verona, 1734), under the title *Divina bibliotheca*, in his edition of the works of Jerome. [A Biblical commission was appointed late in the pontificate of Leo XIII, and Pius X has lately commissioned members of the Benedictine Order to revise the Vulgate. It is intended to restore, so far as possible, the exact text of Jerome.] Among Protestants, Richard Bentley contemplated a new edition of the Latin New Testament together with the Greek (see BIBLE TEXT, II, 2, § 3); about the same time J. A. Bengel (q.v.) did much for it; in the nineteenth century S. Berger in France should have the greatest credit for clearing up the history of the Latin Bible; at last Wordsworth-White have issued what must be called the first critical edition of the Latin New Testament; and in Bavaria P. Thielmann is engaged in publishing those books of the Old Testament which were not translated by Jerome himself.

It is a matter of surprise that a task so easy and interesting as the criticism of the Latin Bible has received so little attention. Berger knew more than 8,000 manuscripts of the Latin Bible; few of them have been properly investigated. What kind of surprises they may offer is shown by the recent discovery of two different translations of the Third Epistle of Paul to the Corinthians in two manuscripts of the tenth and thirteenth centuries at Milan and Laon. The order of the Biblical books in the manuscripts; the prefaces and summaries (cf. on this point *Les Préfaces jointes aux livres de la Bible dans les manuscrits de la Vulgate; mémoire posthume de M. Samuel Berger*, in the *Mémoires de l'Académie des Inscriptions et Belles-Lettres*, ser. i, vol. xi, part 2, 1902); the capitulation and divisions; the illumination and miniatures (many of the manuscripts belong to the most beautiful productions of Christian art); ecclesiastical or private notes; connection with the vernacular versions, influence upon the dialects of Europe; lists of the passages in literature which mention manuscripts of the Latin Bible; and many other points may be named as those which await investigation.

3. Later Latin Translations: That the Latin Vulgate was not sufficient was asserted in the Middle Ages by scholars like Nicolaus de Lyra and Raymond Martini. The English Benedictine Adam Easton (d. 1397) is said to have been one of the first to think of a new translation. It was Erasmus, however, who vindicated the right to place new Latin translations by the side of the Vulgate through his translation of the New Testament (Basel, 1516, 1519, 1522, 1527, 1535, and more than 200 times since the death of Erasmus; see BIBLE TEXT, II, 2, § 1; ERASMUS, DESIDERIUS). He has had many followers who have translated into Latin either the Old or the New Testament or both, as well as separate books of the Bible, even as late as the nineteenth century. But the time has passed when Latin versions were necessary or helpful; since the Reformation translations into the vernacular languages have taken their place.

The more important new translations of the whole Bible are those of the Dominican Sanctes Pagninus (Lyons, 1528; revised and annotated by Michael Servetus, Lyons, 1542), of Arias Montanus in the Antwerp Polyglot (1572), and one prepared under the direction of Cardinal Cajetan (1530 sqq.: see CAJETAN, THOMAS).

The Old Testament was newly translated by the Hebraist Sebastian Münster (Basel, 1534–35 and often); by Leo Jud and (after Jud's death) T. Bibliander, C. Pellican, P. Cholinus, and R. Gualtherus (Zurich, 1543); by Sebastian Castellio (complete ed., Basel, 1551, with a dedication to King Edward VI of England): by Immanuel Tremellius, a Jew of Ferrara, and his son-in-law, Franciscus Junius (du Jon, 5 parts, Frankfort, 1575–79; best ed., with full index, by P. Tossanus, Hanau, 1624. Tremellius's work was well received); by J. Piscator (24 parts, Herborn, 1601–1616; really a revision of Tremellius); by Thomas Malvenda, a Spanish Dominican (left incomplete at Malvenda's death in 1628 and first published with his *Commentarii*, 5 vols., Lyons, 1650); by J. Coccejus (published with his commentaries, *Opera*, vols. i–vi, Amsterdam, 1701; incomplete; contains also most of the New Testament); by Sebastian

Schmid, a Strasburg Lutheran, who worked forty years on the translation (Strasburg, 1696; photographic facsimile, with manuscript notes by Swedenborg, ed. R. L. Tafel, Stockholm, 1872); by Jean Le Clerc (Clericus; Amsterdam, 1693–1731); by C. F. Houbigant (4 vols., Paris, 1753); by J. A. Dathe (Halle, 1773–89); and by H. A. Schott and J. F. Winzer (Leipsic, 1816).

Forty years after the first edition of the New Testament of Erasmus, Beza's Latin New Testament appeared (Geneva, 1556, 1565, 1582, 1588, 1598, and more than 100 subsequent editions; by the *BFBS*, 1896). A translation by H. A. Schott was published at Leipsic in 1805. The latest works of the kind are by F. A. A. Näbe (Leipsic, 1831) and A. Göschen (Leipsic, 1832).

For other translations, including those of separate books of the Bible, cf. the Hauck-Herzog *RE*, iii, 49–58. On translations of the Psalms into Latin verse, cf. Hugues Vaganay, *Les Traductions du Psautier en vers latin au seizième siècle*, in *Compte rendu du quatrième Congrès international des Catholiques* (Freiburg, 1898), part vi, *Sciences philologiques*.

E. Nestle.

Bibliography: On the Latin Bible before Jerome consult: H. Rönsch, *Itala und Vulgata*, Marburg, 1875; idem, in *ZWT*, 1875, pp. 76, 81, 425, 1876, pp. 397, 1881, p. 198; Desjacques, in *Études, religieuses, philosophiques, historiques et littéraires de la compagnie de Jésus*, 1878, pp. 721–724; L. Ziegler, *Die lateinischen Uebersetzungen vor Hieronymus und die Itala des Augustinus*, Munich, 1879; G. Koffmane, *Geschichte des Kirchenlateins bis auf Augustinus-Hieronymus*, Breslau, 1879–81; P. Corssen, *Die vermeintliche "Itala" und die Bibelübersetzung des Hieronymus*, in *JPT*, 1881, pp. 507–519; F. Zimmer, in *TSK*, 1889; F. C. Burkitt, *The Old Latin and the Itala*, in *TS*, iv, 3, Cambridge, 1896; E. Ehrlich, *Beiträge zur Latinität der Itala*, Rochlitz, 1895; idem, *Quæ sit Italæ quæ dicitur verborum tenacitas*, Leipsic, 1889; P. Monceaux, *Les Africains, Étude sur la littérature Latine d'Afrique* and *La Bible Latine en Afrique*, in *REJ*, 1901; *DB*, iii, 47–64; *EB*, iv, 5022–24.

On the Vulgate consult: S. Berger, *Histoire de la Vulgate*, Paris, 1893 (this work was crowned by the Academy, pp. xx–xxiv contain a full list of earlier literature); G. Riegler, *Geschichte der Vulgata*, Sulzbach, 1820; L. Van Ess, *Pragmatisch-kritische Geschichte der Vulgata*, Tübingen, 1824; A. Schmitter, *Kurze Geschichte der hieronymianischen Bibelübersetzung*, Freysing, 1842; F. Kaulen, *Geschichte der Vulgata*, Mainz, 1868; O. Rottmanner, in *Historisch-politische Blätter*, cxiv, 31–38, 101–108; *DB*, iv, 873–890.

On the grammar and the language consult: W. Nowack, *Die Bedeutung des Hieronymus für die alttestamentliche Textkritik*, Göttingen, 1875; J. A. Hagen, *Sprachliche Erörterungen zur Vulgata*, Freiburg, 1863; J. B. Heiss, *Zur Grammatik der Vulgata*, Munich, 1864; V. Loch, *Materialien zu einer lateinischen Grammatik der Vulgata*, Bamberg, 1870; P. Hake, *Sprachliche Bemerkungen zu dem Psalmentexte der Vulgata*, Arnsberg, 1872; H. Gölzer, *Étude de la latinité de St. Jérôme*, Paris, 1884; P. Thielmann, in *Philologus*, xlii, 319, 370; G. A. Saalfeld, *De bibliorum sacrorum Vulgatæ editionis græcitate*, Quedlinburg, 1891; W. M. C. Wilroy, *The Participle in the Vulgate N. T.*, Baltimore, 1892; L. B. Andergassen, *Ueber den Gebrauch des Infinitivs in der Vulgata*, 1891; P. Thielmann, *Beiträge zur Textkritik der Vulgata*, Speier, 1883; S. Berger, in *Revue de théologie et de philosophie*, xvi (1883), 41 sqq.; idem, in *Mémoires de la société des antiquaires de France*, lii, 144; P. Martin, in *Le Muséon*, vii (1888), 88–107, 169–196, viii (1889), 444; H. P. Smith, in *Presbyterian and Reformed Review*, April, 1891; E. von Dobschütz, *Studien zur Textkritik der Vulgata*, Leipsic, 1894 (cf. on it H. J. White, in *Critical Review*, 1896, pp. 243–246); J. Ecker, *Porta Sions, Lexikon zum lateinischen Psalter*, viii, 234, 1,936 columns, Trier, 1904; F. Kaulen, *Sprachliches Handbuch zur biblischen Vulgata*, Freiburg, 1904 (cf. on it Jülicher, in *TLZ*, 1905, no. 6).

On the printed text consult: W. A. Copinger, *Incunabula biblica*, etc., London, 1892; cf. L. Delisle, in *Journal des savans*, 1893, pp. 202–218, where Copinger's 124 editions prior to 1500 are reduced to ninety-nine, and W. Müller, in Dziatzko's *Bibliothekswissenschaftliche Arbeiten*, no. 6, 1894, pp. 84–95); L. Hain, *Repertorium bibliographicum*, 4 vols., Paris, 1826–38, *Index* volume, Leipsic, 1891, *Supplement* by W. A. Copinger, 3 vols., London, 1895–1902, *Appendices* by D. Reichling, fasciculus 1, Munich, 1905 (gives ninety-seven editions prior to 1500). On the first printed Bible consult K. Dziatzko, *Gutenbergs früheste Druckerpraxis auf Grund einer Vergleichung der 42zeiligen und 36zeiligen Bibel*, Leipsic, 1891; L. Delisle, in *Journal des savans*, 1894, pp. 401–413; *British Museum Catalogue*, entry *Bible*.

III. Syriac Versions.—1. The Peshito: According to some Syrians certain of the Biblical books (enumerated by Ishodad, bishop of Haditha, c. 852) were translated into Syriac under Solomon at the request of Hiram, king of Tyre. Another tradition refers this work to a priest Asa or Ezra, who was sent by the king of Assyria to Samaria, and the rest of the Old Testament with the New to the days of King Abgar V of Edessa and the apostle Addai (i.e., Thaddæus; see Abgar. Cf. II Kings xvii, 24, I Chron. xv, 18, in the editions of Lee and Ceriani; J. P. N. Land, *Anecdota Syriaca*, iii, Leyden, 1870, 11; Bar Hebræus on Ps. x; *JA*, 1872, 458).

1. Origin and Name.

Bar Hebræus makes the strange statement that, according to Eusebius (cf. *Hist. eccl.*, VI, xvi, 4, and VI, xvii), Origen found the Syriac version in the keeping of a widow at Jericho; and equally curious is the tradition which refers the translation of the New Testament to Mark. Some manuscripts of the Psalms state that they were translated from Palestinian into Hebrew, from Hebrew into Greek, from Greek into Syriac. Theodore of Mopsuestia (commentary on Zeph. i, 6) rightly says: "These books were translated into Syriac by some one, but who he was no one knows to this day." Some scholars have thought to discover, at least for the New Testament, the influence of the Latin Vulgate; more probable is the supposition that at least some parts of the Old Testament are pre-Christian or certainly Jewish; and the home of the translation is not Jerusalem and Palestine (*JA*, 1872, 458) or Antioch, but Edessa and its neighborhood.

The name which is commonly given to the oldest and most important Syriac version, "Peshito" ("Peshitto"), is first found with Moses bar Kepha (d. 913) and in Masoretic manuscripts of the ninth and tenth centuries (cf. N. P. S. Wiseman, *Horæ Syriacæ*, Rome, 1828, p. 223; J. P. P. Martin, *Introduction à la critique textuelle du Nouveau Testament*, Paris, 1883, p. 101; *ZDMG*, xxxii, 589). It means "the simple" in contradistinction to the more elaborate versions, such as that made from the Greek by Paul of Tella (see below, 2; on the name, cf. K. W. M. Montijn and J. P. N. Land, in *Godgeleerde Bijdragen*, 1882; F. Field, *Origenis Hexapla*, i, Oxford, 1875, p. ix; *ZDMG*, xlvii, 157, 316; A. Mez, *Die Bibel des Josephus*, Basel, 1895, 4; F. C. Burkitt, *Early Eastern Christianity*, London, 1904, chap. ii).

2. The Old Testament.

The Syriac Old Testament is practically the same as that of the Palestinian Jews. Chronicles, however, was missing in the Nestorian canon and, as it seems, also in that of the Jacobites; at least it is not treated in their Masoretic manuscripts, but it is found in very old manuscripts. Ezra-Nehemiah too are not treated in the Masoretic manuscripts nor Esther by the Nestorians, while in Jacobite manuscripts this book together with Judith, Ruth, Susanna, and Thecla forms the "Book of Women" (cf. A. Baumstark, in *Oriens Christianus*, iii, Leipsic, 1901, 353). After the Law there follows as the second part the "Book of Sessions," i.e., Job, Joshua, Judges, Samuel, Kings, Proverbs, Ecclesiasticus, Ecclesiastes, Ruth, Song of Solomon. Among the prophets, Isaiah (sometimes divided at xxv, 2) is followed by the minor prophets, then Jeremiah (with a division at xxxii, 6) with Baruch i–ii and the Epistle of Jeremiah, then Ezekiel and Daniel.

Manuscripts with the Apocrypha are called "catholic" or "pandects"; they do not contain I Esdras, Tobit, or the Prayer of Manasses, but have an Apocalypse of Baruch, IV Esdras, and even the story of Shamuna and Josephus, *War*, V, as IV and V Maccabees. Tobit, as far as chap. vii, 11, is preserved only in the translation of Paul of Tella, but from that point on there is a still later text. Accurate manuscripts give stichometrical lists (cf. Martin, *Introduction*, 677; J. R. Harris, *On the Origin of the Ferrar Group*, London, 1893, 10, 26; *DB*, iv, 650).

The character of the translation is different in various books; it is very literal in the Law, influenced by the Septuagint in Isaiah and the minor prophets, probably also in the Psalms. Ruth is paraphrastic. Chronicles resembles a Jewish targum, while the Syriac Proverbs has been used in the Targum. Ecclesiasticus is taken from the Hebrew.

Up to 1858 only one old version of the New Testament in Syriac was known in Europe; viz., that published for the first time by J. A. Widmanstadt (Vienna, 1555). Textual critics considered it "the queen of the Bible translations."

3. The New Testament. In 1858 W. Cureton published in London, from manuscripts which had come into the British Museum in 1842, *Remains of a very Antient Recension of the Four Gospels in Syriac hitherto Unknown in Europe*. The great value of this recension was soon recognized, and was greatly enhanced when, in 1892, a second manuscript of it was discovered in a palimpsest on Mount Sinai by Mrs. A. S. Lewis and her sister, Mrs. M. D. Gibson, which was published under the title, *The Four Gospels in Syriac Transcribed from the Sinaitic Palimpsest by the Late R. L. Bensly J. R. Harris and F C. Burkitt. With an Introduction by Agnes Smith Lewis* (Cambridge, 1894). Mrs. Lewis published *Some Pages of the Four Gospels Retranscribed from the Syriac Palimpsest with a Translation of the Whole Text* (London, 1894). F C. Burkitt published *Evangelion da-Mepharreshe: The Curetonian Version of the Four Gospels, with the Readings of the Sinai Palimpsest and the Early Syriac Patristic Evidence Edited, Collected, and Arranged* (vol. i, text and translation, vol. ii, introduction and notes, Cambridge, 1904). Burkitt's title is taken from the heading or subscription of the two manuscripts and means "the Gospel of the Separated" (i.e., "the Separated Gospels"), used in contradistinction to the *Diatessaron* of Tatian, which was called among the Syrians "the Gospel of the Combined" ("the Combined Gospels"). Herein is indicated the first problem in the history of the Syriac New Testament. It is well known that a harmony of the Gospels was used in the Syriac Church till the beginning of the fifth century, when Theodoret removed the copies in his diocese, and Rabbulas of Edessa ordered that the "Gospel of the Separated" should be read in church. The great question concerns the relationship of the Peshito, the Mepharreshe, and Tatian. It seems certain that the three are interrelated. It seems further to have been proved by Burkitt that the Peshito is the latest, and is in all probability the revision which Rabbulas of Edessa (d. 435) is said to have undertaken. The decision of the other question, whether the Mepharreshe or Tatian is the earlier, is made difficult by the fact that Tatian's work is not preserved in its original form, and further by the fact that the two representatives of the Mepharreshe, the manuscripts of Cureton and Lewis, differ greatly. But on the whole it seems most probable that Tatian was the first to bring the Gospel to the Syrians in the form of his *Diatessaron*, and that then on the basis of his harmony the version of the separate Gospels originated. Burkitt is inclined to believe that this was toward the end of the second century, perhaps under the influence of the Church of Antioch, through Paul of Edessa. The opposite view, that the Mepharreshe is earlier than Tatian, is taken by Hjelt, who believed he was able to show that the Gospels in the Mepharreshe were translated by different hands, and that the first Gospel especially betrays a Jewish character. Without the discovery of new evidence the question will be very difficult to decide.

No manuscript of an early Syriac version of the Acts and the Pauline Epistles is known. But that there was an older version can be proved from the quotations of such early writers as Aphraates and Ephraem, and perhaps also from readings in the Armenian version. In early times the apocryphal correspondence with the Corinthians was placed with the Epistles of Paul. The Catholic Epistles were at first totally unknown, as is expressly stated by Theodore of Mopsuestia and Theodore bar Koni (cf. A. Baumstark, in *Oriens Christianus*, i, 176, iii, 555). In the Peshito as we have it the three greater of them are found, in accordance with the use of the Church of Antioch. Still later the four others were added. It is strange that the Nestorian inscription of Singan-fu (see NESTORIANS) speaks of twenty-seven books of the New Testament. Revelation never formed part of the canon among the Syrians (cf. on the Syriac canon, T. Zahn, *Grundriss der Geschichte des neutestamentlichen Kanons*, Leipsic, 1904, § 6; J. A. Bewer, *The History of the New Testament Canon in the Syrian Church*, Chicago, 1900; W Bauer, *Der Apostolos der Syrer*, Giessen, 1903), and whether the Pauline collection included Philemon can not be decided.

2. Later Versions: The Nestorian patriarch

Mar Abba (d. 552) is said by Bar Hebræus, Ebed Jesu, and Amru to have translated and explained the Old and New Testaments from the Greek; but nothing more is known about it.

In 508 Philoxenus of Mabug with the help of his coadjutor Polycarp translated at least some parts of the Old Testament and undertook a new version of the New Testament. Parts of Isaiah preserved in a manuscript of the British Museum may belong to this version (ed. A. Ceriani, *Monumenta sacra et profana*, v, 5, Milan, 1873, 1–40). According to Bernstein, the Gospels are contained in manuscript A2 of the Angelican library at Rome. Isaac H. Hall published a *Syriac Manuscript. Gospels from a pre-Harklensian Version, Acts and Epistles of the Peshitto Version, Written (probably) between 700 and 900 A.D. Presented to the Syrian Protestant College* [Beirut] (Philadelphia, 1884). The minor epistles, first published by E. Pococke in 1630 and since often found in editions of the Syriac New Testament, are very likely part of this version, and so is the version of Revelation discovered by J. Gwynn and published by him (Dublin, 1897).

About one hundred years later the work of translation was resumed, for the Old Testament, by Paul of Tella (the so-called Syro-Hexaplar version; see above, I, 1, § 6), and, for the New Testament, by Thomas of Heraclea (Harkel in Mesopotamia). This version was published by J. White under the inappropriate title, *Versio Philoxeniana* (Oxford, 1778–1803). A lacuna in the Epistle to the Hebrews was filled in by R. L. Bensly (*Harklean Version of the Epistle to the Hebrews xi, 28–xiii, 25*, London, 1889). W. Deane began a new edition but was prevented from finishing it. Its completion, especially for the Acts, is much to be desired. For his marginal notes, Thomas made use of a manuscript closely related to the Greek codex D (cf. A. Pott, *Der abendländische Text der Apostelgeschichte*, Leipsic, 1900, and Hilgenfeld, in *ZWT*, xliii, 1900, p. 3). The Syriac text of Revelation published by De Dieu (Leyden, 1627) and now in the common Syriac New Testaments belongs to this version (cf. J. Gwynn, in *Hermathena*, 1898, 227–245).

On the revision of the Old Testament undertaken by Jacob of Edessa in 704–705, cf. Kamphausen, in *TSK*, 1869, 753, and A. Ceriani, *Monumenta sacra et profana*, v, 1 (Milan, 1871).

Mention must also be made of the Palestinian version (used by the Melchite Church in Palestine and Egypt). Of the Old Testament, only fragments remain. The New Testament has been known from an evangeliarium at Rome since 1789 (published by F Miniscalchi-Erizzo, Verona, 1861–1864, and by Lagarde, *Bibliotheca Syriaca*, Göttingen, 1892). Since that time many new texts have been brought to light, especially through Mrs. Lewis. A full list is given in the *Lexicon syropalæstinum* of F. Schulthess (Berlin, 1903), pp. vii–xvi. F. C. Burkitt (*JTS*, ii, 183) gives reasons for believing that this literature may have a connection with the attempts of Justinian in the fifth century to extirpate the Samaritans, and of Heraclius early in the sixth century to harass the Jews. This peculiar dialect is important lexically, as being closely akin to the language spoken in Galilee.

E. Nestle.

Bibliography: The first parts of the Bible printed in Syriac are in Ambrosius Theseus, *Introductio in Chaldaicam linguam, Syriacam atque Armenicam*, Pavia, 1539 (cf. *ZDMG*, lviii, 1904, 601). The Old Testament appeared first in the Paris Polyglot, vols. vi–ix, 1632–45, then in the London Polyglot, vols. i–iv, 1654–57, reprinted by S. Lee for the *BFBS*, London, 1823 (other copies, 1824; on their differences—one set contains Ps. cli, the other not—cf. *ZDMG*, lix, 1905, 31), and at Urumiah (with modern Syriac added), 1852. The text is very bad, resting on a single late manuscript at Paris adapted by Gabriel Sionita, editor of the Paris Polyglot, from which the London Polyglot and Lee took it with scarcely any correction, the Urumiah edition, at least in some parts, with but few corrections (cf. W. E. Barnes, *An Apparatus criticus to Chronicles in the Peshitta Version*, Cambridge, 1897; G. Diettrich, *Ein Apparatus criticus zur Pešitto zum Propheten Jesaia*, Giessen, 1905). Bernstein and Rahlfs have published emendations, the former in *ZDMG*, iii, 1849, 387–396, the latter in *ZATW*, ix, 1889, 161–210. A. M. Ceriani published a photographic reproduction of the *Codex Ambrosianus*, Milan, 1876–83. The Apocrypha was published by Lagarde, Leipsic, 1861. The first critical edition of the Gospels was by P. E. Pusey and G. H. Gwilliam, Oxford, 1901; for the rest of the New Testament there are the editions of the American mission at Urumiah, 1846, New York, 1848, etc. The edition most used in textual criticism hitherto has been that of J. Leusden and C. Schaaf, Leyden, 1709 and 1717, reprinted by Jones, Oxford, 1805 (cf. Tischendorf on Matt. x, 8, with the note of Pusey-Gwilliam). The entire Bible was printed by the Dominicans at Mosul, 1887–91. A list of editions to 1888 is contained in Nestle, *Litteratura Syriaca* (reprinted from *Syrische Grammatik*, Berlin, 1888), 17–30. Consult further: Beck, *Editiones principes Novi Testamenti Syriaci*, Basel, 1771; J. Le Long, *Bibliotheca sacra, emendata . . ab A. G. Masch*, i, part 4, pp. 54–102, 5 vols., Halle, 1778–90; A. M. Ceriani, *Le Edizioni e i manoscritti delle versione Siriache del vecchio Testamento*, Milan, 1869; *Printed editions of the Syriac New Testament*, in *Church Quarterly Review*, July, 1888, 255–297; *Syriac New Testament translated into Eng. by J. Murdock, with a bibliographical Appendix*, by I. H. Hall, 6th ed., Boston, 1893; G. H. Gwilliam, *The Ammonian Sections, Eusebian Canons and Harmonizing Tables in the Syriac Tetraeuangelium*, in *Studia Biblica et Ecclesiastica*, ii, Oxford, 1890; idem, *Materials for the Criticism of the Peshitto*, ib. iii, 1891; Scrivener, *Introduction*, ii, 6–40; F. C. Burkitt, *Evangelion da-Mepharreshe, Introduction*, vol. i, London, 1905. On the Old Testament in the Peshito consult: J. Prager, *De veteris testamenti versione Syriaca quam Peschittho*, Göttingen, 1875; J. Perles, *Meletemata Peschitthoniana*, Breslau, 1860; J. M. Schönfelder, *Onkelos und Peschittho*, Munich, 1869. On parts of the Old Testament: L. Hirzel, *De Pentateuchi versionis Syriacæ indole*, Leipsic, 1815; S. D. Luzzatto, *Philoxenus sive de Onkelosi Chaldaica Pentateuchi versione*, Vienna. 1830; F. Tuch, *De Lipsiensi codice Pentateuchi Syriaco*, Leipsic, 1849; E. Schwartz, *Die syrische Uebersetzung des 1. Samuelis*, Berlin, 1897; J. Berliner, *Die Peschitta zum 1. Buch der Könige*, Berlin, 1897; S. Fränkel, in *JPT*, 1879, pp. 508, 720 (on Chronicles); A. Oliver, *A Transl. of the Syriac Peschito Version of the Psalms*, Boston, 1861; F. Bäthgen, *Untersuchungen über die Psalmen nach der Peschito*, Kiel, 1878; idem, in *JPT*, viii (1882), 405, 593; F. Dietrich, *Commentatio de psalterii usu in ecclesia Syriaca*, Marburg, 1862; B. Oppenheim, *Die syrische Uebersetzung . der Psalmen*, Leipsic, 1891; J. F. Berg, *Influence of the Septuagint upon the Peshitta Psalter*, New York, 1895; Techen, *Glossar*, in *ZATW*, xvii (1897), 129, 280 (on Psalms); Baumann (on Job), in *ZATW*, xviii–xx (1898–1900); J. A. Dathe, *De ratione consensus Syriacæ Proverbiorum*, Leipsic, 1764; A. S. Kamenetzky (on Ecclesiastes), in *ZATW*, xxiv (1904); G. Dietrich, *Die Massorah der östlichen und westlichen Syrer*, London, 1899; idem, *Textkritischer Apparat*, 1905 (Isaiah); C. H. Cornill, *Das Buch des Propheten Ezechiel*, pp. 137–156, Leipsic, 1886; C. A. Credner, *De prophetarum minorum versionis Syriacæ indole*, Göttingen, 1827;

M. Sebök (Schonberger), *Die syrische Uebersetzung der zwölf Propheten*, Breslau, 1887; V. Ryssel, *Untersuchungen über die Textgestalt . des Buches Micha*, Leipsic 1887; J. J. Kneucker, *Das Buch Baruch*, pp. 190–198, Leipsic, 1869; T. Nöldeke, *Die Texte des Buches Tobit*, in *Monatsberichte der Berliner Akademie*, 1879, pp. 45–69.

On the New Testament: *The Peshito Versions of the Gospels*, ed. G. W. Gwilliam, London, 1901. On the Curetonian: C. Hermansen, *De codice evangeliorum Syriaco*, Copenhagen, 1869; Le Hir, *Étude sur une ancienne version syriaque des evangiles*, Paris, 1859; G. Wildeboer, *De waarde der syrische evangelien, door Cureton ontdekt*, Leyden, 1880; Fr. Bäthgen, *Evangelienfragmente*, Leipsic, 1885; H. Harman, *Cureton Fragments*, in *JBL*, 1885, June–Dec., pp. 28–48.

On the Mepharreshe, J. R. Crowfoot, *Fragmenta Evangelica*, London, 1870; idem, *Collation in Greek of Cureton's Syriac Fragments*, ib. 1872. On the Sinai Palimpsest: M. D. Gibson, *How the Codex was found*, Cambridge, 1893; Mrs. R. L. Bensly, *Our Journey to Sinai . with a Chapter on the Sinai Palimpsest*, London, 1896; K. Holzhey, *Der neuentdeckte Codex Syrus Sinaiticus*, Munich, 1896; A. Bonus, *Collatio codicis Lewisiani cum codice Curetoniano*, Oxford, 1896. For further accounts of the Lewis codex consult the files of the *Athenæum*, *Academy*, *Contemporary Review*, *Expository Times*, *Guardian*, *Church Quarterly Review*, *TLZ*, and similar journals for the years 1893–96.

On the Peshito in textual criticism consult: *The Oxford Debate on The Textual Criticism of the New Testament*, London, 1897; T. W. Etheridge, *Horæ Aramaicæ. With a Transl. of . St. Matthew and Hebrews from the . Peshito*, London, 1843; idem, *The Apostolical Acts; Transl. from the Peshito and a later Text*, London, 1849; W. Norton, *A Transl. of the Seventeen Letters . . of the Peshito Syriac*, London, 1890; J. Gwynn, *Older Syriac Version of the four Minor Catholic Epistles*, in *Hermathena*, 1890. On Tatian: A. Hjelt, in T. Zahn, *Forschungen*, vii. 1 (1903); Mrs. Lewis, in *Expositor*, Aug., 1897, June, 1890.

IV. The Samaritan Pentateuch: This must not be confounded with the Hebrew text of the Pentateuch in Samaritan characters or with the Arabic version used by the Samaritans. All three are contained in the famous triglot manuscript in the Barberini Library at Rome of the year 1227 (for facsimile cf. G. M. Bianchini's *Evangeliarium quadruplex*, Rome, 1749, or, on a reduced scale, F. G. Kenyon, *Our Bible and the Ancient Manuscripts*, London, 1896, pl. v). The question of the age of this targum depends on the decision of the question whence the readings are taken which are found under the rubric *to Samaraitikon* in some fifty marginal notes of Origen's Hexapla (to the passages collected by Field add Lev. xv, 8; Deut. viii, 22, xxxiv, 1–3, from the margins of Lagarde's *Bibliotheca Syriaca*). The most probable view seems to be that not Origen but Eusebius took these notes from the Hebrew Pentateuch as used among the Samaritans. On a Samaritan inscription found at Amwas (Emmaus) cf. *Revue Biblique*, 1896, p. 433. E. Nestle.

The Samaritan Pentateuch is essentially the same as the Hebrew The variations, aside from those of a linguistic character, are the following: the narrative of action or declaration by Moses is often preceded by the statement that he acted or spoke by divine direction; Gen. ii, 2a, "seventh" is changed to "sixth"; anthropomorphisms are removed, and in Gen. xx, 13, xxxi, 53, xxxv, 7, Ex. xxii, 8, the plural predicate after Elohim is changed to the singular to avoid a polytheistic implication; "Ebal" (Deut. xxvii, 4) was displaced by Gerizim for national reasons. The Samaritan Pentateuch is proved by these changes to be a revision of the Jewish, but a revision made in early times (possibly pre-Christian), though the modern tendency is to ascribe the text now extant to the second Christian century.

Bibliography: The text was first printed in the Paris Polyglot, 1643, then in Walton's Polyglot, 1657. Other editions of the whole or of parts are: A. Brüll, *Das samaritanische Targum zum Pentateuch*, Frankfort, 1873–75, with two appendices which appeared 1875–76; H. Petermann and C. Vollers, *Pentateuchus Samaritanus* . . ., i, *Genesis*, Berlin, 1872, ii, *Exodus*, 1882, iii, *Leviticus*, 1883, iv, *Numeri*, 1885, v, *Deuteronomium*, 1891; J. W. Nutt, *Fragments of a Samaritan Targum*, London, 1874; F. Field, *Origenis Hexaplorum*, i. p. lxxxii–lxxxiv, Oxford, 1875; S. Kohn, in *Monatsschrift für Geschichte und Wissenschaft des Judentums*, 1894, pp. 1–7, 49–67.

On various phases of the relation to text-criticism consult: J. Morinus, *Exercitationes in utrumque Samaritanorum Pentateuchum*, Paris, 1631; idem, in the Preface of his edition of the Septuagint, 1628; W. Gesenius, *De Pentateuchi Samaritani indole*, . Halle, 1815; G. B. Winer, *De versionis Pentateuchi Samaritanæ indole*, Leipsic, 1817; S. Kohn, *De Pentateucho Samaritano* . , ib. 1865; idem, *Samaritanische Studien*, Breslau, 1868; idem, *Zur Sprache, Literatur und Dogmatik der Samaritaner*, Leipsic, 1876; idem, in *ZDMG*, xxxix (1885), 165–226, A. Cowley, in *JQR*, viii (1896), 562 sqq., and in *JE*, x, 667; idem, *A Supposed Early Copy of the Samaritan Pentateuch*, in PEF, *Quarterly Statement*, Oct., 1904; P. Kahle, *Textkritische und lexikalische Bemerkungen zum samaritanischen Pentateuchtargum*, Leipsic, 1898; J. Skinner, *Notes on a newly acquired Samaritan MS*, in *JQR*, xiv (1901), 26–36; W. E. Barton, *The Samaritan Pentateuch*, in *Bibliotheca sacra*, lx (1903); R. Gottheil, in *JBL*, xxv, part 1, 1906; J. A. Montgomery, *The Samaritans*, Philadelphia, 1907.

V. Aramaic Versions (The Targums): These are Aramaic paraphrases of the Old Testament (*targum* = "interpretation, translation," from *targem*, "to explain, translate"; cf. Ezra iv, 7)

1. Origin and Language.

prepared for use in the synagogue, and took their rise from the custom of repeating and explaining the Hebrew sacred text in the Aramaic tongue, which after the exile became the vernacular of the Jews in Palestine and elsewhere. At first the targum was a free oral exposition; then it gradually acquired fixed form, and at last was reduced to writing. It is frequently found in manuscripts following the Hebrew text verse by verse. When the Law was read, the paraphrase was given after every verse; with the Prophets three verses were allowed to be taken together.

The language of the Targums used to be called Chaldee, because Jerome so named the Aramaic portions of the Hebrew Bible, which are written in a dialect very akin to that of the Targums. In reality, these have preserved the Jewish form of the Aramaic, the next cognate dialect being Syriac, the form of the Aramaic used by the Christians of Edessa, while still other cognate dialects are those of the Palmyrene inscriptions and of the Samaritans (see Semitic Languages). The grammatical and lexicographical use of the Targums is hampered by the fact that no edition has as yet appeared that takes account of all the materials now available. Mercier vocalized the texts after the Syriac, Buxtorf after the Biblical Aramaic; the edition printed by Foa (Sabbionetta, 1557) seems to rest on a manuscript in which the supralinear system of vocalization had been changed into that of Tiberias, but with many faults and inconsistencies. The most original system of vocalization is that preserved in manuscripts from Yemen, on which cf. the works of Merx, Berliner, Landauer, Kautzsch, Margoliouth (*The Superlinear Punctuation*, in *PSBA*, xxiii, 164–205), and Barnstein (*The Targum of Onkelos to Genesis*, London, 1896), and the editions of Prätorius (*Joshua*, Berlin, 1899; *Judges*, 1900).

For the greater part of the Old Testament there is more than one Targum. One on the Pentateuch is attributed in some passages of the Talmud to the helpers of Ezra.

2. Targum Onkelos.

According to the Babylonian Talmud (*Megillot* 3a), Onkelos delivered it orally in Palestine; but this is the result of confusing Onkelos with Aquila, who translated the Old Testament into Greek (see above, I, 2, § 1), and "Judaic Pentateuch-Targum" is a better name than "Targum of Onkelos," which has been in use since Bomberg's Rabbinic Bible of 1517. In the third century its text seems to have been considered fixed, and manuscripts are mentioned several times, but Origen and Jerome apparently did not know a Targum, and hence we may conclude that it did not find official recognition before the fifth century. Its language is different from that of both Talmuds, and seems to render the original into the language of the place and time of its origin (Palestine) as faithfully as a translation which is somewhat paraphrastic can do. The Hebrew text on which it rests is practically our Masoretic text, and it is of interest as representing the exegetical tradition of the Jews. It is quite literal, gives a messianic interpretation of Gen. xlix, 10, and Num. xxiv, 17, additions to Gen. xlix, Num. xxiv, Deut. xxxii, 33, and avoids all anthropomorphisms. Like the Hebrew text, it has been the subject of Masoretic studies, which have been edited by Berliner (*Die Massorah zum Targum Onkelos*, Leipsic, 1877).

The Targum of the Prophets has been ascribed to Jonathan ben Uzziel, Hillel's greatest disciple; others give as its redactor Joseph ben Hiyya of Babylon (d. about 333);

3. Targum Jonathan.

but it did not receive its final written form before the fifth century. It is more paraphrastic than the Targum of the Law, which induced Cornill to think that it is older. Eichhorn and Bertholdt thought they recognized different hands. The paraphrase is greatly influenced by the book of Daniel. Isa. liii is understood of the Messiah, whose suffering atones for Israel. Great enmity is shown against Rome.

The two Targums just described represent the Judaic Aramaic; of a mixed character is the language of Targums Yerushalmi I and II on the Law.

4. Other Targums of the Law and Prophets.

Some verses are missing from the former, and the latter is preserved only in fragments. Certain other fragments found in various manuscripts and editions of the Pentateuch are designated by Dalman (*Grammatik*, § 6, 3) as Yerushalmi III. There are similar fragments of a Targum on the Prophets published by Lagarde from the margins of Reuchlin's codex (on which cf. Bacher, in *ZDMG*, xxviii). Bassfreund (*Das Fragmententargum zum Pentateuch*, Breslau, 1896) and similarly Dalman (*Grammatik*, § 6, 4) see in Onkelos the oldest Palestinian Targum and in Yerushalmi I and II a later development. M. Ginsburger, on the contrary (*Pseudo-jonathan*, Berlin, 1903, preface), and Bacher find in them traces of a very old Palestinian Targum, which has been worked over by Onkelos. The comment in these pieces is sometimes very fantastic.

The Targums of the Hagiographa are not translations, but commentaries; the Targum of the Song of Solomon, for instance, is a panegyric of the Jewish nation with foolish anachronisms,

5. The Hagiographa.

the Targum of the Psalms is in some parts literal, in others explanatory. The Targum of Proverbs is a working over of the Syriac translation (cf. Pinkuss, in *ZATW*, xiv, 65, 161). As the Hagiographa were not read in the Synagogue as regularly as the Law and the Prophets (cf. Lk. iv, 16; Acts xiii, 15; xv, 21), their Targums are to some extent private literary works of differing character. For Ezra-Nehemiah and Daniel no Targum is known, unless the Aramaic parts of Daniel are fragments of a Targum. For Esther there are two Targums. E. NESTLE.

BIBLIOGRAPHY: The best grammar is G. Dalman, *Grammatik des jüdisch-palästinischen Aramäisch*, Leipsic, 1894, *Ausgabe mit Dialektproben*, 1896, 2d ed., 1905 (gives valuable compend of literature). The first special dictionary for the Targum is the *Meturgeman* of Elias Levita, Isny, 1541; quite complete but unsatisfactory linguistically is J. Levy, *Chaldäisches Wörterbuch über die Targumim*, 2 vols., Leipsic, 1867 68. The whole range of Aramaic literature is treated in Nathan ben [illegible]hiel *Sepher he-aruk* (c. 1100 A.D.), first printed without place and date, but before 1480 A.D., new ed., by A. Kohut, Vienna, 1878–92 (cf. *JE*, ix, 180–182). Others are: G. F. Boderianus (1573), printed in the Antwerp Polyglot; J. Buxtorf, *Lexicon chaldaicum*, 1640, new ed., B. Fischer, Leipsic, 1869–75; M. Jastrow, *Dictionary of the Targumim, the Talmud Babli and Jerushalmi and the Midrashic Literature*, 2 vols., New York, 1903 (the most accessible); G. Dalman, *Aramäisch-neuhebräisches Wörterbuch mit Lexikon der Abbreviaturen*, von G. Händler, Frankfort, 1897–1901.

The Targum of Onkelos was first printed Bologna, 1482, with Hebr. text and Rashi's commentary; best edition by Foa, at Sabbionetta, 1557, republished by A. Berliner at Berlin, 1884 (cf. Lagarde, *Mittheilungen*, ii, 163–182); latest edition in the Hebrew Pentateuch *Sefer keter tora* at Jerusalem, 1894–1901. Parts are in A. Merx, *Chrestomathia Targumica*, Berlin, 1883; in E. Kautzsch, *Ueber eine alte Handschrift des Targum Onkelos*, Halle, 1893; and G. Dalman, *Aramäische Dialektproben*, Leipsic, 1896. Translations are that in Eng. by J. W. Etheridge, including Onkelos, Jonathan, and the Jerusalem fragments, 2 vols., London, 1862, and the Latin transl. by P. Fagius, Strasburg, 1546. On the text-critical value and other relations consult: S. Landauer, *Die Masorah zum Onkelos*, Leipsic, 1877; H. Barnstein, *Targum of Onkelos to Genesis*, London, 1896; G. Diettrich, *Grammatische Beobachtungen*, in *ZATW*, xx (1900), 148–159; E. Brederek, in *TSK*, lxxiv (1901), 351–377; A. Merx, *Die Vokalisation der Targume*, in *Verhandlung des 5ten orientalischen Congress*, ii, part 1, pp. 142–188. On the person of Onkelos consult: D. Luzzatto, *Philoxenus*, Cracow, 1895; M. Friedmann, *Onkelos und Akylas*, Vienna, 1896; *JE*, ii, 36–38, ix, 405, xii, 58–59.

The editions of the Targums of Jonathan are: For the "Former Prophets" 1st edition, Leiria, 1494, for the whole, in the first Rabbinic Bible, Venice, 1517; by Lagarde after Reuchlin's MS., 1872 (cf. A. Klostermann, in *TSK*, xlvi, 1873, 731–767); Joshua and Judges by Prätorius from South Arabian MSS., Berlin, 1899-1900; Jonah and Micah by Merx, in his *Chrestomathia*, ut sup.; Nahum by Adler, in *JQR*, vii (1895), 630-657; Jer. i-xii by Wolfsohn, 1903; Ezekiel, i-x by Silbermann, 1902; the Haftaroth in the Hebrew Pentateuch *Sefer keter torah*, ut sup. Consult also: C. W. H. Pauli, *The Chaldee Paraphrase on the Prophet Isaiah*, London, 1871; Z. Frankel, *Zu dem Targum der Propheten*, Breslau, 1872; W. Bacher, in *ZDMG*, xxviii (1874), 1-72, 157, 319; H. S. Levy, *Targum on Isaiah, with Commentary*, London, 1889.

Yerushalmi I and II were first published in Bomberg's Rabbinic Bible, Venice, 1517. The best editions of both are by M. Ginsburger, *Pseudo-Jonathan*, Berlin, 1903, and *Das Fragmententhargum*, 1899 (cf. Barnstein, in *JQR*, xiii, 1899, 167; *ZDMG*, lviii, 1904, 374-378). On both Targums, cf. Dalman, *Grammatik*, § 6, 1-2; on an important manuscript of Yerushalmi II at Nuremberg, cf. Lagarde, *Mittheilungen*, iii, Göttingen, 1889, 87.

The Targum of the Hagiographa: The first edition of Job, Ps., Prov., and the Rolls was in the Rabbinic Bible, Venice, 1517, which books were reprinted by Lagarde in 1873; the best edition of the Targum on Esther is by M. David, Berlin, 1898 (cf. Posner, *Das Targum Rischon zu Esther*, Breslau, 1896); Ecclesiastes, from South Arabian MSS., by A. Levy, ib. 1905. Consult E. Brederek, *Konkordanz zum Targum Onkelos*, Giessen, 1906; H. L. Strack, *Einleitung in das A. T.*, § 84, Munich, 1906.

VI. The Armenian Version: The Armenian translation of the Old Testament rests on the Greek, though it shows in certain passages and books traces of revision either from the Syriac or from the Hebrew. The Greek text used seems to have been dependent on Origen, for in some Armenian manuscripts hexaplaric marks are found. In the manuscripts (not in the printed editions) various pseudepigraphic books appear. The Armenian Psalter printed for the British and Foreign Bible Society at Venice, 1850, was rejected in consequence of these additions. Ecclesiasticus has been translated twice, first in the fifth century, this version being printed in the Venice Bible, 1860; again probably in the eighth century, found in Zohrab's edition of the Armenian Bible of 1805. On the statements of Koriun, Lazar of Parpi, and Moses of Chorene, that the Scriptures were translated by Mesrob, Sahag, Eznik, and others between 396 and 430 from manuscripts brought from Edessa, Constantinople, and Alexandria, cf. Conybeare, *DB*, i, 152 (see ARMENIA, II, §§ 2-3). A collation of the Armenian version was made for Holmes-Parsons (see above, I, 1, § 2), and is being made afresh for the forthcoming Cambridge Septuagint by McLean (cf. Swete, *Introduction*, London, 1900, p. 118). Theodoret states that in his time the language of the Hebrews was translated into that of the Armenians, Scythians, and Sauromatians. A concordance to the Armenian Bible has been printed in the cloister of San Giacomo at Jerusalem (1895). The uncanonical writings of the Old Testament found in Armenian manuscripts in the library of San Lazzaro were translated into English by J. Issaverdens (Venice, 1901); on Ter Moosesjan's *History of the Translation of the Bible into Armenian*, cf. H. Goussen, in *Nouvelle Revue de Théologie*, 1904, p. 9.

For the New Testament Mill used some notes on the Armenian version by W. Guise and L. Piques. For Tregelles C. Rieu collated Zohrab's edition of 1805. His notes were used by Tischendorf in the eighth edition of his New Testament; Gregory catalogued sixty-four manuscripts in Europe (outside of Russia) and America. At Moscow is a copy of the Gospels dated 887, at Echmiadzin is the manuscript 222 written in 989, but with an ivory binding which is much older. Conybeare discovered in this manuscript, after Mark xvi, 8, the words *Ariston eritzou* ("of the presbyter Arist[i]on"), which probably preserve the name of the author of the close of the second Gospel. The Gospels have invariably the so-called Ammonian sections; the Acts and Epistles of Paul, the Euthalian additions (see AMMONIUS OF ALEXANDRIA; EUTHALIUS); at their end is found the apocryphal correspondence of Paul with the Corinthians. After John follows sometimes the apocryphal "Rest of John." The Apocalypse is said to be a recension made by Nerses Lambron in the twelfth century; a much older version is indicated by H. Goussen (cf. Gregory, *Textkritik*, Leipsic, 1902, p. 568). The inclusion of the apocryphal correspondence of Paul with the Corinthians and other characteristics of this version and the whole history of the Armenian Church confirm the view that the Armenian version was first based on the Syriac Bible and afterward revised from the Greek; cf. on this question Conybeare and Burkitt. E. NESTLE.

BIBLIOGRAPHY: The Armenian Bible was first printed, Amsterdam, 1666, from a single MS.; of this the edition by Mechitar, Venice, 1733, was in the main a reprint; the first critical edition was by Zohrab, Venice, 1805. Consult Scrivener, *Introduction*, ii, 148-154; Gregory, *Textkritik*, i, 565-573; F. C. Conybeare, in *DB*, i, 151-154, and in *The Expositor*, 1893, pp. 242 sqq., and Dec., 1895; F. C. Burkitt, in *EB*, iv, 5011, 5028; A. Abeghian, *Vorfragen zur Entstehungsgeschichte der altarmenischen Bibelübersetzungen*, Marburg, 1906; idem, *Zur Entstehungsgeschichte der altarmenischen Bibelübersetzungen*, Tübingen, 1907.

VII. Egyptian Coptic Versions: According to Zosimus Panopolitanus, the Hebrew Bible was translated into Egyptian at the same time as the Septuagint (see above, I, 1, § 6); according to the life of St. Anthony, he heard the Gospel read in church in the Egyptian language. But the latter statement is not certain enough to justify the supposition that the Egyptian version of the New Testament goes back to the middle of the third century. At that time Christianity in Egypt seems to have been restricted to the Greek-speaking towns. Modern scholars distinguish linguistically as many as five or six Coptic dialects; for the textual critic the Coptic versions fall into three divisions, although a former generation knew only one and called it the Coptic, i.e., the Egyptian, version. These divisions are: (1) The Saidic or the version of Upper Egypt, sometimes called the Thebaic; (2) the Fayyumic (formerly called the Bashmuric), with which text the fragments in the Middle-Egyptian dialect agree; (3) the version now in ecclesiastical use among all Copts or Egyptian Christians, called Bohairic. The Bohairah ("Lake") is a district near Alexandria and Lake Mareotis, the modern Beherah. There is a fourth dialect called Akhmimic; but the version of the Catholic Epistles in this dialect, preserved in a very ancient manuscript, is properly classed with the Saidic version. Bashmuric had already died out in the time of Athanasius.

The Bohairic version was for a long time the only one known to European scholars, and is still supposed by some to be the earliest version in any Egyptian dialect; but with better reason others see in it a late recension, characterized by greater faithfulness to the Greek, the basal Greek text being best represented by the Greek Codex L and, among the Fathers, not by Clement and Origen, but by Cyril. Of the Saidic manuscripts some of the more ancient are bilingual, the Greek occupying the page on the left hand of the open book; the Bohairic manuscripts, on the contrary, are often accompanied by an Arabic translation, but there is no instance of a Greco-Bohairic manuscript. When written in two columns the Greco-Saidic manuscripts have both Greek columns on the left and both Saidic on the right, and occasionally the two pages of the codex give different readings. The text of this version generally supports that represented by Codex B, but it has some strange "Western" singularities; for instance, to Luke xxiii, 53, it is added that Joseph placed a stone at the door of the sepulcher, which twenty men were scarcely able to move, and in the parable of the rich man and Lazarus the name of the former is given as "Nineveh." Revelation seems to have been considered uncanonical, for it is not found with the rest of the New Testament. E. NESTLE.

BIBLIOGRAPHY: Ersch and Gruber, *Allgemeine Encyclopädie*, Section 2, vol. xxxix, 12–36; J. P. Martin, in *Polybiblion*, i, 126, Paris, 1886; A. Schulte, *Die koptische Uebersetzung der vier grossen Prophelen*, Münster, 1893; Scrivener, *Introduction*, ii, 91–144; H. Hyvernat, *Étude sur les versions Coptes de la Bible*, in *Revue Biblique*, v (1896), 3, 427–433, 540–569, vi (1897), 1, 48–74; Gregory, *Textkritik*, i. 528–553; *DB*, i, 668–673; *EB*, iv, 5006–11, 5027; W. E. Crum is accustomed to note new Biblical texts in the annual *Archæological Report* of the Egypt Exploration Fund (cf. that for 1905–06, pp. 66 sqq.).

On the Bohairic version of the Old Testament, especially the Pentateuch, cf. A. E. Brooke, in *JTS*, iii, 258–278. For the Bohairic New Testament there is now the fine edition of the Clarendon Press by G. Horner, *The Coptic Version of the N. T. in the Northern Dialect, otherwise called the Memphitic and Bohairic, with Introduction, critical Apparatus, and literal Eng. transl.*, vols. i–ii, Gospels, 1898, vols. iii–iv, Acts and Epistles, 1905.

The Saidic New Testament is edited by P. J. Balestri in *Sacrorum bibliorum fragmenta copto-sahidica Musei Borgiani*, vol. iii, Rome, 1904; the Berlin manuscript of the Psalter, by A. Rahlfs, *GGA*, iv, 4, 1901; cf. also J. O. Prince, *Two Versions of the Coptic Psalter*, in *JBL*, xxi, 92–99; E. O. Winstedt, *Sahidic Biblical Fragments in the Bodleian Library*, in *PSBA*, xxvii., 2; and C. Wessely, *Sahidisch-griechische Psalmenfragmente*, Vienna, 1907. For parts of the Old Testament cf. Lagarde's *Pentateuch*, Leipsic, 1867, *Psalterii versio Memphitica*, Göttingen, 1875, and (for Wisdom, Ecclesiastes, and Psalms) his *Ægyptiaca*, 1883; vols. i and ii of the Borgian Fragments, by Ciasca, 1885–89; on the importance of the Egyptian version of Job, cf. Lagarde, *Mittheilungen*, Göttingen, 1884, i, 203.

VIII. The Ethiopic Version: In Ethiopic there exists a translation of the Bible which has continued the only one authorized among Abyssinian Christians, and even among the Jewish Falashas; and it still maintains its ancient authority, although the Ethiopic long ago ceased to be spoken. There is no reliable information as to the exact time or manner of its origin; but it is certain that it was made from the Septuagint in the early days of Abyssinian Christianity, between the fourth and the sixth century. It is very faithful, being, for the most part, a verbal rendering of the Greek, readable and fluent, and in the Old Testament often renders closely the ideas and the words of the Hebrew.

Dillmann projected an edition of the Ethiopic Old Testament in five volumes, of which he lived to publish vols. i, Gen.–Ruth (1853), ii, Sam.–Kings (1861–71), and v, the Apocrypha (1894). He arranged the manuscripts in three groups: (1) those which contain the original translation from the Septuagint uncorrupted; (2) those the text of which has been revised and completed from the Greek; (3) those which have been corrected from the Hebrew. From the circumstance that the Ethiopic Church was dependent on that in Egypt, it is probable that the particular recension of the Septuagint from which the Ethiopic translation was made was the Hesychian (see above, I, 1, § 5). But the early Aramaic-speaking missionaries influenced the translation, as is shown by the numerous Aramaic words which are employed to convey Christian ideas. Possibly the Bible was translated, at least in part, by these missionaries or their pupils.

The division into chapters was introduced at a later day into Abyssinia, under European influences. The Ethiopic Bible includes the Apocrypha, except the books of Maccabees, which were either not translated or very early lost, and several pseudepigrapha, and puts them upon perfect equality with the canonical writings; and in this way the number of books is given as eighty-one, forty-six for the Old Testament, thirty-five for the New. (See ABYSSINIA AND THE ABYSSINIAN CHURCH.) (F PRÄTORIUS.)

BIBLIOGRAPHY: For lists of Ethiopic MSS. available consult the *Catalogues* by A. T. d'Abbadie, Paris, 1859 (a general list), by C. F. A. Dillmann (for British Museum), London, 1847 (for Bodleian Library), Oxford, 1848, and (for Berlin) Berlin, 1878, by W. Wright (for British Museum), London, 1877, and by H. Zotenberg (for Bibliothèque Nationale), Paris; *ZDMG*, v, 164 sqq. (for those in Tübingen), *ZDMG*, xvi (for Vienna), *Bulletin scientifique publié par l'Académie des Sciences*, ii, 302, iii, 145 sqq. (for those in St. Petersburg), and a general list in C. R. Gregory, *Prolegomena*, iii, 900–912, Leipsic, 1894. On the version consult: C. F. A. Dillmann, in *Jahrbücher der biblischen Wissenschaft*, v (1853), 144–151; Reckendorf, in *ZATW*, vii (1887), 61–90; P. J. Bachmann, *Dodekapropheton æthiopum*, part 1, *Obadiah*, Halle, 1892, part 2, *Maleachi*, 1893, *Die Klagelieder*, 1893, *Jesaia*, 1893; L. Goldschmidt, *Bibliotheca æthiopica*, Leipsic, 1893; Hackspill, in *ZA*, xi (1897), 150–151. The subject is treated also in C. R. Gregory, *Prolegomena*, iii, 894–900, ut sup.; in the *Einleitung* of König, 1893, p 113, of Jülicher, 1894, p. 388, and of Cornill, 1896, p. 338, and the *Introduction* of Scrivener, ii, 154–155.

The best ed. of the Old Testament is that of Dillmann (ut sup.). The New Testament was first printed at Rome in 1548–49 by the Abyssinian Tasfa-Sion or, as he is also called, Peter the Ethiopian, reprinted in the London Polyglot. An ed. was issued by T. P. Platt for the BFBS in 1826–30, reprinted at Leipsic, 1899.

IX. The Georgian (Iberian) Version: The earliest translations of parts of the Bible in the language of the Iberians belong to the fifth century, and seem to betray the influence of the Syriac version. David and Stephen in the eight century are the first names known of men engaged in revision of the Iberian Bible. A papyrus Psalter is assigned to the seventh or eighth century, and a copy of the Gospels is dated a century later (facsimile in Tsagareli). The edition printed at Moscow, 1743, has been retouched from the Slavonic. S. C. Malan in 1862 used this version for his edition of the Gospel of John. On the Georgian manuscripts of the library at Paris there is a recent paper by A. Khakhanov.

E. NESTLE.

BIBLIOGRAPHY: Scrivener, *Introduction*, ii, 156; A. A. Tsagareli, "Information about the Monuments of Georgian Literature" (Russian), parts i–iii, St. Petersburg, 1886–94; C. R. Gregory, *Prolegomena*, iii, 922–923, Leipsic, 1894; idem, *Textkritik*, i, 573; J. M. Bebb, in *DB*, iv, 861; A. Palmieri, *Le Versione Georgiane della Bibbia*, in *Bessarione*, 2 ser., vol. v, 259–268, 322–327, vi, 72–77, 189–194, Rome, 1901–02. On the people consult: A. Leist, *Das georgische Volk*, Dresden, 1903.

X. The Gothic Version of Ulfilas: Ulfilas (q.v.), the Moses of the Goths, as Constantine styled him (cf. *TSK*, 1893, 273), was made bishop probably in 341 at Antioch and died in 381 or 383. He gave to his people the alphabet and the Bible, but, according to Philostorgius (*Hist. eccl.*, ii, 5), omitted to translate the books of Kings because he thought they contained too much about war for the good of his fierce countrymen. Of the Old Testament very few fragments are left; viz., Gen. v, 3–30; Ps. lii, 2–3; Ezra xv (i.e. Neh. v), 13–16, xvi, 14–xvii, 3, xvii, 13–45. The translation follows the recension of Lucian (see above, I, 1, § 5). The Gothic priests Sunnias and Fretela, who were in correspondence with Jerome about the true readings of certain passages in the Psalter some twenty years after the death of Ulfilas (cf. Jerome, *Epist.*, cvi), were perhaps engaged in a revision of the Gothic Psalms. That the Psalms were sung in Gothic at Constantinople is testified by Chrysostom (cf. the dissertation of J. Mühlau, *Zur Frage nach der gotischen Psalmenübersetzung*, Kiel, 1904). On the fragments of Ezra (Nehemiah), cf. E. Langner, *Die gotischen Nehemia-fragmente* (Sprottau, 1903).

More of the New Testament is preserved, thanks to the *Codex Argenteus* now in Upsala, also by a palimpsest from Weissenburg discovered in Wolfenbüttel in 1756, and fragments at Turin discovered by Angelo Mai in 1817 and by Reifferscheid in 1866. The *Codex Argenteus* must have had a very near relationship to *Codex f.* of the Latin Bible (cf. M. Haupt, *Die Vorrede der gotischen Bibelübersetzung*, in his *Opuscula*, vol. iii, Leipsic, 1876; Burkitt, *JTS*, i, 129; Kauffmann, *ZDP*, xxxii, 305–335; Dräseke, *ZWT*, 1907). It was perhaps part of a Greek, Gothic, and Latin Testament. The version is very faithful, following the text used by Chrysostom. More than 100 Greek and Latin words were retained by Ulfilas (cf. C. Elis, *Ueber die Fremdwörter und fremden Eigennamen in der gotischen Bibelübersetzung*, Göttingen, 1903).

E. NESTLE.

BIBLIOGRAPHY: E. Bernhardt, *Kritische Untersuchungen über die gothische Bibelübersetzung*, Meiningen, 1867; K. Weinhold, *Die gothische Sprache im Dienste des Christenthums*, Halle, 1870; A. Kisch, *Der Septuaginta-Codex des Ulphilas*, in *Monatsschrift für Geschichte und Wissenschaft des Judenthums*, xxii (1873), 42–46, 85–89, 215–219; O. Ohrloff, *Die Bruchstücke . . . der gothischen Bibelübersetzung*, Halle, 1873; idem, in *ZDP*, vii (1876), 251–295; A. Schanbach, *Ueber das Verhältnis der gothischen Bibelübersetzung . . . zu der Lutherischen . . .*, Meiningen, 1879; G. Kaufmann, in *Zeitschrift für deutsches Alterthum*, xxvii (1883); K. Marold, *Kritische Untersuchungen über den Einfluss des Lateins auf die gothische Bibelübersetzung*, Königsberg, 1881; C. R. Gregory, *Prolegomena*, iii, 1108, Leipsic, 1894; F. Kauffmann, in *ZDP*, xxix (1896), 306–337; W. Bangert, *Der Einfluss lateinischer Quellen auf die gothische Bibelübersetzung*, Rudolstadt, 1880; W. Luft and F. Vogt, in *Zeitschrift für deutsches Alterthum*, xlii (1898); J. Mühlau, *Zur Frage nach der gotischen Psalmenubersetzung*, Kiel, 1904. On the language consult: G. H. Balg, *Comparative Glossary of the Gothic Language*, 8 parts, New York, 1887–90; J. Wright, *A Primer of the Gothic Language*, London, 1899; on the Gothic alphabet, W. Luft, *Studien zu den ältesten germanischen Alphabeten*, Gütersloh, 1898.

The *Codex Argenteus* was first published by Franciscus Junius (du Jon), Dort, 1665; with the other fragments, glossary, etc., by H. C. de Gabelentz and J. Loebe, Leipsic, 1836 and 1846; in facsimile by A. Uppström, Upsala, 1854, supplemented in 1857 by ten leaves which had been stolen but afterward recovered. The edition most used in Germany is by F. L. Stamm, Paderborn, 1858, 9th ed., with dictionary by M. Heyne and grammar by F. Wrede, 1896. Another ed. with apparatus is by E. Bernhardt, Halle, 1875 (text ed., 1884). There is an American edition by G. H. Balg, *The First Germanic Bible*, Milwaukee, 1891. Partial eds. are J. Bosworth, *The Gothic and Anglo-Saxon Gospels . . . with . . . Wycliffe and Tyndale*, London, 1865, new ed., 1907, and W. W. Skeat, *Mark*, London, 1882.

B. Modern Versions.

I. Arabic Versions: "There are more Arabic versions of the Gospels than can be welcome to theology, with its press of work," wrote Lagarde in the preface of his edition of the four Gospels in Arabic (Leipsic, 1864). There are translations made from Hebrew, Samaritan, Coptic, Latin, Syriac, and Greek. There was not, as it seems, a translation into Arabic before Mohammed (cf. M. J. de Goeje and M. Schreiner, in *Semitic Studies in Memory of Alexander Kohut*, Berlin, 1897, p. 495). John of Seville is said to have produced an Arabic Bible about 737; the chronicle of Michael Syrus mentions an Arabic translation of the Gospels made under direction of John, patriarch of Antioch, at the command of the emir Amru. The "Indians" mentioned by Chrysostom between Egyptians and Persians as in possession of the Scriptures in their mother tongue may be South-Arabians, but there is no additional information about this version.

Of translations from the Hebrew Old Testament, by far the most important is the work of Saadia ben Joseph, the Gaon, from the Fayyum (d. 942; see SAADIA). On Saadia and his translation, cf. H. Ewald and L. Dukes, *Beiträge zur Geschichte der ältesten Auslegung und Spracherklärung des alten Testaments*, ii (Stuttgart, 1844); S. Munk, in *La Bible, traduction nouvelle . . . par S. Cahen*, ix (Paris, 1838), 73–159; M. Steinschneider, *Die arabische Literatur der Juden* (Frankfort, 1902), 56 sqq.; and especially the edition of his collected works by J. H. Derenbourg, vol. i, the Pentateuch (Paris, 1893); iii, Isaiah (1896); iv, Proverbs (1890); v, Job (ed. Bacher, 1899). On the question of the text, cf. P. Kahle, *Die arabischen Bibelübersetzungen . . .* (Leipsic, 1904), no. viii, and against him Bacher, in *TLZ*, 1905, no. 8. Saadia's translation of the Pentateuch was printed first in Hebrew letters with the Hebrew text, Targum and a Persian translation at Constantinople, 1546, then in the Paris and London Polyglots (see BIBLES, POLYGLOT, III, IV). For Genesis and Exodus, cf. Lagarde, in his *Materialien zur Kritik* (Leipsic, 1867). Kahle used for his specimen a manuscript of Florence and Wolfenbüttel, not used by Derenbourg. On Isaiah, cf. Derenbourg, in *ZATW*, 1890, pp. 1–84. Of Job there is an edition by J. Cohn (Berlin, 1889). On the Psalms, cf. the dissertations of Haneberg, in *AMA*, 1841, iii, 2; J. Cohn, in *Magazin für die Wissenschaft des Judentums*, 1881. On Canticles, cf. A. Merx, *Die Saadjanische Uebersetzung des Hohen Liedes ins Arabische* (Heidelberg, 1882). On Proverbs, cf. a dissertation of Jonas

Bondi (Halle, 1888). On Saadia's system of translating, cf. W. Engelkemper, *De Saadiæ Gaonis vita, bibliorum versione, hermeneutica* (Münster, 1897).

There are other Arabic translations made from the Hebrew by Jews such as the *Arabs Erpenii*, a translation of the Pentateuch made by an African Jew in the thirteenth century (published by Erpenius, Leyden, 1622), and a translation of the Psalms made by the Karaite Japhet ben Eli (ed. J. J. L. Bargès, Paris, 1871); a specimen of his commentary on Genesis is in Kahle, viii; his commentary on Deuteronomy was edited by S. Margoliouth, in *Anecdota Oxoniensia*, Semitic series, vol. i, part 3, 1899. Hosea and Joel from an Oxford manuscript were edited by Schröter, in *Archiv für wissenschaftliche Erforschung des Alten Testaments*, i and ii (1869–70). A *Fragment einer arabischen Pentateuchübersetzung* was published by J. Hirsch, Leipsic, 1900.

The first specimen of an Arabic translation of the Samaritan text was published by A. C. Hwiid (Rome, 1780) from the famous triglot in the Barberini library; then by Paulus, 1789 and 1791; better by de Sacy, in *Mémoires de l'Académie des Inscriptions*, xlix, 1–199; S. Kohn, in *Abhandlungen für die Kunde des Morgenlandes*, vol. v, part 4 (Leipsic, 1876), 1–499; J. Bloch, *Die samaritanisch-arabische Pentateuchübersetzung* (Berlin, 1901); and Kahle, ut sup., no. vi. The Samaritans seem to have used at first the translation of Saadia; soon after 1000 they made a translation of their own, which was revised in the middle of the thirteenth century by Abu Said; Genesis, Exodus, and Leviticus of this version were edited by Kuenen, 1851–54 (cf. A. Cowley, in *JE*, x, 677).

Many Coptic manuscripts have an Arabic translation by the side of the Coptic text; in other manuscripts containing only an Arabic version, this is derived from the Coptic (cf. *Arab. 3* in the Greek Pentateuch of Holmes-Parsons; see above, I, 1, § 2); for Job such a translation has been edited by Lagarde, *Psalterium, Job, Proverbia arabice* (Göttingen, 1876); on Psalms, cf. *Psalterium Coptice*, ed. M. G. Schwartze (Leipsic, 1843), v.

From the Latin, either made from it or corrected by it, are the Roman editions such as that of Sergius Risi (Arabic and Latin, 3 vols., Rome, 1671), the Gospels (1591), and Psalms and Prophets (1614). A new recension by Rafael Tuki contains only Genesis–Nehemiah and Tobit (2 vols., 1752). The edition of 1671 without the Apocrypha has been frequently reprinted by the BFBS since 1822 after it had reprinted the Arabic portion of the London Polyglot under the supervision of J. D. Carlyle (Newcastle, 1811). In 1858 the Gospels, in 1860 the New Testament, in 1865 the Old Testament appeared in the new translation begun by the American missionary Eli Smith (q.v.) and finished by C. V. A. Van Dyck at Beirut, with the help of native scholars. It has been frequently reprinted in Beirut, Oxford, London, and New York. In competition with this translation are two from Roman Catholics, the one undertaken by the Dominicans of Mosul under the direction of Joseph David (4 vols., 1875–78), the other by the Jesuits in Beirut (3 vols., 1876–82; reproduced by photolithography in 1 vol., 1897; cf. on these editions Kahle, iii sqq.; A. G. Ellis, *Catalogue of Arabic Books in the British Museum*, London, 1894 sqq.; the Bible Catalogue of the same library; and Darlow-Moule, *Historical Catalogue of the Collection of the BFBS*, ii, London, 1908). Independent translations of the New Testament are those of Salomo Negri (London, 1727) and of Nathanael Sabat (Calcutta, 1816). There is also an edition of the Psalms by Negri (London, 1725; cf. G. A. Freylinghausen, *Memoria Negriana*, Halle, 1764).

From the Syriac Bible is the text of Judges, Ruth, Samuel, I Kings i–xi, II Kings ii, 17 to the end, Chronicles, Neh. ix, 28 to end, and Job in the Paris and London Polyglots. The first four books are, according to Rödiger, by the same author, the rest by different authors. Psalms, Proverbs, and Job have been reissued by Lagarde (*Psalterium*, etc., ut sup.) and the whole with few alterations by the BFBS (1811, ut sup.). A Psalter in Syriac and Arabic in Syriac letters (the so-called Karshunic script; i.e., Gersom's manner of writing) was printed by Maronite monks of Mount Lebanon at Kozchaya, 1610 (perhaps as early as 1585), and reprinted in Arabic type by Lagarde. Leviticus, Numbers, and Deuteronomy in the *Materialien* of Lagarde seem to have been derived from the Syriac Bible. A translation of the Syriac Hexapla of the Pentateuch and Wisdom is the work of Hareth ben Senan ben Sabat (cf. Nestle, in *ZDMG*, 1878, p. 468; Holmes-Parsons, *Præfatio ad Pentateuchum*, and Kahle, ut sup., ix). The fragments of Job were edited by Baudissin, 1870.

From the Greek are translated the prophets and the poetical books (except Job) in the Polyglots, perhaps also the Psalms as edited by Athanasius, patriarch of Antioch (Aleppo, 1706), reprinted by Lagarde with a translation of the tenth century by Abu al-Fath Abdallah ben Fadhl.

Gregory (*Textkritik*, Leipsic, 1902) mentions 137 Arabic manuscripts for the New Testament. On no. 136, cf. Steni), *Die altarabische Uebersetzung der Briefe an die Hebräer, an die Römer und an die Korinther* (Helsingfors, 1901). For the manuscripts on Mount Sinai, cf. the catalogue of Mrs. M. D. Gibson, in *Studia Sinaitica*, iii (Cambridge, 1894), and her publication of a part of an Arabic translation of the Epistles of St. Paul in no. ii (1893) of the same collection; also in no. vii (1899), an Arabic translation of Acts and of the seven Catholic Epistles from an eighth or ninth century manuscript. On the revision of the Arabic made about 250 at Alexandria by Hibath Allah ibn al-Assaly with various readings from the Greek, the Syriac, and the Coptic, cf. D. B. Macdonald, in the *Hartford Seminary Record*, Apr., 1893. Finally, the Arabic version of Tatian's *Diatessaron* (ed. Ciasca, Rome, 1888) must not be forgotten.

E. Nestle.

Bibliography: On the MSS. the one indispensable book is I. Guidi, *Le traduzioni degli evangelii in arabo . . .*, Rome, 1888; and valuable is also C. R. Gregory, *Prolegomena*, iii, 928–947, Leipsic, 1894. On the version and editions consult: Walton's *Polyglot, Prolegomena*, chap. 14, London, 1652; C. F. Schnurrer, *Bibliotheca arabica, de Pentateucho arabico . . .*, Tübingen, 1780; H. E. G. Paulus, *Commentatio critica*, Jena, 1789; R. Holmes, *Vetus Testamentum Græce*, the Preface to the Pentateuch, Oxford, 1798; J. Roediger, *Commentatio . de interpretatione Arabica* , Halle, 1824; idem, *De origine . Arabicæ interpretationis*, ib. 1829; J. Gildemeister, *De evangeliis in Arabicum . translatis*, Bonn, 1865; Gregory, *Textkritik;* Scrivener, *Introduction*, ii, 161–164; F. C. Burkitt, in *DB*, i, 136–138 (a lucid presentation).

II. Celtic Versions: No version of the Bible or of single Biblical books in any of the Celtic dialects has come down from the pre-Reformation period, though a few Biblical extracts in Old Irish (8th–11th centuries) are extant in homilies. After the establishment of the English Church in 1560 as the State Church, Bishop Nicholas Walsh of Ossory and others made an effort toward giving the Bible to the Irish people, and the New Testament, translated by William O'Donnell, archbishop of Tuam, was published at Dublin in 1603 in Irish characters. This edition was republished at London in 1681, and in 1685 the Old Testament, translated by Bishop William Bedell of Kilmore and others, was issued. This edition was often reprinted, especially in a revised form by the British and Foreign Bible Society in 1827. A translation of the New Testament into the modern dialect of Munster by Dr. R. O'Kane appeared at Dublin, 1858. Of the Roman Catholic translation prepared by Archbishop John MacHale of Tuam from the Vulgate, the first volume only (Genesis–Joshua) has appeared (Tuam, 1861). Gaelic, which is spoken in the Highlands and western isles of Scotland, is related to Irish; consequently the Scottish minister Robert Kirke, in order to satisfy the needs of the Protestant Highlanders, had O'Donnell's Irish translation of the New Testament printed in Roman letters and supplied with an Irish-Gaelic glossary (London, 1690). To provide the Gaelic-speaking Highlanders with a Bible of their own, the Society for the Promotion of Christian Knowledge published in 1767 the New Testament translated by James Stuart of

Killin, and in 1783–1801 a translation of the Old Testament prepared by John Stuart, Jr., and John Smith. At the instance of the same society, Dr. Mark Hildesley, bishop of Man, distributed different parts of the Bible among the Manx-speaking clergy of the Isle of Man, with the view of having a translation prepared into this tongue. The whole was revised by P. Moore and his pupil John Kelly. In 1770–72 the Bible in Manx was printed for the above society at Whitehaven under the supervision of J. Kelly, and is the basis of all later editions.

Before the Reformation hardly any parts of the Bible were translated into Cymric. In 1562 the House of Commons resolved to have the Bible and the Book of Common Prayer translated into Cymric within four years, and made the bishops of Bangor, St. Asaph, Hereford, Llandaff, and St. Davids responsible for its execution. The New Testament was published in London in 1567, and in 1588 the whole Bible (revised by Bishop Richard Parry, 1620). All later issues follow Parry's revised text. The Bible has never been translated into Cornish. A manuscript belonging to the first half of the eighteenth century contains a translation of Gen. i, iii; Matt. iv, vi, 9–13, vii; and the ten commandments. Before the beginning of the nineteenth century only short passages of the Bible had appeared in the Breton. The British and Foreign Bible Society published at Angoulême in 1827 the New Testament translated by the Breton scholar Le Gonidec into the dialect of Léon. The translation was made from the Vulgate, and was for other reasons unsuitable. A new translation by the Baptist missionary John Jenkins was printed at Brest in 1847. Le Gonidec's translation of the Old Testament was revised by Troude and Milin, and published at Saint-Brieuc in 1866. In 1883 the Trinitarian Bible Society published a New Testament in the dialect of Tréguier, prepared by the Breton Protestant G. Ar C'hoat, and in 1889 the whole Bible. A Roman Catholic translation of the New Testament was published in Guingamp in 1853, and an edition of the Psalms at Paris in 1873. For linguistic purposes C. Terrien translated the Gospel of Matthew into the dialect of Vannes (Lundayn, 1857) at the instance of Lucien Bonaparte.

(H. Zimmer.)

Bibliography: J. Reid, *Bibliotheca Scoto-Celtica*, Glasgow, 1832; the *Scottish-Celtic Review*, Nov., 1881, pp. 150 sqq.; T. Llewelyn, *An Historical Account of the British or Welsh Versions and Editions of the Bible*, London, 1768; W. Rowland, *Llyfryddiaeth of Cymry*, pp. 10–21, 41–50, 93–97, Llandloes, 1869; *Revue Celtique*, vi, 382, xi, 180–190, 308; *Bible of Every Land*, pp. 151–173, London, 1861; I. Ballinger, *The Bible in Wales*, London, 1906.

III. Dutch Versions: The first printed Dutch version (Delft, 1477), was made, apparently by a layman, probably about 1300 from the Latin. Some parts, which the translator was unwilling to popularize, as Deut. xxii, 13–21, are passed over with a reference to the Latin text. Difficult passages have explanations mostly from the *Historia scholastica* of Peter Comestor. The printed edition omits Psalms and the New Testament, though both are contained in a good manuscript of this version at Vienna. A very good translation of the Psalms is found in several incunabula. About 1,300 translations of the New Testament, or at least of the church lessons or of the life of Christ, began to be made. A translation of the New Testament of Erasmus appeared at Delft in 1524, and two years before at Antwerp a translation of Luther's version was printed by Hans van Roemundt (repeated at Basel, 1525 and 1526, also, a little altered, at Amsterdam, 1526). The Old Testament with the Pentateuch and Psalms translated from Luther, the rest the text of the Delft edition revised, was printed, also by Roemundt, in 1525 in four small vols.; and the first complete Dutch Bible was printed at Antwerp in 1526 by Jacob van Liesvelt. It was reprinted and corrected several times until 1546, when Charles V prohibited the edition.

Roman Catholic editions of the New Testament followed in 1527, 1530, and 1533, in Dutch and Latin in 1539. The whole Bible did not appear until after the meeting of the Council of Trent, at Cologne in 1548 by Alexander Blanckart, and at Louvain in the same year by Nicolaus van Winghe with a sharp preface against the Protestant editions. In 1599 it was revised after the official Vulgate of 1592, again in 1717 by Ægidius Wit of Ghent. After 1820 the Roman Catholics were allowed to use editions without notes, and such an edition of 1599, called the Mörentorf Bible (from its publisher), was circulated by the British and Foreign Bible Society.

The division of Dutch Protestantism into various parties, Lutherans, Mennonites, and Reformed, caused the production of various versions. The Lutherans received a version in 1558 after Bugenhagen's edition in Low German; it has been several times revised and reprinted up to 1851. The Mennonites used a version printed by Nicolaes Biestkens at Emden in 1560, the first Dutch edition with verse divisions. The Reformed received another in 1556, based on the Zurich Bible of 1548–49 (see below, VII, § 5); but in 1562 they adopted a version based on Luther's, called the Deux Aes or Eulenspiegel Bible (from the marginal notes at Neh. ii, 5 and Ecclus. xix, 5). The Remonstrants used at first the *Staatenbibel* (see below) but received a New Testament of their own from Hartsoeker in 1680.

After the beginning of the seventeenth century the necessity of improving the Dutch versions was felt and was shown especially by W Baudartius of Zutphen, who published in 1614 an emended translation. As early as 1594 the States General determined on undertaking a revision. The result is the *Staatenbibel*. At first Philips van Marnix (q.v.) was entrusted with the task of a new translation; in 1596 Johannes Drusius (q.v.) was appointed his assistant. The Synod of Dort discussed the question in eight sessions in Nov., 1618, and May, 1619. The work of translation was completed in 1632, the revision of the Old Testament Sept., 1634, that of the New Testament, Oct. 10, 1635. The first edition was printed, with and without notes, in 1636, but not published before July 29, 1637. An official list of misprints followed in 1655 and in 1711 for the first time an edition was stereotyped. An edition of 500 copies of the New Testament was printed for Peter the Great in 1717.

and of the Old Testament in five parts in 1721, in two columns, one being left blank in order to receive in St. Petersburg the Russian text. Language and orthography raised difficult questions in a revision of 1762, and another by Henry Cats and W. A. van Hengel in 1834. The first impression for the British and Foreign Bible Society was made in 1812.

About the middle of the last century members of the theological faculty of Leyden began a new revision; the New Testament was finished in 1866; work on the Old Testament was interrupted for a time, but was resumed in 1884 by A. Kuenen and his pupils, H. Oort, W H. Kosters, and J. Hooykas. The first instalment appeared at Leyden in 1897, the first part (Gen.-Esther) in 1900, the second part (Job-Malachi) in 1901.

Of other translations that by J. H. van der Palm (1825 and often) is worthy of mention. The New Testament has been translated by G. Vissering, a Mennonite (1854). by S. P Lipman, a Roman Catholic (1861), and by G. J. Vos of the Reformed Church (1895). E. NESTLE.

BIBLIOGRAPHY: The really important work is Isaac Le Long, *Boek-Zaal der nederduitsche Bybels*, Amsterdam, 1732, 2d ed., 1764. Consult also *Bible of Every Land*, pp. 181-186, London, 1861; H. van Druten, *Geschiedenis der Nederlandsche Bijbelvertaling*, 2 vols., Leyden, 1896-97; G. N. De Vooys, *ThT*, March, 1903; J. M. Bebb, in *DB*, extra vol., pp. 414-415.

On the *Staatenbibel* consult N. Hinlopen, *Historie van de Nederlandsche Overzettinge des Bybels*, Leyden, 1777; P. Meyjes, *Jacobus Revius*, Amsterdam, 1895; J. Heinsius, *Klank-en Buigingsleer van de taal des statenbijbels*, Amsterdam, 1897.

IV. English Versions: Setting aside the Biblical poetry that is in the main wrongly ascribed to the Anglo-Saxon Cædmon (q.v.), and the translation of John's Gospel which Bede finished on his death-bed, but of which nothing further is known, the Psalms seem to have been the first part of the Bible to be translated into English.

1. The Earliest Versions. An Anglo-Saxon paraphrase is extant containing the first fifty Psalms in prose, the rest in verse (ed. B. Thorpe, Oxford, 1835), which has been incorrectly attributed to Aldhelm (q.v.), bishop of Sherborne, who died in 709, and to King Alfred; the name of the translator is not known, but he did his work after 778 and used the Latin, not the Greek text, as did all the others down to and including Wyclif. A translation of the four Gospels was made probably in the ninth century (ed. Matthew Parker, 1571; T. Marshall, 1665; B. Thorpe, *Tha halgan Godspel on Englisc. The Anglo-Saxon Version of the Holy Gospels*, London, 1842; Joseph Bosworth and George Waring, *The Gothic and Anglo-Saxon Gospels*, London, 1865; new ed., 1907), and interlinear glosses for the Psalms and the Gospels in the ninth and tenth centuries (*Psalterium Davidis Latino-Saxonicum vetus*, London, 1640). The so-called Vespasian Gospels probably belong to the first half of the ninth century (cf. J. Stevenson, *Anglo-Saxon and Early English Psalter*, 2 vols., London, 1843-47; H. Sweet, *The Oldest English Texts, Early English Text Society*, vol. 83, London, 1885, pp. 183-420; E. Wende, *Ueberlieferung und Sprache der mittelenglischen Version des Psalters und ihr Verhältnis zur lateinischen Vorlage*, Breslau, 1884). There are other similar glosses to the Psalter in the libraries of Cambridge University and Trinity College, Cambridge, in the British Museum, in the Bodleian at Oxford, in Lambeth Palace, and Salisbury Cathedral. For other Gospel versions, cf. G. Stevenson and G. Waring, *The Lindisfarne and Rushworth Gospels* (4 vols., Durham and London, 1854-65); K. W Bouterwek, *Die vier Evangelien in altnorthumbrischer Sprache* (Gütersloh, 1857); W W Skeat, *The Gospel according to Matthew*, etc. (Cambridge, 1887,—*Mark*, 1871; *Luke*, 1871; *John*, 1878); A. S. Cook, *A Glossary of the Old Northumbrian Gospels* (Halle, 1894). Alfric (q.v.) translated the Pentateuch and Joshua in 997-998. The following may also be mentioned: homilies on the lessons by the Augustinian monk Ormin in the twelfth or thirteenth century (the so-called Ormulum): the translation of the Psalms by William de Shorham, vicar of Chart-Sutton, near Leeds in County Kent, about 1325 (the manuscript in Trinity College, Dublin, owned by John Hyde and perhaps written by him, may be a revision of this translation); and the commentary with a translation of the Psalms by Richard Rolle of Hampole near Doncaster, Yorkshire, written about 1330 (cf. H. R. Bramley, *The Psalter by Richard Rolle Edited from Manuscripts*, Oxford, 1884; Heinrich Middendorff, *Studien über Richard Rolle von Hampole*, Magdeburg, 1888).

The language developed and the thoughts of men strode onward. John Wyclif (q.v.) entered the lists to war for the pure truth, and he determined to give the people the Bible. With the help of his pupil Nicholas of Hereford (q.v.) he seems to have translated the whole Bible, and when he was

2. Wyclif. charged with heresy and driven from Oxford in 1382, he withdrew to Lutterworth and revised the whole very carefully. His pupil John Purvey (q.v.) appears also to have revised some things in the Old Testament; he did all he could to spread the translation abroad after Wyclif's death (cf. *The New Testament in English, Translated by John Wycliffe circa 1380, now first printed from a contemporary manuscript. Printed at Chiswick by Charles Whittingham for William Pickering*, London, 1848; Josiah Forshall and Frederic Madden, *The Holy Bible in the Earliest English Versions Made by John Wycliffe and his Followers*, 4 vols., Oxford, 1850, with a list of 170 manuscripts; J. ten Brink, *Geschichte der englischen Litteratur*, vol. ii, by Alois Brandl, Strasburg, 1893, pp. 5-32, especially pp. 27; A. Richter, *Das Wycliffesche Evangelium Johannis im 500. Bde. der Tauchnitzer Collection of British Authors, die Wycliffesche Bibelübersetzung, und das Verhältnis des ersteren zu der letzteren*, programme of the gymnasium at Wesel, Aug. 30, 1862). The first English Bible, the first Bible at all in a modern tongue, was well received by the people, but for a century and a half was the object of attack by priests and nobility. Even long after the discovery of printing no one could think of publishing this translation. It finally came out as a literary necessity in 1731, edited by J. Lewis (reprinted by H. H. Baber, London, 1810, and by Bagster, London, 1841; the edition of 1848 is named above). For another version of this period consult the work of a Swedish lady, Anna C. Paues, *A Fourteenth Century English Biblical Version* (Cambridge, 1904).

The first to translate the New Testament in English from the original Greek was William Tyndale (q.v.). He printed Matthew and Mark first, somewhere on the Continent, in 1524 and 1525, and then the whole New Testament in quarto, partly at Cologne at Peter Quentel's before 1526, partly, it seems, at Worms (at Peter Schöffer's?) in 3,000 copies, and in octavo at Cologne at Schöffer's in 3,000 copies. Both editions were in England by about March, 1526 (cf. *The First Printed English New Testament Translated by William Tyndale. Photolithographed. Edited by E. Arber*, London, 1871; *The First New Testament Printed in the English Language by William Tyndale. Reproduced in facsimile by F. Fry*, Bristol, 1862; James Loring Chenev, *The Sources of Tyndale's New Testament*, Halle, 1883, especially pp. 39, 40; W Sopp, *Orthographie und Aussprache der ersten neuenglischen Bibelübersetzung von William Tyndale*, Marburg, 1889). The hierarchy attacked Tyndale's work violently. The first public burning of the volume appears to have taken place in the autumn of 1526. William Warham (q.v.), archbishop of Canterbury, thought in May, 1527, that his agents had bought up all the copies of all three editions. In 1528 the readers of the New Testament had to take their turn at being burned. Tyndale published the Pentateuch Jan. 17, 1530 (see TYNDALE, WILLIAM), Joshua in 1531.

3. Tyndale.

William Roye, George Joye (afterward a bitter enemy), Miles Coverdale (q.v.), John Rogers (q.v.), and John Frith (q.v.) were among the friends who from time to time worked with Tyndale. Coverdale completed at Antwerp, Oct. 4, 1535, the printing of his translation of the whole Bible "out of Douche and Latyn" (i.e. the German of Luther and the Zurich Bible of 1524-29—see below, VII, § 5—and the Vulgate), using also Tyndale's work. This was the first complete Bible in English; in it the non-canonical books of the Old Testament are in an appendix by themselves, named "Hagiographa." In 1537 the "Matthew" Bible came out, a speculation on the part of the king's printer, although most of it was perhaps printed in Antwerp; it was a combination of Tyndale and Coverdale, made by John Rogers (alias Matthew) in Antwerp. In 1539 appeared the "Taverner" Bible, a revision of the Matthew Bible by Richard Taverner (q.v.). The "Great" Bible was brought out by Cromwell, Earl of Essex, Thomas Cranmer (q.v.), and Thomas More (q.v.), and a committee of prelates and scholars, and was printed under Coverdale's supervision, partly at Paris, till the Inquisitor-General attacked it Dec. 17, 1538, and then in London, where the volume was finished in Apr., 1539; the second edition ("Cranmer's" Bible, 1540) was "apoynted to the vse of the churches"; the Psalter from this Bible still stands in the prayer-book of the English Church. In 1557 William Whittingham published at Geneva an English New Testament with Stephens's verse-division of 1551 (see BIBLE TEXT, III, §§ 2-3) and with many corrections of the translation. In 1558 Coverdale began in Geneva a new Bible, but returned to England in 1559, while Whittingham, Anthony Gilby, and Thomas Sampson finished the printing of the handsome edition known as the "Geneva" Bible in Apr., 1560. Archbishop Parker (q.v.) with eleven bishops and four minor prelates began in 1563 a revision of the edition of 1539, which was completed Oct. 5, 1568, as the "Bishops'" Bible; but it was not especially liked; in the churches they used chiefly the Bible of 1539 and at home the Geneva Bible. See BIBLES, ANNOTATED, AND BIBLE SUMMARIES, II, §§ 1-2.

4. Coverdale. Other Editions.

The Roman Catholic fugitives on the Continent now prepared an English version and published the New Testament at Reims in 1582; the Old Testament followed in two volumes at Douai (q.v.) in 1609-10 (the first edition of the "Douai" Bible; cf. Gregory Martin, *A Discoverie of the Manifold Corruptions of the Holie Scriptures by the Heretikes of our Daies*, etc., Reims, 1582; William Fulke, *A Defence of the Sincere and True Translations of the Holie Scriptures against Gregorie Martin*, London, 1583, ed. C. H. Hartshorne for the Parker Society, Cambridge, 1843). [Both works profess to be "faithfully translated out of the authentical Latin, diligently conferred with the Hebrew, Greek, and other editions in divers languages," and are provided with arguments of books and chapters, annotations, and "other helps for the better understanding of the text, and specially for the discovery of the corruptions of divers late translations, and for clearing the controversies in religion of these days." The New Testament was reprinted at Antwerp in 1600; the two Testaments were united by Richard Challoner (q.v.) in a five volume edition published in London, 1749-50. The version was promoted by Cardinal William Allen (q.v.) and the translation was by Gregory Martin, a former fellow of St. John's College, Oxford, revised by Allen, Richard Bristow, fellow of Exeter College, Oxford, and probably others. The annotations, tables, etc., for the Old Testament were by Thomas Worthington, a graduate of Oxford (Brasenose College) and president of Douai College 1599-1613. The long interval between the publication of the two Testaments was due to lack of means as the translation of both was completed before 1582. The English of the translation is faulty owing to too close following of the Vulgate, and from the critical standpoint it possesses the advantages and defects inherent in that Latin version. An elaborate preface of more than twenty pages explains and justifies the translation. The notes are characterized by the controversial spirit of the time in which they were produced. The Douai version became the standard Bible of the English Roman Catholics and, with extensive changes in language and

5. The Douai Bible.

orthography introduced in Challoner's various editions (see CHALLONER, RICHARD), still remains such. American editions were published in New York in 1854 and 1861. Consult Henry Cotton, *Rhemes and Doway* (Oxford, 1855); F. E. C. Gigot (Roman Catholic), *General Introduction to the Study of the Scriptures* (New York, 1900), pp. 345 sqq.]

6. The Authorized Version.

Puritan dissatisfaction with existing versions, or perhaps with the existence of another version than the one used and approved by themselves, was urged by John Reynolds (q.v.), head of Corpus Christi College, Oxford, at the Hampton Court Conference (q.v.) in Jan., 1604. The idea of a new Bible translation, to be made ostensibly at his instance and under his direction, was congenial to James I. By the summer of 1604 the preliminaries were completed. A commission of six "companies," each of nine scholars (two companies each in Westminster, Oxford, and Cambridge; actually forty-seven members took part; for names of the translators, the division of the work, and much other information about the Authorized Version in convenient form, cf. Mombert's *Hand Book*, chap. xiii; Schaff's *Companion*, chap. vii), was appointed by James and very strict rules were laid down for the work. After years of labor (although some say that the work really began only in 1607 and lasted but two years and a half), during which some passages were wrought over fourteen or even seventeen times, the version appeared in 1611 in two folio editions, set up and printed at the same time so as to have a large number of copies very quickly; in the same year a duodecimo edition came out, of which only one copy (in the Lenox Library, New York City) is said to be known, and in 1613 what is called the second folio edition. The translation was then called "The Authorized Version" (although it does not appear ever to have been "authorized") or "King James's Version," and the title read "Appointed to be read in Churches." The translation was good, clear, dignified, idiomatic, and suited to the people. Of course, like everything new, it was at first and for a long time sharply attacked, but little by little it made its way, and in 1661 the Epistles and Gospels in the English prayer-book were changed to this translation. F. H. A. Scrivener published a critical edition of this version: *The Cambridge Paragraph Bible of the Authorized English Version*, etc. (Cambridge, 1873), in which he compared many of the reprints, as well as the revisions of Dr. Paris in 1762, Dr. Blayney in 1769, and of the American Bible Society in 1867; unfortunately Scrivener does not give the exact text of 1611 or of 1613.

7. The Revised Version.

On Feb. 10, 1870, on motion of Samuel Wilberforce (q.v.), bishop of Winchester, the Convocation of Canterbury determined upon a revision of the Authorized Version (cf. Mombert, *Hand Book*, chap. xiv; Schaff, *Companion*, chap. viii). About thirty-seven scholars were asked to take up the Old Testament, and about twenty-nine the New Testament, although the number really working at any time was less. At least five religious bodies besides the Church of England shared in the work. In like manner two groups of scholars from nine different religious bodies took up the work in America and the results of the deliberations were exchanged across the sea. The Greek text of the New Testament (cf. *The Greek Testament with the Readings Adopted by the Revisers of the Authorized Version*, Oxford, 1881) was thoroughly worked over and the translation made on the basis of the result compared with the translation of 1611, and in every detail filed and polished. The revised New Testament was published in England May 17, 1881, and in America, May 20, 1881; the Old Testament appeared May 19, 1885. Three million copies of the New Testament were sold within a year. The reception, especially in England, was at first, as was to be expected, not very friendly. A very few indeed were dissatisfied because too few alterations had been made. The great mass struggled against the change of old familiar words and found support in one scholar or another. Some conservative scholars condemned the English dress while they approved the changes made in the original text, and others took offense at the new readings in the original text, because they considered the common readings sacred. America had a peculiar reason for complaint, seeing that many an expression which American scholars had preferred was to be found only in the appendix, and they were bound not to issue a new edition within fourteen years. That time was up in 1896, and the American edition, a model of exact work, appeared in New York in 1901. As the years pass the revision gains friends, and gains them more rapidly than did the revision of 1611.

CASPAR RENÉ GREGORY.

8. Minor Versions.

The following is a list (incomplete) of translations of the Bible or parts of it into English or attempts at revision of the Authorized Version by individuals previous to the revision of 1881-85 (see also BIBLES, ANNOTATED, AND BIBLE SUMMARIES, II). Daniel Mace, a Presbyterian clergyman, N. T. (2 vols., London, 1729; Gk. text with a scholarly but eccentric transl.); Anthony Purver, a Quaker, *A New and Literal Transl. of All the Books of the O. and N. T.* (2 vols., London, 1764; has notes); Edward Harwood, *A Liberal Transl. of the N. T.* (2 vols., London, 1768; described as an attempt to translate the sacred writings with the '"freedom, spirit, and elegance" of other translations from the Greek; has notes and includes the First Epistle of Clement); Henry Southwell, entire Bible (London, 1782; the A. V. with notes, "wherein the mistranslations are corrected"); George Campbell, professor in Aberdeen, *The Four Gospels* (2 vols., London, 1789; has dissertations and notes); Gilbert Wakefield, a Unitarian, N. T. (3 vols., London, 1791); James Macknight, *All the Apostolical Epistles* (4 vols., Edinburgh, 1795; has commentary, notes, and life of Paul); William Newcome, archbishop of Armagh, N. T. (2 vols., Dublin, 1796; from Griesbach's text; a Unitarian version based on Newcome's work was issued by Thomas Belsham in 2 vols., London, 1808; Newcome also published "attempts" at improved versions of the Minor Prophets, 1785, and Ezekiel, 1788; his manuscript materials for a revised O. T. are in Lambeth Palace); Nathaniel Scarlett, successively a Methodist, Universalist, and Baptist, N. T. (London, 1798; with notes); David Macrae, *A Revised Transl. and Interpretation of the Sacred Scriptures, after the Eastern manner, from concurrent authorities of the critics, interpreters, and commentators' copies and versions, showing that the inspired writings contain the seeds of the valuable sciences*, etc. (2 parts, London, 1798-99); Charles Thomson, entire Bible, the O. T. from the Septuagint (4 vols., Philadelphia, 1808); John Bellamy, O. T. through

Song of Sol. (London, 1818 sqq.; has notes); Alexander Campbell, founder of the Disciples of Christ, N. T. (1826; see CAMPBELL, ALEXANDER); Rodolphus Dickinson, an American Episcopalian, N. T. (Boston, 1833; has notes); Noah Webster, the lexicographer, the Bible "with amendments of the language" (New Haven, 1833; the amendments were the removal of obsolete words or "those deemed below the dignity and solemnity of the subject, the correction of errors in grammar, and the insertion of euphemisms, words, and phrases which are not very offensive to delicacy"); Nathan Hale, N. T. (Boston, 1836; from Griesbach's text); Granville Penn, N. T. (London, 1836); C. Wellbeloved, a Unitarian, Pentateuch and Job-Song of Sol. (2 vols., London, 1838; "a new transl." with notes); Samuel Sharpe, the Egyptologist, N. T. (London, 1840; from Griesbach's text) and O. T. (3 vols., 1865; there were eight eds. of the former and four of the latter during the author's life; Sharpe's revision is commended for skilful removal of the archaisms of the A. V.); Edgar Taylor, N. T. (London, 1840; from Griesbach's text; a meritorious version); Joshua V. Himes, the "Millerite," N. T. (Boston, 1849); James Murdock, N. T. from the Peshito (New York, 1851); Andrews Norton, Gospels (2 vols., Boston, 1855); Gospel of John (London, 1857) and Pauline Epistles (1861) by Henry Alford, George Moberly, W. G. Humphry, C. J. Ellicott, and John Barrow; L. A. Ambrose, N. T. (Boston, 1858; with chronological arrangement and "improved" chapter and verse divisions); L. A. Sawyer, N. T. (Boston, 1858), entire Bible (New York, 1879 sqq.); Robert Young, author of the concordance, entire Bible (Edinburgh, 1863; very literal); T. S. Green, *The Twofold N. T.* (London, 1864; Gk. text and new transl. in parallel columns); Henry Alford, N. T. (London, 1869); G. R. Noyes, professor in Harvard, N. T. (Boston, 1869; from Tischendorf's text; Prof. Noyes also published translations of Job, 1827, Psalms, 1831, the Prophets, 1833, and Proverbs, Ecclesiastes, and Canticles, 1846); J. N. Darby, N. T. (2d ed., London, 1872); J. B. Rotherham, N. T. (London, 1872; from text of Tregelles, with introduction and notes); Samuel Davidson, N. T. (London, 1875; from Tischendorf's text, with introduction); J. B. McClellan, Gospels (London, 1875; based on A. V. with a "critically revised" text); Julia E. Smith, entire Bible (Hartford, 1876); *The Revised English Bible* (O. T. by F. W. Gotch and Benjamin Davies, N. T. by G. A. Jacob and S. G. Green, London, 1877; with notes, tables, and maps); *The Sunday School Centenary Bible*, by T. K. Cheyne, R. L. Clarke, S. R. Driver, A. Goodwin, and W. Sanday (London, 1880; republished, 1882, as *The Variorum Teacher's Bible*). The American Bible Union, formed in 1850 (see BIBLE SOCIETIES, III, 2), undertook an English version which should reflect Baptist views in the language used, and published the N. T. (2d revision, New York and London, 1869) and certain books of the O. T. Since 1882 the work has been continued by the American Baptist Publication Society of Philadelphia and is now nearing completion. Among the scholars who have collaborated in this version are John A. Broadus, T. J. Conant, H. B. Hackett, William R. Harper, Alvah Hovey, A. C. Kendrick, Ira M. Price, J. R. Sampey, and B. C. Taylor. A present day tendency is represented by *The Bible in Modern English*, translated direct from the original languages by Ferrar Fenton, with critical introduction and notes (St. Paul's epistles, London, 1894; N. T. complete, 1895; O. T., 1903).

The following are by Roman Catholics: John Caryll, a layman, secretary to the queen of James II and intimately associated with the family of James, the Psalms (St. Germains, 1700; a prose version from the Vulgate taking Bellarmine as a guide); Cornelius Nary, parish priest of St. Michan's, Dublin, *The N T . newly Translated out of the Latin Vulgate* (Dublin, 1718; has annotations and notes); Robert Witham, president at Douai, *Annotations on the N. T.* (2 vols., Douai, 1730; explains the "literal sense," "examines and disproves" false interpretations, and gives "an account of the chief differences betwixt the text of the ancient Latin version and the Greek"); "Troy's Bible" (Dublin, 1791; ed. the Rev. Bernard MacMahon, who had already edited three annotated editions of the Reims N. T.; this Bible is annotated and the text of the N. T. differs considerably from Challoner; the name comes from J. T. Troy, titular archbishop of Dublin, who approved the work); Alexander Geddes, Genesis-II Chronicles and the Prayer of Manasses (2 vols., London, 1792-1797) and Psalms i-cviii (1807; see GEDDES, ALEXANDER); the "Newcastle N. T." (1812; differs from every other known edition in the Gospels and Acts); John Lingard, *A New Version of the Four Gospels* (London, 1836; for the most part from the Greek; has notes); F. P. Kenrick, bishop of Philadelphia, later archbishop of Baltimore, N. T. (2 vols., New York, 1849-51; "a revision of the Rhemish translation with notes"); F. A. Spencer, O. P., N. T. (New York, 1898 sqq.; from the Greek). The work of Bishop Challoner has been referred to above (§ 5).

9. Rare and Curious Editions.

The following are certain rare and curious editions of the English Bible with the passage or fact which gives to each its name. *The Breeches Bible:* the Geneva Bible of 1560; Gen. iii, 7 reads "They sewed fig leaves together and made themselves breeches" (also in Wyclif); the *Bug Bible:* an edition of the Matthew Bible in 1551; Ps. xci, 5 reads "So that thou shalt not nede to be afraid for any bugges [i.e., bogies] by night" (also in Coverdale and Taverner); the *Caxton Memorial Bible:* Oxford, 1877; printed and bound in 100 copies in twelve hours; the *Discharge Bible:* London, 1802; I Tim. v, 21, "I discharge [for charge] thee before God"; the *Ears to Ear Bible:* Oxford, 1807; Matt. xiii, 43, "Who hath ears to ear" (also has "good works" for "dead works" in Heb. ix, 14); the *Goose Bible:* Dort editions of the Geneva Bible, because the Dort press had a goose as its emblem; the *He and She Bibles:* the first and the second folio editions of the version of 1611; in Ruth iii, 15, the former reads "He measured six measures of barley and laid it on her: and he went into the city"; the latter "and she went into the city"; both issues were used by printers as copy until in and after 1614 all have "she" (cf. the Revised Version, text and margin); the *Leda Bible:* the first Bishops' Bible (1568): it used a series of initial letters prepared for Ovid's *Metamorphoses* and that for the Epistle to the Hebrews represented Leda and the swan (also called the Treacle Bible, see below); the *Murderers' Bible:* has "murderers" for "murmurers" in Jude 16, also other misprints; the *Placemakers' Bible:* the second edition of the Geneva Bible (1562); has "placemakers" for "peacemakers" in Matt. v, 9; the *Rebekah Bible:* London, 1823; Gen. xxiv, 61, "And Rebekah arose and her camels" (for "damsels"); the *Rosin Bible:* the first Douai Bible (1609-10); Jer. viii, 22, "Is there no rosin in Gilead?" (A. V. "balm"); the *Standing Fishes Bible:* London, 1806; Ezek. xlvii, 10, "The fishes [for fishers] shall stand upon it"; (the error was repeated in editions of 1813 and 1823); the *Thumb Bible:* Aberdeen, 1670; it is about one inch square and half an inch thick; the *To Remain Bible:* Cambridge, 1805; Gal. iv, 29, "Persecuted him that was born after the Spirit to remain even so it is now" (the words "to remain" had been written on the proof in answer to a query whether or not a comma should be deleted; the error was retained in an edition printed for the Bible Society in 1805-06 and in an edition of 1819); the *Treacle Bible:* the first Bishops' Bible (1568; also called the Leda Bible, see above); Jer. viii, 22, "Is there no tryacle in Gilead" (cf. the Rosin Bible); the *Vinegar Bible:* Oxford, 1716-17; has "vinegar" for "vineyard" as the heading to Luke xx (it was printed by J. Baskett, and though the most sumptuous of the Oxford Bibles, soon came to be styled "a basketful of printer's errors"); the *Wicked Bible:* London, 1631; the negative was left out of the seventh commandment (it was printed by the king's printer and there were four editions in the same year; all were suppressed and the printer was fined £300); another Wicked Bible (London, 1653) makes Paul ask, I Cor. vi, 9, "Know ye not that the unrighteous shall inherit the kingdom of God?" the *Wife-Hater Bible:* Oxford, 1810; Luke xiv, 26, "If any man come to me and hate not his father yea, and his own wife [for life] also, he can not be my disciple." The list of misprints might be greatly extended. A Cambridge Bible of 1629, printed and proof-read with great care, introduced "thy doctrine" for "the doctrine" in I Tim. iv, 16, and the error reappeared for many years. An Edinburgh octavo of 1637 has, Jer. iv, 17, "because she hath been religious [rebellious] against me." Perhaps the finest Bible ever printed at Cambridge (1638) has a famous error in Acts vi, 3, which is said to have cost Cromwell £1,000 as a bribe —"whom ye [for we] may appoint." Cotton Mather relates that a Bible printed before 1702 made David complain in Ps. cxix, 161, "Printers [princes] have persecuted me without a cause." The "wicked" Bible of 1631 does not furnish the only instance of an infelicitous omission of a negative; an Edinburgh Bible of 1760 reads, Heb. ii, 16,

"He took on him the nature of angels" (correct reading "he took not"); another (Edinburgh, 1816) has, Luke vi, 29, "Forbid [not] to take thy coat also"; and a London Bible of 1817 reads, John xvii, 25, "O righteous Father, the world hath [not] known thee." On the other hand an Edinburgh edition of 1761 makes the Psalmist's prayer (cxix, 35) "Make me not to go in the path of thy commandments." The errors of an Oxford Bible of 1804 include, Num. xxxv, 18, "The murderer shall surely be put together" (for "to death"), I Kings viii, 19, "out of thy lions [loins]," and, Gal. v, 17, "For the flesh lusteth after [against] the Spirit." A Cambridge Bible of 1819 reads in Mal. iv, 2, "shall the son [sun] of righteousness arise . . . and shall [for ye shall] go forth." An Oxford Bible of 1820 has, Isa. lxvi, 9, "Shall I bring to the birth and not cease [cause] to bring forth?" A Cambridge Bible of 1826 has "heart" for "hart" in Ps. xlii, 1, and the error was repeated in an edition of 1830. A Bible printed at Utica, N. Y., in 1829 begins Jas. v, 17, "Elias was a man possible like unto us" ("subject to like passions as we are"). One of Jesper Harding's early editions, published at Philadelphia, has in I Kings i, 21, "The king shall dagger sleep with his fathers" (the copy read "The king shall † sleep with his fathers"). A Bible published at Hartford in 1837 makes II Tim. iii, 16, read, "All scripture is given by inspiration of God, and is profitable . . for destruction [instruction] in righteousness." An edition printed for the American Bible Society in 1855 has in Mark v, 3, "Who had his dwelling among the lambs [tombs]." The Great Bible in 1539 introduced the mistranslation "fold" for "flock" in John x, 16, and it was not corrected till the Revised Version. Some of the renderings in the early versions are extremely quaint. In Gen. xxxix, 2, Tyndale has, "And the Lord was with Joseph and he was a lucky fellow," and in Matt. vi, 7, "When ye pray, babble not much." Coverdale renders Judges xv, 9, "Then God opened a gome tooth in the cheke bone so the water went out." and I Kings xxii, 34, "Shott the King of Israel between the mawe and the lunges."

English-speaking Jews have used freely the Authorized Version, also, since its appearance in 1885, the revised Old Testament. *The Jewish School and Family Bible* (4 parts, London, 1851–61) has a new translation by A. Benisch, and *The Jewish Family Bible* (London, 1884) has a revision of the Authorized Version by M. Friedländer; the latter was sanctioned by the chief rabbi of the British Jews. Isaac Leeser, a pioneer Jewish rabbi and founder of the Jewish press in America, published a translation of the complete Old Testament at Philadelphia in 1854, giving practically new versions of the Prophets, Psalms, and Job and following the Authorized Version in other parts. In 1898 the Jewish Publication Society of America (Philadelphia) took in hand the preparation of a complete revision, with M. Jastrow, Sr., as editor-in-chief and K. Kohler and F. de Sola Mendes as associate editors. In 1905 Dr. Kohler's translation of the Psalms was issued (cf. the *JE*, iii, 194–195).

Bibliography: The most complete view of the literature on the subject is given in S. G. Ayres and C. F. Sitterly, *The History of the Eng. Bible*, New York, 1898 (a bibliography almost exhaustive, arranged in rubrics). The most complete account up to the time of its publication is J. Eadie, *The Eng. Bible, an External and Critical Hist. of Eng. Translations*, 2 vols., London, 1876. The most recent, and worthy of confidence, is H. W Hoare, *Evolution of the English Bible . 1382–1885*, London, 1902 (exceedingly handy). Consult further: T. J. Conant, *Popular History of the Translation of the Holy Scriptures into the Eng. Tongue*, New York, n.d.; *The English Hexapla*, published by Bagster, London, n.d., has a valuable preface; *The Bible of Every Land*, pp. 189–205, ib. 1861 (contains specimen paragraphs from several versions); C. Anderson, *Annals of the Eng. Bible*, new ed. by H. Anderson, ib. 1862; *Anglo-American Bible Revision, by Members of the American Revision Committee*, New York, 1879; J. Stoughton, *Our Eng. Bible, its Translations and Translators*, London, 1879; B. Condit, *Hist. of the Eng. Bible*, New York, 1882; W F. Moulton, *Hist. of the Eng. Bible*, London, 1882; B. F. Westcott and F. J. A. Hort, *The New Testament in the Original Greek*, vol. ii, *Introduction and Appendix*, London. 1881, New York, 1882; J. I. Mombert, *Handbook of the Eng. Versions*, London, 1907 (valuable); A. S. Cook, *The Bible and Eng. Prose Style*, Boston, 1892; idem, *Biblical Quotations in Old Eng. Prose Writers . . Introduction on Old Eng. Versions*, New York, 1904 (the work of a master, minute and exact); J. Wright, *Early Bibles of America*, ib. 1892 (on printed editions); R. Lovett, *Printed Eng. Bibles 1525–1885*, ib. 1894; T. H. Pattison, *Hist. of the Eng. Bible*, ib. 1894; G. Milligan, *The Eng. Bible, a Sketch of its Hist.*, Edinburgh, 1895; P. Schaff, *Companion to the Greek Testament and the Eng. Version*, 4th ed., New York, 1896 (deals with the A. V and R. V.); J. W. Beardslee, *Bible among the Nations; Study of the great Translators*, ib. 1899; G. L. Owen, *Notes on the Hist. and Text of our Early Eng. Bible*, London, 1901; E. H. Foley, *The Language of the Northumbrian Gloss to the Gospel of St. Matthew*, New York, 1903; R. Demans, *W Tindale: A Biography. Being a Contribution to the Early History of the English Bible*, London, 1904; Anna C. Paues, *Fourteenth Century Eng. Version A. Prologue and Parts of the N. T now first edited from the MSS.*, London, 1904; B. F. Westcott, *General View of the Hist. of the Eng. Bible*, ib. 1905 (the latest ed. of Bishop Westcott's scholarly work); J. R. Slater, *The Sources of Tyndale's Version of the Pentateuch*, Chicago, 1906; S. Hemphill, *Hist. of the R. V of the N. T.*, London, 1906; I. M. Price, *Ancestry of our Eng. Bible*, Philadelphia, 1907. *The Gospels in West Saxon*, ed. J. W. Bright, are appearing in Boston, *Matthew*, 1904, *Mark*, 1905, *Luke*, 1906, cf. *The Gospels, Gothic, Anglo-Saxon, Wycliffe, and Tyndale Versions*, London, 1907.

V. Finnish and Lappish Versions: Although Swedish was formerly the principal language of Finland, which remained a Swedish province till the year 1809, during the period of the Reformation the land acquired a Finnish ecclesiastical language. A young Finn, Michael Agricola (see Finland, § 2) became acquainted with Luther at Wittenberg. Having returned to his native land in 1539, he began to translate religious books into Finnish. His translation of the New Testament was published first in 1548; the Psalms and some of the Prophetical books in 1551–52. In 1642 the entire Bible in Finnish by E. Petræus, M. Stadius, H. Hofman, and G. Favorin was published in Stockholm, Finland having at that time no printing establishment. There were new editions in 1683–85 by H. Florinus, and in 1758 by A. Litzelius; a new translation by A. V Ingman appeared in 1859.

The Lappish and Finnish languages are cognates, the former having several dialects. The Lapps (q.v.) were nominally Christians early in the Middle Ages, but had little real knowledge of Christianity. Thomas von Westen (q.v.) did much for Christian instruction among them during the years 1714–23. Some Christian works were published in Lappish; parts of the Bible were translated and sent to Copenhagen, where they were destroyed by a fire. The Norwegian Bible Society having resolved in 1821 to publish a Lappish translation of the Bible, Provost Kildahl offered his services in 1822 in conjunction with a teacher named Gundersen. Kildahl died the same year, but the work was continued by Gundersen and later by Niels Stockfleth. The first two Gospels were printed in 1838, and the complete New Testament in 1840 (new eds. 1850 and, revised, 1874). Stockfleth translated also parts of the Pentateuch (1840), and the Psalms (1854). A Lapp, Lars Hätta, translated the whole Old Testament, which, after being revised by Prof. J. A. Friis and Seminary-Director Quigstad in Tromsö, was printed in 1875. All these are in the Norwegian-Lapp dialect.

In the Swedish-Lapp dialect a handbook containing the lessons from the Gospels and the Epistles for the church-year, the Psalms, Proverbs, and Ecclesiasticus was published by J. J. Tornäus at Stockholm in 1648. The New Testament was translated by Per Fjellström and published in 1755; a new edition and also the entire Bible was issued at Hernösand in 1811. J. BELSHEIM.

BIBLIOGRAPHY: *Bible of Every Land*, pp. 319–324, London, 1861.

VI. French Versions: The beginnings of a French Bible may be traced at least to the early twelfth century. In all probability pupils of Lanfranc (d. 1089) translated the Psalter for the first time into the French-Norman vernacular. At that time there was scarcely any difference between the Norman and the French (i.e. the dialect used in the Île-de-France, a province having Paris as its capital). The Psalter, together with the canticles used in the Church, was offered to the French-speaking people in a double form; viz., (1) after the *Psalterium Hebraicum*, i.e. the Psalter translated by Jerome directly from the Hebrew (cf. *Le Livre des Psaumes*, ed. from Cambridge and Paris manuscripts, F. Michel, Paris, 1876); (2) after the *Psalterium Gallicanum*, i.e. according to the Psalter carefully revised by Jerome from the Septuagint (cf. *Libri Psalmorum versio antiqua Gallica*, ed. F. Michel, Oxford, 1860; see above A, II, 2, § 2). These translations were made word for word, and are interlinear, the Latin text standing between the lines of the French. The translations from the Gallican Psalter were so well received that down to the Reformation no one ventured on a new rendering. The manuscripts of the French Psalter which are still extant, more than 100 in number, without an exception go back to the old Norman Psalter.

1. The Earlier Versions.

About fifty years later Revelation was translated into French in the Norman provinces; also Samuel and Kings (cf. *Les Quatre Livres des Rois, publiés par le Roux de Lincy*, Paris, 1842). In the twelfth and thirteenth centuries numerous translations originated (cf. G. Paris, *La Littérature française au moyen âge*, Paris, 1890, § 136; J. Bonnard, *Les Traductions de la Bible en vers français*, Paris, 1884). Toward 1170 Peter Waldo, the head of the Poor Men of Lyons, better known later as the Waldenses (q.v.), brought out translations of several parts of the Bible into the vernacular, which had been made by Lyonnaise priests at his expense, and Pope Innocent III did not rest till these suspicious writings were everywhere suppressed by the Inquisition. Nevertheless some remnants of this old Waldensian literature have been saved from the hands of the inquisitors at Metz and Liége.

Of the versions which have been printed, and of which it is possible to give some account, mention may be made of that of Guyard des Moulins, canon of St. Peter's at Aire in Artois, on the borders of Flanders. Taking the *Historia scholastica* of Peter Comestor (q.v.), composed in 1170 and containing a digest of the Bible history with glosses, he made a free translation of it between 1291 and 1295; added a sketch of the history of Job, Proverbs, and probably the other books ascribed to Solomon; substituted for Comestor's history of the Maccabees a translation of Maccabees from the Vulgate; and in general made the whole conform more closely to the text of the Vulgate than Comestor had done. Psalms, the Prophets, and the Epistles and Revelation were not in the work as first issued, and it is uncertain whether Acts was not also omitted; they were added, however, in later issues. These parts, brought together, received the name *Biblium historiale* (*Bible historiale;* see BIBLES, HISTORICAL), and it was printed and reprinted in great numbers. An edition completed by different hands and making thus the first complete Bible, was issued by order of Charles VIII about 1487, edited by the king's confessor, Jean de Rely, and printed by Vérard in Paris. Twelve editions of this appeared between 1487 and 1545. This is called *La Grande Bible* to distinguish it from a work entitled *La Bible pour les simples gens*, a summary of the history of the Old Testament, of which five editions, four undated, one dated 1535, have been examined. Previous to the edition of 1487, an edition of the New Testament of the same translation as that found in the supplemented work of Guyard, but not by Guyard himself, was printed at Lyons by Bartolomée Buyer, edited by two Augustinian monks, Julien Macho and Pierre Farget. It is undated, but is referred to the year 1477, and justly claims to be the *editio princeps* of the French Scriptures.

2. Guyard des Moulins.

In the year 1523 there appeared at Paris, from the press of Simon de Colines, an anonymous translation of the New Testament (often reprinted), to which was added in the same year the Psalter and, in 1528, the rest of the Old Testament, issued at Antwerp in consequence of attempts on the part of the French clergy to suppress the book. There can be no doubt that the well-known humanist Jacques Lefèvre d'Étaples (see FABER STAPULENSIS) was the author of this version. The complete work appeared in one volume at Antwerp, 1530. It was placed on the papal Index in 1546; but in 1550 it was reissued at Louvain, edited by two priests, Nicolas de Leuze and François van Larben, who revised the work, striking out all that savored of heresy. The first Protestant version was prepared by Pierre Robert Olivetan (q.v.) within the space of one year, and printed in 1535 by Pierre de Wingle at Serrières, near Neuchâtel, in Switzerland, at the expense of the Waldensians. It was reprinted several times, in one case with a few emendations from the pen of Calvin, in 1545. The Roman critics had denounced Olivetan's work as of little value because of his supposed ignorance of the languages. But he really knew and used the Hebrew to advantage, and the Old Testament was quite well done; but either through press of time or less accurate knowledge of Greek, the New Testament was inferior. To remedy the defects of Olivetan's version, the "venerable company" of pastors of Geneva undertook a revision of the work and was assisted by Beza, Simon Goulart, Antoine Fay, and others. The editor was Bonaventure Corneille Bertram,

3. Protestant Versions.

who gives an account of his work in the *Lucubrationes Franktallenses* (in Pearson's *Critici Sacri*, vol. viii). This revised edition appeared in 1588. In this as well as in the following editions the divine name Yahweh was translated by *l'Éternel* and this rendering is retained to this day in the Protestant Bible of France.

During the seventeenth century this revision of Olivetan's version, known as the "Geneva Bible," was again revised by different ministers; the editions of G. Diodati (Geneva, 1644), Samuel Des Marets (Amsterdam, 1669), and David Martin (New Testament, Utrecht, 1696; whole Bible, 1707) are the first of such revisions. Martin's Bible was again revised by the Basel minister Pierre Roques (1744), and is to this day disseminated by Bible Societies along with other editions. Twenty years before Roques published Martin's revised text, J. F. Osterwald (q.v.), a pastor at Neuchâtel, published anew the Geneva Bible in 1724, and another and revised edition in 1744, in which he embodied the results of the exegetical science of the time. As Osterwald's translation became the standard version, it was adopted by the British and Foreign Bible Society and issued from time to time. A thoroughly revised version prepared by M. Fossard and other French pastors was published by the French Bible Society in 1887, and this revised text was then adopted by the British and Foreign Bible Society.

The following are other Protestant versions: S. Chastillon (Castalio), complete Bible (2 vols., Basel, 1555); J. Le Clerc (Clericus), N. T. (Amsterdam, 1703); I. de Beausobre and J. Lenfant, N. T. (Amsterdam, 1718; often reprinted in Germany and Switzerland); Charles Le Cène, Bible (Amsterdam, 1741); H. A. Perret-Gentil, professor at Neuchâtel, O. T. (Neuchâtel, 1847 sqq.); E. Arnaud, N. T. (Toulouse, 1858); A. Rilliet, N. T. (Geneva, 1859); M. J. H. Oltramare, N. T. (Geneva, 1872); Louis Segond, O. T. (Geneva, 1874), N. T. (1879), whose work has been printed by the Oxford University press; E. Stapfer, N. T. (Paris, 1889).

4. Roman Catholic Versions.

Of versions by Roman Catholics, the most important are a translation of the New Testament published anonymously (Trévoux, 1702), but ascribed with correctness to Richard Simon (q.v.), and a series of versions which proceeded from Port Royal and the Jansenists. As early as the middle of the seventeenth century, Antoine Godeau (q.v.) published a translation of the Bible, at first in parts, then as a whole. In 1667 the New Testament followed, printed by the Elzevirs at Amsterdam, for a bookseller of Mons, whence it is often called the Mons Testament. The translators were Antoine and Louis Isaac Lemaistre de Sacy (see LEMAISTRE DE SACY, LOUIS ISAAC), aided by Antoine Arnauld, Pierre Nicole, Claude de Sainte-Marthe, and Thomas du Fossé. The Old Testament, translated by Louis Isaac Lemaistre de Sacy, was added later (1671), and the New Testament by Pasquier Quesnel (q.v.) appeared in 1687. These translations exercised great influence, partly on account of the elegance of the language, partly on account of the notes, which served devotional purposes. Their method is not a literal rendering, but is paraphrastic. The translation of the New Testament generally known as that of De Sacy was often republished, and is still widely used in France, being circulated by the British and Foreign Bible Society.

René Benoist (q.v.) published a translation of the Bible in 1566. Jacques Corbin, an advocate of Paris, presented the Vulgate in a translation more Latin than French in 1643. The Latin New Testament of Erasmus was translated into French by Michel de Marolles, abbé of Villeloin (1649), who also published a version of the Psalms (1644). Denys Amelote, a priest of the Oratory, translated the New Testament Vulgate into very good French (1666). Dominique Bouhours, a Jesuit, also issued a French New Testament (1697). In the eighteenth century C. Huré (1702), Augustin Calmet (1707), N. Le Gros (1739), and others made versions, all more or less dependent on the Vulgate. In more recent times the Psalms and Job have been often translated. The entire Bible by E. Genoude (Paris, 1821 sqq.) had great success. The Gospels by Lamennais (Paris, 1846) are a model of style, but because of the notes are really a socialistic polemic. [Other names and works which may be mentioned are: M. Orsini, *La Bible des familles catholiques* (Paris, 1851); H. F. Delaunay, who translated the annotated Bible of J. F. Allioli (q.v.) into French (5 vols., Paris, 1856); J. A. Gaume, *Le Nouveau Testament* (2 vols., Paris, 1863); M. A. Bayle, who furnished the translation for Paul Drach's annotated Bible (Paris, 1869 sqq.); P. Giguet, who translated the Septuagint (4 vols., Paris, 1872); H. Lasserre, *Les Saints Évangiles* (Paris, 1887); the Abbé Boisson (Paris, 1901); the Abbé Glaire, who furnished the French translation for the polyglot Bible of F. Vigouroux (Paris, 1898 sqq.); and the Abbé Crampon, *La Sainte Bible*, revised by the Jesuit fathers with the collaboration of the professors of St. Sulpice (Paris, 1907).]

Translations of the Old Testament by Jews are found in S. Cahen's annotated Bible (18 vols., Paris, 1831–51) [and in the Old Testament translated under the direction of Zadoc Kahn, chief rabbi of France (1901 sqq.)]. (S. BERGER†.)

BIBLIOGRAPHY: The most important contributions on the subject have been produced by S. Berger, as follows: *La Bible française au moyen âge*, Paris, 1884; *Les Bibles provençales et vaudoises*, in *Romania*, xviii (1889); *Nouvelles recherches sur les bibles provençales et catalanes*, ib. xix (1890), cf. P. Meyer, in *Romania*, xvii (1888), 121, and H. Suchier, in *Zeitschrift für romanische Philologie*, iii (1879), 412. For enumeration of French Bibles consult *British Museum Catalogue*, entry "Bibles, French," 175 188, and the *Appendix*, "Bibles, French," 18; O. Douen, *Catalogue de la société biblique de Paris*, 1862; *Bible of Every Land*, pp. 254–260, 281–283, London, 1861 (incomplete, but clear so far as it goes). Consult also J. Le Long, *Bibliotheca sacra*, vol. i, Paris, 1723; E. Reuss, *Fragments littéraires et critiques relatifs à l'histoire de la Bible française*, in *Revue de théologie et philosophie*, ii, iv–vi, xiv, new series, iii–v (1851–67, exceedingly important); idem, *Geschichte der heiligen Schriften des Neuen Testaments*, pp. 465 sqq., Brunswick, 1887; E. Pétavel-Olliff, *La Bible en France, ou les traductions françaises des saintes écritures*, Paris, 1864; É. Cadiot, *Essai sur les conditions d'une traduction populaire de la bible en langue française*, Strasburg, 1868; G. Strümpell, *Die ersten Bibelübersetzungen der Franzosen 1100–1300*, Brunswick, 1872; A. Matter, *Note sur la révision de la bible d'Osterwald*, Paris, 1882; J. Bonnard, *Les Traductions de la bible en vers français au moyen âge*, Paris, 1884; P. Quievreux, *La Traduction du N. T. de Lefèvre d'Étaples*, Paris, 1894; P. Meyer, *Notice du MS. Bibliothèque Nationale F 6447*, Paris, 1897; A. Laune, *La Traduction de l'A. T. de Lefèvre d'Étaples*, Paris, 1895; *Revue de l'histoire des Religions*, xxxii, 56; *DB*, extra vol., pp. 402–406.

VII. German Versions: After the Gothic version of Ulfilas (see above, A, X), the oldest fragment of the Bible in a Germanic tongue is probably the Matthew of Monsee, of the year 738 (twenty-two leaves are in Vienna, two in Hanover; on the left page is the Latin, on the right German), a Bavarian working over of a Frankish or Alsacian original. The best edition is A. Hench, *The Monsee Fragments newly Collated, with Text, Introduction, Notes, Grammatical Treatise, and Exhaustive Glossary and Facsimile* (Strasburg, 1890).

1. Old German Fragments.

The "German Tatian," of which the chief manuscript is at St. Gall (second half of the ninth century, in two columns, left in Latin, right in German), originated about 830 in Fulda. The Latin rests upon a manuscript written about 540 for Bishop Victor of Capua (q.v.), which is still preserved in Fulda, and the German follows the Latin very closely (best edition by E. Sievers, *Tatianus, Lateinisch und Altdeutsch*, Paderborn, 1874, 2d ed., 1892). Heccard, count of Burgundy, in 876 gave as a present an *Evangelium Theudiscum* with other books (cf. P. Lejay, in *Revue des Bibliothèques*, July–Sept., 1896). Walton, in his Polyglot (Prolegomena, p. 34a), asserts that "Rhenanus testifies that Waldo, bishop of Freising [884–906] about the year 800 [sic!] translated the Gospels into German" (cf. Hauck, *KD*, ii, 620, 704, 712). Detached fragments of the Gospels have been published by F. Keinz (*SMA*, 1869, p. 546) and J. Haupt (*Germania*, xiv, 1869, p. 440), which are in a handwriting of the twelfth century, but show the accents used earlier in the school of Notker Balbulus (see NOTKER, 1; cf. W. Walther, *Die deutsche Bibelübersetzung des Mittelalters*, 3 vols., Brunswick, 1889–91, 455–465). For the Heliand and Otfrid's *Liber Evangeliorum* or *Krist*, see HELIAND, THE, AND THE OLD-SAXON GENESIS; OTFRID OF WEISSENBURG).

The first translator after Ulfilas known with certainty is Notker Labeo of St. Gall (d. June 29, 1022; see NOTKER, 5). His Job is lost, but his translation of the Psalms can be almost completely reconstructed from his German and Latin commentary on them (best ed. in P. Piper's *Schriften Notkers und seiner Schule*, 3 vols., Freiburg, 1883–84; facsimile in Vogt and Koch, *Deutsche Litteraturgeschichte*, Leipsic, 1904, and Walther, ut sup., 563). Williram, after 1048 abbot of Ebersberg in Bavaria (see WILLIRAM), made a translation of the Song of Solomon, which found so much favor that nineteen manuscripts are still known, one written as late as 1528 (cf. Walther, 523–536, with facsimile, and J. Seemüller, *Die Handschriften und Quellen von Willirams Paraphrase*, Strasburg, 1877, and *Willirams Paraphrase*, 1878; Hauck, *KD*, iii, 968). An interlinear version of the Psalms from the cloister of Windberg, written 1187, was published by E. G. Graff, *Deutsche Interlinearversionen der Psalmen* (Quedlinburg, 1839; cf. Walther, 566; also A. E. Schönbach, *Bruchstücke einer fränkischen Psalmenversion*, in *ZDAL*, xxiv, 2, pp. 177–186). Other manuscripts of this kind are mentioned by Walther, 568. Some twenty manuscripts and two impressions (the one probably by Knubloczer in Strasburg about 1477, the other by Peter Drach in Worms 1504) have preserved the commentary of Nicolaus de Lyra (see LYRA, NICOLAUS DE), containing translations into German by Heinrich von Mügeln, who was for a time with the emperor Charles IV at Prague and seems to have left him on account of his edict of 1369 against the German books on Holy Scripture (cf. Helm, in Sievers's *Beiträge zur Geschichte der deutschen Sprache*, xxi, 1897, p. 240, xxii, 1898, p. 135).

Especially interesting is Walther's eighth group of translations of the Psalms (which include all Latin-German Psalters printed in the Middle Ages and two or three manuscripts) on account of the fact that the German text does not go back to the Latin Vulgate in common use, but to Jerome's version from the Hebrew (see above, A, II, 2, § 2). To Walther's ninth group belongs the splendid Psalter of St. Florian in three languages, Latin, Polish, and German, which was made either for the Polish queen Marguerite, daughter of the emperor Charles IV, or for Mary, sister of the Polish queen Hedwig of Anjou. Another translation is due to Henry of Hesse, rector of the University of Heidelberg, who died 1427, a Carthusian. On the eve of the Reformation Duke Eberhard I of Württemberg was careful to have translations made for him (cf. *TLZ*, iv, 473; 571).

Besides 202 (203) manuscripts, Walther enumerates between 1466 and 1521 eighteen impressions of complete German Bibles,

2. Printed Bibles before Luther.

twenty-two of Psalters, and twelve of other parts. Of the eighteen complete Bibles, fourteen are in High German. They differ from the common Latin Bible by containing the Epistle to the Laodiceans and by placing Acts after the Epistles of St. Paul. The prayer of Manasses is missing in the first two and placed after Chronicles in the rest. Their correct chronological order is:

(1) Strasburg, Mentel, c. 1466 (Hain, *Repertorium bibliographicum*, no. 3130). (2) Strasburg, Eggestein, c. 1470 (Hain, 3129). (3) Augsburg, Pflanzmann, c. 1473 (Hain, 3131). (4) Augsburg, G. Zainer, c. 1473, a thorough revision of 2 (Hain, 3133). (5) Swiss, 1474 (Hain, 3132). (6 and 7) Augsburg, G. Zainer, and A. Sorg, 1477 (Hain, 3134–3135). (8) Augsburg, A. Sorg, 1480, a repetition of Zainer's impression of 1477 (Hain, 3136). (9) Nuremberg, A. Koburger, 1483 (Hain, 3137). (10) Strasburg, Grüninger, 1485 (Hain, 3138). (11–14) All printed in Augsburg, by H. Schönsperger, 1487, 1490 (Hain, 3139–40), H. Otmar, 1507, and Silvanus Otmar, 1518.

All these editions give in the main one and the same version, but Zainer (4 above) undertook a thorough revision, which had much influence. Koburger (9 above) also made changes. The version was already more than 100 years old when first printed. Its home is not yet ascertained, but there are traces which indicate Bohemia. The Latin text underlying this version is interesting especially in Acts, where it has preserved many Old Latin readings. Led by an entry in a manuscript of Nuremberg, F Jostes tried to prove that a certain Johannes Rellach of Resöm (?) in the diocese of Constance, who he thinks was a Dominican, was the author of this version about 1450 (cf. his *Meister Johannes Rellach, ein Bibelübersetzer des 15. Jahrhunderts*, in *Historisches Jahrbuch*, Munich, 1897, 133–145). Kurrelmeyer (*Die deutsche Bibel*, Tubingen, 1904 sqq.) seems to think the version older than this Rellach, who may have undertaken a revision of it, and he has not pronounced upon the alleged Waldensian origin of the version; the manuscript of Tepl may have been in Waldensian hands, but this does not prove a Waldensian origin. There are certain peculiar readings in which the version agrees with the Provençal translation.

A different translation containing only the Old Testament is represented by the "Wenzel" Bible at Vienna, translated from the Latin at the command of the emperor Wenceslaus by Martin Rotlev later than 1389 (facsimile in Vogt and Koch, ut sup.). A "Bible for the Poor" at Maihingen of 1437 gives a German working over of the 212 hexameters in which Alexander Villadeus summarized all the chapters of the Bible (e.g. Gen. i–vii: *sex, prohibet, peccant, Abel, Enoch, archa fit, intrant*) and counts seventy-six books, fifty-eight prologues, 1,457 chapters, and 1,606 verses in the Psalter. To the same group belongs a manuscript now at Maihingen (1472), beautifully illustrated by Furtmeyer for Albert IV of Bavaria, which has between Deuteronomy and Job Matt. i–v, 44, like a manuscript in the British Museum written by the same copyist in 1465 (cf. the *Athenæum* for May 31, 1884, and R. Priebsch, *Deutsche Handschriften in England*, i, Erlangen, 1896). For other versions, cf. Walther.

The Low German Bibles include the Old Testament of Delft (1477), without Psalms, and the famous Picture Bible of Cologne (about 1478; cf. R. Kautzsch, *Die Holzschnitte der Kölner Bibel von 1479*, in *Studien zur deutschen Kunstgeschichte*, vii, 1896, and G. Gerlach, in Dziatzko's *Arbeiten*, ii, 13, Leipsic, 1896). The Song of Solomon in this Bible is not translated but is given in Latin. The Bible of Lübeck of 1494 gives, up to II Kings vii, an original translation; from that chapter onward text and pictures of the Cologne Bible. The edition of Ludwig Trutebul (Halberstadt, 1522) is very scarce. On the Psalters cf. Walther, 682–703, and Kurrelmeyer, ut sup.

On the "Wenzel" Bible, cf. *AJP*, xxi, 62–75, and F. Jelinek, *Die Sprache der Wenzelbibel*, Görz, 1898–99. On the pre-Lutheran Bibles, cf. A. E. Schönbach, *Miscellen aus Grazer Handschriften, ii. Reihe, Deutsche Uebersetzungen biblischer Schriften*, Graz, 1899; idem, *Ueber ein mitteldeutsches Evangelienwerk aus St. Paul*, Vienna, 1897, and L. J. M. Bebb, in *DB*, extra vol., 411–413.

Contemporaneously with Luther others were engaged in translating parts of the Bible into modern German, e.g., Böschenstein, Lange, Krumpach, Amman, Nachtgal, Capito, and Fröhlich; but their works are forgotten (see also below, § 5). Not contemplating at first the entire Bible, Luther began with the penitential Psalms (Mar., 1517, improved 1525) and followed with the Lord's Prayer and Ps. cx in 1518, the Prayer of Manasses with Matt. xvi, 13–20, in 1519, and other pieces. At the end of 1521 he began with the New Testament. He writes on Dec. 18, 1521: "Meanwhile I am gathering notes, being on the point of translating the New Testament into the vernacular;" two days later: "Now I am laboring on annotating and translating the Bible into the common speech;" on Jan. 13, 1522, to Amsdorff: "Meanwhile I am translating the Bible, though I have undertaken a task beyond my strength. The Old Testament I can not touch unless you lend your aid" (cf. C. Bossert, in *TSK*, 1897, pp. 324, 349, 366). The New Testament was in type Sept., 1522; it was published with woodcuts at Wittenberg without name of printer or of translator (*Das Newe Testament Deutzsch*) and was sold for one and one-half florins. In December a second edition followed (cf. R. Kuhrs, *Verhältnis der Decemberbibel zur Septemberbibel. Kritischer Beitrag zur Geschichte der Bibelsprache M. Luthers. Mit einem Anhang über Joh. Lange's Matthäusübersetzung*, Greifswald, 1901). Of the Old Testament, part i (the five books of Moses) was ready in 1523; parts ii and iii (the historical and poetical books) in 1524; the prophets did not follow until 1532; and the Apocrypha as a whole not until the first complete Bible in 1534. Eleven editions were published during Luther's lifetime, besides numerous reprints. For the Old Testament he used the edition of Brescia, 1494 (the copy is now at Berlin); for the New Testament, the second edition of Erasmus (1519), but he consulted the Vulgate, and for the Old Testament had the assistance of his friends Melanchthon, Bugenhagen, Aurogallus, and all available helps. In the preface to Sirach he mentions the earlier German translation, but he seems on the whole independent of it. The influence of Luther's work was great even outside of Germany. It formed the basis of the Danish translation of 1524, of the Swedish and Dutch of 1526, of the Icelandic of 1540, and, through the mediation of Tyndale, influenced the English Authorized Version of 1611.

3. Luther's Bible.

Large parts of Luther's autograph printer's copy are preserved, and the first part is in print in *D. Martin Luther's Deutsche Bibel*, Weimar, 1906. A catalogue of the original editions of Luther's Bible was published by H. E. Bindseil (*Verzeichniss der Original-Ausgaben*, etc., Halle, 1840), who also, in collaboration with H. A. Niemeyer, issued a critical reprint of the edition of 1545 with a collation of the earlier impressions (7 vols., Halle, 1845–55). J. G. Hagemann, *Nachricht von denen fürnehmsten Uebersetzungen der heiligen Schrift* (Brunswick, 1750), gives a list of editions to 1749. In the Hauck-Herzog *RE*, iii, 74–75, about ninety places are named in which Luther's Bible has been printed, with the date of the first edition in each place. It includes the following towns in America: Germantown, Penn., 1743 (the first Bible in a European language printed in America; see SOWER, CHRISTOPHER) and 1763 (cf. *Basler Bibelbote*, 1899, 52); New York, 1854 (N. T.) and 1857 (complete Bible); Philadelphia, 1846. Reading, Penn., 1813, and Lancaster, Penn., 1819, may be added. A chronological list would show the influence of Pietism. The first Berlin edition (1699), for example, was due to Spener. The first Low German Bible, by J. Boddersen, was printed by L. Dietz at Lübeck in 1533; the last was that of Lüneburg, 1621.

By the middle of the nineteenth century six or seven different recensions of Luther's version were in use in Protestant Germany (cf. C. Mönckeberg, *Tabellarische Uebersicht der wichtigsten Varianten der bedeutendsten gangbaren Bibelausgaben*, New Testament, Halle, 1865, Old Testament, 4 vols., 1870–71). In 1863 a committee was named by the Eisenach Conference (see EISENACH CONFERENCE) to undertake a final revision. As the result of the labors of this committee the revised New Testament appeared in 1867 and again in 1870, Genesis in 1873,

4. Revision of Luther's Version.

the Psalms in 1876, the whole Bible (the so-called *Probebibel*) in 1883. At last, in Jan., 1890, the whole work was finished and the first impression was published at Halle in 1892. The revised edition was adopted in most parts of Germany, though in Mecklenburg it is still opposed. A comparison with the English revision shows that the German was much too timid (cf., on the one side, P. de Lagarde, *Die revidierte Lutherbibel des Halleschen Waisenhauses*, Göttingen, 1885, also in *Mittheilungen*, iii; on the other, E. V. Kohlschütter, *Die Revision der Lutherschen Bibelübersetzung*, 1887, and A. Kamphausen, *Die berichtigte Lutherbibel*, Berlin, 1894; also *TJB*, 1886, where twelve pamphlets for and against the revision are named; O. H. T. Willkomm, *Was verliert unser Volk durch die Bibelrevision?* Zwickau, 1901).

Luther's work was criticized early, especially by his Roman Catholic opponents—e.g., by Hieronymus Emser, to whom Urbanus Rhegius replied in 1524 (see EMSER, HIERONYMUS; RHEGIUS, URBANUS; cf. G. Kawerau's *Hieronymus Emser*, Halle, 1898; for criticism from the modern point of view, cf. P. de Lagarde, *Die revidierte Lutherbibel*, ut sup.). The Wittenberg edition of 1572 introduced the summaries of Veit Dietrich. A. Calovius added in 1661 a "Biblical Calendar" by which it was possible to read the Psalms four times every year, Proverbs twice, and the rest of the Bible with Luther's prefaces once. The Wittenberg faculty added a new preface in 1669. The verse of the "three witnesses" (I John v, 7) was first introduced into a Frankfort edition of 1575, into a Wittenberg impression in 1596. Dietrich's summaries were replaced by those of Leonhard Hutter in 1624; in this edition a Roman Catholic compositor changed "everlasting gospel" in Rev. xiv, 6, to "new gospel," the verse being often applied to Luther, and subsequent editions were printed from the sheet as copy. Several editions gave great offense because of changes in the text or additions—e.g., an edition by N. Funk (Altona, 1815) was asserted to teach a "new faith" because of changes in the indexes and notes. The Bible Institute founded at Halle by Karl Hildebrand, Baron Canstein (q.v.) came to have great influence; after 1717 standing type or stereotyped plates were used and millions of copies of the Halle text were circulated (see BIBLE SOCIETIES, II, 1).

5. Other Versions.

The Anabaptists Hans Denk and Ludwig Hätzer (qq.v.) translated the Prophets before the completion of Luther's version (published by Peter Schöffer, Worms, 1527; many later editions); their work was used by other translators and has been praised for scholarship and style (cf. J. J. I. Döllinger, *Die Reformation*, i, Regensburg, 1846, 199; Heberle, in *TSK*, xxviii, 1855, 832; L. Keller, *Ein Apostel der Wiedertäufer*, Leipsic, 1882, 210 sqq.). The preachers of Zurich published a complete Bible in six parts (1525–1529), using Luther's work so far as available and adding the Prophets (part iv) themselves and the Apocrypha (part v, including III and IV Esdras and III Maccabees but not the Prayer of Azariah, the Song of the Three Children, the Prayer of Manasses, or the Additions to Esther) by Leo Jud (q.v.). The complete Bible was printed in 1530, without prefaces and glosses, the Apocrypha at the end. The edition of 1531 (2 vols.) has a short admonition and introduction for "the Christian reader of these Biblical Books" probably by Zwingli; also summaries, parallel references, woodcuts, and a new translation of the poetical books. The edition of 1548 (2 vols.) professes to have been compared word for word with the Hebrew, but really does not differ from editions of 1542 and 1545; it became the basis of later editions. The verse division was first introduced in 1589. A revision of the Zurich New Testament was undertaken by J. J. Breitinger in 1629, by a *collegium biblicum* in 1817, 1860, 1868, and 1882, and a new revision of the New Testament and Psalms appeared in 1893 (cf. E. Riggenbach, *Die schweizerische revidierte Uebersetzung des Neuen Testaments und der Psalmen*, Basel, 1895).

Besides the Zurich Bible three other "composite" Bibles (i.e., Luther's translation so far as it had appeared with the missing parts supplied from other translations) were published before 1534: (1) Worms, Peter Schöffer, 1529, the so-called "Baptist" Bible, having Hätzer and Denk's version of the Prophets; it was the first Protestant Bible to use the word *Biblia* in the title, retained in Luther's Bible till the eighteenth century; (2) Strasburg, Wolff Köpphl, 1530, Prophets by Hätzer and Denk, Apocrypha by Jud; (3) Frankfort, C. Egenolph, 1534, in which only a part of the Apocrypha was not Luther's. The Epistle to the Laodiceans was included in these editions.

About one hundred years after Luther new versions began to appear. The first complete Bible was that of J. Piscator (Herborn, 1602), called the "Straf mich Gott" Bible because the translator added in smaller type to Mark viii, 12, *Wann disem geschlecht ein zaichen wirdt gegeben werden, so straffe mich Gott* ("If a sign be given to this generation, so strike me God;" cf. R. Steck, *Die Piscatorbibel*, Bern, 1897). The Berleburg Bible (8 vols., 1726–1742) and the Wertheim Bible (1735) were prepared in the interest of mysticism and rationalism respectively (see BIBLES, ANNOTATED, AND BIBLE SUMMARIES, I, §§ 3, 4). Later versions are by J. D. Michaelis (O. T., 13 vols., Göttingen, 1769 sqq.; N. T., 2 vols., 1790); J. H. D. Moldenhauer (O. T., 10 vols., Quedlinburg, 1774 sqq.; N. T., 2 vols., 1787–88); Simon Grynæus (5 vols., Basel, 1776–77; a paraphrase in modern style, the historical books of the O. T. abridged, the Gospels harmonized); and G. F. Griesinger (Stuttgart, 1824). Better than these is the version of W. L. M. de Wette and J. C. W. Augusti (6 vols., Heidelberg, 1809–14; later editions by De Wette alone). Bunsen's annotated Bible (9 vols., Leipsic, 1858–70) has a translation of the Hagiographa by A. Kamphausen, of the Apocrypha and N. T. by H. J. Holtzmann, other portions by Bunsen.

Translations of the New Testament alone include: J. Crell, J. Stegman the elder, and others, the Socinian N. T. (Rakow, 1630); J. Felbinger, also a Socinian (Amsterdam, 1660); J. H. Reitz, Reformed (Offenbach, 1703); C. E. Triller (Amsterdam, 1703); Count Zinzendorf (Ebersdorf, 1727); Timotheus Philadelphus (i.e., J. Kayser, a Stuttgart physician, 1733); C. A. Heumann (Hanover, 1748); J. A. Bengel (Stuttgart, 1753); C. T. Damm (3 vols., Berlin, 1765); C. F. Bahrdt ("the latest revelations of God," 4 vols., Riga, 1773–74); J. C. F. Schulz (vol. i, the Gospels, 1774); P. M. Hahn (Winterthur, 1777); G. W. Rullmann (3 vols., Lemgo, 1790–91); J. A. Bolten (8 vols., Altona, 1792–1806); J. O. Theiss, Gospels and Acts (4 vols., Hamburg, 1794–1800); J. J. Stolz (2 vols., Zurich, 1795; a second ed. of a version by Stolz, J. L. Vögeli, and C. Häfeli, 2 vols., 1781–82); G. F. Seiler (2 vols., Erlangen, 1806); J. C. R. Eckermann (3 vols., Kiel, 1806–08); J. W. F. Hetzel (Dorpat, 1809); C. F. Preiss (2 vols., Stettin, 1811); L. Schuhkrafft (Stuttgart); J. Gossner (Munich, 1815); H. A. W. Meyer (Göttingen, 1829); E. G. A. Böckel (Altona, 1832); J. K. W. Alt (4 parts, Leipsic, 1837–39); K. von der Heydt (Elberfeld, 1852; used by the Plymouth Brethren); F. Rengsdorf (Hamburg, 1860); C. Weizsäcker (Tübingen, 1875; 9th ed., 1900); C. Reinhardt (Lahr, 1878); E. Zittel (3 vols., Carlsruhe, 1880–85); C. Stage (Reclam, Leipsic, 1896; "in present-day speech"); H. Wiese (Berlin, 1905).

Roman Catholic versions have been numerous. Hieronymus Emser's New Testament (Dresden, 1527; see EMSER, HIERONYMUS) was merely a slight revision of Luther after the Vulgate. J. Dietenberger, a Dominican, published the entire Bible at Mainz in 1534 (cf. F. Schneider, *Johann Dietenberger's Bibeldruck*, Mainz, 1901). In the New Testament he followed Emser chiefly, in the Apocrypha Leo Jud, in the Old Testament he took much from Luther. C. Ulenberg revised this version in 1630, and the clergy of Mainz in 1662; thenceforth it was commonly called the "Catholic" Bible. Later Roman Catholic versions are: T. A. Erhard (2 vols., Augsburg, 1722); the Benedictines of the cloister of Ettenheimmünster (Constance, 1751); I. Weitenauer (14 vols., Augsburg, 1777–81); F. Rosalino (3 vols., Vienna, 1781); K. H. Seibt (Prague, 1781); H. Braun (13 vols., Augsburg, 1788–1805; worked over by J. F. Allioli, 6 vols., Nuremberg, 1830–32); D. von Brentano, T. A. Dereser, and J. M. A. Scholz (N. T. by Brentano, 3 vols., Kempten, 1790–91; revised and O. T. added by Dereser and Scholz, 15 vols., Frankfort, 1797–1833); K. and L. van Ess (3 vols., Sulzbach, 1807–22); H. J. Jäck (Leipsic, 1847). Translations of the New Testament alone are: C. Fischer (Prague, 1784); B. B. M. Schnappinger (3 vols., Mannheim, 1787–00); S. Mutschelle (2 vols., Munich, 1789–90); B. Weyl (Mainz, 1789); J. G. Krach (2 vols., Freiburg, 1790); C. Schwartzel (6 vols., Ulm, 1802–05); M. Wittmann (Regensburg, 1809); J. M. Sailer (Graz, 1822); J. H. Kistemaker (Munich, 1825; circulated by the British and Foreign Bible Society, which now also circulates Allioli's translation); B. Weinhart (Freiburg, 1900); A. Arndt, S. J. (Regensburg, 1903); B. Grundl (Augsburg, 1903).

Finally, mention should be made of the scholarly translation of the canonical Old Testament, edited by E. Kautzsch in collaboration with F. Baethgen, H. Guthe, A. Kamphausen, R. Kittel, K. Marti, W. Rothstein, R. Ruëtschi, V Ryssel, K. Siegfried, and A. Socin (Freiburg, 1894; 2d ed., 1896). In the supplementary translation of the Apocrypha and Pseudepigrapha Prof. Kautzsch had the assistance of G. Beer, F. Blass, C. Clemen, A. Deissmann, C. Fuchs, H. Gunkel, H. Guthe, A. Kamphausen, R. Kittel, E. Littmann, M. Löhr, W Rothstein, V. Ryssel, F. Schnapp, K. Siegfried, and P. Wendland. Since 1899 cheap editions called *Textbibel*, both with and without Weizsäcker's New Testament, have been circulated.

German Israelites have translations of the Old Testament prepared under the direction of L. Zunz (Berlin, 1837) and by S. Bernfeld (Berlin, 1902). There are also versions in the Jewish-German (Yiddish). E. NESTLE.

BIBLIOGRAPHY: The one work on early German translations is W. Walther, *Die deutsche Bibelübersetzung des Mittelalters*, 3 vols., Brunswick, 1889–91; cf. *Bible of all Lands*, pp. 178–187, London, 1861, and *DB*, extra vol., pp. 411–414.

The subject of the printed German Bible before Luther has been much elucidated by W. Kurrelmeyer of Baltimore, who has prepared an edition from a collation of all impressions and manuscripts; vols. i and ii, the N. T., have already appeared as nos. 234 and 238 of the *Bibliothek des litterarischen Vereins in Stuttgart*, Tübingen, 1904 and 1905; vols. iii–iv of the O. T., nos. 243, 246, ib. 1907. F. Jostes (Roman Catholic) has long had a history in preparation. Consult L. Hain, *Repertorium bibliographicum*, vol. i, Paris, 1826; L. Keller, *Die Reformation und die älteren Reformparteien*, Leipsic, 1885; idem, *Die Waldenser und die deutschen Bibelübersetzungen*, v, 189, ib. 1886; F. Jostes, *Die Waldenser und die vorlutherische deutsche Bibelübersetzung*, p. 44, Münster, 1885; idem, *Die Tepler Bibelübersetzung*, Münster, 1886; idem, "*Die Waldenserbibeln*" *und . . Johannes Rellach*, in *Historisches Jahrbuch*, xv (1894), 77 sqq.; H. Haupt, *Die deutsche Bibelübersetzung der mittelalterlichen Waldenser* . . ., Würzburg, 1885; idem, in *Centralblatt für Bibliothekswesen*, 1885, pp. 287–290; idem, *Der waldensische Ursprung des Codex Teplensis* . . , Würzburg, 1886; M. Rachel, *Die Freiberger Bibelhandschrift*, Freiburg, 1886; S. Berger, *La Question du codex Teplensis*, in *Revue historique*, xxx (1886), 164, xxxii (1886), 184; K. Schellhorn, *Ueber das Verhältnis der Freiberger und der Tepler Bibelhandschrift*, Freiberg, 1890; W Walther, *Ein angeblicher Bibelübersetzer des Mittelalters*, in *Neue kirchliche Zeitschrift*, viii, 3 (1896), 194–207; Schaff, *Christian Church*, vi, 351 sqq.

On Luther's Bible consult: J. G. Palm, *Historie der deutschen Bibelübersetzung Dr. M. Lutheri, 1517–34*, ed. J. M. Göze, Halle, 1772; G. W. Panzer, *Entwurf einer vollständigen Geschichte der deutschen Bibelübersetzung M. Luthers, 1517–81*, Nuremberg, 1791; J. Janssen-Pastor, *Geschichte des deutschen Volkes*, vii, 531–575, Freiburg, 1893; Schaff, *Christian Church*, vi, 340–368; Moeller, *Christian Church*, iii, 34–35.

On the language of Luther's Bible consult: R. von Raumer, *Einwirkung des Christentums*, Stuttgart, 1845; P. Pietsch, *M. Luther und die hochdeutsche Schriftsprache*, Breslau, 1883; K. Burdach, *Die Einigung der neuhochdeutschen Schriftsprache*, Halle, 1884; B. Lindmeyer, *Der Wortschatz in Luthers, Emsers und Ecks Uebersetzung des N. T.'s*, Strasburg, 1899; F. Dauner, *Die oberdeutschen Bibelglossare des xvi. Jahrhunderts*, Darmstadt, 1898; Böhme, *Zur Geschichte der sächsischen Kanzleisprache*, Reichenbach, 1899; W. W. Florer, *Substantivflexion bei Martin Luther*, Ann Arbor, 1899; H. Byland, *Der Wortschatz des Züricher A. T.'s von 1525 und 1531* . . , Berlin, 1903.

On translations after Luther consult: J. Mezger, *Geschichte der Bibelübersetzungen in der schweizerisch-reformierten Kirche*, Basel, 1876; A. Kappler, *Die schweizerische Bibelübersetzung*, Zurich, 1898; idem, *Die neue Revision der Züricher Bibel*, in *Neue Züricher Zeitung*, Nov. 2 and 27, 1904.

On Roman Catholic versions consult: G. W. Panzer, *Geschichte der römisch-katholischen Bibelübersetzung*, Nuremberg, 1781; J. Janssen-Pastor, ut sup.; G. Keferstein, *Der Lautstand in den Bibelübersetzungen von Emser und Eck*, Jena, 1888.

VIII. Greek Versions, Modern: Parts of the Old Testament were translated by Jews into modern Greek as early as the end of the Middle Ages. A version of the Pentateuch made in 1547 has been edited by C. Hesseling (Leipsic, 1897). On the whole the Greek Church has been anxious to make the people acquainted with the Bible, a fact evinced especially in the sixteenth century by the efforts of Damascenus the Studite (q.v.). But when, at the instance of Cyril Lucar, Maximos Kalliupolites published in 1638 an edition of the New Testament in the original Greek with a modern Greek version, the Church as a whole did not favor it, though the patriarch Parthenios permitted its circulation. This text was reprinted in London in 1703 by the monk Seraphim, also in 1710 at Halle, and by C. Reineccius in his polyglot Bible of 1713 (see BIBLES, POLYGLOT, V). In the East, Seraphim's edition was expressly prohibited by the patriarch Gabriel of Constantinople (1702–04).

A new period began when the British and Foreign Bible Society took the matter in hand. As early as 1810 it published the text of Maximos, and English influence induced the patriarchs Cyril VI and Gregory V to permit its circulation. Other issues followed in 1814, 1819, and 1824. The deficiencies of the old text having been long known, it was decided to bring out a new translation, which should approach more nearly the ancient Greek. For this work the monk Hilarion was employed under the direction of the learned Archbishop Constantius of Sinai, afterward patriarch. But when, in consequence of a controversy over the Apocrypha (1825–27), the society introduced bibles without the Apocrypha, the Greek Church would not circulate them. Moreover, after the war of liberation the desire to be entirely independent of Occidental aid greatly increased and orthodox reaction set in anew. The version of such learned Greeks as Typaldos, Bambas, and others found no more favorable reception. This disposition has continued. The latest version of the New Testament by A. Pallis (Liverpool, 1902), written in common Greek, has not been approved. The patriarch Joachim III has renewed the prohibition of Bible translation. PHILIPP MEYER.

BIBLIOGRAPHY: Korais, in *Atakta*, vol. iii (1830); J. Wenger, *Beiträge zur Kenntnis der griechischen Kirche*, Berlin, 1839; *Bible of Every Land*, pp. 241–244, London, 1861; É. Legrand, *Bibliographie Hellénique*, 3 vols., Paris, 1885–1903 (for 15th and 16th centuries); idem, *Bibliographie Hellénique*, 5 vols., ib. 1894–1903 (for the 17th century); A. D. Kyriakos, *Geschichte der orientalischen Kirchen, 1453–1898*, Leipsic, 1902; *Bible Society Reporter*, Jan. and May, 1902; *DB*, extra vol., p. 420.

IX. Hebrew Translations of the New Testament: The anciently attested Hebrew original of the Gospel of Matthew and the Gospel according to the Hebrews are not to be included in this treatment (see MATTHEW, II; APOCRYPHA, B, I, 19). Of existing Hebrew versions of the New Testament, the more important are the following:

1. Versions by Jews: (1) The *Evangelium Matthaei in lingua Hebraica cum versione Latina*, by Sebastian Münster, appeared at Basel, 1537 (2d ed., Paris, 1541; 3d ed., with Hebrews in Hebrew and Latin, Basel, 1557). (2) The *Evangelium hebraice Matthaei recens e Judæorum penetralibus erutum*, with Latin translation, edited by Jean du Tillet and Jean Mercier (Paris, 1555) is part of a translation of the Gospels by Schemtob Schaprut (1385), which may be preserved in a Vatican manuscript. (3) A complete translation of the New Testament was made by Ezekiel Rachbi (d. 1772), and an assistant from Germany.

2. Versions by Christians: (1) Elias Hutter made a Hebrew translation of the complete New Testament for his polyglot editions (Nuremberg, 1599, 1602; see BIBLES, POLYGLOT, V); a better edition of this version was issued by B. Robertson (London, 1661), and the first part of the same by R. Caddick (London, 1798). (2) Johannes Baptista Jona translated the four Gospels (Rome, 1668). (3) A translation of Matthew by Johannes Kemper (d. 1714), with Latin rendering by A. Borelius, is preserved in manuscript in the library of the University of Upsala. (4) The Epistle to the Hebrews, translated by F. A. Christiani, appeared in Leipsic, 1676, and Luke i, 1–xxii, 14, by I. Fromman at Halle, 1735. (5) The translation of the whole New Testament prepared for the London Society for Promoting Christianity among the Jews appeared in 1821, and in revised form in 1840 and 1866. (6) The edition of the British and Foreign Bible Society, begun in 1864, was made by Franz Delitzsch (Leipsic, 1877, stereotyped ed., 1881; revised ed., 1885; again revised by Delitzsch and edited by G. Dalman, 1892). (7) The translation of the Trinitarian Bible Society, begun by Isaac Salkinson and completed by C. Ginsburg, was issued in London, 1885. (G. DALMAN.)

BIBLIOGRAPHY: On 1: A. Herbst, *Die von Sebastian Münster . Übersetzungen des Evangeliums Matthäi*, Göttingen, 1879; F. Delitzsch, *Brief an die Römer*, pp. 22, 105, 103–109, Leipsic, 1870; S. Schechter, in *JQR*, vi, 144–145. On 2: F. Delitzsch, ut sup., pp. 21–38; *Theologisches Literaturblatt*, 1889–1890; G. Dalman, in *Hebraica*, ix, 226–231 and *Theologisches Literaturblatt*, 1891, pp. 289 sqq.; J. Dunlop, *Memories of Gospel Triumphs*, pp. 378–386, London, 1894.

X. Hungarian (Magyar) Versions: János Erdösi (or Sylvester; b. 1504; died c. 1560) made the first Hungarian translation of the New Testament. After studying in Cracow and Wittenberg (1526–29), he returned to his native land and worked at Sárvár under the patronage of the magnate T. Nádasdi, who erected the first Hungarian printing-press in Uj-Sziget (Neanesis). There Erdösi's translation was printed in 1541. Erdösi was afterward professor of Hebrew in Vienna (1542–52); driven out by the Jesuits, he went to Debreczin and, in 1557, to Löcse (Leutschau) as teacher and preacher. A little later, G. Heltai, pastor at Kolosvár (Klausenburg), and his three colleagues translated the New Testament, with several books of the Old Testament (Kolosvár, 1552–61). Péter Juhász (Melius), pastor and superintendent at Debreczin (1558–72), rendered into Hungarian the books of Job and Kings (Debreczin, 1565), and the New Testament (Szegedin, 1567); of the latter work no copy is known. T. Félegyházi, professor and pastor at Debreczin, published a translation of the New Testament at Debreczin in 1586. Gaspar Károli (d. 1591), a pupil of Melanchthon, pastor at Gönc (not far from Kassa), translated the entire Bible with the Apocrypha and published it at Visoly, 1590. This is styled the Visoly Bible, and it has remained in use to the present. It has passed through many editions with some slight corrections.

1. The First Versions.

2. The Komáromi Bible.

During the religious wars (1604–45) against the Austrian monarchs the Hungarian nation heroically fought for political and religious liberty; to the great Protestant princes of Transylvania, Bocskai, Bethlen, and George (György) Rákóczi the Protestant Church is much indebted, for without them it would have suffered the fate of the Bohemian Church. The victorious Rákóczi family caused 10,000 copies of the Bible to be published at Várad in 1657. The years 1660 to 1781 were a dark period for Hungarian Protestants, during which the Austrian government, under Jesuitical influences, took control of the entire kingdom, and the freedom gained in the Reformation was lost. The crisis came in 1671–81, the so-called "decade of mourning." This grievous situation explains the fact that Hungarian bibles had to be printed in foreign countries. The learned Reformed pastor of Debreczin, György Csipkés Komáromi, an excellent Hebrew scholar, in order to meet the common wish and to make the Bible keep pace with the growth of the language, made a new translation which was approved by the synods in 1681. The city of Debreczin at enormous cost had an edition of 4,000 copies printed at Leyden in 1718. When the edition reached the frontier it was seized by the Jesuits (who had secured from the king an order to that effect) and carried to their house at Kassa. The agitated citizens and council of Debreczin used all means available to recover the books and at length secured a royal edict from King Charles III (June 29, 1723) granting them a free Bible (P. Bod, *Historia Hungarorum ecclesiastica*, iii, 89). So great was the power of the Jesuits, however, that they frustrated the royal edict, and the bishop of Eger, Count F. Barkóczy, carried the Komáromi bibles to his palace and threw them all into damp cellars, where they remained till 1754, when on Nov. 1 he burned them in the court of his palace before a large gathering (cf. *The Bible Society Monthly Reporter*, Mar., 1904, p. 69). A few copies retained in Varsó, hidden in the Prussian ambassador's house, were brought to Debreczin in 1789.

The Roman Catholics, on their part, had the Bible translated by a Jesuit scholar György Káldi, and this translation appeared at Vienna, 1626 (see KÁLDI, GYÖRGY). In the nineteenth century Baron A. Bartakovics, archbishop of Eger, ordered a new translation, which was made by his secretary, the learned Tárkányi (d. 1886); this "Eger Bible" was published at the cost of the archbishop in 1862, and again in 1892.

3. Modern Versions. Samuel Kámori, professor in the Lutheran theological academy at Pozsony (Pressburg), attempted a new translation of the whole Bible with the Apocrypha (Budapest, 1870). Because of the translator's modern style and his inadequate knowledge of the Magyar tongue, notwithstanding its fidelity to the original, this version can not be used by the people. A revision of the old Károli text was proposed as early as 1840, and the British and Foreign Bible Society assumed the task. The first revision of the New Testament was accomplished by J. Menyhárt, professor of exegesis in Debreczin College, and by W. Györi, Lutheran pastor of Budapest. It was issued at Budapest in 1878 and, being sharply criticized, did not gain acceptance. The work of revision began more seriously in 1886, when T. Duka, a native of Hungary and a member of the committee of the Bible society in London, secured the aid of that great organization. Competent men were chosen from among the professors and pastors of both Churches. After many years' labor, the revised Old Testament left the press at Budapest in 1898. This noble work needs further revision, and the Hungarian Church awaits the moment when the second revision, soon to appear, will be ready. Work on the revision of the New Testament is progressing.

After the great revolution of 1848 and between 1851 and 1861, the constitution of Hungary was suspended by the Austrian government and the circulation of the Bible was prohibited. The Bible depot, the property of the British Society, was ordered to be removed, and was located at Berlin; since the coronation of Francis Joseph I all hindrances have been removed, and under the Hungarian state government circulation of the Bible is free. F. BALOGH.

BIBLIOGRAPHY: *Bible of Every Land*, pp. 325–327, London, 1861; F. Verseghi, *Dissertatio de versione Hungarica scripturæ sacræ*, Budapest, 1822; T. Duka, in *Bible Society's Monthly*, London, 1892; *KL*, ii. 770–771; Hauck-Herzog, *RE*, pp. 115–118 (gives the literature in Hungarian); *BD*, extra vol., p. 417.

XI. Italian Versions: Legend has it that Jacobus de Varagine (q.v.), bishop of Genoa, made an Italian translation of the Bible. There can be no doubt that one was prepared as early as the thirteenth century. The earliest printed Italian Bible is that of Nicolò di Malherbi, an abbot of the Camaldolites, based on the Vulgate and published Venice, 1471. In 1530 Antonio Brucciolì published at Venice his translation of the New Testament and in 1532 the entire Bible. In the same year the New Testament by the Dominican Zaccaria was published at Venice, and in 1551 that of Domenico Giglio. After this time Geneva became the home of the Italian Bible. A congregation of refugees settled there about the middle of the sixteenth century, and for their benefit Massimo Teofilo, a former Benedictine of Florence, translated the New Testament from the Greek (Lyons, 1551). For the Old Testament Brucciolì's version was revised and thus in 1562 the first Protestant Bible in the Italian language appeared (at Geneva). It was entirely superseded in 1607 by the translation of G. Diodati (q.v.) of Lucca. This version, made directly from the original texts, stands in high esteem for fidelity and has been repeatedly reprinted by different Bible societies. A version affecting great elegance, but by no means as faithful because made from the Vulgate, is that of Antonio Martini, archbishop of Florence (Turin, 1776). This version has also been repeatedly reprinted by the British and Foreign Bible Society, and in 1889 sqq. an illustrated edition was published by the Catholic publisher Sonzogno at Milan. [A version of the Gospels and Acts in modern Italian prepared under the direction of the St. Jerome Society of Rome by Giuseppe Clementi, a secular priest and professor of Italian literature, with brief notes by Giovanni Genocchi of the Mission of the Sacred Heart, and preface by Giovanni Semeria of the Order of St. Paul (Barnabites), was printed at the Vatican Press with the approbation of Pope Leo XIII in 1902. The work was well received by the public and by scholars, and was approved and circulated by many dignitaries of the Roman Church, although some feared its influence. The completion of the New Testament and translation of the Old, which was contemplated by the Society, has been postponed, as it seemed inadvisable to Pope Pius X to give the Italian people the epistles of St. Paul at the present time. The volume published is sold at a nominal price, and about 500,000 copies, it is claimed, have been distributed.

(S. BERGER†.)

BIBLIOGRAPHY: S. Berger, *La Bible italienne au moyen âge*, in *Romania*, xxiii (1894), 358 sqq. (contains bibliography and list of MSS.); *Bible of Every Land*, pp. 277–279, London, 1861; J. D. Hales, *The Bible or the Bible Society? The Corruption of God's Word in the Italian Version of Martini*, London, 1861; J. Carini, *Le Versione della Bibbia in volgari italiano*, S. Pier d'Arena, 1894; S. Minocci, *Versions Italiennes de la Bible*, in Vigouroux, *Dictionnaire de la Bible; KL*, ii, 741–742; *DB*, extra vol., 406–408.

XII. Lithuanian and Lettish Versions: A forerunner of the Bible translation for Protestant Lithuanians was the rendering of the Scripture lessons from the Gospels and Epistles by B. Willent (Königsberg, 1579) from Luther's text (edited by F. Bechtel, in Bezzenberger's *Litauische und lettische Drucke des 16. Jahrhunderts*, part 3, Göttingen, 1882). The first translator of the Bible in a fuller sense was Jan Bretkun (Bretkunas), minister at Labiau and Königsberg (d. 1602 or 1603). He translated the whole Bible, 1579–90. The manuscript, preserved in the university library at Königsberg, is described by A. Bezzenberger, *Beiträge zur Geschichte der litauischen Sprache* (Göttingen, 1877), pp. vi–vii. Only the Psalms were published (Königsberg, 1625) and the editor, J. Rhesa, introduced many changes.

The Reformed Lithuanians, anxious for a Bible,

in 1657 commissioned Samuel Boguslaw Chylinski to go to England and have the Bible printed there (cf. H. Reinhold, in *Mittheilungen der litauisch-litterarischen Gesellschaft*, vol. iv, part 2, p. 105). The Old Testament as far as the Psalms was presented to the synod at Wilna in print in 1663, other parts in manuscript. Of this Bible impression only three copies, all imperfect, are known to exist. Chylinski was the translator.

The New Testament, translated by Samuel Bythner, was published at Königsberg, 1701, for the benefit of the Lutherans (new ed., Berlin, 1866). A New Testament translated by different ministers was published at Königsberg in 1727. The Old Testament was prepared in the same way and the whole Bible was published at Königsberg, 1735. In the beginning of the nineteenth century the need of a new edition of the Bible was felt, and the work was undertaken, with the help of the British and Foreign Bible Society, by a number of clergymen and especially by L. J. Rhesa. It was based on Luther's version, with comparison of the Hebrew and Greek originals, and was published at Tilsit, 1824.

For the Roman Catholic Lithuanians, Joseph Arnulf Giedraitis (Polish, Giedrojć), bishop of Samogitia, translated the New Testament from the Vulgate (Wilna, 1816).

The oldest specimen of Lettish printing, the *Enchiridion* (Königsberg, 1586–87; called in later editions *Vademecum* and "Hand-Book"), contains among other writings for ecclesiastical use the Scripture lessons for Sundays and festivals for the Evangelical Letts (in later editions enlarged by parts of the Old Testament). The first Lettish Bible, translated by E. Glück and C. B. Witten, was published at Riga, 1685–89. In 1877 A. Bielenstein published at Mitau a thoroughly revised edition. (A. Leskien.)

Bibliography: L. J. Rhesa, *Geschichte der litthauischen Bibel*, Königsberg, 1816; H. Reinhold, *Die sogenannte Chylinskische Bibelübersetzung*, in *Mittheilungen der litauisch-litterarischen Gesellschaft*, vol. iv, part 2, p. 105; Napiersky, *Chronologischer Conspect der lettisch litterarischen Gesellschaft*, vol. iii, 1831; *Bible of Every Land*, pp. 310–313, London, 1861; Bielenstein, *Zum 300jährigen Jubiläum der lettischen Literatur*, Riga, 1886. Consult also the *Annual Reports* of the BFBS.

XIII. Persian Versions: Chrysostom mentions Persians as well as Syrians, Egyptians, Ethiopians, and other nations as being in possession of the Gospel; but it is very doubtful whether there was at that time a version of Scripture in the Persian tongue, since Syrian influence predominated in the Persian Empire. It is said, however, that Chosroes II had the Scriptures brought from Edessa (cf. *TLZ*, 1896, 432, and Theodoret, *Hist. eccl.*, i, 5). All that was known in Europe till 1700 of Biblical and other texts is found in Lagarde, *Persische Studien* (Göttingen, 1884), 3–8.

A translation of the Pentateuch by the Persian Jew Jacob ben Joseph Tawus, printed in Hebrew characters, is contained in a polyglot Pentateuch of Constantinople (1546), and was transcribed into Persian characters with a Latin translation by T. Hyde in vol. iv of Walton's Polyglot. The Gospels, translated from the Greek, were edited by Abraham Wheelocke and, after his death, by Pierson (London, 1657), and another translation from the Syriac was printed in vol. v of Walton's Polyglot, and used by Tischendorf after the edition of C. A. Bode (Helmstadt, 1750–51). In Paris are parts of two different translations of the Old Testament, the one made from the Hebrew, the other from the Aramaic (cf. Zotenberg, *Catalogue des manuscrits Hebreux*, etc., Paris, 1866 sqq., and Lagarde, *Persische Studien*, i, 69, and ii, and his *Symmicta*, ii, Göttingen, 1879, 14–17). On Jewish reports about the Bible in the language of Elam and Media cf. L. Blau, *Einleitung in die heilige Schrift* (Budapest, 1894), 80–94.

E. Nestle.

For partial translations of the Bible, particularly of the Pentateuch, the Psalms, Proverbs, Ecclesiastes, Canticles, the Minor Prophets, Esther, Daniel, Tobit, Judith, Job, and Lamentations, preserved in manuscript, cf. *JE*, iii, 190, vii, 318–319. The oldest fragments of this character are probably those found in the Pahlavi *Shikand-gūmānīg Vijār*, which dates from the latter part of the ninth century (ed. Jamasp-Asana and E. W. West, Bombay, 1887; transl. by E. W West, *SBE*, xxiv, 117 sqq.). These fragments are Gen. i, 2–3, ii, 16–17, iii, 9, 11–16, 18–19, vi, 6; Ex. xx, 5; Deut. xxix, 4, xxxii, 35; Ps. xcv, 10; Isa. xxx, 27–28, xliii, 19; Matt. i, 20, v, 17, vii, 17–18, xii, 34, xv, 13, xviii, 32; Luke v, 31–32, vi, 44, xv, 4; John i, 11, 14, viii, 23, viii, 37–38, 42–45, 47; and Rom. vii, 19–20. They were quoted for anti-Christian polemics, and from the forms of the proper names seem to have been derived from a Syriac original, though traces of the Targum of the pseudo-Jonathan (see above, A, V, § 3) may be discovered in the renderings of Ex. xx, 5 and especially of Gen. iii, 14 (cf. L. H. Gray, in *Actes du XIV congrès international des orientalistes*, i, Paris, 1905, 182–186). Equally interesting are the fragments of the New Testament in Estrangelo script but in an Iranian dialect (probably Sogdhian, thus constituting almost the only known remains of this dialect), discovered in Turfan, Eastern Turkestan, in 1903. These citations are Manichean in origin, and the following passages are thus far known: Matt. x, 14 sqq.; Luke i, 63–80; John xx, 19 sqq.; Gal. iii, 25 sqq., and a number of smaller fragments which are adaptations and compilations rather than translations (cf. F. W. K. Müller, in appendix to the *Abhandlungen der Berliner Akademie*, 1904, pp. 34–37, and *Sitzungsberichte der Berliner Akademie*, 1907, pp. 260–270). Mention may also be made of a Persian version of Gen. i–vi, 6, by Abhichand, a Hindu converted to a mixture of Judaism and Mohammedanism by the Judeo-Persian poet Sarmad early in the seventeenth century, and preserved in the *Dabistan*. This version differs materially from the translation of Jacob Tawus.

Bibliography: Walton's *Polyglot*, Prolegomena, 16, and S. Clericus in vol. iv; S. Munk, *Une version persane MS. de la Bibliothèque Royale*, Paris, 1838; *Bible of Every Land*, pp. 64–71, London, 1861; A. Kohut, *Beleuchtung der persischen Pentateuchübersetzung*, Heidelberg, 1871; T. Nöldeke, in *ZDMG*, li (1893), 548; Horn, *Aus italienischen Bibliotheken*, in *ZDMG*, li (1893); Scrivener, *Introduction*, ii, 163; Gregory, *Textkritik*, i, 575–578.

XIV. Portuguese Versions: Portuguese versions begin with that by João Ferreira d'Almeida, a former Roman Catholic priest (New Testament, Amsterdam, 1681; Old Testament, revised and continued by Danish missionaries, Tranquebar, 1719–1751). A Roman Catholic version, with annotations, by Antonio Pereira de Figueiredo, was published in Lisbon, 1778 sqq. (23 vols.; revised ed., greatly improved, 1794–1819).

A version based on Almeida's translation was made by the Rev. Thomas Boys, and published by the Trinitarian Bible Society (London, 1843–47). The British and Foreign Bible Society has often printed revised editions of both Almeida's and Pereira's versions. The need of a better and more accurate translation of the Bible in the Portuguese language is generally recognized by Protestant missionaries and laborers in Portugal and Brazil. (S. Berger†.)

Bibliography: *Bible of Every Land*, p. 271–276, London, 1861; S. Berger, in *Romania*, xxviii (1899), 543 sqq. (gives a full account of the literature); *DB*, extra vol., pp. 410–411.

XV. Scandinavian Versions: Of the Scandinavian countries, Norway and its colony, Iceland, had at a very early period a national literature in the Old Norwegian tongue (incorrectly called Old Norse). To the earliest period of Bible translation belongs the *Stjorn* ("Dispensation," sc., of God), which includes Gen.–II Kings. This is not a translation but a paraphrase of these books on the basis of the Vulgate, with explanatory remarks from different authors—Josephus, Augustine, Peter Comestor, Vincent of Beauvais, and others. The preface states that it was prepared under the patronage of King Haakon V (1299–1319), and from a note in one of the manuscripts it appears that Brand Jonson, bishop of Hole in Iceland (d. 1264), made the translation. If this note is correct, Jonson probably translated the middle and most ancient part (Ex. xix–Deut. xxxiv). The *Stjorn* was edited by Prof. C. R. Unger (Christiania, 1862). In the Old Norwegian literature there exist many homilies, legends of the saints, and apocryphal Acts of the Apostles which contain many Bible texts; these were put together and published by J. Belsheim under the title *Af Bibelen i Norge og paa Island i Middelalderen* (Christiania, 1884).

1. Before the Reformation.

The earliest traces of a translation of the Bible into Old Swedish appear in the time of St. Bridget. In her "Revelations" as well as in accounts of her life it is said that she had a copy of the Bible made in Swedish. This was undoubtedly only an exposition of the Pentateuch composed by her father confessor Matthias in Linköping (d. 1350; see Bridget, Saint, of Sweden). Joshua and Judges were translated later by Nils Ragnvaldson (d. 1514), while Judith, Esther, Ruth, and Maccabees were translated by Jens Budde of the Nådendal monastery. There is also extant a translation of the Apocalypse, made prior to 1520. All these Biblical works, based on the Vulgate, were edited by G. E. Klemming, in *Svenska Medeltidens Bibelarbeten* (2 vols., Stockholm, 1848–55).

An old Danish version based on the Vulgate, containing the first twelve books of the Old Testament, is contained in a manuscript of the Mariager monastery in Jutland, antedating 1480. The first eight books were edited by Prof. C. Molbech (Copenhagen, 1828). A translation of the Psalms of the same period is extant in different manuscripts. Some of them were edited by C. J. Brandt, in *Gamle danske Læsebog* (Copenhagen, 1857).

In both Denmark and Sweden the entire Bible was first translated in the period of the Reformation. Norway was united with Denmark from 1380 to 1814 and the Danish language, being cognate with the Norwegian, became the common literary language in the two countries. The New Testament was first rendered into Danish by Hans Mikkelsen, formerly burgomaster of Malmö, who followed Christian II into exile in the Netherlands in 1523. This New Testament appeared at Leipsic in 1524. Being a mixture of Danish and German, the language was uncouth. A better translation was made by Christen Pedersen (d. 1554), the first editor of the history of Denmark by Saxo Grammaticus and of other older works. Pedersen's New Testament was printed at Antwerp 1529 and again in 1531, and in the latter year his translation of the Psalms appeared. Previous to this (1528) a translation of the Psalms made by Frans Wormordsen, a Dutchman by birth, was published at Rostock. All these followed the Vulgate closely, but were influenced by Luther and Erasmus. The Danish Reformer Hans Tausen (d. 1561, as bishop of Ribe [Ripen]) translated the Pentateuch from Luther's version (Magdeburg, 1535). Peder Tidemand translated Judges (Copenhagen, 1539), and Wisdom and Ecclesiasticus (Magdeburg, 1541). The first complete Bible in Danish was published at Copenhagen in 1550, following, according to the instructions of Christian III, as much as possible Luther's version. The greater part of the work was done by Christen Pedersen, assisted by a number of professors. A new edition followed, 1589, reprinted 1633. A translation from the original languages, prepared by Hans Paulsen Resen (d. 1638), appeared in 1607, and, revised by Bishop Hans Svane or Svaning (the so-called Svaning Bible), again in 1647 and was used till the middle of the nineteenth century. In 1819 Bishop F. C. K. H. Münter (q.v.) with others undertook a revision of the New Testament, and the whole Bible, revised by C. Rothe, C. Hermansen, and C. Kalkar under the presidency of Bishop H. L. Martensen (q.v.) was published in 1872. There are translations made by other scholars, such as C. Bastholm (New Testament, 1780), O. H. Guldberg (New Testament, 1794), the whole Bible by J. C. Lindberg (1837–56) and C. Kalkar (1847), the four Gospels by K. F. Viborg (1863), and the New Testament by Bishop T. S. Rördam (1886; 2d ed., 1894–95). A Roman Catholic version of the New Testament after the Vulgate was published by J. L. V. Hansen in 1893.

2. Since the Reformation.

After the separation of Norway from Denmark in 1814, three revisions of the New Testament were made (1819, 1830, and 1873), the most important being by Prof. Hersleb in 1830. A new translation of the Old Testament undertaken by Adjunct Thistedahl and Profs. Kaurin, Holmboe, Caspari, and Nissen was published in parts (1857–1869; revised ed. completed 1890), and of the New Testament by Bishops F. W Bugge, A. C. Bang, and others was published in 1904.

The New Testament was rendered into the Norwegian vernacular, which much resembles the Old Norwegian, by Prof. E. Blix, I. Aasen, M. Skard, and J. Belsheim, and published in 1889 (new ed., 1899). A translation of parts of the Old Testament is in preparation and the Book of Psalms was printed in 1904, Genesis in 1905. A translation of the New Testament for the use of Roman Catholics has also been published. During the Reformation period Iceland also received the Bible in its old Norwegian-Icelandic tongue. An Icelander, Odd Gottskalkson, of Norwegian descent, translated the New Testament, which was published at Roskilde, 1540. The whole Bible translated after Luther's version by Bishop Gudbrand Thorlakson appeared in 1584 (revised 1644). A new translation by Bishop Stein Jonson was issued in 1728, but the rendering was not smooth, so the older version of Thorlakson was reprinted at Copenhagen in 1747, and the New Testament again in 1750 and 1807, followed in 1813 by a reprint of the whole Bible. In 1827 a new translation of the New Testament was published, followed by a revised edition of the whole Bible in 1841, and by a revised edition, Oxford, 1863.

When Gustavus Vasa became king of Sweden in 1523, wishing for a Swedish translation, he applied to Archbishop Johannes Magni of Upsala, requesting him with the help of the clergy to prepare a translation of the New Testament. The archbishop devised a plan which, however, was opposed by some of the ministers. Bishop Hans Brask of Linköping said that "it were better for Paul to have been burned, than to be known by every one." The New Testament translated by the chancellor Lorenz Andreä (q.v.) with the assistance of Pastor Olaus Petri (q.v.) was published at Stockholm 1526. The whole Bible, translated by Lars Petri, archbishop of Upsala (d. 1573), was issued 1540–41. This Bible, made after Luther's, was for a long time the church Bible of Sweden. A revised edition by the two bishops Gezelius in Abo (father and son; see GEZELIUS, JOHANNES) was highly praised. Different commissions for translating the Bible were appointed; one, consisting of twenty-three members, spent a long time in preparing a translation with a rationalistic tendency; but the "specimens" published from time to time found no favor. In 1844 the commission was reconstituted, with Prof. A. Knös as one of its most active members. The New Testament prepared by the cathedral provosts C. A. Thoren and H. M. Melin and published in 1853–77 was not favorably received. A better reception met the version of the New Testament prepared by Archbishop Sundberg, Cathedral Provost Thoren, and Bishop Johanson, published in 1882. A new translation of the Old Testament is in preparation. The Bible version of Cathedral Provost Melin was published in 1865–69.

J. BELSHEIM.

BIBLIOGRAPHY: J. Belsheim, *Veiledning i Bibelens Historie*, pp. 252 sqq., Christiania, 1880; J. A. Schinmeier, *Geschichte der schwedischen Bibel-Uebersetzungen und Ausgaben*, Leipsic, 1777; P. W. Becker, *De J. P. Resenii versione Danica*, Copenhagen, 1831; C. Molbech, *Bidrag til en historie af de Danske Bibeloversaettelser*, ib. 1840; *Bible of Every Land*, pp. 214–225, London, 1861; C. W. Bruun, *Bibliotheca Danica*, Copenhagen, 1872; J. P. Häggman, *Forteckning öfver svenska upplagor af Bibeln*, Upsala, 1882; *KL*, ii, 767–769; *DB*, extra vol., pp. 415–416.

XVI. Slavonic Versions: The history of Bible versions in the Slavonic begins with the second half of the ninth century. The oldest translation, commonly called the Church Slavonic, is closely connected with the activity of the two apostles to the Slavs, Cyril and Methodius, in Moravia, 864–885 (see CYRIL AND METHODIUS). The oldest manuscripts are written either in the so-called Cyrillic or the Glagolitic character.

1. The Old Church Slavonic Version.

The former is the Greek majuscule writing of the ninth century with the addition of new characters for Slavic sounds which are not found in the Greek of that time; the latter was a style of the Greek minuscule with the addition of new signs as in the Cyrillic alphabet. The oldest manuscripts are written in the Glagolitic, which is older than the Cyrillic. The oldest manuscripts extant belong to the tenth or eleventh century, and the first complete collection of Biblical books in the Church Slavonic language originated in Russia in the last decade of the fifteenth century. It was made by Archbishop Gennadius of Novgorod, and the Old Testament was translated partly from the Vulgate, and partly from the Septuagint. The New Testament is based upon the old Church Slavonic translation. During the sixteenth century a greater interest in the Bible was awakened in South and West Russia, owing to the controversies between adherents of the Orthodox Church and the Roman Catholics and Uniates. In the second half of the sixteenth century the Gospels, Acts, and Epistles, and parts of the Psalter were often printed at Lemberg and Wilna, though the oldest edition of the Acts and Epistles was issued at Moscow in 1564. In 1581 the first edition of the Slavonic Bible was published at Ostrog, a number of Greek manuscripts, besides the Gennadius Bible, having been used for this edition. But neither the Gennadius nor the Ostrog Bible was satisfactory, and in 1663 a second somewhat revised edition of the latter was published at Moscow. In 1712 the czar Peter the Great issued a ukase ordering the printed Slavonic text to be carefully compared with the Greek of the Septuagint and to be made in every respect conformable to it. The revision was completed in 1724 and was ordered to be printed, but the death of Peter (1725) prevented the execution of the order. The manuscript of the Old Testament of this revision is in the synodal library at Moscow. Under the empress Elizabeth the work of revision was resumed by a ukase issued in 1744, and in 1751 a revised "Elizabeth" Bible, as it is called, was published. Three other editions were published in 1756, 1757, and 1759, the second somewhat revised. All later reprints of the Russian Church Bible are based upon this second edition, which is the authorized version of the Russian Church.

2. Russian Versions.

The Church Slavonic is not intelligible to the Russian people. An effort to produce a version in the vernacular was made by Frantsisk Skorina (d. after 1535), a native of Polotsk in White Russia. He published at Prague, 1517–19, twenty-two Old Testament books in the "Russian language," in the preparation of which he was greatly influenced by the Bohemian Bible of 1506 (see below, § 5). Other efforts were made during the sixteenth and seventeenth centuries, but the Church Slavonic predominated in all these efforts. Peter the Great felt that the mass of the Russian people needed a Bible in the vernacular and authorized Pastor Glück in 1703 to prepare such an edition. Unhappily Glück died in 1705 and nothing is known of his work. It was left to the nineteenth century in connection with the establishment of the Russian Bible Society (founded in 1812 at St. Petersburg, with the consent of Alexander I; see BIBLE SOCIETIES, II, 5) to prepare a Bible in the vernacular. The work was undertaken by Philaret (q.v.), rector of the Theological Academy of St. Petersburg (afterward metropolitan of Moscow), and other members of the faculty of the academy. The Gospels were published in 1818 and in 1822 the entire New Testament. In 1820 the translation of the Old Testament was undertaken, and in 1822 Philaret's translation of the Psalms was published. In 1825 the Pentateuch, Joshua, Judges, and Ruth were issued. The year 1826 saw an end to the activity of the Bible Society in the ban put upon all kinds of private associations, even when non-political. Not before 1858 was the work of translation resumed. In 1876 the entire Bible was published in one volume. The Old Testament books, though based upon the Hebrew, follow the order of the Septuagint and the Church Slavonic Bible. The Apocryphal books also form a part of the Russian Bible. The British and Foreign Bible Society also issued a Russian edition, omitting, however, the Apocrypha.

3. Bulgarian and Servian Versions.

The Bulgarians too were provided during the nineteenth century with translations of Biblical books into the vernacular. In 1828 the New Testament was published at Bucharest (2d ed., 1833), translated by the pastors Sapunov and Seraphim. For the British and Foreign Bible Society the archimandrite Theodosius, abbot of the Bistrica monastery, translated the New Testament, which was printed at London in 1828. The entire edition was sent to St. Petersburg and is said to have been destroyed there. A new translation of the New Testament was published at Smyrna in 1840 (3d ed., Bucharest, 1853, and often). In 1867 the American Bible Society printed in New York a translation of the New Testament and other editions were issued at Constantinople in 1866 and 1872. The Old Testament "translated from the original" was also published there in three parts (1862–64), but without the Apocrypha. An edition of the entire Bible "faithfully and accurately rendered from the original" was published by the same society at Constantinople in 1868 (3d ed., 1874). A translation of the New Testament into Servian was made by Vuk Stefanović Karajić, the founder of modern Servian literature, and published at Vienna in 1847. The Old Testament was translated by Vuk's pupil Dyuro Danichić and issued at Belgrade in 1868. The language in both is excellent. The Servian Bible of Atanasiie Ivanović Stoiković (published by the Russian Bible Society at St. Petersburg, 1824) is not written in the vernacular, but is a mixture of Church Slavonic and Servian.

4. Slovenian and Croatian Versions.

The Bible versions for the Slovenes are most closely connected with the activity of the Reformer of Carniola, Primus Truber (1507–86; see TRUBER, PRIMUS), and his associates and successors; they were intended for the Evangelical Slovenes. Truber translated the Gospel of Matthew, which was printed at Reutlingen in 1555; in 1557 the first part of the New Testament was published at Tübingen, the second part in 1560, and the complete New Testament was issued in 1582; the Psalms appeared in 1566. Dalmatin, who assisted Truber, translated the Old Testament, and an edition of the entire Scriptures in Slovenian was published under his direction at Wittenberg in 1584. Stevan Kuczmics published a New Testament for the Hungarian Slovenians in their dialect at Halle in 1771. An edition published at Güns (Köszeg) in 1848 has the Psalms added. In 1784 a part of the New Testament for the use of Roman Catholics was printed at Laibach, translated from the Vulgate by several hands. The second part of the New Testament was issued in 1786, and the Old Testament between 1791 and 1802. Efforts were also made to prepare a Bible version for the Evangelical Croats or for those who should be brought over to the Evangelical faith. A New Testament translated by Anton Dalmata and Stipan Consul was printed in Glagolitic characters (2 parts) at Tübingen, 1562–63. In the seventeenth century efforts were made to give a translation to the Catholic Croats and Servians in the so-called Illyrian dialect, but nothing was printed till the nineteenth century, when a Bible in Latin letters together with the parallel text of the Vulgate, translated into "the Illyric language, Bosnian dialect" by Petrus Katancsich, was published at Budapest (6 parts, 1831). It followed the Vulgate slavishly.

5. Bohemian Versions.

The Czech literature of the Middle Ages is very rich in translations of Biblical books, made from the Vulgate (cf. the list of manuscripts and prints in J. Jungmann, *Historie Literatury České*, Prague, 1849). During the fourteenth century all parts of the Bible seem to have been translated at different times and by different hands. The oldest translations are those of the Psalter. The New Testament must also have existed at that time, for according to a statement of Wyclif, Anne, daughter of Charles IV, received in 1381 upon her marrying Richard II of England a Bohemian New Testament. It is certain that Huss had the Bible in Bohemian before him as a whole and he and his successors undertook a revision of the text according to the Vulgate. The work of Huss on the Bible antedated 1412. During the fifteenth century the revision was continued. The first complete Bible was published at Prague, 1488; other editions were issued at Kuttenberg, 1489, and Venice, 1506. These prints were the basis of other editions which were published from time to time.

With the United Brethren a new period began for the translation of the Bible. In 1518 the New Testament appeared at Jungbunzlau at the instance of Luke of Prague (q.v.). It was not satisfactory and the same must be said of the edition of 1533. Altogether different was the translation made by Jan Blahoslav from the original Greek (1564, 1568). The Brethren soon undertook the translation of the Old Testament from the original and appointed for this work a number of scholars, who based their translation upon the Hebrew text published in the Antwerp Polyglot. The work began in 1577 and was completed in 1593, and from the place of printing, Kralitz in Moravia, it is known as the Kralitz Bible (6 parts, 1579–93, containing also Blahoslav's New Testament). This excellent translation was issued in smaller size in 1596, and again in folio in 1613 (reprinted at Halle in 1722, 1745, 1766; Pressburg, 1787; Berlin, 1807).

After the year 1620 the publication of non-Catholic Bibles in Bohemia and Moravia ceased, and efforts were made to prepare Bibles for the Catholics. After some fruitless beginnings the work was entrusted to certain Jesuits, who took the Venice edition of 1506 as the basis, but relied greatly, especially for the Old Testament, on the Brethren's Bible. Between 1677 and 1715 the so-called St. Wenceslaus Bible was published at the expense of a society founded in honor of the saint. A new edition appeared at Prague 1769 71. A thoroughly revised edition, using the text of the Brethren's Bible, was published in 1778–80. Still more dependent on the Brethren's Bible was Prochaska's New Testament (Prague, 1786), and his edition of the whole Bible (1804). Editions of Prochaska's text, slightly amended, were issued in 1851 and 1857. The Bible edited by Besděka (Prague, 1860) gives the text of the Brethren's Bible with slight changes. G. Palkovič translated the Bible from the Vulgate into Slovak (2 parts, Gran, 1829).

6. Wendish or Sorbic Versions.

The oldest Sorbic Bible version, that of the New Testament of 1547, is extant in a manuscript in the Royal Library at Berlin. The translator was Miklawusch Jakubica, who employed a dialect (the Lower Sorbic) now extinct. In the eighteenth century Gottlieb Fabricius, a German, made a translation of the New Testament which was printed in 1709. In a revised form this version was published by the British and Foreign Bible Society in 1860. The Old Testament, translated by J. G. Fritz, was printed at Kottbus in 1796. An edition of the entire Bible was published by the Prussian Bible Society in 1868.

Michael Frentzel, pastor in Postwitz (d. 1706), translated the New Testament into the Wendish of Upper Lusatia (Upper Sorbic), and his version was published by his son, Abraham Frentzel (Zittau, 1706). A complete edition of the Bible, the work of different scholars, was first published at Bautzen, 1728. A second revised edition was prepared by Johann Gottfried Kühn and issued in 1742; a third improved edition prepared by Johann Jacob Petschke was published in 1797. Passing over other editions, it is worth while to note that the ninth edition of the complete Bible (Bautzen, 1881) was revised by H. Immisch and others and contains a history of the Upper Lusatian Wendish Bible translation. For the Roman Catholic Wends of Upper Lusatia G. Luščanski and M. Hornik translated the New Testament from the Vulgate, and published it at Bautzen, 1887–92; the Psalms were translated from the Hebrew by J. Laras (Bautzen, 1872).

7. Polish Versions.

The history of the Polish translation of the Bible begins with the Psalter (cf. W. Nehring, *Altpolnische Sprachdenkmäler*, Berlin, 1886). A manuscript of the second half of the fourteenth century, in the abbey of St. Florian, near Linz, in Latin, Polish, and German is probably the oldest. A critical edition of the Polish part was published by Nehring (*Psalterii Florianensis pars Polonica*, Posen, 1883) with a very instructive introduction. Besides the Florian Psalter there is the Psalter of Pulawy (now in Cracow) belonging to the end of the fifteenth century (published in facsimile, Posen, 1880).

Polish Bibles originated after the middle of the fifteenth century. An incomplete Bible, the so-called Sophia Bible (named after Queen Sophia, for whom it was intended, according to a remark from the sixteenth century; also called the Sáros-patak Bible from the place where it is preserved), contains Genesis, Joshua, Ruth, Kings, Chronicles, Ezra, Nehemiah, II (III) Esdras, Tobit, and Judith (ed. A. Malecki, *Biblia Krolowéj Zofii*, Lemberg, 1871). With the Reformation period activity in the work of translation increased as the different confessions endeavored to supply their adherents with texts of the Bible. An effort to provide the Lutherans with the Bible in Polish was made by Duke Albert of Prussia (q.v.) in a letter directed in his name to Melanchthon. Jan Sieklucki, preacher at Königsberg (d. 1578), was commissioned to prepare a translation, and he published the New Testament at Königsberg, 1551 and 1552. The Polish Reformed (Calvinists) received the Bible through Prince Nicholas Radziwill (1515–65). A company of Polish and foreign theologians and scholars undertook the task, and, after six years' labor at Pincow, not far from Cracow, finished the translation of the Bible which was published at the expense of Radziwill in Brest-Litovsk, 1563 (hence called the Brest or Radziwill Bible). The translators state that for the Old Testament they consulted besides the Hebrew text the ancient versions and different modern Latin ones. The Brest Bible was not universally welcomed. The Reformed suspected it of Socinian interpretations; the Socinians complained that it was not accurate enough. The Socinian Simon Budny especially charged against the Brest Bible that it was not prepared according to the original texts, but after the Vulgate and other modern versions, and that the translators cared more for elegant Polish than for a faithful rendering. He undertook a new rendering, and his translation ("made anew from the Hebrew, Greek, and Latin into the Polish") was printed in 1572 at Nešvižh. As changes were introduced in the printing which were not approved by Budny, he disclaimed the New Testament and published another edition (1574). The charges which he made against the Brest Bible were also made against his own, and the Socinian Adam Czechowicz published a new and improved edition of the New Testament (Rakow, 1577). The interesting preface states that Czechowicz endeavored to make an accurate translation, but did not suppress his Socinian ideas; e.g., he used "immersion" instead of "baptism." Another Socinian New Testament was published by Valentinus Smalcius (Rakow, 1606).

The Brest Bible was superseded by the so-called Danzig Bible, which finally became the Bible of all Evangelical Poles. At the synod in Ožarowice, 1600, a new edition of the Bible was proposed and the work was given to the Reformed minister Martin Janicki, who had already translated the Bible from the original texts. In 1603 the printing of this translation was decided upon, after the work had been carefully revised. The work of revision was entrusted to men of the Reformed and Lutheran confessions and members of the Moravian Church (1604), especially to Daniel Mikolajewski (d. 1633), superintendent of the Reformed churches in Great Poland, and Jan Turnowski, senior of the Moravian Church in Great Poland (d. 1629). After it had been compared with the Janicki translation, the Brest, the Bohemian, Pagnini's, and the Vulgate, the new rendering was ordered printed. The Janicki translation as such has not been printed, and it is difficult to state how much of it is contained in the new Bible. The New Testament was first published at Danzig, 1606, and very often during the sixteenth and seventeenth centuries. The complete Bible was issued in 1632, and often since. The Danzig Bible differs so much from that of Brest that it may be regarded as a new translation. It is erroneously called also the Bible of Paliurus (a Moravian, senior of the Evangelical Churches in Great Poland, d. 1632); but he had no part in the work.

For the Roman Catholics the Bible was translated from the Vulgate by John of Lemberg (*Leopolita*, hence this was called the Leopolitan Bible) and published at Cracow, 1561, 1574, and 1577. This Bible was superseded by the new translation of Jakub Wujek (a Jesuit, b. about 1540; d. at Cracow 1593). Wujek criticized the Catholic and non-Catholic Bible versions and spoke very favorably of the Polish of the Brest Bible, but asserted that it was full of heresies and of errors in translation. With the approbation of the Holy See the New Testament was first published at Cracow, 1593, and the Old Testament in 1599, after Wujek's death. This Bible has often been reprinted. Wujek's translation follows, in the main, the Vulgate. (A. LESKIEN.)

BIBLIOGRAPHY: For the beginnings of Slavic versions consult: *Vita sancti Methodii, russo-slovenice et latine*, ed. F. Miklosich, Vienna, 1870; C. Dümmler, *Die pannonische Legende vom heiligen Method*, in *Archiv für Kunde österr. Geschichtsquellen*, vol. xiii; idem and F. Miklosich, *Die Legende vom heiligen Cyrillus*, in *Denkschriften der Wiener Akademie, phil.-histor. Classe*, xix (1870); Jagić, *Zur Entstehungsgeschichte der Kirchenslav-Sprache*, Vienna, 1900. On the history of versions consult: S. W. Ringeltaube, *Nachricht von polnischen Bibeln*, Danzig, 1744; R. G. Ungar, *Allgemeine böhmische Bibliothek*, part 1, *Theologie*, Prague, 1786 (a bibliography of Bohemian versions); J. Dobrowsky, *Ueber den ersten Text der böhmischen Bibelübersetzung*, Prague, 1798; idem, *Glagolitica*, ib. 1807; C. F. Schnurrer, *Slavischer Büchernachdruck in Würtemberg im 16. Jahrhundert*, Tübingen, 1799; G. J. Dlabacz, *Nachricht von einem bisher noch unbekannten böhmischen A. T.*, Prague, 1804; *Bible of Every Land*, pp. 291–310, London, 1861; I. Kostrenčić, *Geschichte der protestantischen Litteratur der Südslaven, 1559–65*, Vienna, 1874; W. R. Morfill, *Slavonic Literature*, London, 1883; *Archiv für Slavische Philologie*, by V. Jagić, especially supplement vol. by F. Pastirnek, Berlin, 1892 (contains bibliographical lists of works on Slavonic subjects for the years 1876–91, including whatever has appeared during that time on the Russian Bible); V. Vondrák, *Die Spuren der altkirchenslavischen Evangelienübersetzung*, Vienna, 1893; F. Ahn, *Bibliographische Seltenheiten der Truberlitteratur*, Leipsic, 1894; L. J. M. Bebb, *The Russian Bible*, in *Church Quarterly Review*, Oct., 1895, pp. 203–225; T. Elze, *Die slovenischen protestantischen Druckschriften des xvi. Jahrhunderts*, Venice, 1896; Scrivener, *Introduction*, ii, 157 sqq.; *BD*, extra vol., pp. 417–420.

XVII. Spanish Versions: It is very difficult to decide at what time the first Spanish version was made. In treating of Spanish Bibles, a distinction should be made between the Catalonian and the Castilian speech. Of Biblical manuscripts in the former there are many from the fifteenth century, one (of the New Testament) from the fourteenth. Report has it that the Dominican Romeu Sabruguera of Mallorca (d. 1313), who translated the Psalms, worked on a translation of the entire Bible; but the report can not be verified. Most of the Catalonian translations of parts of the Bible (Proverbs, the Prophets, Pauline and Catholic Epistles) depend on the Vulgate and early French versions; a translation of the Psalms depends wholly on the French; the Gospels in the oldest manuscripts are not based on the Vulgate but on a text in southern French. Of an alleged translation supposed to have been printed in Valencia, 1478, no bibliographical datum or exemplar is known, only a few fragments being so attributed.

Of the Castilian translations almost as little is known, since no efficient examination of Spanish manuscripts has yet been made. If tradition may be accepted, the oldest version belongs to the thirteenth century, having been made at the request of Alphonso of Castile and John of Leon; but there is no confirmation of this statement. It is a remarkable fact that the early Castilian versions of the Old Testament were made by Jews, and the basis was, naturally, the Hebrew text. Luis de Guzman, grand master of the Order of Calatrava, entrusted in 1422 to the learned rabbi Moses Arragel of Maqueda the work of translating and annotating the Scriptures, but with the help and under the supervision of the Franciscan Arias of Enzinas (Enciena) and others of the clergy. It accords with this that most of the manuscripts follow the order of the Hebrew canon.

Of printed texts the first in chronological order is the New Testament by Francis of Enzinas (Antwerp, 1543); next a Bible printed in two editions (Ferrara, 1553), one for Jews, the other for Christians (reprinted Amsterdam, 1611, 1630; revised ed., 1661). In 1556 Juan Perez published (ostensibly at Venice, really at Geneva) an edition of the New Testament, which follows the original Greek. In 1569 a Bible was published, probably at Basel, in the translation of Cassiodoro de Reina. Another edition with slight changes was published by Ricardo del Campo, 1596, and an entirely revised edition by Cipriano de Valera was published at Amsterdam, 1602. The oldest Jewish-Spanish printed translation of the Pentateuch is that of Constance, 1547. The Old Testament in Hebrew and Spanish was published by Solomon Proops at Amsterdam in 1762. It was not until the end of the eighteenth century that a Roman Catholic scholar undertook to give his Spanish countrymen a new translation, with the Latin text and a commentary. The author of this work (10 vols., Valencia, 1790–93; 20 vols., Madrid, 1794–97) was Felipe Scio de San Miguel, bishop of Segovia. It was often reprinted. A more recent translation, having respect to the original texts, was published by Felix Torres Amat, bishop of Astorga (9 vols., Madrid, 1824–29; 6 vols., 1832–35; reprinted, 17 vols., Paris, 1835). A corrected edition of Amat's version was published under the care of Señor Calderon, by the Society for the Promotion of Christian Knowledge in 1853. In 1893 the American Bible Society published a thoroughly revised edition of Valera's Bible, which may be regarded as practically a new version. The work was done by H. B. Pratt. A New Testament in the Catalan, translated by J. M. Pratt, was issued by the British and Foreign Bible Society. (S. Berger†.)

Bibliography: S. Berger, *Nouvelles recherches sur les bibles catalanes*, in *Romania*, xix, 1890; idem, *Les Bibles castillanes*, ib. xxviii, 1899 (contains bibliography and list of MSS.); J. M. de Egurén, *Memoria de los codices notables*, Madrid, 1859; J. Rodriguez de Castro, *Biblioteca española*, vol. i, ib. 1781; J. L. Villanueva, *De la leccion de la S. Escritura en lenguas vulgares*, Valenzia, 1791; *Bible of Every Land*, pp. 261–267, London, 1861; *The Governor of Madrid's Bible*, ib. 1871; J. E. B. Mayor, *Spain, Portugal, and the Bible*, ib. 1895; G. Borrow, *The Bible in Spain*, latest ed., ib. 1906; *KL*, ii, 743–744; *DB*, extra vol., pp. 408–410.

XVIII. Bible Versions in the Mission Field: Eusebius (*Theophania*, iii, 28) says that the writings of the Apostles were translated in the whole world, in all languages of Greeks and barbarians; and Chrysostom and Theodoret repeat the remark with still greater emphasis. Nevertheless from this early time till the rise of Pietism and the founding of missionary and Bible societies little was done by the official Church or Churches for the translation and circulation of the Bible. The first *Report* of the British and Foreign Bible Society has an account of what was then the most famous collection of Bibles (at Stuttgart) and estimates the number of languages represented there at forty-one. The Bibles presented to the Society in its first year were in forty-six languages, from Arabic and Armenian to Turkish and Welsh. The catalogue of Bibles of the British Museum includes ninety-seven languages. The hundredth *Report* of the British and Foreign Bible Society, in the "Historical Table of Languages and Dialects in which the Translation, Printing, or Distribution of the Scriptures has been at any time promoted by the Society" (pp. 434 sqq.), gives 378 languages; versions in twenty-four languages prepared by other societies have been removed from the list. [The total number of languages into which the Bible, or parts of it, has now been translated is about 500.] The best conspectus is afforded by T. H. Darlow and H. F. Moule, *Historical Catalogue of the Printed Editions of Holy Scripture in the Library of the British and Foreign Bible Society* (2 vols., London, 1903–08).

E. Nestle.

Bibliography: *The Bible of Every Land*, London, 1861; R. N. Cust, *Language as Illustrated by Bible Translations*, ib. 1886; idem, *Essays on the Languages of the Bible and Bible Translations*, ib. 1890; idem, *Three Lists of Bible Translations accomplished to Aug. 1, 1890*, ib. 1890; J. S. Dennis, *Centennial Survey of Foreign Missions*, New York, 1901; E. Wallroth, in *Allgemeine Missionszeitschrift*, xviii, 1901; T. Nicol, *The Bible and the Church and the Mission Field*, in *London Quarterly Review*, Jan., 1904. The *Reports* of the various Bible Societies furnish the sources.

BIBLES, ANNOTATED, AND BIBLE SUMMARIES.

[Under this title certain works are mentioned which give the text of the Bible with annotations aiming to promote its proper use and understanding. They are of the nature of commentaries, and a distinction is not to be sharply drawn. The annotated Bible, however, will always include the text, to which the helps are strictly subordinate; the commentary is published for the sake of the comments and frequently does not include the text.]

I. German: When the Reformation made the Bible the common property of the people, it was not only the source of their faith and piety, but the only literature, the whole intellectual world, of the uneducated classes. The more Luther's Bible was cherished as the compendium of religious and ethical truth and became the daily reading of the people, the more it needed explanatory notes. As early as 1531–33 Luther published his "Summaries of the Psalms," which were incorporated by Bugenhagen in his North Saxon Bible (Lübeck, 1534). In the High German Bible, "summaries and brief contents of all the chapters" are found first appended to the Augsburg edition of 1535. Real annotations appeared as parts of the book only after Luther's death, first as marginal notes or in smaller type under the text (the Wittenberg editions of Lufft, 1551, and Krafft, 1572, the latter containing the arguments and notes of Veit Dietrich, the Nuremberg preacher).

It would be a mistake to imagine that the Reformation early brought the Bible into every house. There were no small cheap editions, and the Thirty Years' War made the earlier ones still scarcer. Duke Ernest the Pious of Saxe-Weimar (d. 1675; see ERNEST I, THE PIOUS) brought about the publication of the famous Ernestine Bible, on which, after plans laid out by him, nearly thirty prominent theologians worked. Every community was to possess a copy; if they were poor, the duke provided it wholly or in part. The actual work of preparation began in 1636, and was completed in 1640. It contained, besides pictures and maps, and a running commentary, tables of weights, coins, etc., the topography of Jerusalem, and the creeds and Augsburg Confession. It was originally sold at six thalers, but the price gradually rose with later improvements and additional illustrations, until its general circulation was impeded. The Tübingen Bible (1730) is an adaptation of this, less firm in its dogmatic stand, by Christoph Matthäus Pfaff (q.v.), professor at Tübingen, and his brother-in-law, Johann Christian Klemm.

1. The Ernestine and Tübingen Bibles.

The same spirit that actuated Duke Ernest induced Eberhard III of Württemberg to publish the "Württemberg Summaries" in 1669, the first attempt to give a clear, precise, and connected paraphrase of the whole Scriptures. A revised and enlarged edition appeared at Leipsic in 1709, followed by others. The complete revision published in 1787 by Magnus Friedrich Roos, Karl Heinrich Rieger, and others of the school of Bengel was less clear, objective, and orthodox. Another Württemberg edition which deserves mention is the New Testament published in 1701 by the court preacher Johann Reinhard Hedinger (q.v.); it was marked by Pietistic deviations from traditional theology, and attracted attention by its sharp rebukes of the sins of the people at large and especially of the clergy.

2. Württemberg Bibles.

The new spirit of mystical Pietism which influenced the last-named work was fully revealed in the Marburg Bible (1712), as might be inferred from the main title, "Mystical and Prophetic Bible." The interpretation of type and prophecy in this follows the federal theology of Coccejus, that of Canticles and Revelation Madame Guyon. It was the forerunner of a larger work in the same spirit, the Berleburg Bible of 1726–42 (8 vols. folio), projected and prepared chiefly by Johann Heinrich Haug (q.v.). The text is a revision of Luther's, with comparison of the English and French versions; the commentary reflects the views of the Philadelphian communities, and quotes the mystical books current among them, especially Madame Guyon's, but its teaching goes back beyond Dippel and Petersen to Jakob Böhme, or even to Origen in some points. It lacks unity of belief and of treatment; it is the work not of a single mystic, giving voice to his inner convictions, but of a propagandist sect with practical tendencies. It is not without value, however, from different points of view; it edifies by its continual application of Scriptural words to the spiritual life, and it prepares the way for historical criticism by an appendix containing apocrypha (Old and New Testament), pseudepigrapha, and postapostolic writings. In the same year (1726) appeared the Ebersdorf Bible, in the preparation of which Zinzendorf shared. Its commentaries are altogether in his spirit, and it was received with favor only by the friends of the Herrnhut community.

3. The Marburg, Berleburg, and Ebersdorf Bibles.

When the emotional mysticism of the Pietists gave way to the prosaic, commonplace conceptions of the age of Enlightenment (q.v.), attempts were made to replace the older commentaries by works conceived in the new spirit. The Wertheim Bible (1735) aroused great excitement in its day, both in Church and State, though its interest now is purely historical. This was only the first part of a projected whole, and contained merely the Pentateuch. The gist of the long, involved preface is that the traditional ideas about the Scriptures rested on prejudice and unscientific conceptions, and that the attempt was now made to found an exposition of their real meaning on adequate grounds of reason and historical evidence. It proposes to give a free translation, adapted to modern comprehension, though faithful in substance, and supplemented by the necessary explanations. The translation is hopelessly bald and commonplace to our taste; the editor showed some originality, however, as for example in venturing to discard the traditional division of chapters and verses. The general philosophical principles, as well as the critical and historical, are those of Wolf; in spite of many blunders, a fair knowledge of Hebrew is displayed. The editor's name is not given, but it was soon known. He was Johann Lorenz Schmidt, a graduate of Jena, personally much respected, who was then tutor to the young Count von Löwenstein at Wertheim in Franconia. He was arrested at the beginning of 1737 and the book was confiscated by the imperial authorities. After a year's close imprisonment, he was allowed more liberty, and escaped to Holland. The literary war which raged around the Wertheim Bible was fierce and not uninteresting. In 1738 Schmidt published a collection of reviews and polemical pamphlets, with his own replies. His work found imitators; another of a similar nature, with modern deistic explanations, appeared in 1756, but had little success; and the excitement over the frankly rationalistic commentary of Nicolaus Funk (Altona,

4. The Wertheim Bible.

1815) was not wide-spread (cf. J. N. Sinnhold, *Ausführliche Historie der Wertheim Bibel*, Erfurt, 1739).

The eighteenth century was not destitute of attempts to carry on the old tradition in a spirit of orthodox edification. The first was that of Christoph Starke (New Testament, 3 vols., 1733 sqq.; Old Testament, 6 vols., 1741 sqq.), which gave Luther's text with extended comments from older expositors and ascetic writers, introductions to each book, and a summary of each chapter. Next came the Hirschberg Bible (1756–63), an excellent work which fell flat at the time and was rescued from oblivion only by a reprint in 1814 under the patronage of Frederick William IV The age was not favorable to the spread of Biblical study, and but a few readers were found for the commentary translated from English expositors by R. Teller, J. A. Dietelmayer, and Brucker (19 vols., 1749–70), or for the edition of Michaelis (1769–92).

5. Later Works.

But the revival of religious devotion ultimately made itself felt in this field. Friedrich von Meyer's revised translation with short, pointed comments and uncritical introductions appeared in 1819. More widely read were Richter's (1834–40) and Lisco's (1833–43). A more learned and thorough work was that of Otto von Gerlach in 6 vols., which is still popular in North Germany, as is the *Calwer Handbuch der Bibelerklärung* (1849) in the South. Other more recent editions which may be mentioned here are those of Bunsen (9 vols., 1858–70), Christian Müller (*Collegium Biblicum*, 6 vols., 1879–84), Johann Peter Lange (36 vols., 1856–77), K. A. Dächsel (illustrated, 7 vols., 1865–80), and R. J. Grau (2 vols., 1877–80). [J. F. Allioli's annotated Bible (6 vols., Nuremberg, 1830–34) has been very popular among Roman Catholics.]

(H. Hölscher.)

II. English: As a rule, Bible societies publish the Scriptures "without note or comment"—a wise plan, for it secures the widest circulation of the Word of God. In early times, however, when a person bought a Bible, he found between the covers not only the Old and the New Testaments, but a commentary in the notes attached, a concordance at the end, and a small dictionary in the introduction and tables. These special editions had their day, and fell into disuse, for very evident reasons. The numerous comments made the volume too bulky for convenience and general use; the notes were likely to be one-sided and subjective, so that a man's theology might be judged by his Bible, from its being supplied with comments by Doddridge, or those of D'Oyly and Mant; however acceptable the annotations might be for a time, eventually they were superseded by later scholarship. Moreover, in the last half-century commentaries, Bible dictionaries, and concordances have grown into great volumes, and constitute a distinct class of literature. They have found their true places apart from the inspired words of the Bible.

Annotated Bibles date back to the time of the Reformation. Matthew's Bible (1537) had annotations, and John Rogers, who was the real translator of this Bible, showed by his notes, especially on the subjects of faith, holy life, and repentance, that he was in full touch with the most advanced Protestantism. The Geneva Bible (1560) attained its great popularity and fame by its prologues and marginal notes. These annotations are so numerous and miscellaneous that it is not easy to give in a brief statement a fair representation of their general tenor. Many are strongly antipapal, and for that reason they were especially acceptable to overzealous Reformers. As might be expected, the Geneva notes are also Calvinistic. When the Geneva Bible was first published, Calvin was the ruling spirit in Geneva. All the features of his theological, ecclesiastical, political, and social system are accordingly reflected in the marginal annotations of the English Bible that issued from the city of his residence. The political doctrine of the book was as much disliked by kings of the absolute order, as were the ecclesiastical notes by infallible popes, and one of the reasons that led King James, in 1604, to agree readily to a new translation of the Scriptures, was his dislike of the politics preached on the margins of the Geneva Bible.

1. Matthew's and the Geneva Bible.

The marginal notes in the Bishops' Bible (1568) are not very numerous, and they are generally not interesting. They were designed mostly for readers of weak capacity. A few, which are valuable and entertaining, are taken verbatim, without acknowledgment, from the Geneva Bible. Some of them, too, remind of Geneva caps and predestination in a way that would scarcely be expected in a Bible issued by a body of prelates. The distribution of notes in the Bishops' Bible is very irregular and unequal. In some books hard to understand, such as the prophecies of Isaiah and Jeremiah, the notes are very sparse, so that five or six consecutive pages may be found here and there without a single annotation; while in other books, such as Genesis, Exodus, Job, and the Epistles of St. Paul, the notes are very frequent.

2. The Bishops' Bible.

In the original edition of the Authorized Version (1611), the number of marginal references to corresponding passages, including those in the Apocrypha, was about 9,000. Large as this number seems, it is but a small fraction of what the references now amount to in some well-edited Bibles. These references, doubtless, have their value, but it can not be denied that many of them obscure the meaning of the statements to which they are attached. It is different, however, with what are called the marginal notes. In the original edition (1611) these notes were nearly as numerous as the marginal references. In the Old Testament there were 6,588 references and 6,637 notes; in the New Testament 1,517 references and 765 notes; in the Apocrypha 885 references and 1,017 notes. These notes are brief and non-polemical, differing in these respects very markedly from the annotations in both Matthew's and the Geneva Bible. They indicate, for the most part, alternative or more literal renderings. In some

3. The Authorized Version.

cases they specify variant readings in the original text, and, in other cases, they give brief explanations of words or expressions. Not a few of the alternative renderings they present have been adopted, either verbatim or substantially, in the revised version of 1881–85. The headings of chapters in the translation of 1611 were new. In the Bishops' Bible, the Geneva Bible, and the Great Bible, all the chapters were headed with a short table of contents; but the King James translators prepared tables of their own. And these tables, drawn up in 1611, appear in many editions at the present day unaltered, save in some twelve instances.

Other Bibles with notes from the pen of annotators appeared and in course of time became very popular. These annotators did not write so much for the learned as for the common people, and their Bibles became household and family books, laying stress more or less on the devotional side.

4. John Canne's Notes, 1647.

John Canne, a Baptist minister (d. 1667?), was the author of three sets of notes which accompanied three editions of the Bible. His great ambition was "to make the Bible its own interpreter." His first authenticated version appeared in 1647 at Amsterdam, under the title, *The Bible, with Marginal Notes, Shewing Scripture to be the Best Interpreter of Scripture.* The work was often reprinted (9 editions, between 1662 and 1754). Orme, in his *Bibliotheca Biblica* (Edinburgh, 1824), says of it, "The marginal references of Canne are generally very judicious and apposite. They still retain a considerable reputation, though most of the latter editions which pass under the name of Canne's Bible are full of errors, and crowded with references which do not belong to the original author."

In 1657 there was published *Annotations upon All the Books of the Old and New Testament. Wherein the text is explained, doubts resolved, Scriptures paralleled, and various readings observed by the labor of certain learned divines thereunto appointed and therein employed, as is expressed in the preface,* 2 vols., London, 1657. This work is usually called the "Assembly's Annotations," from the circumstance of its having been composed by members of the Westminster Assembly.

5. Other Works to 1701.

—Another popular work of the same character was *Annotations upon the Holy Bible wherein the sacred text is inserted, and various readings annexed; together with the parallel Scriptures. The more difficult terms explained; seeming contradictions reconciled; doubts resolved, and the whole text opened. By the Rev. Matthew Poole,* London, 1863, 2 vols., fo. The work was published in many editions. Poole, an eminent non-conformist divine (1624–79), did not finish it; but it was completed after his death.—Not less popular was a work entitled, *The Old and New Testament, with Annotations and parallel Scriptures. By Samuel Clarke, A.M.,* London, 1690. Bishop Lloyd's Bible (London, 1701) was the first to incorporate Archbishop Ussher's chronology.

In 1708 appeared the first volume of Matthew Henry's well-known *Exposition of the Old and New Testament;* four other volumes (to the end of the Gospels) were published in 1710, and a sixth volume (the Book of Acts) from Henry's manuscript after his death (1714); the work was completed by various non-conformist clergymen (see HENRY, MATTHEW).

6. Matthew Henry. Other Works to 1750.

It long enjoyed a high and deserved reputation, and is distinguished, not for depth of learning or originality of views, but for sound practical piety, and the large measure of good sense which it discovers.—Dr. Edward Wells edited between the years 1709 and 1728, *An Help for the more Easy and Clear Understanding of the Holy Scriptures, after the following method: 1. The common English translation rendered more agreeable to the original. 2. A paraphrase wherein the text is explained, and divided into proper sections, and lesser divisions. 3. Annotations. 4. Preface,* 8 vols.—Patrick, Lowth, Whitby, and Arnold's *Commentary on the Bible,* a work of a similar character, appeared in London, 1727–60, 7 vols., and was reprinted as late as 1821. According to Orme, Patrick was "the most sensible and useful commentator on the Old Testament. He had a competent measure of learning for the undertaking, of which he never makes any ostentatious display. The elder Lowth completed the work on the Old Testament, and Whitby commentated on the New Testament. Neither Patrick nor Lowth has so much Arminianism as Whitby, though they all belong to the same theological school. Whitby was superior to both in acuteness and research, but if the reader do not find in them the same talent, he will be exposed to less injury from specious and sophistical reasonings against some important doctrines of Christianity."—John Gill published *An Exposition of the Old and New Testaments, in which the sense of the sacred text is given; doctrinal and practical truths are set in a plain and easy light; difficult passages explained; seeming contradictions reconciled; and whatever is material in the various readings, and the several Oriental versions, is observed. The whole illustrated by notes from the most antient Jewish writings. By John Gill, D.D.,* 9 vols. fo., London, 1748–63; 9 vols. 4to, London, 1809. Gill gives a summary of each chapter. Orme says of him, "Had Dr. Gill fulfilled the promise of his title page, no other commentary on the Bible could have been required. But he moves through his exposition like a man in lead, and overwhelms the inspired writers with dull lucubrations and rabbinical lumber. He is an ultra-Calvinist in his doctrinal sentiments; and often spiritualizes the text to absurdity. If the reader be inclined for a trial of his strength and patience, he may procure the burden of Dr. Gill. He was, after all, a man of undoubted learning, and of prodigious labour."—A very popular work was an English translation of Jean Frédéric Osterwald's *Argumens et réflexions sur l'écriture sainte* (Neuchâtel, 1709–15 and often; see OSTERWALD, JEAN FRÉDÉRIC), which appeared under the title, *The Arguments of the Books and Chapters of the Old and New Testaments, with practical observations. Translated by John Chamberlayne,*

Esq., London, 1749, 3 vols.; fifth edition, enlarged, 2 vols., London, 1779.

Chamberlayne's work was followed by *A New and Literal Translation of all the Books of the Old and New Testaments, with Notes critical and explanatory. By Anthony Purver* (2 vols., London, 1761). Purver was a Quaker and originally a shoemaker. He taught himself Hebrew, Greek, and Latin, in order that he might understand the Bible. His work is often ungrammatical, and unintelligible; the notes are very similar to the text and, what is worse, full of pride and ill-nature.

7. Various Works After 1750.

Notwithstanding these defects, Purver sometimes gives a better rendering than occurs in the Authorized Version. —One year later appeared *The Evangelical Expositor; or a Commentary on the Holy Bible, wherein the Sacred Text is inserted at large, the sense explained, and different passages elucidated, with practical observations, etc. By T. Haweis, LL.B., M.D.*, London, 1765, 2 vols.; Glasgow, 3 vols. 4to, and various editions. Haweis (d. 1820) was rector of Aldwinkle, Northamptonshire; his work had little value.—Next to be mentioned is *The Complete Family Bible: or a Spiritual Exposition of the Old and New Testament; wherein each chapter is summed up in its context, and the sacred text inserted at large, with Notes, spiritual, practical, and explanatory. By the Rev. Mr. Cruden*, London, 1770, 2 vols.—In the same year appeared a similar work under the title, *A Commentary on the Books of Old and New Testaments, in which are inserted the Notes and Collections of John Locke, Esq., Daniel Waterland, D.D., and the Right Hon. Edward, Earl of Clarendon, and other learned persons, with practical improvements. By W Dodd, LL.D.*, London, 1770, 3 vols. This is mostly a compilation, the chief value of which consists in notes furnished from the original papers of John Locke, Dr. Waterland, Lord Clarendon, Gilbert West, and some others. Great use is also made of some of the printed and long-established commentaries on Scripture, such as Calmet, Houbigant, and Doddridge. Adam Clarke said, rather hyperbolically, that it was on the whole by far the best comment that had yet appeared in the English language.—The next work to be mentioned is *The Self-Interpreting Bible, containing the Old and the New Testaments, to which are annexed an introduction, marginal references and illustrations explanatory notes etc., etc. By the late Rev. John Brown, Minister of the Gospel at Haddington*, London, 1778, 2 vols. It was repeatedly reprinted, and proved almost as popular south as north of the Tweed.—Henry Southwell published a *Bible, Authorized Version; with notes etc.; wherein the mis-translations are corrected*, London, 1782.—Another work of a similar character is *The Holy Bible, containing the Books of the Old and New Testaments, carefully printed from the first edition (compared with others) of the present translation; with notes by Thomas Wilson, D.D., Bishop of Sodor and Man, and various renderings, collected from other translations, by the Rev. Clement Crutwell, editor*, London, 1785, 8 vols. Bishop Wilson's notes are merely brief hints either for the explanation or the practical improvement of particular passages. Dr. Thomas Paris, in the Cambridge Bible of 1762, and Dr. B. Blayney, in the Oxford Bible of 1769, added considerably to the number of marginal notes and references.

8. Thomas Scott and Others to 1810.

But far more popular than any of the works already mentioned was the Bible with commentary edited by Rev. Thomas Scott (q.v.). It had the largest circulation and sustained it through many years. It appeared under the title, *The Holy Bible, containing the Old and New Testaments; with original notes, practical observations, and copious marginal references. By Thomas Scott, Rector of Aston Sandford* (London, 1788, and often). As a commentary Dr. Scott's work was superior to any that had appeared before its time. Horne, usually a discriminating judge, speaks of it in high praise (cf. his *Manual of Biblical Bibliography*, London, 1839, p. 259).—In 1799 appeared *A Revised Translation and Interpretation of the Sacred Scriptures, after the Eastern manner, from concurrent authorities of critics, interpreters, and commentators' copies and versions; shewing that the inspired writings contain the seeds of the valuable sciences, being the source whence the antient philosophers derived them, also the most antient histories and greatest antiquities, and are the most entertaining as well as instructing to both the curious and serious* (by David Macrae, or J. M. Ray, J. McRay, or D. McRae; Glasgow, 1799; 2d ed., 1815; 4to, also in 3 vols. 8vo.). The author introduced many approved renderings, but marred the simplicity and dignity of the Authorized Version.—Another noteworthy annotated Bible is that of John Reeves, which appeared in ten volumes in London, 1802. The explanatory notes are based on Wells's *Paraphrase*, and the commentaries of Patrick, Lowth, Whitby, and others. A similar work was the so-called "Reformers' Bible," *The Holy Bible, containing the Old and New Testaments, according to the Authorized Version, with short Notes by several learned and pious Reformers, as printed by Royal Authority at the time of the Reformation, with additional Notes and Dissertations*, London, 1810. The notes in the Old Testament in this edition are taken from the Geneva Bible, the annotations of the New Testament from the Latin of Theodore Beza.

Also in 1810 there began to be published *The Holy Bible, containing the Old and New Testaments: the Text carefully printed from the most correct copies of the present authorized translation, including the marginal readings and parallel texts: with a Commentary, and Critical Notes, designed as a help to a better understanding of the Sacred Writings. By Adam Clarke, LL.D., F.A.S.*, London, 1810–26.

9. Adam Clarke, D'Oyly and Mant, and Bellamy, 1810–34.

The author, a Wesleyan minister (see Clarke, Adam), attained a high reputation as a student of Oriental languages. The scope of the commentary is expressed in its own words: "In this work the whole of the text has been collated with the Hebrew and Greek originals, and all the ancient versions; the most difficult words analyzed and explained; the most important readings in the Hebrew collections of Kennicott and De Rossi on the Old Testament, and in those of Mill, Wetstein, and Griesbach on the New, are noticed; the date of every transaction, as far as it has been ascertained by the best chronologers, is marked; the peculiar customs of the Jews and neighboring nations, so frequently alluded to by the prophets, evangelists, and apostles, are explained from the best Asiatic authorities; the great doctrines of the Law and Gospel of God are defined, illustrated, and defended; and the whole is applied to the important purposes of practical Christianity." A considerable popularity was achieved also by D'Oyly and Mant's commentary, *The Holy Bible according to the Authorized Version, with Notes explanatory and practical, taken principally from the most eminent writers of the United Church of England and Ireland; together with appropriate introductions, tables, indexes, maps, and plans, prepared and arranged by the Rev. G. D'Oyly, B.D., and Rev. Richard Mant, D.D.*, Oxford and London, 1814, 3 vols., and various subsequent editions printed at Cambridge and Oxford. "This work, which was published under the sanction of the venerable Society for Promoting Christian Knowledge, professes to communicate only the results of the critical inquiries of learned men, without giving a detailed exposition of the inquiries themselves. These *results*, however, are selected with great judgment, so that the reader who may consult them on difficult passages will rarely be disappointed. Of the labour attending this publication some idea may be formed, when it is stated that the works of upward of one hundred and sixty authors have been consulted for it, amounting to several hundred volumes. On the fundamental articles of Christian verity—the Deity and atonement of Jesus Christ, and the personality and offices of the Holy Spirit—this work may be pronounced to be a library of divinity" (Horne, ut sup., pp. 261–262).—A work of a similar character was *The Holy Bible, newly translated from the original Hebrew, with Notes critical and explanatory. By John Bellamy*, London, 1818–34. Orme considers it a strange hodgepodge of error, confidence, misrepresentation, and abuse of learned and valuable writers in all the departments of Biblical literature.

Rev. B. Boothroyd edited *A New Family Bible, and Improved Version, from corrected Texts of the Originals, with Notes critical and explanatory; and short Practical Reflections on each Chapter*, Pontefract and London, 1818–23, 3 vols. The author has very happily blended critical disquisition with practical instruction, and an invariable regard to the spirit and design of revelation.—In 1821 there appeared *The Plain Reader's Help in the Study of the Holy Scriptures; consisting of Notes, explanatory and illustrative, chiefly selected or abridged from the Family Bible, published by the Society for Promoting Christian Knowledge. By the Rev. William Thomas Bree, M.A.*, Coventry, 1821–22. The aim was to supply brief and untechnical notes at a moderate price for readers who could not procure or consult larger works.—

10. Other Works 1818-38.

In 1824 appeared *The Holy Bible, arranged and adapted for family reading, with notes, etc. by a Layman of the Church of England* (2 vols., London).—Another popular Bible was the so-called *Cottage Bible and Family Expositor; containing the Authorized Translation of the Old and New Testaments, with Practical Reflections and short Explanatory Notes, calculated to elucidate difficult and obscure Passages. By Thomas Williams*, London, 1825–27, 3 vols., and various subsequent editions. This unassuming but cheap and useful commentary on the Holy Scriptures was professedly designed for persons and families in the humbler walks of life.—There is also to be mentioned *The Comprehensive Bible; containing the Old and New Testaments, according to the Authorized Version, with the various readings and marginal notes usually printed therewith; a general introduction, containing disquisitions on the genuineness, authenticity, and inspiration of the Holy Scriptures,—various divisions and marks of distinction in the sacred Writings,—antient versions,—coins, weights, and measures,—various sects among the Jews; introductions and concluding remarks to each book; the parallel passages contained in the Rev. J. Scott's Commentary, Canne's Bible, Rev. J Brown's Self-Interpreting Bible, Dr. A. Clarke's Commentary, and the English Version of the Polyglott Bible systematically arranged; philological and explanatory notes. With chronological and other indexes* (by William Greenfield, London, 1827).—In 1828 there was published *The Holy Bible principally designed to facilitate the audible or social reading of the Sacred Scriptures; illustrated with notes, historical, geographical, and otherwise explanatory, and also pointing out the fulfilment of various prophecies. By William Alexander*—vol. i—the Pentateuch—York, 1828; two other volumes were planned but did not appear). This Bible owed its origin to efforts of members of the Society of Friends. Passages "unsuitable for a mixed audience" were printed in italics below the text.—C. Girdlestone edited *The Old and New Testament, with a commentary, consisting of short lectures for the daily use of families*, London, 1835–42.—Another Bible of the same style was the *Treasury Bible. First division: containing the authorized English Version of the Holy Scriptures, as printed in Bagster's Polyglott Bible, with the same copious and original selection of references to parallel and illustrative passages, and similarly printed in a centre column. Second division: containing the Treasury of Scripture Knowledge, consisting of a rich and copious assemblage of upwards of five hundred thousand parallel texts, from Canne, Brown, Blayney, Scott, and others, with numerous illustrative notes*, London, 1835.—In 1837 there was published *The Condensed Commentary and Family Exposition of the Holy Bible: containing the best criticisms of the most valuable Biblical Writers, with practical reflections and marginal references; chronology, indexes, etc., etc. By the Rev. Ingram Cobbin, M.A.*, London, 1837. This work is literally a condensed commentary, derived from the best accessible sources. The notes are brief, but well chosen, and are partly critical and explanatory, partly practical. They are taken from nearly two hundred writers, British and foreign.—Another annotated Bible was edited by the Rev. C. Wellbeloved, *The Holy Bible, a New Translation, with introductory remarks, notes explanatory and critical, and practical reflections*, 2 vols., London, 1838. It is Unitarian and designed principally for the use of families.

The standard English version of the Roman Catholics (the "Douai" Bible; see Bible Versions, B, IV, § 5), was provided with notes setting forth and defending the Roman standpoint. The later annotated English Bibles of the Catholics are based chiefly upon these notes. Richard Challoner (q.v.) and George Leo Haydock (*The Holy Bible*, 2 vols., Manchester, 1811–14; revised Reims and Douai text with extensive notes) are well-known Roman Catholic annotators. Most of the "minor versions" enumerated in § 8 of the article on English versions (Bible Versions, B, IV) are annotated.

11. Republication in America. The popular works of England were reissued in America. The first American edition of Scott's commentary was printed and published by W Woodward of Philadelphia in 1804 in 4 vols. Other issues followed by different publishers, most of them from the press of Woodward of Philadelphia, and that of Samuel T. Armstrong of Boston. The most popular form of the book was an octavo of six volumes. Scott's Bible had a continuous sale for more than forty years, and as late as 1844 W E. Dean, 2 Ann Street, New York, published an edition in three volumes.—Adam Clarke's commentary was published by Ezra Sargeant, 86 Broadway, New York, in 1811.—Osterwald's *Observations* appeared in 1813 with this imprint: "New York: Published by Evert Duyckinck, John Tiebout, G. & R. Waite, and Websters & Skinners of Albany. George Long, Printer."—The first American edition of Matthew Henry's *Exposition* appeared in Philadelphia in 1816, published by Towar and Hogan in six volumes. They also issued a stereotyped edition in three volumes in 1829. Burder and Hughes of the same city issued a six volume edition in 1828, with preface by Archibald Alexander.—D'Oyly and Mant's Bible with commentary was reprinted in New York in 1818–20 by T. and J. Swords, 160 Pearl Street. This edition has additional notes from the pen of the Rt. Rev. John H. Hobart, D.D., bishop of New York, who quotes from a large number of Biblical scholars, mainly in the Anglican, Scottish, and American Episcopal Churches, who had not been noticed by the English editors.—Thomas Williams's *Cottage Bible*, reedited by the Rev. William Patton, was printed in two octavo volumes by Conner & Cooke, New York, in 1833. It contains numerous engravings and several maps, and was intended chiefly for the use of Sunday-schools and Bible-classes. The plates were sold by the New York printers, and in after-years the editions were issued at Hartford, Conn.—Greenfield's *Comprehensive Bible* was issued in 1839 with the imprint of "Robinson & Franklin, successors to Leavitt, Lord & Co., 180 Broadway." The book is a thick quarto of 1,460 pages. The American issue was also published by Lippincott, Grambo & Co., Philadelphia, in 1854, and by J. B. Lippincott & Co. in 1857 Canne's marginal notes and references appeared in many editions of American household and family Bibles, and John Brown's *Self-Interpreting Bible* was frequently reproduced. The American Tract Society early published a family Bible with brief notes and instructions and many editions were printed. Eugene Cummiskey, of Philadelphia, published various editions for Roman Catholics, such as *The Holy Bible, translated from the Latin Vulgate, with annotations, references, etc.* Isaiah Thomas, the famous author of the *History of Printing in America*, published and sold the Authorized Version with notes at his press in Worcester Mass.; various editions appeared after 1791.

12. Original American Works. One of the earliest productions of the Philadelphia press was *The Christian's New and Complete Family Bible*, published by William Woodhouse in 1790. It was issued in numbers, and the Rev. Paul Wright, D.D., vicar of Oakley, is supposed to have been the editor.—*The Columbian Family and Pulpit Bible* bears the imprint, "Boston: Published by Joseph Teal, printed by J. H. A. Frost, opposite U. S. Bank, Congress Street, 1822." It claims to be a "corrected and improved American edition of the Popular English Family Bible," supplied "with concise notes and annotations, theological, historical, chronological, critical, practical, moral, and explanatory"; also containing "sundry important received various readings from the most ancient Hebrew and Greek manuscripts and the most celebrated versions of Scripture. Also, sundry corrections and improvements of our excellent English version (generally admitted by learned Christians of every name) with references to authors, versions, and manuscripts; also, an illustrative argument prefixed to each sacred book or epistle, from the best authorities." The volume is a folio, embellished with thirty-six engravings. The book was issued in numbers and had more than three thousand subscribers. The Rev. Jonathan Homer, D.D., of Newton, Mass., revised the observations, and condensed some of the notes and enlarged others.—In 1826 *The Collateral Bible* made its appearance with the following imprint: "Philadelphia: Printed by Samuel F Bradford, and by E. Bliss and E. White, New York. J. Harding, Printer, 1826." This book was edited by William McCorkle, assisted by the Rev. Ezra Stiles Ely, D.D., a Presbyterian minister, and the Rev. Gregory T. Bedell, A.M., rector of St. Andrew's Church, Philadelphia. "In this work the best marginal references are printed at large, and in connection with every passage, by which means every parallel or related phrase in the sacred volume is brought at once under the eye, so as to present the whole scope and subject of every text at a single view" (Horne, *Biblical Bibliography*, p. 86). The three volumes comprised only the Old Testament, and the New Testament part was never attempted.—*The Devotional Family Bible* was edited by the Rev. Alexander Fletcher, D.D., "with practical and experimental reflections on each verse of the Old and New Testaments, and rich marginal references." An edition in quarto with fifty-seven illustrations was published with this imprint: "London and New York: Virtue, Emmins and Company." The title-page has no date, though O'Callaghan assigns the publication to the year 1835.

13. Later Works, English and American.

Of more modern works of a similar character the following may be mentioned: the Lange commentary, translated and edited, with additions, by Philip Schaff and others (25 vols., New York, 1866–88); the work commonly known as the "Speaker's Commentary" (because suggested by the Right Hon. J. Evelyn Denison, speaker of the House of Commons), ed. F. C. Cook (10 vols., London, 1871–81); the *Cambridge Bible for Schools and Colleges*, ed. J. J. S. Perowne (48 vols., Cambridge, 1877 sqq.); Bishop Ellicott's *Commentary for English Readers* (8 vols., London, 1877–84); J. H. Blunt's *Annotated Bible a Household Commentary on the Holy Scriptures* (3 vols., London, 1878); Clark's *Handbooks for Bible Classes*, ed. M. Dods and A. Whyte (47 vols., Edinburgh, 1879 sqq.); the *American Commentary* (Baptist; N. T. complete, ed. Alvah Hovey, 7 vols., O. T., 4 vols.—Lev. and Num., Job, Eccles., Prov. and Song of Songs—published at present, 1881 sqq.); the *International Illustrated Commentary on the New Testament*, ed. Philip Schaff (4 vols., New York, 1889); J. G. Butler, *Bible Work* (11 vols., 1892); the *New Century Bible*, ed. W. F. Adeney (N. T. complete, 13 vols.; O. T., 10 vols. issued, London, 1901 sqq.); and the *Temple Bible* (31 vols., London, 1901–03; especially useful for reading because the text is paragraphed according to the sense, and chapter and verse divisions are relegated to the margin). The so-called "Teachers' Bibles," of which many were published during the last quarter of the nineteenth century, may also be mentioned.

BIBLIOGRAPHY: G. W. Panzer, *Geschichte der deutschen Bibelübersetzung Dr. M. Luthers von 1517–81*, Nuremberg, 1791; J. A. Göz, *Ueberblick über Luthers Dolmetschung der heiligen Schrift und die . . , seiner Zeitgenossen*, Nuremberg, 1824; W. Orme, *Bibliotheca Biblica*, Edinburgh, 1824; F. H. Horne, *Manual of Biblical Bibliography*, London, 1839; M. Göbel, *Geschichte des christlichen Lebens in der rhein-westfälischen evangelischen Kirche*, vols. ii, iii, Coblenz, 1852–60; A. Beck, *Ernst der Fromme*, 2 vols., Weimar, 1865; A. Ritschl, *Geschichte des Pietismus*, vols. i, ii, Bonn, 1880–84; W. Böhne, *Die pädagogischen Bestrebungen Herzog Ernst . von Gotha*, Gotha, 1888; G. Frank, *Die Wertheimer Bibelübersetzung vor dem Reichshofrat in Wien*, in *ZKG*, xii (1891), 2.

BIBLES FOR CHILDREN: Various attempts have been made to present the Bible in the form of a "child's book." The selection of parts best adapted to immature minds and the omission of the unsuitable, with simplification of language, are the chief aims in such attempts. Illustrations, coarse print, and other typographical devices are naturally used freely. Such books spring from the conviction that the Bible contains spiritual truth for all and is the greatest instrument for awakening religious feeling and quickening moral perception, but that its usefulness for these ends is necessarily conditioned upon the form of presentation and that the latter may well be varied for different classes of readers. The following list mentions some noteworthy books of this sort in English, but makes no claim to completeness.

An Abridgement of the Holy Scriptures. By the Rev. Mr. Sellon, late Minister of St. James's, Clerkenwell, published in 1781 and many later eds., at Hartford by Hale and Hosmer, 1813.

The Bible for Children. Arranged from the King James Version. With a Preface by the Rev. Francis Brown, D.D., and an Introduction by the Right Rev. Henry C. Potter, D.D. [compiled by Mrs. Joseph B. Gilder], New York [1902].

The Bible Story Re-told for Young People; the Old Testament Story by W. H. Bennett; the New Testament Story by W. F. Adeney, London, 1897.

The Bible for Young People, translated from the Dutch of H. Oort and I. Hooykas by P. H. Wicksteed, 6 vols., London, 1873–79; 2d ed., 1882.

The Children's Bible, or an History of the Holy Scriptures, to which is added a new manual of devotions for children; by a divine of the Church of England. London, 1759.

The Child's Bible. With plates. By a Lady of Cincinnati, Philadelphia, Henry F. Anners, 1834.

A Compendium of the Religious Doctrines, Religious and Moral Precepts, Historical and Descriptive Beauties of the Bible; with a Separate Moral Selection from the Apocrypha; being a Transcript of the received Text: Intended for the use of Families, but more particularly as a Reading Book for Schools. By Rodolphus Dickinson, Esq., Greenfield, Mass., Horace Graves, Printer, 1814.

A curious Hieroglyphick Bible, or Select Passages in the Old and New Testaments, represented with emblematical figures, for the amusement of youth; designed chiefly to familiarize tender age, in a pleasing and diverting manner, with early ideas of the Holy Scriptures—a very popular work which appeared in many editions (12th ed., London, 1792; Worcester, Mass., Isaiah Thomas, 1788; Dublin, 1789; etc.). It is a child's book, containing short passages of Scripture in which some of the words are represented by small cuts.

The Holy Bible abridged: or the History of the Old and New Testament. Illustrated with Notes, and adorned with cuts. For the Use of Children. To which is added, A Compleat Abstract of the Old and New Testament, with the Apocrypha, in Easy Verse, New York, Hodge, Allen, and Campbell, 1790.

The School and Children's Bible; prepared under the superintendence of the Rev. William Rogers, . London, 1873. It presents the Bible in a shortened form, "adapted for the use of children, and rearranges the matter."

The Bible for Young People, New York, 1902, n. e., 1906.

Scripture Lessons for schools on the British system of mutual instruction. Adopted in Russia by order of the Emperor Alexander I., London, 1820. According to the preface, these selections were originally made in Russian at St. Petersburg in 1818–19, and adopted in Russian schools at the instance of Prince Alexander Galitzin, minister of instruction. The Committee of the British and Foreign School Society then determined to issue them in the chief languages of Europe. The extracts are divided into: (*1*) Historical Lessons from the Old Testament; (2) Lessons on Duty toward God and Man; (3) Lessons from the Evangelists and the Acts.

BIBLES, HISTORICAL (STORY-BIBLES): The usual term applied to a compilation of Holy Scripture which, confining itself chiefly to the historical portions, adapts them to educational purposes. This may be done either by a faithful repetition of the Biblical narratives or by thorough-going changes in the selection of the material, by the representation of facts, and by devotional application. In this article the term is confined to certain medieval works which, written in the language of the people and in popular style, constituted in their time the chief literary media for disseminating the knowledge of Bible history.

It is an interesting fact that the historico-devotional mode of considering the Bible received attention only when the people themselves began their spiritual and religious emancipation. As soon as the vernacular was allowed to become the language of religious instruction, among the Anglo-Saxons and in Germany at the time of Charlemagne,

The Earliest Story-Bibles.

literary phenomena appear which at least to a certain extent fall under the conception of Story-Bibles. It is said that the poetical productions of Cædmon (q.v.) in their original form treated the whole Bible history to the day of judgment; in the *Krist* of Otfrid of Weissenburg (q.v.) and in the Low Saxon *Heliand* (q.v.) not only was sacred history given in poetical form, but in picturesqueness and minuteness of details it appealed directly to the spirit of the people. Several other Story-Bibles in poetical form were subsequently composed, especially in Germany; among them the work of Rudolf of Ems (q.v.) seems to have become most popular. In the Biblical literature of Holland may be mentioned the "Riming Bible" of Jacob of Maerlant. Much older are the poetical compilations of Biblical history in the French language, especially that of Herman of Valenciennes and the popular *Roman de S. Fanuel* which piquantly interweaves evangelical history with apocryphal and miraculous stories. Compilations in prose were also written; it may be said, however, that the strictly literal method of translation made slow progress and fully asserted itself only at the time of the Reformation. It is strange that the history of the Old Testament was treated more frequently than that of the New Testament; probably, being the older and more unknown record, it was better adapted for a free compilation.

The space devoted to Genesis was large in proportion to that given to the other books of the Old Testament. At times an attempt was made to insert in chronological order the few facts known of secular history. As to the sources, many legendary elements from older times may have been incorporated from popular tradition.

Their Character and Sources.

But most of these works presuppose a written source. The material, so far as it can not be traced immediately to the Vulgate, may easily be found in the popular collection of glosses of Walafrid Strabo or in the historical works of Vincent of Beauvais, of Gottfrid of Viterbo, and others. Moreover, later Story-Bibles used earlier works of the same nature. Thus the *Historia scholastica* of Peter Comestor (q.v.) was the source of several German and French works. Similarly, poetical works became the sources of works in prose. A popular Story-Bible of Germany may be traced to the poetical production of Rudolf of Ems, and French literature possesses prose compilations of older riming Bibles; even in the *Quatre Livres des rois* of the twelfth century there are found occasional rimes or even larger passages in verse, all of which clearly show that the original form of the Biblical story in popular literature was poetic. It was only gradually that higher theological education found its way back to the Bible text in its proper form.

In Spain originated the *Historia general*, under the influence of King Alfonso the Wise (1252–84). He entrusted to certain scholars the task of writing a great collective work on the basis of the *Historia scholastica* of Peter Comestor, in which the whole history of the world should be represented in the framework of the Biblical stories with the addition of extensive portions from secular history.

There is a distinction between the French expressions *bibles historiées* and *bibles historiales*. *Histoire* in Old French means "picture," because to people of no education history in the form of pictures was most easily available. Hence *bible historiée* means "illustrated Bible" (see Bibles, Illustrated), while *bible historiale* denotes "Story-Bible." *Bibles historiales* are, then, the works treated above. Of this sort was the translation of the *Historia scholastica* of Peter Comestor into the dialect of Picard by Guyard des Moulins, canon of Aire in Artois (1295), a work which, in connection with a literal translation of the Bible dating from the thirteenth century, formed for hundreds of years one of the most popular Story-Bibles (see Bible Versions, B, VI, § 2).

It was reserved for the Reformation to place in the hands of Christian people the whole Bible according to the original texts, without glosses and additions, and thus with the beginning of that period the Story-Bible had fulfilled its mission.

(S. Berger†.)

Bibliography: M. Güdemann, *Haggadah und Midrasch-Haggadah*, Berlin, 1884; D. H. Müller and J. v. Schlosser, *Die Haggadah von Sarajevo*, Vienna, 1898; T. Mersdorf, *Bibliothekarische Unterhaltungen*, Oldenberg, 1850; E. Reuss, *Die deutsche Historienbibel*, Jena, 1855; idem, *Geschichte der heiligen Schriften des N. T.*, §§ 463–464, Brunswick, 1887; *Les Quatre Livres des rois*, ed. Le R. de Lincy, Paris, 1841; E. Reuss, in *Revue de théologie et philosophie*, xvi (1857), 1 sqq.; H. Palm, *Eine mittelhochdeutsche Historienbibel*, Breslau, 1867; J. Bonnard, *Les Traductions de la Bible en vers français*, Paris, 1884; *Le Roman de S. Fanuel*, ed. C. Chabaneau, ib. 1889; L. Delisle, *Livres d'images destinés à l'instruction religieuse des laïques*, Paris, 1890; S. Berger, *Les Bibles Castillanes*, in *Romania*, xxviii, 1899.

BIBLES, ILLUSTRATED.

The history of illustration goes back beyond the Christian era; the ancients adorned manuscripts of Homer, Vergil, and Livy with drawings and richly painted designs, and illustrations were introduced for educational purposes into the works of Vitruvius on architecture, Aratus on astrology, and Vegetius on the art of war. In like manner, from the time of Constantine and probably earlier, illustration was applied to manuscripts of the Bible.

1. Illustrated Manuscripts, Roman and Byzantine.

Presumably to this decoration may be referred what Jerome and Chrysostom say in reprobation of the luxury which people allowed themselves in the ornamentation of the Scriptures. The high veneration paid to the Bible explains the zeal with which miniature-painting was pursued in the early

Church. The extant illustrated manuscripts do not apparently go further back than the fourth century (the fragment of Genesis in the Vienna library; the Vatican Joshua; the evangeliarium of Rossano; and a Syriac evangeliarium of 586 in the Laurentian library at Florence). In these many features, such as the architecture, costume, action, the introduction of allegorical figures and personifications, indicate the nature of the scene or its locality, which are derived from ancient art and reveal the prevalence of a good tradition. Among them are small pictures executed in body-colors with idyllic artistic feeling, after the manner of the older mural painting. The miniatures of the Vienna Genesis are still partly in the purely illusionist style which had been dominant since the Flavian period, like the paintings in the Baths of Constantine; but the greater part of them are in a style specially adapted to book illustration, more a draftsman's than a painter's. They exhibit the continued influence of the narrative art of the Roman empire in the second and third centuries, as shown in the pictures from the Odyssey on the Esquiline, on Roman sarcophagi, and in the pictures of Philostratus; this defined the specific style of all Christian compositions until the sixteenth century. The illustrations of the Paris Psalter and other manuscripts which may be assigned to the end of the fourth century are characteristic of the end of Greek and the beginning of Roman painting. The Joshua continues the Roman triumphal style, with strong affinity to the reliefs of Trajan's Column. In the Byzantine empire the influence of the ancient civilization was long felt; but a more ornamental tendency came in with the iconoclastic controversy. It is true there are some illustrations of the ninth and tenth centuries, a psalter and a commentary on Isaiah in the Vatican, another psalter and the sermons of Gregory Nazianzen in the Bibliothèque Nationale at Paris, which are worthy to stand by the side of the early Christian specimens; but as a rule the drawing grows harder and stiffer. Ornamentation, on the other hand, is richer; the gold ground becomes more usual, the initial letters are made prominent, and the ornamental borders are more noteworthy. Mosaic and enamel painting set the style for the miniatures as well. The standard of Byzantine painting is laid down in the Mount Athos "Guide to Painting" (1458; translated into German by G. Schäfer, Treves, 1855). The development of illustration in the West was altogether different. Here, too, the influence of the early Christian tradition was operative; but the entrance of the Teutonic nations into the Church brought new impulses and new problems. They were, indeed, barbarians, without any native artistic style; but they brought with them a joyous power of accomplishment, a feeling for nature, and a bold love of truth which had far-reaching effects.

The Roman tradition continued among the Lombards and the Franks; but art became ruder and less refined. In the early Christian and Byzantine manuscripts the decoration had been usually confined to the addition of pictures; the Teutonic peoples extended it to the text itself. The initials are almost buried in bright colors and elaborate decoration, the leaves framed in colored designs.

2. Teutonic and Celtic Manuscripts. The scribe was often the painter. These characteristics appear plainly in the Irish manuscripts—the "Book of Kells" at Trinity College, Dublin, and those of Würzburg, Treves, and St. Gall. The influence of Gregory the Great helped to preserve the early Christian traditions among the Anglo-Saxons and Franks until within the Carolingian period (the Purple Gospel in the British Museum and an evangeliarium at Cambridge, seventh century). An independent conception comes out first in the illustrations proper, without any feeling for perspective, but with an attractive effort to attain truth and naturalness (Ashburnham Pentateuch, seventh century). Under the Carolingians great schools were founded for artistic copying of manuscripts at Tours, Orléans, Metz, Reichenau, St. Gall, Treves, etc. Their work was connected with the old tradition by its sober-minded simplicity and its careful technique (evangeliarium of Godescalc, Paris; another at Vienna; another of St. Médard, 826, at Soissons; another of King Lothair, 843, and the Bible of Charles the Bald, 850, both in Paris). In the provinces the development, though less beautiful, was more independent (Bible of Alcuin, British Museum). Here the draftsman takes precedence of the painter, but the work is marked by originality and poetic imagination and power (Utrecht Psalter, ninth century; a benedictionale at Chatsworth; evangeliaria of Otto I at Aix-la-Chapelle, of Egbert at Treves, c. 980, of Echternach at Gotha, c. 990, and of Otto III at Aix-la-Chapelle). Then the decoration becomes gradually more elaborate, the pictorial and ornamental parts begin to interchange their qualities, the initials and borders are rich and gay.

In the eleventh century the Cluniac mood of struggle and renunciation prevails; the spiritual excitement and vivid fancy of the time are shown in the Bible-illustrations; wasted forms in stiff garments set forth the ascetic ideal of their creators; truth to nature disappears entirely. And yet there is great progress in every domain of the intellectual life—it is the age of Bernard. Even in the miniatures there are signs of the awakening of the individual life; beneath all the passion and combat there are a quiet melancholy and longing for peace.

3. Manuscripts of the Eleventh Century. Henry II endowed his Bamberg foundations with beautifully painted books, and at Hildesheim an important scriptorium, influential throughout the north of Europe, was founded by Bernward, himself a pioneer in painting. Here the forms are hard and traditional, but the content is new and full of deep and animated feeling. After the rise of general civilization under the Hohenstaufens, the bars of form were to a great extent broken down. The joy of living came back, and led the imagination once more into the comprehension of beautiful things, both graceful and dignified. There is a better feeling for outline, and the study of the heritage of antiquity seems to revive. The Bruchsal evangeliarium at Carlsruhe shows surprisingly good drawing and natural movement, as does another of about 1200 in the cathedral library at Treves; best of all is that of Henry the Lion, formerly in the cathedral treasury at Prague but now in the possession of the Duke of Cumberland, and the Merseburg Vulgate. A brilliant period for miniature-painting was opening; but its tone was characterized rather by breadth than by depth, and the more popular it became, the more the profound symbolism of the early times disappeared. Illustration was now bestowed less on Bibles than on books used in public worship, until at the end of the Middle Ages artistic interest once more covered the whole Bible; but new life really came into this branch of illustration with the invention of wood-engraving.

The transition to illustrated Bibles for the people is seen in the *Biblia pauperum* of the thirteenth and fourteenth centuries—short representations of the earthly life of Christ in simple drawings, generally uncolored, ranging in number from thirty-four to fifty. Each event depicted is accompanied by two antitypes from the Old Testament and by four prophets with appropriate citations, and the pictures are explained in Latin or in German. The most important examples of these "Bibles of the Poor" are those of St. Florian in Lower Austria, of the Lyceum library at Constance, in the Vienna and Munich libraries [and in the ducal library at Wolfenbüttel].

4. Biblia Pauperum.

With the invention of printing and engraving, especially wood-engraving, both the Bible and art became common property. Reproductions of the *Biblia pauperum*, which now first became really accessible to the "poor," are among the most celebrated of early block books. The German Bibles before Luther (Augsburg 1477, Cologne c. 1480, Nuremberg 1483, Lübeck 1494) have woodcuts. Finally Dürer, with the wonderful vision which could realize even the majestic pictures of the Apocalypse, raised Biblical illustration to its highest dignity. With the vernacular text, eagerly sought after as it was, a great variety of illustrations went hand in hand. Luther recognized their importance to the Reformation cause and promoted illustration zealously, and Melanchthon drew rough sketches, which he gave to Lucas Cranach for execution. Bible-illustration has never had such a vogue as in the first half of the sixteenth century. The most splendid edition was published by Krafft of Wittenberg in 1576 and 1581. With the middle of the century Biblical illustrating took a new direction, when line-engraving gradually forced wood-engraving into the background. The latter was used mainly for cheap popular editions, while artistic tendencies were mainly displayed by the former. In 1607 the fifty-two pictures from the *logge* of the Vatican, the so-called Raffael Bible, engraved by Badalocchio and Lanfranco, were published, followed by another important series of line-engravings, the *Icones biblicæ* and *Historiæ sacræ* published by Merian at Frankfort, 1625–27, and a long list of similar works in Germany, France, and Italy. In the eighteenth century wood-engraving almost entirely died out, except for cheap ephemeral productions, while line-engraving flourished in the hands of the Dutch school, who shared the renown of the French. German art was mainly imitative, and produced little that is noteworthy in Biblical illustration. Good editions, on the other hand, were published during this period in Holland by Mortier, 1700; Danckers, 1700; Luyken, 1740; Schots, 1749. In France the best were those of Basnage, 1705, and Martin, 1724. In England, besides the Oxford Bible of 1717, there were the editions of Royaumont, 1705; Clarke, 1759; and Fleetwood, 1769. In all these the Dutch-Flemish spirit appears, with its wide, free, joyous life; the fundamental principles of illustration are based on imitation of painting; Rubens, and Rembrandt for etching, are the highest authorities. In the nineteenth century Bible-illustration took a new impulse from England. The modern romantic manner and straining after effect entered into it, largely as a result of the great *Holy Bible with Engravings from Pictures and Designs by the most Eminent Artists*, published in London, 1800. [This, however, had been anticipated by the *Historical Part of the Holy Bible* with illustrations engraved by John Cole (London, 1730) and a volume with the same title illustrated by John Sturt, as well as by the James Tittler Bible (4 vols., 1794-95). It was followed by a series of efforts, such as the *Pictorial Bible* by Charles Knight, with woodcuts (London, 1828–29, New York, 1843), another of the same name, but with steel engravings (London, 1847–49), a numerous series of *Bible Picture Books* issued by the Society for Promoting Christian Knowledge and the Religious Tract Society, and *Bible Illustrations*, issued by Frowde (London, 1896).]

5. Illustrated Bibles of the Reformation and Later.

The interest in the Orient which came up with Napoleon's Egyptian campaign, in alliance with the strong realistic tendency of the century, brought in a wholly new sort of illustrated Bible, like Brown's *Family Bible* (London and New York), with views of towns and landscapes in addition to historical pictures. Later, wood-engraving revived reached once more an unexpected height of excellence, and succeeded in getting in touch with the great masses of the people. Notable products of this revival (in Germany) were Oliver's Bible of 1834; Overbeck's forty fine illustrations to the New Testament (1841); the Cotta edition of 1850, with 175 wood-engravings after the first artists of Germany; and, best of all the German editions, that published by Wigand (Leipsic, 1852–1860), with 240 illustrations by Julius Schnorr von Carolsfeld (Eng. ed., Leipsic, 1855–60; London, 1869). The technically brilliant but too theatrical designs of Doré won great popularity. The Germans have recently published several noteworthy editions, such as the "Pfeilstücker Bible" in 1887, with many explanatory archeological drawings, and the "Star Bible" published by Hinrichs (Leipsic) in 1892, with reproductions of classical pictures for the Old Testament and Hofmann's for the New. [One of the latest attempts at Biblical illustration is the work of the French artist J. J. J. Tissot (d.

6. The Nineteenth Century.

1902), who, during a ten years' residence in Palestine, prepared a series of sketches based upon study of the Biblical places and environment. *The Life of our Lord Jesus Christ*, with 365 compositions in color and black and white, was published in 4 vols. in 1899–1900, and *The Old Testament*, with 396 similar illustrations, in 1904 (2 vols.).] (H. Hölscher.)

Bibliography: A. de Bastard, *Peintures et ornements des MSS.*, especially vol. iii, 8 vols., Paris, 1832–69 (4th–16th centuries, a very complete work); idem, *Peintures, ornements . . de la Bible de Charles le Chauve . à Paris*, ib. 1883; H. Shaw, *Illuminated Ornaments of the Middle Ages*, London, 1833 (6th–17th centuries, elaborate and costly); idem, *Handbook of the Art of Illumination*, ib. 1869; J. O. Westwood, *Illuminated Illustrations of the Bible, copied from Select MSS. of the Middle Ages*, ib. 1846 (with descriptive letterpress); H. N. Humphreys, *Illuminated Books of the Middle Ages*, ib. 1849 (historical and illustrative); H. A. Müller, *Das Evangelistarium Heinrichs III. in der Stadtbibliothek zu Bremen*, Bremen, 1862; W. R. Tymms, *Art of Illuminating*, London, 1866 (noteworthy); J. O. Westwood, *Facsimiles of the Miniatures and Ornaments of Anglo-Saxon and Irish MSS.*, ib. 1868; J. H. Todd, *Descriptive Remarks on Illuminations*, ib. 1869 (deals largely with the Book of Kells); J. E. Wocel, *Die Bilderbibel des Belislav*, Prague, 1871; A. Frind, *Scriptum super Apocalypsin cum imaginibus*, ib. 1872; F. W. Delamotte, *Primer of the Art of Illumination*, London, 1874; W. de G. Birch and H. Jenner, *Early Drawings and Illuminations; Introduction to the Study of Illuminated MSS.*, ib. 1879 ("a handsome book for specialists"); A. Springer, *Psalterillustrationen im frühen Mittelalter*, Leipsic, 1881; idem, *Die Genesisbilder in der Kunst des frühen Mittelalters*, ib. 1884; O. von Gebhardt, *The Miniatures of the Ashburnham Pentateuch*, London, 1883; R. Muther, *Die ältesten deutschen Bilderbibeln*, Munich, 1883; F. X. Kraus, *Die Miniaturen des Codex Egberti . . . zu Trier*, Freiburg, 1884; idem, *Geschichte der christlichen Kunst*, i, 447 sqq., ib. 1896; *Geschichte der deutschen Kunst*, vol. iii, H. Janitschek, *Die Malerei*, Berlin, 1890; K. von Lützow, *Geschichte des deutschen Kupferstichs und Holzschnitts*, vol. iv, ib. 1891; S. Beissel, *Das . . Evangelienbuch im Dome zu Hildesheim*, Hildesheim, 1891; J. Strzygowski, *Das Etschmiadzin Evangeliar*, Vienna, 1891; C. von Kobell, *Miniaturen und Initialen aus MSS. des 4.–16. Jahrhunderts*, Munich, 1892; J. H. Middleton, *Illuminated MSS. in Classical and Modern Times*, London, 1892 (letterpress elaborate and comprehensive); W. von Hartel and F. Wickhoff, *Die Wiener Genesis*, Vienna, 1895; S. Berger, *Les Manuels pour l'illustration du Psautier*, in *Mémoires de la société des antiquités*, 1898, lvii; G. F. Warner, *Illuminated MSS.*, London, 1900; the illustrations of the Evangeliarium of Rossano are reproduced in the exact size of the originals by A. Munoz, Rome, 1907.

On the *Biblia Pauperum* consult: S. L. Sotheby, *Principia typographica*, London, 1858; J. T. Berjeau, *Biblia pauperum*, London, 1859; A. Camesina and G. Heider, *Die bildlichen Darstellungen der Biblia pauperum . in St. Florian*, Vienna, 1863; E. la Roche, *Die älteste Bilderbibel, die sogenannte Biblia pauperum*, Basel, 1881; W. L. Schreiber, *Manuel de l'amateur de la gravure . au xve. siècle*, 7 vols., Leipsic, 1891–1900; F. Laib and F. J. Schwarz, *Biblia pauperum*, Freiburg, 1899; E. M. Thompson, *On a MS. of the Biblia pauperum*, in *Bibliotheca*, iii, 1897; *Biblia pauperum. Unicum der Heidelberger Universitäts-Bibliothek, in 34 Lichtdrucktafeln und 4 Tafeln*, Berlin, 1906.

BIBLES, POLYGLOT.

I. The Complutensian Polyglot.
II. The Antwerp Polyglot.
III. The Paris Polyglot.
IV. The London Polyglot (Walton's Polyglot).
V. Minor Polyglots.

Polyglot Bibles are editions of the Bible presenting the text in several languages side by side. The practical needs of the Jews after Hebrew ceased to be a living tongue led to the preparation of manuscripts giving, with the original Hebrew, translations or paraphrases in Aramaic, Greek, Arabic, Persian, and the languages of Europe. Like conditions in the Church were met in similar manner. Certain manuscripts of the New Testament in both Greek and Latin are mentioned in the article Bible-Text, II, 1, § 9. An edition in the original and in modern Greek was printed in 1638 at the instance of Cyril Lucar (see Bible Versions, B, VIII), and the needs of Syria, Egypt, and Armenia are met in like manner by editions still issued by Rome and by Protestant Bible Societies. The so-called glossaries (see Glosses, Biblical) and interlinear versions giving the Vulgate and the vernacular text of the Middle Ages may also be mentioned in this connection. And there are numerous modern copies of the Vulgate accompanied by an English, German, French, Spanish, or Italian translation.

The name Polyglot, however, can not strictly be given to editions presenting but two languages (Gk. *polys* = "many"), and, in common usage, is restricted to certain particular works, viz.:

I. The Complutensian Polyglot, one of the most noted and rarest of Biblical works, was undertaken under the supervision and at the expense of Cardinal Francisco Ximenez de Cisneros, archbishop of Toledo and chancellor of Castile (d. 1517), and was prepared by the most famous scholars of Spain, such as Demetrius Ducas of Crete, Antonio of Lebrija, Diego Lopez de Stunica, Ferdinand Nuñez de Guzman, and Alphonso of Zamora. After years of labor the work was printed at Alcala (Latin, *Complutum*) between 1513 and 1517, being finished only a few months before the death of the cardinal, and was published in 1520 with the sanction of Pope Leo X. It consists of six folio volumes, the first four including the Old Testament, the fifth the New Testament, and the sixth being a Hebrew-Chaldee lexicon with grammatical and other notes (printed separately as *Alphonsi Zamorensis introductiones artis grammaticæ Hebraicæ*, Alcala, 1526). The languages are (1) the Hebrew of the Old Testament; (2) the Targum of Onkelos; (3) the Septuagint (here printed for the first time and with remarkable alterations of the manuscripts to make the text fit the Hebrew or the Latin); (4) the Vulgate; (5) the Greek New Testament. Latin translations of the Targum and Septuagint are appended. The title-page and last page are given in reduced facsimile in Schaff's *Companion to the Greek Testament* (New York, 1885).

II. The Antwerp Polyglot (*Biblia Regia*) was printed at the expense of Philip II of Spain by the famous Antwerp printer Christophe Plantin (8 vols., folio, 1569–72). Benedictus Arias Montanus (see Arias, Benedictus) had charge of the work, with the help of Spanish, Belgian, and French scholars, among them André Maes, Guy le Fèvre de la Boderie, and François Rapheleng. Volumes i–iv contain the Old Testament, vol. v the New; besides the original texts, the Vulgate, and the Septuagint with Latin translation, Aramaic targums of the Old Testament (with the exception of Daniel, Ezra, Nehemiah, and Chronicles) are given, with Latin translation; also the old Syriac (Peshito) version of the New Testament, lacking II Peter, II and III John, Jude, and the Apocalypse; it is printed with both Syriac and Hebrew characters and has a Latin translation. Volumes vi–vii contain the Hebrew lexicon of Sanctes Pagninus, the Syriac-Chaldee lexicon of Le Fèvre de la Boderie, a Syriac grammar by Maes, a Greek dictionary and archeological treatises by Arias Montanus, and many brief philological and critical notes. The last volume repeats the Hebrew and Greek texts with interlinear Latin translations, by Sanctes Pagninus of the former, and the Vulgate for the latter; this part of the work, especially the New Testament, has often been reprinted. The critical preparation was defective and the manuscripts used were of secondary importance; in many places there is dependence on the Complutensian work.

III. The Paris Polyglot, the most magnificent but scientifically least important of all, was printed at the expense of Guy Michel le Jay in seven languages (10 vols., 1629–45). Volumes i–iv are merely reprints of the Antwerp Bible. Volumes v–vi contain the New Testament from the same edition, augmented by the Syriac Antilegomena and an Arabic version with Latin translation. The other volumes contain (1) the so-called Samaritan Pentateuch with its Samaritan translation (see BIBLE VERSIONS, A, IV); (2) the Syriac; and (3) an Arabic version of the Old Testament, all with Latin translations. The Oratorian Jean Morin prepared the Samaritan texts and the Maronite Gabriel Sionita did most of the Syriac work.

IV. The London Polyglot (Walton's Polyglot), the most scholarly and the commonest of all, was undertaken by Brian Walton (q.v.), afterward bishop of Chester, and completed in 1657 (6 vols., London). Walton had the help of nearly all contemporary English scholars, particularly the Orientalists Edmund Castell, Edward Pococke, Thomas Hyde, Dudley Loftus, Abraham Weelocke, Thomas Greaves, and Samuel Clarke. The excellence of this Polyglot over others consists in the greater number of old Oriental versions and the much greater and more intelligent work of the editor. The first four volumes contain the Old Testament in the Hebrew with the Antwerp interlinear version, the Samaritan Pentateuch, the Septuagint from the Vatican edition of 1587 with the variants of the Alexandrine codex, the fragments of the Itala collected by Flaminius Nobilius, the Vulgate from the Vatican edition with the corrections of Lucas of Brügge, the Peshito augmented by the translation of certain apocrypha, a better edition of the Arabic version, the Targums from Buxtorf, the Samaritan translation of the Pentateuch, and the Ethiopic version of the Psalms and Song of Songs. These texts (nine in all), with Latin translations of the Greek and the Oriental, are arranged side by side or one under the other. Two additional Targums, that of Pseudo-Jonathan and that of Jerusalem, with a Persian translation are given in vol. iv. The New Testament appears in vol. v, the text with few changes from Robert Stephens's folio edition of 1550; then are given Arias's version and the variants of the Alexandrine codex, Syriac, Latin, Ethiopic, and Arabic versions, and the Gospels in Persian, with literal Latin translations. Walton's *Apparatus*, a critical-historical introduction in vol. i, was not superseded for more than a century, and was several times republished. Volume vi contains critical collections to all the texts published. Finally Edmund Castell's *Lexicon Heptaglottum* (2 parts, Cambridge, 1669) is usually counted as an integral part of this Polyglot.

V. Minor Polyglots: Less important are (1) the *Heidelberg Polyglot* (*Polyglotta Sanctandreana*; Old Testament, 1586; New Testament added, 1599), probably edited by Bonaventure Corneille Bertram, professor of Hebrew at Geneva 1566–84, afterward preacher at Frankenthal. It contains the original texts and Septuagint, with Latin translations, and the Vulgate, all from the Antwerp Polyglot. (2) The *Hamburg Polyglot* (1596) consists of six volumes by David Wolder, giving in four columns the Greek texts, the Vulgate, Pagninus's Latin translation of the Old Testament and Beza's of the New, with Luther's German version, to which Elias Hutter's Hebrew Bible of 1587 was added with new title-page bearing the date 1596. (3) The *Nuremberg Polyglot*, the work of Elias Hutter (q.v.), comprises (*a*) an Old Testament in six languages (1599), carried only to the Book of Ruth; (*b*) a Hebrew, Greek, Latin, and German Psalter (1602); (*c*) a New Testament in twelve languages (2 parts, 1599)—Syriac, Italian, Hebrew, Spanish, Greek, French, Vulgate, English, German, Danish, Bohemian, and Polish; (*d*) a New Testament in Hebrew, Greek, Latin, and German, taken from the preceding (1602). (4) The *Leipsic Polyglot* of Christianus Reineccius, rector at Weissenfels, has the New Testament in five languages (1713) and the Old Testament in four (2 vols., 1750–51). (5) The *Bielefeld Polyglot*, ed. R. Stier and C. G. W. Theile (4 vols., ii and iii in two parts, 1846–55), contains the Old Testament in Hebrew, Greek, Latin, and German, the New Testament in the last three languages, with variants of different German versions in the fourth column; there are also copies with the English version in place of the German. Lastly, mention may be made of the *Biblia Hexaglotta* of E. R. de Levante (6 vols., London, 1874–1876), and Bagster's *Biblia sacra polyglotta*, with prolegomena by S. Lee (London, 1831). Other works including only portions of the Bible do not fall within the scope of this article. E. NESTLE.

BIBLIOGRAPHY: J. Le Long, *Bibliotheca Sacra, emendata . . . ab A. G. Masch*, part i, chap. 4, pp. 331–408, Halle, 1778; idem, *Discours historique sur les principales éditions des Bibles polyglottes*, pp. 554 sqq., Paris, 1713; B. Pick, *History of Printed Editions . . and Polyglot Bibles*, in *Hebraica*, ix (1892–93), 47–116.

BIBLES, RABBINIC, called also Great Bibles (*Mikra'ot Gedolot*): Hebrew Bibles containing, besides the original text, the commentaries of sundry Jewish rabbis. The first of these Bibles was published by Daniel Bomberg, edited by Felix Pratensis (4 parts, Venice, 1517–18); it contains, besides the Hebrew, the Aramaic paraphrases and commentaries of eight different writers on certain books, Masoretic notes, and other matter. As the editor was a convert to Christianity, his work did not prove acceptable to the Jews. Its faults induced Bomberg to undertake another edition, for which he employed as editor the celebrated Masoretic scholar Jacob ben Hayyim, who in after-life also embraced Christianity. This edition, the Hebrew title of which means "The Holy Gate of the Lord," was published at Venice (4 vols., 1524–25) and, like the first edition, contains the Hebrew text, the Aramaic commentaries, and the Masoretic notes. The editor's introduction, containing a treatise on the Masorah, has been translated into English by Christian David Ginsburg (*Jacob ben Chajim's Introduction to the Rabbinic Bible*, London, 1865), who based *The Massoretic Critical Text of the Hebrew Bible* (1894) on this edition of Hayyim.

A revised and improved edition of the second Bomberg Bible was published (Venice, 1546–48) under the supervision of Cornelius Adelkind. The changes made in this edition were the omission of some commentaries and the substitution of others. Bomberg's fourth Rabbinic Bible, by J. de Gara, was carried through the press and corrected by Isaac ben Joseph Salam and Isaac ben Gershon Treves (4 vols., Venice, 1568). The correctors remark at the end of the work that they have reinserted in this edition the portion of the Masorah omitted in the edition of 1546–48. Appended to this is the so-called Jerusalem Targum on the Pentateuch.

A Rabbinic Bible (4 vols., Venice, 1617–18) was published by Pietro and Lorenzo Bragadini and edited by the celebrated Leon of Modena. It contains the Aramaic paraphrases, the Masorah, and the Rabbinic commentaries of De Gara's edition. This edition, however, is of less value to the critical student, being censored by the Inquisition.

Buxtorf's Rabbinic Bible or *Biblia sacra Hebraica et Chaldaica cum Masora, quæ critica Hebræorum sacra est, magna et parva ac selectissimis Hebræorum interpretum commentariis* (4 parts, 2 vols., Basel, 1618–19) has a Latin preface by Buxtorf, a table of the number of chapters in the Bible, and a poem of Aben Ezra in the Hebrew language. Besides the Hebrew and the Aramaic paraphrases, it contains the commentaries of Rashi, Aben Ezra, and others, and Buxtorf's *Tiberias sive commentarius masorethicus triplex*. The whole is formed after Jacob ben Hayyim's second edition (1546–48), with some corrections and alterations by Buxtorf. Buxtorf's Bible is imperfect, but in spite of its deficiencies, the student must still thank the editor for his work, which, however, was criticized by R. Simon in his *Histoire critique du Vieux Testament* (p. 513).

The next Rabbinic Bible was the *Sepher Kehillat Moshe*, or "Book of the Congregation of Moses," edited by Moses Frankfurter (4 vols., Amsterdam, 1724–27). This is the most valuable of all the Rabbinic Bibles. It is founded upon the Bomberg editions, and gives not only their contents, but also those of Buxtorf's, with much additional matter.

The latest Rabbinic Bible is the *Mikra'ot Gedolot* published at Warsaw (12 vols., 1860–68) by Lebenson. This gigantic work contains thirty-two commentaries, old and new, among others the critical commentary of Norzi. The Hebrew text is on the whole very correct, the size is more convenient than that of its predecessors, and the edition is recommended by the best Jewish authorities in Poland and Austria. B. PICK.

BIBLIOGRAPHY: The one book for consultation is C. D. Ginsburg, *Introduction to the Massoretico-critical Edition of the Hebrew Bible*, London, 1897; cf. B. Pick, in *Hebraica*, ix (1892–93), 47–116.

BIBLIA PAUPERUM ("Bible of the Poor"). See BIBLES, ILLUSTRATED, § 4.

BIBLIANDER (BUCHMANN), THEODOR: Swiss theologian and teacher; b. at Bischofszell (11 miles s.s.e. of Constance), Switzerland, 1504 (1509?); d. at Zurich Nov. 26, 1564. He studied Hebrew under Jacob Ceporinus in Zurich, in 1526 under Pellican and Œcolampadius at Basel, and later on under Capito. When Duke Frederick II of Liegnitz in 1527 asked for teachers for his high school, the Council of Zurich sent him Bibliander, who served there two years with distinction. He then returned home and was appointed Zwingli's successor in the theological professorship at Zurich in 1531.

Bibliander's specialty was linguistics, and he used to call himself *homo grammaticus*; he was versed in the Semitic dialects and was master of several modern languages. From the beginning his rendering of the Prophets was successful, was indorsed by Bullinger and Pellican, and caused J. H. Hottinger to call him the father of exegetical theology in Switzerland. He wrote also on Hebrew Grammar and on Comparative Linguistics. Perhaps the greatest sensation he caused was that produced by his publication of the Koran (1543, rev. ed., 1550); the magistrates at Basel tried to prohibit the book, but Luther interfered in defense of it and of the translator. Bibliander issued studies on the Gospel of Mark and the *Protevangelium Jacobi*, translating them into Latin. His works betray a rich historical knowledge. Especially worthy of mention in this regard are his *De Ratione Temporum* (1551) and *Temporum Supputatio* (1558). Most of his writings were never published, but are preserved in manuscript at Zurich.

Next to Bullinger, Bibliander appears as the most respected representative of the Church at Zurich. He participated in all theological and ecclesiastical discussions, preserving the heritage of Zwingli. He assisted in the publication of Zwingli's and Œcolampadius's letters (1536). In some treatises he openly attacked the Catholic Church and the Tridentinum (*De Legitima Vindicatione Christianismi*, 1553), and antagonized the Roman propaganda, appealing to England as the land of Christian liberty. He advocated missions to the Jews and Mohammedans, and went so far as to start on mission work, being restrained only by Bullinger's representations. He was made *emeritus* and given a pension in 1560. (EMIL EGLI.)

BIBLIOGRAPHY: A list of the writings of Bibliander is given in H. J. Leu, *Allgemeines Lexicon*, iv, 11–14, 20 vols., Zurich, 1747–65. For his life consult J. J. Christinger, *T. Bibliander, ein biographisches Denkmal*, Frauenfeld, 1867; E. Egli, *Analecta reformatoria*, vol. ii, Zurich, 1901.

BIBLICAL ARCHEOLOGY. See Archeology, Biblical.

BIBLICAL CANON. See Canon of Scripture.

BIBLICAL CRITICISM.

I. Conception and Problem: Criticism, like interpretation, is an art; the two are related to each other as sisters, and both are nourished by science. Interpretation is the art of bringing to the comprehension what has really been handed down and of grasping it as it really is; criticism is the art of rightly estimating what has been actually apprehended according to its real value. Interpretation without criticism befogs and enervates; criticism without interpretation is vague and mere intellectual play. Since man can not understand without exercising the faculty of judgment, in work that deals with spiritual verities the two are not separated, yet the point of view from which they approach the same object is as different as their method. Interpretation proceeds inductively, collecting everything which bears upon the understanding of the matter; criticism proceeds deductively, furnishing the canons by which to value that understanding. While one asks about the fact, the other asks about the truth of it; one builds, the other classifies and estimates the material and tests the building process. Criticism is the inverse of interpretation, and more. While it pronounces upon the results of interpretation, it opens new questions about the trustworthiness or untrustworthiness, the completeness or fragmentariness, the genealogy and the significance of the object; and thus it affords a starting-point for final valuation and definition. It is skill, partly natural, partly acquired, in distinguishing and appropriating true from false, good from bad, beautiful from ugly, whether derived from contemplative perception and revelation or through chance or tradition. Its purpose is positive, though its result may often be negative. It knows no other authority than that of the case before it, no other method than that demanded by the same.

1. The History of the Term. The word has been in use since Plato's time; he distinguished between criticism and construction, the two being employed in the science of knowledge. Aristotle introduced a distinction between the critical and the literary arts, which was taken up by the Alexandrian school in connection with literature and particularly with poetry. Clement of Alexandria established in his review of Greek culture the fact that *grammatikos* as a technical term is later than *kritikos*. Terminology, however, was unstable in the ancient world. *Philologos* was differentiated from *philosophos*, meaning not the independent inquirer but the critic and expounder of classical productions. As the art of valuing, criticism is the product of the eighteenth century. The Encyclopedists called it in particular the restorer of ancient literature, in general the art of open-eyed examination of human productions and of judging them justly.

2. Limitations and Sphere of the Critic. The critic stands in an opposition between subjective and objective. The obscure, the ugly, the disorderly, the arrogant, the artificial—everything which tends to distort a pure impression—arouse the critical function, which manifests itself in simple aversion or blame, or in a deliberate exposition of the causes of distortion. Limitations to understanding lie also in the person. Complex and difficult to grasp are the conditions and impulses which deceive, divert, and suborn the faculty of judgment. Personal taste, inexperience, dogmatic presupposition, arrogance—such hindrances are as numerous as the emotions of the soul. A valuable inheritance sometimes suffers injury by the encroachments of critical ineptitude. Whoever regards a thing as worthy has a sense of loss, even if the criticism be pertinent; much more is that the case if in the critical process insincerity and arbitrariness be present. It is not surprising, therefore, that esthetic and religious natures are filled with aversion to criticism and distrust of it. Goethe once said that a book which had accomplished great results was simply above the operations of criticism, and that criticism is generally a mere habit of moderns. Such an attitude seems to the critic mere obedience to blind authority. Great events and much of literature have rested on fictitious bases. Apocrypha and pseudepigrapha claim genuineness. Such facts are warrant enough for the activities of critical science.

3. Biblical Criticism. The general standards of criticism, like those of interpretation, rest on logic, philosophy, and rhetoric. It applies those standards to the particular case, and the general rules are modified to accord with the demands of the occasion. Since the Scriptures of the Old and the New Testaments have a special importance as a related whole, Biblical criticism is a special and independent branch. It deals with sources, history, and religion; it tests the historical worth of the documents which set forth the religion of the two Testaments. It has as its object the discovery of the religious life operative therein by reason of which this literature has its special meaning. There is a double outlook here; insight into the essence of religion and into the essence of historic fact.

Biblical criticism is on its other side historical criticism. Hence its function is to separate the natural progress of events and the religious limitations of the Biblical exposition of history in order to comprehend their relations upon the basis of this separation. Religious occurrences it must seek to explain upon psychological, pathological, and historico-religious grounds. Lessing says that "the dramatic poet is not a historian; historical verity is not his purpose, only the means to it." Is this poet then a falsifier of history? Similarly for the Biblical writers historical truth is only a means for offering religious truth; it is the channel of the revelation from God. Consequently the task is to examine case by case in order to determine how far historical reality carries revelation. Its own standpoint, therefore, is assured to this science. It asks with what right and under what conditions and limitations the Scriptures exist as a religious collection. It gives historical rating to the contents. Its leading word is—discriminate, which it uses in promoting recognition of worth or its opposite, of fact or mere appearance.

II. The Critical Method: To achieve real service in Biblical criticism appreciation of the religious factor is necessary. The critic, however, may not walk in a rut if he is to attain a right position. After he has through interpretation grasped the object of investigation, he gives it rating according to the conditions and warrant of the facts of the case. He proceeds upon the immanent, not the transcendent. And after the right criterion is found, he has to remember that a complete and not a partial or fragmentary investigation is required, and further that fast hold must be laid upon equipoise between critical acuteness and the perception of what is possible and plain.

1. Fundamental Assumptions.

Eccles. vii, 20 has its application here, "God made man upright, but he has sought out many inventions." What is the inherent standard of Biblical criticism? The historical narratives of the Bible are, so far as they deal with religious life, interpretations of history and testimonies to faith. To express a right judgment the critic must determine the relation between the historical and the religious and decide which is the more prominent. De Wette regarded the Pentateuch as poetry; the opposite view makes the Bible historical only. Between these extremes lies the recognition that the Bible employs history for religious purposes. Is this religious significance to be regarded as expert emphasis upon the worth and force of a real occurrence or was it used to support some dogmatic purpose? Is it found in or read into the case? Is it in the main possible to recognize the fact in the religious dress?

These possibilities the critic must take into account as he holds the scales of truth, testing the composite parts of the Bible and proceeding thence to a consideration of the Bible as a whole. Upon this ground only can the decision be rendered how far the historic facts which the Bible reports stand in organic connection with their religious valuation and whether they may be regarded as history or as legend, fable, or myth. The varying ratio of the admixture of the historical and the religious and the degree of its significance must be observed; and especially the interval between the Old Testament and the New in their historical relations, original limitations, and purposes must be kept in mind. It is one thing to appreciate the essential qualities of Hebrew national literature, covering a thousand years in its development, and another to apprehend the worth and character of the New Testament, which is the literature of a religious propaganda covering but two generations. Yet the critic's methods are essentially the same, corresponding to the varied historical limitations of the subject-matter. When the question of the essence of Christianity arises, the bearing of the Old Testament religion upon Christianity is to be decided and grasped.

The fundamental axiom shows that each literary production, as well as each body of writings which has a common bond, requires its appropriate method both of interpretation and of criticism. Means and end will agree when the character of the whole presents itself in the parts; the last-named will separate and individualize themselves where origins and relations differ.

2. Classification.

The classifications of Biblical criticism arise not out of logical abstractions but out of the demands made by the individualistic Biblical qualities. Criticism of the canon asks how and with what right the two Testaments were united in one book, how and by what methods the correct text of that which has come down is to be ascertained, what was the origin and what is the historical worth and what the relation of the present form of the books to the original form. It draws conclusions from the data furnished by interpretation. On the basis of the recognition (1) of the suitability of means to ends and (2) of the literary individuality, it pronounces upon the worth of a document as a source and upon its relation to the whole to which it belongs and which it serves. The science divides, therefore, into criticism of the text, of the language, of the history, of the style, and constructive criticism.

Since subjectively criticism finds its occasion in the limits of the understanding, its starting-point is doubt about the trustworthiness and the arrangement of what has come down. This doubt proceeds to ask the reason for this impression.

3. Function.

If the reason lies not in the spiritual being of the doubter but in the object, then some defect is understood to exist in expression, contents, or style. The critic has then to discover the kind of defect and to discern its cause. As a means to this, Jerome directs the critic to digest, arrange, deduce, construct. In other words, the critic first diagnoses the case and then applies the remedy. And in this process comparison is constantly employed, holding in view the separate parts and the united whole. The division of the field of the critic into external and internal, higher and lower, does not have any essential truth at its root, and should be rejected for that given at the end of the last paragraph.

III. The Departments of Criticism: That the Old Testament existed as a holy authority for the synagogue and that the New in connection with the Old had the same value for the Church is the fact the success and the right of which criticism has to investigate. It notes the process of formation of the canon and the internal testimony of the canonical writings as related to the authority attributed to them. It asks whether the canon was made or whether it grew, whether and how far its parts are pseudepigraphic. For the Old Testament there is outside testimony only from late Judaism and the Talmud; for the New there is a wealth of evidence arising from the circumstances under which it came into existence by about 150 A.D. One result of criticism is to reveal the motive of canon-formation and also the correctness of the separation of the literature made authoritative by comparison of it with the noncanonical (see CANON OF SCRIPTURE).

1. Criticism of the Canon.

A preliminary in this work is the collection of the text-critical apparatus which shall present an orderly and complete picture of the condition of the text. The documents must be described and their characteristics brought to light. The sources of text-criticism are manuscripts in the original languages, lectionaries of selected parts, translations, citations; for the Old Testament the Masorah, for the Septuagint and the New Testament also patristic commentaries and scholia. The variant readings in this mass of materials are to be arranged and classified, a preliminary to which is the valuation of the text-sources on the basis of age, genealogy, and trustworthiness. In the Old Testament the difference of the Masoretic text from that of the Septuagint proves the two to be independent witnesses; but the fact that the text of the latter is not yet settled makes difficult the task of arbitrating between the two. On the other hand, the New Testament writings were not, before the time of Origen, handled with the care bestowed by the Jews on the text of the law. The collection of apparatus for the New Testament text presents not only an agitated sea of differences in orthography and word-forms which create little or no difference in sense, but also a series of variations which affect the meaning and educed the wail of Origen that they were the result not only of carelessness on the part of the scribes but also of wilfulness and design. The task is to bring order into this mass of variations. There have been discerned three principal types of text, the Alexandrian, the Western, and the Constantinopolitan. The text of the Synoptic Gospels shows the most serious variations, in which purpose is manifest to make parallel passages read in the same way and to supply omissions. The text of Revelation and of the Lucan writings also is in a bad condition. Great differences exist between the text of the Alexandrian and the Greco-Latin types. The last word on relative values has not yet been said, and the matter is still further complicated by the fact that the minuscules have not yet been taken fully into consideration, and they contain very many excellent and independent readings. See BIBLE TEXT.

2. Textual Criticism and Apparatus.

The purpose of comparison of variant texts is approximation to the original. The critic estimates the age of a document. For this much help has been received from the papyri and parchments recovered in Egypt, from which it has been learned that the earliest texts were written in capitals and without accents or marks of punctuation, and that the word or syllable was broken at the end of the line as the demands of space required. Study of the processes of reproduction of manuscripts has shown that errors are either mechanical or designed. The former are illustrated by the doubling of a word or a passage or the omission of the same either by an error of the eye or of the ear, or by the substitution of one word or letter for another which resembles it either in form or sound. Of conscious or designed variations from the original, some were brought about by attempts to smooth a rough passage or to illumine an obscure one, to correct real or supposed errors, to make two parallel passages read in the same way, or to change the reading so as to support some dogmatic interest. The Old Testament was originally written without punctuation or helps to reading and pronunciation; the possibility of error is, therefore, greatly increased as compared with the Greek text, the vowels of which were always written.

After interpretation has set forth the lexicographic and grammatical character of the language, criticism inquires into the relation of expression to thought, unity in the methods of expression, and individual characteristics in writing as related to the general character of the language, and into the various influences which have controlled the form. Dissimilarity in style in parts argues dissimilarity in authorship; disarrangement or disorder suggests interpolation. Especially valuable are the tests which depend upon uniformity in the use of certain fundamental notions such as those of the kingdom of God, life, faith, righteousness, spirit, flesh. Similarly use is made of collection and comparison of idioms which characterize a writing or a group of writings, and in this case critical judgment is of great importance. Individuality is thus discovered, since the idiosyncrasies of writers are in the main unconscious and undesigned. And rhetorical qualities also come into play, the tendency to a type of expression or fondness for certain words or kinds of figures or turns of sentence. Recognition of characteristic ways of using language adds to text-critical apparatus, since it not only presents the facts of different readings and of peculiarities, but also notes their effects, influences, and modifications. So that text-criticism and criticism of the language work together in correcting an unintelligible or corrupt text by employing conjecture. By this is not meant merely subjective sagacity or ineptly used technical skill. Conjecture is the result of study of the causes of error in the text which marks them as mechanical or designed, and then seeks a reading in accordance with the habit and character of the document under examination, a reading which on known principles of error in transmission will produce the particular error.

3. Linguistic Criticism.

Historical criticism is applied not merely to works on history but to any literary product of the past which claims or really has importance for any historical reason. The result of this process is pronouncement upon the worth of any particular document as a source. It deals with the genuineness, unity, integrity, and trustworthiness of a writing, asks whether it is as the author wrote it or whether it has been corrupted or falsified, whether it reflects the habit of the author assumed or of the times in which it is placed.

4. Historical Criticism.

Since it is seldom that explicit external testimony to a document is available, criticism usually proceeds upon internal evidence. But this is not always decisive. Conceivably, the tradition of Israel's sojourn in Egypt might have arisen out of the story of the Babylonian exile. So of the New Testament writings, the decision whether they are really documents of the apostolic age depends finally upon the judgment of their character as a whole and upon appraisement of the distance between them and the postapostolic and apocryphal literature.

The three points upon which the critic is intent are not of equal weight. Thus, though the *authenticity* of a writing be denied on internal grounds, the worth of the writing as a source is not thereby necessarily denied, for the document may have been produced anonymously, may be a genuine witness for the times in which it was written, and yet have had a name wrongly attached to it later. Examples of this are the Books of Samuel, the Gospel of Matthew, and the Epistle to the Hebrews, which last is a genuine document of the apostolic age, though the authorship is undetermined. So *integrity* does not of itself determine source-value. Investigation in this direction discovers gaps or additions and relates them to historic *credibility*. The final test has reference to this quality. Investigation into a writing as a whole leads to the discussion of its composition. Criticism of sources enters here, which on the basis of the linguistic character of the finished work and of its parts decides whether the work is a unit or is composite. In the latter case the questions arise what was the original form and how far it has been changed by the successive hands through which it has passed; whether the parts are in their original form or have been worked over, and in the latter case whether in some dogmatic interest. Such are the problems which arise respecting the Pentateuch and the Gospels. Decision in favor of the trustworthiness of a document in itself a unit and complete is carried a step further toward assurance by comparison with the general whole to which it belongs. This involves consideration of linguistic characteristics, of the circle of ideas in which it moves, the general trend of thought. Account is taken of external testimony. In this case error has to be guarded against, since the trustworthiness and competence of the witness is itself a subject for investigation. The criticism of the Epistle to the Philippians gives an illustration of the difficulties of the process, where irreconcilably different conclusions have been reached by Baur, Holsten, and P. W. Schmidt.

The most important problem affecting credibility arises from the specific character of the Biblical narratives. What attitude shall be assumed toward miracles? How far are the reports legendary or mythical? What is the relation of the religious idea to the question of the historicity of the reports and of their worth as sources? The position taken will depend upon the philosophical position of the critic. The theist does not disavow belief in miracles and values the divine self-consciousness of Jesus as testimony to his living participation in deity. But the historic spirit of the times enters a caveat by noting the limitation placed on the reporters by the characteristics of the times in which they lived. Moreover, he who accepts Jesus as a wonder-worker is not called on as a critic to prove the reports of miracles reliable; nor is he who accepts Jesus as God's son required to prove the stories of the infancy, analogies of which are so abundantly available. But with the recognition that there are obscurities in the reports of miracles and that poetry, legend, and myth are used by the Bible, the last word has not been spoken on the historicity of Biblical narratives. When the English minister Mitchell said in relation to the wars of Frederick the Great that the latter was fighting for the freedom of the human race, he gave an interpretation of history but did not alter the historic fact. It is then possible that without altering the facts the Gospels, under the impression made by the person of Jesus, acknowledge him as Son of God and Savior of the world. If the theologian speaks of salvation as a fact which has become known in history, that is not a dogmatic dislocation but a correct valuation of the historical order in which the Christian religion and its Old Testament precursor reveal themselves.

"Style is only the order and progress in which thought takes form; it supposes the union and exercise of all the intellectual faculties, and it is the man" (Buffon). This utters the final decision in the reaching of which the critical and hermeneutical faculties unite more closely than in the processes named above.

5. Criticism of Style.

It asks the question, what purposes did the writing have and how did it attain them? It takes into account the total impression made by the document, the progress of thought and the conception of history it embodies; it notes clearness and force or indefiniteness and unwieldiness, originality or accord with accustomed forms. And in the background is ever a reference to the historical setting and relationships. Historical criticism may show compositeness in a document and answer the question whether the elements are united by a loose idea or are worked into each other. In the latter case criticism of style shows the relation of the parts to the whole. When historical criticism has thoroughly investigated historical conditions and order, the question of credibility in a new sense arises. Was the purpose objective or personal, did the ideal enter into the personal, did personal interests and passion modify the objectivity of the writing? For documents run to *Tendenz* whenever they are not purely objective narrative.

The results from the processes so far reviewed are now positive, now negative. They produce decisions upon the completeness, reliability, and value of what has been transmitted.

That done, the relation of the product under discussion to the original actuality in particular and in general remains to be investigated. What is historic reconstruction? Niebuhr's *History of Rome* was the first concrete example of the results of the process. It embodied his endeavor to pierce through the displacements and exaggerations of national pride which influenced the historical form of the statements and to discover actuality as it was and developed. His method is and remains the method of constructive criticism. The first step, then, is criticism of sources, which not only reveals their nature and value, but grasps also their connection with the original fact, their original relations, their mutual dependence or independence. In religious literature it is necessary to have regard to the conceptions embodied to see whether these are the original gift of the religion or whether they have entered during the course of the development. Hence the sources have to be traced to their original form, conceptions are abstracted, the historical course of events displayed, and the method by which events have worked out of the objective and essential conditions discovered.

6. Reconstructive Criticism.

The dominant method of source-criticism is literary. It deals with documentary indication, traces backward parallel traditions and distinguishes their relationship, genealogy, and dependence; it shows their original or secondary character, seeks the occasions of their deviations; in documents it would discern the seams of joining, the manner and form of the insertions. And then often the question arises whether an oral or a written source lies in the background. And besides this there is in Biblical literature the complicating factor of the editors; so that modern criticism is well represented graphically by the "Rainbow Bible." In the foreground of interest now is the proving of the relationship of Biblical presentations and conceptions to the original form and sense and the attempt to show their interrelationship. Are the leading Biblical conceptions original and in their original form? Do the terms used carry their original meanings, or has the original sense become detached and connected itself with some other term? The answers to such questions will lead back to the early forms of the religion of the Old Testament and of Christianity, will produce a history of religious ideas; but the work is yet in its infancy. Even the prehistoric cult-motive, found in totemism, animism, and belief in demons will not close the inquiry; there is the background of the self-seeking impulses which led men to placate ghosts and employ magic and sorcery. And the relations of these to the Old Testament and the New are yet under discussion. They indeed point out in which direction criticism must direct its researches.

The highest and most difficult task is the reconstruction of the historic process, the monuments of which are found in the criticized writings. It purposes a presentation of the entire circle of ideas, and seeks to discover from the deficient sources the original connection, and from the reports brought together the original development. The results then are historical, the basis sought is the most ultimate facts attainable, but the degree of assurance necessarily varies. In Biblical science the two objective points are the recovery of the history of Israel and of the history of the origins of the Christian Church. The crux of the first is the relationship of the prophetic literature to the Pentateuch. Is the latter preprophetic or postprophetic and postexilic? Another question still under discussion is the historical value of the body of tradition about the patriarchs and Moses; estimates of the highest importance and bearing upon character hang upon the decision. The reconstruction of New Testament history depends upon the decision as to the existence or non-existence of usable sources of history in the New Testament. The new Dutch school returns a negative answer on the ground that New Testament literature is mostly pseudepigraphic. Everything here depends upon criticism of sources, upon the decision about the bases of the Synoptic Gospels, the Johannine literature, the Christology of the Epistles. Upon decisions rendered here hangs also the estimate of the person and work of the founder of Christianity. For the conception of apostolic times critical valuation of the worth of Acts as a source is required, and a determination of its relation to the Pauline Epistles and of the genuineness of the latter. In this case also conclusions the most opposite are reached with necessarily opposite results in the construction of history. The difficulties of the reconstruction of Biblical history are thus suggested, and in the work only a beginning has been made. Real progress is possible only if the critic is not self-deceived in respect to the continuity and completeness of the sources and the objective basis of his hypotheses, and if he does not forget that the history which he undertakes to reconstruct neither claims to nor can supply the religious force which is operative in history.

IV. History of Criticism: This might be made to embrace all work conducted with critical insight as well as of all branches of Biblical science with the hypotheses and conclusions. Decision must be made between a review of the results and of the conditions and valuations which have given the impulse to a new series of questions. With the latter goes a description of the methods necessitated by the newer conditions. It is also to be remarked that criticism and interpretation, so to speak, alternate and relieve each other. Interpretation flourishes when tradition is accepted at its face value; criticism, when doubt has called in question that value, though indeed criticism is never beyond call.

1. Meaning and Limitations.

The Greeks were the fathers of criticism. No other people of the ancient world employed critical methods; the memory, not judgment, held sway. Judaism was no exception, for the Masorah is text-criticism in a limited sense only. But among the Greeks criticism was the handmaid of interpretation. Homer was their canon, furnishing the model of the completest expression of human relationships. Consequently, text-

2. Hellenistic and Patristic Criticism.

criticism found there its task and elaborated its methods, while interpretation was also at work. The questions of integrity, authenticity, and credibility were raised, but of course the answers were such as the age was qualified to give.

It has often been denied that in the patristic age criticism existed. But patristic literature set itself the task of suppressing the old canon and replacing it by the new canon of the Old Testament and the New. And in this task criticism was a necessary agent. Alexandria and Antioch were the two seats of the new learning, the headquarters where the methods of the Greeks were applied in pursuit of the new object (see ALEXANDRIA, SCHOOL OF; ANTIOCH, SCHOOL OF). Even the fourfold division of the science employed by the Greeks was adopted, though the whole work proceeded from a different standpoint. For the Greeks the esthetic was the principal thing, for the Church Fathers the religious; in both cases criticism served interpretation. The great undertaking of Origen to bring order into the corrupt text of the Septuagint remained incomplete and only introduced further confusion. What opinion is to be entertained of the recensions of Lucian and Hesychius is not yet certain. Jerome's efforts to obtain a better text of the Vulgate advanced text-criticism but little. In the matter of the canon of the New Testament, the genealogy of texts, the public use of the Scriptures, and their genuineness were discussed. Explanations were offered of the differences found in the writings ascribed to John. And in the councils and synods the matter of canonicity was raised for churchly authority to decide.

3. Criticism from the Time of the Reformation.

With the Reformation criticism took a new start upon a basis prepared by humanism, but within the bounds set by patristic criticism. The inspiration of the Bible was assumed, for the need felt was for nourishment of the spirit. Criticism assumed more definite forms after attempts were made to fix the teaching of the Evangelical Church. The early Protestant doctrine of inspiration attempted to exalt into law what had been till then simple religious statement. A wall was built upon the Protestant doctrine of Scripture against the Roman Catholic conceptions. Apologetics and harmonistics were created. The doctrine of verbal inspiration came into play until text-critical apparatus began to accumulate. Then dogmatic pronouncement upon the contents of Scripture, upon its clearness and sufficiency, stumbled over fact, and the earlier dogma of inspiration came to grief.

Under such conditions Biblical criticism developed and became more opposed to dogmatism. Its apostle was Spinoza, who in his *Tractatus theologico-politicus* authoritatively formulated the problem for the future. The skepticism of the seventeenth and the deism and rationalism of the eighteenth centuries changed not the form of the problem, but only the tone of the critic. Spinoza had given a comprehensive description of the exigency produced by a theology benumbed by dogmatics. His desire was to produce an undogmatic Christianity through criticism of the documents. Christianity was to be apprehended as teaching for practical life and not as philosophy. Religion was not to contradict reason. Criticism attacked the problem of the text and proceeded to discussion of the canon and its contents. Meanwhile the view was held that religion was something different from theology.

The first attempts to build up a critical method were in the region of the Roman classics. J. Robertellus (*De arte sive ratione corrigendi antiquorum libros disputatio*, Padua, 1557) defined the sources of error in the text as additions, eliminations, transpositions, extensions, condensations, separations (of parts belonging together), joinings (of parts which should be kept apart), and variations. Caspar Scioppius (1597) argued against the "rash and audacious attempts to better the text." Johannes Clericus (1697) connected criticism of the classics and of the Bible. Perhaps he was the first to see that the canon had a history. L. Cappellus (1634), A. Pfeiffer (1680), and J. G. Carpzov (1728) argued for the unassailable authority of Scripture, but Carpzov's conjectural emendation of the Masoretic text aroused the scorn of the orthodox, who declared this text inviolable, as Ball and Erasmus had that of the Vulgate. But a new turn was given when the Oratorian J. Morinus (1633) exalted the text of the Septuagint over that of the Masoretes because derived from purer sources, though this valuation was discredited by the insecure readings of the Septuagint. Mill (1707) and Wetstein (1751) collected a rich apparatus for the New Testament, and Bengel proposed to alter the *Textus receptus* upon the basis of manuscript readings properly discriminated. The great Bentley's proposal to form a new recension of the Greek text (on the basis of MS. A and of the Vulgate) was wrecked on the rocks of the opposition of the theologians.

The criticism of sources was established in Bentley's disproof of the genuineness of the *Letters of Phalaris*. That method was applied to Biblical literature only in individual instances among the Arminians and Socinians, an example of which is found in H. Grotius's work on Thessalonians. The application of this to the Old Testament was first made in Astruc's discussion of Genesis (1753). The antidogmatic position of criticism became ever more pronounced in the eighteenth century. English deism attacked clumsily the historicity of the Old Testament Scriptures. Skepticism rejoiced over the proof of variety in origin of Biblical writings. Rationalism sought to prove that history is no puzzle and all proceeds in rational order. Lessing's discussion with Goetze over the "Wolfenbüttel Fragments" fathomed deep waters. Against the reckless criticism of English deism appeared Lardner's *Ancient Jewish and Heathen Testimonies to the Truth of the Christian Religion* (1764–67), while through Michaelis and Semler criticism sought to find equipoise.

The modern age of critical research began with the end of the eighteenth century. Its aim is an undogmatic method founded on fact, and its task is reconstruction of history on the basis of a grasp of original conditions and of the actual course of development. It makes use of psychology, linguistics, literary art, and history, and it attempts to guard against the one-sided application of any or all of these, recognizing that subjective criticism would produce results inconsonant with the spirit of the times in which the literature discussed was produced. The historical point of view as applied to the Bible was first expressed by Herder. Schleiermacher and Eichhorn made contributions to it, but not without error. Strauss's intellectual method overlooked criticism of sources. Bruno Bauer's reconstruction of the early history of Christianity on the basis of Philo, Seneca, and Greco-Roman philosophy was bettered by F. C. Baur, who sought a factual basis. Vatke's work on the Old Testament has been confirmed and extended by Reuss, Graf, Wellhausen, and Kuenen. How Biblical criticism has changed its center of gravity is illustrated by the dictionaries. Teller's *Wörterbuch des Alten Testaments* (6th ed., 1805) was ultrarationalistic. Winer's work (3d ed., 1847) expressed the materialistic doubt of De Wette. Schenkel's *Bibellexicon* (1869-75) represented the Tübingen school. Riehm-Baethgen (1897) shut the latter out as much as possible, in which line the new *Dictionary of the Bible* of Hastings follows, while the *Encyclopædia Biblica* occupies the most advanced position and complains that criticism of the New Testament is less advanced than that of the Old.

4. Modern Criticism.

(G. Heinrici.)

V. Biblical Criticism in the Roman Catholic Church: It is a well-known fact that the subject of Biblical criticism has never received so much attention among Roman Catholic as among Protestant scholars. This disparity of interest in a topic so important is doubtless largely due to the fundamentally different attitude of the two Churches toward the Bible itself. While the early Reformers claimed to set aside tradition and church authority, and to make the Bible—and the Bible alone—the foundation-stone of their respective creeds, the Catholic theologians and controversialists, on the other hand, emphasized anew the principle of central organic authority. For Catholics the supreme and ultimate guide in matters of religion, faith, and morals is the infallible authority of the living Church—authority which in their view has been inherited from the Apostles and the Divine Founder of Christianity. This organized society is considered as the divinely appointed custodian of all revelation, whether contained in the Scriptures or in the storehouse of Christian tradition, and to this society belongs, under divine guidance, the official and authoritative interpretation of Holy Writ. The great and exclusive importance given to the Bible in the Protestant communions naturally called for a deep and comprehensive study of the Scriptures, and this, in the nature of things, was bound to develop on critical lines; whereas Catholics, resting content with the principle of church authority, continued to look upon the Bible as something incidental and secondary in comparison with the living, teaching organization. Hence less interest on the part of the latter in the various branches of Biblical investigation, and likewise less alarm at the changes wrought by the so-called destructive criticism in the traditional views concerning the Bible.

But, while the general interest in the topic has been less marked among Catholics, it is true that scholars belonging to that faith have made valuable contributions to the rise and growth of scientific Biblical criticism. The first, perhaps, who deserves mention is the French Oratorian Richard Simon (1638-1712) who, setting aside the abstract, *a priori* methods previously in vogue, began a study at once historical and critical of the principal topics pertaining to the origin and growth of the Bible. The results of his investigations, which were too far in advance of his age to receive intelligent appreciation from his contemporaries, were embodied in a series of volumes, which, however much they may have been superseded by writings of later scholars, are nevertheless extremely interesting as setting forth the true critical method and applying it with a freedom which was bound to provoke opposition and censure on the part of orthodox theologians such as Bossuet (see Simon, Richard). It was the Catholic physician Jean Astruc (q.v.) who gave a valuable key and a starting-point to the modern documentary analysis of the Pentateuch by his essay published in 1753. Another Catholic clergyman who figures prominently among the pioneers in the field of scientific Biblical study is the Scotchman Alexander Geddes (1737-1802; see Geddes, Alexander). Foremost among modern and contemporary Catholic scholars who have distinguished themselves in the field of Biblical criticism must be placed the abbé A. F. Loisy (q.v.), who to a vast erudition and a remarkably keen critical acumen has unfortunately joined a sarcasm of exposition and a rashness of speculation which have brought him into serious disfavor with the authorities of the Church. The more moderate school of Catholic Biblical scholars includes a relatively large and ever growing number of adherents who, always subject to the limitations imposed by church authority, frankly accept the well-authenticated results of scientific critical investigation. Obviously these scholars are not so free and independent in their researches as their non-Catholic brethren, but Catholic apologists claim that while the restrictions imposed do at times curtail unduly the freedom of investigators whose views though correct may not harmonize with traditionally received opinions, they serve, on the other hand, as a salutary check on critical speculations of the more radical and advanced type.

Moved by the acute controversies which within the last quarter of a century have grown up in the field of Bible study and caused so much alarm in most of the orthodox communions, Pope Leo XIII instituted a Biblical Commission which was to be a standing tribunal composed of Scripture specialists and theologians, for the settlement on scientific as well as authoritative grounds of the various knotty questions raised by higher criticism. Under the present pope, however, while the number of members and consultors of this tribunal was greatly augmented, a large majority was conceded to the theologians as distinguished from the Biblical scholars; and the decisions rendered thus far have little or no interest for the scientific world, as they constitute simply a reaffirmation, without specified reasons, of the traditional positions. In the Church at present the trend of authoritative direction as regards the Scriptures is unfavorable to Biblical criticism, as is plain from the Syllabus of Modern Errors and the encyclical against Modernism issued by Pius X in 1907 (see SYLLABUS).

JAMES F DRISCOLL.

BIBLIOGRAPHY: For works on textual criticism see BIBLE TEXT; on the history of criticism consult: H. Cave, *The Battle of the Standpoints; the Old Testament and the Higher Criticism*, London, 1892 (brief and popular); H. S. Nash, *The History of the Higher Criticism of the New Testament*, New York, 1900, new ed., 1907 (an argument for scientific Bible study).

For exposition of methods consult C. A. Briggs, *General Introduction to the Study of Holy Scripture*, New York, 1899 (exhaustive); A. C. Zenos, *Elements of the Higher Criticism*, ib. 1895 (useful); F. Ast, *Wissenschaftliche Darstellung der Grammatik, Hermeneutik und Kritik*, Landshut, 1808; F. Hitzig, *Begriff der Kritik am Alten Testament*, Heidelberg, 1831; F. D. E. Schleiermacher, *Ueber Begriff und Einteilung der philosophischen Kritik*, in his *Sämmtliche Werke*, III. iii, 387–404, Berlin, 1835; A. Kuenen, *Critices et hermeneuticæ librorum Novi Testamenti lineamenta*, Leyden, 1889; F. Blass, *Hermeneutik und Kritik*, in *Handbuch der klassischen Altertumswissenschaft*, I. i, 127–128, Munich, 1891; F. Godet and others, *Higher Criticism, Six Papers*, New York, 1893; C. W Rishell, *Higher Criticism*, Cincinnati, 1893 (needs revision); E. Bernheim, *Lehrbuch der historischen Methode*, Leipsic, 1894; H. Hildebrand, *Die höhere Bibelkritik*, Paderborn, 1902; W. Möller, *Biblical Criticism*, London, 1903; G. W. Gilmore, *Biblical Criticism*, in *The Monist*, xiv (1904), 215 sqq.

For criticism of higher-critical methods and results consult: E. Böhl, *Zum Gesetz und zum Zeugniss, eine Abwehr wider die neu-kritische Schriftforschung im Alten Testament*, Vienna, 1883; O. Naumann, *Wellhausen's Methode*, Leipsic, 1886; F. Vigouroux, *Les Livres saints et la critique rationaliste*, 4 vols., Paris, 1886–90; J. J. Blunt, *Undesigned Coincidences in the Writings of both the Old and the New Testaments*, republished, New York, 1890; R. F. Horton, *Revelation and the Bible*, London, 1892; E. Rupprecht, *Die Anschauung der kritischen Schule Wellhausens*, Erlangen, 1893; A. Zahn, *Ernste Blicke in den Wahn der modernen Kritik des Alten Testaments*, Gütersloh, 1893; F. R. Beattie, *Radical Criticism, an Exposition and Examination of the Radical Critical Theory*, Chicago, 1894; L. Munhall, *Anti-higher Criticism*, New York, 1894 (extreme in its conservatism); S. Leathes, *Claims of the Old Testament*, ib. 1897; W. H. Green, *General Introduction to the Old Testament*, New York, 1899 (Dr. Green was the exponent of the most conservative type of Biblical study, and his strictures on higher criticism will be found in his *Moses and the Prophets*, 1883, *The Hebrew Feasts in their Relation to Recent Critical Hypotheses*, 1886, *Higher Criticism of the Pentateuch*, 1895, and *Unity of the Book of Genesis*, 1895); W. Möller, *Are the Critics Right?* ib. 1903; F. D. Storey, *Higher Criticism Cross-examined*, Philadelphia, 1905; J. Orr, *The Problem of the O. T.*, London, 1906 (conservative). For application and statement of critical methods consult: G. D'Eichthal, *Mélanges de critique biblique*, Paris, 1886; Smith, *OTJC*, cf. R. Watts, *The Newer Criticism and the Analogy of the Faith*, Edinburgh, 1883 (Watts is a reply to Smith); J. P. Smyth, *The Old Documents and the New Bible*, London, 1890; T. K. Cheyne, *Aids to the Devout Study of Criticism*, ib. 1892; W. Sanday, *Inspiration*, ib. 1896 (advanced in dealing with the O. T., conservative as respects the N. T.); idem, *Criticism of the Fourth Gospel*, ib. 1905; W. F. Adeney, *How to Read the Bible*, ib. 1897 (a helpful handbook); G. A. Smith, *Modern Criticism and the Preaching of the Old Testament*, ib. 1901; R. Balmforth, *The Bible from the Standpoint of Higher Criticism*, 2 vols., New York, 1904–05; T. W. Doane, *Bible Myths and their Parallels in Other Religions*, ib. 1905.

On the interrelations of criticism, the Bible, and archeology consult: H. A. Harper, *The Bible and Modern Discoveries*, Boston, 1889; H. E. Ryle, *Early Narratives of Genesis*, London, 1892; T. Laurie, *Assyrian Echoes of the Word*, ib. 1894; A. H. Sayce, *Higher Criticism and the Verdict of the Monuments*, ib. 1894 (archeological, reaching the same conclusions as the critics, yet violently assailing them); W. St. C. Boscawen, *Bible and the Monuments*, ib. 1895; F. Hommel, *Ancient Hebrew Tradition as Illustrated by the Monuments*, ib. 1897 (the standpoint is similar to Sayce's); D. G. Hogarth, *Authority and Archeology*, ib. 1899 (in its Biblical parts sober, and a corrective of Sayce and Hommel); I. M. Price, *Monuments and the Old Testament*, Chicago, 1900; T. G. Pinches, *The Old Testament in the Light of Historical Records and Legends of Assyria and Babylonia*, London, 1902; Schrader, *KAT*.

BIBLICAL HISTORY. See ISRAEL, HISTORY OF, I.

BIBLICAL HISTORY, INSTRUCTION IN: Fundamental to all Christian teaching and attainment, especially according to the Protestant view, is a knowledge of the Bible; and this knowledge naturally begins with the characters, events, and institutions of the Bible—a sum total of knowledge which may be comprehended under the general expression Bible history. Thence the individual is led on to the weightier matters of Christian doctrine and the manner of the Christian life. The organized and premeditated efforts of the earlier Church to impart Christian instruction (see CATECHUMENATE; CATECHESIS, CATECHETICS; CATECHISMS; HOMILETICS; etc.) aimed more directly at the latter, assuming that the former already existed. In the New Testament, knowledge of Old Testament history is presupposed. This knowledge was communicated at home (II Tim. iii, 15) or by readings at the public services (I Tim. iv, 13). The aim of a portion of the New Testament Scripture (the Gospels and Acts) was to keep alive in the congregations the knowledge of the New Testament history. In the primitive Church, besides public service, home training (Eusebius, *Hist. eccl.*, vi, 2; Chrysostom on Eph. vi, 4) and private reading (Cyril, *Catech.*, iv, 35; *Apostolic Constitutions*, vii, 39) were means of imparting Biblical history to beginners in Christianity. During the Middle Ages no systematic school instruction in Biblical history could be furnished for lack of common schools, and self-instruction was not possible for the people because the Bible was commonly in Latin and costly, and but few of the laity could read even the works provided for them in their mother tongue (see BIBLES, HISTORICAL). The great mass were limited to the translations by preachers of the texts of their sermons, or narrations of Bible stories in the sermon; also, scenes especially from the life of Jesus or dramatic spectacles from the Biblical record helped to preserve in the lay world the knowledge of Biblical essentials (see RELIGIOUS DRAMAS). In Reformation time as well as in the following centuries, there was no general systematic schooling in Biblical history; the common-school system was as yet a merely formative conception, and text-books of Bible history (for list cf. Reu) were designed for higher schools or for the home

Conditions Before the Reformation.

Not until Christian common schools were introduced did instruction in Biblical history become a systematized branch of public education. Among the text-books thus used may be mentioned the *Biblische Historien* of Justus Gesenius (1656), and the *Zweimal 52 auserlesenen biblischen Historien* of Johann Hübner (1714). These books are the prototypes of modern German manuals, and such manuals have now generally taken the place of the Bible, from which in earlier times Biblical history was taught by reading aloud. The Roman Catholic Church also teaches Biblical history; a text-book widely in vogue was that of Christoph von Schmid (d. 1850). At present the Bible histories of the Catholics are combined with their diocesan catechisms. Their new catechism, which according to the desire of Pius X is to become the Catholic standard or uniform catechism (*Compendio della dottrina christiana*, 1905), contains a *Breve storia della religione*. It thus appears that modern Churches, in contrast with the primitive Church, have reached the conviction that catechumens should gain the necessary amount of knowledge of Bible history not immediately from the Bible, but from a text-book prepared for this educational object. But the fact is still more significant that the Churches are convinced of the necessity of a knowledge of Biblical history.

Biblical Instruction in Schools.

This conviction rests on the knowledge that Christian belief is the product of a history which came to pass between God and humanity, and that the knowledge and understanding of this salvation on the part of individual Christians must proceed from acquaintance with this history. The selection of Bible stories for catechumens is adapted to this principle. The various manuals of Biblical history deviate from one another in details of selection, but are in substantial agreement in the matter of setting forth the main events of sacred history according to their historical succession. An exception occurs in the case of compilations intended for children who are not yet catechetical scholars; for these there is need of particular Bible narratives adapted to the years of childhood and related to the church festivals. With reference to the connection between instruction in Biblical history and instruction in the catechism, a change has come about, since in earlier times instruction in the former had practically no independent significance, but was designed to subserve the catechism; the contrary situation, however, obtains to-day, certain modern instructors making Biblical history the main issue, while catechetical scholars are confined to the fundamentally illustrative or especially adapted Biblical relations. Concerning the method of instruction, there is a consensus of modern conviction to the effect that the text-book should coincide as far as possible with the wording of the Bible as generally in use. The earlier method of reading the narrative from the Bible, or having it read aloud by a pupil, has been discarded. It is better to have a story related by the teacher; and the preferable method is that his oral discourse should adhere altogether or with close approximation to the phrasing of the text-book. In particular the decisive and striking utterances of the *dramatis personæ* should be reproduced exactly. Opportunity for explanation and application is afforded by the subsequent discussion. The use of maps and pictures, with which modern Biblical text-books are provided, tends to give the matter more of an objective background, but pictures are not so necessary as they formerly were, when pupils had fewer books. [In the United States, religious instruction being necessarily excluded from the public schools, the teaching of Bible history belongs to the Church and the home. See SUNDAY SCHOOLS.]

Methods and Principles.

W. CASPARI.

BIBLIOGRAPHY: C. A. G. von Zezschwitz, *Katechetik*, ii. 2, chaps. 2–4, Leipsic, 1872–74; K. H. Holtsch, *Studien über den biblischen Geschichtsunterricht*, Breslau, 1870; W. H. G. Thomas, *Methods of Bible Study*, New York, 1903; L. Emery, *Introduction à l'étude de la théologie protestante*, pp. 122–132, Paris, 1904; J. M. Reu, *Quellen zur Geschichte des biblischen Unterrichts*, Gütersloh, 1906.

BIBLICAL INTRODUCTION.

I. Old Testament: The science of Old Testament Introduction, like that of Biblical Introduction in general, has developed from indefinite beginnings, and has not yet won the assured and universally recognized form which most other theological disciplines have assumed. The name *eisagōgē* was used in the fifth century by the Syro-Greek monk Adrian, the terms *introductorii libri* and *introductores* in the sixth by Cassiodorus. But these terms carried the meaning of a general and instructive direction how to read the Bible, a guide to its correct understanding, an exposition of the correct principles of exegesis. A complete understanding of the Bible involves, however, a number of auxiliary sciences—linguistics, exegesis, history of literature, general history, archeology, geography, Biblical theology, etc., all useful in obtaining a right apprehension of Scripture. But so large a conception of the science was not reached all at once. It was J. G. Carpzov who first appreciated the comprehensive nature of the discipline and defined it as the precise setting forth of those matters a knowledge of which prepares the approach to the reading of the sacred books. Similarly De Wette understood by Intro-

1. Nature and Scope of the Discipline.

duction all knowledge which contributed to the intelligent reading of the Bible, and which set it forth as a whole and in its parts in relation to history. Keil regarded it as an exposition of those matters the understanding of which prepares for a fruitful reading of Scripture, by which he understands only a history of the text, of the origin of the individual writings, the story of the rise of the canon, and of the general conception of Scripture. A new start was made by H. Hupfeld, who held that Introduction sought to discover what were the writings embraced in the Bible and how they had come to be what they are. In other words, what is sought are the extent and original character of the writings, and a knowledge of the vicissitudes through which they have passed in attaining their present form, unity, worth, and effectiveness. But care is needed in following such a formulation lest one make of Old Testament Introduction simply a history of Hebrew literature, a mistake made by Reuss, who included in his work the letter of Aristeas and the writings of Philo. The first consideration of this science must be its service to theology; its principal concern is with the books of the canon held by the Jews of Palestine, and only secondarily with the circle of writings derived from Hellenistic sources. Care must also be taken not to limit the task of Introduction so as to take away its freedom and to bind it in effect to the pronouncements of tradition as to authorship. On the other hand, Introduction is not what Riehm would make it, the literary-historical characterization of the Bible as the authentification of a divine revelation. It has its own functions to perform in the service of theological science, and its usefulness must not be diminished by setting it at tasks which it may not undertake. Its work is a preparation for that of exegesis and for that of Biblical theology. As Reuss has well expressed the fact, the science of Introduction is not the house itself, but is the set of calculations and estimates necessary for the actual processes of building.

From the preceding it follows that the articulation of this discipline in the general science of theology is fixed. In the arrangement and handling of its subject-matter it demands and requires great freedom; on the other hand, certain lines are laid down along which it must operate. Thus, while the origin of the separate writings and the story of their transmission (history of the text) are its concern, it is a matter of choice whether consideration of the individual writings precede or follow consideration of their collection into a canon.

2. Method of Treatment.

Not unimportant is the question of method of investigating the individual writings. Thus, the chronological order certainly lies near to hand, as in the treatment by Wildeboer and Kautzsch; yet, illuminating as this method is, weighty considerations may be urged for another way of proceeding. If one is disposed to emphasize the theological character of the discipline, concentrating his attention upon the writings received into the canon, the chronological, historical-literary order assumes a complexion of incompleteness, since only a small part of Hebrew literature found place in the canon and that part was not composed with the object of being gathered into a collection. By a simpler grouping the advantage is gained of awakening no expectations which are doomed to disappointment. Then, too, there are practical difficulties attending such a method. Over the origin of most Old Testament writings rests a darkness not yet dispelled and probably never wholly to be banished. Moreover, many of the writings, such as the historical books, are complex in origin, and refer to preceding compositions of which too little is known to admit of their being taken into a history of the literature. These same books also bear traces of being transmitted and worked over by hands the methods of operation of which are altogether uncertain. This historical method consequently leads frequently into a cul-de-sac. It is, therefore, not without reason that many have adopted the literary-historical method, following the grouping of the canon so far as to consider the historical books by themselves, the Prophets in another section, and so on, while the three departments of Introduction are history of the canon, of the separate books, and of the text. Whether a history of exegesis is to be included in this branch of study is debatable. For the history of the Bible in a narrower sense it is not important; yet in itself and its relationship it has such value that there is some justification for including in Introduction what properly belongs in hermeneutics.

3. History.

The history of this science shows in all its phases the same marked trait; viz., that the Church, which would fain remain in restful and thankful enjoyment of the Scriptures as handed down, has been compelled by outside pressure to take up the problems of the origins of those Scriptures and either to modify or discard the traditions regarding them. In the earliest times this pressure came partly from Jewish sources, later from linguistic science and philosophy, and later still from the Roman Catholic Church, which sought to undermine the Protestant principle. Only the salient points of the development of Introduction can be here given.

The beginnings are found in the treatment of the canon in the prologue to Ecclesiasticus, in Josephus and the Talmud, and in the controversy between the Jews and some of the Church Fathers respecting the Palestinian and the Alexandrian canon. This led up to the text-critical labors of Origen. The next name is that of Jerome, about whose time began work on Introduction, but with the limits in treatment already referred to above, by Adrian and Cassiodorus, the latter of whom dealt briefly with the history of the text and of the canon.

4. To the Renaissance.

A slight advance was made in the work of Junilius Africanus (about 550) called *Instituta regularia divinæ legis.* This classified the books according to their contents as history, prophecy, proverbs, and simple teaching, and according to their degree of authority as perfect, medium, or of no authority; it distinguished also between poetical and prose writings. In this connection must be mentioned Augustine's *De doctrina Christiana*, which treated of the extent of the canon and of the use of translations. The Church of the Middle Ages was content with the work done by Cassiodorus, Augustine, and Junilius. But among the Jews there were the stirrings of a more vigorous life, exemplified in the investigations of Ibn Ezra in the region of special introduction.

By the revival of learning the Christians were made familiar with the results of Jewish investigations which were soon to lead to the enrichment of isagogical science. The interest in the Hebrew language grew into a wider concern for Oriental philology, which had a fertile field in the translations of the Old Testament, soon to become of use in the department of text-criticism. The earliest fruits ripened among the Roman Catholics in the work of a convert from Judaism, Sixtus of Sienna (d. 1599), the *Bibliotheca sancta*, which distinguished between protocanonical and deuterocanonical writings, and which dealt also with matters of special introduction. The

5. The Reformation Period.

Reformers did not enter this field, though the exegetical works of Calvin contain materials for special introduction, and Luther necessarily had to do with the extent of the canon. Important was the work of Carlstadt, *De canonicis scripturis* (1520), in which he showed the superiority of the Jewish canon and made the canonicity of a Biblical writing depend not upon the authorship but upon its relation to that canon. The period immediately following the Reformation produced nothing notable. A. Rivetus (d. 1662) represents the standpoint of the age in his definition of Scripture as that which proceeds from God as the special author, who not only impelled (the scribe) to write and gave the thoughts, but even suggested the order and the words.

Out of this dogmatic quiet the theologians were shaken by the newer criticism, which began in the realm of the text. The Reformer Cappellus undertook investigations which showed that the traditional text was not altogether trust-

6. The Seventeenth Century.

worthy, and he was followed by the Catholics Morinus and Richard Simon (d. 1712). The latter's *Histoire critique* was epoch-making in that it employed the literary-historical method, and showed that the Pentateuch could not be wholly the work of Moses and that other historical books had been worked over. Simon had been preceded by Hobbes, whose *Leviathan* had used the method of internal testimony, and Spinoza, whose *Tractatus theologico-politicus* had advanced a number of positions which were to be established later. Simon's book awakened much opposition and was suppressed, only to be reproduced in a Protestant land (Rotterdam, 1685). The ideas of Simon were further established in Protestant regions by the work of Johannes Clericus (q.v.), though the tendencies of Protestantism were conservative, and its supporters came later to hope that the learning of Carpzov would establish firmly the truth of the traditional views.

In the second half of the eighteenth century new doors were opened to Biblical criticism, especially by the researches of Semler. At that time the attitude of criticism toward the Old Testament was unfriendly; it treated the collection from the historical standpoint only, but insisted upon understanding the times in which the writings originated. Of religion little was discovered in the Old Testament. Herder came to the help of

7. The Eighteenth Century.

the defenders of the Bible with his discovery of the poetry it contained, and this newer light was intensified in the work of Eichhorn, which outshone all the works of his predecessors and contemporaries. Special interest attaches to the researches of Eichhorn in general introduction, while the work of special introduction gained from his treatment of the books as constituting a Hebrew national literature. Yet permanent results were lacking from that period, excepting only the discovery by Astruc which forecast the documentary analysis of the Pentateuch.

A new era was opened by De Wette, who combined the literary with the historical method. Ewald carried the process on, not indeed in a work on Introduction, but in exegetical researches in which he employed it, using along with it a sympathetic appreciation rather than a rigid logic. Meanwhile the Pentateuchal problem was pushing to the front in the works of Vatke and Reuss, to receive its most advanced consid-

8. The Nineteenth Century.

eration from Wellhausen and Kuenen. The side of the defense had meanwhile not been inactive, as the works of Hengstenberg, Hävernick, and Keil abundantly prove, all of which contributed something toward the solution of the problems discussed. Between the two extremes represented by the men named come others who approach one or the other tendency, but the general characteristic of their labor is to bring into accord the assured results of criticism and the faith of the Church in revelation. The most notable example of this kind of work is Driver's *Introduction*. But the final solution of the problems raised by the science of Introduction will come not from that discipline but from the other branches of theology which build upon it. (F. Buhl.)

II. New Testament.—1. History of the Discipline: The employment of the term "Introduction" with its present connotation in connection with the New Testament dates in modern times from Michaelis. But as in the case of the Old Testament, beginnings had been made long before. Besides the men mentioned above (I, § 4) as working in this department, Tyconius and Eucherius of Lyons attempted to supply the needed information about the origin, occasion, purpose, and history of the New Testament writings. The antagonism to the apocryphal books and heretical parties such as the Marcionites with their variant canon and the Montanists with their new prophecy enhanced in the second and third centuries the Church's valuation of the Christian books which had come to it from the apostolic age. The Muratorian Canon employed a legendary report of the origin of the Gospels, not to explain individual peculiarities, but to establish the dogmatic unimportance of variations in the Gospel narratives. Similarly, the church practise of using in service the private letters of Paul as well as the public letters and of excluding the spurious ones from use was established. The vacillation of the Church in reference to such writings as the Apocalypse of Peter and the Sheperd of Hermas, the Marcionitic criticism of the canon of the Gospels and of the Pauline epistles, the opposition of the Alogi to the Johannine writings as being the production of a heretic of the apostolic age, the writings of Melitus and Hippolytus about the Fourth Gospel and the Apocalypse—all these suggest the way in which the need for a kind of Introduction made itself felt in even those early times. So a beginning was made in the writing of Dionysius on the Apocalypse, while the sentiments and traditions of the different Churches began to take systematic form in the writings of Origen. Eusebius used considerable space in his works in setting forth the varied views and early testimonies concerning the New Testament books. Jerome followed in the steps of Eusebius, but without contributing much that was new in this particular line of investigation. The doctrinal contests of the fourth and succeeding centuries turned the channel of investigation away from the history of the canon, and for a considerable time there appeared only reproductions of the early opinions about the New Testament books in the prefaces to the commentaries or summaries and synopses which came into being and which gave a general view of the arrangement, contents, and origin of the New Testament writings.

1. To the Reformation.

The silence of the Middle Ages gave place during the Reformation to the utterances of the Catholic scholars Sanctes Pagninus of Lucca (d. 1541), Sixtus of Sienna (d. 1599), and A. Rivetus, who wrote an *Isagoge sive introductio* to both the Old and New Testaments (Leyden, 1627). These works contained much information in this department, along with dogmatic discussions concerning inspiration and the relations of Scripture and tradition. Richard Simon (q.v.) published (at Rotterdam) his three works upon the critical history of the New Testament (*Histoire critique du texte*, 1689, *des versions*, 1690, and *des principaux commentateurs*, 1693, *du Nouveau Testament*), and thus won his place as the father of New Testament Introduction. By "*critique*" he understood the investigations for the establishment of the original text; and, by his history from the sources, he impugned not only the Protestant claim of "a witness of the Spirit," but also the scholastic treatment, which, resting upon imperfect acquaintance with antiquity, could not prove that Christianity was a religion based on facts and that the Bible was the record of those facts. In the effort to establish the New Testament text, he traversed a large part of the province of Introduction.

2. The Sixteenth and Seventeenth Centuries.

The next name is Johann David Michaelis (q.v.), who wrote the *Einleitung in die göttlichen Schriften des Neuen Bundes* (Göttingen, 1750). He disclaimed dependency upon Simon, and yet his work was really, in its first shape, based upon Simon. With each succeeding edition it was greatly improved; but, even in the fourth and last edition (1788), its standpoint was a strongly rational supernaturalism. The differences to be noted between the editions are mainly that his attacks on the "doubters" became milder, and that he gave up the inspiration of the historical books, denied also the inspiration of the non-apostolic books (among which he reckoned apparently the Epistle to the Hebrews), and declared that the "inner witness of the Spirit" was of as little worth as the witness of the Church in proof of the inspiration of any book.

3. Michaelis.

Johann Salomo Semler (q.v.) made the next contribution of importance (in his *Abhandlung von freier Untersuchung des Kanons*, 4 parts, Halle, 1771–75), when he distinguished between the word of God, which contained the doctrines of directly spiritual value, and the Holy Scriptures, which contained them only sporadically. There is, however, no historical proof that any particular passage was the word of God; the inner witness for the truth was the only source of proof. The Church had the right, exercised by the ancient Church and by the Reformers, to say what books should constitute the canon. It can not be said that Introduction was influenced permanently by Semler; the greater impulse was given by Michaelis, who was followed by J. E. C. Schmidt (1804), Eichhorn (1804–14), Hug (1808), Berthold (1812), and De Wette (1826), while in England Horne (1818) had included in his work the domains of Biblical geography and antiquities, which were excluded by the Germans. Schmidt applied the phrase "historico-critical"—since so widely used—to his Introduction; Eichhorn started his fruitful "original Gospel" theory; Hug, in an unexcelled manner, investigated the relations of the synoptists. Schleiermacher (1811) called attention to the need of a reconstruction of this branch of study, declaring that its object was a history of the New Testament, so that its present readers might be, in their knowledge of the origin of the books and their text, on a level with the first. Credner (1832 sqq.) projected a fairly complete scheme for a treatment of the subject, embracing the history of the science of Introduction, history of the origin of the New Testament Scriptures, history of the canon, of translations, of the text, and of interpretation. This scheme he was not permitted to carry out, though his posthumous publications completed the history of the canon. Reuss followed Credner's lead in the *Geschichte der heiligen Schriften des Neuen Testaments* (Brunswick, 1842), while Hupfeld made a contribution in his *Begriff und Methode der biblischen Einleitung* (Marburg, 1844).

4. Semler, Schmidt, and Others.

Ferdinand Christian Baur (q.v.; d. 1860) has had by far the most influence upon New Testament studies of any man of modern times. He attempted nothing less than a reconstruction of all apostolic and postapostolic history and literature, from the four Pauline epistles (Galatians, I and II Corinthians, and Romans) which alone he considered genuine. Starting with the idea that the difference between Paul and the rest of the apostles was fundamental, he declared that those New Testament writings which either put the relations of the apostles in a more favorable light or seemed to ignore their differences altogether were either forgeries or the products of a later time. But his historical considerations were derived from Hegel's philosophy, and his criticism rested upon dogmatic convictions. New discoveries of vital importance in the field of church history and patristics and the recovery of the *Codex Sinaiticus* and of parts of Tatian's *Diatessaron* from Ephraem's commentary have given a new basis for a historical discussion of the New Testament and its origin and contents. It is the irony of history upon Baur's methods that the modern Dutch school have used Baur's methods to discredit the four "genuine" epistles. These four points may be made against Baur: (1) He reasoned in a circle; for he examined critically, first the sources of the history, and then the history of the sources. The reasoning which reduced the genuine Pauline epistles to four reduces the four to none; so that Paul is robbed of his title to have produced any writing which lasted. (2) Baur certainly was extraordinarily familiar with the old Christian literature; but he read it with prejudice, and not with a desire to learn anything different from his preconceptions. (3) He was lacking in the sense of the concrete and the value of the individual, and therefore could not grasp complicated relations and their results. (4) If it is self-evident that one must understand what he criticizes, and that his criticism must rest upon thorough exegesis, then Baur surely was unfitted for his labor; for he was weak as an exegete and his school has done little in exegesis.

5. Baur.

It may, however, be added that the deficiencies in Baur's method of work were supplied by others. B. F Westcott's *General Survey of the History of the Canon* (London, 1855 and often), E. Reuss's *Histoire du canon* (Strasburg, 1863), A. Hilgenfeld's *Kanon und die Kritik des Neuen Testaments* (Halle, 1863), T. Zahn's *Geschichte des neutestamentlichen Kanons* (2 vols., Leipsic, 1888–92), and A. Loisy's *Histoire du canon du Nouveau Testament* (Paris, 1891) are productions of this character. Such works as W M. Ramsay's *Church in the Roman Empire* (London, 1893) have served also as correctives of much of the work which has been accomplished in Germany. The studies of F. Bleek (6th ed., 1893; Eng. transl. of 2d Germ. ed., 1869), Hilgenfeld (1875), Holtzmann (1892), Salmon (1894), S. Davidson (1894), Godet (1893–99; Eng. transl. 1894–99), Zahn (1900), and Jülicher (1901; Eng. transl. 1901), and of the Roman Catholics Trenkle (1897) and Schäfer (1898) in Introduction are important contributions to the science.

6. Later Work.

2. The Conception and the Task: In order to obtain an adequate comprehension of the books which together make up the New Testament as witnesses for a historical movement and to secure for them safe utilization as historic sources, there is required a scientific investigation of their origin. That is, there must be inquiry into the time in which, the circumstances under which, the purpose for which, and the personal relations of the persons by whom they were produced. In other words, the method of research is literary-historical. Whether this can be called a science is debatable, since criticism is the art of distinguishing the genuine from the spurious. But if it be granted that an examination from a historical standpoint of the writings of the New Testament and an adequate exposition of the history of their origin is really scientific, it is none the less a fact that the process has a theological character. For the fact that this literature is Greek and sprang up in the Roman world does not do away with the other fact that it originated in certain communities which had in certain vital respects their existence apart from the world about them. The religious element marks it off from the other productions of the time, and the history of this literature is one side of the history of the Church. If Christianity depends upon the historic reality of a revelation mediated by Christ and authoritatively expounded by the apostles, it is no unimportant result that it can reach historical foundations for the early productions. And those foundations are found in the writings brought together in the New Testament. The supereminent value in this respect of these writings is sufficient justification for considering them apart. But the investigation must not start from a dogmatic conception of what the canon is. The ground fact is that even from the second century this collection has existed in the Church and has been accepted as the one legitimate source for the history of the revelation made through Christ. But if it should appear that there are in the New Testament writings which in general character and in origin separate themselves widely from the rest of the New Testament Scriptures, or if there were outside that collection writings which affiliate themselves with the New Testament Scriptures, Introduction can not content itself with disregarding those facts. It is hardly likely, however, that such discoveries will be made as will compel a radical departure from the accepted procedure, that there will come to light such writings as are referred to in Luke i, 1 sqq., or the correspondence of Paul with the Corinthians implied in I Cor. v, 9, vii, 1. Even such discoveries as those last mentioned would not be likely materially to change accepted results, and the business of the discipline would still be with the New Testament Scriptures.

1. History of New Testament Scriptures.

Along with the history of the separate writings which make up the New Testament goes as a second part the history of the combination of these into the canon in which they have been transmitted to the present time. It is of importance to examine and exhibit the historical antecedents and developments which compassed the formation of this collection, the

2. History of the Canon.

irregularity and vacillation which existed during several centuries, and the adjustment which produced a final and universally accepted result.

The examination of the origins of the individual writings and that of the origin of the collection supplement each other. The one brings to light the common spirit which animated the individual writers, the other reveals the influence which those writers exercised over the churches. And it is noteworthy that the collection was begun almost, if not quite, before the latest writers had finished their work, so that no appreciable interval of time separated the two operations of writing and of collection. And so, notwithstanding the different areas in which these two processes work, they belong together as sections of the one discipline of the literary history of the New Testament.

As to the inclusion of other departments in this branch of study, usage differs. Some have included therein not only the history of the text and of translations, but also the history of the theological handling of the same. But, strictly speaking, neither the story of the vicissitudes of transmission nor the history of translations belongs here. If with Credner and Reuss the history of translations is put as a part of the history of the propagation of the New Testament, its proper place is in the history of missions. So far as the versions assist in the recovery of the original text, the treatment of them belongs in a guide to the exercise of text-criticism or in the prolegomena to editions of the New Testament. To be sure, the history of the earlier text and that of the old versions have importance for the history of the canon because of the fact that not so much individual books as the entire collection or at least great parts of the collection were copied and translated. Were greater certainty than is yet the case attainable concerning the Syriac and the Latin versions, great gains would be made in the history of the canon of the New Testament. But it must be remembered that not all branches which contribute to results in any given line of research are to be included in the department of science in which they are used. (T. ZAHN.)

3. Textual Criticism and Versions.

BIBLIOGRAPHY: On the general introduction to the whole Bible consult: C. A. Briggs, *Study of Holy Scripture*, New York, 1899 (the best book for a comprehensive survey); G. T. Ladd, *Doctrine of Sacred Scripture*, ib. 1883 (full but dry); E. Rapin, *Les Livres de l'Ancien et du Nouveau Testament*, Moudon, 1890; A. Schlatter, *Einleitung in die Bibel*, Stuttgart, 1894 (conservative).

On the Canon of the O. T. it is sufficient to mention: A. Kuenen, *Historisch-kritisch onderzoek naar het onstaan en de verzameling van de boeken des Ouden Verbonds*, 3 vols., Leyden, 1885–93 (the fullest discussion); F. Buhl, *Kanon und Text des Alten Testaments*, Leipsic, 1891, Eng. transl., Edinburgh, 1892 (a model); H. E. Ryle, *Canon and Text of the O. T.*, London, 1892 (reliable, indispensable); G. Wildeboer, *Het Onstaan van den kanon des Ouden Verbonds*, Groningen, 1889, Eng. transl., London, 1885 (all students should have it); E. Kautzsch, *Abriss der Geschichte des alttestamentlichen Schrifttums*, in his *Heilige Schrift des A. T.*, Freiburg, 1896, Eng. transl., *Outline of the Hist. of the Literature of the O. T.*, New York, 1899 (fresh and interesting).

On O. T. Introduction the one indispensable book is Driver, *Introduction*, latest impression, London, 1897. Consult also J. P. P. Martin, *Introduction à la critique générale de l'A. T.*, 3 vols., Paris, 1888–89; A. F. Kirkpatrick, *The Divine Library of the O. T.*, London, 1892 (conservative); S. Davidson, *Introduction to the O. T.*, 3 vols., ib. 1894 (the antithesis of Kirkpatrick); H. L. Strack, *Einleitung in das A. T.*, Munich, 1898; W. H. Green, *General Introduction to the O. T.*, 2 vols., New York, 1898–99 (the extreme in conservatism); W. R. Smith, *O. T. in Jewish Church*, Edinburgh, 1902; C. H. Cornill, *Einleitung in das A. T.*, Freiburg, 1905, Eng. transl., 1907; J. E. McFadyen, *Introduction to the O. T.*, New York, 1905; K. Budde, *Geschichte der althebräischen Litteratur*, Leipsic, 1906; C. L. Gautier, *Introduction à l'A. T.*, 2 vols., Lausanne, 1906.

On the N. T. the works have been sufficiently indicated in the text, though worthy of mention are A. Loisy, *Histoire du Canon du N. T.*, Paris, 1891; *Biblical Introduction; N. T.*, by W. Adeney, London, 1899; B. W. Bacon, *Introduction to N. T.*, New York, 1900; H. von Soden, *Urchristliche Literatur-Geschichte*, i, *Die Schriften des N. T.*, Berlin, 1905, Eng. transl., 1905.

BIBLICAL THEOLOGY.

Biblical theology, or the orderly presentation of the doctrinal contents of Scripture, is a comparatively modern branch of theological science. In general the term expresses not so much the construction of a theology which is Biblical in an especial sense as a method of dealing with the Biblical matter which is midway between exegesis and dogmatics. Its object and limitation can be shown best by tracing its history.

So long as the Church felt or admitted no discord between its tradition and the Biblical tradition, there was no need to compare or contrast the contents of the Bible with the teaching of the Church. On this account the beginnings of a Biblical theology appear in the circles of the theologians of the Reformation, who perceived in Scripture the test by which to try ecclesiastical tradition. Since to them the Bible was the sufficient, self-explaining basis of dogmatics, by this juxtaposition the possibility was given of a separate treatment of the doctrinal contents of the Bible. The first timid effort confined itself to a discussion of the customary quotations (Sebastian Schmidt, *Collegium Biblicum in quo dicta Veteris et Novi Testamenti juxta seriem locorum explicantur*, 1671). Under the influence of Pietism the close connection of dogmatics and the Bible was relaxed, because in the latter was seen less an infallible source of knowledge than a means of grace (A. F. Büsching, *Gedanken von der Beschaffenheit und dem Vorzuge der bibl.-dogm. Theologie von der scholastischen*, Lemgo, 1758, and similar works). When in the eighteenth century J. S. Semler and his school busied themselves in discovering the differences in date and characteristics of the different books of the Bible, and brought to light the dissonance between crystallized dogma and New Testament teaching (a dissonance greater still in the case of the Old Testament), the desire naturally arose to show the essential agreement of the teaching of the Church and that of the Bible by an unprejudiced study of the latter (G. T. Zachariä, *Biblische Theologie oder Untersuchung des biblischen Grundes der vornehmsten kirchlichen Lehren*, 5 vols., Göttingen, 1771–86). The rationalistic school, in

1. Origin and History.

opposition to the formulated dogma of the Church, endeavored to read its own views (those of natural religion) into the Bible (C. F. Ammon, *Entwicklung einer reinen biblischen Theologie*, Erlangen, 1792; G. P. C. Kaiser, *Die biblische Theologie oder Judaismus und Christianismus nach einer freimütigen Stellung in die kritisch-vergleichende Universalgeschichte der Religionen und in die universale Religion*, 2 vols., Erlangen, 1813). In contradistinction to this there was during the nineteenth century an eager desire to give the purely historical results of examination of the Bible. In this way, the fact of differences of conception in the parts of the Bible was fully brought to light.

Probably under the influence of Schleiermacher (q.v.) especial attention was directed to the New Testament, and the "systems" of the different apostles were separately treated (the Pauline by Meyer, 1801, L. Usteri, 1824; the Johannine by K. Frommann, 1839). Along with this an effort was made to show the unity of the Gospel in the very variety of individual conceptions (of the many important works, note A. Neander, *Geschichte der Pflanzung der christlichen Kirche*, Hamburg, 1832; B. Weiss, *Lehrbuch der biblischen Theologie*, Berlin, 1868; W. Beyschlag, *Neutestamentliche Theologie*, Halle, 1891).

2. Study of New Testament Theology.

At the same time another class of theologians was eagerly engaged in tracing the differences of the individual conceptions to their very roots. According to Hegel's formula the crystallized dogma was a synthesis of the two sharp opposites of Paulinism and the primitive apostolate, and this development was followed up in all its details from a literary-historical point of view (F. C. Baur; H. E. G. Paulus; F. C. A. Schwegler, *Nachapostolisches Zeitalter*, Tübingen, 1846; O. Pfleiderer, *Paulinismus*, Leipsic, 1873; C. Holsten, *Evangelium des Paulus und Petrus*, Rostock, 1868; A. Hilgenfeld, *Urchristentum*, Jena, 1854). In like manner the life of Jesus and its sources were treated, in connection with which work there originated a countless number of monographs on the self-consciousness of Jesus and the titles he assumed. The result from this point of view was the conviction that New Testament theology has to deal not with a completed whole, but with a mobile and developing Christianity. Hence "Biblical Theology" and "Introduction" together represent simply a part of the apparatus of general church history (cf. A. Hausrath, *Neutestamentliche Zeitgeschichte*, Heidelberg, 1868; O. Pfleiderer, *Urchristentum*, Berlin, 1887).

Parallel to this development of New Testament theology was that of Old Testament theology. Students came to discern the narrowness and one-sidedness of the Old Testament religion, upon which Hengstenberg vainly insisted in his obliteration of the limits between the Old and the New Testament.

3. The Old Testament.

In acknowledging the principle of slow historical genesis, others sought to understand the development of the Old Testament religion by the principle that no doctrine is completed in the Old Testament, no doctrine in the New Testament is altogether new (G. F. Oehler, *Theologie des Alten Testaments*, Tübingen, 1873–74; similarly Schultz and Riehm). J. Wellhausen (*Prolegomena zur Geschichte Israels*, Berlin, 1886) and A. Kuenen produced a revolution in the treatment of the Old Testament. Under the influence of their religious-historical suppositions and literary-critical conclusions, Old Testament theology served to describe how from the supposed original conditions, from animism and totemism, the prophetic monotheism of the prophets and ultimately the theocratic ceremonialism of postexilic Judaism gradually developed (B. Duhm, *Theologie der Propheten*, Bonn, 1875; R. Smend, *Alttestamentliche Religionsgeschichte*, Freiburg, 1893; S. Kayser and Marti). In this way the Old Testament religion was placed on a level with other religions, and the surprisingly rich discoveries concerning the ancient Orient and the rising science of the history of religion grasped hands with this method of treatment. It was a natural consequence to show that the New Testament possesses a rich heritage of religious fancy common to ethnic religions (cf. especially H. Gunkel, *Schöpfung und Chaos*, Göttingen, 1895; *Religionsgeschichtliche Abhandlung des Neuen Testaments*, 1904). The idea of unity and special individuality of the New Testament thus goes by the board.

In glancing over the development of Biblical theology, it is surprising to see how this branch has worked out its own disintegration. In the beginning the aim was to make the Bible the only and sole source of Christian doctrine in the Reformers' understanding of the phrase, by allowing it to speak for itself without introducing any diluting medium. The investigator sought to penetrate its polymorphous nature, and finally saw that under his touch the uniting bond had disappeared which formerly kept together the disparate parts

4. Limitations.

and made it an undivided object of scientific research. This self-immolation the discipline owes to a one-sided maintenance of the historical and religious-historical method. Biblical theology must indeed be a historical science; but the adjective must not become a noun and the method must not master the subject. For in this study there are fundamental perceptions which can not be obtained by literary criticism and general historical researches. Thus the subject itself—namely, the whole Bible—suggests the question whether the subject-matter is the remains of a religious literature or documents, productions, and descriptions of a history which is fixed by a revelation from God. And the answer to this question is of the greatest import for the investigation. How different must be the verdict of higher criticism, provided the miracles or the declarations of Jesus are regarded as *a priori* historically possible or impossible; how much the selection of the matter decides whether one shall find only religious-ethical views, or historical facts of the "religion of Jesus," or that "the belief in Christ" belongs to the essence of Christianity.

For this reason there has always existed an opposition to the development described above. The history of salvation with its literary deposit ought not to be resolved into a purely human development. The impression is gained rather that the Bible contains a primary life of faith, having the character of uncorrupted self-consistency and unbroken independence, and that consequently there is underneath a uniform and fundamental idea. As standing for this, mention must be made of K. I. Nitzsch, *System der christlichen Lehre* (Bonn, 1829), and H. Ewald, *Lehre der Bibel von Gott* (3 vols., Leipsic, 1871), and particularly of J. C. K. von Hofmann, whose great work (*Die heilige Schrift des Neuen Testaments zusammenhängend untersucht*, completed by Volck, Munich, 1886) culminated in the description of the history of the entire New Testament preaching as a historical development of the uniform word which is not the product of the individual authors. Hermann Cremer (*Biblisch-theologisches Wörterbuch der neutestamentlichen Gräcität*, 8th ed., Gotha, 1895) endeavored in a new way to bring into view the unity of the contents of Scripture by collecting the individual notions of the Bible and following their development from the Hebrew into the Greek. According to him there are not only different modes of expression at different times, but there is a Bible-language, a linguistic body of the divine word, ever developing itself. It is a scientific necessity that Biblical theology regard the individuality of the Bible as the basal principle of its entire activity For the religion of the Bible is not merely a part of the historical past; it is an active factor in the present. In like manner the Bible is not merely a document showing the manner in which the Christian Church originated; it is the authentic tradition of the word of God, out of which the Church is ever originating (M. Kaehler, *Der historische Jesus*, 2d ed., Leipsic, 1896). On this account Biblical theology must always proceed from the unexceptionable agreement, which can only be reached at the end of a development; its way leads, therefore, from the New to the Old Testament, through the whole to the parts. Since, however, that result is nowhere offered in complete form, it is the task of this branch to educe from that which exists what is essential—the entirety—so that the examination of the particular is ever a means to an end, and is always under the control of the final aim of the work.

5. Constructive Work.

Accordingly it is not the task of Biblical theology to criticize the theology of the Bible and to judge it by the measure of a probable understanding of the original to be obtained scientifically, but to show as a matter of fact what the contents of the Bible are and at the same time to bring into view the different forms and shapes in which these contents are offered. It owes to the Church a pure exhibition of the "word" by the preaching of which the Church has lived in all ages. On this account no help is gained by considering some "probable gospel of Jesus," sought behind the sources, but the necessity is that the Jesus Christ of primitive tradition be described, and that in the various forms in which it has been handed down. Again, the highest aim is always to produce a theology of the entire Bible (such an effort is K. Schlottmann, *Kompendium der biblischen Theologie*, 2d ed., Leipsic, 1895). But the separate treatment of the Testaments will generally recommend itself for practical reasons, since a great deal of preliminary work is necessary on the Old Testament, and because the difference of degrees of revelation must be indicated. But the correlation between the two must, after all, never be overlooked. It is a matter of course that the Biblical theology of the whole Bible can never dispense with exegesis. But it raises itself above the purely exegetical by its relation to systematic theology. It is released from the duty of exhibiting all the mazes and changes of development which are not essential to the understanding of the unified whole. On the other hand, it must not be misled into compressing Biblical riches into a narrow, one-sided system, which will take the form of contemporary dogmatics, for the dogmatic interest will take charge of the process of digesting the immense amount of subject-matter. One task of Biblical theology is to open the way of return from contemporary crystallization into formulas in dogmatics to the source itself. In this sense it will be of very great service to evangelical theology, provided it directs us to disclose more clearly and richly God's word in Holy Scripture and thus protests in the name of the document of revelation against every claim of human infallibility, for "God alone is infallible" (Zwingli).

6. The True Aim.

M. KAEHLER.

BIBLIOGRAPHY: Discussions on the methods of the discipline are in: C. A. Briggs, *Study of Holy Scripture*, pp. 569–606, New York, 1899 (historical and critical, discriminating); G. R. Crooks and J. F. Hurst, *Theological Encyclopædia and Methodology*, pp. 249–255, New York, 1894; A. Cave, *Introduction to Theology*, pp. 405–421, Edinburgh, 1896; W Wrede, *Ueber Aufgabe und Methode der sogenannten neutestamentlichen Theologie*, Göttingen, 1897; L. Emery, *Introduction à l'étude de la théologie protestante*, pp. 122–127, Paris, 1904 (the foregoing all contain bibliographies). An excellent review of recent literature is furnished in the *Theologische Rundschau*, May, 1907 (an excellent periodical devoted to the review of works on theology).

Works additional to those in the text which deal with the whole of Biblical theology or of some phase of both the O. and the N. T. are: L. Noack, *Die biblische Theologie*, Halle, 1853; F. Gardner, *The Old and the N. T. in their Mutual Relations*, New York, 1885; H. Schultz, *Alttestamentliche Theologie*, Göttingen, 1885, Eng. transl., Edinburgh, 1892; W. L. Alexander, *A System of Biblical Theology*, 2 vols., Edinburgh, 1888; C. L. Fillion, *L'Idée centrale de la Bible*, Paris, 1888; C. G. Chavannes, *La Religion dans la Bible*, 2 vols., Paris, 1889; C. H. Toy, *Judaism and Christianity*. Boston, 1890 (called by Dr. Briggs "the best book on the subject"); A. Duff, *O. T. Theology*, Edinburgh, 1891 (original); R. H. Charles, *Critical History of the Doctrine of a Future Life in Israel, Judaism and Christianity*, London, 1899 (the one book in the field).

Additional and worthy books on O. T. theology are: C. H. Piepenbring, *Théologie de l'Ancien Testament*, Paris, 1886, Eng. transl., New York, 1893; A. Dillmann, *Handbuch der alttestamentlichen Theologie*, Leipsic, 1895 (posthumous); W. H. Bennett, *Theology of the O. T.*, London, 1896 (a handbook); R. Smend, *Lehrbuch der alttestamentlichen Religionsgeschichte*, Freiburg, 1899; A. B. Davidson, *The Theology of the O. T.*, Edinburgh, 1904 (somewhat disappointing).

Additional works on the N. T. are W. F. Adeney, *Theology of the N. T.*, London, 1894 (corresponds to Bennett on the O. T.); H. J. Holtzmann, *Lehrbuch der neutestamentlichen Theologie*, 2 vols., Tübingen, 1897 (one of the best on the subject); G. B. Stevens, *Theology of the N. T.*, New York, 1899; E. P. Gould, *Biblical Theology of the N. T.*, New York, 1900; D. F. Estes, *An Outline of N. T. Theology*, ib. 1901; J. Bovon, *Théologie du N. T.*, 2 vols., Lausanne, 1893–94, vol. i, 2d ed., 1902.

BIBLICISTS, BIBLICAL DOCTORS: A name sometimes given to those who, during the thirteenth and fourteenth centuries, demonstrated religious truths by the Scriptures and by the authority of the Fathers, in contrast to others, who abandoned Scripture and tradition in order to give full rein to their fancy and philosophy. The most of the latter were Dominican and Franciscan monks who, since their orders held no property, had no libraries, and, owing to their unsettled and vagrant lives, had little opportunity for the study of books. Some of the Biblical doctors were scholars, and produced valuable works; but the majority of them were servile imitators of their predecessors.

BIBRA, NICHOLAS OF. See NICHOLAS OF BIBRA.

BICKELL, GUSTAV: German Roman Catholic theologian and Orientalist; b. at Cassel July 7, 1838; d. at Vienna Jan. 15, 1906. In 1862 he became privat-docent of Semitic and Indo-Germanic philology at Marburg, and in the following year went in the same capacity to Giessen. Two years later he became a convert to Roman Catholicism, was ordained priest in 1866, and from 1867 to 1874 taught Oriental languages in the academy of Münster, where he was appointed associate professor in 1871. From 1874 to 1891 he was professor of Christian archeology and Semitic languages in the University of Innsbruck, and from the latter year until his death was professor of Semitic philology at the University of Vienna. He wrote: *De indole ac ratione versionis Alexandrinæ in interpretando libro Jobi* (Marburg, 1862); *Sancti Ephraemi Syri carmina Nisibena* (Leipsic, 1866); *Grundriss der hebräischen Grammatik* (2 vols., 1869–70; Eng. transl. by S. I. Curtiss, 1877); *Gründe für die Unfehlbarkeit des Kirchenoberhauptes* (Münster, 1870); *Conspectus rei Syrorum literariæ* (1871); *Messe und Pascha* (1872, Eng. transl. by W. F. Skene, Edinburgh, 1891); *Sancti Isaaci Antiocheni opera omnia* (2 vols., Giessen, 1873); *Kalilag und Damnag, alte syrische Uebersetzung des indischen Fürstenspiegels* (text and translation, Leipsic, 1876); *Metrices biblicæ regulæ exemplis illustratæ* (Innsbruck, 1879); *Synodi Brixinenses sæculi quindecimi* (1880); *Carmina Veteris Testamenti metrica* (1882); *Dichtungen der Hebräer* (1882); *Koheleths Untersuchung über den Wert des Daseins* (1884); and *Das Buch Job nach Anlass der Strophik und der Septuaginta auf seine ursprüngliche Form zurückgeführt und im Versmasse des Urtextes übersetzt* (Vienna, 1894).

BICKELL, JOHANN WILHELM: Writer on canon law; b. at Marburg Nov. 2, 1799; d. at Cassel Jan. 23, 1848. He studied law at Marburg and Göttingen; was professor of jurisprudence at Marburg, 1824–34; president of the supreme court of Hesse-Cassel, 1841, and minister of state, 1846. He wrote *Ueber die Entstehung des Corpus Juris Canonici* (Marburg, 1825); *Ueber die Reform der protestantischen Kirchenverfassung* (1831); *Ueber die Verpflichtung der evangelischen Geistlichen auf die symbolischen Schriften* (Cassel, 1839, 2d ed., 1840); of his *Geschichte des Kirchenrechts*, only one volume was completed (part i, Giessen, 1843; part ii, Frankfort, 1849).

BICKERSTETH, EDWARD: The name of three clergymen of the Church of England.

1. A leader of the Evangelicals; b. at Kirkby Lonsdale (60 m. n. of Liverpool), Westmoreland, Mar. 19, 1786; d. at Watton (21 m. w.s.w. of Norwich), Hertfordshire, Feb. 28, 1850. He was at first a lawyer and practised at Norwich, but he was always of deeply religious temperament and in 1815 received priest's orders and was sent to Africa by the Church Missionary Society to inspect the work there. Returning in Aug., 1816, he became one of the society's secretaries and for the rest of his life spent much time traveling in the service of the society; in 1830 he became rector of Watton. He was an active opponent of the Tractarian Movement, and was one of the founders of the Evangelical Alliance and of the Irish Church Missions Society. His published works were numerous and many were very popular; the more important (*A Help to the Study of the Scriptures*, 21st edition; *A Treatise on Prayer*, 14th edition; *A Treatise on the Lord's Supper*, 13th edition; *A Guide to the Prophecies*, 8th edition; and others) were collected in sixteen volumes (London, 1853). He also compiled *Christian Psalmody* (Hereford, 1833), a much-used hymn-book, and edited the *Christian's Family Library* (50 vols.).

BIBLIOGRAPHY: T. R. Birks, *Memoir of E. Bickersteth*, 2 vols., London, 1856 (by his son-in-law); *DNB*, v, 3–4.

2. Dean of Lichfield, nephew of the preceding; b. at Acton (12 m. s. by e. of Bury St. Edmund's), Suffolk, Oct. 23, 1814; d. at Leamington (80 m. n.w. of London) Oct. 7, 1892. He studied at Sidney Sussex College, Cambridge (B.A., 1836; M.A., 1839; D.D., 1864), and at Durham University; became curate of Chetton, Shropshire, 1838; at the Abbey, Shrewsbury, 1839; Penn Street, Buckinghamshire, 1849; vicar of Aylesbury and archdeacon of Buckinghamshire, 1853; honorary canon of Christ Church, Oxford, 1866; dean of Lichfield, 1875; resigned in 1892. In 1864, 1866, 1869, and 1874 he was prolocutor of the lower house of convocation of Canterbury, and as such was a member of the committee of New Testament revisers. He was a High-churchman. He published *Diocesan Synods in Relation to Convocation and Parliament* (London, 1867); *My Hereafter* (1883); edited the fifth edition of R. W. Evans's *Bishopric of Souls* (1877), with a memoir of the author; and contributed the commentary on Mark to the *Pulpit Commentary* (1882).

3. Bishop of South Tokyo, Japan, eldest son of Edward Henry Bickersteth (q.v.); b. at Banningham (10 m. n. of Norwich), Norfolk, June 26, 1850; d. at Chisledon (30 m. n. of Salisbury), Wiltshire, Aug. 5, 1897 He was educated at Cambridge (B.A., 1873), and was ordained priest in 1874. He was curate at Hampstead, London, 1873–75; fellow of Pembroke College, Cambridge, from 1875 till 1877, when he headed the Cambridge Mission for Delhi, India. In this mission he so impaired his health that he was obliged to return to England in 1882, and he became rector of Framlingham, Suffolk. In 1886 he was consecrated bishop of Japan. He was an extreme High-churchman and strove to reproduce this type of church life among the Japanese. The result was the so-called "Catholic Church of Japan" (*Nippon Sei Kokwai*). In 1887 a visit to Korea bore fruit in the establishment of a mission in that country. In 1892 his visit to the Anglican mission stations in Japan convinced him that there should be more bishops; accordingly his diocese was made that of South Tokyo. Again his health gave way and he returned home to die. His lectures for Japanese divinity students were published under the title *Our Heritage in the Church* (London, 1898).

Bibliography: S. Bickersteth, *Life and Letters of Edward Bickersteth, Bishop of South Tokyo*, London, 1905 (by his brother).

BICKERSTETH, EDWARD HENRY: Bishop of Exeter, son of Edward Bickersteth, 1; b. at Islington, London, Jan. 25, 1825; d. in London May 16, 1906. He was educated at Trinity College, Cambridge (B.A., 1847), and was ordered deacon in 1848, and ordained priest in the following year. He was curate of Banningham, Norfolk (1848–51); rector of Hinton Martell, Dorset (1852–55); vicar of Christ Church, Hampstead (1855–85); rural dean of Highgate (1878–85), and dean of Gloucester (1885). He was consecrated bishop of Exeter in 1885, but resigned five years later on account of age. He wrote *Water from the Well Spring* (London, 1852); *The Rock of Ages* (1857); *Commentary on the New Testament* (1864); *Yesterday, To-day, and Forever* (poem in twelve books, 1866; prized as a devout revelation of heaven); *The Spirit of Life* (1869); *Hymnal Companion to the Book of Common Prayer* (1870); *The Two Brothers and Other Poems* (1871); *The Reef and Other Parables* (1873); *The Shadowed Home and the Light Beyond* (1874); *Words of Counsel to the Clergy and Laity of the Diocese of Exeter* (1888); *Charge at Third Visitation* (1895); *From Year to Year* (1895); *The Feast of Divine Love* (1896); and *Charge at Fourth Visitation* (1898). He was the author of a number of well-known hymns.

Bibliography: F. K. Aglionby, *Life of E. H. Bickersteth*, London, 1907.

BICKERSTETH, SAMUEL: Church of England, second son of Edward Henry Bickersteth (q.v.); b. at Hampstead Sept. 9, 1857 He was educated at St. John's College, Oxford (B.A., 1881), and was ordered deacon in 1881 and ordained priest in the following year. He was successively curate of Christ Church, Lancaster Gate (1881–84); chaplain to the bishop of Ripon (1884–87); vicar of Belvedere, Kent (1887–91); and vicar of Lewisham (1891–1905). Since 1905 he has been vicar of Leeds and rural dean. He has written *Life and Letters of Edward Bickersteth, D.D., Bishop of South Tokyo* (his brother, London, 1899), and is the editor of the *Preachers of the Age* series.

BIDDING PRAYER: Originally *bidding of prayers*, signifying "the praying (offering) of prayers," one of the meanings of the verb "to bid" down to the Reformation being "to ask pressingly, to beg, to pray." As this meaning became obsolete the phrase was interpreted to mean "the ordering or directing of prayers"; i.e., an authoritative direction to the people concerning what or whom they should pray for, such directions being not uncommon in England in the sixteenth century. Still later "bidding" was taken as an adjective and the phrase "bidding prayer" came to mean the prayer before the sermon, which the preacher introduced by directing the congregation to pray for the Church catholic, the sovereign and the royal family, different estates of men, etc. (*Constitution and Canons of the Church of England*, § 55). A collect is now usually substituted for it, as the sermon, except on rare occasions, is preceded by the common prayers, which include the petitions prescribed by the canon. When, however, these prayers are not said before the sermon (as at university sermons), and on occasions of more than usual solemnity, the "bidding prayer" is used.

Bibliography: Forms of the Bidding Prayer are to be found in *Manuale et Processionale . ecclesiæ Eboracensis*, ed. W. G. Henderson in Surtees Society Publications, no. 63, Durham, 1875, and in F. Procter, *Hist. of Book of Common Prayer* , *revised by W. H. Frere*, p. 394, London, 1905. Consult C. Wheatley, *Bidding of Prayers before Sermons*, London, 1845; D. Rock, *Church of our Fathers*, 3 vols., ib. 1849–53.

BIDDLE, JOHN: A founder of modern English Unitarianism; b. at Wotton-under-Edge (15 m. s. of Gloucester), where he was baptized Jan. 14, 1615; d. in a London jail Sept. 22, 1662. He was educated at Oxford, and appointed head master of the free school in the parish of St. Mary le Crypt, Gloucester, 1641. Study of the Scriptures led him to disbelieve the doctrine of the Trinity, and, his unsoundness being reported to the city magistrates, he was summoned before them. Fearing imprisonment, he made a confession of faith (May 2, 1644) which was not satisfactory, and so he made a second in which he used more conventional language and was allowed to go free. He then committed to paper *Twelve Arguments Drawn out of Scripture: wherein the commonly received opinion touching the Deity of the Holy Spirit is clearly and fully refuted*, and to these views he was faithful the rest of his life. A friend informed the magistrates of the existence of this paper and so he was cited before the committee of Parliament then at Gloucester, and put in the common jail Dec. 2, 1645. Happily a prominent citizen bailed him out. In 1646 he was summoned to appear before Parliament at Westminster to explain his position, and boldly avowed his belief. He was committed to the custody of one of the officers of the House of Commons and so continued for five years. Meanwhile a committee of the Assembly of Divines sitting at Westminster considered his case and to them he gave a copy of his *Twelve Arguments*. They made answer to it, but did not move him. So in 1647 he published his paper, which makes a tract of thirty-eight small pages. It stirred up great indignation and was suppressed and burned by the common hangman. Next he published *A Confession of Faith Touching the Holy Trinity, according to the Scripture* (1648), a tract of seventy-five small pages, in which in six articles, accompanied by expositions, he plainly states his views, making God the Father the first person of the Holy Trinity; one chief Son of the most high God, with only a human nature, though our God by reason of his divine sovereignty over us, yet subordinate to the most high God, the second person; and one principal minister of God and Christ the third. Next came another tract (eighty-six pages) containing alleged testimonies in favor of his views from the Fathers. In 1648 Parliament, at the instigation of the Westminster divines, made denial of the Trinity a capital offense, yet Biddle was not only not put to death, but in 1649 was released on bail. He became a chaplain and preacher in Staffordshire, but was shortly recalled and remained in prison till Feb., 1651. On his release he publicly advocated his views and continued his publications with *A Two-fold Catechism; the one simply called a Scripture Catechism; the other a brief Scripture Catechism for Children* (1654, the first of 141 small pages, the second of thirty-four, both with a preface). The answers, being entirely in quoted Scripture, could not be gainsaid, but the questions were open to serious criticism. Consequently he was examined by the House of Commons and committed to prison on Dec. 3, 1654, and was not released till May 28, 1655. The *Catechism* was burned by the common hangman Dec. 14, 1654. Again publicly advocating his beliefs on July 3, 1655, he was thrown into prison and a little later was tried for his life on the ordinance above mentioned. Cromwell, unwilling to put him to death, banished him to the Scilly Islands (Oct. 5, 1655), and allowed him 100 crowns a year for maintenance. In 1658 he was released, and resumed preaching. In the latter part of Aug., 1662, he was again imprisoned and after five weeks died.

Bibliography: The principal source of information respecting Biddle is the *Life* by Joshua Toulmin, London, 1789, which analyzes all his writings, including several translations not mentioned above. There are earlier accounts, such as *J. Bidelli Vita*, by J. Farrington, ib. 1682, and *A Short Account of the Life of John Biddle*, ib. 1691. Consult also A. à Wood, *Athenæ Oxonienses*, ed. P. P Bliss, iii. 593–603, 4 vols., ib. 1813–20; J. H. Allen, *Historical Sketch of the Unitarian Movement*, pp. 131–135, New York, 1894; *DNB*, v, 13–16. Some additional information is in Walter Lloyd's *Bicentenary of Barton Street Dissenting Meeting House, Gloucester*, pp. 40–50, Gloucester, 1899.

BIEDERMANN, bī'der-mān, **ALOIS EMANUEL**: Swiss Protestant; b. near Bendlikon, on the west shore of the Lake of Zurich (4 m. from the city), Mar. 2, 1819; d. at Zurich Jan. 25, 1885. He studied at Basel 1837–39, and then at Berlin; became pastor at Mönchenstein (3 m. s. of Basel) 1843; professor extraordinary at Zurich 1850, ordinary 1860, where he lectured at first upon theological encyclopedia and New Testament introduction, later chiefly upon dogmatic theology He was the leading theologian of the neo-Hegelians, and was deeply influenced by the Tübingen school, especially by Strauss. He was a prolific writer for the religious press, but obtained his greatest repute by his *Christliche Dogmatik* (Zurich, 1869; 2d ed., Berlin, 1884–85, vol. ii edited by Rehmke), in which he denies the historicity of the Gospels, yet holds to the eternal ideas which the supposed facts of the Gospels embody; denies Christian doctrine, but advocates Christian practise; denies personality to God and personal immortality to man, yet holds that love to God and man constitutes the essence of religion. He took a deep interest in education and public affairs, preached often and by preference to small and weak congregations, and was tactful and courteous in his associations with men of all classes; he was a lover of athletics and a robust mountain-climber. Many of his briefer publications were collected under the title *Ausgewählte Vorträge und Aufsätze*, with a biographical introduction by J. Kradolfer (Berlin, 1885).

Bibliography: For further notes on Biedermann's life consult J. J. Oeri, *Persönliche Erinnerungen an Biedermann*, in *Kirchenblatt für die reformierte Schweiz*, 1886, nos. 7–18. On his theology and philosophy consult O. Pfleiderer, *Religionsphilosophie*, i, 594, Berlin, 1883; idem, in *Preussische Jahrbücher*, Jan., 1886, pp. 53–76; T. Moosherr, *A. E. Biedermann nach seiner allgemeinen philosophischen Stellung*, Jena, 1893.

BIEL, bīl, **GABRIEL**: One of the most remarkable theologians of the late Middle Ages; b. at Speyer; d. at Tübingen 1495. He studied at Heidelberg, became preacher at St. Martin's Church at Mainz, provost of Urach in Württemberg, and after 1484 professor of theology and philosophy in the newly founded University of Tübingen. In his old age he joined the Brethren of the Common Life (see Common Life, Brethren of the). In theology Biel followed the nominalism of Occam (q.v.), whose system he reproduced in his *Epitome et collectorium ex Occamo super quattuor libros sententiarum* (Tübingen, 1495). In anthropology and soteriology he was a Semi-Pelagian, teaching that "merit depends on man's free will and God's grace" (*sermo* xiv, 7); the sacraments operate not only *ex opere operantis*, but also *ex opere operato*" (*Sent.*, IV, i, 3). The Church, therefore, was for him a mechanically operating sacramental institution; in its priests he glorifies a "mighty dignity." In questions affecting the constitution of the Church, Biel took the position assumed by the councils of Constance and Basel. As a preacher he surpassed his predecessors in the practicality of his views; his knowledge of political economy also deserves recognition. Besides the work already noticed, he wrote *Lectura super canonem missæ* (Reutlingen, 1488); *Expositio canonis missæ* (Tübingen, 1499); *Sermones* (1499); and other works.

Paul Tschackert.

Bibliography: F. X. Linsenmann, *Gabriel Biel der letzte Scholastiker und der Nominalismus*, in *Tübinger theologische Quartalschrift*, 1865, pp. 449 sqq.; idem, in *KL*, ii. 804–808; A. Ritschl, *Die christliche Lehre von der Rechtfertigung und Versöhnung*, i, 102 sqq., Bonn, 1889; H. Plitt, *Gabriel Biel als Prediger*, Erlangen, 1879; Schultz, *Der sittliche Begriff des Verdienstes*, in *TSK*, 1894, pp. 304 sqq.

BIERLING, bī'ār-ling, **ERNST RUDOLF**: German Protestant jurist; b. at Zittau (49 m. s.e. of Dresden) Jan. 7, 1841. He was educated at the universities of Leipsic (1859–63) and Göttingen (1864–65), and after being a lawyer in his native city in 1868–71 was privat-docent at Göttingen for two years. Since 1873 he has been professor of canon and criminal law at Greifswald. In addition to being a member of the Pomeranian provincial synod in 1878–99 and of the general synod in 1875 and 1884–1902, he was a member of the House of Deputies in 1881–85 and of the Upper House after 1889. His publications include *Gesetzgebungsrecht evangelischer Kirchen im Gebiete der Kirchenlehre* (Leipsic, 1869); *Zur Kritik der juristischen Grundbegriffe* (2 vols., Gotha, 1877–82); *Die konfessionelle Schule in Preussen und ihr Recht* (1885); and *Juristische Prinzipienlehre* (3 vols., Tübingen, 1894–1905).

BIGELMAIER, bî″gel-mai′er, **ANDREAS:** German Roman Catholic; b. at Oberhausen (a suburb of Augsburg) Oct. 21, 1873. He was educated at the University of Munich (Th.D., 1899) and was ordained to the priesthood in 1897. From October to November, 1897, he was chaplain at Hörzhausen, in 1904 became privat-docent for church history at the University of Munich; in 1906 professor of church history in the Royal Lyceum of Dillingen. Besides numerous contributions to literary and theological periodicals, he has written *Die Beteiligungen der Christen am öffentlichen Leben in vorkonstantinischer Zeit* (Munich, 1902) and *Zeno von Verona* (1904).

BIGG, CHARLES: Church of England; b. at Manchester Sept. 12, 1840; d. Oxford July 15, 1908. He studied at Christ Church, Oxford (B.A., 1862), where he became tutor. He was master in Cheltenham College (1866–71), head master of Brighton College (1871–81), and rector of Fenny Compton, Leamington, 1887–1901, and honorary canon of Worcester from 1889 to 1901, when he was appointed regius professor of ecclesiastical history in Oxford University. He was examining chaplain to the bishops of Worcester (1889–91), Peterborough (1891–96), London (1897–1901), and Man (1903), Bampton lecturer in 1886, and has been canon of Christ Church, Oxford, since 1901. He has edited a number of Greek classics and the "Confessions" of St. Augustine (London, 1896); the *Didache* (1898); the *De Imitatione Christi* of Thomas à Kempis (1898); and Law's *Serious Call* (1899); and has written *The Christian Platonists of Alexandria* (London, 1886); *Neoplatonism* (1895); *Unity in Diversity* (1899); *Commentary on the Epistles of Peter and Jude* (Edinburgh, 1901); and *The Church's Task under the Roman Empire* (London, 1905).

BIGNE, bîñ, **MARGUERIN,** mār″ge″rañ, **DE LA:** French theologian; b. at Bernières-le-Patry, in Normandy, 1546 or 1547; d. at Paris 1589. He came of noble Norman parentage; studied at Caen and became rector of the university there; went to Paris, where he studied theology at the Sorbonne and received the doctorate. To refute the authors of the Magdeburg Centuries in June, 1576, he undertook to give a fuller edition of the writings of the Fathers of the Church than had been yet made. For this work he was appointed canon of the church of Bayeux, and some time after professor of the chapter-school; resigned to succeed his uncle, François du Parc, who had died, as dean of the church of Mans. In 1576 he was sent as deputy from the clergy of Normandy to the States General of Blois. In 1581 he went as canon of Bayeux to the provincial council there, and defended vigorously his chapter against the usurpation of Bernardin de St. François, bishop of Bayeux. The death of the bishop (July 14, 1582) appeared to end the conflict; but the bishop's successor, Mathurin de Savonnières, eventually forced Bigne to resign. He returned to Paris, where he died the same year. He was a great patristic scholar and an eloquent preacher. G. BONET-MAURY.

BIBLIOGRAPHY: His works were: *Veterum patrum et antiquorum scriptorum ecclesiasticorum collectio* (Paris, 1575–79); *Statuta synodalia Parisiensium episcoporum, Galonis cardinalis, Odonis et Wilhelmi; item Petri et Galteri Senonensium archiepiscoporum decreta primum edita* (1578); *S. Isidori Hispalensis Opera* (1580). Consult: J. Hermant, *L'Histoire du diocèse de Bayeux*, Caen, 1705; P. D. Huet, *Les Origines de la ville de Caen*, Rouen, 1706; Nicéron, *Mémoires*, xxx. 279; J. G. de Chauffepié, *Nouveau dictionnaire historique et critique*, vol. i, Amsterdam, 1750.

BILLICAN, THEOBALD (**Diepold Gernolt** or **Gerlacher**): German theologian; b. at Billigheim (4 m. s.s.w. of Landau), Bavaria, toward the end of the fifteenth century; d. at Marburg Aug. 8, 1554. He took his surname from his birthplace; studied at Heidelberg, where Melanchthon was his fellow student; lectured at Heidelberg; became provost of the college of arts (1520) and had among others Johann Brenz (q.v.) as his pupil. When, in 1518, Luther came to Heidelberg, Billican, Brenz, Schnepff, and Martin Butzer (q.v.) were among his admirers. Billican left Heidelberg in 1522 and went to Weil as preacher. But his sermons against the mediatorship of the Virgin Mary and against purgatory brought about his deposition and he went to Nördlingen (1523), where he remained till 1535. Billican opened there a way for the Reformation and published *Von der Mess Gemein Schlussred* (1524), in which he sharply rebuked the "fraud" of the mass as a sacrifice for the living and the dead. Billican, who corresponded with Luther, Melanchthon, Rhegius, Brenz, Œcolampadius, and Zwingli, was regarded as a leader of the Evangelical cause in South Germany. But future events showed the instability of his character. In his controversy with Carlstadt, who had come to Nördlingen, he sided with Luther against Carlstadt in the doctrine of the Lord's Supper and stated in his *Renovatio ecclesiæ* (1525) that "in the Lord's Supper the flesh and blood of the Lord are present." Induced by Urbanus Rhegius (q.v.) openly to defend the Lutheran doctrine, Billican sent a statement to Rhegius, which the latter published (in mutilated form, as Billican complained) together with his answer Dec. 18, 1525, under the title *De verbis cœnæ dominicæ et opinionum varietate Theobaldi Billicani ad Urbanum Regium* (1526). But while they of Wittenberg were rejoicing over this new ally, Billican changed his views in a letter addressed to Œcolampadius Jan. 16, 1526; and two months later, in letters addressed to Schleupner at Nuremberg and to Pirkheimer, he expressed still other views. While Billican did not fully agree with Zwingli, he stated that he learned more from the Zwinglians than from the Lutherans, and, adopting in part the views of Carlstadt and Œcolampadius, he pretended to teach the only correct doctrine because he stood between the two parties. His vacillating position is best illustrated in a booklet entitled *Epistola Theobaldi Billicani ad Joannem Hubelium qua illo de eucharistia cogitandi materiam conscripsit* (1528) which remained unnoticed.

Billican, of whom so much had been expected, was now avoided by both parties. In 1529 he applied to Heidelberg University for the doctorate, presenting at the same time a confession in which he acrimoniously rejected Lutheran, Zwinglian, and Anabaptist doctrine, and expressed his firm belief in the teachings of the Roman Catholic Church. Being refused by the faculty, he married a woman of wealth, and, regardless of what had taken place, he had the boldness to ask Melanchthon to procure him the doctorate at Wittenberg. The latter replied, "[The authorities] advance no one before he has set forth his doctrinal views" (*CR*, i, 1112). Since he was repelled by the Reformers and not fully trusted by the Roman Catholics, Billican's position became untenable, and so in 1535 he left Nördlingen and went to Heidelberg, where he commenced the study of jurisprudence. He was made licentiate in jurisprudence and for a time took the place of a professor who was disabled on account of sickness. When in 1543 that professor died and Billican sought the position, the entire faculty opposed his nomination, but through the influence of Margaret von der Layen, whose "chancellor" he was considered, he was permitted to give independent lectures on law. On account of his relations with Margaret, the elector Frederick II deposed Billican from his office July 26, 1544, and ordered him to leave Heidelberg. He went to Marburg and was made professor of rhetoric, a position which he held till his death. (T. KOLDE.)

BIBLIOGRAPHY: G. Veesenmeyer, *Kleine Beyträge zur Geschichte des Reichstags zu Augsburg, 1530*, pp. 59 sqq., Nuremberg, 1830; A. Steichele, *Das Bistum Augsburg*, iii. 947 sqq., Augsburg, 1872; T. Keim, *Die Stellung der schwäbischen Kirchen zur zwinglisch-lutherischen Spaltung*, in *TJB*, xiv, 1894; C. Geyer, *Die Nördlinger evangelischen Kirchenordnungen des 16. Jahrhunderts*, Munich, 1896.

BILNEY (BYLNEY), THOMAS: Early English Protestant; b. of a Norfolk family about 1495; burned at the stake at Norwich Aug. 19, 1531. He studied at Trinity Hall, Cambridge, and gave up law for theology and was ordained priest in 1519. He adopted the belief in justification by faith alone and was a leader in a company of Cambridge men who were inclined to the views of the Reformation; Hugh Latimer was added to the number by Bilney's influence and became his lifelong friend. Concerning the mass, transubstantiation, and the powers of the pope and the Church, Bilney remained orthodox; but he preached unremittingly in Cambridge, London, and neighboring counties, denouncing the invocation of saints and relic-worship, pilgrimages and fastings, at the same time leading a most austere life and devoted to deeds of charity. He was arrested and confined in the Tower Nov. 25, 1527; brought to trial, he denied having wittingly taught the doctrines of Luther, but was finally persuaded to abjure his alleged heresies and as penance was kept imprisoned for more than a year. Released in 1529, he went back to Cambridge, suffered much from remorse for his abjuration, and in 1531 resumed preaching, but was immediately arrested, and was executed as a relapsed heretic.

BIBLIOGRAPHY: The sources for a life are in *Letters and Papers of the Reign of Henry VIII.*, vol. v, ed. James Gairdner, in *Record Publications*, London, 1863-80. Consult also C. H. Cooper, *Athenæ Cantabrigienses*, i, 42, ib. 1858; *DNB*, v, 40-43.

BILSON, THOMAS: Bishop of Winchester; b. at Winchester 1546 or 1547; d. there June 18, 1616. He studied at New College, Oxford (B.A., 1566; M.A., 1570; B.D., 1579; D.D., 1581); was made prebend of Winchester 1576, and became warden of the college there; was consecrated bishop of Worcester 1596, translated to Winchester 1597. He was a noted preacher, a man of much learning, and defended the Church of England against both Roman Catholics and Puritans. At the command of Queen Elizabeth he wrote *The True Difference between Christian Subjection and Unchristian Rebellion* (Oxford, 1585), in answer to Cardinal William Allen's *Defence of the English Catholics* (Ingoldstadt, 1584), and *The Survey of Christ's Sufferings for Man's Redemption and of his Descent to Hades or Hell for our Deliverance* (London, 1604), a reply to the Brownist Henry Jacob; in *The Perpetual Government of Christ's Church* (1593; new ed., with memoir, Oxford, 1842) he defended episcopacy. With Dr. Miles Smith he revised the King James translation of the Bible before its publication, and he added the summaries of contents at the head of each chapter.

BIBLIOGRAPHY: A. à Wood, *Athenæ Oxonienses*, ed. P. Bliss, ii, 169-171, 4 vols., London, 1813-20; *DNB*, v, 43-44.

BINDING AND LOOSING, POWER OF. See KEYS, POWER OF THE.

BINDLEY, THOMAS HERBERT: Church of England; b. at Smethwick (3 m. n.w. of Birmingham), Staffordshire, Oct. 21, 1861. He was educated at Brownsgrove College, Worcestershire, and Merton College, Oxford (B.A., 1884), and was ordered deacon in 1889 and ordained priest in the following year. He was assistant curate of Ixworth, Suffolk, in 1889, and since 1890 has been principal of Codrington College, Barbados, and examining chaplain to the bishop of Barbados. He became canon of Barbados in 1893 and archdeacon in 1904, while in the following year he was made vicar-general of the diocese. In theology he is a liberal High-churchman. In addition to numerous contributions to theological periodicals, he has translated *St. Athanasius de incarnatione Verbi Dei* (London, 1887); *Tertullian's Apology* (London, 1889); *Epistle of the Gallican Churches* (1900); and *St. Cyprian on the Lord's Prayer* (1904). He has also edited *Tertulliani Apologeticus* (Oxford, 1889); *Tertulliani De Præscriptione* (1893); and *Œcumenical Documents of the Faith* (London, 1900); and has written *The Creeds* (1896) and *Et incarnatus est* (New York, 1896).

BINGHAM, HIRAM: Congregational missionary; b. at Honolulu, Hawaii, Aug. 16, 1831; d. at Baltimore Oct. 25, 1908. He was educated at Yale College (B.A., 1853) and Andover Theological Seminary (1854-55), and, after acting as principal of the Northampton High School in 1853-54, entered the ervice of the American Board of Commissioners for 'oreign Missions in 1856. He began his missionary ctivity in the Gilbert Islands in 1857, and from 1866 o 1868 was in command of the missionary brig *Iorning Star*. He was corresponding secretary of he board of the Hawaiian Evangelical Association rom 1877 to 1880. From 1880–82 he was Hawaiian overnment protector of South Sea immigrants. In heology he was a conservative. He has written *'tory of the Morning Star* (Boston, 1866); *Gilbertese 'ible* (New York, 1893); *Gilbertese Bible Dictionary* Honolulu, 1895); *Gilbertese Hymn and Tune Book* New York, 1897); *Gilbertese Commentary on Iatthew* (1904); and *Gilbertese Commentary on the 'our Gospels* (1905).

BINGHAM, JOSEPH: Church of England; at Wakefield (9 m. s. of Leeds), Yorkshire, ept., 1668; d. at Havant (6 m. s.e. of Portsmouth), Iampshire, Aug. 17, 1723. He studied at Oxford nd was fellow of University College 1689–95, 'hen he resigned and withdrew from the university ecause his controversial sermon on the Trinity reached before the university had led to the harge, wholly unmerited, of heresy. He was nmediately appointed rector of Headbourn-Vorthy (2 m. n. of Winchester), which made the ich cathedral library accessible to him. In 1712 e was transferred to the better living of Havant. Iis fame rests upon his *Origines Ecclesiasticæ, r the Antiquities of the Christian Church* (8 vols., ondon, 1708-22). This is exhaustive for the field covers and can never be superseded, as it is derived rom the sources and interestingly written. It has een a quarry for many books and itself several imes reprinted; the best edition is by the great-reat-grandson of the author, Rev. Richard Bingam (vols. i-viii of Bingham's *Works*, 10 vols.,)xford, 1855). There is a separate edition of the *ntiquities* in the Bohn Library (2 vols.), a Latin ranslation by Johann Heinrich Grischow (Grischoius; 11 vols., Halle, 1724–38), and an abridged ierman translation by an anonymous Roman 'atholic author (4 vols., Augsburg, 1788–96). 'nfortunately Bingham invested his savings in he South Sea Bubble and so lost them in 1720.

IBLIOGRAPHY: Bingham's biography by his great-grandson is given in the Oxford ed. of his works. Consult also: J. Darling, *Cyclopædia Bibliographica*, pp. 312–315, London, 1854; S. S. Allibone, *Critical Dictionary of Eng. Literature*, i, 189–190, Philadelphia, 1891; *DNB*, v, 48–50.

BINNEY, THOMAS: English Congregationalist; at Newcastle-upon-Tyne Apr. 30, 1798; d. at 'lapton, London Feb. 24, 1874. He was for seven ears a bookseller's clerk at Newcastle, during which ime he learned Greek and Latin and accomplished onsiderable reading. He studied at the theological eminary at Wymondley, Hertfordshire, and was ninister for a year at Bedford; became minister t Newport, Isle of Wight, 1824, of the King's Veigh-House Chapel, Eastcheap, London, 1829, nd remained there forty years. After retiring rom his pastorate he was professor of homiletics nd pastoral theology at New College, London. Ie was chairman of the Congregational Union in 848. He was strongly opposed to an established 'hurch, and in 1833 at the laying of the corner-stone of a new chapel for the Weigh-House congregation expressed himself on the subject in language which led to a long and bitter controversy. He felt that the sermon occupied too large a place in the service of the non-ritualistic Churches and favored the introduction of responsive readings and similar changes in the form of worship; his *Service of Song in the House of the Lord* (London, 1848) exercised much influence in the development of a richer and better musical service, and he enriched the hymnals by the hymn "Eternal light, eternal light." He edited Charles W Baird's *Chapter on Liturgies*, adding a preface and an appendix, "Are Dissenters to Have a Liturgy?" (1856). His other publications include a *Memoir of Stephen Morell* (1826); *Dissent Not Schism* (1835); a life of Sir Thomas Fowell Buxton (1849); *Is it Possible to Make the Best of Both Worlds?* (1853); *Lights and Shadows, or Church Life in Australia*, observations made during a visit in 1857–59 (1860); *Money, a Popular Exposition in Rough Notes* (1864); *St. Paul, his Life and Ministry* (1866); *Micah the Priest Maker, a handbook on ritualism* (1867); *From Seventeen to Thirty*, a book for young men (1868). Two series of his *Sermons Preached in the King's Weigh-House Chapel, 1829–69*, were published, the second with biographical sketch by the Rev. H. Allon (1869–75).

BIBLIOGRAPHY: Besides the sketch in the volume of his sermons, the following may be consulted: *A Memorial of the late Rev. Thomas Binney*, ed. J. Stoughton, London, 1874; E. P. Hood, *Thomas Binney, his Mind, Life and Opinions*, ib. 1874; *DNB*, v, 57–59.

BINTERIM, ANTON JOSEF: German Catholic theologian; b. at Düsseldorf Sept. 19, 1779; d. at Bilk (s. suburb of Düsseldorf) May 17, 1855. After receiving his first education in his native city, he entered the Franciscan order in 1796 and studied philosophy and theology at Düren and Aachen for five years and a half. Returning to Düsseldorf, he was ordained priest at Cologne (Sept. 19, 1802). The suppression of the monasteries on the right bank of the Rhine in the following year, however, obliged him to become a secular priest, and in 1805, after passing the required examination, he was appointed to the ancient and extensive parish of Bilk, where he remained until his death. Binterim was an enthusiastic propagandist of ultramontanism, and to this cause he devoted the greater part of his prolific literary activity. He also defended the Jesuits and upheld the authenticity of the Holy Coat of Treves, while with equal consistency he opposed the followers of Georg Hermes (q.v.) and Catholic "rationalism." In 1837, with his elder brother, he had founded and endowed the vicarage of St. Anthony of Padua at Bilk, and in honor of his jubilee the first impulse toward the establishment of the Historischer Verein für den Niederrhein was given in 1852. In his devotion to the Church he was imprisoned for six months in 1838 for opposing mixed marriages.

(VICTOR SCHULTZE.)

BIBLIOGRAPHY: Among the numerous publications of Binterim special mention may be made of the following: *Ueber Ehe und Ehescheidung nach Gotteswort und dem Geiste der katholischen Kirche* (Düsseldorf, 1819); *Calendarium ecclesiæ Germanicæ Coloniensis sæculi noni* (Cologne, 1824); *Die vorzüglichsten Denkwürdigkeiten der christ-katholischen Kirche* (7 vols., Mainz, 1825–41); *Die katholische Kirche, ein Gegensatz des Rationalismus und Aftermysticismus* (Düsseldorf, 1827); *Die alte und neue Erzdiocese Köln* (4 vols., 1828–30); *Ueber die zweckmässige Einrichtung des uralten katholischen Gottesdienstes und den heilsamen Gebrauch der lateinischen Sprache bei demselben* (1832); *Ueber den Gebrauch des Christenblutes bei den Juden* (1834); *Pragmatische Geschichte der deutschen Concilien* (7 vols., 1835–49); *Der katholische Bruder- und Schwesterbund zu einer rein katholischen Ehe* (1838); *De proepiscopis sive suffraganeis Coloniensibus extraordinariis* (Mainz, 1843); *Zeugnisse für die Echtheit des heiligen Rockes zu Trier* (3 parts, Düsseldorf, 1845–46); *Die geistlichen Gerichte vom 13.–19. Jahrhundert* (2 parts, 1849); *Der heilige Hilarius* (Leipsic, 1851); *Hermann II., Erzbischof von Köln* (Düsseldorf, 1851); *Ueber den Hostienhandel in Deutschland und Frankreich* (2d ed., 1852); and *Die geheimen Vorschriften der Jesuiten (Monita Secreta), ein altes Lügenwerk* (1853).

For his life consult: *ADB*, vol. ii; K. Werner, *Geschichte der katholischen Theologie seit dem Trienter Konzil bis zur Gegenwart*, pp. 391–393; *KL*, ii, 848–854 (in considerable detail).

BIRCH, THOMAS: Church of England clergyman and author; b. in London Nov. 23, 1705; d. there Jan. 9, 1766. He was ordained priest in 1731, although of Quaker parentage and without a university education; was an ardent Whig and, having influential patrons, received many good preferments, holding at the time of his death the rectories of St. Margaret Pattens, London, and Depden, Suffolk. He was an indefatigable writer, and his works have been criticized as showing more industry than judgment; they include a number of volumes relating to English history; lives of Robert Boyle (London, 1744), Archbishop Tillotson (1752), and others, as well as most of the English biographies in the *General Dictionary* (10 vols., 1734–41); editions of Milton's prose (1738), Sir Walter Raleigh's works (1751), and the works and letters of Lord Bacon (1765); *History of the Royal Society of London* (4 vols., 1756–57); numerous communications in the "Philosophical Transactions" and other periodical publications.

Bibliography: J. Nichols, *Literary Anecdotes of the Eighteenth Century*, i, 585–637, ii, 507, iii, 258, v, 40–43, 53, 282–290, London, 1812–15; *DNB*, v, 68–70.

BIRD, FREDERIC MAYER: Protestant Episcopalian; b. at Philadelphia June 28, 1838; d. in South Bethlehem, Pa., Apr. 3, 1908. He was educated at the University of Pennsylvania (B.A., 1857) and Union Theological Seminary (1860). He was ordained to the Lutheran ministry in 1860, and after serving as an army-chaplain in 1862–63, held several pastorates. In 1870 he became Protestant Episcopal rector of Spotswood, N. J., from 1870 to 1874. Seven years later he was appointed professor of psychology, Christian ethics, and rhetoric in Lehigh University, remaining there in this capacity, as well as in that of chaplain, until 1886. He was also acting chaplain there in 1896–98, and from 1893 to 1898 was editor of *Lippincott's Magazine*. In the latter year be became associate editor of *Chandler's Encyclopedia*. In addition to numerous contributions to periodicals and encyclopedias, including most of the American matter in Julian's *Dictionary of Hymnology* (London, 1892), he has edited *Charles Wesley Seen in his Finer and Less Familiar Poems* (New York, 1867); the *Hymns* of the Lutheran Pennsylvania ministerium (Philadelphia, 1865; in collaboration with S. M. Schmucker); and *Songs of the Spirit* (New York, 1871; in collaboration with Bishop W. H. Odenheimer). He made a noteworthy collection of hymnology, now in Union Theological Seminary, New York City.

BIRETTA. See Vestments and Insignia, Ecclesiastical.

BIRGITTA, ST., AND THE BIRGITTINE ORDER. See Bridget, Saint, of Sweden.

BIRINUS, SAINT: First bishop of the West Saxons; d. Dec. 3, 650. He was a Benedictine monk at Rome and was given a missionary commission by Pope Honorius I. After being consecrated bishop at Genoa by Asterius, archbishop of Milan, he landed in Wessex about 634. He baptized its king, Cynegils, in 635, Oswald of Northumbria standing as sponsor. He fixed his see at Dorchester (now a small village, 8 m. s.e. of Oxford), and gained influence in Wessex and Mercia. Cwichelm, the son of Cynegils, was baptized in 636; Cuthred, Cwichelm's son, in 639; Cenwalh, the brother and successor of Cynegils, in 646.

Bibliography: Bede, *Hist. eccl.*, iii, 7.

BISHOP: A spiritual overseer in the Christian Church. The origin of the office, its historic development, and theories of its relative dignity will be found discussed in the article Polity; for views of different communions concerning the office, see Episcopacy; this article will deal mainly with the selection of bishops and their duties.

Election and Consecration.

In the Roman Catholic Church the bishop holds the first place in the hierarchy, not as belonging to a separate order, but as having the fulness of the priesthood. Conditions for consecration are the following: legitimate birth, the age of thirty years, eminent learning, and moral probity. In the ordinary case the candidate is supposed also to be a native of the country and acceptable to the government. The choice of the person belongs, on the curialist theory, to the pope; but in practise it is generally left to the chapter, either by election, or when there are canonical impediments to be removed, as when translation from another see is required, by Postulation (q.v.); or it may occur through nomination by the government. The candidate must then receive the papal confirmation, after examination as to his fitness. This is made first by a papal delegate in the place of the election (*processus informativus in partibus electi*), after which a second investigation takes place at Rome, by the committee of cardinals appointed for the purpose (*congregatio examinis episcoporum*); this second examination is called *processus electionis definitivus in curia*. If both prove favorable to the candidate, he is confirmed, preconized, and put in possession of his powers of jurisdiction, though not, of course, of those pertaining to orders until his consecration, which is supposed to occur within three months. It is administered by a bishop designated by the pope, with the assistance of two other bishops or prelates, in the cathedral of the new bishop's diocese. The candidate takes the ancient oath of fidelity to the pope (substantially the same as that prescribed by Gregory VII in 1079), signs the profession of faith, and then, after he has been duly consecrated according to the form laid down in the Roman Pontifical, is solemnly enthroned. An oath of allegiance to the government of the country is also usually administered before consecration.

The rights or powers of a bishop may be considered under three heads—as pertaining to his orders, to his jurisdiction, and to his dignity. As to the first, he has all the *jura ordinis* of the fulness of the priesthood, including, besides those powers which every priest shares with him, the special episcopal prerogatives of administering ordination and confirmation, of consecrating the holy oils, churches, and sacred objects in general, of benediction of abbots and abbesses, and of anointing sovereigns. The rights of jurisdiction, in the broad sense, embrace the bishop's whole power of ruling his diocese as its chief pastor. Sometimes, however, the term *lex jurisdictionis* is applied specially to his legislative and executive functions (for the *jurisdictio contentiosa* and *coercitiva*—i.e., the power of hearing cases and pronouncing and enforcing judgment—see AUDIENTIA EPISCOPALIS; JURISDICTION, ECCLESIASTICAL), while the expression *lex diœcesana* refers to his right to the various church taxes. These rights belong to the bishop as bishop, and in regard to them he is *judex ordinarius*, "the ordinary"; but he often holds other powers specially delegated to him as representative of the pope (see FACULTIES). Finally, in regard to his dignity, he takes ecclesiastical rank, in virtue of his exalted office, immediately after the cardinals, and bears various customary titles of honor, being addressed as "Right Reverend," "My Lord," etc. In many places he also enjoys secular precedence; and he has his special insignia and vestments (see VESTMENTS AND INSIGNIA, ECCLESIASTICAL). To these prerogatives corresponding duties are attached, including not only the cure of souls, but residence in his diocese, and a visit to Rome to report upon its condition at fixed intervals, varying with the distance. Since the bishop is naturally unable to exercise all the rights and duties above described in person throughout his entire diocese, he has always had special assistants—in early times the archdeacons and archpriests, later his chapter and variously designated functionaries, vicars-general and the like, as well as, for those things which pertain to the power of orders, coadjutor or assistant bishops. See the articles under these titles.

Rights and Duties.

In the Protestant Churches the episcopate in the Roman Catholic sense has not been preserved. In the early days of the Reformation in Germany, the assaults of the Reformers were directed not so much against the episcopal power in itself as against abuses in its exercise; until 1545 the question was debated on what conditions the adherents of the evangelical doctrine could agree to submit to the existing bishops of the old Church. The Lutheran confessions of faith recognize as of divine right only the pastoral function in the bishop's office; all else is of merely human institution, and may be abolished by the same power that created it. Since, however, they laid down no definite form of ecclesiastical polity as ordained by God, they could and did declare themselves willing to recognize these powers still, so long as the bishops would allow freedom to teach the pure doctrine and tolerate the priests who preached it. Some bishops fulfilled the condition and accepted the evangelical doctrine; but this semblance of episcopal government had clearly nothing in common with the pre-Reformation episcopate except the name and certain forms. Elsewhere, as in Schwerin and later at Osnabrück and Lübeck, the name bishop was definitely used for an official appointed by the ruling power, in no sense ecclesiastical. The attempt to prove that the German Reformation deliberately intended to retain episcopal government is quite useless, though the tendency which it represents has had adherents, among whom were Frederick William IV and Bunsen. Where the title has been employed in the modern evangelical Church of Germany, it represents nothing more than a general superintendent. The bishops of England, Sweden, and Denmark are also not bishops in the strict sense understood by the Roman Catholics; their institutions rest on special historical grounds which are beyond the scope of this article.

(E. FRIEDBERG.)

In the Church of England there are three classes of bishops: the diocesan bishops, taking their titles (with a few exceptions of recently founded sees) from the old pre-Reformation dioceses; suffragan bishops, bearing likewise territorial titles; and assistant bishops. The diocesan bishops are nominally elected by the chapters of their cathedrals, but practically are appointed by the Crown, which sends a nomination to the chapter with the *congé d'élire*. Suffragan bishops are also nominated by the Crown, while assistant bishops are appointed by the prelate under whom they are to serve. Their appointment is revocable at his pleasure; that of suffragans is for life. None of these classes has any jurisdiction independent of its superior. With the first extension of the Anglican colonial episcopate, the English government attempted to claim the same right of nomination as at home; but this claim was abandoned, and the colonial bishops are now elected either by the clergy or by the deliberative assemblies of their dioceses. In the Episcopal Church of the United States, bishops are elected by the diocesan conventions: their election must then be confirmed by a majority of the other bishops and "standing committees." Assistant bishops in this Church are now known as bishops-coadjutor, and have the right of succession on the death of the diocesan bishop. In England bishops are frequently "translated" from one see to another; in the United States, bishops of missionary jurisdictions may be elected to a diocesan see, but this is all. Throughout the Anglican communion consecration by three other bishops is required. Every English bishop at his consecration takes the oaths of allegiance to the sovereign and canonical obedience to his metropolitan; in the United States each bishop is independent, subject only to the general law of the Church as formulated by the

General Convention, the office of presiding bishop being almost purely honorary. Throughout the Anglican communion the administration of certain quasisacramental rites (confirmation, ordination, consecration of churches, etc.) is strictly reserved to the bishop, who also has a power of ordinary jurisdiction in some measure resembling that exercised by the Roman Catholic prelates. The two English archbishops, the bishops of London, Winchester, and Durham, and most of the other bishops (the number corresponding to that of the more ancient sees), as "spiritual lords," have seats in the upper house of parliament. The American Methodist Episcopal Church also has its bishops, who are elected in any number required by the General Conference. They have joint jurisdiction throughout the Church, being confined to no diocese or districts, though for practical reasons the General Conference designates episcopal residences at its quadrennial sessions. Their functions are purely executive—they preside at conferences, arrange districts for presiding elders, fix appointments of preachers, and, especially, travel throughout the Church to promote its spiritual and temporal interests. No distinction of order is recognized between them and other ministers.

Bibliography: Consult Bingham, *Origines*, books iv, v, ix, xvi, xvii, for the election of bishops and the exercise of discipline; P. Hergenröther, *Lehrbuch des katholischen Kirchenrechts*, Freiburg, 1905. On the general subject consult works cited in Church Government.

BISHOP, NATHAN: Baptist layman; b. of New England stock at Vernon, Oneida County, N. Y., Aug. 12, 1808; d. at Saratoga Aug. 7, 1880. He was graduated at Brown 1837, and elected tutor; was superintendent of schools in Providence 1838–51, in Boston 1851–57 Removing to New York, he became an active member of the Sabbath Committee, manager of the American Bible Society, a member of the Christian Commission during the Civil War, and of the Indian Commission appointed by President Grant in 1869; he was also a member of the New York State Board of Charities, a delegate of the Evangelical Alliance to the Czar of Russia in behalf of religious liberty in the Baltic provinces in 1871, a trustee of Brown University from 1842, and one of the original board of trustees of Vassar College. For two years he served gratuitously as secretary of the Amerlean Baptist Home Mission Society, and he was chairman of the finance committee of the American Bible Revision Committee till his death.

(P Schaff†) D. S. Schaff.

BISHOP (EPISCOPUS) IN PARTIBUS INFIDELIUM. See Bishop, Titular.

BISHOP, TITULAR: According to the old law of the Church, only one bishop was consecrated for a diocese; and none was conscerated at large or without a definite diocese (First Council of Nicæa, canon viii). If, therefore, occasion arose for the designation of a representative to perform episcopal functions in the place of an incapacitated bishop, it was necessary to call upon some neighboring bishop or one who happened to be in those parts (see Coadjutor). In the ninth and tenth centuries, certain Spanish bishops who had been driven from their sees by the Saracens, and in the tenth some from Prussia and Livonia who were in a similar position, served in this capacity. The same service was rendered in the fourteenth century by the bishops of sees founded in the East during the crusades and afterward occupied by the Mohammedans. So, even after all hope of the recovery of these territories had been abandoned, bishops continued to be consecrated for these dioceses, called *episcopi in partibus infidelium* ("bishops in the regions of the unbelieving") until 1882, when Leo XIII ordered the use of the designation *episcopi titulares*. Their functions are various. In the first place, they serve as auxiliary or coadjutor bishops in dioceses where the need exists, when the diocesan makes a request to the pope for such an assignment, naming a suitable person, and giving assurance for his support. The coadjutor of course possesses all the *jura ordinis* like any other bishop, but exercises them only at the direction of his superior, and he has not, *ex officio*, the other prerogatives of a diocesan bishop (see Bishop). Apostolic vicars, who administer missionary districts not formed into dioceses, are usually consecrated bishops, and so are certain Roman functionaries who are members of the great congregations, and papal nuncios and other diplomatic representatives. Titular bishops are also consecrated for certain special purposes, such as the administration of holy orders to the Uniat Greeks of Italy, and the spiritual oversight of the military and naval forces of certain countries (see Exemption). (P Hinschius†.)

Bibliography: L. Thomassin, *Vetus et nova ecclesiæ disciplina*, part I, book i, chaps. 27–28, Lucca, 1728; A. H. Andnucci, *Tractatus de episcopo titulari*, Rome, 1732; J. C. Möller, *Geschichte der Weihbischöfe von Osnabrück*, Lingen, 1887.

BISHOPRIC, or DIOCESE: The territory over which the jurisdiction of a bishop extends. The origin of such divisions goes back to the foundation and growth of the very early Christian communities. When the apostles founded a church in a city, the faithful living there (Gk. *paroikoi*, *parepidēmoi*; cf. Eph. ii, 19; I Pet. ii, 11) formed a community (*paroikia*) which gradually took more definite shape under the leadership of the presbyters or bishops, and gained adherents outside the town. At first these latter attended divine service in the city, until their numbers increased sufficiently to form a separate dependent community, the term *paroikia* being applied to the larger territory equally. In the West the name *parochia* retained this sense until the ninth century, when it became restricted to single parishes in the modern sense, the bishop's jurisdiction being known as *diœcesis* (already in use to designate a civil governor's jurisdiction). The latter word in the East, following the analogy of civil divisions, was applied to the district ruled by a patriarch. In Gaul the ecclesiastical unit was constituted out of the chief town of a district and its annexed territory (*conventus*, Gk. *dioikēsis*), which in the Frankish period corresponded to the jurisdiction of a count. In Germany the original diocese was larger, and the *Gau* was coterminous with its subdivision of archdeaconry or deanery. The erection or redistribution of dioceses was from the fourth century a function of the metropolitan and the provincial synod; in Germany from the eighth century it was carried out under papal supervision. From the eleventh century it has been reserved to the pope; but in Germany the joint action of the state has been required, the matter being considered a *causa mixta*.

(E. Friedberg.)

Bibliography: L. Thomassin, *Vetus et nova ecclesiæ disciplina*, part I, book iii, Lucca, 1728; R. Hooker, *Ecclesiastical Polity*, book viii, chap. 8, best ed., by Keble, 3 vols., Oxford, 1845; H. Milman, *History of Christianity*, book iv, London, 1867; W. T. Arnold, *Roman System of Provincial Administration*, London, 1879; Bingham, *Origines*, Books iv–v, ix; *KL*, ii, 878–888.

BISHOPS' BOOK, THE: A work published at London in 1537, compiled by a commission of English bishops and clergymen, of which the full title is *The Institution of a Christian Man, containing the exposition or interpretation of the common creed, of the seven sacraments, of the x commandments and of the pater noster, and of the ave maria, justification, and purgatory.* It reflects the conditions of the time in maintaining that the authority of the pope is a human institution, while not denying that the Church of Rome is a part of the Church Universal. It is reprinted in *Formularies of Faith Put Forth by Authority during the Reign of Henry VIII*, edited by C. Lloyd, bishop of Oxford (Oxford, 1825). Consult C. Hardwick, *A History of the Christian Church during the Reformation* (6th ed., London, 1877).

BISSELL, EDWIN CONE: American Congregationalist; b. at Schoharie, N. Y., Mar. 2, 1832; d. at Chicago Apr. 10, 1894. He was graduated at Amherst 1855, and at Union Theological Seminary, New York, 1859; was pastor of Congregational churches at Westhampton, Mass., 1859–64, San Francisco, 1864–69, Winchester, Mass., 1871–73; missionary of the American Board in Austria 1874–79; became Nettleton professor of Hebrew and Old Testament exegesis in the Hartford Theological Seminary 1881, and of Old Testament exegesis and literature in McCormick Theological Seminary, Chicago, 1892. During his pastorate at Westhampton he raised a company of the fifty-second regiment, Massachusetts volunteers, and served as its captain under Gen. Banks at Port Hudson 1862–63. In 1869–70 he supplied the pulpit of the Congregational Church at Honolulu, Sandwich Islands. He published *The Historic Origin of the Bible* (New York, 1873); *The Apocrypha of the Old Testament* (a revised translation, introduction, and notes, vol. xv of the American Lange series, 1880); *The Pentateuch, its origin and structure* (1885); *Biblical Antiquities* (Philadelphia, 1888); *A Practical Introductory Hebrew Grammar* (Hartford, 1891); *Genesis Printed in Colors, showing the original sources from which it is supposed to have been compiled, with introduction* (1892).

BITHYNIA. See Asia Minor in the Apostolic Time, VI.

BIZOCHI. See Fraticelli.

BJÖRLING, biör'ling, **CARL OLOF:** Swedish theologian; b. at Westerås (60 m. w.n.w. of Stockholm), Sweden, Sept. 16, 1804; d. there Jan. 20, 1884. He studied at the University of Upsala; became bishop of Westerås, 1866, having long been connected as teacher and rector with the Gefle gymnasium. He was the author of several learned works, including a treatise on Christian dogmatics (2 parts, 1847–75), which attracted considerable attention in Germany, and shows his firm adherence to the Augsburg Confession.

BLACK FATHERS. See Holy Ghost, Orders and Congregations of the, 11, 6.

BLACK FRIARS: A name given in England to Dominican monks because of the color of their dress.

BLACK, HUGH: Scotch Presbyterian; b. at Rothesay (40 m. w of Glasgow), Buteshire, Mar. 26, 1868. He was graduated from Glasgow University in 1887 and the Free Church College, Glasgow, in 1891, and was ordained to the Presbyterian ministry in the latter year. He was pastor of Sherwood Church, Paisley, 1891–96, and became associate pastor of St. George's Free Church, Edinburgh, 1896. He lectured on homiletics at Union Theological Seminary, New York, in 1905, and in 1906 became professor of practical theology in that institution. He has written *The Dream of Youth* (London, 1894); *Friendship* (1897); *Culture and Restraint* (1901); *Work* (1903); *The Practice of Self-Culture* (1904); and *Comfort* (1906).

BLACK JEWS. See Church of God, 2.

BLACK RUBRIC: The popular name for the declaration enjoining kneeling at the end of the order for the administration of the Lord's Supper in the prayer-book of the Church of England, so called because it was printed in black letter in the prayer-book as revised by William Sancroft (q.v.) in 1661. It is not, strictly speaking, a rubric at all as it is intended for the direction of the people and not for the officiating clergy. Nor did Sancroft originate it, as it dates back to the second prayer-book of Edward VI (1552), whose council ordered that the communicants should receive the elements kneeling, and explained in the "rubric" that this attitude was not used to express belief in transubstantiation. The "rubric" was omitted in the Elizabethan prayer-book of 1559, and this omission was one of the cherished grievances of the Puritans. In the Savoy Conference of 1661 the Presbyterians demanded its restoration, but the bishops were not at the time inclined to grant it; at the last moment, however, it was replaced and so it appears in the revised prayer-book of Charles II and is still retained in the English prayer-book. It was removed from the prayer-book as revised for the American Episcopal Church in 1789.

BLACKWOOD, WILLIAM: Presbyterian; b. at Dromara, County Down, Ireland, June 1, 1804; d. in Baltimore, Md., Nov. 13, 1893. He was graduated at the Royal College, Belfast, 1832; became pastor successively of the Presbyterian churches of Holywood, near Belfast, 1835; of

Trinity Church, Newcastle-on-Tyne, 1843; and of the Ninth Church, Philadelphia, Penn., 1850. He was secretary to the Education Committee of the Irish Presbyterian Church, 1834–40; mathematical examiner of students under care of the Synod of Ulster, 1839–43; and was moderator of the Presbyterian Church in England, 1846. He published, with other works, essays on *Missions to the Heathen* (Belfast, 1830); *Atonement, Faith, and Assurance* (Philadelphia, 1856); *Bellarmine's Notes of the Church* (1858); and edited the papers of the late Rev. Richard Webster, with introduction and indexes, and published them under the title *Webster's History of the Presbyterian Church* (Philadelphia, 1857); also the *Biblical, Theological, Biographical, and Literary Encyclopædia* (2 vols., 1873–76).

BLAIKIE, WILLIAM GARDEN: Free Church of Scotland; b. at Aberdeen Feb. 5, 1820; d. at North Berwick June 11, 1899. He studied at Marischal College and at Edinburgh (M.A., Aberdeen, 1837); was ordained minister of the Established Church at Drumblade, Aberdeenshire, 1842; joined the Free Church of Scotland, 1843; was minister of Pilrig, Edinburgh, 1844–68; professor of apologetics and pastoral theology in New College, Edinburgh, 1868–97. With the Rev. William Arnot he was delegate from the Free Church of Scotland to the General Assembly of the Presbyterian Church of the United States at Philadelphia in 1870 to convey congratulations on union; he took a leading part in the Alliance of the Reformed Churches; was deeply interested in measures to improve the condition of the poor and the working classes; and active in behalf of home missions, temperance, church extension, and all the work of the Free Church. In 1892 he was moderator of the General Assembly. He edited *The Free Church Magazine* 1849–53, *The North British Review* 1860–1863, *The Sunday Magazine* 1873–74, and *The Catholic Presbyterian* 1879–83.

Bibliography: The more important of his many books were *Bible History in Connection with the General History of the World*, London, 1859; *Better Days for the Working People*, 1863 (originally published as *Six Lectures Addressed to the Working Classes on the Improvement of their Temporal Condition*, Edinburgh, 1849); *Heads and Hands in the World of Labor*, 1865; *For the Work of the Ministry, a Manual of Homiletical and Pastoral Theology*, 1873; *Glimpses of the Inner Life of our Lord*, 1876; *The Personal Life of David Livingstone*, 1880; *The Public Ministry and Pastoral Methods of our Lord*, 1883; *Leaders in Modern Philanthropy*, 1884; *Robert Rollock, first Principal of the University of Edinburgh*, 1884; *The Preachers of Scotland from the Sixth to the Nineteenth Century* (Cunningham Lectures for 1888); *Thomas Chalmers*, Edinburgh, 1896; *David Brown, a Memoir*, London, 1898. He also edited *Memorials of the Late Andrew Crichton*, 1868, and James Walker's *Theology and Theologians of Scotland*, 1872; wrote five of the *Present Day Tracts*, 1883–1885; contributed the "Expositions and Homiletics" for the Epistle to the Ephesians in the *Pulpit Commentary*, and prepared the Books of Joshua and Samuel for the *Expositor's Bible*. For his life consult his *Autobiography*, edited with introduction by N. L. Walker, London, 1901, and *DNB*, supplement vol. i, 212–213.

BLAIR, HUGH: Church of Scotland; b. in Edinburgh Apr. 7, 1718; d. there Dec. 27, 1800. He studied in the local university; became minister of Colessie, Fifeshire, 1742; second minister of the Canongate Church, Edinburgh, 1743; minister of Lady Yester's 1754; was transferred to the High Church 1758. From 1759 he lectured in the University so acceptably on rhetoric and belles-lettres, that in 1760 he was appointed the town council professor in that department, and from 1762 to 1783 was the royal professor; when on resigning he published his lectures (2 vols.) he became one of the most famous authors of works on rhetoric in the English language and retained the position for a century. In 1780 he received a pension of £200 a year. To his own generation he was a most acceptable preacher and his sermons continued to be read and to be translated far into the nineteenth century. Their simplicity, excellent style, and high morality account for their vogue, but their lack of depth in thought and spirituality have caused them to lose popularity.

Bibliography: Sketches of Blair's life were appended to vol. v of his sermons by J. Finlayson, London, 1801; consult also John Hill, *An Account of the Life and Writings of H. Blair*, Edinburgh, 1807; *DNB*, v, 160–161.

BLAIR, JAMES: Virginia colonial Episcopal clergyman; b. in Scotland in 1656; d. at Williamsburg, Va., Apr. 18, 1743. He was graduated M.A. at Edinburgh in 1673; became a clergyman of the Episcopal Church of Scotland and was rector of Cranston in the diocese of Edinburgh. In the latter part of the reign of Charles II he went to England and was persuaded by Dr. Compton, bishop of London, to emigrate to Virginia, where he arrived in 1685; he was minister of Henrico parish till 1694, at Jamestown till 1710, and at Williamsburg the rest of his life. In 1689 he was appointed by the bishop of London commissary for Virginia, the highest church office in the colony, the duties of which were practically those of a bishop exclusive of ordination. After 1793 he was member of the colonial Council and for many years its president. He was a man of sterling character and great ability, and worked with persistent zeal and energy to promote the religious and material welfare of Virginia. He did much to elevate the character of the colonial clergy. With several of the governors he had bitter disputes and was influential in securing their removal. He was founder and first president of William and Mary College, for which he procured a charter in England in 1693, and which he made a success in spite of great difficulties and discouragements. He published four volumes containing 117 sermons on *Our Savior's Divine Sermon on the Mount* (London, 1722) and with Henry Hartwell and Edward Chilton prepared *The Present State of Virginia and the College* (London, 1727).

Bibliography: D. E. Motley, *The Life of Commissary James Blair*, in *Johns Hopkins University Studies in Historical and Political Science*, series xix, no. 10, Baltimore, 1901; *DNB*, v, 161–162.

BLAIR, SAMUEL: American Presbyterian; b. in Ireland June 14, 1712; d. at Londonderry, Penn., July 5, 1751. He came early to America; studied at Tennent's "Log College" at Neshaminy; was ordained pastor of Middletown and Shrewsbury, N. J., 1734; in 1739 removed to Londonderry or Fagg's Manor (40 m. w.s.w. of Philadelphia),

Chester County, Penn., and established there a school after the model of the "Log College." He was an adherent of Gilbert Tennent in the controversies of his time. His principal writings were collected by his brother, Rev. John Blair (Philadelphia, 1754); they include sermons, a treatise on predestination and reprobation, and an account of a revival in his congregation at Londonderry.

BIBLIOGRAPHY: Consult the biographical sketch in A. Alexander, *The Founder and Principal Alumni of the Log College*, pp. 164-196, Philadelphia, 1851.

BLAIR, WILLIAM: United Free Church of Scotland; b. at Cluny (23 m. s.w. of St. Andrews), Fifeshire, Jan. 13, 1830. He studied at the University of St. Andrews (M.A., 1850), and in 1856 was ordained to the United Presbyterian ministry at Dunblane, Perthshire. He was clerk to the Stirling Presbytery for twenty-five years, and to the United Presbyterian Synod 1894–1900; since 1900 he has been clerk to the United Free Church General Assembly, and was moderator of the United Presbyterian Synod in 1898-99. He has been chaplain to the famous Black Watch since 1892, a member of the University Court of St. Andrews University since 1903. In theology he adheres strictly to the Westminster Confession. He has written *Chronicles of Aberbrothoc* (Arbroath, 1853); *Rambling Recollections; or, Scenes worth Seeing* (Edinburgh, 1857); *Archbishop Leighton, Life with Selections* (London, 1883); *Jubilee Memorial Volume* (Edinburgh, 1887); *History and Principles of the United Presbyterian Church* (1888); and *Robert Leighton, Extracts and Introduction* (London, 1907).

BLAISE, SAINT. See HELPERS IN NEED.

BLAKESLEE, ERASTUS: Congregationalist; b. at Plymouth, Conn., Sept. 2, 1838; d. at Brookline, Mass., July 12, 1908. While a sophomore at Yale in 1861 he enlisted as a cavalryman. He was mustered out in 1865 as brevet brigadier-general of volunteers. After a business career he studied in Andover Theological Seminary from 1876 to 1879, and entered the Congregational ministry. He had three charges, at Greenfield, Mass., Fairhaven, Conn., and at Spencer, Mass. (1887–92), and resigned the last that he might give his whole time to the preparation and publication of the "Bible Study Union Lessons," which are not only widely used in this country, but translated into several missionary languages. With the teachers' aids, issued separately, more than 160 volumes of lessons were published. FRANK SANDERS.

BLANCKMEISTER, FRANZ THEODOR: German Lutheran; b. at Plauen (21 m. s.w. of Zwickau) Feb. 4, 1858. After studying at Leipsic from 1877 to 1880 and teaching for a year, he entered the ministry, and has been, since 1897, pastor of Trinity Church in Dresden. In theology he is extremely Protestant and an adverse critic of the Roman Catholic Church. Of his numerous publications may be mentioned *Alte Geschichte aus dem Sachsenlande* (3 vols., Barmen, 1886–89); *Sachsenspiegel* (Dresden, 1897; 2d ed., 1902); and *Sächsische Kirchengeschichte* (1899; 2d ed., 1906).

BLANDINA, SAINT: A martyr who was among the victims of the persecution in Lyons under Marcus Aurelius. In the account of that persecution given by the Christian community there, and preserved by Eusebius (*Hist. eccl.*, v, 1), the courage of the young slave girl is specially extolled; and she is singled out for mention by name, an honor which she shares with only seven of the other martyrs, including the bishop Pothinus. (A. HAUCK.)

BLANDRATA, GEORGIUS: Italian Unitarian; b. about 1515 at Saluzzo (17 miles n.w. of Coni), Piedmont; d. after 1585. He migrated to Poland, where he became physician to Sigismund I, then went to Transylvania and served the widow of Jan Zapolya in a like capacity. Having returned to Italy, he went to Pavia, and became an object of suspicion on account of his radical utterances on theology, but escaped the Inquisition by going to Geneva. There he debated with Martinenghi, the preacher of the Italian congregation, also with Calvin, especially concerning the doctrine of the Trinity, which he regarded as endangering the doctrine of the unity of God. He regarded speculation on the relation of the three persons as unnecessary (F. Trechsel, *Protestantische Antitrinitarier*, 4 parts, Bern, 1841–42, ii, 467; *CR*, xvii, 2871). Calvin replied in his *Responsum ad quæstiones G. Blandratæ* (Geneva, 1559). As some members of the congregation sided with Blandrata, Calvin had a confession signed which condemned the antitrinitarian doctrine. Blandrata went to Zurich, then again to Poland, where he was received by Prince Radziwill and took part in several synods (cf. H. Dalton, *Lasciana*, Berlin, 1898, iv), but Calvin's repeated warnings against him, stigmatizing him as "a foul pest," prevented any lasting activity. In 1563 Blandrata went again to Transylvania and openly professed Unitarianism, being assisted by Prince Stephen Bathori, afterward king of Poland. Faustus Socinus accused Blandrata of having separated from his coreligionists out of avarice; at any rate, tired of the conflict, he ceased to take part in public affairs. K. BENRATH.

BIBLIOGRAPHY: Many of the letters of Blandrata are printed in *CR*, vols. xvii–xxi. Sources for a biography are: C. Sandius, *Bibliotheca antitrinitariorum*, Freistadt, 1684; S. Lubienski, *Historia reformationis Polonicæ*, ib. 1685. Consult V. Malacarne, *Commentario delle opere e della vicendi di G. Biandrata*, Padua, 1814; O. Fock, *Der Socinianismus*, Kiel, 1847; and J. H. Allen, *Historical Sketch of the Unitarian Movement*, New York, 1894.

BLASPHEMY (Gk. *blasphēmia*, "a speech or word of evil omen"): Properly any species of calumny and detraction, but technically limited to evil-speaking of God or things held sacred. The conception that such an act is a crime may be traced back to Judaism, whose code imposed death by stoning as a punishment (Lev. xxiv, 15–16; Matt. xxvi, 65; John x, 33). The later Roman law also attached the death penalty (*Nov. Justin.*, LXXVII, i, 1–2). In the earlier church law, blasphemy is not mentioned as a punishable offense. Pope Gregory IX (1227–41) prescribed penance for public blasphemy against God, the saints, or the Virgin; the guilty person must stand for seven Sundays at the church porch during the mass, on the last of the seven without cloak or shoes; he must fast the Fridays preceding on bread and water, and give alms according to his means. The civil authorities were also admonished to impose a fine. By the end of the century the offense came to be more definitely defined as any depreciatory or opprobrious expression concerning God, Christ, or the Holy Spirit, such as the denial of a divine attribute, or the ascription of something unseemly (as falsehood or revenge), or wishing ill to or in any way dishonoring God, the saints, or the Virgin. Leo X (1513–21) imposed fines according to the ability of the offender and bodily punishments which included flogging, boring the tongue, and condemnation to the galleys in extreme cases. Later a tendency to substitute admonition and exhortation for severe penalties becomes apparent. By the common law of England, and in many of the United States by statute law, blasphemy is an indictable offense; prosecutions, however, have become infrequent. (P. Hinschius†.)

The blasphemy against the Holy Ghost which is pronounced unpardonable (Matt. xii, 31; Mark iii, 29; Luke xii, 10) is best understood to be wilful and persistent resistance to the influences and warnings of God, which renders the subject incapable of repentance and pardon. See Holy Spirit, II.

Bibliography: J. D. Michaelis, *Mosäisches Recht*, part v, § 251, Frankfort, 1770–75, Eng. transl., London, 1810; P. Hinschius, *Das Kirchenrecht in Deutschland*, iv, p. 793, n. 3, v, 184, 318–319, 325, 699, vi, 188, Berlin, 1869–98; Blackstone, *Commentaries*, IV, 4, iv; Sir J. F. Stephen, *History of the Criminal Law of England*, ii, 469–476, London, 1883; Bishop, *Commentaries*, X, x; *DB*, i, 305–306; *EB*, i, 589–590.

BLASS, FRIEDRICH WILHELM: German Protestant classical scholar; b. at Osnabrück (30 m. n.e. of Münster) Jan. 22, 1843; d. at Halle Mar. 5, 1907. He studied in Göttingen (1860–61) and Bonn (1861–63; Ph.D., 1863), and after being a teacher in gymnasia at Bielefeld (1864–66), Naumburg-an-der-Saale (1866–70), Magdeburg (1870–73), and Stettin (1873–74), became privatdocent at Königsberg in 1874. Two years later he was appointed associate professor at Kiel, where he was promoted to the rank of full professor in 1881. From 1892 he was professor of classical philology at Halle. Besides editions of Greek authors and inscriptions, and several works on strictly classical themes, he published *Philology of the Gospels* (London, 1898) and *Grammatik des neutestamentlichen Griechisch* (Göttingen, 1896; Eng. transl. by H. St. J. Thackeray, London, 1898), and edited *Acta Apostolorum* (Göttingen, 1895; minor edition, Leipsic, 1896); *Evangelium secundum Lucam* (Leipsic, 1897); *Evangelium secundum Matthæum* (1901); *Evangelium secundum Johannem* (1902); and (*Barnabas*) *Brief an die Hebräer* (Halle, 1903).

BLASTARES, MATTHÆUS: At first a secular priest and later a monk of the order of St. Basil, who made about 1335 a collection of laws, both civil and ecclesiastical, known as "Alphabetical Collection," *Syntagma alphabeticum rerum omnium quæ in sacris canonibus comprehenduntur*. The civil part ("political laws") is based upon the *Novellæ* of Justinian, the ecclesiastical ("canons") upon the collection of Photius, with the commentaries of Zonaras and Balsamon. Such a dictionary of law filled a practical want, and so was universally used by the Eastern clergy, and even translated into Slavic. A complete reprint is found in Beveridge's *Synodicon*, ii, 2, and in vol. vi of the *Syntagma tōn theiōn kai hierōn kanonōn* (Athens, 1859). (E. Friedberg.)

BLAURER (BLARER, BLAARER), AMBROSIUS: German Reformer; b. at Constance Apr. 12, 1492; d. at Winterthur (12 miles n.e. of Zurich), Switzerland, Dec. 6, 1564. He studied at Tübingen, where he became acquainted with Melanchthon; about 1510 he entered the monastery at Alpirsbach, and continued his studies at Tübingen till 1513. Through study of the Bible and of Luther's writings, to the reading of which he was led by his brother Thomas, who while studying at Wittenberg had become intimate with Luther and Melanchthon, he embraced the principles of the Reformation, which he tried to introduce into the monastery. Being opposed by the abbot, he went to Constance July 5, 1522, and at the instance of the council of the city began to preach in 1525. He became the leader of the Reformation there. From 1528, Blaurer labored for the Reformation outside of his native city. He was present at the colloquy in Bern (Jan. 6, 1528), was at Memmingen Nov., 1528–Feb., 1529, and presided over the convention of the friends of the Reformation in Upper Germany which met in Memmingen Feb. 27–Mar. 1, 1531. From May to July, 1531, he was at Ulm with Œcolampadius and Butzer, afterward at Geislingen, and (Sept. 1531–July, 1532) at Esslingen. He everywhere displayed ability in organization. In July, 1532, his native city recalled him, and in 1533 he married a former nun.

In 1534 he was called by Duke Ulrich, together with the Lutheran Erhard Schnepf, to further the cause of the Reformation in the duchy of Wurttemberg. The two men came to an agreement, Aug. 2, 1534, concerning the doctrine of the Lord's Supper paving thereby the way for the coming union of the German Evangelical Church. To Blaurer was assigned the south of Württemberg with residence at Tübingen. He encountered there certain difficulties: (1) the agreement with Schwenckfeld, 1535; (2) the reformation at the University of Tübingen, which Brenz had undertaken; (3) the image-question, which Blaurer solved by removing all of them from the churches, but the "idol-diet" at Urach left the decision to the duke. At Schmalkald Blaurer refused in Feb., 1537, to sign the articles of Luther, but approved those of Melanchthon. Court intrigues brought about Blaurer's dismissal in June, 1538. Not till 1556 did Duke Christopher compensate him for his four years' services. He was at Augsburg June 27–Dec. 6, 1539, where he earnestly labored against the luxury of the rich, pleaded for benevolence to the poor, and for the cause of morality. He went to Kempten and labored there (Dec., 1539, to the end of Jan., 1540) for the peace of the Church, and also at Isny, 1544–55.

By the Interim, Constance lost its independence. The Spaniards took the city Aug. 6, 1548, and made it an Austrian town, speedily crushing the Reformation. Blaurer left there Aug. 28, and preached in Biel (1551–59), Leutmerken, and finally at Winterthur, where he died. He declined calls to Bern, Augsburg, Memmingen, and the Palatinate, and influenced large circles by his correspondence. His twenty-two hymns give evidence of poetical power and fervor.

G. Bossert.

Bibliography: D. C. Pfister, *Denkwürdigkeiten der württembergischen und schwäbischen Reformationsgeschichte*, part i, Tübingen, 1817; T. Keim, *Ambr. Blarer der schwäbische Reformator*, Stuttgart, 1860; T. Pressel, *Ambrosius Blaurer's Leben und Schriften*, ib. 1861; *Leben und ausgewählte Schriften der Väter der reformierten Kirche*, vol. xiv, Elberfeld, 1861; E. Schneider, *Württembergische Reformationsgeschichte*, Stuttgart, 1887; E. Issel, *Die Reformation in Konstanz*, Freiburg, 1898; F. Roth, *Augsburgs Reformationsgeschichte*, vols. i, ii, Munich, 1901, 1904; *Zwingliana*, 1900, no. 2, p. 163, 1902, no. 2, p. 317.

BLAURER, MARGARETHA: Sister of Ambrosius Blaurer (q.v.), one of the most intelligent and deeply religious women of the Reformation time; d. in Constance 1542. She became deeply interested in the person and work of Pilgram Marbeck (q.v.) during his residence in Strasburg (1528–1532) and, whether she sympathized with his antipedobaptist teaching or not, reproached Butzer for his intolerant proceedings against Marbeck and refused to be convinced by Butzer's arguments that Marbeck was a heretic or a hypocrite. She died while ministering to the plague-stricken poor of Constance, and has the honor of being one of the first Protestant women to engage in diaconal service.

A. H. Newman.

Bibliography: J. W. Baum, *Capito und Butzer*, passim, Elberfeld, 1860; C. Gerbert, *Geschichte der Strassburger Sectenbewegung zur Zeit der Reformation, 1524–1534*, pp. 97 sqq., Strasburg, 1889; and literature under Blaurer, Ambrosius.

BLAVATSKY, HELENA PETROVNA: Theosophist; b. at Ekaterinoslav (250 m. n.e. of Odessa), Russia, July 31 (O. S.), 1831; d. in London May 8, 1891. Supposed to have been the child of a Russian officer named Peter Hahn, she married, at the age of seventeen, a Russian official, Nicephore Blavatsky, from whom she separated after a very few months. For the next twenty years her life was a wandering one, mixed with spiritualism and similar cults. During this time she visited Paris, Cairo, New Orleans, Tokyo, and Calcutta, and she claimed to have resided for seven years in Tibet, whence she pretended to draw the mysteries of theosophy (q.v.). In 1858 she started a spiritualistic movement in Russia, and in 1873 was again in the United States. In 1875 she founded at New York, in collaboration with Col. Henry Steel Olcott, the Theosophical Society. Her chief works, which have run through repeated editions and have been translated into many languages, both in Europe and India, are *Isis Unveiled: The Master Key to Ancient and Modern Mysteries*, the standard text-book of the Theosophists (2 vols., New York, 1877); *Secret Doctrine: The Synthesis of Science, Religion, and Philosophy* (2 vols., 1888); *Voice of the Silence* (1889); *Key to Theosophy, in the Form of Question and Answer* (1889); and the posthumous *From the Caves and Jungles of Hindostan* (1892; originally contributed to the Russian *Russky Vyestnik*); *Nightmare Tales* (London, 1892) *Theosophical Glossary* (1892); and *Modern Panarion Collection of Fugitive Fragments* (1899).

Bibliography: E. Coulomb, *Some Account of my Intercourse with Madame Blavatsky from 1872 to 1884*, London, 1885; A. P. Sinnett, *Incidents in the Life of Madame Blavatsky*, ib. 1886; C. Wachtmeister, *Reminiscences of H. P. Blavatsky and "the Secret Doctrine,"* ib. 1893; A. Lillie, *Madame Blavatsky and her "Theosophy": A Study*, ib. 1895; V. S. Solovyoff, *Modern Priestess of Isis*, from the Russian, by W. Leaf, ib. 1895 (an *exposé*); H. Freimark, *Helena Petrovna Blavatsky*, Leipsic, 1907.

BLAYNEY, BENJAMIN: Church of England Hebrew scholar; b. 1728; d. at Poulshot (22 m. n.w. of Salisbury), Wiltshire, Sept. 20, 1801. He studied at Worcester and Hertford Colleges, Oxford (B.A., 1750; M.A., 1753; B.D., 1768; D.D., 1787); was appointed regius professor of Hebrew in 1787 and was made canon of Christ Church. He revised the text of the Authorized Version of the Bible to secure typographical accuracy and added to the marginal references; the edition appeared in 1769 and is the standard for the Oxford press. He also published *A Dissertation by Way of Inquiry into the True Import and Application of the Vision Called Daniel's Prophecy of Seventy Weeks* (Oxford, 1775); two sermons, on *The Sign Given to Ahaz* (1786) and *Christ the Greater Glory of the Temple* (1788); translations of Jeremiah and Lamentations (1784) and Zechariah (1797); and an edition of the Samaritan Pentateuch (1790).

BLEDSOE, ALBERT TAYLOR: American Southern Methodist; b. at Frankfort, Ky., Nov. 9, 1809; d. at Alexandria, Va., Dec. 8, 1877. He was graduated at West Point, 1830, became lieutenant of infantry, and resigned 1832; he became assistant professor of mathematics at Kenyon College, Gambier, O., 1834; entered the ministry of the Protestant Episcopal Church, was rector at Hamilton, O., and professor of mathematics at Miami University, Oxford, O., 1835–36; practised law in Springfield, Ill., and in the United States Supreme Court at Washington, 1840–48; was professor of mathematics in the University of Mississippi, 1848–54, and in the University of Virginia, 1854–1861; he entered the Confederate service as a colonel, but was soon made assistant secretary of war; lived in England 1863–66; after 1867 published *The Southern Review* at Baltimore, which under his management became one of the leading periodicals of the Methodist Church, South. He was ordained a Methodist minister in 1871, but never took charge of a church. He was a strenuous advocate of the doctrine of free will and a stern opponent of atheism and skepticism; the doctrine of predestination he considered a reflection upon the divine glory, and a cause of unbelief; his views are set forth in his *Examination of Edwards on the Will* (Philadelphia, 1845) and his *Theodicy, or Vindication of the Divine Glory* (New York, 1853). He also published *Liberty and Slavery* (Philadelphia, 1857); *The Philosophy of Mathematics* (1868); *Is Davis a Traitor? or was secession a constitutional right previous to the war of 1861?* (Baltimore, 1866).

BLEEK, FRIEDRICH: Protestant theologian and exegete; b. at Ahrensbök, Holstein, July 4, 1793; d. at Bonn Feb. 27. 1859. He studied theology and philology at Kiel and Berlin, 1812–17, and began to lecture as repetent in theology in the latter place in 1818. His lectures on the Old and the New Testaments attracted attention, and in 1821 he was made extraordinary professor; he succeeded Lücke as professor at Bonn, 1829, receiving the same year his doctorate from Breslau. For thirty years Bleek lectured at the university in Bonn. He was extremely painstaking in the preparation of his lectures, which were so carefully written that after his death they could easily be used for publication, and continue in much larger circles the influence they had already exerted. His works printed during his lifetime include: *Ueber die Entstehung und Zusammensetzung der Sibyllinischen Orakel, Ueber Verfasser und Zweck des Buches Daniel,* and *Beitrag zur Kritik und Deutung der Offenbarung Johannis,* three valuable essays published in the theological review edited by Schleiermacher, De Wette, and Lücke (Berlin, 1819–22); *Versuch einer vollständigen Einleitung in den Brief an die Hebräer* (Berlin, 1828), followed in 1836 and 1840 by a translation of Hebrews and commentary on the book; *Beiträge zur Evangelienkritik* (Berlin, 1846). Of his posthumous works mention may be made of *Einleitung in das Alte Testament* (edited by his son J. F Bleek and A. Kamphausen, Berlin, 1860; 3d ed., by Kamphausen, 1870; 4th, 5th, and 6th ed., by J. Wellhausen, 1878, 1886, 1893; Eng. transl. by G. H. Venables, 2 vols., London, 1869; on the last three editions cf. H. L. Strack, *Einleitung in das Alte Testament,* Munich, 1895, 11); *Einleitung in das Neue Testament* (1st and 2d editions by his son, J. F Bleek, 1862, 1866; 3d and 4th editions by W Mangold, Berlin, 1875, 1886; Eng. transl. by W Urwick, London, 1870); *Synoptische Erklärung der drei ersten Evangelien* (ed. H. Holtzmann, 2 vols., Leipsic, 1862); *Vorlesungen über die Apokalypse* (ed. T. Hossbach, Berlin, 1862; Engl. transl., London, 1871); *Vorlesungen über die Briefe an die Kolosser, den Philemon und die Epheser* (ed. F Nitzsch, Berlin, 1865); *Vorlesungen über den Hebraerbrief* (ed. A. Windrath, Elberfeld, 1868). Bleek's writings are especially distinguished for thoroughness in investigation and clearness of expression. His standpoint in criticism was conservative.

A. Kamphausen.

BLEMMYDES, NIKEPHOROS: Greek monk; b. at Constantinople about 1197; d. (near Ephesus?) 1272. He founded a monastery near Ephesus, and became its archimandrite. His many writings were philosophical treatises, discourses on the procession of the Holy Spirit, on the Trinity, on Christology, on the duties of the king, and an exposition of the Psalms. [He is principally noted for his defense of the Roman doctrine of the procession of the Spirit from Father and Son before the emperor John III Vatatzes at Nicæa.] Blemmydes was honest and incorruptible, but harsh in character. Out of devotion to the ascetic life, he declined the patriarchate.

Philipp Meyer.

Bibliography: The works of Blemmydes are in *MPG,* cxlii, and also in A. Heisenberg's *N. Blemmydæ, curriculum vitæ et carmina,* Leipsic, 1896, which contains the newly discovered autobiography. Consult Krumbacher, *Geschichte,* pp. 445 sqq., et passim.

BLESSEDNESS.

Biblical Basis (§ 1).	In Communion with God (§ 3).
Foundation in Ethics (§ 2).	Degrees of Blessedness (§ 4).

The term "blessedness" is the usual rendering in the English Bible for the idea of the Hebrew *asher* and Greek *makarios*. The German *Seligkeit* represents besides the content of those words also the idea of the Greek *sōzein,* "to save." The Latin equivalent of *makarios* is *beatus*, which has, however, passed in usage to designate the state of Christians who have fallen asleep (cf. Rev. xiv. 13); while *beatitudo* in scholastic usage designates the aim and the highest good of the Christian. The union of two Biblical conceptions in one expression gives to the latter its unique Christian content, as is realized when the two ideas are traced to their junction. Illuminative of this point is Paul's use (Rom. iv, 7–8) of Ps. xxxii, 1-2. The Old Testament passage bases "blessedness" on forgiveness of sin, and goes to the root of human felicity or its opposite. The Reformed theology traced the idea of blessedness to the salvation implied in that forgiveness, and the fact is evinced in Luther's use of *Seligkeit* to express the state consequent upon forgiveness. Thus the union of the ideas of blessedness and salvation is manifest.

1. Biblical Basis.

The term suggests also the idea of a condition of abiding satisfaction fully realized in consciousness. This is attributed to God in I Tim. vi, 15–16 (cf. i, 11), with which dogmatics agrees on the ground of his absoluteness and completeness. In this respect, to man may be attributed only a relative blessedness. By reason of his constitution man may pursue and attain a sort of arbitrary satisfaction; and in consequence of his being a creature he can attain full satisfaction only in a way in accord with his inner nature. A purpose which for him reaches beyond the present life involves a blessedness not to be reached here, where only a conditioned form is for him attainable. This is the point of view of the Biblical presentation. Man holds, on the one hand, relations with God, and on this depends his blessedness; he is also, as a member of the race of Adam, a sinner and so under the impress of evil, and his blessedness is contingent upon salvation from this condition.

On the foregoing basis is built Christian usage, in which "eternal life," "eternal blessedness," and "blessed eternity" are variant expressions for the same concept. Life in its fulness is the idea. The Bible and philosophy agree in the ethical as the source of blessedness (Jas. i, 25; Acts xx. 35), but the former annexes also a religious relationship (Jas. i, 27). If the most significant limitation in life, that which distinguishes man from God, viz., guilt, be removed, on this line of thought blessedness may be attributed to man. Out of this comes the emphasis constantly laid in the language of the Gospels upon the identity of salvation and blessedness, the latter resting upon freedom from guilt and from the proscription ari-

2. Foundation in Ethics.

sing from sin. Thus blessedness and life, in this way reaching its fulness, are regarded as equivalents.

A special dogmatic terminology has developed from this usage, as when Schleiermacher (*Christliche Glaube*, Berlin, 1821, §§ 100, 101, 108, 110) describes the activity of Christ in that he receives believers up into his own God-consciousness and into participation in his serene blessedness, into the "peace" of the New Testament. Similarly J. C. K. von Hofmann (*Theologische Ethik*, Nördlingen, 1878, p. 89) asserts that "faith as obedience is freedom, faith as certainty is blessedness." So the term designates the religious side of the Christian's condition as distinct from the ethical. The eudemonistic side is expressed by J. Kaftan (*Wesen der christlichen Religion*, Bielefeld, 1881, pp. 67, 292) in the form "blessedness is enjoyment of the highest good." Into Christian usage there has come a transcendent element, implying the satisfaction of all needs which present themselves to the people of God. If among these needs is classed complete communion with God in the completely realized kingdom of God, or intercommunion of mankind made one in God, the satisfaction of this need goes on to God as the source, and to communion with him as the means of attaining such satisfaction. Hence in Biblical representations intimate communion with him is the highest privilege of which man may think in his Godward relations. Companionship with God appears therefore as an implicit ground of blessedness, and the Old Testament conception comes out in the manifestation of theophanies and in the intimate intercourse had by Moses with God (Ex. xxxiii, 11; Num. xii, 8; Deut. xxxiv, 10). The idea is still further carried out in later books, as in Ps. xvii, 15, cxl, 14 ("I shall be satisfied"), and is expressed by Job as a desire (xix, 26). The opposite effect is the result of separation from God (Isa. xxxviii, 11). Ps. lxxxiv exuberantly sets forth the blessedness arising from this companionship with God. In the New Testament the same notion of the consciousness of God's presence and of faith in him is in evidence (John xiv, 9; II Cor. iv, 6; I Pet. i, 8). Yet in this life knowledge of God and communion with him is but partial (I Cor. xiii, 12, cf. II Cor. v, 7; Matt. xi, 27). It is the sons who see the father, and so the sons of the Heavenly Father are called blessed (Matt. v, 9). This intimacy, which is conditioned upon ethical oneness with God, is the source throughout the development of the man of God from which he draws the completion of his happiness.

3. In Communion with God.

A difficulty has been encountered in the question whether there are steps or grades of blessedness or glory. To this an affirmative answer is given on the basis of such passages as Matt. x, 41, xiv, 28–29, xxv, 14–15. Such a conclusion is fortified by the consideration that blessedness includes within itself a kingdom whose subjects are men of God, and that such a conception involves diversity in which differences must exist in relation to blessedness. Such differences imply variety in order of felicity to accord with personal gifts and individuality.

4. Degrees of Blessedness.

The figurative language of Heb. iv, 10 makes mention of a final Sabbath rest. The question has been raised whether by this is meant a state of inactivity or of continued activity. It will be noted that the passage refers to the rest following upon creation; therefore, not the stagnation of absence of life is represented, but the quietude of the achievement of an end. And in the Christian imagery of Rev. xxi, 3–4, what is implied is the absence of evil, grief, and toil with the unrest which they entail. Similarly the conception of the restoration of all things (*apokatastasis pantōn*), in which there is stated an eternity of punishment as well as of satisfaction or peace, raises the question whether the latter will not be marred because of pity on account of the misery of the condemned. Relief is afforded by the consideration that the region is one in which ethical measures apply, not those of emotion. Dante has the blessed look into the mirror of God's heart, which last is the source from which the ethical world draws its being and order. In ancient times Tertullian (*De spectaculis*, xxx), in modern times Jonathan Edwards held that among the causes of the blessedness of the redeemed will be the sight of the misery of the wicked. Edwards declared that the "sight of hell torments will exalt the happiness of the saints forever" (*Works*, vol. vi, pp. 120, 426).

Bibliography: H. L. Martensen, *Dogmatik*, §§ 283 284, Berlin, 1856, Eng. transl., Edinburgh, 1865; E. Riehm, *Lehrbegriff des Hebräerbriefs*, Basel, 1867; B. Weiss, *Theologie des N. T.*, §§ 144, 149, 157, Berlin, 1880, Eng. transl., Edinburgh, 1882–83; I. A. Dorner, *System der christlichen Glaubenslehre*, ii, 864, Berlin, 1887; H. Schultz, *Alttestamentliche Theologie*, pp. 370–371, Göttingen, 1896, Eng. transl., London, 1892.

BLESSIG, JOHANN LORENZ: German Protestant; b. at Strasburg Apr. 15, 1747; d. there Feb. 17, 1816. He studied at the university of his native city; traveled extensively in Italy, Hungary, and Germany; began to preach, and was continually promoted till he was in charge of the principal Protestant church of Strasburg; became professor in the philosophical faculty in 1778, and in the theological, 1787. He was three times rector; his lectures covered Greek literature, history of philosophy, Old Testament exegesis, dogmatics, and homiletics, and in them all he made the practical dominate. His activities carried him into the field of politics also, and he was elected to the city council. The French Revolution brought upon him exile, a fine, and imprisonment for eleven months. Robespierre's downfall restored his liberty and he returned to his labors. Church and school were reorganized, Blessig's influence being felt everywhere. He left no great work, but not less than forty minor writings, including several memorial addresses, which were highly esteemed in their time. Worthy of special mention are: *Ueber Unglauben, Aberglauben und Glauben* (Strasburg, 1786); *De censu Davidico pesteque hunc censum secuta* (1788); and *De evangeliis secundum Ebræos, Ægyptios atque Justini Martyris* (1807). (A. Erichson†.)

Bibliography: C. M. Fritz, *Leben Dr. J. L. Blessigs*, 2 vols., Strasburg, 1819; A. Froelich, *Dr. J. L. Blessig. Ein Vorkämpfer des religiösen Liberalismus im Elsass*, in *Schriften des protestantischen liberalen Vereins in Elsass-Lothringen*, no. 36, ib. 1891.

BLESSING AND CURSING.

Ethnic Conceptions (§ 1). In the Old Testament (§ 2). Higher and Lower View (§ 3).

The conception of blessing and cursing has a large part in every religion. It refers to the supernatural or divine promotion or hindrance to human action and welfare. Sometimes it is predicated of man himself as possessing through his connection with deity the ability to exercise over another the power originally possessed only by deity (cf. Gen. xii, 3; Num. vi, 24, 27). In this latter case, the power is often exercised by means of verbal expression, though it is not confined to that means. It is apparent that in the religion of the peoples who were neighbors of the Hebrews as well as elsewhere the conception of blessing and cursing belonged in the sphere of magic. Wizards commanded the blessing and furthering force of deity, which they could exercise at a given point for good and still more often the power resident in a host of evil spirits, to damage or to cause damage at the desired place and time. While often power to bless comes not from an equipment gained for a special occasion and then lost, continuance of power and conditions for evil are especially frequent. The curse lurks in the background of earthly existence, enshrined in the form of harmful and malicious demons, into whose power a careless word or heedless step may instantly cast the unfortunate. According to ethnic belief, only the most painstaking care, the most punctilious caution, observance of a host of rules and practises can enable one to escape danger. Frequently without any overt act, by merely mentioning these spirits or by entering their domain without adequate protection, the spirits are summoned and their power let loose on man, animal, and possessions.

1. Ethnic Conceptions.

Within the Old Testament there are many traces of the contact of Israel with such conceptions. The prophetic religion was especially emphatic in its opposition to witchcraft, necromancy, and the like, and, especially in the Babylonian age, was not successful in combating them. Earlier examples are found in Saul's resort to the witch of Endor and the cases suggested by Deut. xviii, 10–14, and Isa. ii, 6. It is, then, not surprising that the conceptions of blessing and cursing are found together among the Hebrews, though they come to have a more spiritual content. It is noticeable that the tendency of the development was toward a narrowing of the region in which the idea was operative, and it was thrust more and more into the background.

2. In the Old Testament.

In examining the cases presented in the Old Testament, it becomes evident that use was made both of the word of power and of an instrument. The staff was used frequently, its use being attributed to Moses and Aaron and to the Egyptian magicians (Ex. iv, 2, vii, 8 sqq.), while in Hos. iv, 12, it seems to have been used to obtain oracles, and possibly it was a magical staff which Balaam carried (Num. xxii, 27). It is possible that the origin of the staff is to be connected with the idea of the tree as the seat of deity (cf. the Asherah and the stake customary at the grave). A branch from a tree was either the seat of deity or the symbol of his power. A farther means of operating, especially for evil, was the glance of the eye (cf. the common notion of the "evil eye"). Cases of this in the Old Testament are suggested by Prov. xxiii, 6, xxviii, 22 (cf. Ecclus. xiv, 3; *Pirke Abot* v, 13). The laying on of hands seems to have had close connection with the operation of blessing (Gen. xxvii, xlviii, 14 sqq.), the idea being that in this way the person bestowing the blessing caused to pass to the recipient some of the power which was his, especially if he were a man of God.

Blessing and cursing were often connected with things holy, particularly with sacrifice. By means of these a blessing or a curse were often bespoken. So in Judges ix, 27 the cursing of Abimelech was evidently closely bound up with the feast in the temple of the deity. The episode of Balaam also makes evident the connection between sacrifice and curse (or blessing, Num. xxiii, 1 sqq.), and the same fact has been noted among Arabs of ancient and modern times. A special case is that of the ordeal by water, narrated in Num. v, 11 sqq. Blessing and curse operate also through the spoken word, which may take either the phase of a magical formula or of a prayer of which the content is spiritually pure. The latter is of very frequent occurrence in the Old Testament, where the blessing, or equally the curse, is besought of God.

This practise of seeking blessing or curse had continuing vogue in the common religious ideas of Israel, remaining in evidence down to prophetic times. As elsewhere, so among the Hebrews, superstition and the practise of magic never completely died out, and not only deity but the spirits of the dead (I Sam. xxviii) and of ancestors were invoked to give effect to the invocation or the imprecation. The deity is in mind in Samuel's blessing of the meal (I Sam. ix, 13), in Eli's blessing of Hannah (I Sam. i, 17), in the blessing of Rebecca by her brothers (Gen. xxiv, 60), and in Solomon's blessing (I Kings viii, 15 sqq.). There is every reason to assume that on occasions of gatherings such as sacrifices and feasts the priests besought a blessing for the people. While such invocations did not always take a fixed form, there must have been a tendency in that direction, as is proved by the priestly blessing in Num. vi, 24–26. And there is a suggestion of a fixed formula for the curse in I Kings viii and in the alternate words of blessing and cursing in Deut. xxviii.

If it be asked who are the persons who may bless or curse, it is always found that they are those in especially close relation to deity, either seer or priest or man of God. Of these Moses, Balaam, Joshua (Josh. vi, 26), Elisha (II Kings ii, 24–25) are examples. And like persons are among the Arabs conceived as possessing the power. Special power in this matter is also ascribed to the dying, who are already on the border between the human and the divine. Thus Moses when dying blesses his people (Deut. xxxiii), and the dying patriarchs Isaac and Jacob distribute both blessing and its opposite when on the eve of dissolution (Gen xxvii, 10 sqq., xlviii, 8 sqq., xlix, 2 sqq.). Under special stress the power to bless or curse, especially the latter, is attributed to almost any one, as when the Arabs assert that one influenced by anger may effectively pronounce a curse. Such a case is presented in II Sam. xvi, 5 (cf. verse 10), and another in the narrative of II Sam. xxi, 1 sqq. Prov. xxvii, 14 presents a peculiar case, in which the early and loud call may be thought of as arousing the spirits of malice and letting them loose on the object of the call. A similar conception is involved in Amos vi, 10. The name of Yahweh, who lingers near occupied in the work of the plague, is not to be spoken lest by the mere utterance he be summoned to the spot and slay the only surviving member of the household.

3. Higher and Lower View.

Investigation into the way in which blessing and cursing operate in the Old Testament shows a lower and a higher view. Not infrequently the mere vocal expression of the wish works out the fulfilment in a kind of blind compulsion such as takes place in ethnic magic (cf. Gen. xxvii, 33 sqq.—the blessing has been uttered over Jacob and can not be recalled—and Num. xxii sqq., especially xxii, 6, "I know that he whom thou blessest is blessed, and he whom thou cursest is cursed," the words of Balak to Balaam). An illuminating case is given in the connection of Josh. vi, 26 with I Kings xvi, 34, in which the ancient curse pronounced upon him who should rebuild Jericho works itself out in the death of the youngest and the eldest sons of Hiel the Bethelite. And a similar instance is Saul's breach of the treaty with the Gibeonites in which the curse operates after his death until reparation is made with blood (II Sam. xxi). David's charge to Solomon (I Kings ii, 5 sqq.; cf. II Sam. xvi, 13) furnishes other examples. Solomon is to take vengeance on Shimei and on Joab. The former had pronounced a heavy curse on David. Since it was yet operative but had not fallen on David himself, it must work itself out on his house. But it can be so diverted as to fall on the head of its formulator and become changed into a blessing for David's family. On the other hand, Joab's deeds of blood laid David, Joab's lord, under a curse which could be relieved only by expiation exacted from the perpetrator of the deeds [cf. on this *EB*, i, 1034, note 1].

While this inevitability is to be recognized in the Old Testament as inherent by the mere formulation of blessing and cursing or curse, the act takes on more and more the character of the expression of a wish to be fulfilled by Yahweh, and so it becomes distinguished in form and character from magic and witchcraft. And while the method of operation is thus transferred, the character of the blessing sought changes from the material to the spiritual. Thus in the priestly blessing of Num. vi, 24–26 there is doubtless in mind the highest good of God's grace and peace, and in this light is to be construed verse 27. A similar content is to be recognized in Gen. xii, 3 and parallel passages: "In thee shall all families of the earth bless themselves," i.e., shall wish for themselves the very blessing which Abraham had obtained.

As oracles were quoted among the heathen, so sayings attributed to Yahweh or spoken in his name were cited among the Hebrews, and blessings and curses appear almost in profusion in the Old Testament, derived from prophetic or ancestral authority. These take on often a cryptic character and anticipate the more extended apocalyptic writings of later times (cf. the sayings ascribed to Moses and to Jacob in Gen. xlix and Deut. xxxiii).

The uncertainty of the original significance of the practise is disclosed by an examination of the etymology of the words used. The technical Hebrew term for cursing is *arar*, the meaning of which was evidently to press heavily upon one. Alongside this was used for the curse a word derived from *alah*, connected with the word *el*, "God." This last implies a calling upon deity or a reference to him as agent, a meaning which recalls the idea in the German *segnen*, "to (make the) sign (of the cross over one)." But another root also used, *ḳalal*, had no inherent reference to the deity, meaning simply "to vilify." So the original sense of the word *ḳababh*, meaning "to curse," is uncertain. Not less obscure is the original meaning of the word for blessing, *berakhah*. It has been referred to *berekh*, "knee," suggesting the meaning "to bow the knee." But that the idea of worship was originally connected with the word or that it meant "to pray" does not appear probable. It is possible to relate it to *berēkhah*, meaning an accumulation of the growth and fruitfulness attributed to water and then the attainment of prosperity.

A noteworthy expression is that which appears quite frequently (e.g., Gen. ix, 26), "Blessed be Yahweh." Is this only a manner of speech equivalent to "Yahweh be praised"? While this may be the sense in later ages, it was hardly so in early times. It has doubtless come down as a survival of the conception that even deity might be blessed by the utterance of some highly endowed individual.

(R. Kittel.)

Bibliography: P. Scholz, *Götzendienst und Zauberwesen bei den Hebräern*, Regensburg, 1877; C. F. Keil, *Biblical Archæology*, ii, 457, Edinburgh, 1888; R. Smend, *Alttestamentliche Religionsgeschichte*, § 334, Freiburg, 1893; *DB*, i, 307, 534–535; *EB*, i, 591–592; *JE*, iii, 242–247. For ethnic parallels consult: E. B. Tylor, *Primitive Culture*, pp. 112–132, New York, 1877; I. Goldziher, *Muhammidanische Studien*, 2 vols., Halle, 1889–90; Wellhausen, *Heidentum;* F. T. Elworthy, *The Evil Eye*, London, 1895; F. B. Jevons, *Introduction to Hist. of Religion*, chaps. iii–iv, ib. 1896; G. B. Frazer, *Golden Bough*, i, 97, ib. 1900; S. I. Curtiss, *Primitive Semitic Religion*, New York, 1902.

BLISS, DANIEL: Congregational missionary; b. at Georgia, Vt., Aug. 17, 1823. He was graduated at Amherst College in 1852 and Andover Theological Seminary in 1855. He was ordained to the Congregational ministry in 1855, and immediately went to Syria as a missionary of the American Board of Commissioners for Foreign Missions, remaining there in this capacity until 1862. Four years later he was appointed president of the Syrian Protestant College, Beirut, and retained this position until 1902, when he resigned and became president emeritus. He is the author of a number of works in Arabic, particularly a text-book of mental philosophy and another of natural philosophy.

BLISS, EDWIN MUNSELL: Congregationalist; b. at Erzerum, Turkey, Sept. 12, 1848. He was educated at Robert College, Constantinople, High School, Springfield, Mass., Amherst College (B.A., 1871), and Yale Divinity School (B.D., 1877). He was assistant agent of the American Bible Society for the Levant in 1872–88 (excepting 1875–77, when he was completing his theological studies in America), and after his return to America in 1888 edited *The Encyclopedia of Missions* (New York, 1889–91) and was associate editor of *The Independent* in 1891–1901. He was an editorial writer on *Harper's Weekly* and *The New York Times* in 1901–02. and was field secretary of the American Tract Society for New England in 1903–04. He was then pastor of the Congregational church at Sanford, Fla., in 1904–05, and general secretary of the Foreign Missions Industrial Association in 1905–06. In 1907 he became connected with the United States Census Bureau in Washington. In theology he is liberal-orthodox. He has written *Turkey and the Armenian Atrocities* (Philadelphia, 1896); *The Turk in Armenia, Crete, and Greece* (1896); and *Concise History of Missions* (Chicago, 1897).

BLISS, FREDERICK JONES: American archeologist; b. at Mount Lebanon, Syria, Jan. 22, 1859. He was educated at Amherst College (B.A., 1880), and was for three years principal of the preparatory department of the Syrian Protestant College, Beirut, Syria. He then studied at Union Theological Seminary, where he was graduated in 1887. Returning to Syria, he was an independent explorer until his appointment, in 1890, as explorer to the Palestine Exploration Fund (London). During the ten years in which he held this position, he excavated the mound of Tell-el-Hesy (Lachish) in 1891–93, and from 1894 to 1897 was engaged in excavations at Jerusalem. In 1898–1900 he excavated four Palestinian cities. In addition to numerous briefer contributions, he has written *A Mound of Many Cities; or Tell-el-Hesy Excavated* (London, 1894); *Excavations at Jerusalem, 1894–1897* (1898); *Excavations in Palestine during 1898–1900* (1902; in collaboration with R. A. S. Macalister); and *The Development of Palestine Exploration*, the Ely lectures at Union Seminary for 1903 (New York, 1906).

BLISS, HOWARD SWEETSER: Congregational missionary; b. at Mount Lebanon, Syria, Dec. 6, 1860. He was educated at Amherst College (B.A., 1882), Union Theological Seminary (1884–1887), and the universities of Oxford (1887–88), Göttingen, and Berlin (1888–89). He taught at Washburn College, Topeka, Kan., in 1883–84, and after his return from Europe to the United States was successively assistant pastor of Plymouth Church, Brooklyn, N. Y. (1889–94), and pastor of the Christian Union Congregational Church, Upper Montclair, N. J. (1894–1902). Since 1902 he has been president of the Syrian Protestant College, Beirut, Syria.

BLISS, ISAAC GROUT: Congregational foreign missionary; b. at Springfield, Mass., July 5, 1822; d. at Assiut, Egypt, Feb. 16, 1889. Educated at Amherst College (B.A., 1844) and at Yale and Andover (1847) theological seminaries, he served as missionary of the American Board at Erzerum, Eastern Turkey, 1847–52, when the failure of his health compelled his return to the United States. In 1857 he returned to the foreign field as agent for the Levant of the American Bible Society, with residence in Constantinople.

BLISS, WILLIAM DWIGHT PORTER: American Protestant Episcopalian; b. at Constantinople Aug. 20, 1856. He was educated at Robert College, Constantinople, Phillips Academy, Andover, Mass., Amherst College (B.A., 1878), and Hartford Theological Seminary (1882). He was ordained to the Congregational ministry, but after holding pastorates in Denver, Col., and South Natick, Mass., he entered the Protestant Episcopal Church in 1885, and was ordered deacon in 1886 and ordained priest in the following year. He was minister at Lee, Mass., in 1885–87, and was then successively rector of Grace Church, South Boston (1887–90), Linden, Mass. (1890), Church of the Carpenter, Boston, Mass. (1890–94), Church of Our Savior, San Gabriel, Cal. (1898–1902), and Amityville, L. I. (since 1902). He has taken an active interest in social reform, and in 1889 organized the first Christian Socialist Society in the United States, and has since been its secretary, while he has been president of the National Social Reform League since 1899, and was the Labor candidate for lieutenant-governor of Massachusetts in 1887 He has also been secretary of the Christian Social Union since 1891, and in 1905 was a member of the United States Labor Department on the Unemployed. In theology he is a radical Broad-churchman. He edited *The Dawn* (1889–96), *The American Fabian* (1895–96), *The Civic Councillor* (1900), and the *Encyclopedia of Social Reform* (New York, 1898; 1908); and has written *Hand-Book of Socialism* (London, 1895).

BLODGET, HENRY: Congregational foreign missionary; b. at Bucksport, Me., July 13, 1825; d. at Bridgeport, Conn., May 23, 1903. Educated at Yale College (B.A., 1848) and at Yale Divinity School, he was a missionary in China of the American Board from 1854 to 1894, living in Peking from 1864 on. He shared in the translation of the New Testament into the Mandarin colloquial of Peking, and independently translated much in prose and verse.

BLOMFIELD, CHARLES JAMES: Bishop of London; b. at Bury St. Edmunds, Suffolk, May 29, 1786; d. at Fulham Palace Aug. 5, 1857 He was educated at Trinity College, Cambridge (B.A., 1808); was ordained 1810; became chaplain to Bishop Howley of London 1819; archdeacon of Colchester 1822; bishop of Chester 1824; bishop of London 1828. He retired from office in 1856 after a vigorous and effective administration. He was a noted Greek scholar, edited a Greek grammar (Cambridge, 1818), and a number of Greek texts (the dramas of Æschylus, 1810–24; Callimachus, 1815; Euripides, 1821; fragments of Sappho, Alcæus, and Stesichorus for Gaisford's *Poetæ minores Græci*, 1823), and wrote much for the reviews on classical subjects. His theological works comprise *Five Lectures on John's Gospel* (1823); *Twelve Lectures on the Acts* (1828); several collections of sermons; and *A Manual of Private and Family Prayers* (1824).

Bibliography: A. Blomfield, *A Memoir of C. J. Blomfield, with Selections from his Correspondence*, 2 vols., London, 1863 (by his son); G. E. Biber, *Bishop Blomfield and his Times*, London, 1857; *DNB*, v, 229–230. The *British Museum Catalogue* devotes five pages to a list of Blomfield's works.

BLOMFIELD, WILLIAM ERNEST: English Baptist; b. at Rayleigh (24 m. s.w. of Colchester), Essex, Oct. 23, 1862. He was educated at Regent's Park College, London (B.A., University of London, 1883), and after being assistant (1884–85) and sole minister (1885–86) of Elm Road Baptist Church, Beckenham, was pastor of Turret Green Church, Ipswich, 1886–95 and of Queen's Road Church, Coventry, 1895–1904. Since 1904 he has been president of the Baptist College, Rawdon, Leeds.

BLOMMAERDINE, blem″mār-dī'ne, **HADEWICH** or **HADEWIJCH:** A heretical mystic whose religious activity and writings caused great excitement in Brussels early in the 14th century. Her adherents venerated her as a saint and her writings as divine revelations; her opponents charged her with heretical teaching on the freedom of the spirit, and with mingling religious devotion and sensual passion. During his stay in Brussels (1317–43), Ruysbroeck conducted a strong polemical campaign against her, which, however, did not prevent people from coming after her death to seek the cure of diseases by touching her shroud. The scanty notices which Ruysbroeck's biographer gives of her life and writings have been recently filled out by the scholarly investigations of K. Ruelens and P Fredericq. They have shown it to be extremely probable that the mystic was identical with the important Flemish poetess Hadewijch (erroneously called "Sister Hadewijch"), whose remains in prose and verse, known only in part heretofore, have been published in full by J. Vercoullie (Ghent, 1877). The principal theme of all these writings is love (*Minne*) for God. The specimens given by Fredericq display the tempestuous, sometimes actually sensual, passion with which she longs for mystical union with him. In describing her numerous visions the poetess boasts of very intimate relations with Christ and the saints, and claims the gift of prophecy and the power of working miracles. She expresses herself bitterly in regard to the persecutions set on foot by her enemies, the *vremden*, against herself and her adherents, whom she calls *vriende*, the *nuwen* or *volmaakten der Minne* (*perfecti*). In one place she gives the number of her then living followers (principally nuns or Beguines) as ninety-seven, of whom twenty-nine were outside the Netherlands. Apparently the *domicella Heilwigis dicta Blommardine*, the daughter of William Blommaert, a rich and noble citizen of Brussels, who died about 1336, is the same as the mystic and the poetess. It appears that as late as the beginning of the fifteenth century the Inquisition in Brussels was still obliged to proceed against adherents of the heresies promulgated by her, which were not far removed from the views of the Brethren of the Free Spirit (q.v.). (Herman Haupt.)

Bibliography: Henricus Pomerius, *De origine monasterii Viridisvallis*, in *Analecta Bollandiana*, iv, 286, Paris, 1886; H. C. Lea, *History of the Inquisition*, ii, 377, Philadelphia, 1888; P. Fredericq, *Corpus documentorum inquisitionis . . . Neerlandicæ*, I, 185 sqq., 266 sqq., The Hague, 1889; idem, *De geheimzinnige ketterin Blæmardinne en de secte der "Nuwe" te Brussel*, in *Verslagen en Mededeelingen der koninkl. Akademie van Wetenschappen te Amsterdam*, series 3, xii (1895), 77 sqq.; W. A. Jonckbløet, *Geschiedenis der Nederlandsche letterkunde*, ii, 270 sqq., 1889; A. Auger, *Étude sur les mystiques des Pays-Bas au moyen âge*, in *Mémoires couronnés . . . par l'académie royale de Belgique*, xlvi (1892), 149 sqq., 164.

BLONDEL, DAVID: French Protestant theologian; b. at Châlons-sur-Marne 1590; d. at Amsterdam 1655. He belonged to a noble family of Champagne; studied classics at the College of Sédan and theology at the Academy of Geneva; was called as pastor to Houdan (Île de France), then to Roucy on the estate of La Rochefoucauld. Because of his great knowledge of the Scriptures and of ecclesiastical history, he was chosen more than twenty times secretary of the provincial synod of Île de France. His writings in defense of the Protestants against their Roman Catholic opponents won for him a great reputation for scholarship. In 1631 he was appointed professor of divinity at Saumur, but his parish of Roucy declined to give him up. For his contributions to the history of the Reformation, the National Council of Charenton allowed him an annuity of 1,000 livres, enabling him to devote himself to his studies without fear of want. After the death of Vossius in 1650, he was appointed professor of history at the *École Illustre* at Amsterdam. Pierre Bayle said of him: "He was a man who had an unbounded knowledge of religious and profane history" He was accused by the orthodox party of Arminianism and of indifference to his church; he also endured much from political opponents on account of an article against Cromwell written during the war between Great Britain and Holland. His works were in part: *Modeste déclaration de la sincérité et vérité des Églises réformées de France* (Sédan, 1619); *Pseudo-Isidorus et Turrianus vapulantes* (Geneva, 1628); *Eclaircissements familiers de la controverse de l'Eucharistie* (Quevilly, 1641); *De la primauté en l'Église* (Geneva, 1641); *Des Sibylles, célébrées tant par l'antiquité payenne que par les Saints-Pères* (Charenton, 1649); *Actes authentiques des Églises réformées de France, Germanie, Grande-Bretagne* (Amsterdam, 1655).

G. Bonet-Maury.

BLOOD-BROTHERHOOD. See Comparative Religion, VI, 1, b, § 6.

BLOOD-REVENGE: A custom nearly universal in the tribal or clan stage of society, often surviving later, binding the kin of a murdered man to secure satisfaction for the murder by the death of the slayer or of one of his clan. The custom depends upon two fundamentals of that stage of civilization: (1) the sacredness of life and the solidarity of the clan; (2) the *lex talionis*. Its essence is execution of the slayer or some of his kin by the representatives of the slain, not by public authorities; it belongs therefore to private as opposed to public justice. In nomadic society the perpetuation of the clan depends upon its fighting strength and its sense of unity. Hence assault upon a member of the clan, if attended with even unintended fatal results, involves the tribe, clan, or family of the slain in what is felt to be a sacred duty, the avenging of the shedding of blood. The custom is important from the standpoint of utilitarian ethics, since the knowledge that reparation will be demanded by the clan of the assailed restrains a potential assailant from wanton attack and makes men more careful in ordinary intercourse. The duty set by the institution is binding, and so close is the relationship in the clan (see COMPARATIVE RELIGION, VI, 1, b, § 1) that all its members may become involved, the result being a blood-feud between the clans of the assailant and the victim. Usually, however, the duty devolves upon the next of kin. Refusal on his part to exercise his right and perform his duty subjects him to utter contempt and even to outlawry.

In the advance of civilization the State assumes exclusively the function of Capital Punishment (q.v.) and the custom becomes obsolete. The Hebrew legislation furnishes an example of an intermediate condition, by which the right of the family of a man deliberately (not wantonly) murdered to execute justice was recognized and the murderer, when captured, was delivered by the authorities to the avenger of blood (*go'el haddam*, Lev. xix, 11–13; Num. xxxv, 19, 21, 27; for the general law of murder among the Hebrews consult Gen. ix, 6; Ex. xxi, 12; Lev. xxiv, 17; Josh. xx). Even in the case of accidental killing, the avenger of blood might kill the slayer if before the death of the high priest he found him outside the city of refuge in which he had taken sanctuary. See LAW, HEBREW, CIVIL AND CRIMINAL, III.

GEO. W. GILMORE.

BIBLIOGRAPHY: A. H. Post, *Studien zur Entwicklungsgeschichte des Familienrechts*, pp. 113-137, Oldenburg, 1889; Smith, *Kinship* (invaluable for the Semitic peoples, cf. also his *Rel. of Sem.*); and for modern savage practise, Spencer and F. J. Gillen, *Native Tribes of Central Australia*, London, 1899; idem, *Northern Tribes of Central Australia*, ib. 1904; *DB.* ii, 222–224; *EB.* ii, 1746–47.

BLOUNT, CHARLES. See DEISM, I, § 3.

BLUMHARDT, CHRISTIAN GOTTLIEB: German Protestant; b. in Stuttgart Apr. 29, 1779; d. in Basel Dec. 19, 1838. He studied at Tübingen; in 1803 became secretary of the *Deutsche Christentumsgesellschaft* in Basel; minister at Bürg, Württemberg, 1807; returned in 1816 to Basel as director of the missionary school. From 1816 he edited the *Missionsmagazin*, and from 1828 also the *Heidenbote;* he published *Versuch einer allgemeinen Missionsgeschichte der Kirche Christi* (5 vols., Basel, 1828–37), reaching down to the time of the Reformation.

BLUMHARDT, JOHANN CHRISTOPH: German Lutheran; b. at Stuttgart July 16, 1805; d. at Boll (5 miles s.w. of Göppingen) Feb. 25, 1880. He studied at Tübingen; became teacher at the missionary institution at Basel 1830; succeeded Pastor Barth at Möttlingen, near Calw, 1838. By the reported cure by prayer of a girl named Gottliebin Dittus, supposed to be a demoniac, which cure was effected after a two years' struggle, Blumhardt gained great fame. A revival followed, attended by so many people from so large an area that on Good Friday, 1845, no less than 176 localities were represented at the service. At his services, so it is reported, healing of physical infirmities resulted from Blumhardt's laying on of hands in token of absolution. Blumhardt received calls to other places, but felt that his gifts and time belonged to the "distressed"; in order to be able to devote himself entirely to them, he bought in 1853 the royal watering-place Boll, which became an asylum for sufferers of all kinds, and from all ranks of society. The girl he had cured went with him as an assistant, accompanied by a brother and a sister whom Blumhardt had also cured. In 1869 and 1872 his sons joined him in the work. From all countries the afflicted flocked to his asylum, where his unique treatment seemed to give them new vital energy. At last sickness attacked him, and he ordained his son to the work with the words, "I consecrate thee to victory." In 1899 this son withdrew from the clergy, but continued to maintain the establishment at Boll. (J. HESSE.)

BIBLIOGRAPHY: F. Zündel, *Pfarrer J. C. Blumhardt*, Zurich, 1887; T. H. Mandel, *Der Sieg von Möttlingen im Licht des Glaubens und der Wissenschaft*, Leipsic, 1895; C. Blumhardt, *Gedanken aus dem Reiche Gottes im Anschluss an die Geschichte von Möttlingen und Bad Boll und unsere heutige Stellung*, Bad Boll, 1895.

BLUNT, JOHN HENRY: Church of England scholar; b. in Chelsea, London, Aug. 25, 1823; d. in London Apr. 11, 1884. He gave up a business career for the ministry, studied at University College, Durham (M.A., 1855), and was ordained priest in 1855; after filling a number of curacies, he became in 1868 vicar of Kennington, near Oxford, and in 1873 rector of Beverston, Gloucestershire. He was a pronounced High-churchman, and an indefatigable writer both of articles for the periodicals and of books; among his works are a number of useful theological and Biblical compends, such as *The Annotated Book of Common Prayer* (2 vols., London, 1866; new ed., 1895); *Dictionary of Doctrinal and Historical Theology* (1870); *The Book of Church Law* (1872; 9th ed., revised by W. G. F. Phillimore and G. E. Jones, 1901); *Dictionary of Sects, Heresies, Ecclesiastical Parties, and Schools of Religious Thought* (1874); *The Annotated Bible: being a household commentary upon the Holy Scriptures, comprehending the results of modern discovery and criticism* (3 vols., 1879–82); *A Companion to the New Testament* (1881); *A Companion to the Old Testament* (1883); also an important history of *The Reformation of the Church of England* (2 vols., 1869–82). At the time of his death he was working upon a *Cyclopædia of Religion* (1884).

BLUNT, JOHN JAMES: English theologian; b. at Newcastle-under-Lyme (15 m. n.n.w. of Stafford), Staffordshire, 1794; d. at Cambridge June 18, 1855. He studied at St. John's College, Cambridge (B.A., and fellow, 1816; M.A., 1819;

B.D., 1826); traveled in Italy and Sicily; became curate to Reginald Heber at Hodnet, Shropshire, in 1821; rector of Great Oakley, Essex, 1834; Lady Margaret professor of divinity at Cambridge 1839. He wrote many books and contributed much to the periodical press; some of his works have passed through many editions. They include *A Sketch of the Reformation in England* (London, 1832); *Undesigned Coincidences in the Writings both of the Old Testament and New Testament an Argument for their Veracity* (1847); *A History of the Christian Church during the First Three Centuries* (1856); *The Duties of the Parish Priest* (1856); *Two Introductory Lectures on the Study of the Early Fathers* (with memoir, Cambridge, 1856).

BLYTH, GEORGE FRANCIS POPHAM: Anglican bishop in Jerusalem and the East; b. at Beverley (9 m. n.n.w. of Hull), Yorkshire, in 1832. He was educated at Lincoln College, Oxford (B.A., 1854), and was ordered deacon in 1855, and ordained priest in the following year. He was successively curate of Westport St. Mary's, Wiltshire (1855–61), and Sigglesthorne, Yorkshire (1861–63), and chaplain to the earl of Kimberley (1863–66). He then went to India, was chaplain of the ecclesiastical establishment at Allahabad (1866–67), and was attached to the cathedral of Calcutta and chaplain to the bishop of Calcutta (1867–68). He was then stationed successively at Barrackpur, Bengal (1868–74), Naini-Tal, North-West Provinces (1874–77), and Fort William, Bengal (1877–1878), after which he was archdeacon of the pro-cathedral at Rangoon from 1879 to 1887. In the latter year he was consecrated bishop in Jerusalem and the East. He has written *The Holy Week and Forty Days* (2 vols., London, 1879).

BOARDMAN, GEORGE DANA: **1.** Baptist foreign missionary; b. at Livermore, Me., Feb. 8, 1801; d. at Tavoy, Burma, Feb. 11, 1831. In 1824 he was a resident licentiate in Andover Theological Seminary. In 1825 he went out to Burma under the Baptist Board of Missions, which had accepted his services in 1823, but owing to the Burmese war he could not reach that country till 1827. After a year at Maulmain he opened the new station at Tavoy, 150 miles north, and there he immersed the first Karen convert—Ko Tha Byu. From this center he prosecuted a very successful missionary work, but pulmonary disease caused his death after less than three years.

BIBLIOGRAPHY: A. King, *Good Fight, or G. D. Boardman and the Burman Mission*, Boston, 1875.

2. American Baptist, son of the preceding; b. at Tavoy, Burma, Aug. 18, 1828; d. at Atlantic City, N. J., Apr. 28, 1903. He was graduated at Brown in 1852 and at the Newton Theological Institution 1855; was pastor in South Carolina 1855–1856; in Rochester, N. Y., 1856–64; of the First Baptist Church, Philadelphia, 1864–94. He was president of the American Baptist Missionary Union (1880–84), and of the Christian Arbitration and Peace Society of America. His publications were for the most part studies of Biblical texts of an exegetical character and include *Studies in the Creative Week* (New York, 1877), *in the Model Prayer* (1879), and *in the Mountain Instruction* (1881); *Epiphanies of the Risen Lord* (1879); *The Divine Man from the Nativity to the Temptation* (1887); *University Lectures on the Ten Commandments* (1889); *The Kingdom* (1899); *The Church* (1901); *Our Risen King's Forty Days* (Philadelphia, 1902).

BIBLIOGRAPHY: *Life and Light. Thoughts from the Writings of George Dana Boardman, with Memorabilia*, Philadelphia, 1905.

BOARDMAN, GEORGE NYE: American Congregationalist; b. at Pittsford, Vt., Dec. 23, 1825. He was graduated at Middlebury College, Vt. (B.A., 1847), and Andover Theological Seminary (1852). He was tutor at Middlebury College, in 1847–49, and after the completion of his theological studies was appointed professor of rhetoric and English literature in Middlebury College, also acting as temporary professor of intellectual philosophy. Six years later (1859), he accepted a call to the pastorate of the First Presbyterian Church at Binghamton, N. Y., where he remained until 1871, when he was chosen professor of systematic theology in Chicago Theological Seminary. He resigned from this position in 1893, with the title of professor emeritus. He was the first moderator of the new synod after the reunion of the Old School and New School Presbyterian Churches, being also chairman of the committee for the formation of new presbyteries. He was also moderator of the Congregational General Association of Illinois in 1881, and has been a corporate member of the American Board of Commissioners for Foreign Missions since 1869. He prepared the section on systematic theology in the seven volumes of *Current Discussion*, issued by the faculty of the Chicago Theological Seminary (Chicago, 1883–89), and has also written *Lectures on Natural Theology* (1881); *Congregationalism* (1889); *Regeneration* (1891); and *History of New England Theology* (New York, 1899).

BOCHART, bō″shār′, SAMUEL: French Protestant; b. at Rouen 1599; d. at Caen 1667. His father was the learned René Bochart, pastor at Rouen, and his mother Esther du Moulin. At the age of fourteen he made Greek verses in honor of his masters. He studied philosophy at Sédan, theology at Saumur under Cameron, whom he accompanied to London in 1621. He did not stay long, but soon returned to Leyden, where he took up theology and the study of the Arabic language under Erpenius. He was appointed Protestant minister at Caen, but gave private lessons in a Roman Catholic family. His controversy with the Jesuit Véron, in 1628, gave him a great name, and he edited an account of it (2 vols., Saumur, 1630) to refute Véron's teachings. In 1652 Queen Christina of Sweden wished his presence and he followed her call, accompanied by his pupil Huet, later bishop of Avranches. He remained in Stockholm one year, studying Arabic texts in the queen's library. Returning to Caen, he became the representative of Normandy at the National Calvinist Synod of Loudun. He died suddenly during a session of the academy at Caen. His works include *Theses theologicæ de verbo Dei* (Saumur, 1620); *Actes de* *la conférence tenue à Caen entre Samuel Bochart et Jean Baillehache, ministres de la parole de Dieu en l'Église réformée et François Véron* (2 vols., 1630); *Réponse à la lettre du père de la Barre, Jésuite, sur la présence réelle* (1661); *Hierozoicon sive historia animalium S. Scripturæ* (London, 1663); *Opera omnia, hoc est, Phaleg, Canaan, et Hierozoicon, quibus accessere variæ dissertationes* (Leyden, 1675). G. Bonet-Maury.

Bibliography: P. D. Huet, *Les Origines de la ville de Caen*, Rouen, 1706; Nicéron, *Mémoires*; W. R. Whittingham, *The Life and Writings of S. Bochart*, in *Essays on Biblical Literature*, London, 1829; Smith, *Samuel Bochart*, Caen, 1833; E. and É. Haag, *La France protestante*, ed. H. L. Bordier, vol. ii, Paris, 1879; *KL*, ii, 950–952.

BOCKHOLD, JOHANN (JAN BEUKELSZOON). See Muenster, Anabaptists in.

BOD, bed, **PETER:** Hungarian theologian and ecclesiastical historian; b. at Felső-Csernáton (a village of Transylvania) Feb. 12, 1712; d. at Magyar-Igen (40 m. s.w. of Klausenburg) Mar. 3, 1769. He was educated at the Reformed college of Nagy-Enyed and the University of Leyden, and in 1743 became pastor at Héviz, whence he was called, six years later, to Magyar-Igen. He was the author of fifty-six works, of which twenty-three were printed, but by a decree of Maria Theresa restricting the liberty of the press certain of his books of a patriotic and Protestant tendency were confiscated. Among his works in Hungarian special mention may be made of the following, the titles being translated into English: "*History of the Holy Bible*" (Hermannstadt, 1748); "*History of the Church of God*" (Basel, 1760); "*History of the Reformed Bishops of Transylvania*" (Enyed, 1766); "*The Magyar Athens*" (Hermannstadt, 1767); biographies of 485 Hungarian authors, and "*The Hungarian Phenix*" (Enyed, 1767); biography of the printer Kiss; while his Latin works include: *Historia Unitariorum in Transylvania* (Leyden, 1776), a vivid description of the struggles of the Socinians in Hungary; *Historia Hungarorum ecclesiastica* (ed. Rauwenhoff and Prins, 3 vols., 1888–1890, from a manuscript recently discovered in the library of the university); and two treatises on the promoters and defenders of the Hungarian Reformation (in Gerdes, *Scrinium Antiquarium*, ii, Groningen, 1763). F. Balogh.

Bibliography: G. D. Teutsch, *Korrespondenzblatt des Vereins für siebenb. Landeskunde*, no. xi, 1888, nos. v, vi, 1891; *Presbyterian and Reformed Review*, vols. i–ii, 1891–92.

BODELSCHWINGH, bō'del-shving, **FRIEDRICH VON:** German Lutheran; b. near Tecklenburg (20 m. n.n.e. of Münster), Westphalia, Mar. 6, 1831, son of Ernst von Bodelschwingh-Velmede, a distinguished Prussian statesman. After gaining practical experience of mining and agriculture, he studied theology (from 1854) in Basel, Erlangen, and Berlin, and in 1858 became pastor of the German congregation in Paris, at Dellwig in Westphalia 1864. During the wars of 1866 and 1870–1871 he served as army chaplain. Since 1872 he has devoted himself to the work of the *Innere Mission* (q.v.) at Bielefeld, and the following institutions have been founded by his exertions: the Bethel house for epileptics with 1,800 inmates; the Sarepta deaconesses' house with 980 sisters located in 326 stations, of which eleven are in foreign countries; the Nazareth house for training male nurses with 350 deacons in 120 stations, six not in Europe and six more outside Germany; the "workingmen's colony" Wilhelmsdorf (a practical attempt to deal with the tramp problem), the first of its kind in Germany, having at present five branches and 400 inmates; a "workingmen's home" with 164 houses and 400 dwellings; a missionary seminary for candidates in theology.

Bibliography: M. Siebold, *Kurze Geschichte und Beschreibung der Anstalten Bethel bei Bielefeld*, Bethel publishing house, 1898, and the annual reports.

BODENSTEIN, ANDREAS RUDOLF VON. See Carlstadt.

BODY, CHARLES WILLIAM EDMUND: Protestant Episcopalian; b. at Clapham (a suburb of London) Oct. 4, 1851. He was educated at St. John's College, Cambridge (B.A., 1875), where he was fellow from 1877 to 1881. In the latter year he was chosen provost and vice-chancellor of Trinity University, Toronto, where he remained until 1894, when he was appointed professor of Old Testament literature and interpretation in the General Theological Seminary, New York City. He has written *The Permanent Value of Genesis* (the Paddock Lectures for 1894; New York, 1894).

BODY, GEORGE: Church of England; b. at Cheriton Fitzpaine (9 m. n.w. of Exeter), Devonshire, Jan. 7, 1840. He was educated at St. John's College, Cambridge (B.A., 1862), and was curate of St. James's, Wednesbury, Staffordshire (1863–65), Sedgley, Staffordshire (1865–67), and Christ Church, Wolverhampton (1867–70). From 1870 to 1884 he was rector of Kirby-Misperton, Yorkshire; and since 1883 he has been canon of Durham. He was proctor in convocation of York for Cleveland in 1880–85 and was select preacher to the University of Cambridge in 1892, 1894, 1896, 1900, and 1904, as well as lecturer on pastoral theology in the same university in 1897. He was warden of the Community of the Epiphany, diocese of Truro, in 1891, and is also chaplain to the bishop of St. Andrews and vice-president of the Society for the Propagation of the Gospel. He has written: *Life of Justification* (London, 1884); *Life of Temptation* (1884); *The Appearances of the Risen Lord* (1890); *The School of Calvary* (1891); *Activities of the Ascended Lord* (1891); *The Life of Love* (1893); *The Guided Life* (1894); and *The Work of Grace in Paradise* (1896).

BOECKENHOFF, bök'en-hof, **WILHELM BERNARD ALOYSIUS KARL:** German Roman Catholic; b. at Schermbeck (37 m. s.w. of Münster) July 10, 1870. He was educated at Münster (1890–93), the Gregorian University, Rome (1897–1900; Doctor Juris Canonici, 1899), and the University of Berlin (1900–01; D.D., Münster, 1901). He was ordained to the priesthood in 1894 and was a *vicar* in Dolberg from that year until 1897, when he resumed his studies. He became a privatdocent at Münster in 1902, but three years later went in a similar capacity to Strasburg, where he was appointed associate professor of canon law in the following month. In addition to contributions to theological periodicals, he has written *De individuitate matrimonii* (Berlin, 1901) and *Das apostolische Speisegesetz in den ersten fünf Jahrhunderten* (Paderborn, 1903).

BOEGNER, bōg'ner, **ALFRED ÉDOUARD:** French Protestant; b. at Strasburg Aug. 2, 1851. He was educated at the university of his native city and at the theological faculty at Montauban, after which he studied at the German universities of Leipsic, Erlangen, and Tübingen in 1873–74. From 1876 to 1879 he was pastor of the Protestant church at Fresnoy-le-Grand, and in the latter year became subdirector of the Paris Society of Evangelical Missions, of which he has been director since 1882. In this capacity he made tours of inspection of South Africa in 1883, Senegal and the West Coast in 1890–91, and Madagascar, the Transvaal, Orange Free State, and Cape Colony in 1898–99. He is also director of the Paris House of Evangelical Missions, and in addition to editing the *Journal des missions évangéliques de Paris* since 1879 and publishing or editing a number of minor contributions, has written *Patterson, le missionnaire de la Mélanésie* (Paris, 1881); *Le Missionnaire de Methlakatla* (1882); *Les Bassoutos, autrefois et aujourd'hui* (1885); *Quelques réflexions sur l'autorité en matière de foi* (1892); and *Rapport sur la délégation à Madagascar* (in collaboration with P. Germond; 1900).

BOEHL, bōl, **EDUARD:** German theologian; b. at Hamburg Nov. 18, 1836; d. at Vienna Jan. 24, 1903. He was educated at Berlin (1855), Halle (1856–58), and Erlangen (1858–60), and became licentiate and privat-docent at Basel in 1860, whence he was called to Vienna four years later as professor of Reformed dogmatics and symbolics, and also of pedagogics, philosophy of religion, and apologetics, in the Protestant faculty of theology. In 1864 he also became a permanent member of the Synod of the Reformed Church of Austria, and was in 1883 president of its fourth General Synod. He edited the *Evangelische Sonntagsboten für Oesterreich*, and published *De Aramaismis libri Koheleth* (Erlangen, 1860); *Vaticinium Jesajæ c. 24–27 commentario illustratum* (Leipsic, 1861); *Zwölf messianische Psalmen erklärt; nebst einer grundlegenden christologischen Einleitung* (Basel, 1862); *Confessio Helvetica posterior* (Vienna, 1866); *Allgemeine Pädagogik* (1870); *Forschungen nach einer Volksbibel zur Zeit Jesu und deren Zusammenhang mit der Septuaginta-Uebersetzung* (1873); *Die alttestamentlichen Citate im Neuen Testament* (1878); *Christologie des Alten Testaments, oder Auslegung der wichtigsten messianischen Weissagungen* (1882); *Zum Gesetz und zum Zeugniss; eine Abwehr wider die neukritischen Schriftforschungen im Alten Testament* (1883); *Von der Incarnation des göttlichen Wortes* (1884); *Christliche Glaubenslehre* (Amsterdam, 1886); *Dogmatik; Darstellung der christlichen Glaubenslehre auf reformirtkirchlicher Grundlage* (1887); *Zur Abwehr: etliche Bemerkungen gegen Prof. Dr. A. Kuyper's Einleitung zu seiner Schrift "Die Incarnation des Wortes"* (1888); *Von der Rechtfertigung durch den Glauben* (Leipsic, 1890); *Beiträge zur Geschichte der Reformation in Oesterreich* (Jena, 1902).

BOEHM, HANS: A popular preacher of the fifteenth century, known as the Drummer of Niklashausen; executed July 19, 1476. He was originally a shepherd at Helmstadt, between Würzburg and Wertheim. Up to the beginning of 1476, he had been used to play the drum and fife for rustic dances, but what he heard of the preaching of the Franciscan Capistrano (see CAPISTRANO, GIOVANNI DI) worked a great change in him. He alleged that the Virgin Mary had appeared to him and called him to be a prophet and preacher of repentance. In the village of Niklashausen near his home there was a picture of her already reputed miraculous and visited by pilgrims. Here, at the end of March, he began to preach, having burnt his drum in token of conversion. Lacking not only secular education but even elementary religious knowledge, he yet made a deep impression on his hearers by the innocence and purity of his nature. He did not stop with calling the peasants to repentance, but showed increasing bitterness against the clergy and nobles, who, he said, would find no place in the kingdom announced to him by the Virgin; taxes were to be abolished, no one was to have more than another, and all men were to live as brothers. His fame soon spread throughout central and southern Germany, and crowds of pilgrims, put as high as 40,000, thronged to hear him. He seems to have intended to lead them in an armed rising; but Bishop Rudolf of Würzburg had him arrested on July 12, and warded off the danger of a great peasants' war. Two days later, 16,000 of his followers appeared to rescue him, but were dispersed; and on the 19th, a recantation having been extorted from him, he perished on the scaffold as a heretic and enchanter.

(HERMAN HAUPT.)

BIBLIOGRAPHY: C. A. Barack, *Hans Böhm und die Wallfahrt nach Niklashausen im Jahre 1476*, Würzburg, 1858; C. Ullmann, *Reformers before the Reformation*, i, 377–392, Edinburgh, 1877 (a very detailed account); E. Gothein, *Politische und religiöse Volksbewegungen vor der Reformation*, pp. 10 sqq., Breslau, 1878; H. Haupt, *Die religiösen Sekten in Franken vor der Reformation*, pp. 57 sqq., Würzburg, 1882.

BOEHME, bō'me, JAKOB.

The famous German mystic Jakob Böhme (often written Behmen or Boehme in English), born at Alt-Seidenberg, near Görlitz, Nov., 1575; d. at Görlitz Nov. 17, 1624. His parents were peasants, from whom he inherited, it seems, a strain of visionary mysticism. Unable to bear the rough outdoor life of the farm, he was put to shoemaking in the little town of Seidenberg, where he had a hard apprenticeship with a family that had no Christian principles, and got an early insight into the controversies of the age. With diligent reading of the Bible and prayer for

1. Early Tendency Toward Mysticism.

the illumination of the Holy Spirit he combined eager study of the works of fanatical visionaries, such as Paracelsus, Weigel, and Schwenckfeld, by means of which he felt himself elevated above the strife of tongues around him into the light and joy of the contemplation of God. He settled, as master of his trade, at Görlitz in 1599. He had his shop there until 1613, and must have prospered to a certain extent, since he bought a house in 1610 and had fully paid for it in 1618. He married a master butcher's daughter in 1599, and had four sons and two daughters, passing as a model husband and father among his neighbors. All these things go to show that he had a practical hold on life, and was far from being a mere crazy visionary.

A visionary, however, he remained. He tells the story of a stranger coming into his shop and calling him by name, taking him aside to tell him he should be so great that the world should wonder at him, and warning him to remain true to the Word of God and to a life of virtue. Other visions followed.

2. Mystic Visions. One day the reflection of the sun from a bright metal vessel in his shop seemed to infuse such spiritual light into his soul that the inner mysteries of things were laid open to his sight. He went out into the fields to seek the revelation of God's will in earnest prayer, and found his peace and joy only grow the deeper. None the less, ten years passed before he ventured to put down in writing what he had seen, and then he did so only on the encouragement of a new vision and as a memorandum for himself. The incomplete manuscript, written in great haste, which he called *Aurora oder die Morgenröte im Aufgang*, began to circulate among his acquaintances at the instance of Karl von Ender, a friendly nobleman who was an adherent of Schwenckfeld's. In this way it came under the notice of Gregorius Richter, the pastor of Görlitz, who at once began a fanatical war upon the presumptuous shoemaker, and urged the local magistrate to suppress him, lest the wrath of God should fall upon the town.

3. Opposition to his First Book. Böhme was minutely examined before the council, and only dismissed on promising to write no more books. The observance of this promise, however, was not only made difficult by the insistence of his friends, but by his own inner feeling that the fear of men had driven him to deny the grace of God that was in him. The bitter abuse of Richter, too, still continued, and after five years of silence, during which he had learned a good deal and developed more, Böhme could bear it no longer, and, encouraged by a fresh vision, again took up his pen. His new writings were at first circulated only in manuscript copies. Richter, who thought himself the appointed guardian of orthodoxy, thundered against him from the pulpit and attacked him in a vulgar lampoon, which Böhme answered in a tone naturally excited, but still showing a nobler spirit than the absurdly haughty and unchristian contempt of the attack. Far from having broken with the word of God and the sacraments, he was trying to live as an upright Christian, in strict self-discipline; and although among his twenty-eight works there are some which directly attack the visible Church as Babel, the city of confusion, and set forth Christ in us as the mystical ideal, his general attitude by no means justifies the scornful "Shoemaker, stick to thy last" of his opponent. In 1624 he was obliged to leave Görlitz, and went to Dresden, where he found shelter in the house of the director of the Elector's chemical laboratory and enjoyed the society of many of the most intellectual people of the court and the capital.

4. Finds Sympathy in Dresden. In May he had a hearing before several distinguished clerics and professors, who fully recognized his mental endowments, and encouraged him to go home, especially as his family, deprived of its head, had been exposed to no little suffering in the confusion of the Thirty Years' War. He returned to Görlitz, but his end was near. When he asked for communion upon his death-bed, the successor of Richter, a man like-minded, would only give it to him after a searching examination, of which the report is still extant. Full of confidence, however, and with heavenly voices ringing in his ears,

5. Death of Böhme. Böhme took leave of his wife and children and died with the joyful cry "I go to Paradise!" In spite of clerical opposition, a befitting funeral was provided by the town authorities; a cross was put up over the grave by his friends, to be defiled and thrown down by the populace.

Thus despised and rejected in his own day, Böhme has been honored by some of the greatest minds of Germany in a later age; such men as Friedrich von Hardenberg, Jung-Stilling, Friedrich Schlegel and Ludwig Tieck, Hegel and Schelling received valuable intellectual impulses from his works, which also attracted much attention in England, where a complete translation appeared between 1644 and 1662. Besides those already named, the most important are *Von den drei Principien göttlichen Wesens; Vom dreifachen Leben des Menschen; Vierzig Fragen von der Seele; Von wahrer Busse; Das Gespräch einer unerleuchteten Seele;* and *Der Weg zu Christo;* including two against predestinarianism and two

6. His Writings. against pantheism. Böhme's influence has never been a popular one, because his train of thought is frequently difficult and sometimes almost impossible to follow. This is due partly to his lack of education, which prevented him from expressing himself clearly, but partly also to the depth and intensity of his thought, which has to struggle for adequate representation in words. With sincere longing, with real hunger of the soul he plunges into the depths of God's being. The traditional theology of the schools, with its strife about the letter, could not content him. "As the many kinds of flowers grow in the earth near each other, and none

7. His Transcendentalism. contends with the other about color, smell, or taste, but they let the earth and the sun, rain and wind, heat and cold, do what they will with them, while they grow each according to its own nature, so is it with the children of God." And he was simply a child of God, that longed to grow and approach more closely to God. In this effort he studied the Bible and clung to it, but nature and life, to say nothing of the writings of earlier enthusiasts, contributed their part. He held fast to the fundamental doctrines of his Church, the Trinity, the Incarnation, the Atonement. "That which is said of God, that he is Father, Son, and Holy Ghost, is truly said; but it must be explained, or the unenlightened can not comprehend it." "Thou must not think the Son is another God from the Father, or that he is outside the Father, as when two men stand side by side. The Father is the source of all forces, and all forces are in each other as one force; and thus he is called one God. The Son is the Father's heart, the heart or center of all the powers of the Father. From the Son rises the eternal heavenly joy, having its source in all the powers of the Father, a joy that no eye has seen, and no ear heard." Christ, the Father's heart, descended into the midst of the conflagration which had broken out in the world, extinguished it by his death, and by his resurrection, the resurrection of the God-Man, raised man to participation in the Godhead. The Scripture is the receptacle of the truth; he holds to it, and its sense alone (cf. Col. i, 15–20) teaches a cosmic, universal conception of Christianity; baptism and the Lord's supper are means of grace to him. He remains, in spite of all obscurities, a man of inspiration who raised Protestant mysticism to a great height, and not only endowed it with the riches of his own meditations but, through his "theosophic Pentecostal school, in which the soul is taught by God," has shown many others the way to a deep and abiding happiness.

8. His Essential Orthodoxy.

(F. W. Dibelius.)

Bibliography: The works of Böhme were collected in Germany by J. G. Gichtel, 1682, and an edition in 7 vols. was edited by Schiebler, Leipsic, 1831–47. The Eng. ed. is mentioned in the text. Early accounts in Eng. of his life were by D. Hotham, London, 1654, and by F. Okeley, Northampton, 1780; in Germ. by J. A. Calo, Wittenberg, 1707. For later accounts consult: J. Classen, *J. Böhme. Sein Leben und seine theosophischen Werke*, 3 vols., Stuttgart, 1885; H. L. Martensen, *J. Böhme*, Copenhagen, 1882, Eng. transl., London, 1885; R. A. Vaughan, *Hours with the Mystics*, vol. ii, ib. 1888; Schönwälder, *Lebensbeschreibung J. Böhmes*, Görlitz, 1895. More nearly concerned with his philosophy are: J. Hamberger, *Die Lehre des deutschen Philosophen J. Böhme*, Munich, 1844; C. F. Baur, *Zur Geschichte der protestantischen Mystik*, in *Theologische Jahrbücher*, vii–viii, 1848–49; A. Peip, *J. Böhme, der Vorläufer christlicher Wissenschaft*, Leipsic, 1860; idem, *J. Böhme ... in seiner Stellung zur Kirche*, Hamburg, 1862; J. Tulloch, *Rational Theology and Christian Philosophy in the Seventeenth Century*, Edinburgh, 1874; F. von Baader, *Vorlesungen über J. Böhme*, in *Sämmtliche Werke*, vol. xiii, Leipsic, 1855; F. Hartmann, *Life and Doctrines of Böhme, the God-taught Philosopher*, London, 1893; J. F. Hurst, *History of Rationalism*, chap. i, New York, 1902. McClintock and Strong, *Cyclopædia*, ii, 842, gives in Eng. complete list of his works.

BOEHMER, bō'mer, **EDUARD**: German theologian and Romance scholar; b. at Stettin May 24, 1827; d. at Lichtental Feb. 5, 1906. He was educated at the universities of Halle and Berlin, and in 1854 became privat-docent for theology in Halle. He later turned his attention to Romance, and in 1866 was appointed associate professor in that subject in Halle, and full professor two years later. In 1872 he went to Strasburg in the same capacity, but retired, as professor emeritus, in 1879. Died at Lichtental (a suburb of Baden) Mar. 1, 1906. His theological writings are *Ueber Verfasser und Abfassungzeit der johanneischen Apokalypse* (Halle, 1855); *Das erste Buch des Thora* (1862); *Franzisca Hernandez und Fraі Franzico Ortiz* (Leipsic, 1866); *Bibliotheca Wiffeniana: Spanish Reformers of two Centuries from 1520* (2 vols., Strasburg, 1874–83); and *Des Apostels Paulus Brief an die Römer* (Bonn, 1886).

BOEHMER, JUSTUS HENNING: A jurist who made important contributions to the study of Roman and still more of canon law; b. at Hanover Jan. 29, 1674; d. at Halle Aug. 23 or 29, 1749, as chancellor of the duchy of Magdeburg and head of the faculty of law at Halle. He rendered a great service to the continuity of Protestant church law in that he was the first to show the adaptability of the older canonical principles to post-Reformation conditions. This was made possible by his profound knowledge of church history and his extensive theoretical and practical acquaintance with both the common and the statute law. In the question of the relation of Church and State he declared for the territorial system. Out of the large number of his writings may be mentioned the *Duodecim dissertationes juris ecclesiastici ad Plinium Secundum et Tertullianum* (2d ed., Halle, 1729); *Entwurf des Kirchenstaats derer ersten drey Jahrhundert* (1733); *Institutiones juris canonici* (5th ed., 1770); *Jus ecclesiasticum Protestantium* (6 vols., 1714); and an edition of the *Corpus juris canonici* (2 vols., 1747), valuable for its notes, index, and appendices. He also made some contributions to church hymnody. He was the founder of a family of jurists, two of whom deserve mention for their contributions to the study of canon law. These are his son, **Georg Ludwig**, b. 1715; d. 1797, as head of the law faculty at Göttingen; author of *Principia juris canonici* (Göttingen, 1762), which was used in the revision of the Prussian laws; and Georg Ludwig's son, **Georg Wilhelm** (1761–1839), who published *Grundriss des protestantischen Kirchenrechts* (Göttingen, 1786) and other cognate works.

(E. Friedberg.)

Bibliography: Nicéron, *Mémoires*; C. G. Haubold, *Institutiones juris Romani literariæ*, p. 153, Leipsic, 1819; *ADB*, iii, 79 sqq., 1876; J. F. Schulte, *Geschichte der Quellen und Litteratur des canonischen Rechts*, vol. iii, part 2, pp. 92 sqq., Stuttgart, 1880; W. Schrader, *Geschichte der Friedrichs-Universität zu Halle*, i, 146 sqq., Berlin, 1894.

BOEHRINGER, bō-ring'er, **GEORG FRIEDRICH**: Swiss Protestant (Tübingen school); b. at Maulbronn, Württemberg, Dec. 28, 1812; d. at Basel, blind and crippled, Sept. 16, 1879. He studied at Tübingen, took part in the insurrectionary movements in 1833, and was in consequence compelled to flee to Switzerland; became pastor at Glattfelden, Canton Zurich, 1842; resigned, 1853; removed to Zurich, and then to Basel. He wrote, from the sources and in a scholarly manner, a series of biographies which constituted a church history down to pre-Reformation times, under the general title *Die Kirche Christi und ihre Zeugen* (24 vols., Zurich, 1842–58; 2d ed., 1860–79).

BOËTHIUS, bō-ī'thi-us, **ANICIUS MANLIUS SEVERINUS:** Statesman and philosopher; b. at Rome, of wealthy and influential family, c. 480; executed at Pavia 525. He received as good an education as the time could give, and acquired a close acquaintance with Greek philosophy. In 510 he was consul, and for several years occupied a prominent position in the Roman world, equally revered by the people and esteemed by the Ostrogothic king, Theodoric, the ruler of Italy (489–526). After the decree of the Emperor Justin I (518–527) against the Arians, Theodoric became suspicious of all Romans and Catholics; he imprisoned Boëthius at Pavia on a charge of desiring to restore the old Roman freedom, and finally put him to death. By his translations and commentaries (including the entire six books of the *Organon* of Aristotle and the *Isagoge* of Porphyry) and by his independent works (*Introductio ad categoricos syllogismos, De syllogismo categorico, De syllogismo hypothetico, De divisione, De definitione, De musica, De arithmetica*, etc.), Boëthius became the connecting link between the logical and metaphysical science of antiquity and the scientific attempts of the Middle Ages. His influence on medieval thought was still greater through his *De consolatione philosophiæ* (written while in prison at Pavia) and the theological writings attributed to him. Whether Boëthius was a Christian has been doubted; and it is certain that the *Consolatio* makes no mention of Christ, and all the comfort it contains it owes to the optimism of the Neoplatonic school and to the stoicism of Seneca. Nevertheless, for a long time the book was read with the greatest reverence by all Christendom, and its author was regarded as a martyr for the true faith. Having advanced from a mere logician to a moralist, he next came to be regarded as a theologian; but it is not probable that he wrote any of the theological works attributed to him. The tradition is very old, however; he is mentioned by Alcuin as the author of *De sancta trinitate*, and by Hincmar of Reims as author of a treatise, *Utrum pater et filius et spiritus sanctus de divinitate substantialiter prædicentur.*

BIBLIOGRAPHY: The complete works of Boëthius first appeared at Venice, 1492; again at Basel, 1546 and 1570; they are reproduced in *MPL*, lxiii–lxiv. The *Consolatio philosophiæ* was first printed at Nuremberg, 1473; a good edition is by Peiper, Leipsic, 1871; there have been many English translations, beginning with King Alfred's Anglo-Saxon version, and including one by Chaucer and one ascribed to Queen Elizabeth; a late translation is by H. R. James, London, 1897. The translations from Aristotle were published by C. Meiser, 2 vols., Leipsic, 1877–80; the *De arithmetica, De musica*, and *De geometrica* by G. Friedlein, ib. 1867. The theological writings appeared at Louvain in 1633 and are in Peiper's edition of the *Consolatio* (ut sup.). Consult: F. Nitzsch, *Das System des Boethius*, Berlin, 1860; Jourdain, *De l'origine des traditions sur le christianisme de Boëce*, Paris, 1861; A. Hildebrand, *Boethius und seine Stellung zum Christenthum*, Regensburg, 1885; H. F. Stewart, *Boethius: an Essay*, Edinburgh, 1891 (valuable; an analysis of the *Consolation* and other theological tracts, discusses the question of Boëthius's Christianity, gives literature at head of each chapter); E. K. Rand, *Joh. Scottus*. I. *Der Kommentar des Johannes Scottus*, II. *Des Remigius von Auxerre zu den opuscula sacra des Boethius*, Munich, 1906.

BOGATZKY, KARL HEINRICH VON: German Pietist; b. at Jankowe (a village of Lower Silesia) Sept. 7, 1690; d. at Halle June 15, 1774. When fourteen years of age, he entered the ducal court of Saxe-Weissenfels as a page, but at the instance of the pious count Henry XXIV of Reuss-Köstritz, he began to complete his education in his twentieth year. From 1713 to 1715 he studied law at Jena and then devoted himself to theology at Halle, where Francke, Anton, Freylinghausen, and other Pietists greatly influenced him. After completing his theological studies in 1718, he lived for several years among the nobility of Silesia, and exercised much influence as a spiritual leader. He also resided for a number of years at the Silesian village of Glaucha, where he aided in building an orphan-asylum, and from 1740 to 1746 he lived at the ducal court of Saalfeld, and finally at Halle, engaged in literary work of a devotional character and in the practical furtherance of Pietistic life. The most popular of his many works was his *Güldenes Schatzkästlein der Kinder Gottes*, which he composed for his own edification while at the university (Breslau, 1718; 65th ed., Halle, 1904; Eng. transl., London, 1745, and many subsequent editions); while among his other books special mention may be made of his *Tägliches Hausbuch der Kinder Gottes* (2 vols., Halle, 1748–49) and of his *Betrachtungen und Gebete über das Neue Testament* (7 parts, 1755–61). Several of his hymns obtained a place in the popular hymnals of the German people, and were collected in his *Uebung der Gottseligkeit in allerlei geistlichen Liedern* (Halle, 1749), while a selection of 160 was published by Johannes Claassen, (Stuttgart, 1888), together with a biography of Bogatzky. (GEORG MÜLLER.)

BIBLIOGRAPHY: Bogatzky's autobiography was published by Knapp, Halle, 1801, Eng. transl. by S. Jackson, London, 1856. Consult: G. Frank, *Geschichte der protestantischen Theologie*, iii, 201–202, Leipsic, 1875; *ADB*, iii, 37–39, Leipsic, 1876; A. F. W. Fischer, *Kirchen-Lieder-Lexikon*, ii, 430–431, Gotha, 1879; Julian, *Hymnology*, p. 152.

BOGERMAN, bō'ger-mān, **JAN:** Dutch theologian; b. at Oplewert, East Friesland, 1576; d. at Franeker Sept. 11, 1637 He was professor of divinity at Franeker after 1633. He took an active part in the Arminian controversy and presided at the Synod of Dort (q.v.). He was one of the workers on the Old Testament of the *Staatenbibel* (see BIBLE VERSIONS, B, III). He wrote a polemic against Grotius, *Annotationes contra H. Grotium*, and translated Beza's *De la punition des hérétiques*, under the title *Van het-ketter straffen* (Franeker, 1601).

BOGOMILES. See NEW MANICHEANS, I.

BOGUE, DAVID: English Congregationalist; b. at Hallydown, near Coldingham (10 m. n.w. of Berwick), Berwickshire, Feb. 18, 1750; d. at Brighton Oct. 25, 1825. He studied at Edinburgh (M.A., 1771), was licensed to preach, and taught school in England; in 1780, while minister of a Congregational chapel at Gosport (opposite Portsmouth), he undertook the instruction of young men for the ministry, and from this beginning was developed the London Missionary Society. He was also active in founding the British and Foreign Bible Society and the Religious Tract Society. In 1796 with two other ministers and Robert Haldane he offered to go to India as a missionary, but the plan was not approved by the East India Company. Besides sermons and tracts he published *An Essay on the Divine Authority of the New Testament* (London, 1801), and with James Bennett wrote the *History of Dissenters from the Revolution to 1808* (4 vols., 1808–12; 2d ed., 2 vols., 1833).

BIBLIOGRAPHY: James Bennett, *Memoirs of the Life of Rev. David Bogue*, London, 1827; *DNB*, v, 302–303.

BOHEMIA. See AUSTRIA.

BOHEMIAN BRETHREN.

I. Origin and History to 1496: The Compactata of Prague, which marked the political end of the Hussite Wars in 1433 (see HUSS, JOHN, HUSSITES), proved unsatisfactory to the religious and ecclesiastical demands of the majority of the Bohemians. Many scattered communities accordingly arose throughout the country, seeking to carry out the Reformation in life and doctrine, independent of the Waldensians who had long been settled in Bohemia. In 1453–54, moreover, the preaching of the Utraquistic archbishop Rokycana (pastor of the *Teinkirche* at Prague after 1448) resulted in the formation of a community at Prague, headed by his nephew Gregory. The conviction that the validity of the sacraments, sermons, prayer, and the like depended on the moral and religious character of the priest caused them to seek for "good" pastors, and this congregation, together with others and at the suggestion of Rokycana, became closely allied with the Chelčic Brethren, the followers of a layman named Peter of Chelčic, who first appeared at Prague in 1419 and seems to have died before 1457. He had refused to join any of the Hussite parties, since he rejected all temporal defense of the Gospel, and recorded his peculiar views in his writings, of which the most important were his *Netz des wahren Glaubens* (1455) and his *Postilla* (1434–36). His ideal of Christian life, the fulfilment of the "law of Christ" (Matt. xxii, 37–39; Gal. vi, 2) in public and in private life without regard to consequences, and his rejection of all that could not be reconciled with this law, such as temporal power, wealth, war, and trade, made a profound impression on Gregory and his followers, and inspired them to attempt to realize this ideal. At their request their friend and counselor Rokycana secured permission from King George Poděbrad for them to settle in the village of Kunwald in the district of Lititz, which belonged to him, and they accordingly established their colony there in 1457 or 1458, Michael, the pastor of the neighboring town of Senftenberg, becoming their spiritual head. How large it was, whether including only individuals or entire families, is not known, although the latter seems to have been the case. At all events, families were soon attracted to Kunwald, for the oldest document of the Brethren, a synodical resolution of 1464, presupposes the existence of households with civil occupations, as well as of widows and orphans.

1. Origin of the Sect.

This sketch of the origin of the Bohemian Brethren renders it clear that the current view which represents them as remnants of the Taborites is incorrect. In 1471 they designated themselves as disciples of Rokycana and his colleagues, and declared that they had been developed from the older communities mentioned above. The main outlines of the organization are contained in certain synodical resolutions of 1464–67. The community was divided into three groups: beginners or penitents, comprising children under the age of twelve and all who sought to enter the community from the time they made profession of their desire until they were received; the advanced, forming the majority of the community and devoting themselves to various civil callings, with masters and matrons appointed to supervise and counsel them; and the perfected (also called priests, although the community then had no specially appointed priesthood), who had renounced private property and given their possessions to the poor, particularly to those who "journey for the sake of the word of God." It was the duty of the perfected to proclaim the word and to hear confessions; they were required to travel in pairs, instead of alone, to earn a livelihood by the work of their hands, and to collect alms regularly, which were destined partly for the poor and partly for themselves, in case their work was insufficient to support them. Those of the laity, either male or female, who had voluntarily chosen poverty, also belonged to this class. At the head of the communities stood one or more elders, although no details of their duties are known, and information is equally scanty regarding the composition of their frequent synods. The Brethren at Kunwald gained an increasing number of adherents in Bohemia and Moravia, while their opposition to the dominant Church became stronger and stronger, especially as a result of the persecution instituted against them by King George in 1460. They accordingly felt themselves obliged, seven years later, to break entirely with the Church by the creation of an independent priesthood, the historical course of events being as follows, according to Goll's proposed combination of the sources, which are not always in entire agreement.

2. Early Organization.

By a meeting with the Waldensians and their "bishop" Stephen, with whom they had become acquainted through Rokycana, the Bohemian Brethren had entered into relations with the Waldensians previous to 1467. These negotiations proved fruitless, however, since the Waldensians as a body would not countenance an open break with the Roman Catholic Church. Some of them, on the other hand, joined the Brethren, and among this number was an old Waldensian priest, who was present, together with certain representatives of the German Waldensians, at a conference of about sixty Brethren from various parts of Bohemia and Moravia which was held, according to a later tradition, at Lhotka, a village near Reichenau, in 1467 to choose and ordain priests of their own. Fully aware of the momentous nature of their proceeding, they wished God himself to decide by lot whether the time had come for them to venture the step, and which persons should be the first priests. Nine candidates were proposed, each of whom was required to draw one of twelve slips, nine blank and three containing the word *jest* ("he is"). In case all the candidates drew blanks, the synod was to be adjourned for a year. Thomas, Matthias, and Elias, however, drew the three written slips, whereupon they were "confirmed" by the laying on of hands by the old Waldensian priest, apparently assisted by the priest Michael (?), in the name and authority of the synod. By a more restricted lot Matthias was chosen from the three to have "the first place in authority," or as "bishop," as Michael called himself in a conference with the Utraquistic consistory in 1478. It was not until May of the following year (1468) that the Brethren informed Rokycana of what had occurred, and they then seem to have broken definitely with him. They themselves, however, were soon divided as to "whether it should so remain," and the result was the decision that Matthias should be consecrated bishop by the Waldensian bishop Stephen. Strangely enough, the priest Michael was sent, instead of Matthias himself. Michael met Stephen in southern Moravia, received consecration from him, and gave it, when he returned, to Matthias, whereupon he resigned both the authority of bishop, which he had received only for this purpose, and also his Catholic priesthood, having himself reordained by Matthias as a priest of the Brethren, while the new bishop likewise ordained Thomas and Elias. This is the account of Michael and other eye-witnesses, while later sources, even of the early sixteenth century, present many deviations, partly in an endeavor to conceal the cooperation of the Waldensians so far as possible.

3. First Priests of the Brethren.

The members of this newly constituted community called themselves "Brethren," and were known in different portions of the country by the names of their chief centers, such as Kunwalders, Bunzlau Brethren, and the like. As a whole they termed themselves *Jednota Bratrská*, which they later rendered into Latin as *Unitas Fratrum*. Their characteristic designation was Brethren, which had already been current in various older Bohemian communities. The name *Fratres legis Christi* first arose in the second half of the sixteenth century, but never became general. Their opponents usually termed them Waldensians or Pickards (a corruption of Beghards), and this designation, found even in the royal decrees, became so general that they themselves employed it in the titles of many of their writings, terming themselves "the Brethren who for envy and hatred are called Waldensians or Pickards." The first result of the events of 1467 was a renewal of the persecutions, which lasted until the death of George and Rokycana in 1471, and which also involved the Waldensians, Stephen being burned at the stake in Vienna during this period. This persecution may also have been the cause of the renewed attacks on them in Brandenburg, and about 1478 two Waldensians accordingly went from that country to the Brethren, thus inaugurating an intercommunication between the two sects which resulted in a number of Waldensians joining the Brethren after 1480 and settling at Landskron in Bohemia and at Fulneck in Moravia. In the latter country both sects were tolerated under King Matthias, until the end of his reign, when a decree of expulsion was issued in 1488, although it was soon revoked at the petition of some patrons of high rank. A portion of the Brethren had already emigrated to Moldavia, but apparently returned within a few years.

4. Relations with the Waldensians.

Internal strife, centered about the ideal of Peter mentioned above, was more perilous to the maintenance of unity than external oppression. A "small" party clung to this ideal, and accordingly rejected temporal power, law, service in war, the oath, and the like as unchristian, while a "great" party regarded all these as dangerous, yet not to be rejected unconditionally. The controversies ended in 1494 with the victory of the "great" party, the "small" party, who called themselves Amosites after their leader Amos, separating as an independent community and preserving an existence for several decades. During these dissensions two leaders of the "great" party, Lukas and Thomas, journeyed to North Italy to visit the Lombard Waldensians in their own homes, possibly seeking, in view of their disagreement with the "small" party, to make a final effort to induce the Waldensians to break openly with Rome. A correspondence between the Brethren and the Waldensians was associated with this journey, the three Waldensian treatises, preserved either entire or in fragments, *La epistola al serenissimo Rey Lancelau; Ayczo es la causa del nostre departiment de la gleysa Romana;* and *De l'Antichrist*, as well as the catechism *Las interrogations menors*, being apparently translations or revisions of Bohemian writings composed by the Brethren, although the mutual relations are not yet altogether clear.

II. The Brethren under Lukas: The period between 1496 and 1528 is marked by the activity of Lukas. Although he was not appointed presiding bishop until 1517, his influence was potent during the administration of his predecessors in office, Procopius (1507) and Thomas of Přelouč (1517). His special task was the restoration of the Unity which had become necessary in consequence of the secession of the "small" party. A mass of ordinances, touching on all the relations of life, was prepared to build up the Christian community on the principles newly won. The doctrines, which had thus far been formulated but feebly, were now systematized on other foundations, and from these various points of view Lukas developed a noteworthy literary activity. The external existence of the Unity was seriously threatened at the beginning of the sixteenth century, when Vladislav, who had tolerated them hitherto, was induced to proceed against them by Bohuslav of Lobkowitz, the foremost representative of Bohemian humanism, who saw the roots of manifold evils in religious disunion. At the same time Alexander VI sent the Dominican Heinrich Institoris to Olmütz as censor of books for Bohemia and Moravia (bull of Feb. 4, 1500), and he, after a fruitless disputation with certain representatives of the Brethren, preached against them with extreme severity. The overtures toward a reconciliation between Rome and the Utraquists (1501) led the latter to make common cause in opposition to the Brethren, and a decree of the king, dated July 5, 1503, forbade all further toleration of the sect in Prague and the royal cities, while the Roman Catholic estates voluntarily enforced this prohibition in their districts. A conference held at Prague between the Utraquistic clergy and some of the Brethren failed to convince the latter of their "errors," nor did a Latin creed given them by the king in 1503 meet with their approval. He was still more incensed at them by two venomous letters of the Olmütz canon Augustine Käsebrot, so that he issued a sharp decree against them in 1507. These decrees, however, could not become valid until accepted by the diet, and Vladislav accordingly proposed a law against the Brethren at the diet convoked on July 25, 1508. This was accepted by the estates and placed on the code, as in force throughout the country. It forbade all public and private gatherings of the "Pickards," and ordered the destruction of all their books and writings, while they were commanded to attend Roman Catholic or Utraquistic churches, their clergy and teachers being prisoners of the king unless they should consent, after receiving instruction, to join one of these religious bodies. The law is said to have been obeyed by all estates until Christmas, and those who still tolerated "Pickards" were mulcted. This measure conditioned the position of the Brethren in Bohemia for almost the entire period of their existence, but the Moravian diet refused to accept it. In 1541 the code was destroyed by a fire at Prague, so that it became necessary to draft the laws anew at following diets. Thereupon the Brethren endeavored to secure the abolition of the law, but in vain; nor was it repealed until an imperial letter of Rudolf II in 1609. It is strikingly suggestive of the political conditions of Bohemia in the sixteenth century, however, that a community which was legally prohibited, like the Brethren, could attain such wide extension and importance. This was possible only because the nobles obeyed the laws as they pleased, for the king was generally too much occupied with foreign affairs to be able to insist rigidly on compliance with his statutes, and in case he did attempt to execute them, he was resisted by a coalition of the estates, who sought to check all growth of the royal power. At first the law was strictly observed, and the Brethren were severely oppressed, their meeting-places being closed, their priests expelled, and imprisonment and even occasional execution serving as deterrent measures. Lukas himself was imprisoned, and was freed only by the death of Vladislav on Mar. 13, 1516. This event lessened the severity of a persecution which had been opposed by some estates from the very beginning. During the reign of Vladislav's son Louis, which marked a further decay of the royal power, the persecution of the Brethren ceased altogether, and the governmental center of the Unity, which had been transferred to Prerau in Moravia during the period of oppression, was again removed to Bohemia, and located at Jungbunzlau, the residence of Lukas. While he was presiding bishop, the Brethren first came into contact with the German Reformation, when Luther learned of their short catechism, of which he seems to have received a German translation in 1521.

1. Oppressive Measures of Vladislav.

Although Luther at first declared himself at least in sympathy with their doctrine of the Lord's Supper, he became estranged from the Brethren after 1524, while their tendency to remain aloof, so far as possible, from the Lutheran movement was strengthened by the vagaries of Gallus Cahera in Prague (1523–29), especially since it resulted in the enforcement by the diet of the decree of Vladislav (1525). The Brethren also sent a fruitless deputation to Erasmus, apparently in 1520. In the closing years of his life Lukas found himself obliged to break with the Habrovanites or Lultish Brethren in Moravia, who were closely associated with the "small" party, and rejected celibacy, spiritual and temporal authority, and the taking of oaths, in addition to following Carlstadt in the doctrine of the Lord's Supper, and wishing to substitute baptism of the spirit for baptism by water. After a fruitless conference, letters were exchanged with considerable frequency for a number of years, while an effort made by the Anabaptists who had emigrated from the Tyrol to Moravia to unite with the Brethren ended in 1528 in a complete schism. Lukas died at Jungbunzlau on Dec. 11, 1528, and was buried in the local house of the Brethren, which had formerly been a monastery. The organization, however, which he had given the Unity remained unchanged until its end.

2. Overtures to the Protestants.

In principle the supreme judicial power was lodged with the synod, which consisted of all the clergy, although it contained no delegates chosen from the communities. It was, at the same time, the supreme court of appeal, although the chief administrative body, the "Close Council" (*úzká rada*), which was composed of some ten members chosen by the synod for life, apparently constituted the real government. The legal relation of the "Close Council" to the synod seems never to have been accurately defined. At the Synod of 1497 the "Close Council" was treated with all submission and obedience, and was empowered to make whatever changes and ordinances it deemed best without awaiting a decision of the synod. According to tradition, it never abused its privileges, and held a general council yearly whenever this was possible, while other synods also existed in individual districts. The presiding officer of the "Close Council" was called a "judge" (*sudí*), and this office was originally united with that of bishop in the person of Matthias, although he proved himself unequal to the position in the strife with the "small" party, so that Procopius was appointed *sudí*, Matthias retaining only the episcopal power of ordination. Authorized by the "Close Council," he associated Thomas and Elias, whom he had already ordained priests, and after the death of Matthias and the resignation of Procopius in 1500, the power of direction and ordination was again united, and given to four newly chosen Brethren, Thomas, Elias, Lukas, and Ambrose, the first two already possessing the episcopal ordination and the last two now receiving it. Each of them was placed over a diocese which he controlled and in which he ordained the priests. The priest next in age to these four was called the judge, and had special functions. Jafet, writing in 1605, sought to show that this organization existed from the first and that four bishops had ruled simultaneously since 1467, and this erroneous view was so widely disseminated by Wengierski (Regenvolscius) that it is still found sporadically. At the head of each community stood the priest or director (*správce*), who lived in the "house of the Brethren" and supported himself as an artisan or farmer. He might possess property, although he was bound by certain restrictions, so that when, for example, he received a legacy, he was required to deposit it with the "Close Council," which deprived him of it in case of need or inability to discharge his office. While there was no insistence on the celibacy of the clergy, it was regarded as desirable, in view of the unsettled position of the community, and was the rule until the second half of the sixteenth century. With the priest lived his assistant or deacon, who aided him both in his daily toil and in teaching school, and especially in the instruction of the acolytes (young men in training for the priesthood), who resided in the "house of the Brethren." The deacon accompanied the priest in all his pastoral journeys, and was permitted to preach, to baptize in case of need, and to aid in the Lord's Supper, although he could neither consecrate the elements nor pronounce the benediction at the close of the service of the community. A council of the community aided, and in part supervised, the priest in controlling the property of the congregation and in distributing alms. The income consisted, in addition to gifts and foundations, of two collections, taken at Christmas and St. John's Day. Three persons were deputed to oversee the giving of alms, while the council of the community was required to reconcile antagonistic members of the congregation with each other or with the priest, to control morals, and to maintain the discipline of the church. The bodies next in rank were the "Close Council" and the synods. The council of the community found its counterpart in a committee of aged widows and spinsters appointed to supervise the morals and the conduct of the sisters. This organization, the genesis of which is known chiefly from the *Dekrety*, remained unchanged after Lukas. It was first described in full detail by Lasicius in the eighth book of his history of the Brethren, and was officially formulated by them at the General Synod of Žeravic in Moravia, held in 1616.

3. Later Organization.

III. Development from 1528 to 1621: The independent development of the *Unitas Fratrum* closed with the death of Lukas. The Lutheran party among the Brethren, headed by such men as Johann Horn (Roh), Michael Weisse, Johann Augusta, and Mach Sionsky, now became more prominent and assumed the leadership. After the brief administration of the insignificant Martin Skoda, Horn became judge in 1532, but was surpassed in importance by his colleague Johann Augusta, a man characterized by meager education, yet of great firmness, energy, and eloquence, and deeply impressed with a sense of the peculiar advantages of the community. He sought to associate the Brethren with the foreign Evangelicals, and found a favorable opportunity shortly after 1530, when the margrave George of Brandenburg requested Conrad of Krajek to instruct him in the doctrines of his sect. A confession was prepared, and Luther was induced to have it printed at Wittenberg with a eulogistic preface. At the same time, however, Augusta made overtures to the Strasburg theologians, and Matthias Červenka, his envoy to Butzer, unexpectedly met Calvin. On the other hand, his relations with the Utraquistic Church of Bohemia were strained, especially during the administration of Mistopol. Another trait which characterizes the history of the Brethren after Lukas (1528–47) is the prominence of their nobility. The country estates were required to take part in the country diets just as the estates of the kingdom shared in the royal diets, and it thus became necessary for the estates of the Brethren to enter the former to defend the existence of their ecclesiastical union. In 1535, therefore, they gave King Ferdinand the creed of the Brethren, signed by all members of the nobility among them, twelve lords and thirty-five knights. Since ten of the twenty-six nobles tried by Ferdinand after the suppression of the so-called Bohemian revolt in 1547 were members of the Unity, he found a long-desired pretext to crush the community so far as possible. The decree of Vladislav was reenforced, certain estates which had been the centers of the brotherhood were confiscated by the king, and the former protectors of the Brethren were no longer able to evade the execution of the decree under the existing circumstances. The community was practically destroyed in Bohemia. Its seat of government was transferred to Moravia, but the majority of the Brethren were banished from the entire kingdom. Augusta himself was betrayed to Ferdinand, and regained his freedom only after repeated tortures and an imprisonment of sixteen years.

1. Johann Augusta.

The sixth decade of the century ushered in a period of comparative peace for the Brethren, and they now sought, under the leadership of Johann Blahoslav, to gain state recognition of their Church, their chances seeming especially favorable in view of the supposed Protestant tendency of Maximilian. In 1555 and the following years they accordingly endeavored to win the favor of the archduke through repeated conferences between Blahoslav and Maximilian's court preacher, Pfauser of Vienna, but their efforts to secure definite promises for the future bore little fruit. The same object was pursued by Utraquism, which had now become essentially Lutheran, and which had prepared a new creed for the Lutheran Church in Bohemia in 1575, after the compacts had been annulled by the diet of deputies in 1567 as antiquated.

2. Cessation of Persecution.

Through their representatives the Brethren sought to have their independence clearly expressed in the preface of the new creed, but their chance of recognition by the side of the "Neo-Utraquists" steadily decreased, while their essential community of interest with the new body became more and more clear. In 1609, when the estates forced Rudolf to issue his charter, the Brethren shared the religious liberty which it granted by joining in the Bohemian Confession of 1575, after having already given a full explanation of its acceptance in the previous year.

All special names were now to cease, and the members of the united Bohemian Evangelical Church were henceforth to be called "Utraquistic Christians." The Brethren were represented in the common consistory, but despite the abolition of a separate name, this was, strictly speaking, not a union, but rather a confederation between the *Unitas Fratrum* and the Bohemian Church. The Brethren, therefore, retained their own organization and regulations, and even their independent creed (1564), while the Bohemian Lutherans, in like manner, held to the Augsburg Confession, although both creeds are declared to be in full harmony with the Bohemian Confession of 1575. Definitive form was accordingly given the church discipline of the Brethren at the Synod of Žeravic in 1616 under the title *Ratio disciplinæ ordinisque ecclesiastici in unitate fratrum Bohemorum*, but the plan of making this valid for the whole Bohemian Church was not realized. This organization, however, had but a brief period of prosperity, for the battle at the White Hill (Nov. 8, 1620) destroyed Protestantism in Bohemia and Moravia for more than a century and a half.

3. The Brethren Merged in the Utraquists.

IV. The Brethren in Prussia and Poland: The Brethren expelled from Bohemia in 1547 in consequence of the Schmalkald War emigrated partly to Moravia and partly to Prussia, where they were received by Duke Albert. After his death in 1568 they returned to Moravia and Poland, exercising an important influence on the introduction of the Reformation in the latter country, and attempting to establish friendly relations between the various Evangelical bodies at a synod held at Sendomir in 1570. Their scanty remnants still exist in the five so-called communities of Unity in the Prussian province of Posen: Posen, Lissa, Lasswitz, Waschke, and Orzeszkowo. JOSEF MUELLER.

BIBLIOGRAPHY: For full bibliography of the subject consult W. G. Malin, *Catalogue of Books relating to or illustrating the History of the Unitas Fratrum or United Brethren now generally known as the Moravian Church*, Philadelphia, 1881.

For general history consult: J. Camerarius, *Historica narratio de fratrum orthodoxorum ecclesiis in Bohemia, Moravia, et Polonia*, Heidelberg, 1605; J. Lasicius, *De origine et institutis Fratrum libri viii* (only the eighth book was published, ed. J. A. Comenius, 1649); *Historia persecutionum ecclesiæ Bohemicæ*, Amsterdam, 1648, Eng. transl., London, 1650; J. A. Comenius, *Ecclesiæ Slavonicæ historiola*, Amsterdam, 1660; idem, *Historia fratrum Bohemorum*, ed. Buddeus, Halle, 1702; *Martyrologium Bohemicum, oder die böhmische Verfolgungsgeschichte, 894–1632*, Berlin, 1766; D. Cranz, *Alte und neue Brüder Historie*, Barby, 1771, Eng. transl., London, 1780; *The Reformation and Anti-Reformation in Bohemia*, ib. 1845; V. Krasinski, *Religious History of the Slavonic Nations*, Edinburgh, 1851; A. Gindely, *Geschichte der böhmischen Brüder*, 2 vols., Prague, 1857; A. Bost, *Hist. of the Bohemian and Moravian Brethren*, London, 1863; E. W. Cröger, *Geschichte der alten Brüderkirche*, Gnadau, 1865; D. Benham, *Notes on the Origin and Episcopate of the Bohemian Brethren*, London, 1867; B. Czerwenka, *Geschichte der evangelischen Kirche in Böhmen*, 2 vols., Bielefeld, 1870; E. Jane Whately, *Sketches of Bohemian Religious History*, London, 1876; E. de Schweinitz, *Hist. of the Church known as the Unitas Fratrum*, Bethlehem, 1885.

For the church order consult: *Ratio disciplinæ ordinisque ecclesiastici in unitate fratrum Bohemorum*, Leszno, 1632, Amsterdam, 1660, and Halle, 1732; B. Seifferth, *Church Constitution of the Bohemian and Moravian Brethren. The Original Latin with a Transl.*, London, 1866.

The original text of the *Confession* is reproduced in A. Gindely, *Quellen zur Geschichte der böhmischen Brüder*, p. 354 sqq., Vienna, 1861, and in de Schweinitz, *History*, ut sup., pp. 648 sqq. Consult also J. C. Koecher, *Die drey letzten und vornehmsten Glaubensbekenntnisse der böhmischen Brüder*, Leipsic, 1741; H. A. Niemeyer, *Collectio confessionum*, pp. 771 sqq., ib. 1840.

For catechisms consult: J. G. Ehwalt, *Die alte und neue Lehre der böhmischen Brüder*, Danzig, 1756; C. A. G. von Zezschwitz, *Die Katechismen der Waldenser und böhmischen Brüder*, Erlangen, 1863; J. Müller, *Die deutschen Katechismen der böhmischen Brüder*, Berlin, 1887.

On the Hymnology consult: P. Wackernagel, *Das deutsche Kirchenlied*, iii, 229–368, iv, 346–485, Berlin, 1870–75; J. Zahn, *Die geistlichen Lieder der Brüder in Böhmen, Mähren und Polen*, Nuremberg, 1875; Julian, *Hymnology*, pp. 153–160.

BOIS (BOYS), JOHN: Church of England scholar; b. at Nettlestead, near Hadleigh (35 m. e.s.e. of Cambridge), Suffolk, Jan. 3, 1561; d. at Ely Jan. 14, 1644. He studied at St. John's and Magdalen Colleges, Cambridge, was elected fellow of the former in 1580, and was Greek lecturer 1584–1595; became rector of Boxworth (5 m. n.w. of Cambridge) 1596, and prebendary of Ely 1615. He was one of the translators of the Authorized Version, belonging to the Apocrypha company, and when his own part was done is said to have assisted the other Cambridge company on the section from Chronicles to Canticles; he was one of the delegates engaged in the final revision. He assisted Sir Henry Savile (who calls him "most ingenious and most learned") in his edition of Chrysostom (8 vols., Eton, 1612 [1610–13]), and left many manuscripts, but his only published work was *Veteris interpretis cum Beza aliisque recentioribus collatio in quattuor evangeliis et apostolorum actis* (London, 1655).

Bibliography: The life of Bois, founded partly on his diary and written by Anthony Walker, is printed in Francis Peck's *Desiderata curiosa*, ii, 325–342, London, 1779, and additions to it by T. Baker are appended to Peck's *Memoirs of . . . Oliver Cromwell*, London, 1740. Consult also *DNB*, v, 311–313.

BOLINGBROKE, HENRY SAINT-JOHN, VISCOUNT. See Deism, I, § 8.

BOLIVIA: A republic of western South America, bounded on the north and east by Brazil; on the south by Paraguay and Argentina; and on the west by Chile and Peru. The area is estimated at from 520,000 to 600,000 square miles, the population from 1,900,000 to 2,500,000, of whom 1,250,000 are Indians and over 500,000 half-breeds. The constitution adopted in 1826 after independence had been attained recognized Roman Catholicism as the state religion and prohibited the public exercise of any other form of faith, toleration existing only in new colonies. Nevertheless, the properties of the Church were confiscated and sold, only the bishops being allowed a moderate annual sum. Complete religious liberty was granted by the government in 1905.

In its hierarchical organization, Bolivia forms the province of La Plata, under the archbishop of La Plata (Chuquisaca de la Plata) or Sucre (diocese since 1551; archdiocese since 1609 with 135 parishes). The suffragan bishoprics are those of Cochabamba, La Paz, and Santa Cruz de la Sierra. Cochabamba, founded in 1847, has fifty-six parishes; La Paz, founded 1608, has thirty-eight; and Santa Cruz, founded 1605, fifty-four. In addition to the secular clergy, members of orders, including the Jesuits, are actively engaged in missionary labors among the Indians, of whom some 200,000 still cling to their pagan faith. The schools among the converted Indians are under religious control. There are four seminaries for the clergy, six "universities," and sixteen higher schools.

The inaccessibility of Bolivia renders immigration, especially from Europe and North America, scanty. The number of Protestants in the country is accordingly small. There is a Presbyterian chapel in Sucre. Canadian Baptists have been engaged in missionary work in the country since 1898 and have organized churches at Oruro, La Paz, and Cochabamba. More recently the Methodist Episcopal Church of the United States has entered the field with headquarters at La Paz. An interdenominational mission is being conducted at Cochabamba by Australians. The educational system is being reorganized under the direction of an American missionary.

Bibliography: *Bolivia*, issued by Bureau of American Republics, Washington, 1891, cf. the *Annual Reports* of the Bureau since then; A. Bellessont, *La Jeune Amérique. Chili et Bolivie*, Paris, 1897; C. Matzenauer, *Bolivia in historischer, geographischer und cultureller Hinsicht*, Vienna, 1897, J. S. Dennis, *Centennial Survey of Foreign Missions*, New York, 1902; T. C. Dawson, *The South American Republics*, vol. ii, New York, 1904; J. Lee, *Religious Liberty in South America; with special Reference to recent Legislation in Peru, Ecuador and Bolivia*, Cincinnati, 1907.

BOLLAND, JAN, AND THE BOLLANDISTS: The founder of the monumental hagiographical work known as the *Acta Sanctorum Bollandistarum* (see Acta Martyrum, Acta Sanctorum), and his associates. Bolland was born at Julemont, near Liége, Aug. 13, 1596; d. at Antwerp Sept. 12, 1665. He entered the Jesuit order in 1612, was ordained priest before 1625, and in 1630 was sent to Antwerp, where he began what was to prove his life-work, making use of the mass of accumulated material left by Héribert Rosweyde (q.v.), the originator of the idea, but largely extending the space contemplated by him. After working for thirteen years on the two volumes of January, he called to his aid two other Jesuits, Gottfried Henschen and Daniel Papebroch (qq.v.), who visited numerous libraries of Germany, Spain, and Italy in quest of material, and laid the foundation of the magnificent collection of 120,000 volumes which the Bollandists now possess. The first volume appeared at Antwerp in 1643, and the work went on without interruption until the suppression of the Jesuits in 1773. Their house at Antwerp was to be turned into a military school, and there seemed little prospect of continuing their task until in 1776 the empress Maria Theresa made arrangements to help them, and two years later assigned them the Caudenberg monastery in Brussels as a home. Here they labored on as a company of secular priests until Joseph II interfered arbitrarily with their plans and finally, in 1788, forbade them to continue the publication, as a mere collection of old documents which could have but little interest for educated men. In the following year the Premonstratensians of the abbey of Tangerlo in Brabant offered to buy their library and continue the work. The sixth volume of October appeared there in 1794; but in 1796 the French Republic took possession of Belgium and dissolved the abbey; the manuscripts, however, were preserved in the Royal Library at Brussels. Though both Napoleon and the French Academy desired the continuation of the work, it was not found possible until 1837, when, under the inspiration of De Ram, rector of the University of Louvain, the Belgian Jesuits once more took it up, with the promise of an annual subsidy of 6,000 francs from the government. The editors are now at work on the month of November, and at the present rate of progress, it is hoped that the end of the twentieth century may see the completion of the gigantic work. The present Bollandists are also publishing (since 1882) an annual volume of *Analecta Bollandiana*, containing additional Latin, Greek, and Syriac texts, new dissertations, and corrections to the earlier part of the work; and since 1890 they have also published a *Bulletin de publications hagiographiques*, a review of all new books bearing on the subject. They have published, in addition, two complete bibliographies (Greek, 1 vol., Latin, 2 vols.) of all the printed texts and other works on hagiography.

Bibliography: A memoir of Bolland is prefixed to vol. i for March of the *ASB*. Consult further J. M. Neale, *Essays on Liturgiology*, pp. 89–97, London, 1863; C. Dehaisnes, *Les Origines des Acta Sanctorum*, Douai, 1869; G. T. Stokes, *The Bollandists*, in *Contemporary Review*, xliii (1883), 69–84; R. Aubé, *Les Derniers Travaux des Bollandistes*, in *Revue des deux mondes*, lxviii (1885), 169–199.

BOLSEC, JÉRÔME HERMÈS: French controversialist and physician; b. at Paris in the early part of the sixteenth century; d. probably at Lyons 1584. He entered the Carmelite order, but was driven from Paris for the boldness of his sermons and fled to Ferrara. In 1550 he was physician to M. de Falais, a nobleman residing near Geneva, who was a friend of Calvin. Bolsec was fond of dabbling in dogmatics, but was repeatedly admonished by the *compagnie des pasteurs* that his objections to the doctrine of predestination were contrary to the Bible. He seemed to submit, but on Oct. 16, 1551, he provoked a new discussion at Geneva on the same subject and was imprisoned, whereupon he charged Calvin with ignorance of the Bible and of teaching contrary to it, and the council, in their perplexity, accepted the proposition of the clergy to ask the advice of the Swiss churches. Their condemnation of Bolsec was mild, but the clergy of Basel declared that Bolsec was heretical in many respects, while the pastors of Neuchâtel declared that he was an instrument of Satan. On Dec. 22 he was sentenced to perpetual banishment for publishing offensive doctrines, as well as for slandering the clergy and charging them with preaching false dogmas. He was expelled from Thonon (Chablais) by Calvin, and from Lausanne by Beza, after having again accused the former of "making God the author of sin." He then returned to France and abjured Protestantism. He was the author of three works: *Le Miroir, envoyé de Vérité au Roi Charles neufième* (1562), addressed to the king to bring about a reformation; *Histoire de la vie, mœurs, actes, doctrine, constance et mort de Jean Calvin, jadis ministre de Genève* (Lyons, 1577), which made the author infamous; and *Histoire de la vie, mœurs, doctrine et déportemens de Th. de Bèze, dit le Spectable, grand ministre de Genève* (Paris, 1582), written in a tone of moderation. The entire life of Bolsec shows him to have been a restless, vain spirit, not overscrupulous in getting revenge or in winning patrons. EUGÈNE CHOISY.

Bolsec may easily be represented in a more favorable light as an honest opponent of Calvinistic dogma, and an advocate of liberty of conscience and freedom of speech. Persecution (defamation, repeated imprisonment, banishment from Geneva and from other places where he attempted to settle by the persistent efforts of Calvin, Beza, and others) embittered his spirit and no doubt led to exaggerated representations of the tyranny and cruelty of his opponents, and at last drove him back to the Roman Catholic Church. A. H. N.

BIBLIOGRAPHY: *CR, Opera Calvini*, viii, 141; E. and É. Haag, *La France protestante*, ed. H. L. Bordier, vol. ii, Paris, 1879; E. Choisy, *La Théocratie à Genève au temps de Calvin*, Geneva, 1897; J. A. Gautier, *Histoire de Genève*, iii, 432 sqq., ib. 1899.

BOLSENA, MIRACLE OF: A miracle which, according to an account strongly affirmed in local tradition, occurred in 1264 in the town of Bolsena (the ancient Vulsinius; 7 m. s.w. of Orvieto) in Umbria, Italy. The details of the story vary in different accounts, but the substance of the occurrence is as follows: A priest, who had been long troubled with doubts as to the real presence of Christ in the Eucharist, accidentally let fall upon the linen corporal, while saying mass, some drops from the consecrated chalice. While endeavoring to conceal this mishap, he was amazed to perceive that the stain was no longer as of wine but resembled fresh blood, and had not the irregular trace of a few spilled drops, but the form and contour of the consecrated host or wafer. The miracle produced a great sensation throughout the surrounding country. Pope Urban IV, at that time staying in Orvieto with the pontifical court, caused the stained corporal to be brought to the city, where it has ever since been carefully preserved. This miracle was the determining reason which caused Urban to make general the celebration of the feast of Corpus Christi (q.v.). The composition of the liturgical office of the feast was entrusted to Thomas Aquinas, but in it there is no allusion to the miracle.

The miracle of Bolsena has been immortalized by the genius of Raffael, who made it the subject of one of his frescoes in the second sala of the Vatican. The painting idealizes the scene and introduces, not Urban IV but Julius II, under whose pontificate the fresco was executed, as present at the mass. The present cathedral church of Orvieto was built on the site of an earlier structure to commemorate the miracle, and much of the elaborate decoration refers to it. The corporal is preserved in a silver shrine enriched with many figures in relief and subjects in translucent colored enamels. The shrine was begun by Ugolino Veri of Sienna in 1338 and is one of the most important specimens of medieval silversmith work in Italy. The feast of Corpus Christi is celebrated with extraordinary solemnity each year in Orvieto and the corporal is carried in procession through the town together with the Blessed Sacrament.

JAMES F DRISCOLL.

BIBLIOGRAPHY: *Dictionnaire des prophéties et des miracles*, vol. i, in Migne's *Encyclopédie théologique*, vol. xxiv, Paris, 1852.

BOLZANO, bel-tsā'nō, BERNHARD: German Roman Catholic theologian, and noted mathematician; b. at Prague Oct. 5, 1781; d. there Dec. 18, 1848. He took orders and was made professor of the philosophy of religion in Prague 1805. He was soon suspected of heterodoxy, was accused at Rome by the Jesuits, and in 1820, on a charge of connection with certain student societies, was compelled to resign his professorship; he was also suspended from his priestly functions. Thenceforth he devoted himself to study and literary work. He sought to reconcile the teachings of the Church with reason and, it was said, considered the reasonableness of a doctrine of more importance than its traditional belief. In philosophy he was influenced by Leibnitz and Kant. His contributions to mathematical science were original and important. His works were numerous; the most noteworthy are *Lehrbuch der Religionswissenschaft* (4 vols., Sulzbach, 1834), a philosophic presentation of the dogmas of Roman Catholic theology; *Wissenschaftslehre; Versuch einer neuen Darstellung der Logik* (4 vols., 1837).

BIBLIOGRAPHY: *Lebensbeschreibung des Dr. Bolzano*, new ed., Vienna, 1875 (an autobiography); *Dr. Bolzano und seine Gegner. Ein Beitrag zur neuesten Literaturgeschichte*, ib. 1839; A. Wisshaupt, *Skizzen aus dem Leben B. Bolzanos*, Leipsic, 1850.

BOMBERGER, JOHN HENRY AUGUSTUS: Reformed (German); b. at Lancaster, Penn., Jan. 13, 1817; d. at Collegeville, Penn., Aug. 19, 1890. He was graduated at Marshall College, 1837, and at the Theological Seminary, Mercersburg, Penn., 1838; served as pastor of German Reformed Churches in Pennsylvania till 1870, when he became president of Ursinus College at Collegeville. He began a condensed translation of the first edition of Herzog's *Realencyklopädie* of which two volumes were published (Philadelphia, 1856–60), embracing vols. i–vi of the original; he issued a revised translation of Kurtz's *Text-book of Church History* (Philadelphia, 1860), and edited *The Reformed Church Monthly* (in opposition to the "Mercersburg theology"), 1868–77. He also published *Infant Salvation in its Relation to Infant Depravity, Infant Regeneration, and Infant Baptism* (1859); *Five Years at the Race Street Church* [Philadelphia], *with an ecclesiastical appendix* (1860); *The Revised Liturgy, a history and criticism of the ritualistic movement in the German Reformed Church* (1867); *Reformed, not Ritualistic; a reply to Dr. Nevin's "Vindication"* (1867).

BONA, GIOVANNI: Roman Catholic theological writer; b. at Mondovi (55 m. w. of Genoa), Piedmont, Oct. 19, 1609; d. in Rome Oct. 28, 1674. He came of an old French family, and in his fifteenth year entered the Italian congregation of reformed Cistercians, becoming later prior, abbot, and general. Clement IX made him a cardinal in 1669, and he acquired a great reputation for both piety and learning. His most important writings are ascetical and liturgical. To the latter class belong his *Psallentis ecclesiæ harmonia* (Rome, 1653), a historical, symbolic, and ascetic treatise on the psalmody of the Church, and the still better known *Rerum liturgicarum libri ii* (Rome, 1671), a sober and learned investigation of liturgical antiquities. The first complete edition of his works appeared at Antwerp, 1677, followed by several others.

BONALD, LOUIS GABRIEL AMBROISE, VICOMTE DE: French political and philosophical writer; b. at Monna, near Millau (130 m. w.n.w. of Marseilles), Aveyron, Oct. 2, 1754; d. there Nov. 23, 1840. He emigrated in 1791 and settled at Heidelberg; returned to France in 1797, lived in concealment for a time, and then was allowed to proceed to his estates; in 1808 he was appointed councilor of the Imperial University, and, after the Restoration, member of the Council of Public Instruction; from 1815 to 1822 he was member of the chamber of deputies, in 1822 minister of state, and in 1823 was made a peer of France; after 1830 he retired to private life. He was one of the leaders of the reactionary school to which belonged De Maistre, D'Eckstein, Ballanche, Lamennais, and others, which started with the principle that revelation and not observation is the true ground of philosophy; absolutism in politics and ecclesiastical despotism in religion were in his view the natural and desirable order of things. The most noteworthy of his many writings were *Théorie du pouvoir politique et religieux* (3 vols., Constance, 1796); *La Législation primitive* (3 vols., Paris, 1802); *Recherches philosophiques sur les premiers objets des connaissances morales* (2 vols., 1818). His collected works were published in twelve volumes in 1817–19 and again in three volumes in 1859. His second son, **Louis Jacques Maurice,** b. at Millau Oct. 30, 1787, d. at Lyons Feb. 25, 1870, became bishop of Puy in 1823, archbishop of Lyons in 1839, cardinal in 1841; he was a strong Ultramontane.

BIBLIOGRAPHY: Victor de Bonald, *De la vie et des écrits du vicomte de Bonald*, Avignon, 1853 (by his son); J. Blanchon, *Le Cardinal de Bonald , sa vie et ses œuvres*, Lyons, 1870.

BONAR, ANDREW ALEXANDER: Free Church of Scotland; b. at Edinburgh May 29, 1810, youngest brother of Horatius Bonar (q.v.); d. in Glasgow Dec. 30, 1892. He studied at Edinburgh; was minister at Collace, Perthshire, 1838–56, of the Finnieston Church, Glasgow, 1856 till his death. He joined the Free Church in 1843, and was its moderator in 1878. He was identified with evangelical and revival movements and adhered to the doctrine of premillenialism. With the Rev. R. M. McCheyne he visited Palestine in 1839 to inquire into the condition of the Jews there, and published *A Narrative of a Mission of Inquiry to the Jews from the Church of Scotland in 1839* (Edinburgh, 1842); he also published a *Memoir* of Mr. McCheyne (1845); a *Commentary on Leviticus* (1846); *Redemption Drawing Nigh, a defence of Premillenialism* (1847); *Christ and his Church in the Book of Psalms* (1859); edited Samuel Rutherford's *Letters* (1863); and wrote many tracts, pamphlets, and minor biographies.

BIBLIOGRAPHY: *A. A. Bonar, Diary and Letters*, edited by his daughter, Marjory Bonar, London, 1895, who published also a volume of *Reminiscences*, ib. 1895.

BONAR, HORATIUS: Free Church of Scotland; b. in Edinburgh Dec. 19, 1808; d. there July 31, 1889. He studied at Edinburgh; became minister at Kelso 1837, at the Chalmers Memorial Church, Edinburgh, 1866; with his congregation he joined the Free Church in 1843. He was a premillenarian and expressed his views in books, such as *Prophetical Landmarks* (London, 1847), and in the *Quarterly Journal of Prophecy*, which he founded in 1849. He is best known for his poems and hymns which include "What a friend we have in Jesus," "I heard the voice of Jesus say," and others equally familiar. The best known collections of his verse are *Hymns of Faith and Hope* (3 vols., 1857–66); *The Song of the New Creation and other pieces* (1872); *Hymns of the Nativity* (1878); *Songs of Love and Joy* (1888); *Until the Daybreak and other hymns left behind* (1890). His prose publications, besides sermons, tracts, etc., include *The Night of Weeping, or words for the suffering family of God* (1846); *God's Way of Peace* (1862); *The White Fields of France, or the story of Mr. McAll's mission to the working-*

men of Paris and Lyons (1879); *Life and Work of G. T. Dodds* (1884).

BIBLIOGRAPHY: *Horatius Bonar, a Memorial*, London, 1889; S. W. Duffield, *English Hymns*, pp. 168–169 and passim, New York, 1886; Julian, *Hymnology*, pp. 161–162; *DNB*, supplement vol. i, 231–232.

BONAVENTURA (Giovanni di Fidanza, called *Doctor Seraphicus*): Theologian; b. at Bagnorea (50 m. n.n.w. of Rome) 1221; d. at Lyons July 15, 1274. He entered the order of St. Francis probably in 1238; went to Paris, 1242 or 1243, and studied under Alexander of Hales; lectured there on the "Sentences" of Peter Lombard and on the Holy Scriptures till the university suspended lectures in 1255; was chosen general of his order, 1257; cardinal bishop of Albano, 1273. His last public act was an impressive speech delivered before the Council of Lyons in May, 1274, for the union of the Eastern and Western churches. He was canonized by Sixtus IV in 1482. In defense of his order, before he became its general, during the contest between the Sorbonne and the mendicant monks, he wrote his *De paupertate Christi*, in reply to William of St. Amour's *De periculis novissimorum temporum* (1256); by a somewhat forced and sophistical argumentation he represents voluntary poverty as an element of moral perfection. Of his general views on monastic life he has given an exposition in his *Determinationes quæstionum circa regulam Francisci*. In his administration he was mild yet firm. As a teacher and author he occupies one of the most prominent places in the history of medieval theology; not so much, however, on account of any strongly pronounced originality as on account of the comprehensiveness of his views, the ease and clearness of his reasoning, and a style in which still linger some traces of the great charm of his personality. His mystical and devotional writings—as, for instance, *De septem itineribus æternitatis*—are almost imitations of Hugo of St. Victor. His dialectical writings are more independent. His *Breviloquium* (ed. Da Vicenza, 2d ed., Freiburg, 1881) is one of the best expositions of Christian dogmatics produced during the Middle Ages.

BIBLIOGRAPHY: Bonaventura's works have been published in many editions, of which the best are that by Peltier, 15 vols., Paris, 1863–71, and that prepared by the Franciscans, 10 vols., Clairac, 1882–93. Of his real or supposititious works accessible in English translation, the following may be mentioned: *The Mirror of the Blessed Virgin Mary*, Dublin, 1849; *Psalter of the Blessed Virgin*, London, 1852; *The Life of Christ*, ib. 1881; *The Month of Jesus Christ*, ib. 1882; *The Life of St. Francis of Assisi*, 4th ed., ib. 1898; *St. Bonaventura's Instructions for the Season of Lent*, ib. 1884; *The Soul's Progress in God* (transl. of the *Itinerarium mentis in deum*) is in the *Journal of Speculative Philosophy*, vol. xxi (1887).

For his life consult: *ASB*, July 14, vol. iii, pp. 838–860; *Histoire littéraire de la France*, xix, 266–291; A. M. da Vicenza, *Der heilige Bonaventura . . . in seinem Leben und Wirken*, Germ. transl. from the Italian, Paderborn, 1874; *Le Cardinal S. Bonaventure . . . sa vie, sa mort et son culte à Lyon*, Lyons, 1875; L. C. Skey, *Life of St. Bonaventure*, London, 1889.

On his works consult: A. de Margerie, *Essai sur la philosophie de S. Bonaventure*, Paris, 1855; W. A. Hollenberg, *Studien zu Bonaventura*, Berlin, 1862; J. Richard, *Étude sur le mysticisme spéculatif de S. Bonaventure*, Paris, 1873; Fidelis a Fauna, *Ratio nova collectionis operum omnium . . . Bonaventuræ*, Paris, 1874; A. Maria a Vicetia et Johannes a Rubino, *Lexicon Bonaventurianum philosophico-theologicum*, Venice, 1880; J. Krause, *Die Lehre des heiligen Bonaventura über die Natur der körperlichen und geistigen Wesen*, Paderborn, 1888.

BOND, WILLIAM BENNETT: Anglican archbishop of Montreal and primate of all Canada; b. at Truro (8 m. n.n.e. of Falmouth), Cornwall, England, Sept. 10, 1815; d. at Montreal Oct. 9, 1906. He came to Newfoundland while in early youth and was educated at Bishop's College, Lennoxville, P. Q., being ordered deacon in 1840 and ordained priest in the following year. After being successively a traveling missionary in 1840–42 and a missionary at Lachine, P. Q., in 1842–48, he was curate of St. George's, Montreal, from 1848 to 1860 and rector of the same church from 1860 to 1878. He was likewise archdeacon of Montreal in 1870–72 and dean in 1872–78. In the latter year he was consecrated archbishop of Montreal, and in 1901 was elected metropolitan of Canada, while in 1904 he became primate of all Canada. He was also president of the theological college of the diocese of Montreal.

BONET-MAURY, AMY GASTON CHARLES AUGUSTE: French Protestant; b. at Paris Jan. 2, 1842. He was educated at the Lycée Napoléon (now Collège Henri IV), the Sorbonne (baccalauréat ès lettres, 1860) and the universities of Geneva and Strasburg (1868). He was successively pastor of the Walloon Reformed Church at Dort in 1868–72 and of the French Reformed Church at Beauvais (Oise) in 1872–79. In 1879 he became professor of church history in the faculty of Protestant theology of the University of Paris, and now holds the same position in the Independent Divinity School of Paris. From 1885 to 1889 he was librarian of the Musée Pédagogique. In theology he is a liberal evangelical. He wrote: *Les Origines de la réforme à Beauvais* (Paris, 1874); *Gerard de Groote, un précurseur de la réforme au quatorzième siècle* (1878); *E quibus fontibus Nederlandicis hauserit scriptor libri cui titulus est De Imitatione Christi* (1878); *Des Origines du christianisme unitaire chez les Anglais* (1881; Eng. transl., London, 1883); *Arnauld de Brescia, un réformateur au douzième siècle* (Paris, 1881); *De opera scholastica fratrum vitæ communis in Nederlandia* (1889); *G. A. Bürger et les origines anglaises de la ballade littéraire en Allemagne* (1890); *Ignace Dœllinger, 1799–1890* (1892); *Lettres et déclarations de J. J. I. Dœllinger au sujet des décrets du Vatican, traduites de l'Allemand* (1893); *Le Congrès des religions à Chicago en 1893* (1895); *Histoire de la liberté de conscience depuis l'Édit de Nantes jusqu'à juillet 1870* (1900); *Les Précurseurs de la réforme et de la liberté de conscience dans les pays latins du douzième au quinzième siècle* (1904); *Edgar Quinet, son œuvre religieuse et son charactère moral* (1903); and *L'Islamisme et le christianisme en Afrique* (1906).

BONIFACE: The name of nine popes.

Boniface I: Pope 418–422. After the death of Zosimus, a part of the clergy and people chose the archdeacon Eulalius to succeed him (Dec. 27, 418); he was recognized by the prefect Symmachus and consecrated in the Lateran two days later. But another faction held an election on the 28th, and chose Boniface, the son of the priest Jocundus, consecrating him on the following day. In accordance with the report of Symmachus, the emperor Honorius recognized Eulalius, and Boniface had to leave Rome. His supporters appealed to the emperor, representing him as the choice of the majority. Honorius called a council to meet at Ravenna, Feb. 8, 419, to decide the matter, but it reached no conclusion, and another was summoned for May 1, both candidates being forbidden to enter Rome in the mean time. Eulalius, however, entered the city on Mar. 18, and had to be removed forcibly; and Honorius now recognized Boniface, who took up his duties on Apr. 10. This contest caused Honorius to decree that in any subsequent case of a contested election, both candidates should be set aside and a new choice made.

When Boniface I intervened in any ecclesiastical disputes, he showed great justice and moderation. The clergy of Valence accused their bishop Maximus of grievous crimes; Boniface referred the matter to a Gallic synod, reserving to himself the right to review its decision. Considering the privilege granted by Pope Zosimus (417) to Bishop Patroclus of Arles, to consecrate bishops for the provinces known as *Viennensis, Narbonensis prima,* and *Narbonensis secunda*, to be an infringement of earlier canonical provisions, he did not hesitate to withdraw it so far as to allow the bishop of Narbonne this metropolitan privilege for the *Provincia Narbonensis prima*. He was involved in long-drawn-out negotiations with the patriarch of Constantinople. Certain Illyrian bishops, wishing to bring charges against Bishop Perigenes of Patras, who had been chosen metropolitan of Corinth, getting satisfaction neither from the papal delegate for Illyria, Bishop Rufus of Thessalonica, nor from the pope himself, turned to Atticus of Constantinople for redress. The latter procured an edict from the emperor Theodosius II (421), placing Illyria under the jurisdiction of Constantinople. Boniface made strong representations to the Byzantine court (Mar., 422), but would probably not have been successful had not the influence of the Western emperor Honorius prevailed with Theodosius, who withdrew the edict. Finally, Boniface had inherited from his predecessor a difficult controversy with the African church (see ZOSIMUS): he had no better success than Zosimus in securing the recognition in Africa of the right of appeal to Rome. On the contrary, the Synod of Carthage in 419 confirmed the seventeenth canon of the synod of 418, which positively forbade to priests and lower clergy any such appeals, and tolerated them for bishops only on condition that the prescription appealed to could be shown to be Nicene; as a matter of fact, it came from the Council of Sardica. Boniface died Sept. 4, 422, and is reckoned among the saints of the Roman Catholic Church. (A. HAUCK.)

BIBLIOGRAPHY: *Liber pontificalis*, ed. Duchesne, i. 227, Paris, 1886; *ASB*, Oct., xi. 605-616; F. Gregorovius, *Geschichte der Stadt Rom*, i, 170 sqq., Stuttgart, 1875, Eng. transl., London, 1900; J. Langen, *Geschichte der römischen Kirche bis Leo I.*, pp. 763 sqq., Bonn, 1881; Jaffé, *Regesta*, i, 52; Hefele, *Conciliengeschichte*, ii, 122, Eng. transl., ii, 466; Bower, *Popes*, i, 162-166; Neander, *Christian Church*, ii, 208, 235, 652.

Boniface II: Pope 530-532. After the death of Felix IV (middle of Sept., 530), a contested election followed. The minority, in obedience to the dying charge of Felix, chose the archdeacon Boniface, a Goth; the majority elected Dioscurus, a Greek, and both were consecrated on the same day (Sept. 22). The Roman senate took cognizance of the matter, forbidding under heavy penalties any proceedings in the lifetime of a pope looking toward the elevation of a successor. The schism was soon ended by the death of Dioscurus, Oct. 14. The *Liber pontificalis* asserts that Boniface proceeded with great violence against his adherents; and we have evidence that five years later the bitterness caused by this was not extinct among the Roman clergy. The close of the Semi-Pelagian controversy falls in the pontificate of Boniface II. In a letter to Cæsarius of Arles he pronounced against the opinion that man could attain faith in Christ by his own resources, without the help of divine grace; and at the same time, in accordance with the wishes of Cæsarius, he confirmed the decisions of the Synod of Orange. He was always zealous in maintaining, if it was not possible to extend, the papal claims to jurisdiction. When Bishop Stephen of Larissa in Thessaly appealed to him from a sentence of deposition pronounced by the patriarch of Constantinople, Boniface endeavored to reassert the old rights of the Roman See over Illyria, which had been obsolete for a hundred years. The proceedings of a synod held in Rome for this purpose (Dec., 531) seem to have been fruitless, for soon afterward the see of Larissa was filled by a nominee of Constantinople. After attempting in vain to designate the deacon Vigilius as his successor, Boniface died in Oct., 532. (A. HAUCK.)

BIBLIOGRAPHY: *Liber pontificalis*, ed. Duchesne, i, 281, Paris, 1886; F. Gregorovius, *Geschichte der Stadt Rom*, i, 329, Stuttgart, 1875, Eng. transl., London, 1900; L. Duchesne, *La Succession du pape Félix IV.*, Rome, 1884; J. Langen, *Geschichte der römischen Kirche von Leo I. bis Nikolaus I.*, p. 305, Bonn, 1885; R. Baxmann, *Die Politik der Päpste von Gregor I. bis auf Gregor VII.*, i, 20 sqq., Elberfeld, 1868; Jaffé, *Regesta*, i, 111; Schaff, *Christian Church*, iii, 326, 869; Neander, *Christian Church*, ii, 711; Hefele, *Conciliengeschichte*, ii, 737-742, Eng. transl., iv, 165, 167, 171 sqq.; Bower, *Popes*, i, 331-333.

Boniface III: Pope 607. He was a Roman by birth, previously a deacon and *apocrisiarius* at the court of Constantinople, to which he had been sent by Gregory the Great in 603. Apparently he was still there when the election took place, as nearly a year elapsed between the death of his predecessor and his consecration (Feb. 19, 607). As (in modern language) nuncio at Constantinople, he had apparently maintained friendly relations with the usurper Phocas, which would account for the favorable decision made by the latter on a point of great importance to the papal claims. One of the commissions given to him by Gregory was the settlement of the strife over the title of "universal bishop" claimed by the patriarch of Constantinople, John the Faster; Gregory did not claim it for himself, but he was unwilling that it should be borne by another. The *Liber pontificalis*, Paulus Diaconus, and Bede all assert that Phocas recognized Rome as *caput omnium ecclesiarum*. Though the fact is not denied, it is to be regarded rather as a triumph of papal politics, which did not disdain the alliance of a base and criminal ruler, than as a historical justification of the claims of Rome. Boniface died Nov. 12, 607. (A. HAUCK.)

BIBLIOGRAPHY: *Liber pontificalis*, ed. Duchesne, i, 316, Paris, 1886; Paulus Diaconus, *Hist. Langobardorum*, iv, 36, in *MGH, Script. rer. Langob.*, ed. G. Waitz, Hanover, 1878, Eng. transl., p. 177, Philadelphia, 1907; F. Gregorovius, *Geschichte der Stadt Rom*, ii, 102, Stuttgart, 1876, Eng. transl., London, 1900; J. Langen, *Geschichte der römischen Kirche . . . bis Nikolaus I.*, p. 500, Bonn, 1885; Bower, *Popes*, i, 425–427; Mann, *Popes*, I, i, 259–262.

Boniface IV: Pope 608–615. He was the successor of Boniface III after an interregnum of ten months. He kept up the same friendly relations with Phocas, from whom he acquired the Pantheon in Rome, built as a heathen temple, and transformed it into a church. When Heraclius, who overthrew Phocas in 610, was endeavoring to find a way to reconciliation with the Monophysites, Boniface seems to have approved of his plans; which probably accounts for a letter of Columban (q.v.) written from Bobbio (c. 613), informing him that people call him a receiver and protector of heretics who deny the double nature of Christ, and warning him that his power will remain only so long as he maintains the true faith. Boniface died May 25, 615. (A. HAUCK.)

BIBLIOGRAPHY: *Liber pontificalis*, ed. Duchesne, i, 317, Paris, 1886; Jaffé, *Regesta*, i, 220; Paulus Diaconus, *Historia Langobardorum*, iv, 36, in *MGH, Script. rer. Langob.*, ed. G. Waitz, Hanover, 1878, Eng. transl., p. 178, Philadelphia, 1907; Bede, *Hist. eccl.*, ii, 4, ed. Plummer, vol. i, p. 88, Oxford, 1896; R. Baxmann, *Die Politik der Päpste*, i, 150, Elberfeld, 1868; F. Gregorovius, *Geschichte der Stadt Rom*, ii, 102, Stuttgart, 1876, Eng. transl., London, 1900; J. Langen, *Geschichte der römischen Kirche . . . bis Nikolaus I.*, p. 501, Bonn, 1885; Neander, *Christian Church*, iii, 32, 34, 134; Bower, *Popes*, i, 428–429; Mann, *Popes*, I, i, 268.

Boniface V: Pope 619–625. The *Liber pontificalis* tells that he was a Neapolitan, that he distinguished himself as pope by his love of peace and kindness, and that he issued a number of decrees affecting the functions of the different orders of the clergy. Bede and William of Malmesbury mention several letters addressed to English personages; the most important is that preserved by the latter, a letter to Justus, archbishop of Canterbury (625), confirming for all time the position of his diocese as the metropolitan see of Britain, and extending his powers. Boniface died Oct. 25, 625. (A. HAUCK.)

BIBLIOGRAPHY: *Liber pontificalis*, ed. Duchesne, i, 321, Paris, 1886; Jaffé, *Regesta*, i, 222; Bede, *Hist. eccl.*, ii, 7, ed. Plummer, vol. i, pp. 93–95, Oxford, 1896; F. Gregorovius, *Geschichte der Stadt Rom*, ii, 122, Stuttgart, 1876, Eng. transl., London, 1902; Mann, *Popes*, I, i, 294; Bower, *Popes*, i, 430–432.

Boniface VI: Pope 896. He was the son of Hadrian, a Roman, and was elevated to the papal throne in April or May, 896, by a popular movement, on the death of Formosus, although he had twice been deposed from his spiritual functions by John VIII on charges affecting his moral character, and apparently was never canonically restored. He maintained his position only for fifteen days, as the party hostile to Formosus carried through the election of Stephen VI, who drove him out. Others say that he died fifteen days after his election. (A. HAUCK.)

BIBLIOGRAPHY: Jaffé, *Regesta*, i, 439; *Annales Fuldenses*, ed. G. H. Pertz, in *MGH, Script.*, i, 412, Hanover, 1826; R. Baxmann, *Die Politik der Päpste*, ii, 70, Elberfeld, 1869; J. Langen, *Geschichte der römischen Kirche . . . bis Gregor VII.*, p. 303, Bonn, 1892; Bower, *Popes*, ii, 229.

Boniface VII: Pope 974, 984–985. After the downfall of Benedict VI, Crescentius, the leader of the nobles, caused the election of the deacon Boniface, called Franco (June, 974). One of his first acts was to order his predecessor to be put to death. But he was able to hold his own only for six weeks, after which he fled to Constantinople. Here he remained for more than nine years—or as long as Otto II lived to protect the popes set up by him, Benedict VII and John XIV. Otto died Dec. 7, 983, and the fugitive Boniface immediately asserted his claims. He reappeared in Rome, and in the following April defeated John XIV, imprisoned him in the castle of Sant'Angelo, and had him either poisoned or starved to death there. Eleven months later, this "horrible monster" (as a contemporary calls him) met a like fate, dying, it seems probable, by assassination in the summer of 985; his body was mutilated and insulted by the infuriated populace. Gfrörer's hypothesis that his murder was caused by the empress Theophano has no support in the original authorities. (A. HAUCK.)

BIBLIOGRAPHY: Jaffé, *Regesta*, i, 485; Herimannus Augiensis, *Chronicon*, ed. G. H. Pertz, in *MGH, Script.*, v, 116 sqq., Hanover, 1844; Gerbert, *Acta concilii Remensis*, ed. G. H. Pertz, *MGH, Script.*, iii, 672, ib. 1839; L. C. Ferucci, *Investigazioni . . . su la persona ed il pontificato di Bonif. VII.*, Lugo, 1856 (attempts to clear Boniface of the charges); J. M. Watterich, *Pontificum Romanorum vitæ*, i, 66, Leipsic, 1862; J. Langen, *Geschichte der römischen Kirche . . . bis Gregor VII.*, Bonn, 1892.

Boniface VIII (Benedetto Gaetani): Pope 1294–1303. He was born at Anagni [c. 1235], and probably studied civil and canon law at Paris. He began his ecclesiastical career as canon of Todi, held benefices in Lyons and Rome, and became notary of the Curia. Martin IV made him a cardinal in 1281, and under Nicholas IV and Celestine V he was one of the most prominent members of the sacred college, being employed in the most varied missions. He encouraged Celestine V in his project of retirement to ascetic seclusion, and even drew up the formula of abdication, by which he was to profit; for, less than a fortnight after Celestine had laid down the papal dignity, it was bestowed upon his adviser (Dec. 24, 1294). Even before his consecration, the new pope asserted his prerogatives by revoking many appointments of his two predecessors, deposing archbishops and bishops appointed by Celestine without the consent of the cardinals, and leaving Naples for Rome with all his court, in spite of the efforts of Charles II to detain him there. He was consecrated and crowned in St. Peter's, Jan. 23, 1295, and soon took an active part in the conflicts of the time, offering to mediate between Genoa and Venice in February. Sicily occupied him next; it had freed itself from

Policy and Successes in Italy.

French domination in 1282, chosen Peter III of Aragon as king, and thus dissolved the feudal connection with Rome. Peter's son and heir, James II, showed himself ready to abandon Sicily after Aragon had fallen to him by the death of his elder brother. Another brother, however—Frederick—stepped in and assumed the Sicilian crown, and neither repeated papal anathemas nor an armed league against him could make him renounce it; in 1302 he obtained favorable terms of peace, and in 1303 papal recognition. Boniface also intervened in the strife between the Blacks and Whites of Florence, in favor of the former, and sent a legate to Tuscany. From the sojourn of Dante in Rome as the ambassador of the *Bianchi* dates the bitter hatred which he displays for Boniface VIII. In agreement with the *Neri*, Boniface brought Charles of Valois to Tuscany in 1301 as governor; but his five months' rule accomplished nothing but the alienation of the last sympathizers of the pope there. Boniface had real power only in the south of Italy and some central cities. Charles II of Naples became the obedient servant of the Curia, while Pisa, Velletri, Orvieto, and Terracina chose Boniface as their ruler. But a hostile party was forming in Rome, led by the two Colonna cardinals, who disapproved of the close alliance with Charles II and secretly supported the pretensions of the house of Aragon in Sicily. In 1297 the pope stripped them of all their ecclesiastical dignities; and on the same day they formally renounced their allegiance to him, declaring Celestine's abdication to have been invalid and appealing to a general council. Boniface deprived the whole family of their possessions, one after another, and soon Palestrina alone held out against the papal army. The Colonna submitted in 1298; but when, the next year, Boniface destroyed Palestrina, contrary, they asserted, to a promise of ultimate restitution, they took up arms once more against him. Again they were defeated, and their estates divided between their enemies, the Orsini and the Gaetani.

Denmark, Hungary, and Poland.

Soon after his accession, Boniface became involved in complications beyond the boundaries of Italy. Eric VIII of Denmark had imprisoned the archbishop of Lund in 1294, really to extort money from him, but nominally on the ground of conspiracy. In 1295 Boniface sent a legate to demand his release on pain of excommunication and interdict. These penalties were imposed in 1296, but Eric held out until 1302, though even then the pope did not succeed in restoring the deposed archbishop. In the contest for the throne of Hungary, on the ground that he had been "set over princes and kingdoms, to put down iniquity," and that Hungary belonged on special grounds to the Apostolic See, he claimed the deciding voice; in 1300 he sent Charles Robert, grandson of Mary of Sicily, to the Hungarians as their king; but they first clung to Andrew III, and after his death elected the son of Wenceslaus II of Bohemia as Ladislaus V. At the moment of Boniface's death, Wenceslaus was preparing to unite with Philip the Fair against him, and his interests clashed with the pope's in another place as well—in Poland, which had elected Wenceslaus in 1300, to take the place of the deposed King Ladislaus. Again Boniface claimed suzerain rights supported the exiled king, who had sought his aid and forbade Wenceslaus to assume the crown without the papal sanction; but, as in Hungary, his words were not heeded.

Germany.

He met with somewhat greater success in Germany. The undertaking given by Adolf of Nassau in the Treaty of Nuremberg (Aug. 21, 1294), to support Edward I of England against Philip IV, displeased the pope, who wished to see peace between France and England. He wrote to Adolf forbidding him to take up arms, and reproaching him for not having announced his election to him. Adolf returned a submissive answer, and received some privileges in return, but the papal legates were bidden still to insist on peace. He even went so far as to impose a year's truce on all three kings (1295), which, at its expiration, he renewed for another two years. In 1296 he commanded them to submit their differences to his decision; but only Adolf sent his representatives to Rome. On June 27, 1298, Boniface decided that neither Philip nor Adolf must overstep his boundaries, and that these must be restored where they had been violated. Adolf never heard of this decision; four days before it was rendered, he had been deposed by the electoral princes, and on July 2 he fell in battle against his rival Albert of Austria. Boniface took a lofty tone with Albert, summoning him to appear within six months and submit his claims to the throne, since it belonged to the pope to examine the person chosen king of the Romans, and reject him if unsuitable. Albert delayed until he made his position secure in Germany, and then sent his ambassadors (Mar., 1302) with liberal promises and the required evidence. Boniface needed his help against France too badly to raise any objection, and recognized him as king of the Romans and future emperor. Albert, in return, renounced his alliance with Philip, and made all possible theoretical and practical concessions.

England.

But a more stubborn obstacle was found in the king and parliament of England. When Edward I had conquered Scotland for the second time in 1298, Boniface claimed that country also as a fief of the Holy See, and summoned Edward before his tribunal for having ventured to lay hands upon it. Edward laid the bull before Parliament in 1301; the reply of the English people was that Scotland had never been a papal fief, that their king should not answer the summons, and that, even if he wished to, they would not permit it. On May 7 Edward informed the pope that he would not give up Scotland; and Boniface was obliged to be content with the answer, because in the mean time the memorable conflict with France had broken out.

Philip the Fair was a ruler after the very pattern of Macchiavelli's later description, knowing no law but self-interest, and sticking at nothing to accomplish his ends. His relations with Boniface had at first been friendly, but he was probably offended by the pope's above-mentioned interference with his designs against England. When in 1296 the clergy of both France and England complained to Boniface of the taxes laid upon them by their sovereigns for warlike purposes, he answered by the bull *Clericis laicos* (Feb. 25, 1296). It opened with the offensive assertion that the laity had always been and still were hostile to the clergy, and proceeded to forbid all princes to tax the clergy of their dominions without papal sanction, under pain of excommunication. Edward, though at first protesting, declared in 1297 that no further tax should be laid upon the clergy without their consent; but Philip responded by forbidding all exportation of gold and silver, coined or uncoined, from France (Aug., 1296). This cut off so large a portion of the papal revenue that Boniface modified his attitude in the bull *Ineffabilis amoris* (Sept. 25), and yielded more completely in three briefs (Feb. and July, 1297) extremely conciliatory in tone; in the same spirit he completed the canonization of Louis IX in August, and the discord seemed in a fair way to be removed. But it was not long in breaking out again. Philip had welcomed to his court some of the exiled Colonna family, and had lent a willing ear to their unmeasured abuse of the pope, which did not spare his moral character. The king's misuse of the *droit de régale* (see RÉGALE), on the other hand, had been giving increasing provocation to the pope since 1299. An open rupture came in 1301; and by that time both contestants had increased their pretensions and were ready to wage a more bitter war than ever. Boniface chose to send as legate to Paris a Frenchman, Bernard de Saisset, bishop of Pamiers, who was for several reasons *persona non grata* at the French court, and his haughty tone at this time made him no better liked. Philip refused to see him; and, then, when he had returned to Pamiers, brought him back to Paris, and had him tried and condemned on a charge of treason and lese-majesty. On Dec. 5, 1301, Boniface demanded that his ambassador should immediately be set free to come to Rome; and at the same time he summoned the principal French churchmen and jurists to assemble in Rome Nov. 1, 1302, to take counsel with him in the difficulties of the French question. Notifying Philip of this, amid the most passionate reproaches, in the bull *Ausculta fili*, he commanded him also to appear in person or by proxy at this assembly; the assertions were repeated that God had set the Vicar of Christ over princes and kingdoms, thus giving him charge to ordain what might be needed for the removal of scandals and for the welfare of the kingdom of France. To meet this, Philip summoned his estates to Paris for Apr. 10, 1302, and laid before them not the bull *Ausculta fili*, but a document purporting to be the pope's utterance, which far surpassed even the real one in matter of offense. The estates, stirred up by this, voted to stand by the king. Toward the end of the year, Philip notified the pope that he would have none of his arbitration in the struggle with England; and Boniface now urged Edward to war instead of peace. Peace, however, was made in 1303. Meantime, as a result of the synod which the pope opened on Oct. 30, 1302, at which not a few French prelates were present in spite of Philip, the bull *Unam sanctam* was drawn up, asserting in the most definite terms the theory of "the two swords," and the necessity to salvation of submission to the pope. Some futile attempts at conciliation took place in the early part of 1303, but Philip was declared on Apr. 13 to have rendered himself liable to excommunication. Two months later, the king assembled his nobles, prelates, and jurists, and his answer came in the form of a definite accusation against Boniface under twenty-four separate heads of the most appalling nature. Impressed by this, the assembly resolved to appeal to a general council against him; but since he would have to be forced to attend it, the collection of funds for this purpose was begun. William of Nogaret, the king's vice-chancellor, went to Italy and struck up an alliance with Sciarra Colonna, who had the wrongs of his family to avenge. They enlisted a number of the nobles of the Campagna, and used money freely, winning adherents even among Boniface's fellow townsmen of Anagni, where he was then holding his court. He had resolved to make formal publication of the anathema against Philip on Sept. 8; but early on the morning of the 7th, William and his adherents, a few hundred strong, gained an entrance into the town, penetrated even into the sleeping apartments of Boniface, and when he refused all concessions made him a prisoner in his own palace. On the 9th the citizens rose and liberated him; Nogaret and Sciarra Colonna were forced to flee, while Boniface returned to Rome Sept. 25. But, worn out by the long strife, he died Oct. 11.

Character and Achievements of Boniface.

His defeat is to be seen not in the circumstances of his captivity and his death, but in the fact that the spiritual weapons he wielded proved utterly unequal to the conquest of the aroused national feeling of France. The national spirit showed itself more powerful than the ecclesiastical. This defeat inflicted a staggering blow upon the authority of the papacy. Yet Boniface was no ordinary man. Though he was between seventy and eighty when he became pope, he showed no trace of the weakness of age; his will was unbending, his mind clear and logical. But his whole heart was set on power. In some ways he reminds of Gregory VII, and he could no more hope to escape conflicts than could the unflinching Hildebrand. But he did not in the conflict show the moral loftiness of Hildebrand—to say nothing of that of such men as Nicholas I and Innocent III. Nor is his personality without moral flaws. He had no scruple in using the funds he had raised for the recovery of the Holy Land in his own wars; nor is the reproach unfounded that he used the privileges of his position to surround his own family with princely splendor. When he strove for peace, as between England and France, his determining motive was plainly the desire to show himself the supreme arbiter of nations; when he had nothing to gain, he was ready enough to set them against each other, as he set Albert I and

Edward I against Philip. Fair criticism must, however, reject the accusations of debauchery entirely, since they rest on no trustworthy testimony; and quite as groundless is the charge of heresy brought against him by his foes. Clement V had good foundation for the doubtful praise which he bestows upon Boniface when he calls him a destroyer of heretics; for he not only confirmed, but even strengthened the laws passed against heresy by Frederick II. He had a great influence on the development of the canon law by the issue in 1298 of his so-called *Liber sextus*, —a continuation of the five books which Gregory IX had put together in 1234; it contains his own decrees as well as those of his predecessors since Gregory's time. It must be mentioned to his credit that he erected higher schools at Avignon and at Fermo in the March of Ancona, modeled after the University of Bologna, for the study of theology, civil and canon law, medicine, and the liberal arts; and he has a special title to the gratitude of Rome for the refounding of the Roman University, originally established by Charles of Anjou in 1265. (A. HAUCK.)

BIBLIOGRAPHY: Walter de Hemingbburgh, *Chronicon de gestis regum Angliæ*, ed. H. C. Hamilton, pp. 39 sqq., London, 1848; Rishanger, *Chronica*, ed. H. T. Riley, pp. 145 sqq., 483 sqq., ib. 1865; *Annales Parmenses majores*, in *MGH, Script.*, xviii (1863), 715 sqq.; *Chronicon Colmar*, ib. xvii (1861), 263; Guilelmus de Nangiaco, *Chronicon*, ib. xxvi (1882), 647 sqq. The bulls *Clericis laicos* and *Unam sanctam* are translated in Thatcher and McNeal, *Source Book*, pp. 311–313, 314–317, and other relevant documents on pp. 276, 313; the bulls are also in Henderson, *Documents*, pp. 435–437; *Unam sanctam* is in Robinson, *European History*, i, 346–348; the *Clericis laicos* is also in Gee and Hardy, *Documents*, pp. 87–88; the Lat. text is in Reich, *Documents*, pp. 191–195. Valuable for sources is also G. Digard, M. Faucon, and A. Thomas, *Les Régistres de Boniface VIII. Recueil des bulles de ce pape . d'après les MSS. originaux des archives du Vatican*, 5 vols., Paris, 1884–90; T. H. Finke, *Aus den Tagen Bonifaz VIII.*, Münster, 1902.

For Boniface's life and activities consult: L. Tosti, *Storia di Bonifazio VIII.*, 2 vols., Monte Cassino, 1846; Jorry, *Histoire du pape Boniface VIII.*, Plancy, 1850; W. Drumann, *Geschichte Bonifacius VIII.*, 2 vols., Königsberg, 1852 (critical); A. von Reumont, *Geschichte der Stadt Rom*, ii, 618, Berlin, 1868; A. Potthast, *Regesta pontificum Romanorum*, ii, 1923–2024, 2133, Berlin, 1875; F. Gregorovius, *Geschichte der Stadt Rom*, v, 502, Stuttgart, 1878, Eng. transl., London, 1898; W. Wattenbach, *Geschichte des römischen Papsttums*, 216 sqq., Berlin, 1876; Balan, *Il Processo di Bonifazio VIII.*, Rome, 1881; F. Rocquain, *La Papauté au moyen âge. . Boniface VIII.*, Paris, 1881; idem, *Philippe le Bel et la bulle Ausculta fili*, in *Bibliothèque de l'école des chartes*, 1883, pp. 393–394; B. Jungmann, *Dissertationes selectæ*, vol. vi, Regensburg, 1886; J. Berchtold, *Die Bulle Unam sanctam*, Munich, 1887; W. Martens, *Das Vaticanum und Bonifaz VIII.*, Freiburg, 1888; Neander, *Christian Church*, iv, 67, 632, v, 1–13 and passim; Hefele, *Conciliengeschichte*, vi, 281 sqq.; Bower, *Popes*, iii, 43–55, 64; R. Scholz, *Die Publizistik zur Zeit Bonifaz VIII.*, Leipsic, 1903.

On his relations to the various European states consult: F. C. Dahlmann, *Geschichte von Dänemark*, i, 425 sqq., Hamburg, 1840; R. Pauli, *Geschichte von England*, vol. iv, Gotha, 1855; E. Boutaric, *La France sous Philippe le Bel*, pp. 88 sqq., Paris, 1861; A. Baillet, *Histoire des démêlés du pape Boniface VIII. avec Philippe le Bel*, Paris, 1818; E. Engelmann, *Der Anspruch der Päpste auf Konfirmation bei den deutschen Königswahlen*, Breslau, 1886; Fessler, *Geschichte von Ungarn*, i, 451 sqq., ii, 3 sqq., Leipsic, 1867–69; J. B. Sägmüller, *Die Thätigkeit und Stellung der Cardinäle bis Bonifaz VIII.*, Freiburg, 1896; J. Caro, *Geschichte Polens*, Gotha, 1863.

Boniface IX (Pietro Tomacelli): Pope 1389–1404. He came of a noble Neapolitan family, and was made a cardinal by Urban VI, whom he succeeded Nov. 2, 1389. He is said to have been judicious, affable, and pious, but without learning or knowledge of affairs. His principal aim was the restoration of the papal authority in Rome and the States of the Church, for which he labored not unsuccessfully. The Romans, it is true, expelled him from the city in 1392, but fearful that he might fix his residence permanently elsewhere, they recalled him in the following year. He returned on condition of the surrender of a great part of the civic liberties; and another rising in 1398 gave him the opportunity to limit them still further. He was fortunate also in regard to Naples, where things were in a condition very unfavorable to the papacy, owing to the confused policy of Urban VI. Clement VII and Louis II of Anjou thought the time had come to make a thorough conquest of the kingdom, but Boniface made a close alliance with King Ladislaus and finally gained a complete victory over the French, holding Naples in the Roman obedience. By the aid of his political influence, Boniface hoped to succeed in ending the great schism, at first depending on the German king Wenceslaus, whom he invited to Rome for coronation as emperor; but matters were in too critical a state in Germany for him to leave. An appeal to Charles VI of France in 1392 to abandon his allegiance to Clement had no good result; nor had a similar attempt in Castile. The hope of accommodation raised by the death of Clement VII (Sept. 16, 1394) was destroyed by the action of the Avignon cardinals, who elected Benedict XIII. In the contests resulting in the deposition of Wenceslaus and the attempt to put the count palatine Rupert in his place, Boniface wavered from side to side, and only expressed his willingness to recognize Rupert in 1403 from a fear that he would be thrown into the arms of the king of France. Boniface acquired an unenviable reputation for avarice, nepotism, and simoniacal transactions. He died Oct. 1, 1404. (A. HAUCK.)

BIBLIOGRAPHY: Some of the sources for a history of Boniface IX are the following: The bulls are in O. Raynaldus, *Annales ecclesiastici*, ed. Baronius, continued by A. Theiner, Paris, 1864 sqq.; the *Diplomata* are in *Monumenta vaticana historiam Hungariæ illustrantia*, vol. iii, Budapest, 1888; Dietrich von Nieheim, *De Schismate*, book ii, chap. 6 sqq., ed. G. Erler, pp. 129 sqq., Leipsic, 1880; Gobelinus Persona, *Cosmodromium*, in H. Meibom, *Rerum Germanicarum*, i, 316 sqq., Helmstadt, 1688; and a *Vita* in L. A. Muratori, *Rerum Italicarum script.*, III, ii, 830, 25 vols., Milan, 1723–38. Consult further: M. Jansen, *Papst Bonifatius IX.*, Freiburg, 1904; *Historia de Bonifacio nono*, Venice, 1613; N. Valois, *La France et le grand schisme*, ii, 157, Paris, 1896; Creighton, *Papacy*, i, 111–183; Pastor, *Popes*, i, passim; Neander, *Christian Church*, vol. v, passim; Bower, *Popes*, iii, 143–152; Hefele, *Conciliengeschichte*, vi, 812.

BONIFACE, SAINT: The apostle of the Germans; b. at Crediton (8 m. n.w. of Exeter), Devonshire, between 675 and 683; d. a martyr on the banks of the Borne near Dokkum (13 m. n.e. of Leeuwarden), in Friesland, June 5, 755. He was an Englishman of a distinguished family of Wessex, and was originally named Winfrid or Wynfrith. His studies were begun at the monastery of Adescancastre (Exeter?), and continued at Nutshalling or Nursling, near Winchester. Here he won distinction for learning and practical wisdom, and at an early age was made master of the monastic school.

Disregarding brilliant prospects at home, from 717 Boniface gave himself to missionary work on the Continent. After a brief effort in Friesland—the field of his countryman Willibrord (q.v.)—he went to Rome and received a commission from the pope (Gregory II) as missionary to Central Germany. He began his labor in Thuringia and Hessia, the easternmost of the lands of the Franks, where he found not only heathen but Christians and priests who knew nothing and wanted to know nothing of Roman discipline and order. They were probably converts and disciples of Iro-Scottish and British monks, who had long been laboring among the tribes from the Rhine to the Saale and southward to the Alps (see Celtic Church in Britain and Ireland, II, 2, § 3, III, 2, § 2). For two or three years Boniface's activity was diverted to Friesland, but then he returned to the Franks, and, with the help of two landed proprietors, founded a central settlement for himself and companions at Amöneburg on the Ohm in Hessia. His success was great and led to a summons to Rome from Gregory II. There he was consecrated bishop and swore fidelity to the canons of the Church; he was charged to be on his guard against heretical priests and anti-Roman bishops. About 724 he returned to Germany, provided with letters of recommendation to the major domus, Charles Martel, to the clergy, chieftains, and people. Charles Martel granted him protection, and, after confirming recent converts in Hessia, and felling the sacred oak of Thor near Geismar, Boniface went eastward into Thuringia, and established its first monastery at Ohrdruf. He founded many churches, converted the heathen, expelled the anti-Roman priests, and in ten years had won a new province for the Church and the pope.

Early Missionary Work.

Being promoted to the dignity of archbishop, Boniface organized his Church by founding the sees of Würzburg, Buraburg, and Erfurt, and by building monasteries and nunneries, which he filled with monks and nuns from England and endowed and improved with the help of English money. Bavaria next claimed his attention. Anti-Roman influence was strong there and among the neighboring Alemanni (q.v.), but, with the authorization of Gregory III, in a few years, Boniface placed men in sympathy with Rome in the sees of Regensburg, Passau, Salzburg, and Freising, and substituted the Benedictine rules for those of Columban in the monasteries. On the death of Charles Martel (741), his sons Karlman and Pepin, who had been brought up under monkish influence, succeeded to his power. In 742 Karlman called upon the papal legate to regulate the affairs of the Church for the East Franks. Under the guiding influence of Boniface two synods were held and measures were adopted concerning the monastic and scholastic discipline, the restoration of church estates which had been lost, the introduction of Roman marriage laws, celibacy of the clergy, the expulsion of the old British itinerant priests and bishops, the extirpation of remnants of heathenism, the establishment of the hierarchical order, and the like. There was some opposition from the nobles, certain of the bishops, and the people, who were attached to their old customs, but at court and in the Council the adversaries of the "reformation of the Church" lost all authority.

Organization.

In 744 Pepin followed the example of his brother. A synod was held at Soissons, and Boniface was given a free hand, notwithstanding resistance from the Frankish clergy. For a long time, however, he was unable to alienate the people from their old priests and bishops, such as Adalbert and Clement (qq.v.). A general Frankish synod in 745 published new agenda for both divisions of the country and promised Boniface the metropolitan see at Cologne. In 747 the Frankish bishops with Boniface at the head signed in due form a bill of submission in which they acknowledged the papal rights, laws, and power, and promised obedience and faithfulness. By this action the bond between the Frankish empire and Rome was sealed; the "Prince of the Apostles" was to be head and master in the countries north of the Alps. Pope Zacharias had every reason to be grateful to his legate. Instead of Cologne, Boniface received Mainz as his see. Here he was near his old mission field in Hessia and Thuringia, and from Mainz he could direct the building of his favorite foundation, the abbey of Fulda (q.v.). Worldly affairs now occupied him little. After the death of Willibrord he desired strongly to continue the Friesian mission. In 754 he spent some time in Friesland. The next year he again descended the Rhine with a large following and pitched his camp on the little river Borne, expecting the newly baptized would come thither for confirmation. But the camp was attacked by night by a band of heathen and Boniface and his entire company were massacred. He is buried at Fulda. An English synod shortly after his death proclaimed him patron of the English Church by the side of Gregory the Great and Augustine. Pius IX in 1875 ordered to invoke his name because of troubles in Germany and England. Many churches in Germany are dedicated to him. [A number of writings have been attributed to Boniface. Those most commonly regarded as genuine are letters, a collection of ecclesiastical statutes, a Latin poem called *Ænigmata de virtutibus*, and several shorter poems.] A. Werner.

Archbishop.

Bibliography: *S. Bonifacii opera quæ extant omnia*, ed. J. A. Giles, 2 vols., London, 1844, contains, besides the genuine and supposed works of Boniface, his life, written within ten years of his death by Willibald, a presbyter of Mainz. The works, Willibald's life, and a life by Othlo, a monk of St. Emmeram's at Regensburg, written at Fulda between 1062 and 1066, are in *MPL*, lxxxix. Better editions are: Of the letters, Willibald's life, the so-called *Passio S. Bonifatii* (11th century), and extracts from Othlo and a life by an unknown writer of Utrecht in *Monumenta Moguntina*, ed. P. Jaffé, *Bibliotheca rer.*

Germ., vol. iii. 1866; the biographical matter also issued separately with title, *Vitæ S. Bonifatii*, Berlin, 1866; cf. also *Vitæ S. Bonifatii*, ed. W. Levison, Hanover, 1905; of the letters, ed. E. Dümmler, in *MGH*, *Epist.*, iii (1892), *Epistolæ Merovingici et Carolini ævi*, i; of the poems, ed. idem, in *MGH*, *Poet. Lat. ævi Car.*, i (1881), pp. 1–23; of Willibald's life, ed. A. Nürnberger, Breslau, 1895, and, with Othlo's prologue, in *MGH*, *Script.*, ii (1829). For the letters consult F. Loofs, *Zur Chronologie der auf die fränkischen Synoden des heiligen Bonifatius bezüglichen Briefe der bonifazischen Briefsammlung*, Leipsic, 1881; G. Pfahler, *Die bonifatianische Briefsammlung chronologisch geordnet*, Heilbronn, 1882.

For modern accounts in German from the Roman Catholic standpoint, consult: J. C. A. Seiters, *Bonifacius, . . . nach seinem Leben und Wirken geschildert*, Mainz, 1845; G. Pfahler, *St. Bonifacius und seine Zeit*, Regensburg, 1880; F. J. von Buss, *Winfred Bonifacius*, ed. R. von Scherer, Graz, 1880. From the Protestant standpoint: J. P. Müller, *Bonifacius. Eene kerkhistorische Studie*, 2 vols., Amsterdam, 1869–70; A. Werner, *Bonifacius.. und die Romanisirung von Mitteleuropa*, Leipsic, 1875; O. Fischer, *Bonifatius der Apostel der Deutschen*, ib. 1881; J. H. A. Ebrard, *Bonifatius, der Zerstörer des columbanischen Kirchenthums auf dem Festlande*, Gütersloh, 1882, cf. his *Iroschottische Missionskirche des 6ten–8ten Jahrhunderts*, ib. 1873; G. Traub, *Bonifatius. Ein Lebensbild*, Leipsic, 1884. For life in Eng. consult: G. W. Cox, *Life of Boniface*, London, 1853; Mrs. Hope, *Boniface and the Conversion of Germany*, ib. 1872; G. F. Maclear, *Apostles of Mediæval Europe*, pp. 110–128, London, 1888; I. G. Smith, *Boniface*, in *Fathers for English Readers*, ib. 1896; J. M. Williamson, *Life and Times of St. Boniface*, ib. 1904. Consult also: H. Hahn, *Bonifaz und Lul*, Leipsic, 1883; G. Woelbing, *Die mittelalterlichen Lebensbeschreibungen des Bonifatius untersucht*, ib. 1883; Moeller, *Christian Church*, ii, 74–83; Schaff, *Christian Church*, iv, 92–100; *DCB*, i, 324–327; *DNB*, v, 346–350; Neander, *Christian Church*, iii, 46–96 et passim.

BONIFATIUS-VEREIN ("Boniface Society"): A Roman Catholic society of Germany, having as its object "to promote the spiritual interests of Catholics living in Protestant parts of Germany, and the maintenance of schools" (by-laws, § 1). The tendency toward freer relations between different confessions and shifting of confessional connections in Germany in the earlier years of the nineteenth century aroused the anxiety of the Church of Rome. According to a statement in the Ultramontane *Münchener historisch-politische Blätter* (lxviii, 45) the Roman Church lost between 1802 and 1870 more than 500,000 souls in South Germany, whereas the loss in North Germany between 1802 and 1850 was estimated at one million. The "Francis Xavier Society," which had its headquarters at Lyons in France, and properly speaking was a missionary society, took care of the "missions" in Germany as far as possible; but until 1848 no Roman Catholic church or school could be established in Germany without the consent of the government. These restrictions were done away with in 1848, and when the third convention of Roman Catholics met at Regensburg, Oct. 4, 1849, at the suggestion of Döllinger, at that time an ardent champion of Rome, and of Count Josef von Stolberg, son of the famous convert Frederick Leopold von Stolberg, the Bonifatius-Verein was founded. Paderborn was chosen as the center of operation. Pius IX approved the society, Apr. 21, 1852, and Leo XIII favored the priests belonging to it with indulgences, Mar. 15, 1901. In Bavaria the society was not favorably received at first on account of similar societies already existing, and in North Germany it seemed to be a failure by 1853. But after 1857, owing to the exertions of Bishop Martin of Paderborn and of Alban Stolz, it progressed rapidly and in 1899 celebrated the golden jubilee of its successful activity.

The society obtains the means necessary for carrying on its work in various ways: (1) from collections in the churches; (2) from private persons who obligate themselves to pay for a number of years the minister's salary in a certain congregation; (3) from donations to a permanent endowment fund; (4) from societies which collect seemingly worthless objects, as cigar ends, corks, and the like; the income from these societies, used particularly for orphan asylums and like institutions, amounted from 1885 to 1891 to 1,190,539 marks; (5) from the profits of the Bonifatius printing-house and the Bonifatius second-hand book-stall at Paderborn; (6) from periodicals and pamphlets; (7) from academical Bonifatius societies, which built the Catholic church at Greifswald; (8) from societies of a like character, as the "Boniface Society of the Catholic Noblemen of Silesia," the "Boniface Society of Catholic Ladies for Church Vestments and Furniture," and others. The aggregate receipts from all these sources between 1849 and 1899 were 36,000,000 marks; and between 1849 and 1901 more than 29,000,000 marks were expended for 2,240 stations. In 1902 the revenues aggregated 442,000 marks, and expenditures 310,000 marks.

The territory of the Bonifatius-Verein comprises Germany, Austria with Bosnia and Herzegovina, Switzerland, Denmark, and Luxembourg. In Germany special attention is paid to the Protestant parts of Prussia, above all Berlin; Saxony, Brunswick, and Mecklenburg are also regarded as missionary fields. In Bavaria, Nuremberg, formerly wholly Protestant, is especially an object of the propaganda in order to connect the northern and southern parts of Bavaria. C. FEY.

BIBLIOGRAPHY: A. J. Kleffner and F. W. Woker, *Der Bonifacius-Verein. Seine Geschichte, seine Arbeit und sein Arbeitsfeld, 1849–1899*, 2 parts, Paderborn, 1899; *Bonifaciusblatt*, ib. 1853 sqq.; *Schlesisches Bonifacius-Vereins-Blatt*, Breslau, 1860 sqq.

BONI HOMINES: A name borne by several monastic brotherhoods, particularly by the Grammontensians (see GRAMMONT, ORDER OF), the *Fratres saccati*, or Sack Brethren (q.v.), and an order of canons regular founded in Portugal by John Vicenza (d. 1463), physician and professor at Lisbon, afterward bishop of Lamego, and later bishop of Vizeu. In 1425 Vicenza and his followers, who had made pilgrimages throughout Portugal, received the Benedictine cloister of San Salvador in Villar de Frades. They adopted the dress and statutes of the canons regular of San Giorgio in Alga, at Venice, and received papal confirmation under this title. In another house near Lisbon they received the name Canons Regular of the Congregation of St. John the Evangelist. The *Boni homines* of San Salvador were later included under this title. They gradually attained a strength of fourteen houses in Portugal, and also maintained missions in India and Ethiopia.

After the Minims (q.v.) had come into possession of the house of the Grammontensians at Vincennes they, too, came to be called *bons hommes.* Even at an earlier date it seems that the Minims in Paris had been contemptuously called *bons hommes.* The same name was also appropriated by certain heretical sects, for instance, by the Cathari (see New Manicheans) and by the Brethren of the Free Spirit. In Florence, in the thirteenth century, the twelve men elected to restore order after the withdrawal of the Ghibellines were called *buoni uomini*, likewise the overseers of the thirteen city districts in Rome in the fourteenth century.

BONIZO (BONITHO): Bishop of Sutri; b. at Cremona c. 1045; d. at Piacenza July 14, probably 1090. As a young cleric he joined the Patarene movement (see Patarenes) in Cremona and Piacenza. He came to Rome in 1074, possibly in consequence of his conflict with Bishop Dionysius of Piacenza, and was himself made bishop of Sutri in 1075 or 1076. In the spring of 1078 he was in Lombardy as legate, and back in Rome by November, when he took part in the synod that discussed Berengar's teachings. A zealous partizan of Gregory VII, he was imprisoned by Henry IV in 1082 and entrusted for safe-keeping to the antipope Guibert of Ravenna (Clement III). He contrived to escape, but never returned to his see. In 1085 he found shelter with Countess Matilda, and in the summer of 1086 was chosen bishop of Piacenza by the Patarene party. His election being uncanonical, Anselm of Milan, the metropolitan, refused to install him; but he succeeded in gaining the approval of Pope Urban II in 1088 or 1089. He did not long enjoy his triumph, meeting a violent death in a rising of the imperialist party. The most important of his writings, the *Liber ad amicum* (ed. E. Dümmler, *MGH, Libelli de lite*, i, 1891), composed between the death of Gregory VII and the accession of Victor III (1085–86), besides discussing the question whether a Christian may bear arms in the defense of the Church (which he answers in the affirmative), shows by an extended historical sketch that the Church grows under persecution. The chief value of the work is due to its presentation of the ideas of Gregory and his adherents; it informs us how the papal camp judged of the numerous theological and ecclesiastico-political controversies of the time, and as a whole is one of the most noteworthy productions of the Gregorian party. Often as it has been appealed to as a contemporary source, it has to be used with caution, owing not only to carelessness and errors of detail, but to demonstrable perversions of history, as in the account of the Canossa episode. In fact, it is colored throughout by the author's subjective standpoint. The *Liber in Hugonem schismaticum* (presumably Cardinal Hugo Candidus) has unfortunately been lost. As a canonist Bonizo left a large *Decretum* in ten books, from which Mai published extracts in 1854. Carl Mirbt.

Bibliography: H. Saur, *Studien über Bonizo*, in *Forschungen zur deutschen Geschichte*, viii, 397–464, Göttingen, 1868; E. Steindorff, *Jahrbücher des deutschen Reichs unter Heinrich III.*, i, 457–462, ii, 478–482, Leipsic, 1874, 1887; W. Martens, *Ueber die Geschichtschreibung Bonizos*, in *Tübinger theologische Quartalschrift*, 1883, pp. 457–483; idem, *Gregor VII.*, 2 vols., Leipsic, 1894; H. Lehmgrübner, *Ueber des Leben des Bonizo . . .*, in *Benzo von Alba*, pp. 129–151, Berlin, 1887; G. Meyer von Knonau, *Jahrbücher des deutschen Reichs unter Heinrich IV.*, vols. i, ii, Leipsic, 1890–94; C. Mirbt, *Die Publizistik im Zeitalter Gregors VII.*, ib. 1894; idem, *Die Wahl Gregors VII.*, Marburg, 1892.

BONNER, EDMUND: Bishop of London; b., probably at Hanley, Worcestershire, about 1500; d. in the Marshalsea prison, at Southwark, near London, Sept. 5, 1569. He studied at Pembroke College (then called Broadgate Hall), Oxford (B.C.L., 1519; D.C.L., 1525), and was ordained about 1519. He received his first preferment from Cardinal Wolsey; after the death of Wolsey (1530) he served the king, received a number of benefices, and was employed at different times as ambassador to the pope, to the king of France, and to the emperor; he was made bishop of London in 1539. He fell out with the privy council, which undertook to govern under Edward VI (1547), and in 1549 was reprimanded for not enforcing the use of the new prayer-book, deprived of his bishopric, and imprisoned. The accession of Mary (1553) brought his release and reinstated him in his see. He is remembered chiefly by his connection with the religious persecutions of the reign of Mary and it is said that in three years he condemned more than two hundred persons to the stake. In 1559, after the accession of Elizabeth, he refused to take the oath of supremacy and was imprisoned and kept in confinement till his death. It has been usual to represent Bishop Bonner as unprincipled and cruel; yet his firmness in following the unpopular course and the suffering undergone in consequence do not indicate a lack of principle; to judge and condemn heretics was one of the duties of his position, and it is not clear that he took delight in undue severity; there is documentary evidence that he acted under pressure from the queen and her husband (Philip II of Spain). He was unpopular in London apart from the persecutions. He wrote a preface for the second edition of Gardiner's *De vera obedientia* (Hamburg, 1536) and published a collection of *Homilies* for his diocese (London, 1555, and many later editions).

Bibliography: The sources for a life are in the *State Papers of Henry VIII*, in the *Rolls Series*, 15 vols., ed. by various hands, London, 189–. Consult also: S. R. Maitland, *Subjects Connected with the Reformation in England*, London, 1849; *DNB*, vi, 356–360.

BONNET, bon"nê', ALFRED MAXIMILIEN: French classical scholar; b. at Frankfort Nov. 3, 1841. He was educated at Bonn University, and, after being a professor at the academy of Lausanne in 1866–74 and at the École Monge and the École Alsacienne at Paris in 1874–81, was successively lecturer and instructor in the faculty of letters at Montpellier. Since 1890 he has been professor of Latin in the same institution. In 1898 he was elected a corresponding member of the Academy of Inscriptions, and has written, among other works, *Narratio de miraculo a Michaele archangelo Chonis patrato, adjecto Symeonis Metaphrastæ de eodem re libello* (Paris, 1890) and *Le Latin de Grégoire de Tours* (1890); and has prepared editions of the *Liber de miraculis beati Andreæ apostoli*, in *MGH, Script. rer. Merov.*, i (1885), 821–846, the Acts of Thomas (Leipsic, 1883) and of Andrew (1895), and the *Acta apostolorum apocrypha* (1891 sqq.; in collaboration with R. A. Lipsius).

BONNET, JULES: French Protestant layman; b. at Nimes (40 m. n.e. of Montpellier) June 30, 1820; d. there Mar. 23, 1892. He was educated as a lawyer, but became a professor in the University of France and gained recognition by his works on the history of the Reformation. He was also secretary of the Société d'Histoire du Protestantisme Français and editor of its publications. Among his works special mention may be made of the following: *Olympia Morata, épisode de la renaissance en Italie* (Paris, 1850; Eng. transl., Edinburgh, 1852); *Lettres françaises de Calvin* (2 vols., 1854; Eng. transl., 4 vols., Edinburgh, 1855–57); *Calvin au val d'Aoste* (1861); *Aonio Paleario, étude sur la réforme en Italie* (1863; Eng. transl., London, 1864); *Récits du seizième siècle* (1864); *Nouveaux récits du seizième siècle* (1869); *La Réforme au château de Saint Privat* (1873); *Notice sur la vie et les écrits de M. Merle d'Aubigné* (1874); *Derniers récits du seizième siècle* (1875); *Quelques souvenirs sur Augustin Thierry* (1877); *Famille de Curione, récit du seizième siècle* (Basel, 1878); *Histoire des souffrances du bienheureux martyr Louis de Marolles* (Paris, 1882); *Souvenirs de l'Église réformée de la Calmette* (1884); and *Récits du seizième siècle, troisième série* (1885). He also edited the *Mémoires de la vie de Jean de Parthenay-Larchevêque, sieur de Soubise* (Paris, 1879), while his own letters from 1851 to 1863 have been edited by E. de Bude (Geneva, 1898).

BONNIVARD, bən″nî″vār′, **FRANÇOIS DE:** The "Prisoner of Chillon"; b. at Seyssel on the Rhone (21 m. s.w. of Geneva) c. 1493; d. at Geneva 1570. As a younger son he entered the Church and became prior of St. Victor near Geneva; certain other benefices to which he thought he was entitled he failed to receive through the intrigues of Charles III, duke of Savoy; in consequence he joined the party of the young Genevan patriots who were resisting the duke's attempts to gain control of the city. When the duke entered Geneva in 1519, Bonnivard fled, but fell into the hands of the duke, and was imprisoned for twenty months. On May 26, 1530 he was arrested near Lausanne, taken to the castle of Chillon at the east end of Lake Geneva, and kept there for six years. It is this imprisonment which Byron has immortalized in verse more musical than truthful. The first two years were tolerable; but after a visit from the duke in 1532 he was put in the dungeon now shown to visitors. It is only a local tradition that he was chained to a pillar. In the spring of 1536 the Bernese took the castle and freed Bonnivard. During his incarceration the priory and church of St. Victor had been razed and the income of the estates applied to the city hospital. As indemnification he was pensioned and given a liberal sum to pay his debts. He adopted the Reformation and married four times, but no time happily. He made the city of Geneva his heir on condition that it should pay his debts; but his estate consisted only of certain books which formed the beginning of the city library. Bonnivard's literary activity was the chief reason for the forbearance which his contemporaries showed him; his career was somewhat wavering, time-serving, and dishonorable. In 1517 he was entitled "poet-laureate," and after his liberation he was commissioned by the magistracy to write a history of the republic of Geneva. This work, *Les Chroniques de Genève* (published at Geneva, 2 vols., 1831), ends with 1551, is full of anecdotes and interesting, but unreliable. Other works which have been published are: *Advis et devis des langues* (Geneva, 1849); *Advis et devis de la source de l'idolatrie et tyrannie papale* (1856); *De l'ancienne et nouvelle police de Genève* (1865).

Bibliography: J. J. Chaponnière, *Mémoire sur Bonnivard*, Geneva, 1846; F. Gribble, *Lake Geneva and its Literary Landmarks*, London, 1901.

BONNUS, HERMANNUS (Hermann Gude?): German Reformer; b. at Quackenbrück, in Osnabrück, 1504; d. at Lübeck Feb. 12, 1548. He was educated apparently first at Münster, then in Bugenhagen's school at Treptow, but certainly entered the University of Wittenberg in 1523, coming under the influence of Luther and Melanchthon. In 1525, probably, he migrated to Greifswald, and about two years later went to Gottorp to act as tutor to the six-year-old son of Frederick I of Denmark. Thence he was called to Lübeck in 1530, and (on Bugenhagen's oganization of the Evangelical Church there) made superintendent in the following February. Here he remained until his death, in spite of calls to Hamburg in 1532 and to Lüneburg in 1534. He represented his town in the conference of the six free cities of Lübeck, Bremen, Hamburg, Rostock, Stralsund, and Lüneburg, held at Hamburg in 1535 to concert measures for dealing with Papists, Anabaptists, and Sacramentarians. In 1543 he visited Osnabrück to take part in the establishment of a Reformed system and liturgy which received the approval of the bishop, Franz von Waldeck, and was later extended to the whole diocese. The attempt to carry it into that of Münster was forcibly resisted by the chapter, but met with partial success in the country districts. His influence was extended by his Low German catechism (1539) and by his services to the hymnody of this dialect. He certainly edited and revised several collections of both German and Latin hymns, and probably contributed some of his own. He took a courageous part against the democratic revolution in Lübeck under Wullenweber, and in his *Chronika der kaiserlichen Stadt Lübeck* (1539) pointed out the dangers of innovating tendencies. After the formal adoption of the Augsburg Confession in 1535, he contended successfully against the efforts of the Roman Catholic party to regain control and against the propaganda of the Anabaptists. His office required him to expound the Scriptures, and his discourses on the Acts and on the liturgical epistles for the Sundays were published. In accordance with the Hamburg decisions, which had required preachers to dwell upon the examples of the saints, he published in 1539 a compilation of hagiographical extracts. The king of Denmark tried to secure him for an important office (probably the bishopric of Sleswick), but he refused to leave Lübeck, where his body was deposited amid universal mourning in St. Mary's church. (G. KAWERAU.)

BIBLIOGRAPHY: H. Spiegel, *Hermann Bonnus*, Göttingen, 1892; G. Bossert, in *TLZ*, 1892, pp. 260 sqq.

BONOSUS AND THE BONOSIANS.

From a letter written to Anysius of Thessalonica and the other Illyrian bishops, soon after the Synod of Capua (winter of 391–392), by either Pope Siricius or an unknown Italian bishop, we learn certain facts about a bishop Bonosus, whose see is not given. He had been accused, apparently by neighboring bishops, but of what does not clearly appear in the letter, except that he had asserted that Mary bore other children to Joseph, after the birth of Jesus. The case came before this synod at Capua, called by the emperor Theodosius to put an end to the schism at Antioch (see MELETIUS OF ANTIOCH); but the synod referred it to the bishops whose dioceses bordered on those of both parties, especially the Macedonian prelates. The decision was in favor of suspension, a temporary provision being made for the administration of Bonosus's diocese. He wrote to St. Ambrose to know whether he was bound to heed this sentence, and Ambrose counseled patience. Meantime the bishops hesitated to make the sentence absolute, and would have been glad of the opinion of the writer of the letter. He, however, whether Siricius or some one else, declared that it did not belong to him "to decide as if by authority of a synod"; the responsibility, he told them, rested on them of forming such a decision that neither the accused nor the accusers should be able to evade it. So much consideration was not usually shown to "heretics"; there may have been circumstances connected with the case which we do not know. But to deny the perpetual virginity of Mary was a serious offense from the standpoint of the time (see HELVIDIUS). Ambrose speaks (*De instit. virg.*, v, 35) of a bishop being accused of this "sacrilege"—probably meaning Bonosus. It is, therefore, evident that at this time Bonosus was accused of no worse or further heresies.

1. Heresy and Suspension of Bonosus.

Some twenty years later we hear more of Bonosus in two letters of Innocent I—one to Marcian of Naissus, northwest of Sardica, and a later one to the bishops of Illyria. From them it appears that Bonosus had been definitely condemned by his fellow bishops, and had then founded a separate ecclesiastical organization of his own. For the avoiding of scandal, those who had been ordained by him were, if they wished it, received back into the Church as clerics. Innocent allows this only in the case of those ordained by Bonosus before his condemnation; but here again his heresy is not specified. Twenty years later still (431), Marius Mercator names Marcellus, Photinus, "and lately the Sardican bishop, Bonosus, who was condemned by Pope Damasus, among the followers of Ebion." There is practically no doubt that this is the same Bonosus; in this case, and accepting the statement of Marius, we have learned that Bonosus was bishop of Sardica, and that his errors had grown, after 392, into dynamistic Monarchianism. We have no further information as to the fate of his following in the Balkan peninsula. The mention of him in the so-called *Decretum Gelasii*, even if it was written by Gelasius, and the anathemas pronounced against him by Vigilius in 552 and 553 prove nothing on this point. If Gregory I in his *Epistola ad Quiricum* really named the *Bonosiaci* with the Cataphrygians as heretics who needed rebaptism because they did not believe in Christ the Lord, this is not very strong evidence for the continued existence of the body, and tells nothing of its locality.

2. Final Condemnation of Bonosus.

The case is different with the repeated mentions of *Bonosiaci* or *Bonosiani* by the writers of Spain and southern Gaul. Gennadius quotes the Spanish bishop Audentius (end of fourth century) as having specially written against them, which proves at least that Gennadius knew them; he speaks in another place of "Photinians, who now are called Bonosians." A little later Avitus of Vienne mentions them in two well-known passages; in one he expresses himself in relation to King Gundobad (see BURGUNDIANS) as willing to accept their baptism. The 17th canon of the so-called Second Synod of Arles (generally placed 443–452) shows the same conciliatory attitude; but the Third Synod of Orléans (538) tells us that the Bonosians rebaptized their converts, which may be taken to show that their baptism was not then recognized by the other side. About the same time, according to Isidore of Seville, Justinian of Valencia was writing against them his lost *Liber responsionum contra Bonosianos, qui Christum adoptivum filium et non proprium dicunt*. While for Gaul the latest reference is given by the Synod of Clichy in 626 or 627, showing thus their gradual extinction there, in Spain they were attracting attention fifty years later; the Synod of Toledo in 675, declaring that Christ was the Son of God by nature, not by adoption, was plainly directed against them. On the other hand, the mention of Bonosus—not of the Bonosians—in the Adoptionist controversy (see ADOPTIONISM) does not prove that they lasted to the eighth century in Spain, nor is the medieval view that Adoptionism was a revival of the heresy of Bonosus worth considering. They really disappear with the end of the seventh century.

3. Bonosians in Spain and Southern Gaul.

That these mentions of Bonosians from the fifth to the seventh centuries are not merely the survival of an old term of opprobrium, but that they really existed in Spain and southern Gaul at that period has long been justly accepted. It is still further confirmed by a passage of Avitus, whose true reading (*Bonosiacorum* for *bonorum*) has only lately been established. Writing to Sigismund, his convert, son of the Arian king Gundobad, he gives the information that the latter had formally promised to set up a Bonosian community in his kingdom by the establishment of a bishop of their faith, and that this body was recruited from the Arians. This would explain the attitude of Gennadius toward their baptism. Avitus took an opposite view, either to conciliate the king, who at that time gave hopes of his conversion, or from motives of general policy.

4. Sympathy between Bonosians and Arians.

The Bonosians began to be absorbed into the Arian body; toward the end of Gundobad's reign Avitus had hopes that they would entirely disappear, if the king could be induced to let his promises to them lapse into oblivion. The later history shows that this hope proved false, because the sect was not confined to Burgundian territory; and it is not surprising that sharp measures were taken against those who remained obdurate in their heresy under Catholic rule. Only one thing can be urged against the correctness of the account here given—the recognition of the validity of Bonosian baptism by the synod said to have been held at Arles about 450; but this really tells the other way, for general support is now accorded to the theory put forth in the eighteenth century that this second synod of Arles never had any existence, the canons attributed to it being nothing but a collection of various older synodical decisions made toward the end of the fifth century, and canon xvii having then first been heard of. Accordingly it is safe to say that the Bonosians in the generally Arian territories of the Burgundians and the West-Goths were the followers of Bonosus of Sardica, though the name Bonosus was not an uncommon one.

5. Relation between Bonosus and the Bonosians.

Isidore of Seville says expressly that they had sprung "from a certain bishop Bonosus," and the "plague of the Bonosians" did not begin in the Burgundian kingdom, since Avitus speaks of it as *ab infernalibus latebris excitata*. The district in which Bonosus of Sardica labored bordered on territories held in his time by the West-Goths, and relations may well have remained close between that region and the West-Goths of the south of Gaul; so that the passage of his teaching from the Balkan peninsula into the Burgundian kingdom, which was in close contact with the West-Goths, is perfectly possible, and we may safely conclude to accept the statement of Marius Mercator. (F. Loofs.)

The wide-spread acceptance of the Adoptionist view of the person of Christ from the apostolic time throughout the Middle Ages and beyond (Ebionites, *Shepherd* of Hermas, Theodotas of Rome, Paul of Samosata, the Paulicians, most medieval sects, many Anabaptists, and others) makes it easy to account for this aspect of the teaching of the Bonosians as well as for the Spanish Adoptionism of the eighth century without the supposition of its independent origin in either case. For much valuable information on the early origin and the persecution of Adoptionist Christology cf. F. C. Conybeare, *The Key of Truth: A Manual of the Paulician Church of Armenia. The Armenian Text edited and translated with illustrative Documents and Introduction* (Oxford, 1898). A. H. N.

Bibliography: Ceillier, *Auteurs sacrés*, v. 708–711; C. W. F. Walch, *Historie der Ketzereien*, iii. 598–625, Leipsic, 1766; A. Helfferich, *Der westgothische Arianismus*, Berlin, 1860; C. Binding, *Das burgundisch-romanische Königreich*, vol. i, Leipsic, 1868; Hefele, *Conciliengeschichte*, vols. ii, iii; *DCB*, i, 330–331.

BONWETSCH, ben″vetch′, **GOTTLIEB NATHANAEL**: German Protestant theologian; b. at Nortla, Russia, Feb. 17, 1848. He was educated at the universities of Dorpat (1866–70), Göttingen (1874–75), and Bonn (1877–78), the time between his residence at these universities being spent in practical pastoral work. He became privat-docent at Dorpat in 1878 and associate professor of church history four years later, while from 1883 to 1891 he was full professor in the same university. Since 1891 he has been professor of church history at Göttingen. In addition to numerous contributions to theological journals and religious encyclopedias, he edited Thomasius's *Dogmengeschichte der alten Kirche* (Erlangen, 1886) and the *Studien zur Geschichte der Theologie und Kirche* in collaboration with R. Seeberg (Leipsic, 1897 sqq.), and has written *Die Schriften Tertullians untersucht* (Bonn, 1878); *Die Geschichte des Montanismus* (Erlangen, 1881); *Unser Reformator Martin Luther* (Dorpat, 1883); *Kyrill und Methodius, die Lehrer der Slaven* (Erlangen, 1885); *Methodius von Olympus*, i, *Schriften* (Leipsic, 1891); *Studien zu den Kommentaren Hippolytus zum Buche Daniel und Hohenliede* (1897); *Hippolytus Werke* (Berlin, 1897; in collaboration with H. Achelis); and *Die Apokalypse Abrahams, das Testament der vierzig Märtyrer* (1898). He also edited, in collaboration with P. Tschackert, the thirteenth and fourteenth editions of J. H. Kurtz's *Lehrbuch der Kirchengeschichte* (2 vols., Leipsic, 1899, 1906).

BOOS, MARTIN: Roman Catholic priest; b. at Huttenried near Schongau, Bavaria, Dec. 25, 1762; d. at Sayn, near Coblenz, Aug. 29, 1825. He studied at Dillingen under Sailer, Zimmer, and Weber. He followed the extreme practises of asceticism as a penance for sin, all to no avail, as he believed, and then developed a doctrine of salvation by faith which came very near to pure Lutheranism. This he preached with great effect. He was driven from Bavaria by the opposition of the ecclesiastical authorities and other priests and lived in Austria from 1799 to 1816, when he was compelled to leave that country. His last years were spent at Düsseldorf and Sayn.

Bibliography: His autobiography was edited by J. Gossner, Leipsic, 1831, Eng. transl., London, 1836, who also issued two volumes of his sermons, Berlin, 1830. Consult also F. W. Bodemann, *Gesammelte Briefe von, an und über Martin Boos*, Frankfort, 1854.

BOOTH, BALLINGTON: General-in-chief and president of the Volunteers of America; b. at Brighouse (4 m. s.s.e. of Halifax), Yorkshire, England, July 28, 1859. He was educated at a private school in Bristol and subsequently at Trenton Collegiate Institute and Nottingham Seminary, Nottingham, England. He was commander of the Salvation Army in Australia from 1885 to 1887, and held the same office in the United States from

1887 to 1896. In the latter year his connection with the Salvation Army ceased, however, and he established a similar though not identical organization known as the Volunteers of America (q.v.), of which he has since been the head. He was ordained at Chicago in August, 1896, a presbyter in the Christian Church.

BOOTH, CATHERINE (MUMFORD): "Mother of the Salvation Army"; b. at Ashbourne (13 m. n.w. of Derby), Derbyshire, England, Jan. 17, 1829; d. at Clacton-on-Sea (13 m. s.e. of Colchester), Essex, Oct. 4, 1890. She was educated chiefly at home, and in 1844 removed with her parents to London. In the same year she joined the Wesleyan congregation at Brixton, but four years later was debarred from that organization, together with others. These "Reformers," as they called themselves, then formed a separate congregation, and in 1851 she became acquainted with her future husband, William Booth (q.v.), likewise an excommunicated "Reformer." Four years later they were married, and in 1858 she first took public part in her husband's pastoral work at Gateshead, Durham, where he was then located. Two years later, after the publication of a pamphlet defending the right of women to preach, she delivered her first sermon in her husband's pulpit, and within the next three years began to conduct independent religious meetings, leading successful missions at Margate in 1867 and at Portsmouth in 1873. Meanwhile the plan which resulted in the formation of the Salvation Army (q.v.) was maturing, and the new organization was definitely formulated in 1877. Mrs. Booth herself took an active part in the work, especially among women and children. Her greatest work as a revivalist was done in 1886–87, but in the following year she was stricken with cancer, which ultimately caused her death. She wrote *Papers on Practical Religion* (London, 1879); *Papers on Aggressive Christianity* (1881); *Papers on Godliness* (1882); *Life and Death* (1883); *The Salvation Army in Relation to the Church and State* (1883); and *Popular Christianity* (1887).

Bibliography: F. St. G. de L. Booth Tucker, *The Life of Catherine Booth*, 2 vols., London and Chicago, 1892; J. Chappell, *Four Noble Women and their Work*, ib. 1898.

BOOTH, WILLIAM: Commander-in-chief of the Salvation Army; b. at Nottingham, England, Apr. 10, 1829. He was educated by a private theological tutor of the Methodist New Connexion Church, and began his career as an open air preacher at the age of fifteen. He entered the ministry of the Methodist New Connexion Church in 1852, and was successively a traveling evangelist and a circuit preacher until 1861, when he left the denomination to devote himself entirely to evangelistic work. In 1865 he founded at London the Christian Mission for the amelioration of the condition of the destitute and vicious population of the eastern portion of London, and this developed, in 1878, into the Salvation Army (q.v.). He has traveled extensively in the interests of his Army, and has written *Salvation Soldiery* (1890); *In Darkest England and the Way Out* (1890); and *Religion for Every Day* (1902).

Bibliography: F. St. G. de L. Booth Tucker, *Life of General William Booth*, Chicago, 1898; T. F. G. Coates, *The Prophet of the Poor; the Life Story of General Booth*, London, 1905.

BOOTH TUCKER, EMMA MOSS: Salvation Army worker; b. at Gateshead, Durham, Jan. 8, 1860; d. near Dean Lake, Mo., Oct. 28, 1903. She was the daughter of William Booth (q.v.), the founder of the Salvation Army, and from 1880 to 1888 was in charge of the international training homes of that organization. In the latter year she married Frederick St. George de Lautour Tucker (see the following article), and went with him successively to India and London, whence she came to the United States in 1896. She held the rank of consul in the Salvation Army, and had equal powers with her husband in its control. She died from injuries received in a railroad accident. A volume of selections from her writings has been published under the title *The Cross and Our Comfort* (London, 1907).

BOOTH TUCKER, FREDERICK ST. GEORGE DE LAUTOUR: Secretary for Foreign Affairs of the Salvation Army; b. at Monghyr (80 m. e. of Patna), Bengal, Mar. 21, 1853. He was educated at Cheltenham College, England, and passed the examinations for the India Civil Service in 1874. After two years of additional study, he was appointed to the Punjab, where he was successively assistant commissioner and treasury officer. He resigned from the service, however, in 1881 to join the Salvation Army, which he established in India in the following year. He remained in command of the Army there until 1891, when he was transferred to London as secretary for international work. He held this office for five years, and from 1896 to 1904 was commander of the Army in the United States. Since the latter year he has been Secretary for Foreign Affairs of the Salvation Army, with headquarters in London, and is thus responsible to General William Booth (q.v.) for all work of the organization outside of the British Isles. In 1888 he married the daughter of Gen. William Booth (see the preceding article) and subsequently assumed the name of Booth Tucker. He has written *In Darkest India and the Way Out* (Bombay, 1891); *The Life of Catherine Booth* (2 vols., Chicago, 1892); *Life of General William Booth* (1898); and *Favorite Songs of the Salvation Army* (1899).

BOOTHS, FEAST OF. See Tabernacles, Feast of.

BORA, KATHARINA VON: Luther's wife; b. of an old family of Klein-Laussig, near Bitterfeld in Meissen, Jan. 29, 1499; d. at Torgau Dec. 20, 1552. She was placed in the Cistercian convent of Nimpsch at Grimma (17 m. s.e. of Leipsic) when a child and became a nun in 1515; with the cognizance of Luther she and eight other nuns fled from the convent Apr. 4, 1523, and repaired to Wittenberg. She is said to have refused an offer of marriage from Dr. Kaspar Glatz, vicar at Orlamünde. and at the same time to have expressed a preference for Amsdorf or Luther. She was married to the latter June 13, 1525, and bore him six children. She proved a true wife, was a good housekeeper, and the marriage was a happy one. After Luther's death (Feb. 18, 1546) she remained at Wittenberg, much of the time in poverty. Her death was due to an accident which occurred as she was on the way, with her children, to Torgau to escape the plague at Wittenberg.

BIBLIOGRAPHY: W. Beste, *Die Geschichte Katharinas von Bora*, Halle, 1843; F. G. Hofmann, *Katharina von Bora oder Luther als Gatte und Vater*, Leipsic, 1845; A. Stein, *Katharina von Bora, Luthers Ehegemahl*, Halle, 1897; A. Thoma, *Katharina von Bora*, Berlin, 1900. Consult also the various biographies of Luther. The chief of the many libels concerning Luther's marriage is Eusebius Engelhard's (Michael Kuen) *Lucifer Wittenbergensis*, 2 vols., Landsberg, 1747–49.

BORBORITES, BARDELITES. See GNOSTICISM.

BORDELUMIANS: A separatistic sect formed at Bordelum, a village of Sleswick, about 1739, under the leadership of a pietistic Saxon theological student named David Bähr. They originally consisted of fifteen or twenty persons, and claimed to be saints who had advanced further than Paul according to Rom. vii, 24. Since they believed that they had received special gifts from God, they decried the Church as the house of the devil, and despised the sacramants. As being pure, to whom all things were pure, they rejected marriage in favor of free love, and instituted a communism of property for their financial support. An edict of Christian VI, issued June 11, 1739, condemned the leaders to imprisonment; those who had led an immoral life were punished according to the laws, and the remainder were admonished. The leaders managed to escape the punishment, however, Bähr, who had seduced a married woman, fleeing to Jena. Expelled from that city, he returned to Holstein, and was imprisoned at Glückstadt. Having become a cripple in consequence of the rough treatment to which he had been subjected in prison, he was released, and died wretchedly, still unconverted, at Bredstädt in 1743. His adherents caused much trouble to the pastor of Bordelum.

PAUL TSCHACKERT.

BIBLIOGRAPHY: *Acta historico-ecclesiastica*, vol. v, part 29, p. 653 sqq., and Supplement, pp. 1014 sqq., 20 vols., Weimar, 1734–38, continued in 13 vols., till 1790.

BORDIER, bōr"dyê', HENRI LÉONARD: Reformed Church of France; b. in Paris Aug. 8, 1817; d. there Aug. 31, 1888. He was educated at the École de Droit and the École des Chartes in Paris, and licensed in law and as paleographic archivist in 1840; thereafter he devoted himself to historical studies. He was successively assistant to the historian Augustin Thierry; assistant in the Academy of Inscriptions; secretary *par interim* of the École des Chartes; a member of the commission on the departmental archives of the minister of the interior (1846); archivist of the national archives (1850), and dismissed on the establishment of the Empire. He was, during the siege of Paris, on the commission upon the papers of the Tuileries; and in 1872 was nominated honorary librarian in the department of manuscripts in the Bibliothèque Nationale. He was for many years on the committee of the Société d'Histoire du Protestantisme Français, and prepared numerous works, noted for their accuracy. Among them may be mentioned: various notices in the *Bibliothèque de l'École des Chartes* (Paris, 1841–86); *Histoire générale de tous les dépôts d'archives existant en France* (1855); *Les Églises et monastères de Paris* (1856); an edition of the *Libri miraculorum aliaque opera minora* of Gregory of Tours, Latin text with French translation (4 vols., 1857–64); a French translation of the *Historia Francorum* of Gregory of Tours (2 vols., 1859–61); *Les Inventaires des archives de l'Empire* (1867); *Une Fabrique de faux autographes* (1869); *Chansonnier huguenot du seizième siècle* (1869); *L'Allemagne aux Tuileries, de 1850 à 1870, collection de documents tirés du cabinet de l'Empereur* (1872); *La Saint-Barthélemy et la critique moderne* (Geneva, 1879); *L'École historique de Jérôme Bolsec* (Paris, 1880); *Nicolas Castellin de Tournay, réfugié à Genève, 1564–1576* (1881); *Description des peintures et autres ornements contenus dans les manuscrits grecs de la Bibliothèque Nationale* (1885). With E. Charton he published in 1860: *Histoire de France d'après les documents originaux et les monuments de l'art de chaque époque*. At the time of his death he was engaged upon a new and enlarged edition of the brothers Eugène and Émile Haag's *La France protestante* (originally 12 vols., Paris, 1845–59), and had brought out the first five volumes (1877–86).

BOREEL, bo"rêl', ADAM: Preacher and sectary; b. at Middelburg, in Zealand, 1603; d. in Amsterdam 1666. He was pastor of a Reformed congregation, but resigned his office, and became the leader of a separatistic party, which acknowledged no other religious authority than the Scripture. His work, *Ad legem et testimonium* (1645), attracted great attention. Here he developed that the written word of God, without any human commentary, was the sole means of awakening faith; that the Church had fallen completely away from the Lord; that the Christian ought to shun all connection with the Established Church, and confine himself to his private devotion, etc. His minor writings, fifteen in number, were collected at Amsterdam, 1683. His followers, known as Boreelists, never attained to much importance.

BORNEMANN, bōr'ne-mān, FRIEDRICH WILHELM BERNHARD: German Lutheran theologian; b. at Lüneburg (68 m. n.n.e. of Hanover) Mar. 2, 1858. He was educated at the universities of Göttingen (Ph.D., 1879) and Leipsic, and was successively tutor at Bremen (1879) and Medingen (1880). Two years later he became inspector of the seminary at Göttingen, and in 1884 was privatdocent for church history in the same university. In 1886 he was appointed inspector of the seminary for theological candidates at Magdeburg, where he became professor in the following year. From 1898 to 1902 he was professor of theology at Basel, and since the latter year has been pastor of the Luther Church at Frankfort. His works include *In investiganda monachatus origine quibus de causis ratio habenda sit Origenis* (Göttingen, 1886); *Die Unzulänglichkeit des theologischen Studiums* (Leipsic, 1886; anonymous); *Kirchenideale und Kirchenreformen* (1887); *Schulandachten* (Berlin, 1889); *Bittere Wahrheiten* (5th ed., Göttingen, 1891); *Unterricht im Christentum* (1891); *Die Thessaloni-*

cherbriefe (1894; in *Kritisch-exegetischer Kommentar uber das Neue Testament*); *Historische und praktische Theologie* (Basel, 1898); *Die Allegorie in Kunst, Wissenschaft und Kirche* (Freiburg, 1899); *Einführung in die evangelische Missionskunde* (Tübingen, 1902); and *Bete und Arbeite!* (Leipsic, 1904; a collection of sermons). He likewise translated the "Confessions" of St. Augustine (Gotha, 1889).

BORNHAEUSER, bōrn-hei'zer, **KARL BERNHARD**: German Lutheran; b. at Mannheim (43 m. s.w. of Frankfort) May 19, 1868. He was educated at the universities of Halle and Greifswald, and was pastor at Sinsheim (1890–94) and Carlsruhe (1894–1902). In 1902 he became associate professor of systematic and practical theology at Greifswald, and in 1905–06 was also assistant to the professor of practical theology at Halle. Became professor of systematic and practical theology at Marburg, 1907. He has written *Vergottungslehre des Athanasius und Johannes Damascenus* (Gütersloh, 1903); and *Wollte Jesus die Heidenmission?* (1903).

BORNHOLMERS: Danish sect of the nineteenth century. During the first part of the century different parts of Sweden were permeated with sects which emphasized the gospel of the free and unmerited grace of God in Christ. About 1805 the *Nya Läsare* ("New Readers") originated in the congregation at Piteå in Norrbotten, deviating from the old *Läsare*, who adhered to the Lutheran doctrines, by asserting that saving faith may be found in those whose hearts are still attached to sin and the world, and by regarding the importance attributed to the law as a temptation to pharisaical self-righteousness. In the course of time this party, headed by a soldier named Erik Stålberg, broke with the State Church, and finally the "New Readers" declared that the ministers of the latter preached the doctrine of the devil. In the fifth decade of the century, the Finnish preacher Frederik Gabriel Hedberg, afterward provost and preacher at Kimito in the archbishopric of Abo, evolved similar views in a work on "Pietism and Christianity," in which he accused Spener and his followers of teaching that man must be holy and pure before he can rely on the unmerited grace in Christ, whereas Hedberg seems to have regarded man as a soul hungering for grace, but utterly unable to aid himself in the attainment of salvation. In 1846 a party of Hedbergians was formed at Stockholm and Helsingland which rejected all preaching of repentance. A like tendency was manifested by the sect headed by Karl Olof Rosenius (b. 1816; d. 1868), who had been greatly influenced by the Methodist George Scott, who labored in the Swedish capital. Rosenius, who sought to remain a true Lutheran throughout his life, emphasized the grace of God in Christ. His sermons and his magazine, which he entitled *Pietisten*, although he was opposed to the legalism of the Pietists, exercised an important influence on the religious life of Sweden. Hedbergianism and the writings of Rosenius gave rise between 1850 and 1870 to a new evangelical party in many parts of Sweden, whose sole dogma was the forgiveness of sins without merit of the sinner, and whose watchword, "the world is justified in Christ," won them many proselytes not only in Sweden and Norway, but also in the American Synod of Missouri.

The new evangelism found a fertile soil in the Danish island of Bornholm (in the Baltic Sea, 90 m. e. of Zealand), which became the center of propaganda for a part of Denmark. The movement was inaugurated by P. C. Trandberg, a powerful preacher of repentance, who had broken with the State Church, and by 1863 had gathered about him almost a thousand followers. Trandberg sent out lay preachers, and the "Bornholmers," as they were called, were soon found in North Zealand, Copenhagen, Lolland, Falster, and West Jutland. His adherents gradually lost confidence in him, however, and in 1877 he resigned. Later he became professor in the Dano-Norwegian department of Chicago Theological Seminary and died in 1896. As a rule, the Bornholmers are pious and earnest, and their antinomistic theory usually becomes nomistic, and even quasipietistic in practise, thus forming a bond of union between them and the "Inner Mission" in Denmark, and making them one of the means to awaken spiritual life in many of the Danish people. F. NIELSEN†.

BOROWSKI, bo-rov'ski, **LUDWIG ERNST VON**: A prominent Prussian evangelical preacher; b. at Königsberg June 17, 1740, of a well-to-do Polish family which had emigrated on account of its religion; d. in Berlin Nov. 10, 1831. In his fourteenth year he went to the University of Königsberg, where he was one of Kant's earliest pupils, practised oratory, and showed an inclination toward literature. His theological convictions were not influenced by Kant, despite a lasting personal devotion, but rather by the supernaturalist school. In 1758 Kant recommended him to General von Knobloch as a tutor in his family; but before long Field-marshal von Kunheim, impressed by Borowski's oratorical gifts, urged him to become a military chaplain. This career he finally took up in 1762, being ordained by Süssmilch, and joining his regiment in the camp at Sorau soon afterward. He remained with the army until 1770, when Süssmilch had him appointed superintendent of the district of Schaaken in East Prussia. Here he labored diligently for twelve years, until he was called to a pastoral charge in his native town. The development of his preaching powers and theological knowledge won him increasing prominence; in 1793 the king appointed him a member of the special commission on churches and schools, and he received the title of consistorial councilor in 1804. When the storms of war burst over Germany, he rose to the height of the occasion, and his eloquent exhortations had a deep effect on Frederick William III and his queen, who resided in Königsberg from 1807 to 1809. The king's warm affection and respect continued to be shown through the years that followed. In 1812 he made Borowski general superintendent, in 1815 first court preacher, in 1816 a bishop, and in 1829 archbishop of the Prussian Evangelical Church. These last years of his life, old as he was, were full of incessant activity;

he was president of the Bible Society and of the Missionary Union founded in 1822. Outside of his preaching, however, he gave more thought to the training of his candidates for ordination than to anything else, and even in the wanderings of his last illness his mind was occupied with them.

(HERMANN HERING.)

BIBLIOGRAPHY: Selected sermons and lectures, with sketches of his activities by von Kahle and E. Oesterreich, were published by his grandson, K. L. Volkmann, Königsberg, 1833. Consult also *ADB*, iii, 177.

BORRHAUS, MARTIN (generally known as **CELLARIUS**): German theologian; b. at Stuttgart 1499; d. at Basel Oct. 11, 1564. Being educated and adopted by his kinsman Simon Cellarius, he called himself Cellarius until about forty years of age, although the name of his parents seems to have been Burress or Borrhus. In 1515 he was made *magister artium* at Tübingen, where he became intimately acquainted with Melanchthon, two years his senior. He was made bachelor of theology under Reuchlin at Ingolstadt in 1521, and became a friend of Marcus Stübner at Wittenberg. The eight sermons delivered by Luther after his return from the Wartburg impressed Cellarius deeply, but his zeal in defense of Stübner was such that he left Wittenberg, where he had treated Luther with rudeness, and went to Switzerland, whence he traveled by way of Austria and Poland to Prussia, which had just embraced the Evangelical faith. There he was tried, and required to sign a bond in which he promised to return at once to Wittenberg. His interview with Luther in 1526 filled the latter with respect for Cellarius, who now settled in southern Germany, winning the hearts of Capito and Butzer in Strasburg. In 1527 he published his first work, *De operibus Dei*, and in 1544 he was appointed professor of the Old Testament at Basel, where, in collaboration with Castello and Curio, he composed a polemical treatise under the name of Martin Bellius, directed against Calvin in the Servetus controversy. He rejected infant baptism, but was a firm believer in predestination.

CARL ALBRECHT BERNOULLI.

BIBLIOGRAPHY: *ADB*, iii (1876), 381; E. Egli, *Zwingliana*, i, 30-31, Zurich, 1904; C. Gerbert, *Geschichte der Strassburger Sektenbewegung zur Zeit der Reformation, 1524-34*, Strasburg, 1889. References will be found in the lives of the Reformers Luther, Melanchthon, Butzer, Zwingli.

BORROMEO, CARLO: Italian prelate and reformer; b. at Arona (on the s.w. shore of Lago Maggiore, 37 m. n.w. of Milan) Oct. 2, 1538; d. at Milan Nov. 3, 1584. He was the nephew of Giovanni Angelo Medici (afterward Pope Pius IV), and even in his boyhood showed an inclination for the priesthood, receiving his first benefice at the age of twelve through the resignation of an uncle. Four years later he went to Pavia, where he studied law, and had just taken his degree in 1559, when the newly elected Pius IV invited him to Rome. His rise was extraordinary, and at the age of twenty-two he was a cardinal and the archbishop of Milan. When the Council of Trent was reopened on Jan. 18, 1562, Borromeo used his influence in securing the sharp formulation of questions relating to discipline and faith. He also governed the Romagna and the March, both of which had been added to the papal dominions in the course of the fifteenth century. In foreign politics nothing took place without him and he was also an active member of the Congregation of the Inquisition, besides being the protector of the Franciscans, the Knights of Malta, and the Carmelites. He could maintain such an activity, however, only while he lived at Rome; conforming to the decision of the Council which required all bishops to reside in their own dioceses, he removed to Milan, where he had already prepared a house for the Jesuits, who acted as his instruments in reorganizing his diocese of Milan. Borromeo's activity here had scarcely begun when Pius IV died, but his successor Pius V assisted the archbishop in the reorganization of the largest of the Italian dioceses, which was to be a model for all. Borromeo founded seminaries for the better education of the clergy in the strictest ecclesiastical spirit, and also introduced rigid church discipline, beginning with the clergy; his efforts to popularize synodical work and to improve the existing orders, as well as his introduction of others, such as the Theatines, into Italy were all designed to further the same object. In revenge, some degenerate monks who had been affected by his reform, planned his murder, but by a miracle, as it was claimed, he escaped the bullet of his would-be assassins. Hand in hand with the reform within the Church went a merciless severity against every form of "heresy" in Lombardy, the Valtellina, and the Engadine, as well as against "witches" in Valcamonica. During the plague of 1576 he heroically cared for the sick and buried the dead, while the officials fled in terror from the city His statue near Arona still recalls the memory of Borromeo, who became, by his canonization in 1610, the saint of the Counter-reformation.

K. BENRATH.

BIBLIOGRAPHY: The *Opera omnia* appeared in Milan, 1747. The earlier biographies are antiquated by the works of A. Sala: *Documenti circa la vita e le opere di San C. Borromeo*, 3 vols., Milan, 1857-61, and *Biografia di C. Borromeo*, ib. 1858; *The Life of St. Charles Borromeo*, ed. E. H. Thompson, London, 1858, new ed., 1893; *St. Charles and his Fellow Labourers*, ib. 1869; C. Sylvain, *Histoire de S. Charles Borromée*, 3 vols., ib. 1884; C. Camenisch, *Carlo Borromeo und die Gegenreformation im Veltlin*, Chur, 1901; F. Wymann, *Der heilige Karl Borromeo*, Stans, 1903.

BORROW, GEORGE (HENRY): English adventurer and writer; b. at East Dercham (15 m. w.n.w. of Norwich), Norfolk, July 5, 1803; d. at Oulton (15 m. s.e. of Norwich), Suffolk, July 26, 1881. His boyhood was unsettled, his father, a soldier, moving about the country with his regiment. In 1819 he was articled to a solicitor at Norwich, but abandoned the work, went to London, and lived as a hack writer for the publishers. Then he took to wandering about England, and visited France, Spain, and Italy. In 1833 he was sent by the British and Foreign Bible Society to St. Petersburg to superintend the publication of a Manchu translation of the New Testament (published in eight volumes, 1835); he continued in the service of the Society, most of the time in Spain, till 1840. Then he married and adopted a more settled life in England. He had much aptitude for languages and acquired a knowledge, though not scientific, of many tongues, being particularly noted for his acquaintance with the Romany, the dialect of the Gipsies, with whom he associated much both on his wanderings and after his return to England. He published a Romany word-book (London, 1874), translations, and romances which tell the story of his life with more or less fiction interwoven. He edited a translation of the New Testament into Spanish (Madrid, 1837) and translated the Gospel of Luke into the dialect of the Gitanos (Spanish Gipsies; 1837) and into Basque (1838). Complete editions of his works were published in five volumes in London and New York. The best known of them are *The Zincali; or an Account of the Gipsies in Spain* (2 vols., London, 1841) and *The Bible in Spain* (3 vols., 1843).

Bibliography: W. I. Knapp, *The Life, Writings, and Correspondence of George Borrow*, 2 vols., London, 1899; W A. Dutt, *George Borrow in East Anglia*, ib. 1896; *DNB*, v, 407–408.

BOSCHI, bos'ki, **GIULIO:** Cardinal; b. at Perugia, Italy, Mar. 2, 1838. He was educated in his native city and completed his studies at Rome, where he became the secretary of Cardinal Pecci (afterward Pope Leo XIII) in 1861. In 1888 he was consecrated bishop of Todi, and seven years later was translated to the see of Sinigaglia. In 1900 he was elevated to the archbishopric of Ferrara, and in the following year was created cardinal priest of S. Lorenzo in Panisperna.

BOSNIA AND HERZEGOVINA: Two provinces of the Austro-Hungarian monarchy. Previous to the Treaty of Berlin (1878) they formed the extreme northwestern part of Turkey in Europe, but since 1908 they have been part of Austria. Bosnia has the Hungarian and Austrian provinces of Croatia, Slavonia, and Dalmatia on the north and west, Servia to the east, and to the south Herzegovina, which is bounded on the east by Montenegro and on the south and west by Dalmatia. The capital is Sarajevo in Bosnia, the chief town and former capital of Herzegovina, Mostar. The area is about 16,200 and 3,500 miles respectively; the population (1896) 1,591,036, of whom 219,511 are credited to Herzegovina. The natives are nearly all Slavs of the Servian branch. The number of foreigners living in the land is estimated at 71,000, most of them having entered the country since the Austrian occupation.

The religious statistics for 1895 were as follows: Greek-Orientals, 673,246 (43 per cent.); Mohammedans, 548,632 (35 per cent.); Roman Catholics, 334,142 (21 per cent.); Jews, 8,213; other religions (mostly Protestants), 3,859. The Mohammedans, in the main converts from Christianity since the Turkish conquest in the fifteenth century, are not of the most rigid kind, although they made a brave stand against the Austrian government. They are the landed proprietors of the country and merchants in the towns. They are under the Sheik ul Islam in Constantinople and a Rais al Ulama in Sarajevo. They have a large endowment fund for mosques, schools, hospitals, and the like, which is now administered under government supervision. The free exercise of their religion is guaranteed to them. The Roman Catholics are descendants of the older population and constitute the larger number of the artisans in the cities and the farmers. They are most numerous in the districts of Travnik and Mostar. The Franciscans have been active among them since the thirteenth century and have done much for them. Their condition has much improved since the Austrian occupation. There is an archbishop of Bosnia, who since 1881 has resided at Sarajevo, and there are suffragan bishops of Banjaluka, Mostar and Duvno, and Marcana and Trebinje. The provincial seminary is at Banjaluka, where there are also four schools for boys and four for girls and an orphan asylum under the charge of Trappist monks. The adherents of the Greek Church are under the patriarch of Constantinople and the metropolitans of Sarajevo, Dolnja Tuzla, and Mostar. They are most numerous in the north, are farmers and traders, and are inferior to both the Latins and Mohammedans in education. Less than ten per cent. of the entire population can read or write, and the church schools are poor. Public schools are being established and there are three higher schools (two gymnasia and a *Realschule*), ten trade schools, and a normal school.

Bibliography: The church statistics are included in those for Austria (q.v.). Consult: V Klais, *Geschichte Bosniens bis zum Zerfall des Königreichs*, Leipsic, 1885; *Bosniens Gegenwart und nächste Zukunft*, Leipsic, 1886; *Die Lage der Mohammedaner in Bosnien*, Vienna, 1900 (answered by *Kallay und Bosnien-Herzegovina*, Budapest, 1900).

BOSO: Third English cardinal; d. after 1178. His name was Boso Breakspear and he was a nephew of Pope Adrian IV (Nicholas Breakspear). He belonged to the Benedictine monastery of St. Albans, but went to Rome probably under Eugenius III. From Nov. 6, 1149, to May 3, 1152, he calls himself *Romanæ ecclesiæ scriptor*. Adrian IV made him his chamberlain early in his pontificate, probably therefore in 1154, and later made him cardinal deacon of Sts. Cosmas and Damian; under Alexander III he became cardinal priest of St. Pudentiana. With the latter title his signature appears to a number of papal bulls from March 18, 1166, to July 10, 1178, soon after which he appears to have died. He was a strong supporter of the policy of Adrian and Alexander. He wrote nine poetical lives of female saints, which are still in manuscript and was a poet of considerable merit. For the papal biographies composed by him see Liber Pontificalis.

Bibliography: The sources for a life are in Thietmar of Merseburg, *Chronicon*, *MGH*, *Script.*, iii (1839), 750. Consult Migne, *Encyclopédie théologique*, vol. xxxi, *Dictionnaire des Cardinaux*, s.v.; T. Greenwood, *Cathedra Petri*, London, 1856; *DNB*, v, 421; *KL*, ii, 1129–30. Consult also the biographies of Adrian IV and Alexander III.

BOSSE, FRIEDRICH: German Lutheran; b. at Rossla (38 m. w. of Halle) Aug. 23, 1864. He was educated at the universities of Tübingen, Berlin (Ph.D., 1886), Marburg, Heidelberg, and Greifswald, completing his studies in 1890. In the following year he became privat-docent at the University of Greifswald, and from 1892 to 1894 was provisional professor in Königsberg, thereafter becoming associate professor of church history at Kiel. In 1899 he returned in a similar capacity to Greifswald. Became first librarian in the Kaiser Wilhelm Library at Posen, 1909. He has written *Prolegomena zu einer Geschichte des Begriffes "Nachfolge Christi"* (Berlin, 1895).

BOSSUET, bos"sü"é', **JACQUES BÉNIGNE**: Bishop of Meaux (about 27 m. e.n.e. of Paris); b. at Dijon Sept. 27, 1627; d. in Paris Apr. 12, 1704. He began his studies in the Jesuit school of Dijon, and finished at the Collège de Navarre, Paris. He became priest and doctor of theology, 1652; after some time spent in retirement at St. Lazare, he went to Metz, where he was canon and archdeacon, acquired great fame as a preacher, and engaged in controversy with representatives of the Reformed Churches. At the request of his bishop he published his first work (1655), a *Réfutation* of the catechism of Paul Ferry (q.v.). In 1669 he was made bishop of Condom, Gascony, but resigned this office after he was appointed tutor to the dauphin (1670). When the education of his pupil was finished, in 1681, he was made bishop of Meaux. Bossuet adopted the Cartesian philosophy, to which he added the Thomist theology and a great admiration for Augustine. He is generally considered the foremost of French preachers; and, in so far as the art of eloquence is concerned, his six *Oraisons funèbres* (best collected eds., by Lequeux, Paris, 1762, and, with notes, etc., by A. Gasté, 1883) must be ranked among the finest specimens of Christian oratory, though they reflect the splendor and greatness of Louis Quatorze more vividly than the power and humility of the Gospel. As tutor to the dauphin he wrote *De la connaissance de Dieu et de soi-même* (1722; better ed., 1741) and *Discours sur l'histoire universelle depuis le commencement du monde jusqu'à l'empire de Charlemagne* (1681; 5th ed., enlarged, 1703; the continuation to 1661, published 1806, was printed from his notes), the latter of which is a strikingly original attempt to construct a Christian philosophy of history on the principle that the destinies of nations are controlled by providence in the interest of the Roman Catholic Church. Among his controversial writings against the Protestants, the two most remarkable are *Exposition de la doctrine de l'Église catholique sur les matières de controverse* (1671) and *Histoire des variations des Églises protestantes* (2 vols., 1688; best ed., 4 vols., 1689). The latter was sharply criticized by Jurieu and Basnage, and involved its author in a long and vehement controversy. He characterized the revocation of the Edict of Nantes (1685) as "le plus bel usage de l'autorité," but he was no ultramontanist. He presided in 1682 over the assembly of the French clergy which the king had convened to defend the royal prerogatives and the liberties of the Gallican Church against the claims of the pope. Nor was he in the least tainted by mysticism. His attacks on Fénelon and the Quietists approached very near to persecution. He was one of the greatest of the many distinguished men who lent brilliancy to the century of Louis XIV, but he was a representative of his time, and his ideas of church polity corresponded to, if they were not dictated by, the king's "l'état, c'est moi."

Bibliography: There have been many editions of his works; the basis of most of them is that prepared by the Abbé Pérau, at government expense, 20 vols., Paris, 1743-1750; three volumes of *Œuvres posthumes*, ed. by C. F. Leroy were published in 1753; the best edition is the *Œuvres complètes*, by F. Lechat and others, 31 vols., 1862-66; with appendix of *Œuvres inédites*, 2 vols., 1881-1883. Besides many single sermons accessible in English translation, the following works may be mentioned: *Select Sermons and Funeral Orations*, 1801; *A Survey of Universal History*, 1819; *A Conference* [between Bossuet and J. Claude, Mar. 1, 1679] *on the Authority of the Church*, London, 1841; *An Exposition of the Doctrine of the Catholic Faith*, 1841; *Elevations to God*, 1850; *The History of the Variations of the Protestant Churches*, 2 vols., Dublin, 1836; *Meditations*, London, 1901.

For a bibliography consult H. M. Bourseaud, *Histoire et description des MSS. et des éditions originales des ouvrages de Bossuet*, Paris 1898 (includes translations).

For his life and writings and his relations to Fénelon, Jansenism, Quietism, etc., consult: L. F. de Bausset, *Histoire de Jacques Bénigne Bossuet*, 4 vols., Paris, 1814, Besançon, 1846; M. M. Tabaraud, *Supplément aux histoires de Bossuet . composé par . . de Bausset*, Paris, 1822; F. le Dieu (his secretary), *Mémoires et journal sur la vie et les ouvrages de Bossuet*, 4 vols., ib. 1856-57; A. Réaume, *Histoire de J.-B. Bossuet et de ses œuvres*, 3 vols., ib. 1869; Mrs. H. L. (Farrer) Lear, *Bossuet and his Contemporaries*, London, 1874; C. A. Sainte-Beuve, *Essays on Men and Women*, ib. 1890; R. de la Broise, *Bossuet et la Bible*, Paris, 1891; G. Lanson, *Bossuet*, ib. 1[illegible] (a study of the writings); A. Rébelliau, *Bossuet, historien du protestantisme*, ib. 1891; Sir J. F. Stephen, *Horæ Sabbaticæ*, vol. ii, London, 1892; C. E. Freppel, *Bossuet et l'eloquence sacrée au xvii. siècle*, Paris, 1893; J. Denis, *Querelle de Bossuet et de Fénelon*, ib. 1894; L. Crouslé, *Fénelon et Bossuet. Études morales et littéraires*, 2 vols., ib. 1894-95; A. M. P. Ingod, *Bossuet et jansénisme*, ib. 1897.

BOST, PAUL AMI ISAAC DAVID: Swiss evangelist; b. at Geneva June 10, 1790; d. at La Force (6 m. w. of Bergerac), France, Dec. 14, 1874. He devoted four years to theology at the University of Geneva, but gained little spiritual profit from his studies, and was ordained in 1814 in a spirit of empty formalism. In 1816 he accepted a call as assistant pastor at Moutiers-Granval in the Canton of Bern, where he remained two years, ascribing to this period his firm belief in the doctrines of grace and justification. A parish proved too small for his energies, however, and in 1818, under the auspices of the "London Continental Society," he began the missionary journeys which were to occupy almost thirty-five years of his life. After the first of these trips, he withdrew from the Church of Geneva, and in the following year was in Colmar. He was expelled from France, however, and began a roving life, oppressed by poverty and burdened with a large family, yet preaching in Offenbach, Frankfort, Hanau, Friedrichsdorf, and Carlsruhe.

In 1825-26 Bost was in Geneva as the pastor of the free church of Bourg-de-Four. In answer to the attacks of the State Church, he published his *Défense de ceux des fidèles de Genève qui se sont constitués en églises indépendantes* (Geneva, 1825), charging the national Church with abandoning the Gospel and adopting Arianism. He was accordingly tried for slander, but was acquitted, although he was fined 500 francs for his libelous statements regarding the "Compagnie des pasteurs." Despite the fact that this trial marked a union of the divergent elements of the Free Church, Bost resigned his pastorate at Bourg-de-Four and founded a new congregation at Carouge near Geneva, which he dissolved after two years in favor of a more diversified activity, establishing the religious and political magazine *L'Espérance* in 1838. Two years later he successfully sought readmission to the clergy of Geneva, without retracting any of his views. After a brief pastorate at Asnières and Bourges in France, he was appointed chaplain of the prison of the Maison Centrale at Melun, where he remained until 1848, then living successively at Geneva, Nîmes, Neuchâtel, Jersey, and Paris, and spending his last years at La Force. The chief works of Bost, who also gained a certain amount of reputation as a writer of hymns, are as follows: *Genève religieuse* (Geneva, 1819); *Histoire des frères moraves* (2 vols., 1831; abridged Eng. transl., London, 1834); *Sur la primauté de Pierre et son Épiscopat* (3 pamphlets, 1832); *Histoire générale de l'établissement du Christianisme* (a revised translation of Blumhardt's *Versuch einer allgemeinen Missionsgeschichte der Kirche Christi*, 4 vols., Valence, 1838); *Les prophètes protestants* (Melun, 1847); and *Mémoires pouvant servir à l'histoire du réveil religieux* (Paris, 1854–55).

(E. Barde†.)

Bibliography: E. Guers, *Premier réveil à Genève*, Paris, 1871; Lichtenberger, *ESR*, ii, 373–374.

BOSTON, THOMAS: Church of Scotland; b. at Dunse (13 m. w. of Berwick-upon-Tweed), Berwickshire, Mar. 17, 1677; d. at Ettrick (40 m. s. of Edinburgh), Selkirkshire, May 20, 1732. He studied at the University of Edinburgh; became minister at Simprin, Berwickshire, 1699; at Ettrick, 1707 By circulating the *Marrow of Modern Divinity* among his friends he started the Marrow Controversy (q.v.). He wrote much and has exercised great influence in the Presbyterian Churches both of Scotland and England. The works by which he is now best known are *Human Nature in its Fourfold State of Primitive Integrity, Entire Depravation, Begun Recovery, and Consummate Happiness or Misery* (Edinburgh, 1720), commonly called "Boston's Fourfold State"; *The Sovereignty and Wisdom of God Displayed in the Afflictions of Men* (1737; reprinted as *The Crook in the Lot*, with memoir, Glasgow, 1863). He left an autobiography published as *Memoirs* (Edinburgh, 1776; ed. G. H. Morrison, 1899), and printed from Boston's manuscript, with introduction, notes, and bibliography by G. L. Low, under the title *General Account of my Life* (Edinburgh, 1907). His *Whole Works* edited by S. McMillan were published in twelve volumes at Aberdeen in 1848–52.

Bibliography: Besides the autobiography mentioned above, consult: A. à Wood, *Athenæ Oxonienses*, ed. P. Bliss, iii, 407–409, 4 vols., Oxford, London, 1813–20; Jean L. Watson, *Life and Times of Thomas Boston*, Edinburgh, 1883; A. Thomson, *Thomas Boston*, London, 1895; *DNB*, v, 424–426.

BOTTOME, MARGARET (McDONALD): Founder of the King's Daughters; b. in New York City Dec. 29, 1827; d. there Nov. 14, 1906. She was educated at a private school in Brooklyn, and in 1850 married the Rev. Frank Bottome. She had already become interested in religious and philanthropic work, and in 1876 began to give Bible talks in the homes of prominent New York women, continuing them for twenty-five years. In 1886 she organized the order of King's Daughters, basing her system on Edward Everett Hale's *Ten Times One is Ten*. In the following year the society was enlarged to include men, and the name was changed to the present International Order of the King's Daughters and Sons. In 1896 she was elected president of the women's branch of the International Medical Mission. She was also an associate editor of the *The Ladies' Home Journal*, and in addition to a few pamphlets and a large number of contributions to religious magazines wrote *The Guest Chamber* (New York, 1893); *Crumbs from the King's Table* (1894); and *A Sunshine Trip to the Orient* (1897).

BOUDINOT, bū″dī″nō′, **ELIAS:** American man of affairs and philanthropist; b. at Philadelphia May 2, 1740; d. at Burlington, N. J., Oct. 24, 1821. He was a lawyer and eminent in his profession; represented New Jersey in the Continental Congress 1778–79 and 1781–84, was chosen president in 1782, and, as such, signed the treaty of peace with Great Britain; he was member of the first three national congresses, and director of the United States mint 1795–1805. He was a member of the American Board of Commissioners for Foreign Missions (1812–21), and first president of the American Bible Society (1816–21). He was wealthy and gave liberally for philanthropic purposes during his life and in his will. He wrote *The Age of Revelation; or the age of reason shown to be an age of infidelity* (Philadelphia, 1801), in reply to Thomas Paine; *The Second Advent or Coming of the Messiah in Glory shown to be a scriptural doctrine and taught by divine revelation* (Trenton, N. J., 1815); and *A Star in the West; or a humble attempt to discover the long lost tribes of Israel* (1816), in which he advocated the view that the American Indians are the ten lost tribes. He also published anonymously in the *Evangelical Intelligencer* for 1806 a memoir of William Tennent (reprinted New York, 1847). His *Journal or Historical Recollections of American Events during the Revolutionary War* was printed at Philadelphia in 1894.

Bibliography: *The Life, Public Services, Addresses, and Letters of Elias Boudinot*, edited by Jane J. Boudinot, 2 vols., Boston, 1896.

BOUHOURS, bū″hūr′, **DOMINIQUE:** Jesuit; b. in Paris May 15, 1628; d. there May 27, 1702. He entered the Society of Jesus at sixteen, and acquired such renown as a teacher that the young Longueville princes and the son of Colbert were put under his care. Besides a number of biographical and other works, he made (with two other Jesuits, Tellier and Bernier) a translation of the New Testament from the Vulgate into French (Paris, 1697–1703).

BOUQUET, bū″kē′, **MARTIN:** Benedictine of St. Maur; b. at Amiens Aug. 6, 1685, d. in Paris Apr. 6, 1754. He entered the Benedictine order at St. Faron, Meaux, in 1706, and was ordained priest. His knowledge of Hebrew and Greek secured his appointment as special assistant to Montfaucon in his editorial labors. When the great edition of the *Scriptores rerum Gallicarum et Francicarum* came to be made (it had been projected by Colbert as early as 1676, and was entrusted to the Benedictines of St. Maur in 1723), he was placed in charge of it. Difficulties were encountered owing to his opposition to the bull *Unigenitus*, which caused the king to banish him from Paris; but he succeeded in preparing the first eight volumes for publication (1738–52). Other members of the congregation brought out five more after his death (1757–86). Interrupted by the Revolution, the work was taken up again by the Institute, and later by the Academy of Inscriptions, by whom ten more volumes were published in the nineteenth century.

BOUQUIN, bū"kañ', **PIERRE (PETRUS BOQUINUS):** French Calvinist; b. either in the province of Saintonge or in that of Guienne; d. at Lausanne 1582. The first certain date in his life is his taking the degree of doctor of theology at the university of Bourges Apr. 23, 1539. He was a Carmelite monk at Bourges and rose to be prior; but, embracing the Reformation, he left his monastery in 1541 and went first to Basel, then to Leipsic and Wittenberg, where he had letters to Luther and Melanchthon. The latter recommended him to Butzer when a theologian was required to continue the lectures which Calvin had delivered in Strasburg. Here he began to lecture on Galatians in September, 1542. Later he returned to Bourges, where he lectured on Hebrew and the Scriptures, gaining protection and a pension from Margaret of Navarre, and being allowed by the archbishop to preach in the cathedral. The Protestant leaders, Calvin, Farel, and Beza, seem to have suspected him of intending to desert the Reformation; but his teaching brought him again into conflict with the Roman authorities, and he left Bourges once more for Strasburg in 1555. Here he remained until the elector Otto Henry appointed him in 1557 to a provisional professorship in the University of Heidelberg, which was made permanent the next year. In the internal dissensions of Protestantism he took an increasingly decided Calvinistic stand, and in the reign of Frederick III was thus the only Heidelberg theologian to retain his position, and was made head of the faculty and a member of the new Reformed church council (1560). This period of prosperity ended, however, with the death of Frederick III, after which he was deprived of his position (1577), and became, a year later, professor and preacher at Lausanne. His numerous works are mainly polemical treatises against the Lutherans and Roman Catholics.

(E. F. Karl Müller.)

Bibliography: Biographical material is found in his *Brevis notatio . de cœna domini*, pp. 140–179, Heidelberg, 1582. Consult further: M. Adam, *Vitæ eruditorum*, ii, 72 sqq., Heidelberg, 1706; E. and É. Haag, *La France protestante*, ed. H. L. Bordier, ii, 875 sqq., Paris, 1879.

BOURDALOUE, būr"da"lū', **LOUIS:** Jesuit preacher; b. at Bourges Aug. 20, 1632; d. in Paris May 13, 1704. He was for some time a teacher in literature and philosophy; in 1665 he was sent to preach in the provinces, in 1669 was recalled to Paris; after the revocation of the Edict of Nantes, he was sent to Languedoc to preach to the Protestants; his last years he devoted to the service of the poor and unfortunate in Paris. As a man he was justly esteemed and loved; as a preacher his strength is in the clearness of his argument, its readiness and its cogency. The first edition of his works was edited by Bretonneau (16 vols., Paris, 1707–34); a good recent edition is that of Lille, 1882 (6 vols.).

Bibliography: L. Pauthe, *Bourdaloue, d'après les documents nouveaux*, Paris, 1900; A. Feugère, *Bourdaloue, sa prédication et son temps*, ib. 1874; M. Lauras, *Bourdaloue, sa vie et ses œuvres*, 2 vols., ib. 1881; E. de Ménorval, *Bourdaloue*, Paris, 1897; F. Castets, *La Vie et la prédication d'un religieux au xvii. siècle*, vol. i, Montpellier, 1901.

BOURIGNON, bū"rī"ñyoñ', **DE LA PORTE, ANTOINETTE:** Fanatical enthusiast; b. at Ryssel (Lille), then in the Spanish Netherlands, Jan. 13, 1616; d. at Franeker, Friesland, Oct. 30, 1680. She grew up neglected and solitary on account of a facial deformity, afterward removed by an operation, and came to love isolation and communion with God. For a time her older sister drew her into the world; but she shrank from marriage, and once thought she heard the voice of God asking her, "Canst thou find a lover more perfect than I?" She thought of becoming a Carmelite, but concluded that the true Christians were not to be found in the cloisters, and sought another way to leave the world. Her father tried to force a marriage upon her in 1636; she fled in a male disguise, and after many romantic adventures was brought home, but took refuge at Mons under the protection of the archbishop. When her plans for founding an ascetic community on a primitive model were hindered, she went to Liége and made another unsuccessful attempt. On her father's death she brought suit against her stepmother for his entire property and won it. Now she fell under the influence of a doubtful friend of mysticism, Jean de St. Saulieu, who induced her to take charge of a home for orphan girls (1653), which she put under the Augustinian rule and made cloistered (1658). Her rule there came to an untoward end in 1662, when she took flight under serious accusations of cruelty. She went first to Ghent and then to Mechlin, where she found an adherent in the superior of the Oratorians, Christian de Cort. Soon she developed a fantastical system, based on alleged revelations. As the "woman clothed with the sun" of the Apocalypse, she was to revive the teachings of the Gospel and gather her spiritual children around her into a communistic, priestless brotherhood; she was the second revelation of the Son of Man on earth.

The books which Antoinette now began to publish contain the bitterest condemnation of the Roman Catholic Church, reject infant baptism, and the Trinity was exchanged for a sacred triad of truth, mercy, and justice. She had dealings with the Jansenists, but rejected their teaching on predestination. In 1667, with De Cort, she went to Amsterdam and lived for a while in the happy exchange of views with the most various heretics and fanatics. The following years are occupied with the history of the attempt to find a home for her elect on the island of Nordstrand in the North Sea, which De Cort had discovered as the destined place. His financial troubles, which make up a large part of the story, ended only with his imprisonment at Amsterdam and his death in 1669. Antoinette, as his heir, was for several years more much occupied with courts of justice, not without danger of imprisonment, and went from Amsterdam to Haarlem, thence to Sleswick, and finally to Husum to be as near as possible to Nordstrand. Here she might have been left in peace if she would have given up her claims. But she set up a printing-press and carried on the liveliest literary controversy, until her press was confiscated by the government. So her story proceeds, amid quaint and vivid details too numerous to give here, until she is found at Hamburg in 1679 formally charged with sorcery by a former adherent, an eccentric colonel of artillery named La Coste. She fled to escape arrest, and remained in hiding until her death the next year. The points of her quietistic mysticism need no discussion; for herself the important one was her own position as bride of the Holy Ghost and channel of revelation. Though she was probably more of an adventuress than even an enthusiast or an insane woman, the solemn prophetic tone of her visions and divine messages continued for some time to attract readers who believed in her inspiration; but her community seems to have been entirely scattered at her death. (G. KAWERAU.)

Antoinette had many followers in Scotland, more, it is said, than in any other country. Prominent among them were the Rev. James Garden (1647–1726), who rose to be professor of divinity at King's College, Aberdeen, and was deprived in 1696 because he had refused to sign the Westminster Confession of Faith, and his younger brother, Rev. George Garden (1649–1733), who after being one of the ministers of St. Nicholas, the town parish of Aberdeen, was "laid aside" by the privy council in 1692 because he refused to pray for William and Mary and in 1701 was deposed from the ministry because he had advocated Bourignonianism in his book, *An Apology for M. Antonia Bourignon* (1699), a reply to books by his brother-in-law, the Rev. John Cockburn (1652–1729), entitled *Bourignianism Detected; or, the Delusions and Errors of A. Bourignon and her Growing Sect. Narrative i.* (London, 1698), *Narrative ii.* (1698), and *A Letter to his Friend giving an account why the other Narratives about Bourignianism are not yet published, and answering some Reflections passed upon the first* (1698).

The General Assembly of the Church of Scotland in 1701, 1709, and 1710 passed deliverances against Bourignonians in which their views are thus described: I. They denied (1) the divine permission of sin and that divine vengeance and eternal damnation were inflicted upon it; (2) the decrees of election and reprobation; and (3) the doctrine of the divine foreknowledge. II. They asserted (1) that Christ had a twofold human nature, one produced of Adam before the woman was formed, and the other born of the Virgin Mary; (2) that in each soul before birth are a good and an evil spirit; (3) that the will is absolutely free, and there is in man some infinite quality which makes it possible for him to unite himself to God; (4) that Christ's nature was sinfully corrupt, so that by nature he was rebellious to the will of God; (5) that perfection may be attained in this life; and (6) that children are born in heaven.

Notwithstanding these deliverances, the views of Antoinette Bourignon continued to exist in Scotland and in 1711 Bourignonianism was put among the heresies which candidates for the ministry were required formally to disown when applying for ordination.

BIBLIOGRAPHY: An edition of the works of Antoinette Bourignon was published in 19 vols., at Amsterdam, 1680–86. She wrote two accounts of her life: *La Parole de Dieu, ou sa vie intérieure* (1634–63), Mechlin, 1663; and *La Vie extérieure* (1616–61), Amsterdam, 1668. These were continued by her disciple, Pierre Poiret, in *Sa Vie continuée, reprise depuis sa naissance et suivie jusqu'à sa mort*, appended to a later edition of the preceding. Her autobiography in Eng. transl. under the title *The Light of the World; a Most True Relation of a Pilgrimess Travelling Towards Eternity*, 3 parts, London, 1696, reprinted, ib. 1863; abridged, ib. 1786. Consult especially A. van der Linde, *Antoinette Bourignon, Das Licht der Welt*, Leyden, 1895 (cf. on this G. Kawerau, in *GGA*, 1895, pp. 426 sqq.).

BOURNE, FRANCIS: Roman Catholic archbishop of Westminster; b. at Clapham (a suburb of London) Mar. 23, 1861. He was educated at St. Cuthbert's College, Ushaw (1869–75), St. Edmund's, Ware (1875–80), St. Thomas's Seminary, Hammersmith (1880–81), St. Sulpice, Paris (1881–1883), and the University of Louvain (1883–84). He was ordained to the priesthood in 1884, and after serving as assistant at Blackheath, Mortlake, and West Grinstead for five years, was appointed rector of Southwark Diocesan Seminary, holding this position until 1898, also acting for several years as professor of moral theology and Holy Scripture. He was named domestic prelate to the pope in 1895, and in the following year was consecrated titular bishop of Epiphania and coadjutor to the bishop of Southwark. He was bishop of Southwark from 1897 to 1903, and since the latter year has been archbishop of Westminster. He practically refounded St. John's Seminary at Wonersh, and has been most active in movements for social reform in the diocese of Southwark. He represented the Roman Catholics of England at the St. Augustine celebrations at Arles in 1897, as well as the English Roman Catholic bishops at Autun in 1899, and led the English pilgrims to Lourdes in 1902.

BOURNE, HUGH. See METHODISTS, I., 4.

BOUSSET, bū″set′, JOHANN FRANZ WILHELM: German Protestant; b. at Lübeck Sept. 3, 1865. He was educated at Erlangen, Leipsic, and Göttingen (Th.Lic., 1890) and became privat-docent at the latter university in 1890, being made associate professor of New Testament exegesis six years later. Theologically he belongs to the liberal historical school. In addition to minor contributions, he has written *Evangeliencitate Justins des Märtyrers* (Göttingen, 1891); *Jesu Predigt im Gegensatz zum Judentum* (1892); *Textkritische Studien* (Leipsic, 1894); *Antichrist* (Göttingen, 1895;

Eng. transl. by A. H. Keane, London, 1896); *Kommentar zur Offenbarung des Johannes* (in the *Kritisch-exegetischer Kommentar zum Neuen Testament*, 1896); *Religion des Judentums im neutestamentlichen Zeitalter* (Berlin, 1903; 2d ed., 1906); *Das Wesen der Religion* (Halle, 1903); *Was wissen wir von Jesus?* (1904); *Jesus* (Halle, 1904; Eng. transl., London, 1906); and *Erklärung des Galater- und ersten und zweiten Korintherbriefes*, in J. Weiss's *Schriften des Neuen Testaments neu übersetzt* (Göttingen, 1905). Since 1897 he has edited the *Theologische Rundschau* in collaboration with W Heitmüller, and the *Forschungen zur Religion und Literatur des Alten und Neuen Testaments* in collaboration with H. Gunkel since 1903.

BOUTHILLIER, bū"tîl"lyê', **DE RANCÉ, ARMAND JEAN LE.** See TRAPPISTS.

BOWEN, GEORGE: Methodist Episcopal foreign missionary; b. at Middlebury, Vt., April 30, 1816; d. in Bombay, India, Feb. 5, 1888. He was graduated at Union Theological Seminary, New York City, in 1847; was ordained by the presbytery of New York, and the same year went to Bombay under the American Board. He spent the rest of his life in that city, but severed his connection with the American Board in 1855 and was an independent missionary till 1872 when he connected himself with the Methodist Episcopal missionary society. He edited the Bombay *Guardian* from 1854 on; and was also the secretary of the Religious Tract Society of Bombay. By the volumes which have been made up from his writings he has helped many spiritually. They are: *Daily Meditations* (Philadelphia, 1865); *Discussions by the Seaside* (Bombay, 1857); *Love revealed. Meditations on the parting words of Jesus with his disciples in John xiii. to xvii.* (Philadelphia, 1872); *Verily, Verily. The Amens of Christ* (1879).

BOWEN, JOHN WESLEY EDWARD: Methodist Episcopalian; b. at New Orleans, La., Dec. 3, 1855. He was educated at the University of New Orleans (B.A., 1878) and Boston University (Ph.D., 1887). After acting as professor of ancient languages at Central Tennessee College, Nashville, Tenn., from 1878 to 1882, he held successive pastorates at Boston (1882–85), Newark, N. J. (1885–1888), and Baltimore and Washington (1888–92), while during the latter incumbency he was likewise professor of church history and systematic theology in Morgan College, Baltimore, and also professor of Hebrew in Howard University, Washington, in 1891–92. Since 1893 he has been president and professor of historical theology in Gammon Theological Seminary, Atlanta, Ga. He was a member and examiner of the American Institute of Sacred Literature in 1889–93, as well as secretary and librarian of the Stewart Missionary Foundation for Africa. He was likewise a member of the general conferences of 1896, 1900, and 1904, and from 1892 to 1900 was a member of the board of control of the Epworth League. He is the editor of *The Voice*, *The Negro*, and the *Stewart Missionary Magazine*, and has written *National Sermons*, *Africa and the American Negro* (Philadelphia, 1891); *University Addresses* (Atlanta, 1893); *Discussions in Philosophy and Theology* (1893); and *The United Negro* (1902).

BOWER, ARCHIBALD: Professed convert from Roman Catholicism to Protestantism; b. at Dundee Jan. 17, 1686; d. in London Sept. 3, 1766. He was educated at Douai, went to Italy, became a Jesuit 1706, and in 1723 was made a counselor of the Inquisition at Macerata, Italy. In 1726 he fled secretly to England, and, after some years, joined the Established Church; he gained influential patrons, who procured him employment in literary work and teaching. In 1745 he was readmitted into the Society of Jesus, but, after two years, again professed to leave the Church of Rome. His principal publication was the *History of the Popes* (7 vols., London, 1748–66; reprinted with a continuation by S. H. Cox, 3 vols., Philadelphia, 1844–45), which was attacked by Alban Butler and John Douglas as a mere translation of Tillemont and earlier writers without proper acknowledgment. Bower's character for virtue as well as veracity is not above suspicion.

BIBLIOGRAPHY: The *DNB*, vi. 48–51, furnishes a succinct account of his life and the charges against him, with a list of literature upon him.

BOWMAN, THOMAS: The name of two contemporary American bishops.

1. Methodist Episcopal bishop; b. at Berwick, Pa., July 15, 1817. He was educated at Dickinson College (B.A., 1837), and two years later entered the Baltimore conference of the Methodist ministry. He taught in the grammar-school of Dickinson College in 1840–43, and five years later founded Dickinson Seminary, Williamsport, Pa., of which he was the president until 1858, when he was chosen president of Asbury (now De Pauw) University, Greencastle, Ind. In 1864–1865 he was also chaplain of the United States Senate. He resigned the presidency of Asbury University in 1872, when he was elected bishop, and since that time has officially visited all the conferences of his denomination in the United States, Europe, India, China, Japan, and Mexico.

2. Bishop of the Evangelical Association; b. in Lehigh township, Northampton County, Pa., May 28, 1836. He studied at the Vanderveers Seminary, Easton, Pa., and entered the ministry of the Evangelical Association. He was pastor in the eastern Pennsylvania conference 1859–75, and was presiding elder of the same conference 1870–75. He has been a bishop since 1875, and since 1890 principal of the Union Biblical Institute at Napersville, Ill., which is the theological seminary of the Evangelical Association. He characterizes his theological position as "Arminian-evangelical." He has published a revision of the catechism of his Church, also an account of the disturbance in the Evangelical Association.

BOWNE, BORDEN PARKER: American educator; b. at Leonardville, N. J., Jan. 14, 1847 Died at Brookline, Mass., Apr. 1, 1910. He was educated at the University of New York (B.A. 1871), and studied at Halle, Göttingen, and Paris From 1876 he was professor of philosophy at Boston University. He was chairman of the Philosophical Department at the St. Louis World's Fair in 1904 and an honorary member of the Imperial Education Society of Japan. His writings are: *The Philosophy of Herbert Spencer* (New York, 1874); *Studies in Theism* (1879); *Metaphysics* (1882); *Philosophy of Theism* (1887); *Introduction to Psychological Theory* (1887); *Principles of Ethics* (1892); *Theory of Thought and Knowledge* (1897); *The Christian Revelation* (Cincinnati, 1898); *The Christian Life* (1899); *The Atonement* (1900); *Theism* (Deems lectures for 1902; New York, 1902); and *The Immanence of God* (Boston, 1905).

BOWRING, SIR JOHN: English Unitarian; b. at Exeter Oct. 17, 1792; d. there Nov. 23, 1872. He served his country as member of Parliament (1835–37 and 1841–49), in the public service in China and the Far East (1849–59), and as member of various governmental commissions; he was an ardent Utilitarian and first editor of the *Westminster Review* (1825). He was a remarkable linguist and an enthusiastic student of literature. His writings relate to public affairs, give the results of his travels, and include numerous translations, particularly of the popular poetry of Eastern Europe; he edited the works of Jeremy Bentham with biography (11 vols., London, 1838–43). He is mentioned here for his hymns, many of which are in general use, as "God is love, his mercy brightens," "From the recesses of a lowly spirit," "In the cross of Christ I glory," "Watchman, tell us of the night," "We can not always trace the way," and others.

Bibliography: *Autobiographical Recollections, with Memoir* by [his son] Lewin Bowring, London, 1877; *DNB*, vi, 76–80; S. W. Duffield, *English Hymns*, pp. 260–263, New York, 1886; J. Julian, *Dictionary of Hymnology*, pp. 166–167, London, 1907.

BOY-BISHOP: A popular custom of the Middle Ages to provide a diversion for the boys of a church or cathedral choir or school, and to reward the most deserving. One of the number was chosen "bishop," most commonly on St. Nicholas's day (Dec. 6), and in episcopal dress and attended by his fellows as priests, he went through the streets bestowing his blessing. Often he entered into the church and conducted some part of the service, at times delivering a sermon, prepared for the purpose by an older head (cf. the *Concio de puero Jesu* of Erasmus, edited by S. Bentley, London, 1816, which was spoken by a boy of St. Paul's School, London, on such an occasion). The boys occupied the seats of the clergy while the latter sat in the lowest places. In some localities the game lasted from St. Nicholas's day until Holy Innocents' day (Dec. 28). It was very popular in England, where it was observed not only in the churches and schools, but at the court and in the castles of the nobility; the boys were called "St. Nicholas's clerks." The custom was forbidden in 1542 but was restored under Mary. It was also common in France, although repeatedly forbidden there (by the papal legate, 1198; the synods of Paris 1212, Cognac 1260, Nantes 1431; the chapter of Troyes 1445). In some places, as Reims and Mainz, it lasted till the eighteenth century. See Fools, Feast of, and consult the works mentioned in the bibliography of that article.

BOYCE, JAMES PETIGRU: American Baptist; b. at Charleston, S. C., Jan. 11, 1827; d. at Pau, France, Dec. 28, 1888. He was graduated at Brown University 1847; studied theology at Princeton Theological Seminary, 1849–51; became pastor of the Baptist church at Columbia, S. C., 1851; professor of theology in Furman University, Greenville, S. C., 1855; chairman of the faculty, and professor of systematic theology in the Southern Baptist Theological Seminary, opened at the same place in 1859. He was opposed to secession, but went with his State into the Civil War; was chaplain of the Sixteenth South Carolina volunteers 1861–62; member of the legislature 1862–65; of the State council and on the staff of Gov. A. G. Magrath 1864–65; member of the State convention for reconstruction 1865. At the close of the war he returned to his duties in the seminary, reopened it and reestablished it with much labor, and made considerable contributions to its support from his own means. In 1872 he was transferred to the chair of church government and pastoral duties, but was absent much of the time for the next few years arranging for the removal of the seminary to Louisville, Ky., which was accomplished in 1877. In 1887 he returned to his old department of systematic theology. He was president of the Southern Baptist Convention 1872–79 and in 1888. Besides sermons, speeches, and articles he published *Three Changes in Theological Education* (Greenville, 1856); *A Brief Catechism of Bible Doctrine* (Memphis, 1872); *An Abstract of Theology* (Louisville, 1882; rev. and enlarged ed., Baltimore, 1887; rev. and annotated by F. H. Kerfoot, Philadelphia, 1898).

Bibliography: J. A. Broadus, *Memoir of James Petigru Boyce*, New York, 1893.

BOYD, ANDREW KENNEDY HUTCHISON: Established Church of Scotland; b. at Auchinleck (28 m. s. of Glasgow), Ayrshire, Nov. 3, 1825; d. at Bournemouth, Hampshire, England, Mar. 1, 1899. He studied at King's College and the Middle Temple, London, and at the University of Glasgow (B.A., Glasgow, 1846); was ordained minister of Newton-on-Ayr 1851; minister of Kirkpatrick-Irongray, near Dumfries, 1854–59; of St. Bernard's, Edinburgh, 1859–65; first minister of the city of St. Andrews from 1865. He won distinction both as a clergyman and a writer (over the signature A. K. H. B., and the *sobriquet* "The Country Parson"), and was perhaps the most widely known minister of the Scottish Church. In 1866 he was made chairman of a committee to prepare a new collection of hymns and filled the place with much judgment and tact. He was moderator of the General Assembly in 1890. The most notable of his many books were *Recreations of a Country Parson* (3 series, London, 1859–78); *Leisure Hours in Town* (1862); *Graver Thoughts of a Country Parson* (3 series, 1862–75); *The Commonplace Philosopher in Town and Country* (1862–64); *Counsel and Comfort Spoken from a City Pulpit* (1863); *The Autumn Holidays of a Country Parson*

(1864); *Critical Essays of a Country Parson* (1865); *Sunday Afternoons in the Parish Church of a University City* (1866); *Lessons of Middle Age* (1867); *Changed Aspects of Unchanged Truths* (1869); *Present Day Thoughts* (1870); *Seaside Musings* (1872); *A Scotch Communion Sunday* (1873); *Landscapes, Churches, and Moralities* (1874); *From a Quiet Place* (1879); *Our Little Life* (2 series, 1881–84); *Towards the Sunset, Teachings after Thirty Years* (1882); *What Set him Right, with other chapters to help* (1885); *Our Homely Comedy and Tragedy* (1887); *The Best Last, with other papers* (1888); *To Meet the Day through the Christian Year* (1889); *East Coast Days and Memories* (1889); *Twenty-five Years of St. Andrews* (2 vols., 1892), autobiographical reminiscences, continued in *St. Andrews and Elsewhere* (1894), and *Last Years of St. Andrews* (1896).

BIBLIOGRAPHY: Consult, besides the autobiographical sketches mentioned above: A. Lang, in *Longman's Magazine*, May, 1899; *DNB*, supplement vol. i, 244–245.

BOYLE, ROBERT, AND THE BOYLE LECTURES: Robert Boyle was born at Lismore Castle (30 m. n.e. of Cork), Waterford, Ireland, Jan. 25, 1627, son of Richard Boyle, earl of Cork; d. in London Dec. 30, 1691. He studied at Eton and (1638–44) at Geneva and elsewhere on the Continent; on his return to England he lived at first on his estate, Stalbridge, Dorsetshire, after 1654 in Oxford, and after 1668 in London. As a scientist he holds a high rank and has been considered the heir to both the methods and abilities of Francis Bacon. He was one of the founders of the Royal Society (1662), and was constantly engaged in investigations which resulted in numerous publications. He wrote many theological, moral, and religious essays, gave freely for the translation of the Bible into various languages, and was liberal in private charity. He was governor of the Corporation for the Spread of the Gospel in New England (see ELIOT, JOHN). In his will he left an endowment of £50 annually for the Boyle Lectures, a series of 8 sermons, to be delivered each year in some church, against unbelievers. For the lectures St. Paul's was used in 1690 and 1701, the parish church of St. Mary le Bow 1711–1805, Westminster Abbey 1852–53, the Chapel Royal, Whitehall, 1864–85, while the lectures of 1903–05 were delivered in the Church of St. Edmund, Lombard St. The first course was given by Richard Bentley (1692); his successors have included some of England's most prominent theologians. A selection from the sermons was published by Gilbert Burnet, vicar of Coggeshall, in 4 vols., London, 1737 A partial list of the published Boyle Lectures down to 1892–93 is given in J. F Hurst, *Literature of Theology* (New York, 1896). Since then there have been published the lectures for 1895, W C. E. Newbolt, *The Gospel of Experience* (London, 1896), and for 1903–05 by R. J. Knowling, *The Testimony of St. Paul to Christ* (London, 1905).

Boyle's complete works with life were published by Thomas Birch (5 vols., London, 1744; 2d ed., 6 vols., 1772).

BIBLIOGRAPHY: Aside from the Life by Birch there are available: A. à Wood, *Athenæ Oxonienses*, ed. P. Bliss, ii, 286, 4 vols., London, 1813–20; A. C. Brown, *Development of the Idea of Chemical Composition*, pp. 9–14, Edinburgh, 1869; *DNB*, vi, 118–123.

BRACE, CHARLES LORING: American philanthropist; b. at Litchfield, Conn., June 19, 1826; d. at Campfer in the Engadine, Switzerland, Aug. 11, 1890. He was graduated at Yale 1846; studied at the Yale Divinity School 1847–48 and at Union Theological Seminary, New York, 1848–1849; traveled and studied in Europe for two years; in 1853 he became first secretary and executive agent of the Children's Aid Society of New York, and remained such till his death. He planned and developed the work and supported it in the earlier days with much self-sacrificing labor; industrial and night schools were established, lodging-houses provided for newsboys and for girls, reading-rooms opened, summer charities instituted, and nearly 100,000 boys and girls were assisted to new homes and occupations with healthful and moral surroundings. By thus removing incipient criminals a marked diminution in juvenile crime was shown in the police reports of New York. The history of the work was given by Mr. Brace in his annual reports and in his two books, *Short Sermons to Newsboys, with a history of the formation of the Newsboys' Lodging House* (New York, 1866); and *The Dangerous Classes of New York, and twenty years' work among them* (1872; enlarged ed., 1880). He published several works of travel of a popular character such as *Home Life in Germany* (1853); *The New West* (1869); and as results of considerable thinking and study, *Gesta Christi, a history of humane progress under Christianity* (1882; 4th ed., 1884); and *The Unknown God, or inspiration among pre-Christian races* (1890).

BIBLIOGRAPHY: *C. L. Brace, His Life, chiefly told in his own Letters*, edited by his daughter, Emma Brace, New York, 1894.

BRACKMANN, ALBERT: German Protestant historian; b. at Hanover June 24, 1871. He was educated at the universities of Tübingen, Leipsic, and Göttingen, and occupies the position of associate professor of history at the University of Marburg. He is a collaborator of the Royal Academy of Sciences at Göttingen for the publication of early papal documents, and in addition to a number of contributions to historical periodicals has written: *Urkundliche Geschichte des Halberstädter Domkapitels im Mittelalter* (Wernigerode, 1898).

BRADFORD, AMORY HOWE: American Congregationalist; b. at Granby, N. Y., Apr. 14, 1846. He was educated at Genesee College, Hamilton College (B.A., 1867), Andover Theological Seminary (1870), and Oxford University. Since 1870 he has been pastor of the First Congregational Church, Montclair, N. J. He was associate editor of *The Outlook* from 1894 to 1901, member of the American Board of Commissioners for Foreign Missions deputation to Japan in 1895, and moderator of the National Council of Congregational Churches in 1901–04. He is also first secretary and second president of the American Institute of Christian Philosophy, and was elected president of the American Missionary Association in 1904. He was Southworth Lecturer at Andover Theological Seminary in 1902–03 and George Sheppard Lecturer at Bangor Theological Seminary in 1906. In theology he is a liberal evangelical. He has written *Spirit and Life* (New York, 1888); *Old Wine, New Bottles* (1892); *The Pilgrim in Old England* (1893); *Heredity and Christian Problems* (1895); *The Growing Revelation* (1897); *The Sistine Madonna* (1897); *The Holy Family* (1899); *The Art of Living Alone* (1899); *The Return to Christ* (1900); *The Age of Faith* (Boston, 1900); *Spiritual Lessons from the Brownings* (New York, 1900); *Messages of the Masters* (1902); *The Ascent of the Soul* (1905); and *The Inward Light* (1905).

BRADFORD, JOHN: Church of England Protestant martyr; b. at Manchester about 1510; burned at Smithfield July 1, 1555. He was in the service of Sir John Harrington, the king's paymaster in France; began to study law in the Temple 1547, but the next year turned to divinity and entered St. Catherine's Hall, Cambridge (M.A., by special grace, 1549); was elected fellow of Pembroke Hall 1549; became prebendary of Kentish Town in the church of St. Paul, 1551; was chaplain to Bishop Ridley, in 1552 one of the king's six chaplains in ordinary, and preached in many localities with great fervor and earnestness. In August, 1553 (six weeks after the accession of Mary), he was arrested on the charge of preaching seditious sermons and committed to the Tower; he was examined before Bishops Gardiner, Bonner, and others in January, 1555, and condemned as a heretic. His writings (chiefly sermons, letters, and devotional pieces) were edited for the Parker Society by Aubrey Townsend (2 vols., Cambridge, 1848–53).

Bibliography: W. Stephens, *Memoirs of John Bradford*, London, 1832; *The Life of John Bradford*, vol. iii of *Library of Christian Biography*, London, 1855; *DNB*, vi, 157–159.

BRADLAUGH, CHARLES: English freethought advocate and politician; b. at Hoxton (a suburb of London) Sept. 26, 1833; d. at London Jan. 30, 1891. He was educated in local schools until the age of twelve, when his business life began. A few years later he became an advocate of freethought, and rapidly achieved notoriety for his propaganda. His attitude seriously affected his career, and at the age of seventeen he enlisted as a private soldier, remaining in the army three years. He then entered a solicitor's office, and soon rose to a position of responsibility. Meantime he had resumed his campaign for freethought, and in 1858 began a platform tour of the provinces, advocating not only radicalism in religion, but also in politics. From 1862 until his death, excepting in 1863–66, he was the proprietor of the republican *National Reformer*, and in his advocacy of radical politics was secretary of the fund raised in 1858 to defend E. Truelove for publishing a vindication of Orsini's attempt to assassinate Napoleon III. He was likewise a member of the parliamentary reform league of 1866, and drew up the first draft of the Fenian proclamation issued in the following year, while three years later he was the envoy of the English republicans to the Spanish republican leader Castelar, and was likewise nominated as candidate for a division of Paris on the foundation of the French republic in the same year. He then attempted to go to Paris on the outbreak of the Commune to be an intermediary between Thiers and the insurrectionists, but was arrested at Calais and forced to return to England.

In 1868 Bradlaugh's attempts to gain a seat in the House of Commons began, but his avowed principles caused his defeat both in that year and in 1874. Six years later, however, he was returned, and by his refusal to take the required oath on the Bible initiated a struggle which involved him in repeated scenes in the House of Commons and in eight legal actions. He was again and again excluded from the House, his willingness to take the oath as a mere matter of form, or to affirm, being overruled by the plea that he was an avowed freethinker. Nevertheless, he was reelected for Northampton by special elections after his expulsion in 1881 and 1882, and at the general election in 1886 was once more returned, being permitted this time to take his seat, which he retained until his death. During this troubled period of his life he was also involved in a contest for the abolition of all restrictions on the press, beginning with his refusal, in 1868, to give security to the government against the publication of blasphemy and sedition in his *National Reformer*. In the following year another legal contest resulted in the passage of the Evidence Amendment Act, by which the evidence of freethinkers was declared admissible, a judge having refused to take his testimony on the ground that he was a freethinker. A few years later, in 1874, he became associated with Annie Besant (q.v.), who was assistant editor of the *National Reformer* until 1885, when she resigned on account of his opposition to socialism. In 1876 they were sentenced to six months' imprisonment and a fine of £200 for the publication of the *Fruits of Philosophy*, which advocated the artificial restraint of the increase of population. The sentence was suspended, however, and the contest resulted in the passage of an act removing the remaining restrictions on the press.

In Parliament Bradlaugh was active in securing the passage of a number of measures, of which the chief was one permitting the substitution of an affirmation for the oath both in the House of Commons and in the courts. In 1889 he visited India, and during his final illness the resolutions of his expulsion from the House of Commons were unanimously expunged. The writings of Bradlaugh were chiefly brief controversial pamphlets and contributions to the press. Among them the most important are *The Impeachment of the House of Brunswick* (London, 1872); *Autobiography* (1873); *Land for the People* (1877); *The New Life of David* (1877); *Genesis, its Authorship and Authenticity* (1882); and *The True Story of my Parliamentary Struggle* (1882).

Bibliography: A. S. Headingley, *Biography of Charles Bradlaugh*, London, 1880; C. R. Mackay, *Life of Charles Bradlaugh* ib. 1888; H. Bonner (his daughter), *Charles Bradlaugh: A Record of his Life and Work*, 2 vols., ib. 1894.

BRADLEY, GEORGE GRANVILLE: Dean of Westminster; b. at High Wycombe (30 m. w.n.w.

of London), Buckinghamshire, Dec. 11, 1821; d. in London Mar. 12, 1903. He studied at Rugby under Arnold (1837–40), and at University College, Oxford (B.A., 1844; M.A., 1847); was fellow of University College 1844–50; became assistant master at Rugby 1846; head master of Marlborough College, Wiltshire, 1858; master of University College, Oxford, 1870; dean of Westminster, London, succeeding Arthur Penrhyn Stanley, 1881; resigned his deanery 1902. He edited and revised Arnold's *Latin Prose Composition* (London, 1881), and published *Aids to Writing Latin Prose* (1884); *Recollections of Arthur Penrhyn Stanley* (1883); *Lectures on Ecclesiastes* (Oxford, 1885; new ed., 1898); *Lectures on the Book of Job* (1887); and assisted R. E. Prothero in preparing the *Life and Correspondence of Arthur Penrhyn Stanley* (2 vols., London, 1894).

BRADSHAW, WILLIAM: Puritan; b. at Market Bosworth (12 m. w. of Leicester), Leicestershire, 1571; d. at Chelsea 1618. He studied at Emmanuel College, Cambridge, and became fellow of Sidney Sussex College in 1599; took orders but never received a living owing to his Puritan principles, and spent much of his time in retirement in Derbyshire, whence he made many journeys in behalf of the cause to which he was devoted. His chief work was *English Puritanism : containing the main opinions of the rigid sort of those that are called Puritans in the Realm of England* (London, 1605; Latin transl., by William Ames, Frankfort, 1610; an abstract is given in Neal's *History of the Puritans*, part ii, chap. i). The main point of his system was that he would subject no congregation to any ecclesiastical jurisdiction "save that which is within itself." He would have the members delegate their powers to pastors and elders, retaining that of excommunication. No clergyman should hold civil office. He was strongly opposed to "ceremonies." He was not a separatist and held that the king as "the archbishop and general overseer of all the churches within his dominions" had the right to rule and must not be resisted except passively. He published many other works and tracts, most of them anonymously.

Bibliography: A fair biography and references to the somewhat abundant literature may be found in *DNB*, vi, 182–185.

BRADWARDINE, THOMAS: Archbishop of Canterbury; b. probably at Chichester, Sussex, 1290; d. in London Aug. 26, 1349. His name is variously spelled (Bragwardin, Brandnardin, Bredwardyn, etc.), in public documents he is usually called Thomas de Bradwardina, and a title often given him is *Doctor profundus*. He studied theology, philosophy, mathematics, and astronomy at Merton College, Oxford; lectured there; became chancellor of St. Paul's Church at London; in 1339 accompanied Edward III as his confessor in his campaigns in France; in 1349 was chosen archbishop of Canterbury, was consecrated at Avignon, and died a few weeks afterward. He was highly esteemed by Wyclif, Jean Gerson, and Flacius. He was the author of a large work entitled *De causa Dei contra Pelagium* [ed. Sir Henry Savile, London, 1618], in which he attempted to show that the theology as well as the Church of his time were Pelagian. He gave the name Cainites to those who gave up hope in God and depended upon their own merits; his personal experience gave him a different conception: "In the schools of the philosophers I rarely heard a word concerning grace, but I continually heard that we are the masters of our own free actions." Rom. ix, 16 had seemed to him to be wrong; "but afterward . I came to see that the grace of God far preceded all good works both in time and in nature—by grace I mean the will of God." Bradwardine wished to support this position on theoretical grounds. He acknowledged Augustine as his master. The sum of his teaching is as follows: God is complete perfection and goodness, is good action itself, free from the potentiality of imperfection. He is not limited by mentality. He is the first cause, the absolute principle of being and motion. Therefore, no one can act nor can anything "happen"; God works or orders events. Divine foreknowledge is will exercised long before, or predestination of [man's] will. God's will, moreover, is unchanging. Everything takes place by virtue of the immutable antecedent necessity caused by the divine volition. Hence man can say nothing "more useful or efficacious than 'thy will be done.'" The effects of predestination are the gift of grace in the present, justification from sin, award of merit, perseverance to the end, and unending bliss in the world to come. The result of this line of thought is, of course, determinism of a Thomistic type. In spite of this theory, Bradwardine, like Augustine, asserted the reality of free will. His historical importance consists in the fact that he was one of the most powerful champions of the Augustinian movement which took place toward the end of the Middle Ages. This movement contributed to the dissolution of scholasticism and to a new understanding of Christian doctrine from the point of view of personal faith. R. Seeberg.

Bibliography: The scanty notices of his life are collected by Sir Henry Savile in the preface to his edition of the *Causa Dei*. For his mathematical works consult M. Cantor, *Geschichte der Mathematik*, ii, 102 sqq., Leipsic, 1892. Consult further G. V. Lechler, *De Thoma Bradwardino*, Leipsic, 1862; idem, *Johann von Wiclif und die Vorgeschichte der Reformation*, i, 220 sqq., Leipsic, 1873; Eng. transl., pp. 88–96, London, 1878; K. Werner, *Der Augustinismus in der Scholastik des späteren Mittelalters*, pp 337 sqq., Vienna, 1883; R. Seeberg, *Dogmengeschichte*, ii, 192, Leipsic, 1898; *DNB*, vi, 188 190.

BRADY, NICHOLAS: Church of England clergyman and poet; b. at Bandon (20 m. s.w. of Cork), County Cork, Ireland, Oct. 28, 1659; d. at Richmond, Surrey, May 20, 1726. He studied at Christ Church, Oxford (B.A., 1682), and Trinity College, Dublin (B.A., 1685; M.A., 1686; B.D. and D.D., 1699); took orders in Ireland and received two livings in the diocese of Cork. He was a zealous promoter of the Revolution of 1688 and soon thereafter removed to England; became lecturer at St. Michael's, Wood Street, London; minister at St. Catherine Cree, 1691; rector of Richmond, 1696, and of Clapham, 1706. He was also rector of Stratford-on-Avon, 1702–05, and conducted a school at Richmond. He was chaplain to William

III, to Mary, and to Queen Anne. He published a tragedy, *The Rape, or the Innocent Imposters* (London, 1692), a translation of the Æneid of Vergil (4 vols., 1726; now extremely rare), and two volumes of sermons (1704–06); but is remembered chiefly for his share in the *New Version of the Psalms of David*, produced jointly by himself and Nahum Tate (q.v.).

BRAHMANISM.

Brahmanism is the orthodox religion of India, the most ancient of all Indo-Germanic faiths of which there is record. In itself the most catholic and elastic of cults, its test is the recognition of the divine authority of the Vedas; its outward sign is reverence for the gods, some of whom are comparatively late and foreign in origin; and, for the Brahmans, its end is emancipation from the sorrow of existence and the misery of reincarnation through reabsorption into the divine essence of the All-Soul.

Brahmanism may be divided into three periods: I. The Age of the Vedas and their Ancillary Literature; II. Brahmanism and the Pantheism of the Upanishads; III. The Age during which the Buddhistic and Jainistic Heresies Prevailed. The two phases which are included in the Brahmanistic counterreformation and rise of the Hindu sects, and modern Hinduism and the unitarian movements are treated under Hinduism (q.v.).

I. Vedism, the Age of the Vedas and their Ancillary Literature (the Brahmanas and Sutras—the former a sort of Hindu Talmud; the latter brief verses in technical language, a favorite form of expressing rules): At a period of remote antiquity, possibly between 2000 and 1500 B.C., a section of the Indo-Germanic peoples known by various names, of which the most common are Indians and Aryans, broke off from the kindred Iranian stock and wandered southward and eastward through Afghanistan into the Punjab or the "Five Waters," in the extreme northwest of the Indian peninsula.

1. The People of the Vedas and their Gods.

Like the Iranians of Persia, they were divided into the three classes of priests, warriors, and husbandmen, whence were to be formed later the three higher castes, and were a nomadic and agricultural people, filled with the joy of living, valiant in war, daring freebooters, hot in love and reveling in wine, almost everything, in short, that the later Hindus were not. Their gods were like themselves, concrete and strong: Surya, the bright deity of the sun; Indra, the blinding lightning which ushers in the rainy season; Agni, the god of fire; and Soma, the deified inspiration of strong drink and of the divine courage which it gives. Few are the deities which show the softer side of the early Aryan mind, such as Ushas, the goddess of the dawn, or Varuna, the god of the sky-ocean, who watches over all and even later in this period receives praises which almost savor of monotheism.

The beliefs of the Aryans of this period are contained in the Rig-Veda, a book of hymns, the earliest literary records of the Indo-Germanic race, to which the most probable date assigned is 1500–500 B.C. This Veda is divided into ten books

2. The Rig-Veda.

containing 1,022 hymns. Books ii–vii form the "family books," composed by successive generations of families of bards. Book ix is restricted to the Soma hymns, while i and viii, and especially x, the latest of all, are more diverse in contents and authorship. Within this range of space and time are represented many phases of religious thought, ranging from crass polytheism through intricate henotheism or syncretism to a quasi-monotheism, or rather pantheism; varying from earnest faith to incipient skepticism; touching, too, on daily life as well as on worship and sacrifice.

It must not be supposed, however, that the faith of the Veda is naive or childlike. It is, on the contrary, quite developed and occasionally even corrupt. Many of the hymns were undoubtedly composed for the ritual, although it is scarcely possible to regard the entire collection as subservient to the liturgy. Untenable also is the theory of the French school which reduces the entire Rig-Veda to a mass of allegory, nor are the conclusions of the realistic school, which regards this Veda as entirely Indic and interprets it rationalistically, altogether free from criticism. To the elucidation of a collection so extended both in space and time no single method of interpretation is adequate. Naiveté and mature thought, liturgy and hymnology, allegory and realism must each be recognized as occasion demands, must even be combined at times to give a true representation of the Vedic Hinduism.

The basis of the Vedic religion is nature-worship. Each element is deified, the fire as Agni, the dawn as Ushas, the sky as Varuna, and the lightning of the storm as Indra. A single object in nature may be represented by many gods, as when the sun is venerated under the names of Surya, "the glowing one"; Savitar, "the enlivener"; Bhaga, "the bestower of boons"; Pushan, "he who causeth to flourish"; and Vishnu, "the mighty one." While these names may represent the deity in different aspects, as do the Egyptian Ra and Tum, the gods of the rising and the setting sun, it must not be forgotten that variance in name and even in concept of the same divinity may have been in its origin mere local divergence in expression for one and the same god, for the Rig-Veda was composed by many minds, at many places, in many periods. Behind nature-worship doubtless lay the earlier phase of animism, although its traces are obscured in the Vedic texts. Still more scanty are the evidences of ancestor-worship, or the cult of ghosts, though this phase was perhaps rather officially ignored than popularly absent. The eschatology of the Rig-Veda is comparatively simple, and resembles in its meagerness the poverty of early Semitism as represented by the Assyro-Babylonian religion. Allusions to the future state of the dead are practically confined to the late tenth book. Yama, the first of men to die, is the king of the dead; and apparently the blessed, i.e., the brave and generous, go when they die to the sun, where they engage in revelry like that of the Norse heroes of Asgard. The unblessed dead merely disappear, for hell is, in Indian thought, a late theological invention, devised to counterbalance the joys of heaven. In the latest portion of the Rig-Veda, moreover, appear the chief hymns later rubricized in the ritual, if indeed they were not, at least in part, designedly composed for an already existing liturgy.

3. The Sama- and Yajur-Vedas.

Beside the Rig-Veda exist two other canonical Vedas, and a fourth which is uncanonical. The Sama or "Song" Veda is composed of verses taken chiefly from the eighth and ninth books of the Rig-Veda and arranged for the liturgy. Far more important is the Yajur or "Sacrificial" Veda, which exists in several recensions, the chief being the Vajasaneyi or "White" Yajur-Veda, so called from being composed only in verse, and the Taittirya and Maitrayani, which are termed "black," since the verse of the text is intermingled with a quasi-commentary and amplification in prose.

The arena implied is no longer the Punjab but the "middle district," around the modern Delhi, which the Aryans had reached in their slow migration eastward. The change of locality, however, is dwarfed into insignificance by the alteration in religious tone. The frank delight in life which characterizes the Rig-Veda is changed to mysticism and an ever-increasing ritualism. Religion has given place to magic. The principle of henotheism which is so marked a feature of the Rig-Veda, through which poetic enthusiasm comes to attribute to one divinity the names and attributes of another, thus elevating him for the nonce into the supreme and only object of adoration, becomes in the Yajur-Veda symbolism carried to its limit. A thing is no longer *like* something else, it *is* something else. The Brahman is no longer merely a priest, he is a god with all the attributes of divinity, while prayer and sacrifice are now means of compelling the deity to perform the will of his worshipers, instead of being modes of propitiation or bargaining. The religion of India now centers in the sacrifice, and a ritual is developed which is perhaps the most elaborate that the world has ever seen. While the power of the Brahmans was thereby increased until they were apotheosized, the view is antiquated which regards the development of the liturgy as the ecclesiastical device of a cunning and self-interested priesthood, despite the enormous fees which were given for the performance of sacrifice.

The pantheon of this period suffers little diminution as compared with the epoch of the Rig-Veda, but the gods have declined in power, although some have been greatly magnified, such as Kala (Time), who played no part in the earliest Veda. The epithets and the functions of the gods become separate divinities in many cases, and an All-God now gains the full recognition which is only suggested even in the latest portions of the Rig-Veda. The legends of the deities, on the other hand, are richly developed, though their quantity is more admirable than their quality. This, however, is a recrudescence of popular beliefs previously not officially recognized, rather than new speculations of the Brahmans, though this faith of the people finds its application in the explanation and proof of the sacrifice. The rules for the Brahmanic ritual are contained not only in the various recensions of the Yajur-Veda, but in the still more important Brahmanas, of which each school of each of the Vedas has at least one, while the Tandin recension of the Sama-Veda has three. Additional details are contained in the Srautasutras, and the ritual for daily life may be found in the various Grihyasutras.

4. The Atharva-Veda.

Beside the three canonical Vedas and their ancillary literature, representing the official religion of the Vedic and Brahmanic periods, stood a Veda of magic—the uncanonical Atharva-Veda. The pantheon of the Rig-Veda is here a jumbled confusion of divinities, at their head a supreme god of all, while eschatology has so far developed as to recognize a place of torment for the malignant dead. The predominant note of the Atharva-Veda is magic. It is filled with all manner of charms and incantations for wealth and for children, for long life and good health, for love and for revenge, charms for plants, animals, and diseases, curses and maledictions for the destruction of enemies and for counteracting the enemy's black magic. Linguistically and chronologically far later than the Rig-Veda, the material of the Atharva-Veda is in all probability as old in some of its parts as the most ancient portions of the Rig. It is an invaluable document for early Hindu religion as the oldest monument of its popular faith.

II. Brahmanism and the Pantheism of the Upanishads: The enormous structure of ritualism erected by the Yajur-Veda, the Brahmanas, and the Sutras gradually became a burden too heavy to be borne; liturgy was then undermined by philosophical speculation. Traces of this are already evident in the later portions of the Rig-Veda, as in the famous hymn (x, 121) whose refrain runs: "To whom (as) god shall we offer sacrifice?" thus affording a basis for the Brahmanas to create a god "Who." By this time, moreover, an All-God was definitely recognized in Prajapati, "the lord of creatures," but it was reserved for the close of the Brahmanic period to ignore the gods and arrive at God.

The Upanishads, the literary records of this phase of thought, represent a perfection of pantheism which has never been equaled, and their influence is a mighty factor in Hindu thought of the present day. Salvation is no longer to be attained by works, but by knowledge, and the entire teaching of the Upanishads may be comprised in the one famous phrase found in the Chandogya Upanishad: *Tat tvam asi*, "That art thou," or, in other words, "Thou art the Infinite." Though the *summum bonum* of the Upanishads is this saving knowledge and the reunion with the All-Soul which it brings, such a consummation is not requisite for all, since there are many who do not desire it, and for them minor blessings are reserved in a future life. The existence of the gods is not denied, though they be but phases of the All-Soul, nor is the advantage of sacrifice denied, for such offerings are still imperative. Herein lies, perhaps, the secret of the origin of the Upanishads.

1. The Upanishads.

The concluding portion of each Brahmana is an Aranyaka, or "forest-book," designed for the use of those forest hermits who had passed beyond the need of sacrifice, and in each Aranyaka is an Upanishad. Primarily, therefore, the Upanishads represented the text-books of those who had passed through the sacrificial stage of their religious life and were henceforth free to meditate on sacred things as seemed best in their own eyes. Later, however, the Upanishads became a special form of the sacred writings of the Hindus; and served as the basis of the most lofty of all their six orthodox systems of philosophy. To see in them a religious revolt of the second, or warrior, caste against Brahman control, as certain scholars have sought to do, seems, on the whole, scarcely warranted.

Somewhat subsequent to the Upanishads were developed the six orthodox systems of Indian philosophy, the Samkhya and Yoga, the Vaiseshika and Nyaya, and the Purvamimamsa and Vedanta.

2. The Six Orthodox Systems of Philosophy.

Of these the Vaiseshika and Nyaya are systems of logic rather than of philosophy; the Samkhya and Yoga, which supplement each other, are essentially dualistic; while the Purvamimamsa and Vedanta, of which the former is the least important of all the systems, represent the spiritual aftermath of the Upanishads, and are, accordingly, rigidly pantheistic.

III. The Age of the Buddhistic and Jainistic Heresies: Beneath the excessive ritual of the Brahmanistic period and the pantheistic speculations of a chosen few still lay the popular faith of the Aryan invaders of India. Meanwhile, however, the course of immigration had moved still further to the east and become centered about the holy city of Benares. The doctrine of the misery of all earthly existence was by this time accepted by all, and the teachings of metempsychosis were fully established. The worship of Siva, originally a local godling of some aboriginal western tribe, was attaining such popularity that he was opposed as the Destroyer to the Vedic sun-god Vishnu, who was worshiped as the Preserver (of the universe). For the sake of symmetry, *brahma*, denoting in the Rig-Veda "prayer," was developed by the priestly theologians into Brahma, the Creator, who, though on the whole a pale abstract deity, respected rather than worshiped, formed the third member of the *trimurti*, or triad.

The religious texts of this period are comparatively few, though from them may be gleaned data of the greatest importance for a knowledge of India's faith. The principal sources are the law books, especially the famous code of Manu, and the Mahabharata, the great epic of India and the longest poem of all literature. From the point of view of orthodox Hinduism, however, the epoch, possibly because of the comparative scantiness of material, presents less of interest than any of the others. It was, on the other hand, essentially the age of heresy, this term denoting in India simply a formal denial of the divine authority of the three canonical Vedas. There had, of course, been heretics and infidels long before this period; traces of them occur as early as the tenth book of the Rig-Veda, but it was not until the period under consideration that heresies of lasting importance were able to develop. In the sixth century B.C. arose two independent teachers, both from the Kshatriya, or warrior, class and both accordingly more or less antagonistic to the Brahmans. Forebodings of such a struggle between the two upper castes are not lacking in the Upanishads, where, in more than one instance, a warrior rose superior to a Brahman in theological learning.

Rebelling against Brahman supremacy, ignoring salvation by sacrifice, rejecting the authority of the Vedas, teaching emancipation from the pain of life and the misery of rebirth by personal service to all living creatures however lowly, and choosing, moreover, with pointed significance, as their linguistic medium the despised popular dialects instead of the hallowed Sanskrit of the Brahmans, Sakya Muni (Buddha) and Mahavira founded the religions which still exist as Buddhism and Jainism (qq.v.). When, after the lapse of nearly a millennium, those two religions lost their hold upon India, a new form of Brahmanism arose in what is known as Hinduism (q.v.), the basis of which was a compromise between the orthodox and philosophical Brahmanism of pre-Buddhistic times and the religions of the Dravidian and other non-Aryan peoples of southern India. See INDIA.

BIBLIOGRAPHY: The literature of India itself is enormous, and that upon it is almost as great. A bibliography of India is much needed. The most accessible and convenient body of sources for the English reader is the *SBE*, more than half of which is devoted to translations from the various departments of Indian literature. Outside of this collection, the following texts and translations are important: *Sanskrit Texts, Sacred Hymns*, 6 vols., London, 1849–74, new ed., 1890–92; H. H. Wilson, *Rig Veda Sanhita*, 6 vols., ib. 1850 sqq. (a translation); *Rig Veda*, a transl. by P. Peterson, ib. 1888; H. Grassmann, *Rigveda übersetzt*, 4 vols., Leipsic, 1876–77; *Rig-Veda*, by A. Ludwig, in 6 vols., Prague, 1875–88 (Germ. transl., introduction and commentary); *Sama-Veda*, T. Benfey, Leipsic, 1848 (text and Germ. transl.); R. T. Griffith, *Hymns of the Rigveda, Transl. with Commentary*, 4 vols., Benares, 1889–92; idem, *Hymns of the Samaveda, Transl. with Commentary*, ib. 1893; idem, *Hymns of the Atharva-Veda*, ib., 2 vols., 1895–96; *Atharvaveda*, by A. Ludwig, 2 vols., Prague, 1876 (Germ. transl.); *Atharva-Veda, livre vii (viii, xiii) traduit* . par V Henry, Paris, 1891–1892; *The Aitareya-Brahmana*, transl. by M. Haug, 2 vols., Bombay, 1863; the *Brahmanas* of the *Sama Veda* have been edited by A. C. Burnell, 6 vols., London, Trübner, n.d.; *Atharva-Veda Samhita, Translation and . Commentary* by W. D. Whitney, ed. C. R. Lanman, 2 vols.,

Boston, 1906; *The Vedantasara, A Manual of Hindu Pantheism*, transl. by G. A. Jacob, ib. 1881. Parts of some of the *Upanishads* have been edited and translated by E. Roer, 19 parts, Calcutta, n.d., and by E. B. Cowell, 2 parts, ib. 1861. Important is J. Muir, *Original Sanskrit Texts*, 5 vols., London, 1868-73. The *Sutras* are represented in the Germ. transl. by A. F. Stenzler, Leipsic, 1876, in the Eng. transl. of W. D. Whitney, New Haven, 1871, and of G. Thibaut, London, Trübner, n.d.

On the history of Indian literature consult: A. Weber, *The White Yajur Veda*, Berlin, 1849; idem, *A Hist. of Indian Literature*, London, 1882 (critical and brief); F. Max Müller, *Hist. of Ancient Sanskrit Literature*, ib. 1860 (now out of print); A. Kaegi, *Der Rigveda*, Leipsic, 1881, Eng. transl., London, 1886; F. Nêve, *Les Époques littéraires de l'Inde*, Paris, 1887; J. C. Oman, *The Great Indian Epics*, London, 1884 (a condensation of the stories, with notes); A. A. Macdonell, *Hist. of Sanskrit Literature*, ib. 1900; E. W. Hopkins, *The Great Epic of India*, New Haven, 1901.

On the philosophy the best single book is F. Max Müller, *Six Systems of Indian Philosophy*, London, 1899, cf. his *Three Lectures on the Vedanta Philosophy*, ib. 1894. Other works are J. Davies, *The Sankhya Karika of Iswara Krishna. An Exposition of the System of Kapilà*, ib. 1881; A. E. Gough, *Philosophy of the Upanishads*, ib. 1882; Ram Chandra Bose, *Hindu Philosophy popularly Explained*, Calcutta, 1888; M. Williams, *Indian Wisdom*, London, 1893; R. Garbe, *Philosophy of Ancient India*, Chicago, 1897 (an excellent " first book "); J. Kreyher, *Die Weisheit der Brahmanen und des Christentums*, Gütersloh, 1901; P. Deussen, *Philosophy of the Upanishads*, Edinburgh, 1905; idem, *Die Geheimlehre des Veda*, Leipsic, 1907; idem, *Outlines of Indian Philosophy*, Berlin, 1907; L. D. Barnett, *Some Sayings of the Upanishads*, London, 1906; S. A. Desai, *A Study of the Indian Philosophy*, ib. 1907.

On the religion of India the best single book is R. W Frazer, *Literary Hist. of India*, New York, 1898. H. T. Colebrooke, *Essays on the Religion and Philosophy of the Hindus*, 2d ed. by his son, 3 vols., London, 1873, is a classic, with which should be put C. Lassen, *Indische Alterthumskunde*, 4 vols., Bonn, 1847-61. Of high value is J. H. Wilson, *Essays on the Religion of the Hindus*, 2 vols., London, 1861-62. Other treatises are: S. Johnson, *Oriental Religions, India*, Boston, 1872; F. Max Müller, *Lectures on . Religions of India*, London, 1879; A. Barth, *Religions of India*, ib. 1882; W J. Wilkins, *Hindu Mythology, Vedic and Puranic*, ib. 1882; A. W Wallis, *Cosmology of the Rig Veda*, ib. 1887; M. Williams, *Religious Life and Thought in India*, ib. 1887; G. A. Jacob, *Hindu Pantheism*, ib. 1889; J. Dowson, *Classical Dictionary of Hindu Mythology and Religion*, ib. 1891; *Religious Systems of the World*, ib. 1893; H. Oldenberg, *Die Religion des Veda*, Berlin, 1894; idem, *Ancient India, its Language and Religions*, London, 1896; E. W. Hopkins, *Religions of India*, Boston, 1895 (very useful, systematic and clear, gives list of works); idem, *India, Old and New*, New York, 1902; M. Phillips, *The Teaching of the Vedas*, London, 1895; Z. A. Ragozin, *Vedic India*, ib. 1895; A. Weber, *Vedische Beiträge*, Berlin, 1895; A. Hillebrandt, *Vedische Mythologie*, 3 vols., Breslau, 1902; J. C. Oman, *Mystics, Ascetics and Saints of India*, London, 1903; J. M. Mitchell, *Great Religions of India*, New York, 1905; E. B. Havell, *Benares the Sacred City. Sketches of Hindu Life and Religion*, London, 1906.

BRAHMO SOMAJ: A Hindu theistic society. Its aim is the monotheistic reform of the Hindu polytheistic religion. The founder, Rammohan Roy (b. 1774), of Brahman descent, through the study of the Koran and the Bible became estranged from his ancestral belief, and was attracted by Christianity, without, however, getting beyond a rationalistic pantheism. He endeavored to formulate a universal monotheism based upon various ancient scriptures. He denounced ethnic impurities, but maintained the institution of caste. In 1816 he gathered a small community at Calcutta, the *Atmiya Sabha*, of which he was the leader till his death, Sept. 26, 1833, at Bristol, England, where he acted as political agent.

The weakened reform party was strengthened in 1839 by the founding of the *Tatwabodhini Sabha*, whose leader was Babu Devendranath Tagore. He held aloof from Christian influences in the patriotic effort to restore (what he regarded as) the pure religion of the Vedas, but finally conceived a deistic system on the basis of reason, rejecting all scriptures. In 1862 the religious community was reorganized as the *Adi Somaj*. Meanwhile a follower named Dayanand Saraswati had turned again to the Vedas, which he regarded as teaching a purely theistic religion, and as anticipating also the results of modern culture. He founded the *Arya Somaj*, the adherents of which came afterward under spiritualistic influences. The two societies last named found a competitor in the adherents of Babu Keshav Chandra Sen (b. Nov. 19, 1838, at Calcutta), who, through European culture had become dissatisfied with the religion of his ancestors, and attempted to find rest in philosophy. But this brought no satisfaction to his religiously disposed mind. After much study of the Bible he came to a decision, and in 1858 joined the *Adi Somaj*. For a time he cooperated with Devendranath Tagore, but finally found himself at variance with this conservatively disposed leader, who did not approve his bold denunciation of the shameful practises of heathenism, and even of caste. After the rupture which naturally resulted, in 1863 he founded the *Brahmo Somaj* of India, which soon developed an activity that almost rivaled the Christian propaganda. He went to England in 1870, where he was much honored. Many Christian ideas tending to promote his cause were brought back by him to India, and the *Brahmo Somaj* found many adherents. But he grew more conservative and gradually drew away from Occidental influences. The representatives of progress separated and founded the *Sadharan Brahmo Somaj*. Only the less important members of the former community adhered to Chandra Sen, who lost himself more and more in a dark mysticism. Finally he appeared as the founder of a world-religion (" The New Dispensation "), as he claimed by divine command. For the new Church he prepared a ritual and teaching. Nevertheless, his success was not striking, though by his small circle of adherents he was almost worshiped. He died January 8, 1884. His successor, Babu Protap Chandra Mozumdar, had great difficulty in preventing the further disruption of the community, and little progress was made. In 1891 it numbered 3,051 members, mostly in Bengal.

The *Arya Somaj* had a larger success, developing especially in the United Provinces and the Punjab, numbering some 40,000 members. But few of the Brahmo Somaj have accepted Christianity. See INDIA, III, 1. R. GRUNDEMANN.

BIBLIOGRAPHY: Sources: *Indian Mirror*, Calcutta, 1861-1880; *Sunday Mirror*, ib. 1880-82; *The Liberal and the New Dispensation*, ib. 1881 sqq.; *Theistic Annual*, ib. 1872 sqq.; *Theistic Quarterly Review*, ib. 1879. Consult also: Mary Carpenter, *Last Days in England of Ramohun Roy*, London, 1866; K. Chunder Sen, *Brahmo Somaj*, ib. 1870; J. Hesse, *Der Brahmo Somaj . .* , in *Basler Missions Magazin*, 1876, pp. 385 sqq.; Kesavachandra, *Brahmo Somaj*, Calcutta, 1883; F. Max Müller, in *Biographical Es-*

says, London, 1884 (gives accounts of recent religious movements); T. E. Slater, *Keshab Chundra Sen and the Brahma Samaj*, Madras, 1884; P. C. Mozoomdar, *Life and Teachings of Chunder Sen*, Calcutta, 1887; H. Baynes, *Evolution of Religious Thought in India*, London, 1889 (a full account); L. J. Frohneyer, *Neuere Reformbestrebungen in Hinduismus*, in *Basler Missions Magazin*, 1888, pp. 129 sqq.; *The Offering of Devendranath Tagore*, transl. by M. M. Chatterji, Calcutta, 1889; Rammohun Roy, *English Works*, 2 vols., London, 1888; Navakanta Chattopadhyaya, *Life and Character of Ram Mohun Roy*, Dacca, 1890; C. N. Aitchison, *The Brahmo Somaj*, in *Church Missionary Intelligencer*, 1893, pp. 161 sqq.

BRAIG, KARL VON BORROMAEO: German Roman Catholic; b. at Kanzach (a village near Buchau, 30 m. s.w. of Ulm) Feb. 10, 1853. He was educated at the University of Tübingen (Ph.D., 1877), where he was instructor in dogmatic theology in 1879–83, and was parish priest at Wildbad and district inspector of schools, except for tours of Austria, Germany, France, Italy, and England, from 1883 to 1893. In the latter year he was appointed associate professor of apologetics and dogmatics at the University of Freiburg, and four years later was promoted to his present position of full professor of the same subjects. He is also director of the dogmatic seminar in the university, and has written *Zukunftsreligion des Unbewussten* (Freiburg, 1882); *Kunst des Gedankenlesens* (Frankfort, 1886); *Encyklopädie der theoretischen Philosophie* (Stuttgart, 1886); *Gottesbeweis oder Gottesbeweise?* (1888); *Apologie des Christentums* (Freiburg, 1889); *La Matière* (Paris, 1891); *Die Freiheit der philosophischen Forschung* (Freiburg, 1894); *Vom Denken* (1896); *Vom Sein* (1896); *Vom Erkennen* (1897); *Leibniz, sein Leben und die Bedeutung seiner Lehre* (Frankfort, 1901); *Zur Erinnerung an Franz Xavier Krauss* (Freiburg, 1902); *Wesen des Christentums* (1903); and *Der Papst und die Freiheit* (1903).

BRAINERD, DAVID: Missionary to the American Indians; b. at Haddam, Conn., Apr. 20, 1718; d. at the home of Jonathan Edwards (to whose daughter Jemima he was engaged), Northampton, Mass., Oct. 9, 1747 He entered Yale College in 1739 and was expelled in his junior year; it was the time of the Great Awakening and Brainerd, who was "sober and inclined to melancholy" from childhood, sympathized with the "New Lights" (Whitefield, Tennent, and their followers); he attended their meetings when forbidden to do so, and criticized one of the tutors as having "no more grace than a chair"; as a consequence he was expelled. He was licensed at Danbury, Conn., July 29, 1742; was approved as a missionary by the New York correspondents of the Society in Scotland for Propagating Christian Knowledge, Nov. 25, 1742, and labored among the Indians at Kaunaumeek (Brainerd, Rensselaer County, N. Y., 18 m. s.e. of Albany) Apr., 1743–Mar., 1744; was ordained as a missionary at Newark, N. J., June 12, 1744; ten days later began work at what was intended to be his permanent station, at the forks of the Delaware, near Easton, Penn.; in October he visited the Indians on the Susquehanna, and June 19, 1745, began to preach at Crossweeksung (Crosswick, 9 m. s.e. of Trenton), the scene of his greatest success. His life among the Indians was one of hardship and suffering borne with heroic fortitude and self-devotion; his health gave way under the strain and he relinquished the work, Mar. 20, 1747, dying from consumption. The portions of his diary dealing with his work at Crossweeksung (June 19–Nov. 4, 1745, and Nov. 24, 1745–June 19, 1746) were published before his death by the commissioners of the Society (*Mirabilia dei inter Indicos : or the rise and progress of a remarkable work of grace among a number of the Indians in the provinces of New Jersey and Pennsylvania ;* and *Divine Grace Displayed : or the continuance and progress of a remarkable work of grace*, etc., both published at Philadelphia, 1746, and commonly known as "Brainerd's Journal"). All of his papers, including an account of his early life and the original copy of his diary, were left with Jonathan Edwards, who prepared *An Account of the Life of the Late Rev. David Brainerd* (Boston, 1749), omitting the parts of the diary already published. The life and diary entire, with his letters and other writings, were edited by S. E. Dwight (New Haven, 1822) and by J. M. Sherwood (New York, 1884). His place as missionary was taken, at his request, by his brother **John** (b. at Haddam, Conn., Feb. 28, 1720; d. at Deerfield, N. J., Mar. 18, 1781). He was graduated at Yale, 1746. His work was hindered by disputes about title to Indian lands, war, and opposition from the Quakers; he was dismissed by the Society in Scotland in 1755, reengaged in 1756, again dismissed in 1757, and again asked to return in 1759; the funds provided by the Society and by the Synod of New York and New Jersey were insufficient, and he gave freely from his own scanty means; he served the whites no less faithfully than the Indians and was at the same time both foreign and home missionary; after 1777 he had charge of a church at Deerfield. Consult his life by Thomas Brainerd (Philadelphia, 1865).

BRAINERD, THOMAS: American Presbyterian; b. at Leyden, Lewis County, N. Y., June 17, 1804; d. at Scranton, Penn., Aug. 22, 1866. He gave up the study of law for theology, and was graduated at Andover in 1831; was pastor of the Fourth Presbyterian Church, Cincinnati, 1831–33; of the Pine Street (Third) Presbyterian Church, Philadelphia, 1837 till his death. He was a leader of the New School branch of the Presbyterian Church, a personal friend of Lyman Beecher and Albert Barnes; was distinguished for patriotic ardor and services during the Civil War. He wrote much for religious periodicals, edited the *Cincinnati Journal*, a Presbyterian religious paper (1833–36), and a young people's paper, and wrote the *Life of John Brainerd* (Philadelphia, 1865). His great-great-grandfather was an uncle of David and John Brainerd, the missionaries.

Bibliography: Mary Brainerd, *Life of Rev. Thomas Brainerd*, Philadelphia, 1870.

BRAMHALL, JOHN: Protestant archbishop of Armagh; b. at or near Pontefract (22 m. s.s.w. of York), Yorkshire, 1594; d. at Omagh (30 m. s. of Londonderry), County Tyrone, Ireland, June 25, 1663. He studied at Sidney Sussex College, Cambridge (B.A., 1612; M.A., 1616; B.D., 1623;

D.D., 1630); took orders about 1616 and distinguished himself in Yorkshire, where he received several appointments. In 1633 he went to Ireland as chaplain to Wentworth (afterward Earl of Strafford); became archdeacon of Meath, and, in 1634, bishop of Derry. He did much to increase the revenues of the Irish Church, and tried to establish episcopacy more firmly. Most of the time from the Irish insurrection of 1641 till the Restoration he spent on the Continent, was made archbishop of Armagh in 1661, and as such displayed a commendable moderation in striving to secure conformity. His works were collected by John Vesey, archbishop of Tuam, and published at Dublin in 1677; they include five treatises against Romanists, three against sectaries, three against Hobbes, and seven miscellaneous, in defense of royalist and Anglican views. The works are reprinted in the *Library of Anglo-Catholic Theology* (5 vols., Oxford, 1842–45) with life.

BRANDENBURG, BISHOPRIC OF: A diocese established by Otto the Great in 948, including the territory between the Elbe on the west, the Oder on the east, and the Black Elster on the south, and taking in the Uckermark to the north. It was originally under the archiepiscopal jurisdiction of Mainz, but in 968 was transferred to that of Magdeburg. The disturbances of 983 practically annihilated it; bishops continued to be named, but they were merely titular, until the downfall of the Wends in the twelfth century and the German settlement of that region revived the bishopric. Bishop Wigers (1138–60) was the first of a series of bishops of the Premonstratensian order, which chose the occupants of the see until 1447; in that year a bull of Nicholas V gave the right of nomination to the elector of Brandenburg, with whom the bishops stood in a close feudal relation. The last actual bishop was Matthias von Jagow (d. 1544), who took the side of the Reformation, married, and in every way furthered the undertakings of Elector Joachim II (q.v.). There were two more nominal bishops, but on the petition of the latter of these, the electoral prince John George, the secularization of the bishopric was undertaken and finally accomplished, in spite of legal proceedings to have the bishopric declared immediately dependent on the empire and so to preserve it, which dragged on into the seventeenth century.

BRANDENBURG, CONFESSIONS or CONFESSIONS OF THE MARK (*Confessiones marchicæ*, i.e., *Brennoburgenses*): The confessions of the mark Brandenburg during the Reformation. They are three in number: (1) the Confession prepared by order of Johann Sigismund, elector of Brandenburg, 1614, which was intended to reconcile the views of Luther with those of Calvin (see SIGISMUND, JOHANN); (2) the Leipsic Colloquy, 1631, i.e., the declarations of the theologians who took part in the Colloquy of Leipsic (q.v.), 1631; (3) the Declaration of Thorn, 1645 (see THORN, CONFERENCE OF).

BIBLIOGRAPHY: The text of the three confessions is in J. C. W. Augusti, *Corpus librorum symbolicorum*, pp. 369 sqq., Elberfeld, 1827, and in H. A. Niemeyer, *Collectio confessionum in ecclesia reformata publicatarum*, pp. 642 sqq., Leipsic, 1840. Consult Schaff, *Creeds*, ii. 554–563.

BRANDES, brän'dez, FRIEDRICH HEINRICH: German Reformed; b. at Salzuflen (48 m. s.w. of Hanover) Apr. 25, 1825. Educated at the University of Berlin, he was successively second preacher and rector at Salzuflen from 1853 to 1856, and pastor at Göttingen from 1856 to 1901. Since the latter year he has been court-preacher at Bückeburg. Among his numerous writings those of theological interest are: *Wir werden leben, Gespräche über Unsterblichkeit* (Göttingen, 1858); *John Knox, der Reformator Schottlands* (Elberfeld, 1862); *Katechismus der christlichen Lehre* (Göttingen, 1865); *Verfassung der Kirche nach evangelischen Grundsätzen* (2 vols., Elberfeld, 1867); *Zur Wiedervereinigung der beiden evangelischen Kirchen* (Göttingen, 1868); *Des Apostel Paulus Sendschreiben an die Galater* (Wiesbaden, 1869); *Geschichte der kirchlichen Polizei des Hauses Brandenburg* (2 vols., Gotha, 1872–73); *Blicke in das Seelenleben des Herrn* (Gütersloh, 1888); *Unser Herr Christus, i, Seine Person* (1901); and *Einigungen der evangelischen Kirchen ein Befehl des Herrn* (Berlin, 1902).

BRANDT, WILHELM: Dutch Protestant; b. at Amsterdam July 22, 1855. He was educated for the ministry of the Dutch Reformed Church and was a pastor until 1891, when he went to Berlin, where he resided for two years. Since 1893 he has been professor of New Testament exegesis and the history of religions at the University of Amsterdam. In theology he belongs to the historico-critical school, and has written *Die mandäische Religion* (Leipsic, 1889); *Mandäische Schriften* (Göttingen, 1893); and *Die evangelische Geschichte und der Ursprung des Christenthums* (Leipsic, 1893).

BRANN, HENRY ATHANASIUS: Roman Catholic; b. at Parkstown (27 m. s.w. of Drogheda), County Meath, Ireland, Aug. 15, 1837 He came to the United States at the age of ten, and was educated at St. Mary's College, Wilmington, Del., St. Francis Xavier's College, New York City (B.A., 1857), St. Sulpice, Paris (1857–60), and the American College, Rome (D.D., 1862). He was ordained to the priesthood at Rome in 1862, being the first priest of the American College, and from 1862 to 1864 was vice-president of Seton Hall College, South Orange, N. J., where he also taught theology. Four years later he became director of an ecclesiastical seminary at Wheeling, W Va., where he remained until 1870, when he was appointed rector of St. Elizabeth's Church, Fort Washington, N. Y. Twenty years later he became rector of St. Agnes's Church, New York City, where he still remains. He is archdiocesan censor of books and has written *Curious Questions* (Newark, N. J., 1867); *Truth and Error* (New York, 1871); *Essay on the Popes* (1875); *The Age of Unreason* (1881); *The Immortality of the Soul* (1882); and *Life of Archbishop Hughes* (1892).

BRANN, MARCUS: German Jewish historian; b. at Rawitsch (64 m. s. of Posen) July 9, 1849. He was educated at the University of Breslau (Ph.D., 1873) and the rabbinical seminary in the same city, from which he was graduated in 1875. He was then a rabbi in various cities of Germany until 1891, when he was appointed to succeed H. Graetz as professor of history and Biblical exegesis in the Jewish theological seminary at Breslau, where he still remains. He has written: *De Herodis Magni filiis patrem in imperio secutis* (Breslau, 1873); *Die Söhne des Herodes* (1873); *Geschichte der Gesellschaft der Brüder in Breslau* (1880); *Geschichte der Juden und ihrer Literatur* (2 vols., 1893–94); *Geschichte des Rabbinats in Schneidemühl* (1894); *Geschichte der Juden in Schlesien* (3 parts, 1895–1901); *Ein kurzer Gang durch die jüdische Geschichte* (1895); *Ein kurzer Gang durch die Geschichte der jüdischen Literatur* (1896); *Lehrbuch der jüdischen Geschichte* (4 vols., 1900–03); and *Geschichte des jüdischen theologischen Seminars* (1904). He has likewise edited the *Jahrbuch zur Belehrung und Unterhaltung* since 1890, and from 1892 to 1899, in collaboration with D. Kaufmann, edited the *Monatsschrift für Geschichte und Wissenschaft des Judentums*, becoming its sole editor on Kaufmann's death in the latter year. He likewise collaborated with F. Rosenthal in editing the *Gedenkbuch zur Erinnerung an David Kaufmann* (Breslau, 1900).

BRANT, brünt, **SEBASTIAN:** German satirist; b. at Strasburg 1457; d. there May 10, 1521. He was but ten years old when his father died, and, after being educated privately, entered the University of Basel in 1475, where the strife between realism and nominalism had been revived as a struggle between humanism and scholasticism. There Brant devoted himself half-heartedly to the study of law, but his preference for philosophy and poetry proved too unremunerative to yield him a livelihood, so he was obliged to take up the study of jurisprudence in earnest, and finally received the degree of doctor of civil and canon law in 1489. Meanwhile he had developed a literary activity which led him, in addition to the lectures which he delivered after 1484, to write book upon book, partly on jurisprudence, both in Latin and the vernacular, and partly in verse, chiefly in German. Filled with longing for his native city, he applied for the vacant position of syndic, and secured it in the early part of 1501, both through his own reputation and through the recommendation of Johann Geiler. Two years afterward he was appointed secretary of the municipality, and later was made imperial councilor to the emperor Maximilian.

Though Brant was either the author or the editor of a long series of books, there is but one which has preserved his fame to the present day, the *Narrenschiff* (Basel, 1494). The end of the Middle Ages, which marked the wreck and ruin of all the ancient conditions in Church and State, as well as in moral and social life, was felt most keenly in Germany, where it evoked a spirit of satire which spared neither life nor death. The most striking representative of this tendency, next to the Dance of Death, is the *Narrenschiff* of Brant. Wherever the poet looked, he saw only folly, regardless of sex, age, or estate, and as at carnival the mummers ran through the streets in the guise of fools, often with ships on wheels, he regarded life as a great carnival, where fool on fool took his seat in the ship of fools to voyage to Narragonia, the land of fools. Brant was, therefore, in this sense the spokesman of his time, and his work has become immortal in that it is a mirror of the period. He remained true, moreover, to the genius of the German people, despite his attraction toward humanism and his numerous sentiments and parallels drawn from the classics. His views and his habits of thought were taken from the life around him, and his German, though evidently based on his Latinity, is neither as awkward nor as unintelligible as that of Niclas of Wyle immediately preceding him or that of his successor Hutten. He was so far from intending to restrict his work to the learned that he even considered those who did not know how to read, and accordingly adorned his book with pictures as a substitute for the letters. The *Narrenschiff*, therefore, alternates between picture and text, thus giving a double representation of folly, an arrangement which divides the poem into disjointed fragments succeeding each other by chance rather than by design, although the diversity of the material would scarcely have permitted the author to mold it into a homogeneous whole. Yet Brant was swayed by two opposing tendencies, and while, on the one hand, he did not hesitate to expose the faults in the external life of the Church with its lack of faith, and its lack of morality, he feared to touch its inner and higher teachings, and lamented the wavering bark of St. Peter, upbraiding the heretics and regarding the printer as an unmixed evil. (E. Steinmeyer.)

His "Ship of Fools."

Bibliography: The *Narrenschiff* was reprinted many times and was as frequently revamped, especially in the Latin translation of Jakob Locher Philomusus (1497). In 1497 it was translated into French, four years later into Latin verse by Jodocus Badius Ascensius, in 1519 into Low German, and in 1635 into Dutch, while in 1509 it was rendered into English by Alexander Barclay (q.v.) under the title of the *Ship of Fools*. The best German edition is by F. Zarncke, Leipsic, 1854, next to it is that by K. Goedeke, ib. 1872. In 1498 a series of sermons was based upon the *Narrenschiff* by Geiler of Kaisersberg, and it was repeatedly imitated, as in the *Von S. Ursulen-Schifflein*, by the Brotherhood of St. Ursula (Strasburg, 1497), and by Brant's compatriot, Thomas Murner, in his *Narrenbeschwörung* (1512). Bibliographies are given by C. Schmidt, *Histoire littéraire de l'Alsace*, i, 189–333, ii, 340–373, Paris, 1879, and K. Goedeke, *Grundriss zur Geschichte der deutschen Dichtung*, i, 383–392, Dresden, 1884. The best accounts of the life of Brant are to be found in the introductions to the editions of the *Narrenschiff* by Zarncke and Goedeke, ut sup. Consult also C. Schmidt, *Notice sur Sébastian Brant*, in the *Revue d'Alsace*, new series, vol. iii, 1874.

BRASTBERGER, IMMANUEL GOTTLOB: Popular German preacher; b. at Sulz (40 m. s.w. of Stuttgart), Württemberg, 1716; d. July 13, 1764, as *Spezialsuperintendent* at Nürtingen. His sermons on the Gospels, *Evangelische Zeugnisse der Wahrheit zur Aufmunterung im wahren Christenthum* (Stuttgart, 1758) are still read, the eighty-fifth edition having appeared at Reutlingen in 1883, and a translation into Polish in 1905.

BRASTOW, LEWIS ORSMOND: Congregationalist; b. at Brewer, Me., Mar. 23, 1834. He was educated at Bowdoin College (B.A., 1857) and

Bangor Theological Seminary (1860), and held successive pastorates at the South Congregational Church, St. Johnsbury, Vt. (1860–73), and the First Congregational Church, Burlington, Vt. (1873–84), in addition to being chaplain of the Twelfth Vermont Volunteers in the Civil War. Since 1885 he has been professor of practical theology in Yale Divinity School. He was a member of the Constitutional Convention of the State of Vermont in 1870. In theology he is a conservative liberal, and in addition to numerous briefer contributions has written *Representative Modern Preachers* (New York, 1904) and *The Modern Pulpit* (1906).

BRATKE, EDUARD: German Protestant; b. at Neuhaus (a village near Waldenburg, 43 m. s.w. of Breslau), Silesia, Feb. 26, 1861; d. at Breslau Jan. 30, 1906. He was educated at the universities of Berlin, Göttingen (Ph.D., 1883), and Breslau (licentiate of theology, 1885). In 1886 he became privat-docent of the latter university, but four years later was called to Bonn as associate professor of church history, remaining there until 1903, when he returned to Breslau as full professor of the same subject. He wrote *Justus Gesenius und seine Verdienste um die hannoverische Landeskirche* (Göttingen, 1883); *Luthers fünfundneunzig Thesen und ihre dogmenhistorischen Voraussetzungen* (1884); *Wegweiser zur Quellen- und Literaturkunde der Kirchengeschichte* (Gotha, 1890); *Das neuentdeckte vierte Buch des Danielkommentars des Hippolytus* (Bonn, 1891); *Das sogenannte Religionsgespräch am Hof der Sasaniden* (Leipsic, 1900); *Die Weisheit des Todes* (Gütersloh, 1902); and *Euagrii altercatio legis inter Simonem Judæum et Theophilum Christianum* (Vienna, 1904; text and commentary).

BRATTON, THEODORE DU BOSE: Protestant Episcopal bishop of Mississippi; b. at Winnsboro, S. C., Nov. 11, 1862. He studied at the University of the South, Sewanee, Tenn., but withdrew in 1882, a few months before graduation, because of trouble with his eyes. He was at once appointed proctor of the university, and in 1883 became a teacher in the preparatory school attached to the same institution. He pursued theological studies in St. Luke's Theological Hall, the seminary of the University, and was graduated in 1887. He was ordered deacon in the same year and was priested in 1888, after having been a missionary in his native State in the interval. He was then rector of the Church of the Advent, Spartanburg, S. C., 1888–99, also being professor of history in Converse College, Spartanburg, 1890–99, after which he was rector of St. Mary's School for Girls at Raleigh, N. C. In 1903 he was consecrated third bishop of the diocese of Mississippi.

BRAUN, JOHANN WILHELM JOSEF: Roman Catholic theologian and scholar; b. at Gronau (30 m. n.w. of Münster) Apr. 27, 1801; d. at Bonn Sept. 30, 1863. He was associated with the University of Bonn as a student from 1821 to 1825, adjunct professor from 1829 to 1833, and professor of theology from 1833. For the part which he took in the Hermesian controversy see HERMES, GEORG. With J. H. Achterfeld, he published the *Zeitschrift für Philosophie und katholische Theologie* from 1832 to 1852. His *Bibliotheca regularum fidei* (Bonn, 1844) and a number of occasional archeological studies should also be mentioned.

(A. HAUCK.)

BRAY, GUIDO DE. See BRÈS.

BRAY, THOMAS: Church of England; b. at Marton, near Cherbury (17 m. s.w. of Shrewsbury), Shropshire, 1656; d. in London Feb. 15, 1730. He studied at Oxford (B.A., All Souls, 1678; M.A., Hart Hall, 1693; B.D. and D.D., Magdalen, 1696), took orders about 1678, and soon won friends and advancement by his "exemplary behaviour and distinguished diligence." In 1690 he became rector of Sheldon, Warwickshire. In 1696 Bishop Compton of London appointed him commissary for Maryland. He was unable to sail for the colony until Dec., 1699, landed in Mar., 1700, but after a residence of less than six months returned to England, finding he could better promote the interests of the province there. From 1706 he was rector of St. Botolph Without, Aldgate, London.

Bray's Varied and Effective Activity.

Bray's life furnishes a striking example of what can be accomplished by energy, good judgment, and disinterested benevolence. As soon as he was appointed commissary for Maryland he took up the work, and, while detained in England, tried to find there suitable men to send out as missionaries and formed a plan to provide them with books. He did not limit his good services to Maryland, and his plan grew into a scheme for a "Protestant congregation *pro propaganda fide* by charter from the king." When this failed in spite of persistent endeavor, he organized a voluntary society to provide libraries at home and abroad and to support schools and missions for the colonies and the heathen. The first meeting was held Mar. 8, 1699, and this was the beginning of the Society for the Promotion of Christian Knowledge (q.v.). In June, 1701, he divided its work and procured a royal charter for a second society—the Society for the Propagation of the Gospel in Foreign Parts (q.v.). From his appointment as commissary till he was able to sail he bore his own expenses and he paid the costs of his voyage. By his return he forfeited his salary, which was available only when he was in Maryland. A present of £400 he devoted to public use. He collected and managed a fund for the instruction of the negroes in the provinces, and, at the age of seventy-one, became interested in the prisoners in the London jails and undertook to ameliorate their condition. It is believed that he influenced General Oglethorpe to found the colony of Georgia. His benefactions were continued by numerous bequests in his will.

Libraries in America.

Bray's exertions resulted in the foundation of nearly forty libraries in America. In 1699, just before he sailed for Maryland, he wrote that he had sent books to the value of £2,400 into the plantations, "whereby thirty libraries have been already advanced, and a foundation is laid of seventy libraries more." The greater number were in Maryland, but there were several in Virginia, two in North Carolina, and one each in Boston, Rhode Island, New York City, Albany, New Jersey, Philadelphia, and Charleston. That at Annapolis, Md., was the largest collection of books at the time in the plantations and was the first lending library in the British colonies. Its remains are now in the possession of St. John's College, Annapolis. The remnant of the Boston library is in the Boston Athenæum.

After a severe illness in 1723 Bray chose four friends to assist in the management of the negro schools and continue his work after his death. Thus originated "Dr. Bray's Associates for Founding Clerical Libraries and Supporting Negro Schools," an association which has continued to exist and in 1906 reported 130 libraries maintained in England and Wales and 153 in sixty-seven colonial and missionary dioceses; during the year two new libraries were founded and negro schools were maintained in Nova Scotia and the Bahama Islands. The total number of libraries founded in Great Britain and the colonies is over 500. About eighty of the total number were founded by Dr. Bray, exclusive of those established in America. A reorganization of the "Associates" was effected in 1905, and a division of the funds was made whereby the income of an endowment amounting to about £7,000 will be applied to the support of the schools; the remainder of the funds, amounting to about £4,500, will be used to establish, maintain, or augment theological libraries in Great Britain or elsewhere for the use of clergymen of the Church of England and students who are candidates for holy orders.

The Bray Associates.

While at Sheldon, Bray planned *A Course of Lectures upon the Church Catechism, in 4 volumes*, and completed vol. i, twenty-six lectures, *On the Preliminary Questions and Answers* (Oxford, 1696); the book proved popular, brought him upward of £700, extended his reputation to London, and helped to secure his appointment as commissary; vols. ii–iv were not completed. In connection with his library plans he published: *Bibliotheca parochialis, or a scheme of such theological heads as are requisite to be studied by every pastor of a parish, with a catalogue of books* (London, 1697; 2d ed., much changed, 1707); *An Essay towards Promoting All Necessary and Useful Knowledge* (1697), closing with a catalogue of sixty-three books "designed to lay the foundation of lending-libraries to be fixed in all the market-towns in England"; *Bibliotheca catechetica, or the country curate's library* (1702); and *Primordia bibliothecaria* (1726), in which he gives "several schemes of parochial libraries" and outlines a method "to proceed by a gradual progression from strength to strength, from a collection not much exceeding in value £1 to £100." *Several Circular Letters to the Clergy of Maryland* (1701) treats of the "work of catechising" and the "duty of preaching," with many practical directions for the use of books; a list for a "layman's library" is appended. Of interest as Americana are: a sermon on *Apostolic Charity*, preceded by *A General View of the English Colonies in America with Respect to Religion* (London, 1698); a sermon on *The Necessity of an Early Religion*, preached before the Assembly of Maryland (Annapolis, 1700; the earliest extant work printed in Maryland); *The Acts of Dr. Bray's Visitation at Annapolis, May 23–25, 1700* (London, 1700; reprinted in F. L. Hawks's *Contributions to the Ecclesiastical History of the United States*, vol. ii, New York, 1839, pp. 497–523); *A Memorial Representing the Present State of Religion on the Continent of North America* (1700). He was a strong Anti-Romanist, and another noteworthy publication was *Papal Usurpation and Persecution* (1712), intended as a supplement to Fox's *Book of Martyrs*. The materials gathered for this volume and a continuation of it, which he did not complete, he left to Sion College, London.

Writings.

Bibliography: Bray's *Life and Designs*, written probably by Richard Rawlinson (d. 1755) and preserved in manuscript in the Bodleian Library, has been made the basis of all subsequent accounts (such as *Public Spirit Illustrated in the Life and Designs of the Rev. Thomas Bray*, London, 1746, 2d ed., with notes and the report of the "Associates" for 1807, by Henry J. Todd, 1808), and has been printed in full, with valuable notes and *Selected Works Relating to Maryland*, by B. C. Steiner, *Maryland Historical Society Fund Publication no. 37*, Baltimore, 1901. An article by Mr. Steiner in *The American Historical Review*, ii (1897), 59–75, gives an account of Bray's American libraries. Some information concerning the fate of those in England may be found in the *Transactions and Proceedings of the First Annual Meeting of the Library Association of the United Kingdom*, pp. 51–53, 145–150, London, 1879. A paper by J. F. Hurst on *Parochial Libraries in the Colonial Period*, in *Papers of the American Society of Church History*, vol. ii, part 1, New York, 1890, deals with the Bray libraries. The "Associates" (address, 19 Delahay St., London, S. W.) publish an annual report which contains a brief *Memoir of Dr. Bray*.

BRAZIL: A republic of eastern South America; area, 3,218,100 square miles; population, 15,000,000. Brazil became independent of Portugal by the creation of the Empire of Brazil in 1822, which was superseded without war in 1889 by the United States of Brazil, forming a republic with a new constitution framed in 1891. Each of twenty states sends representatives to the senate and house of deputies, but retains a large measure of self-government. It is expressly forbidden to "create, support, or prevent religious denominations," the basal principle being the free exercise of all religions, so far as they are not prejudicial to the public welfare. No religion, therefore, receives aid from the State, and civil marriage before a magistrate is legal, while instruction in the schools is required to be secular, the religious orders being suppressed. Simultaneously with the promulgation of this constitution, and partly in consequence of it, there was a rapid increase in immigration from Europe to Brazil, although for many years previously a considerable number of Italians had been coming to the country. This, however, made little change in religious conditions, although in more recent times the German immigration has somewhat increased, and a small number of North Americans has been added to the Italians, particularly in the cities; this increase, predominantly Protestant, is almost negligible in comparison with the numbers of Italians, Portuguese, and Spaniards. Non-German Protestant denominations are also represented, especially in the maritime towns, where there are English churches, which, however, do not always have permanent rectors. The Presbyterians, particularly from North America, have settled in considerable numbers in São Paulo, where they have established a college, and the American Seaman's Friend Society has an agent in the capital, Rio de Janeiro. In 1899 the Protestant Episcopal Church made the Rev. Lucien Lee Kinsolving (q.v.) bishop of southern Brazil, with residence at Rio Grande do Sul (São Pedro). In 1907 his diocese was made an integral part of the American Episcopal Church.

German Protestantism is represented over an extensive territory and has numerous centers, as is shown by the existence of two great ecclesiastical bodies, the "Evangelical German Synod," subject to the jurisdiction of the higher church council of Berlin since 1869, and the "Evangelical Synodical Union" of 1884. The latter receives its clergy not only from Berlin, but also through the missionary societies of Barmen and Basel, especially in view of the number of Swiss immigrants to Brazil. Many German evangelical communities, as well as scattered members of the Evangelical Church are found both in Rio de Janeiro itself and the state of the same name (including Petropolis) and the state of Espirito Santo (including Leopoldina), and especially in the four southern states of São Paulo, Paraná, Santa Catharina, and Rio Grande do Sul. In the latter state there are forty congregations, while in Santa Catharina 7,500 Protestants live in the German city of Blumenau alone, and of the 100,000 Germans in the state about two-thirds are evangelical. All the districts with a German population are richly provided with schools, even though all branches of instruction are not as thorough as might be desired. Evangelical schools, however, are not infrequently replaced by interdenominational religious schools. In the Roman Catholic German communities careful provision is made for schools, and in a number of colonies the educational activity of the clergy is such that they receive salaries from the State.

The Roman Catholic Church has two archdioceses in Brazil: (1) Bahia or São Salvador (founded as a bishopric in 1555, made an archbishopric in 1676), with the suffragan bishoprics of Alagoas (founded 1900; residence at Maceió), Amazon (1893; residence Manáos), Belem or Pará (1719), Fortaleza or Ceará (1854), Goyaz (1826; residence Uberava), São Luiz (1677; residence Maranhão) Olinda (1676), Parahyba (1893), and Piauhy (1902; residence Therezina); and (2) São Sebastião or Rio de Janeiro (1676; made an archbishopric 1893), with the suffragan bishoprics of Curitiba (1893), Cuyabá (1745), Diamantina (1854), Marianna (1745), São Paulo (1745), Petropolis (1893), São Pedro (1848; residence Porto Alegre), Pouso Alegre (1900), and Espirito Santo (1896; residence Vitoria). There is also the exempt prelature of Santarem (1903).

While secular priests are chiefly employed in the service of the Church, they are lacking in many districts and their training is defective. Despite the suppression of the orders, therefore, many of the larger ones have numerous representatives. Although they have few stations, they are actively engaged in the conversion of the Indians, among whom the Jesuits worked with great success in the seventeenth and eighteenth centuries in the ranges of the Cordilleras and along the Upper Amazon. In 1767 the Portuguese expelled the Jesuits from Brazil. The aborigines in the interior of Brazil still remain uninfluenced by any missionary activity.

WILHELM GOETZ.

BIBLIOGRAPHY: On the country and people consult: J. C. and D. P. Kidder, *Brazil and the Brazilians*, New York, 1896; [Miss M. R. Wright], *The New Brazil, its Resources and Attractions*, London, 1901; Santa-Anna Néry, *The Land of the Amazons*, New York, 1901; *United States of Brazil: a Geographical Sketch, with special Reference to Economic Conditions and Prospects of Future Development*, Bureau of Am. Republics, Washington, 1901; T. C. Dawson, *The South American Republics*, vol. i, New York, 1903 On religious matters consult: F. Badaro, *Les Couvents au Brésil*, Florence, 1897; H. P. Beach, *Protestant Missions in South America*, New York, 1900; J. S. Dennis, *Centennial Survey of Foreign Missions*, ib. 1902; H. C. Tucker, *Bible in Brazil*, ib. 1902. An exhaustive work of reference is A. L. Garraux, *Bibliographie brésilienne*, Paris, 1898.

BREAD AND BAKING: Bread was for the Hebrews the chief article of diet, as it is for modern Palestinian peasants. In early times it was made from barley, which was later displaced by wheat, except as it remained the staple for the poorer classes, though now it is not regarded as altogether wholesome. Primitive usage was to roast the ears of grain, which were so eaten especially at harvest time (Ruth ii, 14), and, thus prepared, still form a convenient food for travelers. In primitive preparation of grain for food, a sort of mortar was used to crush it into the coarser meal, a handmill for the flour. The latter, of primitive form, is still used in the East and consists of two stones, the lower one the harder, the middle surfaces not flat, but respectively concave and convex, the upper with a hole in the center in which the post of the lower is set and into which the grain is poured for grinding. The work of grinding fell to the women or to slaves, though the later and larger mills were turned by beasts. The preparation of meal or flour was a daily task, done as there was need for the product. The dough was mixed in a wooden kneading-trough, and in early times was unleavened, as is the case generally with the modern Bedouin. The dough was made up round, flat or disk-shaped, and baked on a layer of heated stones from which the coals were removed when the dough was placed upon the stones to bake and then replaced. Mention is made (Lev. ii, 5) of an iron plate or pan for baking. There came to be finally two forms of oven, both in common use among the modern peasantry, one of which is heated from the outside, the other from the inside. The art of baking was developed with the other arts till it became a handicraft or trade, and gave its name to a street in Jerusalem (Jer. xxxvii, 21; cf. Hos. vii, 4). Bread was used in sacred offerings at first either leavened or unleavened; later the former was excluded (Ex. xxiii, 18; Lev. ii, 11).

(I. BENZINGER.)

BIBLIOGRAPHY: An excellent account, perhaps the best, is to be found in *DB*, i, 315–319. Consult also: E. Robinson, *Biblical Researches*, ii. 416–417, New York, 1856; C. M. Doughty, *Arabia Deserta*, i. 131 and passim, London, 1888; Benzinger, *Archäologie*, pp. 62–66, 2d ed.; H. Vogelstein, *Die Landwirtschaft in Palästina*, Berlin, 1894; *EB*, i. 604–605.

BRECKINRIDGE, JOHN: American Presbyterian; b. at Cabell's Dale, near Lexington, Ky., July 4, 1797; d. there Aug. 4, 1841. He studied at Princeton and was tutor there 1820–21; was chaplain of Congress 1822–23; was ordained Sept. 10, 1823, and was pastor of the Second Presbyterian Church, Lexington, Ky., 1823–26; of the Second Presbyterian Church, Baltimore, 1826–31; corresponding secretary of the Board of Education of the Presbyterian Church at Philadelphia 1831–36; professor of pastoral theology in Princeton Seminary 1836–38; secretary of the Presbyterian Board of Foreign Missions 1838–40. He was president of the American Colonization Society, and at the time of his death was president-elect of Oglethorp University, Georgia. He was a leader of the Old School party and an ardent controversialist. He published a discussion with Archbishop Hughes of New York under the title *Roman Catholic Controversy* (Philadelphia, 1836) and some minor controversial essays.

BRECKINRIDGE, ROBERT JEFFERSON: Presbyterian minister, brother of John Breckinridge (q.v.); b. at Cabell's Dale, near Lexington, Ky., Mar. 8, 1800; d. at Danville, Ky., Dec. 27, 1871. He was graduated at Union College, 1819; practised law in Kentucky, 1823–31, and was a member of the State legislature, 1825–29; studied theology at Princeton, 1831–32, was ordained Nov. 26, 1832, and was pastor of the Second Presbyterian Church, Baltimore, 1832–45; president of Jefferson College, Pennsylvania, 1845–47; pastor of the First Presbyterian Church, Lexington, Ky., and at the same time State superintendent of public instruction, 1847–53; professor of theology at Danville Seminary, 1853–69. He was a stanch Old School Presbyterian and the author of the "Act and Testimony" (1834), complaining of the prevalence of doctrinal errors, the relaxation of discipline, and the violation of church order, which played an important part in the disruption of the Presbyterian Church; he opposed the reunion in 1869. He was a bitter opponent of the Roman Catholic Church. During the Civil War he defended the Union cause and was president of the national Republican convention at Baltimore in 1864 which renominated Abraham Lincoln for the Presidency. During his residence in Baltimore he edited *The Literary and Religious Magazine* (1835–43), and *The Danville Review* at Danville (1861–65); his principal literary work is two volumes, *The Knowledge of God*, objectively and subjectively considered (New York, 1857–59).

BRECKLING, FRIEDRICH: A forerunner of the Pietistic school; b. at Hanved near Flensburg, Sleswick, 1629; died at The Hague Mar. 16, 1711. He studied at Rostock, where he imbibed the theology of Arndt; then at Königsberg, where syncretism was dominant, at Helmstädt, where his relation Calixtus then was, at Wittenberg, Leipsic, Jena, and Giessen. Here his thesis for the master's degree (1653) was criticized as savoring of Weigelianism, but he refused to alter it, and published it at Amsterdam under the title *Mysterium magnum, Christus in nobis* (1662). He became closely allied with Tackius, and went deeper into theosophy by the aid of Hermes Trismegistus, Paracelsus, and Böhme. Going to Hamburg, he read Betke's *Antichristentum*, and was much influenced by its conception of priestless Christianity. After some years of wandering in search of knowledge, he was ordained to be his father's assistant and ultimate successor; but violent attacks on the local clergy caused his deposition and imprisonment in 1660. Escaping, he went to Amsterdam and got a charge at Zwolle, where he spent eight years of comparative quiet, but was again deprived of his office, and lived in retirement at Zwolle (1668–72), Amsterdam (1672–90), and The Hague (1690–1711). He maintained a correspondence with Spener and with Gottfried Arnold, whom he helped in his church history, and was busily engaged as a writer. In spite of his weaknesses, he deserves remembrance as a link in the chain of mystical natures who prepared the way for Spener and the Pietistic movement. (F. Nielsen†.)

Bibliography: G. Arnold, *Kirchen und Ketzergeschichte*, iii. 148–149, iv. 1103–04, Frankfort, 1729; A. Ritschl, *Geschichte des Pietismus*, ii. 1, 128, 146, Bonn, 1884; L. J. Moltesen, *F. Breckling, et Bidrag til Pietismens Udviklingshistorie*, Copenhagen, 1893.

BREDENKAMP, KONRAD JUSTUS: German Lutheran; b. at Basbeck (a village near Stade, 22 m. w.n.w. of Hamburg) June 26, 1847; d. at Verden (21 m. s.e. of Bremen) Mar. 25, 1904. He was educated at the universities of Erlangen, Bonn, and Göttingen, and was pastor at Kuppentin, Mecklenburg, from 1872 to 1878. He then resided at Göttingen for a year, and from 1880 to 1883 was privat-docent at Erlangen. In the latter year he accepted a call to Greifswald as professor of theology, and remained there until 1889, after which he was honorary professor of Old Testament exegesis at Kiel until his death. He wrote *Der Prophet Sacharja erklärt* (Erlangen, 1879); *Vaticinium quod de Immanuele edidit Jesaias (vii, 1–ix, 6)* (1880); *Gesetz und Propheten* (1881); and *Der Prophet Jesaia erläutert* (1887).

BREECHES BIBLE. See Bible Versions, B, IV, § 9.

BREED, DAVID RIDDLE: Presbyterian; b. at Pittsburg, Pa., June 10, 1848. He was educated at the Western University of Pennsylvania, Hamilton College (B.A., 1867), and Auburn Theological Seminary (1870), and was pastor of the House of Hope Presbyterian Church at St. Paul, Minn., from 1870 until 1885, when he organized the Church of the Covenant, Chicago, of which he was pastor until 1891. In the latter year he accepted a call to the First Presbyterian Church of Pittsburg, and since 1898 has been professor of practical theology in the Western Theological Seminary, Allegheny, Pa. In theology he is conservative. In addition to numerous pamphlets, he has written *Abraham, the Typical Life of Faith* (Chicago, 1886); *History of the Preparation of the World for Christ*

(1891); *Heresy and Heresy* (1891); and *The History and Use of Hymns and Hymn Tunes* (1903).

BREITHAUPT, brait'haupt, **JOACHIM JUSTUS:** First professor of theology at Halle; b. at Nordheim (12 m. n. of Göttingen), Hanover, Feb. 1658; d. at the monastery of Berge (Kloster Bergen, s. of Magdeburg; the site is now a public park) Mar. 16. 1732. He studied at Helmstädt, became corector in Wolfenbüttel in 1680, and went thence to Kiel, where he continued theological studies under Christian Kortholt (q.v.) and became privat-docent. Then he lived for some time in Frankfort and came completely under Spener's influence. He returned to Kiel as professor of homiletics, became court preacher at Meiningen in 1685, went to Erfurt in 1687 as preacher at the Dominican Church and became professor of theology in the university. His Pietistic tendencies aroused much opposition, and in 1691 he removed to Halle, where with August Hermann Francke and Paul Anton (qq.v.) he gave the theological study of the new university its peculiar character and direction. In 1705 he added to his other duties those of superintendent of the duchy of Magdeburg and in 1709 was made abbot at the monastery of Berge (then transformed into a school). He was a man of much faith, prayerful, and took a deep interest in poor students. Besides minor writings, he published *Institutiones theologicæ* (2 vols., Halle, 1694; 2d enlarged ed., 1723; vol. iii, *Institutiones theologiæ moralis*, 1732); *Theses credendorum et agendorum fundamentales* (1700). He was not without poetic talent and published a collection of *Poemata miscellanea* (Magdeburg, 1720). Some of his hymns are still found in the German hymn-books.

(GEORG MÜLLER.)

BIBLIOGRAPHY: The Memorial, ed. G. A. Francke, Halle, 1736, contains the *Lebensbeschreibung* by C. P. Leporin and Baumgartens *Memoria incomparabilis theologi J. J. Breithaupt*. Consult also A. Ritschl, *Geschichte des Pietismus*, iii, 385 et passim, Bonn, 1884; Julian, *Hymnology*, pp. 169–170; W. Schrader, *Geschichte der Friedrichs-Universität zu Halle*, vol. i, passim, Halle, 1894; *ADB*, iii. 291.

BREITINGER, brai'tin-ger, **JOHANN JAKOB:** Swiss theologian; b. at Zurich Apr. 19, 1575; d. there Apr. 1. 1645. Not until his seventeenth year did his spiritual gifts begin to manifest themselves, but from 1593 to 1596 he studied at Reformed seminaries in Germany and Holland, and in 1597 became a member of the clergy of his native city. His prominence during the pestilence of 1611 proved him worthy of the appointment of deacon to the church of St. Peter. Two years later he was made pastor of the *Grossmünster*, thus becoming the most important clergyman in Zurich, and in 1614 he was appointed school-rector. His importance was not due, however, to his religious or theological originality, but rather to his political intelligence and practical skill in organization and execution, combining shrewd circumspection and patience with a versatile initiative. His sermons, though not deep, were characterized by warmth of feeling, clearness, pithiness, and charm. The most important of his works are his synodical addresses, in which he sought to exalt the position of the clergy. These sermons, delivered at the semiannual sessions of the synod and collected by him in the latter years of his life, are models of pastoral wisdom, and received practical application in Breitinger's own activity. The status of the preachers was revolutionized on the basis of two of his speeches before the council in 1628, and he secured the general adoption of music in the churches, which Zurich had lacked altogether until 1598. He likewise enriched the liturgy with sections which are still in use, as with the prayer for the dead and the morning prayer after the sermon of 1638. Breitinger also successfully urged the need of religious instruction of the young, as is shown by repeated ordinances of 1613, 1628, 1637–1638, and 1643. He was, likewise, the ultimate author of the custom by which the Swiss Confederations celebrate the days of thanksgiving, repentance, and prayer at the same time, and it was he who introduced the rule of making a public announcement of marriage. In 1634 he introduced into the churches of Zurich and eastern Switzerland the use of parochial registers, which were to be returned every three years to the head of the clergy and thus served as a sort of census-report. Four years later he instituted parochial visitations, and finally established the ecclesiastical archives of Zurich.

Breitinger was deeply interested in education, and was also active in the establishment of scholarships for poor students. He was no less enthusiastic in his patronage of charity, and prepared statistics of the poor as early as 1621, while in 1623, at the request of the mayor, he published *Gutachten der Bettler und Armen halber*. Three years later, on the basis of further studies, Breitinger made noteworthy proposals for houses of correction for neglected youth, and was also active in the improvement of prisons and hospitals. Ever watchful over the morals of the people, he opposed lack of refinement and excess, and sought to obviate the evil influences of the war in the neighboring kingdom, in addition to restricting lavish expenditure in clothing (1616, 1628), and in weddings and funerals (1621, 1628, 1640), as well as the drinking of toasts (1632), and occasionally even the stage and the cultivation of art. A watchful opponent of the hopes and propaganda of Catholicism and Anabaptism, he refrained from excessive hostility, contenting himself with remaining a constant protector of the Reformed. His personal preeminence and his interest in his church frequently involved him in political problems, and during the Thirty Years' War he was the leader of a Swedish party in Zurich. The fortification of the city was due, strictly speaking, to him, and had he had his way, Switzerland would have been involved in the struggle. (EMIL EGLI.)

BIBLIOGRAPHY: The chief work is by J. C. Mörikofer, *J. J. Breitinger und Zürich*, Leipsic, 1874. Consult also G. R. Zimmermann, *Die Zürcher Kirche*, pp. 143–184, Zurich, 1877–78.

BREMEN: A free city and state of the German Empire. The city is situated on the Weser, about forty-six miles from its mouth and 215 miles by rail w.n.w. of Berlin. The state includes also the harbor-cities of Vegesack and Bremerhaven and about ninety-nine square miles of contiguous territory. The total population in 1900 was 224,-697, of whom 163,292 belonged to the city of Bremen. Ninety-four per cent. are reported as Evangelical Protestants, 4.9 per cent. as Roman Catholics; the number of Jews is about 1,000. Of the Protestants nearly one-third are Reformed. The Protestants have no ecclesiastical organization, the government standing at the head of the Church and managing its affairs through a commission, which is also the school board. The various congregations are independent one of the other, but, individually, take a warm interest in missionary and benevolent work.

Bibliography: W. von Bippen, *Geschichte der Stadt Bremen*, 2 vols., Bremen, 1892–98; *Jahrbuch für bremische Statistik*, ib. 1905.

BREMEN, BISHOPRIC OF: A former diocese of Germany, whose foundation belongs to the period of the missionary activity of Willehad (q.v.) on the lower Weser. He was consecrated July 15, 787, at Worms, on Charlemagne's initiative, his jurisdiction being assigned to cover the Saxon territory on both sides of the Weser from the mouth of the Aller, northward to the Elbe and westward to the Hunte, and the Frisian territory for a certain distance from the mouth of the Weser. Willehad fixed his headquarters at Bremen, though the formal constitution of the bishopric took place only after the subjugation of the Saxons in 804 or 805, when Willehad's disciple, Willerich, was consecrated bishop of Bremen, with the same territory. The diocese was probably at that time ecclesiastically subject to Cologne. When, after the death of Bishop Leuderich (838–845), it was given to Ansgar, it lost its independence (see Ansgar), and from that time was permanently united with Hamburg. The new combined see was regarded as the headquarters for missionary work in the north, and new sees to be erected were to be subject to its jurisdiction. Ansgar's successor, Rimbert, the "second apostle of the north," was troubled by onslaughts first of the Normans and then of the Wends, and by renewed claims on the part of Cologne. The see of Bremen attained its greatest prosperity and later had its deepest troubles under Adalbert (see Adalbert of Hamburg-Bremen). The next two archbishops, Liemar and Humbert, were determined opponents of Gregory VII. Under the latter the archbishopric of Lund (q.v.) was erected, and Bremen had suffragan sees only in name, the Wendish bishoprics having been destroyed. Schisms in Church and State marked the next two centuries, and in spite of the labors of the Windesheim and Bursfelde congregations (qq.v.), the way was prepared for the Reformation, which made rapid headway, partly owing to the fact that the last Roman Catholic archbishop, Christopher of Brunswick, was also bishop of Verden and resided there. By the time he died (1558), nothing was left of the old religion outside of a few monasteries and the districts served by them. The title of archbishop, with the secular jurisdiction, was borne for a time by Protestant princes. The Peace of Westphalia (1648) secularized it and made it (with Verden) a duchy and an appanage of the crown of Sweden. In 1712 it passed into the possession of Denmark, and three years later was sold to Hanover, to which it was restored in 1813 after the Napoleonic disturbances. Its former territory was distributed ecclesiastically at this time among the neighboring dioceses of Hildesheim, Osnabrück, and Münster, the imperial city of Bremen and the surrounding district being administered by the vicar-apostolic of the northern missions.

BRENDAN, SAINT, OF CLONFERT (called "the Navigator"): Irish saint; b. at Tralee (on Tralee Bay, west coast of Ireland, County Kerry) 484; d. at the monastery of his sister, Brigh, at Annadown (on the east shore of Lough Corrib, County Galway), 577. After studying with the most distinguished Irish masters, he was ordained presbyter, and then undertook the expedition or expeditions which form the basis of "The Navigation of St. Brendan," one of the most popular legends of the Middle Ages. In 552 or 553 (according to others in 556 or 557) he founded the monastery of Clonfert (in the barony of Longford, County Longford) and ruled it for twenty years, during which time it was the most famous school in West Ireland. He is said also to have founded a monastery in Brittany. A visit to Columba on Hinba Island, near Iona, is recorded, which must have been after 563, and he is last heard of in 570, when he acted as bard at the inauguration of the first Christian king of Cashel.

According to an Irish life of St. Brendan, when he was ordained he pondered on the words in Luke xviii, 29–30, and determined to forsake country and brethren and seek a mysterious unknown land which he saw in visions. Under angelic guidance he set forth in a coracle of wicker work and hides, but after seven years was directed to return, as work was waiting for him at home. Some years later the impulse to travel again sent him forth, this time in a fine ship, fully equipped, and with a crew of sixty. "The whole story of the saint's adventures bears neither repetition nor criticism: but in the midst of much crude fiction we find occasional touches which have evidently been derived from the reports of genuine voyagers. In the course of their seven years' adventures they visit the Isle of Sheep, a full fair island full of green pasture: another fair island, full of flowers, herbs, and trees, where they thank God of his good grace: a little island wherein were many vines full of grapes: they meet with great tempests, in which they are greatly troubled long time and sore forlaboured; at other times calm airs and water so clear that they might see all the fishes that were about them, whereof they are full sore aghast: again they behold an hill all of fire and a foul smoke and stink coming from thence: and finally reach an attemperate land, ne too hot ne too cold, the fairest country that any man might see, in which the trees are charged with ripe fruit and flowers. Here they walk forty days, but find no end thereof, and at length lade their ships with its fruits and return home" (E. J. Payne,

History of the New World, i, Oxford, 1892, 106–107). The story was known in France, Spain, and Holland in the eleventh century, and was very popular with all classes. It exists in translation into eight languages. Some of its incidents are derived from classical sources; others resemble the *Arabian Nights*. An expedition to the Hebrides and northern islands may have furnished the basis of fact.

Bibliography: Lanigan, *Eccl. Hist.*, ii. 28–28; *St. Brandan*, a metrical and a prose life, in English, ed. T. Wright, in Percy Society Publications, vol. xiv, London, 1844; W. J. Rees, *Lives of the Cambro-British Saints*, pp. 251–254, 575–579, Llandovery, 1853; W. Reeves's *Adamnan's Life of St. Columba*, p. 221, Dublin. 1857; C. Schröder, *Sanct Brandan, ein lateinischer und drei deutsche Texte*, Erlangen, 1871; A. P. Forbes, *Kalendars of Scottish Saints*, pp. 284–287, Edinburgh, 1872; F. Michel, *Les voyages merveilleux de S. Brandan*, Paris, 1878; J. Healy, *Insula sanctorum et doctorum*, pp. 209 sqq., Dublin, 1890; D. O'Donoghue, *Brendaniana*, Dublin, 1893; T. Olden, *The Church of Ireland*, pp. 63–64, London, 1895; C. Plummer, *Some New Light on the Brandan Legend*, in *Zeitschrift für celtische Philologie*, v (1904), 124–141; J. O'Hanlon, *Lives of the Irish Saints*, v, 389–472, Dublin, n.d.

BRENT, CHARLES HENRY: Protestant Episcopal missionary bishop of the Philippines; b. at Newcastle, Ont., Apr. 9, 1862. He was graduated at Trinity College, Toronto, in 1884, and was ordered deacon in 1886 and priested in 1887. He was then curate of St. Paul's Cathedral, Buffalo, N. Y., 1887–88, and of St. John the Evangelist, Boston, 1888–91, and associate rector of St. Stephen's, in the same city, 1897–1901, being also a member of the editorial staff of *The Churchman* from 1897 to 1900. In 1901 he was consecrated first bishop of the missionary district of the Philippine Islands. On May 6, 1908, he was elected bishop of the diocese of Washington. He has written *With God in the World* (New York, 1899); *The Consolations of the Cross* (1902); *The Splendor of the Human Body* (1904); and *Liberty and Other Sermons* (1906).

BRENZ, JOHANN.

Johann Brenz, the German theologian and Swabian Reformer, was born at Weil (8 m. s. of Stuttgart) June 24, 1499; d. at Stuttgart Sept. 11, 1570. He received his education at Heidelberg, where, shortly after becoming magister and regent of the Realistenbursa in 1518, he delivered philological and philosophical lectures. He also lectured on the Gospel of Matthew, only to be prohibited on account of his popularity and his novel exegesis, especially as he had already been won over to the side of Luther, not only through his ninety-five theses, but still more by personal acquaintance with him at the disputation at Heidelberg in Apr., 1518.

1. Early Advocacy of the Reformation.

In 1522 Brenz was threatened with a trial for heresy, but escaped through a call to the pastorate of Hall. In the spring of 1524 he received a strong ally in his activity as a Reformer in Johann Isenmann (q.v.), who became pastor of the parish-church at Hall. The feast of Corpus Christi was the first to be discarded, and in 1524 the monastery of the Discalced Friars was transformed into a school. In the Peasants' War, on the other hand, Brenz deprecated the abuse of evangelical liberty by the peasants, pleading for mercy to the conquered and warning the magistracy of their duties. At Christmas the Lord's Supper was administered in both kinds, and at Easter of the following year the first regulations were framed for the church and the school. Brenz himself prepared in 1528 a larger and a smaller catechism for the young, both characterized by simplicity, warmth, and a childlike spirit.

He first attained wider recognition, however, when he published his *Syngramma Suevicum* on Oct. 21, 1525, attacking Œcolampadius, and finding the explanation of the creative power of the word of Christ in the theory that the body and blood of Christ are actually present in the sacrament. Henceforth Brenz took part in all the important conferences on the religious situation. In Oct., 1529, he attended the Colloquy of Marburg, and in the following year, at the request of the Margrave George of Brandenburg, he was present at the diet in Augsburg, where he seconded Melanchthon in his efforts to reach an agreement with the adherents of the ancient faith, but refused all association with the followers of Zwingli.

2. Activity in behalf of the New Movement.

In 1532 he collaborated in the church-regulations of Brandenburg and Nuremberg, and furthered the Reformation in the margravate of Brandenburg-Ansbach, Dinkelsbühl, and Heilbronn, while three years later Duke Ulrich of Württemberg called him as an adviser in the framing of regulations for the church, visitations, and marriage. In Feb., 1537, he was at Schmalkald, and two months later undertook the difficult but successful task of the reformation of the University of Tübingen. He likewise attended the conference on the use of images held at Urach, Sept., 1537, where he urged their abolition. Brenz returned to Hall in April of the following year, in June, 1540, attended the conference at Hagenau, was at Worms in the latter part of the same year, and in Jan., 1546, was at Regensburg, where he was obliged to deal with Cochlæus, although, as he had foreseen, he was unsuccessful. He devoted himself with great zeal to his pastoral duties, and side by side with his sermons was evolved a valuable series of expositions of Biblical writings.

After the last remnants of the ancient regulations of the church of Hall had been abolished, his new rules appeared in 1543. Calls to Leipsic in 1542, to Tübingen in 1543, and to Strasburg in 1548 were declined in favor of his position at Hall. Brenz had long opposed the adherence of Hall and the margrave to the Schmalkald League, since he regarded resistance to the temporal authorities as inadmissible.

3. Opposed by the Emperor.

Gradually, however, his views changed, through the hostile attitude of the emperor. In 1538 Hall entered the League, and after its defeat Charles V came to the city (Dec. 16, 1546), and obtained possession of papers, letters, and sermons of Brenz, who, despite the bitter cold, was obliged to flee, although he returned Jan. 4, 1547. The new Interim of the emperor (see INTERIM), which Brenz called *interitus* ("ruin"), recalled him to the scene of action, and he earnestly opposed its adoption. The imperial chancellor, Granvella, demanded his surrender, and Brenz, warned by a note reading: "Flee, Brenz, quickly, more quickly, most quickly!" escaped on the evening of his forty-ninth birthday, June 24, 1548. He hastened to Duke Ulrich, who concealed him in the castle of Hohenwittlingen near Urach, where, under the pseudonym of Joannes Witlingius, he prepared an exposition of Ps. xciii and cxxx. As the emperor was everywhere searching for him, Ulrich sent him by way of Strasburg to Basel, where he was kindly received and found time to write an exposition of the prophecy of Isaiah. Duke Christopher called him to Mömpelgard, where, in Jan., 1549, Brenz was notified of the death of his wife. The condition of his children induced him to go to Swabia, but owing to the pursuit of the emperor, he was often in great danger, and the duke sheltered him in the castle of Hornberg near Gutach. There he spent eighteen months under the name of Huldrich Engster (Encaustius), always active for the welfare of the Church, both by his advice to the duke and his theological labors. He declined calls to Magdeburg, Königsberg, and England. In Aug., 1549, he ventured to go to Urach, where his friend Isenmann was now minister, in order to take counsel with the duke, his advisers, and Matthæus Alber (q.v.) regarding the restoration of the evangelical divine service. In the autumn of 1550 he married for his second wife Catharine, the oldest daughter of Isenmann.

4. Activity, 1550–53. After Ulrich's death Brenz was asked to prepare the *confessio Wirtembergica* for the Council of Trent, and with three other Wittenberg theologians and Johann Marbach of Strasburg, he went to Trent, Mar., 1552, to defend his creed (see BEURLIN, JAKOB). Great was the surprise of the fathers of the council, but they refused to be instructed by those who were to obey them. The Interim was abolished. Brenz who had thus far lived at Stuttgart, Tübingen, Ehningen, and Sindelfingen as counselor of the duke, was made provost of the Cathedral of Stuttgart, Sept. 24, 1554, and appointed ducal counselor for life. He was now the right hand of the duke in the reorganization of ecclesiastical and educational affairs in Württemberg. The great church order of 1553–59, containing also the *confessio Wirtembergica*, in spite of its dogmatism, is distinguished by clearness, mildness, and consideration. In like manner, his *Catechismus pia et utile explicatione illustratus* (Frankfort, 1551) became a rich source of instruction for many generations and countries. The proposition made by Kaspar Leyser and Jakob Andreä in 1554 to introduce a form of discipline after a Calvinistic model was opposed by Brenz, since he held that the minister should have charge of the preaching, the exhortation to repentance, and dissuasion from the Lord's Supper, whereas excommunication belonged to the whole church. At the instance of the duke, Brenz moved in 1553 to Neuburg, to arrange the church affairs of the Palatinate.

5. Controversies. The Osiandric controversy about the doctrine of justification in 1551 and the following years, which caused a scandalous schism in Prussia, was a cause of much annoyance and defamation to Brenz, who saw in this controversy nothing but a war of words. In 1554–1555 the question of the Religious Peace of Augsburg occupied his mind; in 1556 the conference with Johannes a Lasco, in 1557 the Frankenthal conference with the Anabaptists and the Worms Colloquy; in 1558 the edict against Schwenckfeld and the Anabaptists, and the Frankfort Recess; in 1559 the plan for a synod of those who were related to the Augsburg Confession and the Stuttgart Synod, to protect Brenz's doctrine of the Lord's Supper against Calvinistic tendencies; in 1563 and 1569 the struggle against Calvinism in the Palatinate (Maulbronn Colloquy) and the crypto-Calvinistic controversies. The attack of the Dominican Peter a Soto upon the Württemberg Confession in his *Assertio fidei* (Cologne, 1562) led Brenz to reply with his *Apologia confessionis* (Frankfort, 1555). In 1558 he was engaged in a controversy with Bishop Hosius of Ermland. The development of the Reformation in the Palatinate led the aged man to a vehement renewal of his negotiation with Bullinger, with whom he had been forced into close relation through the Interim. The question concerned the doctrine of the Lord's Supper and also involved a peculiar development of Christology, which was opposed by the Lutheran theologians outside of Württemberg, since Brenz carried to its logical conclusion the concept of "personal union," thus favoring an absolute omnipresence (ubiquity) of the body of Christ, which did not begin with the ascension but with the incarnation.

6. Later Years. Brenz took a lively interest in the Waldensians and the French Protestants. But all efforts in behalf of the latter, the journey of the Württemberg theologians to Paris to advise King Antony of Navarre in 1561 (see BEURLIN, JAKOB), the meeting of the duke and Brenz with Cardinal Guise of Lorraine at Zabern, the correspondence and the sending of writings, all ended in bitter disappointment. The Protestants of Bavaria, who had to suffer under Albert, also had his full sympathy. To the citizens of Strasburg Brenz expressed his doubts as to the advisability of following the procession with the monstrance and advised them not to attend mass. He was also deeply interested in the Protestants in Austria, for whom the first Slavic books were then printed at Urach. His last Reformatory activity was the correspondence with Duke William of Jülich and Julius of Brunswick-Wolfenbüttel (1568–69). In addition to this he continued his exposition of the Psalms and other Biblical books, which he had commenced at Stuttgart. In 1569 he was paralyzed, and his strength was broken. He was buried beneath the pulpit of the cathedral; but the Jesuits demolished his grave.

G. BOSSERT.

BIBLIOGRAPHY: An index of the works, printed and in MS., of Brenz, and of works about him is furnished in W. Köhler, *Bibliographia Brentiana*, Berlin, 1904. There is no complete ed. of Brenz's productions, though selected works, in 8 vols., were published, Tübingen, 1576–90. The letters are given in T. Pressel, *Anecdota Brentiana*, ib. 1868, and in *Beiträge zur bayerischen Kirchengeschichte*, ed. T. Kolde, i. 273, ii, 34. The earliest sketch of his life is by J. Heerbrand, *Oratio funebris*, Tübingen, 1570. For later accounts consult: J. Hartmann and C. Jäger, *Johann Brenz*, 2 vols., Hamburg, 1840–42 (still the best account); J. Hartmann, *Johann Brenz*, Elberfeld, 1862; G. Bossert, *Das Interim in Württemberg*, Halle, 1895; E. Schneider, *Württembergische Geschichte*, Stuttgart, 1896.

On the theology of Brenz consult: H. Schmid, *Der Kampf der lutherischen Kirche um Luther's Lehre vom Abendmahl im Reformationszeitalter*, Leipsic, 1868; A. Hegler, *J. Brenz und die Reformation im Herzogtum Wirtemberg*, Freiburg, 1899; C. W. Kügelgen, *Die Rechtfertigungslehre des J. Brenz*, Leipsic, 1899; G. Traub, *Beitrag zur Geschichte des Rechtfertigungsbegriffs*, in *TSK*, lxxiii, 1900.

BRÈS, brê, GUY DE (Guido de Bray): Reformer in the Netherlands; b. at Mons 1522; executed at Valenciennes May 31, 1567. He was brought up strictly by his Roman Catholic mother, but before his twenty-fifth year had become a thorough Protestant. When persecution broke out in 1548, he fled to England, where he spent four years. Then he came back and settled at Ryssel (Liége), where he won great popularity as a preacher. In 1556 his congregation was dispersed by a fresh persecution, and he was obliged to flee, going apparently for a while to Ghent, then to Frankfort, and probably to Switzerland. Early in 1559 he returned to the southern Netherlands, with Tournai for his headquarters, but serving also Ryssel and Valenciennes, and visiting Antwerp and Mons in the cause of his religion, often in disguise for safety's sake. The public singing of Marot's psalms in Sept., 1561, gave rise to a judicial investigation, which exposed Brès to fresh danger. Undaunted, he undertook to secure justice for his comrades by laying before the authorities his confession of faith (known as the Belgic Confession, q.v.) in thirty-seven articles, on the model of that adopted by the French Reformed churches in 1559. This modest, sober, positive statement, which he hoped would show the authorities that his friends were not revolutionary Anabaptists, failed to stop the persecution; but the frequent editions of it show that it met with popular approval; it won thousands to the cause of the Reformation, and was soon recognized as a standard formula. Once known, however, as its author, the Reformer was obliged to escape from Tournai to Amiens, and thence possibly to Antwerp. In 1564 he was in Brussels for a conference with William of Orange, and took part in the negotiations at Metz for a union of the Lutherans and Calvinists. Then he found a refuge at Sedan with Henri Robert de la Marck, Sieur de Bouillon, but was called back to a post of danger in the summer of 1566 by the consistory of Antwerp. In August he settled at Valenciennes, where by this time more than two-thirds of the inhabitants were in sympathy with the Reformation. At first he preached in the open air, but after the iconoclastic outbreak of Aug. 24 took possession of St. John's church. The governor's attempts to suppress the movement led to the siege of the city in December, and its surrender in the following March. Once more Brès was forced to flee, but he and his fellow preachers were captured a few hours later at Saint-Amand, and sent as prisoners to Tournai and then back to Valenciennes. The letters which he wrote to comfort his wife and his aged mother give an insight into his faith and the nobility of his character. He was sentenced to be hanged in front of the town hall, and thus ended a life full of toil and peril, which is one of the glories of the Reformation in the southern Netherlands.

(L. A. van Langeraad.)

Bibliography: L. A. van Langeraad, *Guido de Bray; zyn leven en werken. Bydrage tot de geschiedenis van het zuid-Nederlandsche Protestantisme*, Zieziksee, 1884; W. C. van Manen, *Guy de Bray; opsteller van de Belydenisse des geloofs der gereformeerde Kercken in Nederland*, Amsterdam, 1885.

BRESLAU, BISHOPRIC OF: A diocese which is shown to be already in existence at the date of the foundation of the archbishopric of Gnesen (1000). Probably it was established not long before that date, presumably not by Otto III, but by Duke Boleslav Chrobry of Poland. The original extent of the diocese can not be determined, but in later times it was nearly coextensive with the present province of Silesia, including also the Meissen district on the western side of the Queis.

(A. Hauck.)

A line of unusually excellent bishops administered the see with success until the sixteenth century; but Jacob von Salza (1520–39) was too weak to stand against the rising tide of the Reformation, and his successor, Balthasar von Promnitz, was even inclined to Lutheran doctrines. From 1608 to 1664 the see was occupied by three archdukes of Austria and a prince of Poland, who had little care for religion, and when Silesia came under Frederick II of Prussia Protestantism was still more encouraged. In 1821 the diocese, which is now partly in Germany and partly in Austria and numbers about two million souls, was made an exempt bishopric.

BRETHREN, BOHEMIAN; BRETHREN OF THE COMMON LIFE, and similar titles. See Bohemian Brethren; Common Life, Brethren of the, etc.

BRETSCHNEIDER, bret'shnai"der, KARL GOTTLIEB: German theologian; b. at Gersdorf (40 m. e. of Dresden), Saxony, Feb. 11, 1776; d. at Gotha Jan. 22, 1848; studied at Leipsic; appointed minister at Schneeberg, 1807, superintendent at Annaberg, 1808, and superintendent-general at Gotha, 1816. He was a prolific writer and took an active part in controversies. Among his principal works may be mentioned: *Lexicon manuale Græco-Latinum in libros Novi Testamenti* (Leipsic, 1824; 3d ed., 1840); *Systematische Entwickelung aller in der Dogmatik vorkommenden Begriffe* (1805; 4th ed., 1841); *Handbuch der Dogmatik* (1814; 4th ed., 1838). He founded the series of reprints called the *Corpus reformatorum* (Halle, 1834 sqq.), in which the works of Melanchthon and Calvin have appeared, to which Zwingli will be added. His standpoint was that of the so-called rational supernaturalism—a rather untenable ground between rationalism and supernaturalism.

Bibliography: K. G. Bretschneider, *Aus meinem Leben; Selbstbiographie*, ed. H. Bretschneider (his son), Gotha, 1852.

BREVIARY: The name of the Roman Catholic service-book containing what is called the "divine office" or the services for the canonical hours, as distinguished from the missal, which contains the altar-service, and the ritual, which has the rites for the administration of the sacraments, etc. It is a practically arranged, well-divided collection of prayers with numerous brief extracts from Scripture, and the Fathers and ancient hymns. From the subdeacon upward every Roman cleric is bound to recite the whole office daily.

The breviary is based on the idea of realizing, in the spirit of the Church, at least symbolically, the apostolic command to "pray without ceasing"; the whole life of the Christian is to appear as a continuous prayer, not only in heart and works, but also in words; at all hours and places of the earth the prayer of the Church is to ascend to God. The custom of the synagogue (Dan. vi, 10, 13; Ps. iv, 18) in regard to morning and evening hours (I Chron. xxiv, 30) as well as other times of prayer (Ps. cxix, 62, 64) was taken as a standard. At first there were the three hours, the third, sixth, and ninth, or 9 A.M., noon, and 3 P.M. (cf. Acts ii, 15, 46; iii, 1; x, 9). To these were added midnight, the hour when Paul and Silas prayed in the prison (Acts xvi, 25), and the beginning of the day and the night. This arrangement of prayer is mentioned in Tertullian, Cyprian, Justin Martyr, Clement of Alexandria, and the Apostolic Constitutions. In the fourth century, Athanasius (*De virginitate*, xii–xx) knows of seven hours; Gregory Nazianzen speaks with approval of the nightly vigils and the antiphonal singing. All these hours were adopted in the monasteries especially, as Jerome (*Epist.*, vii, cviii, cxxx), Basil, and Augustine attest. From the monasteries these hours of prayer (called canonical as a part of canonical life) spread to the cathedral and collegiate chapters. Benedict added the seventh (compline, *completorium*), and since the sixth century the order and number of hours have not varied. The day-hours are prime (normally at 6 A.M.), terce (9 A.M.), sext (noon), none (3 P.M.), and vespers (6 P.M.); nowadays compline and lauds are usually reckoned with them. (See the articles under these titles.)

The Canonical Hours.

Matins, answering to the three Roman vigils, is divided into three nocturnes, and was originally followed by the present lauds.

The bulk of the prayers for all these hours was taken from the Psalms, to which antiphons were added, giving the psalms a special meaning appropriate to the occasion. Afterward collects were added, which were intended to prevent distraction and excite devotion, and are accordingly brief. The posture varied between standing, sitting, and kneeling. The whole structure was enriched and completed by the addition of other prayers, responsories, versicles, etc. The musical element was provided for by official books known as antiphonaries, especially that composed under Gregory I, and the so-called *Micrologus* (twelfth century). Cassian attests that each three psalms at matins were followed by three lessons, taken from Scripture, on Sunday only from the New Testament; later on the lives of the saints and exegetical passages from the most prominent teachers of the Church were inserted. The introduction of metrical hymns was long opposed (Council of Braga, 553), especially in Rome. So many arbitrary additions made the offices too long, and Gregory VII reduced them; other revisions were made under Gregory IX, Clement VII, who had the assistance of the Franciscan general, Cardinal Quignonez (1536), Clement VIII (1602), and Urban VIII (1631). The late Vatican Council also introduced some changes.

Sources and Revisions of the Breviary.

At present the Roman breviary, which has at last succeeded in supplanting the many local or diocesan uses, consists of four parts, corresponding to the four seasons of the year. Each part again has four divisions: (1) The psalter, or ordinary week-day service for each day and hour; (2) the "proper of the season," the service for the festivals of Christ and the Sundays of the various seasons; (3) the "proper of saints," the special service for the festivals of particular saints; and (4) the "common of saints," providing, under separate classes, services for those saints who have no special one. Appendices contain the office for the dead, the gradual and penitential psalms, prayers for the dying and for travelers, and grace before and after meals.

Contents of the Roman Breviary.

The analogous service-book in the Greek Church is called *Horologium*. In the Evangelical Church a similar service was often retained in cathedral and collegiate chapters, for which Luther's suggestions of 1523 and 1526 furnished a basis. The matins and vespers were especially retained. Attempts have lately been made, with varying success, to restore the other hours; but the problem can not be considered as solved. The Anglican Church, in its Book of Common Prayer, has made skilful use of important portions from the ancient order.

M. HEROLD.

The calendar of the Roman breviary is a complicated affair, especially since the multiplication of festivals in the last two or three centuries. These are classed as double or simple. The simple form the lowest class, and have no second vespers. The double (so called from the antiphons being doubled, or recited entire both before and after the psalms and canticles at lauds and vespers) are classed in order of importance as doubles of the first class (with or without an octave), second class, greater, and lesser. Where two feasts occur, i.e., fall on the same day, or concur, i.e., the first vespers of one conflict with the second vespers of the other, the difficulty is met, according to detailed rules based on the rank of the feasts, either by "transferring" the less important to the first unoccupied day, or by "commemorating" it with the recitation of its chief antiphon, versicle and response, and collect, after the collect for the day at lauds and vespers.

BIBLIOGRAPHY: A complete Eng. transl. of the Roman Breviary was made by John Marquess of Bute, 2 vols., London, 1879. Consult also: C. H. Collette, *The Roman*

Breviary, London, 1880; G. Schober, *Explanatio critica breviarii Romani*, Regensburg, 1891; S. Bäumer, *Geschichte des Breviers*, Freiburg, 1895, Fr. transl., Paris, 1905; P. Batiffol, *Histoire du bréviaire Romain*, Paris, 1893, Eng. transl., London, 1898; Bingham, *Origines*, book xiii, chap. 9; J. Baudot, *Le Bréviaire romain, ses origines, son histoire*, Paris, 1906.

On the Scripture reading consult E. Ranke, *Das kirchliche Perikopensystem aus den ältesten Urkunden der römischen Liturgie*, Berlin, 1847.

On the hymns consult: F. Probst, *Brevier und Breviergebet*, Tübingen, 1868; J. Kayser, *Beiträge zur Geschichte und Erklärung der alten Kirchenhymnen*, 2 vols., Paderborn, 1881–86; Julian, *Hymnology*, pp. 170–181. A rich bibliography of Breviaries is to be found in the *British Museum Catalogue*, s.v. Liturgies.

BREWER, LEIGH RICHMOND: Protestant Episcopal bishop of Montana; b. at Berkshire, Vt., Jan. 20, 1839. He was educated at Hobart College (B.A., 1863) and the General Theological Seminary (1866), and was ordered deacon in 1866 and ordained priest in the following year. He was successively rector of Grace Church, Carthage, N. Y. (1866–72), and Trinity Church, Watertown, N. Y. (1872–80), and in 1880 was consecrated missionary bishop of Montana.

BREWSTER, CHAUNCEY BUNCE: Protestant Episcopal bishop of Connecticut; b. at Windham, Conn., Sept. 5, 1848. He was educated at Yale College (B.A., 1868) and Berkeley Divinity School, Middletown, Conn. (1872). He was a tutor at Yale in 1870–71, was ordered deacon in 1872, and was advanced to the priesthood in the following year. He was curate of St. Andrew's, Meriden, Conn., in 1872, and was then rector in succession of Christ Church, Rye, N. Y (1873–81), Christ Church, Detroit, Mich. (1881–85), Grace Church, Baltimore (1885–88), and Grace Church, Brooklyn Heights (1888–97). In 1897 he was consecrated bishop-coadjutor of Connecticut, and became bishop in 1899. His theological position is that of a High-churchman with liberal sympathies. He has written *The Key of Life* (New York, 1894); *Aspects of Revelation* (1901; the Baldwin lectures for 1900); and *The Catholic Ideal of the Church* (1904).

BREWSTER, WILLIAM: Leader of the "Pilgrim Fathers"; b. of good family probably at Scrooby (37 m. s. of York), Nottinghamshire, England, 1560; d. at Plymouth, Mass., Apr. 10, 1644. He matriculated at Peterhouse, Cambridge, but apparently did not graduate. From 1584 till 1587 he was in the service of William Davison, ambassador to the Low Countries and afterward secretary of state. About 1587 he retired to Scrooby, where he lived in the manor-house and was keeper of the post, a position of considerable importance at that time. He was a prominent member of a separatist congregation of which Richard Clifton (q.v.) was pastor, holding its meetings regularly at Brewster's house. Because of persecution in England they made an unsuccessful attempt to flee to Holland in 1607, and in 1608 escaped to Amsterdam with John Robinson (q.v.) as "teacher" and Brewster as "elder." In 1609 they settled at Leyden, where Brewster, having exhausted his means, gave lessons in English and also set up a printing-press. He favored the emigration to America, was influential in securing a grant of land in 1619, and sailed with the first company in the *Mayflower*, Sept., 1620. He continued as elder of the congregation at Plymouth, and preached regularly until the first ordained minister, Ralph Smith, came in 1629, but as he was not ordained, he never administered the sacraments. See CONGREGATIONALISTS, I, 1, §§ 5–7; 4, § 1.

BIBLIOGRAPHY: *Memoir*, written by his colleague, William Bradford, the governor and historian of the Plymouth colony (b. 1590; d. 1657), in Young's *Chronicles of the Pilgrims*, Boston, 1841, and in the *Collections of the Massachusetts Historical Society*, series 5, vol. iii; A. Steele, *Chief of the Pilgrims. Life and Time of W. Brewster*, Philadelphia, 1857; J. Savage, *Genealogical Dictionary of the First Settlers of New England*, 4 vols., Boston, 1860–62; W. Walker, *History of Congregational Churches*, pp. 56, 59, 61–74, 77, 227, New York, 1894; *DNB*, vi, 304–305.

BREYFOGEL, brai'fo-gel, **SYLVANUS CHARLES:** Bishop of the Evangelical Association; b. at Reading, Pa., July 20, 1851. He was ordained to the ministry of the Evangelical Association in 1873, was elected presiding elder of the same organization in 1886, and has been bishop since 1891. In this capacity he has made tours of inspection throughout the United States, Canada, and Europe, as well as China and Japan. He is chancellor of the Correspondence College of the Evangelical Association at Reading, Pa., has lectured frequently before the Ocean Grove School of Theology, the Winona Assembly, and similar summer assemblies, and has written *Landmarks of the Evangelical Association* (Cleveland, 1887).

BRICONNET, bri"son"né', **GUILLAUME:** French prelate; b. at Paris 1470; d. at Esmans (near Montereau, 20 m. e.s.e. of Melun) Jan. 24, 1534. He was a descendant of a noble family of Touraine, and, after completing his theological studies at the college of Navarre, was appointed bishop of Lodève and was also made abbot of St. Germain-des-Près in 1507. Four years later he attended the Council of Pisa, and during his absence a spirit of licentiousness spread among his monks, whom he was unable to control. Francis I then appointed him bishop of Meaux and sent him on a mission to Rome, where he remained two years. On his return, he sought to improve the morals and customs of his diocese, and accordingly convoked several synods, and also extended invitations to a number of evangelical preachers, such as Lefèvre, Roussel, and Farel, who preached in thirty-two different places in his diocese, and introduced French translations of the Gospels and Epistles. When Farel attacked Rome, however, Briçonnet deprived him of his office and convoked two synods, the first condemning the teachings of Luther and forbidding the purchase or the reading of his works, and the second prohibiting all heterodox interpretations of the Gospel. Briçonnet found himself between two factions; one turning against Rome by denying the authority of the pope, the worship of the Virgin and of the saints; and the other clinging to the old traditions. In his effort to avoid extremes, he published certain proclamations between Dec., 1524, and Jan., 1525, threatening to excommunicate those who had burned the bull of Clement VII and destroyed images of the Virgin. Notwithstanding this, he was charged by the Cordeliers before the Parliament of Paris with being in sympathy with the Lutherans (Mar., 1525–Oct., 1526), whereupon a commission ordered that Lefèvre's translations be burned, and forbade evangelical preaching. The preachers accordingly fled to Strasburg, although Briçonnet himself was acquitted. Taking advantage of the absence of Francis I, who was held captive in Madrid, the Cordeliers renewed their charges, and two of the new preachers, Jacobus Pauvan and Matthæus Saunier, were convicted of heresy by the Sorbonne and burned at the stake. Briçonnet wrote a letter of submission to the Parliament, and Francis quashed the case. His works were as follows: *Synodalis oratio* (Paris, 1520); *Synodalis oratio* (1552); and a correspondence with Margaret of Navarre, some of which, with other fragments, is contained in Génin, *Lettres de Marguerite d'Angoulême* (1841) and *Nouvelles lettres de la reine de Navarre* (1842), and Herminjard, *Correspondance des réformateurs* (Geneva, 1878).

G. Bonet-Maury.

Bibliography: G. Bretonneau, *Histoire généalogique de la maison des Briçonnet*, Paris, 1620; M. T. C. Duplessis, *Histoire de l'Église de Meaux*, ib. 1731; V. Duruy, *Histoire de France*, i, 575 sqq., ib. 1856; A. L. Herminjard, *Correspondance des réformateurs*, vol. i, ib. 1878; E. and É. Haag, *La France protestante*, ed. H. L. Bordier, ib. 1877 sqq.; Lichtenberger, *ESR*, ii, 423 429; S. Berger, in *Bulletin de la société du protestantisme français*, 1895.

BRICTINANS (Brittinans, Brittinians, so named from S. Blasius de Brictinis, a desolate region not far from Fano in Umbria): An Italian hermit-society founded during the pontificate of Gregory IX, who confirmed it in 1234 by an edict, enjoining upon the members the most rigorous asceticism, especially as to fasting and the total abstinence from flesh in any form between Sept. 14 and Easter of every year. Innocent IV sought, apparently with success, to merge them, as well as the anchorite orders of the Williamites and John-Bonites (qq.v.), in the new order of the Augustinians (q.v.). A bull of Alexander IV, however, dated in 1260 (Potthast, *Regesta*, no. 17,915), assures them the right of independent existence. O. Zöckler†.

BRIDAINE (BRYDAINE), JACQUES: French Roman Catholic preacher; b. at Chusclan (15 m. n.n.w. of Avignon), Department of Gard, Mar. 21, 1701; d. at Roquemaure, near Avignon, Dec. 22, 1767. He studied at the Jesuit College and the Mission Seminary of St. Charles de la Croix in Avignon; visited as a missionary preacher or evangelist nearly every city and village of France, producing a profound impression by his somber and vehement sermons. He almost always preached extemporaneously, appealed to the emotions of his hearers, and sought to terrify them. He prepared a volume of *Cantiques spirituels* (Montpellier, 1748), which has passed through fifty editions. Certain works have been published from his manuscripts, including *Lectures et méditations* (Avignon, 1821); *Réglement de vie pour une pieuse demoiselle* (1821); and five volumes of sermons (1823).

Bibliography: Abbé Carron, *Le Modèle des prêtres*, Paris, 1804.

BRIDEL, bri"del', PHILIPPE LOUIS JUSTIN: Swiss Protestant; b. at Lausanne Nov. 27, 1852. He was educated at the Academy (now the University) of his native city and in the theological faculty of the Free Church of the same institution, being graduated from the former in 1870 and from the latter in 1876. He also studied at the University of Göttingen, and after the completion of his education held successive pastorates in the Canton of Vaud (1875–78), Paris (1879–87), and Lausanne (1887–94). Since 1894 he has been professor of philosophy and the history of theology in the theological faculty of the Free Church at Lausanne. He has been associate editor of the *Revue de théologie et de philosophie* since 1895 and of the *Liberté chrétienne* since 1898. In theology he is, to a certain extent, a follower of C. Secrétan and A. R. Vinet, and has written *La Philosophie de la religion d'Immanuel Kant* (Lausanne, 1876); *La Palestine illustrée* (4 vols., 1888–91); *Roger Hollard, pasteur à Paris* (1902); and *Charles Renouvier et la philosophie* (1905).

BRIDGE, WILLIAM: Puritan; b. in Cambridgeshire about 1600; d. at Clapham, near London, Mar. 12, 1670. He was a fellow of Emmanuel College, Cambridge, and, as rector at Norwich, was silenced by Bishop Wren for non-conformity (1637), and excommunicated; he remained in Norwich, however, till the writ *de excommunicato capiendo* came out against him, when he fled to Holland and became pastor of the English Church at Rotterdam, succeeding Hugh Peters and associated with Jeremiah Burroughs; he returned to England in 1642 and was a member of the Westminster Assembly; was minister at Great Yarmouth till ejected in 1662, and spent the rest of his life at Clapham. He was an Independent (Congregationalist) and Calvinist, a learned man, and had a library rich in the Fathers and schoolmen. His collected works in three volumes were published at London, 1649, and, with memorial, in five volumes, 1845.

BRIDGET (Brigit, Brigida, Bride), SAINT, OF KILDARE: Patron saint of Ireland; b. at Fochart (Faugher, 2 m. n. of Dundalk), Leinster, c. 453; d. at Kildare (30 m. w.s.w. of Dublin) Feb. 1, 523. She was the daughter of a certain Dubhthach and his bondmaid or concubine named Brotsech. At the age of fourteen she received the veil in Meath from the hand of Bishop Machille (Mel), and during a long life won renown for piety and benevolence, and as a founder of monasteries. Her first and most important foundation was Kildare (*cill dara*, so named from a large oak under which her cell was first placed), which was followed by Breagh in Meath, Hay in Connaught, Cliagh in Munster, and others. She was buried at Kildare, where the nuns of her monastery (the "fire-house") kept the so-called "St. Bridget's fire" continually burning in her honor till 1220, when the bishop of the time ordered it extinguished to make an end of the many superstitions connected with it. Thus far the notices of her life are well authenticated; but in very early times legend began to associate marvels of the wildest sort with her name—a tendency not unknown to her oldest biographers. An aged seer foretold her future greatness to her mother before she was born.

While still a child Bridget prophesied her coming spiritual rule over Ireland by stretching her arms over the green fields and crying "it will be mine." As nun and monastery-head she performs numerous miracles of benevolence and love like those of Elijah at Zarephath and Jesus in feeding the multitude. The milk which she gives to a poor man, instead of making it into butter, is restored in a wondrous way; so likewise the bacon which she gives to a hungry dog instead of cooking it. She gives seven sheep, one after the other, to a beggar who comes to her in seven different forms, but the number of her flock is not diminished. She changes the water drawn from a spring for a sick man into a delicious liquor. She satisfies a whole company of episcopal guests with the milk of a single cow which had already been milked three times the same day.

Some of her dream-miracles and visions are more credible; but here, on the one hand, a Roman-clerical tendency is easily recognized—as when she finds herself transported to Rome and hears a mass read there which awakens in her the desire to transplant the same to Ireland—and, on the other hand, we meet with characteristics of a benevolent nature-deity, which the legends mentioned above also indicate by ascribing to her manifold miracles connected with the giving of food and drink. It is thus not unlikely that the old heathen nature-goddess Ceridwen (the Ceres of the Celts), transformed into a Christian saint, survives in Bridget. The fire also which was kept burning in her honor at Kildare speaks for this supposition. It is said that the foundations of a temple of Ceridwen, with great vaults for the storing of fruits, have been found beneath the chapel of the monastery (cf. *Transactions of the Royal Irish Academy*, iii, 1789, *Ant.*, 75–85). In old Irish legend and song, Bridget is likened to the Virgin Mary, or even extolled as the Mary of the Irish by expressions such as "mother of Christ," "mother of the Lord," and the like. A hymn, attributed to Bishop Ultan (d. 656) and in any case very old, calls her "beloved queen of the true God," and the old *Officium S. Brigidæ* (printed at Paris, 1622) speaks of her as "another Mary," "like to Mary," etc. The monasteries, churches, and villages named after her are almost without number.

O. Zöckler†.

Bibliography: The three oldest lives (by Brogar Cloen, Cogitosus, and Ultan), dating from the sixth and seventh centuries, with three later lives, from the ninth to the twelfth centuries, were published by J. Colgan in his *Trias thaumaturga*, pp. 515–626, Louvain, 1647; the *ASB* gives three of these lives with two others and a preface, Feb., i, 99–185. The life by Cogitosus is in *MPL*, lxxii. For later presentations consult J. Lanigan, *Ecclesiastical History of Ireland*, i, 68, 335, and chaps. viii and ix, passim, Dublin, 1829; J. H. Todd, *The Book of Hymns of the Ancient Church of Ireland*, i, 64–70, Dublin, 1855; idem, *St. Patrick*, pp. 10–26, Dublin, 1864; A. P. Forbes, *Kalendars of Scottish Saints*, pp. 287–291, Edinburgh, 1872; J. Healy, *Insula sanctorum*, pp. 106–121, Dublin, 1890; T. Olden, *The Church of Ireland*, pp. 38–48, London, 1895; J. O'Hanlon, *Lives of the Irish Saints*, ii, 1–224, Dublin, n.d.

BRIDGET, SAINT, OF SWEDEN AND THE BRIGITTINE ORDER.

Bridget's Early Life (§ 1).
Bridget's Revelations and Later Life (§ 2).
Her Works (§ 3).
The Brigittine Order (§ 4).

Bridget, the famous Scandinavian mystic and monastic founder, was born probably at Finstad, not far from Upsala, in 1303; d. in Rome July 23, 1373. Her father, Birger Persson, was one of the principal landowners of the district, and charged with both administrative and judicial functions. Her family on both sides had been distinguished for religious devotion, and the child received a careful education in spiritual things. Her imagination, nourished on the lives of the saints, brought her her first vision at the age of seven. Others followed, the reality of which neither she nor her parents doubted.

1. Bridget's Early Life.

After her mother's death, Bridget was entrusted to an aunt at Aspanäs, whose strict discipline laid the foundation of her asceticism and strength of will. In 1316 she was married, in pursuance of her father's political plans, to Ulf, son of the governor of the province of Nerike, and took up her residence at Ulfåsa in that province, where she acquired great influence by the renown of her piety and unselfishness. By degrees she collected around her a group of devout and learned men—Nicolaus Hermanni, renowned as a Latin poet, and later bishop of Linköping, who was the instructor of her children; Matthias, her confessor, the foremost theologian of the time in Sweden; Prior Peter of Alvastra; and another Peter, who succeeded Matthias as her confessor. Through Matthias, who was the author of a commentary on Revelation, she gained an insight into the religious movements and the rich apocalyptic literature of the day. After King Magnus Ericsson's marriage with Blanche of Namur, Bridget became chief lady-in-waiting to the queen, and soon acquired a great influence at the court.

No remarkable visions or revelations seem to have marked this period. When, however, she was approaching the age of forty (probably between 1341 and 1343), she and her husband made a pilgrimage to the shrine of St. James at Compostella (see Compostella). On the way back, Ulf fell ill at Arras; and as she watched by his bedside, she thought she saw St. Denis, the protector of France, who told her that she was under the special care of heaven. Her husband's recovery, which was indicated as a sign of this, was only temporary. He died in 1344, and Bridget believed the last tie which bound her to earth had been broken. Not long afterward, she thought she saw

2. Bridget's Revelations and Later Life.

Christ himself, who said to her: "Thou art my spouse, and the link between me and mankind; thou shalt see and hear marvelous things, and my Spirit shall be upon thee all thy days." This was her first revelation, strictly so called. She and those around her were fully convinced of the reality and the divine origin of these revelations. She used to write or dictate them in Swedish; later they were somewhat freely put into Latin by Matthias, by Prior Peter, and after 1365 by the Spanish prelate Alphonsus, formerly bishop of Jaen. Bridget felt herself called to be a divine instrument for the religious and moral awakening of her age. Soon she was convinced that she should found a new order in honor of the Savior, and dictated to Peter the rules revealed to her. King and nobles joined in building and endowing a home for the order; the approval of the archbishop of Upsala was secured. To obtain that of the pope, Bridget undertook the long journey to Rome in 1349, arriving in the jubilee of the following year. Here she spent the rest of her life, except for pilgrimages, in works of mercy and in warning great and small against sin. She did not gain the papal sanction for her order until 1370, when her rule was confirmed by Urban V A pilgrimage to Palestine in 1372 was the last notable event in her life. She was canonized by Boniface IX in 1391. The connection between Sweden and the South was much furthered by her fame and by the permanent use of her Roman house by monks from her convent of Vadstena (on the east shore of Lake Vettern, 110 m. s.w. of Stockholm); its head in the Reformation period was Peter Magnus, who, after his return to Sweden, consecrated the Lutheran bishops there, affording a basis for a claim to apostolic succession.

3. Her Works.

The authorized edition of Bridget's works contains eight books of revelations, besides another of *Revelationes extravagantes*, or supplement, from the collection of Prior Peter, with his own notes; the rule of her order; and a collection of edifying readings for the community, with certain prayers (known as the *Quattuor orationes*). The works were first printed at Lübeck in 1492 from the official copy preserved at Vadstena; the Roman edition of 1628 is considered the best. The "Revelations" have been translated into most European languages and into Arabic. With much that is superstitious and fantastic, they contain a pure mysticism, rich in thought, and marked by deep insight into the inner mysteries of the devout life. Bridget's views are of course medieval and those of a submissive daughter of the Roman Catholic Church. None the less, they show traces of admirable anticipations of Reformation ideas. The conception of the universal priesthood appears here and there; in her personal devotion, she goes back to the eternal source of life and truth; and her rule commends the preaching of the Word to the people in the vernacular.

4. The Brigittine Order.

The Brigittine Order (*Ordo Sancti Augustini sancti Salvatoris nuncupatus*) was intended by her as an instrument for spreading the Kingdom of God upon earth. Its convents (as, e.g., at Fontévraud) were for both monks and nuns, though their dwellings were separate. The age of entrance was twenty-five for men and eighteen for women. The convent was to be ruled by an abbess selected by the community. Originally the monks were governed by a prior independent of the abbess, but before long the pope subjected them also to her rule, the former prior being called only confessor-general. At the same time they were placed under immediate papal jurisdiction, though provision was made for a yearly visitation by the bishop. They were strictly cloistered; silence was observed, except at certain hours, but the rule of fasting was not rigorous. The monks were admitted to the nuns' convent only to administer the sacraments to the dying or to carry out the dead. The rich endowments of the convent of Vadstena, which remained the mother house, show the popularity of this national foundation among all classes. Not a few Brigittine convents, however, sprang up in other countries, prominent among which were Nådendal in Finland, Munkaliv near Bergen, Mariendal near Reval, Marienwald near Lübeck, Marienkron near Stralsund, and Sion House, Richmond, near London. The importance of the order during the later Middle Ages for the civilization of the North, and especially of Sweden, can hardly be overestimated. Vadstena has been called the first high-school of the North; on it and on its daughter house at Nådendal the literary life of Sweden before the Reformation depended. Vadstena had the largest library in Sweden; and here were made the first attempts toward a complete Swedish version of the Bible. In 1495 a printing-press was set up; but it was destroyed by fire the same year, and published nothing so far as known.

The order was so deeply rooted in Sweden that it survived the Reformation, though with diminished strength. Not even Gustavus Vasa's hatred of the "popery" of the Brigittines could entirely destroy the devotion of all classes to them. During the sixteenth century his wife, sons, and daughters, and many others of the highest nobility, as well as numbers from other classes are found among the benefactors of Vadstena, which, however, was suppressed by Duke Charles in 1595. The Reformation abolished most of the houses outside of Sweden, but an attempt was made to revive it in the Counterreformation, to which period belong the *Fratres novissimi Birgittini* in Belgium, confirmed by Gregory XV, and the reformed order for women introduced only into Spain by the visionary Marina de Escobar (d. 1633) and confirmed by Urban VIII. This is said to have a few houses in Spain now; and four convents of the original order still exist—at Altomünster in Bavaria, St. Bridget's Abbey in Devonshire, and two in Holland.

(HERMAN LUNDSTRÖM.)

BIBLIOGRAPHY: The two earliest lives, by the two confessors of Bridget in the year of her death, were published by Dr. C. Annerstedt in *Script. rerum Svecicarum medii ævi*, III, ii, 188-206, Upsala, 1876. The *Vita sive chronicon* by Margareta Clausdota was published in *Script. Suecici medii ævi*, ed. J. E. Rietz, pp. 193-240, Lund, 1844. Early material is found also in *ASB*, Oct. 4th, pp. 368-560. The best modern accounts are in H. Schück, *Svensk Literaturhistoria*, pp. 129 sqq., Stockholm, 1890, and in *Illusterad Svensk Litteraturhistoria*, i, 84 sqq., ib. 1896. Consult also L. Clarus, *Das Leben der heiligen Birgitta*, Regensburg, 1856; J. B. Schwab, *Johannes Gerson*, pp. 364 sqq., Würzburg, 1858; F. Hammerich, *St. Birgitta, die nordische Prophetin und Ordensstifterin*, Gotha, 1872 (Germ. transl. from the Swedish); Bettina von Ringseis, *Leben der heiligen Birgitta*, Regensburg, 1890; G. Binder, *Die heilige Birgitta von Schweden und ihr Kloster-*

orden, Munich, 1891; Comtesse Flavigny, *Ste. Brigitte de Suède*, Paris, 1892; A. Brinkmann, *Den hellige Birgitta*, Copenhagen, 1893.

For the order consult: *Rerum Suevicarum script. medii ævi*, ed. E. M. Fant, I, i, 1818 sqq., Upsala, 1818; *History of the Eng. Brigittine Nuns*, Plymouth, 1886; *Gesammelte Nachrichten über die einst bestandenen Kloster vom Orden der heiligen Birgitta*, Munich, 1888; Binder, ut sup., and *Geschichte der bayrischen Birgitten-Klöster*, ib. 1896; Helyot, *Ordres monastiques*, ii, 146 sqq., Currier, *Religious Orders*, pp. 185–187; Heimbucher, *Orden und Kongregationen*, i, 440, 505–510.

BRIDGETT, THOMAS EDWARD: English Roman Catholic; b. at Derby (35 m. n.n.e. of Birmingham), Derbyshire, Jan. 20, 1829; d. at Clapham (a suburb of London) Feb. 17, 1899. His parents were Baptists, but in 1845 he was baptized into the Church of England. Two years later he matriculated at St. John's College, Cambridge, but just before taking his degree in 1850 he refused to take the oath of supremacy and was received into the Roman Catholic Church. He then studied for six years on the Continent, and was ordained priest in 1856, after having joined the Redemptorist Order. His life-work lay in the mission field to which his order is particularly devoted, and in 1868 he established the Confraternity of the Holy Family connected with the Redemptorist church at Limerick, Ireland. In addition to his activity as a missioner, he wrote *The Ritual of the New Testament* (London, 1873); *Our Lady's Dowry, or, how England Gained and Lost that Title* (1875); *The Discipline of Drink* (1876); *History of the Holy Eucharist in Great Britain* (2 vols., 1881); *Life of Blessed John Fisher, Bishop of Rochester* (1888); *The True Story of the Catholic Hierarchy Deposed by Queen Elizabeth* (in collaboration with T. F Knox; 1889); *Blunders and Forgeries: Historical Essays* (1890); *The Life and Writings of Sir Thomas More* (1891); and *Sonnets and Epigrams on Sacred Subjects* (1898). He likewise edited a number of works, of which the most important were Bishop T. Watson's *Sermons on the Sacraments* (London, 1876); R. Johnson's *The Suppliant of the Holy Ghost* (1878); Cardinal W. Allen's *Souls Departed* (1886); *The Wit and Wisdom of Blessed Thomas More* (1892); *Lyra Hieratica: Poems on the Priesthood* (1896); *Poems on England's Reunion with Christendom* (1896); and *Characteristics from the Writings of Nicholas Cardinal Wiseman* (1898).

BRIDGEWATER TREATISES: A series of books written in accordance with the will of Francis Henry, eighth earl of Bridgewater (d. Feb. 11, 1829), who left eight thousand pounds to the Royal Society, to be paid to one or several authors, selected by the president, for writing a treatise "On the power, wisdom, and goodness of God, as manifested in the Creation." The following eight authors were selected, and their treatises published (12 vols., London, 1833–36): (1) Thomas Chalmers, *The Adaptation of External Nature to the Moral and Intellectual Condition of Man*; (2) John Kidd, *The Adaptation of External Nature to the Physical Condition of Man*; (3) William Whewell, *Astronomy and General Physics considered with Reference to Natural Theology*; (4) Charles Bell, *The Hand, its Mechanism and Vital Endowments as Evincing Design*; (5) Peter Mark Roget, *Animal and Vegetable Physiology considered with Reference to Natural Theology*; (6) William Buckland, *Geology and Minerology considered with Reference to Natural Theology*; (7) William Kirby, *The Habits and Instincts of Animals with Reference to Natural Theology*; (8) William Prout, *Chemistry, Meteorology, and the Function of Digestion considered with Reference to Natural Theology*.

BRIDGMAN, ELIJAH COLEMAN: Congregational foreign missionary; b. at Belchertown, Mass., Apr. 22, 1801; d. in Shanghai, China, Nov. 2, 1861. He was graduated at Amherst College in 1826 and at Andover Theological Seminary in 1829 and that year on October 14 sailed for Canton under the appointment of the American Board. He arrived there on Feb. 25, 1830, and lived there till 1847, when he removed to Shanghai to supervise the translation of the Bible. In 1832 he began, as a labor of love, the valuable monthly *The Chinese Repository* and was its editor till 1851. In 1841 he brought out his Chinese chrestomathy. In 1844 he was one of the two secretaries of legation to Hon. Caleb Cushing when on his special mission to China and rendered important services. In February, 1852, he left Shanghai for a visit to America, arrived there June 16; on his return he left New York on October 12, and arrived at Shanghai on May 3, 1853.

Bibliography: E. G. Bridgman, *Life of E. C. Bridgman*, New York, 1864.

BRIEFS, BULLS, AND BULLARIA: Written mandates of the pope, differing in form, the bull being more solemn than the brief; bullaria are collections of both kinds of documents. At first the Roman bishops sealed documents with a ring, but from the end of the sixth century seal-boxes or seal-forms (*bullæ*), usually of lead, began to be attached to all public documents, whereas for the others the signet stamped in wax by the ring was used. Since the thirteenth century it has borne the same device, the apostle Peter casting a net into the sea (Matt. iv, 18, 19), whence it is known as the "ring of the fisherman" (*annulus piscatoris*, q.v.). The oldest *bullæ* have on one side the name of the pope, on the other the word *Papa*. The present form has on the obverse the heads of Peter and Paul with the distinguishing inscription S. P A.—S. P E. (i.e., *Sanctus Petrus* or *Paulus Apostolus*, *Sanctus Petrus* or *Paulus Episcopus*); on the reverse, the name of the pope with his number. The string by which they are attached is of red and yellow silk or hemp. From designating the seal, the word *bulla* passed to the document itself.

The bull is written upon strong parchment; the brief on thin parchment or paper. Instead of having the seal attached to it, it is issued *sub annulo piscatoris*, which to-day is only a stamp on the paper. Both begin in an invariable form with the name of the pope and a salutation. In the brief the number is added to the name, in the bull the title *Episcopus servus servorum Dei* takes the place of the number. At the close of the brief merely the place and date are given; the bull gives the date according to both the ancient Roman and the Christian calendars and the year of the pope's reign. The most solemn form is used for bulls issued in the consistory (*bullæ consistoriales*). They are signed by the pope and the cardinals, and are sent out not in the original but in an authorized copy (*transcriptum*). Of other bulls (*non consistoriales*) the pope signs only the minute (*minuta*), and the completed document is signed by the various papal officers who helped in its preparation. The briefs are signed only by the secretary of briefs. Briefs are drawn up in accordance with the special rules of the department in the apostolic secretariate or dataria (see CURIA); bulls in the chancery. Leo XIII simplified the procedure in 1878 by ordering that bulls other than consistorial should be written in ordinary script on parchment and sealed only with a red stamp containing the pictures of Peter and Paul and the name of the reigning pope.

The more important briefs and bulls are contained in collections known as *bullaria*. The oldest collections contained mostly only a small number. To these belong: *Bullæ diversorum pontificorum a Joanne XXII ad Julium III a bibliotheca Ludovici Gomes* (Rome, 1550), containing only some fifty documents; another from Boniface VIII to Paul IV (1559), with about a hundred and sixty; and one from Gregory VII to Gregory XIII (1579), with 723 documents. The *Magnum bullarium Romanum*, covering the period from Leo I to the year 1585, was published in 1586, and since has been continued in revised and completed editions. The latest as well as most convenient and complete edition is the *Bullarium magnum Romanum*, published at Turin by order of Pius IX and under the auspices of Cardinal Gaude (1857–72, 24 vols., covering the years 440–1740). For delimiting bulls (*bullæ circumscriptionis*), see CONCORDATS AND DELIMITING BULLS.

E. FRIEDBERG.

BIBLIOGRAPHY: M. Marini, *Diplomatica pontificia*, Rome, 1841; H. Bresslau, *Handbuch der Urkundenlehre*, i, 67 sqq., Leipsic, 1888; G. Phillips, *Kirchenrecht*, iii, 640 sqq., Regensburg, 1889; E. Friedberg, *Lehrbuch des katholischen und evangelischen Kirchenrechts*, Leipsic, 1895.

BRIEGER, brī'ger, **JOHANN FRIEDRICH THEODOR**: German Protestant; b. at Greifswald June 4, 1842; educated at the universities of Greifswald, Erlangen, and Tübingen from 1861 to 1864 (Ph.D., Leipsic, 1870). He became privat-docent at Halle in 1870, and was appointed associate professor of church history in the same university three years later. In 1876 he was called to Marburg as full professor of the same subject, and since 1886 has been professor of church history at Leipsic. In addition to numerous contributions to theological periodicals, he has written *Gasparo Contarini und das Regensburger Concordienwerk des Jahres 1541* (Gotha, 1870); *De formulæ Ratisbonensis origine atque indole* (Halle, 1870); *Constantin der Grosse als Religionspolitiker* (Gotha, 1880); *Die angebliche Marburger Kirchenordnung von 1527* (1881); *Luther und sein Werk* (Marburg, 1883); *Aleander und Luther, 1521* (Gotha, 1884); *Die Torgauer Artikel* (Leipsic, 1888); *Die theologischen Promotionen auf der Universität Leipzig 1428–1539* (1890); *Der Glaube Luthers in seiner Freiheit von menschlichen Autoritäten* (1892); *Die fortschreitende Entfremdung von der Kirche im Licht der Geschichte* (1894); *Das Wesen des Ablasses am Ausgange des Mittelalters* (1897); and *Zur Geschichte des Augsburger Reichstages von 1530* (1903). He was also one of the founders of the *Zeitschrift für Kirchengeschichte* in 1876, and has been its editor to the present time.

BRIESSMANN, bris'mān, **JOHANN**: Reformer; b. at Cottbus (on the Spree, 43 m. s.s.w. of Frankfort), Brandenburg, Dec. 31, 1483; d. at Königsberg Oct. 1, 1549. He belonged to a prominent family, and as a Franciscan he studied after 1518 at Frankfort-on-the-Oder, and after 1520 at Wittenberg, where he was promoted in 1521 as licentiate and in 1522 as doctor of theology. Influenced by Luther's appearance at the Leipsic disputation with Eck (1519), but more especially by Luther's great reformatory writings of the year 1520, he soon found himself one in the Evangelical faith with his beloved friend. When the Franciscans had to leave Wittenberg, Briessmann went to Cottbus, but on the initiative of Luther he was able to return in 1522. He addressed a reformatory epistle to the congregation at Cottbus, *Unterricht und Ermahnung* (Cottbus, 1523), and at the instance of Luther wrote a powerful refutation of the attacks of the Franciscan Schatzgeyer upon Luther's *De votis monasticis* (Wittenberg?, 1523), stating in his declaration to Spalatin that he could not refuse the wish of Luther, "since he felt himself in agreement not so much with a Luther as with the Evangelical truth."

Preacher in Königsberg, 1523–27.

On the recommendation of Luther, he was called in 1523 as preacher to Königsberg by Albert, the grand master of the Teutonic order (see ALBERT OF PRUSSIA). A Königsberg chronicler thus describes his life and work: he preached the word with gentleness but with all seriousness; many became pious Christians and better men; "on account of his godly, honorable, moral life he was beloved by many and his sermons were gladly heard." About the time when he entered upon his pastoral duties he published his *Flosculi de homine interiore et exteriore de fide et operibus* (ed. P. Tschackert, Gotha, 1887), containing 110 verses in which, following Luther's work "Concerning Christian Liberty," he defends the Evangelical doctrine against Rome and the fanatics. His influence upon Bishop George of Polentz (q.v.) is seen in the latter's sermon delivered on Christmas day, 1523, in which he publicly expressed his belief in the Evangelical teaching of justification by faith alone. As the bishop did not preach himself, he appointed as his substitute "the learned Dr. Johann Briessmann, a man well versed in the holy scripture." In 1524 the bishop issued his first reformatory mandate, enjoining the ministers to use only the German language in their ministerial acts, and to read Luther's writings, especially his translation of the Bible. Of lasting effect were also certain writings of Briessmann, as his *Umschreibung und Erklärung des Vater Unsers als Anleitung zum wahrhaft evangelischen Gebetsleben im Gegensatz gegen die Mariengebete;* a *Sermon von dreierlei heilsamer Beichte*, as guide to Evangelical confession in opposition to auricular confession; and his sermon *Von der Anfechtung des Glaubens und der Hoffnung*, with reference to the Gospel-lesson on the woman of Canaan (Matt. xv. 21–28). For the benefit of the more cultured members of the congregation he delivered lectures on the epistle to the Romans. He laid stress upon the inwardness of the Christian life in opposition to the impetuous zeal of Amandus in forcibly doing away with ancient usages and forms. With Luther, who greatly rejoiced over the rapid progress of the Reformation in Prussia, he entertained a lively correspondence, and on June 12, 1524, one day before Luther, he was married, being the first married minister of Prussia.

After the secularization of the territory of the Teutonic Order (q.v.) in 1525 under Polish feudal supremacy, Briessmann and his colaborers, Speratus and Poliander, faithfully assisted Duke Albert at the diet, Dec., 1525. He accepted a call from the citizens of Riga to complete the reformatory movement there, with the consent of the duke, Oct., 1527 By preaching and teaching he brought about the necessary reformation and published in 1530 *Kurze Ordnung des Kirchendienstes sammt einer Vorrede von Ceremonien.*

In Riga, 1527–31.

After four years of faithful work he returned to Königsberg in 1531 as cathedral preacher. With his colleagues he had soon to oppose the fanatical tendencies of Schwenckfeld, which the ill-advised duke had favored at first. As he labored for the purity of Evangelical doctrine, he also labored for the upbuilding of the inner life of the Church by the new *Landesordnung* (1540), by the articles concerning the appointment and support of the ministers (1540), by the introduction of a new order of marriage and divine service (1544). He recommended the *lectio continua*, or continuous reading of the whole Bible in divine service, thus making the congregations acquainted with Holy Scripture, and a thorough instruction in the catechism besides the preaching; he introduced church-singing by the use of a hymn-book, the first in Prussia. Repeated calls to Rostock he declined. He also devoted his energies to the development of the schools and higher education. He formed the plans for the university which was founded in 1544. During the sickness of Bishop Polentz in 1546, the business of the episcopal see was entrusted to Briessmann, and in 1547 he made a tour of inspection to correct abuses which still existed in the diocese. He opposed especially teachings brought thither by refugees from the Netherlands, represented by the humanist Gulielmus Gnaphæus (or Fullonius, q.v.), a sympathizer with Carlstadt. It was also due to Briessmann's energy that the troubles caused by the first rector of the university, Georg Sabinus, had no lasting influence. Against Andreas Osiander, whom the duke had called to Königsberg, he defended the genuine Lutheran doctrine and confession. Painful as was this Osiandrian controversy for Briessmann, yet he rejoiced toward the end of his life that the Moravian Brethren, driven from Poland by the intrigues of the Polish-Catholic clergy, were in 1548 received into the Prussian state church, after being settled in Prussia with the permission of the duke. In opposing the Osiandrian errors, Briessmann also opposed the duke who at first adhered to Osiander. To the suggestion of the duke to hear the opinion of churches from abroad, Briessmann replied: "Since the present controversy concerns doctrinal points which have been preached in Prussia for over twenty-four years, the opinion and judgment of others is not to be awaited." These are the last words from his mouth and pen, "the testament of the first Reformer of Prussia, and therefore especially valuable for the history of the Prussian Reformation" (Tschackert). In the spring of 1549 he retired from his arduous duties. He is buried in the choir of the cathedral at Königsberg. David Erdmann.

Activity in Königsberg 1531–49.

Bibliography: P. Tschackert, *Urkundenbuch zur Reformationsgeschichte des Herzogtums Preussen*, vols. i., ii., in *Publikationen aus den königlichen preussischen Staatsarchiven*, vols. xliii.–xlv., Leipsic, 1890.

BRIGGS, CHARLES AUGUSTUS: Protestant Episcopalian; b. at New York City Jan. 15, 1841. He was educated at the University of Virginia (1857–60), Union Theological Seminary (1861–63), and the University of Berlin (1866–69). From 1863 to 1866 he was in business with his father. He was ordained to the Presbyterian ministry and was pastor at Roselle, N. J., from 1870 to 1874, when he was appointed professor of Hebrew at Union Theological Seminary. In 1891 he was transferred to the chair of Biblical theology, and since 1904 has been professor of theological encyclopedia and symbolics. In 1892 he was tried for heresy by the Presbytery of New York, but was acquitted, although in the following year he was suspended by the General Assembly. In 1899 he was ordained to the priesthood in the Protestant Episcopal Church. He is a member of the American Oriental Society, the Deutsche Morgenländische Gesellschaft, and the Society of Biblical Literature and Exegesis. He was editor of the *Presbyterian Review* from 1880 to 1890, and collaborated with S. D. F. Salmond in editing the *International Theological Library* (New York, 1891 sqq.), with S. R. Driver and A. Plummer in editing the *International Critical Commentary* (1895 sqq.), and with F Brown and S. R. Driver in preparing the *Hebrew and English Lexicon of the Old Testament* (12 parts, Oxford, 1891–1906). In addition to numerous studies in various theological periodicals, he has written *Biblical Study* (New York, 1883); *American Presbyterianism* (1885); *Messianic Prophecy* (1886); *Whither? A Theological Question for the Times* (1889); *The Authority of Holy Scripture* (1891); *The Bible, the Church, and the Reason* (1892); *The Higher Criticism of the Hexateuch* (1893); *The Messiah of the Gospels* (1894); *The Messiah of the Apostles* (1895); *General Introduction to the Study of Holy Scripture* (1899); *The Incarnation of the Lord* (1902); *New Light on the*

Life of Jesus (1904); *Ethical Teachings of Jesus* (1904); and *Critical Commentary on the Psalms* (1906).

BRIGHT, WILLIAM: English church historian and patristic scholar; b. at Doncaster (30 m. s. of York), Yorkshire, England, Dec. 14, 1824; d. at Oxford Mar. 6, 1901. He studied at Rugby and University College, Oxford (B.A., 1846; M.A., 1849), and became fellow 1847; was theological tutor in Trinity College, Glenalmond, Perthshire, 1851–58; tutor of University College, Oxford, 1862; appointed regius professor of ecclesiastical history and canon of Christ Church, Oxford, 1868. His publications were very numerous and have gone through many editions; besides sermons and addresses, poems, and devotional works they include: *Ancient Collects and Other Prayers selected from various rituals* (London, 1857); *A History of the Church from the Edict of Milan, A.D. 313, to the Council of Chalcedon, A.D. 451* (1860); *Eighteen Sermons of St. Leo I, surnamed the Great, on the Incarnation*, translation and notes (1862); *Eusebius's Ecclesiastical History*, text and introduction (1872); *Orations of St. Athanasius against the Arians*, text, with life (1873); *Socrates's Ecclesiastical History*, text and introduction (1878); *Chapters of Early English Church History* (1878; 3d ed., 1897); *Select Anti-Pelagian Treatises of St. Augustine* (1880); St. Athanasius's *Historical Writings* (1881); *Later Treatises of St. Athanasius*, translation, notes, and an appendix of St. Cyril (vol. xlvi. of *A Library of the Fathers*, ed. E. B. Pusey and others, 1881); *Notes on the Canons of the First Four General Councils* (1882); *Lessons from the Lives of Three Great Fathers* (1890); *Morality in Doctrine* (1892); *Waymarks in Church History* (1894); *The Roman See in the Early Church and Other Studies in Church History* (1896); *The Law of Faith* (1898); *Some Aspects of Primitive Church Life* (1898). With P. G. Medd he edited a Latin translation of the English prayer-book (1865), and he contributed the section on the Litany to J. H. Blunt's *Annotated Book of Common Prayer* (1866).

Bibliography: *W. Bright, Selected Letters*, ed. B. J. Kidd, with *Memoir* by P. G. Medd. London, 1903.

BRIGHTMAN, FRANK EDWARD: Church of England; b. at Bristol June 18, 1856. He was educated at University College, Oxford (B.A., 1879), and was ordered deacon in 1884 and ordained priest in the following year. He was chaplain of University College from 1884 to 1887 and assistant curate of St. John the Divine, Kennington, in 1887–88, while from 1884 to 1903 he was Pusey Librarian. He was also examiner in the Theology School in 1899–1901, and since 1902 has been fellow and tutor of Magdalen College, Oxford, as well as prebendary of Carlton with Thurlby in Lincoln Cathedral. He has written *Liturgies Eastern and Western* (vol. i., Oxford, 1896) and *What Objections have been made to English Orders?* (London, 1896), and has also translated the *Preces Privatæ* of Lancelot Andrewes (1903).

BRIGHTMAN, THOMAS: Puritan and Presbyterian; b. at Nottingham 1562; d. at Hawnes (5 m. s. by e. of Bedford) Aug. 24, 1607. He studied at Queen's College, Cambridge (B.A., 1581; M.A., 1584; B.D., 1591), became a fellow there in 1584, and rector of Hawnes in 1592. He was one of the fathers of Presbyterianism in England; as Thomas Cartwright says, "The bright star in the Church of God." He subscribed the Presbyterian Books of Discipline. He was a famous expositor of Revelation (*Apocalypsis Apocalypseos*, Frankfort, 1609, Heidelberg, 1612, Eng. transl., *A revelation of the Revelation*, Amsterdam, 1615, Leyden, 1616) and of Daniel from xi. 36 to end of xii. (Basel, 1614, which edition has notes on Canticles; Eng. transl., London, 1644). He opened up a new path in the exposition of the Apocalypse by making two distinct millenniums: the first, from Constantine until 1300, in this corresponding with the common orthodox view; the second, from 1300 to 2300, which was a new departure, by which he was enabled to find a place for the future conversion of the Jews, and a more glorious condition of the Church on earth, which he gains by a symbolical interpretation of Rev xxi. and xxii. His views greatly modified the Puritan interpretation of the Apocalypse, and were expounded by different writers and reproduced in different forms long after his death. His collected works appeared London, 1644.

BRIGIDA, SAINT, BRIGITTINES. See Bridget, Saint, of Sweden.

BRILL, JAKOB: Mystic; b. at Leyden Jan. 21, 1639; d. there Jan. 28, 1700. He was a follower of Pontiaan van Hattem; between 1685 and 1699 he published about forty works of a mystical-devotional character, which were much read; but spiritualizing Christ to such a degree that the historical Christ almost disappeared, and the sacrifice on the cross became a mere symbol of the sacrifice which shall take place in us, he at last got lost in a mystical pantheism, far away from Christianity.

Bibliography: A eulogy of Brill is found in Poiret's *Catalogue des écrivains mystiques* (Lat. transl., Amsterdam, 1708). Consult also Ypey en Dermont, *De hervormde Kerk in Nederland*, vol. iii., Breda, 1824.

BRINCKERINCK, JAN: A popular preacher and spiritual director in connection with the Brethren and Sisters of the Common Life; b. near Zütphen, Guelderland, 1359; d. at Deventer Mar. 26, 1419. Thomas à Kempis, who wrote his life, says that he came of a good family, but tells nothing further of his early life except that, living in the days of the great religious awakening under Groote's influence, he was profoundly impressed by it. He came into intimate personal relations with Groote and his disciples, and devoted himself to forwarding the "new devotion" and the education of the young. He was ordained priest in 1393, and not long afterward took charge as rector of the house for women founded at Deventer by Groote, "Meester Geertshuis" as it was commonly called (see Common Life, Brethren of the). He introduced a strict discipline into the life of the inmates, and was practically the founder of the sisters whose houses afterward became so numerous. Under his direction the numbers grew so considerably that new buildings were needed. After three years the church and convent were ready for occupancy; at first of wood, they were rebuilt of stone in 1407. The foundation was placed under the Windesheim chapter, who named Brinckerinck as its confessor. Numbering in that year twelve sisters and novices, by the middle of the century the community had grown to considerably over a hundred, including all classes. It was self-supporting; the sisters copied and illuminated manuscripts, or occupied themselves profitably in other ways according to their gifts. In 1408 a new house was erected at Diepenveen, a few miles away, in the choir of whose church Brinckerinck was buried. He was known far and wide for his popular preaching, which, according to the testimony of Rudolf Dier, one of his hearers, and of the Brethren of the Common Life, gave to all the impression that he had sat at the feet of Jesus. From a manuscript biography by Elizabeth of Delft, one of the twelve first sisters, we learn that she wrote down some of his sermons, and Rudolf Dier adds that out of such materials eight vernacular "collations" were formed, containing his admonitions to the sisters. These were discovered not long ago, and published by Moll in 1866. They read like notes of spoken discourses, sometimes apparently combinations of different ones. Like the usual "collations" of the Brethren of the Common Life, they were not formal sermons following a rhetorical method, but simple and artless talks which pass readily from one topic to another, and are rich in short, pithy sentences of a kind to be easily understood and remembered by his hearers. L. SCHULZE.

BIBLIOGRAPHY: The *Vita* by Thomas à Kempis is in the *Chronicon monasterii S. Agnetis*, ed. H. Rosweyde, Antwerp, 1615; another by J. Buschius is in the latter's *Chronicon Windeshmense*, ed. K. Grube, Halle, 1886. Consult: G. Dunbar, *Analecta*, vol. i., Deventer, 1719; idem, *Het Kerkelyk en Wereltlyk Deventer*, ib. 1732-88; W. Moll, *Kerkgeschiedenis van Nederland voor de Hervorming*, ii. 2, 209 sqq., Utrecht, 1871.

BRISTOL, FRANK MILTON: Methodist Episcopal bishop; b. in Orleans Co., N. Y., Jan. 4, 1851; elected bishop, 1908.

BRITISH CHURCH. See CELTIC CHURCH.

BRITISH HONDURAS. See CENTRAL AMERICA.

BRITTINANS, BRITTINIANS. See BRICTINANS.

BRIXEN, BISHOPRIC OF: A diocese which takes its name from Brixen, a town of the Tyrol, situated 40 m. s.s.e. of Innsbrück. The present Tyrol became a part of the Roman Empire 15 A.D., and the rapid spread of Christianity in north Italy gives ground for the supposition that it penetrated comparatively early into the Alpine region. The earliest authentic mention of a bishopric in southern Rhætia, however, dates from the end of the sixth century. Among the bishops of Venetia and Rhætia Secunda who addressed a letter to the emperor Maurice in 591 appears the name of a certain Ingenuinus, whom Paulus Diaconus and the author of the *Versus de ordine comprovincialium pontificum* describe as bishop of Sabiona, the present Seben. The existence of the bishopric seems to have been continuous from this time. It embraced to the south of the Brenner the upper Eisackthal and the Pusterthal, to the north of the Brenner almost the whole of what is now the Tyrol. Probably under Otto II., the see was removed from Seben to Brixen; in a document of 967 Bishop Richpert is designated as *Prihsinensis ecclesiæ episcopus*. (A. HAUCK.)

Brixen counts among the most ancient examples of exemption from the secular jurisdiction, having received it from Charlemagne and Louis the Pious. Its territory increased largely by donations from successive emperors, and Frederick I. (1179) gave its incumbent the princely title and rights. Henceforth the bishops received investiture immediately from the emperor, and had a seat and a voice in the imperial diet. The secular privileges, however, were gradually absorbed by the powerful magnates of the Tyrol, and at the Peace of Lunéville the principality was formally suppressed, to be conferred the next year on the house of Austria. Brixen was the meeting-place in 1080 of a council of imperialist prelates who undertook to depose Gregory VII. and elect Guibert of Ravenna pope in his place. Cardinal Nicholas of Cusa occupied the see from 1450 to 1464, and Caspar Ignatius, Count Künigl (1702-1747), was among the greatest and most active prelates of his day. The nomination to the see is vested in the emperor of Austria.

BROAD CHURCH. See ENGLAND, CHURCH OF.

BROADUS, JOHN ALBERT: American Baptist; b. in Culpeper County, Va., Jan. 24, 1827; d. in Louisville, Ky., Mar. 16, 1895. He was graduated at the University of Virginia 1850, and was assistant professor of Latin and Greek there, 1851-53, chaplain to the University 1855-57, pastor of the Baptist church in the place until, in 1859, on its organization, he became professor of the interpretation of the New Testament and of homiletics in the Southern Baptist Theological Seminary, then in Greenville, S. C. In 1877 the seminary was removed to Louisville, and in 1888 he became its president. He attained high rank as teacher, preacher, and scholar, and published two notable volumes in the field of homiletics, *The Preparation and Delivery of Sermons* (Philadelphia, 1870; 25th ed., by E. C. Dargan, New York, 1905) and *Lectures on the History of Preaching* (New York, 1876); also *Sermons and Addresses* (1886; 6th ed., 1905); a commentary on Matthew (Philadelphia, 1887); *Jesus of Nazareth* (New York, 1890); *Harmony of the Gospels according to the Revised Version* (1893); *Memoir of James Petigru Boyce* (1893). He also prepared a commentary on Mark (Philadelphia, 1905), and edited and revised the Oxford translation of Chrysostom's homilies on Philippians, Colossians, and Thessalonians, with an essay on St. Chrysostom as a homilist, in vol. xiii. of Philip Schaff's *Nicene and Post Nicene Fathers* (New York, 1889).

BIBLIOGRAPHY: A. T. Robertson, *Life and Letters of John Albert Broadus*, Philadelphia, 1901.

BROCHMAND, brek'mānd, **JESPER RASMUSSEN:** Bishop of Zealand; b. at Köge (20 m. s.w.

of Copenhagen), Zealand, Aug. 5, 1585; d. at Copenhagen Apr. 19, 1652. He studied at Herlufsholm, Copenhagen, Leyden, and Franeker; became rector of Herlufsholm academy 1608; professor pædagogicus, University of Copenhagen, 1610; professor of Greek 1613; member of the theological faculty 1615. In 1617 he was appointed teacher to Prince Christian, son of King Christian IV., but returned to the university three years later. At this time Denmark was disturbed by Roman Catholic propaganda, and Brochmand made the controversy with Rome a subject of his public lectures. In 1626–28 he published *Controversiæ sacræ* (3 parts), a reply to Bellarmine's attacks on the Lutheran Church, and in 1634, at the king's order, he engaged in a polemic with the Jesuits, who endeavored to defend the conversion of Margrave Christian William of Brandenburg to Catholicism. In their final reply the Jesuits stigmatized Brochmand as a "disturber of the Roman empire, the boldest despiser of His Imperial Majesty and the Catholic rulers, a poisonous spider, and a degenerate Absalom." Against this pamphlet Brochmand delivered a series of lectures which after his death were collected and published under the title *Apologiæ speculi veritatis confutatio* (Copenhagen, 1653). He was ordained bishop of Zealand in 1639, and during his long and fruitful activity in this office reorganized the Danish church service, especially by abolishing the Latin choir, and by introducing Wednesday services during Lent. His reputation as a dogmatist was established by his *Universæ theologiæ systema* (2 vols., 1633) in which he proved himself a bitter opponent, not only of the Roman Catholics, but also of the Reformed, whom he calls "enemies of God and of truth." He wrote several devotional works, of which his *Sabbati sanctificatio* for more than two centuries was a favorite collection of sermons with the Danish people. (F. NIELSEN†.)

BROEMEL, brū'mel", **ALBERT ROBERT:** German Lutheran pastor and author; b. at Teichel (15 m. s.s.e. of Erfurt), Schwarzburg, Apr. 27, 1815; d. at Ratzeburg (12 m. s.e. of Lübeck), Prussia, Oct. 28, 1885. He was educated at Göttingen, Jena, and Berlin, and after spending two years helping Otto von Gerlach (q.v.) in both educational and pastoral duties in the last-named place, was called in 1846 to be pastor of Lassahn in the duchy of Lauenburg. In 1854 he became superintendent of the whole district, with special charge of the principal church of Ratzeburg. Besides the multifarious duties which occupied him during the next thirty years, he found time for a considerable literary activity. His principal work was his *Homiletische Charakterbilder* (2 vols., Berlin, 1869–1874), which is practically a history of preaching, especially the post-Reformation and German. As is natural from the character of his life, his writings generally are more practical than theoretical. (WILHELM GLAMANN.)

BROMLEY, THOMAS: English mystic; b. in Worcester 1629; d. 1691. He held a fellowship in Oxford until 1660, when, as a non-conformist, he refused to accept the Anglican Liturgy. But previously he had become a follower of Jakob Boehme the mystic (q.v.), and with John Pordage and Jane Lead had founded the Philadelphian Society (see LEAD, JANE); when he left Oxford he came to Pordage, and lived with him many years. He rejected the outward church and advocated virginity for all. *The Way to the Sabbath of Rest* (last ed., 1802) is his most important work.

BROOKE, FRANCIS KEY: Protestant Episcopal bishop of the missionary district of Oklahoma and Indian Territory; b. at Gambier, O., Nov. 2, 1852; graduated at Kenyon College, 1874. He was successively rector at College Hill, Portsmouth, Piqua, and Sandusky, Ohio; St. Louis, Mo.; and Atchison, Kan., and was consecrated bishop in 1893.

BROOKE, STOPFORD AUGUSTUS: English Unitarian; b. at Letterkenny (16 m. s.w. of Londonderry), County Donegal, Nov. 14, 1832. He was educated at Trinity College, Dublin (B.A., 1856), and was ordained priest in the Church of England in 1857 He was successively curate of St. Matthew's, Marylebone (1857–59) and Kensington Church (1860–63). He was then chaplain to the princess royal, Berlin (1863–65), and after his return to England was minister of St. James's Chapel, York Street (1866–75), and of Bedford Chapel (1876–94). He was appointed chaplain to the queen in 1872, but in 1880 he withdrew from the Church of England, finding himself unable to accept the orthodox teaching concerning miracles. Among his writings special mention may be made of the following: *Life and Letters of the late Frederick W Robertson* (2 vols., London, 1865); *Freedom in the Church of England* (1871); *Sermons* (1868–77); *Theology in the English Poets* (1874); *A Fight of Faith* (1877); *Spirit of the Christian Life* (1881); *Unity of God and Man* (1886); *The Early Life of Jesus* (1887); *History of Early English Literature* (1892); *Short Sermons* (1892); *History of English Literature* (1894); *Study of Tennyson* (1894); *God and Christ* (1894); *Jesus and Modern Thought* (1894); *Old Testament and Modern Life* (1896); *The Gospel of Joy* (1898); and *Poetry of Robert Browning* (1902).

BROOKS, ELBRIDGE GERRY: American Universalist; b. at Dover, N. H., July 29, 1816; d. at Philadelphia Apr. 8, 1878. He was licensed at Portsmouth. N. H., 1836; became pastor in West Amesbury, Mass., 1837; in East Cambridge, 1838; in Lowell (First Universalist Church), 1845; in Bath, Me., 1846; in Lynn, Mass. (First Universalist Church), 1850; in New York (Church of our Savior), 1859; in Philadelphia (Church of the Messiah), 1868. He was general agent of the board of trustees of the General Convention, 1867–1868. He was an eloquent preacher, courageous and energetic, an advocate of the Maine liquor law and of the cause of the Union during the Civil War, as well as of the doctrine of remedial punishment in the future world. He published *Universalism in Life and Doctrine and its Superiority as a Practical Power* (New York, 1863) and *Our New Departure, or the methods and works of the*

Universalist Church of America as it enters on its second century (Boston, 1874).

BIBLIOGRAPHY: E. S. Brooks, *Life-Work of Elbridge Gerry Brooks*, Boston, 1881.

BROOKS, PHILLIPS: American preacher and bishop; b. in Boston Dec. 13, 1835; d. there Jan. 23, 1893. He was of distinguished New England ancestry being descended on his father's side from John Cotton and on his mother's side from Samuel Phillips, the founder of Phillips Academy, Andover. He was graduated at Harvard, 1855; studied at the Protestant Episcopal Theological School, Alexandria, Va., 1856–59; became rector of the Church of the Advent, Philadelphia, 1859; of Holy Trinity Church, Philadelphia, 1862; of Trinity Church, Boston, 1869; he was consecrated bishop of Massachusetts, 1891. He was one of the most eloquent, spiritual, successful, and highly esteemed clergymen of his time, and held this position both by intellectual power and an engaging personality. His preaching was preeminently the product of his own experience; he was of broad sympathies and tactful in his dealings with men. He was particularly courteous in cultivating cordial relations with those of other than his own denomination. He gave the Lyman Beecher lectures on preaching before the Yale Divinity School in 1877 (published as *Lectures on Preaching*, New York, 1877), and was Bohlen lecturer at the Philadelphia Divinity School in 1879 (*The Influence of Jesus*, 1879). He published five volumes of *Sermons* during his life (1878–90), and five have been added since his death (1893–1905). His *Letters of Travel written to his family* appeared in 1893, and a volume of *Essays and Addresses, religious, literary, and social*, edited by his brother, John Cotton Brooks, in 1894. Individual sermons, addresses, etc., have been printed in many forms and the number of books of extracts from his preaching is very large.

BIBLIOGRAPHY: The best biography is his *Life and Letters* by A. V. G. Allen, 2 vols., New York, 1900, condensed into 1 vol., ib. 1907.

BRORSON, HANS ADOLF: Bishop of Ribe; b. at Randrup, on the west coast of northern Sleswick, June 20, 1694; d. at Ribe, Jutland, June 3, 1764. He studied at the University of Copenhagen (1712–17), devoting himself more to history and literature than to theology, and acted as tutor in the house of an uncle at Lögum in Sleswick, where he caught the spirit of the religious revival at that time making itself felt in this province. In 1722 he was appointed minister at Randrup, and in 1729 he was called as deacon to Töndern. Here he began collecting Danish hymns for the use of his congregation, to replace the German ones previously sung before and after the Danish sermon. In 1732 he published a small volume of Christmas hymns which contains some of his most excellent compositions; later he published other booklets, and in 1739 the first edition of his *Troens rare Klenodie* ("The Faith's Rare Jewel"), a collection of 250 hymns, mostly translations from the German. In 1737 King Christian VI. appointed him dean of Ribe stift, and two years later he succeeded to the bishopric. Brorson was one of the greatest of Danish hymn-writers, and is preeminently the poet of Christmas. His hymns are associated with the melodies of the people, and he was essentially a singer for those who worship in the privacy of their homes. While not unable to write original hymns, it was especially the hymns and melodies of German Pietism that he transplanted into the church of Denmark. The best edition of his hymns is by P. A. Arland (Copenhagen, 1867). (F. NIELSEN†.)

BIBLIOGRAPHY: A. D. Jörgensen, *H. A. Brorson*, Copenhagen, 1887.

BROTHERHOODS, RELIGIOUS. See CONFRATERNITIES.

BROTHERS OF THE CHRISTIAN SCHOOLS. See CHRISTIAN BROTHERS.

BROUGHTON, brau'tun, HUGH: Church of England Hebrew scholar; b. at Oldbury (near the border of Wales, 20 m. s.w. of Shrewsbury), Shropshire, 1549; d. in Tottenham, London, Aug. 4, 1612. He was helped in his efforts to obtain an education by Bernard Gilpin (q.v.), and became fellow of St. John's and Christ's colleges, Cambridge (B.A., 1570). In London he gained fame as a preacher of Puritan doctrine. In 1588 he published *A Consent of Scripture*, a treatise on Bible chronology; it was attacked at both universities and Broughton undertook lectures in its defense at London. In 1589 or 1590 he went to Germany and thenceforth spent most of his life on the Continent, where he disputed with Jews, Roman Catholics, and Protestants who did not agree with him, and wrote letters to England asking for appointments. His learning and ability were unquestioned, but his unhappy temper and bad manners prevented his advancement. He was long anxious to assist in preparing a new version of the Bible, but when the translators were appointed by King James in 1604 he was not one of them, and when their work was done he made a bitter attack upon it. His writings were collected by Lightfoot, with the pompous title *The Works of the Great Albionean Divine, Renowned in Many Nations for Rare Skill in Salem's and Athens's Tongues and Familiar Acquaintance with all Rabbinical Learning, Mr. Hugh Broughton* (London, 1662); a sketch of his life is included.

BIBLIOGRAPHY: Besides the life prefixed to his works, there are available sketches in: B. Brook, *Lives of the Puritans*, ii. 215 sqq., London, 1813; A. à Wood, *Athenæ Oxonienses*, ed. P. Bliss, ii. 308 sqq., 4 vols., ib. 1813–20.

BROUSSON, brū"sōn', CLAUDE: French Protestant; b. at Nîmes 1647; executed at Montpellier Nov. 4, 1698. He practised as a lawyer at Castres, Castelnaudary, and, after 1679, in Toulouse, and employed his talent with courage and self-sacrifice to defend his coreligionists against the rigorous measures of the government. In 1683 he was compelled to leave France and lived for a time in Lausanne. He visited Berlin and Holland to bring about a coalition between the Protestant princes against Louis XIV In 1689 he returned to France and traveled through the southern part of the country admonishing and exhorting his brethren, though a price was put on his head, and he was hunted by the officials like a beast of prey.

In 1693 he again retired to Lausanne, and was ordained there (1694). In 1695 he reentered France through Sédan, and visited most of the Reformed congregations north of the Loire, finally escaping through Franche-Comté into Switzerland. Once more, in 1697, he visited France, but was caught at Oloron, and sentenced to death by strangling. Among his works, of which a list is given in *La France protestante*, vol. iii., the most prominent are: *État des réformés de France* (The Hague, 1685); *La Manne mystique du désert* (Amsterdam, 1695); *Lettres pastorales sur le cantique des cantiques* (Delft, 1697).

Bibliography: A. Borrel, *Biographie de C. Brousson*, Nîmes, 1852; H. S. Baynes, *The Evangelist of the Desert. Life of C. Brousson*, London, 1853.

BROWN, ARTHUR JUDSON: Presbyterian; b. at Holliston, Mass., Dec. 3, 1856. He was educated at Wabash College (B.A., 1880) and Lane Theological Seminary (1883). He was ordained to the Presbyterian ministry in 1883, and held successive pastorates at Ripon, Wis. (1883–1884), First Presbyterian Church, Oak Park, Ill. (1884–88), and First Presbyterian Church, Portland, Ore. (1888–95). Since 1895 he has been one of the secretaries of the Presbyterian Board of Foreign Missions. In addition to numerous contributions to periodicals, he has written *The New Era in the Philippines* (Chicago, 1903) and *New Forces in Old China* (1904).

BROWN, CHARLES REYNOLDS: Congregationalist; b. at Bethany, W. Va., Oct. 1, 1862. He was graduated from the University of Iowa (B.A., 1883; M.A., 1886) and the School of Theology of Boston University (1889). He was pastor of Wesley Chapel Methodist Episcopal Church, Cincinnati, O. (1889–92); of Winthrop Congregational Church, Boston (1892–96); since 1896 he has been pastor of the First Congregational Church, Oakland, Cal. He was special lecturer on ethics in Leland Stanford University in 1900–06, Lyman Beecher lecturer at Yale in 1905–06, and lecturer on ethics in Mills College in 1906–08. In 1897 he made a tour of Egypt and Palestine, and has been president of the board of trustees of Mills College since 1902 and a director of the Oakland Associated Charities since 1899, and chairman of the committee for the reconstruction of the San Francisco churches after the earthquake of 1906. In theology he is a liberal, and in addition to pamphlets and sermons, has written *Two Parables* (Chicago, 1898); *The Main Points: A Study in Christian Belief* (San Francisco, 1899); and *The Social Message of the Modern Pulpit* (Yale lectures, New York, 1906).

BROWN, CHARLES RUFUS: Baptist; b. at East Kingston, N. H., Feb. 22, 1849. He was educated at Phillips Exeter Academy (1863–65) and the United States Naval Academy (1865–69), and attained the rank of master. He resigned from the navy, however, and continued his studies at Newton Theological Institution (1874–75, 1877–1878), Harvard University (B.A., 1877), Union Theological Seminary (1878–79), and the universities of Berlin (1879–80) and Leipsic (1880–81). He was ordained to the Baptist ministry at Franklin, N. H., in 1881, and remained there as pastor until 1883. He was appointed associate professor of Biblical interpretation, Old Testament, in the Newton Theological Institution in 1883, and since 1886 has been professor of Hebrew and cognate languages there. He was also librarian of the institution in 1884–85, 1889–97, and 1900–06, secretary of the faculty in 1887–92, and registrar in 1892–95. He has been a member of the Society of Biblical Literature and Exegesis since 1883, and was formerly a member of the American Oriental Society (1886), the Archeological Institute of America (1899), and the department of archeology in the University of Pennsylvania (1902). He has written *An Aramaic Method* (2 parts, Chicago, 1884–86); in 1893–94 edited the course of Sunday-school lessons in the Bible Study Minor Graded Lesson System, and made a critical translation of Jeremiah (Philadelphia, 1907).

BROWN, DAVID: Free Church of Scotland; b. at Aberdeen Aug. 17, 1803; d. there July 3, 1897. He studied at the University of Aberdeen (M.A., 1821); was licensed 1826, and was assistant to Edward Irving in London 1830–32; was ordained minister of a country chapel six miles southwest of Banff 1836; he went with the Free Church 1843, and the same year became minister of St. James's, Glasgow; was elected professor of apologetics, church history, and exegesis of the Gospels at the Free Church College, Aberdeen, 1857; elected principal 1876, and resigned his professorship 1887. He was a director of the National Bible Society of Scotland, one of the founders of the Evangelical Alliance, was deeply interested in the Alliance of the Reformed Churches and a member of the third General Council at Belfast, 1888. He was an opponent of Robertson Smith in the controversy which resulted in the dismissal of the latter from Aberdeen, and as a member of the New Testament revision company took a highly conservative position. He was moderator of the General Assembly of the Free Church in 1885. Besides numerous contributions to the periodicals, he published *Christ's Second Coming: Will it be Premillenial?* (Edinburgh, 1846; 6th ed., 1867), a classic; *Crushed Hopes Crowned in Death*, a memorial of his son, Alexander Brown, of the Bengal civil service, d. Jan., 1860 (London, 1861); *The Restoration of the Jews: the History, Principles, and Bearings of the Question* (Edinburgh, 1861); *Life of the late John Duncan* (1872); *The Apocalypse: its structure and primary predictions* (London, 1891). He collaborated with R. Jamieson and A. R. Fausset in preparing the *Commentary, Critical, Experimental, and Practical, on the Old and New Testaments* (6 vols., Glasgow, 1864–70), furnishing the portion devoted to the Gospels, the Acts, and the Epistle to the Romans; wrote the commentary on the Epistles to the Corinthians for Schaff's *Popular Commentary on the New Testament* (1882); and prepared the Epistle to the Romans for Dods and Whyte's *Handbooks for Bible Classes* (Edinburgh, 1883).

Bibliography: W. G. Blaikie, *David Brown, A Memoir*, London, 1898.

BROWN, FRANCIS: Presbyterian; b. at Hanover, N. H., Dec. 26, 1849. He was educated at Dartmouth College (B.A., 1870), Union Theological Seminary (1877), and the University of Berlin (1877–79). He was assistant master in Ayers' Latin School, Pittsburg, Pa., in 1870–72, and tutor in Greek in Dartmouth College in 1872–74. He became instructor in Biblical philology in Union Theological Seminary, New York City, 1879; associate professor of the same, 1881; professor of Hebrew and the cognate languages, 1890; and also president, 1908. He was president of the Society of Biblical Literature and Exegesis in 1895–96 (member since 1881); president of the Society of Historical Theology (Oxford) in 1899–1900 (member since 1891; member of the American Oriental Society since 1881). He was Ely lecturer in Union Theological Seminary in 1907; head of the American School for Oriental Study and Research in Palestine, 1907–08. He has written: *The Teaching of the Twelve Apostles* (New York, 1884; in collaboration with R. D. Hitchcock); *Assyriology, its Use and Abuse in Old Testament Study* (1885); *A Hebrew and English Lexicon of the Old Testament* (12 parts, Oxford, 1891–1906; in collaboration with S. R. Driver and C. A. Briggs); and *The Christian Point of View* (New York, 1902; in collaboration with A. C. McGiffert and G. W. Knox).

BROWN, HUGH STOWELL: English Baptist; b. at Douglas, Isle of Man, Aug. 10, 1823; d. at Liverpool Feb. 24, 1886. He learned surveying, and became a railroad engineer; at twenty-one entered King William's College, Castletown, Isle of Man, to study for the ministry of the Established Church; doubts concerning the baptismal teachings of the Church and the relations of Church and State led him to think of returning to his trade; in 1846 he joined the Baptists, in 1847 became minister of the Myrtle Street Chapel, Liverpool, and remained there till his death. He inaugurated Sunday afternoon lectures for workingmen, with whom, owing to his early experiences, he had great influence. He was president of the Baptist Union 1878, an active member of the Baptist Missionary Society, and president of the Liverpool Peace Society. He published numerous lectures and sermons.

Bibliography: *Hugh Stowell Brown, his Autobiography, his Commonplace Book, and Extracts from his Sermons and Addresses, a memorial Volume*, edited by his son-in-law, W. S. Caine, London, 1887; *DNB*, supplement vol., i. 300–301.

BROWN, JAMES BALDWIN: English Congregationalist; b. in London Aug. 19, 1820; d. there June 23, 1884. He studied at London University (B.A., 1839); studied law for two years and then studied theology at Highbury College; became minister of London Road Chapel, Derby, 1843; of Claylands Chapel, Clapham Road, London, 1846, and remained with this congregation till his death; a new church on Brixton Road (Brixton Independent Church) was occupied in 1870. He was distinguished for the breadth of his theological views and strongly opposed to Calvinism. He took an active interest in public movements such as the relief of the laboring classes during the Lancashire cotton famine. He favored the opening of the Crystal Palace on Sundays, and was a warm advocate of the admission of dissenters to the universities. He strenuously opposed the doctrine of conditional immortality as a deadly error. In 1878 he was chairman of the Congregational Union; at this time a movement to discover some common ground on which Christians of various ways of thinking might unite in independence of dogma and of the historic side of Christianity had made such progress as to call for repressive action on the part of the Union in the opinion of many; he strongly opposed such action, but was overruled and outvoted. His more important books were: *The Divine Life in Man* (London, 1859), which brought upon him a charge of heterodoxy; *The Soul's Exodus and Pilgrimage* (1862); *The Divine Treatment of Sin* (1864); *The Home Life in the Light of its Divine Idea* (1866); *Idolatries, Old and New, their Cause and Cure* (1867); *The First Principles of Ecclesiastical Truth* (1871); *The Higher Life, its Reality, Experience, and Destiny* (1874); *The Doctrine of Annihilation in the Light of the Gospel of Love* (1875); *Home, its Relation to Man and Society* (1883).

Bibliography: For his life consult Elizabeth B. Brown, *J. Baldwin Brown, Minister of Brixton Independent Church*, London, 1884 (by his wife).

BROWN, JOHN: English Congregationalist; b. at Bolton-le-Moors (12 m. n.w. of Manchester), Lancashire, June 19, 1830. He was educated at Owens College, Manchester, and the Lancashire Independent College, Manchester (B.A., London University, 1853), and was minister of Park Chapel, Manchester, from 1855 to 1864, and of Bunyan Church, Bedford, from 1864 to 1903, when he became pastor emeritus. He was chairman of the Congregational Union of England and Wales in 1891, Congregational Union lecturer in 1898, and Lyman Beecher lecturer at Yale in 1899. He was also president of the County Association of Free Churches in Bedfordshire from 1878 to 1902, and chairman of the committee of the Congregational Union of England and Wales, 1893–95. He represented the latter body at the Triennial Union of the United States at Minneapolis in 1892, and at the Congregational Union of Ontario and Quebec at Toronto in 1905. In Biblical criticism he is a liberal conservative, and in theology belongs to the evangelical school. In addition to numerous pamphlets and magazine articles, he has written: *Lectures on the Book of Revelation* (London, 1866); *God's Book for Man's Life* (1881); *John Bunyan, his Life, Times, and Work* (1885); *The Pilgrim Fathers of New England* (1895); *The Bedfordshire Union of Christians* (1896); *Apostolical Succession in the Light of History and Fact* (Congregational Union lectures, 1898); *The Present Crisis in the Church of England* (1899); *Puritan Preaching in England* (Yale Lectures for 1899, New York, 1900); *Eras of Nonconformity* (2 vols., London, 1904). He likewise edited Bunyan's *Pilgrim's Progress, Holy War*, and *Grace Abounding* (3 vols., London, 1887–88), and the same author's complete works for the Cambridge University Press (2 vols., Cambridge, 1905–06).

BROWN, JOHN: The name of several Scotch ministers, the most noteworthy being:

1. John Brown of Edinburgh: Scotch Burgher minister, eldest son of Rev. John Brown of Whitburn (21 m. w.s.w. of Edinburgh), Linlithgowshire (b. 1754; d. 1832), and grandson of John Brown of Haddington (q.v.); b. at Whitburn July 12, 1784; d. at Edinburgh Oct. 13, 1858. He studied at Edinburgh and the divinity hall of the Burgher Church at Selkirk; was licensed 1805 and ordained minister of the Burgher Church of Biggar, Lanarkshire, 1806; became minister of the Rose Street Church, Edinburgh, 1822, and of the Broughton Place Church in the same city 1829; was professor of exegetical theology to the United Associate Synod after 1834. He was strongly in favor of the separation of Church and State, and in 1845 was tried (and acquitted) before the synod on a charge of holding unsound views concerning the atonement. He was a fine orator and a voluminous writer; the most prominent of his works are: *Expository Discourses on First Peter* (3 vols., Edinburgh, 1848); *Exposition of the Discourses and Sayings of our Lord Jesus Christ* (3 vols., 1850); *The Resurrection of Life*, an exposition of I Cor. xv. (1852); *Expository Discourses on Galatians* (1853); *Analytical Exposition of the Epistle of Paul to the Romans* (1857). He was the father of the well-known John Brown, M.D. (b. 1810; d. 1882), author of *Rab and his Friends* (Edinburgh, 1859).

Bibliography: J. Cairns, *Memoirs of John Brown*, Edinburgh, 1861; *DNB*, vii. 18–19.

2. John Brown of Haddington: Scotch Burgher minister; b. at Carpow, near Abernethy (on the Frith of Tay, 6 m. s.e. of Perth), Perthshire, 1722; d. at Haddington (12 m. e. of Edinburgh) June 19, 1787. He was poor and self-taught, but acquired no small amount of learning; was a herd-boy, pedler, soldier, and school-teacher; studied theology under Ebenezer Erskine and James Fisher of Glasgow; was licensed in 1750, and in 1751 settled as pastor of the Burgher branch of the Secession Church of Haddington, where he remained till his death, declining a call as professor of divinity in Queen's College, N. J. After 1768 he was professor of theology to the Associate Synod. His yearly income from his church never exceeded £50, and his professorship had no salary; nevertheless he brought up a large family, gave freely in charity, and wrote books (which brought him no pecuniary profit) not only popular but valuable. They include: *Two Short Catechisms Mutually Connected* (Edinburgh, 1764); *A Dictionary of the Bible* (2 vols., 1769; revised ed., 1868); *The Self-interpreting Bible* (2 vols., 1778; often reprinted); and *A Compendious History of the Church of England and of the Protestant Churches in Ireland and America* (2 vols., Glasgow, 1784; new edition by Thomas Brown, Edinburgh, 1823).

Bibliography: Sketches of his life are prefixed to various editions of his works; the best is that by his son, prefixed to his *Select Remains, ed. his Sons, J. and E. Brown*, this edited by W. Brown, Edinburgh, 1856. Consult also *DNB*, vii. 12–14.

BROWN, JOHN NEWTON: American Baptist; b. at New London, Conn., June 29, 1803; d. at Germantown, Penn., May 15, 1868. He was graduated at Hamilton Institute (Colgate University), Hamilton, N. Y., 1823; preached at Buffalo, N. Y., Providence, R. I., Malden, Mass., and Exeter, N. H.; was professor of theology and church history in the New Hampton (New Hampshire) Theological Institution, 1838–45; pastor at Lexington, Va., 1845–49; editorial secretary of the American Baptist Publication Society 1849 till his death. He prepared (1833) and revised (1852) the "New Hampshire [Baptist] Confession of Faith." His most important literary work was the *Encyclopædia of Religious Knowledge* (Brattleboro, 1835).

BROWN, PETER HUME: Scotch historian, layman; b. at Haddington (18 m. e. of Edinburgh), Haddingtonshire, Dec. 17, 1850. He was educated at Edinburgh University (M.A., 1873), and had originally intended to enter the Church. He gave up this plan, however, and ultimately turned his attention to history. In 1898 he was made editor of the Register of the Privy Council of Scotland, and three years later was appointed to his present position of professor of ancient (Scottish) history and paleography in the University of Edinburgh. He has written: *George Buchanan, Humanist and Reformer* (Edinburgh, 1890); *Early Travellers in Scotland* (London, 1891); *Scotland before 1700, from Contemporary Documents* (Edinburgh, 1893); *John Knox: a Biography* (2 vols., 1895); *History of Scotland* (2 vols., Cambridge, 1898–1902); *Scotland in the time of Queen Mary* (Rhind Lectures for 1903; London, 1904); and *George Buchanan and his Times* (1906).

BROWN, PHŒBE ALLEN (HINSDALE): Hymn-writer; b. at Canaan, Columbia County, N. Y., May 1, 1783; d. at Marshall, Henry County, Ill., Oct. 10, 1861. She was left an orphan at the age of two, and in early life suffered great hardship and even cruel treatment at the hands of strangers; she first learned to write at the age of eighteen. In 1805 she married Timothy Brown (d. 1853) and moved to East Windsor, Conn. In 1813 the family went to the neighboring village of Ellington, and in 1818 to Monson, Mass. Her husband was a village mechanic, the family was poor, and her life was hampered by care; nevertheless she read much, kept up systematic Bible study, and found money to devote to Christian work, especially to the cause of missions. She wrote for her own amusement, but published newspaper articles, tracts, and a volume of tales, *The Tree and its Fruits* (New York, 1836); she left an autobiography in manuscript. Her best known hymn,

"I love to steal awhile away
From every cumbering care,"

is said to have been written at Ellington at a time when poverty and domestic duties left little opportunity for meditation at home and she was in the habit of going out for a walk every day at dusk; some thoughtless remarks of neighbors being reported to her, she wrote "An Apology for my Twilight Rambles." The second line originally read "From little ones and care." The poem was first printed (abridged and revised) in Nettleton's *Village Hymns* (New York, 1824). The tune "Monson," to which it is often sung, was written by her son, Samuel Robbins Brown (q.v.).

Bibliography: F. M. Bird, in *The Independent* for Jan. 6, Jan. 20, and April 14, 1881; S. W. Duffield, *English Hymns*, pp. 242–246, New York, 1886 (gives original text of the hymn mentioned in the text); Julian, *Hymnology*, p. 185.

BROWN, SAMUEL ROBBINS: The first American appointed missionary to Japan; b. at East Windsor, Conn., June 16, 1810, son of Phœbe (Hinsdale) Brown (q.v.); d. at Monson, Mass., June 20, 1880. He was graduated at Yale, 1832; studied at the Theological School, Columbia, S. C., 1835–37, and at Union Theological Seminary, New York, 1837–38; went to China in 1838 and took charge of a school founded and maintained by the Morrison Education Society (see Morrison, Robert), located first at Macao, in 1842 removed to Hongkong. He returned to America in 1847 bringing with him three Chinese boys, one of whom was Yung Wing, afterward at the head of the Chinese Education Commission; he taught at Rome, N. Y., 1848–51, and was pastor of the Reformed (Dutch) Church and principal of a successful school at Owasco Outlet (Sand Beach), near Auburn, N. Y., 1851–59; was one of the incorporators (1851) and first chairman of the executive committee of Elmira College, the first chartered woman's college in America. In May, 1859, he sailed for Japan as missionary of the Reformed (Dutch) Church, and located at Kanagawa till 1863, when he removed to Yokohama; returned to America in 1867 and for two years preached for his old church at Owasco Outlet; was again in Japan 1869–79. Dr. Brown arrived in Japan immediately after the opening of the country; during the difficult transition period which followed he labored with rare judgment and unfailing zeal for both natives and foreign residents. His views and his methods were free from narrowness and he considered the advancement of civilization a part of the work of the Christian missionary. He wrote many articles and newspaper letters on Chinese and Japanese subjects; prepared school books for his pupils; published *Colloquial Japanese* (Shanghai, 1863), and *Prendergast's Mastery System Adapted to the Study of Japanese or English* (Yokohama, 1878); and assisted in the Japanese translation of the New Testament, completed just before his death and published the same year.

Bibliography: W. E. Griffis, *A Maker of the New Orient, Samuel R. Brown*, New York, 1902.

BROWN, WILLIAM ADAMS: Presbyterian; b. in New York City Dec. 29, 1865. He was educated at Yale University (B.A., 1886), Union Theological Seminary (1890), and the University of Berlin (1890–92). He was successively instructor in church history (1892–93) and systematic theology (1893–95) in Union Theological Seminary, where he was provisional professor of systematic theology from 1895 to 1898, and has been Roosevelt professor of the same subject since 1898. He is a member of the Society of Biblical Literature and Exegesis, and has written, in addition to contributions to Hastings's *Dictionary of the Bible*, *Musical Instruments and their Homes* (New York, 1888); *The Essence of Christianity* (1892); *Christ the Vitalizing Principle of Christian Theology* (1898); and *Christian Theology in Outline* (1907).

BROWN, WILLIAM MONTGOMERY: Protestant Episcopal bishop of Arkansas; b. near Orrville, O., Nov. 6, 1855. He was educated at Seabury Hall, Faribault, Minn., and by private tutors, and graduated from Bexley Hall, the theological seminary of Kenyon College, Gambier, O., 1884. He was ordered deacon in 1883, and priest, 1884. He was in charge of Grace Mission, Galion, O., 1883–91, and during this period established seven other missions in adjacent places. In 1891 he was chosen general missionary and archdeacon of the diocese of Ohio, and in this capacity founded many new parishes, besides building twenty-one mission chapels. He was likewise secretary of the Diocesan Missionary Committee and of the Diocesan Board of Trustees. In 1898 he was consecrated bishop-coadjutor of Arkansas, and on the death of Bishop Henry N. Pierce in 1899, became bishop of the diocese. He has written *The Church for Americans* (New York, 1896).

BROWNE, EDWARD HAROLD: Bishop of Winchester; b. at Aylesbury (35 m. n.w. of London), Buckinghamshire, Mar. 6, 1811; d. at Shales, near Bitterne (2 m. n.e. of Southampton), Hampshire, Dec. 18, 1891. He studied at Emmanuel College, Cambridge (B.A., 1832; M.A., 1836; B.D., 1855); became fellow and tutor of his college, 1837; curate of Stroud, Gloucestershire, 1840; perpetual curate of St. James's, Exeter, 1841; perpetual curate of St. Sidwell's, Exeter, 1842; vice-principal and professor of Hebrew in St. David's College, Lampeter, Wales, 1843; vicar of Kenwyn-cum-Kea, Cornwall, and prebendary of Exeter, 1849; vicar of Heavitree and canon of Exeter, 1857; in 1854 he was appointed Norrisian professor of divinity at Cambridge; in 1864 was consecrated bishop of Ely; in 1873 translated to Winchester; resigned 1890. He took a deep interest in the "Old Catholic" movement and attended the congress at Cologne in 1872; was a member of the Old Testament company of revisers; was prominent on the conservative side in the beginning of the controversy concerning Bible criticism and issued *The Pentateuch and the Elohistic Psalms, in Reply to Bishop Colenso* (London, 1863). He also published: *The Fulfilment of the Old Testament Prophecies Relating to the Messiah* (1836); *An Exposition of the Thirty-nine Articles* (2 vols., 1850–53; new ed., 1886)—the work by which he is best known; and *Position and Parties of the English Church* (1875). He also contributed to *Aids to Faith* and wrote the introduction to the Pentateuch and the commentary on Genesis for the "Speaker's Commentary."

Bibliography: G. W. Kitchin, *Edward Harold Browne. . . A Memoir*, London, 1895; *DNB*, supplement vol., i. 304.

BROWNE, GEORGE: First Protestant archbishop of Dublin; d. 1556. He is first heard of in 1534, when, as provincial of the order of Austin Friars, he was employed to administer the oath of succession to the friars of London and the south of England; he was nominated to the see of Dublin, vacant by the murder of Archbishop Allen, was consecrated the same year, and arrived in Ireland in 1536. He worked diligently to introduce the Reformation in Ireland and to further the cause of the king; he was deposed under Mary. His opponents have described him as avaricious, profligate, and unlearned.

BIBLIOGRAPHY: A sketch and useful references to sources are in *DNB*, vii. 43–45.

BROWNE, GEORGE FORREST: Bishop of Bristol; b. at York Dec. 4, 1833. He was educated at St. Catherine's College, Cambridge (B.A., 1856), where he was fellow and lecturer in 1863–1865. He was ordained to the priesthood in 1859, and after being chaplain of St. Catherine's College and theological tutor at Trinity College, Glenalmond, Scotland, was rector of Ashley, Hants, from 1869 to 1875. He was a member of the Council of the Senate of Cambridge University in 1874–1878 and again in 1880–92, and was Disney professor of archeology in the same university from 1887 to 1892. He was treasurer of St. Paul's in 1891–99 and canon in 1892–97, and in 1895 was consecrated bishop suffragan of Stepney, being translated to the see of Bristol two years later. He was also Bell lecturer in the Scottish Episcopal Church in 1862 and secretary to the Cambridge Local Examinations seven years later, and is president of the Alpine Club. He has written: *Ice Caves of France and Switzerland* (London, 1865); *The Venerable Bede* (1879); *University Sermons; The Ilam Crosses* (1889); *Lessons from Early English Church History* (1893); *The Church at Home before Augustine* (1894); *Augustine and his Companions* (1895); *Off the Mill* (1895); *Conversion of the Heptarchy* (1896); *Theodore and Wilfrith* (1897); *History of St. Catherine's College* (1902); and *Life and Works of St. Aldhelm* (1903).

BROWNE, JOHN: English Congregationalist; b. at North Walsham (15 m. n. of Norwich), Norfolk, Feb. 6, 1823; d. at Wrentham (33 m. n.e. of Ipswich), Suffolk, Apr. 4, 1886. He studied at Coward College and University College, London 1839–44 (B.A., London University, 1843); was minister at Lowestoft, Suffolk, 1844; at Wrentham, 1848 till his death. His chief publication was the *History of Congregationalism and Memorials of the Churches in Norfolk and Suffolk* (London, 1877), which is of great importance for the beginnings of English Congregationalism.

BROWNE, PETER: Protestant Irish bishop; b. in County Dublin soon after 1660; d. Aug. 25, 1735. He studied at Trinity College, Dublin; was consecrated bishop of Cork and Ross 1710. He opposed the custom of drinking healths in a series of pamphlets (1713 sqq.) which won him much notoriety, but has more enduring fame as an anti-deistical writer; in reply to John Toland he published *A Letter in Answer to a Book Entitled Christianity not Mysterious* (Dublin, 1697), and afterward elaborated his argument in *The Procedure, Extent, and Limits of Human Understanding* (London, 1728), a critique of Locke's *Essay;* in *Things Divine and Supernatural Conceived by Analogy with Things Natural and Human* (1733) he asserts that knowledge of God's essence and attributes can be only "analogical" and not direct.

BROWNE, ROBERT: Leader of the English Separatists (from whom they received their popular name of Brownists), and generally considered the founder of the Congregationalists; b. at Tolethorp (3 m. n. of Stamford), Rutlandshire, about 1550; d at Northampton after June 2, 1631. He was of good family and had influential relatives on both his father's and his mother's side, including the great chancellor, Lord Burghley. He studied at Corpus Christi College, Cambridge (B.A., 1572). It is said that in 1571 he was domestic chaplain to Thomas Howard, duke of Norfolk, and that the duke took his part in some obscure trouble with the ecclesiastical authorities; but this is doubtful. He taught school for three years (seventeenth century writers say in or near London) and made "enemics" by freely speaking his mind concerning "many things amiss, and the cause of all to be the woeful and lamentable state of the Church." In 1578 or 1579 he returned to Cambridge. At this time his views seem to have ripened. Holding that the true Church consisted only of such as led Christian lives and did not properly include all baptized persons, he declared that "the kingdom of God was not to be begun by whole parishes, but rather of the worthiest, were they never so few." He publicly harangued against "the calling and authorizing of preachers by bishops," preached constantly to Puritan audiences (acceptably, it would appear) although he had no bishop's license, and, when his brother obtained a license for him, disdained it. Naturally he was silenced, and illness compelled him temporarily to comply with the bishop's mandate.

About 1580 Browne went to Norwich, attracted thither by a friend, Robert (or Richard) Harrison (q.v.), who became his coworker. Here he organized his first church and soon extended the field of his operations as far as Bury St. Edmunds. The bishop of Norwich complained of him as a preacher of "corrupt and contentious doctrine" and likely to mislead "the vulgar sort of people," but Burghley protected him. Nevertheless Norwich was made so uncomfortable for the little band that about Jan., 1582, most of them, with their pastor, emigrated to Middelburg in Zealand. Browne's impulsive and imperious character, as well as the principles of the congregation, did not promote unity. After two years of continual discussion and division, with four or five families, he left for Scotland. They arrived in Edinburgh Jan., 1584, and at once commenced the propagation of their peculiar doctrines. They "held opinion of separation from all kirks where excommunication was not rigorously used against open offenders not repenting; they would not admit witnesses [sponsors] in baptism, and sundry other opinions they had." Within a week Browne was summoned before the session of the kirk; he was imprisoned, but only for a short time; and soon, unhindered, if not covertly encouraged by the secular authorities, he traveled over Scotland. He returned to England, and, possibly, again visited Holland.

It has generally been supposed that Browne kept on as zealously and offensively as ever so far as his strength—which was beginning to break owing to imprisonments and hardships—permitted, continually harassed by the authorities and favored by Burghley, until 1586; that in that year the bishop of Peterborough excommunicated him, and this so wrought upon him that he changed completely, submitted to the Church, and thenceforth lived quietly, and, after a few years, in the enjoyment of a good benefice. Mr. Burrage transfers the excommunication to a later period and gives the date of Browne's submission Oct. 7, 1585. In Nov., 1586, he was elected master of St. Olave's Grammar-school in Southwark, binding himself to abstain from propagating his peculiar doctrines and to live as a member of the Church. His controversial powers were now employed against his former associates, Henry Barrow and John Greenwood. In Sept., 1591, he received the living of Achurch-cum-Thorpe, Northamptonshire; he was ordained deacon and priest on Sept. 30, and he remained at Achurch for forty uneventful years. For a period of ten years (1616–26) the entries in the parish register are not in his handwriting. Mr. Burrage thinks that this was the time when he was under sentence of excommunication by the bishop of Peterborough, and that the cause was a manifestation of Separatist tendencies encouraged by Browne in his parish. If this be so he made submission a second time, for his handwriting reappears in the register. His last entry is dated June 2, 1631, and in Nov., 1633, a new rector took his place. He died in Northampton jail, committed for striking a constable who came to him to collect a debt, and having shown something of his early fervid manner when brought before a justice in consequence.

Browne's biographers have been much puzzled to explain or extenuate his extraordinary conduct in making terms with the Church. It has been urged that he was broken physically and mentally in 1586; but he can not have been forty years old at that time and he lived forty-five years afterward. Dr. Dexter's suggestion that he was naturally of unsound mind with a tendency to insanity which at times became acute has found wide acceptance. It would explain not only Browne's own conduct but also the long forbearance and continued kindness which he enjoyed from Burghley and others. Mr. Burrage thinks that "at last he had become wearied of the continual criticism to which his views in the past had subjected him, and probably had honestly come to feel that he might be of really more service to the world, as it was, not by wearing himself out by combating established ideas, but rather by accepting what the world offered him and by using the advantage he had thus gained to the furtherance of his higher ideals."

The starting-point of Browne's views and system seems to have been his conviction that the spiritual welfare of true Christians required their separation from others who were Christians in name only. It was futile to hope that such separation would be brought about by the bishops and clergy of the Established Church or by the civil rulers. Yet the necessity for it was immediate. Hence the only course possible was for the faithful to secede and organize themselves. A voluntary association or covenant of true believers constituted a church, and each church had the exclusive right of discipline and the choice of its own officers. Two kinds of officers are designated in the New Testament: apostles, prophets, evangelists are temporary and belong to the past; the abiding officers are the pastor, teacher, elders, deacons, and widows who have their charge in one church only. The presence of these officers does not release any member from the duty of watching and helping the others, and a similar responsibility exists between churches. The civil authorities should have nothing to do with spiritual matters, and it is not their province to enforce conformity to any ecclesiastical system. He was thus the first Englishman to express the Anabaptist doctrine of complete separation of Church and State. See CONGREGATIONALISTS, I., 1, §§ 1–2.

Browne published three treatises at Middelburg (1582), entitled respectively: (1) *A Book which Sheweth the Life and Manners of All True Christians, and how unlike they are unto Turks and Papists and heathen folk; also the points and parts of all divinity that is of the revealed will and word of God are declared by their several definitions and divisions in order* (extracts in Walker, pp. 18–27); (2) *A Treatise of Reformation without Tarrying for Any, and of the wickedness of those preachers which will not reform till the magistrate command or compel them* (reprinted, Boston, "Old South Leaflet, no. 100"; with biographical introduction by T. G. Crippen, London, 1903); (3) *A Treatise upon the 23d of Matthew, both for an order of studying and handling the Scriptures and also for avoiding the popish disorders and ungodly communion of all false Christians, especially of wicked preachers and hirelings* (extracts in Burrage, pp. 21–25). These were intended primarily to further his cause in England and were spread abroad by his followers; two men were hanged in 1583 for disseminating them (see COPPIN, JOHN). Several other publications or manuscripts of Browne's are mentioned (Mr. Burrage, *True Story*, pp. 74–75, enumerates twenty-five) and the following are known to be preserved: (4) *A True and Short Declaration both of the Gathering and Joining together of Certain Persons, and also of the lamentable breach and division which fell among them* (1584?; reprinted in *The Congregationalist*, London, 1882), the story of Browne's early life; (5) *An Answer to Master Cartwright's Letter for joining with the English Churches* (London, n.d.; extracts in Burrage, pp. 31–36); (6) *A Reproof of Certain Schismatical Persons* [Henry Barrow and John Greenwood] *and their doctrine, touching the hearing and preaching of the word of God* (manuscript written probably in 1588, discovered by Mr. Burrage and published by him, Oxford, 1907); (7) A letter addressed "My good Uncle," and dated "the last of December, 1588" [Jan. 10, 1589], discovered and published with introduction by Champlin Burrage under the title *A New Years Guift* (London, 1904). The letter is quoted by Richard Bancroft, afterward archbishop of Canterbury, in a sermon at Paul's Cross, Feb. 9, 1588, and the manuscript discovered by Mr. Burrage is indorsed in what is believed to be Brancroft's handwriting "Mr. Browne's Answer to Mr. Flower's Letter." One sheet (4 pages) is lacking, but the part preserved contains more than 6,000 words, discusses the subject of church government at considerable length, and is particularly interesting for the idea which it gives of Browne's views concerning the Church of England at the time of writing; (8) A letter to Burghley, Apr. 15, 1590, printed by Strype in the *Life and Acts of John Whitgift*, appendix, bk. iii., no. xlv. (appendix, pp. 133–134, ed. London, 1718).

BIBLIOGRAPHY: T. Fuller, *Church History of Great Britain*, book ix., cent. xvi., sect. vi., §§ 1–7, 64–69, ed. J. S.

Brewer, 6 vols., London, 1845; C. H. Cooper, *Athenæ Cantabrigienses*, ii. 177-178, London, 1858-61; H. M. Dexter, *Congregationalism of the Last Three Hundred Years*, New York, 1880; W. Walker, *Creeds and Platforms of Congregationalism*, pp. 1-27, ib. 1893; idem, *History of the Congregational Churches in the United States*, 31-41, ib. 1894; *DNB*, vii. 57-61; C. Burrage, *The True Story of Robert Browne (1550-1603), Father of Congregationalism*, Oxford, 1906.

BROWNE, SIR THOMAS: Author of the *Religio Medici;* b. in Cheapside, London, Oct. 19, 1605; d. at Norwich Oct. 19, 1682. He attended Winchester College and Broadgate Hall (Pembroke College), Oxford (B.A., 1626; M.A., 1629); studied medicine and practised in Oxfordshire; traveled in Ireland, France, and Italy, continued his medical studies at Montpellier and Padua, and received his degree of doctor of medicine at Leyden about 1633; settled at Norwich in 1637, where he gained much repute as a physician and still more as a man of universal knowledge. The *Religio Medici* was probably written about 1635 and not intended for publication; two unauthorized editions appeared in 1642, which led to an edition with the author's approval, but anonymous, in 1643. The work is peculiar from its blending of deep religious feeling and skeptical views. "It appears to have been composed as a *tour de force* of intellectual agility, an attempt to combine daring skepticism with implicit faith in revelation." The style is metaphorical and artificial, with many Latinized words, but striking and impressive. Browne also published: *Pseudodoxia Epidemica, or Enquiries into very Many Received Tenets and commonly Presumed Truths, which Examined prove but Vulgar and Common Errors* (London, 1646); *Hydriotaphia or Urnburial* and *The Garden of Cyrus* (1658); many of his manuscripts were published posthumously. The best edition of his complete works is by Simon Wilkin (4 vols., London, 1835-36; reprinted, abridged, by Bohn, 3 vols., 1851-52). The *Religio Medici*, with *A Letter to a Friend upon Occasion of the Death of his Intimate Friend* (first published 1690) and *Christian Morals* (1716), and the *Hydriotaphia* and *Garden of Cyrus*, have been carefully edited by W. A. Greenhill (London, 1881 and 1896); and the *Religio Medici* is ed. with introduction by C. H. Herford (New York, 1907).

Bibliography: A rather extended sketch of Browne's life and writings is given in *DNB*, vii. 64-72, where the literature and list of works is given at some length. Consult also E. Gosse, in *English Men of Letters*, London, 1905.

BROWNISTS. See Browne, Robert.

BROWNLEE, WILLIAM CRAIG: American (Dutch) Reformed clergyman; b. at Torfoot, Lanarkshire, Scotland, 1783; d. in New York Feb. 10, 1860. He was graduated at Glasgow University; was licensed and emigrated to America in 1808; was pastor at Mt. Pleasant, Washington County, Penn., Philadelphia (1813), and Baskingridge, N. J. (1819); professor of languages in Rutgers College 1825; called to the Collegiate Reformed Dutch Church, New York, 1826; made pastor emeritus after a paralytic stroke in 1843. He was a strong opponent of Roman Catholics and Quakers. He published *Inquiry into the Principles of Quakers* (New York, 1824); *The Roman Catholic Controversy* (Philadelphia, 1834); *Lights and Shadows of Christian Life* (New York, 1837); *Popery an Enemy to Civil and Religious Liberty* (1836); *Romanism in the Light of Prophecy and History* (1857).

Bibliography: A *Memorial* was published by the consistory of his Church (New York, 1860).

BROWNSON, ORESTES AUGUSTUS: Roman Catholic convert; b. at Stockbridge, Vt., Sept. 16, 1803; d. at Detroit, Mich., Apr. 17, 1876. His religious career is marked by its many changes. The influences of his boyhood were of the strictest New England orthodoxy; at nineteen he joined a Presbyterian church at Ballston, N. Y.; in 1826 he was ordained (at Jaffrey, N. H.) a Universalist minister; after two or three years he left the Universalists, and, influenced by Robert Dale Owen and his projects, became a socialist, entered politics, and helped form a "Workingmen's Party" in New York. He soon despaired of reform by means of political organization, and in 1831 again began preaching at Ithaca, N. Y., this time as an independent, attracted by the writings of William Ellery Channing. Later he had Unitarian parishes at Walpole, N. H., and Canton, Mass. In 1836 he organized in Boston "The Society for Christian Union and Progress" and continued its minister till 1843, when he gave up preaching. In Oct., 1844, he was received into the Roman Catholic Church in Boston, and did not again change his faith, although he continued independent and combative within the Church and received a recommendation from Rome to be more guarded in his language. He wrote with great zeal and no small ability in advocacy of all of his successive beliefs. He started *The Boston Quarterly Review* in 1838 and wrote nearly all its numbers till it was merged in *The Democratic Review* of New York in 1843; from 1844 to 1864 and again 1873-75 he published *Brownson's Quarterly Review*, at first in Boston, later in New York, where he lived 1855-75. His books were: *New Views of Christianity, Society, and the Church* (Boston, 1836); *Charles Elwood, or the Infidel Converted* (1840); *Essays and Reviews* (New York, 1852); *The Spirit Rapper; an Autobiography* (Boston, 1854); *The Convert, or Leaves from my Experience* (New York, 1857); *The American Republic, its Constitution, Tendencies, and Destiny* (1865).

Bibliography: His son, Henry F. Brownson, has published a collected edition of his *Works*, 20 vols., Detroit, 1882-87, and his *Life*, 3 vols., 1898-1900.

BRUCE, ALEXANDER BALMAIN: Church of Scotland; b. at Aberargie (a hamlet in the parish of Abernethy, 7 m. s.e. of Perth), Perthshire, Jan. 30, 1831; d. at Glasgow Aug. 7, 1899. He was educated at the University of Edinburgh (1845-49) and the Divinity Hall of the Free Church of Scotland, which he entered in 1849. After the completion of his theological studies, he was an assistant minister at Ancrum, Roxburghshire, and Lochwinnoch, Renfrewshire, until 1859, when he accepted a call to the pastorate of Cardross, Dumbartonshire, where he remained nine years. He was then minister of the East Free Church, Broughty Ferry, Forfarshire, from 1868 to 1875, and in the latter year was appointed professor of apologetics and New Testament exegesis in the Free Church Hall, Glasgow, a position which he held until his death. In theology he declared himself to be "in sympathy with modern religious thought, while maintaining solidarity with all that is best in the theology of the past; in favor of freedom in critical inquiries on the basis of evangelic faith, and of a simplified and more comprehensive creed." The boldness of his views brought him to the notice of the General Assembly of his denomination in 1890, but after consideration his writings were pronounced to be, on the whole, in accord with orthodox standards. He was Cunningham Lecturer in 1874, Ely Lecturer in Union Theological Seminary, New York, in 1886, and Gifford Lecturer in Glasgow University in 1896–97, and after 1894 collaborated with T. K. Cheyne in editing the *Theological Translation Library*. In addition to minor contributions, he wrote *The Training of the Twelve* (Edinburgh, 1871); *The Humiliation of Christ* (1876); *The Chief End of Revelation* (London, 1881); *The Parabolic Teaching of Christ* (1882); *The Galilæan Gospel* (Edinburgh, 1884); *F. C. Baur and his Theory of the Origin of Christianity and of the New Testament* (London, 1885); *The Miraculous Element in the Gospels* (the Ely lectures for 1886; 1886); *The Life of William Denny* (1888); *The Kingdom of God, or, Christ's Teachings according to the Synoptic Gospels* (Edinburgh, 1889); *Apologetics: or, The Cause of Christianity defensively stated* (1892); *St. Paul's Conception of Christianity* (1894); *With Open Face: or, Jesus mirrored in Matthew, Mark, and Luke* (London, 1896); *The Providential Order of the World* (Gifford lectures for 1897; 1897); a commentary on the synoptic Gospels in *The Expositor's Greek Testament* (1897); *The Epistle to the Hebrews: the first Apology for Christianity* (Edinburgh, 1899); and *The Moral Order of the World in Ancient and Modern Thought* (Gifford lectures for 1898; London, 1899).

Bibliography: *DNB*, supplement i., 321–322.

BRUCH, bruh, **JOHANN FRIEDRICH**: German theologian; b. at Pirmasens (13 m. e.s.e. of Zweibrücken), Rhenish Bavaria, Dec. 13, 1792; d. at Strasburg July 21, 1874. He was educated at the gymnasium of Zweibrücken and the Protestant academy of Strasburg, after which he was successively tutor at Cologne (1812), vicar at Lohr in German Lotharingia, and private tutor in Paris (1815). In Nov., 1821, he was appointed professor at the Protestant seminary at Strasburg, and a few months later became full professor in the theological faculty. His position, both then and later, was rationalistic. His conception of revelation, miracles, Christ and his works, sin, and salvation, therefore, frequently diverged widely from the teachings of the Church and of tradition. His lectures were at first restricted to Christian ethics and the synoptic Gospels, but later embraced also systematic theology and the New Testament, in addition to practical homiletics. After 1831 he was preacher at the Nicholaikirche, where he sought to instruct and calm the religious excitement caused by the attacks of orthodox Pietism on liberal theology, aiming to further a faith based on reason and a life of true Christianity, as well as unity and peace within the Church.

Bruch's influence was also felt in the development of the religious life of his city, and in the foundation and administration of religious and ecclesiastical projects. The first infant schools, the evening schools for poor children, Sunday lectures for workingmen, the society for the improvement of young criminals, and the society for the evangelization of Protestants scattered in the departments of the East were among those inspired and called into existence by him. He was also the president of the Strasburg Bible Society and until his death conducted the pastoral conference of his city. After 1828 he likewise acted as the director of the Protestant gymnasium. In 1849 he was appointed inspector of the district of St. Thomas, in 1852 a member of the supreme consistory, and in 1866 of the directory. Amid all these tasks he found time and strength to treat the most obscure problems of theology and philosophy, although he was obliged, for lack of sympathy, to abandon his plan of writing in French to supply the deficiency of Protestant theological literature in France. The Franco-Prussian War brought devastation into Church and school, and Bruch was accordingly appointed rector of the new university and placed in control of the provisional direction of ecclesiastical affairs, the final efforts of his life being devoted to a reorganization of the theological faculty and of the ecclesiastical situation, which he sought to protect against the domination of the system prevailing at Berlin.

Bruch was a prolific writer, his works, in addition to numerous pamphlets and articles in learned periodicals, being as follows: *Lehrbuch der christlichen Sittenlehre* (2 vols., Strasburg, 1829–32); *Christliche Vorträge* (2 vols., 1838–42); *Études philosophiques sur le christianisme* (Paris, 1839); *Ideen zur Abfassung einer den Bedürfnissen der deutsch-protestantischen Kirche Frankreichs entsprechenden Liturgie* (Strasburg, 1839); *Die Lehre von den göttlichen Eigenschaften* (Hamburg, 1842); *Zustände der protestantischen Kirche Frankreichs* (1843); *Betrachtungen über Christenthum und christlichen Glauben in Briefen* (2 vols., Strasburg, 1845–46); *Weisheitslehre der Hebräer, ein Beitrag zur Geschichte der Philosophie* (1851); *Das Gebet des Herrn* (1853); *Ueber das Prinzip der weltüberwindenden Macht des Christenthums* (Gotha, 1856); *Die protestantische Freiheit* (Strasburg, 1857); *Die Lehre von der Präexistenz der menschlichen Seele* (1859); and *Theorie des Bewusstseins* (1864).

T. Gerold.

Bibliography: Bruch's life-story is told in *Kindheit- und Jugenderinnerungen von Dr. Fr. Bruch*, Strasburg, 1889, and *Johann Friedrich Bruch, seine Wirksamkeit in Schule und Kirche, 1821–72*, 1890, both edited from his remains by his son-in-law, T. Gerold.

BRUECK, brük (**PONTANUS**, real name **HEINSE, HENISCH, HEINCZ**), **GREGORIUS**: German jurist; b. at Brück (22 m. n. of Wittenberg) c. 1484; d. at Jena Feb. 15, 1557. He studied at Wittenberg and Frankfort-on-the Oder, and became so famous as the secretary and representative of the jurist Hennig Göde that princes and critics sought his advice. Frederick the Wise invited him to his court, and after the death of the electoral councilor Degenhard Pfeffinger (1519), Brück seems to have taken his place. He was soon interested in Luther, and it was not without significance that he accompanied the elector to Cologne and Worms. Having returned to Wittenberg, Brück received the degree of doctor of law, and soon afterward was appointed chancellor. His tact and ability greatly helped the cause of the Reformation, and the development of the Evangelical Church. He was instrumental in bringing about the Torgau-Magdeburg confederations; he advised the elector at the diets held at Speyer in 1526 and 1529, and it was due to him, next to Luther, that the Pack-disturbances did not lead to a general war. But his greatest services were rendered at the Diet of Augsburg in 1530. He not only gave the first impulse to the composition of the Augsburg Confession, but he took part in the preparation of its details, wrote the introduction to it, caused it to be read in public, and gave to the emperor the Latin copy in the name of the Evangelical estates. He would not be intimidated, but, on the contrary, encouraged the timid, and acted as spokesman in all public debates, so that his eloquence and ability were even recognized by his opponents. Cochlæus, well aware of the importance of Brück, vainly tried to induce him to abandon the Lutherans by an "Admonition to Peace and Unity." Brück's reply is unknown, for at the time he was engaged in writing a true account of events at the Diet of Augsburg, 1530, which was first printed in Förstemann's *Archiv für die Geschichte der kirchlichen Reformation* (Halle, 1831). Brück attended all diets held during his lifetime, and he also strove for the consolidation of the Church, finally succeeding in 1542 in forming a permanent consistory. For a time he resided at Wittenberg, but after the disastrous end of the Schmalkald War, which he had consistently opposed, he followed the sons of the Elector to Weimar, remaining a loyal friend of the imprisoned Frederick. Still later Brück retired to Jena, where he died.

(T. Kolde.)

Bibliography: *CR*, xii. 351 contains the *Oratio de Gregorio Pontano* (by Melanchthon); J. A. Wimmer, *Vita Gregorii Pontani*, Altenburg, 1730; T. Kolde, in *ZHT*, 1874, pp. 34 sqq.

BRUECKNER, brük'ner, **BENNO BRUNO:** German Protestant; b. at Rosswein (23 m. w. of Dresden) May 9, 1824. He was educated at the University of Leipsic, and after serving as pastor at Hohburg from 1850 to 1853 was appointed associate professor and second university preacher at Leipsic. Two years later he was made full professor, and in the following year was appointed university preacher and director of the seminary for practical theology. He became canon of Meissen and consistorial councilor in 1860, and nine years later went to Berlin as provost of St. Nicholas and St. Mary, honorary professor, university preacher, and member of the high consistory, of which he became clerical vice-president in 1877 In 1872 he was chosen general superintendent of Berlin, and in the following year was appointed canon of Brandenburg. He became high consistorial councilor in 1880, a member of the Prussian council of state in 1884, and president of the united synods of the district of Berlin in 1889. His works include *Epistola ad Philippenses Paulo auctori vindicata contra Baurium* (Leipsic, 1848); *Betrachtungen über die Agende der evangelisch-lutherischen Kirche in Sachsen* (1865); and numerous sermons, both individual and collected, many of which ran through several editions. He also edited the second and third editions of W M. L. De Wette's commentary on the Catholic Epistles (Leipsic, 1853–67) and the fifth edition of his commentary on the Gospel of John (1863).

BRUEGGLERS. See Kohler, Christian and Hieronymus.

BRUGMANN, brūg'mān, **JAN:** A theologian and reformer of the Franciscan order in the Netherlands and Germany. The date of his birth is unknown, but from the way in which he speaks of his age in 1473, the year of his death, he was probably born about 1400, at Kempen. He was educated and admitted to the clerical state in a monastery of the northwestern Netherlands, perhaps Groningen. He joined the Franciscans at Saint-Omer in Artois, where the community was full of the spirit of St. Bernardin of Sienna, the founder of the strict or Observant Franciscans. Here he taught theology, until in 1439 he was charged, at the request of the town council of Gouda, with the erection of an Observantine house there, and later took part in a similar work at Stuis, Leyden, and Alkmaar. Learning to know the moral and spiritual condition of the people while discharging these missions, he set himself to elevate it by popular preaching, at the same time effecting a reform in the convents of Gronigen, Gorinchem, Haarlem, Warnsveld, and Nymwegen between 1450 and 1455. At Amsterdam he founded a house in 1462, and composed a bitter factional strife among the citizens. He brought about the foundation of the Observantine province of Cologne, of which he was provincial for several years. Feeling his end approaching, he retired to Nymwegen, where he died. His influence went far beyond the reform of the Franciscan houses; he ranks with the great popular preachers of the Netherlands at that time, such as Groote and Florentius Radewyns, with whom he was in close alliance. A few of his sermons have been printed (see below). He wrote also a life of Christ, which in some particulars resembles those of Bonaventura and Ludolf of Saxony, though adhering more closely to the Gospel narrative. In spite of its frequently erroneous exegesis and its arbitrary mystical interpretations, it is so full of simple piety and warm devotion that it awakens respect. He wrote also, in three different versions, the life of Lidwina of Schiedam, a mystical ascetic considered a saint in the Netherlands (1350–1443); it has recently been discovered that he was a vernacular spiritual poet of no slight importance.

L. Schulze.

Bibliography: The one book is W. Moll, *Joh. Brugmann, en het Godsdienstig Leven*, Amsterdam, 1854. One of his sermons is given in Moll's biography, but other sermons and writings of his appear in *Handelingen Mantschappij der Nederlandsche letterkunde*, The Hague, 1887; *De Katholiek*, xx.; *Archief voor Nederlandsche Kerkgeschiedenis* i. (1885), iv. (1892–93).

BRULLY, brü''yî' (**BRUSLY**), **PIERRE** (*Petrus Brulius*): The successor of Calvin in Strasburg; b. at Mersilhaut (Mercy-le-Haut, about 2 m. s.e. of Metz) c. 1518; burned at the stake at Tournai (14 m. e. of Lille), Flanders, Feb. 19, 1545. Educated for the Church, he became lector in the Dominican convent at Metz and was expelled in 1540 or 1541 for sympathizing with the Reformation. In July, 1541, he was in Strasburg and intimate with Calvin, in whose house he lived, and when Calvin was recalled to Geneva (1541) succeeded him in the pastorate. In September, 1544, he undertook a missionary journey to Flanders on the invitation of persons in Tournai who wished instruction in the Reformed faith; preached there and in neighboring cities with earnestness and success, but necessarily in secret, as to preach Protestant doctrine was forbidden. He was arrested at Tournai in November, condemned, and executed, notwithstanding efforts made to save him from Strasburg and by the Protestant princes of Germany.

Bibliography: C. Paillard, *Le Procès de Pierre Brully*, Paris, 1878; E. Reuss, *Pierre Brully*, Strasburg, 1879.

BRUNETIÈRE, brü''ne-tyär', **MARIE FERDINAND**: French Roman Catholic critic; b. at Toulon (42 m. e.s.e. of Marseilles) July 19, 1849; d. in Paris Dec. 9, 1906. Educated at Marseilles and at the Lycée Louis le Grand, Paris, he became secretary of the editorial board of the *Revue des deux mondes* in 1875 and editor in 1893. He was appointed professor of the French language and literature at the École Normale Supérieure, Paris, and in 1893 became a lecturer at the Sorbonne. He delivered a course of lectures in the United States in 1897. In 1887 he was made a chevalier of the Legion of Honor, and in 1893 was admitted to the French Academy, while in 1895 he was appointed a commander of the Order of Pius IX. His theological attitude was noteworthy in that, like Coppée, Huysmans, and other distinguished literary men of France, he became convinced of the truth of the teachings of the Roman Catholic Church, abandoning the agnosticism which he had formerly professed. His writings, which mark a new epoch in French criticism, include *Études critiques sur l'histoire de la littérature française* (7 vols., Paris, 1880–1903); *Histoire et littérature* (3 vols., 1884–86); *Questions de critique* (2 vols., 1889–90); *Évolution des genres dans l'histoire de la littérature* (1890); *Nouvelles questions de critique* (1890); *Les Époques du théâtre français 1636–1850* (1892); *Essais sur la littérature contemporaine* (2 vols., 1892–95); *L'Évolution de la poésie lyrique en France au dix-neuvième siècle* (2 vols., 1894); *Éducation et instruction* (1895); *La Moralité de la doctrine évolutive* (1896); *La Renaissance de l'idéalisme* (1896); *Le Roman naturaliste* (1896); *Manuel de l'histoire de la littérature française* (1897; Eng. transl., New York, 1898); and *Discours académiques* (1901); *Les motifs d'espérer* (1902); *Cinq lettres sur Ernest Renan* (1903); *Les difficultés de croire* (1904); and *Sur les chemins de la croyance* (1904).

BRUNFELS, OTTO: German humanist and Reformer. The date of his birth can not be determined; d. at Bern Nov. 23, 1534. His father was an artisan at Mainz. At an early age he entered the Carthusian order, but the spirit of the age soon drew him out of his convent into the polemics of the time. At first he was a follower of Hutten, for whom he broke a lance with Erasmus, and whose library he used in compiling a small collection of the writings of Huss, which he published in 1524, with a dedication to Luther. He served the Reformation as a preacher, first at Steinheim, and then at Neuenburg in the Breisgau. When the attitude of the imperial government made his position there insecure, he went to Strasburg, where he supported himself by teaching, wrote against tithes, and studied medicine. He was a friend of Luther and also of Carlstadt, but was still more strongly attracted by Zwingli, whose influence procured him a medical position at Bern. His importance lies chiefly in the fact that he was a successful botanist, and a pioneer in this science for Germany, with his extensive illustrated *Herbarium* (Strasburg, 3 vols., 1530–40, translated into German, 2 parts, 1532–37, 2d ed., 1546). (W. Vogt.)

BRUNNER (FONTANUS), LEONHARD: German Reformer; b. probably at Esslingen (7 m. e.s.e. of Stuttgart) c. 1500; d. at Landau (18 m. n.w. of Carlsruhe) Dec. 20, 1558. In 1527 he was called from Strasburg, where he was a deacon, to Worms, as pastor of the congregation. By his discretion he soon restored harmony in the community, which had been endangered for a time by the activities of the Anabaptists Denk, Hetzer, and Kantz. In 1531 he published his *Christliche Betrachtung, wie man sich bei den Kranken und Sterbenden halten soll*; and in 1543 he prepared a *Catechismus und Anweisung zum christlichen Glauben*, of which the few fragments still extant show his catechetical ability. In the doctrine on the Lord's Supper he followed the Strasburg theologians. Through the Interim he was obliged in 1548 to resign his office at Worms and fled to Strasburg, where he soon became assistant pastor. With the other Strasburg ministers he adopted the Lutheran teaching, and remained faithful to it in Landau, whither he was called in 1553 by the Treaty of Passau. Here he contributed much toward the amelioration of the moral and religious life of the people. Besides the works already mentioned, he published *Concordantz des Neuen Testaments* (Strasburg, 1524) and *Concordantz und Zeiger aller biblischen Bücher* (1530).

Julius Ney.

Bibliography: A. Weckerling, *L. Brunner*, Worms, 1895; A. Becker, *Beiträge zur Geschichte von Worms*, pp. 54 sqq., ib. 1880.

BRUNO OF COLOGNE: Archbishop of Cologne 953–965; b. in the spring of 925, the youngest son of Henry I., the Fowler; d. at Reims Oct. 11, 965. He was educated from his fourth to his fourteenth year in the cathedral school of

Utrecht. His brother Otto I. recalled him in 939 to the court. As early as 940 he was invested with the functions of chancellor, and ordained deacon a year or two later. In 951 he was made *archicapellanus* and thus exercised a great influence on the administration of the whole kingdom. In 947 he took part in the Synod of Verdun, where German ecclesiastics settled the question of the archbishopric of Reims, important to the later history of France. In 951 he went with Otto to Italy, and supported his brother faithfully in the disturbances of the next year. Otto had him chosen archbishop of Cologne ir 953, and added to his spiritual sovereignty the government of Lorraine. He was consecrated Sept. 25. Lorraine was a very troublesome possession; it was not until after the banishment of Count Raginar of Hainault in 958 that he succeeded in establishing peace and order there. The relations with France often offered difficult problems, too. After the death of King Louis d'Outremer and Duke Hugh the Great, Bruno was made a sort of supreme judicial arbiter for France in his brother's name. Peace was his constant aim, together with the assertion of Carolingian sovereignty. On Otto's second absence in Italy (961), the administration of the empire was confided to Bruno and William of Mainz. Bruno's importance is mainly political, as a representative of the close alliance of the episcopate and the crown which marked Otto's policy. As a bishop, however, he did much to promote a real and living piety and to encourage education. (A. HAUCK.)

BIBLIOGRAPHY: The *Vita Brunonis*, by Ruotger, ed. G. H. Pertz, is in *MGH, Script.*, iv. 252–275, Hanover, 1841; and another *Vita* by an unknown author, ib., pp. 275–279. Consult: Pieler, *Erzbischof Bruno I. von Köln*, Arnsberg, 1851; E. Meyer, *De Brunone I. archiepiscopo Coloniensi*, Berlin, 1867; C. Martin, *Beiträge zur Geschichte Bruno I. von Köln*, Jena, 1878; Hauck, *KD*, iii. 40 sqq.

BRUNO, (FILIPPO) GIORDANO: Italian philosopher of the Renaissance; b. at Nola (14 m. e.n.e. of Naples), Campania, 1548; burned at the stake at Rome Feb. 17, 1600. He joined the Dominicans at Naples at the age of fourteen or fifteen, but study and reflection and particularly the influence of the works of Nicholas of Cusa and Raymond Lully made him doubtful of dogma and restive under the strict rules of his order. In 1576 he fled to Rome and thenceforth led a wandering life. He first visited various cities of North Italy; about 1580 he reached Geneva, stayed there two years, and went on to Paris through Lyons and Toulouse; at Paris he gave lectures on philosophy; from 1583 to 1585 he was in England, where he had the friendship of such men as Sir Philip Sidney, and composed his most important works; between 1586 and 1588 he was lecturing at Wittenberg; he visited Prague, Helmstädt, Frankfort, Zurich, and Padua, and reached Venice early in 1592. Here he was arrested in May, tried before the Inquisition, and his case adjourned to Rome, Jan., 1593. On Jan. 7, 1600, after a confinement of seven years, he was condemned as an apostate and heretic and given over to the civil authorities for execution. He was the first philosopher to espouse the Copernican hypothesis; in his metaphysical interpretation of it he radically opposed the philosophy and science of his time, and subverted also the most cherished teachings of the Church. His fundamental principle, as against Aristotle, was the absolute boundlessness of the universe. The supernatural in its traditional sense was thus eliminated. No heaven existed separate from the universe. The world—the phenomenal aspect of the universe—and God are not the same, but God is identified with the universe; or God may be designated as matter conceived of in extended substance, essentially immaterial, the immanent cause or soul of the world. Later philosophers, Descartes, Spinoza, Leibnitz, Boehme, and Hegel owe much to Bruno. Just three hundred years after his execution, Feb. 17, 1900, on the very spot where he was burned, a monument was dedicated to his memory.

Bruno's most important works were the *Spaccio della bestia trionfante* (Paris, 1584); *Della causa, principio ed uno*, and *Del infinito universo e mondi* (Venice, 1584); *De triplici minimo et mensura*, and *De monade numero et figura* (Frankfort, 1591). His Italian works were edited by Wagner (2 vols., Leipsic, 1830) and by Paul de Lagarde (2 vols., Göttingen, 1888); his Latin works by Fiorentino (2 vols., Naples, 1879–91) and by Tocco (Florence, 1889). The *Della causa* has been translated into German by Lasson (3d ed., Leipsic, 1902), and a German translation of his collected philosophical works begun by L. Kuhlenbeck (Jena, 1904, vol. v., 1907), who has also edited *Lichtstrahlen aus Giordano Bruno's Werken* (Leipsic, 1891). There is an English translation of "The Expulsion of the Triumphant Beast" by W. Morehead (London, 1713; only 50 copies printed and now extremely rare), and of the "Heroic Enthusiasts" (*Gli eroici furori*, Paris, 1558) by L. Williams (London, 1887); a general account and synopsis of the "Infinite Universe," written by Bruno in his dedication of the work to Lord Castelnau, was translated by John Toland and printed, with a Latin essay on the death of Bruno (in *A Collection of Several Pieces of Mr John Toland*, vol. i., London, 1726, pp. 304–349).

BIBLIOGRAPHY: On the life of Bruno a noteworthy production is J. L. McIntyre, *Giordano Bruno*, London, 1903. Phases of his life and philosophy are presented in F. J. Clemens, *Giordano Bruno und Nicolaus von Cusa, eine philosophische Abhandlung*, Bonn, 1847; C. J. G. Bartholmess, *Jordano Bruno*, 2 vols., Paris, 1846–47; D. Berti, *Vita di Giordano Bruno*, Milan, 1868; Mrs. Besant, *Giordano Bruno*, London, 1877; R. Mariano, *Giordano Bruno, la vita e l'uomo*, Rome, 1881 (important); M. Carriere, *Die philosophische Weltanschauung der Reformationszeit*, Leipsic, 1887 (the work of a specialist); Miss I. Frith, *Life of Giordano Bruno*, London, 1887; D. Berti, *Giordano Bruno, sua vita e sua dottrina*, Turin, 1889; R. Landseck, *Bruno der Märtyrer der neuen Weltanschauung*, Leipsic, 1890; J. Owen, *Giordano Bruno*, in *Skeptics of the Italian Renaissance*, London, 1893; H. Brunnhofer, *Giordano Bruno's Weltanschauung und Verhängniss*, Leipsic, 1899; G. Louis, *Giordano Bruno. Seine Weltanschauung und Lebensauffassung*, Berlin, 1900; A. Riehl, *Giordano Bruno*, Leipsic, 1900, Eng. transl., London, 1905. Consult also the works on the History of Philosophy, by Ueberweg, Ebrard, etc.

BRUNO (BONIFATIUS) OF QUERFURT: Missionary to the Slavs and Prussians, among whom he suffered martyrdom, Feb. 14, or Mar. 16, 1009.

He was a Saxon nobleman, educated at the cathedral-school at Magdeburg, and accompanied his cousin, the Emperor Otto III., to Rome (996), where he took holy orders. Pope Sylvester II. entrusted to him a missionary expedition to the Slavs in the east, which the Polish duke Boleslav had asked for, and he was raised to the rank of archbishop. His chief task was to be the conversion of the heathen Prussians, to whom Adalbert of Prague (q.v.) had fallen victim but a short time before. Being detained at Magdeburg by wars between Germans and Poles, he wrote the *Vita S. Alberti*. Peace being reestablished, he went to Poland and was gladly received by Boleslav, but being unable to enter into Prussia, he converted the Petchenegs and organized their church affairs. Remaining for some time in Poland, he wrote the *Vita quinque fratrum Poloniæ*, Christian martyrs slain in 1003 near Meseritz, and when at last he took upon him the task he was entrusted with, he and his companions, like St. Adalbert, lost their lives by the swords of the heathen not far from Braunsberg. Boleslav, who was deeply afflicted, ordered the remains of the martyrs to be gathered and brought to Poland, where they were solemnly buried and became an object of most devoted reverence. A. WERNER.

BIBLIOGRAPHY: The sources for a life are: the *Chronicon* of Dietmar, ed. J. M. Lappenberg, Hanover, 1889; Damian's *Vita St. Romualdi*, ed. G. H. Pertz, in *MGH, Script.*, iv. 850–854, ib. 1841; *Chronicon Magdeburgense*, ed., Meibom, in *Script. rer. Germ.*, pp. 269–378. Consult: W. von Giesebrecht, *Geschichte der deutschen Kaiserzeit*, ii. 104, 192 sqq., Brunswick, 1875; idem, *Erzbischof Brun-Bonifatius* in *Neue preussische Provinzialblätter*, i. (1859); Hauck, *KD*, vol. iii.; *ADB*, iii. 433.

BRUNO, SAINT: Founder of the Carthusian order. See CARTHUSIANS.

BRUNO OF SEGNI: Bishop of Segni (28 m. s.e. of Rome); b. at Solero (6 m. w. of Alessandria), Lombardy, between 1045 and 1049; d. at Segni July 18, 1123. He was educated in a monastery near his birthplace and at Bologna, became a canon at Sienna, and came to Rome in 1079. Here he came in contact with the leaders of the Church, and must have soon attracted the attention of Gregory VII., if it is true that it was at his request that he disputed with Berengar on the Eucharist. In any case he accomplished his task so well that the pope made him bishop of Segni in the Campagna the same year. He was even more closely connected with Urban II., whom he accompanied to France in 1095. In 1099 he entered the monastery of Monte Cassino, but without resigning his see or severing his relations with the outside world. He undertook an important mission to France for Paschal II. in 1106, and remained with the pope for some time after his return, finally going back to his cloister, where he was elected abbot in 1107 Paschal made no objection to this pluralism until in the conflicts of 1111 Bruno took the part of the antipope Maginulf (Sylvester IV.), and was forced to resign his abbacy and return to Segni. Lucius III. canonized him in 1181. His works (in *MPL*, clxiv., clxv.) are principally exegetical. His *Libellus de symoniacis*, written before 1109, is important for its discussion of the meaning of simony, and especially for its attitude on the sacraments of a simoniacal priest. CARL MIRBT.

BIBLIOGRAPHY: Sources for a life are the *Chronicon Cassinense*, book iv., chaps. 31–42, ed. W. Wattenbach, in *MGH, Script.*, vii. 776–783, Hanover, 1846, and an anonymous *Vita* in *ASB*, 18 July, iv. 478–488. The fullest and best modern treatment is by B. Gigalski, *Bruno, Bischof von Segni, ... sein Leben und seine Schriften*, Münster, 1898. Consult also Hefele, *Conciliengeschichte*, vol. v.; C. Mirbt, *Die Publizistik im Zeitalter Gregors VII.*, pp. 384–385, 423–424, 522–523, Leipsic, 1894; Meyer von Knonau, *Jahrbücher des deutschen Reichs unter Heinrich IV.*, pp. 92 sqq., ib. 1904.

BRUNO OF TOUL. See LEO IX., Pope.

BRUNO OF WÜRZBURG: Bishop of Würzburg 1034–45. He was the son of Duke Conrad I. of Carinthia, and thus a nephew of Pope Gregory V. and a cousin of the emperor Conrad II. The latter made him bishop of Würzburg in 1034. In the spring of 1045 he accompanied Henry III. to Hungary, and died May 26 from the results of injuries received in the fall of a building at Persenbeug in what is now Upper Austria. As a theologian he is remembered for his commentary on the Psalms, made up mainly of extracts from older authors, especially Cassiodorus, but including Augustine, Gregory the Great, the pseudo-Bede, and the *Breviarium in Psalmos* ascribed to Jerome. A catechetical exposition of the Lord's Prayer and the Apostles' and Athanasian Creeds attributed to him is probably older. (A. HAUCK.)

BIBLIOGRAPHY: Bruno's Commentary is in *MPL*, cxlii. Consult: J. Baier, *Der heilige Bruno ... als Katechet*, Würzburg, 1893; *ADB*, iii. 435.

BRUNSWICK: A North German duchy, consisting of three larger territories and six small exclaves, bounded on the north by Hanover, on the east by Saxony, on the south by Hanover, and on the west by Westphalia; area, 1,424 square miles; population (1900), 464,333, of whom 432,570 (93.1 %) are Lutherans; 4,406 (.9 %) Reformed; 24,175 (5.2 %) Roman Catholics; 1,358 of various sects; and 1,824 (.39 %) Jews. The Lutheran Church was established in the duchy in 1568, but received its first official organization in 1657 and 1709, while in 1755 and 1764 the administration was placed under six general superintendencies, which are now located at Wolfenbüttel, Brunswick, Helmstädt, Blankenburg, Gandersheim, and Holzminden. The act of Oct. 12, 1832, emphasized the ecclesiastical power of the duke, which is enforced with the cooperation and counsel of an evangelical consistory composed of both clergy and laity. At the same time the appointment of church-directors for the administration of individual churches was considered, but these officials were not actually created until Nov. 20, 1851. Where the congregation has the right of electing its pastors, these "church-deputies," together with an equal number of representatives elected by the community, choose the ministers, and in other cases extend the invitation to the candidates proposed by the duke or by patrons. The congregations, however, have the right to reject candidates who are deficient either in morality or in ability. The number of deputies has increased with the population from four to sixteen, and they are chosen by secret ballot, serving for a term of six years.

About twenty years after the organization of the parishes, a general synod was created (May 31, 1871), consisting of twelve clergymen and sixteen laymen from seven electoral districts, in addition to two clerical and two lay delegates appointed by the duke. This synod, which holds its sessions in public, controls all modification, interpretation, and promulgation of laws for the churches, except in matters of doctrine. The committee of the synod is composed of two clerical and two lay members with a fifth chosen from one of the two main bodies, and is required to decide, together with the consistory, on the rejection of candidates by individual congregations, and to discipline pastors and teachers of religion.

Shortly after the creation of this synod, inspectoral synods were introduced by a law of Jan. 6, 1873, which enacted that each parish should be inspected every two years, and that this must take place annually for the city of Brunswick in one of the local churches. A lay inspector may also be appointed by the duke in addition to the regular synod. These regulations control twenty-eight superintendencies with 230 parishes and 428 buildings for religious purposes, of which 333 are churches. A seminary for preachers is conducted at Wolfenbüttel by the consistory, and numerous institutions and associations exist in the duchy. Among the latter special mention may be made of a missionary society, a house of deaconesses, the sisterhoods at Marienberg near Helmstädt, and, above all, of the "Evangelical Association for the Duchy of Brunswick," with its many affiliated interests. Few sectaries have found their way into Brunswick, although Baptists and Mennonites are found here and there, the latter having an establishment for missions in the capital itself.

(WILHELM GOETZ.)

BIBLIOGRAPHY: J. Beste, *Geschichte der braunschweigischen Landeskirche*, Wolfenbüttel, 1889; *Entwurf einer Verfassungs-Urkunde für die evangelisch-lutherische Kirche des Herzogtums Braunschweig*, Brunswick, 1850; J. Bugenhagen, *Bugenhagens Kirchenordnung für die Stadt Braunschweig, 1528*, Leipsic, 1885; F. Koldewey, *Beiträge zur Kirchen- und Schulgeschichte des . . . Braunschweig*, Wolfenbüttel, 1888; *Beiträge zur Statistik des Herzogtums Braunschweig*, Brunswick, part xx., 1907.

BRUSTON, brü"stōṅ', **CHARLES AUGUSTE**: French Reformed; b. at Bordeaux (90 m. n. of Marseilles) Mar. 6, 1838. He was educated at the lyceum of Grenoble (bachelier ès lettres, 1854), the seminary at Montauban (bachelier en théologie, 1859), and the universities of Geneva, Halle, Berlin, Göttingen, and Heidelberg. He was then successively pastor of Reformed churches at Châtillon-en-Diois in 1861–62, Die in 1862–64, Bordeaux in 1864–68, and Orléans in 1868–74. In the latter year he was appointed professor of Hebrew in the Protestant faculty of theology of Montauban, and since 1894 has been dean of the same faculty. He is a member of the synodical committee of studies and other committees, and was elected a corresponding associate of the Société des Antiquaires de France. In theology he is progressive, but is opposed to arbitrary speculations. He has written: *De l'authenticité des Actes des Apôtres* (Toulouse, 1859); *Les Psaumes traduits de l'Hébreu* (Paris, 1868); *Du Texte primitif des Psaumes* (1873); *De lapsu hominis* (Orléans, 1873); *Histoire critique de la littérature prophétique des Hébreux* (Paris, 1881); *Les Quatre sources des lois de l'Exode* (1883); *Études sur l'Apocalypse* (1884); *Les Deux Jéhovistes, études sur les sources de l'histoire sainte* (Montauban, 1885); *Les Origines de l'Apocalypse* (Paris, 1888); *La Vie future d'après l'enseignement de Jésus-Christ* (1890); *La Sulammite, mélodrame en cinq actes* (1891); *Les Cinq Documents de la loi mosaïque* (1892); *Le Parallèle entre Adam et Jésus-Christ, étude exégétique sur Rom. v. 12–21* (1894); *La Vie future d'après St. Paul* (1895); *Le Dixième congrès des Orientalistes et l'Ancien Testament* (1895); *Études sur Daniel et l'Apocalypse* (1896); *La Descente de Christ aux enfers d'après les Apôtres et d'après l'Église* (1897); *Les Paroles de Jésus découvertes en Égypte* (1898); *Les Prédictions de Jésus* (1899); *Le Cantique de Débora* (1901); *Études phéniciennes* (2 vols., 1903 06); *L'Inscription de Siloé et celle d'Eshmoun-azar* (1904); *Vraie et fausse critique biblique* (1905); *Fragments d'un ancien recueil de paroles de Jésus* (1905); and *L'Histoire sacerdotale et le Deutéronome primitif* (1906), in addition to numerous contributions to theological periodicals and works of reference.

BRUYS, PIERRE DE. See PETER OF BRUYS.

BRYANT, JACOB: English antiquarian; b. at Plymouth 1715; d. at Cypenham, in Farnham Royal (4 m. n. of Windsor), Nov. 14, 1804. He studied at King's College, Cambridge (B.A., 1740; M.A., 1744), and became fellow; was tutor and in 1756 became secretary to the Duke of Marlborough, and enjoyed the patronage of the family during his life and had free access to their famous library at Blenheim. He was a learned man, but his fondness for paradox and other eccentricities render his writings of slight permanent value. He published works upon a variety of subjects, classical literature and antiquities, the gipsy language, the Marlborough collection of gems, etc. Those which have religious interest are *Observations and Enquiries Relating to Various Parts of Ancient History* (Cambridge, 1767), in which he defends the reading *Euroclydon* in Acts xxvii. 14, and maintains that Melita was not Malta; *A New System or an Analysis of Ancient Mythology* (3 vols., London, 1774–76; 3d edition with account of the author, 6 vols., 1807), an attempt to substantiate the Bible by a study of the traditional remains of all nations; *Vindiciæ Flavianæ: a Vindication of the Testimony of Josephus concerning Jesus Christ* (1777); *A Treatise on the Authenticity of the Scriptures* (1791); *Observations on a Controverted Passage in Justin Martyr;* also upon *the Worship of Angels* (1793); *Observations upon the Plagues Inflicted upon the Egyptians*, with maps (1794); *The Sentiments of Philo Judæus concerning the Logos* (1797); *Observations upon Some Passages in Scripture* (relating to Balaam, Joshua, Samson, and Jonah, 1803).

BIBLIOGRAPHY: *Literary Anecdotes of the Eighteenth Century* (9 vols., London, 1812–15) and *Illustrations of the Liter-*

ary History of the Eighteenth Century (8 vols., ib. 1817–58), both by John Nichols, contain very numerous references to Bryant. Consult also *DNB*, vii. 155–157.

BRYCE, GEORGE: American Presbyterian; b. at Mount Pleasant, Ont., Apr. 22, 1841. He was educated at the University of Toronto and Knox College Toronto (B.A., 1871), and was examiner in natural history in the former institution in 1870–1872. In 1871 he was chosen by the General Assembly of the Presbyterian Church of Canada to organize a church and college in Winnipeg, and accordingly established Manitoba College in the same year and Knox Church, Winnipeg, in 1872. Five years later he was one of the founders of Manitoba University, where he was examiner in science and chairman of the faculty of science until 1904. In the following year he was appointed to his present position of professor of English literature and financial agent in Manitoba College. For many years he has been active in Presbyterian home missions in Manitoba, and was moderator of the general Assembly of the Presbyterian Church in Canada in 1902–03. He has written: *Manitoba; Infancy, Progress, and Present Condition* (London, 1882); *Short History of the Canadian People* (1887); *The Apostle of Red River* (Toronto, 1898); *Remarkable History of the Hudson's Bay Company* (London, 1900); and *Makers of Canada* (Toronto, 1903).

BRYENNIOS, bri-en"ni'os, **PHILOTHEOS,** fi"lo-thé'es: Greek metropolitan of Nicomedia; b. at Constantinople March 26 (old style), 1833. He was educated at the "Theological School in Chalce of the great Church of Christ" (1856), and the universities of Leipsic, Berlin, and Munich. In 1861 he became professor of ecclesiastical history, exegesis, and other studies at Chalce, of which he was appointed master and director in 1863, although he soon resigned the latter positions. In 1867 he was called to Constantinople to be the head of the "Great School of the Nation" in the Phanar, or Greek quarter of Constantinople, and remained there until in 1875 he was sent by the Most Holy Synod of metropolitans and patriarchs to the Old Catholic conference at Bonn, where he received the patriarchal letter announcing his appointment as metropolitan of Serrae in Macedonia. In 1877 he was transferred to the metropolitan see of Nicomedia, and three years later went to Bucharest as commissioner of the Eastern Orthodox Patriarchal and other independent churches, to decide concerning the Greek monasteries which had been plundered in Moldavia and Wallachia. In 1882, at the instance of the Holy Synod of Metropolitans in Constantinople, and the patriarch Joachim III., he wrote a reply to the encyclical letter of Pope Leo XIII. concerning the Slavic apostles Cyrillus and Methodius, which was published at Constantinople in 1882 with the approbation and at the expense of the Holy Synod. His fame rests upon his discovery in 1873 in the Jerusalem Monastery of the Most Holy Sepulcher in the Greek quarter of Constantinople of a manuscript containing (1) a synopsis of the Old and New Testaments in the order given by St. Chrysostom; (2) The Epistle of Barnabas; (3) The First Epistle of Clement of Rome to the Corinthians; (4) The Second Epistle of Clement to the Corinthians; (5) The Teaching of the Twelve Apostles; (6) The spurious letter of Mary of Cassoboli; and (7) Twelve pseudo-Ignatian Epistles. He edited the Epistles to the Corinthians with prolegomena and notes at Constantinople in 1875, and published the "Teaching of the Twelve Apostles" in the same city in 1883. See Didache.

Bibliography: P. Schaff, *Teaching of the Twelve Apostles*, pp. 8–9, 289–295, New York, 1890.

BUCER, MARTIN. See Butzer.

BUCHANAN, CLAUDIUS: A pioneer of modern Anglican missionary work in India; b. at Cambuslang, near Glasgow, Mar. 12, 1766; d. at Broxbourne (5 m. s.e. of Hertford), Hertfordshire, Feb. 9, 1815. At sixteen he went to the University of Glasgow, intending to study law, but, after finishing his course, spent three years in a careless wandering life. Smitten by repentance, he placed himself under the care of John Newton, the celebrated evangelical preacher in London, one of whose friends enabled him to spend four years at Cambridge. In 1796 he went to Calcutta as a chaplain in the East India Company's service. He found the conditions there very unfavorable for earnest work. All the Company was willing to do for sixty millions of souls was to place a chaplain here and there, who was told not to meddle with the native population. While Buchanan was waiting for a chance to do real work, he learned Hindustani and Persian. In 1800, being transferred to Calcutta itself, he found a like-minded helper in Lord Mornington (later Marquis of Wellesley), the Governor-general, who founded a college in Calcutta for the teaching of the Oriental languages and placed Buchanan in charge of it. It was closed, however, three years later, and all looked as dark as ever. But after a while a new institute was founded, on a smaller scale, and Buchanan took hope once more. In 1805 he published his *Expediency of an Ecclesiastical Establishment for India*, in which he developed the first plan for the establishment of regular dioceses and bishops While waiting for his seed to bear fruit, he translated the New Testament into Hindustani and Persian, and founded an institute for such work. In 1806 he made an extended journey along the Malabar coast, partly for his health and partly in the missionary interest, publishing his observations in *Christian Researches in Asia* (Cambridge, 1811, new ed., London, 1840). He returned to Calcutta in 1807, full of plans for which the time was once more unfavorable. Lord Wellesley had been recalled, and his successor, Lord Minto, looked coldly on such projects, as did the Company in general. To push his views in England was the most necessary thing, and Buchanan returned thither in 1808 to press upon the ministry the setting up of a theological seminary in each presidency, the granting of licenses to missionaries, and the appointment of bishops. Lord Liverpool approved this plan, but the House of Commons agreed to the appointment of only one bishop. Middleton, the first bishop of Calcutta, was consecrated in 1816, and when his successor was provided with suffragans for Madras and Bombay, Buchanan's plan had been realized in its essentials, though he did not live to see it.

BIBLIOGRAPHY: H. Pearson, *Memoirs of the Life and Writings of Claudius Buchanan*, 2 vols., London, 1819; R. Vormbaum, *H. Martyn, D. Brown und C. Buchanan*, Elberfeld, 1865; *DNB*, vii. 182–184.

BUCHANAN, GEORGE: Scotch scholar; b. in the parish of Killearn (44 m. w.n.w. of Edinburgh), Stirlingshire, early in Feb., 1506; d. in Edinburgh Sept. 28, 1582. He studied in Paris, 1520–22, at St. Andrews, 1525, and again in Paris, where he became teacher in the College of Ste. Barbe, 1528; returned to Scotland 1535. He inclined toward Protestant views and wrote two satires on the monks, the *Somnium* and the *Franciscanus et fratres*, for which he was obliged to leave his country in 1539. He taught at Paris, Bordeaux, and Coimbra, and was active in the production of literary works; to this period belong his translations into Latin of the *Medea* and of the *Alcestis* and his Latin tragedies, *Jephthes* and *Baptistes* (translated into English verse by A. Gibb, Edinburgh, 1870; and by A. Gordon Mitchell, Paisley, 1903–04); he began his translation of the Psalms into Latin (published at Paris, 1566) while confined in a monastery by the Inquisition at Coimbra. In 1562 he was acting as tutor to Mary Stuart in Scotland; he now openly embraced Protestantism and became influential in both Church and State; was an ardent supporter of Moray (who made him principal of St. Leonard's College, St. Andrews, in 1566), and an active opponent of the queen. In 1570 he became tutor to the young James VI. and keeper of the privy seal; his royal pupil he undertook to make "the greatest scholar in the land." During the last period of his life he wrote his two greatest works, the *De jure regni apud Scotos* (Edinburgh, 1579; Eng. transl., 1680), a defense of limited monarchy, suppressed by act of parliament in 1584 and again in 1664 and burned at Oxford in 1683; and the *Rerum Scoticarum historia* (1582; 19th ed., 1762; Eng. transl., 1690). His works have been edited by Ruddiman (2 vols., Edinburgh, 1715; reprinted by Burman, Leyden, 1725).

BIBLIOGRAPHY: The Leyden ed. of the *Works* contains a full bibliography. The *Life*, by David Irving, Edinburgh, 1817, is an excellent literary history of the times. Consult also: P. H. Brown, *George Buchanan, Humanist and Reformer*, Edinburgh, 1890; idem, *George Buchanan and his Times*, ib. 1906; D. Macmillan, *George Buchanan, a Biography*, London, 1906; D. A. Millar, *George Buchanan, a Memorial, 1506–1906*, London, 1907; *DNB*, vii. 186 193.

BUCHANITES: The followers of Elspat (or Elspeth) Simpson, wife of Robert Buchan, a journeyman potter at Greenock, Scotland. She was born at Fatmacken, between Banff and Portsoy, 1738; was brought up in the Scottish Episcopal Church; while a servant at Greenock she married and followed her husband into the Burgher Succession Church. In 1781 she separated from him and removed with her children to Glasgow. In 1783 she joined the Dowhill Relief church at Irvine, whose pastor was the Rev. Hugh White. She had already adopted fantastic views as to religion and claimed to be a teacher sent from heaven. She got a hearing, her chief converts being Mr. White, who proclaimed that she was the woman spoken of in Rev. xii. 1 sqq. and that he was the man-child she had brought forth. The Relief presbytery deposed Mr. White from the ministry, and when converts to Mrs. Buchan's pretensions began to gather, the parish authorities in May, 1784, compelled the whole band to leave. They settled on a farm at New Cample, near Closeburn, Dumfriesshire, and there the sect grew to about fifty members, some of whom were superior persons. Mrs. Buchan was called "spiritual mother" by her followers, and professed to be able to impart the Holy Spirit by breathing on the candidate; also to be a prophetess, and as such foretold that neither she nor her followers would ever die but would meet the Lord in the air in the advent which she taught was at hand, basing her teaching on I Thess. iv. 17. The usual charge of sexual immorality was brought against the sect, the most distinguished witness being the poet Robert Burns, who is said to have had a lady-love in the sect (see his letter to John Burness, dated August, 1784). His song "As I was a walking" was set to an air which was a favorite with the Buchanites. In May, 1791, Mrs. Buchan died. This, being in direct contradiction to her teaching, had a disastrous effect on her sect which then began to disintegrate, but the last adherent of it did not pass away till 1848.

BIBLIOGRAPHY: Joseph Train, *The Buchanites from First to Last*, Edinburgh, 1846; *Eight Letters between the People called Buchanites and a Teacher* (J. Purves): *Three of which are written by Mr. White, and one by Mrs. Buchan, together with two Letters from Mrs. Buchan and one from Mr. White to a Clergyman in England*, ib. 1785.

BUCHEL, ANNA VON. See RONSDORF SECT.

BUCHWALD, būн'vält, **GEORG APOLLO:** German Protestant; b. at Grossenhain (19 m. n.n.w. of Dresden) July 16, 1859. He was educated at the University of Leipsic (Ph.D., 1882), and was successively a teacher in the real-school of Mittweida (1882–83) and the royal gymnasium of Zwickau (1883–85), after which he was *diaconus* at Zwickau (1885–92) and Leipsic (1892–96). Since 1896 he has been pastor of the Michaeliskirche, Leipsic. In addition to numerous minor contributions to theological periodicals and to collaborating on the Weimar and Erlangen editions of the works of Luther, he has written *Luther und die Juden* (Leipsic, 1881); *Nachklang der Epistolæ obscurorum virorum* (Dresden, 1882); *Logosbegriff des Johannes Scotus Erigena* (Leipsic, 1884); *Lutheri Scholæ in librum Judicum* (1884); *Ungedruckte Predigten D. Martin Luthers 1530 auf der Coburg gehalten* (Zwickau, 1884); *Sechs Predigten Johannes Bugenhagens* (Halle, 1885); *Andreas Poachs handschriftliche Sammlung ungedruckter Predigten D. Martin Luthers aus den Jahren 1528–46* (2 vols., Leipsic, 1884–85); *Allerlei aus drei Jahrhunderten* (Zwickau, 1887); *Eine sächsische Pilgerfahrt nach Palästina vor vier hundert Jahren* (Barmen, 1889); *Elf ungedruckte Predigten Luthers gehalten in der Trinitatiszeit, 1539* (Werdau, 1888); *Luthers letzte*

Streitschrift (Leipsic, 1893); *Zur Wittenberger Stadt- und Universitätsgeschichte in der Reformationszeit* (1893); *Entstehung der Katechismen Luthers und die Grundlage des grossen Katechismus* (1894); *Wittenberger Ordinierten-Buch* (2 vols., 1894); *Selige Pilgerschaft* (1896; extracts from the writings of Luther); *Philipp Melanchthon* (1897); *Luthers grosser Katechismus* (1897); *Paul Eber* (1897); *Geschichte der evangelischen Gemeinde zu Kitzingen* (1898); *Luthers deutsche Briefe ausgewählt und erläutert* (1899); *Reformationsgeschichte der Stadt Leipzig* (1900); *Konrad Stürtzel von Buchheim* (1900); *Die evangelische Kirche im Jahrhundert der Reformation* (1900); *Dr. Martin Luther* (1901); *So spricht Dr. Martin Luther* (Berlin, 1903; selections from the writings of Luther); *Deutschlands Kirchengeschichte für das evangelische Haus* (Bielefeld, 1904); *Lutherlesebuch* (Hamburg, 1905); and *Ungedruckte Predigten aus den Jahren 1537–1540* (Leipsic, 1905).

BUCK, CHARLES: English Independent; b. at Hillsley (15 m. n.e. of Bristol), Gloucestershire, 1771; d. in London Aug. 11, 1815. He held pastorates at Sheerness and London. He is mentioned for his *Theological Dictionary, containing definitions of all religious terms; a comprehensive view of every article in the system of divinity; an impartial account of all the principal denominations which have subsisted in the religious world from the birth of Christ to the present day; together with an accurate statement of the most remarkable transactions and events recorded in ecclesiastical history* (2 vols., London, 1802; many subsequent editions and reprints). He also published *Anecdotes, Religious, Moral, and Entertaining* (1799), which proved a highly popular work.

Bibliography: Buck's *Memoirs and Remains* were edited by J. Styles, London, 1817.

BUCKLAND, AUGUSTUS ROBERT: Secretary of the Religious Tract Society; b. at Newport (20 m. n.w. of Bristol), Monmouthshire, Apr. 18, 1857 He was educated at Pembroke College, Oxford (B.A., 1881), and was ordained to the priesthood of the Church of England in 1881. He was curate of Spitalfields, London, in 1880–84. In 1887 he became editor of the *Record* and has since engaged largely in journalistic work. He has also been morning preacher in the Foundling Hospital, London, since 1890, and was chosen secretary of the Religious Tract Society in 1902. He has written: *Strayed East* (London, 1889); *The Patience of Two* (1894); *The Heroic in Missions* (1894); *John Horden, Missionary Bishop* (1894); *Women in the Mission Field* (1895); *The Confessional in the English Church* (1900); and *The Missionary Speaker's Manual* (1901; in collaboration with J. D. Mullins). In addition, he has edited many works for the Religious Tract Society, notably its *Devotional Commentary*.

BUCKLEY, JAMES MONROE: Methodist Episcopalian; b. at Rahway, N. J., Dec. 16, 1836. He was educated at Wesleyan University, Middletown, Conn., but did not graduate, and he also studied theology at Exeter, N. H. He held various pastorates in New Hampshire (1859–63), Central Church, Detroit (1863–66), Brooklyn, N. Y. (1866–1869, 1872–75, and 1878–80), and Stamford, Conn. (1869–72 and 1875–78). Since 1880 he has been editor of the *New York Christian Advocate*. His general theological position is that of his denomination, although he reserves all rights to individual judgment concerning non-essentials. He has written: *Appeals to Men of Sense and Reflection to begin a Christian Life* (New York, 1869); *Christians and the Theatre* (1875); *Supposed Miracles* (Boston, 1875); *Oats or Wild Oats?* (New York, 1885); *The Midnight Sun, the Czar and the Nihilist* (Boston, 1887); *Faith Healing, Christian Science, and Kindred Phenomena* (New York, 1892); *Travels in Three Continents* (1895); *History of Methodism in the United States* (1897); *Extemporaneous Oratory for Professional and Amateur Speakers* (1899); and *The Fundamentals of Religion and their Contrasts* (1906).

BUCKMINSTER, JOSEPH STEVENS: New England clergyman; b. at Portsmouth, N. H., May 26, 1784; d. in Boston June 9, 1812. He was graduated at Harvard, 1800; studied theology while teacher at (Phillips) Exeter Academy and private tutor at Waltham; was called to the Brattle Street Church, Boston, 1804; appointed lecturer on Biblical criticism at Harvard, 1811. In theology he was liberal, a forerunner of the Unitarian movement; he belonged to the "Anthology Club," was a frequent contributor to the *Monthly Anthology*, and one of the founders of the literary reputation of Boston. He superintended the publication of the American edition of Griesbach's Greek Testament (1808); two volumes of sermons, with memoir by Rev. S. C. Thacher, were published after his death (Boston, 1814; 1829), and his *Works* appeared in two volumes in 1839.

Bibliography: His *Memoir* (together with that of his father, Rev. Joseph Buckminster of Portsmouth, N. H.; b. 1751; d. 1812) was published by his sister, Eliza B. Lee, Boston, 1851.

BUDDE, būd'de, KARL FERDINAND REINHARD: German Protestant; b. at Bensberg (9 m. e. of Cologne) Apr. 13, 1850. He was educated at the universities of Bonn, Berlin, and Utrecht from 1868 to 1873, although his studies were interrupted in 1870–71, when he served in the Franco-Prussian War. He became privatdocent for the Old Testament at Bonn in 1873, and was also teacher at the Schulbring'sche höhere Töchterschule in 1873–89 and inspector of the theological seminary of the university in 1878–85. In 1879 he became associate professor of Old Testament theology at the same university, and in 1889 was called to Strasburg in a like capacity, shortly thereafter being promoted to full professor. Since 1900 he has been professor of Old Testament theology at Marburg. Chosen rector of the University of Marburg for 1910–11. He has written: *Beiträge zur Kritik des Buches Hiob* (Bonn, 1876); *Die biblische Urgeschichte untersucht* (Giessen, 1883); *Die Bücher der Richter und Samuel, ihr Aufbau und ihre Quellen* (1890); *The Books of Samuel, Critical Edition of the Hebrew Text* (in the *Polychrome Bible*, Leipsic, 1894); *Das Buch Hiob* (in the *Handcommentar zum Alten Testament*, Göttingen, 1896); *Das Buch* *der Richter* (in the *Kurzer Handcommentar zum Alten Testament*, Freiburg, 1897); *Hohelied und Klagelieder* (in the same series, 1898); *The Religion of Israel to the Exile* (The American Lectures on the History of Religions for 1898–99, New York, 1899); *Die sogenannten Jahvelieder und die Bedeutung des Knechtes Jahves in Jesaija 40–55, ein Minoritätsvotum* (Giessen, 1900); *Der Kanon des Alten Testaments* (1900); *Die Bücher Samuel* (in *Kurzer Handcommentar zum Alten Testament*, Freiburg, 1902); *Das Alte Testament und die Ausgrabungen* (Giessen, 1903); *Die Schätzung des Königtums im Alten Testament* (Marburg, 1903); *Was soll die Gemeinde aus dem Streit um Babel und Bibel lernen?* (Tübingen, 1903); and *Hebräische Litteraturgeschichte* (Leipsic, 1906). He also translated A. Kuenen's *National Religions and Universal Religions* (Hibbert Lectures for 1882, London, 1882) under the title *Volksreligion und Weltreligion* (Berlin, 1883), and a number of the same scholar's monographs as *Gesammelte Abhandlungen zur biblischen Wissenschaft* (Freiburg, 1894). He has likewise edited the eighth and ninth editions of J. Hollenberg's *Hebräisches Schulbuch* (Berlin, 1895, 1900) and *Eduard Reuss' Briefwechsel mit seinem Schüler und Freunde Karl Heinrich Graf* (in collaboration with H. J. Holtzmann, Giessen, 1904).

BUDDENSIEG, bŭd″den-sîg′, **OSKAR GOTTLIEB RUDOLF:** German Lutheran; b. at Greussen (25 m. n.w. of Weimar) Sept. 5, 1844. He was educated at the universities of Leipsic and Berlin (1864–67; Ph.D., Berlin, 1871), and studied in London in 1867–73. Returning to his native country, he was a teacher successively at the Andreanum in Hildesheim (1873–74) and at the Vitzthum gymnasium in Dresden (1874–87), declining a call to a professorship in the University of Vienna in 1886. From 1887 to 1894 he was director of a normal school for young men in Dresden, and thereafter held a similar position in a normal school for young women there. In 1883 he founded the Wyclif Society in London. He wrote: *Die assyrischen Ausgrabungen und das Alte Testament* (Heilbronn, 1880); *Johann Wiclifs lateinische Streitschriften zum ersten Male aus den Handschriften herausgegeben* (2 vols., Leipsic, 1883; Eng. ed., under the title *John Wiclif's Polemical Works*, 2 vols., London, 1884–85); *Johann Wiclif und seine Zeit* (Halle, 1884); *John Wiclif, Patriot and Reformer* (London, 1884); and *Johann Wiclifs De veritate sacræ scripturæ* (3 vols., Leipsic, 1904; Eng. ed., 3 vols., London, 1905–07). Died at Dresden Oct. 13, 1908.

BUDDEUS, bŭd″dê′ŭs, **JOHANNES FRANCISCUS** (Johann Franz Budde): German theologian and philosopher; b. at Anclam (47 m. n.w. of Stettin), Pomerania, where his father was pastor, June 25, 1667; d. at Gotha Nov. 19, 1729. He early received a thorough education in classical and Oriental languages, and had read the Bible through in the original before he went to the University of Wittenberg in 1685. He was appointed adjunct professor of philosophy there soon after taking his master's degree in 1687, and in 1689 exchanged this for a similar position at Jena, where he also paid much attention to the study of history. In 1692 he went to Coburg as professor of Greek and Latin, and the next year to the new University of Halle as professor of moral philosophy. Here he remained until 1705, when he went to Jena as second professor of theology. His lectures embraced all branches of this science, and frequently touched on philosophy, history, and politics. Respected by all as a man and a Christian, he remained at Jena for the rest of his life, several times acting as rector of the university temporarily and being head of his department and an ecclesiastical councilor from 1715. He was considered the most universally accomplished German theologian of his time. In philosophy he professed an eclecticism which rested on a broad historical foundation; but he recognized in Descartes the originator of a new period, and in attacking the "atheist" Spinoza followed especially the upholders of the law of nature, such as Hugo Grotius, Puffendorf, and Thomasius. His theological position was determined by the tradition of Musæus at Jena, partly through his close relations with Baier; but on another side he was inclined toward Pietism. His association with Spangenberg, Spener, and Zinzendorf brought him under suspicion and actually gave rise to a formal investigation of his doctrine. In certain ways, too, he was influenced by the federalist theology, but without allowing it to lead him beyond the bounds of Lutheran orthodoxy. In all departments he showed himself a man of sound learning and scholarly instincts. His work was epoch-making in church history, especially that dealing with the Old Testament and the apostolic age. Taken as a whole, the life of Buddeus belongs to the transition period which follows that of simple orthodoxy; the influence of a new age and new leading interests appears in him, and at times he seems to be conscious of the change. Yet in his Biblical criticism he did not get so far as to make the slightest concession; not a verse of a canonical book can be touched without injuring the perfection of the whole. As an academic teacher he attained great success, and he had the gift of a striking and pregnant style, especially in Latin. His works, great and small, number over a hundred. Of those published in the Halle period may be mentioned *Elementa philosophiæ practicæ* (1697) and *Elementa philosophiæ eclecticæ* (1703). To the second Jena period belong among others the *Institutiones theologiæ moralis* (1711; German transl., 1719), a work strictly in accordance with his philosophical ethics; the *Historia ecclesiastica veteris testamenti* (1715–18); *Theses theologicæ de atheismo et superstitione* (1716), which, directed especially against Spinoza, attracted much attention; *Institutiones theologiæ dogmaticæ* (1723), a work once very influential, obviously founded on Baier's Compendium; *Historische und theologische Einleitung in die vornehmsten Religionsstreitigkeiten* (1724, 1728), edited by Walch; *Isagoge historico-theologica ad theologiam universam* (1727), dealing with the problems, methods, and history of theology in a way remarkable for that time; and *Ecclesia apostolica* (1729), intended as an introduction to the study of the New Testament.

(JOHANNES KUNZE.)

BIBLIOGRAPHY: Buddeus himself issued a *Notitia dissertationum . scriptorumque a J. F. Buddeo editorum*, Jena, 1728 (a list of his writings); and the *Ehrengedächtniss des J. F. Buddeus*, ib. 1731, also contains a catalogue of his productions. Consult: W. Schrader, *Geschichte der Friedrichsuniversität zu Halle*, i. 60, Berlin, 1894; W. Gass, *Geschichte der protestantischen Dogmatik*, iii. 30, 149 sqq., 214 sqq., Berlin, 1862; G. Frank, *Geschichte der protestantischen Theologie*, ii. 148, 214 sqq., Leipsic, 1865; C. E. Luthardt, *Geschichte der christlichen Ethik*, ii, 203 sqq., ib. 1893.

BUDDHISM.

Buddhism is the religion established in India by Buddha in the sixth century B.C., and having, according to a conservative estimate, upward of 100,000,000 adherents at the present time, chiefly in Ceylon, Nepal, Tibet, Farther India, China, and Japan. While frequently regarded as a new religion, it is, strictly speaking, only a reformation of Brahmanism, and can not be understood without some knowledge of the conditions preceding it. The religious system of India as outlined in its oldest religious books, the Vedas, had reached in the Brahmanas and Sutras a degree of ritualism such as, perhaps, never existed elsewhere (see BRAHMANISM). This formalism produced a revolt, and from time to time arose various teachers, philosophers, and reformers, of whom the most influential was Siddhartha, also known as Sakya, Sakyamuni, Gautama, and, most frequently, as Buddha.

1. Life of Buddha. Buddha, the son of Suddhodana, king of Kapilavastu, a city in the district of Gorakhpur, Oudh, was born in 557 B.C. in the grove of Lumbini, two miles from the capital. He was, therefore, like Mahavira, the founder of the rival system of Jainism (q.v.), a member of the Kshatriya or warrior caste. The details of the life of the Buddha, or "The Enlightened One," so far as they may be verified historically, are comparatively few. He lost his mother, whom the later texts name Maya, at a very early age, and he married while still young, according to Hindu custom, and had a son called Rahula. At the age of twenty-nine (528 B.C.), he renounced his succession to the throne and became a hermit. Herein there is nothing extraordinary, for Brahmanism divided life into the four stages of student, householder, hermit, and ascetic. Two of these the prince had already performed; two more yet remained for him, and he went forth to win knowledge of the truth by penance and meditation. From the first he gained nothing, nor could his teachers help him, while his five companions abandoned him as unfitted to receive a knowledge of the truth. In his wanderings he came to Uruvela, the modern Buddha Gaya in Bengal. There, in 521 B.C., after seven years of struggle, he received illumination while sitting in meditation beneath the sacred bo-tree (*Ficus religiosa* or pipul-tree). Thus the Bodhisattva, or potential Buddha, became a true Buddha or Tathagata, "the Perfected One." He now entered upon the fourth and the last stage of life, and became a wandering ascetic and teacher. His earliest followers were the five monks who had turned from him before, and as other converts were made they were sent as apostles of the doctrine. Favor was his in high places also, for Bimbisara, king of Magadha, became an adherent of the faith. Over all ranks and classes Buddha exercised a powerful influence, due, it is very possible, rather to his personal charm of manner than to any essential novelty of the doctrine which he taught. It was undoubtedly in great part the result of his disregard of the fundamental Hindu principle of caste that he won for himself so large a following. Peaceably and calmly the life of Buddha passed, with little opposition, save from his cousin Devadatta, who attempted, from motives of personal ambition, to rouse hostility against his kinsman. At the age of eighty the Buddha felt that his end was drawing near, and for the first time in his life severe illness befell him. At the village of Kusinara, about thirty miles west of Kathmandu, the capital of Nepal, the master passed away (477 B.C.).

About the life here outlined the mythopeic tendencies of the Oriental mind wove a web of legend. In course of time Buddha no longer stands alone. He is the successor of twenty-seven Buddhas and himself received recognition from twenty-four of them, passing through a hundred thousand world cycles and countless reincarnations before he reached the perfection which was requisite for his high mission. When in him all perfection and all knowledge was united, the gods besought him to be born on earth, and in answer to their prayer he entered the womb of Maya in the form of a white elephant, while thirty-two signs of wonder appeared and the ten thousand worlds trembled at the coming of the savior of the world.

2. Legendary Additions. At the end of ten months, the Buddha was born beneath a sal-tree in the grove of Lumbini, while gods and men did homage unto him. On the fifth day of his life the Brahman Kondanna prophesied to Suddhodana the king that the child was destined to become a Buddha when he should see four signs of evil omen, an old man, a sick man, a corpse, and a monk. By every means within his power the father sought to keep his son from seeing these sights, surrounding him with every luxury, and marrying him in his sixteenth year to his cousin Yasodhara, the daughter of Suprabuddha. It was all in vain, however, for Siddhartha beheld the four signs, realized the misery of life, and abandoned the palace. On the expiration of his seven years of wandering, he realized that he was at last to gain Buddhahood, and amid many marvels he sat down beneath the bo-tree facing the East. Fruitlessly did Mara, the leader of the host of evil, endeavor to terrify the Bodhisattva. The blandishments of his daughters, Desire, Pining, and Lust, and his more subtle temptation that the Buddha should at once enter Nirvana without proclaiming his saving knowledge to mankind, failed ignominiously. From the time of his illumination until his death few myths gather about the Buddha, but when he was about to die there were marvels, and the course of nature was again disturbed, until the Tathagata passed to Nirvana.

The key-note of Buddhism is the transitoriness and vanity of life, which is conditioned by karma, the fruit of deeds done in countless previous lives; nor can existence be ended before the expiration of many reincarnations devoted to works of holiness and spent in unceasing efforts to gain Nirvana. Three elements common to all post-Vedic Hindu thought are at once discernible in this teaching; viz., transmigration, karma, and the dissolution of individuality.

3. Buddha's Teaching.

In its shortest form Buddha's teaching may be summarized as follows: Birth is sorrow, age is sorrow, sickness is sorrow, death is sorrow, clinging to earthly things is sorrow. Birth and rebirth, the chain of reincarnation, result from the thirst for life together with passion and desire. The only escape from this thirst is to follow the Eightfold Path: Right belief, right resolve, right word, right act, right life, right effort, right thinking, right meditation.

The goal of Buddhism is Nirvana. A definition of this term is almost impossible for the simple reason that Buddha himself gave no clear idea, and in all probability possessed none, of this state. He was indeed asked by more than one of his disciples whether Nirvana was postmundane or postcelestial existence, or whether it was annihilation.

4. Nirvana.

To all these questions, however, he refused an answer, for it was characteristic of his teachings that they were practically confined to the present life, and concerned themselves but little either with problems of merely academic philosophy or with the unknowable. Some measure of light, however, may be gained from the orthodox systems of Indian philosophy which are based upon the doctrine of the divine inspiration of the Veda. According to all of these, the *summum bonum* is release from karma and reincarnation, a goal which is to be attained by knowledge, and which consists in absorption into or reunion with the Over-Soul. This involves the annihilation of individuality, and in this sense Nirvana is nihilism, so that with the tacit ignoring of any real conception of the divine in the teachings of Buddha, Nirvana seems to imply the annihilation of the soul rather than its absorption. It is noteworthy, furthermore, that the word Nirvana etymologically denotes "a blowing out," the extinguishing of the fires of hatred, infatuation, and all passions. Nirvana seems to have been twofold, a secondary condition which may be reached by the righteous in this life, and the blessed state of freedom from rebirth.

Surpassing the teachers who had preceded him, Buddha denied both the authority of the Vedas, whose recognition, however formal, constitutes orthodoxy in India, and the power of sacrifice, while he practically ignored the existence of the divine. He rejected the entire system of caste, thus unconsciously preparing his doctrines to be potentially a world-religion instead of an ethnic faith. In the later Buddhist theology an elaborate cosmology is developed, with thirty-one worlds inhabited by fourteen classes of beings, of which the three highest are the supreme Buddhas, Pratyekabuddhas, and Arhats, the latter being those who are almost ready to attain Nirvana, while the Pratyekabuddha has attained the knowledge necessary to Nirvana but does not preach it. In addition to these must be noted the Bodhisattva, a potential Buddha who will attain to Buddhahood in due time.

Even in his lifetime Buddha established an order, thus forming the "triple jewel," Buddha, Dhamma (the law), and Sangha (the congregation). In this order were gathered the followers of the teacher, who were bound by the ten vows: neither to kill nor to steal, to abstain from impurity, falsehood, and intoxicating drinks, not to eat at forbidden times, to abstain from the folly of dancing, singing, music, and the theater, to use no manner of adornment, not to sleep in a high or a broad bed, and to receive neither gold nor silver.

5. Buddhist Monks.

The monks, who were bound to celibacy and poverty, and were called, in old Hindu fashion, *bhikkus*, or beggars, might be received as novices at the age of seven or eight, although they could not be ordained before their twentieth year. Twice a month the monks of each monastery assembled for the confession of sins, and annually in the rainy season a retreat was held both for rest from the pilgrimages of the preceding year and to gain new strength for the coming season. Even in the lifetime of Buddha women were admitted to the order and nunneries were built for their accommodation.

The history of Buddhism is a curious bit of irony; the founder who had ignored the existence of a god himself became a god. In Southern India, however, the religion remained relatively pure, although some heretical doctrines crept in at an early period and a number of councils were held to maintain the faith in its integrity. The first of these took place at Rajagaha in the year of Buddha's death, the second at Vaisali about a century later, the third, a sectarian meeting, at Pataliputra about 246 B.C., and the fourth at Jalandhara under the Indo-Scythian king Kanishka in 78 A.D.

6. Development after Buddha's Death.

The religion gained royal approval at an early date, its great kingly adherent being Asoka, who was crowned at Pataliputra in Madagha about 259 B.C. and reigned thirty-seven years. Not only did he spread the faith throughout his dominions, but his son Mahendra carried the new creed to Ceylon. In the second century B.C. the Indo-Scythian kings of Cabul and Bactria established Buddhism in their lands, whence it was promulgated in Northwestern India. Thus the faith spread by degrees over all the country north of the Vindhyas, existing side by side with Brahmanism and Jainism in harmony and peace. Its downfall in the land of its birth was due to two causes, the conflict of the sects which arose within itself and the Mohammedan invasion of India, but there was no persecution by the other Hindu sects. In Ceylon, on the other hand, Buddhism still exists, especially in the southern part of the island, and it is there that the purest Buddhism is found.

It was but natural that divergent opinions should arise within the faith itself. These remained comparatively unimportant, however, until the schism into the Mahayana and Hinayana, or the "Great Vehicle" and "Little Vehicle." The latter still adhered strictly in the main to the original tenets of Buddhism, although it was subdivided into the Vaibhashikas and the Sautrantikas, **7. Buddhist Sects.** the former laying special stress on the "Abhidhammapitaka" or metaphysical section of the sacred books of the religion, and the latter on the "Suttapitaka" or discourses of the Buddha. The Mahayanists, on the contrary, who form by far the larger sect, devoted themselves to all manner of speculation, being influenced not only by Hinduism but at a later period by Shamanism (q.v.) as well. The Mahayana postulates the existence of a thousand Buddhas with a supreme god, the Adibuddha, and prefers beneficent activity to the passivity of the Buddha's own doctrines, although both the principal subdivisions of this sect, the Yogacaras and the Madhyamikas, are strictly idealistic, and in so far are orthodox Hindus.

Buddhism was introduced into Tibet about the seventh century A.D., when it was already permeated by Saivaite and Tantric Hinduism and by Mahayanism, while under the influence of Mongolian Shamanism it departed still more from its original ideal. Here is evolved the concept of the Dhyani-Buddhas, the celestial types of the **8. The Dhyani-Buddhas.** Buddhas which appear on earth as men (Manushi-Buddhas). These Dhayani-Buddhas, who are five in number, watch over the welfare of the world between the incarnations of the Manushi-Buddhas, although they themselves never become incarnate. Three of them correspond to the three Buddhas who preceded Gautama in the present age of the world; one, Amitabha, to the historical Buddha, whose earthly reincarnation is the lesser Lama of Tibet; and the fifth is the Dhyani-Bodhisatva Padmapani or Avalokitesvara, who is represented on earth by the Dalai-Lama at Lhassa, and is the type of the Bodhisatva Maitreya, the future earthly Buddha and the savior of the world. See LAMAISM.

Buddhism was introduced into China in its Mahayanistic form by the emperor Mingti in 61 A.D., and despite persecutions, especially under the Tang dynasty (620–907), it has survived there until the present day, although overlaid with superstition and consisting in great part in the worship of pictures and relics. It has gained, however, only a subordinate place in China, being unable to compete either with the popular Taoism or the cultured Confucianism, despite the fact that the three religions exist peaceably side by side. From China Buddhism was carried to Japan, where numerous sects have arisen, although the results have been little more than a further departure from the original faith (see CHINA, I., 3; JAPAN, I., II., 2).

Some scholars would like to derive the gospel narrative from Buddhism, but it is a significant fact that an overwhelming majority of Oriental scholars have decided that the story of Buddha has had no influence on the canonical life of Christ. They reach this conclusion by a comparison of elements of the Buddha legend composed long after the death of the teacher with the Gospels. The Buddhist parallels are drawn, moreover, in the main, from the texts of the Northern school, which are confessedly late and mythopeic to a degree which almost totally obscures the figure of the historic Buddha, while some of the so-called cogent Christian **9. Buddhism and Christianity.** parallels are based upon the apocryphal Gospels. Considering the canonical Gospels on the one hand and the texts of the Southern Buddhism on the other, the parallels between the lives of Jesus and Buddha seem to resolve themselves into those which are natural in the case of great religious teachers. Thus of five parallels mentioned by Seydel, the ablest advocate of the theory of Buddhistic influence on Christianity, the three most important are the presentation of the infant Jesus in the temple compared with that of the infant Buddha; the fast of Jesus and that of Buddha; and the preexistence of Jesus and of Buddha in heaven. Of these the presentation of Buddha is found neither in the writings of the Southern school nor in the ancient text of the Northern, while at the time of Jesus it was usual for a pious mother to attend the temple for the redemption of the first-born and her own ritual purification. The account of the fasting and temptation is not entirely harmonious in both accounts. Buddha first overcomes Mara and then fasts forty-nine days, while Jesus fasts forty days and is then tempted by the devil. Not only is the account of the Gospels the more accurate psychologically, but it may be paralleled with similar events in the lives of Moses and Elijah, while the story of the temptation is found not only in Buddhism and Christianity, but also in Zoroastrianism. The third parallel of the preexistence of Jesus and Buddha is equally discrepant. Jesus existed in heaven from all eternity and is unique in such existence, while Buddha merely shares the history of all other Buddhas and was reincarnated on earth countless times. It must be borne in mind that the spirit of the two religions as of their founders is entirely divergent. The tragedy and the majesty of the Christ is very different from the peacefulness and the sweetness of Buddha. Jesus sought to save the world, not himself. Buddha began by saving himself and then taught the world. The aim of Jesus is faith and individual existence in heaven in the presence of God; the *summum bonum* of Buddha is knowledge and the annihilation of self in Nirvana. In the face of such essential divergencies, the parallels alleged to exist between Buddha and Jesus seem to be cases of accidental coincidence, and it is almost certain that, despite the travel between Palestine and India, which may have influenced to some degree the apocryphal Gospels on the one hand and late Northern Buddhism on the other, Christianity and Buddhism developed to all intents and purposes independently. For esoteric Buddhism (so called), see THEOSOPHY.

BIBLIOGRAPHY: The literature on Buddhism is enormous, and it is possible to cite here only a few out of the many books on the subject, while reference may be made for more complete bibliographies to the works of Kern and Aiken mentioned below.

General works and Indian Buddhism: K. Köppen, *Die Religion des Buddha*, Berlin, 1857-59; Barthélemy Saint-Hilaire, *Le Bouddha et sa Religion*, Paris, 1860; R. Hardy, *Manual of Buddhism in its Modern Development*, London, 1860; E. Burnouf, *Introduction à l'histoire du Bouddhisme Indien*, Paris, 1876; H. Oldenberg, *Buddha, sein Leben, seine Lehre, seine Gemeinde*, Berlin, 1897, Eng. transl. by W. Hoey, London, 1882; E. Senart, *Essai sur la légende du Bouddha*, Paris, 1882; M. Williams, *Buddhism in its Connection with Brahmanism and Hinduism and its Contrast with Christianity*, London, 1889; T. W. Rhys Davids, *Buddhism, its History and Literature*, New York, 1896; idem, *Buddhism*, London, 1899; H. Kern, *Geschiedenis van het Buddhisme in Indië*, Haarlem, 1884; idem, *Manual of Indian Buddhism*, Strasburg, 1896; E. Hardy, *Der Buddhismus nach älteren Pali-Werken*, Münster, 1890; idem, *Buddha*, Leipsic, 1903; R. Copleston, *Buddhism, Primitive and Present, in Magadha and Ceylon*, London, 1892; K. Neumann, *Buddhistische Anthologie*, Berlin, 1892; idem, *Die Reden des Gotama Buddhas*, Leipsic, 1897; idem, *Theragatha und Therigatha*, Berlin, 1899; H. Warren, *Buddhism in Translation*, Cambridge, Mass., 1896; J. Dahlmann, *Buddha*, Berlin, 1898; and for special topics consult, among other works: S. Hardy, *Eastern Monachism*, London, 1860; A. Bastian, *Der Buddhismus in seiner Psychologie*, Berlin, 1882; idem, *Der Buddhismus als religions-philosophisches System*, ib. 1893; J. Dahlmann, *Nirvana*, ib. 1896; W. St. C. Tisdall, *The Noble Eightfold Path*, London, 1903; A. Menzies, *The Religions of India, Brahmanism and Buddhism*, ib. 1904.

Exceedingly important for the legendary development of Buddhism is the *Jataka: or Stories of the Buddha's Former Births*, Pali text edited with its commentary by V. Fausböll, 8 vols., London, 1877-97; translation by various hands edited by E. B. Cowell, vols. i.-v., ib. 1895-1905. Consult also *Portfolio of Buddhist Art, Historical and Modern*, Chicago, 1906 (a collection of 31 plates).

Extra-Indian Buddhism: H. Alabaster, *The Wheel of the Law*, London, 1871; P. Bigandet, *The Life or Legend of Gaudama, the Buddha of the Burmese*, ib. 1880; E. Schlagintweit, *Buddhism in Tibet*, Leipsic, 1863; W. Rockhill, *The Life of the Buddha*, London, 1884; L. A. Waddell, *The Buddhism of Tibet or Lamaism*, ib. 1895 (contains bibliography, pp. 578-583); A. Grünwedel, *Mythologie des Buddhismus in Tibet und der Mongolei*, Leipsic, 1900; J. Edkins, *Chinese Buddhism*, London, 1880; S. Beal, *Buddhism in China*, ib. 1884; idem, *Si-yu-ki, Buddhist Records of the Western World, from the Chinese*, ib. 1906; B. Nanjio, *Twelve Japanese Buddhist Sects*, Tokyo, 1887; R. Fujishima, *Le Bouddhisme Japonais*, Paris, 1887.

Buddhism and Christianity: R. Seydel, *Das Evangelium von Jesus in seinen Verhältnissen zu Buddha-Sage und Buddha-Lehre*, Leipsic, 1882; idem, *Die Buddha-Legende und das Leben Jesu*, ib. ed. 1897; Rhys Davids, *Buddhism and Christianity*, London, 1888; R. Falke, *Buddha, Mohammed und Christus*, Gütersloh, 1900; C. Aiken, *The Dhamma of Gotama the Buddha and the Gospel of Jesus the Christ*, Boston, 1900; A. Bertholet, *Buddhismus und Christentum*, Tübingen, 1902.

Reference may also be made to the general works on comparative religion and the religions of India, especially E. Hopkins, *Religions of India*, Boston, 1895, pp. 298-347; Chantepie de la Saussaye, *Lehrbuch der Religionsgeschichte*, 3d ed., Freiburg, 1905; C. von Orelli, *Allgemeine Religionsgeschichte*, pp. 448-493, Bonn, 1899, and the bibliographies there given.

BUDÉ, bü″dé′, **GUILLAUME**: French humanist; b. at Paris 1467; d. there Aug. 23, 1540. He studied law at Orléans, and, after leading a dissipated life for several years, began to apply himself to Greek, philosophy, theology, and science. Well received at court, he was repeatedly entrusted with diplomatic missions to Rome. On Aug. 21, 1522, Francis I. appointed him librarian of the royal library at Fontainebleau and royal councilor, and it was owing to Budé's initiative that the king enlarged the Royal Library of Paris and also the Royal College, which afterward became the Collège de France. Long before Luther, Budé had felt the necessity of reforms in the Church, but, like many scholars and bishops of his day, he feared a rupture with Rome. Among his numerous works, special mention may be made of the following: *De Asse et partibus ejus* (Paris, 1514); *De Studio bonarum litterarum recte et commode instituendo* (1527); *Commentarii linguæ græcæ* (1529); *De transitu Hellenismi ad Christianismum* (1535); *Forensia quibus vulgares et vere latinæ jurisconsultorum loquendi formulæ dantur* (1548); and *Lexicon græco-latinum* (Geneva, 1554 etc.). G. BONET-MAURY.

BIBLIOGRAPHY: The best account of his life is by E. de Budé, *Vie de Guillaume Budé*, Paris, 1884. Consult also E. and É. Haag, *La France protestante*, ed. H. L. Bordier, ib. 1877-86; Rebitté, *G. Budé, essai historique*, Paris, 1846; A. Moquet, *Les Seigneurs de Marly*, Paris, 1882.

BUDER, bü′der, **PAUL VON**: German Protestant; b. at Leutkirch (40 m. s. of Ulm) Feb. 15, 1836. He was educated at the University of Tübingen (Ph.D., 1858), and, after being lecturer at the theological seminary attached to that institution from 1861 to 1865, was successively deacon and inspector of schools at Backnang from 1865 to 1868 and second court-preacher, as well as assistant in the consistory and a member of the theological examining board, in Stuttgart from 1868 to 1872. In the latter year he became associate professor of dogmatics and New Testament exegesis and supervisor of the theological seminary of the University of Tübingen, where he was full professor from 1877. Retired from active duties, 1910. He has written *Ueber die apologetische Aufgabe der Theologie der Gegenwart* (Tübingen, 1876).

BUECHNER, büн′ner, **GOTTFRIED**, got′frid. German Lutheran theologian; b. at Rüdersdorf (the district of Saxe-Altenburg) 1701; d. at Querfurt (18 m. w. of Merseburg) 1780. He studied at Jena, and lectured there from 1725 until he was called as rector to Querfurt, where he died. He is best known as the author of *Biblische Real- und Verbal-Hand-Concordanz* (Jena, 1740; 23d ed., Berlin, 1899; ed. H. L. Heubner, Philadelphia, 1871). A list of Büchner's other theological works is given in Jöcher and Adelungs *Allgemeines Gelehrten-Lexikon*, s.v.

BUECHSEL, büн′sel, **KARL**: German Lutheran theologian: b. at Schönfeld (a suburb of Prenzlau, 71 m. n.n.e. of Potsdam) May 2, 1803; d. at Berlin Aug. 14, 1889. After completing his studies, he became minister in his native place, superintendent at Brüsson, and in 1846 pastor of St. Matthew's at Berlin. In 1853 he was made superintendent general, but retired from the ministry in 1884. He belonged to the most prominent and influential preachers of the German capital, and was the author of *Erinnerungen aus dem Leben eines Landgeistlichen* (5 vols., Berlin, 1888-97), which went through many editions.

BUELL, MARCUS DARIUS: Methodist Episcopalian; b. at Wayland, N. Y., Jan. 1, 1851. He was educated at New York University (B.A., 1872) and the Boston University School of Theology

(1875). He entered the Methodist ministry in 1875, and held successive pastorates at Portchester, N. Y., Brooklyn, N. Y., and Hartford, Conn., in 1875–84. In the latter year he studied at the universities of Cambridge, Berlin, and Heidelberg, and returned to the United States as professor of New Testament Greek and exegesis in Boston University, a position which he still holds. He was also assistant dean in 1885–89 and dean in 1889–1904. He is a member of the Society of Biblical Literature and Exegesis and of the Harvard Biblical Club, and has written, in addition to a number of minor contributions, *Studies in the Greek Text of the Gospel of Mark* (Boston, 1890).

BUG BIBLE. See BIBLE VERSIONS, B, IV., § 9.

BUGENHAGEN, bū″gen-hê′gen, **JOHANN:** A leader of the German Reformation; b. at Wollin (29 m. n. of Stettin), Pomerania, June 24, 1485; d. at Wittenberg Apr. 20, 1558. He was educated at the University of Greifswald, paying special attention to the Latin classics. In his eighteenth year he was placed in charge of the school at Treptow on the Rega, which he made famous far and wide by the thorough Renaissance devotion to study which he inculcated. In 1509 he was ordained priest, though without any special theological training. Humanism, in fact, strongly influenced his theology. He turned away from the schoolmen to seek a purer doctrine in the early Fathers, and by Erasmus, whom he considered to represent them, was brought to a deep study of the Bible. In 1517 he was appointed to lecture on the Bible and the Fathers in the new monastic school of Belbuck. A journey throughout Pomerania in search of documents to aid in Spalatin's historical work led to the publication of its results in his *Pomerania* (1518), in which he foreshadows his later career by incidental attacks on the preachers of indulgences; and a sermon delivered before a clerical assembly in 1519 (or 1520) is even more outspoken in its reproof of abuses. Not long after, Luther's writings fell into his hands. He was at first shocked by the *Captivitas Babylonica*, but further reading convinced him of its truth. An earnest correspondence with Luther followed, and in 1521 Bugenhagen went to Wittenberg, sending back to Treptow a long letter in which he declared his adhesion to his new master's doctrines.

Early Life.

He matriculated at the university, made friends with Melanchthon, and began to expound the Psalms to an increasing audience. The swift development of practical reform carried him with it, and he married in 1522, in spite of the uncertainty of his future. Luther exerted himself to find a position for him, and, a vacancy occurring in the principal church of Wittenberg, put his useful follower in, despite the protests of the capitular body to whom the right of nomination really belonged. Here Bugenhagen busied himself in many practical pastoral works, finding time for literary activity also; he helped in the Low German edition of Luther's New Testament (1524), and in the same year published his lectures on the Psalms and Latin commentaries on several other books of Scripture. These, as well as some German treatises on practical piety, made his name known, and he was called to St. Nicholas's church at Hamburg. The town council objected, and the proposal fell through. Bugenhagen came, however, to the help of the evangelical community in Hamburg in the following year by his tractate *Von dem Christenloven und rechten guden Werken* (published 1526; High German version in Vogt), which is one of the best popular presentations of the Lutheran teaching. In 1525 he officiated at Luther's marriage, and wrote a defense of the married clergy. Besides his faithful pastoral labors, continued even through the plague of 1527, he took part in the general movement of the Reformation by a letter "to the Christians in England" (1525), by taking a prominent part against Zwingli and Butzer in the eucharistic controversy, and by new exegetical works.

At Wittenberg.

Bugenhagen's forte, however, was organization, which he carried forward in many parts of North Germany, in both ecclesiastical and educational matters. The results of his activity were seen, for example, in the new church constitutions of Brunswick, Hamburg, Lübeck, and Pomerania. In 1535 he came back to spend two years in his duties at Wittenberg, and became a member of the theological faculty. He was called away once more in 1537 to superintend the carrying out of the reforming movement in Denmark, which had been begun the year before, when Christian III. had broken the power of the bishops and confiscated their property. He revised the proposed constitution, crowned the king and queen at Copenhagen, ordained seven evangelical theologians as superintendents to take the place of the expelled bishops, and reorganized the university, which he governed for a time as rector, working meanwhile at his great commentary on the Psalms, not completed till 1544. Returning home in the spring of 1539, he took part in the thorough revision of Luther's Bible, and stood by him in the conflict with Agricola (see ANTINOMIANISM AND ANTINOMIAN CONTROVERSIES, II., 1, § 3). He declined a call to the bishopric of Sleswick, and another to the University of Copenhagen; but he visited Holstein in 1542, at the king's invitation, to assist in the adoption and adaptation of the Danish church constitution for the duchies. No sooner had he returned than the success of the arms of the Schmalkald League against Henry of Brunswick laid a new task upon him, together with Corvinus and Görlitz; viz., that of organizing an Evangelical Church in the conquered territory. The constitution for Brunswick-Wolfenbüttel which appeared in the autumn of 1543 is mostly his work, and that adopted for Hildesheim in the following year is practically derived from it. Yet the difficulties which he had experienced in this visitation were sufficient, it would seem, to make him reluctant to accept the invitation of the duke of Pomerania to take the place of the deceased bishop of Kammin; and when the duke would have no conditional acceptance, he declined abso-

His Ability as an Organizer.

lutely, though professing his willingness to assist for a time in organization.

Bugenhagen remained, accordingly, at Wittenberg, a help and strength to Luther in his last years, and preached his funeral sermon on Feb. 22, 1546. In the troublous times that followed, he adhered undauntedly to the cause of the Wittenberg church, encouraged the citizens during the siege, and went on preaching even after the emperor had entered the city as conqueror. The consideration with which he was treated by Charles V and the new elector Maurice, and his desire to serve the university and to remain connected with it, combined to reconcile him to the new state of things more readily than some ardent evangelicals thought fitting. There was much criticism of his action from his own side, and calumny even went so far as to accuse him of venality. He was drawn into the policy of the Interim still further, as conducted by Maurice of Saxony and represented theologically by Melanchthon. His personal share in the negotiations was, indeed, a slight one; he was in the opposition at Alten-Zelle, and was consequently not summoned to Jüterbogk. But the concessions made to the Roman Catholic ceremonial found a sympathizer in the man who had impressed upon North German Lutheranism a conservative approximation to the old forms; he overlooked the fact that, as Hering has truly said, what had originally been consideration for the weak brethren might now be only obsequious deference to the powerful. His attitude cost him the confidence of the deposed elector and of Albert of Prussia, and not a few of his old friends turned from him. As an attempt to set himself right, he published in 1550 his commentary on Jonah, in which he gave vigorous expression to his undiminished protest against the Roman Catholic Church, undertaking to derive its doctrines and practises from the Montanist heresy. He raised his voice during the troubles of 1556 in a warning to all pastors to prepare for the end of the world by confession of sin and firm adherence to their faith. Decaying bodily strength forced him to give up preaching in 1557, and a year later he went to his long rest, being buried near the altar in the church he had served so long. He left behind him many a trace of his organizing abilities throughout northern Germany, especially in Lower Saxony, of his wisdom in practical matters, his sensible views on education, and his liturgical institutions, which substantially determined the abiding character of North German Lutheranism.

Last Years.

(G. Kawerau.)

Bibliography: His *Briefwechsel*, ed. O. Vogt, appeared Stuttgart, 1888. The best treatment is to be found in H. Hering, *Doktor Pomeranus, J. Bugenhagen*, Halle, 1888. Special treatises are: G. H. Goetze, *De J. Bugenhagii meritis . . . oratio*, Leipsic, 1704; J. D. Jäncke, *Lebensgeschichte J. Bugenhagens*, Rostock, 1757; R. F. L. Engelken, *J. Bugenhagen, ein biographischer Aufsatz für die evangelische Kirche*, Berlin, 1817; J. H. Zietz, *J. Bugenhagen. Ein biographischer Versuch*, Leipsic, 1834; M. Meurer, *J. Bugenhagen's Leben*, ib. 1862; K. A. T. Vogt, *J. Bugenhagen Pomeranus*, Elberfeld, 1867. Consult further: J. Köstlin, *Martin Luther*, ed. G. Kawerau, passim, 2 vols., Berlin, 1903; Schaff, *Christian Church*, vi. 347, 467, 567, 621–622; Moeller, *Christian Church*, vol. iii. passim; *KL*, ii. 1453–58. Bugenhagen's *Vermahnung an die Böhmen* was published in *Zeitgemässe Traktate aus der Reformationszeit*, part 2, ed. C. von Kügelgen, Leipsic, 1903.

BUHL, būl, **FRANTS PEDER WILLIAM MEYER:** Danish Semitic scholar; b. at Copenhagen Sept. 6, 1850. He was educated at the University of Copenhagen (Ph.D., 1878), and was successively professor of Old Testament exegesis at Copenhagen (1882–90) and Leipsic (1890–98). In 1898 he was recalled to the University of Copenhagen as professor of Semitic languages, a position which he still holds. In theology he is dogmatically conservative, but liberal in isagogics. Since 1900 he has been a member of the Royal Society of Sciences at Copenhagen. In addition to numerous briefer contributions, he has written: *Jesaja oversat og fortolket* (8 parts, Copenhagen, 1889–94); *Gennesaret Sö og dens Omgivelser* (1889); *Palästina i kortfattet geografisk og topografisk Fremstilling* (1890); *Kanon und Text des Alten Testaments* (Leipsic, 1891; Eng. transl. by J. Macpherson, Edinburgh, 1892); *Det israelitiske Folks Historie* (Copenhagen, 1892); *Geschichte der Edomiter* (Leipsic, 1893); *De messianske Forjættelser i det Gamle Testament* (1894); *Til Vejledning i de gammeltestamentlige Undersögelser* (1895); *Geographie des alten Palästina* (Freiburg, 1896); *Hebraisk Syntax* (Copenhagen, 1897); *Die socialen Verhältnisse der Israeliten* (Berlin, 1899); *Psalmerne oversatte og fortolkede* (12 parts, Copenhagen, 1898–1900); and *Muhammeds Liv* (1903). He has also collaborated in editing the twelfth, thirteenth, and fourteenth editions of the *Hebräisches und aramäisches Handwörterbuch über das Alte Testament* of Gesenius (Leipsic, 1895–1905).

BULGARI (BOURGES): Name of a heretical sect. See New Manicheans, II.

BULGARIA: A principality under the suzerainty of Turkey in the northeastern part of the Balkan Peninsula, bounded on the north by Rumania, on the east by the Black Sea, on the south by Turkey, on the west by Servia. It was created by the Treaty of Berlin in 1878 and attained its present extent in 1885 by the addition of Eastern Rumelia (the territory south of the Balkan Mountains) after a revolt of the Bulgars there; in 1908 it proclaimed its independence; area, 38,080 square miles; population (1900), 3,744,283.

In race and religion the population is very diverse. The majority are the Bulgars, who number some 2,880,000 and belong to the Oriental Orthodox Church, their prince Boris having adopted Christianity in 864, two centuries after they had entered the region south of the Danube (see Bulgarians, Conversion of the). Simeon, the successor of Boris as prince or czar, established an autonomous Church for his extensive domains, placing at its head a bishop, or exarch, who had his seat at Ochrida on the frontier of Albania. This diocese lapsed after the fall of the Bulgarian state, nor was it revived when the principality was reorganized. The Slavic bishoprics were gradually replaced with Greek, and the Bulgarian Church was first restored in 1870–72, when, through the insistence of Russian diplomats, the Sultan permitted the Bulgarian Church to separate from

Bulgarian Church.

the patriarchate and to appoint an exarch in Constantinople who should be the Slavic head of all those communities which might wish to join the new ecclesiastical body. Although condemned by the patriarch in 1872 as schismatic, large numbers of Slavs in the Turkish provinces soon declared themselves Bulgarians.

The governing body of this Church is the Holy Synod, which consists of four bishops chosen for four years by secret ballot of all the bishops and presided over by the exarch; it meets annually in May. The rights and external organization of the Bulgarian Church are recognized throughout the principality by the constitution, which declares it to be the State Church. Other religions are tolerated, however, while the exarch can issue commands to his bishops only after reaching an agreement with the minister of foreign affairs.

Organization. According to the exarchial statute of 1883, the laity exercise a considerable influence on the election of bishops, and, with the Turkish districts of the Bulgarian Church, even on the choice of the exarch. In each eparchy, or diocese, three clerical and three lay members form a committee which selects two names from a large list of candidates, sending these names to the Holy Synod, by which the list in question is drawn up and constantly renewed.

In the principality of Bulgaria there are eleven dioceses, or eparchies, at Varna, Rustchuk (Cherven and Dorostol), Tirnova, Lovatz, Vratsa, and Widin north of the Balkans, and Sofia, Philippopolis, Stara Saghra, and Sliven south of this mountain range. These dioceses receive from the State an annual revenue of 800,000 francs, while the monasteries supply the funds for twenty-four archimandrites. One of the richest monasteries is that of St. John in the Rilo mountains, and other important cloisters are those of St. Nicholas near the Shipka Pass and Tcherepis at the northern end of the Isker gap. The majority of the parish clergy lack the requisite education, and the monks are very inferior in education to those of Servia. The parish priests are accordingly reverenced but little by the peasants and citizens. They number nearly 2,000, and there are 240 monks in seventy-eight monasteries.

Not all the Slavs recognize the authority of the exarch, and in the southeast 60,000 Greeks have the four small dioceses of Varna, Mesembria, Sozopolis, and Anchiolo, as well as the metropolitanate of Philippopolis. Roman Catholicism has but scant representation in Bulgaria. Nicopolis is the name of the bishopric for Danubian Bulgaria, but in reality the bishop resides at Rustchuk. In the

Other Churches. south is the apostolic vicariate of Sofia and Philippopolis, in charge of the Capuchins since 1841. The majority of the Roman Catholics are Bulgars, partly descended from the Paulicians, who were formerly numerous (see PAULICIANS). The minority are immigrants from Austria-Hungary and other Roman Catholic countries, and have churches and small congregations in various cities along the Danube, as well as in Sofia, Philippopolis, and Burgas. The Armenians have their own bishop in Rustchuk. Bulgarian Protestants are mainly the result of American missionary propaganda. [The Methodists entered the country north of the Balkans in 1857 and the American Board commenced work south of the Balkans at about the same time. The educational work of Robert College near Constantinople has done much for the Bulgarians.] There are also Protestant communities of some 500 Germans in Sofia and Rustchuk.

The Jews in Bulgaria are for the most part descendants of exiles from Spain in the sixteenth century. The Gipsies number about 50,000, although some of them declare themselves Orthodox.

Non-Christian Religions. The great majority of the Mohammedans are Turks; the number has decreased owing to extensive emigration since 1878. They have many schools, including a theological school at Shumla.

[The religious statistics of the census of 1900 are: Orthodox Greeks, 3,019,296; Mohammedans, 643,300; Jews, 33,663; Roman Catholics, 28,569; Armenian Gregorians, 13,809; Protestants, 4,524; Unknown, 1,122.] WILHELM GOETZ.

BIBLIOGRAPHY: C. Jireček, *Geschichte der Bulgaren*, Prague, 1876 (authoritative); idem, *Das Fürstentum Bulgarien*, Vienna, 1891; J. Samuelson, *Bulgaria, Past and Present*, London, 1888 (best general account in English); L. Lamouche, *La Bulgarie dans le passé et dans le présent*, Paris, 1892; A. Strausz, *Die Bulgaren, ethnographische Studien*, Leipsic, 1898; *Acta Bulgariæ ecclesiastica, 1565–1799*, *collegit* C. Fermendziu, Agram, 1868; A. d'Avril, *La Bulgarie chrétienne*, Paris, 1898; J. S. Dennis, *Centennial Survey of Foreign Missions*, New York, 1902.

BULGARIAN NATIONAL CHURCH IN THE UNITED STATES, THE: There are, according to moderate calculations, about 25,000 Bulgarians in the United States and Canada, the immigration of Bulgarians becoming greater since 1903. They have settled in large numbers at Granite City and Madison, Ill.; Hopkins, Mich.; and St. Louis, Mo., and are scattered also farther westward, while a considerable number of them are to be found in New York City, and also in Toronto and parts of northern Canada. The first Bulgarian church in the United States was built in 1907 in Madison, Ill., being followed by those at Granite City and St. Louis. There are at present three Bulgarian priests in the United States. A. A. STAMOULI.

BULGARIANS, CONVERSION OF THE: According to Jireček, who follows Schafarik, the Bulgarians were originally related to the Finns. Jordanis says that they lived on the shores of the Black Sea in the fifth century, clashing frequently with the Ostrogoths in the reign of Theodoric, who, according to Ennodius, checked their victorious advance toward the west in 487; Cassiodorus mentions another victory in 504. But their attacks were directed also against the Byzantine Empire. Under Constantine Pogonatus a Bulgarian horde established itself in 679 between the Danube and the Balkans, extending their conquests gradually as far as the mouth of the Save. This territory seems to have been inhabited by people of Slavic race, who first gave their language to the conquerors and then gradually amalgamated with them. The race formed by this fusion was so strongly pagan that it resisted the introduction of Christianity, which had its martyrs in the first half of the ninth century. A change set in under Bogoris (c. 852–888), who in his contests with both Franks and Greeks held out hopes of a conversion as an inducement for peace. In 864 he seems to have entered the Greek Church, and received in return a considerable slice of territory. In Constantinople his conversion was considered genuine, and Photius took pains to instruct him at some length in the duties of a Christian prince. The Bulgarians were apparently less delighted, and rose in armed revolt. The wily barbarian, however, had one eye on the West, and at the same time sent an embassy to Pope Nicholas I., with a number of questions on which he sought enlightenment from Rome. Nicholas immediately sent two bishops to take possession of the Bulgarian territory for the Church, and answered the questions of Bogoris with much more painstaking seriousness than they deserved. Another embassy went to Louis the German to ask that Christian missionaries might be sent. In 867 Louis commissioned Bishop Ermanrich of Passau and a numerous retinue of priests to set out for the Danube. Charlemagne followed by raising a large sum to provide books and church utensils for the Bulgarians. But all this interest was thrown away. When Ermanrich reached Bulgaria, he found the field already occupied by priests from Rome, and returned to Germany. The communion with Rome lasted but a few years longer. Bogoris requested the appointment of Formosus of Porto (one of the two original Roman missionaries) as archbishop, and proposed another candidate when Nicholas declined; when this second nomination was rejected by Adrian II. he lost patience and turned to Constantinople. His envoys took part there in the final session of the Eighth Ecumenical Council (870), and after its close, in spite of the protests of the Roman legates, declared that Bulgaria belonged to the patriarchate of Constantinople. The Roman clergy were obliged to leave and the patriarch Ignatius organized the church by the consecration of a metropolitan and several bishops. Adrian II. protested (871), but in vain, and the efforts of John VIII. to reopen the question were equally fruitless; Bulgaria remained, as, indeed, its geographical situation demanded, a part of the Greek Church. (A. HAUCK.)

BIBLIOGRAPHY: C. Jireček, *Geschichte der Bulgaren*, Prague, 1876; idem, *Das Fürstentum Bulgarien*, ib. 1891; *La Bulgarie chrétienne. Étude historique*, Paris, 1861; *Légendes religieuses bulgares, traduites par Lydia Schischmanoff*, ib. 1896.

BULGARIS, bul-gū'ris, **EUGENIOS**, ē"ū-gē'nī-os: Russian prelate; b. in the island of Corfu Aug. 10, 1716; d. at St. Petersburg June 10, 1806. He was educated at Padua, and taught in various schools and at the academy of Athos from 1755 to 1759. His orthodoxy being impugned, he went to the West, and was recommended by Frederick the Great to Catharine II. of Russia, who appointed him bishop of Slovensk and Kherson. In 1801 he retired to the monastery of Alexander Nevsky. Bulgaris was a very gifted and learned man, and contributed toward making Western culture accessible to his people. Together with Koraïs, he may be regarded as the founder of modern culture in Greece. He was an eclectic in philosophy, and was familiar with all branches of theology. Among his numerous works (in Greek), special mention may be made of his "Orthodox Confession" (Amsterdam, 1767), written against the Jesuit Leclerc, but also opposing the Protestants; and his "Address on Tolerance" (1768), denying the State the right of intolerance toward adherents of other creeds than that of the national church. His principal work was the "Dogmatic Theology" (ed. Lontopulos, Venice, 1872), the first real Greek treatise on dogmatics since the Middle Ages. It is divided into four parts, treating of God, the Trinity, anthropology, and Christology. Among his historical writings the most important was the "First Century from the Incarnation of Christ the Saviour" (Leipsic, 1805), while to the department of practical theology belongs the "Pious Talk" (2 vols., 1801), a moralistic exposition of the Pentateuch. He also translated several writings of Augustine, and such works as the *De processione Spiritus sancti* of Zoernikau (St. Petersburg, 1797). He likewise edited the works of Joseph Bryennius, and assisted in the editing of the works of Theodoret (Halle, 1768). PHILIPP MEYER.

BIBLIOGRAPHY: P. Strahl, *Das gelehrte Russland*, Leipsic, 1828 (from Russian sources); A. P. Vretos, *Biographie de l'archevêque E. Bulgari*, Athens, 1860; A. D. Kyriakos, *Geschichte der orientalischen Kirchen*, Leipsic, 1902.

BULL, GEORGE: Bishop of St. David's; b. at Wells, Somersetshire, Mar. 25, 1634; d. at Brecon, Wales, Feb. 17, 1710. He studied at Oxford but did not take a degree; became minister of St. George's, near Bristol, 1655; rector of Suddington St. Mary's, near Cirencester, 1658, to which was joined the vicarage of the adjoining parish of St. Peter's 1662; rector of Avening, Gloucester, 1685. From 1678 to 1686 he was a prebendary of Gloucester; from 1686 to 1705 archdeacon of Llandaff. He became bishop of St. David's, Wales, in 1705. His fame rests upon his *Defensio fidei Nicænæ*, published originally in Latin in 1685 and received with marked approval by Protestant and Roman Catholic (e.g., Bossuet and Jurieu) scholars everywhere; it is still a classic. In English translation, it appears in the Library of Anglo-Catholic Theology, together with his *Harmonia Apostolica* (4 vols., Oxford, 1851–53).

BIBLIOGRAPHY: His complete works appeared in 7 vols., 1827, with the life by Robert Nelson (originally 1713, separately 1840). The *DNB*, vii. 238–238, gives a very satisfactory account of his life.

BULL, PAPAL. See BRIEFS, BULLS, AND BULLARIA.

BULLINGER, bul'lin-ger, **HEINRICH.**

Heinrich Bullinger was a Swiss Reformer; b. at Bremgarten ($14\frac{1}{2}$ m. e.s.e. of Aargau) July 18, 1504; d. at Zurich Sept. 17, 1575. He was the son of a priest, who looked after his bringing up. After receiving his elementary education in the schools of his native town, he was sent to Emmerich on the Lower Rhine to the Brethren of the Common Life, and in 1519 he went to Cologne. There, in the seat of opposition to the Reformation, Bullinger gradually became a convert to the new doctrines. When he began the study of theology, his text-books were the *Sententiæ* of Peter Lombard and the *Decretum* of Gratian, but noting that these were based on the Church Fathers, he resolved to study the latter more closely, thus learning from Chrysostom, Ambrose, Origen, and Augustine how widely the scholastics had diverged in their treatment of Christian truths. At the same time he came into possession of some pamphlets of Luther which convinced him that the Wittenberg Reformer marked an advance over the scholastics. Since, however, Luther, like the Church Fathers, appealed to the Scriptures, Bullinger obtained a New Testament, which nourished his opposition to Roman doctrine. He was also strongly influenced by Melanchthon's *Loci communes*, and by 1522, despite a bitter inward struggle, he had broken definitely with the Roman Catholic Church. Being thus debarred from an ecclesiastical career, he resolved to become a teacher, and after nine months he secured a position in the Cistercian monastery at Kappel, where he remained from Jan., 1523, to Pentecost, 1529. Not only did he introduce his pupils to the classics, but he also interpreted a portion of the Bible to them daily, in addition to lecturing on other theological subjects in the presence of the abbot, the monks, and many of the residents of the city. Through his preaching of a reformation of doctrine and life the movement was completed in 1525–26, although Bullinger's life was imperiled by the hostility of the adherents of the ancient faith. In the early part of 1527 the monastery was transferred to the authorities of Zurich and the monastery church became the parish church of the community, with Bullinger as the preacher. In close harmony with Zwingli, whom he had known since the end of 1523, and in consultation with Leo Jud, he began the active preparation of a large number of tracts designed to work for the Reformation in central Switzerland. After being invited by Zwingli in Jan., 1525, to attend a conference with the Anabaptists, he combated them, and in 1528 he accompanied Zwingli to the Disputation of Bern, where the leading Reformers of Switzerland and South Germany became acquainted with each other.

1. Conversion to Protestantism.

2. Friendship with Zwingli.

In June, 1529, Bullinger succeeded his father as pastor of Bremgarten, but his position was a perilous one, and the Reformed strongholds were fortified in expectation of the war between the Confederates, which threatened to break out in 1529. Despite the so-called "land-peace" and the sermons delivered by Bullinger at the diets held at Bremgarten in the summer of 1531, in which he urged upon his hearers the horrors of civil war and sought to reconcile the adherents of both creeds by the weapons of the spirit and the word of God without the effusion of blood, the Reformation had long been political rather than religious, and on Oct. 11, 1531, the battle of Kappel was fought, in which the leaders of the Zurich Reformation fell. The progress of the entire movement was checked, and at Bremgarten at heavy cost a peace was made from which the clergy were excepted. In the night of Nov. 20 Bullinger fled to Zurich. The difficult task of the reconstruction of the Reformed Church and the maintenance of Zwingli's life-work now devolved upon him, and on Dec. 9, 1531, he was chosen pastor of the Grossmünster to succeed the great Swiss Reformer. At the same time, however, a controversy arose between the adherents of the ancient conditions, who advocated peace at any price, and the evangelical party, resulting in a decision to prohibit the clergy from touching on political questions in their sermons. After consultation with his colleagues, Bullinger declared himself ready to promote peace, but declined to refrain from political problems which were connected with religion. The liberty which he demanded was granted him after long deliberation, and the clergy accordingly placed themselves in opposition to the reactionaries. The sermons of Bullinger and Jud, however, resulted in their being cited before the council. They were honorably discharged, but were requested in future to lay their political complaints before the council on the chance that they might be settled without the necessity of publicity. Through this recognition of the spheres of Church and State as distinct but not opposed, Bullinger sustained a more healthy relation to the political body than Zwingli, and he also avoided the struggles made by Calvin to make the State subservient to the Church. A still more difficult task was the stemming of the Catholic reaction, and it was chiefly due to him that the disaster of Kappel had no worse results. The evangelical communities, however, suffered severely, and turned to Zurich for help, and the council, in their eagerness to refute the charge of Roman tendencies, unwisely inserted in their manifesto words which the Catholics claimed were an insult to the mass. In the controversy which ensued, Zurich was cited before the council of the Confederation, whereupon Bullinger, while blaming the city for its folly, advised the mutual surrender of the old letters of confederation, the peaceable division of the common territories, and the formation of a new union with such bodies as held to the word of God. Although it proved possible to preserve peace without this dissolution of the Confederation, the result was a partial humiliation of Zurich.

3. The Successor of Zwingli.

4. Political Activity.

In the earlier years of his pastoral activity Bullinger was an indefatigable preacher, delivering between six and eight sermons each week, nor was it until 1542 that his labors were lessened to two addresses, on Sunday and Friday. Like Zwingli, he was accustomed to interpret entire books of the Bible in order, and his sermons were esteemed far and wide, especially in England. He was also active in education, and brought the schools of

Zurich to a high standard of excellence, proposing an admirable scheme, which comprised both teachers and pupils and prescribed their duties. He likewise promoted theological training by the establishment of scholarships and secured the canons' fund for the maintenance of the schools, in addition to preparing regulations for preachers and synods. The first of these, drawn up by him and Leo Jud, remained unchanged for almost three centuries.

5. Pastoral and Educational Activity.

The synod met twice annually, and had as representatives of the State a non-officiating burgomaster and eight members of the great council. The chief duty of the synod was a complete report of the activity, qualifications, and conduct of each and every pastor. Bullinger was highly esteemed as a pastor, especially in time of pestilence, while his *Quo pacto cum ægrotantibus et morientibus agendum sit parænesis* (1540) is a work of unusual excellence. A generous friend and patron of fugitives from Germany, Locarno, and England, he also wrote an enormous mass of letters, numbering among his correspondents Lady Jane Grey, Henry II. and Francis II. of France, Henry VIII. and Edward VI. of England, Elizabeth, Christian of Denmark, Philip of Hesse, and the palsgrave Frederick III.

Bullinger took part in the controversy over the Lord's Supper as the chief representative of German-Swiss doctrine. After the death of Zwingli both the Romanists, headed by Johann Faber, and Luther assailed the doctrines of his followers, only to be answered by Bullinger in his *Auf Johannsen wienischen Bischofs Trostbüchlein tröstliche Verantwortung* (Zurich, 1532) and in the introduction to Leo Jud's translation of the treatise *De corpore et sanguine Domini* of Ratramnus, a monk of Corvey. Even in these earlier works he emphasized the objective side of the sacrament, the work of Christ in the faithful, whereas Zwingli

6. Eucharistic Teachings.

had taught rather the subjective aspect as a memorial. The controversy involved the Protestant party in Germany, and in the ensuing efforts for reconciliation Butzer and Bullinger were active figures, the latter preparing a confession for the former, showing how far a union with Luther was possible. This confession was sent in Nov., 1534, to the remaining Swiss cities and was gladly accepted by the majority, Bern alone refusing to subscribe to it until after the Conference of Brugg in Apr., 1535. This was, however, little more than an agreement of the clergy, and the desirability of an understanding with Luther, as well as the expectation of a general council, rendered it advisable for the Swiss Church to make an official formulation of its creed. The result was the First Helvetic Confession (see HELVETIC CONFESSIONS), framed at Basel in 1536, Bullinger being one of its authors. Meanwhile Butzer had framed the Wittenberg Concord (q.v.), which was accepted by the cities of Upper Germany, but was opposed by Bullinger in Zurich and rejected by Bern. The Swiss responded with an elucidation of the Helvetic Confession prepared by Bullinger and addressed directly to Luther (Nov., 1536), seeking the middle way between transubstantiation and the concept of a mere memorial meal. The reply was conciliatory, but the peace was soon broken by Luther, who bitterly attacked the Zwinglian doctrines of the Lord's Supper in 1544. Bullinger replied in the Zurich Confession of 1545, and, though no understanding was reached between the Swiss and the Lutheran churches, the French and German sections of the Swiss Church were drawn together all

7. The Helvetic and Zurich Confessions and the Consensus Tigurinus.

the closer, a matter which was the more momentous since the Reformed had found a second center in Geneva, thus giving rise to the danger of a schism like that headed by Luther and Melanchthon in Germany. The peril was averted, however, by the *Consensus Tigurinus*, which was quietly prepared by Bullinger and Calvin in 1549 and which was in complete harmony with the previous views of Bullinger on the Lord's Supper, while it emphasized the divine work of grace, though it restricted it to the elect. In his later years he was involved in a controversy with Brenz, who defended the doctrine of the ubiquity of the sacraments but reached no definite conclusion. The views concerning the Lord's Supper were closely connected with the doctrine of predestination. While still in Kappel, Bullinger had maintained that free will was incompatible with the foreknowledge of God, but later he was gradually led to accept the Calvinistic doctrine of predestination, his views finding their ultimate expression in the famous Second Helvetic Confession, which he prepared in consultation with his friend Peter Martyr to serve as a posthumous testimony of his own belief and that of his church. It was published, however, in 1566, when Frederic III., who was accused of Calvinism, wished to defend himself before the Diet of Augsburg. At his request Bullinger sent him the confession, which he printed

8. His Part in the Second Helvetic Confession.

and which was accepted not only by all Swiss churches with the exception of Basel, but also by the Reformed in France, Scotland, and Hungary and highly praised in Germany, England, and Holland. It was, strictly speaking, the bond uniting the scattered members of the Evangelical-Reformed churches.

In the controversies concerning the relation of Church and State, Bullinger regarded the two as united, Christian citizens forming both Church and State, and temporal officials being likewise the servants of God. The chief duty of the Church was the unrestricted preaching of the word, and the power of admonishing the authorities, when necessary, of their obligations. Neither Church nor State, however, should interfere in

9. Views on the Relation of Church and State.

each other's affairs. External administration of the property of the Church, on the other hand, was to be left to the State, which was also to execute ecclesiastical punishments. With this was closely connected his attitude toward heretics. While in his earlier career he had expressed the utmost tolerance, he later reached the conclusion that preaching and writing against heresy must be supplemented by state punishment. Roused by Anabaptism, he urged in 1535 that no heretics should be admitted to the city and that, if all efforts at conversion proved fruitless, they should be punished by the secular arm, though with due consideration of the circumstances of each individual case. This position did not exclude capital punishment, and while Bullinger did not avail himself of it in the case of the Anabaptists, it is easy to see how he could counsel the execution of Servetus and the exile of Ochino.

The years 1564–65 were marked with sorrow for Bullinger, who lost many of his relatives and closest friends by death, and was himself so seriously ill with the plague that his life was despaired of. Even after his apparent recovery his health was shattered, and his sufferings from calculi increased until he was repeatedly near death. His last sermon was delivered on Whitsuntide, 1575, and four months later he died.

Bullinger's works are extraordinarily numerous but have never been published in collected form and some are extant only in manuscript. The catalogue of the municipal library of Zurich lists about 100 separate works, and this number is raised to 150 by J. J. Scheuchzer. Especially noteworthy are his Latin expositions of all the books of the New Testament with the exception of the Apocalypse, which were prepared up to 1548, when their place was taken by collections of sermons, the majority also in Latin, comprising 100 on the Apocalypse, sixty-six on Daniel, 170 on Jeremiah, and 190 on Isaiah. His sermons on the decalogue, the Apostles' Creed, the sacraments, etc., were highly esteemed and published under the title, *Sermonum decades quinque* (Zurich, 1557; translated into Dutch and French; Eng. transl., *The Decades*, London, 1577, ed. for the Parker Society by T. Harding, Cambridge, 1849–1851). Among his theological works special mention may be made of his *De providentia* (Zurich, 1553); *De gratia Dei justificante*, and *De scripturæ sanctæ auctoritate et certitudine deque episcoporum institutione et functione* (1538, Eng. transl., *Woorthynesse, authoritie, and sufficiencie of the holy Scripture*, London, 1579). He was likewise the author of a drama on Lucretia and Brutus and of a hymn beginning: "O holy God, have mercy now!" Bullinger also wrote a chronicle and description of Kappel, and later prepared a similar work entitled *Antiquitates aliquot ecclesiæ Tigurinæ*, which is preserved in manuscript in the municipal library. An important source for the history of the Anabaptists is found in his *Der Wiedertaüfern Ursprung, Fürgang, Sekten* (Zurich, 1560), but his chief historical work was his detailed chronicle of the Swiss, the most valuable part being the history of the Reformation up to 1532 (ed. J. J. Hottinger and H. H. Vögeli, 6 vols., Frauenfeld, 1838–40).

10. The Works of Bullinger.

(Emil Egli.)

Bibliography: Sources: Bullinger's autobiography was printed in *Miscellanea Tigurini*, iii. 1–171, Zurich, 1722; valuable also is his *Reformationsgeschichte*, 3 vols., Frauenfeld, 1838–40. Other early sources are: J. W Stucki, *Oratio funebris*, Zurich, 1575; J. Simmler, *De ortu, vita, et obitu Heinrici Bullingeri*, ib. 1575; *Archiv für die schweizerische Reformationsgeschichte*, vol. i., Solothurn, 1868. For his life consult: J. F. Franz, *Merkwürdige Züge aus dem Leben des . H. Bullinger*, Bern, 1828; S. Hess, *Lebensgeschichte Bullingers*, 2 vols., Zurich, 1828–1829; G. Friedländer, *Beiträge zur Reformationsgeschichte. Sammlung ungedruckter Briefe des Bullinger*, Berlin, 1837; C. Pestalozzi, *Heinrich Bullinger*, Elberfeld, 1858; R. Christoffel, *H. Bullinger und seine Gattin*, Zurich, 1875; G. R. Zimmermann, *Die Zürcher Kirche und ihre Antistes*, ib. 1877; Schaff, *Christian Church*, vii. 206–214, 514, 618; Moeller, *Christian Church*, vol. iii, passim.

BUNBURY, THOMAS: Protestant bishop of Limerick; b. at Shandrum, County Cork, 1832. He was educated at Trinity College, Dublin (B.A., 1852), ordered deacon 1854, and priest the following year. He was curate of Clonfert, County Galway (1855–58), and of Mallow, County Cork (1858–1863), rector of Croom, County Limerick (1863–72), rector of St. Mary's, Limerick, and dean of Limerick (1872–99). From 1895 to 1899 he was also chaplain to the bishop of Limerick, and in the latter year was himself consecrated to that see. Died at Shandrum Jan. 19, 1907.

BUND, EVANGELISCHER ("Evangelical Union"): An alliance of German Protestants for maintaining Protestant interests in Germany. The occasion of the formation was the modern aggressions of the papacy (leading to the *Kulturkampf*) and the arrogance of Ultramontanism, the dream of which is to reestablish Catholicism in Germany. Its founder was Prof. W Beyschlag of Halle who, finding others interested in the scheme, called a preliminary meeting at Erfurt, October 5, 1886, which was attended by seventy men representing different types of Protestant theology. After a thorough discussion, an organization was effected under the presidency of Count von Wintzingerode-Bodenstein. The confessional basis of the alliance is: "Belief in Jesus Christ, the only begotten Son of God, as the only mediator of salvation, and adherence to the principles of the Reformation." In the beginning of the year 1887 a circular containing 243 names was sent out, and when the alliance held its first annual meeting in Frankfort, August 15–17, 1887, 10,000 members were reported. The ecclesiastical authorities, who were at first indifferent, soon perceived the great importance of the Bund and expressed their approval of the purposes of the alliance, which in various ways has developed a great activity in opposition to the Roman propaganda. In public lectures the burning religious questions of the day are treated with the intention of sharpening and strengthening the Protestant consciousness. As the Bund has its own publication house at Leipsic, it publishes not only a monthly in behalf of Protestant interests, but also pamphlets intended to expose and to refute the claims of Ultramontanism and to repel attacks, especially directed against the memory and work of Luther and Gustavus Adolphus. The Bund has also the practical end of affording material help to weak institutions in the "Diaspora." The effect of the Bund is felt by the Ultramontanes, and their attacks upon it only show its necessity.

(W Beyschlag†.)

Bibliography: G. Warneck, *Der evangelische Bund und seine Gegner*, Leipsic, 1889; H. Meyer-Herrmann, *Der Kampf des evangelischen Bundes gegen Rom und seine Wirksamkeit in der evangelischen Kirche*, Barmen, 1890;

Nippold, *Ziele und Vorgeschichte des evangelischen Bundes*, 1890; L. Witte, *Der evangelische Bund, sein gutes Recht und sein gethanes Werk*, Barmen, 1896; Blankmeister, *Das Reich muss uns doch bleiben*, Leipsic, 1896; also the pamphlets published by the Bund.

BUNGENER, bün"je-né' (LAURENT LOUIS), FÉLIX: Swiss Protestant; b. at Marseilles Sept. 14, 1814; d. in Geneva June 14, 1874. He was graduated B.L. at Marseilles, 1832, B.S. at Geneva, 1834, studied theology at Geneva and was graduated at Strasburg, 1838; ordained in Geneva, 1839, and lived there as teacher, writer, and occasional preacher. His books and articles were very numerous and exerted a wide influence, especially those of a controversial character against the Church of Rome. From 1849 till his death he was one of the editors of *Étrennes religieuses*, an annual chronicle of religious events, particularly those connected with Geneva. His more noteworthy books were: *Un sermon sous Louis XIV* (Paris, 1843; Eng. transl., *The Preacher and the King, or Bourdaloue in the Court of Louis XIV*, London and Boston, 1853); *Histoire du concile de Trente* (2 vols., 1847; Eng. transl., Edinburgh, 1852; by J. McClintock, New York, 1855); *Trois sermons sous Louis XV* (3 vols., Paris, 1849; Eng. transl., *The Priest and the Huguenots, or Persecution in the Age of Louis XV*, 2 vols., London, 1853); *Voltaire et son temps* (2 vols., 1850; Eng. transl., Edinburgh, 1854); *Julien ou la fin d'un siècle* (4 vols., Paris, 1854; Eng. transl., London, 1854); *Christ et le siècle* (Paris, 1856); *Rome et la Bible* (1858); *Calvin, sa vie, son œuvre et ses écrits* (1862; Eng. transl., Edinburgh, 1863); *Trois jours de la vie d'un père*, written after the death of his two years old daughter (Paris, 1863; Eng. transl., Edinburgh, 1864, New York, 1867); *Lincoln, sa vie, son œuvre et sa mort* (Lausanne, 1865); *Saint Paul, sa vie, ses œuvres et ses épîtres* (Paris, 1867; Eng. transl., London, 1870); *Pape et concile au xix. siècle* (Paris, 1870; Eng. transl., Edinburgh, 1870). A volume of "Sermons" was published after his death (1875).

BIBLIOGRAPHY: Jean Gaberel, in *Étrenne religieuse* for 1875; Henri Gambier, *Félix Bungener*, Geneva, 1891.

BUNSEN, bun'zen, CHRISTIAN KARL JOSIAS: Baron; German scholar and diplomat; b. at Korbach (28 m. s.w. of Cassel) Aug. 25, 1791; d. at Bonn Nov. 28, 1860. He studied theology and philology in Marburg and Göttingen (1808–13). Resigning his hopes of journeying to India, Bunsen followed his friend Brandis to Rome in 1816, first as secretary to the Russian embassy, over which Niebuhr presided. Two years later he succeeded Brandis in the diplomatic service, and represented Prussia at Rome (where he became a close friend of Tholuck and Rothe) from 1823 to 1839. In the latter year he was sent as minister to Bern, and in 1841 to London as minister plenipotentiary and envoy extraordinary of his Majesty Frederick William IV at the Court of St. James. In 1854 he returned to Germany and was ennobled by the king of Prussia. In the same year he retired to Heidelberg, devoting himself to literary pursuits. Shortly before his death he moved to Bonn, where he continued his studies until the last. Bunsen's influence and position enabled him to assist not only scholars like Birch, Cureton, Max Müller, Richard Lepsius, and Hoffmann, but also to found institutions, like the German hospitals in Rome and London, and the archeological institute at Rome. He helped to establish the Anglo-Prussian bishopric at Jerusalem (see JERUSALEM, ANGLICAN-GERMAN BISHOPRIC IN) as a basis of a larger union between the German evangelical and the Anglican churches. A complete list of his writings would include contributions to Roman and Egyptian Antiquities, as well as to politics, liturgy, and hymnology. His chief works of theological interest are as follows: *Ignatius von Antiochien und seine Zeit* (Hamburg, 1847); *Hippolytus and his Age* (4 vols., London, 1851), which, together with his *Analecta Ante-Nicæna* and *Outlines of the Philosophy of Universal History as Applied to Language and Religion*, form his great work *Christianity and Mankind* (7 vols., 1854), for which many scholars wrote contributions. Soon after his return to Germany he published *Die Zeichen der Zeit* (2 vols., Leipsic, 1855; Eng. transl., *Signs of the Times*, London, 1856), in which he assailed the anarchy existing in political, religious, and intellectual life, advocating toleration and liberty of conscience, and opposing the sophistical and fanatical doctrines of Stahl and Ketteler. Another work which involved Bunsen in controversy was his *Gott in der Geschichte, oder der Fortschritt des Glaubens an eine sittliche Weltordnung* (3 vols., 1857–58; Eng. transl., *God in History*, 3 vols., London, 1868–70), but his most important book was his *Vollständiges Bibelwerk für die Gemeinde* (9 vols., 1858–70). Bunsen lived to see the publication of vols. i., ii., and v.; after his death Adolf Kamphausen, continued the work with the help of Johannes Bleek, H. Holtzmann, and others; the work gave a marked impetus to the revision of Luther's Bible version, and was diligently consulted by the German revisers. A. KAMPHAUSEN.

BIBLIOGRAPHY: The chief work on Bunsen's life is by his widow, *Memoir of Baron C. C. J. Bunsen*, 2 vols., London, 1868–69, translated and enlarged by Nippold, 3 vols., Leipsic, 1868–71. Consult also A. J. C. Hare, *Life and Letters of Baroness Bunsen*, London, 1878, Germ. transl. by F. A. Perthes, Gotha, 1885. Both works have had a large circulation on both sides of the Atlantic.

BUNTING, JABEZ: The "second founder of Methodism"; b. at Manchester May 13, 1779; d. in London June 16, 1858. He received a good school education in Manchester, and began to preach at the age of nineteen; was stationed first in Manchester, then at Macclesfield (1801), London (1803), Manchester (1805), Sheffield (1807), Liverpool (1809), Halifax (1811), Leeds (1813), London (1815), Manchester (1824), Liverpool (1830); from 1833 he lived in London and filled the most important positions at the denominational headquarters. He was one of the founders of the Wesleyan Missionary Society and its secretary for eighteen years; was first president of the Wesleyan Missionary Institute in London, from 1835 till his death; was president of the conference in 1820, 1828, 1836, and 1844. He perfected the Methodist organization, and it was his influence which gave steadily increasing powers to laymen. He edited the seventh edition of *Cruden's Concordance* (Liverpool, 1815) and *Memoirs of the Early*

Life of William Cowper (1816). Two volumes of sermons, edited by his eldest son, W. M. Bunting, appeared posthumously (1861–62).

BIBLIOGRAPHY: His *Life* was written by T. P. Bunting (brother of W. M. Bunting, above), vol. i., London, 1859, vol. ii., completed by G. S. Rowe, 1887. Consult also *DNB*, vii. 273–275, where other literature is given.

BUNYAN, JOHN: "The immortal dreamer of Bedford jail;" b. at Harrowden (1 m. s.e. of Bedford), in the parish of Elstow, christened Nov. 30, 1628; d. in London Aug. 31, 1688. He had very little schooling, followed his father in the tinker's trade, was in the parliamentary army, 1644–47; married in 1649; lived in Elstow till 1655, when his wife died and he moved to Bedford. He married again 1659. He was received into the Baptist church in Bedford by immersion in the Ouse, 1653. In 1655 he became a deacon and began preaching with marked success from the start. In 1658 he was indicted for preaching without a license; kept on, however, and did not suffer imprisonment till Nov., 1660, when he was taken to the county jail in Silver Street, Bedford, and there confined, with the exception of a few weeks in 1666, till Jan., 1672. In that month he became pastor of the Bedford church. In March, 1675 (the original warrant, discovered in 1887, is published in facsimile by Rush and Warwick, London), he was again imprisoned for preaching and this time in the Bedford town jail on the stone bridge over the Ouse. In six months he was free and was not again molested In Aug., 1688, on his way to London he caught a severe cold from being wet, and died at the house of a friend on Snow Hill.

All the world knows that Bunyan wrote *The Pilgrim's Progress*, in two parts, of which the first appeared at London in 1678, and was, at all events, begun during his imprisonment in 1676; the second in 1684. The earliest edition in which the two parts were combined in one volume was in 1728. A third part falsely attributed to Bunyan appeared in 1693, and was reprinted as late as 1852. *The Pilgrim's Progress* is the most successful allegory ever written, and like the Bible is adapted to man in every clime. It is indeed commonly translated by Protestant missionaries after the Bible. It is thus read in all literary languages and is a world-classic. Two other works of Bunyan's would have given him fame, but not as wide as that he now enjoys; viz., *The Life and Death of Mr. Badman* (1680), an imaginary biography, and the allegory *The Holy War* (1682). The book which lays bare Bunyan's inner life and reveals his preparation for his appointed work is *Grace Abounding to the chief of sinners* (1666). It is very prolix, and being all about himself, in a man less holy would be intolerably egotistic, but his motive in writing being plainly to exalt the grace of God and to comfort those passing through experiences somewhat like his own, his egotism makes no disagreeable impression.

The works just named have appeared in numerous editions, and are accessible to all. There are several noteworthy collections of editions of the Pilgrim's Progress, e.g., in the British Museum, and in the New York Public Library, collected by the late James Lenox.

Bunyan was a popular preacher as well as a very voluminous author, though most of his works consist of expanded sermons. In theology he was a Puritan, but not a partizan; nor was there anything gloomy about him. The portrait which his friend Robert White drew, which has been often reproduced, is a most attractive one and this was his true character. He was tall, had reddish hair, prominent nose, a rather large mouth, and sparkling eyes. He was no scholar, except of the English Bible, but that he knew thoroughly. Another book which greatly influenced him was Martin Luther's *Commentary on the Epistle to the Galatians*, in the translation of 1575.

[Some time before his final release from prison Bunyan became involved in a controversy with Kiffin, D'Anvers, Deune, Paul, and others. In 1673 he published his *Differences in Judgement about Water-Baptism no Bar to Communion*, in which he took the ground that "the Church of Christ hath not warrant to keep out of the communion the Christian that is discovered to be a visible saint of the word, the Christian that walketh according to his own light with God." While he owned "water-baptism to be God's ordinance," he refused to make "an idol of it," as he thought those did who made the lack of it a ground for disfellowshiping those recognized as genuine Christians. Kiffin and Paul published a rejoinder in *Serious Reflections* (London, 1673), in which they ably set forth the argument in favor of the restriction of the Lord's Supper to baptized believers, and received the approval of Henry D'Anvers in his *Treatise of Baptism* (London, 1674). The result of the controversy was to leave the question of communion with the unbaptized an open one so far as the Particular (Calvinistic) Baptists were concerned. Bunyan's church admitted pedobaptists to fellowship and finally became pedobaptist (Congregationalist). A. H. N.]

BIBLIOGRAPHY: The best edition of Bunyan's *Complete Works* is by G. Offor and R. Philip, 3 vols., London, 1853, new ed., 1862. The best biography is by John Brown, London, 1885, new ed., 1902, the author of which was for many years the minister of the Bunyan chapel at Bedford. Other good biographies are: J. A. Froude, in *English Men of Letters*, 1887; E. Venables, in *Great Writers Series*, 1888; and W. H. White, in *Literary Lives Series*, 1904.

BURCHARD OF WORMS: Bishop of Worms; d. Aug. 20, 1025. He was a Hessian by birth, and was educated at Coblenz and under the famous Olbert in the Flemish monastery of Laubach. Willigis of Mainz ordained him, and employed him in a number of important affairs. Otto III. gave him the bishopric of Worms (1000), which had fallen into a bad condition. He improved the city in many ways; established the episcopal power more firmly and even increased it; demolished the fortress of Duke Otto and built a monastery with the stones from it, placing over the door the inscription *Ob libertatem civitatis*. In 1014 Henry II. gave him secular jurisdiction over the inhabitants, which he used to promote uniformity and security of law. He rebuilt the cathedral, consecrating it in 1016; but his fame rests chiefly on his collection of canon law, which had a very wide circulation not only in Germany but in Italy. (A. HAUCK.)

BIBLIOGRAPHY: The *Decretorum libri viginti* are in *MPL*, cxl. Materials for a life are in *Lex familiæ Wormatiensis ecclesiæ*, *MGH*, *Legum*, section iv., *Constitutiones et acta*, ed. L. Weiland, i. (1893) 639, no. 438; and the anonymous *Vita*, ed. G. H. Pertz in *MGH*, *Script.*, iv. (1841) 829–846, and *MPL*, cxl. 507–536. Consult: Hauck, *KD*, iii. 435; H. G. Gengler, *Das Hofrecht des Burchard von Worms*, Erlangen, 1859; A. M. Königer, *Burchard I. von Worms*, Munich, 1903.

BURCHARD OF WÜRZBURG: Bishop of Würzburg 741–754. He was an Anglo-Saxon who left England after the death of his kinsfolk and joined Boniface in his missionary labors, some time after 732. When Boniface organized bishoprics in Middle Germany, he placed Burchard over that of Würzburg; his consecration can not have occurred later than the summer of 741, since in the autumn of that year we find him officiating as a bishop at the consecration of Willibald of Eichstädt. Pope Zacharias confirmed the new bishopric in 743. Burchard appears again as a member of the first German council in 742, and as an envoy to Rome from Boniface in 748. With Fulrad of Saint-Denis, he brought to Zacharias the famous question of Pepin, whose answer was supposed to justify the assumption of regal power by the Merovingians.

(A. HAUCK.)

BIBLIOGRAPHY: Two anonymous lives, one of the ninth or tenth, the other of the twelfth century, ed. Holder-Egger, are in *MGH*, *Script.*, xv. (1887) 47–62. Consult: A. Nürnberger, *Aus der litterarischen Hinterlassenschaft des . Burchardus*, Neisse, 1888; Rettberg, *KD*, ii. 313; Hauck, *KD*, i. 487 and passim; Neander, *Christian Church*, iv. 203.

BURDER, GEORGE: English Congregationalist; b. in London June 5, 1752; d. there May 29, 1832. He was trained for an artist, but began preaching under the influence of Whitefield and his associates; became minister at Lancaster, 1778; Coventry, 1783; Fetter Lane, London, 1803. He was one of the founders of the London Missionary Society (1795), of the Religious Tract Society (1799), and of the British and Foreign Bible Society (1804), and from 1803 to 1827 served gratuitously as secretary of the first-named, besides editing *The Evangelical Magazine* for many years. The most successful of his many publications were *Village Sermons* (7 vols., London, 1798–1816), and *A Collection of Hymns, Intended as a Supplement to Watts* (1784), which went through some fifty editions and contained three or four hymns of his own.

BIBLIOGRAPHY: There are *Memoirs* by his son, H. F. Burder, London, 1833, and by I. Cobbin, 1856. Consult also *DNB*, vii. 294–295, and for his hymns, S. W. Duffield, *English Hymns*, pp. 121. 508, New York, 1886; Julian, *Hymnology*, p. 194.

BURDINUS, MAURITIUS. See GREGORY VIII., Antipope.

BURGER, KARL HEINRICH AUGUST VON: German theologian; b. at Baireuth (126 m. n. of Munich) May 1, 1805; d. at Schönau (a village near Berchtesgaden, 12 m. s. of Salzburg) July 14, 1885. He studied theology and philology at the University of Erlangen (1823–27), and in 1827 was appointed teacher at the gymnasium there. Eleven years later he became curate at Fürth near Nuremberg, and in 1846 he was transferred in the same capacity to Munich, where he was appointed dean in 1849 and councilor of the high consistory in 1855, holding this office until his resignation in 1883. Under the guidance of his father-in-law, Johann Christian Krafft, of Erlangen, he gained a thorough knowledge of the Bible which was evinced by his *Die Briefe Pauli an die Korinther* (2 vols., Erlangen, 1859–60); *Die Evangelien nach Matthäus, Marcus und Lucas* (Nördlingen, 1865); *Das Evangelium nach Johannes* (1868); and *Die Offenbarung St. Johannis* (Munich, 1877). Interpreting the Bible by the Bible, he sought to render his work available for the educated laity, while clergymen also find it valuable in the preparation of sermons. His interpretation of Revelation has met with special favor in Württemberg. While his sermons were not couched in popular style, and while they demanded close attention on account of their logic and depth, they appealed effectually to serious auditors, and two collections of them were published, *Predigten in der protestantischen Stadtpfarrkirche zu München gehalten* (Erlangen, 1857) and *Predigten für alle Sonn- und Festtage des Kirchenjahres* (2 vols., Nördlingen, 1864). As a member of the high consistory, Burger aided the Bavarian Church to surmount rationalism and to become a true evangelical Lutheran body, and his task was facilitated by his thorough knowledge of philosophy, history, and theology, as well as by his tact and discretion. Despite his reserved and quiet nature, which shunned all publicity, he enjoyed the deep esteem and gratitude of the clergy and their congregations, as well as the confidence of the three kings of Bavaria under whom he served, Louis I., Maximilian II., and Louis II.

KARL BURGER†.

BURGES, bŭr′jes, CORNELIUS: Presbyterian; b. in Somersetshire (date undetermined, probably 1589); d. at Watford (7 m. s.w. of St. Albans), buried there June 9, 1665. He was educated at Oxford in Wadham and other colleges; was vicar of Watford (1613–45), also (1626–41) rector of St. Magnus Church in London, holding the two charges at the same time. On the accession of Charles I. (1625), he was appointed one of the chaplains in ordinary. He was appointed a member of the Westminster Assembly in 1643. July 8 he was chosen by them assessor with Dr. White, and generally occupied the chair on account of the illness of Dr. Twisse. He was chairman of the first of the three grand committees of the Assembly, and one of the most energetic members of the body, being active especially in the discussion of Church Government and the Directory for Worship. He was energetic in political as well as ecclesiastical affairs. On the Restoration his handsome property was confiscated, and he died in want. His chief works are: *A Chain of Graces Drawn out at Length for Reformation of Manners* (London, 1622); *The Fire of the Sanctuary newly Discovered or a Compleat Tract of Zeal* (1625); and *Baptismal Regeneration of Elect Infants* (Oxford, 1629). In the latter he maintains: "It is most agreeable to the Institution of Christ that all elect infants that are baptized (unless in some extraordinary cases doe, ordinarily, receive, from Christ, the Spirit in

Baptism, for their first solemn initiation into Christ, and for their future actual renovation, in God s good time, if they live to yeares of discretion, and enjoy the ordinary means of grace appointed of God to this end." He delivered a large number of sermons before Parliament and other civil bodies, which were published from time to time. He is credited also with the paper subscribed by the London ministers, entitled *A Vindication of the ministers of the Gospel in and about London from the unjust Aspersions cast upon their former Actings for the Parliament, as if they had promoted the Bringing of the King to Capital Punishment*, London, 1648. C. A. Briggs.

Bibliography: A. à Wood, *Athenæ Oxonienses*, ed. P. Bliss, iii. 681; D. Neal, *History of the Puritans*, ii. 365, 368, iv. 332, Dublin, 1759; *DNB*, vii. 301-304 (quite detailed).

BURGESS, ANTHONY: Non-conformist clergyman. He entered St. John's College, Cambridge, in 1623 and became fellow of Emmanuel; was vicar of Sutton Coldfield, Warwickshire, in 1635; member of the Westminster Assembly; ejected by the Uniformity Act of 1662 after the Restoration, and lived afterward in retirement at Tamworth (14 m. n.w. of Birmingham). He wrote: *Vindiciæ Legis* (London, 1646); *The True Doctrine of Justification Asserted* (1648); *Spiritual Refining*, 120 sermons (1652; 2d ed., 161 sermons, 1658); *Expository Sermons* (145) on John xvii. (1656); *The Scripture Directory* (a commentary on I Corinthians iii.), *to which is Annexed the Godly and Natural Man's Choice*, upon Psalm iv. 6-8 (1659); *The Doctrine of Original Sin Asserted* (1659).

BURGESS, DANIEL: English Presbyterian; b. at Staines (15 m. w.s.w. of London), Middlesex, 1645; d. in London Jan. 26, 1713. He studied at Magdalen Hall, Oxford, but would not conform and so did not graduate; went to Ireland in 1667 with Roger Boyle, earl of Orrery, and became master of a school founded by his patron at Charleville, County Cork; was ordained by the Dublin presbytery; in 1685 he settled in London, where he gained influential friends and preached to a large congregation attracted by his lively and witty style. Besides preaching he took pupils and was tutor to Henry St. John (Lord Bolingbroke). His publications were numerous, mostly sermons; they include: *Directions for Daily Holy Living* (London, 1690); *The Golden Snuffers; or Christian Reprovers and Reformers Characterized, Cautioned, and Encouraged* (1697); *Proof of God's Being and of the Scriptures' Divine Original, with Twenty Directions for Reading them* (1697).

BURGESS, FREDERICK: Protestant Episcopal bishop of Long Island; b. at Providence, R. I., Oct. 6, 1853. He was educated at Brown University (B.A., 1873), the General Theological Seminary (1874-75), and Oxford University (1876), and was successively rector of Grace Church, Amherst, Mass. (1878-83), Christ Church, Pomfret, Conn. (1883-89), Grace Church, Bala, Pa. (1889-96), Christ Church, Detroit (1896-98), and Grace Church, Brooklyn (1898-1902). In 1902 he was consecrated bishop of Long Island.

BURGESS, GEORGE: First Protestant Episcopal bishop of Maine; b. at Providence, R. I., Oct. 31, 1809; d. at sea while returning from the West Indies Apr. 23, 1866. He was graduated at Brown 1826; tutor there 1829-31; studied at Bonn, Göttingen, and Berlin 1831-34; was rector of Christ Church, Hartford, 1834-47; consecrated bishop Oct. 31, 1847 He published a translation of the Psalms into English verse (New York, 1840), *Pages from the Ecclesiastical History of New England between 1740 and 1840* (Boston, 1847), and other works.

Bibliography: *Memoir of Life of Rev. Geo. Burgess*, by his brother, A. Burgess, Philadelphia, 1869.

BURGESS, HENRY: Church of England clergyman and scholar; b. in Newington, London, Jan. 29, 1808; d. Feb. 10, 1886. He studied at the Dissenting College, Stepney; after graduation (1830) was for a time a Baptist minister, but decided to join the Church of England in 1849, was ordained deacon 1850, and priest 1851; became curate at Blackburn 1851; perpetual curate of Clifton Reynes, Buckinghamshire, 1854; vicar of St. Andrew, Whittlesea, Cambridgeshire, 1861. His principal works were translations from the Syriac of the *Festal Letters of St. Athanasius* (London, 1852) and of *Select Metrical Hymns and Homilies of Ephraem Syrus, with an introduction and historical and philological notes* (1853); *The Reformed Church of England in its Principles and their Legitimate Development* (1869); *Essays, Biblical and Ecclesiastical, relating chiefly to the authority and interpretation of the Holy Scriptures* (1873); *The Art of Preaching and the Composition of Sermons* (1881). He edited *The Clerical Journal* 1854-68, *The Journal of Sacred Literature* 1854-62, and the second edition of Kitto's *Cyclopædia of Biblical Literature* (2 vols., Edinburgh, 1856).

BURGHERS AND ANTIBURGHERS. See Presbyterians.

BURGON, JOHN WILLIAM: Church of England scholar; b. at Smyrna (the son of a Turkey merchant) Aug. 21, 1813; d. at Chichester Aug. 4, 1888. He studied at London University (University College) 1829-30 and then entered his father's counting-house; matriculated at Worcester College, Oxford, 1841, and was graduated B.A., 1845; elected fellow of Oriel 1846, graduated M.A., 1848, B.D., 1871; ordained deacon 1848 and held curacies in Berkshire and Oxfordshire; became vicar of St. Mary's Oxford, 1863; Gresham professor of divinity 1867; was installed dean of Chichester 1876. He has been described as "a High-churchman of the old school," and he won distinction at Oxford as a vehement "champion of lost causes and impossible beliefs." He was the ablest and most learned as well as the bitterest adverse critic of the Revised New Testament and of the revised Greek text. His publications, including sermons, articles in the periodicals, and controversial tracts, were very numerous; among the most noteworthy of his books were: *The Life and Times of Sir Thomas Gresham* (2 vols., London, 1839); *A Plain Commentary on the Four Holy Gospels* (8 vols., 1855); *Ninety Short Sermons for Family Reading* (2 series, each 2 vols., 1855, 1867); *Historical Notices of the Colleges of Oxford* (1857); *Portrait of a Christian Gentleman, a Memoir of P. F. Tytler* (1859); *Inspiration and Interpretation*, seven sermons in answer to *Essays and Reviews* (Oxford, 1861); *The Last Twelve Verses of the Gospel according to St. Mark Vindicated and Established* (1871); *The Revision Revised*, articles reprinted from *The Quarterly Review* against the Revised Version of the New Testament (London, 1883); *The Lives of Twelve Good Men* (2 vols., 1888). *The Traditional Text of the Holy Gospels Vindicated and Established* and *Causes of the Corruption of the Traditional Text*, edited by Edward Miller, appeared in 1896.

Bibliography: E. M. Goulburn, *John W. Burgon: a Biography, with Letters and Journals*, 2 vols., London, 1891; *DNB*, supplement vol. i. 335-338.

BURGUNDIANS: A Germanic race, akin to the Goths and Vandals, whose earliest known home was on the Baltic between the Oder and the Vistula. In the middle of the second century they had begun to move southward; in the middle of the third they were driven further to the southwest, and occupied what is now Franconia, north and east of Lyons. With their neighbors on the southwest, the Alemanni, they had many conflicts, and summoned the aid of the Romans; they are found cooperating on the Rhine with Valentinian I. against them in 370. Next they occupied the right bank of the river, and the Vandal invasion of Gaul in the fifth century carried them across with it, to receive an allotment of land in *Germania prima*, a province of Gaul, in 413, and become subject to the empire. By this time they had adopted the religion of their Roman neighbors, probably almost in a body. Peaceful relations with the Romans did not last long, however. In 435 King Gundicar attacked the first Belgian province, but was driven back by Aëtius. A year later they were again defeated by the Huns, acting with the Romans, and lost their king and much of their power. But they must have recovered before many years, for in 457, with the consent of the West-Goths, they occupied the province *Lugdunensis prima;* in the following decade they extended their rule over the *Provincia Viennensis;* and about 472 they added the greater part of the *Maxima Sequanorum*. After Gundicar's death, his sons Gunduic and Chilperic I. shared the kingship, and the latter reigned alone after his brother's death. Gunduic's son, Gundobad, succeeded Chilperic; he had three brothers, Godegisel, Chilperic II., and Godomar. Godegisel appears as a partaker of his sovereignty; Chilperic was said to have been put to death by his order, but this is not certain, as Avitus speaks of Chilperic's death and Godomar's (which happened early in his reign) as a great blow to him. Gundobad was succeeded by his son Sigismund, who was captured by the Frankish kings in 523 and put to death in the next year. His brother Godomar II. maintained himself against the Franks for ten years; but he also succumbed, and in 534 the Burgundian territory became part of the Frankish kingdom.

The religious development of the Burgundians during the progress of these events is peculiar. They had come from the Rhine to the Rhone as Catholic Christians; but most of them joined the Arians in their new home. The royal house seems to have been slow to change; Gunduic and Chilperic II. were Catholics; but Gregory of Tours mentions Gundobad, with his brother Godegisel, as Arians. The change to Arianism seems to have followed from the feudal relations of the Burgundians to their more powerful West-Gothic neighbors. Gundobad was not a persecutor, though some churches were taken from the Catholics; Avitus of Vienne seems even to have had hopes of his conversion. But, though the bishop failed with the father, he succeeded with the son; Sigismund returned to the Church in his father's lifetime, followed by many of the people. But not until Gundobad's death did the decisive movement away from Arianism occur. Sigismund's son Sigeric followed his father's example, and Godomar had become a Catholic even earlier. In 517 a synod was held at Epao, the present Albo, south of Vienne (see Epao, Synod of), the decrees of which plainly show that Arianism was no longer dangerous, and that the time for its total suppression was believed to have come. Certainly it disappeared from that time, though no exact date can be assigned. By the union with the Frankish kingdom, the Burgundian Church lost its independence and became merely a part of the Frankish ecclesiastical organization. (A. Hauck.)

Bibliography: Sources are to be found in *MGH, Legum*, section iii., *Concilia*, vol. i., ed. F. Maassen, 1893; *MGH, Leges*, ed. G. H. Pertz, vol. iii., 1863; *Chronica Minora sæc. iv-vii*, ed. T. Mommsen, in *MGH, Auct. ant.*, vols. ix. (1892), xiii., part i. (1894); G. S. A. Sidonius, *Epistolarum libri, Carmina*, ed. C. Lütjohann, in *MGH, Auct. ant.*, viii. (1887) 1-204; A. E. Aviti, *Opera*, ed. R. Pieper, in *MGH, Auct. ant.*, vii., part 2 (1883). Consult: H. Derichsweiler, *Geschichte der Burgunden*, Münster, 1863; A. Jahn, *Die Geschichte der Burgundionen*, 2 vols., Halle, 1874; P. Milsand, *Bibliographie bourguignonne*, 2 vols., Dijon, 1885-88; L. M. J. Chaumont, *Histoire de Bourgogne*, Lyons, 1887; Rettberg, *KD*, vol. i.; Hauck, *KD*, vol. i.; Neander, *Christian Church*, vols. iii., iv., passim.

BURIAL.

I. Hebrew: In all periods interment was the customary Hebrew method of disposing of the dead. I Sam. xxxi. 12 and Amos vi. 10, in spite of the corrupt condition of the text, show that burning was exceptional; indeed, incineration implied something discreditable to the dead and in ancient custom and the priest-code was an intensification of the death-penalty (Josh. vii. 25; Lev. xx. 14). Aversion to incineration accompanied ancient belief in the existence of a bond between soul and body even after death. The spirits of the unburied dead wandered restless on the earth, and in Sheol their lot was pitiable, driven as they were into nooks and corners (Ezek. xxii. 23). The grave confined the soul to the body so as to give it repose and save it from injury. Consequently it was not merely an awful disgrace but a terrible misfortune not to be buried (I Kings xiv. 11; II Kings ix. 10; Isa. xxxiii. 12). Hence it was a sacred duty to inter a body found unburied. In the case of criminals stoned to death a heap of stones over the body served as a grave (Josh. vii. 26).

The climate of Palestine necessitated the quickest possible disposition of the corpse; interment, therefore, took place on the day of death (Deut. xxi. 23). In the time of Christ the body was washed, anointed with fragrant spices, and more or less completely wrapped in linen (Acts. ix. 37; Mark xvi. 1; John xi. 44). The Old Testament makes no allusion to this custom. The belief that the dead in Sheol might be recognized by the habit implies that in early times the corpse was buried in the apparel of daily life. Later, royalty and officials were buried with costly spices, ornaments, gold, and silver (Josephus, *Ant.*, XIII. viii. 4; XV. iii. 4). And if the account by Josephus of the plundering of David's tomb by Hyrcanus and Herod may be trusted, this custom reached back into antiquity. Embalming was a custom foreign to the Hebrews; cases of it are Jacob and Joseph (Gen. l. 2, 26) and Aristobulus (Josephus, *Ant.*, XIV. vii. 4). The use of coffins was post-exilic.

1. Preparation for Burial.

The place of burial was determined by the belief that the ties of kinship lasted beyond death. The value of a family burying-place was in part due to the fact that burial therein involved union with kin in Sheol (Gen. xxv. 8, 17; II Sam. xxi. 14). Therefore, family tombs were in the earliest ages on the estate and near the house (I Sam. xxv. 1). Therein might be laid only members of the family. A public cemetery was provided for the very poor, for foreigners, and for criminals (Jer. xxvi. 23; Isa. liii. 9; Matt. xxvii. 7). The kings of Judah had tombs in Jerusalem, and Ezekiel charges them with the serious offense of laying their dead next to the precincts of the sanctuary. To miss burial with one's kin was dire misfortune or divine punishment. For practical reasons people began quite early to locate tombs outside the cities, and graves came to be regarded as ceremonially impure. In the time of Christ tombs were whitewashed in order that their character might be known at a distance and defilement avoided (Matt. xxiii. 27; Luke xi. 44).

2. Place.

The grave was simple in its appointments. Wherever in Jewish tombs rich ornamentation is found, foreign influence (generally Greek) is recognized. Apart from the general lack of artistic sense displayed by the Hebrews, a religious consideration comes in to explain this: the stern opposition of the Yahweh-cult to ancestor-worship discouraged adornment of burial-places, which thus differed widely from Egyptian and Phenician tombs. This and the lack of inscriptions make it difficult to determine the date of Jewish graves. For situation, rocky chambers, natural or artificial, were preferred.

Four kinds of graves are known: (1) recess-graves, oblong, rock-hewn, about six feet long by one and a half square, hewn lengthwise into the wall of the chamber, into which the body was placed from the end; (2) sunken-graves, like those used in the Occident, but covered with stone; (3) bench-graves, set bench-like in the walls of the chamber, twenty-two inches high, often arch-roofed and hewn sidewise into the chamber-wall; (4) trough-graves, a combination of (2) and (3) above. Of the chambers there are three varieties: (1) single chambers with a single sunken grave in the floor; (2) single chambers with several graves of one or more of the above-mentioned kinds; (3) larger burial-places with more than one chamber. All of the third variety so far found belong to a late date, as is proved by the architecture. The oldest and commonest are of the second type, single chambers with recess-graves, which are so typical that they may be named specifically Hebrew. Such allow the largest number of interments in a given chamber. Shaft-tombs of the Egyptian pattern have so far not been discovered in Palestine.

3. Varieties of Graves.

The Phenician custom of marking an excavated grave by a grave-stone other than the stone-heap piled on it was not adopted by the Hebrews. The tombs built above ground date from the Greek period, or later, and are of foreign origin.

(I. Benzinger.)

Bibliography: F. I. Grundt, *Die Trauergebräuche der Hebräer*, Leipsic, 1868; W. M. Thomson, *The Land and the Book*, New York, 1886; F. Schwally, *Das Leben nach dem Tode nach den Vorstellungen des alten Israel und des Judentums*, Giessen, 1892; Benzinger, *Archäologie*, pp. 136–137; Nowack, *Archäologie*, i. 187; H. B. Tristram, *Eastern Customs in Bible Lands*, London, 1894; A. P. Bender, *Beliefs, Rites and Customs of the Jews connected with Death, Burial and Mourning*, in *JQR*, 1894–95; G. M. Mackie, *Bible Manners and Customs*, London, 1895; *KL*, ii. 182–189; *DB*, i. 331–333.

II. Christian: From the beginning the Christians regarded the final disposal of the dead as a congregational matter, and, when possible, they had burial-places, in which only those who were their members might be buried and which were called *cœmeteria* ("resting-places"), in allusion to the resurrection (see Cemeteries). In deference to the body as the organ of the spirit and in the expectation of the resurrection, they were careful that the funeral should take place in a proper manner. The corpse was carried to the grave by bearers whom the Christian congregation had appointed, and the fact that the funeral took place, if possible, in day-time, was designed to express joy and hope that the departed had been set free and had entered into eternal life. The pagan lamentation for the dead, as well as the crowning of the corpse, was not approved, but torches were carried in front, as befitting the victorious combatant, and hymns and psalms were sung, in praise of God. A memorial address was doubtless made on special occasions, but a funeral sermon in the modern sense seems to have been unknown. Prayers were

1. Early Practise and Ceremonies.

offered at the grave, and the survivors gave food and money to the poor. Prayers were made for the deceased, not only in private, but also in public. The third, seventh (or ninth), thirtieth (or fortieth) day were memorial days, on which the church ceremony for the dead took place, as well as on the anniversary of death (see CEMETERIES, II., 6). These prayers and offerings were believed to have a beneficial effect for the dead, provided he belonged to the saved.

2. The Greek Church. The Greek Church preserves a remnant of the idea that the death of a Christian invites to praise, and on this account uses the Hallelujah in the celebration at the church The requiem-mass is unknown, but additional prayers are offered for the dead. The ceremony at the grave is very brief, the priest throwing earth upon the corpse with the spade and sprinkling it with oil from the holy lamp or ashes from the censer.

3. The Medieval Church. The Western Church of the Middle Ages also knew only of burial as a means of disposal of the dead. Charlemagne forbade the conquered Saxons to cremate corpses on pain of death. The place in which a Christian was buried was considered holy ground, but patrons or spiritual dignitaries were entombed in churches in token of distinction. Every Christian was to be buried in consecrated ground, but if special emergencies, like war or shipwreck, necessitated a burial in unconsecrated ground, the grave had to be provided with a cross. The dead was washed, dressed in linen or penitential robes, or, in case of one in holy orders, in official dress. On the day of the funeral he was carried by his peers, the layman by laymen, and the clergy by clergy, first to the church, where mass was celebrated, and afterward to the grave, in which he was laid, with his face turned toward the East. Various ceremonies had their meaning; the holy water sprinkled on the body protected it from demons; charcoal indicated that there was a grave there and thus kept it from profanation; incense kept away the odor of decay, and was a symbol of prayer for the dead, as implying that he was a sacrifice well pleasing to God; ivy and laurel symbolized the imperishable life of those who die in Christ. The custom of throwing three shovelfuls of earth upon the body was known in the Middle Ages, although the present Roman ritual does not mention it. The modern Roman Catholic Church has retained the old Christian view that the death of little children who have been baptized is a joyful event and that their burial should have the character of joy.

4. The Reformation Burial Service. The Reformation made a clean sweep of the existing burial rites, in so far as they presupposed the doctrines of purgatory, mass, and the mediation of the Church, but it adhered to the view that the dead body is not a worthless thing but is to rise again, no matter how it has decayed. On this account it should have a Christian burial, and the burial-places must have a fitting appearance. The burial was a matter of the church, and the congregation should take part in it, if possible, and should also attend the funerals of the poor. Accordingly, the bells called the congregation together. The church was represented by the minister and the school-children, or at least by the sexton and grave-digger. As the procession was passing to the cemetery, the children or the mourners sang Christian funeral hymns, and at the grave such Biblical passages as I Thess. iv. 13–18 or John xi. were read and prayer was offered, while basins were also placed to receive alms for the poor. The burial service of the Reformed was similar. In some countries the congregation recited the creed after the closing prayer.

The desire to instruct the congregation on every occasion was expressed in the burial service by the reading of Scripture and the singing of hymns. A short discourse on death and the resurrection was read in the home, in the church, or at the grave, although a special sermon might be requested of the minister if he was specially paid for it, and in such cases he referred particularly to the life and death of the subject of his address. Thus arose the funeral sermon, which was originally designed to instruct the congregation in eschatology, and to honor the memory of the departed.

5. Modern Developments. In modern times the burial rites were extended by carrying the cross before the procession, by casting earth upon the body thrice, and by pronouncing the benediction. The first two ceremonies were known even among the Protestants in former centuries and were occasionally used, although they were generally regarded with distrust, and were even directly prohibited. The blessing is connected with the prayer for the dead. The Reformed rejected prayers for the dead unconditionally, while Luther and the Augsburg Confession permitted it, and Johann Gerhard endeavored to prove its validity by dogmatics. From this developed the blessing of the dead, which, despite vehement opposition since the middle of the nineteenth century, has spread more and more. That the dead is addressed by "thou," may perhaps be explained on the ground that, according to the ancient Christian view, the congregation regards the departed as still belonging to it. The meaning of the solemn declaration: "I bless thee," however, is very uncertain, and the blessing should take the form of a wish.

It should be noted that the Church of Rome prohibits cremation, whereas the Protestant Churches have not yet reached a uniform conclusion.

W CASPARI.

BIBLIOGRAPHY: On the general question consult C. Martène, *De antiquis ecclesiæ ritibus*, Antwerp, 1736–37; F. X. Kraus, *Realencyklopädie der christlichen Alterthümer*, articles *Tod*, *Totenbestattung*, Freiburg, 1880–96; T. Kliefoth, *Liturgische Abhandlungen*, vol. i., part 2, *Vom Begräbniss*, Halle, 1869; Bingham, *Origines*, book xxiii. On the antiquarian and legal sides of English custom consult: J. Stutt, *A Compleat View of the Manners, Customs . . . of the Inhabitants of England*, 3 vols., London, 1775–1776; C. A. Cripps, *Law of Church and Clergy*, ib. 1886; T. Baker, *Law of Burials*, 6th ed., by E. L. Thomas, ib. 1898; *Encyclopædia Britannica*, xxvi. 466–468.

BURIDAN, bur'i-dan or French bü"rî"dān', **JEAN** (*Johannes Buridanus*): Medieval French philosopher; b. at Béthune (25 m. n.w. of Douai), in the latter part of the thirteenth century; d. after 1358. He was educated at Paris, and was made rector in 1327 The story of his expulsion from the city, like his love affair with a queen of France, seems to be a myth, for it is clear that he occupied a prominent position at Paris between 1348 and 1358. He was the author of the *Summula de dialectica*, or *Compendium logicæ* (Paris, 1487), and also wrote on the "Politics," "Ethics," and other Aristotelian writings, but he paid no attention to theology. As an admirer and follower of Occam, he was a consistent nominalist, and hence felt a special interest in ethical and psychological questions, in which he showed the characteristic union of skepticism and dogmatism. He became famous by his thorough research into the problem of the freedom of the will, but his works contain ingenious investigations rather than clear decisions, so that it is doubtful whether he was a determinist or an indeterminist. His psychology allowed no decision of the will without a motivating judgment of the understanding. The famous aphorism of the ass standing between two hay-stacks, and obliged either to starve or to decide deterministically for one or the other, is not found in his writings, and it is uncertain whether either he or his opponents used it, or whether later legend ascribed to him the example already found in Aristotle. His collected works were first edited at Paris by J. Dullardus in 1500, and were frequently reprinted.

R. SCHMID.

BIBLIOGRAPHY: Sketches of his life and philosophy will be found in the works on the history of philosophy by Ueberweg, Ritter, and Erdmann. Consult also A. Stöckl, *Geschichte der Philosophie des Mittelalters*, ii. 1023–28, 3 vols., Mainz, 1864–66.

BURKE, THOMAS MARTIN ALOYSIUS: Roman Catholic bishop of Albany, N. Y.; b. in County Mayo, Ireland, Jan. 10, 1840. He came to the United States in childhood, and was educated at St. Michael's College, Toronto, St. Charles' College, Md. (B.A., 1861), and St. Mary's Seminary, Baltimore (B.T., 1864). He was ordained to the priesthood in 1864, and was successively assistant and rector at St. John's Church, Albany, N. Y. (1864–74), and rector of St. Joseph's Church in the same city (1874–94). He was appointed vicar-general of the diocese of Albany in 1887 and consecrated bishop in 1894. He was created a Knight of the Holy Sepulcher in 1890, and a Knight of the Grand Cross in 1894.

BURKITT, FRANCIS CRAWFORD: Church of England theologian and Syriac scholar; b. at London Sept. 3, 1864. He was educated at Trinity College, Cambridge (B.A., 1886), where he was appointed University lecturer in paleography in 1904–05. Since 1905 he has been Norrisian professor of divinity in the same university. He was elected fellow of the British Academy in 1905, and was also president of the Cambridge Philological Society in 1904–05 and Jowett lecturer in 1906. In addition to numerous contributions to theological periodicals and encyclopedias, he has written: *The Rules of Tyconius* (Cambridge, 1894); *The Old Latin and the Itala* (1896); *Fragments of Aquila* (1897); *Hymn of Bardaisan* (London, 1899); *Early Christianity outside the Roman Empire* (Cambridge, 1899); *Two Lectures on the Gospels* (London, 1900); *Gospel Quotations of St. Ephraim* (Cambridge, 1901); *Evangelion da-Mepharreshe* (2 vols., 1904); and *Early Eastern Christianity* (London, 1905). He also made an English translation of the *Lehrbuch der ägypto-arabischen Umgangssprache* of K. Vollers (Cairo, 1890) at Cambridge in 1895, and collaborated with R. L. Bensly and J. R. Harris in editing *The Four Gospels in Syriac transcribed from the Sinaitic Manuscript* (Cambridge, 1894), and with G. H. Gwilliam and J. F. Stenning in the *Biblical and Patristic Relics of the Palestinian Syriac Literature from Manuscripts in the Bodleian Library* (Oxford, 1896).

BURKITT, WILLIAM: Church of England; b. at Hitcham (12 m. n.w. of Ipswich), Suffolk, July 25, 1650; d. at Dedham (10 m. s.w. of Ipswich), Essex, Oct. 24, 1703. He studied at Pembroke Hall, Cambridge (B.A., 1668; M.A., 1672); became curate at Milden, Suffolk, about 1672, and vicar of Dedham, 1692. He is remembered for his *Expository Notes with Practical Observations on the New Testament* (the Gospels, London, 1700; Acts–Revelation, 1703; many subsequent editions). It is a compilation and bears some resemblance to the commentaries of Matthew Henry.

BURMA: [At present the largest and easternmost province of British India, having been gradually annexed after three wars in 1826, 1852, and 1885. It extends southward from Tibet into the Malay peninsula a distance of 1,250 miles, with a breadth from east to west varying from 30 or 10 to 550 miles. According to the census of 1901 the area is 236,738 square miles, the population 10,490,624 persons, classed by religions as follows: Hindus 457,391; Sikhs 3,147; Buddhists 8,951,649 (85.3 per cent.); Mohammedans 533,973; Christians 248,628; Animists 294,787; other religions 1,049. The native peoples are of Malay-Chinese stock, belonging to many tribes. The capital is Rangun. Buddhism appears at its best in Burma; the prevailing form is of the southern type, most closely approximating the teachings of Gautama, and it has done much to uplift the people, who are better educated (by the Buddhist monks) than the people of India. Temples and shrines are numerous and have been built at much expense. The monasteries are well organized.]

Baptist Missions: The earliest attempt at Protestant missionary work in Burma was at Rangun, where Messrs. Chater and Mardon, of the Baptist Missionary Society of England, opened a mission in 1807. During a service of four years Chater translated the Gospel of Matthew into Burmese. Felix Carey, son of William Carey (q.v.), came soon after Chater and Mardon, remaining until 1814, when he entered the service of the Burman Government and removed to Ava. The London Missionary Society sent two missionaries to Rangun in 1808, but within a year one died and the other left.

The first permanent Protestant mission in Burma was that of the American Baptist Missionary Union, which began work at Rangun in 1813. The first missionary was Adoniram Judson (q.v.), who translated the Bible into Burmese. Six years after he landed in Rangun the first convert was baptized, and then the work among the Burmans progressed, although slowly.

The Karens, a hill tribe, early attracted the attention of the missionaries. They had strange traditions that they once had known of the true God, and that foreigners would restore to them the lost knowledge and the book containing it. In 1828 the first Karen convert, a slave redeemed by Dr. Judson, was baptized by Rev. George Dana Boardman (q.v.). The Karens have been more receptive of the Gospel than any other race in Burma. They are divided into many tribes; the chief dialects are the Sgaw and the Pwo, into which the Bible has been translated. Self-support has been a marked feature of the Karen churches. They are distinctly missionary in spirit, representatives having gone from them to many other races. A remarkable development in the Karen mission is an independent evangelistic movement inaugurated and directed by a native leader, Ko San Ye. Large buildings have been erected and an institutional work is carried on. In one year over 2,500 converts were baptized in two stations alone as a result of this movement.

.Work is conducted also among the Shans, the Chins, the Kachins, the Talains, the immigrants from peninsular India (mostly Telugus and Tamils), the Chinese, and the Eurasians and other English-speaking peoples. A movement of large proportions is taking place among the Lahu and other hill tribes about Kengtung, in eastern Burma, where over 2,000 were baptized in 1905. They have peculiar traditions similar to those of the Karens.

Educational work has been emphasized, village day-schools, station boarding-schools, and the Rangun Baptist College being conducted in cooperation with the government. The college has over 1,000 students in all departments. There are two theological seminaries at Insein, for Karens and Burmans respectively. The American Baptist Mission Press, at Rangun, has a fine equipment, and prints literature in most of the languages and dialects of the province.

Statistics (1906): Stations, 29; churches, 843; members, 58,642; baptisms, 7,069; missionaries, 192, including 13 physicians; native workers, 1,909; schools, 696, pupils, 24,807: Sunday-schools, 518, pupils, 19,730; college, 1; theological seminaries, 2; high schools, 3; boarding-schools, 31; hospitals, 3; in-patients, 77, out-patients, 23,093; dispensaries, 7; receipts in medical fees, $1,155; total contributions, $91,101 (benevolence, $19,666).

American Methodist Episcopal Missions: American Methodists entered Burma in 1879, when a church was organized by Bishop Thoburn. The mission has now grown to nine stations, where work is conducted for English-speaking peoples, Burmese, Tamils, Telugus, and Chinese. Emphasis is placed upon schools, colportage, and street preaching. The European high school in Rangun, for boys and girls, is the only one for non-conformists in the city and has a well-earned reputation for thoroughness and moral training. Anglo-vernacular schools are conducted in several stations. A number of strong schools are now being equipped with new and larger buildings. A training institute is held during the summer months. At Thandaung a successful orphanage is conducted. A monthly paper for Telugus is published.

Statistics (1905): Missionaries, 17; native helpers, 44; members, 561; probationers, 370; baptized adults, 46, children, 28; high schools, 4; day-schools, 10; pupils, 943; Sunday-schools, 26; Sunday-school pupils, 986; churches and chapels, 3; contributions on field, 44,319 rupees [= $21,494].

Society for the Propagation of the Gospel: This society conducts work among English-speaking peoples, Burmese, Karens, Tamils, Telugus, and Chins. Educational work is vigorously pushed, the leading institution being St. John's College, at Rangun, whose graduates take high rank. A printing-press at Toungoo provides Bibles, prayer-books, and other literature. There are 35 missionaries, 13 being European.

Statistics (1905): Outstations, 196; churches, 15; boarding-schools, 75; teachers, 125 (14 non-Christian); boarders, 549; pupils in all schools, 3,366; catechists, 139; readers, 4; baptisms, adult 722, children 753; baptized persons, 10,403; communicants, 4,047; catechumens, 3,531; confirmed during year, 273; native contributions, 11,759 rupees, 12 annas [= $5,703].

Wesleyan Methodist Missions: English Wesleyans began work in 1889 and have now four stations, with seven missionaries. Special features are the work among soldiers, evangelistic-educational work, and a lepers' home, at Mandalay, which has 140 in its wards.

Statistics (1903): Chapels and other preaching places, 26; catechists, 5; local preachers, 19; teachers (day-school), 62; members, 270; on trial, 61; Sunday-schools, 19; pupils in Sunday-schools, 1,065; day-schools, 25; pupils in day-schools, 1,181; raised locally, £3,450 17s. 3d. The average attendance at public worship is 1,550.

Roman Catholic Missions: Roman Catholic missionaries have been on the ground for several centuries, and are about equally divided between French and Italian. Their work is in various parts of Burma. The statistics for the French Foreign Missionary Society, including those for Laos, are as follows (1906): Missionaries, 70; native workers, 3; charities, 65; total Roman Catholic population, 56,600.

Miscellaneous: Besides the organizations mentioned, the Young Men's Christian Association and the Young Women's Christian Association have work at Rangun. The Mission to Lepers, the Missionary Pence Association, and the Leipsic Missionary Society also have work in Burma. The China Inland Mission has one missionary in Bhamo.

STACY REUBEN WARBURTON.

BIBLIOGRAPHY: *The Life of Adoniram Judson*, by F. Wayland, Boston, 1853, and by E. Judson, Philadelphia, 1898; Mrs. M. Wylie, *Story of the Gospel in Burmah*, New York, 1860; Mrs. Mason, *Civilizing Mountain Men*, . *Mission Work among the Karens*, ib. 1862; C. J. S. F. Forbes, *British Burmah and its People*, . *Manners, Customs and Religion*, London, 1878; J. H. Titcomb, *British Burmah and its Mission Work*, ib. 1880; Mrs. I. B. Bishop, *Golden Chersonese*, ib. 1883; C. H. Carpenter, *Self Support in Bassein*, Boston, 1884; A. R. Colquhoun, *Amongst the Shans*, London, 1885; L. P. Brockett, *Story of the Karen Mission in Bassein*, Philadelphia, 1891; W. N. Wythe, *Missionary Memorials, Ann H. Judson, Sara B. Judson, Emily C. Judson*, 3 vols., New York, 1892; E. D. Cuming, *With the Jungle Folk*, London, 1897;

A. Bunker, *Soo Thah, . Making of the Karen Nation*, New York, 1902; Julius Smith, *Ten Years in Burmah*, Cincinnati, 1902; W. C. Griggs, *Odds and Ends from Pagoda Land*, Philadelphia, 1906.

BURMANN, FRANS: Dutch theologian; b. at Leyden 1628; d. at Utrecht Nov. 12, 1679. At twenty-three he took the pastoral charge of a new Dutch church at Hanau; in 1661 he became vice-rector of the college at Leyden, and the next year professor of dogmatic theology at Utrecht, combining this position with a pastoral charge there, and teaching church history also from 1671. His principal work, *Synopsis theologiæ* (2 vols., Utrecht, 1671–72), shows him to have been the clearest systematic thinker of the school of Cocceius (q.v.). He also wrote Dutch commentaries on all the historical books of the Old Testament (collected edition Amsterdam, 1740), and several minor works.
(E. F. KARL MÜLLER.)

BURN, RICHARD: Legal writer; b. at Winton (37 m. s.e. of Carlisle), Westmoreland, 1709; d. at Orton, Westmoreland (10 m. w. of Winton), Nov. 12, 1785. He studied at Queen's College, Oxford (B.A., 1734); became vicar of Orton 1736, and was justice of the peace for Westmoreland and Cumberland; chancellor of Carlisle 1765. His works include two standard treatises, *The Justice of the Peace and Parish Officer, comprehending all the law to the present time* (2 vols., London, 1755; 29th edition, enlarged, edited by Chitty and Bere, 6 vols., 1845; 30th ed., 1869); and *Ecclesiastical Law* (2 vols., 1763; 9th edition, with additions, by Phillimore, 4 vols., 1842).

BURNET, GILBERT: Bishop of Salisbury; b. in Edinburgh Sept. 18, 1643; d. at Salisbury Mar. 17, 1715. He was educated at Aberdeen; became a probationer 1661; studied and traveled in England, Holland, and France till 1664; became minister at Saltoun 1665; professor of divinity at Glasgow 1669; removed to London 1674 and was made chaplain at the Rolls Chapel, and lecturer at St. Clement's, 1675. The popularity he enjoyed in Scotland did not forsake him in London, but his intimacy with Lord William Russell, whom he attended on the scaffold (July 21, 1683), cost him the court favor and he was dismissed from both these positions. On the accession of James II. he left England and, after visiting France and Italy, settled at The Hague and was active in promoting the accession of William and Mary. He returned to England with William in 1688 and by him was made in 1689 bishop of Salisbury, in which office he was a model. His family connections, wealth, and ambition, his scholarship, friendships, and positions, his employment in diplomacy and honorable politics, all qualified him to write his admirable *History of his own Time* (i., London, 1723; ii., 1734; best ed. by M. J. Routh, 6 vols., Oxford, 1833; Part I. *The Reign of Charles the Second*, edited by Osmund Airy, 2 vols., 1897–1900; a *Supplement* to the *History* was edited by Miss H. C. Foxcroft, 1902), a work of great accuracy and fairness. Other works worthy of mention are: *History of the Reformation of the Church of England* (i., 1679; ii., 1681; iii., 1714; ed. N. Pocock, 7 vols., 1865); his works against the Roman Catholic Church, *The mystery of iniquity unveiled* (1673); *Rome's glory, or a collection of divers miracles wrought by popish saints*, (1673); *Infallibility of the Roman Church confuted* (1680); also his life of William Bedell (1685); *Exposition of the XXXIX. Articles* (1699), which was censured by the Lower House of Convocation.

BIBLIOGRAPHY: The *Life*, by his son, Thomas B. Burnet, is prefixed to the Oxford edition of his works, in 6 vols., 1833, which contains also a list of the bishop's writings. A detailed account is given in *DNB*, vii. 394–405. Consult also S. A. Allibone, *Critical Dictionary of English Literature*, i. 296–298, Philadelphia, 1891. Further sources are the *History*, and the *Letters* to Herbert in the Egerton MSS. in the British Museum.

BURNET, THOMAS: Church of England; b. at Croft (40 m. n. of York), Yorkshire, about 1635; d. in London Sept. 27, 1715. He studied at Clare Hall and Christ's College, Cambridge (fellow of Christ's, 1657; M.A., 1658; LL.D., 1685?); became master of the Charterhouse 1685, and in 1686 incited the first stand made by any society in England against the royal dispensing power in the reign of James II., and thereby prevented the illegal admission of a pensioner at the king's demand. He wrote fine English and excellent Latin, and was the author of several books which created much commotion. The *Telluris theoria sacra* (part i., London, 1681; Eng. version, revised, *The Sacred Theory of the Earth*, 1684; part ii. and Eng. version of the entire work, 1689; 7th ed., with life by Ralph Heathcote, 1759) was a fanciful attempt to explain the structure of the earth, and of no scientific value. In the *Archeologiæ philosophicæ sive doctrina antiqua de rerum originibus* (1692; Eng. transl., 1692) he interpreted the account of the Fall as an allegory, and the work cost him his position as clerk of the closet to William III. and marred his hope of advancement. In later life he wrote *De fide et officiis Christianorum*, in which "he regards the historical religions as based upon the religion of nature and rejects original sin and the 'magical' theory of the sacraments"; and *De statu mortuorum et resurgentium*, in which he defended the doctrine of the middle state, the millennium, and the limited duration of future punishment; these works were first authoritatively printed in 1727 (Eng. translations, 1727–28).

BIBLIOGRAPHY: R. Heathcote, *Life of Thomas Burnet*, prefixed to the 7th ed. of *The Sacred Theory*, 1759; *DNB*, vii. 408–410.

BURNETT PRIZES AND LECTURES: A foundation by John Burnett, a merchant of Aberdeen, Scotland (b. 1729; d. 1784), who bequeathed his entire estate for charitable and philanthropic purposes. One of the provisions of his will vested a portion of his property in trustees to provide prizes for the best and the next best essay intended to prove "that there is a Being, all-powerful, wise, and good, by whom everything exists; and particularly to obviate difficulties regarding the wisdom and goodness of the Deity; and this, in the first place, from considerations independent of written revelation, and, in the second place, from the revelation of the Lord Jesus; and, from the whole, to point out the inferences most necessary for, and useful to mankind." It was provided that the competition should be open to the whole world;

that the prizes should be of not less than £1,200 and £400 respectively, and should be offered at intervals of forty years; and that three appointees of the trustees of the testator's estate, the ministers of the Established Church of Aberdeen, and the principals and professors of King's and Marischal Colleges should act as judges. The first competition was in 1815, when fifty essays were submitted and the first prize was given to William Laurence Brown (b. 1755; professor at Utrecht, 1788–95; at Marischal College, 1795, principal from 1796; d. 1830) for a treatise *On the Existence of a Supreme Creator* (2 vols., Aberdeen, 1816), and the second to John Bird Sumner (q.v.), afterward archbishop of Canterbury, for an essay entitled *Records of Creation* (2 vols., London, 1818). In the second competition, 1855, out of 208 essays the judges selected *Christian Theism* (2 vols., London, 1855) by Robert Anchor Thompson (b. 1821; curate of Binbrook, Lincolnshire, 1854–58; from 1858 master of the Hospital of St. Mary the Virgin, Newcastle-on-Tyne; d. 1894) for the first prize, and *Theism* (Edinburgh, 1855) by John Tulloch (q.v.) for the second prize. In 1881 the use of the fund was changed by being applied to the support of a lectureship at Aberdeen, the lecturer to be appointed at intervals of five years and hold office for three years, and the subject to be either that prescribed by Mr. Burnett or some topic of history, archeology, or physical or natural science, so treated as to illustrate the theme originally suggested. Lecturers and subjects have been as follows:

1883–86. George Gabriel Stokes, professor of mathematics at Cambridge, *On Light* (London, 1887).

1888–91. W. Robertson Smith, professor of Arabic at Cambridge, *On the Religion of the Semites* (1st series only published, *Fundamental Institutions*, London, 1889; 3d ed., 1907).

1891–94. William L. Davidson, minister of Bourtie, Aberdeenshire, *Theism as Grounded in Human Nature historically and critically Handled* (London, 1893).

The funds are now devoted toward the endowment of a chair of history and archeology in the university.

BURNS, WILLIAM CHALMERS: Missionary; b. at Dun (6 m. w. of Montrose), Forfarshire, Scotland, Apr. 1, 1815; d. at Niu-chwang, China, Apr. 4, 1868. He studied at Marischal College, Aberdeen; began the study of law, but decided to become a minister and reentered the university in 1832; studied theology at Glasgow and was licensed in 1839; preached first in Dundee, and then traveled through the British Islands and visited Canada (1844–46) as an evangelist, meeting with much success. On June 9, 1847, he sailed as first missionary to China of the English Presbyterian Missionary Society; he adopted the Chinese dress and life and lived in Hongkong, Canton, Amoy, Shanghai, Peking, and Niu-chwang, choosing not to stay long in one place. He was one of the most devoted missionaries of modern times and won the respect of both the natives of China and the foreign residents. He translated Bunyan's *Pilgrim's Progress* into Chinese.

Bibliography: I. Burns, *Memoir of W. C. Burns*, London, 1870 (by his brother); W. G. Blaikie, in *Leaders in Modern Philanthropy*, New York, 1884.

BURNT OFFERING. See Sacrifice.

BURR, ENOCH FITCH: Congregationalist; b. at Westport, Conn., Oct. 21, 1818; d. at Hamburg, Conn., May 8, 1907. He was educated at Yale College (B.A., 1839), and devoted several years of study in New Haven to science and theology. He then traveled extensively, and after his return to the United States was called in 1850 to the pastorate of the Congregational church at Lyme, Conn., which he held till his death. He lectured on the scientific evidences of religion at Amherst College, Williams College, the Sheffield Scientific School, and other institutions, and wrote: *The Mathematical Theory of Neptune* (New Haven, 1848); *Spiritualism* (New York, 1859); *Ecce Cœlum* (Boston, 1867); *Pater Mundi* (1869); *Ad Fidem* (1871); *Evolution* (1873); *Sunday Afternoons for Little People* (New York, 1874); *Toward the Strait Gate* (Boston, 1876); *Work in the Vineyard* (1876); *Dio the Athenian* (New York, 1880); *Tempted to Unbelief* (1882); *Ecce Terra* (Philadelphia, 1884); *Celestial Empires* (New York, 1885); *Theism as a Canon of Science* (London, 1886); *Universal Beliefs* (New York, 1887); *Long Ago, as Interpreted by the Nineteenth Century* (1888); *Supreme Things* (1889); *Aleph the Chaldean* (1891); *Fabius the Roman* (1897); and *Autumn Leaves from the Mansewood* (Andover, Mass., 1905).

BURRAGE, HENRY SWEETSER: Baptist; b. at Fitchburg, Mass., Jan. 7, 1837. He was educated at Brown University (B.A., 1861), and entered Newton Theological Institution, but left it in 1862 and served in the 36th Massachusetts Volunteers throughout the Civil War, rising from private to brevet major and acting assistant adjutant-general, first brigade, second division, ninth army corps. He was wounded at Cold Spring Harbor, June 3, 1864, and was a prisoner of war from Nov. 1, 1864, to Feb. 22, 1865. On the conclusion of the war, he resumed his studies at Newton Theological Institution (1867) and the University of Halle (1868–69), and was successively pastor of the Baptist church at Waterville, Me. (1870–74), and editor of *Zion's Advocate*, Portland, Me. (1874–1905). Since 1905 he has been chaplain of the eastern branch of the National Home for Disabled Volunteer Soldiers, Togus, Me. From 1875 to 1905 he was recording secretary of the Maine Baptist Missionary Convention, and since 1876 has held a similar office in the American Baptist Missionary Union. Since 1889 he has been recorder of the Maine Commandery of the Military Order of the Loyal Legion of the United States, and chaplain-in-chief of the entire organization since 1899, while he was secretary of the Maine Society of the Sons of the American Revolution from 1891 to 1905, when he was elected its president for 1906–1907. He was secretary of the Maine Society of Colonial Wars in 1899–1905, and is the president of the Maine Baptist Historical Society. He is a trustee of Colby College and Newton Theological Institution, and was also a trustee of Brown University from 1889 to 1903, when he was chosen one of the board of fellows. In addition to numerous articles in magazines and reviews, he has written:

Brown University in the Civil War (Providence, R. I., 1868); *The Act of Baptism in the History of the Christian Church* (Philadelphia, 1879); *History of the Anabaptists in Switzerland* (1882); *Rosier's Relation of Waymouth's Voyage to the Coast of Maine, 1605* (Portland, Me., 1887); *Baptist Hymn Writers and their Hymns* (Boston, 1888); *History of the Baptists in New England* (1894); *History of the Baptists in Maine* (Philadelphia, 1904); and *Gettysburg and Lincoln* (New York, 1906). He has also edited *Early English and French Voyages* (N. Y., 1907) and a number of works relating chiefly to the history of Maine.

BURRELL, DAVID JAMES: Reformed (Dutch); b. at Mount Pleasant, Pa., Aug. 1, 1844. He was educated at Yale University (B.A., 1867) and Union Theological Seminary (1870), and after serving as a missionary in Chicago for four years, held successive pastorates at the Second Presbyterian Church, Dubuque, Ia. (1876–87), Westminster Presbyterian Church, Minneapolis, Minn. (1887–91), and the Marble Collegiate Church, Manhattan, New York City (since 1891). Since 1903 he has also been acting professor of homiletics in Princeton Theological Seminary. He has been on the board of regents of the Theological Seminary of the Northwest, Bennett Female Seminary, Elmira Female College, and McCormick Theological Seminary; and is at present a member of the board of managers of the American Tract Society, the Pan-Presbyterian Council, and the American Sabbath Union; president of the New York State Sabbath Association, a vice-president of the National Temperance Society, and of the Evangelical Alliance; and a trustee of the United Society of Christian Endeavor and the Board of Domestic Missions of the Reformed Church. He is also a member of the New York and Pennsylvania Historical Societies. In theology he is a conservative. He has written: *The Religions of the World* (Philadelphia, 1888); *Hints and Helps* (3 vols., New York, 1891–93); *Gospel of Gladness* (1892); *Morning Cometh* (1893); *Religion of the Future* (1894); *Spirit of the Age* (1895); *For Christ's Crown and Covenant* (1896); *The Golden Passional* (1897); *The Early Church* (1897); *The Wondrous Cross* (1898); *God and the People* (1899); *The Gospel of Certainty* (London, 1899); *The Unaccountable Man* (Chicago, 1900); *The Church in the Fort* (1901); *The Wonderful Teacher* (1902); *The Verities of Jesus* (New York, 1903); *Christ and Progress* (1903); *Teachings of Jesus Concerning the Scriptures* (1904); *Christ and Men* (1906); *The Wayfarers of the Bible* (1906); and *The Evolution of a Christian* (1906).

BURRITT, ELIHU: American Congregational layman, scholar, and philanthropist; b. at New Britain, Conn., Dec. 8, 1810; d. there Mar. 6, 1879. While earning his living by his trade of blacksmith, he acquired before the age of thirty some acquaintance with most of the languages of Europe, and also with Hebrew, Samaritan, and Ethiopic. So although modest and deprecating notoriety, he became known as "the learned blacksmith." In 1841 he was invited to lecture, and prepared an address on "Application and Genius," in which he argued that all attainments are the result of persistent will and application alone. His lecturing was successful, and thenceforth he was prominent before the public as orator, editor, and philanthropist. In 1846 he went to England. For the next twenty-five years he spent most of his time abroad. He organized "The League of Universal Brotherhood" to work for the abolition of war and to promote friendly feelings between different peoples, and was active in connection with the first Peace Congress at Brussels in 1848 and similar gatherings afterward. He developed the idea of an "ocean penny postage," i.e., the reduction of the high rates then charged on international letters to a sum not more than double the domestic rate. After the outbreak of the Crimean War he returned to America and advocated the emancipation of the negro slaves, with compensation to the owners. From 1865 to 1869 he was consular agent of the United States at Birmingham. After 1870 he lived in retirement at New Britain, but was busy with his pen. He was always active in church work and strove to promote Christian fellowship between different creeds and confessions. He published many works, including: *Sparks from the Anvil* (London, 1847); *Thoughts and Things at Home and Abroad* (Boston, 1854); *Walk from London to John O'Groat's House* (London, 1864); *Walk from London to Land's End and Back* (1865); *Walks in the Black Country and its Green Border Lands* (1866); *Lectures and Speeches* (1866); *The Mission of Great Suffering* (1867); *Prayers and Meditations from the Psalms* (New York, 1869); *Sanskrit Handbook* (London, 1874). He founded and edited a number of periodicals for the promotion of his plans, of which the most important were *The Christian Citizen*, devoted to "peace, freedom, temperance, and every good cause" (Worcester, Mass., 1844–51), and *Bonds of Brotherhood* (London, 1846–68).

Bibliography: C. Northend, *Elihu Burritt; Sketch of his Life and Labors*, New York, 1882.

BURROUGHES (BURROUGHS), JEREMIAH: English Congregationalist; b. about 1600; d. in London Nov. 13, 1646. He studied at Emmanuel College, Cambridge, and was graduated M.A. in 1624, but left the university because of non-conformity; was assistant to Edmund Calamy (q.v.) at Bury St. Edmunds; in 1631 became rector of Tivetshall, Norfolk; suspended for non-conformity in 1636 and soon afterward deprived, he went to Rotterdam (1637) and became "teacher" of the English church there; returned to England in 1641 and served as preacher at Stepney and Cripplegate, London. He was a member of the Westminster Assembly and one of the few who opposed the Presbyterian majority. While one of the most distinguished of the English Independents, he was one of the most moderate, acting consistently in accordance with the motto on his study door: *Opinionum varietas et opinantium unitas non sunt ἀσύστατα* ("Difference of belief and unity of believers are not inconsistent"). His publications were many, the most important being *An Exposition with Practical Observations on the Prophecy of Hosea* (4 vols., London, 1643–57).

BURROUGHS (BURROUGH), GEORGE: The most prominent victim of the Salem witchcraft delusion; b. about 1650; executed on Gallows Hill, Salem, Mass., Aug. 19, 1692. He was graduated at Harvard, 1670; preached at Casco (Portland), Me.; at Salem Village (Danvers), Mass., 1680–83, where he suffered because of a church quarrel antedating his pastorate; was in Casco again in 1685, and when the town was destroyed by the French and Indians in May, 1690. In 1692, while acting as preacher at Wells, Me., he was accused of witchcraft by certain of his old parishioners at Salem and arrested; was brought to trial at Salem Aug. 5 and convicted on all indictments against him; before his execution he made an address which moved the hearers to tears and led Cotton Mather to remind the crowd that the devil often appeared as an angel of light.

Bibliography: J. L. Sibley, *Harvard Graduates*, vol. ii., Cambridge, 1881; C. W. Upham, *Salem Witchcraft*, ib. 1867.

BURROWS, WINFRID OLDFIELD: Church of England; b. at London Nov. 9, 1858. He was educated at Corpus Christi College, Oxford (B.A., 1881) and Christ Church, Oxford (M.A., 1885), and was ordered deacon in 1886 and priested two years later. He was a tutor of Christ Church from 1884 to 1891, after which he was principal of Leeds Clergy School until 1900. He was then vicar of Holy Trinity, Leeds, for three years (1900–03), and since 1903 has been vicar of St. Augustine's, Edgbaston, Birmingham. He was commissioner for North China in 1894 and for Natal in 1901, as well as surrogate for the diocese of Ripon in 1900–1903 and examining chaplain to the bishop of Wakefield in 1888–1905. Since 1904 he has been archdeacon of Birmingham, and since 1905 has also been examining chaplain to the bishop of Birmingham. In addition to briefer contributions, he has written *The Mystery of the Cross* (London, 1896).

BURSFELDE, CONGREGATION OF: An association of reformed Benedictine monks, taking its name from the abbey of Bursfelde on the Weser, about 10 m. west of Göttingen, founded by Count Henry of Nordheim and his wife Gertrude in 1093. It had been richly endowed, but by the beginning of the fifteenth century was so far fallen into decay that only a single monk lived there, and he in great poverty, while the church was used by traveling merchants as a stable. Johann of Minden, abbot of Rheinhausen, with Rembert ter List, prior of the Windesheim monastery of Wittenberg, was charged with reforming monastic life in Saxony and Brunswick after the Council of Basel; and the case of Bursfelde was specially commended to him by Duke Otto of Brunswick. He took up the task in 1433, and obtained the monks he needed from the abbey of St. Matthias at Treves. Dying in 1439, he left an equally energetic successor in Johann Hagen, who thoroughly completed the task in the thirty years of his rule, and founded the Congregation, including four other monasteries, with a view to the strict observance of the monastic rule, after the model of the Windesheim Congregation (q.v.). The spirit grew until Hagen could number thirty-six monasteries, besides some nunneries, under his leadership. The movement spread into the Netherlands also, under the influence of Jan Busch and Nicholas of Cusa. A yearly chapter of the whole congregation was held, always under the presidency of the abbot of Bursfelde. It received numerous privileges from the provincial council held by Nicholas of Cusa in 1451, and was confirmed by Pius II. in 1458 and 1461. It grew after Hagen's death until it numbered 142 monasteries; but in the sixteenth century it began to decline, though there was a brief revival about 1629 and during the Thirty Years' War. Many of the monasteries came into the possession of Protestant princes, including Bursfelde itself, whose Catholic abbot was replaced in 1579 by a Lutheran. Since the foundation of the University of Göttingen, the senior professor of the theological faculty has borne the title of abbot of Bursfelde, with an income derived from the revenues of the foundation. The last head of the Congregation was Bernhard Bierbaum, abbot of Werden, who was elected in 1780 at a chapter held in Hildesheim and died in 1798.

L. Schulze.

Bibliography: Sources are: The *Chronicon Windeshemense* by J. Busch, ed. with introduction by K. Grube, Halle, 1886; J. G. Leuckfeld, *Antiquitates Bursfeldenses*, Leipsic, 1713; Ewelt, *Die Anfänge der Bursfelder Benediktiner-Kongregation*, in *Zeitschrift für vaterländische Geschichte*, 3d series, vol. v., Münster, 1865. Consult Heimbucher, *Orden und Kongregationen*, i. 141–144, 159, 196.

BURT, WILLIAM: Methodist Episcopal bishop; b. at Padstow (38 m. n.w. of Plymouth), Cornwall, England, Oct. 23, 1852. He was educated at Wesleyan University, Middletown, Conn. (B.A., 1879), and Drew Theological Seminary, Madison, N. J. (1881). He entered the New York East Conference in 1881, and after being successively pastor of St. Paul's Church, Brooklyn (1881–83), and the De Kalb Avenue Church in the same city (1883–86), he was transferred to the Italy Conference and made presiding elder of the Milan district. He then resided in Florence from 1888 to 1890, when he removed to Rome, where he remained fourteen years, having charge of the Methodist Episcopal churches and schools of Italy and establishing several churches and schools, as well as a publishing house and two colleges. He was a delegate to the Ecumenical Methodist Conference at London in 1901, and to the General Conference of the Methodist Episcopal Church in 1892, 1896, 1900, and 1904. He was also a fraternal delegate to the Irish Conference at Belfast in 1906 and to the British Conference at Nottingham in the same year. In theology he is an orthodox, though liberal, member of his denomination. In 1904 he was elected bishop by the General Conference at Los Angeles, Cal. Since that time he has resided in Europe, with special jurisdiction over the Methodists of the Continent. He was created a cavalier of the Order of Mauritius and Lazarus in 1903, and is the author of several works in Italian, and in 1889 founded the Italian weekly *L'Evangelista*.

BURTON, ASA: Congregational minister; b. at Stonington, Conn., Aug. 25, 1752; d. at Thetford, Vt., May 1, 1836. He was graduated at

Dartmouth, 1777; ordained minister at Thetford, 1779, and spent his life there, laboring for the spiritual, social, and material welfare of the community in the way of the old-fashioned New England clergyman. It is said that he trained sixty young men for the ministry. He published *Essays on Some of the First Principles of Metaphysics, Ethics, and Theology* (Portland, Me., 1824).

BIBLIOGRAPHY: A *Memoir* by Thomas Adams was printed in *The American Quarterly Register*, x. 321-341, Boston, 1838.

BURTON, EDWARD: Church of England patristic scholar and church historian; b. at Shrewsbury Feb. 13, 1794; d. at Ewelme (10 m. s.e. of Oxford) Jan. 19, 1836. He studied at Christ Church, Oxford (B.A., 1815; M.A., 1818; D.D., 1829); became curate of Pettenhall, Staffordshire, 1815; went to the Continent in 1818 and worked in the libraries of France and Italy; took up his residence at Oxford 1824, and in 1829 became regius professor of divinity. Among the more important of his works are: *Testimonies of the Ante-Nicene Fathers to the Divinity of Christ* (Oxford, 1826); *Inquiry into the Heresies of the Apostolic Age* (Bampton lectures, 1829); *The Greek Testament with English Notes* (2 vols., 1831); *Testimonies of the Ante-Nicene Fathers to the Doctrine of the Trinity and of the Divinity of the Holy Ghost* (1831); *Lectures on the Ecclesiastical History of the First Three Centuries* (2 vols., 1831-33). His edition of the *Historia ecclesiastica* of Eusebius appeared after his death (text, 1838; again 1856 and 1872; notes by Heinichen, Leipsic, 1840).

BIBLIOGRAPHY: His collected works, with memoir, were published at Oxford in 5 vols., 1846.

BURTON, ERNEST DE WITT: Baptist; b. at Granville, O., Feb. 4, 1856. He was educated at Denison University, Granville, O. (B.A., 1876), and Rochester Theological Seminary (1882), and also studied at the universities of Leipsic (1887) and Berlin (1894). He was an instructor in Kalamazoo College, Kalamazoo, Mich., in 1876-77, and a teacher in the public schools of Xenia and Norwood, O., in 1877-79. In 1882 he was appointed instructor in New Testament Greek in Rochester Theological Seminary, but in the following year was called to Newton Theological Institution as associate professor of New Testament interpretation, and was full professor there from 1886 to 1892. In the latter year he went to the University of Chicago as professor of New Testament literature and interpretation, and head of the department of Biblical and patristic Greek, a position which he still holds. He has been a member of the Society of Biblical Literature and Exegesis since 1883 and of the Chicago Society of Biblical Research since 1892. In theology and Biblical criticism his attitude is that of a conservative progressive. He has been associate editor of the *Biblical World* since 1892 and of the *American Journal of Theology* since 1897 He has also written: *Syntax of the Moods and Tenses in New Testament Greek* (Chicago, 1893); *Harmony of the Gospels for Historical Study* (New York, 1894; in collaboration with W. A. Stevens); *Handbook of the Life of Christ* (1894; in collaboration with W. A. Stevens); *Records and Letters of the Apostolic Age* (1895); *Handbook of the Life of Paul* (Chicago, 1899); *Constructive Studies in the Life of Christ* (1901; in collaboration with S. Mathews); *Principles and Ideals of the Sunday School* (1903; in collaboration with S. Mathews); *Short Introduction to the Gospels* (1904); *Studies in the Gospel of Mark* (1904); and *Some Principles of Literary Criticism and their Application to the Synoptic Problem* (1904).

BURTON, LEWIS WILLIAM: Protestant Episcopal bishop of Lexington, Ky.; b. at Cleveland, O., Nov. 9, 1852. He was educated at Kenyon College, Gambier, O. (B.A., 1873), and at the Divinity School of the Protestant Episcopal Church, Philadelphia, from which he was graduated in 1877. He was ordered deacon in 1877 and was priested in 1878. He was successively curate and rector of All Saints', Cleveland, 1877-80, of St. Mark's, Cleveland, 1881-84, rector of St. John's, Richmond, Va., 1884-93, and rector of St. Andrew's, Louisville, Ky., 1893-96. In 1896 he was consecrated bishop of Lexington. While in Virginia, he was an examining chaplain to the bishop of that diocese. He is now a trustee of Kenyon College and of the University of the South, as well as a member of the Joint Commission of the General Convention on Christian Education. In theology he belongs to the conservative school. His publications include sermons, charges, contributions to periodicals, and the section on the annals of Henrico Parish, Va., in J. S. Moore's *Virginiana* (Richmond, 1904).

BURTON, ROBERT: Author of the *Anatomy of Melancholy*; b. at Lindley (20 m. e.n.e. of Birmingham), Leicestershire, Feb. 8, 1577; d. at Oxford Jan. 25, 1640. He studied at Brasenose and Christ Church, Oxford (B.D., 1614); became vicar of St. Thomas, in the west suburbs of Oxford, 1616, and in addition, about 1630, rector of Segrave, Leicestershire. His life was spent among his books at Oxford; Anthony Wood, a generation after his death, describes him as a good mathematician, a philologist, and astrologer, a hard student and well-read scholar, considered by some melancholy and morose, but by those who knew him better esteemed for honesty and charity, and as a merry and genial companion. His famous work (Oxford, 1621), which is a vast collection of quotations and allusions, abundantly proves his learning. Five editions appeared during Burton's life, each with many alterations and additions and a sixth was printed from his annotated manuscript (1651-52). The edition of 1800 contains an account of the author. There is a modern edition by A. R. Shilleto, with introduction by A. H. Bullen (London, 1893). The *Philosophaster* is a Latin comedy written in 1606 and acted at Christ Church on Shrove Monday (Feb. 16), 1618; with certain Latin *poemata* it was printed for the Roxburghe Club (London, 1862).

BIBLIOGRAPHY: Besides the *Memoir* in the ed. of 1800, consult: A. à Wood, *Athenæ Oxonienses*, ed. P. Bliss, ii. 652-653, 4 vols., London, 1813-20; J. Nichols, *History and Antiquities of the County of Leicester*, vol. iii., part i., pp. 415-419, 4 vols., London, 1795-1811. The account in *DNB*, viii. 12-14 describes rather the book than the man.

BURWASH, NATHANIEL: Methodist Episcopalian; b. at Argenteuil, Quebec, July 25, 1839. He was educated at Victoria College, Cobourg, Ont. (B.A., 1859), Yale College, and Garrett Biblical Institute, Evanston, Ill. (B.D., 1871). He entered the Methodist Episcopal ministry in 1860, and after acting as classical tutor in Victoria College in 1860–1861, held pastorates until 1866, when he was recalled to Victoria College as professor of natural science. He was made dean of the theological faculty in the same institution in 1873, and since 1887 has been its president and chancellor. He is also a member of the senate and council of the University of Toronto and of the council of education for the province of Ontario. He has been a member of successive general conferences of his denomination since 1874, and was president of the one held in 1889–90, in addition to being secretary of education for the Methodist Episcopal Church in Canada from 1874 to 1886. He has written: *Memorials of Edward and Lydia Jackson* (Toronto, 1876); *Genesis, Nature, and Results of Sin* (1878); *Wesley's Doctrinal Standards* (1881); *Relation of Children to the Fall, the Atonement, and the Church* (1882); *Handbook on the Epistle to the Romans* (1887); *Inductive Studies in Theology* (1896); *Manual of Christian Theology* (1900); *Life and Times of Egerton Ryerson* (1902); and *The Development of the University of Toronto as a Provincial Institution* (1905).

BURY, RICHARD DE: Bishop of Durham; b. at Bury St. Edmunds (61 m. n.e. of London) 1281, the son of Sir Richard Aungerville; d. at Auckland (11 m. s.w. of Durham) Apr. 14, 1345. He studied at Oxford, then entered the Benedictine order at Durham, became tutor to the future Edward III., who on his accession (1327) entrusted various offices to him, and sent him twice to Pope John XXII. as ambassador, and later in the same capacity to Paris, Hainault, and Germany, and as commissioner for the affairs of Scotland. He was made dean of Wells, and the same year (1333) bishop of Durham. Useful as he was to the king and his country as a diplomat, and able as he was as an ecclesiastic, he is remembered solely as a bibliophile, perhaps the earliest in England worthy of the name. He has no claim to be considered a scholar, but he loved books and used all his personal and official influence in their accumulation. Wherever he was, he was on the lookout for MSS., and he also had agents on the Continent in the search for them. So he had more books than all the other English bishops put together. Some of these MSS. he stored in his palace, others he is said to have deposited in the library he founded in Oxford in connection with Durham College (on the site of the present Trinity College). His love of books comes out in that bibliophile's delight, the *Philobiblon* (first published at Cologne, 1473, next at Speyer, 1483, and in Paris, 1500). It has been often republished, the best edition, having both the Latin text and an English translation, being by Ernest C. Thomas (London, 1888), and Mr. Thomas's translation was reprinted 1902.

BIBLIOGRAPHY: Sources for a biography are: H. Wharton, *Anglia Sacra*, i. 765 sqq., London, 1691; *Historiæ Dunelmensis*, edited for the Surtees Society by J. Raine, Durham, 1839; T. Rymer, *Fœdera*, vol. ii., best ed., London, 1816. Consult also *DNB*, viii. 25–27.

BUSCH, JAN: Dutch monastic reformer; b. at Zwolle (52 m. e.n.e. of Amsterdam) Aug. 9, 1399; d. at Sülte, near Hildesheim, c. 1480. Educated first in the school of Zwolle, which then, under its famous rector Cele, numbered about a thousand students, he went to Erfurt at the age of eighteen to study law; but his inclination was for the monastic life, and in 1419 he entered the Windesheim house, of which Vos was then prior. He labored diligently to overcome theoretical doubts by study of the Scriptures and spiritual writers, and to form himself practically in the devout life. Vos, on his death-bed, exhorted him to constancy in reforming zeal, and he was soon sent to Bödingen near Cologne, where he was ordained priest. He remained four years at Bödingen, and then, after a short stay in the mother house, received a more difficult commission, being sent to Ludinkerken in East Friesland, where conditions of shocking laxity prevailed, but the great papal schism, a contested episcopal election, and his own weak health prevented him from accomplishing much there. After some years of comparative rest, he began his more important work in 1437 as subprior of the reformed monastery of Wittenberg near Hildesheim, which was to extend over a large part of Germany and to embrace especially, in the spirit of the Council of Basel, the reform of the Augustinian convents of both sexes, particularly in Saxony. Working in harmony with the Bursfelde Congregation (q.v.), he began with the neighboring monastery of Sülte, of which he took charge himself, with the title of provost, commonly used in Saxony instead of prior. His success in restoring discipline there induced the archbishop of Magdeburg in 1446 to place in his hands the Premonstratensian house of Our Lady in the same city. In the following year he became provost of the rich *Neuwerkstift* at Halle, combining with it the office of archdeacon, which gave him authority over 700 secular priests. After the plague of 1450, he went on to Glauchau, where he enjoyed the powerful support of his friend Nicholas of Cusa, who had been sent to Germany as cardinal-legate with special reference to monastic reform. After a provincial synod at Bergen, the legate entrusted Busch with the oversight of this work in the entire province, giving him full power to inspect all monasteries and reform whatever disorders he found, taking the Windesheim statutes as a standard. He went vigorously to work in Halle, Leipsic, and Halberstadt, but in 1452 the opposition aroused by his zeal led to demands for his removal being laid before the pope and the archbishop. At first they were fruitless, but when Busch found the archbishop cooling toward him, he resigned his office of provost, still retaining his powers as visitor. In 1456 he went to attend a general chapter at Windesheim, and remained there several years, living as a simple brother and employing the time in literary work. He wrote the lives of the first twenty-four brothers and of his teacher Cele (*Liber de viris illustribus de Windeshem*), as well as a chronicle of the house and congregation. He took up active work again as provost of Sülte, and exercised his visitatorial powers over a still wider field, at the same time writing an account of his work which is of some value. He resigned his office as provost in 1479, and probably died in the following year. His *Chronicon Windeshemense* was first printed by Heribert Rosweyde at Antwerp in 1621, and an incomplete edition of his four books *De reformatione monasteriorum* was prepared by G. W. von Leibnitz, in *Scriptores rerum Brunsvicensium* (3 vols., Hanover, 1707–11); an excellent modern edition, with introduction and notes, is that of K. Grube (Halle, 1886). A few smaller works, letters, and sermons, have recently been discovered and published by J. M. Wüstenhoff (Ghent, 1890).

L. Schulze.

Bibliography: The sources for a life are best discovered in his own writings: *Chronicon Windeshemense*, ed. K. Grube, Halle, 1886; *Liber de reformatione monasteriorum*, ed. Grube, with the *Chronicon*, ut sup. (contains a brief life by the editor). Consult also: K. Grube, *Johannes Busch, Augustinerpropst zu Hildesheim*, Freiburg, 1881; W. Moll, *Kerkgeschiedenis van Nederlande voor de Hervorming*, II., ii., pp. 115, 221 sqq., 349, Utrecht, 1871; J. G. R. Acquoy, *Het Klooster te Windesheim en zijn invloed*, 3 vols., ib. 1875; L. Schulze, *Des Johannes Busch bisher unbekannte Schriften*, in *ZKG*, xi. (1890) 586–596.

BUSEMBAUM (BUSENBAUM), HERMANN: German Jesuit, casuist; b. at Nottelen (a village of Westphalia) 1600; d. at Münster Jan. 31, 1668. He was a teacher at Cologne, and afterward rector at Hildesheim and Münster. His text-book of casuistry, entitled *Medulla theologiæ moralis* (Münster, 1645), in seven books, ran through 200 editions before 1776, although it caused offense when it was published with a commentary in 1710. The book contained the Jesuitic teachings on regicide, and in France, when an attempt was made to assassinate Louis XIV., the matter was brought before the courts. The Paris parliament was satisfied with simply condemning the book, while that of Toulouse had it publicly burned and held the principals of institutions who used it responsible. Meanwhile the moral theology of the *Medulla* was incorporated in the classical text-book of the order of Redemptorists, edited by Liguori. Busembaum's *Lilium inter spinas* (Cologne, 1660) is ascetic in character.

K. Benrath.

Bibliography: J. J. I. Döllinger and F. H. Reusch, *Geschichte der Moralstreitigkeiten*, vol. i., Stuttgart, 1890; F. H. Reusch, *Index der verbotenen Bücher*, ii. 826, 896, 898, 920.

BUSH, GEORGE: American Swedenborgian; b. at Norwich, Vt., June 12, 1796; d. at Rochester, N. Y., Sept. 19, 1859. He was graduated at Dartmouth, 1818; studied at Princeton Theological Seminary, 1820–22; was tutor in Princeton College, 1822–23; went to Indiana for the Home Missionary Society in 1824 and was pastor of a Presbyterian church at Indianapolis 1825–28; professor of Hebrew and Oriental literature in the University of the City of New York 1831–47; instructor of sacred literature in Union Theological Seminary in the same city 1836–37. In 1845 he connected himself with the Swedenborgians and was preacher of the New Church Society in New York 1848–52, in Brooklyn 1854–59. He was an active defender of the tenets of his faith with both pen and voice, and edited the *New Church Repository and Monthly Review* 1848–55. His writings on other subjects include: *Life of Mohammed* (New York, 1832); *A Treatise on the Millennium* (1832); *A Grammar of the Hebrew Language* (1835); *Notes Critical and Practical on the Old Testament* (Genesis–Judges, 8 vols., 1840 sqq.); *Anastasis* (1845), against the doctrine of the resurrection of the body. He was justly esteemed as a Hebrew scholar.

Bibliography: *Memoirs and Reminiscences of George Bush*, a collection of contributions from friends, edited by Woodbury M. Fernald, Boston, 1860.

BUSHNELL, HORACE: Congregationalist; b. at Litchfield, Conn., Apr. 14, 1802; d. in Hartford, Conn., Feb. 17, 1876. He was graduated at Yale College, 1827; after an interval spent in teaching and journalism, he returned (1829) to study law in the Yale Law School, but after two years, during which he was a tutor in the college, was converted and studied for the ministry in the Yale Divinity School and graduated in the class of 1833. He was pastor of the North Church, Hartford, Conn., from May 22, 1833, till Nov. 22, 1859, when he resigned on account of his health, though he continued his ministrations with undiminished power. His distinction rests upon several great works: (1) His *Christian Nurture* (Hartford, 1846)—a contribution of the first rank to religious thought—in which he drew attention away from revivals to the training of children in Christian households as the law of growth in the Church. (2) His doctrine of the "Instrumental Trinity" (*God in Christ*, New York, 1849), showing affinities with Sabellianism, but lifting the idea of the Trinity out of the region of speculation and making it available for actual life (see Christology, IX., 3, § 4). (3) His supreme emphasis on ethical and religious values and his refusal of metaphysics; here he anticipates the Ritschlian attitude, the ground of which for him lay not in philosophy, but in a theory of language ("Dissertation on Language," in *God in Christ*: "Our Gospel a Gift to the Imagination," in *Building Eras*, New York, 1881) and in a profound Christian experience. (4) His moral view of the Atonement (q.v.), "grounded in principles of universal obligation" and universal vicariousness, later modified by the idea of God as propitiating himself in the forgiveness of the sinner (*The Vicarious Sacrifice*, New York, 1865; *Forgiveness and Law*, ib. 1874—the two volumes published under the title *The Vicarious Sacrifice*, 1877). (5) In apologetics Bushnell related "Miracles" to "Law," and drew his matchless picture of "The Character of Jesus Forbidding his Possible Classification with Men" (*Nature and the Supernatural*, New York, 1858). (6) Many of his sermons are unsurpassed for insight, feeling, imagination, noble thought, and splendor of diction. Yet by his own generation he was generally called a heretic; and for his condemnation there was a demand throughout the American orthodox churches! In 1849 and 1851 he was actually accused of heresy in formal fashion, and still more savagely attacked after 1866, but his congregation stood by him and he was not tried. The present generation in America venerates him as one of the molders of religious opinion, and has been influenced by him more perhaps than it knows. A centenary edition of his works appeared in twelve volumes (New York, 1903).

Bibliography: H. C. Trumbull, in *My Four Religious Teachers*, Philadelphia, 1903; M. B. Cheney, *Life and Letters of Horace Bushnell*, New York, 1880 (by his daughter); T. T. Munger, *Horace Bushnell, Preacher and Theologian*, Boston, 1899. His *Spirit in Man, Sermons and Selections* was published in a centenary ed., with classified and annotated literature, by H. B. Learned, New York, 1903.

BUTLER, ALBAN: English Roman Catholic; b. at Appletree (70 m. n.w. of London), Northamptonshire, Oct. 24, 1710; d. at St. Omer (22 m. s.e. of Calais), France, May 15, 1773. He was educated at Douai and became professor there of philosophy and divinity; was ordained priest, 1735; traveled through France and Italy, 1745–46, and then was sent for a short time to the Roman Catholic mission in Staffordshire. Later he was tutor to Edward Howard, duke of Norfolk, and accompanied him to Paris; about 1766 he became president of the English college at St. Omer. He labored for thirty years on his chief work, *The Lives of the Fathers, Martyrs, and Other Principal Saints*, which was published anonymously in four volumes (vol. iii., 2 parts) at London, 1756–59. The second edition, with notes and other matter omitted in the first edition, edited by Dr. Carpenter, archbishop of Dublin, appeared at Dublin in twelve volumes in 1779–80. It has appeared in several later editions and abridgments (as by F. C. Husenbeth, with omission of the notes and most of the shorter lives, 2 vols., London, 1857–60), and was translated into French and Italian. His nephew, Charles Butler (q.v.), prepared a continuation (London, 1823). A complete general index was published in 1886.

Bibliography: Charles Butler, *An Account of the Life and Writings of Alban Butler*, Edinburgh, 1800, contained also in vol. iii. of the works of Charles Butler, London, 1817, and in many editions of the *Lives*; *DNB*, viii. 33–34.

BUTLER, ALFORD AUGUSTUS: Protestant Episcopalian; b. at Portland, Me., Sept. 23, 1845. He was educated at Griswold College, Davenport, Ia., where he completed his theological education in 1873. He was ordered deacon in the same year, and was ordained priest in 1874. He was successively assistant in Grace Cathedral, Davenport, Ia. (1873), and rector of Grace Church, Cedar Rapids, Ia. (1873–77), Trinity Church, Bay City, Mich. (1877–84), Church of the Epiphany, New York City (1884–91), and Christ Church, Red Wing, Minn. (1891–94). Since 1894 he has been warden and professor of homiletics, liturgics, and religious pedagogy in Seabury Divinity School, Faribault, Minn. He was active in organizing the Parochial Mission Society of the United States, and was chosen secretary of its executive committee, and also took a prominent part in establishing the first deaconess school in the Protestant Episcopal Church. He is likewise a member of the Joint Commission on Sunday Schools and of the General Convention of the Protestant Episcopal Church. He has written: *How to Study the Life of Christ* (New York, 1902); *How shall we worship God?* (1904); and *The Churchman's Manual of Sunday School Methods* (Milwaukee, 1906).

BUTLER, ALFRED JOSHUA: Church of England layman; b. at Loughborough (10 m. n.n.w. of Leicester), Leicestershire, Sept. 21, 1850. He was educated at Trinity College, Oxford (B.A., 1874), and after being assistant master at Winchester from 1874 to 1879, was tutor to the Khedive of Egypt in 1879–81. He was elected fellow of Brasenose College, Oxford, in 1877, and was appointed bursar four years later, both of which positions he still holds. He has written: *Amaranth and Asphodel, Verses from the Greek Anthology* (London, 1880); *Ancient Coptic Churches of Egypt* (2 vols., Oxford, 1884); *Court Life in Egypt* (London, 1887); *The Churches and Monasteries of Egypt and some neighboring Countries attributed to Abu Salih, the Armenian* (1895, in collaboration with B. T. A. Evetts); and *The Arab Conquest of Egypt* (London, 1902).

BUTLER, CHARLES: English Roman Catholic layman; nephew of Alban Butler (q.v.); b. in London Aug. 14, 1750; d. there June 2, 1832. He studied at Douai, and for many years was a leading lawyer of London. He was prominent in the movement to secure the repeal of the laws against Roman Catholics; in regard to the hierarchy and the relations of English Catholics to the pope he was an extreme Gallican, and found bitter opponents in the vicars-apostolic in England. He was a voluminous writer; among the more important of his works are *Horæ biblicæ* (2 pts., London, 1797–1802); *Historical Memoirs respecting the English, Irish, and Scottish Catholics from the Reformation* (4 vols., 1819–21); *Reminiscences* (1822); *The Book of the Roman Catholic Church* (1825); biographies of Alban Bulter (1800), Fénelon (1811), Erasmus (1825), Grotius (1826), and others. He continued his uncle's *Lives of the Saints*.

BUTLER, CLEMENT MOORE: American Episcopalian; b. at Troy, N. Y., Oct. 16, 1810; d. in Philadelphia Mar. 5, 1890. He was graduated at Washington (Trinity) College 1833, and at the General Theological Seminary, New York, 1836; was rector of various churches in New York, the District of Columbia, Massachusetts, and Ohio 1837–61, and from 1849 to 1853 chaplain of the United States Senate; chaplain of the United States embassy at Rome 1861–64; professor of church history in the Protestant Episcopal Divinity School, Philadelphia, 1864–84. Besides occasional sermons, he published: *The Year of the Church, hymns and devotional verse for the Sundays and Holy Days of the ecclesiastical year for young persons* (Utica, N. Y., 1839); *The Book of Common Prayer Interpreted by its History* (Boston, 1845; 2d ed., enlarged, Washington, 1849); *Addresses and Lectures on Public Men and Public Affairs delivered in Washington City* (Cincinnati, 1856); *The Flock Fed, catechetical instruction preparatory to confirmation* (New York, 1862); *Inner Rome, political, religious, and social* (Philadelphia, 1866); *The Ritualism of Law* (1867); *A Manual of Ecclesiastical History* (from the first to the nineteenth century: 2 vols., 1868–72); *History of the Book of Common*

Prayer (1880); *History of the Reformation in Sweden* (New York, 1883).

BUTLER, HENRY MONTAGUE: Master of Trinity College, Cambridge; b. at Gayton (4 m. n. of Towcester), Northampton, July 2, 1833. He was educated at Trinity College (B.A., 1855), and was ordained priest in 1859. He was fellow of his college in 1855–60, and was head master of Harrow School from 1859 to 1885. He was honorary chaplain to the queen in 1875–77 and chaplain in ordinary in 1877–85, as well as examining chaplain to archbishops Tait and Benson of Canterbury from 1879 to 1887. He was also prebendary of Holborn in St. Paul's Cathedral in 1882–85, dean of Gloucester in 1885–86, and vice-chancellor of Cambridge in 1889–91. Since 1886 he has been master of Trinity College, and honorary canon of Ely since 1898. He was select preacher at Oxford in 1877–78, 1878–80, 1882, and 1899, and at Cambridge in 1879, 1885, 1893, 1896–98, 1901, and 1903, while in 1871 he was created a commander of the Order of the Crown of Italy. He is also a governor of Haileybury College, Harrow School, Cheltenham College, Wellington College, and Westminster School, and has written: *Sermons preached in the Chapel of Harrow School* (2 vols., London, 1861–69); *Belief in Christ and other Sermons preached in Trinity College* (1898); *"Lift up your Hearts": Words of Good Cheer for the Holy Communion* (1898); *University and other Sermons* (1899); and *Public School Sermons* (1899).

BUTLER, JAMES GLENTWORTH: Presbyterian; b. at Brooklyn, N. Y., Aug. 3, 1821. He was educated at New York University (did not graduate), Union Theological Seminary (1846–47), and Yale Divinity School, being graduated from the latter in 1849. After being a resident licentiate at the same institution in 1849–50, he was ordained to the Presbyterian ministry late in 1852 and was pastor of the Walnut Street Presbyterian Church, Philadelphia, Pa., until 1868. He was then elected corresponding secretary of the American and Foreign Christian Union, a position which he retained three years, after which he was pastor of the First Presbyterian Church, Brooklyn, for two years (1871–73). In 1874 he retired from the active ministry, and has since lived the life of a private scholar. In addition to a number of briefer contributions, he prepared *The Bible Reader's Commentary, New Testament* (2 vols., New York, 1879), which was afterward enlarged under the title *Bible Work* (11 vols., 1892) and made to include the Old Testament; and *Vital Truths respecting God and Man* (Philadelphia, 1904).

BUTLER, JOHN GEORGE: Lutheran; b. at Cumberland, Md., Jan. 28, 1826. He was educated at Pennsylvania College (1846) and Gettysburg Theological Seminary, Gettysburg, Pa (1847–1849), and was pastor of St. Paul's English Lutheran Church, Washington, D.C., from 1849 to 1873. From the latter year he was pastor of the Luther Place Memorial Church in the same city. He also served throughout the Civil War as a chaplain in and near Washington, was chaplain of the House of Representatives from 1869 to 1875, and of the Senate from 1866 to 1893. He was likewise professor of homiletics and church history in Howard University, Washington, from 1871 to 1891, and for many years was Washington correspondent of the *Lutheran's Observer* and the *Lutheran Evangelist*, and editor of the latter paper from 1893. Died in Washington, D. C., Aug. 2, 1909.

BUTLER, JOSEPH: Bishop of Durham; b. at Wantage (14 m. s.w. of Oxford) May 18, 1692; d. at Bath June 16, 1752. He was the youngest of the eight children of Thomas Butler, a retired linen-draper and stanch Presbyterian, but was allowed to enter Oriel College, Oxford, and in 1718 the ministry of the Church of England. From 1719 to 1726 he was preacher at the Rolls Chapel, London, where most of the congregation were lawyers and the pay small; from 1721 to 1738 he was prebendary of Salisbury; from 1721 to 1725, rector of Haughton-le-Skerne (2 m. n.e. of Darlington); and from 1725 to 1740 of Stanhope (26 m. n. of Darlington). From 1733 to 1740 he was a prebendary of Rochester; from 1733 to 1736 chaplain to the lord chancellor; from 1736 to her death in 1737 clerk of the closet to Caroline, queen consort of George II.; from 1738 to 1750 bishop of Bristol, the poorest see in England; from 1740 to 1750 dean of St. Paul's with a prebend and residentiary canony; from 1746 to 1750 clerk of the closet to the King (George II.); from 1750 till his death, bishop of Durham, the richest see in England. As appears from the above, he was a pluralist. He was not, however, avaricious, but generous to a fault. He was shy, reticent, sensitive, more of a thinker than a reader, and he never married. His one great aim was to combat the current Deism and contempt for religion. This he did with unrivaled force. He had the very expensive taste of building and spent much money in reconstructing his episcopal residences.

His reputation rests upon his writings, all published by himself or in his lifetime, as his literary remains were destroyed at his death, according to his direction. These writings are few in number but weighty in matter. This is the full list: *Fifteen Sermons Preached at the Rolls Chapel* (1726); *The Analogy of Religion Natural and Revealed to the Constitution and Course of Nature* (1736); six occasional sermons of various dates; a part of his episcopal charge at Bristol in 1749, and his episcopal charge at Durham in 1751; and the correspondence, down to 1714, between himself and Samuel Clarke, which the latter published in the fourth edition (1716) of his Boyle lectures on the *Being and Attributes of God*, and separately the same year, but which has received additions.

To understand and appreciate these writings of Butler one must bear in mind two facts: Butler lived in the "golden age of English Deism," when Christianity, as he himself says, was "not so much as a subject of inquiry; but that it is, now at length, discovered to be fictitious"; and secondly that he was intensely practical. He wrote his famous *Fifteen Sermons*, as J. H. Bernard says, "not to propound a new basis for speculative ethics, but to justify to practical men the practice of the common virtues, benevolence, compassion, and the like. He desires to take human nature as an existing fact, and to analyze its constituents just so far as is necessary to bring to light the obligations to right living." His *Six Sermons* are likewise practical: The first is a defense of foreign missions; the second is an appeal for the London hospitals; the third is on the true way to safeguard liberty; the fourth is a plea for charity schools; the fifth is upon the uses to which the union of Church and State should be put, and the sixth upon the proper management of infirmaries. Of like practicality is his more famous *Analogy*. He took the Deists on their own ground and strove to cut the ground from under their feet in order that he might bring them to the Christian foundation. To quote Bernard again: "We find in Butler's works no attempt to construct a philosophy of religion nor . an analysis of the religious consciousness. Religion is treated altogether from the historical point of view. Its main doctrines are facts and are susceptible of proof, just like any other facts. It is an *argumentum ad hominem* all through, and is not intended to present an absolute and consecutive statement of the grounds of faith. His point was, not that the difficulties of revelation repeat the difficulties of nature, but rather the difficulties of revelation, admitted to be embarrassing in themselves, cannot be counted destructive of religious belief, inasmuch as difficulties of a similar nature beset the recognition of nature as a coherent and systematic whole."

The first part of the *Analogy*, consisting of seven chapters, is the Analogy of Natural Religion to the constitution and course of Nature; and is generally considered more successful than the second part, in eight chapters, on the Analogy of Revealed Religion to the constitution and course of Nature (or a kind of evidences of Christianity). But both parts are very hard reading, because, though perfectly clear, the argument is very profound. It has been a college and university text-book for nigh 175 years and the quarry of innumerable works.

There are many editions of Butler. Two of remarkable excellence are that by the late W. E. Gladstone (two vols., Oxford, 1896, with a volume of Gladstone's *Studies subsidiary to Butler's works*) and that by J. H. Bernard (2 vols., London, 1900).

BIBLIOGRAPHY: The earliest *Life* appeared in the *Biographia Britannica*, in the Supplement, London, 1753, and the *Life* by Kippis, which appeared in his ed. of the *Biographia*, London, 1778–93, is often prefixed to the *Works* or to the *Analogy*. Consult further: T. Bartlett, *Memoirs of Joseph Butler*, London, 1839; John Hunt, *Religious Thought in England*, vols. ii., iii., ib. 1871–73; C. J. Abbey and J. H. Overton, *English Church in the Eighteenth Century*, 2 vols., ib. 1878; T. R. Pynchon, *Bishop Butler, a Sketch of his Life with an Examination of the Analogy*, New York, 1889; *Bishop Butler, An Appreciation, with the best passages of his Writings*, London, 1903; *DNB*, viii. 67–72.

BUTLER, WILLIAM: Methodist; b. in Dublin, Ireland, Jan. 31, 1818; d. at Old Orchard, Me., Aug. 18, 1899. He was graduated at Didsbury College, near Manchester, Eng., 1844, and the same year became a member of the Irish Wesleyan Conference. In 1850 he came to America and joined the New England Conference. In 1856 he was sent to India to be superintendent of a mission to be founded in that country. He located it in Oudh, Northwest India, but had scarcely begun work before the Sepoy rebellion broke out and he was for a time in extreme peril. Quiet being restored, he conducted the mission very successfully, making his headquarters at Bareilly. In 1865 he returned to America because, the mission being organized into a conference, no superintendent was needed. He resumed his pastoral labors till in 1869 he became secretary of the American and Foreign Christian Union, in New York. In 1873 he was for the second time selected by his Church to found a mission, this time in Mexico, and was its superintendent till 1879. He revisited India in 1883 and 1884, and saw the great success which had attended the mission he had founded. His last days were passed at Newton Centre, Mass. He wrote: *Compendium of Missions* (Boston, 1852); *The Land of the Veda* (New York, 1872); *From Boston to Bareilly and Back* (1885); *Mexico in Transition* (1892).

BIBLIOGRAPHY: Clementina Butler, *William Butler, the Founder of Two Missions of the M. E. Church*, New York, 1902.

BUTLER, WILLIAM ARCHER: Church of Ireland; b. at Annerville (2 m. e. of Clonmel), County Tipperary, 1814; d. at Raymoghy (5 m. n. of Raphoe), County Donegal, July 5, 1848. He studied at Trinity College, Dublin, and was professor of moral philosophy there from 1837 to his death. From 1837 to 1842 he was minister at Clondehorka, diocese of Raphoe, County Donegal, and then rector of Raymoghy in the same diocese. He was a brilliant and profound thinker, but his works are all posthumous and prepared for the press by others. They are *Letters on the Development of Christian Doctrine in Reply to Mr Newman's Essay* (ed. Thomas Woodward, Dublin, 1850); *Lectures on the History of Ancient Philosophy* (ed. William Hepworth Thompson, 2 vols., Cambridge, 1856, 5th ed., 1 vol., London, 1874); *Sermons Doctrinal and Practical* (1st series, ed. with memoir by Thomas Woodward, Dublin, 1849, 3d ed., Cambridge, 1855; 2d series, ed. James Amiraux Jeremie, Cambridge, 1856), each series having twenty-six sermons; the two series with his lectures were reprinted in New York, 1879.

BUTTERBRIEFE, BUTTERWOCHE. See LACTICINIA.

BUTTLAR, EVA VON: The leader in a disgraceful aberration externally connected with Pietism, which is in no way responsible for it; b. at Eschwege (26 m. e.s.e. of Cassel), Hesse, 1670; d. at Altona after 1717 Educated without religious instruction, she married at seventeen a French dancing-master in Eisenach, named De Vésias. After ten years of a gay court life, she was touched by the Pietistic movement, left her husband, stopped going to church, and in 1702, with a group of friends, founded at Allendorf in Hesse a new Christian-Philadelphic society, like several others which had sprung up in the Netherlands and western Germany. The esoteric doctrine of these societies included the expectation of an approaching millennium, the rejection of marriage as degrading, and the extinction of carnal desires by unrestrained indulgence. Eva and her friends are said to have practised the most lawless excesses, as sanctioned by their beliefs. Driven from Allendorf, they sought refuge in Wittgenstein, the common asylum of the persecuted; but even there the tribunals were obliged to interfere. Eva and her special intimates, the theologian Winter and the physician Appenfeller, embraced Catholicism at Cologne *pro forma* as a means of protection, and then settled at Lüde near Pyrmont, where their blasphemous insanity reached its height in 1706. They were all again arrested, but escaped. Appenfeller, who had been legally married to Eva, settled with her in Altona as a practising physician; and she is said finally to have lived a decent, regular life with him there as a member of the Evangelical Lutheran Church.

(F. W. Dibelius.)

Bibliography: Thomasius, *Gedanken über allerhand gemischte philosophische und juristische Händel*, iii. 208–624, Halle, 1725; Keller, *Die Buttlarische Rotte*, in *ZHT*, 1845, part 4; M. Goebel, *Geschichte des christlichen Lebens in der rheinisch-westphälischen Kirche*, Coblenz, 1852.

BUTTZ, HENRY ANSON: American Methodist Episcopalian; b. at Middle Smithfield, Pa., Apr. 18, 1835. He was educated at Princeton College (B.A., 1858), and held pastorates at Millstone, N. J. (1858–59), Irvington, N. J. (1859–60), Woodbridge, N. J. (1860–61), Mariner's Harbor, Staten Island (1862–63), Prospect Street Church, Paterson, N. J. (1864–66), and Morristown, N. J. (1867–1869). He was also instructor in Drew Theological Seminary, Madison, N. J., in 1867, becoming adjunct professor of Greek and Hebrew in 1868, and professor of New Testament Greek and exegesis two years later. Since 1880 he has been president of the seminary. He has edited, in addition to a number of briefer studies: *The New Life Dawning* by B. H. Nadal (New York, 1873) and *The Epistle to the Romans in Greek* (1876).

BUTZER, MARTIN.

Martin Butzer (Bucer) was born at Schlettstadt (26 m. s.w. of Strasburg) Nov. 11, 1491; d. at Cambridge, Eng., Feb. 28, 1551. He received his first education at the excellent Latin school of his native town, and in 1506 joined the order of the Dominicans. In 1517 he was at Heidelberg, where he studied the writings of the humanists, the Bible, and also the writings of Luther, whose personal acquaintance he made in 1518 and with whom he began to correspond in 1520. Being suspected by his order and accused at Rome, Butzer, who favored the evangelical cause, left the monastery in 1520 to avoid further difficulties, and became an associate of Hutten and Sickingen. The latter called him in 1522 to the pastorate of Landstuhl, and in the same year he married, being one of the first priests to break his vow of celibacy. When Sickingen was defeated by the elector of Treves, however, Butzer had to leave the city, and for a year he acted as evangelical preacher at Wissenburg in Alsace, supported by the council and citizens, but attacked by the Franciscan monks. In 1523 he went to Strasburg, where the Reformation, prepared in different ways, was already in progress. Together with Zell, Capito, and Hedio, Butzer became the soul of the Strasburg Reformation, and by preaching and writing, by letters and journeys, and by personal relations with ecclesiastics and statesmen, he exerted a reformatory and organizing activity, not only in Alsace but also in different countries. He was pastor of St. Aurelia 1524–31, and pastor of St. Thomas 1531–40, having already become in 1530 president of the newly founded church council which was the supreme ecclesiastical authority in Strasburg. As spiritual spokesman of the Strasburg citizens, who were eager for the Reformation, and as leader of the evangelical ministers, he appeared before the council, which proceeded cautiously and advisedly. He accomplished the abolition of the mass on Feb. 20, 1529, by a decree of the lay assessors, and thus the introduction of the Reformation into the free imperial city Strasburg was made a matter of history. But long before this the reorganization of the divine service and of ecclesiastical life began. Butzer's *Ordnung und Inhalt deutscher Messe* (1524) was typical of the Reformed order of worship. He devoted special attention to catechetics and published three catechisms between 1524 and 1544, while by the church ordinance of 1534 he introduced the lay presbytery into Strasburg, and in 1539 he inaugurated confirmation in the same city. Together with his friend Johannes Sturm, he laid the foundations of the Protestant educational system in Strasburg, founding the gymnasium in 1538, and the seminary in 1544. In the interest of ecclesiastical discipline he energetically opposed the Anabaptists and such radicals as Carlstadt, Hetzer, Denk, Sebastian Frank, Schwenckfeld, Melchior Hofmann, and Clemens Ziegler.

1. Early Activity in the Protestant Cause.

2. The Reformation in Strasburg.

Outside of Strasburg Butzer brought about the introduction of the Reformation into Hanau-Lichtenberg (1544), while Württemberg, Baden, and especially Hesse owed him much. For the elector of Cologne, Archbishop Hermann of Wied, Butzer, together with Melanchthon, composed an order of reformation (1543). His influence even reached as far as Belgium, Italy, and France.

Butzer's activity in ecclesiastical organization is treated too lightly in most works on church history, which lay their main stress on his efforts toward a union of the two main streams of the Reformation, and especially on his endeavors to reconcile Luther and Zwingli in the eucharistic controversy, which significantly interrupted the course of the main events in the period of the Reformation. When Carlstadt had to leave Strasburg in 1524, Butzer addressed a writing to Luther in the name of the Strasburg ministers, in which he and they expressed their position in regard to

Carlstadt. Concerning the sacrament of the altar, they taught that the bread is the body of Christ and the wine his blood, but that greater importance should be attached to the commemoration of the death of Jesus than to the question what one eats and drinks. At first Luther answered reassuringly, but in his work *Wider die himmlischen Propheten* (1525) he attacked the Strasburg theologians.

3. Endeavors to Reconcile Luther and Zwingli.

The latter sent an envoy to appease Luther, but he emphasized the bodily presence of Christ in the Lord's Supper more than ever, and gave the Strasburgers to understand that they should not be deceived by the light of reason. The Strasburgers now saw themselves driven more and more to the side of the Swiss, so far as the doctrine of the sacrament was concerned. At the Disputation of Bern (q.v.) in 1528 Butzer made the personal acquaintance of Zwingli, with whom he had been corresponding since 1523. Luther again attacked his opponents in his *Grosses Bekenntnis vom Abendmahl* (1528), but Butzer did not lose hope of coming to an understanding by a personal interview. Together with the landgrave Philip of Hesse, who was animated by the same interest in the union and agreement of the Protestants, he brought about the religious conference of Marburg (q.v.) in 1529. Concerning the question whether the true body and blood of Christ are actually present in the bread and wine, no agreement could be reached; nevertheless, each party was to show Christian love toward the other, so far as the conscience of each allowed. Butzer visited Luther at Coburg in Sept., 1530, and received the promise to examine a new confession which Butzer intended to prepare. Butzer now endeavored to induce the Protestants, at least in southern Germany, to prepare a declaration which should approximately satisfy Luther, since the Swiss opposed every further advance, an additional incentive being the threatening attitude of the emperor toward the Protestants at this time. The outcome of these endeavors wa the Wittenberg Concord (q.v.), which was agreed upon with Luther in 1536 by a delegation of Upper German theologians under the direction of Butzer.

4. The Wittenberg Concord.

In this Concord the concession was made to Luther that the body and the blood of Christ are truly and essentially present with the bread and with the wine and are so given and received, the only modification being that the unworthy, but not the unholy, actually receive the body of the Lord. By this agreement a certain sort of theological understanding was reached between Luther and the South Germans, but the rupture between Butzer and the Swiss was accomplished.

Whatever views be held of Butzer's efforts for union, especially in the eucharistic controversy, his honest intention and his unselfish zeal to serve the Church are beyond all question. His diplomatic tactics were not always such as to inspire confidence, and they gave offense to other parties besides Luther. Butzer himself felt it afterward and honestly acknowledged that he had not always interfered in a discreet manner. The whole subject of controversy was of less interest for Butzer than for Luther, hence Butzer's

5. Critique of Butzer's Attitude in the Controversy.

readiness to make concessions and ever new formularizations. The real success of his endeavors was that the South Germans were not only induced to make common political cause with the North Germans, but were also drawn into the communion of Lutheranism, in spite of their peculiar doctrine of the Lord's Supper. The fact that Melanchthon, influenced partly by Butzer, took an intermediate position, and was thus drawn nearer to Calvin, was also far-reaching in its importance for the future formation of the Evangelical Church in Germany. The outcome of the Schmalkald War and the defeat of the Protestants (1547) gave the emperor power to settle the religious troubles by the Augsburg Interim (see INTERIM) in 1548, which was accepted by the majority of the intimidated diet and was to be forced upon the city of Strasburg. This was most energetically opposed by Butzer and his younger colleague, Paul Fagius, on the ground of the Romanizing character of the document. But when the council, yielding to the force of circumstances, accepted the Interim, Butzer perceived that he could remain in Strasburg no longer, and he accepted a call to England, whither he had been invited, together with Fagius, by Thomas Cranmer, archbishop of Canterbury, the soul of the Reformation in England.

6. Butzer in England.

In Apr., 1549, both arrived at London, and were met by Cranmer and King Edward VI. The king wished them to translate the Bible from the original into Latin, this version being intended to serve as the basis of an English version for the people. The work was commenced at once. At the end of the summer of 1549 Butzer and Fagius were to go to Cambridge as teachers and assist in the education of candidates for the ministry. Fagius arrived first, but died of a slow fever (Nov., 1549). In Jan., 1550, Butzer commenced his lectures at Cambridge, which were attended by large crowds of students, some of whom afterward exercised a powerful influence in the Anglican Church. Butzer was directed to examine the Book of Common Prayer, and was thus led into a public disputation held on Aug. 6, 1550, to expose the opposition of the English bishops (who still leaned toward Rome) to evangelical principles and innovations. At the request of the young king, Butzer wrote his *De regno Christi*, which he prepared in less than three months. This work was intended to teach the true nature of God's kingdom and the means by which it might be realized in earthly form in a country like England. This work was Butzer's last.

7. Death of Butzer.

Scarcely had the king expressed his warm approval and the university conferred the degree of doctor of divinity unconditionally, a thing which never happened before, when Butzer died after a short illness. He was buried with great honor in the principal church at Cambridge; but in 1556 his body was exhumed and publicly burnt. Four years afterward, however, Queen Elizabeth again honored his memory.

PAUL GRUENBERG.

BIBLIOGRAPHY: A complete collection of Butzer's works has never been made, that begun by his associate K. Hubert never getting beyond the first volume, Basel, 1577 (known as *Tomus Anglicanus* because it contained mostly writings published in England). A bibliography of Butzer's published works and literature about him was issued by F. Mentz and A. Erichson in *Vierhundertjährige Geburtsfeier M. Butzer's*, Strasburg, 1891. Consult: J. W. Baum, *Capito und Butzer, Strassburgs Reformatoren*, Elberfeld, 1860 (from the sources); J. B. Rady, *Die Reformatoren in ihrer Beziehung zur Doppelehe des Landgrafen Philipp*, Frankfort, 1890; C. Conrad, *Martin Butzer*, Strasburg, 1891; A. Erichson, *Die calvinistische und die Altstrassburger Gottesdienstordnung*, ib. 1894; H. von Schubert, in *Beiträge zur Reformationsgeschichte*, pp. 192–228, Gotha, 1896; A. Ernst and J. Adam, *Katechetische Geschichte des Elsasses bis zur Reformation*, pp. 42–72, Strasburg, 1897; F. Hubert, *Strassburger Katechismen aus den Tagen der Reformation*, in *ZKG*, xx. (1899) 395–413; A. Lang, *Der Evangelienkommentar Butzers und die Grundzüge seiner Theologie*, in *Studien zur Geschichte der Theologie und Kirche*, vol. ii., Leipsic, 1900; S. M. Jackson, *Huldreich Zwingli*, passim, New York, 1903; J. Köstlin, *Martin Luther*, ed. G. Kawerau, passim, 2 vols., Berlin, 1903; J. M. Reu, *Quellen zur Geschichte des kirchlichen Unterrichts*, Gütersloh, 1904; J. Ficker, *Thesaurus Baumianus*, Strasburg, 1905; Moeller, *Christian Church*, vol. iii., passim; Schaff, *Christian Church*, vol. vi., passim.

BUXTORF: A family of scholars at Basel, noteworthy for their services in the study of the Old Testament and Hebrew language and literature.

1. Johann Buxtorf the Elder: Orientalist; b. at Camen (8 m. s.w. of Hamm), Westphalia, Dec. 25, 1564; d. at Basel Sept. 13, 1629. He received his earliest education in the schools of Hamm and Dortmund, and then went to Marburg and Herborn, where he began his Hebrew studies under Piscator. Leaving Herborn, he studied successively at Heidelberg, Basel, Zurich, and Geneva, returning to Basel and taking his degree in 1590. In the following year, after much hesitation, he accepted the chair of Hebrew at the University of Basel, and later added other duties to this position, including the direction of the gymnasium. In 1610, however, he declined an appointment to a professorship of theology, as well as calls to Leyden and Saumur. Buxtorf was the greatest rabbinical student among the Protestants, availing himself not only of the Hebrew commentaries on the books of the Old Testament and the writings of learned Jews, but also carrying on an active correspondence with Jewish scholars in Germany, Poland, and Italy. His close relations with Jews, however, frequently exposed him to suspicion, and on one occasion he was fined 100 florins for attending the circumcision of a son of a Jew who resided in his house as his assistant in the printing of his Hebrew Bible. He devoted his Hebrew knowledge to the defense of the original text of the Old Testament against the Roman Catholics, who regarded the Vulgate and the Septuagint as the more reliable authorities, and also against the doubts cast upon it by such Reformers as Luther, Zwingli, and Calvin, his services being the more important in view of the necessity of appeal to the purity of the Hebrew text in Protestant polemics against Catholicism. His chief works are as follows: *Manuale Hebraicum et Chaldaicum* (Basel, 1602); *Juden-Schül* (1603; Latin transl., *Synagoga Judaica*, by H. Germberg, Hanau, 1604); *Lexicon Hebraicum et Chaldaicum* (1607); *De abbreviaturis Hebraicis* (1613); *Biblia Hebraica cum paraphrasi Chaldaica et commentariis rabbinorum* (4 vols., 1618–19); and *Tiberias, sive commentarius masorethicus* (1620); but he did not live to complete his *Concordantiæ Bibliorum Hebraicæ* or his *Lexicon Chaldaicum, Talmudicum et Rabbinicum*, both of which were edited by his son (Basel, 1632, 1639).

2. Johann Buxtorf the Younger: Orientalist; son of the preceding; b. at Basel Aug. 13, 1599; d. there Aug. 17, 1664. After receiving his first education from his father, he attended the high school of his native city, and in 1617 went to Heidelberg, where he remained two years, then going to Dort, where he attended the synod. After its conclusion he made a tour of Holland, England, and France, in company with the delegates of the city, and then returned to Basel. At the age of twenty-three he published his *Lexicon Chaldaicum et Syriacum* (Basel, 1622), and in the following year studied at Geneva, but declined a call to the professorship of logic at Lausanne, preferring to remain in his native city, where he served as a deacon from 1624 to 1630. Delicate health, however, obliged him to resign all hopes of becoming a preacher, and in 1630 he succeeded his father as professor of Hebrew. He declined calls to Groningen and Leyden, and in 1654 accepted the chair of Old Testament exegesis, as being closely associated with the one which he already held. It was his task to defend the views of his father on the purity of the transmitted Masoretic text of the Old Testament against many attacks, particularly by Cappel (q.v.), who assailed the credibility of rabbinical tradition and regarded the Hebrew text as inferior in places to the ancient versions. In this and kindred controversies Buxtorf wrote *De punctorum, vocalium atque accentuum in libris Veteris Testamenti Hebraicis origine, antiquitate et auctoritate* (Basel, 1648), and *Anticritica, seu vindiciæ veritatis Hebraicæ adversus Ludovici Cappelli criticam quam sacram vocat* (1653), but though the logical victory rested with Cappel, who could appeal both to the judgment of Elias Levita (q.v.), who exercised a powerful influence on the development of Old Testament studies among the Protestants, and could also claim the support of many of the Reformers, he was regarded as a dangerous man, who sought to deny the divinity of the Scriptures, while his opponent was looked upon as a defender of orthodoxy, and won the formal verdict. In a minor controversy with Cappel on the Eucharist he wrote his *Vindiciæ exercitationis Sanctæ Cœnæ contra Cappellum* (Basel, 1646) and his *Anticritica contra Cappellum* (1653). He likewise made a Latin translation of the *Moreh Nebukim* of Maimonides (Basel, 1629) and edited, with notes and a translation, the *Liber Cosri, sive colloquium de religione* of Judah ha-Levi (1660).

3. Johannes Jakob Buxtorf: Orientalist; son of the preceding; b. at Basel Sept. 4, 1645; d. there Apr. 1, 1704. He was educated at the university of his native city, and succeeded his father as professor of Hebrew in Nov., 1664. In the following year he received leave of absence and visited Geneva, France, Holland (wintering at Leyden), and London. The general suspicion of foreigners in London just after the great fire, however, caused Buxtorf to take refuge in a neighboring village, whence he later went to Oxford and Cambridge. In 1669 he returned to Basel and resumed his duties at the university, in addition to acting as librarian Although regarded as an excellent scholar and a diligent student, he wrote little with the exception of a preface to his edition of his grandfather's *Tiberias* (Basel, 1665), and his emendations to the *Synagoga Judaica* (1680).

4. **Johann Buxtorf**: Nephew of the preceding; b. at Basel Jan. 8, 1663; d. there June 19, 1732. After completing his education at Basel, he went to Holland to continue his Oriental studies. In 1694 he was appointed preacher at Aristdorf, a village near Basel, and in 1704 he succeeded his uncle as professor of Hebrew at the University, holding this position until his death. His most noteworthy book was his *Catalecta philologico-theologica cum mantissa epistolarum virorum clarorum ad Johannem Buxtorffium patrem et filium scriptarum* (Basel, 1707). (Carl Bertheau.)

Bibliography: *Athenæ Rauricæ*, Basel, 1778 (contains biographies and catalogues of their publications); K. R. Hagenbach, *Die theologische Schule Basels*, pp. 27 sqq., ib. 1860; C. H. H. Wright, *Introduction to the O. T.*, London, 1891; C. D. Ginsburg, *Introduction to the Massoretico-critical Edition of the Hebr. Bible*, ib. 1897; C. A. Briggs, *Study of Holy Scripture*, passim, New York, 1899; Buxtorf-Falkeisen, *Johannes Buxtorf Vater*, Basel, 1860; E. Kautzsch, *J. Buxtorf der ältere*, ib. 1879. On the younger Johannes, L. Diestel, *Geschichte des alten Testaments in der christlichen Kirche*. pp. 330 sqq., Jena, 1868. On Johannes Jakob, S. Werenfels, *Vita J. J. Buxtorfii*, Basel, 1705.

BYFIELD, ADONIRAM: Puritan and Presbyterian; b. probably at Chester, before 1615, the son of Nicholas Byfield (q.v.); d. in London 1660. He was educated at Emmanuel College, Cambridge, and chosen chaplain to a regiment of Parliament's army in 1642. In 1643 he was appointed one of the two scribes of the Westminster Assembly, but was not a member of that body. The manuscript minutes (edited by Mitchel and Struthers, 1874), now in the Williams Library, University Hall, Gordon Square, London, are in his handwriting. He also edited, by authority of Parliament, the various papers in the controversy between the Westminster Assembly and the Dissenting Brethren, published London, 1648, including *Reasons Presented by the Dissenting Brethren against Certain Propositions concerning Presbyterian Government, The Answer of Assemby of Divines, Papers for Accumulation,* and *The Papers and Answers of the Dissenting Brethren and the Committee of the Assembly of Divines.* He was rector of Fulham in Middlesex (1644?) and vicar of Fulham (1645?–1657), subsequently rector of Collingbourn-Ducis in Wiltshire. C. A. Briggs.

BYFIELD, NICHOLAS: Puritan and Presbyterian, b. in Warwickshire in 1579; d. at Isleworth (2 m. s. of Brentford), Middlesex, Sept. 8, 1622. He was educated at Exeter College, Oxford; was for seven years pastor of St. Peter's Church at Chester, when (1615) he became vicar of Isleworth in Middlesex, where he remained until his death. William Gouge describes him as "a man of a profound judgment, strong memory, sharp wit, quick invention, and unwearied industry." His works were numerous, and greatly esteemed. His *Marrow of the Oracles of God* (London, 1620), containing six treatises previously published apart, reached an eleventh edition in 1640. *The Principles, or, the Pattern of Wholesome Words,* dedicated in 1618, reached a seventh edition in 1665, and is a valuable compend of divinity. His expository sermons on the Epistle to the Colossians were published 1615, and several series on the First Epistle of Peter at various times, finally collected and enlarged in a *Commentary upon the Whole First Epistle of St. Peter* (1637). *The Rule of Faith, or an Exposition of the Apostles' Creed* was issued by his son Adoniram, after his death (1626), and is an able and instructive work. He must be numbered among the Presbyterian fathers in England.

C. A. Briggs.

BYROM, JOHN: Author of "Christians awake, salute the happy morn," a Christmas hymn in almost universal use in England; b. at Kersall Cell, Broughton, near Manchester, Feb. 29, 1692; d. there Sept. 26, 1763. He entered Trinity College, Cambridge, 1708 (B.A., 1712; M.A., 1715), and became fellow, 1714; contributed to the *Spectator;* invented a system of shorthand and taught it with success; became F.R.S., 1724; succeeded to the family estate at Kersall, 1740, and spent his later years there. He was a mystic and a Jacobite; took deep interest in religious speculations, and knew most of the celebrities of his time; he wrote some of the best epigrams in the language. His *Poems,* written in easy, colloquial style for his own and his friends' amusement, were printed posthumously (2 vols., Manchester, 1773; again, with life and notes, London, 1814); the Chetham Society of Manchester has published his *Private Journal and Literary Remains,* ed. R. Parkinson (2 vols., 1854–1857), and the *Poems,* ed. A. W. Ward (2 vols., 1894–1895).

BYRUM, ENOCH EDWIN: American clergyman and editor of *The Church of God;* b. near Union City, Ind., Oct. 13, 1861. He was educated in the public schools, and also studied elocution and oratory in the Northern Indiana Normal School (1886) and Sunday-school work in Otterbein University (1887). He was ordained a minister of "The Church of God" in 1892, and in addition to editing *The Gospel Trumpet* and *The Shining Light* since 1890, has written: *The Boy's Companion* (Moundsville, W Va., 1890); *Divine Healing of Soul and Body* (1892); *The Secret of Salvation* (1896); *The Prayer of Faith* (1899); *The Great Physician* (1900); *Behind the Prison Bars* (1901); *What shall I do to be Saved?* (1903); *Ordinances of the Bible* (1904); and *Travels and Experiences in other Lands* (1905).

C

CABALA, cab'a-la.

The term Cabala designates the esoteric doctrines of Judaism. Although it claims to be a product of the tannaitic period and to be the work of such sages as Ishmael ben Elisha, Simeon ben Yoḥai, and Neḥunya ben ha-Ḳanah, modern investigation has proved that it is purely a product of the Middle Ages. Nor does the name *ḳabbalah* (from *ḳibbel*, "to receive") occur with this special connotation before the thirteenth century, the term *ḳabbalah* denoting in the Talmud the Hagiographa and the Prophets in contradistinction to the Torah, or Pentateuch.

The Cabala originated at a period when a crassly anthropomorphic concept of God prevailed in Judaism. In Maimonides rationalism had reached its climax, the literal meaning alone being accepted, while all allegorical interpretation was rejected. The study of the Talmud had become purely legalistic, and worship had degenerated into formalism. Against this stereotyped faith born of Aristotelianism arose a reaction, the Cabala. This sought to give the soul the nourishment it craved by an esoteric interpretation of the Scriptures, vivid presentation, and dramatic narrative, even though, in its speculative fervor, it became involved only too often in hopeless haze, and evoked a dark superstition through its juggling with the names of God. Arising in Provence, the reaction against rationalism passed to Spain, the real home of the Cabala. Thence, with the expulsion of the Spanish Jews, it was carried to Palestine, whence it spread throughout Europe. The fundamental doctrines of the Cabala are derived from the Hellenistic Judaism, Neoplatonism, and Neo-Pythagoreanism, with occasional traces of Gnosticism. These elements are so interwoven, however, with the Bible and with a midrashic method of presentation, that the whole has been stamped with the seal of Judaism.

1. Origin and Spread of the Cabala.

According to the Cabala, God is the eternal and boundless principle of all, and is therefore called *En Sof* ("The Infinite"). The attributes given him are general, rather than specific. He is absolutely perfect, and is free from all blemish; he is unity and immutability; he is boundless and naught exists beside him; and since he may be known neither by wisdom nor by understanding, no definition can be given of him, no concept be formed regarding him, and no question asked concerning him. To all beings he is the concealed of all concealed, the hidden of all hidden, the ancient of the ancient; the first of all first, and the primal principle.

2. Doctrine of God.

The cardinal cosmogonic doctrine of the Cabala is creation *e nihilo*. The reconciliation of the imperfect and transitory phenomenal world with the perfection and immutability of God, and the mutual relation of the two formed never-ending problems for the cabalists. To explain the riddle they assumed the existence of a series of independent and spiritual primeval potentialities, which were intelligible substances or demiurges emanating from the deity. These demiurges (*sefiroth*) are mentioned as early as the *Sefer Yeẓirah*, where their number is given as ten. According to this work, the first emanation was the spirit of the living God, from which proceeded the entire phenomenal world. This same spirit, futhermore, caused ether, water, and fire to emanate from each other. From ether arises the intellectual world, from water the material (the *tohu wa-bohu* of Gen. i. 2), and from fire the spiritual (the angels and the throne of God). These four *sefiroth* are followed by the six bounds of space, height, depth, east, west, north, and south. There is, however, no consistent view concerning the nature of the *sefiroth*, which are sometimes regarded as intermediaries between God and the visible world, and at other times as the manifestations of the powers and properties of God; and there is an equal divergence of opinion as to whether they are actual creations which form, in a sense, the basis of later creations, or emanations whereby God emerges from his concealment and assumes form. All attempts to reconcile these conflicting views by postulating the existence of God both in and above phenomena proved unsuccessful. The issuance of the *sefiroth* from God was regarded by the cabalists as imperiling the doctrine of his immutability and infinity. The first difficulty was obviated by the hypothesis that God's design to manifest himself had existed from all eternity. Since, however, God in his infinity filled the entire universe, no room was left for the *sefiroth*, until Moses ben Jacob Cordovero (1522–70) and Isaac Luria (1533–72) postulated two concentrations, one a contraction and the other a retraction. Many cabalists, however, felt themselves unable to accept this theory of concentration, which was closely connected, moreover, with the Gnosticism of Valentinian and Basilides, and preferred to assume that the emergence of God from his retirement was to be understood in terms of concept rather than of space, and some regarded the entire process as metaphorical.

3. Creation and the Sefiroth.

The first *sefirah* was *Kether* ("Crown"), the primal source of all existence. The second was *Ḥokmah* ("Wisdom"), which, though enveloped in God, generated the ideas. The third was *Binah* ("Intelligence"), which carries out the ideas of development of the Cabala, and that it was not fully developed until the thirteenth century.

The Messianic teachings of the Cabala are closely connected with the doctrine of the realm of the evil *sefiroth*. When through their piety and virtue mankind shall steadily have diminished the kingdom of the *ḳelifoth*, the Messiah will appear and restore all things to their original condition. Under his rule all will turn to the divine light, and idolatry will cease. In its account of the nature and task of the Messiah the Cabala diverges a little from the views advanced by the Talmud and the Midrash.

8. Doctrine of the Messiah.

In its anthropology the Cabala generally adopts the tenets of Talmudic and Gaonic mysticism, so that its new developments may be summarized briefly. Earthly man is a type of the prototype *Adham ḳadhmon*, and thus comprises within himself all that the ideal creation contains. He is, therefore, a microcosm. The Cabala also teaches the dual nature of man, who consists of body and soul. Every member has its symbolic meaning, while the body, as the garment of the soul, typifies the *merkabah* (the heavenly Throne-Chariot of Ezek. i., x.). The soul, however, is far superior to the body, since it is derived from the divine all-soul, and through the "canals" (*ẓinnoroth*) can influence the intellectual world and draw down its blessings to the lower world. It appears under the three designations of *nefesh*, *ruaḥ*, and *neshamah*. The first is blind impulse, the second is the seat both of good and evil impulses, and the third is able to unite with God and the kingdom of light.

9. Doctrines of the Soul.

The Cabala also teaches the preexistence of the soul. All souls destined to enter human bodies have existed from all eternity in a fixed number, nourished by the sight of the divine radiance of the Shekinah. The entrance of the soul into a body is a misfortune, and it implores God to spare it such imprisonment. Before their entrance into human bodies souls are androgynous, while marriage unites the severed halves to a single whole. This doctrine, like the preceding, is reminiscent of Plato and Philo, as is the cabalistic doctrine that all earthly learning is but a reminiscence of what the soul had known before it came to earth. Of special interest is the cabalistic doctrine of reincarnation. Each soul which is united with a body is to undergo a period of trial in this world, and if it is found able to preserve its original purity it returns immediately at death to its place of heavenly origin. If, on the other hand, it falls into sin, it is subjected to a purification, and is obliged to remain in lower forms of existence, such as animals, trees, stones, and rivers, until it has fully atoned for its evil and has regained the purity requisite for its return to its celestial home. Occasionally, however, the sin-laden soul wanders in the world with its fellows, naked and ashamed, until it finally receives its purification in hell. New souls are seldom born, the greater number being reincarnations. This is a proof of the corruption of the human race, and though exalted spirits sometimes descend to earth for the welfare of man and assume human form, all the souls created from the beginning have not yet been able to be born on account of the number of reincarnations necessitated by human wickedness, and the Messiah consequently has not come. During sleep the souls of the righteous frequently leave their bodies, ascend to the celestial regions, hold converse with the spirits there, and receive revelations of future mysteries. Evil souls, on the other hand, descend to the realms of darkness and impurity and converse with demons, who give them false and lying words. To enable mankind to hold communication with the world of light during terrestrial existence, the cabalists exacted a scrupulous observance of the ceremonial law and, above all, prayer, to which was ascribed an influence over God himself. Among other agencies stress was laid on asceticism, flagellation, retirement from the world, the practise of all good works, the wearing of white garments, and the use of the phylacteries and the prayer-mantle.

10. Metempsychosis.

Aristotelian scholasticism gave rise in Judaism to a system of exegesis which resulted in a view of religion as a matter of the head, rather than the heart. Yet at this very time the increasing persecution of the Jews evoked a need for spiritual strength and revivification, and these requirements were met by the cabalistic opposition to the purely intellectual interpretation of the Bible and by the substitution of a new method of hermeneutics, which sounded the depths of the Scriptures and thus strengthened the sinews of religion. As early as the Talmudic and Mishnaic period the feeling had prevailed in certain quarters that in addition to the literal meaning of the Bible (*peshat*) there was an allegorical meaning (*derush*). The cabalists went still further, and regarded the letters, words, and names of the Bible as possessed of deeply hidden divine mysteries, while such accounts as those of Hagar, Esau, and Balak contained far more than mere history. They therefore laid little stress on the literal sense of the Bible, though not a letter might be added to it or taken from it. In their endeavor to unlock the divine mysteries they employed various systems of exegesis. Of these the chief was the *gematria*, or study of letters. As early as the *Sefer Yeẓirah* the twenty-two letters of the Hebrew alphabet were divided according to sound, form, and numerical value. To the first class belonged the three "mothers," *aleph*, *mem*, and *shin*, which represented the three primal elements, *aleph* standing for air (*awwer*), *mem* for water (*mayim*), and *shin* for fire (*esh*). The seven "double" letters which formed the second division (*beth*, *gimel*, *daleth*, *kaph*, *pe*, *resh*, and *taw*) were symbolic of the seven planets, the seven days of the week, the seven gates of the soul, the seven seas, and the like; while in virtue of their twofold pronunciation, either aspirated or unaspirated, they typified the seven antitheses of man: life and death, wisdom and folly, riches and poverty, peace and war, beauty and hideousness, fertility and desolation, power and slavery. The twelve "simple" letters, which

11. Mystic Biblical Exegesis of the Cabala.

12. Biblical Interpretation by Gemaṭria.

constituted the remainder of the alphabet, symbolized the twelve activities of man: sight, hearing, smell, speech, eating, cohabitation, toil, walking, wrath, laughter, reflection, and sleep. The numerical value of the letters, moreover, rendered numbers sacred, so that twelve, for example, typified the twelve tribes, the twelve months, and the twelve signs of the zodiac. Subsequently *gematria* was divided into arithmetical and figurative, the first considering the letters according to their numerical value and the latter devoted to the mode of writing the letters.

A second exegetical system was the *notarikon*, the acrostic use of the letters in such a way that each letter of a word formed the initial letter of a new word. The third method was *ẓiruf*, the combination of letters, and the fourth was *temurah*, the creation of new words by the permutation and interchange of letters. The names of God were special subjects of cabalistic jugglery, since they were no longer the means whereby God had emerged from his concealment and become manifest to the understanding, but were now agencies to work upon the intelligible powers and to perform miracles of all kinds. The most marvelous powers were ascribed to the divine tetragrammaton YHWH. Whosoever possessed the true pronunciation of this name might come into relation with the upper world and receive revelations from the All-Soul. Each letter of the name was portentous. The *yodh* represented the Father as creator, and the double *he* the upper and lower Mother, while the *waw* typified the creation. Through permutation of the letters of the tetragrammaton was obtained a wealth of divine names, to which, in like manner, were ascribed miraculous powers. In the "practical" Cabala these new names played an important part, being used in formulas, amulets, and conjurations, their correct enunciation and the gestures with which they were spoken being leading factors in all these operations. In like manner, the twelve-lettered, twenty-two-lettered, twenty-four-lettered, and seventy-two-lettered name contained great mysteries, influenced the Supreme Being and averted threatening doom, while the names of the angels were subjected to similar manipulation. The net result was the total loss of any comprehension of the actual meaning of the text of the Bible.

13. Magic Powers of the Tetragrammaton.

The history of the Cabala comprises a period of a thousand years, since its beginnings may be traced to the seventh century, while its last adherents belonged to the eighteenth. This lapse of time may be divided into two periods, the first from the seventh to the thirteenth century, and the second from the fourteenth to the eighteenth.

14. The Early Period of the Cabala.

From the seventh to the ninth century flourished the mysticism of the *Merkabah*, devoted to descriptions of "the great and small halls," and describing the throne of God and his court of angels according to Byzantine models. God the Infinite, the *sefiroth*, and transmigration are still unknown, and the authority cited on all occasions is the Tanna Ishmael ben Elisha, who flourished in the first and second centuries A.D. The juggling with the alphabet is represented by the "Alphabet of Rabbi Akiba," which treats of the letters according to name and form, and connects them with all manner of moral and religious teachings. With the appearance of the *Sefer Yeẓirah* ("Book of Creation") in the eighth century, the mystery of the Throne-Chariot gave place to the mystery of the creation, and a cosmogonic element was introduced which increased steadily in importance in the subsequent period. Here the doctrine of emanation appears in the form in which it had originated in Alexandria. The twenty-two letters are connected, moreover, with the ten divine emanations, and thus form the thirty-two paths of esoteric wisdom and constitute the basis of all things. God is not only the creator, but also the sustainer and ruler of the world.

15. The Sefer Yeẓirah.

The letters of the alphabet are "real powers" which underlie all phenomena, while their permutation and their evaluation, like their connotation, are of importance. The *Sefer Yeẓirah* is the earliest work which unites cabalistic speculation in a systematic whole. According to it there are four basal principles, emanating in order from each other—spirit, spirits, primeval water, and primeval fire, all united by the three dimensions and their antitheses into a decade. All things are in continual flux, dissolving old combinations and forming new ones, while throughout phenomena rules the law of antitheses, which are united by the mean between them. A remarkable work of the same period is the *Sefer Raziel*, which teaches the influence of the planets and the figures of the zodiac on the earth. The angel Raziel here takes the place of Meṭaṭron, the angel of the presence, as he who possesses and communicates astrological and astronomical mysteries.

16. Crystallization of the Cabala.

In the thirteenth century the crystallization of the Cabala began and the doctrine of the *sefiroth* was fully developed. To the same period probably belongs the composition of the "Luminous Book," also called the "Midrash of Neḥunya ben ha-Ḳanah," which teaches the main outlines of metempsychosis, while the ten divine emanations, which are not yet called *sefiroth*, but *ma'amarim* ("commands"), appear as categories possessed of creative force and connected with the attributes of God. A tendency toward visionary prophecy was impressed upon the Cabala by Abraham ben Samuel Abulafia (d. about 1304), who laid special stress on a knowledge of the divine name as determined by the exegetical methods of *gemaṭria*, *noṭarikon*, *ẓiruf*, and *temurah*, while his pupil Joseph ben Abraham Gikatilla devoted himself to the mysteries of the alphabet, which he brought into close association with the doctrine of the *sefiroth*. The cabalistic speculation begun by Isaac the Blind reached its climax in the *Zohar*, apparently written by Moses ben Shem-Ṭob of Leon (d. 1305). If the *Sefer Yeẓirah* be called the Mishnah of the Cabala, the *Zohar* is its Talmud. Ostensibly it is a midrashic commentary on the pericopes of the Pentateuch, but practically it is eternal Wisdom. The fifth was *Ḥesedh* ("Love"; sometimes called *Gedhulah*, "Magnitude"), the fifth *Din* ("Law"; also called *Gebhurah*, "Might," or *Paḥadh*, "Fear"), the sixth *Tifereth* ("Beauty"; also called *Raḥamim*, "Mercy"), the seventh *Neẓaḥ* ("Firmness"), the eighth *Hodh*

4. Names of the Sefiroth. ("Splendor"), and the ninth *Yesodh* ("Foundation"). The tenth *sefirah* was *Malkhuth* ("Kingdom"; also called *Shekhinah*, "Royalty"), and was united in marriage with the God who rules the world. The number of the *sefiroth* was doubtless influenced by the fact that astronomy then postulated the existence of ten spheres, and also by the sanctity ascribed to the number ten.

As early as the eleventh century Hai Gaon (998–1038) classified the ten primal potentialities into two groups, the first including three which produced the spiritual world, and the second comprising two triads which were united by a seventh, and these formed the source of the material world. The main outlines of this classification were retained by later cabalists. Azriel (1160–1238) distinguished three groups—intellectual, spiritual, and material, a classification evidently due to Neoplatonic influence. Each group forms a triad, and its members stand in the mutual relation of thesis, antithesis, and synthesis. The first two members, moreover, sustain a polar relation to each other, and are united by the third. Thus, in the first triad, which consists of "Crown," "Wisdom," and "Intelligence," "Intelligence" forms the connecting link. In the second triad, which consists of "Love," "Law," and "Beauty," "Beauty" (or "Mercy") forms the bond of union, while in the third triad of "Firmness," "Splendor," and "Foundation," the last recon-

5. Triads of Sefiroth. ciles the first two. All three triads are subject to the tenth *sefirah*, "Kingdom," which binds them into a harmonious whole. The first triad, moreover, contained the "authors of the plan of the world," the second the "arrangers," and the third the "creators." Although the *sefiroth* are by no means comparable with God and do not condition his independence, they partake of his infinity and transmit his streams of blessings to the various worlds. For this purpose, on which their existence and activity depend, they are united with God by invisible canals (*ẓinnoroth*) which proceed from the throne of the divine majesty.

In so far as the *sefiroth* are the earliest manifestations of God, they form an ideal world which bears no relation to the material world, and in this aspect they are termed either "primeval man" (*adham ḳadhmon*) or "superman" (*adham 'ilai*), who is sometimes considered to be the *sefiroth* collectively, and sometimes regarded as the first manifestation whereby God revealed himself as the creator and ruler of the world. In this aspect he seems to be a revelation interposed between God and the universe, and thus a second god, as it were, or the Logos.

According to a later view, various grades of emanation produced four worlds, in each of which the ten *sefiroth* were repeated. The first of these was the *'Olam ha-Aẓilah* ("World of Radiation"), which contains the powers of the divine plan of the worlds. These powers have the same nature as the world of the *sefiroth* or the *Adham ḳadhmon*, while, according to the Zohar, it also contains the throne of the Shekinah and God's mantle of light. From the *'Olam ha-Aẓilah* emanated the *'Olam ha-Beriah* ("World of Creation"), the home of the organizing powers and potencies. There were the treasuries of blessing and life,

6. The Four Worlds. and there was the throne of the glory of God, as well as the halls of all spiritual and moral perfection, where the souls of the righteous dwelt. In its turn, the *'Olam ha-Beriah* produced the *'Olam ha-Yeẓirah* ("World of Creation") with the angels and Meṭaṭron as their chief. To him are subject the evil spirits (*ḳelifoth*, "husks"), who dwell in the planets and other heavenly bodies, or in the ether. The fourth world is the present material and phenomenal *'Olam ha-'Assiyah* ("World of Action"), which is subject to constant change and delusion. Like the *sefiroth*, the four worlds are closely connected with God as the primal principle, and receive continual streams of divine blessing. This cosmology of four worlds is based on the theophany of Ezek. i. and seems to be first mentioned in the *Massekheth Aẓiluth*, a small treatise of the first half of the thirteenth century. The anthropomorphic tendencies of the cabalists led them to make distinctions of sex among the *sefiroth*. The masculine principle, which is white in color, appears chiefly in "Love," although it underlies both the other two *sefiroth* of the right side ("Wisdom" and "Firmness"); while the passive red female principle, which owes its existence to the male, dwells chiefly in "Law," yet also forms the basis of the other *sefiroth* of the left side ("Intelligence" and "Splendor").

Side by side with the heavenly *sefiroth* exist the *sefiroth* of evil, and *Adham ḳadhmon*, in like manner, has his counterpart in *Adham Beliyya'al*. The realms are related to each other as the right and the left wing. In the kingdom of evil, as in the realm of good, there are ten grades. Under the leadership of Samael and his queen, the great adulteress, the dark *sefiroth* toil unceasingly for the destruction of the world. Since, however, the *sefiroth* of darkness, like the *sefiroth* of light, were regarded as emanations, there was danger that the Infinite might be considered the author of evil. To obviate this, the older cabalists advanced the hypothesis that the origin of evil was to be sought in the distances of the emanations from

7. Origin of Evil. their divine author, since the further they went from God into the material world, the more degenerate they became. The younger cabalists like Luria, on the other hand, held that the vessels of the *sefiroth* were unable to contain and conduct the fulness of the divine blessing and burst, thus giving rise to evil. Penance, self-mortification, prayer, and rigid observance of the prescribed ceremonies, however, would gradually reconcile the upper and lower realms and restore the original harmony of the universe. It is noteworthy that this doctrine of the opposition of the two kingdoms is a late filled with a mass of cabalistic and other mystical speculations, and with allegorism run mad, especially concerning the names of God, the accents, and the vowel-points. In like manner, the kingdom of evil, with its demons and evil spirits which continually oppose the realm of righteousness, is described in terms of wildest fantasy. Its statements are placed in the mouth of Simeon ben Yohai, a Tanna of the second century A.D., who, according to the Talmud, lived in association with the angel Meṭaṭron, who communicated to him the divine mysteries. Yet it is by no means a uniform work, among its older components being the "Book of Mystery," which is devoted to the creation and the events which preceded it; the "Great Holy Assembly," which forms a compend of cabalistic speculation and finds the type of all *sefiroth* in man, through whose mental processes the upper world of light is united with the lower world of sense, while the anthropomorphisms of the Old Testament are declared to be mere metaphors; and the "True Shepherd," which explains the nature of the primal emanations. The later elements of the *Zohar* are as follows: the "Small Holy Assembly," which gives a clearer exposition of the subjects treated in the "Great Holy Assembly"; the "Book of the Mystery of Mysteries," devoted to physiognomy and cheiromancy; the "Book of the Halls," which describes the abodes of the souls in the Garden of Eden and in hell; the "Hidden Midrash," which recounts the return of the souls to their new and perfect human forms after the resurrection, and portrays the meal prepared for the righteous; the "Ancient," which describes the transmigration of souls and the punishments of hell; the "Young," an exposition of various cabalistic teachings; and "Mishnas and Tosefta," which is devoted chiefly to the mystical meanings of the divine names. Despite the opposition of Talmudists and philosophers the *Zohar* gained an enormous following and was regarded as a revelation from heaven. Through it Spain became the real home of the Cabala, and even to the present day it is considered authoritative in some Judaistic quarters.

17. The Zohar.

With the exile of the Jews from Spain the Cabala was carried into all lands, and Safed in Palestine became its new center. There, in the sixteenth century, Moses ben Jacob Cordovero and Isaac Luria systematized the Cabala and filled many a gap which had existed in the *Zohar*, the former emphasizing the metaphysical and speculative, and the latter the ascetic and ethical side. Through them the *Zohar* was well-nigh deified, and in a like spirit many cabalists of the seventeenth century, such as Shabbathai Ẓebi and Jacob Frank, proclaimed themselves prophets or asserted that the Shekinah or the soul of the Messiah had become incarnate in them. From this time on, however, the Cabala has steadily declined, and the names of its representatives are too unimportant to require mention here.

18. Closing Period of the Cabala.

Though the Cabala was devoted to a spiritualization of religion, the pagan elements which it adopted brought to Judaism a view of the universe which was entirely foreign to it, and worked it grave injury. The Biblical concept of a monotheistic God was superseded by a vague Gentile theory of emanation with a pantheistic tendency, and the doctrine of the unity of God was thrust into the background by the ten *sefiroth*, who were regarded as divine in essence. Since prayer was no longer addressed immediately to God but to the *sefiroth*, a genuine *sefiroth*-cult was evolved. The Talmud and philosophy were disdained by the cabalists, and even the study of the Bible was neglected, since it was no longer read for its own sake, but solely with the aid of cabalistic methods of hermeneutics. Nor did the ritual escape change and mutilation, and the phylacteries and the prayer-mantles were now put on to the accompaniment of various cabalistic formulas, especially prominent being the prayers to the *sefiroth*. Worst of all was the growth of superstition. That the soul might attain to the realm of light after death, the severest mortification of the flesh was practised, while the mysterious names of God were believed to heal the sick and quench the flames, and God altered his divine will at the prayer of the cabalist. The very kingdom of darkness was subject to the proper formulas of prayer, and the damned were freed from their torments by use of the magic names of God.

19. Influence of the Cabala on Judaism.

During the period of the Reformation the Cabala attracted wide attention because of the alleged kinship and agreement of its doctrines with the dogmas of the Christian Church. The opinion accordingly prevailed that it formed the means by which Judaism and Christianity might easily be united, especially as it was believed to contain the doctrines of the Trinity, the Messiah as the Son of God, and his work of atonement. In his missionary zeal for the Saracens in the thirteenth century Raymond Lully (q.v.) considered the Cabala a divine revelation, and after the converted Jew Paulus de Heredia (about 1480) had shown in his "Letter of Secrets" that all the chief truths of Christianity were contained in the Cabala, Christian scholars became rivals in their eagerness to study esoteric Judaism. In 1486 Pico de Mirandola published at Rome his *Septuaginta-duæ conclusiones cabballisticæ*, and invited all scholars to Rome to attend a disputation to convince themselves of the kinship between the Cabala and Christianity. The first German to investigate this subject was Reuchlin, who devoted to it his *De verbo mirifico* (Basel, 1494) and his *De arte cabbalistica* (Hagenau, 1517). Latin translations of various portions of cabalistic works were made by Baruch of Benevento at the request of Cardinal Ægidius of Viterbo and by the convert Paul Riccio, physician in ordinary to the emperor Maximilian I., but the most important work which sought the truths of Christianity in the Cabala and gave translations from it was the *Kabbala denudata* of Christian Knorr von Rosenroth (4 vols., Sulzbach and Frankfort, 1677–84), the source for all subsequent scholars.

20. Relation of the Cabala to Christianity.

It is now recognized that the concepts of God and the creation are entirely divergent in the Cabala and Christianity; the first triad of the *sefiroth* does not actually correspond to the Trinity, nor does the Christian doctrine of Christ as the Son of God find an analogue in the *Adham ḳadhmon* of the Cabala. According to Christianity, redemption is possible only through Christ, while the Cabala postulates that man can save himself by his mystic influence on God and the world of light through rigid observance of the law, asceticism, and similar agencies. (AUGUST WÜNSCHE.)

BIBLIOGRAPHY: The literature up to about 1860 is arranged in J. Fürst, *Bibliotheca judaica*, iii. 329–335, Leipsic, 1863. The best book in Eng. is C. D. Ginsburg, *The Kabbalah, its Doctrines, Development, and Literature*, London, 1865. A most valuable work is A. Franck, *La Kabbale, ou la philosophie religieuse des Hébreux*, 3d ed., Paris, 1892 (Germ. transl., Leipsic, 1844). Of older literature the following may be mentioned: J. F. Buddeus, *Introductio ad historiam philosophiæ Hebræorum*, Halle, 1721; J. Basnage, *Histoire de la religion des Juifs*, vol. iii., Rotterdam, 1707–11; J. F. Kleuker, *Ueber die Natur und den Ursprung der Emanationslehre bei den Kabbalisten*, Riga, 1786; F. A. Tholuck, *De ortu Cabbalæ*, vol. i., Hamburg, 1837. Of later literature the following are suggested as worthy of study: A. Jellinek, *Beiträge zur Geschichte der Kabbala*, 2 vols., Leipsic, 1852 (of great value) idem, *Auswahl kabbalistischer Mystik*, ib. 1853; J. W. Etheridge, *Jerusalem and Tiberias, Sora and Cordova*, London, 1856; S. Munk, *Mélanges de philosophie juive et arabe*, pp. 461–511, Paris, 1857; G. des Mousseaux, *Le Juif*, pp. 509 sqq., ib. 1869; C. Siegfried, *Philo . . als Ausleger des Alten Testaments*, Jena, 1872; F. Ueberweg, *History of Philosophy*, i. 417, New York, 1876; F. Weber, *System der altsynagogalen palästinischen Theologie*, Leipsic, 1880; L. Wogue, *Histoire de l'exégese biblique*, Paris, 1881: *Die Kabbala. Ihre Hauptlehre*, Innsbruck, 1885; Simeon ben Yochai, *Kabbala denudata, Kabbalah Unveiled*, London, 1887; I. Meyer, *Qabbalah; Philosophical Writings of Solomon . Gebirol or Avicebron and their Connection with the Hebrew Qabbalah*, Philadelphia, 1888; P. Bloch, *Geschichte der Entwickelung der Kabbala*, Trier, 1894; J. Hamburger, *Real-Encyklopädie für Bibel und Talmud*, Leipsic, 1896–1901; *The Canon; an Exposition of the Pagan Mystery Perpetuated in the Cabala*, London, 1897; M. Mielziner, *Introduction to the Talmud*, Cincinnati, 1897; J. H. Weldon, *The Cabbala of the Bible*, 1897–1900; C. A. Briggs, *Study of Holy Scripture*, chap. xviii., New York, 1899; W. Begley, *Biblia cabalistica*, London, 1903; E. Bischoff, *De Kabbala Inleiding tot de joodsche mystiek*, Amsterdam, 1906; S. A. Binion, *The Kabbalah*, in *World's Best Literature*, ed. C. D. Warner, pp. 8425–42; *JE*, iii. 456–479, where other literature is mentioned. At the head of the article in Hauck-Herzog, *RE* is a very full list of works, including periodical literature.

CADALUS: Antipope. See HONORIUS II., antipope.

CADMAN, SAMUEL PARKES: Congregationalist; b. at Wellington (30 m. n.w. of Birmingham), Shropshire, England, Dec. 18, 1864. He was educated at Richmond College, London, graduating in theology and classics in 1889, and held successive Methodist pastorates at Millbrook, N. Y. (1890–1893), Yonkers, N. Y. (1893–95), and the Metropolitan Temple, New York City (1895–1900). He then became pastor of the Central Congregational Church, Brooklyn. His theological position is that of a liberal-conservative.

CADOC (*Cadocus, Docus*): A Welsh saint, called "the Wise," son of a chieftain of South Wales and cousin of St. David of Menevia; d., according to one account, at his monastery of Llancarven (near Cowbridge, 10 m. w.s.w. of Llandaff, Glamorganshire), according to others, as a martyr at Beneventum, 570 (?). He early devoted himself to the religious life, refused to succeed his father in his principality, studied under Irish scholars at home, and visited Ireland, Scotland, Rome, and Jerusalem in quest of instruction. He founded the monastery at Llancarven and made it a famous center of learning. Tradition associates him with David and Gildas (who was one of the teachers at Llancarven) as training the "second order of Irish saints" (see CELTIC CHURCH IN BRITAIN AND IRELAND, II., 2, § 1) and thus influencing the church life of Ireland. One of the earliest monuments of the Welsh language is *The Wisdom of Cadoc the Wise*, a collection of proverbs, maxims, and the like (in *The Myvyrian Archaiology of Wales*, ed. O. Jones, E. Williams, and W. O. Pugh, iii., London, 1807; new ed., Denbigh, 1870, 754 sqq.). *The Fables of Cadoc the Wise* may be found in *Iolo Manuscripts*, ed. E. Williams (London, 1848).

BIBLIOGRAPHY: Lanigan, *Eccl. Hist.*, i. 489–492; W. J. Rees, *Lives of the Cambro-British Saints*, 22–96, 309 395, 468, 587, Llandovery, 1853; A. P. Forbes, *Kalendars of Scottish Saints*, pp. 292–293, Edinburgh, 1872.

CÆCILIANUS. See DONATISM.

CÆDMON: The first Christian poet of England and, with the exception of Cynewulf (q.v.), the only Anglo-Saxon versifier whose name is known; d. about 680. All information concerning him comes from Bede, who states (*Hist. eccl.*, iv. 24) that he was a brother in Hilda's monastery at Streanæshalch (see HILDA, SAINT) and learned the art of song, not from men, but from God. Till well advanced in years he lived a secular life, and he often left a merry company where all were called on to sing in turn, feeling his inability to comply. On one such occasion he went from the hall to the stable, it being his duty that night to watch the animals, and in his sleep he saw some one standing before him and commanding him to sing of the Creation—which he thereupon was enabled to do, reciting an original poem, which Bede gives in Latin translation.[1] On awaking Cædmon remembered the poetry of his dream, and proceeded to add more of the same purport. Being brought before the abbess Hilda, he related his vision, and, at the request of the learned men there present, put passages of Scripture which they repeated to him into excellent verse. Thereupon he was received into the monastery and instructed in the Biblical stories, large portions of which he subsequently versified. Among these were the creation of the world, the origin of man, and the whole history of Genesis; the departure of the children

[1] "Now ought we to praise the founder of the heavenly kingdom, the power of the Creator, and his wisdom, the deeds of the Father of Glory; how he, since he is God eternal, is the author of all things wonderful, and the one who first created the heaven as a roof for the sons of men, then the earth the almighty guardian of the human race." Bede explains that he gives the sense, not the order of words, and wisely remarks that no verses can be transferred *verbatim* from one language to another, no matter how well it may be done, without losing much of their beauty and power.

of Israel from Egypt and their entrance into the land of promise; the incarnation, passion, resurrection, and ascension of Christ; the descent of the Holy Ghost and the preaching of the apostles; the terror of future judgment, the horror of hell, and the blessedness of heaven; and many other things by which he sought to lead men from the love of the world and to the choice of a good life. He was a very religious man and the manner of his death was in complete accord with his devout and tranquil life. Bede was born before Cædmon's death and lived not far from his monastery; hence his account is worthy of belief. The attempt of Sir Francis Palgrave to show that the story is a mere monk's tale is to be rejected. No doubt a monk named Cædmon lived at Streanæshalch and wrote poetry there, and evidently he was of low origin and unlearned. Several poems from a manuscript now in the Bodleian Library—a paraphrase of Genesis of more than 2,900 lines; Exodus, about 600 lines; Daniel, about 800 lines; and portions of the New Testament, including the lament of the fallen angels, Christ's visit to hell, and the temptation of Christ, formerly known as the Christ and Satan—were published by Franciscus Junius (François du Jon) at Amsterdam in 1655 and attributed to Cædmon. At present it is conceded that only the first of these poems has any claim to be considered the production of Cædmon, and that even this has been transmitted in an interpolated and much modified form (see HELIAND, THE, AND THE OLD-SAXON GENESIS); many think that it contains no work of Cædmon's at all. The hymn mentioned by Bede, however, is preserved in the Northumbrian dialect (Cædmon's own) by a Cambridge manuscript of the *Historia ecclesiastica* and is the oldest extant Christian poem in a Germanic tongue. (R. WÜLKER.)

BIBLIOGRAPHY: Besides the edition of Junius, the poems of the Bodleian manuscript have been published by the Society of Antiquaries of London—*Cædmon's Metrical Paraphrase of Parts of the Holy Scripture in Anglo-Saxon, with an English Translation, Notes, and a verbal Index by B. Thorpe*, London, 1832. The same society also published in their *Archæologia*, xxiv. (1832), fifty-two plates illustrative of the manuscript, including the illuminations, reissued separately London, 1833. Later editions are by K. W. Bouterwek, 2 vols., Gütersloh, 1849–54, and C. W M. Grein, in his *Bibliothek der angelsächsischen Poesie*, ii. 316–562, new ed. by R. Wülker, Leipsic, 1894. Grein has also furnished a German translation in alliterative verse in *Dichtungen der Angelsachsen stabreimend übersetzt*, Göttingen, 1863. Consult further: Sir Francis Palgrave, in *Archæologia*, xxiv. (1832) 341–343, reprinted by Cook, pp. 12–13 (see below); W H. F. Bosanquet, *The Fall of Man or Paradise Lost of Cædmon Translated in Verse*, London, 1860; E. Sievers, *Der Heliand und die angelsächsische Genesis*, Halle, 1875; R. S. Watson, *Cædmon, the First English Poet*, London, 1875; B. ten Brink, *Geschichte der englischen Litteratur*, i., 2d ed., Strasburg, 1899, Eng. transl., London, 1883; J. Earle, *Anglo-Saxon Literature*, London, 1884; R. Wülker, *Grundriss zur Geschichte der angelsächsischen Litteratur*, Leipsic, 1885; idem, *Geschichte der englischen Litteratur*, Leipsic, 1896; A. Ebert, *Allgemeine Geschichte der Litteratur des Mittelalters*, vol. iii., Leipsic, 1887; A. S. Cook, in the *Publications of the Modern Language Association of America*, vol. vi., part 1, pp. 9–28, Baltimore, 1891; Plummer's *Bede*, ii. 248–258, Oxford, 1896; W. Bright, *Early English Church History*, pp. 311–316, Oxford, 1897; R. T. Gaskin, *Cædmon, the First English Poet*, London, 1902. For the striking resemblance between parts of the Genesis and Milton's Paradise Lost, consult I. Disraeli, *Amenities of Literature*, pp. 37–50, ed. B. Disraeli, London, 1875; S. H. Gurteen, *The Epic of the Fall of Man, a Comparative Study of Cædmon, Dante, and Milton*, London, 1896 (gives reduced facsimiles of the illuminations of the Bodleian manuscript).

CÆLESTIUS. See PELAGIUS, PELAGIANISM.

CÆRULARIUS, MICHAEL: Patriarch of Constantinople 1043–58. The exact date and place both of his birth and death are unknown, and few details of his life are certain. During the reign of Michael the Paphlagonian (1034–41) he was banished for conspiracy, but he was raised to the patriarchate by Constantine Monomachus, who hoped to find in him a firm ally. Cærularius, however, strenuously defended the rights of the Church, and his chief importance is due to the fact that his course resulted in the complete cleavage between the Greek and Roman Churches. At the very time when the Norman War gave the Byzantine court and the pope an opportunity to draw more closely together, the patriarch violently suppressed the Latin ritual observed in many cloisters and churches, and renewed the ancient charges of Photius (q.v.) in a letter to the bishop of Trani in Apulia, reserving his special attack for the Roman use of unleavened bread in the Sacrament, which he condemned as Jewish. Leo IX. replied with a haughty defense of the primacy of Rome, and at Constantine's request an embassy was sent to Constantinople, headed by the Cardinal Bishop Humbert. Their letters were intended to win over the emperor and humble the patriarch, and the feeble Constantine, overawed by Humbert's attacks on the Greek Church, had neither the courage to protect Cærularius nor to oppose him openly. The patriarch, however, refused to yield, and on July 16, 1054, the embassy excommunicated him and all his adherents. After the departure of the envoys, Cærularius regained his prestige with Constantine, and maintained it during the reign of Theodora. Isaac Comnenus, on the other hand, banished him on account of his arrogance in 1058, and he seems to have died shortly afterward. In addition to the letters already mentioned, Cærularius was the author of some decretals (*De episcoporum judiciis, De nuptiis in septimo gradu non contrahendis, De sacerdotis uxore adulterio polluta*; edited by Rhalles and Potlis, "Collection of Canons," v. 40–47) and a few writings still preserved in manuscript (*De missa, Opus contra Latinos*; listed by Fabricius, *Bibliotheca Græca*, ed. Harles, xi. 195–197). (PHILIPP MEYER.)

BIBLIOGRAPHY: C. Will, *Acta et scripta ... de controversia ecclesiæ ...*, Marburg, 1861; J. Hergenröther, *Photius*, vol. iii., Regensburg, 1869 (rich in original matter); A. Pichler, *Geschichte der kirchlichen Trennung zwischen dem Orient und Occident*, 2 vols., Munich, 1864–65; R. Baxmann, *Die Politik der Päpste*, vol. ii., Elberfeld, 1868–69; W Fischer, *Studien zur byzantinischen Geschichte des elften Jahrhunderts*, Plauen, 1883; K. Krumbacher, *Geschichte der byzantinischen Litteratur*, passim, Munich, 1897.

CÆSARIUS OF ARLES: Bishop of Arles; b. at Châlon-sur-Saône (33 m. n. of Mâcon) 469 or 470; d. at Arles (44 m. n.w. of Marseilles) Aug. 27, 542. Little is known of his life before his eighteenth year, but at the age of twenty he went to the famous cloister on the island of Lérins, although it was now declining under the weak abbot Porcarius. There Cæsarius became acquainted with the writings of Faustus, who had been abbot of Lérins for some thirty years, and these works exercised an influence on him throughout his life. Porcarius appointed him master of the refectory, but the discontent of the monks caused his removal, and he thereupon devoted himself so rigidly to fasting that it became necessary to send him to Arles in search of health. He there became acquainted with Firminus, and at his request began the study of rhetoric with Pomerius of Africa, who is now generally regarded as identical with the author of the *De vita contemplativa*. Pomerius was, moreover, a follower of Augustine, and seems to have won his pupil over to this teacher. Recognizing in Cæsarius a fellow countryman and kinsman, Æontius, bishop of Arles, not only ordained him and placed him in charge of a monastery, but also induced the clergy, citizens, and king to appoint him his successor. In 502, therefore, Cæsarius became bishop of Arles, though sorely against his will.

Early Life.

His first measure was to make daily attendance at church agreeable to the laity, largely by singing, and he also required them to learn passages from the Bible, in addition to the Creed and the Lord's Prayer. The administration of funds was entrusted to laymen and deacons, and he strove to maintain firm discipline, being apparently the author of the first Occidental manual of ecclesiastical law, the *Statuta ecclesiæ antiqua*. In 505 Cæsarius was charged with high treason by his secretary Licinianus, and was banished to Bordeaux by Alaric II., although he quickly proved his innocence and was permitted to return. On Sept. 11, 506, he resumed the long interrupted series of Gallic synods with the Synod of Agde (q.v.), and the canons, evidently written by Cæsarius, are important documents for ecclesiastical history. Particularly noteworthy among them are the resolutions on ecclesiastical jurisdiction, slavery, celibacy, and church-property which was to be regarded as set aside for the poor. The death of Alaric shortly after the close of the synod ended the kingdom of Toulouse, and in 508 the Franks and Burgundians began the siege of Arles. A relative of the bishop deserted to the enemy, and Cæsarius himself was charged with treason and imprisoned, escaping only when the treason of the Jews who had accused him became known. In 510 the city was relieved, and Cæsarius cared for the captives without regard to creed, in addition to ransoming many with the money and ornaments of the churches. Three years later, however, he was cited to appear before Theodoric at Ravenna, probably because of his expenditures of church funds for the foundation of a nunnery at Arles and similar purposes, but he won the king completely to his side, and received such rich gifts from all quarters for the ransom of Burgundian captives that he was able to bring to Arles 8,000 solidi (about $56,000). From Ravenna he went to Rome, and in October gave the pope a petition, in which he requested permission to employ church funds for cloisters; to abrogate, in view of the lack of clergy in Gaul, the hieratic *cursus honorum*, on which strict stress was laid at Rome; and also asked information regarding the marriage of widows and nuns, bribery in the election of bishops, and the prohibition against naming a bishop without the knowledge of the metropolitan. On Nov. 6, 513, the petition was granted with a few reservations, Symmachus allowing only the usufruct to be devoted to cloisters and the like.

Bishop, 502.

Little is known of the life of Cæsarius between 514 and 523, although the canons of the Council of Gerunda in 516–517 show that his influence was traceable in Spain. In 523, however, it became possible for him to exercise his metropolitan functions, since the peaceable intervention of Theodoric in the Franko-Burgundian War brought ten cities of Burgundy under the sway of the Ostrogoths. Cæsarius now held five synods: Arles, 524; Carpentras, 527; Orange and Vaison, 529; and Marseilles, 533. The disciplinary and legislative activity of Cæsarius accordingly lies in the *Statuta ecclesiæ antiqua* and in the canons of the six synods, to which should probably be added the decrees of what is commonly considered the second synod of Arles. Stress should also be laid on his care for the rural communities and for the erection of schools for the education of the clergy. As early as the *Statuta*, moreover, Cæsarius had taken for granted the right and duty of preaching, and he insisted on it again in the *Admonitio*, which seems to have appeared at the synod of Vaison. The Council of Orange (June 3, 529) was the only one devoted to a dogmatic question, and also the only one which received papal sanction as an ecumenical council. This was apparently the conference of bishops of Vienne (mentioned in the *Vita*), who, as Semi-Pelagians, attacked the doctrine of grace taught at Arles, while Cyprian, bishop of Toulon, represented Cæsarius, who was prevented by illness from attending, and defended the dogma of prevenient grace. The epilogue of its resolutions, apparently written by Cæsarius himself, ascribes free will to all the baptized, and rejects predestination to damnation. His own position toward this problem first became clear in 1896, when Morin edited the treatise *Quid dominus Cæsarius senserit contra eos qui dicunt quare aliis det Deus gratiam, aliis non det*, in which he maintains that divine grace works without regard to the merits of man, while God acts according to his will and pleasure.

Synods after 523.

The close of the second decade of the sixth century saw the climax of the activity of Cæsarius, and his relations with Rome changed for the worse. Pope Agapetus charged him with cruelty and injustice in his proceedings against Contumeliosus, bishop of Riez, although he had acted simply in accord with Gallican usage and had defended the discipline of the Church. Under Pope Vigilius he was obliged, as vicar of the Roman See, to render a decision in a question of marriage, which was disregarded. Old and sickly, he took no personal part in the French synods, although the ecclesiastical influence of his pupils remained important. He lived, however, to see the cloister which he had founded on Aug. 26, 512 or 513, in a flourishing condition, and to complete a bishopric of forty years.

No collected edition of the works of Cæsarius exists as yet, although the Benedictine Germaine Morin has long been preparing one, but the places in which his scattered writings may be found are given by Arnold, 435–450 (cf. 491–496), Malnory, v.–xviii., and Fessler-Jungmann, 438, 452. In addition to the works already mentioned, his most important writings are his sermons. His chief sources, often noted in his manuscript, were Augustine, Rufinus, Faustus, Salvianus, and Eucherius, and his generosity in giving of his treasures to others has resulted in the ascription of many of his sermons to Augustine, Faustus, and similar authors. On the other hand, he prepared homiliaries, represented by *Cod. Laon. 121* (ninth century) and *Parisin. 10605 fol. 71* (thirteenth century). A similar collection contains forty-two admonitions, and a third is devoted to sermons for the cloister. A special category is formed by the homilies for the Old Testament lessons for each fast, and these are supplemented by interpretations of texts of the New Testament. Another group of sermons is eschatological and a third is important for the history of penance. His monastery rules are extremely valuable for the history of asceticism, and his regulations for nuns, based on Augustine's letter *Ad sanctimoniales*, the so-called rules of Macarius, and his own monastic rules, received their final form in 534 and clearly show the various strata of their development. Of the other writings of Cæsarius, only the letters need be considered, for the *Testamentum beati Cæsarii* (*MPL*, lxvii. 1139–42) is now recognized as spurious.

Works.

(F Arnold.)

Bibliography: Sources for a life are: *Epist. Arelatenses*, in *MGH, Epist.*, iii. 1–83, ed. W. Gundlach, Hanover, 1891; *Concilia ævi Merovingici*, in *MGH, Leg.*, sectio iii., part 1, pp. 37–61, ed. Maassen, ib. 1893. The early lives are in *MGH, Script. rer. Merovingicarum*, iii. 457–501, ed. B. Krusch, ib. 1896, and in *ASB*, 27 Aug., vi. 64–83, with comment by Stilting, pp. 50–64. Consult: A. Malnory, *S. Césaire évêque d'Arles*, Paris, 1894; C. F. Arnold, *Cäsarius von Arelate und die gallische Kirche seiner Zeit*, Leipsic, 1894; *Histoire littéraire de la France*, iii. 190, iv. 1, x., p. xv., xii., p. vii.; J. M. Trichaud, *Histoire de S. Césaire, évêque d'Arles*, Arles, 1858; U. Villevieille, *Histoire de S. Césaire*, Aix-en-Provence, 1884; P. Lejay, *Les Sermons de Césaire d'Arles*, in *Revue biblique*, iv. (1895) 593–610; J. Fessler, *Institutiones patrologiæ*, ed. B. Jungmann, ii. 438–452, Innsbruck, 1896; G. Pfeilschifter, *Der Ostgothen König Theoderich der Grosse und die katholische Kirche*, pp. 123–136, Münster, 1896; Hefele, *Conciliengeschichte*, ii. 68–77, Eng. transl., iv. 131, 143 sqq.

CÆSARIUS OF HEISTERBACH, hais'ter-bɑH: Monk; b. probably at Cologne c. 1180; d. at Heisterbach (20 m. s. of Cologne) c. 1240. He received an excellent education at Cologne and gained a good knowledge of the Church Fathers and classical writers. In 1198 or 1199 he entered the monastery of the Cistercians at Heisterbach and spent his life there in quiet seclusion. He became master of the novices, and also prior according to Henriquez (*Monologium Cisterciense*, ad diem 25 Sept.). His literary activity is closely connected with his monastic duties. Only sixteen of his many writings are extant and most of these are still in manuscript. One of the best known is the *Dialogus miraculorum* or *De miraculis et visionibus sui temporis* (ed. J. Strange, 2 vols., Cologne, 1851; index, Coblenz, 1857; see bibliography below for title of German select transl.). As master of the novices Cæsarius had to acquaint the future monks with the regulations, opinions, and decisions of the order, and he believed the best way to accomplish this was by means of examples. At the request of his abbot he committed his instructions to writing and the copiousness and variety of his material, drawn from the recent past as well as more remote antiquity, is surprising. His written sources belong mostly to the Cistercian order, but he also drew from oral communications. Each narrative is intended to have a religious or moral practical application, but Cæsarius knew how to include everything under these heads, and thus it happens that his stories contain many points of interest for contemporaneous history and the history of civilization. In a series of pictures he brings before us the life on the Lower Rhine, especially at Cologne, and we often meet with popular beliefs and superstitions in which survivals of old Germanic mythology may still be discovered. The *Dialogus* is especially important for information concerning ecclesiastical customs and conditions, especially in the monastic life. The regulations of the monasteries, especially among the Cistercians, the chorus-singing and work, the eating and sleeping, the fasting and bloodletting of the monks—all comes before us in living examples. Cæsarius is much in earnest about the evils of confession; he suppresses the worst, but what he tells is bad enough and his judgment upon it is severe (cf. iii. 41 and 45). For the rest the dialogue from beginning to end is a witness to the mania for miracles and the belief of the time in the marvelous. One finds everywhere an interference of partly divine, partly demonic powers with earthly happenings, and when it takes place the most incredible becomes credible. Here is the weak point of the book which must not be overlooked, despite the poetic charm of many narratives and the morally pure personality of Cæsarius. He contributed his share to cause the belief in witchcraft and sorcery, in incubi and succubi, and all sorts of devilish intervention, to be regarded as a constituent part of Christian belief. The praise bestowed on the *Dialogus* induced Cæsarius to prepare a second work of the kind, not however in the form of dialogue, the *Libri VIII miraculorum*, of which only three books are preserved (ed. Aloys Meister, Rome, 1901, supplementary vol. to the *Römische Quartalschrift*). Cæsarius's historical works include a *Catalogus episcoporum Coloniensium* (in J. F Böhmer, *Fontes rerum Germanicarum*, ii., Stuttgart, 1845, 272–282, and, ed. H. Cardauns, in *MGH, Script.*, xxiv., 1879, 345–347; Germ. transl. by M. Bethany, Elberfeld, 1898) and a *Vita sancti Engelberti*, an archbishop of Cologne who was murdered by a relative in 1225 (in Böhmer, ut sup., 294–329). This work insures to Cæsarius a place among the most prominent biographers of the Middle Ages. The first book describes the personality of Engelbert; the second describes in dramatic manner the dangers with which the arrogance of insubordinate vassals threatened the archbishop, and ends with a thrilling account of the final catastrophe. The third book treats of the miracles of Engelbert, who was revered as martyr. Lastly, Cæsarius deserves no minor place among the preachers of his time. His homilies (edited by the Dominican J. A. Koppenstein, 4 parts, Cologne, 1615–28) are indeed monastic, not popular, sermons, like those of Bernard of Clairvaux. But both have in common the rich application of Holy Writ, the connection of moral and allegorical exposition, and the endeavor to edify their hearers. In spite of their simplicity they reveal an indeed unsought for, but not unconscious art in their plan. Peculiar to Cæsarius and corresponding to his method, already noted, is the very copious intertwining of historical examples from modern times. He was a true child of his time, and belongs to its best. In him still lives the spirit of the old Cistercians, as Bernard impressed it on the order. He unites an earnest orthodoxy with fervent piety and a highly moral sentiment. Though implicitly devoted to the Church, nevertheless he has a keen eye for its obvious defects, and his judgment was incorruptible. Though a zealous monk, he did not lose all interest in the events of the world, and the political disorders of the time, with all the misery which they brought, concern him. S. M. Deutsch.

Bibliography: A. Kaufmann, *Cäsarius von Heisterbach*, Cologne, 1850, 2d ed., 1862; W. Cave, *Scriptorum ecclesiasticorum historia literaria*, year 1225, 2 vols., London, 1688–98; J. Hartzheim, *Bibliotheca Coloniensis*, pp. 42–46, Cologne, 1747; *Histoire littéraire de la France*, xviii. 194–201, Paris, 1835; Braun, in *Zeitschrift für Philosophie und katholische Theologie*, pp. 1–27, Bonn, 1846 (contains a list of his writings prepared by himself); A. W. Wybrands, *De Dialogus miraculorum van Cæsarius van Heisterbach*, in *Studien en Bijdragen*, ii. 1–116, Amsterdam, 1871; K. Unkel, *Die Homilien des Cäsarius von Heisterbach und ihre Bedeutung für die Kultur und Sittengeschichte des zwölften und dreizehnten Jahrhunderts*, in *Annalen des historischen Vereins für den Niederrhein*, xxxiv. (1879) 1–67; A. Kaufmann, *Wunderbare und denkwürdige Geschichten aus den Werken des Cäsarius von Heisterbach*, in *Annalen des historischen Vereins für den Niederrhein*, Cologne, 2 parts, 1884–91; Wattenbach, *DGQ*, ii. 412, 485.

CÆSARIUS OF SPEYER. See Francis, Saint, of Assisi, and the Franciscan Order, I., § 4; II., § 1.

CÆSAROPAPISM: A name applied to the conception of the relations between Church and State which contemplates the secular ruler's exercising spiritual power also. It is thus the converse of the theocratic system which the popes have attempted to carry into effect (i.e., in regard to the world at large, not to their limited states), which also underlies Calvin's teaching as to the relations of Church and State. Its principles are met with as early as 355, when Constantine addressed the Synod at Milan in the words: "Whatever *I* will, let that be acknowledged as a 'canon'" (Athanasius, *Hist. Arian.*, xxxiii.; *NPNF*, 2d ser., iv. 281). It developed more rapidly in the Eastern Church because of the absence of the counterpoise which the papacy formed in the West. Justinian may be regarded as a typical representative of it; but the Church managed during the iconoclastic controversy to free itself in a large measure from imperial dictation. Since that time the term has not borne any strict application, though it is sometimes applied in a modified sense to the position of the Czars since Peter the Great in the Russian Church, and has sometimes, though with still less justice, been used of the German evangelical princes who have exercised authority in spiritual things, though even the territorial system recognizes a sphere for religion independent of the State.[1] See Erastus, Thomas. (E. Friedberg.)

CAIAPHAS, cai'a-fas (more exactly Joseph, who also was called Caiaphas; cf. Josephus, *Ant.*, XVIII. ii. 2): The Jewish high priest who held office during the ministry and death of Jesus. He was the last of the four high priests whom the Roman procurator Valerius Gratus appointed successively to this dignity. As Valerius was procurator from 15 to 26 A.D., his appointment of Caiaphas must have occurred at the latest in 26 A.D.; most likely it happened c. 18 A.D., as Valerius Gratus probably appointed Ishmael, the first of the four high priests, immediately after his own inauguration, and as the next two remained in office only about one year, Caiaphas held his office until c. 36 A.D., when he was removed by Vitellius, the legate of Syria. His administration, therefore, lasted about eighteen years—a long term when compared with that of most other high priests of the Roman period. For this he was probably indebted less to his ability than to his submissiveness to the anti-Jewish policy of the Roman government. Probably he belonged to the party of the Sadducees and shared their fondness for foreign ideas, as did his father-in-law Annas (Acts iv. 1, 6; v. 17) and the latter's son Annas the Younger (Josephus, *Ant.*, XX. ix. 1). See Annas. F. Sieffert.

Bibliography: A. Edersheim, *Life and Times of Jesus the Messiah*, ii. 547, London, 1885; D. F. Strauss, *Leben Jesu*, iv. 30 sqq., Bonn, 1895; Schürer, *Geschichte*, ii. 204, 218, Eng. transl., II. i. 182, 199; *DB*, i. 338; *EB*, i. 171–172; *JE*, ii. 493; and, in general, commentaries on the Gospels.

CAILLIN, SAINT, OF FENAGH: Irish saint of the "second order" who flourished about 560. His alleged history is a typical one among the stories of the Irish "saints," and is also noteworthy for the light it throws on the conditions of the time and the progress of Christianity in pagan Ireland. Caillin's kinsmen of Dunmore (County Galway) had determined to slay a part of their number, the land having become overpopulated; but, on the advice of the saint, who had received Christian education in Rome, they

[1] The term Cæsaropapism is somewhat opprobrious in its implications; but if it is to be kept in use at all it is applicable to all monarchical governments in which union of Church and State, with civil control, prevails. In a limited monarchy like Great Britain it is not as much the king as the cabinet, representing a majority of the representatives of the people, that exercises authority in religious matters. Where imperial authority is less limited, as in Germany, ecclesiastical control by the sovereign or his representative is more complete. Where imperial authority is absolute, as in Russia until recently, the term Cæsaropapism is applicable without qualification. A. H. N.

desisted, and Caillin undertook to find more land. In the course of the search he came to Fenagh (County Leitrim, 3 m. s.w. of Ballinamore), where he converted the king's son, Hugh, and a band of warriors sent to drive him away. The prince then gave the saint his fortress and the latter built a church there. When the druids came, at the king's behest, to expel Caillin, he restrained his Christian followers from attacking them, and turned them into stones. Hugh succeeded to the throne on his father's death; he was known as "the Dark" from his personal appearance, but Caillin made him of fair complexion. Notwithstanding his love of peace, Caillin is said to have given the tribe a *cathach* or standard, a mighty talisman in battle.

Bibliography: *The Book of Fenagh*, ed. D. H. Kelly and W. M. Hennessy, Dublin, 1875; T. Olden, *The Church of Ireland*, pp. 65–67, London, 1892.

CAIN, KENITES: The Hebrew word *Ḳayin* occurs in the Old Testament as the name of a stock of nomads, associated with Midian, Amalek, and Israel, mentioned in Judges iv. 11 and Num. xxiv. 22, probably also to be read in I Sam. xv. 6b. More often the form *Ḳeni*, "Kenite," is met (Gen. xv. 19; Num. xxiv. 21; Judges iv. 11, 17, etc.). In the time of Moses this stock seems to have been dependent on the Midianites, since Hobab, Moses's father-in-law, appears (Judges i. 16) as the head of a Kenite family, and in Num. x. 29 is designated as a Midianite, as is Jethro in Ex. iii. 1 and Reuel in Ex. ii. 16. Midianites is most likely the larger term and includes the Kenites as one of the branches. The Kenites attached themselves to the Israelites during the wandering; at the time of Barak and Deborah the Kenite Heber was near the plain of Jezreel, detached from the rest of his tribe (Judges iv. 11). In Saul's time the Kenites were associated with the Amalekites. It is noteworthy that in I Chron. ii. 55 the Kenites are brought into connection with the Rechabites, who retained primitive customs, suggesting their adherence to a nomadic form of life and to the primitive Yahweh-religion of the desert (Jer. xxxv.).

The Kenites.

This stock of Cain was apparently intended to be brought into connection with the patriarchs of the race (Gen. iv. 1–16); the conclusion of Wellhausen, Budde, and Stade, however, is that originally the story of Cain had nothing to do with the Kenites for the following reasons: Gen. iv. 17 sqq. deals with the world at large (verses 17, 20–22); Gen. iv. 1–16 with the land of Israel and neighboring deserts. The *Adhamah*, "ground," of Gen. iv. 14 can be only the land inhabited by Israel from which Cain was banished. Gen. iv. 20 makes Jabal the ancestor of nomads, while Cain's nomadic condition resulted from his sin (iv. 14–16). Abel, too, was a shepherd of small cattle who dwelt in Yahweh's land. The story of Cain in this passage can not be understood to deal with the earliest ages of mankind because of the advanced civilization it implies. Its region is the southern part of Palestine; it explained the separation of a people whose God was the same as Israel's by the commission of murder which is named fratricide because of the close connection of Kenites and Hebrews. The mark for Cain, worn on the forehead, must have denoted adherence to the worship of Yahweh (cf. Ex. xiii. 9, 16; Isa. xliv. 6; I Kings xx. 38, 41), and implied the same limits in exacting blood-revenge as were obligatory on the Israelites.

Their Relation to Cain.

The word *Ḳayin* also occurs as the name of an ancestor of a part of mankind. The name stands in J at the head of the so-called Cainite table, Gen. iv. 17 In its present form this includes seven generations, and in the seventh four branches appear—Jabal and Jubal, sons of Lamech by Adah, and Tubal-cain and Naamah, son and daughter of Lamech by Zillah. Cain built the first city and named it after his son Enoch; Jabal was the ancestor of nomads, Jubal of musicians, and Tubal-cain of artisans. The table evidently is an account of supposed origins of civilization, so is to be related to Gen. ix. 20–27. Then Noah's earlier connection with the Cainite table through Lamech is probable, though in Gen. v. 28 (P) he is a Sethite. That the narratives are doublets appears on comparison (cf. Cain and Kenan, Methusael and Methuselah, Ired and Jared, as well as the fact that *Adam* and *Enos* both mean "man"). The Sethite and the Cainite tables are both traced to a single original, and the Cainite line of J is believed to have been originally a Sethite line, while Gen. iv. 25–26 originally preceded iv. 17.

Cain in Gen. iv.

The present form of the text is probably attributable to the editor of the work of J who inserted the flood story. He borrowed the material from an old Sethite table, and setting Cain at the head formed a Cainite table and inserted the Cain-story (Gen. iv. 1–16) and the sword-song of Lamech. He thus brought into juxtaposition the killing by Lamech and that by Cain, completed the identification of Cain [father of the Kenites and Cain brother of Abel] through Cain, founder of the city. Thus he secured a contrast between the godless Cainites and the pious Sethites on which was founded the ecclesiastical tradition that alienation from God was in the Cainite blood, while in the Sethite piety was instinctive.

Of the other names in the table little need be said. In II Sam. xxi. 16 *Ḳayin* means "a spear," in Arabic and Syriac "a smith," and possibly (Gen. iv. 1) is to be connected with the word to "make." Enoch (*Hanokh*) is the name of a Reubenite (Gen. xlvi. 9) and a Midianite (Gen. xxv. 4) stock (cf. the Annakus who was king of Phrygia, mentioned by Stephen of Byzantium). With Jubal should be connected the Hebrew for "ram's horn" (Joshua vi. 5). Tubal is the Tibareni of Asia Minor (Gen. x. 2), while the addition of Cain, "smith," goes well with their reputation for metalwork. A goddess Adah was worshiped by Babylonians, and one named Naamah by the Phenicians.

(H. Guthe.)

Bibliography: The subject is treated more or less adequately in the commentaries on Genesis, best in A. Dillmann's, Edinburgh, 1897, and in H. Gunkel's, Göttingen, 1902. Consult further: I. Goldziher, *Der Mythos bei den Hebraern*, Leipsic, 1876, Eng. transl., London, 1877; K. Budde, *Biblische Urgeschichte*, pp. 117 sqq., Giessen, 1883; F. Lenormant, *Les Origines de l'histoire d'après la Bible*, vol. i., Paris, 1880, Eng. transl., *Beginnings of History*, London, 1883; J. Wellhausen, *Die Komposition des Hexateuchs*, pp. 10 sqq., 305, Berlin, 1889; H. E. Ryle, *Early Narratives of Genesis*, pp. 78-83, London, 1892; B. Stade, in *ZATW*. xiv. (1894) 250 sqq.; *EB*, i. 622-628, iv. 4411-17; *DB*, i. 338-339. On the later Jewish mythology, J. A. Eisenmenger, *Entdecktes Judenthum*, i. 462, 471, 832, 836, Frankfort, 1700.

CAINITES: According to Irenæus (*Hær.*, i. 31), a sect of the Ophites (q.v.) who worshiped Cain as an instrument of the Gnostic Sophia, treated with hostility by the demiurge. They saw in Judas the one who best of all knew the truth, celebrated his treason as a mystery, and had a "Gospel of Judas." The notices of Pseudo-Tertullian (*Hær.*, vii.), Philastrius (*Hær.*, ii.), and Epiphanius (*Hær.*, xxxviii.) accord with these statements. Cain was generated of higher power than Abel, and Judas was the benefactor of the human race, either because by his treason he frustrated Christ's intention to destroy truth (Philastrius), or because he compelled the archons to kill Christ, and so assisted in obtaining the salvation of the cross (Epiphanius). When Tertullian (*Præscriptio hæreticorum*, xxxiii.; cf. *De baptismo*, i.) mentions "Gaiana heresis" he probably refers to the Cainites. Cf. also Clement, *Strom.*, vi. 108; Theodoret, *Hær.*, i. 15; Hippolytus, *Phil.*, viii. 20. For Cainites, descendants of Cain, see CAIN, KENITES. G. KRÜGER.

BIBLIOGRAPHY: Neander, *Christian Church*, i. 448, 476, 646; Harnack, *Litteratur*, II. i. 538 sqq.; see literature under GNOSTICISM; OPHITES.

CAIRD, JOHN: Church of Scotland; b. at Greenock (23 m. w.n.w. of Glasgow), Renfrewshire, Dec. 15, 1820; d. there July 30, 1898. He was educated at the University of Glasgow (1837-1838, 1840-45; M.A., 1845), interrupting his studies in 1838-39 while engaged in his father's engineering works. After the completion of his education he was minister successively at Newton-on-Ayr (1845-1847), Lady Yester's, Edinburgh (1847-49), Errol, Perthshire (1849-57), and the Park Church, Glasgow (1857-62). In 1862 he was appointed professor of theology in the University of Glasgow, where he became principal and vice-chancellor in 1873, retaining both positions until his death, although he announced his intention of resigning early in 1898. He was Croall Lecturer at Edinburgh in 1878-79 and Gifford Lecturer at Glasgow in 1890-91 and 1896, though a stroke of paralysis forced him to discontinue this second course. He wrote: *Sermons* (Edinburgh, 1858); *Introduction to the Philosophy of Religion* (Croall lectures for 1878-79; Glasgow, 1880); *Spinoza* (Edinburgh, 1886); and the posthumous *University Addresses* (Glasgow, 1898); *University Sermons* (1898); and *The Fundamental Ideas of Christianity* (Gifford lectures; 2 vols., 1899; ed., with a memoir of the author, by E. Caird).

BIBLIOGRAPHY: E. Caird, memoir prefixed to his edition of *The Fundamental Ideas of Christianity*, 2 vols., Glasgow, 1899; *DNB*, supplement, i. 368-369.

CAIRNS, JOHN: United Presbyterian Church, Scotland; b. at Ayton Hill (7 m. n.w. of Berwick-on-Tweed) Aug. 23, 1818; d. in Edinburgh Mar. 12, 1892. After being the wonder of his first school, he became the wonder of the University of Edinburgh, where he studied arts (1834-40), and of Secession Hall, where he studied theology (1840-43). In 1843-44 he studied and traveled on the Continent and received impressions and made acquaintances, especially in Germany, which affected his life. From 1845 till 1876 he was minister of the Golden Square United Presbyterian Church, Berwick-on-Tweed. In frame he was massive, and he had apparently great powers of endurance, but he toiled too much, responded to too many calls in every direction, and on all sorts of errands, and so in 1855 broke down and after that was frequently laid aside. He early became one of the leaders of his denomination, and developed into one of the foremost Scotchmen. He was from 1867 to 1876 professor of apologetics in the theological hall of his denomination in Edinburgh; in 1872 moderator of its general assembly. In 1876 he gave up his pastoral charge, and moving to Edinburgh received the joint professorship (with the principal) of systematic theology and apologetics—the terms of which had been lengthened from seven weeks to five months. In 1879 he succeeded to the principalship. In 1880 he visited America and was a prominent character in the second council of the Alliance of the Reformed Churches held in Philadelphia. He died of heart disease after a brief illness. He never married.

His best work was done upon the platform and in the pulpit. The great respect felt for him there and as a man of affairs and counsel withheld criticism of him as an educator, for as such he was less successful. He had considerable learning and remarkable gifts, especially in the way of language, and he acquired foreign languages readily, even such tongues as Assyrian and Arabic when in middle life. He was sprung from the common people, undersood how to address them, and was reverenced by them. His nature was genial, free from affectation and hauteur, and he was untiring in the service of others. He made a deep impression on his own generation by his broad-mindedness, moral courage, and fervent eloquence.

The topics upon which he spoke with convincing power, springing from deep conviction, were the freedom of the Church from the State; home and foreign missions; temperance, and (after 1874) in advocacy of total abstinence; modification of the Confession of Faith, by a declaratory statement (adopted 1879); union of the United Presbyterian, the Free Church, and the Church of Scotland (realized as far as the first two are concerned in 1900); and the disestablishment of the Church of Scotland.

His literary work was small in amount. He published aside from pamphlets a memoir of Rev. John Brown, of the United Presbyterian Church, father of the author of *Rab and his Friends* (Edinburgh, 1860); *Unbelief in the Eighteenth Century*, Cunningham lectures for 1881; and after his death came a volume of his sermons, *Christ the Morning Star, and Other Sermons* (London, 1892).

BIBLIOGRAPHY: A. R. Macewen, *Life and Letters of John Cairns*, London, 1895; *Principal Cairns*, in the *Famous Scots Series*, Edinburgh, 1903.

CAIUS, kē'us: The name of several characters in Roman history, of whom only two need be included here.

1. Roman author early in the third century, mentioned by Hippolytus, Dionysius of Alexandria, and Eusebius. What Theodoret and Jerome tell of him rests on Eusebius; Photius's account is worthless, as the tradition from which he derived it confused Hippolytus and Caius. It is doubtful whether he was a Roman presbyter, to say nothing of the title of "bishop of the nations" given him by Photius from tradition. In the library at Jerusalem Eusebius found a work of his, the "Dialogue with Proclus" (the head of the Roman Montanists); but this is the only one known. From the quotations of Eusebius it appears that Caius rebuked the audacity of the Montanists in manufacturing new Scriptures, that he rejected millenarianism and with it the Apocalypse, and that he recognized only thirteen epistles of Paul. Ebed Jesu (in Assemani, *Bibl. Orient.*, III. i., p. 15) says that Hippolytus wrote some *Capita adversus Caium;* and this statement is now confirmed by the discovery of John Gwynn, who found in the British Museum and published five fragments of these very *Capita* (*Hermathena*, vi., Dublin, 1888). From the statements of Caius here attacked it is clear that he spoke strongly against the contents of the Apocalypse (presumably in the "Dialogue"), and considered it as unworthy of credence and conflicting with the Holy Scriptures. Thus from one of Eusebius's references (*Hist. eccl.*, III. xxviii. 1-2) the conclusion is almost certainly justified that Caius held the Apocalypse to be the work of Cerinthus. Since this view is also that of the Alogians of Asia Minor, and since the method of his polemic against the book strikingly suggests theirs, a connection between them is a plausible hypothesis. (A. Harnack.)

Bibliography: A. Harnack, *Die Gwynn'schen Cajus und Hippolytusfragmente*, in *TU*, vi. 3 (1891), 121-128; idem, *Litteratur*, i. 601-603; Krüger, *History*, pp. 320-321 (gives further literature); *DCB*, i. 384-386; *NPNF*, i. 129, 160, 163, 268.

2. Pope 283-296. These dates, Dec. 17 for his election and Apr. 22 for his death, are given in the *Catalogus Liberianus;* Eusebius (*Hist. eccl.*, VII. xxxii. 1) ascribes to him a pontificate of about fifteen years. In any case, his rule falls in the peaceful period before the outbreak of the persecution of Diocletian, and for this reason, if for no other, the tradition that he died a martyr is incredible. According to the *Depositio episcoporum* he was buried in the cemetery of St. Calixtus. (A. Hauck.)

CAJETAN, cā'jĕ-tān or caj'e-tan, **THOMAS**: Italian cardinal; b. at Gaeta Feb. 20, 1469; d. at Rome Aug. 9, 1534. His real name was Jacopo Vio, he took the monastic name Thomas, and his surname is from his birthplace. At the age of fifteen he entered the Dominican order, and, devoting himself to studies in the Thomist philosophy, became, before he was thirty, one of its noted teachers; he was made general procurator in 1507 and general a year later. Faithful to the traditions of the Dominicans, he appears in 1511 as a supporter of the pope against the claims of the Council of Pisa, composing in defense of his position the *Tractatus de Comparatione auctoritatis Papæ et conciliorum ad invicem.* At the Fifth Lateran Council (1512-17) which Julius II. set up in opposition to that of Pisa, Cajetan played the leading rôle; and it was he who during the second session of the council brought about the decree recognizing the infallibility of the pope and the superiority of his authority to that of the council. For his services Leo X. made him in 1517 cardinal presbyter of Saint Sisto, Rome, and bestowed on him in the following year the bishopric of Palermo. This he resigned in 1519 to take the bishopric of Gaeta granted him by the emperor Charles V., for whose election Cajetan had labored zealously. In 1518 he was sent as legate to the Diet of Augsburg and to him, at the wish of the Saxon elector, was entrusted the task of examining and testing the teachings of Luther. Treatises of his own, written, without knowledge of Luther's theses, in 1517 show that Luther was justified in his assertion that on the doctrine of dispensation the Church had as yet arrived at no firmly established position; the doctrine of confession Cajetan seemed also to regard as a subject open to controversy. Yet more than investigator and thinker he was politician and prelate, and his appearance at Augsburg in all the splendor of ecclesiastical pomp only served to reveal him to Luther as the type of Roman curialist, hateful to Germans and German Christianity. Cajetan was active in furthering the election of Adrian VI., retained influence under Clement VII., suffered a short term of imprisonment after the storming of Rome by the Constable of Bourbon and by Frundsberg (1527), retired to his bishopric for a few years, and, returning to Rome in 1530, assumed his old position of influence about the person of Clement, in whose behalf he wrote the decision rejecting the appeal for divorce from Catharine of Aragon made by Henry VIII. of England (March 23, 1534: printed in *Records of the Reformation*, ed. N. Power, Oxford, 2 vols., 1870, ii. 532-533). Of the Reformation he remained a steadfast opponent, composing several works directed against Luther, and taking an important share in shaping the policy of the papal delegates in Germany.[1] Learned though he was in the scholastics, he recognized that to fight the Reformers with some chance of success a deeper knowledge of the Scriptures than he possessed was necessary. To this study he devoted himself with characteristic zeal, wrote commentaries on the greater part of the Old and the New Testament, and, in the exposition of his text, which he treated critically, allowed himself considerable latitude in departing from the literal and traditional interpretation. In the very field of Thomist philosophy he showed striking independence of judgment, expressing liberal views on marriage and divorce, denying the existence of a material hell and advocating the celebration of public prayers in the vernacular. The Sorbonne found some of these views heterodox, and in the

[[1] Cajetan bore witness to Luther's ability when he exclaimed, "Ego nolo amplius cum hac bestia colloqui: habet enim profundos oculos et mirabiles speculationes in capite suo." (I do not want to have any further parley with that beast; for he has sharp eyes and wonderful speculations in his head.)]

1570 edition of his celebrated commentary on the *Summa* of Thomas Aquinas (counted among the best; new ed., Lierre, 1892 sqq.) the objectionable passages were expunged. A complete edition of his works with life appeared in five volumes at Lyons, 1639. (T. Kolde.)

Bibliography: Besides the Life prefixed to his works, consult: R. Simon, *Histoire critique du Vieux Testament*, p. 319, Rotterdam, 1678; idem, *Histoire des principaux commentateurs du N. T.*, p. 537, 1639; C. F. Jäger, in *ZHT*, 1858, p. 431.

CAJETANS. See Theatines.

CALAH. See Assyria, IV., § 3.

CALAMY: The name of an English family which produced several distinguished clergymen in the seventeenth century.

1. Edmund Calamy the Elder: Presbyterian; b. in London Feb., 1600; d. there Oct. 29, 1666. He was educated at Pembroke Hall, Cambridge; became (1626) vicar of St. Mary's in Swaffham Prior, Cambridgeshire; thence in the same year removed to St. Edmund's Bury in Suffolk as lecturer, where he remained ten years, until compelled to retire on account of his opposition to the *Book of Sports*, thereby identifying himself with the Puritan party. He accepted from the Earl of Warwick the rectory of Rochford in Essex, where he remained until in 1639 he was chosen pastor of St. Mary Aldermanbury Church in London, where he labored until 1662. He composed in 1641 with others "*An Answer to a Book entitled, An Humble Remonstrance in which the original of Liturgy and Episcopacy is discussed: and Queries proposed concerning both. The Parity of Bishops & Presbyters in Scripture demonstrated. The occasion of their Imparity in Antiquity discovered. The Disparity of the Ancient & our modern Bishops manifested. The Antiquity of Ruling Elders in the Church vindicated. The Prelatical church bounded. Written by Smectymnuus* [i.e., S(tephen) M(arshall), E(dmund) C(alamy), T(homas) Y(oung), M(atthew) N(ewcommen), and W(illiam) S(purstow)]. This reply to Joseph Hall's *Humble Remonstrance* became the platform of the Presbyterians, as that became the platform of the Episcopal party, each side claiming *jure divino*. Several other tracts were issued in the controversy *pro* and *con*. Calamy was chosen a member of the Westminster Assembly of Divines (1643), and took an active part in its proceedings, being moderate in doctrinal position, and inclined to a union with both Independents and Episcopalians in some comprehensive polity. He also became one of the most energetic members of the Provincial Assembly of London; took part in the composition of the *Vindication of the Presbyterian Government and Ministry*, 1649; was the author of the *Jus Divinum Ministerii Evangelici*, 1654, both adopted by that body. He had opposed the execution of Charles I. and was active in restoring Charles II. to the kingdom in 1659; was one of the divines sent to Holland to treat with him. At the Restoration in 1660 he was made one of the king's chaplains, and offered the bishopric of Coventry and Lichfield, which, however, he declined. With Baxter, Reynolds, and others, he gave his energies for a comprehension of Presbyterians and Episcopalians through a revision of the Liturgy, and a reduction of Episcopacy on Archbishop Ussher's model. He took part in drawing up the *Exceptions* against the Liturgy, and reply to the *Reasons* of the Episcopal clergy. He was a great preacher, frequently delivering sermons before Parliament and the lord mayors on public occasions; and his lectures were frequented by the best people of London. A number of these have been published. His most popular work is *The Godly Man's Ark* (London, 1657; 18th ed., 1709; reprinted, 1865). He was the compiler of *The Souldier's Pocket Bible*, issued for the use of the Commonwealth army in 1643; reprinted in facsimile 1895. He was a practical man of affairs, rather than a scholar and writer. He was ejected for non-conformity in 1662, and imprisoned in Newgate for a short time for having preached after his ejection. But the king interposed, on account of great public indignation, and he was released. C. A. Briggs.

Bibliography: The *DNB*, viii. 227-230, contains an excellent account of his life, and adds details of references to literature.

2. Edmund Calamy the Younger: Non-conforming minister, eldest son of Edmund Calamy the elder; b. at Bury St. Edmunds about 1635; d. at Totteridge, near Barnet, May, 1685. He studied at Sidney Sussex College and Pembroke Hall, Cambridge (B.A., 1654; M.A., 1658); was made rector of Moreton, Essex, 1658; ejected on the passage of the Uniformity Act (1662), and thenceforth lived a retired life in London, preaching occasionally in private or to friends.

Bibliography: *Biographia Britannica*, ed. A. Kippis, iii. 136, London, 1784; *DNB*, viii. 230-231.

3. Benjamin Calamy: Church of England, second son of Edmund Calamy the elder; b. in London on or before June 8, 1642; d. there Jan., 1686 (buried Jan. 7). He studied at Catherine Hall, Cambridge (B.A., 1661; M.A., 1668; D.D., 1680); became curate of St. Mary Aldermanbury, London, 1677, from which his father was ejected fifteen years earlier; king's chaplain 1680; vicar of St. Lawrence Jewry, with St. Mary Magdalene, Milk Street, annexed, 1683; prebendary of St. Paul's 1685. Unlike his father and elder brother, he was a High-churchman; he lived on very friendly terms, however, with his non-conformist brother and befriended the latter's son. He published many sermons which are commended for beauty of language and excellent sentiments. His *Discourse about a Doubting* (in the second edition, *Scrupulous*) *Conscience* (1683) made a great sensation, it was directed against dissenters and called forth a reply from Thomas de Laune, a Baptist schoolmaster (*A Plea for the Non-Conformists*, 1684). His brother James Calamy edited a volume of his sermons, containing also his funeral sermon by Dean Sherlock (London, 1690; several subsequent editions).

Bibliography: *Biographia Britannica*, ed. A. Kippis, iii. 137, London, 1784; *DNB*, viii. 226-227.

4. Edmund Calamy: The historian of non-conformity, son of Edmund Calamy the younger;

b. in London Apr. 5, 1671; d. there June 3, 1732. He studied at several schools kept by ejected ministers in England, and at the University of Utrecht, 1688–89; then spent nine months at Oxford; became assistant to Matthew Sylvester at Blackfriars, London, 1692; was ordained 1694; in 1703 settled as pastor of a church in Westminster, London. He was a man of winning manners and much tact, and succeeded in accomplishing his purposes without making enemies. His publications were numerous, for the most part sermons; those which have permanent value are his historical works on English non-conformity. He edited Baxter's *Narrative* (*Reliquiæ Baxterianæ*) and supplied an index and table of contents (1696); six years later he published an abridgment of the same work, adding a history of ministers ejected for non-conformity down to the close of Baxter's life in 1691. The publication provoked much criticism, to which Calamy replied in a second edition (2 vols., 1713) bringing the history down to 1711; and in 1727 he published a continuation of the work in two volumes. Calamy's four volumes were condensed into two by Samuel Palmer, with the title *The Non-Conformist's Memorial* (1775), and a three-volume edition was issued in 1803. He left an autobiography, *An Historical Account of my Own Life, with some reflections on the times I have lived in*, edited by John Towill Rutt (2 vols., London, 1829). Calamy was well qualified by his moderation and catholicity to be the fair-minded historian of non-conformity.

Bibliography: Besides the autobiography mentioned above, consult: *Biographia Britannica*, ed. A. Kippis, iii. 140, London, 1784; *DNB*, viii. 231–235 (quite in detail).

CALAS, cɑ̈'lɑ̈', JEAN. See Rabaut, Paul.

CALASANZE, JOSÉ. See Piarists.

CALATRAVA, ORDER OF: A knightly order, founded about the middle of the twelfth century, to defend the frontiers of Christian Spain against the Moors. The fortress of Calatrava (on the Guadiana, 65 m. s.e. of Toledo), on the borders of Andalusia, commanded the passes into Castile and was hotly contested. After being bravely held for several years by a company of monks and knights under the lead of a Cistercian monk and former soldier, Velasquez, and the abbot Raymond of Fitero, it was presented to the band by Sancho III., king of Castile, in 1158. The general chapter of the Cistercians gave the order a rule under the oversight of the monastery of Morimund, and prescribed as dress a white scapulary (or white cloak) with a garland of red lilies. The rule was confirmed by Pope Alexander III. in 1164. The knights of the order captured Cordova in 1177 and performed other noteworthy deeds of arms. After 1195 a long period of decline began. Calatrava was lost and the seat of the order was transferred to Salvatierra (*Mons Salutis*) in the Sierra Morena. In 1212 Calatrava was again occupied, but was abandoned for New Calatrava, eight miles farther south, in 1218, the Order of Alcantara (q.v.) undertaking the defense of Calatrava. Toward the end of the Middle Ages the grand master possessed such wealth and power that he became an object of suspicion to the crown. At the instigation of Ferdinand and Isabella, Pope Innocent VIII. in 1486 deprived the order of the right of choosing its master, and after 1523 the office was united with the crown. Since 1808 the order has been merely one of merit. Nuns of Calatrava were instituted by the grand master Gonzalez Yanes in 1219 at the time of the removal to New Calatrava. They had their convent at Barrios near Amaya, later at Burgos, but never attained to importance. (O. Zöckler†.)

Bibliography: Helyot, *Ordres monastiques*, vi. 34–53, 66 sqq.; W. H. Prescott, *History of the Reign of Ferdinand and Isabella*, i. 308–309, Philadelphia, 1873; P. B. Gams, *Kirchengeschichte Spaniens*, iii. 54, Regensburg, 1879; Heimbucher, *Orden und Kongregationen*, i. 226–227; Currier, *Religious Orders*, p. 216.

CALDECOTT, ALFRED: Church of England; b. at Chester Nov. 9, 1850. He was educated at the University of London (B.A., 1873) and at St. John's College, Cambridge (B.A., 1879), and was ordered deacon in 1880, and ordained priest two years later. He was curate of Christ Church, Stafford, in 1880, fellow of St. John's College, Cambridge, in 1880–86, and fellow and dean of the same college in 1889–95, in addition to being curate of St. Paul's, Cambridge, in 1881–82, vicar of Horningsey, Cambridgeshire, in 1882–84, and principal of Codrington College, Barbados, and examining chaplain to the bishop of Barbados in 1884–86. He was organizing secretary of the Society for the Propagation of the Gospel at Cambridge in 1889–1905, and was rector of North cum South Lophan, Norfolk, in 1895–98. Since the latter year he has been rector of Frating cum Thorington, Essex, and has also been examining chaplain to the bishop of St. Albans since 1903. He was examiner in Moral Science Tripos in Cambridge in 1884, 1888–89, and 1893–94, and was select preacher in the same university in 1884, 1890–91, and 1894, while in 1891–1892 he was junior proctor. In addition to his duties as rector, he has been professor of moral and mental philosophy in King's College, London, since 1891, and examiner in theology in the University of London since 1902, as well as Cambridge Extension Lecturer in 1880–82 and 1886–87 He has likewise been senior secretary of St. John's Cambridge Mission in South London in 1883–86 and 1889–95, vice-president of the Cambridge Ethical Society in 1890–1905, governor of Colchester Grammar School in 1900–05, a member of the committee of the Christian Evidence Society since 1903, and a member of the Senate of the University of London since 1904. In 1906 he was elected a fellow of King's College, London. He has written: *English Colonisation and Empire* (London, 1891); *The Church in the West Indies* (1898); and *The Philosophy of Religion in England and America* (1901).

CALDERWOOD, DAVID: The historian of the Church of Scotland; b. probably at Dalkeith (7 m. s.e. of Edinburgh) 1575; d. at Jedburgh (40 m. s.e of Edinburgh) Oct. 29, 1650. He studied at Edinburgh, and in 1604 was ordained minister of Crailing, near Jedburgh. He was a determined opponent of the scheme of King James to introduce prelacy into the Church of Scotland; in 1617 he presented a remonstrance to the king, and argued so boldly and successfully in support of his position that he was imprisoned and ultimately ordered to leave the country. He went to Holland (1619), where he lived in quiet and obscurity; at one time it was rumored that he was dead and a false *Recantation Directed to Such in Scotland as Refuse Conformity to the Ordinances of the Church* was published and ascribed to him (London, 1622). After the death of James (1625) he returned to Scotland, but did not obtain a charge until 1640, when he was appointed minister at Pencaitland, East Lothian. Gradually he came again into prominence and, with David Dickson and Alexander Henderson, was employed in drawing up the "Directory for Public Worship." In 1648 the General Assembly voted him an annual pension of £800 Scots (£66 13s. 4d. sterling) to enable him to complete his great work, the history of the Kirk of Scotland. He died, however, leaving it still in manuscript, and in three forms; the first and longest is now partially preserved in the British Museum; the second, "a digest of the first," was published with a *Life* by Thomas Thomson by the Wodrow Society in eight volumes, Edinburgh, 1842–49; the third, another abridgment, was published in 1678 with the title *The True History of the Church of Scotland from the Beginning of the Reformation unto the End of the Reign of King James VI.* These histories have slight literary merit, but are invaluable as sources, their material having been collected with diligence and fidelity. The most notable of Calderwood's other publications was his *Altar of Damascus, or the pattern of the English hierarchy and church obtruded upon the Church of Scotland* (Leyden, 1621; Lat. transl., *Altare Damascenum*, with considerable additions, 1623; 2d ed., 1708), which became later the great storehouse of arguments in favor of Presbyterianism.

Bibliography: Besides the *Life*, by T. Thomson, prefixed to the Wodrow ed. of the *History*, and the *Preface* to vol. viii. of the same, by D. Laing, consult: G. Grub, *Ecclesiastical History of Scotland*, vols. ii., iii., Edinburgh, 1861; J. Walker, *Theology and Theologians of Scotland*, ib. 1872; *DNB*, viii. 244–246.

CALDERWOOD, HENRY: United Presbyterian Church of Scotland; b. at Peebles (21 m. s. of Edinburgh) May 10, 1830; d. at Edinburgh Nov. 19, 1897. He studied at the University of Edinburgh and the theological hall there of the United Presbyterian Church; was ordained minister of Greyfriars Church, Glasgow, 1856; was appointed professor of moral philosophy, Edinburgh, 1868. As a philosopher "he tried to discover and explain the bearings of physiological science on man's mental and moral nature. He believed it to be demonstrated by physiology that the direct dependence of mind on brain was confined to the sensory-motor functions, the dependence of the higher forms of mental activity being, on the other hand, only indirect. He endeavored to establish the thesis that man's intellectual and spiritual life, as we know it, is not the product of natural evolution, but necessitates the assumption of a new creative cause." His interests were not confined to his professional work; he was chairman of the Edinburgh school board, chairman of the North and East of Scotland Liberal Unionist Association, was a member of the mission board of his Church, and advocated temperance reform, Presbyterian union, and other philanthropic and religious movements. He edited *The United Presbyterian Magazine*, and published *The Philosophy of the Infinite* (London, 1854), a criticism of Sir William Hamilton prepared during his student days; *Handbook of Moral Philosophy* (1872); *On Teaching, its Means and Ends* (1874); *The Relations of Mind and Brain* (1879); *The Parables of our Lord* (1880); *The Relations of Science and Religion*, Morse lectures before Union Theological Seminary, New York, 1880 (1881); *Evolution and Man's Place in Nature* (1893; enlarged ed., 1896); several of these works have appeared in many editions.

Bibliography: His *Life* was written by his son, W. L. Calderwood, with David Woodside, with chapter on his philosophical works by A. S. Pringle-Pattison, London, 1900.

CALEB, CALEBITES: One of twelve scouts whom Moses sent from the Wilderness of Sin to spy out the promised land (Num. xii. 16–xiii. 17a, 21, 25), and his descendants. According to Num. xiii. 6 he represented the tribe of Judah. Joshua xiv. 6, 14 designates him as "the Kenizzite," with which Joshua xv. 17 agrees in making Othniel, the brother of Caleb, the "son of Kenaz." The Kenizzites were a branch of the Edomitic stock, Kenaz being a grandson of Esau (Gen. xxxvi. 11, 15). Then Caleb, and Othniel were originally not Israelites, but had left their people and united with the Hebrews, and this agrees with the location of their settlements in Hebron and Debir (Josh. xiv. 6–15, xv. 13–19; Judges i. 12–15, 20). I Chron. ii. 42–49 puts into the possession of Caleb Maresha, Hebron, Tappuah, Maon, Jokdeam, and Beth-zur (Madmannah, verse 49, is a city of the Negeb, Josh. xv. 31). The Calebites occupied the same region in the time of Saul and David, and to them belonged a part of the Negeb (I Sam. xxx. 14). There David lived long as a freebooter, his first wife was of Calebite stock, and Abigail was from Maon-Carmel. After Saul's death David occupied Hebron and its Calebite neighborhood and was there made king. His realm included the territory of Caleb and Judah, though the latter gave the name to his kingdom. In spite of the formal union of the two peoples, the Calebites maintained a practical independence with a residence in Judahitic territory. This explains Absalom's resort to Hebron in his insurrection against David.

The name Caleb was then originally that of a stock, and, personified, became that of the eponymous ancestor (see Eponym). With this the story of Achsah (Judges i. 12–15, Josh. xv. 15–19) is seen to agree when it is remembered that tribally "daughter" means a weaker stock which has lost its independence to a stronger.

The Calebites remained in the district mentioned till exilic times, when the Edomites drove them, weakened by Nebuchadrezzar's measures, northward to the neighborhood of Jerusalem—a change explained in customary genealogical phrasing (I Chron. ii. 18–19), and the Calebites were reckoned to Judah (I Chron. ii. 5, 9, 18, 50–55).

An early age can not be ascribed to the narrative which gives the story of the spies, since Caleb is there reckoned as a Judahite without any discrimination of stocks such as other passages cited above make necessary. The assumption in the representation of P in Num. xiii.-xiv., and of the Chronicler, of the assimilation by the Hebrews of the Calebites is good for postexilic times. (See JUDEA.) (H. GUTHE.)

While advanced scholarship generally takes the position indicated in the text (so, for example, J. A. Selbie in *DB*, i. 340), conservative criticism insists that Caleb was originally a personal name and declines altogether the idea of eponymity; cf. J. D. Davis, *Dictionary of the Bible*, Philadelphia, 1898, pp. 103–104.

BIBLIOGRAPHY: J. Wellhausen, *De gentibus et familiis, I Chron. ii. 4*, Göttingen, 1870; idem, *Die Komposition des Hexateuchs*, pp. 336–338, Berlin, 1889; H. Grätz, *Die Kelubaiten oder Kalebiten*, in *Monatsschrift für Geschichte und Wissenschaft des Judentums*, xxv. (1876) 461 sqq.; W. R. Smith, *Kinship and Marriage*, pp. 200, 219, London, 1885; idem, in *Journal of Philology*, ix. (1876) 89; E. Meyer, *Die Entstehung des Judentums*, pp. 114 sqq., 147–148, Halle, 1896.

CALENDAR BRETHREN (Fratres Calendarii): A fraternity which arose in the second half of the Middle Ages, especially in lower Saxony, but also in other portions of Germany and occasionally in the neighboring countries. It might be termed a clerical gild, for though men who were not members of the clergy were admitted, they were restricted to a minor position, and the statutes of many communities termed only the clergy "full brothers." The first fraternity of Calendar Brethren which is definitely known to have existed was that of Laer in Westphalia in 1279, but it was not until the fourteenth century that they became numerous. They seem to have originated in the official conferences held by the clergy of each archdiaconate on the first day of the month (Latin, *Kalendæ*). They centered about religious worship, the members being required to say mass for the repose of each other's souls or have it said, and to pray for one another. They were likewise bound, as in the gilds, to mutual support and social elevation. With the accession of wealthy laymen, the fraternities gained in importance and wealth, and became famous for their banquets. They made a firm resistance to the Reformation, since they refused to allow their wealth to be diverted to other purposes. Some maintained themselves for a considerable length of time in Evangelical districts, but they were finally suppressed even in Roman Catholic countries. (G. UHLHORN†.)

BIBLIOGRAPHY: L. von Ledebur, *Die Kalandsverbrüderungen in den Landen des sächsischen Volksstammes*, in *Märkische Forschungen*, iv. 7 sqq., Berlin, 1850; Bierling, *Die Kalandsbruderschaften*, in *Zeitschrift für Altertumskunde und Geschichte in Westphalen*, series 10, iii. 178 sqq.

CALENDAR, THE CHRISTIAN.

The Christian calendar is an index of the year arranged according to months and weeks, and giving a list of feasts, fasts, and saints' days, to which data of a more miscellaneous character may be added. The dependence of the feasts on chronology renders it necessary to consider the systems of reckoning time, especially as both the chronological and liturgical portions of the calendar were established by the Church, and remained in the hands of the clergy throughout the Middle Ages. In its most general aspect of an annual list of days and feasts, the Christian calendar dates from the primitive Church, which found its model in classical antiquity, particularly among the Romans. Numerous Roman calendars of the imperial period have been preserved either in whole or in part, designed for public use within areas ranging from a town to an entire country. These calendars contain astronomical information as well as lists of religious feasts and civic celebrations, some of which were connected with the cult, such as many of the public games, while others commemorated historic events. The transition from pagan to Christian usage may be seen in two calendars from the middle of the fourth and fifth centuries (ed. T. Mommsen, *CIL*, i. 332 sqq.). One of these was drawn up at Rome in the reign of Constantine II. and is evidently a revision of a pagan calendar, omitting all feasts of a distinctively religious character, both heathen and Christian, but retaining the purely civic feasts.

1. The Origin of the Christian Calendar.

Christian influence is visible, however, in the recognition of the Christian weeks beside the Roman system, since the year, which here begins with Jan. 1, falls in two regular divisions, one of eight days each (the *nundinæ*) represented by the letters A–H, and the other of seven days, indicated by A–G. The second calendar was prepared in 448, during the reign of Valentinian III., and, though pagan in basis, contains for the first time a small number of Christian feasts, having five festivals of Christ and six saints' days. The oldest exclusively Christian calendar is a Gothic fragment, apparently prepared in Thrace in the fourth century, containing the last eight days of October and the entire month of November. Seven days have the names of saints attached to them, two from the New Testament, three from the general Church, and two from the Goths.

2. The Calendar in the Early Church.

Even before the inclusion of Christian feasts in the Roman calendar, however, the Church had lists of saints' days arranged according to the date of their celebration, although not yet incorporated in a formal calendar. Allusions to such lists of memorial days are found in Tertullian and Cyprian, but the earliest one extant was prepared at Rome in the middle of the fourth century. It consists of an enumeration of twelve Roman bishops and a list of martyrs for twenty-four days, including feasts in commemoration of the birth of Christ and of St. Peter (Feb. 22), all the remainder being festivals of martyrs, generally of local origin. The next oldest calendar is a list of the festivals of the Church of Carthage, which apparently dates from the end of the fifth or the beginning of the sixth century, and contains the names of bishops and martyrs, the most of whom were natives of Carthage. From such beginnings a wealth of calendars soon developed throughout the Latin world, and the lists of the days of the month received an increasing proportion of martyrological, hagiological, and heortological material. The active intercourse of the churches, especially of Rome with Africa, Gaul, Spain, and England, resulted in the addition of such numbers of foreign saints that those who received honor throughout the Church exceeded the saints of local fame, and finally there was no day of the year which did not have one or more saints.

Since martyrs were commemorated in the early Church especially in the place where they had suffered, each community originally had its own list of feasts and its own calendar. This usage was of long duration, despite the frequent interchange of names and despite the increasing prestige of the Roman calendar and list of feasts. The diversity of calendars was augmented, moreover, by the reverence paid to the local saints of individual countries and dioceses, while a still more important factor was the discrepancy in the dating of the beginning of the year. The first of the year was reckoned from no less than six days: (1) the Feast of the Circumcision (Jan. 1; used in conformity to the Julian calendar); (2) Mar. 1 (Merovingian France, the Lombards, Venice, and, for a time, Russia); (3) the Feast of the Annunciation (Mar. 25; first in Florence and Pisa, whence it extended to France, Germany, England, and Ireland, being retained in the latter two countries until the eighteenth century); (4) Easter (especially in France); (5) Sept. 1 (Byzantine Empire, and, until modern times, Russia); (6) Christmas (Carolingian France, the Anglo-Saxons, Scandinavia, Prussia, Hungary, and portions of Holland, Switzerland, etc.). The problem was further complicated by the various methods of indicating the day of the month, of which at least five systems were used contemporaneously: (1) the ancient Roman method of calends, ides, and nones; (2) the Greco-Christian consecutive numbering of the days of the month, now generally used; (3) the *consuetudo Bononiensis*, which divided the month into two halves, in one of which (*mensis intrans*) the days were numbered forward from 1, while in the other (*mensis exiens*) they were reckoned backward from 30 or 31; (4) the method of Cisiojanus or Cisianus, which designated the days of the month by the syllables of arbitrary mnemonic verses (long popular in Poland and North Germany); (5) the designation of the day by the feast celebrated on it. This confusion was worse confounded by the various reckonings of Easter, while the movable feasts based upon it and running side by side with the fixed festivals, or even crossing them, added their quota of perplexity.

3. Complications in Dating.

In the Middle Ages calendars were multiplied, partly in consequence of the chronological intricacies already noted and partly because of the universal need for ecclesiastical data of this character. It is true that there are few calendars still extant which were prepared previous to the eighth century, but this deficiency is made good in various ways, especially by the sacramentaries which give the list of feasts, while liturgical books, particularly manuscripts of the Psalter, frequently have a calendar prefixed to them. Such calendars are usually perpetual, that is, available for any year, but are usually provided with methods for the determination of the movable feasts of any particular year. Not only are the letters A–G repeated in them from Jan. 1 to designate the days of the week, but they also contain the numbers I.–XIX. to denote all new moons which fall, in the course of a cycle of nineteen years, on the day of the month designated by one of these numbers. By means of such a calendar, when the Dominical Letter and the Golden Number (qq.v.) of the cycle are known, may be obtained the day of the week of any date and all new moons throughout the year. From the latter is derived the date of the spring new moon, which gives, when the day of the week on which it falls is determined by the Dominical Letter, the date of Easter. An Easter table for a series of years is also frequently added to the calendars.

4. Early Medieval Calendars.

All calendars of the Greek and Slavic churches begin their ecclesiastical year, as already noted, with Sept. 1. The great majority of their immovable feasts are consecrated to the saints and the Virgin, while a number of the movable feasts are consecrated to Christ. The latter, like the Sundays of the year, are divided into three periods: *Trioidion* (beginning with the tenth Sunday before Easter), *Pentēkostarion* (from Easter to the close of the second week after Whitsuntide), and *Oktoēchos* (extending from the second Sunday after Whitsuntide into the Western Epiphany). The calendar of the Greek Church is characterized by numerous fasts, partly of single days and partly of several weeks. To the latter belong the four "great fasts." Two of these are movable, the Easter fast of seven weeks, and the Fast of the Apostles, the latter lasting from the Feast of All Martyrs on the Sunday after Whitsuntide to the day of SS. Peter and Paul (June 29). The other two, the Fast of the Virgin (August 1–15) and the Fast of Advent (Nov. 24–Dec. 24), are immovable. In a number of the more important feasts the Greek calendar harmonizes with the Western, but it deviates in numerous instances from the latter in its dating of the feasts of saints and martyrs.

5. Greek and Slavic Calendars.

In the Western Church the majority of calendars were written in Latin until the end of the Crusades. Among them special mention may be made of the ancient list of feasts prepared at Rome during the reign of Gregory II. or Gregory III., and noteworthy as giving the Roman stations in which the feasts were celebrated and the lessons from the Gospels. Other noteworthy calendars include one prepared in 781 by Godesscalc at the command of Charlemagne, a calendar from Luxeuil of the latter part of the seventh century, a marble **6. Later Medieval Calendars.** calendar drawn up at Naples by Bishop John IV between 840 and 850, and a calendar of Bishop Gundekar II. of Eichstätt (1057–79). Among other German calendars mention may be made of one from Freising of the latter part of the tenth century, from Salzburg in the eleventh century, from Regensburg in the twelfth, and from Passau and Augsburg in the thirteenth. Toward the end of the Middle Ages the Latin calendars began to be translated into the vernacular, although a metrical calendar had been written in Anglo-Saxon before the close of the tenth century. A French calendar of the thirteenth century is still extant in manuscript, but German calendars, which are tolerably numerous, are not found until a hundred years later. The invention of printing in the fifteenth century wrought important changes in the calendar, although the first printed specimens resemble those in manuscript and, like them, are perpetual. The first calendar for a definite year was printed at Nuremberg in 1475 in German and Latin. It was designed for the years 1475, 1494, and 1513 as the first of a triple cycle of nineteen years each, and was so constructed that the dates for other years might be derived from these three, so that it really extended from 1475 to 1531. The ecclesiastical portions, however, were in perpetual form, since the calendar contained, in addition to the letters A–G for the days of the week, only the names of the saints for a limited number of days without a division into weeks and without the movable feasts. It was not until the middle of the sixteenth century that calendars arranged according to the weeks and feasts of a definite year came into general use.

The reckoning of Easter hitherto employed had long been recognized as inadequate, and the elimination of the errors which this system had caused was one of the most urgent tasks which awaited solution after the close of the Middle Ages. Since the second half of the third century the rule had been adopted by the Alexandrian Church, and confirmed by the Council of Nicæa, that Easter should fall on the Sunday after the spring full moon, that is, on the first Sunday after the full moon on or next after the vernal equinox. The date of this equinox was to be Mar. 21, while the **7. Errors in Calculating Easter.** full moon was to be reckoned according to a cycle of nineteen years. This system of reckoning was introduced into the Roman Church in 525 by Dionysius Exiguus, and spread thence throughout Italy, Gaul, and Spain, and was given to the Anglo-Saxon churches by Bede in 729. This method, however, was vitiated by two faults which could not fail to become evident in the course of time. In the first place, by its assumption that the vernal equinox falls on Mar. 21 it adopted the entire Julian system which makes the year 365¼ days in length and intercalates a day every four years. In reality this year is eleven minutes too long, so that an extra day is intercalated every 128 years. In the second place, by its reckoning of the spring full moon according to a nineteen-year cycle of 235 months or 6,939¾ days, it made the cycle an hour too long, thus making a discrepancy of the day between the real and the theoretical new moon every 210 years. It was not until the thirteenth century that this error attracted attention, the first works to note it being the *Computus* of Master Conrad in 1200 (extant only in a revision of 1396 in a Vienna manuscript) and the similar work of an anonymous author of 1223 (preserved in great part by Vincent of Beauvais). The problem was likewise taken up by Johannes de Sacro-Busto about 1250 in his *De anni ratione* and by Roger Bacon in a treatise addressed to Clement IV., *De reformatione calendarii,* while among the Greeks the monk Isaac Argyros wrote on the problem in 1272. In the fifteenth century the reformation of the calendar was discussed in the great councils of the Roman Catholic Church, especially by Pierre d'Ailly at Kostnitz in 1414 and by Nicholas of Cusa at Basel in 1436, the latter proposing to begin the correction of the calendar in 1439.

The actual reform of the calendar was first carried out by Gregory XIII. (1572–85) in conformity with a resolution of the Council of Trent. In 1577 the pope appointed a committee which held its sessions at Rome to carry out the plan proposed by the Calabrian astronomer Aloigi Ligli, and confirmed this reformed calendar, which was called the Gregorian in his honor, by a bull of Feb. 24, 1582. The reform was designed, on **8. The Gregorian Reform.** the one hand, to regulate Easter with reference to the solar and lunar revolutions, thus restoring the year of the lunar cycle according to the date and intention of the Nicene Council, and, on the other, to avoid any future shifting of the vernal equinox and the spring full moon. To restore the vernal equinox to Mar. 21, the ten days between Oct. 4 and 15 were dropped, while for the correction of the spring full moon the new moons were set back three days from Jan. 3 to Dec. 31. These corrections were assured by retaining the Julian system of intercalation and the nineteen-year lunar cycle for a century. The intercalary day was to be omitted thrice in four centuries, and the new moon was to be retarded one day eight times in twenty-five centuries (seven times after each three hundred years and the eighth time after four hundred). For the correction of the lunar cycle the reckoning of epacts, or the age of the moon on Jan. 1, was introduced according to the cycle proposed by Ligli.

The Gregorian calendar was adopted in Roman Catholic countries either immediately or in the course of a few years. The Protestant districts, on the other hand, opposed it, partly on account of their hostility to Rome and partly on account of its chronological discrepancies. Its inaccuracies were recognized by the landgrave **9. Opposition to the Gregorian Calendar.** William IV. of Hesse-Cassel, and the Calvinistic Joseph Justus Scaliger issued repeated warnings against it. After the end of the sixteenth century the Julian calendar existed in Germany side by side with the Gregorian, the two being designated as old and new style, respectively. The movable feasts of the two faiths accordingly differed, and the advocates of the new style dated the days of the month ten days in advance of the old until the end of the seventeenth century. In view of the discrepancies between the two systems the German Protestants devised a third calendar, which was to agree neither with the Gregorian nor the Julian and was to take effect in 1700. In its reckoning of time it agreed with the Gregorian, but its feasts were calculated astronomically according to the meridian of Uraniborg and the Rudolphinian Tables of Kepler. The result was increased confusion and embitterment between Roman Catholics and Protestants, particularly in 1724, 1744, and 1788, when there was a divergency of a week between the Gregorian and the astronomical Easter. This Protestant calendar was finally suppressed by Frederick the Great in 1775, and the Gregorian calendar became supreme throughout Germany. German Protestants have sought in recent years to transform Easter into an immovable feast, but the plan as yet remains inchoate.

10. Attempts to Reform the Calendar.

The evangelical reforms of the calendar thus far considered were concerned only with chronology, without regard to the traditional Christian lists of saints and martyrs. There is, however, a tendency among the Lutherans to revise the hagiology of the Church, in view of the Protestant skepticism regarding the existence of many of the saints of tradition and the Christianity ascribed to others. They are offended, furthermore, by the names of such heroes of the Counterreformation as St. Ignatius Loyola and other opponents of their sect, while prominent Protestants, it is felt, should be recognized in an ecclesiastical calendar designed for Lutheran use. Such an attempt was made by Ferdinand Piper in his *Evangelischer Kalender* (published from 1850 to 1870), in which he sought to transform the hagiology of the Western Church according to evangelical ideas. To increase the interest of the laity in this new list of names, brief biographies were added, and these, 399 in number, were later published separately under the title *Zeugen der Wahrheit* (4 vols., Leipsic, 1874; Eng. transl., by H. M. MacCracken, 3 vols., Boston, 1879). Piper's calendar, however, failed to secure official recognition in any German church, although in various revisions it has been included in a number of popular calendars in Germany. It is self-evident that only partial success can be attained by any Protestant hagiological calendar in view of the diversity of Protestant conditions and requirements. Apparently, the most that can be done is to add new dates and names, whether these be supplementary or corrective, to the traditional hagiology of the Church, so that, according to the requirements of time or place, a choice may be made from the names associated with any particular day.

(O. Zöckler†.)

Bibliography: On the general subject consult: L. Ideler, *Handbuch der Chronologie*, 2 vols., Berlin, 1825–26; A. J. Weidenbach, *Calendarium historico-christianum medii et novi ævi*, Regensburg, 1855; W. S. B. Woolhouse, *Analysis of the Christian, Hebrew and Mahometan Calendars*, London, 1881; Ledouble, *La Connaissance des années et des jours. Traité du calendrier*, Soissons, 1887; E. Mahler, *Fortsetzung der Wustenfeld'schen Vergleichungs-Tabellen der muhammedanischen und christlichen Zeitrechnung*, Leipsic, 1887; J. C. Macdonald, *Chronologies and Calendars*, London, 1897; F. Rühl, *Chronologie des Mittelalters und der Neuzeit*, Berlin, 1897; B. M. Lersch, *Einleitung in die Chronologie*, 2 vols., Freiburg, 1899 (vol. ii. on Christian Calendar); *Encyclopædia Britannica*, iv. 664–682 (gives comparative tables); *DCA*, i. 256–258.

On the origin of the Christian calendar consult: T. Mommsen, *Der Chronograph vom Jahre 354*, in *Abhandlungen der sächsischen Gesellschaft der Wissenschaften*, ii. (1850) 547 sqq.; A. J. Binterim, *Denkwürdigkeiten*, i. 20 sqq., 7 vols., Mainz, 1837–41; L. Coleman, *Ancient Christianity*, chap. xxvi., § 5, Philadelphia, 1852; F. Piper, *Der Ursprung der christlichen Kalendarien*, in *Königlicher preussischer Staatskalender*, 1855, pp. 6–25; A. Lechner, *Mittelalterliche Kalendarien in Bayern*, Freiburg, 1891; E. Berfried, *Die Ausgestaltung der christlichen Osterberechnung*, Mittelwalde, 1893.

On calendars of the Middle Ages useful works are: N. Nilles, *Kalendarium manuale utriusque ecclesiæ*, 4 vols., Innsbruck, 1879–85, vols. i., ii., 2d ed., 1897 (a most valuable collection for the Eastern Churches); A. Cave, *Scriptorum ecclesiasticorum historia literaria*, Appendix, part ii., London, 1698 (describes Eastern calendars); F. Piper, *Kirchenrechnung*, pp. vi. sqq., Berlin, 1841; idem, *Karls des Grossen Kalendarium*, ib. 1858; W. L. Krafft, *Kirchengeschichte der germanischen Völker*, I. i. 371, 385–387, ib. 1854; F. Kaltenbrunner, *Die Vorgeschichte der gregorianischen Kalenderreform*, Vienna, 1876; O. E. Hartmann, *Der römische Kalender*, Leipsic, 1882; J. Weale, *Analecta liturgica*, 2 vols., London, 1889; H. Grotefend, *Taschenbuch der Zeitrechnung des deutschen Mittelalters und der Neuzeit*, Hanover, 1898; A. von Maltzew, *Menologien der orthodox-katholischen Kirche des Morgenlandes*, part i., Berlin, 1900 (Sept.–Feb., German and Slavic and reference to original Gk. text).

For the history of the Gregorian reform consult: F. Kaltenbrunner, *Die Polemik über die gregorianische Kalenderreform*, Vienna, 1877; J. B. J. Delambre, *Histoire de l'astronomie moderne*, i. 1–84, Paris, 1821; G. S. Ferrari, *Il calendario Gregoriano*, Rome, 1882; the literature under Gregory XIII.

For modern Protestant calendars the following may be consulted: F. Piper, *Die Verbesserung des Kalenders*, in *Evangelischer Kalender*, 1850, pp. 1–11; idem, *Die Verbesserung des evangelischen Kalenders*, Berlin, 1850; W. Löhes, *Martyrologium. Zur Erklärung der herkömmlichen Kalendernamen*, pp. 1–12, Nuremberg, 1868; E. Scharfe, *Die christliche Zeitrechnung und der deutsch-evangelische Kalender*, pp. 18–28, Stuttgart, 1893.

CALENDAR, HEBREW AND JEWISH. See Day, the Hebrew; Moon, Semitic Conceptions of; Year, the Hebrew; Synagogue.

CALF, THE GOLDEN, AND CALF-WORSHIP.

The story of the worship of the golden calf during the desert journey is given Ex. xxxii. and Deut. ix. 7–21; cf. Neh. ix. 18; Ps. cvi. 19–20; Acts vii. 39–40. The authorized calf-worship of Northern Israel is mentioned I Kings xii. 28–33; II Kings x. 29, xvii. 16; Hos. viii. 5–6, x. 5–6, xiii. 2; II Chron. xi. 15, xiii. 8. The Hebrew term generally applied to the calf is *'egel*; *'eglah* in Hos. x. 5 is probably a mistake for *'egel*.

It has generally been supposed that the Israelites borrowed calf-worship from the Egyptians, a supposition thought to be supported by the fact that Jeroboam had been recalled from Egypt. But the Egyptian animal-worship was essentially different from the Semitic type, since the Egyptian worship was paid to living animals. The bulls or calves of Jeroboam—the classical example in Israel—were, on the other hand, intended to be symbols of Yahweh. In any case Jeroboam would not have introduced a foreign cult to strengthen his new and precarious government. The Hebrew calf-worship did not reproduce the cult of Apis and Mnevis, which were living animals, one black, the other white, dedicated to Osiris, and he was believed to be incarnated in them (J. G. Wilkinson, *Manners and Customs of the Ancient Egyptians*, iii., London, 1878, 86–95, 306–307). Suggestions of bull-worship among the Hebrews are found in the horns of the altar, in the oxen under the lavers (I Kings vii. 25), and possibly in the cherubim. While examples of Hebrew bull-worship are rare, the proof of its existence among neighboring nations is abundant. In the Babylonio-Assyrian and Syro-Phenician religions, the bull represented the masculine type of divinity, as was natural to a pastoral people. The primitive Aryans also explained the heavenly phenomena by comparisons drawn from the life of their herds. The Zendavesta makes mention of "the first bull." The bull represented power and strength, and at the same time the destructive and the reproductive omnipotence of the deity. The sun-god is hardly to be recognized in the bull, as has been supposed. The gold of the Hebrew bull idols does not necessarily point to the splendor of the sun, for the images of other gods were also of gold or gilded. Still less credible is the assertion that the strength of the bull represented the scorching blaze of the sun. Among the Babylonians the bull was sacred to the thunder-god *Ramman* (Syrian *Rimmon*), Assyrian *Adad* (Syrian *Hadad*), who is represented in Layard's *Monuments*, plate 65, as having four horns and holding the lightnings in one hand and a battle-ax in the other. The bull is also the emblem of Ramman-Adad on the stele of Esarhaddon found at Zingirli in Northern Syria, as well as in the procession of the gods depicted on the rock at Maltai (cf. G. Perrot and C. Chipiez, *Histoire de l'art dans l'antiquité*, ii., Paris, 1881 sqq., 642–643). An image of the Syrian Jupiter of Doliche, which was carried from Syria to Rome, represents him standing upon a bull (cf. F. Hettner, *De Jove Dolicheno dissertatio philologica*, Bonn, 1877; A. H. Kan, *De Jovis Dolicheni Cultu dissertatio*, Groningen, 1901). The Jupiter of Hierapolis in Syria was pictured sitting upon bulls (Lucian, *De dea Syria*, xxxi.). The classical tale of the seduction of Europa is a form of the Baal myth, in which the god, in the shape of a bull, journeys with Astarte (q.v.) to Crete (for the identity of Astarte with Europa, cf. *De dea Syria*, iv.). The sacredness of cattle among the Philistines also is demonstrated by the story of the return of the ark on a new cart drawn by two milch kine, on which there had come no yoke (I Sam. vi. 7 sqq.).

1. Origin of Calf-worship among the Hebrews.

2. Bull-worship among Other Semites.

That bull-worship among the Hebrews was ancient the foregoing makes quite possible. It was, however, hardly practised before the final settlement in Canaan, since it was always characteristic of peoples who had either reached or passed the agricultural stage. The prohibition of the Book of the Covenant (Ex. xx. 23, cf. xxxiv. 17) is, therefore, the first warning against this type of worship. Ex. xxxii. assumes, however, that it was practised during the journey in the wilderness. The leading features of the narrative are as follows: The people had become impatient under the continued absence of their leader, and Aaron made for them an image of the god who had led them out of Egypt. With the material furnished by the golden earrings of the women and children, "a molten calf" was fashioned, before which an altar was built, and to it divine honors were paid. The rest of the chapter tells of Yahweh's anger, of Moses's energetic intervention, of Aaron's apology, and finally of the destruction of the calf and of 3,000 of its worshipers. The narrative—a composite of J and E—has been, however, considered by many modern critics as unhistorical and really a polemic against Jeroboam's newly instituted worship. The cardinal passage on calf-worship is I Kings xii. 28–29 (cf. II Chron. xi. 15), where the story is told of the bulls set up by Jeroboam I., who ordained a non-levitical priesthood, and did not pretend to do more than return to the Yahweh-worship of the past. That he did thus return is proved by his success. When Jehu destroyed the Baal-worship, he did not touch the bulls, a clear proof that he acknowledged the bull-worship as Yahweh-worship (II Kings x. 29). Yet the spiritual prophets opposed the bull-worship from the beginning. Indirect testimony to this may be seen in Amos (v. 5). Direct testimony is first found in Hosea. This younger contemporary of Amos is the only one of the prophets who alludes to bull-worship; and to him the worship of an image is the worship of an idol (viii. 5–6, xiii. 2, cf. x. 5–6). With regard to the precise form and structure of Jeroboam's bulls there is no direct information. Gold being scarce and precious, it is probable that the images were small—an assumption supported by the fact that they are called calves. Naturally these royal statues would be of pure gold and not merely gilded.

3. Bull-worship in Israel.

In the kingdom of Judah bull-worship does not seem to have flourished, for nowhere is found a reference to Judaic worship of this kind, and the polemics of Hosea exclusively against the calf of Samaria at Bethel would be unintelligible, had he been aware of the same cult in Judah. The Deuteronomic redactor of the book of Kings saw in the bull-worship the special sin of Jeroboam, wherewith he caused Israel to sin (I Kings xiv. 16, xv. 26).

4. Bull-worship in Judah.

Bibliography: W. Baudissin, *Studien*, vol. i., Leipsic, 1878; J. Selden, *De dis Syris*, pp. 45–64, London, 1617; C. T. Beke, *The Idol of Horeb . . . the Golden Image . . . a Cone . . . not a Calf*, ib. 1871; A. Kuenen, *Religion of Israel*, i. 73–75, 235–236, 260–262, 345–347, ib. 1874; E. König, *Hauptprobleme der altisraelitischen Religionsgeschichte*, pp. 53–92, Leipsic, 1884; idem, *Bildlosigkeit des legitimen Jahwehcultus*, ib. 1886; F. Baethgen, *Bei-*

träge zur semitischen Religionsgeschichte, pp. 198 sqq., Berlin, 1889; J. Robertson, *Early Religion of Israel*, chap. ix., Edinburgh, 1892; F. W. Farrar, *Was there a Golden Calf at Dan?* in *Expositor*, viii. (1893) 254–265; S. Oettli, *Der Kultus bei Amos und Hosea*, in *Greifswalder Studien*, 1895, pp. 1–34; *DB*, i. 340–343; *EB*, i. 631–632. Consult also the works on O. T. Theology, especially that by H. Schultz, Eng. transl., Edinburgh, 1892, and the works mentioned under IDOLATRY; IMAGES AND IMAGE-WORSHIP.

CALIXTINES. See HUSS, JOHN, HUSSITES.

CALIXTUS, ca-lix'tus: The name of three popes and one antipope.

Calixtus (Callistus) **I.:** Pope 217–222. Through the discovery of the work of Hippolytus (q.v.) on heresies, a new aspect, differing in many particulars from the traditional one, has been assumed by the story of this early bishop. The old account ascribed to him the building of the church of Santa Maria in Trastevere. The Pseudo-Isidorian Decretals (q.v.) contain two in which, among other things, regulations are laid down for the ember fasts. He was called a martyr, but the acts of his martyrdom are purely legendary, probably composed in the seventh century. The picture given by Hippolytus, though bitterly hostile, is at least clear and sharp in its outlines. According to it, Callistus was the slave of a Christian official named Carpophorus, who entrusted him with considerable sums of money, which he lost. Taking flight to avoid a reckoning, he was pursued by his master, and jumped into the sea to escape him, but was pulled out and condemned to the treadmill. Then he got into a quarrel with the Jews in Rome, and was beaten and sent to the mines of Sardinia, from which he was released by the influence of Marcia, the mistress of Commodus. It is impossible to determine how far Callistus was morally blameworthy in this chequered career · probably not as much as Hippolytus says. The events recited are said to have happened in the pontificate of Victor. The next bishop, Zephyrinus, brought Callistus back to Rome, probably already in orders, and gave him charge of the large cemetery which later bore his name. Under Zephyrinus he came into conflict with Hippolytus on the dogma of the Incarnation (see MONARCHIANISM); and at the next vacancy a schism occurred, each party electing its own leader as bishop (see HIPPOLYTUS). Callistus seems to have been, like Zephyrinus, a Modalist; it was he who excommunicated Sabellius. The question of discipline also brought him into conflict with Hippolytus, according to whom he laid down the principle, unacceptable to the rigorists of the time, that all sins might be forgiven, and denied the necessity of deposing a bishop who should be guilty of deadly sin. Hippolytus accuses him of taking this position so as to increase the numbers of his own church; but it is undeniable that a clear-sighted man could hardly fail to see the defects and inconsistencies of the then existing church discipline, and Callistus was probably seeking to establish a more logical system. The *Catalogus Liberianus* is authority for placing his death in 222. [The largest of the Roman catacombs is the Cemetery of St. Callistus; and De Rossi says it was the first common cemetery, given to the pope by some noble family for the use of the whole Christian community. Thirteen out of the next eighteen popes after Zephyrinus are said to have been buried there.] (A. HAUCK.)

BIBLIOGRAPHY: The *Epistolæ* are in *MPG*, vol. x. An anonymous *Translation*, ed. Holder-Egger, is in *MGH, Script.*, xv. (1887) 418–422. Consult: C. K. J. Bunsen, *Hippolytus and his Age*, 2 vols., London, 1852–56; J. J. I. von Döllinger, *Hippolytus und Callistus*, Regensburg, 1853; K. J. Neumann, *Der römische Staat und die allgemeine Kirche*, i. 312–313, Leipsic, 1890; T. E. Rolffs, *Das Indulgenz-Edikt des Kallist*, in *TU*, xi. (1894) 3; H. Achelis, *Hippolytstudien*, Leipsic, 1897; Harnack, *Litteratur*, i. 603–605; Jaffé, *Regesta*, i. 12–13, ii. 731; Milman, *Latin Christianity*, i. 75–79; Bower, *Popes*, i. 20–21.

Calixtus II. (Gui, or Wido, son of Count William of Burgundy): Pope 1119–24. He was made archbishop of Vienne in 1088, and under Paschal II. was legate in England, with little success. In the investiture controversy he was one of the leaders of the French opposition to the compromise of 1111 with Henry V. A synod called by him at Vienne in that year condemned lay investiture without reserve and excommunicated Henry, threatening the pope with renunciation of allegiance if he did not confirm its decrees. When he was elected pope by the cardinals assembled at Cluny (Feb. 2, 1119), Henry had reason to fear the accession of a second Hildebrand. He made conciliatory overtures to the new pontiff, offering to submit the controversy to a council called by Calixtus, and approved an agreement with the papal representatives by which, in return for the revocation of his excommunication, he surrendered his claims to the right of investiture. But the agreement proved impossible of execution, and soon, in a great council held at Reims (Oct. 29 and 30, 1119), Calixtus renewed his denial of the right and his excommunication of Henry and of Antipope Gregory VIII. Though the sentence remained ineffective in Germany, Calixtus strengthened his authority in France during his stay there, finding a firm ally in Louis the Fat. He went to Italy in the spring of 1120, and entered Rome in triumph, Gregory VIII. fleeing to Sutri, whose citizens delivered him up to his victorious rival in the following April. This strengthened Calixtus's position still more against the emperor; but the final decision of the contest was brought about by the intervention of the German princes, assembled at Würzburg in the autumn of 1121. They counseled Henry to acknowledge Calixtus and the canonically elected bishops, undertaking in return to arrange a peace with the Church, and proposing the convocation of a general council, in which they promised to defend the honor of the Empire. Calixtus appointed Lambert of Ostia and two other cardinals to conduct the negotiations, which began at Worms in Sept., 1122. Archbishop Adalbert of Mainz continued to urge the strict Hildebrandine position, and it was due to Lambert's work alone that the discussion, instead of being fruitless, led to the Concordat of Worms (see CONCORDATS AND DELIMITING BULLS, I., § 1). This was solemnly confirmed by Calixtus in the First Lateran Council, opened on Mar. 18, 1123, which also renewed the canons against simony and clerical marriage, and proclaimed a "truce of God" and a new crusade. While the plans for this undertaking were being made, Calixtus died, Dec. 13 or 14, 1124. (A. HAUCK.)

BIBLIOGRAPHY: The *Epistolæ et Privilegia* are in *MPL*, clxiii.; An *Epistola spuria*, ed. W. Grundlach, is in *MGH, Epist.*, iii. (1891) 108–109. The *Vita* by Cardinal Pandulfus Aletrinus, a contemporary, is in *ASB*, May, v. 14–15, and in *MPL*, clxiii. Consult: *Liber pontificalis*, ed. Duchesne, ii. 322, 376, Paris, 1892; H. Witte, *Forschungen zur Geschichte des Wormser Concordats*, Göttingen, 1877; M. Maurer, *Papst Calixt II.*, Munich, 1889; F. Gregorovius, *Geschichte der Stadt Rom*, iv. 369 sqq., Stuttgart, 1890, Eng. transl., iv. 390–402, London, 1896; U. Robert, *Histoire du pape Calixte II.*, Paris, 1891; idem, *Bullaire du pape Calixte II.*, ib. 1891; Jaffé, *Regesta*, i. 270; Milman, *Latin Christianity*, iv. 130–149; Bower, *Popes*, ii. 456–460.

Calixtus III. (Johannes de Struma): Antipope 1168–73, in opposition to Alexander III. (q.v.). After the peace of Venice, he maintained himself for a while at Albano, but on Aug. 29, 1178, he made his submission to Alexander and was restored to the communion of the church, being entrusted with the government of Benevento. (A. HAUCK.)

BIBLIOGRAPHY: Jaffé, *Regesta*, ii. 429, 430; Milman, *Latin Christianity*, iv. 431–437; Bower, *Popes*, ii. 514–515.

Calixtus III. (Alonso de Borja or Borgia): Pope 1455–58. Born at Xativa in Valencia [Dec. 31, 1378]. After a legal education he became bishop of Valencia in 1429 and cardinal in 1444. On Apr. 8, 1455, being then seventy-seven years old, he was elected pope. He was a man of simple and blameless life, but too weak to cope with the disorders of the time, some of which arose directly from his own partiality for his relatives. Immediately after his accession, he took a vow to carry forward a war against the Turks and atone for the manner in which Europe had looked on supinely at the fall of Constantinople. Legates were sent throughout the Continent to preach a crusade and collect troops and money. Money, indeed, came in, especially through the help of the mendicant orders, in large sums; but the old crusading zeal had died down too far to be rekindled. The tithes which were required, on behalf of the undertaking, from the clergy of France and Germany aroused universal discontent. The doctors of the University of Paris and the clergy of Rouen appealed in 1456 to a general council against the tax, and a similar appeal was made in Germany, not only on this ground but on that of the failure to observe the Vienna Concordat of 1448 in regard to the system of clerical benefices. While endeavoring to put down this rebellious spirit, Calixtus succeeded in assembling a small fleet which sailed (May 31, 1456) to help the Knights of St. John in their dangerous position at Rhodes. The fleet, under the command of the cardinal legate Scarampo, occupied some small islands of the Grecian archipelago, without venturing on a decisive engagement. The Greeks had not the courage to rise in force, and the Christian princes and Italian cities took but a languid interest in the crusade. It was a piece of luck that the victory of the heroic Hunyadi at Belgrade (July 14 and 21, 1456) averted the most pressing peril. The pope was hindered by the consequences of his hostility to Alfonso of Naples, after whose death (June 27, 1458) he refused to acknowledge the claim of Alfonso's natural son Fernando, asserting that the kingdom reverted as a fief of the papacy to himself. This attitude was the outcome of his desire to advance his own nephews, one of whom, Rodrigo (the future Alexander VI.), he had made cardinal and vice-chancellor of the Roman Church in spite of his being below the canonical age; another, Pedro, he had made duke of Spoleto, destining the Neapolitan crown for him. Calixtus died, however (Aug. 6, 1458), before his unscrupulous designs could break the peace of Italy. His nephews and their Spanish followers left Rome, where, in alliance with the Colonna family, they had been guilty of incessant crimes and violence. (A. HAUCK.)

BIBLIOGRAPHY: B. Platina, *The Lives of the Popes*, ii. 250–257, London, n.d. Consult: A. von Reumont, *Geschichte der Stadt Rom*, iii, 126 sqq., Berlin, 1868; F. Gregorovius, *Geschichte der Stadt Rom*, vii. 146 sqq., Stuttgart, 1870, Eng. transl., London, 1900; Pastor, *Popes*, ii. 317–479; Creighton, *Papacy*, iii. 178–201; Milman, *Latin Christianity*, viii. 120 sqq.; Bower, *Popes*, iii. 238–240.

CALIXTUS, GEORG: The most influential continuator of Melanchthon's theology in the seventeenth century, spokesman of the so-called "syncretism" in Germany at that time; b. at Medelbye (in the district of Tondern, 115 m. n.n.w. of Hamburg), Schleswig, Dec. 14, 1586; d. at Helmstädt, Brunswick, March 19, 1656. His father, pastor at Medelbye, a pupil of Melanchthon, wished to have his son educated in the same way, and after due preparation sent him to the university at Helmstädt, where like-minded friends of Melanchthon, e.g., the humanist Caselius, were still in office. From 1603 to 1607 he studied philology and philosophy, then theology, paying especial attention to the study of early patristics. From 1609 to 1613 he traveled in Germany, Belgium, England, and France, enlarging his ideas, and becoming acquainted with the conditions of the Reformed and Roman Catholic churches, comparing them with those of the Lutheran Church to which he belonged. Thus he developed an irenic tendency which he retained all his life. He was appointed in 1614 professor of theology at Helmstädt, and remained there until his death. A memorial tablet on his house in the little city in the duchy of Brunswick commemorates the activity of this enlightened mind. His life fell in the age of the Counterreformation and the Thirty Years' War, when the hatred of the confessions toward each other had reached its height. The main effort of this irenic theologian was inspired by the idea that theology must have for its prime object not so much pure doctrine as Christian life. Thus he became the creator of theological ethics as a special theological discipline, and therein undoubtedly marks an epoch in the progress of theology; most moral philosophers still follow him in this formal principle. But the danger was thereby incurred of detaching ethics from dogmatics and building the former without the necessary religious foundation. In the second place he endeavored to bring about a union of all Christian churches, taking the Apostles' Creed and the consensus of the first five centuries as a dogmatically and ecclesiastically sufficient norm. He aspired to a union of all Christian confessions. For this reason he took part in the Conference of Thorn (see THORN, CON-

FERENCE OF) in 1645, where, however, he found that the Lutherans would not work with him, since they felt justifiably that from his point of view the Reformation lost its essential importance: a religious indifferentism would be the obvious sequence, and it is certainly no accident that during the seventeenth century many princes and princesses left the Lutheran Church and joined the Roman Catholic (John Frederick of Hanover, Christine of Sweden, the daughter of Gustavus Adolphus, and some others). On the other hand the orthodox, not altogether from combativeness, endeavored to maintain the religious content of the Reformation; this is their merit against all syncretism. Finally Calixtus made himself a name in scientific dogmatics by introducing the analytical method. After his death the syncretistic controversies continued till they lost their interest through the Pietistic movement. Among his numerous writings those of most interest are his academical orations *Orationes selectæ* (Helmstädt, 1660); his influential exegetical writings, *Expositiones* and *Lucubrationes* on New and Old Testament books; and, of his irenic writings, the *Judicium de controversiis theologicis quæ inter Lutheranos et Reformatos agitantur, et de mutua partium fraternitate atque tolerantia propter consensum in fundamentis* (1650). His son and successor, **Friedrich Ulrich Calixtus** (b. 1622; d. 1701), tried to continue the work of his father, but met with no approval among the Lutherans. They rather tried to supplant syncretism in the Lutheran Church by a new orthodox confession, *Consensus repetitus fidei vere Lutheranæ*. But this confession, which would have turned the Church into an orthodox school, was nowhere officially accepted. The syncretistic controversy remained for a long time of such importance that no interest was felt in the Pietistic principles which soon sprang up. This can be understood only from the course of the syncretistic controversies. See SYNCRETISM.

PAUL TSCHACKERT.

BIBLIOGRAPHY: Account should be taken of Calixtus's *Briefwechsel*, ed. E. L. T. Henke, Halle, 1883, cf. issues of Jena, 1833, Marburg, 1840. Consult: W. Gass, *G. Calixt und der Synkretismus*, Breslau, 1846; E. L. T. Henke, *G. Calixtus und seine Zeit*, 2 vols., Halle, 1853–1856; W. C. Dowding, *German Theology during the Thirty Years' War; Life and Correspondence of G. Calixtus*, London, 1863; H. Friedrich, *Georg Calixtus, der Unionsmann des 17. Jahrhunderts*, Anklam, 1891; *ADB*, iii. 696 sqq.

CALLAWAY, HENRY: Church of England, missionary bishop of St. John's, Kaffraria; b. at Lymington, Somerset, Jan. 17, 1817; d. at Ottery Saint Mary (12 m. e.n.e. of Exeter) Mar. 26, 1890. In early life he was a Quaker, and after teaching from 1835 to 1839, was successively a chemist's assistant and a surgeon's assistant. He then studied surgery and was licensed by the Royal College of Surgeons in 1842 and by the Apothecaries' Society two years later. In 1852, however, failing health obliged him to sell his lucrative practise and to spend a year in France. In the following year he graduated M.D. at King's College, Aberdeen, and determined to be a physician, but his interest in missions becoming active, he was ordered deacon in 1854, having left the Society of Friends for the Church of England two years previously, and went as missionary to Africa. He was first stationed at Ekukanyeni near Pietermaritzburg, but on being priested in 1855 was made rector of St. Andrew's, Pietermaritzburg. Three years later he obtained a grant of land beyond the Umkomanzi River and settled at Insunguze, which he renamed Spring Vale. There he began his studies of Zulu religion and customs, but was recalled to England in 1873 to be consecrated first missionary bishop of St. John's, Kaffraria. In the following year he left England, and in 1876 removed the seat of the diocese to Umtata, where he founded St. John's Theological College in 1879. His fragile health, however, had already necessitated the consecration of Bransby Key as bishop-coadjutor in 1873, and in 1886 Callaway resigned his see and returned to England in the following year, settling at Ottery Saint Mary, where he spent the remainder of his life. He wrote: *Immediate Revelation* (London, 1841); *Memoir of James Parnell* (1846); *Nursery Tales, Traditions, and Histories of the Zulus* (Spring Vale, 1868); *The Religious System of the Amazulu* (Natal, 1868–70); and *Missionary Sermons* (London, 1875). He likewise translated the book of Psalms (Natal, 1871) and the Book of Common Prayer (1882) into Zulu.

BIBLIOGRAPHY: M. S. Benham, *Henry Callaway, M.D., D.D., first Bishop of Kaffraria; his Life-History and Work*, London, 1896.

CALLEGARI, cāl"lé"gā'rī, GIUSEPPE: Cardinal priest; b. at Venice Nov. 4, 1841. He was ordained to the priesthood in 1864, and, after being successively a teacher and a parish priest, was consecrated bishop of Treviso in 1880, and two years later was translated to the see of Padua. He was created cardinal priest of Santa Maria in Cosmedin in 1903, and still retains his bishopric. He is likewise a member of the Congregations of Bishops and Regulars, the Council, Rites, and Studies.

CALLENBERG, cāl'len-berH, JOHANN HEINRICH: German theologian; b. at Molschleben (a village of Gotha) Jan. 12, 1694; d. at Halle July 16, 1760. He was educated at Halle, where in 1727 he was appointed associate professor of philology, becoming full professor in 1735 and being transferred to the faculty of theology four years later. His deep interest in Protestant missions among the Jews and Mohammedans of the East led him, in 1728, to found the *Institutum Judaicum* for the education of missionaries. To this institution, which lasted until 1791 and was instrumental in the conversion of a large number of Jews, he later attached, at his own expense, a press for the promotion of the cause. Europe, as well as parts of Asia and Africa, was traversed by his pupils, for whom he printed Arabic translations of portions of the Old Testament, the whole of the New Testament, "The Imitation of Christ," and other works. His propaganda among the Mohammedans, however, met with little success. His independent works, which are of minor importance, include: *Kurze Anleitung zur jüdisch-teutschen Sprache* (Halle, 1733); *Berichte von einem Versuch das jüdische Volk* *zur Erkenntniss des Christlichen anzuleiten* (3 vols., 1728–30); and *De conversione Muhammedanorum ad Christum expetita tentaque* (1733).

BIBLIOGRAPHY: J. M. H. Doering, *Die gelehrten Theologen Deutschlands*, i. 221 sqq., Neustadt, 1831; J. C. F. Hoefer, *Nouvelle Biographie générale*, vii 202, 46 vols., Paris, 1851–66.

CALLING (vocation; Lat. *vocatio*, Gk. *klēsis*): In dogmatic language as well as in the practical usage of the Church that act of divine grace (*gratia applicatrix*) with which the *ordo salutis* (see ORDER OF SALVATION) begins.

Biblical Usage. The Greek terms *kalein, klētos, klēsis* are often used both in the Septuagint and in the New Testament in the sense of calling (e.g., Matt. ix. 13; Acts iv. 18), then of summoning to court, of inviting to dinner, etc. (e.g., III Macc. v. 14; Matt. xxii. 4. 8; Rev. xix. 9). But even in the Old Testament usage the Hebrew *ḳara'* or the Greek *kalein* has the meaning of calling some one effectually for some purpose (cf. Isa. xlii. 6, xlviii. 12, xlix. 1, li. 2), which may signify "to call into existence" (Wisd. of Sol. xi. 25; Baruch iii. 33, 34; cf. Ps. xxxiii. 9). From this point the solemn usage of the New Testament takes its departure. The call proceeds from God; it comes to man through the word of preaching, which is not the word of man but of God (I Cor. i. 9; II Pet. i. 3; I Thess. ii. 13; II Thess. ii. 14). Inasmuch as the call comes from God, it is a "holy calling" (II Tim. i. 9), a "heavenly calling" (Heb. iii. 1), a "high calling of God in Christ Jesus" (Phil. iii. 14). The call is a free act of the grace of God (Rom. ix. 11), in which the divine election and predestination realize themselves (II Thess. ii. 13, 14; II Tim. i. 9–10; Rom. viii. 30). From this it is clear that it is always the effectual calling that is thought of; indeed it is precisely the divine election of grace which is made manifest in the call. Hence those who became Christians were "called to be saints" (Rom. i. 7; I Cor. i. 2, cf. Jude 1: "called and kept"). That to which the Christians are called, or that which constitutes the content of the call is the blessing of the New Testament salvation, and this is expressed in the most diverse terms: to communion with Christ (I Cor. i. 9); to salvation (II Thess. ii. 14); to the peace of Christ (Col. iii. 15); to the kingdom and glory of God (I Thess. ii. 12); out of the darkness into a wonderful light (I Pet. ii. 9); to eternal life, to his glory and his inheritance (I Tim. vi. 12; I Pet. v. 10; Heb. ix. 15); to the hope of his calling (Eph. i. 18, iv. 4).

Inasmuch as the call indicates the New Testament salvation, it also procures the moral change comprehended in that blessing. As on the human side obedience corresponds to the call (Heb. xi. 6), so we are called "not for uncleanness, but in sanctification" (I Thess. iv. 7); the Christian's life is to be holy "as he who called you is holy" (I Pet. i. 15). If, therefore, the call is the effectual invitation of God to man, conveyed through the Word, for the kingdom and its blessings, so that every one possessing these came by them through the call, the call, on the other hand, points beyond itself to the realization through God or through man: "Faithful is he that calleth you who also will do it" (I Thess. v. 24) and "give the more diligence to make your calling and election sure" (II Pet. i. 10).

Luther's use of the expression in the exposition of the third article of his Shorter Catechism is important for the history of the conception. But the term did not immediately receive on that account an independent place in dogmatics. In the older Protestant literature it is used in connection with election and the Church.

By the Reformers. It seems to have received a firm place in dogmatics for the first time in Hutter (*Compendium*, XIII. v. 8). According to Calovius it opens the *ordo salutis*, and he defines it (*Systema*, x. 1) as an "effectual bringing in to the Church" (*ad ecclesiam efficax adductio*), whereas Hollaz (*Examen theologicum*, III. i. 4, quæstio 1) makes it an offer of benefits by Christ. Moreover, a distinction is made between the *vocatio generalis*, which through nature, etc., comes to all men, and the *vocatio specialis*, which comes through the Gospel. The latter may be *ordinaria*, i.e., through the Word, or *extraordinaria*, and that *immediata* or *mediata*. The call is *seria* and *efficax* (in opposition to the view of the Reformed), inasmuch as the Spirit regularly becomes effectual in the Word. It is, moreover, *universalis*. That many peoples do without it is their own fault. Then comes the doubtful contention that since Adam all peoples in one way or another have been given the opportunity of hearing the Gospel (the above is from Hollaz; for a full discussion cf. H. Schmid, *Die Dogmatik der evangelisch-lutherischen Kirche*, Gütersloh, 1893, 320 sqq.).

In Dogmatics. Dogmatically considered, the doctrine of vocation is only the application of the doctrine of the Word of God to conversion. Therefore, this conception will disclose no new dogmatic knowledge, but will only offer a confirmation of such things as have been acquired elsewhere. But because the Scriptures often apply the term and because it has through the catechism gone over into the popular religious consciousness, its right to a special treatment in dogmatics is not to be denied. The call takes place the very moment a person—be he a non-Christian or be he externally connected with Christianity—becomes aware that the heard (or read) Word as the Word of God efficaciously works in him the divine will unto salvation, and as there is no conceivable moment in the Christian life in which that revelation of salvation in the Word becomes superfluous, the vocation will be a continual one and the Christian will always remain a *vocatus*. We may, therefore, confine the conception to the opening of the new life; but, starting from the thought of the Word of God, we must define the call as that influence of God upon man, through the medium of the Word, which makes the beginning of the new life and conditions its continuation and its completion. The call brings us the whole salvation, as the passages of Scripture above cited show. If dogmaticians as a rule, in speaking of vocation, think only of the first influence of God, this must be supplemented by the fact that this term comprehends within itself the further divine activities. If now the call embraces the whole of salvation in its relation to us, it is plain that its content is the Gospel; as the old writers rightly perceived. But since "law" and Gospel stand in close connection, the law also must be indirectly included in the call. R. SEEBERG.

CALLING, EARTHLY: The position in life occupied by each individual, and the duties toward society which appertain to such a position. These duties are primarily social rather than ethical, and may be hedonistic in motive, as when they are performed for the sake of livelihood. The calling may be ethicized, however, if the ends of the social organism be served expressly for the glory of God, thus transforming the calling into divine worship. Since the calling conditions the class of services rendered to society, it must form the basis of an ethical activity. Each function resulting from the divinely created nature of man may develop into a calling, although the variety in callings does not necessarily imply a distinction in the value of personalities. Nor is it unethical to have no calling, but only to desire to have none, since those who are so conditioned that, through no volition of their own, they are without a calling do not become unethical for that reason.

In the rich development of Christian ethics in the New Testament the earthly calling is comparatively neglected. yet, from the point of view of love toward one's neighbor, he who disregards his duties to his family, and toward society and the Church, must be considered unethical. The earthly calling is, accordingly, individualistic rather than universal in its obligations to society, and represents one of the forms of Christian ethics. Wilful neglect of the calling is immoral, since it is the only means of intercommunication in society, which would otherwise be incoherent and disorganized. The bodily and mental gifts of man are fruitless unless they are devoted to the welfare of society through a definite calling, and their neglect is not only contrary to nature but also to the will of God.

The ethical signification of the earthly calling forms an important chapter of philosophical ethics. Through its recognition of the dignity of labor and the worth of the individual, Christianity revolutionized the ethics of the pagan world, although the full ethical evaluation of the calling began only at the Reformation. Since God is served less by self-chosen cults than by the ethical obedience which he himself has commanded (Isa. i. 11–17; Hos. vi. 6; Matt. ix. 13, xii. 7), the believing Christian performs a true worship corresponding to his estate as a child of God in his faithful performance of his calling. In a certain sense the principles of the ethical value of the fulfilment of the calling are merely a renewal of the New Testament doctrine that the Christian confirmation of faith through love bears a distinct and active relation to society (I Cor. vii. 20–24; Eph. vi. 5 sqq.; I Pet. ii. 12 sqq.), even though nowhere in the New Testament is earthly calling specifically mentioned. The distinction of callings begins in the family, whence it develops successively into the acquisition and control of temporal benefits and into the charge over intellectual and spiritual blessings in religion, science, and art, the culmination being the constitution of society as a whole. Yet the individual can not make free choice of his own calling, but is restricted by certain social limitations; still, other things being equal, that calling should be chosen which is most in harmony both with talents and inclination. External conditions, however, frequently render impossible the development of the most gifted talent, yet in such cases there is no reason for the formation of a religious and moral personality to suffer injury, since such adverse circumstances demand full and complete fidelity to the calling, and thus strengthen true Christian piety, instead of impairing it. (L. LEMME.)

CALMET, AUGUSTIN: French Roman Catholic theologian and author; b. at Mesnil-la-Horgne (a village near Commercy, 25 m. e. of Bar-le-Duc) Feb. 26, 1672: d. at Senones (7 m. n.e. of St. Dié) Oct. 25, 1757. He was a Benedictine monk of the congregation of St. Vannes, and studied at the priory of Breuil, while he learned Hebrew from the Protestant clergyman Favre. After 1698 he instructed the pupils of the order in theology and philosophy at the abbey of Moyen-Moutier in the Vosges, and in 1704 was appointed subprior at Münster. Fourteen years later the general chapter of his order made him abbot of St. Leopold at Nancy, whence he was transferred in 1728 to Senones, and there he passed the remainder of his life. His numerous works give evidence of extraordinary reading and erudition, but lack critical ability and insight. His best writings are devoted to the interpretation of the Bible according to the principles of the Council of Trent. To this category belongs his *La Sainte Bible en latin et en français avec un commentaire littéral et critique* (23 vols., Paris, 1707–16), the French translation being that of Sacy and the commentary giving simply a grammatical exegesis. The excursuses on each book, dealing with chronology, history, antiquities, and similar topics, were the most valuable portion of the work, and were published separately under the title *Dissertations qui peuvent servir de prolégomènes à l'Écriture Sainte* (3 vols., 1720), and the *Trésor d'antiquités sacrées et profanes des commentaires du P. Calmet* (13 vols., Amsterdam, 1722) is the same work with a different arrangement. The notes scattered in the commentaries are collected in alphabetical order in the *Dictionnaire historique et critique, chronologique, géographique et littéral de la Bible* (2 vols., Paris, 1722, supplement, 1728; Eng. transl., 3 vols., London, 1732), which long remained the quarry for similar works. Less important are the *Histoire sainte de l'Ancien et du Nouveau Testament et des Juifs* (2 vols., 1718) and the *Histoire universelle sacrée et profane* (17 vols., Strasburg, Senones, and Nancy, 1735–71). Calmet's works are now little read, with the exception of the *Histoire ecclésiastique et civile de la Lorraine* (4 vols., Nancy, 1728), which is based on archives and accompanied with valuable documents. (C. PFENDER.)

BIBLIOGRAPHY: The autobiography is contained in his *Histoire de Lorraine*, vol. iv., ut sup. Consult: A. Fangé, *Vie de Calmet*, Senones, 1762 (by his nephew; contains a complete list of Calmet's works); A. Digot, *Notice biographique et littéraire sur A. Calmet*, Nancy, 1861; *KL*, ii. 1717–21. New material is presented in *Documents inédits sur les correspondances de Dom Calmet*, ed. P. É. Guillaume, ib. 1875.

CALOVIUS, cā-lō′vi-us (**KALAU**), **ABRAHAM**: Lutheran dogmatic theologian; b. at Mohrungen (62 m. s.s.w. of Königsberg), Prussia, Apr. 16, 1612; d. at Wittenberg Feb. 25, 1686. He was driven away by the plague from the first two schools he attended, at Thorn and at Königsberg, but he prosecuted his studies at home to such good purpose that when barely fourteen he was able to enter the University of Königsberg. Here he took his master's degree six years later, and was at once taken into the philosophical faculty. He lectured on philosophy and mathematics, while eagerly continuing the study of theology. His polemical activity began with a tractate against the Reformed court preacher Berg (1635). In 1634 he migrated to the University of Rostock, of which he became a doctor in 1637. Then he returned to Königsberg,

Education and Early Professorial Activity.

was made assessor to the theological faculty, and resumed his lectures. Two years later he became adjunct professor, and visitor of the Samland district; in 1643 he went to Danzig as rector of the gymnasium there and pastor of Trinity Church. He was a delegate to the Thorn Conference of 1645, where he came in contact with Calixtus. From this time on a great part of his life was devoted to polemical activity, especially against Syncretism (q.v.) and Calvinism. In 1650, at the invitation of the elector John George I., he went to Wittenberg, where the rest of his life was to be spent. He began there as third professor and preacher at the parish church, of which he became pastor in 1652 and general superintendent of the district, and by 1660 he was head professor and dean of the faculty. The university increased considerably in numbers through the attraction of his teaching, though the increase fell off when the elector of Branden-

Calovius at Wittenberg.

burg forbade his subjects (1662) to go there for theology or philosophy, on account of the opposition of the *principia Caloviana* to the Reformed teaching. An iron constitution enabled him to work incessantly at his books and lectures, as well as to support the loss of five wives and thirteen children and to marry again at the age of seventy-two. A complete record of his activity is left in his books, since he nearly always expanded his lectures into that form. His polemical activity was directed chiefly against the Syncretistic school of Helmstädt and its Königsberg allies Behm, Dreier, and Latermann, as well as later against the Hessian friends of Calixtus. He had paid his compliments to the latter's teaching even in his Danzig days, and in his *Institutionum theologicarum prolegomena* (2 parts, 1649–50). More important onslaughts on this school were *Synopsis controversiarum potiarum* (1652), with an introduction specially directed against Calixtus; *Syncretismus Calixtinus* (1653); and *Harmonia Calixtina-haretica* (1655), in which he accuses the "innovators" not merely of tolerating false doctrine but of teaching it themselves, and proves his point by attempting to show their "harmony" with Calvinists and Papists, Arminians and Socinians. By the date of this publication Calovius thought the time was ripe for a step which he had been urging for four years. The *Consensus repetitus fidei veræ Lutheranæ* is undoubtedly in its essence the work of Calovius, in its first as well as in its final form. The purpose of this new dog-

His Controversial Writings.

matic standard, the exclusion of the Syncretists from the Church and so from the protection of the religious truce, was not attained; in fact, after 1655, and still more after 1669, when definite instructions were conveyed to the Wittenberg theologians to restrain their polemical ardor, there is a noticeable slackening of anti-Syncretist activity; and Calovius turned his attention rather to the Jena school, and especially to Musæus. In 1682, finally, he published a complete account of the whole controversy in his *Historia syncretistica*. Owing to the prohibition of polemical publications, it appeared without any author's name or place of printing, described merely as the work of "D. A. C. [Dr. Abraham Calovius], a distinguished theologian." The elector John George III., who objected on political grounds to such literature, had all the copies bought up, so that this edition is very rare. A second edition appeared in 1685, with Calovius's approval and with his name on the title-page. He attacked the Roman Catholics in his *Matæologia papistica* (1647), and the Socinians in several small works, which when collected (1684) filled two folio volumes. As if the conflict within his own Church did not give him enough to do, he interposed in the controversies of the Calvinists with his *Consideratio Arminianismi* (1655) and his *Theses theologicæ de Labbadismo* (1681). His last work, the *Anti-Bœhmius* (1684), directed against Jakob Böhme, shows a failure in power.

In the way of constructive theology, his *Systema locorum theologicorum* (12 vols., 1655–77) is, with the possible exception of Gerhard's, the most important dogmatic production of the century—the true exemplar of what has been called Lutheran scholasticism. It takes the Lutheran doctrine, as it had developed on the basis of the *Formula Concordiæ* and the Scriptural principles, pushed to their extreme since the Regensburg conference of 1601, and defends it with unyielding logic and firmness against the intellectual forces of a new age. Even his principal exegetical work, the

His Constructive Theology.

Biblia illustrata (4 vols., 1672–76), has a polemical bearing, being intended to correct the *Annotata* of Hugo Grotius, which is incorporated in it. He accomplishes his task with great acuteness, wonderful learning, and more feeling for the sense of Scripture than his opponent, whose preference was for secular authors, but with his inevitable dogmatic limitations. The circumstances of his life render it difficult to pronounce a summary judgment on the man and his career.

The party of Calixtus naturally hated and despised him; but the fact that they found it necessary to spread absurd fictions about his horrible end shows clearly enough that nothing could justly be said against his personal character. In his own day he compelled the respect and admiration of a great variety of men, and his talents have been fully recognized by some who were far from agreeing with him, like Buddeus, Walch, and Stäudlin. His incessant controversial activity has left a misleading impression of him; he himself says of this branch of his work, "I come to this kind of writing unwillingly and by force; my disposition inclines me rather to stick to positive doctrinal work." As a theologian he was a faithful member of the Wittenberg school. No one has insisted more on the necessity of a Scriptural basis for all teaching. It is true, of course, that the defects of Lutheran orthodoxy—its hardness and its extremes—are to be found in him. Faith is essentially the acceptance of the orthodox system; not only the essentials (and they covered a great deal of ground in those days), but every derived article must be accepted, for the faith is one. The standard books of doctrine are theoretically subordinate to the Scriptures; but the student is required to accept them not hypothetically but categorically—not in so far as, but because, they agree with the Bible. His firm conviction of the truth of his system gives, however, a certain dignity to his polemics; but his untiring activity never reached its aim—he did not succeed in raising the *Consensus repetitus* to the dignity of a creed, and a new era had dawned before he went to his rest.

Estimate of Calovius.

(JOHANNES KUNZE.)

BIBLIOGRAPHY: The sources for a life of Calovius are: his own *Historia syncretistica*, 1682; a funeral discourse by his colleague J. F. Mayer, 1686; and C. S. Schurzfleisch, *Orationes panegyricæ*, pp. 71 sqq., Wittenberg, 1697. Consult: H. Pipping, *Memoria theologorum*, pp. 108–136, Leipsic, 1705; J. C. Erdmann, *Lebensbeschreibungen von den wittenbergischen Theologen*, pp. 88 91, Wittenberg, 1804; A. Tholuck, *Der Geist der lutherischen Theologen Wittenbergs*, pp. 185–211, Gotha, 1852; E. L. T. Henke, *Georg Calixtus und seine Zeit*, 2 vols., Halle, 1853–1856.

CALVARY. See HOLY SEPULCHER.

CALVARY, MOUNT, ORDERS OF: Three religious orders taking their name from the Mount of Crucifixion.

1. **The Calvarists or Priests of Mt. Calvary:** An association of secular priests founded by Hubert Charpentier at Mt. Bétharam, diocese of Lescar (4 m. n.w. by w. of Pau), France, in 1633 "in commemoration of the sufferings of Christ and for the spread of the Catholic faith," five years later united with a similar association formed in Paris by a Capuchin named Hyacinthe, primarily to convert Protestants. The chief seat of the united orders was Mont Valérien, Paris (hence popularly called *Colline du Calvaire*). They perished in the French Revolution.

2. **The Nuns of Mt. Calvary** (*Bénédictines de Notre-Dame du Calvaire*): Founded by Antoinette d'Orléans (d. 1618) and the Capuchin Joseph de Clerc de Tremblay in 1617 at Poitiers, properly a branch of the Order of Fontévraud (q.v.). In the seventeenth century they had about twenty houses which were destroyed in the French Revolution. Since then the order has been revived and has a number of convents mostly in western France.

3. **The Daughters of Mt. Calvary** (*Figlie del Calvario*): Founded at Genoa in 1619 by Virginia Centurione (d. 1651), daughter of the doge of Genoa and wife of Grimaldi Bracelli, who undertook the care of abandoned children in a time of great distress from famine. She received help from the Marchese Emanuele Brignole, from whom the members of the order were called *Le suore Brignole* in Genoa. They spread in North Italy, were given a house in Rome by Gregory XVI. in 1833, and later established orphan asylums at Rieti and Viterbo.

(O. ZÖCKLER†.)

BIBLIOGRAPHY: Helyot, *Ordres monastiques*, vi. 355–370; Heimbucher, *Orden und Kongregationen*, i. 197, ii. 362, 427. Consult also A. M. Centurione, *Vita di Virginia Centurione-Bracelli*, Genoa, 1873.

CALVERT, JAMES: Wesleyan foreign missionary; b. at Pickering, 25 m. n. by e. of York, England, Jan. 3, 1813; d. at Torquay, England, Mar. 8, 1892. When appointed by the Wesleyan Missionary Society in 1838 to go to Fiji he was master of the printing and bookbinding trades and had been in 1837 a student in the Hoxton Academy. His industrial training stood him in good stead for he was able to do his own printing in Fiji and issue many books, among them a translation of the New Testament into the vernacular. He lived to see the complete abandonment of heathenism by the Fijians, a result to which his heroic labors contributed largely. From 1865 to 1872 he was supernumerary minister at Bromley, Kent, England, thence he went as missionary to the South African diamond fields. He returned in 1881 and settled at Torquay. In 1885 he paid a visit to Fiji and rejoiced in the marvelous change.

BIBLIOGRAPHY: G. S. Rowe, *James Calvert of Fiji*, London, 1893.

CALVIN, JOHN.

John Calvin the Reformer, b. at Noyon (60 m. n.e. of Paris), Picardy, July 10, 1509; d. in Geneva, Switzerland, May 27, 1564, was the son of Gérard Cauvin, or Caulvin, of which Calvin is the Latinized form, a registrar of the government of Noyon, solicitor in the ecclesiastical court, fiscal agent of the county, secretary of the bishopric, and attorney of the cathedral chapter. Calvin's mother was Jeanne Le Franc of Cambrai, noted for personal beauty and great religious fervor and strictness. Of the five sons of his parents he was the second, and but one of his younger brothers survived childhood. His mother died while he was still young and his father married a widow, whose name is unknown, who bore him two daughters. His father's position and ambition for his sons was such that he secured for them the best educational advantages at home, association with the children of prominent families, and ecclesiastical patronage; so that Calvin on May 19, 1521, when only twelve years of age, received the chaplaincy attached to the altar of La Gésine in the cathedral of Noyon, which gave him a regular income. It was expected that he would become a priest and so he was given the tonsure.

1. Childhood.

In 1523 he was sent to Paris to prepare for the priesthood. He attended for a few months the Collège de la Marche, wherein Mathurin Cordier grounded him in Latin; next the Collège de Montaigu, where he remained till the opening of 1528. The high grade of his childish friendships and of those of maturer years reveals his own character, and refutes the insinuations his detractors have dared to whisper. That he stood well with the ecclesiastics in his native city is shown by their giving him on Sept. 27, 1527, in addition to the chaplaincy mentioned, the (nominal) curacy of Saint Martin de Martheville, eight leagues from Noyon, which he exchanged on June 5, 1529, for the curacy of Pont l'Évêque, a village 1 m. w. of s. of Noyon, associated with his ancestors, who were boatmen on the Oise (not to be confounded with Pont l'Évêque, 25 m. e.n.e. of Caen). On Apr. 30, 1529, he resigned his chaplaincy in favor of his younger brother, but resumed it on Feb. 26, 1531, and held it till May 4, 1534.

2. Student of Theology.

As a student Calvin showed rare ability and was rapidly acquiring the priestly training when in 1528 his father, who had fallen out with the ecclesiastical authorities in Noyon, ordered him to change his studies to law. He meekly obeyed and left Paris for Orléans, whose university was then a famous law center, as there Pierre Taisan de l'Estoile lectured, and the next year went to Bourges, where Andrea Alciati, a rival of equal eminence, and more to Calvin's taste, was the great attraction. In both universities he came under the influence of Melchior Wolmar, a humanist of the front rank and favorable to the Reformation. On May 26, 1531, his father died, and Calvin left Bourges and returned to Paris, to classical study and the study of Hebrew, except that from the summer of 1532 to that of 1533 he was again a student of law at Orléans and there "annual representative" of the dean of the Picard students, another indication of his moral standing and popularity with the students, for students do not honor of their own accord dubious or disagreeable characters.

3. Student of Law and the Classics.

In Apr., 1532, he published in Paris at his own expense, and at a pecuniary loss, the text of Seneca's *De Clementia*, with a commentary, which showed that he was still a humanist within the Roman Church. But the Reformation was making headway in France among the humanistic class to which he belonged, and so must have often been a topic of his conversation. Step by step he approached the position of the Reformers, but slowly, for, as he says himself, in the partly autobiographic preface to his commentary on the Psalms (and it is about all that is known on the subject), he "was too obstinately devoted to the superstitions of popery to be easily extricated from so profound an abyss of mire." But, some time in 1533, "God by a sudden conversion subdued and brought [his] mind to a teachable frame. Having thus received some taste and knowledge of true godliness, [he] was immediately inflamed with so intense a desire to make progress therein, that although [he] did not altogether leave off other studies, [he] yet pursued them with less ardor. [He] was quite surprised to find that before a year had elapsed, all who had any desire after purer doctrine were continually coming to [him] to learn, although [he himself] was as yet but a mere novice and tyro."

4. His First Publication. Conversion.

Among those with whom he discussed Reformed doctrine was his bosom friend Nicolas Cop, and when Cop was elected rector of the university of Paris it seemed to them a splendid opportunity to commend the Reformation to the cultured and brilliant audience which would be gathered in the Church of the Mathurins to hear the inaugural address. Accordingly they planned it together and on Nov. 1, 1533, Cop delivered it. He announced his theme as "Christian Philosophy," and proceeded to speak in a manner which greatly amazed his audience. By "Christian Philosophy" he meant the Gospel. The phrase and the treatment in the opening part of the address were derived from Erasmus. The burden of it was on the relation of Law and Gospel, and here Luther's influence appears. The concluding part was more independent, and in it was struck that note of certainty as to salvation, which was to be a feature of Calvinism.

5. Cop's Inaugural Address.

Perhaps all would have gone well, for there must have been many secret sympathizers with their views in the audience, had Cop not criticized the theologians of the Sorbonne as "sophists." This infuriated them, and they stirred up the government against the audacious speaker, and Cop had to fly. Calvin also fled, because his intimacy with Cop was known, although it is not certain whether it was ever suspected that he had any share in the composition of the address as it is now certain that he had. Being assured that his fears of personal injury were groundless, he ventured to return shortly afterward. But his sympathy with the Reformation could not be hidden, and so he did not feel safe in the city where so many already had been imprisoned for their faith's sake, and in Jan., 1534, he went forth a wanderer, usually living under an assumed name.

6. Years of Wandering. Second Publication.

These wanderings lasted for two years and a half. As well as they can be made out their course was this: he went first to Angoulême, where he studied in the excellent library of his friend Louis du Tillet and began his "Institutes"; next to Nérac in Apr., 1534, where Marguerite d'Angoulême, duchess of Berry and sister of King Francis I. of France, held her court; in May he was at Noyon, where he resigned his benefices, and where he was for some reason imprisoned; in the closing part of the year he was at Paris again, and then it was he met Servetus for the first time. Next he appeared at Orléans, whence he issued his second publication, his *Psychopannychia*, a refutation of the theory that the soul sleeps between death and the Last Judgment. In Dec., 1534, he was at Angoulême, and thence with Du Tillet he removed to Strasburg to escape threatened persecution.

7. Publication of his "Institutes."

In Jan., 1535, he was at Strasburg, and the same month at Basel. There he put the finishing touches on his "Institutes of the Christian Religion," and issued it Mar., 1536. The persecution of the Reformed in France was its immediate occasion. He thus speaks of this famous book in the preface to his commentary on the Psalms: "My objects were, first, to vindicate my brethren whose death was precious in the sight of the Lord; and next that, as the same cruelties might very soon after be exercised against many unhappy individuals, foreign nations might be touched with at least some compassion toward them and solicitude about them. When it was then published it was not the copious and labored work which it is now, but only a small treatise, containing a summary of the principal truths of the Christian religion; and it was published with no other design than that men might know what was the faith held by those whom I saw basely and wickedly defamed by those flagitious and perfidious flatterers. That my object was not to acquire fame appeared from this, that immediately after I left Basel, and particularly from the fact that nobody there knew that I was the author." It was prefaced by a letter to King Francis I. of France, who was an archpersecutor of Protestants in his kingdom while cultivating friendly relations with them outside, which ranks as one of the masterpieces in apologetic literature.

8. First Residence in Geneva and in Strasburg.

After publishing it he went to Ferrara to stay a while in the court of the Duchess Renée, wife of Ercole II. In May 1536 he was in Aosta and a little later in Paris once more. There he met his younger brother Antoine and his half-sister Marie, and with them left for Strasburg. The war then going on compelled him to make a détour and so he arrived in Geneva in the latter part of July, 1536, intending only to spend the night there. But Farel (see FAREL, GUILLAUME), who was trying with zeal not always directed by discretion to keep the Genevans whom he won for the Reformation at peace among themselves, learned of his presence and seeing in the young scholar, who wanted nothing so much as to be allowed to pursue his studies in quiet, a valuable ally, besought him to stay with him, and then, as Calvin himself says in the preface mentioned above, "finding that he gained nothing by entreaties proceeded to utter an imprecation that God would curse [his] retirement and the tranquillity of the studies which [he] sought if [he] should withdraw and refuse to give assistance when the necessity was so urgent." Calvin felt as if "God had from heaven laid his mighty hand upon [him] to arrest [him]." Unable to resist, he laid aside all his plans and stepped to Farel's side. But the city could not brook the drastic reforms which the Reformers would institute, and so on Easter Monday (Apr. 23), 1538, less than two years from his arrival, he and Farel were ordered by the General Assembly to leave the city within three days. Calvin went to Basel, and then to Strasburg where on Sept. 8, 1538, he became minister to the French refugees, in the Church of St. Nicolas aux Oudes. He married early in Aug., 1540, Idelette de Bure, widow of Jean Stordeur of Liége, an Anabaptist whom Calvin had converted to the pedobaptist position. She had had a son and daughter by her first husband, but they had died in infancy. To Calvin she bore a son on July 28, 1542, but he lived only a few days. She herself passed away on Mar. 29, 1549, and Calvin did not marry again.

9. Rising Fame. Recall to Geneva.

When Calvin went to Strasburg he thought he had done with Geneva. He was very poor, and his position was comparatively obscure, but his abilities soon brought him into prominence and appeals for advice from friends in Geneva kept him in touch with that city. He utilized his position to study and also to put into practise certain reforms he could not carry out in Geneva. And his fame rapidly spread. He was asked to share in the cathedral lecture course, next he was sent as delegate of the city to the Colloquies of Worms and Regensburg. When on Mar. 18, 1539, Cardinal Jacopo Sadoleto wrote a letter to the city of Geneva which was a plea for it to return to the Roman obedience and it was sent to Bern, it was Calvin who was requested by the Bern government to answer, and he did in his masterly fashion. A change took place in the government in Geneva and the friends of Calvin got the upper hand. Then his virtues and extraordinary powers were remembered, and on Sept. 21, 1540, the Little Council voted to try to induce him to return. More and more the impression spread that he was the man to rule the city. There was no intention of going back to Rome, but the city was torn by faction and contained many unruly elements which needed an iron hand to hold in check. On Oct. 19 and 20 the Two Hundred and the General Assembly formally invited him to return, but the invitation was unwelcome and he would give no decided answer. But when in Feb., 1541, the impetuous Farel urged him to go, he found him as irresistible as before, and so on Sept. 13, 1541, he entered again the city of Geneva and took up the heavy task of ordering her affairs according to his high standards. He came without illusions, knowing that he was not even the choice of a majority, that he had many personal enemies, and would encounter many difficulties; but he believed that God had called him and would sustain him.

He received an honorable reception from the government, and was given a house to live in, and, for salary, five hundred florins, twelve measures of wheat, and two tubs of wine. From that time on, Geneva was his home and his parish, his center of activity, but by no means his circumference of influence. Under his firm rule the city assumed a new aspect. Immorality of every sort was sternly suppressed. It was well for the success of this system that Geneva was a refuge for the persecuted in every land. Hollanders, English, Italians, Spaniards, and more particularly Frenchmen, settled in the town, and readily lent their aid in maintaining Calvin's peculiar methods. But not refugees alone came: his lectures and those of Beza attracted many thousands of students, and thus spread their fame far and wide. But incessant study, a vast correspondence, "the care of all the churches," his sedentary life—these conspired to make him the victim of disease, and at fifty-five years of age he breathed his last. He had spent little on himself, but given generously both in money and service, so he left behind him only a hundred and seventy dollars, but an incalculable fortune in fame and consecrated influence; and from him Geneva inherited faith, education, government, brave citizens, and pride in an honored name.

10. Second Residence in Geneva.

Calvin based his system upon the Apostles' Creed, and followed its lines. Ethics and theology were handled in the closest connection. His reformation in theology was preeminently a practical affair. Even the doctrine of predestination was developed, not as a speculation, but as a matter of practical concern. By the extraordinary emphasis put upon it, the Genevans were taught to consider it almost the corner-stone of the Christian faith. In opposition to the lax views of sin and grace which the Roman Church inculcated, he revived the Augustinian doctrine in order by it to conquer Rome. In so doing he was one with Zwingli, Œcolampadius, Luther, and Melanchthon. But in his supralapsarian views he stood alone among the Reformers. His views of ecclesiastical authority and discipline are also important. He allowed to the Church a greater authority than any other Reformer. Here, again, the influence of Augustine is seen. He says, "The Church is our mother" ("Institutes," IV. i. 1). Outside of the Church there is no salvation. Her ministry is divinely constituted, and to it believers are bound to pay deference. Her authority is absolute in matters of doctrine; but, when civil cases arise, she hands the offenders over to the State for punishment. State and Church have, therefore, separate and exclusive jurisdiction; yet they exist side by side, and cooperate. They mutually support each other. The ideal government embraced a democracy, an aristocracy, and a king or autocrat. Calvin taught obedience to the powers that be. In this scheme he had in mind the Israelites. He aimed at a theocracy. He bowed before the majesty of the righteous Judge. His fear of God led him to unquestioning submission. In a sense it was his very breath; and so in his system justice is more prominent than love. God as the ruler, rather than as the lover of all in Christ, was the object of his reverence.

11. Calvin's Fundamental Ideas.

In accordance with his principles was his work. During his first residence in Geneva he showed his determination to separate Church and State; and therefore he and his fellow preachers protested against the interference of the State in the matter of the use of fonts, of unleavened bread in the Lord's Supper, and in the celebration of the church-festivals, as these were properly within the ecclesiastical province. When, also, he refused the Eucharist unto the city, because of its immorality, he asserted for the Church freedom from the civil authority. This determined stand cost him temporarily his position; but, when he resumed his work in Geneva, he and the citizens knew that he aimed to rule absolutely. The reforms he instituted are famous, and often condemned as infamous. They are, however, not only defensible, but commendable, if judged by the standard of that age. We can not withhold our admiration of the moral courage, the self-forgetfulness, the stern morality, and the uncompromising zeal with which Calvin addressed himself unto the apparently hopeless task of curbing the passions of the loose populace, and gaining the cordial cooperation of the upper classes. He succeeded. Geneva came to be regarded as a normal school of religious life. Religion was the life of the greater part of the inhabitants. With a correct insight into the necessities of the case, Calvin declared immediately after his victorious reentry that he could not take up work without a reorganization of the Church; viz., by the formation of a church-court, which should have full authority to maintain discipline. On Nov. 20, 1541, at a popular meeting, the scheme he drew up was ratified. This provided for a consistory, composed of the pastors of the city churches, who were five in number, and three assistants, and twelve elders—one of the latter to be a syndic and their president—which met every Thursday, and put under church-discipline, without respect of persons, every species of evil-doers. The rigor and vigor of this administration quickly awakened natural indignation, in part even among those who on the whole favored Calvin. His life was at times in danger. Some showed their terrified contempt for him by naming their dogs after him. In a city like Geneva, full of refugees of every description, there were many who looked upon all restraint as oppression; others who objected to Calvin's measures as going too far, or criticized his methods. In order still further to increase the authority of the church-court, Calvin secured (1555) an important modification of the city government, whereby the *Conseil Général* (the "General Council"), the highest law-making body, was only called twice a year—in February to elect syndics, and in November to fill some

12. His Reforms.

minor offices, and fix the price of wine. But nothing might be discussed in this meeting which had not been previously determined upon in the Council of Two Hundred; nor in the latter which the Council of Sixty did not approve of; nor could this council take up anything not previously agreed to in the highest council, which thus practically governed the State. The General Council became in this way a superfluity, without the power of initiative. It had, however, accomplished its mission—accepted the Reformation.

Most prominent among the means Calvin used to reform the city was preaching. Every other week he preached every day in plain, direct, convincing fashion, without eloquence, but still irresistibly; and the life that the preacher led constituted his strongest claim to attention. The reports of his sermons are probably from notes made by his hearers; which was the easier done, because, being asthmatic, he spoke very slowly. Every Friday the so-called "Congregation" was held, in which questions were answered, and debates even carried on. Minors were carefully instructed in a catechism originally prepared by Calvin in French and Latin 1545. In 1537 he had issued a French, and in 1538 a Latin catechism, which was a mere abridgment or syllabus of his "Institutes," and was not in the form of question and answer; but the catechism of 1545 was in the usual form.

Calvin has the credit of first introducing congregational singing into the worship of the Reformed Church in Geneva. The first songs were some of his own metrical renderings of the Psalms. Like Zwingli and Luther, Calvin had his difficulties with the Anabaptists. He met them in public debate Mar. 16–17, 1537, and in the opinion of the Council of Two Hundred effectually disposed of their arguments. So on Mar. 19 it passed a sentence of perpetual banishment against them.

But he had personal controversies, the chief of which were—(1) first with Pierre Caroli, a French refugee and pastor in Lausanne, a religious chameleon, whose latest hue was that of a stickler for orthodoxy. Calvin was very indifferent to the terminology of theology, so long as the truth was expressed. In discussing the nature of the Godhead during his first residence in Geneva, he avoided using the words "Trinity" and "Person," although he had no particular objection to them; and so they did not occur in the Confession of Faith which he drew up, and to which the citizens of Geneva were compelled to assent; nor did the Geneva Church subscribe formally to the Athanasian Creed. Caroli accused Calvin and his fellow divines of Arianism and Sabellianism; and so plausible was the charge, that Calvin was greatly troubled. However, in the synod of 1537, held in Bern, the Genevan divines fully cleared themselves, and Caroli was deposed and banished. (2) Philibert Berthelier, the son of a martyr for freedom, was forbidden the communion (1553) by the consistory. The council absolved the ban. Calvin from the pulpit, two days before the September Communion (one of the four yearly occasions), declared that he would die sooner than give the Lord's holy things to one under condemnation for despising God. Perrin, who was then syndic for the second time, ordered Berthelier to stay away from communion, and so ended a dispute from which the enemies of Calvin had hoped a great deal. (3) Jérôme Hermès Bolsec (q.v.), whose presumption in denying predestination, and abusing the ministers at a "Congregation," drew upon him, not only Calvin's indignant reply at the time, but also imprisonment and banishment (1551). (4) Sebastian Castellio (q.v.), a learned but arrogant man, won Calvin's opposition because of his denial of the inspiration of the Canticles and of the descent of Christ into hell. (5) But by far the most famous of all Calvin's opponents was Michael Servetus (q.v.), who seems to have been a rather flippant person. It is said he desired Calvin's banishment in order that he might be installed in his place. To this end he accused Calvin of perfidious, tyrannical, and unchristian conduct. It is no wonder, therefore, that Calvin treated him harshly. It is idle to shield Calvin from the charge of bringing about Servetus's death, although it is true that the mode adopted (burning) did not meet with his approval—he wished to have him beheaded; but at the same time it is easy to excuse him on the ground of the persecuting spirit of his age. The Protestants who had felt the persecution of Rome were ready to persecute all who did not follow them. The burning of Servetus (Oct. 27, 1553) for the crime of heresy, specifically antitrinitarianism, was approved by the Helvetic Church, and, what is more remarkable, by the mild Melanchthon; but it failed even then to win universal approval, and now it is usually considered a sad, ineffaceable blot upon Calvin's character. Many who know nothing else of either Calvin or Servetus are very indignant over the tragedy, and apparently reject Calvinism because of it. We ought rather to mourn than to censure. Servetus knew the danger he braved in coming to Geneva. He had as early as 1534 been in debate with Calvin, although they did not meet personally. On his intimating an intention to visit Geneva, Calvin gave him fair warning, that, if he came, he would prosecute him to the death.[1] While, therefore, Calvin may be held responsible for Servetus's death, he must be cleared of the charges of having allured Servetus to Geneva, and of rejoicing in his death on personal grounds.

13. His Opponents.

No good came of the execution, only evil—ridicule from the Roman Catholics, and the adverse criticism from many friends. It likewise failed to check the antitrinitarian heresy. Calvin defended himself, and Beza aided him; but no defense could excuse the facts. In 1903 a penitential monument was erected on the place of his burning.

By his lectures Calvin attracted students from every quarter. He often had as many as a thou-

[1] "Nam si modo valeat mea auctoritas vivum exire nunquam patiar (I shall never permit him to depart alive if my authority is great enough)." Calvin to Farel, Feb. 13, 1546 (cf. Calvin's Letters, Eng. transl., ii. 33).

sand: therefore his influence was constantly spreading. As was natural, it was most formative in France, whence most of his pupils came, and to whose Protestants Calvin was leader

14. His Ecclesiastical Influence.

and spiritual father. But in other lands he exerted his power. In Italy he came to the aid of the troubled duchess of Ferrara. To England he sent his commentary on Isaiah, with a dedication to the youthful king, Edward VI. To Cranmer he wrote letters; and through Knox he molded Scotland. He counseled the Moravian Brethren. He helped the Poles in the Trinitarian controversy, and likewise the Reformed cause in Hungary. He also prepared, in his way, the present interest in foreign missions by his unfortunate mission to Brazil in 1555 (see VILLEGAGNON, NICOLAS DURAND DE).

Calvin's relations with Switzerland and Germany were unpleasant. He strove most earnestly to unite the different branches of the Protestant Church. But unhappily he was suspected by many Swiss of Lutheran views on the Lord's Supper—for this was the controverted point and by many Germans of too much Zwinglianism; so that he made but an indifferent mediator. He had high hopes of the Consensus of Zürich (1549), which harmonized the Swiss churches; but the controversy with the Lutherans was violently renewed by Hesshus.

The common conception of Calvin is erroneous. He was not the stony-hearted tyrant, the relentless persecutor, the gloomy theologian, the popular picture represents him to have been. Men, by a blessed inconsistency, are often kinder than their creeds. So, at all events, was Calvin. To the superficial observer he is not attractive; but it is the opinion of every one who has studied him that he improves upon acquaintance. Granted that he was constitutionally intolerant; that he did draft and sternly carry out regulations

15. His Character.

which were vexatious and needlessly severe; that he knew no other standpoint in government, morals, or theology than his own—he had qualities which entitle him to respect and admiration. He was refined, conscientious, pure, faithful, honest, humble, pious. He attracted men by the strength of his character, the loftiness of his aims, and the directness of his efforts. He had the common human affections. He loved his wife, and mourned her death. He grieved over his childlessness. He took delight in his friends; and they were the noblest in the Protestant Church. Somewhat of the forbidding aspect of his life may perhaps be accounted for by the unnatural life he was forced to lead. He desired to spend his days in study; whereas he was forced to incessant, multifarious, and most prominent labor. Experience shows there is no harder master than a timid man compelled to lead. Again, his ill-health must be taken into account. He was a chronic invalid. Such men are not apt to be gentle. The wonder rather is that he showed so patient a spirit. The popular verdict has been given against him; but *vox populi* is not always *vox dei*. What Beza, his biographer, wrote is nearer truth: "Having been an observer of Calvin's life for sixteen years, I may with perfect right testify that we have in this man a most beautiful example of a truly Christian life and death, which it is easy to calumniate, but difficult to imitate." Ernest Renan finds the key to his influence in the fact that he was "the most Christian man of his generation" (*Studies of Religious History and Criticism*, New York, 1864 pp. 286 sqq.).

Calvin was of middle stature, and, through feeble health, of meager and emaciated frame. He had a thin, pale, finely chiseled face, a well-

16. His Personal Appearance.

formed mouth, a long, pointed beard, black hair, a prominent nose, a lofty forehead, and flaming eyes. He was modest, plain, and scrupulously neat in dress, orderly and methodical in all his habits, temperate, and even abstemious, allowing himself scarcely food and sleep enough for vigorous work. (The famous portrait by Ary Scheffer is too much idealized.)

Leaving out of view his correspondence, the writings of Calvin divide themselves into the theological and the exegetical. In regard to the latter it suffices now to say that they have never been excelled, if, on the whole, they have been equaled. He possessed all the requisite qualifications for an exegete—knowledge of the original tongues, good common sense, and abundant piety. His expositions are brief, pithy, and clear.

17. His Literary Labors.

His theological writings are remarkable for their early maturity and their unvarying consistency. Besides his minor writings, we possess that masterpiece of Protestantism, the "Institutes of the Christian Religion." He produced at twenty-six a book in which he had nothing essential to change at fifty-five. The repeated enlargements were mere developments of its germinal ideas. The first edition (Basel, 1536) contained 519 pages, measuring $6\frac{1}{4}$ by 4 inches, was divided into six chapters, and was intended merely as a brief apology of the Reformed doctrine: (1) Of law, with an exposition of the decalogue; (2) Of faith, with an exposition of the Apostles' Creed; (3) Of prayer, with an exposition of the Lord's Prayer; (4) Of the sacraments of baptism and the Lord's Supper; (5) Of the other so-called sacraments; (6) Of Christian liberty, church government and discipline. The French translation made by Calvin himself appeared in Basel, 1541. The final form was given to the "Institutes" in the Latin edition of Geneva, 1559, when it was made into a treatise of four books, divided into a hundred and four chapters.

BIBLIOGRAPHY: For a comprehensive bibliography, giving full details as to the successive publications of Calvin, their later editions, also of books written on Calvin's life and theology, consult A. Erichson, *Bibliographia Calviniana*, Berlin, 1900.

The complete edition of Calvin's Works, superseding previous editions, is *Joannis Calvini Opera quæ supersunt omnia*, vol. i.–lix., ed. J. W. Baum, E. Cunitz, E. Reuss, P. Lobstein, and A. Erichson. The last was assisted by W. Baldensperger and L. Horst. The edition was begun by the three first-named, Berlin, 1860, and finished by Erichson in 1900. There is an excellent translation of the commentaries, his *Institutes*, and his *Tracts relating to the Reformation*, by H. Beveridge, published by the Calvin Translation Society, 52 vols., Edinburgh, 1844–55. The fullest collection of Calvin's letters is in the Berlin edition. In 1854 in Paris Jules Bonnet published a collection, and this has been translated, volumes i., ii., by D. Constable, Edinburgh, 1855–57; volumes iii., iv., by M. R. Gilchrist, Philadelphia, 1858. The four volumes are now published by the Presbyterian Board of Publication, Philadelphia. The letters to correspondents living in French-speaking lands are given in their original Latin or French with careful and scholarly annotations by A. L. Herminjard (d. 1900) in the nine volumes of his *Correspondance des réformateurs dans les pays de langue française, 1512–44*, Geneva, 1866–97. The first letter of Calvin's is no. 310 in vol. ii., 2d ed., 1878.

For the life of Calvin the original source is the sketch by his friend and coadjutor Theodore Beza, Geneva, 1564, 2d ed., Lausanne, 1575; edited by Neander, Berlin, 1841, Eng. transl., by H. Beveridge, in *Tracts relating to the Reformation*, in the Calvin Society translation, vol. i., Edinburgh, 1844. Much information comes out incidentally in his correspondence.

Modern lives of Calvin, derived from independent study of the works and other sources, which can be commended are those by T. H. Dyer, London, 1850; F. Bungener, 2 vols., Paris, 1862–63, Eng. transl., Edinburgh, 1863; E. Stähelin, 2 vols., Elberfeld, 1863; F. W. Kampschulte, ed. W. Goetz, 2 vols., Leipsic, 1899; P. Schaff, *Christian Church*, vii. 257–844; E. Doumergue, Lausanne, 1899 sqq. (to be in five volumes, of which the second appeared in 1902 and the third in 1905, a life-work, aims at being exhaustive, is illustrated by numerous reproductions of old drawings, plans, pictures, etc., and hundreds of special sketches by H. Armand-Delilée); A. M. Fairbairn, in *The Cambridge Modern History*, vol. ii., *The Reformation*, chap. xi., pp. 342–376, New York, 1904; by W. Walker, in the *Heroes of the Reformation Series*, New York, 1906; and by A. Bossert, Paris, 1906. Mention should also be made of the material on Calvin and French church history generally constantly appearing in Paris in the *Bulletin de la société de l'histoire du protestantisme français*, under the editorship of the learned Nathanael Weiss, secretary of the Society.

CALVINISM.

1. Meaning and Uses of the Term. Calvinism is an ambiguous term in so far as it is currently employed in two or three senses, closely related indeed, and passing insensibly into one another, but of varying latitudes of connotation. Sometimes it designates merely the individual teaching of John Calvin. Sometimes it designates, more broadly, the doctrinal system confessed by that body of Protestant Churches known historically, in distinction from the Lutheran Churches, as "the Reformed Churches" (see PROTESTANTISM); but also quite commonly called "the Calvinistic Churches" because the greatest scientific exposition of their faith in the Reformation age, and perhaps the most influential of any age, was given by John Calvin. Sometimes it designates, more broadly still, the entire body of conceptions, theological, ethical, philosophical, social, political, which, under the influence of the master mind of John Calvin, raised itself to dominance in the Protestant lands of the post-Reformation age, and has left a permanent mark not only upon the thought of mankind, but upon the life-history of men, the social order of civilized peoples, and even the political organization of States. In the present article, the term will be taken, for obvious reasons, in the second of these senses. Fortunately this is also its central sense; and there is little danger that its other connotations will fall out of mind while attention is concentrated upon this.

On the one hand, John Calvin, though always looked upon by the Reformed Churches as an exponent rather than as the creator of their doctrinal system, has nevertheless been both reverenced as one of their founders, and deferred to as that particular one of their founders to whose formative hand and systematizing talent their doctrinal system has perhaps owed most. In any exposition of the Reformed theology, therefore, the teaching of John Calvin must always take a high, and, indeed, determinative place. On the other hand, although Calvinism has dug a channel through which not merely flows a stream of theological thought, but also surges a great wave of human life—filling the heart with fresh ideals and conceptions which have revolutionized the conditions of existence—yet its fountain-head lies in its theological system; or rather, to be perfectly exact, one step behind even that, in its religious consciousness. For the roots of Calvinism are planted in a specific religious attitude, out of which is unfolded first a particular theology, from which springs on the one hand a special church organization, and on the other a social order, involving a given political arrangement. The whole outworking of Calvinism in life is thus but the efflorescence of its fundamental religious consciousness, which finds its scientific statement in its theological system.

2. Fundamental Principle. The exact formulation of the fundamental principle of Calvinism has indeed taxed the acumen of a long series of thinkers for the last hundred years (e.g., Ullmann, Semisch, Hagenbach, Ebrard, Herzog, Schweizer, Baur, Schneckenburger, Guder, Schenkel, Schöberlein, Stahl, Hundeshagen; for a discussion of the several views cf. H. Voigt, *Fundamentaldogmatik*, Gotha, 1874, pp. 397–480; W Hastie, *The Theology of the Reformed Church in its Fundamental Principles*, Edinburgh, 1904, pp. 129–177). Perhaps the simplest statement of it is the best: that it lies in a profound apprehension of God in his majesty, with the inevitably accompanying poignant realization of the exact nature of the relation sustained to him by the creature as such, and particularly by the sinful creature. He who believes in God without reserve, and is determined that God shall be God to him in all his thinking, feeling, willing—in the entire compass of his life-activities, intellectual, moral, spiritual, throughout all his individual, social, religious relations—is, by the force of that strictest of all logic which presides over the outworking of principles into thought and life, by the very necessity of the case, a Calvinist. In Calvinism, then, objectively speaking, theism comes to its rights; subjectively speaking, the religious relation attains its purity; soteriologically speaking, evangelical religion finds at length its full expression and its secure stability. Theism comes to its rights only in a teleological conception of the universe, which perceives in the entire course of events the orderly outworking of the plan of God, who is the author, preserver, and governor of all things, whose will is consequently the ultimate cause of all. The religious relation attains its purity only when an attitude of absolute dependence on God is not merely temporarily assumed in the act, say, of prayer, but is sustained through all the activities of life, intellectual, emotional, executive. And evangelical religion reaches stability only when the sinful soul rests in humble, self-emptying trust purely on the God of grace as the immediate and sole source of all the efficiency which enters into its salvation. And these things are the formative principles of Calvinism.

3. Relation to Other Systems.

The difference between Calvinism and other forms of theistic thought, religious experience, evangelical theology is a difference not of kind but of degree. Calvinism is not a specific variety of theism, religion, evangelicalism, set over against other specific varieties, which along with it constitute these several genera, and which possess equal rights of existence with it and make similar claims to perfection, each after its own kind. It differs from them not as one species differs from other species; but as a perfectly developed representative differs from an imperfectly developed representative of the same species. There are not many kinds of theism, religion, evangelicalism, among which men are at liberty to choose to suit at will their individual taste or meet their special need, all of which may be presumed to serve each its own specific uses equally worthily. There is but one kind of theism, religion, evangelicalism; and the several constructions laying claim to these names differ from each other not as correlative species of a broader class, but as more or less perfect, or more or less defective, exemplifications of a single species. Calvinism conceives of itself as simply the more pure theism, religion, evangelicalism, superseding as such the less pure. It has no difficulty, therefore, in recognizing the theistic character of all truly theistic thought, the religious note in all actual religious activity, the evangelical quality of all really evangelical faith. It refuses to be set antagonistically over against any of these things, wherever or in whatever degree of imperfection they may be manifested; it claims them in every instance of their emergence as its own, and essays only to point out the way in which they may be given their just place in thought and life. Whoever believes in God; whoever recognizes in the recesses of his soul his utter dependence on God; whoever in all his thought of salvation hears in his heart of hearts the echo of the *soli Deo gloria* of the evangelical profession—by whatever name he may call himself, or by whatever intellectual puzzles his logical understanding may be confused—Calvinism recognizes as implicitly a Calvinist, and as only requiring to permit these fundamental principles—which underlie and give its body to all true religion—to work themselves freely and fully out in thought and feeling and action, to become explicitly a Calvinist.

4. Calvinism and Lutheranism.

It is unfortunate that a great body of the scientific discussion which, since Max Göbel (*Die religiöse Eigenthümlichkeit der lutherischen und reformirten Kirchen*, Bonn, 1837) first clearly posited the problem, has been carried on somewhat vigorously with a view to determining the fundamental principle of Calvinism, has sought particularly to bring out its contrast with some other theological tendency, commonly with the sister Protestant tendency of Lutheranism. Undoubtedly somewhat different spirits inform Calvinism and Lutheranism. And undoubtedly the distinguishing spirit of Calvinism is rooted not in some extraneous circumstance of its antecedents or origin—as, for example, Zwingli's tendency to intellectualism, or the superior humanistic culture and predilections of Zwingli and Calvin, or the democratic instincts of the Swiss, or the radical rationalism of the Reformed leaders as distinguished from the merely modified traditionalism of the Lutherans—but in its formative principle. But it is misleading to find the formative principle of either type of Protestantism in its difference from the other; they have infinitely more in common than in distinction. And certainly nothing could be more misleading than to represent them (as is often done) as owing their differences to their more pure embodiment respectively of the principle of predestination and that of justification by faith. The doctrine of predestination is not the formative principle of Calvinism, the root from which it springs. It is one of its logical consequences, one of the branches which it has inevitably thrown out. It has been firmly embraced and consistently proclaimed by Calvinists because it is an implicate of theism, is directly given in the religious consciousness, and is an absolutely essential element in evangelical religion, without which its central truth of complete dependence upon the free mercy of a saving God can not be maintained. And so little is it a peculiarity of the Reformed theology, that it underlay and gave its form and power to the whole Reformation movement; which was, as from the spiritual point of view, a great revival of religion, so, from the doctrinal point of view, a great revival of Augustinianism. There was accordingly no difference among the Reformers on this point: Luther and Melanchthon and the compromising Butzer were no less jealous for absolute predestination than Zwingli and Calvin. Even Zwingli could not surpass Luther in sharp and unqualified assertion of it: and it was not Calvin but Melanchthon who gave it a formal place in his primary scientific statement of the elements of the Protestant faith (cf. Schaff, *Creeds*, i. 451; E. F. Karl Müller, *Symbolik*, Leipsic, 1896, p. 75; C. J. Niemijer, *De Strijd over de Leer der Predestinatie in de IX. Eeuw*, Groningen, 1889, p. 21; H. Voigt, *Fundamentaldogmatik*, Gotha, 1874, pp. 469–470). Just as little can the doctrine of justification by faith be represented as specifically Lutheran. Not merely has it from the beginning been a substantial element in the Reformed faith, but it is only among the Reformed that it has retained or can retain its purity, free from the tendency to become a doctrine of justification on account of faith (cf. E. Böhl, *Von der Rechtfertigung durch den Glauben*, Amsterdam, 1890). Here, too, the difference between the two types of Protestantism is one of degree, not of kind (cf. C. P. Krauth, *The Conservative Reformation*, Philadelphia, 1872). Lutheranism, the product of a poignant sense of sin, born from the throes of a guilt-burdened soul which can not be stilled until it finds peace in God's decree of justification, is apt to rest in this peace; while Calvinism, the product of an overwhelming vision of God, born from the reflection in the heart of man of the majesty of a God who will not give his glory to another, can not pause until it places the scheme of salvation itself in relation to a complete world-view, in which it becomes subsidiary to the glory of the Lord God Almighty. Calvinism asks with Lutheranism, indeed, that most poignant of all questions, What shall I do to be saved? and answers it as Lutheranism answers it. But the great question which presses upon it is, How shall God be glorified? It is the contemplation of God and zeal for his honor which in it draws out the emotions and absorbs endeavor; and the end of human as of all other existence, of salvation as of all other attainment, is to it the glory of the Lord of all. Full justice is done in it to the scheme of redemption and the experience of salvation, because full justice is done in it to religion itself which underlies these elements of it. It begins, it centers, it ends with the vision of God in his glory: and it sets itself before all things to render to God his rights in every sphere of life-activity.

One of the consequences flowing from this fundamental attitude of Calvinistic feeling and thought is the high supernaturalism which informs alike its religious consciousness and its doctrinal construction. Calvinism would not be badly defined, indeed, as the tendency which is determined to do justice to the immediately supernatural, as in the first, so also in the second creation. The strength and purity of its belief in the supernatural Fact (which is God) saves it from all embarrassment in the face of the supernatural act (which is miracle). In everything which enters into the process of redemption it is impelled by the force of its first principle to place the initiative in God. A supernatural revelation, in which God makes known to man his will and his purposes of grace; a supernatural record of this revelation in a supernaturally given book, in which God gives his revelation permanency and extension—such things are to the Calvinist almost matters of course.

5. Soteriology of Calvinism. And, above all, he can but insist with the utmost strenuousness on the immediate supernaturalness of the actual work of redemption itself, and that no less in its application than in its impetration. Thus it comes about that the doctrine of monergistic regeneration or as it was phrased by the older theologians, of "irresistible grace" or "effectual calling"—is the hinge of the Calvinistic soteriology, and lies much more deeply embedded in the system than the doctrine of predestination itself which is popularly looked upon as its hall-mark. Indeed, the soteriological significance of predestination to the Calvinist consists in the safeguard it affords to monergistic regeneration—to purely supernatural salvation. What lies at the heart of his soteriology is the absolute exclusion of the creaturely element in the initiation of the saving process, that so the pure grace of God may be magnified. Only so could he express his sense of men's complete dependence as sinners on the free mercy of a saving God; or extrude the evil leaven of Synergism (q.v.) by which, as he clearly sees, God is robbed of his glory and man is encouraged to think that he owes to some power, some act of choice, some initiative of his own, his participation in that salvation which is in reality all of grace. There is accordingly nothing against which Calvinism sets its face with more firmness than every form and degree of autosoterism. Above everything else, it is determined that God, in his Son Jesus Christ, acting through the Holy Spirit whom he has sent, shall be recognized as our veritable Savior. To it sinful man stands in need not of inducements or assistance to save himself, but of actual saving; and Jesus Christ has come not to advise, or urge, or induce, or aid him to save himself, but to save him. This is the root of Calvinistic soteriology; and it is because this deep sense of human helplessness and this profound consciousness of indebtedness for all that enters into salvation to the free grace of God is the root of its soteriology that to it the doctrine of election becomes the *cor cordis* of the Gospel. He who knows that it is God who has chosen him and not he who has chosen God, and that he owes his entire salvation in all its processes and in every one of its stages to this choice of God, would be an ingrate indeed if he gave not the glory of his salvation solely to the inexplicable elective love of God.

Historically the Reformed theology finds its origin in the reforming movement begun in Switzerland under the leadership of Zwingli (1516). Its fundamental principles are already present in Zwingli's teaching, though it was not until Calvin's profound and penetrating genius was called to their exposition that they took their ultimate form or received systematic development. From Switzerland Calvinism spread outward to France, and along the Rhine through Germany to Holland, eastward to Bohemia and Hungary, and westward, across the Channel, to Great Britain. In this broad expansion through so many lands its voice was raised in a multitude of confessions; and in the course of the four hundred years which have elapsed since its first formulation, it has been expounded in a vast body of dogmatic

6. Consistent Development of Calvinism. treatises. Its development has naturally been much richer and far more many-sided than that of the sister system of Lutheranism in its more confined and homogeneous environment; and yet it has retained its distinctive character and preserved its fundamental features with marvelous consistency throughout its entire history. It may be possible to distinguish among the Reformed confessions, between those which bear more and those which bear less strongly the stamp of Calvin's personal influence; and they part into two broad classes, according as they were composed before or after the Arminian defection (c. 1618) demanded sharper definitions on the points of controversy raised by that movement (see ARMINIUS, JACOBUS, AND ARMINIANISM; REMONSTRANTS). A few of them written on German soil also bear traces of the influence of Lutheran conceptions. And, of course, no more among the Reformed than elsewhere have all the professed expounders of the system of doctrine been true to the faith they professed to expound. Nevertheless, it is precisely the same system of truth which is embodied in all the great historic Reformed confessions; it matters not whether the document emanates from Zurich or Bern or Basel or Geneva, whether it sums up the Swiss development as in the Second Helvetic Confession, or publishes the faith of the National Reformed Churches of France, or Scotland, or Holland, or the Palatinate, or Hungary, Poland, Bohemia, or England; or republishes the established Reformed doctrine in opposition to new contradictions, as in the Canons of Dort (in which the entire Reformed world concurred), or the Westminster Confession (to which the whole of Puritan Britain gave its assent), or the Swiss Form of Consent (which represents the mature judgment of Switzerland upon the recently proposed novelties of doctrine). And despite the inevitable variety of individual points of view, as well as the unavoidable differences in ability, learning, grasp, in the multitude of writers who have sought to expound the Reformed faith through these four centuries—and the grave departures from that faith made here and there among them—the great stream of Reformed dogmatics has flowed essentially unsullied, straight from its origin in Zwingli and Calvin to its debouchure, say, in Chalmers and Cunningham and Crawford, in Hodge and Thornwell and Shedd.

It is true an attempt has been made to distinguish two types of Reformed teaching from the beginning; a more radical type developed under the influence of the peculiar teachings of Calvin, and a (so-called) more moderate type, chiefly propagating itself in Germany, which exhibits rather the influence, as was at first said (Hofstede de Groot, Ebrard, Heppe), of Melanchthon, or, in its more recent statement (Gooszen), of Bullinger. In all that concerns the essence of Calvinism, however, there was no difference between Bullinger and Calvin, German and Swiss: the Heidelberg Catechism is no doubt a catechism and not a confession, but in its presuppositions and inculcations it is as purely Calvinistic as the Genevan Catechism or the catechisms of the Westminster Assembly.

7. Varieties of Calvinism. Nor was the substance of doctrine touched by the peculiarities of method which marked such schools as the so-called Scholastics (showing themselves already in Zanchius, d. 1590, and culminating in theologians like Alsted, d. 1638, and Voetius, d. 1676); or by the special modes of statement which were developed by such schools as the so-called Federalists (e.g., Coccelus, d. 1669, Burman, d. 1679, Wittsius, d. 1708; cf. Diestel, *Studien zur Federaltheologie*, in *Jahrbücher für deutsche Theologie*, 1862, ii.; G. Vos, *De Verbondsleer in de Gereformeerde Theologie*, Grand Rapids, 1891; W Hastie, *The Theology of the Reformed Church*, Edinburgh, 1904, pp. 189-210). The first serious defection from the fundamental conceptions of the Reformed system came with the rise of Arminianism in the early years of the seventeenth century (Arminius, Uytenbogaert, Episcopius, Limborch, Curcellæus); and the Arminian party was quickly sloughed off under the condemnation of the whole Reformed world. The five points of its "Remonstrance" against the Calvinistic system (see REMONSTRANTS) were met by the reassertion of the fundamental doctrines of absolute predestination, particular redemption, total depravity, irresistible grace, and the perseverance of the saints (Canons of the Synod of Dort). The first important modification of the Calvinistic system which has retained a position within its limits was made in the middle of the seventeenth century by the professors of the French school at Saumur, and is hence called Salmurianism; otherwise Amyraldism, or hypothetical universalism (Cameron, d. 1625, Amyraut, d. 1664, Placæus, d. 1655, Testardus, d. c. 1650; see AMYRAUT, MOÏSE). This modification also received the condemnation of the contemporary Reformed world, which reasserted with emphasis the importance of the doctrine that Christ actually saves by his spirit all for whom he offers the sacrifice of his blood (e.g., Westminster Confession, Swiss Form of Consent).

If "varieties of Calvinism" are to be spoken of with reference to anything more than details, of importance in themselves no doubt, but of little significance for the systematic development of the type of doctrine, there seem not more than three which require mention: supralapsarianism, infralapsarianism, and what may perhaps be called in this reference, Postredemptionism; all of which (as indeed their very names import) take their start from a fundamental agreement in the principles which govern the system. The difference between these various tendencies of thought within the limits of the system turns on the place given by each to the decree of election, in the logical ordering of the "decrees of God."

8. Supralapsarianism and Infralapsarianism. The Supralapsarians suppose that election underlies the decree of the fall itself; and conceive the decree of the fall as a means for carrying out the decree of election. The Infralapsarians, on the other hand, consider that election presupposes the decree of the fall, and hold, therefore, that in electing some to life God has mankind as a *massa perditionis* in mind. The extent of the difference between these parties is often, indeed usually, grossly exaggerated: and even historians of repute are found representing infralapsarianism as involving, or at least permitting, denial that the fall has a place in the decree of God at all: as if election could be postposited in the *ordo decreto-*

rum to the decree of the fall, while it was doubted whether there were any decree of the fall; or as if indeed God could be held to conceive men, in his electing decree, as fallen, without by that very act fixing the presupposed fall in his eternal decree. In point of fact there is and can be no difference among Calvinists as to the inclusion of the fall in the decree of God: to doubt this inclusion is to place oneself at once at variance with the fundamental Calvinistic principle which conceives all that comes to pass teleologically and ascribes everything that actually occurs ultimately to the will of God. Accordingly even the Postredemptionists (that is to say the Salmurians or Amyraldians) find no difficulty at this point. Their peculiarity consists in insisting that election succeeds, in the order of thought, not merely the decree of the fall but that of redemption as well, taking the term redemption here in the narrower sense of the impetration of redemption by Christ. They thus suppose that in his electing decree God conceived man not merely as fallen but as already redeemed. This involves a modified doctrine of the atonement from which the party has received the name of Hypothetical Universalism, holding as it does that Christ died to make satisfaction for the sins of all men without exception *if*—if, that is, they believe: but that, foreseeing that none would believe, God elected some to be granted faith through the effectual operation of the Holy Spirit.

9. Postredemptionism.

The indifferent standing of the Postredemptionists in historical Calvinism is indicated by the treatment accorded it in the historical confessions. It alone of the "varieties of Calvinism" here mentioned has been made the object of formal confessional condemnation; and it received condemnation in every important Reformed confession written after its development. There are, it is true, no supralapsarian confessions: many, however, leave the questions which divide supralapsarian and infralapsarian wholly to one side and thus avoid pronouncing for either; and none is polemically directed against supralapsarianism. On the other hand, not only does no confession close the door to infralapsarianism, but a considerable number explicitly teach infralapsarianism which thus emerges as the typical form of Calvinism. That, despite its confessional condemnation, Postredemptionism has remained a recognized form of Calvinism and has worked out a history for itself in the Calvinistic Churches (especially in America) may be taken as evidence that its advocates, while departing, in some important particulars, from typical Calvinism, have nevertheless remained, in the main, true to the fundamental postulates of the system. There is another variety of Postredemptionism, however, of which this can scarcely be said. This variety, which became dominant among the New England Congregationalist Churches about the second third of the nineteenth century (e.g., N. W. Taylor, d. 1858; C. G. Finney, d. 1875; E. A. Park, d. 1900; see NEW ENGLAND THEOLOGY), attempted, much after the manner of the "Congruists" of the Church of Rome, to unite a Pelagian doctrine of the will with the Calvinistic doctrine of absolute predestination. The result was, of course, to destroy the Calvinistic doctrine of "irresistible grace," and as the Calvinistic doctrine of the "satisfaction of Christ" was also set aside in favor of the Grotian or governmental theory of atonement, little was left of Calvinism except the bare doctrine of predestination. Perhaps it is not strange, therefore, that this "improved Calvinism" has crumbled away and given place to newer and explicitly anti-Calvinistic constructions of doctrine (cf. Williston Walker, in *AJT*, Apr., 1906, pp. 204 sqq.).

It must be confessed that the fortunes of Calvinism in general are not at present at their flood. In America, to be sure, the controversies of the earlier half of the nineteenth century compacted a body of Calvinistic thought which gives way but slowly: and the influence of the great theologians who adorned the churches during that period is still felt (especially Charles Hodge, 1797–1878, Robert J. Breckinridge, 1800–71, James H. Thornwell, 1812–62, Henry B. Smith, 1815–77, W. G. T. Shedd, 1820–94, Robert L. Dabney, 1820–98, Archibald Alexander Hodge, 1823–86). And in Holland recent years have seen a notable revival of the Reformed consciousness, especially among the adherents of the Free Churches, which has been felt as widely as Dutch influence extends, and which is at present represented in Abraham Kuyper and Herman Bavinck, by a theologian of genius and a theologian of erudition worthy of the best Reformed traditions. But it is probable that few "Calvinists without reserve" exist at the moment in French-speaking lands: and those who exist in lands of German speech and Eastern Europe appear to owe their inspiration directly to the teaching of Kohlbrügge. Even in Scotland there has been a remarkable decline in strictness of construction ever since the days of William Cunningham and Thomas J. Crawford (cf. W. Hastie, *The Theology of the Reformed Church*, Edinburgh, 1904, p. 228).

10. Present Fortunes of Calvinism.

Nevertheless, it may be contended that the future, as the past, of Christianity itself is bound up with the fortunes of Calvinism. The system of doctrine founded on the idea of God which has been explicated by Calvinism, strikingly remarks W. Hastie (*Theology as a Science*, Glasgow, 1899, pp. 97–98), "is the only system in which the whole order of the world is brought into a rational unity with the doctrine of grace. It is only with such a universal conception of God, established in a living way, that we can face, with hope of complete conquest, all the spiritual dangers and terrors of our time. But it is deep enough and large enough and divine enough, rightly understood, to confront them and do battle with them all in vindication of the Creator, Preserver, and Governor of the world, and of the Justice, and Love of the Divine Personality." See FIVE POINTS OF CALVINISM.

BENJAMIN B. WARFIELD.

BIBLIOGRAPHY: The Reformed Confessions have often been collected; the fullest collection is E. F. K. Müller, *Die Bekenntnisschriften der reformierten Kirche*, Leipsic, 1903. For Eng. readers the most convenient is Schaff, *Creeds*, vol. iii. (vol. i. contains a history of creeds). An older collection is H. A. Niemeyer, *Collectio Confessionum in ecclesiis reformatis publicatarum*, Leipsic, 1840. Consult also: M. Schneckenburger, *Vergleichende Darstellung des lutherischen und reformierten Lehrbegriffs*, Stuttgart, 1855; G. B. Winer, *Comparative Darstellung des Lehrbegriffs der verschiedenen christlichen Kirchenparteien*, Berlin, 1866, Eng. transl., Edinburgh, 1873; and the various works on Symbolics, especially E. F. K. Müller, *Symbolik*, Erlangen, 1896. Attempts more or less successful have been made to present the Reformed system from the writings of its representative theologians. For examples of these consult: A. Schweizer, *Die Glaubenslehre der evangelisch-reformierten Kirche*, 2 vols., Zurich, 1844–1847; J. H. Scholten, *De Leer der Hervormde Kerk in hare Grondbeginselen*, Leyden, 1848, 2d ed., 1870; H. Heppe, *Die Dogmatik der evangelisch-reformierten Kirche*, Elberfeld, 1861; cf. B. de Moor, *Commentarius perpetuus in Johannis Marckii compendium theologiæ christianæ*, 7 vols., Leyden, 1761.

For the "principle" of Calvinism consult: H. Voigt, *Fundamentaldogmatik*, pp. 397–480, Gotha, 1874; W Hastie, *The Theology of the Reformed Church in its Fundamental Principles*, Edinburgh, 1904; cf. Scholten and Schneckenburger, ut sup., where lists of the literature are given. A good history of the Reformed theology is still a desideratum. Sketches have been given in: W Gass, *Geschichte der protestantischen Dogmatik*, Berlin, 1854–67; G. Frank, *Geschichte der protestantischen Theologie*, 3 vols., Leipsic, 1862–75; I. A. Dorner, *Geschichte der protestantischen Theologie*, Munich, 1867, Eng. transl., 2 vols., Edinburgh, 1871. Contributions have been made by: C. M. Pfaff, *Introductio in historiam theologiæ literariam*, pp. 255 sqq., Tübingen, 1724; B. Pictet, *Theologia christiana*, part iii., Leyden, 1733–34; J. G. Walch, *Bibliotheca theologica selecta*, i. 211 sqq., Jena, 1757–68; A. M. Toplady, *Historic Proof of the Doctrinal Calvinism of the Church of England*, London, 1774; A. Ypey (Ijpeij), *Beknopte letterkundige geschiedenis der system. godgeleerd* (Utrecht?), 1793–98; A. Schweizer, *Die protestantischen Centraldogmen in ihrer Entwicklung innerhalb der reformierten Kirche*, Zurich, 1854; J. H. Scholten, ut sup., i. 67 sqq.; H. Heppe, *Die confessionelle Entwicklung der altprotestantischen Kirche Deutschlands*, Marburg, 1854; idem, *Dogmatik des deutschen Protestantismus im sechzehnten Jahrhundert*, Gotha, 1857; W. Cunningham, *The Reformers and the Theology of the Reformation*, Edinburgh, 1862; idem, *Historical Theology*, 2 vols., ib. 1864; J. H. A. Ebrard, *Christliche Dogmatik*, i. 44, Königsberg, 1863; J. Walker, *The Theology and Theologians of Scotland*, Edinburgh, 1872; C. Sepp, *Het Godgeleerd onderwiis in Nederland , 16e en 17e eeuw*, Leyden, 1873–74; A. Milroy, *The Church of Scotland, Past and Present*, ed. R. H. Story, London, n.d.; idem, *Scottish Theologians and Preachers, 1610–1638*, Edinburgh, 1891. Consult also on the general subject: A. Kuyper, *Calvinism*, New York, 1890 (an admirable statement, summing up a series of brochures in Dutch); J. A. Froude, *Calvinism*, London, 1871, and in *Short Studies on Great Subjects*, second series, ib. 1871; J. L. Girardeau, *Calvinism and Evangelical Arminianism*, Columbia, 1893; B. B. Warfield, *The Significance of the Westminster Standards as a Creed*, New York, 1898; E. W. Smith, *The Creed of Presbyterians*, ib. 1901. Some of the chief Calvinistic dogmatists find mention in the text; a list of the more important is given in Heppe and Schweizer, ut sup., at the beginning. The series may be fairly represented by the following names: Calvin, Ursinus, Zanchius, Polanus, Alsted, Voetius, Burman, Turretin, Heidegger, Van Mastricht. The brief compends of Bucanus (*Institutiones theologicæ*, Geneva, 1609), Wollebius (*Compendium theologiæ*, Cambridge, 1648), Ames (*Medulla theologica*, Amsterdam, 1656, Eng. transl., London, 1642), and Marck (*Compendium theologiæ*, Amsterdam, 1705) present the system in briefest form. The more recent theologians are indicated in the text.

CAMALDOLITES (called also **Camaldolensians, Camaldolese, Camaldules, Camaldulians,** from the monastery at Camaldoli near Arezzo): A religious order springing from the movement for monastic reform which also gave rise to the congregations of Cluny and Lorraine, with which it is allied in some respects, though it differs from them in others. The Italian movement is wholly independent of the French, and began later—not before the close of the tenth century, after the Cluniac monks had already reformed numerous monasteries in upper and central Italy. It was more enthusiastic than the French, and had for its object not so much the strict enforcement of the Benedictine rule as the commendation, in opposition to the moral corruption which was even deeper in the south than in the north, of the severest form of the ascetic life, that of hermits. This recalls the Greek monastic originators; and the fact is easily explicable by the strong influence of Greek traditions in Italy, especially in the south.

St. Romuald is the most prominent, but by no means the only, representative of this idea. Before or with him were working for the same end the Armenian hermit Simeon, St. Dominic of Foligno, the founder of Fonte Avellana, and the Greek Nilos of Rossano. Romuald was born at Ravenna, of the ducal family there, about 950. He was startled out of a worldly life when his father Sergius killed a kinsman in a duel arising out of a dispute over a piece of property, and retired to the monastery of S. Apollinare in Classe near Ravenna to do penance forty days on his father's behalf. His ascetic zeal was not satisfied here, although the monastery had been reformed not long before by Majolus of Cluny. He began to live a hermit's life near Venice, continued it in Catalonia, and then returned to the neighborhood of Ravenna. Wherever he went, a group of disciples formed around him; but as soon as they were sufficiently numerous in any one place, he gave them into the charge of a superior and left them. Most of these colonies were in central Italy; the three most important were Val di Castro, Monte Sitrio in Umbria, and Camaldoli, where he established a monastery in 1012.

St. Romuald.

His organization shows a combination of the Western cenobite system with the Eastern anchorite life. The brothers lived in single cells, with an oratory in the midst. The whole Psalter was recited every day; the only written memorial left by Romuald was an exposition of the Psalms, which, however, is taken almost word for word from that of Cassiodorus. Meals were taken in common, but they were exceedingly scanty; the brothers went barefoot and wore their hair and beards long; the rule of silence was strictly observed. They busied themselves with agriculture and various handicrafts, those near the sea especially with the making of baskets and nets. We meet for the first time in these hermit colonies with *famuli*, the later lay brothers, who relieved the monks of the more burdensome household duties. The rule of fasting and silence was not so strict for them, but apparently, as at Fonte Avellana, they had to take lifelong monastic vows. This institution was borrowed by Gualberto, a disciple of Romuald's, for his order of Vallombrosa and further developed by him (see GUALBERTO, GIOVANNI). Romuald's activity was not confined to the founding of these communities. He made a deep impression upon the most varied classes, and exercised a great influence over the emperor Otto III., who, it is asserted not improbably, promised him to exchange the crown for the cowl after he had conquered Rome. Though Romuald disclaimed any intention of taking part in ecclesiastical politics, he raised his voice loudly in Italy against simony and the marriage of the clergy. His zeal called him to the mission-field; disciples of his penetrated into Russia and Poland, there to meet death for their faith, and the desire of the martyr's crown finally took the aged hermit himself to Hungary. Ill health hindered his work there, and he returned to die in 1027.

His zeal for a reform of monasticism remained active in his followers. They did not, however, emphasize the hermit ideal to the same extent, and the Italian movement gradually approximated to that of Cluny. Romuald's spirit was best followed in the community of Camaldoli, which received papal confirmation from Alexander II. in 1072. Its rule was first written in 1080 by the fourth prior, Rudolph, who modified in some respects the extreme strictness of Romuald's prescriptions, and also founded (1086) the first convent of nuns under this rule, San Pietro di Luco at Mogello. Camaldoli received many rich gifts, and the congregation spread throughout Italy, without, however, producing any very notable men except the famous jurist Gratian (q.v.). The transition from the hermit to the community life became more marked, in spite of the efforts of Ambrose the Camaldolite (q.v.) of Portico, "major" or head of the congregation in 1431, supported by Pope Eugenius IV., to restore the old ideals. In 1476 the community of St. Michael at Murano near Venice renounced the obedience of Camaldoli, and formed a group of distinctly cenobitic Camaldolese houses, confirmed as a congregation by Innocent VIII. In 1513 Leo X. reunited all the Camaldolese monks under the headship of Camaldoli, providing that the major should hold office for but three years, and be chosen alternately from the hermits and the cenobites. But in 1520 he allowed Paolo Giustiniani to draw up new statutes and to form the new communities of hermits which he was to found into an independent congregation of St. Romuald. This new congregation, which took its name from Monte Corona near Perugia, had a very strict rule; it spread through Germany, Austria, and Poland. A fourth congregation, that of Turin, was founded in 1601 by Alessandro di Leva (d. 1612), to take in the hermits of Piedmont. A branch of this became practically a separate congregation on account of the political views of Richelieu, who was unwilling that the French hermitages should be subject to Italian superiors. By a brief of Urban VIII. (1635), its head was always to be a Frenchman, and directly subject to the pope. From 1642 Gros-Bois near Paris was its mother house. All the French communities perished at the Revolution. The congregation of Camaldoli has now six houses, including Camaldoli itself and one famous for its picturesque site high above Naples. The principal house of the Murano congregation is San Gregorio in Rome, from which came the only Camaldolese monk who has occupied the papal throne, Gregory XVI. (1831–46). Outside of Italy there is only the community of Bielany in the diocese of Cracow, belonging to the congregation of Monte Corona. The total membership of the order is not more than 200. Convents of nuns exist only in Rome and Florence.

The Camaldolese.

(G. GRÜTZMACHER.)

BIBLIOGRAPHY: Petrus Damianus, *Vita Romualdi* is in Damianus, *Opera*, ed. C. Cajetanus, ii. 255 sqq., Rome, 1608, and *MPL*, cxliv. 953 sqq. Another *Vita* is in *ASB*, 7th Feb., ii. 124–140. Consult: G. B. Mittarelli and G. D. Costadoni, *Annales Camaldulenses*, 9 vols., Venice, 1755–1773; W. Wattenbach, *Deutschlands Geschichtsquellen*, i. 436, Berlin, 1893; C. W. Currier, *Hist. of Religious Orders*, pp. 118–123, New York, 1896; P. Helyot, *Ordres monastiques*, vol. v.; Heimbucher, *Orden und Kongregationen*, i. 203–208.

CAMBRAI, cān″brê′: An ancient archbishopric in the north of France. As early as the beginning of the fifth century, when the Franks invaded Gaul, Cameracum was an important town, as is evident from Gregory of Tours (*Hist. Francorum*, ii. 9). On the death of Lothair II. it passed to Charles the Bald. Later its possession was contested by the emperors, the counts of Flanders, and the kings of France. It was taken from the French by the Spaniards in 1595, but has been a part of France since 1677.

The traditional list of its bishops begins with Diogenes, said to have been sent by Pope Siricius (384–398); but this is untrustworthy. Firm historical ground is reached first with St. Vedast, who was consecrated bishop of St. Remigius, bishop of Reims, and presided over the churches of Arras and Cambrai until his death in 540. The see was transferred to Cambrai under Vedulf (545–c. 580), but the two remained united until Arras received a bishop of its own in 1093. Among later incumbents of the see of Cambrai may be mentioned the holy Odo (1105–06), the unfortunate Cardinal Robert of Geneva (bishop from 1368, antipope 1378–94), the renowned Pierre d'Ailly (1397–c. 1425); and, after its elevation in 1559 to the rank of an archbishopric, Fénelon (1695–1715), and Cardinal Dubois (1720–23). The Revolution deprived Cambrai of its metropolitan dignity, subjecting it as a simple bishopric to the see of Paris, but in 1842 it was once more made an archbishopric, with Arras as suffragan. Its magnificent ancient cathedral was destroyed in the Revolution, with the exception of the tower, which fell in a great storm in 1809. The present cathedral was formerly the Benedictine church of the Holy Sepulcher.

BIBLIOGRAPHY: M. A. le Glay, *Recherches sur l'église metropolitaine de Cambrai*, Cambrai, 1825; idem, *Cameracum christianum*, Lille, 1849; H. J. P. Pisquet, *La France pontificale*, s.v. Cambrai, 22 vols., Paris, 1864–71; *KL*, ii. 1750–55.

CAMBRIDGE PLATFORM. See CONGREGATIONALISTS, IV., § 1.

CAMBRIDGE PLATONISTS: The name usually given to a succession of distinguished English divines and philosophers of the seventeenth century, also known to their contemporaries as "Latitude Men," from the breadth and comprehensiveness of their teaching. The most important of them were Benjamin Whichcote, John Smith, Ralph Cudworth, and Henry More. Other members of the school were Simon Patrick, Nathanael Culverwel, John Worthington, George Rust, and Edward Fowler; while Joseph Glanvill and John Norris, though Oxford men, were so intimately associated with it as to be sometimes included. Starting with many of the same thoughts as their immediate predecessors in the development of liberal or rational thought, Hales and Chillingworth, they aimed less than these at ecclesiastical comprehension; their purpose was to find a higher organon of Christian thought, and to vindicate the essential principles of Christianity against both dogmatic excesses within the Church and philosophical extravagances without it. Unlike the former, too, they all came from the Puritan side; with the exception of More, their leaders were members of the famous Puritan college of Emmanuel, and thus closely bound together into a definite group or school. The main source of their inspiration was the study of the Platonic philosophy, not only in Plato himself but in his Alexandrian and modern disciples. This Platonic revival was important as evoking the only force adequate to meet the development of naturalism in a direction which threatened the distinctive principles of religion. But if Platonism was the positive determinant factor in the movement, the negative influence which formed the school was opposition to the destructive reasoning of Hobbes, whose materialistic tendency they met not only, like Clarendon and others, by polemical criticism, but by a well-ordered scheme of thought, whose principles had been already worked into unison with Christian philosophy. Of their permanent achievements, not the least important was their inculcation of the doctrine of toleration, at that time so novel and unpopular. They solved the religious problem, not by giving it up, but by pushing it to its legitimate conclusion and drawing the essential distinction between dogma and religion, which is one of their chief contributions to modern thought. Against the materialism of their time, they labored to prove that religion was a transcendent reality, a substantive power binding the soul to God and revealing God to the soul. Their writings are frequently obscure and involved, and they show a lack of critical and historical judgment in their confusion of Platonism and Neoplatonism, in their speculative fancifulness, and in their misappreciation of evidence. But their services to their age can scarcely be overrated. The exponents and advocates of a comprehensive Church, the purifiers of the popular theology, they were at the same time the great champions of the reality of religion at a time when the excesses of its partizans were driving so many of their contemporaries into unbelief. See the separate articles on the various men named above.

Bibliography: The best account is by J. Tulloch, *Rational Theology and Christian Philosophy in England*, vol. ii., Edinburgh, 1872. The early prospectus was a pamphlet by S. P (Simon Patrick?), *Brief Account of the New Sect of the New Latitude Men*, London, 1662. Consult further: E. Fowler, *Practices of Certain Divines Abusively Called Latitudinarians*, ib. 1671; G. Dyer, *History of the University of Cambridge*, ii. 91–101, ib. 1814; W. E. H. Lecky, *History of Rationalism in Europe*, 2 vols., ib. 1875 (an ill-balanced estimate); F. Greenslet, *Joseph Glanvill*, New York, 1900; E. T. Campagnac, *The Cambridge Platonists; being Selections from Whichcote, Smith, and Culverwel*, Oxford, 1901.

CAMEL: The most valuable possession of the nomads of the desert.

The Syrian and Egyptian camel is the single-humped, lank, and long-legged *Camelus dromedarius*. Its foremost utility is that of common carrier ("ship of the mainland" was its poetical designation even prior to Islam). Great bodily strength and endurance fit it for this service. Its very voracity is content with the meanest fodder of the driest pasture grasses, half-dried acacia twigs, dry straw, and the like; and it can toil days at a time upon an exceedingly small stint of forage. At such times the fatty hump, which when in good condition weighs as much as thirty pounds, almost entirely disappears. It is no less easily satisfied in the article of water. In spring it feeds on freshly dewed grasses, and can dispense with watering several weeks running. In the dry season it can hold out three or four days without water; and then, when it reaches a watering-place, it swallows the water in enormous quantities. Its broad, fleshy, cushioned foot prevents it from sinking deeply into the desert sand.

The carrier camel bears ordinarily from two to three hundredweight; still more on occasion (cf. II Kings viii. 9). Its gait at a walk is about two and one-half miles an hour, and it maintains this pace right along with alacrity and freshness for twelve or fourteen hours and even longer. The riding camel differs from the foregoing, just as a noble race-horse from the heavy draft-horse. It can cover as much as ninety miles a day, and this for several days together. The camel saddle is a trough-shaped wooden seat fastened over the hump with a tight gearing both front and back. This is covered with a cushion. The rider sits as on a side-saddle. For women and children palanquins are likewise in use, with seats and curtains (Gen. xxiv. 61, xxxi. 17). The camel ministers to the Bedouins' every-day needs. The rather thick and fatty camel's milk is their beverage; and their horses often drink it. The flesh of the camel, except that of the hump, which is esteemed a peculiar delicacy, is said to be hard and tough; but still it is a feast for the Bedouin to kill one of the herd and eat meat. They also occasionally bleed the camel a little in times of scarceness. The Israelites accounted camel's flesh unclean. The Bedouins' coarse cloaks are woven of camel's hair (Matt. iii. 4), and also their thick tent-rugs. The hide is worked into sandals, thongs, water-skins, and the like. The dung is dried and then serves for fuel.

The camel naturally is less important in agricultural Palestine. Yet even here it has its usefulness as beast of burden; and when heavy loads and great distances are in question, horses and mules are not to be compared with it. In the Old Testament the breeding of camels on a large scale is found under the patriarchs (Gen. xii. 16, xxiv. 10, xxx. 43) and David (I Chron. xxvii. 30). But in every era there is reference to the manifold uses of camels (e.g., II Kings viii. 9; Isa. xxx. 6; I Chron. xii. 40; Ezra ii. 67; Neh. vii. 69). To the poet the camel in its wild raging during the rutting season is an image of the nations which in their blind passion are devoted to strange gods (Jer. ii. 23). I. BENZINGER.

BIBLIOGRAPHY: H. B. Tristram, *Natural History of the Bible*, p. 58 sqq., London, 1867; idem, *Survey of Western Palestine, Fauna and Flora*, ib. 1884; H. Blackburn, *Bible Beasts and Birds*, ib. 1886; J. G. Wood, *Bible Animals*, ib. 1883; idem, *Domestic Animals of the Bible*, ib. 1887; H. C. Hart, *Animals of the Bible*, ib. 1888; A. E. Knight, *Bible Plants and Animals*, ib. 1890; *DB*, i. 344-345; *EB*, i. 633-636.

CAMERA APOSTOLICA. See CURIA, § 2.

CAMERARIUS, cā″mē-rā′ri-us **(CAMERMEISTER), JOACHIM:** Protestant humanist; b. at Bamberg Apr. 12, 1500; d. at Leipsic Apr. 17, 1574. He was descended from an old Bamberg family and was educated there till his thirteenth year, when his parents sent him to the University of Leipsic, where he devoted himself chiefly to the study of Greek under Richard Crocus, Johann Metzler, and Peter Mosellanus. Subsequently he removed to the University of Erfurt, where he joined the circle of the humanists, became master of arts (1520), and was highly esteemed and admired for his knowledge of Greek. In 1521 he went to the University of Wittenberg, where he became intimately acquainted with Melanchthon. In 1525 he accompanied Melanchthon on his journey to the Palatinate, and thence proceeded to Basel to pay homage to Erasmus. In the same year he left Wittenberg and went to Bamberg. From here he accompanied Canon Fuchs on a journey to Prussia (1525) and in 1526 was called, upon recommendation of Melanchthon, to the gymnasium of Nuremberg as teacher of Greek and expounder of the Latin historians. A visit to Melanchthon at Speyer in 1529 during the diet held at that city brought him into immediate contact with the ecclesiastical and political affairs of the time; he also took part in the Diet of Augsburg in 1535. Conditions at Nuremberg did not satisfy him, although he had intercourse with men like W. Pirkheimer, W Linck, Osiander, Lazarus Spengler, and Albrecht Dürer. As early as 1528 he complained of the coldness and indifference toward the humanistic sciences on the part of his contemporaries. His school also did not make progress, and in 1535 he gladly followed a call to Tübingen, where he found a fruitful field for his activity as teacher. In 1541 he removed to Leipsic. Although Camerarius took part in the ecclesiastical dissensions of the time, his chief importance lies in the field of humanism and pedagogics. In his first pedagogical treatise *Præcepta honestatis atque decoris puerilis* (1528) he emphasized as a true disciple of Melanchthon humanistic education as a necessary preparation for all later vocations, but humanistic education, as he holds, has its foundation in the reverence of God. In accordance with his view that the Christian religion should be taught alongside of the rudiments of the languages, he edited the chief articles of Christianity in Greek hexameters, translated the Augsburg Confession into Greek and composed a catechism in the same language. His biographical works are of great value as sources, and show that he was a keen observer, especially his *Narratio de Eobano Hesso*, etc. (Nuremberg, 1553), *Narratio de Georgio Principe Anhaltino* (Leipsic, 1555), and his famous writing *De Philippi Melanchthonis ortu, totius vitæ curriculo et morte, implicata rerum memorabilium temporis illius hominumque mentione narratio* (Leipsic, 1566; best ed. with copious notes by S. T. Strobel, Halle, 1777; the text reprinted by A. F. Neander, Berlin, 1841). Another prominent work, measured by the standards of his time, is his *Historica narratio de Fratrum Orthodoxorum ecclesiis in Bohemia, Moravia et Polonia*, which was first edited in 1605 by his grandson Joachim Ludwig Camerarius and is still valuable. Camerarius also edited (though badly) the letters of Melanchthon (Leipsic, 1569), and rendered great services to historical research by his collection of letters from the time of the Reformation, which was continued by his son. (T. KOLDE.)

BIBLIOGRAPHY: E. C. Bezzel, *Joachim Camerarius*, Nuremberg, 1793; H. J. Kämmel, *Joachim Camerarius in Nürnberg*, Zittau, 1862; F. Seckt, *Ueber einige theologischen Schriften des J. Camerarius*, Berlin, 1888; *KL*, ii. 1758-1761; *ADB*, iii. 720 sqq.

CAMERLINGO (CAMERLENGO). See CURIA, § 1.

CAMERON, GEORGE GORDON: Free Church of Scotland; b. at Pluscarden (a village near Elgin, 71 m. n.w. of Aberdeen), Elginshire, Sept. 13, 1836. He was educated at University and King's College, Aberdeen (M.A., 1860), Free Church College, Aberdeen (1860-62), and New College, Edinburgh (1863-65). He was a tutor on the Continent in 1862-63 and in 1865-66 was assistant minister in Leghorn, Italy. He was then assistant minister in Dundee, Scotland, for a year and at Kuthrieston, Aberdeen, in 1867-69, and after another year as temporary professor of Hebrew in Free Church College in 1869-70 was assistant minister for brief periods at St. Andrews, Edinburgh, London, and North Leith in 1870-71. In the latter year he was ordained associate minister of St. John's Free Church, Glasgow, and retained this position until 1882, when he was appointed to the chair of Old Testament language and literature in the United Free Church College, Aberdeen, where he still remains. He is a member of various committees for the general work of his sect, and has written, in addition to contributions to periodicals, *Memorials of John Roxburgh* (Glasgow, 1881).

CAMERON (CAMERO), JOHN: Scottish theologian; b. at Glasgow c. 1579; d. at Montauban, France, 1625. He studied at Glasgow and began to give lessons in Greek there at the age of twenty. In 1600 he went to Bordeaux and was soon appointed professor of the humanities at Bergerac. From 1601 to 1603 he was professor of divinity at Sédan. Then he returned to Bordeaux and received a scholarship enabling him to complete his theological studies. He became tutor in the family of Calignon and went with his pupils to Paris, Geneva, and Heidelberg. At the university of the last-named place on Apr. 4, 1608, he supported in a a public discussion theses *de triplici Dei cum ho-*

mine fœdere. Later in the same year he became a minister at Bordeaux and had great success as a preacher. When the Protestants were driven from the town after eight years he took refuge at Tonneins. He was appointed professor at the Academy of Saumur in 1618. In 1620 he participated in a discussion at Orléans with Tilenus, formerly professor at Sédan, and controverted his Arminian propositions. In 1622 James I. of England called him to London and appointed him principal and professor of theology at Glasgow. But the jealousy of many of his colleagues forced him to leave his native town and in 1623 he returned to Saumur. The following year the king authorized him to teach at Montauban. He arrived there at a time when there was violent contention on the question of obedience to the king and took sides with the party of passive obedience. On May 15, 1625, he was injured in a public tumult and died in consequence a few months later. His works are: *Discours apologétique pour ceux de la religion réformée* (Bergerac, 1614); *Traité auquel sont examinés les préjugés de ceux de l'Église romaine contre la religion réformée* (La Rochelle, 1616; Eng. transl., Oxford, 1624); *Theses de gratia et libero arbitrio* (Saumur, 1618); *Amica collatio de gratiæ et humanæ voluntatis concursu in vocatione* (Leyden, 1621); *Defensio sententiæ de gratia et libero arbitrio* (Saumur, 1624); and *Prælectiones* (3 vols., 1626–28).

G. Bonet-Maury.

Bibliography: Sources for a life are: the memoir by Cappel prefixed to Cameron's *Opera*, Geneva, 1642; Robert Baillie, *Letters and Journals*, passim, 2 vols., Edinburgh, 1775. Consult also: D. Irving, *Scottish Writers*, i. 333–346, London, 1850; R. Chambers, *Biographical Dictionary of Eminent Scotchmen*, i. 273–275, Edinburgh, 1868; *DNB*, viii. 295–296.

CAMERON, RICHARD, CAMERONIANS: Scotch covenanting leader (b. at Falkland, Fifeshire; killed at Ayrsmoss or Airdsmoss, Ayrshire, July 22, 1680), and his followers. Brought up in the Church of Scotland, early impressed by the services of those ministers who, ejected by the Act of Uniformity (q.v.) of 1662, continued to preach in the fields, Cameron adopted and advocated their view that it was wrong to accept the Declaration of Indulgence (q.v.) of 1662, although it mitigated their lot. Licensed by these field preachers, although without university training, he soon became a leader. In 1679 he went to Holland, whither many of his persecuted countrymen had gone after the defeat in the battle of Bothwell Bridge, June 22, 1679; in 1680 he returned and with Donald Cargill (q.v.) and Thomas Douglas headed the party, which after him was called "Cameronians," or impersonally "Society People." Their platform was the Declaration of Sanquhar (published June 22, 1680), drawn up by Cameron and others. In it the royal authority was disowned because of its tyranny. This action brought Cameron and his followers immediately into trouble. A band with him at its head was attacked by the royal troops and literally cut to pieces.

The party lived in and were united in "societies," which had become somewhat numerous before the Revolution. They welcomed King William; but they did not approve of the Revolution settlement, and did not join the Established Church. They objected to the Church, which had made many unworthy compromises; were displeased at the want of recognition of the covenants; did not consider that the independence of the Church was secured; and generally believed that God was not sufficiently honored in the new settlement. They objected, too, to the recognition of Erastianism in England. In 1706 the Rev. John Macmillan of Balmaghie joined the societies, and was their first minister. In 1743, another minister having joined them, they constituted "the Reformed Presbytery." In 1774 a similar presbytery was formed in the United States. A presbytery was constituted likewise in Ireland. About 1863 most of the Scotch synod came to be of opinion that there was nothing in their principles requiring them to abstain from countenancing the political institutions of the country, e.g., from voting for a member of Parliament; but, a small minority having a different opinion, a disruption took place. In 1876 a union took place between the larger body and the Free Church of Scotland. Although "Cameronians" has always been a common name given to those who refused to accept the settlement of Church and State under William and Mary, they repudiated it themselves, preferring to be called "Reformed Presbyterians." See Covenanters; Presbyterians.

Bibliography: *Biographia presbyteriana*, vol. i., Edinburgh, 1827 (life of Cameron); R. Wodrow, *Hist. of the Sufferings of the Church of Scotland*, 2 vols., ib. 1721–22; T. McCrie, *Sketches of Scottish Church Hist.*, ib. 1875; J. Cunningham, *Church Hist. of Scotland*, 2 vols., ib. 1883; *DNB*, viii. 301–302.

CAMILLUS DE LELLIS. See Agonizants.

CAMISARDS, cam'i-zārds: The name generally applied to those French Protestants who, in the reign of Louis XIV., rose in arms in Languedoc and waged a bloody war (1702–05) for the purpose of restoring their Church. Their name was derived from the jacket (*camisia*) which they wore over their clothes during their night attacks. Neither the dragonades nor the revocation of the Edict of Nantes (1685) succeeded in destroying Protestantism in France; but, though private worship was never forbidden, new laws were continually enacted by Louis XIV. in his attempt to enforce conformity in religion throughout France, which made it more and more difficult, and at last almost impossible, for a French citizen to adhere to the Reformed confession. In 1686 and the following years the gatherings in the desert were forbidden, and fines, imprisonment, demolition of homes, the galleys, and the wheel were employed as punishments. Nevertheless, with the pressure grew the power of resistance. Religious meetings were held by night in secluded places, originally presided over by refugee clergy, and later by men of little learning, but fervent in prayers and exhortations.

Origin.

As was natural, the miseries of the time produced a corresponding hope of the future; and books like Pierre Jurieu's *L'Accomplissement des prophéties* (Rotterdam, 1686) and *Suite de l'accomplissement* (1687), in which he predicted the speedy downfall of the papacy, contributed to give shape and direction to this unconscious movement. A girl appeared as prophetess in Dauphiné in 1688. Other prophets arose in Vivarais. The number increased rapidly, especially in the Cévennes after 1700, where almost a fourth of the population was Protestant. Despite the creation of new bishoprics for their conversion and notwithstanding the military aid given by the State to the ecclesiastical authorities, ecstatic phenomena increased throughout the district, sparing neither old nor young. In the trance, when seized by convulsions, and pouring forth words of repentance and admonition, often in pure French instead of the local dialect, those "possessed by the spirit" saw troops from far-off garrisons come marching toward the place, they singled out those among their comrades who should fall in the encounter, they recognized the traitors among them; and these predictions were always accepted with reverence and confidence, and often proved true; although, on the other hand, the power of prophecy later steadily declined. Without this apocalyptic factor, diseased yet sincere, the enthusiasm and obstinacy of the Camisards is unintelligible. Terming themselves "children of God," and their camp the "camp of the Eternal," they relied with absolute trust on divine guidance and aid, while their fanaticism in destroying churches, like their cruelty in killing priests, finds its explanation in the fact that they believed themselves called of God to extirpate "Babylon and Satan," as they designated the Roman Catholic priests and their Church.

Fanatical Disorders.

Open revolt broke out in 1702, when a priest named François de Langlade du Chayla undertook to punish the refractory. In his house at Pont de Montvert, in the present department of Lozère, he built a cell in which he shut up his recalcitrant parishioners, and tortured them. On the night of July 23, hearing a rumor that the abbé intended to put certain prisoners to death, the Camisards assembled at the instigation of the prophets Séguier, Couderc, and Mazel, burned the house, liberated the prisoners, and slew the priest. Bâville, the intendant of Languedoc, felt a particular satisfaction in pursuing the guilty. Séguier was caught and burned at the stake Aug. 12; but the rest escaped among the mountains, where they were soon reenforced by new throngs formed by Castanet, Catinat, Roland, and others. In Jean Cavalier (b. at Ribante, department of Gard, Nov. 28, 1681) they found an able leader, and the war began which was to depopulate and devastate the provinces of Languedoc, Vivarais, Gevaudan, and Rouergue. The Camisards never numbered more than five thousand, and they had no military organization. But they fought with brutal fury, even when they marched into battle with psalms on their lips, while the royal troops punished them with torture and imprisonment. In their camps they lived as in a church, preaching, praying, and fasting; and they won brilliant victories, particularly at Sainte-Chatte, Mar. 15, 1704. Bâville was unable to make head against them, and in Feb., 1703, Marshal Montreval was sent with a large body of troops. He defeated the Camisards repeatedly (La Jonguière, Mar. 6; La Tour de Bélot, Apr. 29), but the cruelties practised by the troops won new adherents to the Protestant cause, even though he razed all the houses and villages in the upper Cévennes, thus rendering 20,000 homeless. The confusion was increased by a bull of Clement XI. (May 1, 1703), proclaiming a crusade against the heretics and creating bands which equaled their opponents in savagery. In Apr., 1704, Montreval was replaced by Marshal Villars. Before Villars began active operation, he surrounded the whole district with a line of strong military posts, thus cutting off all communication between the rebels and the outside world; and then he offered pardon to all who, within a certain time, laid down arms and surrendered. Cavalier, who saw that further resistance was useless, left the country, afterward fought against his countrymen in Holland, Italy, and Spain, and settled finally in England. There he was appointed governor of Jersey, and later governor of the Isle of Wight. He died in Chelsea, London, May 18, 1740. His former comrades branded him as a traitor and continued the hopeless struggle. Roland fell Aug. 14, 1704. Castanet, Catinat, Joanni, and others fled to Geneva. Without leaders, the Camisard army gradually melted away. In 1705 Catinat, Ravanel, and some of their colleagues returned and conspired to raise a new revolt, only to die at the stake or on the wheel. A last attempt, made by Mazel, Coste, and Claris in 1709 in Vivarais was quenched in blood, and the French Reformed Church was definitely blotted out. [In England the Camisards were known as the French Prophets (q.v.).]

The Camisard Wars.

(Theodor Schott†.)

Bibliography: For sources from the Roman Catholic standpoint consult: C. J. de la Baume, *Rélation historique de la révolte des Camisards*, ed. Goiffon, Nîmes, 1874; J. B. Louvreleuil, *Le Fanatisme renouvelé*, Avignon, 1704–1707; *Lettres choisies de Fléchier avec une rélation des fanatiques du Vivarez*, Paris, 1715 (partizan); *Mémoires de l'intendant Bâville*, Amsterdam, 1734 (serviceable); *Mémoires de Villars*, The Hague, 1734 (brief but impartial). Written from the Protestant side are: M. Misson, *Le Théâtre sacré des Cévennes*, London, 1707 (by an eyewitness, but partizan and unreliable); J. Cavalier, *Memoirs of the Wars of the Cévennes*, ib. 1712 (inaccurate). In the *Bulletin de la société de l'histoire du protestantisme français* are *Le Camp des enfants de Dieux*, 1867, pp. 273 sqq., and the memoirs of *Monbonnoux*, 1873, pp. 72 sqq. Read also *Mémoires de Rossel d'Aigaliers*, ed. G. Frostérus, in *Bibliothèque Universelle*, March–May, 1866, and A. Jäger, *Spiritus miraculosus in provincia Sevennensi regnans*, Tübingen, 1712. Consult further: A. Court, *Histoire de troubles des Cévennes*, Villefranche, 1760, ed. Alais, 1819 (rich and reliable); I. C. K. Hofmann, *Geschichte des Aufruhrs in den Sevennen unter Ludwig XIV.*, Nördlingen, 1837 (also valuable); N. Peyrat, *Histoire des pasteurs du désert*, Paris, 1842 (picturesque but unreliable); G. Frostérus, *Les Insurgés protestants sous Louis XIV.*, ib. 1868 (of importance); E. Bonnemère, *Histoire des Camisards*, Paris, 1869; S. Smiles, *Huguenots in France After the Edict of Nantes*, London, 1877; C. Tylor, *Huguenots in the Seventeenth Century*, pp. 255 sqq., London, 1892; H. M. Baird, *The Camisard Uprising*, in *Papers of the American Church Hist. Society*, ii. 13–34, New York, 1890; idem, *Huguenots and the Revocation of the Edict of Nantes*, vol. ii., ib. 1895.

CAMPANELLA, TOMASO: Italian monk and philosopher; b. at Stilo (30 m. n.e. of Reggio), Calabria, Sept. 5, 1568; d. in Paris May 21, 1639. He entered the Dominican order at the age of fifteen; studied philosophy and theology at Cosenza and Naples, and added to his other accomplishments a knowledge of medicine, astrology, alchemy, and magic. He boldly rejected the Aristotelian system and chose to study nature rather than authority, whereby he made many and powerful opponents. After wandering through Italy for a number of years he returned to Cosenza in 1598, and the next year was arrested by the government, charged, probably truthfully, with being implicated in a conspiracy to free Naples from the Spanish dominion. His political and social views were undeniably dangerous. He was kept in prison till 1626, when Pope Urban VIII. succeeded in having him transferred to the Inquisition, and in 1629 set him free. For a few years he lived at Rome, but, not feeling secure there, in 1634 he went to Paris, where he was received with favor by Cardinal Richelieu. His last years were spent in preparing a complete edition of his works, of which, however, only one or two volumes appear to have been published. The philosophy which Campanella would substitute for that of Aristotle was incomplete and fantastic, influenced by Thomas Aquinas, Bernardino Telesio (b. at Cosenza 1508), Raymund Lully, and the Cabala, but in part independent and in certain points anticipatory of the work of more modern thinkers. He held that God has made a twofold revelation of himself, in nature and in the Bible; on the one rests philosophy, on the other theology. These have nothing to do the one with the other. He was thus able to take a very conservative position in theology, and stoutly defended Roman Catholicism and the papacy (as in his *Monarchiæ Messiæ* and *Discorsi della liberta e della felice suggettione allo stato ecclesiastico*, Jesi, 1633). Certainty, he taught, is found only in immediate intuitions; the first truth is that I exist; then that I can, that I know, and that I want or will; these three activities indicate the fundamental qualities of all being (*potentia, sapientia, amor*). He believed that matter is eternal and that the world was created through emanations from the deity. His views concerning society and the State were communistic; they are set forth in his *Civitas solis, idea reipublicæ philosophicæ*, printed as an appendix to part iii. (*politica*) of his *Realis philosophiæ epilogisticæ partes iv, hoc est, de rerum natura, hominum moribus, politica, et œconomica* (Frankfort, 1623); there is an English translation (incomplete) by T. W. Halliday in *Ideal Commonwealths*, vol. xxiii. of "Morley's Universal Library" (London, 1885).

BIBLIOGRAPHY: Campanella is said to have written eighty-two works, most of them during his long imprisonment. He gives some account of them in his *De libris propriis et recta ratione studendi syntagma*, ed. G. Naudé, Paris, 1642. Among the more important of those which have been published, besides the ones already mentioned, are: *Philosophia sensibus demonstrata*, a defense of Telesio, Naples, 1590; *Prodromus philosophiæ instaurandæ*, Frankfort, 1617; *De sensu rerum et magia*, 1620; *Apologia pro Galileo*, 1622; *Astrologicorum libri vii*, 1630; *Atheismus triumphatus*, Rome, 1631; *Medicinalium libri vii*, Lyons, 1635; *De gentilismo non retinendo* and *De prædestinatione contra Thomisticos*, Paris, 1636; *Philosophiæ rationalis partes v, videlicet grammatica, dialectica, rhetorica, poetica, historiographia*, 1638; *Universalis philosophiæ seu metaphysicarum rerum juxta propria dogmata partes iii, libri xviii*, 1638; *De monarchia hispanica*, Amsterdam, 1640, Eng. transl., *A Discourse Touching the Spanish Monarchy*, London, 1654. A selection from his works by A. d'Ancona appeared in 2 volumes at Turin, 1854. His sonnets have been translated into English by J. A. Symonds with the sonnets of Michelangelo, London, 1878. For his life and criticism of his writings and teachings consult: Cyprian, *Vita et philosophia T. Campanellæ*, Amsterdam, 1705, 2d ed., 1722; M. Baldacchini, *Vita e filosofia di T. Campanella*, Naples, 1840; Berti, *La vita e le opere di T. Campanella*, Rome, 1878; L. Amabile, *Fra Tommaso Campanella, la sua congiura, i suoi processi, e la sua pazzia*, 3 vols., Naples, 1882; idem, *L'andata di Fra T. Campanella a Roma dopo la lunga prigionia di Napoli*, ib. 1886; idem, *Fra T. Campanella ne' castelli di Napoli, in Roma ed in Parigi*, 2 vols., ib. 1887; idem, *Del carattere di Fra T. Campanella*, ib. 1890; E. Nys, *T. Campanella et ses théories politiques*, Brussels, 1889; G. S. Felici, *Le dottrine filosofico-religiose di T. Campanella*, Lanciano, 1895; P. Lafargue, in *Die Vorläufer des neueren Socialismus*, pp. 469–506, Stuttgart, 1895; von Koslowski, *Die Erkenntnislehre Campanellas*, Leipsic, 1897.

CAMPANUS, cam-pā'nus, **JOHANNES:** Reformer; b. at Maeseyck (17 m. n.e. of Maestricht) in Belgium; d. at Jülich (Juliers, 15 m. n.e. of Aachen) c. 1575. He studied at Cologne, whence he was expelled in 1520 for opposing the scholastic doctors; went to Jülich and was noted for his vehement Lutheranism; went to Wittenberg in 1527; was present at the Conference of Marburg in 1529, and surprised both sides by his presentation of the view that the bread is indeed bread and at the same time the body of Christ because he makes it so. He was not, however, allowed to take part in the debate. This snub and others incurred by his tendency to unorthodox views turned him against the Reformers and them against him. He was called insane because he would not yield to their arguments. So he was repeatedly imprisoned and died a prisoner. In 1530 he prepared a book in Latin and German "Against All the World Since the Apostles" and circulated it in manuscript—no complete or printed copy is known to exist, but extracts have been preserved in a manuscript by Bugenhagen (cf. *ZHT*, 1846, pp. 495 sqq.). In 1532 one of his followers, Franz von Streitten, published a popular restatement of his views which he dedicated to King Frederick of Denmark. He taught that the Holy Spirit was not the Third Person but the common essence of the two, while the Son was not coeternal with the Father but, created out of his essence, before all creatures. He was likewise an Anabaptist and in general a radical.

(A. HEGLER†) K. HOLL.

BIBLIOGRAPHY: F. S. Bock, *Historia antitrinitariorum* ii. 244 sqq., Leipsic, 1784; G. J. Dlabacz, *Biographie des J. Campanus, mit einem Verzeichnisse seiner Schriften*, Prague, 1804; K. Reinbert, *Die "Wiedertaufer" im Jülich*, Berlin, 1899; J. Köstlin, *Martin Luther*, vol. ii. passim, Berlin, 1903.

CAMPBELL, ALEXANDER: Founder of the Disciples of Christ (q.v.); b. near Ballymena (a mile from Shane's Castle on the northern shore of Lough Neagh), County Antrim, Ireland, Sept. 12, 1788; d. at Bethany, W. Va., Mar. 4, 1866. He was the son of Thomas Campbell, a Seceder minister, and Jane Carneigle. Educated at Glasgow University, he went to America in 1809, whither his father had preceded him two years earlier, and settled in western Pennsylvania. While at Glasgow he had come in contact with James Alexander and Robert Haldane (q.v.) and was greatly impressed by their teaching. On joining his father, he found Providence had guided him into the same liberal and independent views. Thomas Campbell's fraternity with other Christians, his indifference to ecclesiastical rules, and his pleadings in behalf of Christian liberty and brotherhood had brought upon him the censure of his brethren; consequently he withdrew from them and continued to plead for Christian liberty and union, dwelling upon the evil of divisions in religious society, urging the Sacred Word as an infallible standard and all-sufficient and alone-sufficient basis of union, and setting forth one rule to govern himself and his associates: "Where the Scriptures speak, we speak; and where the Scriptures are silent, we are silent." On Sept. 7, 1809, he formed The Christian Association of Washington and issued his famous *Declaration and Address* (see DISCIPLES OF CHRIST). In May, 1811, The First Church of the Christian Association of Washington Co., Pa., was organized at Brush Run with twenty-nine members; here Alexander Campbell was ordained to the ministry Jan. 1, 1812.

His Father, Thomas Campbell.

Mr. Campbell's marriage in 1812 to Margaret Brown, a Presbyterian, turned his attention to the subject of baptism. After diligent study of the Scriptures and critical examination of the words "baptize" and "baptism," he became satisfied they could mean only "immerse" and "immersion," and that believers only could be the proper subjects of this ordinance. With his father and five others he was immersed by Mathias Luse, June 12, 1812. "I have set out," he said, "to follow the Apostles of Christ and their master, and I will be baptized only into the primitive Christian faith." From this time Thomas Campbell conceded to his son the guidance of the movement he had originated. The Brush Run church joined the Redstone Baptist Association after full statement of their views, using the primitive Confession of faith instead of a religious experience, and breaking bread weekly without restricted communion. A second church on the same basis was organized in Wellsburg, W. Va.

Adopts Baptist Views.

In 1820 Mr. Campbell held his first public discussion. He was not disputatious, and at first declined a challenge, but it was forced upon him. The debate was with the Rev. John Walker, a Presbyterian, and the chief point debated was the identity of the covenants upon which the Jewish and Christian institutions rested. His later discussions with Rev. N. L. Rice on baptism, the Holy Spirit, and human creeds as bonds of union, a debate which lasted sixteen days and over which Henry Clay presided (1843), with Robert Owen on the claims of Christianity (at Cincinnati, 1829), and with Archbishop Purcell on the claims of Roman Catholicism (also at Cincinnati, 1837) are masterpieces of discussion which created a profound impression in their time and did much to extend the principles advocated by Mr. Campbell.

Public Debates.

In 1823 Mr. Campbell began the publication of *The Christian Baptist*. In the first seven years from his little country printing-office he issued 46,000 volumes of his works. His writings were read far and wide. His views began to influence large numbers of people. He was assailed as a disorganizer, but it was not his aim merely to overthrow the existing order of religious society. He was well aware of the vast benefit resulting to mankind from Christianity even in its most corrupt forms. He desired simply to dethrone the false that he might reestablish the true, to replace the traditions of men by the teachings of Christ and the Apostles; to substitute the New Testament for creeds and human formularies. His work was positive, not negative. In 1825 he published in *The Christian Baptist* a series of articles entitled *A Restoration of the Ancient Order of Things*, in which he argued for the abandonment of everything not in use among the early Christians, such as creeds and confessions, unscriptural words and phrases, theological speculations, etc., and for the adoption of everything sanctioned by primitive practise, as the weekly breaking of the loaf, the fellowship, the simple order of worship, and the independence of each church under the care of elders and deacons. His plea was not for a reformation, but for a restoration of the original Church.

His Views and Aims.

In 1826 Mr. Campbell published *The Sacred Writings of the Apostles and Evangelists of Jesus Christ, Commonly Styled the New Testament*, with notes. In this work he Anglicized the Greek words commonly rendered "baptism," "baptize," etc., being the first to do so in an English version. The principles taught by the Campbells were now widespread, especially among the Baptists; but in 1827 Baptist Associations began to declare non-fellowship with the brethren of "the Reformation" and from this time dates the rise of the people known as the Disciples of Christ.

In 1829 Mr. Campbell began to publish the *Millennial Harbinger*, a magazine which he continued to issue monthly until his death. In October of the same year he sat in the Virginia State Constitutional Convention. Ex-President Madison, one of his fellow delegates, said of him afterward: "I regard him as the ablest and most original expounder of Scripture I ever heard." In 1840 he founded Bethany College with the Bible as a text-book. In 1847 he traveled and preached in Great Britain. This was his busiest period; he traveled thousands of miles, lectured and preached constantly, edited, presided over the College, and held public discussions. In June, 1850, he spoke before both houses of Congress at the Capitol at Washington. He was gifted with a fine presence, with great ease and skill of utterance,

His Most Active Years.

with fine argumentative powers, and with a great fund of information. He was a man of profound piety and broad philanthropy. "Surely," said George D. Prentice, "the life of a man thus excellent and gifted is a part of the common treasure of society. In this essential character he belongs to no party, but to the world." His publications include sixty volumes. F. D. POWER.

BIBLIOGRAPHY: Robert Richardson, *Memoirs of Alexander Campbell*, Cincinnati, 1888; B. B. Tyler, in *American Church History Series*, xii. 34-59, New York, 1894.

CAMPBELL, ARCHIBALD EAN: Anglican bishop of Glasgow and Galloway, Scotland; b. at Skipness, Argyll, June 1, 1856; graduated B.A. at Cambridge, 1880; became vicar of the Walter Farquhar Hook Memorial Church in Leeds, 1891; was consecrated bishop 1904.

CAMPBELL, GEORGE: Church of Scotland divine; b. at Aberdeen Dec. 25, 1719; d. there Apr. 6, 1796. He was educated at Marischal College, Aberdeen, and began the study of law in Edinburgh, but changed to theology, which he pursued there and in Aberdeen; was ordained minister of Banchory Ternan (on the Dee, 20 m. from Aberdeen), 1748; became one of the ministers of Aberdeen, 1757; principal of Marischal College, 1759, professor of divinity, 1771; resigned on account of ill health, 1795. He was one of the founders in 1758 of a famous philosophical society of Aberdeen, which included among its members Thomas Reid, John Gregory, James Beattie, and other distinguished men. His publications were sermons and *A Dissertation on Miracles*, an answer to Hume's *Essay* (Edinburgh, 1762; 3d ed., with corrections and additions and correspondence between Hume and Campbell, 2 vols., 1797); *The Philosophy of Rhetoric*, long considered a standard work (2 vols., London, 1776; many subsequent editions); *The Four Gospels, translated from the Greek, with preliminary dissertations and notes, critical and explanatory* (2 vols., 1789). Posthumous publications were *Lectures on Ecclesiastical History*, with a brief *Life* by G. S. Keith (2 vols., London, 1800), and *Lectures on Systematic Theology and on Pulpit Eloquence* (1807). A collected edition of his *Theological Works* appeared in six volumes at London, 1840.

CAMPBELL, JOHN McLEOD: Scotch clergyman; b. at Kilninver (on the w. coast of Scotland, 60 m. n.w. of Glasgow), Argyllshire, May 4, 1800; d. at Roseneath, near Helensburgh (20 m. n.w. of Glasgow), Dumbartonshire, Feb. 27, 1872. He studied at Glasgow 1811-20, and continued his theological course at Edinburgh; became minister of Row (near Helensburgh), Dumbartonshire, 1825. Here he preached "assurance of faith" and an "unlimited atonement," and in consequence was tried for heresy and deposed by the General Assembly in 1831 (cf. the volume of his *Sermons and Lectures*, Greenock, 1832, and *The Whole Proceedings Before the Presbytery of Dumbarton and the Synod of Glasgow and Ayr in the Case of the Rev. John McLeod Campbell*, 1831). He retired to Kilninver, preached in the Highlands for a year or two, and in 1833 became pastor of an independent congregation in Glasgow and remained there till compelled to retire by ill health in 1859. His services were given gratuitously and were very successful. He was recognized as one of the intellectual leaders of Scotland and was highly esteemed for his personal qualities. His theory of the atonement, by which he was best known outside of Glasgow, he expressed in this sentence in the book on the Atonement mentioned below: "It was the spiritual essence and nature of the sufferings of Christ, and not that these sufferings were penal, which constituted their value as entering into the atonement made by the Son of God, when he put away sin by a sacrifice of himself." He published *Christ the Bread of Life* (Glasgow, 1851), a book on the Eucharist suggested by the Roman Catholic controversy of the time; *The Nature of the Atonement and its relation to remission of sins and eternal life* (Cambridge, 1856; 4th ed., 1873); *Thoughts on Revelation* (1862), called forth by *Essays and Reviews* (q.v.).

BIBLIOGRAPHY: A volume of *Reminiscences and Reflexions*, begun in 1871 and left unfinished at his death, appeared in London in 1873, edited by his son, Donald Campbell, who also edited his *Memorial*, 2 vols., London, 1877; J. Vaughan, in *Contemporary Review*, June, 1878 (an account of Dr. Campbell's views); *DNB*, viii. 388-389.

CAMPBELL, REGINALD JOHN: English Congregationalist; b. at London Jan. 29, 1867. He was educated at University College, Nottingham, and Christ Church, Oxford (B.A., 1895), and entered the Congregational ministry in 1895. After being pastor of Union Church, Brighton, from 1895 to 1903, he succeeded Joseph Parker as minister of the City Temple, London, a position which he still retains. In theology he is a liberal evangelical. He has written: *The Restored Innocence* (London, 1898); *The Making of an Apostle* (1898); *A Faith for Today* (1900); *City Temple Sermons* (1903); *Sermon to Young Men* (1904; American edition under the title *The Choice of the Highest*, Chicago, 1904); *Sermons Addressed to Individuals* (1905); *Song of Ages* (1906); *The New Theology* (1907); *New Theology Sermons* (1907); *Religion and Social Reform* (1907).

BIBLIOGRAPHY: A. H. Wilkerson, *Reginald John Campbell, the Man and his Message*, London, 1907.

CAMPBELLITES. See CAMPBELL, ALEXANDER; DISCIPLES OF CHRIST.

CAMPEGGIO, cām-ped'jō **(CAMPEGI, CAMPEGGI, CAMPEGIUS), LORENZO:** Italian cardinal and statesman; b. at Milan Nov. 7, 1474; d. at Rome July 25, 1539. His father was a noted professor of law at Pavia, Padua, and Bologna, and the son, adopting his father's career, became lecturer on imperial and papal law and the Decretals at Bologna after 1499. He participated in the political life of the university town and won the attention of the Curia by his ardent advocacy of the papal cause against the imperial family of Bentivogli. The loss of his wife hastened his entrance into the priestly state, for which he had long cherished a strong inclination. Julius II. made him representative for Bologna at the tribunal of the Rota in Rome in the early part of 1511. In August he went as nuncio to the court of the emperor Maximilian to win that ruler away from his support of the Pisan council and for the pope's scheme of a Lateran council. Returning successful in 1512 he was made bishop of Feltre and sent as nuncio to the court of Maximilian Sforza at Milan, but was recalled to be entrusted with a second mission to the imperial court with the object, this time, of furthering the papal plan for the reestablishment of general peace in Europe. At this post he remained till 1517, when on account of his "preeminent services to the Apostolic chair" and for a fee of 24,000 ducats he was created cardinal in company with thirty others. Once more Campeggio was sent on a mission of universal peace, this time to England, where he shared the dignity of papal legate with Cardinal Wolsey and participated in the formation of the General League of Peace concluded in October, 1518. In the same year he returned to Rome, bearing with him many royal gifts and the promise of the succession to the bishopric of Salisbury. He became bishop of Bologna in 1523, but resigned the office two years later on acquiring possession of the promised English see and retained it till 1535. He enjoyed at the same time the profits from a Spanish bishopric and from other churches, though it is difficult to determine precisely which. Alone among the cardinals he seems to have won the confidence of Adrian VI. and to him (not to Egidio of Viterbo) must be attributed the authorship of the reform memorial addressed to the pope. After the ill success of the papal cause at the first diet of Nuremberg, Campeggio was sent to Germany to work for the enforcement of the Edict of Worms. At the second Nuremberg diet he met the demands of the German princes with insulting pride, but by all his efforts could not prevent the assembly from expressing the demand for a meeting of the representatives of the German nation to consider means for the settlement of the religious question. It was Campeggio who was primarily responsible for the league concluded at Regensburg in the summer of 1524 by the enemies of the Reformation, the first of the partizan confederations that were to result in the dismemberment of the nation. At Regensburg, too, a scheme of reform for the clergy was formulated by Campeggio with the aid of Nausea and Cochlæus, a scheme, however, which never attained practical effect. An unsuccessful mission to England in 1528–29 in the matter of the divorce of Henry VIII. was followed by an appointment to the imperial court, where he is known to have advised Charles V. in case a policy of conciliation toward the Protestants proved ineffective "to eradicate the poisonous growth with fire and sword." At the same time he did not disdain to attempt the milder means of bribery, notably in the case of Melanchthon. In 1532 Campeggio returned to Rome. His last phase of activity was in connection with the plans of Paul III. for a general council. A memorial on the *Centum gravamina Germanorum*, written in 1536, shows that by that time Campeggio had arrived at a different view of the claims and rights of the German nation.

(T. Brieger.)

Bibliography: C. Sigonius, *De vita Laurentii Campegii*, Bologna, 1581, republished in *Sigonii Opera omnia*, iii. 531–576, Milan, 1733; S. Ehses, *Römische Dokumente zur Geschichte der Ehescheidung Heinrichs VIII., 1527–34*, pp. xvi.–xxxi., Paderborn, 1893.

CAMPELLO, COUNT ENRICO DE: Roman Catholic; b. at Rome in the year 1831; d. in the year 1903. Brought up in the Roman Catholic Church, he became priest 1855, and canon of St. Peter's, Rome, 1868. Feeling himself unable, however, to accept the dogma of papal infallibility, he resigned his office in 1881 and became a member of the Methodist Episcopal Church. Later he joined the Protestant Episcopal Church, and founded the Reformed Italian Catholic Church, of which he was consecrated bishop by Bishop E. Herzog in Switzerland. He worked for many years, first in Rome without success and later in Umbria, but in 1902 returned to the Roman Catholic faith. He wrote: *Cenni autobiografici che rendono ragione dell' uscita di lui dalla chiesa papale* (Rome, 1881).

Bibliography: A. Robertson, *Count Campello and Catholic Reform in Italy*, London, 1891.

CAMPION, EDMUND: Jesuit; b. in London Jan. 25, 1540; hanged there at Tyburn Dec. 1, 1581. He won much distinction for ability and scholarship at school in London, and had a brilliant career at St. John's College, Oxford (B.A., 1561; M.A., 1565); in 1567 he was ordained deacon in the Church of England, but, having always been a Roman Catholic at heart, in 1569 or 1570 he went to Ireland, hoping to find employment in a new university to be located in Dublin. The scheme fell through and he returned to England, went thence to Douai, where he openly renounced Protestantism, finished his theological studies, and took the degree of B.D. In 1573 he joined the Jesuits in Rome, and was sent to Prague, where he was ordained deacon and priest in 1578. In June, 1580, he entered England as a missionary of his order, and preached and worked there with success until July, 1581, when he was arrested and committed to the Tower. He was treated with much severity, was several times examined under torture, and in November was condemned, after an unfair trial, upon a charge of having conspired to dethrone the queen. He is described by Protestants as well as Roman Catholics as a man of uncommon ability, an eloquent orator, of much diplomatic skill, and amiable in disposition and life. His chief work was the *Decem rationes*, in which he challenges the Protestants to meet him in debate and professes himself ready to prove the falsity of Protestantism and the truth of the Roman Catholic religion by argument upon any one of ten topics, finished about Easter, 1581, and printed ostensibly at Douai, but really in or near London, the same year; it was spread broadcast at commencement at Oxford in June (best edition by Silvester Petra-Sancta, Antwerp, 1631; Eng. transl., 1606, 1632, 1687, 1827). While in Ireland he wrote a history of the country which was used by Holinshed in compiling his *Chronicles* (1577), and was printed by Sir James Ware in his *History of Ireland* (Dublin, 1633; reprinted in *Ancient Irish Histories*, 1809).

Bibliography: R. Simpson, *Edmund Campion, a Biog-*

raphy, London, 1867 ("perhaps the most able monograph of Catholic history"); J. A. Froude, *History of England*, vol. xi., chap. xxviii., London, 1870; E. L. Taunton, *The History of the Jesuits in England, 1580–1771*, ib. 1901; J. Gillow, *Bibliographical Dictionary of the English Catholics*, i. 370–392, London, n.d. (a full list of his works is appended); *DNB*, viii. 398–402.

CAMP-MEETINGS: Religious gatherings held in a grove, usually lasting for several days, during which many find shelter in tents or temporary houses. The main features are the open-air preaching, the night prayer-meetings, and the freedom of the life. They are not now so common as formerly. The first meeting of the kind is said to have taken place in Kentucky, on the banks of the Red River, in 1799, under a Presbyterian and a Methodist minister. These denominations at first used them in common; but gradually the Presbyterians withdrew, and they became almost exclusively Methodist and Baptist gatherings. In recent times the Methodists have purchased tracts of land in desirable locations on the seaboard or inland, and turned them into parks, with comfortable houses, streets, post-offices, meeting-places, Biblical models, etc., and there in the summer many persons live, and there the religious gatherings of different kinds are held daily. Thus the primitive camp-meeting is continued in an improved form. The credit of introducing camp-meetings into England is due to the Rev. Lorenzo Dow (q.v.), an eccentric though able minister of Methodist views, who in 1807 proposed it in Staffordshire. Two Methodists, William Clowes and Hugh Bourne, were so impressed with the advantages of this style of service that they persisted in holding them after they were disapproved by the Wesleyan Conference in 1807; for doing which they were finally expelled. In 1810 they founded the Primitive Methodists, which body uses the camp-meeting The Irish Wesleyans commenced using them in 1860.

Bibliography: S. C. Swallow, *Camp-Meetings: their Origin, Hist., and Utility, also their Perversion*, New York, 1878.

CAMUS, cä''mü', de Pont Carré, JEAN PIERRE: French prelate; b. in Paris Nov. 3, 1584; d. there Apr. 25, 1652. He became successively bishop of Belley 1609, abbot of Aulnay in Normandy 1629, but retired to the Hospital des Incurables in Paris 1651. He was an extremely prolific writer. The catalogue of his writings (Paris, 1653) contains 186 titles. Among them are many moral romances, which were admired in his time, and some translated into English, but are now forgotten. He is still remembered for his satirical pamphlets against the mendicant orders, e.g., *Désappropriation Claustrelle* and *Pauvreté Evangélique*, which were elaborately refuted in *Anti-Camus* (Douai, 1634), and especially for the fruit of his great intimacy with Francis of Sales, *L'Esprit du bien-heureux François de Sales* (6 vols., Paris, 1641, new ed., 3 vols., 1840, abridged by Collot, 1737; Eng. transl. of abridgement, *The Spirit of S. Francis de Sales*, London, 1880). His dogmatic work in the Latin translation *Appropinquatio Protestantium ad Ecclesiam Catholico-Romanam* is in vol. v. of Migne's *Cours de théologie*.

Bibliography: F. Boulas, *Camus*, Lyons, 1879.

CANA. See Galilee, II., § 4.

CANAAN, CANAANITES.

Canaan, Canaanites, are names given in the Old Testament and elsewhere to the land acquired by the Hebrews and to the pre-Hebraic people who occupied it. Apart from a few cases of personification, Canaan is the general name applied to the country (Judges v. 19; in JE, Gen. xlii.; in P, Gen. xi. 31). It is formed from *Kana'* with the addition of the *n* denoting place; the simple form does not occur in the Old Testament, but there is abundant evidence in the Amarna tablets and elsewhere that it was used. It is also clear that it was not originally a proper name. The significance of the word is not clear, though many attempts to discover it have been made. It seems in some places to have the signification of "Lowland" (Num. xiii. 29; Josh. v. 1; Zeph. ii. 5).

1. The Name.

In some of the Egyptian inscriptions the word is used to denote the part of Asia under Egyptian control, including Phenicia; but the general custom of Egyptians was to designate southern Syria by *Haru* and northern Syria by *Rutennu*. In the Amarna tablets it means what is now understood by Syria. Old Testament usage varies. In Gen. x. 19 (JE) it includes Phenicia, the land of Israel, and Philistia, with boundaries undefined on the north, a usage followed generally by D, though Deut. xi. 24 extends the eastern boundary to the Euphrates. The general statement is justified that in the Old Testament the name is used to designate what is now meant by Syria, without very definite boundaries, generally excluding lands east of the Jordan. And Canaanites designated the people who inhabited the land of Canaan, except that E uses "Amorites" (q.v.) to express this meaning.

The question is suggested whether the Canaanites had anything in common apart from their dwelling in the land so designated. Isa. xix. 18 mentions "the language of Canaan," a phrase which implies that a common language was there used. Of course there were dialectical differences, say, between the north and the south, but these were not such that the inhabitant of one part could not understand the inhabitant of another. Historic and inscriptional evidence bears this out. Besides unity of language there was a common conception of religion. The deities were originally nature-powers such as the sun, the heavens, the moon, thunder and lightning.

2. Language and Religion.

With advance of civilization they blended, and while worship was still offered at numerous local shrines. At these the proper names of the deities were not generally used, the gods were spoken of as the *Ba'al* "Lord" or the *Ba'alah* "Mistress" of the place, e.g., Baal-Hermon, "Lord of Hermon." The places of worship were the tops of the hills (see High Places). Near the altar stood a sacred stone or tree or pillar. If there were an image of the deity, there was also a temple or a house and a priest. The customs of worship were in the closest connection with the work of daily life, the offerings were of the products of field, garden, vineyard, or pasture. In the cities more developed forms took their place. The myth was everywhere employed, at first in local form, later in philosophical and poetical development in which origins, destinies, beginnings of human customs, and the beginnings of cities and holy localities had their place. In some places prostitution for religious purposes was practised, also self-mutilation and infant-sacrifice. There were also numerous practises which were survivals from primitive worship, from animism, totemism, and fetishism. The culture of the people had in general a common stamp. Babylonian influence had advanced by the third millennium B.C. at least as far south as central Syria. Egypt's influence was first felt about 1500 B.C. While northern Syria immediately bordered on the Euphrates, a desert stretched between southern Syria and Egypt. The fact that the Amarna tablets, which are classed as Egyptian documents, are in the cuneiform shows that Babylonian ideas were dominant, though some admixture of Egyptian ideas must be allowed.

The middle position of Syria, between the east and the west, between the desert and the sea, introduces another occupation besides those mentioned in which the inhabitants engaged, commerce. Before the sea was traversed by ships, the roads from the Euphrates to Egypt passed through north and south Syria. Sea-travel later opened up routes which included the Mediterranean and the Red Sea. The products of Canaan proper were small in proportion to those resulting from commercial operations. These became, therefore, the favorite employment of the Canaanites, and their name became synonymous with merchant (Ezek xvi. 29, R. V. margin).

3. Commerce.

There were no great states built up in Canaan (the Hebrews are not here under discussion) except that of the Hittites (q.v.), who possessed a great kingdom in northern Syria. Apart from this only small states are mentioned. The Amarna tablets make known a number of these as at war with each other and as accused of unfaithfulness to the Pharaohs Amenophis III. and IV. Egyptian overlordship was maintained more or less completely 1500–1200 B.C. The sons of the local kings were sent to Egypt for their education, and their enthronement when they succeeded to power was the deed of the Pharaoh. The topography of the country, cut up by mountain ranges with intervening valleys and wadis, is not favorable to the formation and maintaining of great states; even those of Damascus and of Israel were not long-lived.

4. Political Relations.

According to the representation in Gen. x. 18b, the Canaanites had spread from the central part toward the south. This can not be proved, but the course of subsequent historical movements makes it probable. The custom of E in using "Amorites" to connote the inhabitants of the land and the known course of the progress of this people is one of these indications. Only faint recollections of the primitive dwellers are preserved in the Old Testament, in such passages as Deut. ii. 10–11; II Sam. xxi. 16, 18, 20, 22, where they appear as "giants," a mythical term (cf. Amos ii. 9). From them the Plain of Rephaim west of Jerusalem received its name. In the passages from Samuel quoted above *Raphah*, "the Giant," is named as their ancestor. Deut. ii. 11 reckons the Anakim as belonging to them, and Num. xiii. 33 is an expression of their physical stature; their chief town is named as Kirjath-arba, the latter part of which name is explained as the name of the ancestor and the greatest of the Anakim (Josh. xiv. 15, xv. 13).

5. The Earlier Inhabitants.

The Old Testament employs the term Canaanites not only in the sense explained in the foregoing as the common name of the inhabitants of Canaan, but also in an ethnographical sense of one of the stocks included. But from the preceding discussion the doubt is raised whether this usage is original or has ethnological worth. For decision of this question it is important to note that the Canaanites are mentioned among other peoples of Canaan when the author wishes to note a great number of peoples whom the Hebrews had subdued. In this case a settled form was employed with an alternative form. The common form was "Canaanite, Hittite, Amorite, Perizzite, Hivite, and Jebusite" (in eleven passages), in which the intention is clear to place the more important peoples first in the arrangement. The alternative form is "Amorite, Perizzite, Canaanite, Hittite, Girgashite, Hivite, and Jebusite" (Josh. xxiv. 11). This last is varied by the insertion of Kenites, Kenizzites, and Kadmonites (Gen. xv. 19–21), or by the omission of one or more from the list (for Kenites see CAIN, KENITES; for Kenizzites see CALEB, CALEBITES, and see also AMORITES and JEBUS, JEBUSITES).

6. Peoples Mentioned in the Bible.

The Hittites have become more familiar through the decipherment of the hieroglyphs and cuneiform inscriptions than through the Old Testament. Thothmes III. (c. 1500 B.C.) first came into contact with them in the district later known as Commagene on the northern boundary of Syria. A hundred years later they were in possession of a kingdom which stretched from the Euphrates to the middle Orontes, including Hamath within its bounds. Rameses II. (c. 1300–1230 B.C.) waged a long war with them, and in the twenty-first year of his reign made a treaty in which a demarcation of the boundaries of their respective realms was agreed upon. About 1200 B.C. this kingdom fell apart into a number of small states. In the ninth and eighth centuries the Assyrians mention a small Hittite kingdom encountered in their campaigns, that of Carchemish on the Euphrates. They also use the phrase "land of the Hittites" to denote the region between the Euphrates and the Taurus range and south as far as Palestine. But this can not be held to prove that the Hittite power extended so far. They left numerous inscriptions, in the attempt to decipher which P. Jensen is particularly engaged, and he thinks he can discover in the Hittites the forerunners of the Armenians. The Egyptians call the Hittites *Hata*, the Assyrians call them *Hatti*. Old Testament passages locate them in North Syria in close connection with the Arameans (I Kings x. 29) and II Kings vii. 6 associates them with the Syrian kingdom of Muṣri (according to Winckler, misread "Egypt," see ASSYRIA, VI., 2, 3, § 7). And the Table of Nations in Gen. x. 15 with its context leaves no doubt that the intention was to locate them in North Syria. The Hittites in the service of David (I Sam. xxvi. 6; II Sam. xi. 3) were probably soldiers of fortune who had come south. Some few Old Testament passages coincide with the late Assyrian usage and speak of the land far south as Hittite. See HITTITES.

7. The Hittites.

The Hivites are associated with the Amorites in the LXX. text of Isa. xvii. 9 (cf. R. V. margin), but, apart from the stereotyped formulas mentioned above, seldom appear in Scripture. II Sam. xxiv. 7 locates them among the Canaanites dwelling south of Tyre. According to Judges iii. 3, cf. Josh. xi. 3, their country was in Lebanon between "Baal-hermon and the entering in of Hamath." Josh. xi. 3 is not in accord with II Sam. xxiv. 7, and it does not lighten the difficulty to substitute Hittites for Hivites.

8. The Hivites.

The Horites according to Gen. xxxvi. 30 inhabited Mt. Seir, that is the district east and west of the valley (the wadi Arabah) south of the Dead Sea. They were destroyed by the Edomites (Deut. ii. 12, 22). Gen. xxxvi. 20–30 counts seven branches of the Horites. Gen. xiv. 6 assigns to them the mountain east of the wadi Arabah. Nowadays the custom prevails to connect them with the people named *Haru* by the Egyptians, who mean by it South Palestine.

9. The Horites.

The Perizzites are seldom mentioned except in the stereotyped formulas; in three J passages, Gen. xiii. 7, xxxiv. 30; Judges i. 4, they are associated with the Canaanites, and in Josh. xvii. 15 with the *Rephaim*, "Giants." The last passage would make of them pre-Canaanites, for which the J passages give no occasion, but locate them about Bethel, Shechem, and Bezek, within the boundaries of the Joseph territory.

10. The Perizzites.

The Geshurites are in Deut. iii. 14; Josh. xii. 5, xiii. 11, 13 placed in the Aramaic district of Geshur, in the northern part of the Jaulan east of the Jordan; but Josh. xiii. 2 and I Sam. xxvii. 8 locate them in southern Philistia. Since Wellhausen, the last passage has been made to read "Gezerites" instead. But it must be concluded that the name Geshurites was applied to nomads in southern Palestine. Besides the foregoing there appear the Girgashites (Gen. x. 16, etc.), to be connected, perhaps, with names known to be Phenician; the Avvim (Deut. ii. 23; Josh. xiii. 3), whose residence was south of Gaza; and the Kadmonites (Gen. xv. 19), of whom nothing is known.

11. The Geshurites.

The conquest of Canaan by the Hebrews was rendered easy by several circumstances. The overlordship of the Egyptians became about 1250 B.C. a mere name. Moreover, about 1400 B.C., according to the Amarna Tablets (q.v.), a people called the Ḥabiri had crossed the Jordan westward, partly because the chiefs there were employing them as soldiers and partly to better their lot. These, related to the Israelites, were indeed their predecessors along the same route, who by establishing themselves gave the invitation to others to settle there. But the light-armed Israelites, who established themselves in the more open country, had a more difficult task against the Canaanites armed with iron weapons and chariots of the same material. The assault of the Hebrews was not made with their united force and at one time, as the narrative in Joshua asserts, but in two divisions, and not at the same time. The first attack was made by Simeon, Levi, and Judah, the second by the Joseph tribes under the leadership of Joshua (Judges i. 1–3, 22). A series of victories, reported in Josh. ii.–x., made it possible for the Joseph tribes to settle between Bethel and the Plain of Jezreel. According to the first part of Joshua, the Hebrews put the ban on the Canaanites, i.e., exterminated them. But this does not agree with other statements. While indeed those foes were perhaps exterminated who were taken in actual contest, the universal application of the ban does not accord with many other passages of Scripture. The Canaanites were pressed back; progress in possession was made partly by subjecting the earlier inhabitants, partly by peaceful means. In the former case the Canaanites became slaves; in the latter, union of stocks was brought about. The victory at Taanach under Deborah and Barak assured to the Hebrews the control of the Plain of Jezreel. The northern districts of Naphtali and Asher retained their non-Israelitic population (see GALILEE). The southern stock of Judah in time allied itself with many peoples of alien race (see CALEB, CALEBITES, and cf. Gen. xxxviii.). The remainder of the non-Hebraic population was put to service by Solomon.

12. The Conquest by the Hebrews.

It is this reduction of the Canaanites to servitude which is at the basis of the narrative in Gen. ix. 20–27, which deals with Noah and his three sons. Wellhausen has made it plain that in ix. 22 the words "Ham the father of" are an intrusion by the editor to bring the section into harmony with its context. Canaan is the younger brother who is there subjected to his brethren. Shem no doubt, in the passage, means Israel, and Japhet the Phenicians, and Shem and Japhet are both ruling peoples. Canaan's position in the Table of Nations (q.v.) is quite other than that in Gen. ix. 20–27.

(H. GUTHE.)

BIBLIOGRAPHY: K. Budde, *Die biblische Urgeschichte*, Giessen, 1883; A. H. Sayce, *Races of the Old Testament*, London, 1891 (brief, needs bringing up to date); idem, *The 'Higher Criticism' and the Monuments*, ib. 1894; idem, *Patriarchal Palestine*, ib. 1895 (the last two books are damaged by their polemic aim); G. F. Moore, in *JAOS*,

xv. (1893), pp. lxvii.-lxx. (on the etymology); J. Benzinger, *Hebräische Archäologie*, § 12, Freiburg, 1894; E. Schrader, *Das Land Amurru*, in *Sitzungsberichte der Berliner Akademie*, Dec. 20, 1894; idem, *KAT*, Index s.vv. "Amoriter," "Amurru," "Kanaan"; J. F. McCurdy, *History, Prophecy and the Monuments*, vols. i.–ii., New York, 1895-96; F. Buhl, *Geographie des alten Palestina*, § 46, Tübingen, 1896; F. Hommel, *The Ancient Hebrew Tradition*, London, 1897; G. A. Smith, *Historical Geography of the Holy Land*, pp. 4–5, ib. 1897 (on the etymology); L. B. Paton, *Early History of Syria and Palestine*, New York, 1901 (an antidote for the works of Sayce and Hommel); W. Erbt, *Die Hebräer. Kanaan im Zeitalter der hebräischen Wanderung und hebräischen Staatengründungen*, Leipsic, 1906; H. Vincent, *Canaan d'après l'exploration récente*, Paris, 1907; *DB*, i. 347–348; *EB*, i. 638–643. The literature on the Amarna Tablets usually discusses the subject.

CANADA: A country of North America occupying the entire continent north of the United States except Alaska; area, 3,745,574 square miles; population (1901), 5,371,315 (estimated in 1909 at 6,100,000).

Political Divisions and Government.

The Dominion of Canada, the official designation of the country, was formed in 1867 by a confederation of the eastern provinces of Upper and Lower Canada (now Ontario and Quebec), New Brunswick, and Nova Scotia, the coalition being recognized by an Act of Parliament of the mother country. A governor-general, appointed by the king of England, and a privy council administer the government. The legislative power is a parliament consisting of a senate, whose members are appointed for life by the crown on nomination of the ministry, and a house of commons elected every five years at the longest. The Dominion now comprises, in addition to the provinces already named, Manitoba (admitted 1870), British Columbia (1871), Prince Edward Island (1873), Alberta (1905), Saskatchewan (1905), and the Northwest Territories comprising the districts of Assiniboia, Athabasca, Keewatin, Yukon, Mackenzie, Ungava, and Franklin. Each province has its own "lieutenant-governor," executive council, and legislative assembly. Nearly three-quarters of the entire population is in the two provinces of Ontario and Quebec, and almost ninety per cent in the five eastern provinces. The increase during the last decade was a little more than eleven per cent. There is no State Church, but the Roman Catholics of Quebec are guaranteed the privileges which they enjoyed previous to the English occupation.

History and Statistics.

The Frenchman Jacques Cartier took possession of the Labrador region in the name of his king in 1534, and in 1535–36 he ascended the St. Lawrence as far as Montreal. The first permanent settlement was at Quebec in 1608 under the lead of Champlain. The gain in French colonists was slow, and the stream flowed westward toward the Mississippi. English conquest and the peace of 1763 brought Canada under English control. The English and Protestant inhabitants were considerably increased by immigration of English loyalists from the United States after 1783, and the Roman Catholics received a large increment during the nineteenth century by immigration from Ireland; the French population also was augmented after 1871 by a noteworthy number of Alsatians.

The following is the table of religious statistics from the census of 1901:

Adventists	8,058	Latter-day Saints (Mormons)	6,891
Agnostics, Atheists, etc.	3,613	Lutherans	92,524
Anglicans	680,620	Mennonites	31,797
Baptists	292,189	Methodists	916,886
Baptists, Free	24,288	Mohammedans	47
Brethren	8,014	New Church (Swedenborgians)	881
Buddhists	10,407	Non-sectarian	215
Catholic Apostolic (Irvingites)	400	No Religion	4,810
Christadelphians	1,030	Pagans	15,107
Christians	6,900	Plymouth Brethren	2,774
Christian Scientists	2,619	Presbyterians	842,442
Church of Christ	2,264	Protestants	11,612
Church of God	351	Reformed Episcopalians	874
Confucians	5,115	Roman Catholics	2,229,600
Congregationalists	28,293	Salvation Army	10,308
Deists	78	Spiritualists	616
Disciples	14,900	Theosophists	107
Dukhobors	8,775	Tunkers	1,528
Evangelicals	10,193	Unitarians	1,934
Friends (Quakers)	4,100	United Brethren	4,701
Greek Church	15,630	Universalists	2,589
Holiness Movement (Hornerites)	2,775	Unspecified	43,222
Jews	16,401	Various Sects	2,795
		Zionites	42

The Roman Catholics constitute 41.5 per cent of the entire population. They are most numerous in Quebec (1,429,260; 86.7 per cent of the population of the province); in Ontario their number is 390,304 (1.8 per cent). The total number of Protestants is about 3,000,000 (56.2 per cent). Nearly all of the Buddhists and Confucians are in British Columbia, whither they have come as a result of the active trade with eastern Asia. The adherents of the Greek Church are mostly immigrants from Russia to Manitoba, Alberta, and Assiniboia; the Dukhobors (q.v.), who may be regarded as a schismatic branch of this Church, are in Assiniboia and Saskatchewan. Of the Jews almost half (7,498) are in Quebec and 5,321 in Ontario. Nearly all the Mormons are in Ontario (3,377) and Alberta (3,212). Of the Mennonites, 15,246 are in Manitoba, 12,208 in Ontario, and 3,683 in Saskatchewan. The "pagans" are the Eskimos and unconverted Indians; according to some authorities their number is much larger than that given by the census. All the large denominations are actively engaged in missionary work in the wide domain of Canada, operating through permanent stations and itinerant missionaries. The Roman Catholic Church has from the first been particularly successful in this work, and the majority of the Indians converted to Christianity belong to this Church. The "various sects" are 110 in number and include seventy-nine which reported less than ten members each.

The Roman Catholic Church in Canada dates from the discovery. Huguenots were allowed to settle, only on conditions that soon proved fatal to their religion. In 1615 three Recollect priests settled in Quebec, forming the earliest regular establishment. In 1625 the Jesuits arrived, and began their missionary and educational labors. In 1657

François Xavier de Laval-Montmorency (q.v.) was named vicar apostolic of New France, becoming first bishop of Quebec in 1674. Under him the church system was fully organized. For some time after the conquest, the see of Quebec remained vacant, as the English Government would recognize its occupant only as the head of the Roman Church in Canada, and not as the bishop of that city. The difficulty was, however, overcome. In 1819 Joseph Octave Plessis (bishop of Quebec from 1806) became the first Canadian archbishop.

The Roman Catholic Church.

As organized at present the Roman Catholic Church of Canada has an apostolic delegate (first appointed by Leo XIII.), who resides at Ottawa. There are eight provinces, twenty dioceses, and four vicariates apostolic, as follows:

Province of Halifax (Nova Scotia, Prince Edward Island, and New Brunswick; the Bermuda Islands also form a part of the archdiocese of Halifax); archdiocese, Halifax (founded as the vicariate apostolic of Nova Scotia, 1817; diocese, 1842; archdiocese, 1852); dioceses, Antigonish (founded as the diocese of Arichat, 1844; transferred to Antigonish, 1886), Charlottetown (Prince Edward Island and the Magdalen Islands, 1829), Chatham (1860), and St. John (1842).

Province of Kingston (Eastern and Northern Ontario); archdiocese, Kingston (diocese, 1826; archdiocese, 1889); dioceses, Alexandria (1890), Peterborough (1882), and Sault Ste. Marie (1904).

Province of Montreal (Southern and Western Quebec); archdiocese, Montreal (diocese, 1836; archdiocese, 1886); dioceses, Joliette (1904), St. Hyacinthe (1852), Sherbrooke (1874), and Valleyfield (1892).

Province of Ottawa (parts of Ontario and Quebec in the neighborhood of the city of Ottawa and the region about James Bay); archdiocese, Ottawa (diocese, 1847; archdiocese, 1886); diocese, Pembroke (vicariate apostolic, 1882; diocese, 1898).

Province of Quebec (Eastern Quebec); archdiocese, Quebec (vicariate apostolic, 1657; diocese, 1674; archdiocese, 1844); dioceses, Chicoutimi (1878), Nicolet (1885), Rimouski (1867), and Three Rivers (1852); vicariate apostolic of the Gulf of St. Lawrence (prefecture apostolic, 1882; vicariate, 1905).

Province of St. Boniface (the extreme western part of Ontario, Manitoba, Saskatchewan, Alberta, and Northwest Territories); archdiocese, St. Boniface (diocese, 1847; archdiocese, 1871); diocese, St. Albert (1871); vicariates apostolic, Athabasca (1862), and Saskatchewan (1890).

Province of Toronto (Southwestern Ontario); archdiocese, Toronto (diocese, 1841; archdiocese, 1870); dioceses, Hamilton (1856), and London (1856).

Province of Victoria (British Columbia, the Klondike and Great Slave regions); archdiocese, Victoria (1847); diocese, New Westminster (vicariate apostolic of British Columbia, 1863; diocese, 1890); vicariate apostolic of Mackenzie (1901).

The *Official Catholic Directory* for 1906 gives the following figures: number of priests of religious orders, 1,116; secular priests, 2,613; churches, 2,495; seminaries, 17, with 1,183 students; universities and colleges, 45; charitable institutions, 202. One hundred and ten Catholic papers are named, and the list of religious orders includes twenty-seven for men and thirty-five for women, the larger number of which are actively engaged in missionary and charitable work. Laval University was founded at Quebec in 1852 and has faculties of theology, law, medicine, and arts.

The Anglican Church in Canada dates from its conquest by England. The first congregation was organized in Montreal in 1766, service being held in the chapel of the Recollects at such hours as the building was not required for mass. In 1774, while the Roman Catholic Church was secured in all its previous rights, it was restricted to collecting its church-dues from members of its own communion, and the purpose was intimated of establishing a Protestant Church. In 1791, when Canada first received a constitution, one-seventh of all the land in the colony disposed of by sale or grant to colonists was "reserved" for the support of a Protestant clergy. In 1787 Charles Inglis was appointed by the English Crown bishop of Nova Scotia—the first of the colonial bishops; in 1793 Jacob Mountain was appointed bishop of Quebec. The present organization includes two provinces and twenty-three bishoprics, as follows:

The Anglican Church.

Province of Canada (the Maritime Provinces, Quebec, and Ontario); archdiocese, Montreal (founded 1850; archdiocese, 1901; since 1904 the archbishop has borne the title primate of all Canada); dioceses, Algoma (with the bishop's seat at Sault Ste. Marie, 1873), Fredericton (1845), Huron (London, 1857), Niagara (Hamilton, 1875), Nova Scotia (Halifax, 1787), Ontario (Kingston, 1861), Ottawa (1896), Quebec (1793), Toronto (1839).

Province of Rupert's Land (the territory west of Ontario and south and east of Hudson Bay); archdiocese, Rupert's Land (1849; archdiocese, 1893; the cathedral is at Winnipeg); dioceses, Athabasca (1884), Calgary (1888), Keewatin (1901), Mackenzie River (1874), Moosonee (1872), Qu'Appelle (1884), Saskatchewan (1874), Selkirk (1891).

Dioceses not forming part of any province: Caledonia (1879), Columbia (1859) Kootenai (1901), New Westminster (1879).

There are theological schools at Lennoxville, Que., Montreal, Toronto, and Winnipeg.

For the history and information about other religious bodies of Canada, see the articles on the different denominations.

Canada has a good system of public instruction, each province managing its own affairs without centralized system for the entire dominion. Elementary schools, high schools or collegiate institutes, and normal schools lead up to the university, and a good education is within the reach of all. The expenses are met by government grants, local assessments, and school fees. Roman Catholic schools are entitled to a share in the public educational funds by the agreement of 1763, and the religious question has led to complications in some localities. In Quebec there are two distinct boards of school commissioners, Protestant and Roman Catholic, each having its portion of the public funds and managing its schools as it sees fit. In Manitoba there are no separate schools, but religious instruction may be given in the school buildings by Protestant or Catholic teachers.

Education.

BIBLIOGRAPHY: Statistics and other information may be gathered from the *Canadian Almanac*, Toronto, the *Statistical Year Book of Canada*, Ottawa, and *Le Canada ecclésiastique*, Montreal, all annuals, the last Roman Catholic. On the English Church consult: E. R Stimson, *History of Separation of Church and State in Canada*, Toronto, 1888; J. Langtry, *History of the Church in Eastern Canada*, London, 1892. There is also a *Cyclopædia of Methodism in Canada*, Toronto, 1881. For early Catholic relations consult the monumental work, ed. R. G. Thwaites, *Jesuit Relations and Allied Documents*, 74 vols., Cleveland, 1896–1901.

CANARY ISLANDS. See AFRICA, III.

CANDIDUS, cŏn-dĭ'dŭs (WEISS), PANTALEON: Reformed theologian; b. at Ybbs (60 m. w. of Vienna), Austria, Oct. 7, 1540; d. at Zweibrücken

(55 m. n.w. of Carlsruhe), in the Palatinate, Feb. 3, 1608. He was sent in his tenth year to Andreas Cupicius, Evangelical preacher at Weissenkirchen, for instruction. When his teacher was persecuted by the Jesuits on account of his faith and thrown into prison, Candidus attended him as *famulus* and fled with him to Hungary. Returning to his native land, he continued his studies with the aid of Vitus Nuber, abbot of Säussenstein (near Ybbs), and when he also was persecuted, Candidus accompanied him to Duke Wolfgang of Zweibrücken. He received a scholarship from the duke which enabled him to acquire a thorough humanistic and theological education at the University of Wittenberg, where he spent about seven years from 1558; he became amanuensis of Hubert Languet and was on intimate terms with Melanchthon. In 1565 he left Wittenberg, and, after having taught a short time in the Latin school of Zweibrücken, became pastor at Hinzweiler, then deacon at Weisenheim and Zweibrücken, and in 1571 town preacher and general superintendent in Zweibrücken.

The Church of Zweibrücken had been founded by Johannes Schweblin in accordance with the Lutheran doctrine by the acceptance of the Augsburg Confession and the Wittenberg Concord (q.v.) of 1536. Duke Wolfgang, after the death of Melanchthon, took vigorous measures against the Philippists and Calvinists by employing strict Lutherans like Marbach, Andreä, and Hesshus. His son, John I., continued the same policy, and the most influential positions were filled with trustworthy Lutherans such as Jacob Heilbrunner and Jacob Schopper. But a change of conditions was brought about under the influence of the Count Palatine John Casimir, who sent his cousin John a statement of the conflicting opinions of Reformed princes and theologians. Thereupon the latter demanded in 1578 a general convention for the discussion of these questions. Candidus, who had always leaned toward Calvinism, became now one of the most influential advocates of the Reformed cause, and the duke himself openly confessed the Calvinistic doctrine, although he had signed the Formula of Concord. The remonstrances of the Lutheran electoral princes were of no avail, nor was a Lutheran embassy which was sent in 1580, consisting of men like Marbach and Osiander. Candidus accepted the Reformed Christology and the Calvinistic doctrine of the Lord's Supper, and in 1585 edited a catechism which contributed considerably to the eradication of the Lutheran doctrine. Moreover, he entered into negotiations with the Reformed theologians of Heidelberg and completed the work of Calvinism in 1588 by his *Christliche und notwendige Erklärung des Catechismi aus Gottes Wort*, etc., which in its wording and sense follows closely the Heidelberg catechism. The Reformed Church service was introduced in the same way. The dissensions were renewed in 1593 at the religious colloquy of Neuburg, where the Zweibrücken theologians protested against any innovations and attempted to show their agreement with the Augustana. Since the beginning of the seventeenth century the Church of Zweibrücken has been counted among the Reformed Churches. Candidus was also active in the literary field and has left twenty works, written mostly in Latin. He was especially prolific in Latin poetical productions and handled the elegiac measure with ability.

(J. Schneider.)

Bibliography: F. Butters, *Pantaleon Candidus, ein Lebensbild*, Zweibrücken, 1865; L. Häusser, *Geschichte der rheinischen Pfalz*, Heidelberg, 1856; *ADB*, s.v., vol. iii.

CANDLEMAS: The popular English name for the feast of the Purification of the Virgin Mary or the Presentation of Christ in the Temple, Feb. 2, derived from the ancient custom of blessing candles on that day for use in church and elsewhere. See Mary.

CANDLEMAS DAY. See Mary, Festivals of.

CANDLER, WARREN AKIN: Bishop of the Methodist Episcopal Church, South; b. near Villa Rica, Ga., Aug. 23, 1857. He was educated at Emory College, Oxford, Ga. (B.A., 1875), and entered the North Georgia Conference of the Methodist Episcopal Church, South, in 1875, holding various pastorates until 1886. From the latter year until 1888 he was editor of the *Christian Advocate*, Nashville, Tenn., the official organ of his denomination, and from 1888 to 1898 was president of Emory College. Since 1898 he has been a bishop of the Methodist Episcopal Church, South. In theology he is a Wesleyan Arminian. He has written: *History of Sunday Schools* (New York, 1880); *Georgia's Educational Work* (Atlanta, Ga., 1893); *Christus Auctor* (Nashville, Tenn., 1900); *High Living and High Lives* (1901); and *Great Revivals and the Great Republic* (1904).

CANDLES. See Lights, Use of, in Divine Service.

CANDLISH, ROBERT SMITH: One of the founders and a leader of the Free Church of Scotland; b. in Edinburgh Mar. 23, 1806; d. there Oct. 19, 1873. He studied at Glasgow (M.A., 1823), and at the divinity hall 1823–26; was licensed in 1828 and served as assistant of St. Andrews, Glasgow, and of Bonhill, Dumbartonshire; in 1834 he became minister of St. George's, Edinburgh, where his talent as a preacher soon made him famous. In 1839 he publicly identified himself with the party in the Church of Scotland which afterward became the Free Church, and in all the public proceedings prior to the disruption in 1843, especially in the debates in the General Assembly, took a leading part; after the disruption he was foremost in organizing and developing the Free Church. His eloquence in debate, his business tact, and his high character enabled him to retain the high position he had gained in spite of a somewhat sharp and abrupt manner, and a tendency to what some considered diplomatic management. On the death of Dr. Chalmers in 1847 he was appointed to succeed him as professor of divinity in New College, Edinburgh, but declined the appointment, preferring to continue minister of St. George's; in 1862, however, he became principal of New College, the duties involving little labor. He was the chief organizer and extender of the school system of the Free Church, which was afterward incorporated with the national system of education; and one of the founders of the Evangelical Alliance in 1845. He was a voluminous author, although his books did not attain a very large circulation; among his writings were: *Contributions Towards the Exposition of the Book of Genesis* (3 vols., Edinburgh, 1843–62; rev. ed., 2 vols., 1868); *Scripture Characters and Miscellanies* (London, 1850); *Examination of Mr. Maurice's Theological Essays* (1854): *Life in a Risen Saviour*, discourses on I Cor. xv. (Edinburgh, 1858); *The Two Great Commandments*, sermons on Romans xii. (London, 1860); *The Atonement, its Reality, Completeness, and Extent* (1861); *The Fatherhood of God*, the first course of Cunningham lectures at New College, Edinburgh, 1864 (5th ed. enlarged, 2 vols., Edinburgh, 1890); *The First Epistle of John Expounded in a Series of Lectures* (1866); *Discourses Bearing upon the Sonship and Brotherhood of Believers* (1872); *Sermons*, with memoir (1873); and *The Gospel of Forgiveness*, a series of discourses (1878).

Bibliography: W. Wilson, *Memorials of R. S. Candlish*, Edinburgh, 1880 (with a concluding chapter on his character as a theologian by Robert Rainy, his successor as principal of New College); Jean L. Watson, *Life of R. S. Candlish*, London, 1882.

CANISIUS, ca-nī'si-ūs *or* ca-nī'shus, **PETRUS** (**Peter Kanis, Canis, Canijs**): A Jesuit to whom the order owes its spread in Germany; b. at Nymwegen, in the Netherlands, May 8, 1521; d. at Freiburg, Switzerland, Dec. 21, 1597. He studied at Cologne from 1535 to 1544 and obtained the degrees of bachelor of theology, licentiate of arts, and master of arts (i.e., doctor of philosophy). In 1543 he went to the Jesuit Pierre Favre (q.v.) at Mainz, made the "spiritual exercises" (see Jesuits) under his guidance, and entered the order as a novice. With nine like-minded companions he founded secretly at Cologne the first Jesuit colony, but the city council dissolved the body, though at the intercession of the university the members were permitted to remain in the city, as individuals. In 1545 Canisius began his lectures, preached, and prepared an edition of the works of Cyril of Alexandria, with a Latin translation, the first volume of which was published at Cologne in 1546. In the mean time, the fervent orator, who had agitated especially against the archbishop Hermann of Wied, who inclined toward Protestantism, had obtained such authority among the strictly Catholic party that at the beginning of the Schmalkald War it delegated him as mediator to the imperial camp at Ulm. Here he came into close relations with Cardinal Otto Truchsess, bishop of Augsburg, who was destined to open the way for him into Bavaria and insure the activity of his order. Ignatius Loyola perceived the talent of Canisius, and, to perfect him in the spirit and nature of the order and make him a chosen vessel, called the young man to Rome and employed him for two years in Italy at Messina. Upon his return, Canisius commenced his work in Bavaria in 1549, in 1552 at Vienna and in the Austrian territories, in 1555 at Prague with the two objects in view, to permeate the German Catholics with the Jesuitic spirit of piety, and to repel Protestantism. At Vienna he composed the *Summa doctrinæ Christianæ*, the "catechism," which an imperial edict soon introduced into all Austria; in four hundred editions published during 130 years, it proved an excellent means of mental training (Eng. transl., Paris, 1588). His other literary productions include two volumes (*De Johanne Baptista*, Dillingen, 1571, and *De Maria Virgine*, Ingolstadt, 1577), written against the "pestilentissimum opus," the Magdeburg Centuries (q.v.). But his literary activity against Protestantism was unimportant compared with what he accomplished as teacher in Vienna, Dillingen, and Ingolstadt, as adviser of Catholic princes, and as preacher and pastor of very large circles. Besides the colleges already mentioned, the order owes to him the establishment of the important colleges of Augsburg, Munich, and Innsbruck, and its spread to Poland. When at the height of his successes he attended the Council of Trent in 1562. And yet in the long run he did not retain the confidence of the leaders of his order. The general stopped him when he was on the point of preparing a third volume for the refutation of the "Centuries" (*De potestate Petri et successorum*). His last achievement was the founding of a new college at Freiburg in Switzerland. K. Benrath.

Bibliography: F. Riess, *Der selige Petrus Canisius*, Freiburg, 1865; M. Philippson, *La Contre-Révolution religieuse*, Brussels, 1880; Delplace, *L'Établissement de la compagnie de Jésus dans les Pays Bas*, ib. 1887; P. Drews, *Petrus Canisius, der erste deutsche Jesuit*, Halle, 1892; *Epistulæ et acta P. Canisii*, ed. O. Braunsberger, 4 vols., Freiburg, 1896–1905.

CANO, cā'nō (**Canus**), **MELCHIOR**: A scholastic Dominican of the University of Alcala; b. at Tarancón (38 m. w. of Cuenca), Spain [Jan. 1, 1509; d. at Toledo Sept. 30, 1560]. He took part in the deliberations of the Council of Trent, especially in those concerning the doctrine of the Eucharist, opposing the efforts made at the instance of the emperor Ferdinand that the cup should be given to the laity. Having returned from Trent, Philip II. made him bishop of the Canaries, without residence there, as he became provincial of his order in Castile. His principal works are: *Prælectiones de pœnitentia* and *De sacramentis* (both Salamanca, 1550), and his *Loci theologici* (1563), consisting of twelve books about the sources whence doctrinal proofs may be derived; the "*authoritas*" has its place before the "*ratio*," and the principal source is of course tradition. Although an opponent of the Jesuits, Cano was a thoroughgoing papal theologian, and he was a scholastic, although he opposed "false" scholasticism. For his opposition to the Jesuits he had to suffer denunciations which caused his citation to Rome in 1556 as "perditionis filius, Melchior Canus, diabolicis motus suasionibus, non erubuit prædicare, antichristum venisse." By the exertions of the Spanish government the citation was not heeded. But the *Loci theologici* were placed on the Lisbon index in 1624, and were much altered by the expurgator. K. Benrath.

Bibliography: F. H. Reusch, *Der Index der verbotenen Bücher*, i. 303 et passim, Bonn, 1883; F. Caballero, *Co-*

quenses illustres. II. *Melchior Cano,* pp. 279, 382, Madrid, 1871.

CANON: A word used in a variety of senses in ecclesiastical terminology, all more or less related to the primary meaning of the Greek word *kanōn,* "a straight rod or bar, rule, standard." (1) The decisive list of the books considered as forming part of the Holy Scriptures (see CANON OF SCRIPTURE). (2) In ancient usage, any official church list, as of those who were to be commemorated in the liturgy, whence the term canonization, or of the clergy attached to a certain church, whence (3) A member of a body of clergy living together under a more or less definite rule in connection with a cathedral or collegiate church or in a quasimonastic organization as canons regular (see CHAPTER; AUGUSTINIANS; PREMONSTRATENSIANS). (4) The decree or decision of a council for the regulation of doctrine or discipline (see CANON LAW). (5) The fixed, most important portion of the mass, from the *Sanctus* to the *Pater noster.* (6) In the hymnology of the Eastern Church, an important class of long and elaborate hymns usually sung in the morning office, founded mainly on the Old Testament canticles then used, and composed of either eight or nine odes.

CANONESS: A member of a company of women under the rule of an abbess and bound by vows of celibacy and obedience, but not by one of poverty. Some canonesses were "secular," and the houses they lived in were homes for ladies of the nobility; but others were "religious" and lived in nunneries of the Benedictine or Augustinian order. Few of these establishments survived the Reformation, and their inmates generally became Protestants. Some of the houses became Protestant homes for noble ladies, as those at Gandersheim, Herford, and Quedlinburg in Germany.

CANON LAW.

I. Definition and General Discussion.
II. Collections of Canons and Decretals.
1. Early History.
2. First Codification.
3. Earliest Western Collections.
   The *Quesnelliana* (§ 1).
   The *Prisca* (§ 2).
   Collections of Dionysius (§ 3).
4. Next period, by Countries.
   Africa (§ 1).
   Spain (§ 2).
   British Isles (§ 3).
   Frankish Empire (§ 4).
5. Further Systematization.
   Forerunners of Gratian (§ 1).
   Grarian (§ 2).
6. Collections of Decretals.
   Before Gregory IX. (§ 1).
   Collection of Gregory (§ 2).
   Supplements to It (§ 3).
7. Corpus Juris Canonici.

Canon law is the sum total of the legal enactments of the Church.

I. Definition and General Discussion: In modern times the differences between various Christian Churches have brought about a variance of law, since it springs in the first instance from the development of the ecclesiastical consciousness; and it is thus possible to speak of Roman Catholic and Protestant canon law. While the expression is most commonly used in connection with the former, it is not quite coextensive or identical with the law of the Roman Catholic Church, but designates rather the content of the *Corpus juris canonici* (see below, II., 7), in contrast with the newer regulations based on the decisions of the Council of Trent, the concordats and bulls of circumscription of the nineteenth century, and the Vatican Council. These have in many particulars modified or superseded the older law, until a new codification of the whole mass of enactments has become necessary, and is now contemplated under the direction of Pope Pius X.

The canon law, in the sense thus assigned to the term, contains a large number of regulations pertaining to matters which, according to modern constitutions, have been withdrawn from ecclesiastical jurisdiction and placed under the ordinary secular tribunals. These provisions have thus ceased to be operative. They include the relations between Church and State, the legal status of heretics, ecclesiastical jurisdiction, etc. The Roman Catholic Church, it is true, still maintains in theory the permanent validity of these enactments, and claims the same preeminent power and independence of the State as it possessed in the Middle Ages. Since the Reformation and the upbuilding of modern nationalities, however, the principle of the unity of jurisdiction and the authority of the law has proved irreconcilable with these claims. The freedom and independence conceded to the Church in the ordering of its own internal affairs by no means involves the absolute supremacy and validity of the canon law when it comes into conflict with the civil law, or releases the ecclesiastical authorities from their responsibility and their obedience to the State; for the freedom of the Church, like all other freedom in the modern world, is a freedom within the bounds of the law. But while the Roman Catholic Church appeals to divine mission and inalienable rights in support of its protest against these limitations, and has occasionally provoked serious conflicts by insistence upon its position in this matter, Protestantism from the very start took a much more restricted view of the extent of ecclesiastical operations and of the authority of its own law, sometimes, where it is established, working directly with the State, but always submitting without question to civil ordinances. The difference is seen again in the fact that while Roman Catholicism recognizes only one Church, and thus only one valid church law, Protestantism, though holding its own interpretation of the Christian faith for the true one, does not claim exclusive jurisdiction over all creatures, and concedes to the various bodies which it conceives as forming an invisible unity the right to their own independent action in matters of legislation.

Canon law, the outcome of the Church's development, rests upon positive enactment, and the attempt to construct a natural ecclesiastical law on rational principles must necessarily fail, setting as it does arbitrary and subjective views in place of the positive data of church history. A philosophical treatment of church law is, on the other hand, of great importance. It grasps in their entirety the fundamental principles on which as a basis the actual development has taken place, correlates them with the objective conceptions and principles of the Church itself, and in this way discovers not only the errors and deviations but the inevitable tendencies and direction of the development. In modern times, since the delimitation of the boundary between Church and State, doubt has been cast upon the independence of the church law, as if there could be no law without the action of the State, and what passed for law outside this action was only an ethical standard, not a juridical. The law of the State, however, in its essence, is a product not so much of the State as of the national consciousness of what is just, and really precedes rather than follows the operation of the State; its standards do not have to wait for sanction until the State declares its readiness to enforce them by pains and penalties. The Church as a distinct moral order is qualified to regulate and develop its own internal functions and institutions of its own motion. It is true that until recently Protestant churches have to a large extent been organized, especially in England and Germany, by secular legislation; but this state of things is really an anomalous one, not corresponding to the essential idea and meaning of the Church. The result of the modern settlement has been in most cases to leave the Church free to develop independently its own system, without the need of any special permission or privilege from the State in order to give such regulations the force of law within the Church. Its members realize that they are bound to the fulfilment of such ordinances because they have come into being in a regular and legal manner, and so long as they are not repealed in the same manner. This obligation is not a mere matter of conscience, but rests on a basis of positive law, because the standards of action imposed by it are the expression of the will of the Church in its corporate capacity. Nor does the Church lack means to enforce obedience by the withdrawal of blessings which it alone is empowered to impart and equally empowered to withhold. According to the Protestant conception, it is true, the binding force of ecclesiastical regulations is to a great extent dependent upon the will of the individual to be and remain a member of the church fellowship. E. Sehling.

II. Collections of Canons and Decretals.—1. **Early History**: In the first three centuries the term canon was applied to the standard of right living accepted in the Church, resting partly on written and partly on oral tradition. When the synods, especially the general ones, became the main agents in the development of church life, their decisions on points of practise were also known as canons—though this name was not usually applied to the decrees of local synods until the sixth century, after their inclusion in the great and widely circulated collections had given them a status and an authority in a measure analogous to those of the ecumenical councils. With the development of the primatial power of the pope, the name came at the beginning of the ninth century to be applied also to his decrees, and finally its use was extended in medieval terminology to any ecclesiastical enactment. The collections of canons were made up at first of the decrees of councils and of popes; later collections include, in addition to these, excerpts from the Fathers, from letters and regulations of bishops, from Scripture, and even from Roman law, Frankish capitularies, and ordinances of German emperors. The Council of Trent employed the word exclusively for dogmatic propositions couched in juridical form and followed by an anathema.

2. **First Codification**: During the primitive age of the Church, when its constitution and discipline rested quite simply upon the precepts of Christ and the Apostles, and the new problems which were later to make the Christian life more complicated had not yet come up, there was no need for a codification of the laws. It is hardly necessary to say that the so-called Apostolic Constitutions and Canons (q.v.) are the product of a later age. The systematic formulation of law began with the closer organization of the Church and the holding of synods. The earliest mention of a *Codex canonum* is found in the acts of the Council of Chalcedon (451), at which certain canons were read to the assembly from a collection. These, though numbered consecutively in the collection, can be identified as the sixth of Nicæa (325) and the fourth, fifth, sixteenth, and seventeenth of Antioch (332). This collection, accordingly, seems to have contained the canons of several councils, beginning with the twenty of Nicæa and possibly closing with those of Antioch, including between these twenty-five of Ancyra (314), fourteen of Neocæsarea (314), and twenty of Gangra (c. 365). There were undoubtedly other collections known in this period; one, which is still recognizable in the oldest Western Latin version, which omitted the canons of Antioch; others which included those of Laodicea (between 347 and 381), Constantinople (381), and Chalcedon (451); and still others which had also those of Sardica (347) and Ephesus (431). There is, however, no basis for the supposition that either the collection read from at the Council at Chalcedon or any other of these collections had an official character.

3. **Earliest Western Collections**: Of these Greek canons, only those of Nicæa were at first accepted in the West, and those of Sardica in the Latin original. As early as the fifth century, however, there were collections here also of Greek canons in a Latin version, through which the Eastern decrees gradually acquired authority. Of these three deserve special mention.

1. The *Quesnelliana.*

(1) The **Isidorian** version, incorrectly so called because it is found in the great collection long ascribed to Isidore of Seville, is the oldest. It seems to have included originally only the canons comprised in the oldest Greek collection, to which those of Antioch, Laodicea, and Constantinople were added later. It was probably made in Italy; its date can not be determined, but its version of the Nicene canons was known in Gaul as early as 439. It was first published in 1675 by Paschasius Quesnell, from a manuscript at Oxford of a collection apparently made in Gaul at the end of the fifth century. (2) The *Versio prisca*, made in Italy in the latter half of the fifth century, which contains the canons of Ancyra, Neocæsarea, Nicæa, Antioch, Gangra, Constantinople, and Chalcedon; frequent use was

made of it for the completion of the Isidorian version and for other collections, especially Italian. **2. The Prisca.** It was first published by Justeau in the *Bibliotheca juris canonici* from an imperfect manuscript, then more fully and accurately by the Ballerini brothers. (3) That made by Dionysius Exiguus, probably in Rome at the end of the fifth century, and revised early in the sixth. It contains fifty "apostolic canons"; those of Nicæa, **3. Collections of Dionysius.** Ancyra, Neocæsarea, Gangra, Antioch, Laodicea, and Constantinople from a Greek collection; from another twenty-seven of Chalcedon in a new version; twenty-one of Sardica in the Latin original; and the acts of the Synod of Carthage (419). Somewhat later, probably under Pope Symmachus (498–514), Dionysius made another collection of all the decrees of popes known to him, including those of Siricius, Innocent I., Zosimus, Boniface I., Celestine I., Leo I., Gelasius I., and Anastasius II. Of a third collection made by order of Pope Hormisdas (514–523), and containing the original text of Greek canons with a Latin version, only the prologue is extant. The first two, however, combined into one, soon acquired preeminent consideration; Cassiodorus (d. 536) says that they were universally preferred in the Roman church of his time; they were used in Africa, the Frankish church, Spain, England, and Ireland. They were supplemented in course of time by the decretals of Hilary, Simplicius, Felix, Symmachus, Hormisdas, and Gregory II. A codex thus enlarged was presented by Adrian II. to Charlemagne in 774; this was taken, after the *Capitulare ecclesiasticum* of 789, as the basis of the Frankish capitularies, and probably sanctioned at the Synod of Aachen in 802 as the official code of the Frankish church.

4. Next Period, by Countries: The canonical collections of the succeeding period may most conveniently be grouped under their respective countries. In Africa discipline rested primarily on the decrees of home councils, special weight **1. Africa.** being given to the Synod of Carthage in 419, with whose acts those of the synods held under Aurelius from 393 were incorporated. These are the canons included, though imperfectly, in the collection of Dionysius; they were later translated into Greek and received into Oriental collections. Of other African collections only two require special mention—that made before 546 by Fulgentius Ferrandus, a Carthaginian deacon, under the name of *Breviatio canonum*, containing some of the Greek canons in the Isidorian version and African canons down to 523, and the *Concordia canonum*, compiled c. 690 (?) by Cresconius, possibly a bishop.

Spain had its collections of canons and decretals in the sixth century, as is shown by the acts of the **2. Spain.** Council of Braga in 563 and the Third of Toledo in 579. The enforcement of order and discipline required a completer codification, and a large collection seems to have been made at the Fourth Council of Toledo (633). By later additions it acquired the form in which it is now printed (Madrid, 1808). Its first or conciliar part contains the Greek canons found in the Isidorian version, those of Sardica, those of the Third Council of Constantinople (681), and two letters of Cyril under the name of the Council of Ephesus; nine African councils; sixteen Gallic councils, from 314 to 549; and thirty-six Spanish, from 305 (?) to 694. In this last division, to the canons of the Second Council of Braga is appended a collection made by Martin, archbishop of Braga, a native of Pannonia (d. about 580), by free translation and selection of Greek, African, Gallic, and Spanish canons. The second part contains decretals of the popes from Damasus to Gregory I., including all that Dionysius had placed in his. The compiler of this great collection, usually cited as *Hispana*, is unknown. There is no evidence to show that Isidore of Seville had any direct hand in it; his name was first connected with it by the compiler of the False Decretals, who incorporated the older and genuine collection with them.

In the British Isles the Celtic church developed a disciplinary system of its own in synods of whose proceedings scarcely anything has been preserved. For certain fifth- and sixth-century canons of a penitential nature, see PENITENTIAL BOOKS. The Anglo-Saxon church in like manner relied for a long time on its own legislative resources, **3. British Isles.** though the collection of Dionysius was known here in the seventh century. Except the penitential ordinances of Theodore, Bede, and Egbert, no Anglo-Saxon canons are extant. There is, however, an Irish collection of the seventh century or beginning of the eighth, compiled from Scripture, the Fathers, numerous Greek, African, Gallic, Spanish, and Irish synods, and papal decretals. The large number of Irish canons gives a specially interesting insight into the conditions of church life there.

The Frankish empire, before the period mentioned above, possessed a number of collections of Greek, Gallic, and Spanish canons and papal decretals, which, however, need no detailed consideration. Besides the enlarged Dionysian collection, the *Hispana* was also known at the end of the eighth century, and was used to complete the Codex sent by Adrian. The large extent of this material and its lack of chronological arrangement soon brought about attempts at selection and systematic arrangement, which were frequent in the eighth and ninth **4. Frankish Empire.** centuries, and of which some deserve special mention. (1) A collection in 381 chapters, sometimes found independently, sometimes as a fourth book to the canonical work erroneously ascribed to Archbishop Egbert of York. It dates from the end of the eighth century, and is important because of the use made of it by Regino (see below, 5) and of the help which it gives toward explaining a number of erroneous titles which passed over into this and the *Decreta* of Burchard and Gratian. (2) The *Collectio Acheriana*, so called from its first publisher D'Achéry, extant in numerous manuscripts and belonging to the end of the eighth or beginning of the ninth century. Its canons, divided into three books, are taken without exception from Adrian's edition of Dionysius and from the

Hispana. (3) The Penitential of Halitgar of Cambrai, compiled between 817 and 831 at the request of Archbishop Ebbo of Reims. Of its five books the first two are taken from the writings of Gregory I. and Prosper of Aquitaine, while the larger part of the last three, as well as the prologue, come from the two collections just named, especially the second. All three of these collections are constructed with special regard to the penitential system of the time; and the same is true of the collections made by Rabanus Maurus, particularly the *Liber pœnitentium ad Otgarium* of 841 and the *Epistola ad Heribaldum* of 853, the main purpose of which is to restore the ancient discipline by appeals to the writings of the Fathers and the old canons and decretals. A somewhat similar character is seen in the *Capitula episcoporum*, or small collections made by individual bishops, sometimes with the assent of diocesan synods, for the regulation of their own subjects, usually from larger works, but occasionally including their own edicts and the provisions of local law.

5. Further Systematization: The great influence of the secular power on ecclesiastical action in the Carolingian period tended to add to the earlier church law a large amount of material, frequently covering matters of church discipline, in the capitularies of the Frankish kings. Efforts at systematization were soon called forth in this field also by practical needs. The first was that of Abbot Ansegis, which, however, as it contains nothing but capitularies, does not need further consideration here. It is different from the work which Benedict Levita of Mainz compiled in three books. Its purpose, according to him, was the completion of the work of Ansegis, but the imperial laws form only a small part of its contents, which are far more largely taken from the Bible, the Fathers, the ancient canons, with Roman statute and German common law. The special interest of this collection is the relation in which it stands, or has been thought to stand, to the Pseudo-Isidorian Decretals (q.v.).

1. Forerunners of Gratian.

Between the ninth and twelfth centuries a large number of compilations came into being, with the purpose of bringing the wealth of material scattered throughout the older works into practical relation with the more modern ecclesiastical principles. Unlike the smaller collections described above, which usually served rather local interests, these are as a rule of considerable size and sufficiently general to be used outside the limits of the diocese in which they originate. Some of them attained a wide currency and no little practical importance; but only a few of them need be mentioned for the purpose of this article. (1) The as yet unpublished *Collectio Anselmo dedicata*, taking its name from an Archbishop Anselm, probably Anselm II. of Milan (883–897). It is certainly Italian in origin; its material is taken partly from Adrian's edition of Dionysius enlarged by the addition of Carthaginian, Gallic, and Spanish councils from the *Hispana*, and partly from the False Decretals, the *Registrum* of Gregory I., two Roman synods under Zacharias (743) and Eugenius II. (826), the laws of Justinian, and the *Novellæ* of Julian—though probably this last part was interpolated afterward. It is important not only as being the first to make a thorough use of the code of Justinian, but as being the source of a large part of the *Decretum* of Burchard, and through it of that of Gratian. (2) The *Libri duo de causis synodalibus et disciplinis ecclesiasticis*, compiled by Regino, abbot of Prüm about 906, at the request of Rathbod, archbishop of Treves, to be used by him and his representatives in the administration of the diocese. This work, interesting as another source of Burchard's as well as for its immediate relation to the synodal courts and the practise of its time, was later enlarged, revised, and borrowed from in a whole series of similar collections. (3) The *Decretum* (*Liber decretorum*, *Collectarium*) of Bishop Burchard of Worms, compiled between 1012 and 1023. The important material contained in its twenty books embraces the whole range of church discipline and order. A peculiarity of Burchard is that he frequently ascribes canons of councils and excerpts from Roman law, the capitularies, or penitential ordinances to one of the older popes or councils, evidently with the view of assuring their reception as authoritative—thus misleading later compilers, especially Gratian. (4) The *Collectio duodecim partium*, still unprinted; apparently made by a German very soon after the completion of Burchard's. Theiner, who was the first to call attention (in his *Disquisitiones criticæ*, Rome, 1836) to the importance of this collection, was under the erroneous impression that it was a source of Burchard's; but the relation is exactly the reverse. It contains, however, a number of interesting Frankish and German canons, some of them probably copied directly from the original documents. (5) The collection of Bishop Anselm of Lucca (d. 1086), which was incorporated almost bodily in the *Decretum Gratiani*, and which contains a number of papal decretals not previously known, and probably taken from the Roman archives. (6) The collection of Cardinal Deusdedit, dedicated to Pope Victor III. (1086–87), in four books, of which the last deals with the freedom of the Church from secular interference, and thus introduces an element new to these collections. The ample use made of the Lateran archives gives a special interest to his collection, much of which is also in Gratian. (7) and (8) are two collections attributed to Bishop Ivo of Chartres (d. 1117)—the *Decretum* in seventeen books and the *Pannormia* in eight. The relation of these two works has been the subject of much controversy; and if Ivo's authorship of the *Pannormia*, at one time often denied, is now considered certain, the *Decretum*, on the other hand, has been recently thought not to be his. Both, however, were abundantly drawn upon by Gratian, as was also, though not to the same extent, another unpublished collection (9), known under the name of *Collectio trium partium*. Its first part contains papal decretals down to Urban II. (d. 1099) in chronological order, though not complete; the second, canons of councils, similarly arranged; the third, a separate collection of canons taken from the *Decretum* of Ivo. (10) A work frequently used by the *Correctores Romani* (see below, 7) is that compiled by a certain Cardinal Gregory in 1144, principally from the two collections *Anselmi* and *Anselmo dedicata.* It is usually cited as *Polycarpus,* from the designation given to it by the compiler himself in his preface, addressed to Bishop Didacus of Compostella.

These collections, from such diverse countries and periods, had many defects when it came to a question of practical use. There was no sort of general arrangement, but ecclesiastical and secular, universal and local law were inextricably mixed up; discrepancies and contradictions were numerous; many regulations had become obsolete, and been replaced in actual practise by others. There was great need for the compilation of a new work which should give a comprehensive survey of the law that was in force. This was undertaken by Gratian, a brother of the Camaldolite monastery of St. Felix at Bologna. Between 1139 and 1142 he compiled a work entitled *Concordantia discordantium canonum,* though since the end of the twelfth century it has usually been known simply as the *Decretum Gratiani.* It is composed principally of the material found in (3) and (5) to (10) of the works named in the last section, and is divided into three parts. The first twenty "distinctions" in the first part contain propositions as to the sources of law, which Gratian designates as a treatise on decretals, followed by other treatises on qualifications for ordination, on ordination, and on ecclesiastical promotion. The second part, though other subjects occasionally come in, is mainly devoted to ecclesiastical jurisdiction, offenses, and legal proceedings, dealing in the last nine *causæ* with the law of matrimony, with a separate treatise on penance put into the thirty-third. The last part, entitled "Of consecration," deals with religious functions, and especially the sacraments, in five distinctions. The feature most characteristic of the work as a whole is that Gratian did not content himself with collecting canons to illustrate and enforce the principles to which they related and arranging them after a certain rather unsatisfactory system, but in the first two parts himself elucidated these principles in (generally short) explanations to which he appended the canons as *pièces justificatives.* In these *dicta* of his the attempt is frequently visible to reconcile or eliminate the discrepancies appearing in the canons as they stand.

2. Gratian.

The extent to which the *Decretum,* in spite of all its defects, met a practical want of its day is seen by the approval and currency which it attained. The older collections were superseded by it; the work which Cardinal Laborans put together in 1182, containing much the same material with a really better arrangement, failed to attract attention. The wide popularity of Gratian's work is to be explained partly by the fact that it appeared at a time when Bologna was the headquarters for the study of law. The laborious activity of the glossators of the Roman law afforded a model for the application of the same learned method to Gratian's material. He himself lectured upon it, and thus became the founder of a new school of canonists who, in addition to their lectures, like the civil jurists, expounded separate passages of the *Decretum* by glosses or commentaries (see GLOSSES AND GLOSSATORS OF CANON LAW). In this way it became known far and wide; and its authority was further strengthened by the fact that the popes made use of it and cited it. It was never, indeed, expressly confirmed by any pope, or received in the Church as an official codex; but the influence of the university insured its respectful acceptance and its application in practise. It was not long before others, particularly a pupil of Gratian's named Paucapaleo, added canons here and there to make it more complete—at first in the form of marginal glosses, but later as a part of the text, with the designation *Palea,* which must have referred originally to the above-named scholar (though other interpretations have been attempted) and then have been adopted as a specific term for these additions. That they must early have crept into the text is shown by the fact that the majority of them are accepted in the work of Cardinal Laborans, a few years later.

6. Collections of Decretals: Great as was the popularity and the practical importance which the *Decretum* acquired at the outset, it appeared, none the less, in a period characterized by great legislative activity on the part of the popes, who were now approaching the height of their power. The decretals issued from the twelfth century on contained an extraordinary wealth of new material for ecclesiastical law, which in many particulars altered and further developed the previous discipline of the Church; and thus it was not long before the work of Gratian, which, when it was compiled, represented practically the whole extant canon law, came inevitably to be regarded as antiquated or incomplete, and the need of new collections was felt. These, because they were composed almost wholly of papal decrees and the canons of councils held under the pope's eye, were usually known as *collectiones decretalium.*

Of such collections made before Gregory IX., five deserve special mention. (1) The *Breviarium extravagantium,* completed about 1191 by Bernard, dean of Pavia. The title comes from the fact that the laws included in it, principally new ones, were such as were not found in the *Decretum,* but, so to speak, wandered about homeless (*extra Decretum vagantes*). Bernard took his material partly from some older collections, of which he names explicitly the *Corpus canonum* (probably the *Collectio Anselmo dedicata*) and Burchard, and partly, especially for the newer decretals, from collections made after Gratian. In the division and arrangement of his work, he evidently took the code of Justinian for a model. The first book deals with ecclesiastical offices and prerequisites for judgment; the second, with judicial tribunals and their procedure; the third, with the clergy and religious orders; the fourth, with marriage, and the fifth with crime and its punishment. The work was accepted by the Bolognese teachers, and, as the first of its kind, became known as *Compilatio prima.* (2) By order of Innocent III. the papal notary Petrus Col-

1. Before Gregory IX.

livacinus of Benevento made a collection of the decretals of that pope, issued in the first eleven years of his pontificate, to 1210, based upon two earlier ones which had not been received at Bologna because they contained unauthentic documents. Innocent, sending the new work to the universities, guaranteed its fidelity to the *Regesta*, thus making it the first codification of canon law expressly authorized by any pope. This *Compilatio tertia*, as it is called, marks a turning-point in the history of canon law. The action of Honorius III., and still more of Gregory IX., shows how the development of ecclesiastical law had by their time become an exclusive privilege of the pope. (3) Though written after the last-named, that which contains the decretals of the popes from Alexander III. to Innocent III is known as *Compilatio secunda* from its place in the chronological order. These particular decretals had already been compiled by two Englishmen at Bologna, Gilbert and Alan, but the university had not approved their work, and it was now done over by Johannes Galensis (John the Welshman), his collection being accepted. (4) The Lateran Council of 1215 gave occasion for another compilation, known as *Quarta*, which included the decrees of the council and the papal pronouncements of the years following 1210. Its compiler is unknown. (5) In 1226 Honorius III. sent to Bologna a collection of his own decretals and the constitutions of Frederick II. It was accepted as *Compilatio quinta*, but was soon superseded, with the other four, by the official collection of Gregory IX.

2. Collection of Gregory.

In 1230 Gregory entrusted his chaplain Raymond of Peñaforte with the preparation of a new collection which should reduce all that had gone before to a consistent and intelligible whole. Raymond omitted a number of sections from the older compilations in order to avoid repetitions or discrepancies, revised some older decretals to bring them into harmony with the most recent legislation, condensed some long documents, and divided others into parts which could be classified by their subjects. This compilation was sent to Bologna by the pope in 1234 as the only authorized collection.

The legislative activity of the succeeding popes soon made supplements necessary, which were sent by them to the universities as separate compilations, but were intended to be added to the Gregorian collection. Thus Innocent IV in 1245 sent to Bologna and Paris a list of the initial words of his bulls, desiring that they, as well as the decrees of the Council of Lyons, should be inserted in their proper places in the decretals of Gregory IX.; thus too the decretals of Alexander IV., Urban IV., and Clement IV. were put together in special collections. Gregory X. communicated to the universities the acts of the Second Council of Lyons (1274), and the same was done with a collection of five decretals of Nicholas III.

3. Supplements to It.

The same reasons which had influenced Gregory IX. induced Boniface VIII. to combine all the post-Gregorian decretals with his own numerous bulls into a single whole. In his bull of publication addressed to the universities of Bologna and Paris, he emphasized the uncertainty which had prevailed in regard to the authenticity of some decretals, to eliminate which he had had a thorough revision and verification made. He promulgated the new compilation in 1298 under the name of *Liber sextus*, as being a completion of the five books of the Gregorian collection. The decretals subsequently issued by Boniface himself (including the famous bull *Unam sanctam*) and by his successor, Benedict XI., sixteen in number, were frequently appended to the *Liber sextus*, though without official authority. Clement V. had the decisions of the Council of Vienne (1311) and his own decretals collected (according to the traditional system) into five books, which he promulgated in 1313, apparently under the title of *Liber septimus*, and sent to the University of Orléans. Then, however, he stopped its further circulation and had it revised, so that it was sent to Paris and Bologna only by his successor John XXII. in 1317. This collection ultimately became known as the Clementine Constitutions. The difference between it and the other post-Gregorian compilations was that while they had borne to a certain extent the character of exclusive codes, it did not exclude the other *Extravagantes* which had appeared since the *Liber sextus*, and that it contained, besides the canons of Vienne, nothing but Clement's own decretals.

The reason for this abandonment by Clement V and John XXII. of the system of their predecessors was the difficult situation in France, and the desire to avoid provoking a rejection of their compilation by including in it matter which was certain to excite violent opposition there. This accounts for the fact that no further official collections of decretals were published. The increasing difficulties of the papacy with the secular power and with national churches made the reception of such things problematical, at the same time that it claimed the best energies of the popes for other matters. Of collections subsequently published, though no longer by the popes themselves, with the title of *Extravagantes*, two have retained some importance to the present day, because of their inclusion in the *Corpus juris canonici*. When at the end of the fifteenth century the booksellers Gering and Remboldt in Paris undertook an edition of all the parts of the *Corpus*, they entrusted the editing of the *Decretum*, the *Liber sextus*, the *Clementina*, and the *Extravagantes* to Jean Chappuis, who made a new arrangement of the last-named, preserved in all subsequent editions. He divided them into two collections; the first, *Extravagantes Johannis Papæ XXII.*, contained twenty decretals of that pope, put together by himself in a chronologically consistent whole and glossed by Zenzelinus de Cassianis in 1325; the second, seventy-four (originally seventy) decretals of popes from Urban IV. (1261–64) to Sixtus IV (1471–84), known as *Extravagantes communes*, not because they belong to a number of popes, but because they are the commonly cited ones—though no single previous edition had contained more than thirty-three of these. In 1590 Petrus Matthæus published at Lyons a *Liber septimus* containing decretals from Sixtus IV to Sixtus V. (1585–90); but this, though printed as an appendix to many old editions of the *Corpus juris canonici*, never met with much recognition or use. Gregory XIII. appointed a commission to prepare an official *Liber septimus*, but the work, which finally included the dogmatic decrees of Florence and Trent, was not completely printed until 1598, in the pontificate of Clement VIII., under whose name it appeared; and then Clement, for some reason now unknown, refused to approve it. No further systematic collection of later decretals has been undertaken, though frequent chronological arrangements of them have been published under the title of *Bullaria* (see BRIEFS, BULLS, AND BULLARIA).

7. Corpus Juris Canonici: It remains to give an account of the *Corpus juris canonici*, by which name it has been customary since the sixteenth century to designate the collection formed by combining the *Decretum Gratiani*, the decretals of Gregory IX., the *Liber sextus*, the *Clementina*, and the two collections of *Extravagantes* made by Chappuis. The name was applied to Gratian's work in the twelfth century, and by Innocent IV to the Gregorian collection; Pierre d'Ailly, in his treatise *De necessitate reformationis*, written at the opening of the Council of Constance, speaks of the reservations prescribed " in corpore juris canonici," where there is no doubt that he means the sum of the collections named above, with the exception of the as yet non-existent *Extravagantes*. During the council the term *Corpus juris* or *jus scriptum* was constantly employed in contradistinction to the post-Clementine *Extravagantes*, and similarly at the Council of Basel. The legal authority of the *Extravagantes* was, in fact, frequently contested, and the thesis of the independent validity of every papal pronouncement, which had had practical effect since Innocent III., no longer recognized. So far, then, this distinction was justified, and while no new accepted collection was added to the *Clementina* the previously accepted *Corpus* might be considered as closed. The name does not occur in the oldest printed editions, which is to be explained by the fact that the component parts were usually printed separately. In the sixteenth century it became usual for these parts, together with Chappuis's two collections of *Extravagantes*, to be published by the same house in three volumes, the first containing Gratian's work, the second the decretals of Gregory IX., and the third the remainder with the glosses. In the latter half of this century, however, it was more common to omit the glosses and bind the whole in one volume, so that the inclusive title now becomes usual. The edition of Demochares (Paris, 1550, 1561) showed a certain amount of critical spirit, but with little result. During the sessions of the Council of Trent the need of revision was clearly apparent, and Pius IV in 1563 established a commission of cardinals and other scholars for this purpose. Under his successors, Pius V. and Gregory XIII., it was confirmed and enlarged to thirty-five members. The work of these *Correctores Romani*, as they are called, was completed in 1580, and the resulting revised edition published at Rome in 1582. Though they had rendered valuable service, much remained to be done, as was made evident by the editions of Antonius Augustinus and Berardus—to say nothing of the modern ones. The earlier editions usually contained a number of appendices, including the *Institutiones juris canonici* of Paul Lancelot, professor at Perugia under Paul IV (1555-59), the *Liber septimus* of Petrus Matthæus, etc.

For the internal relations of the Roman Catholic Church the *Corpus juris canonici* is still the authority in common law, though with some limitations. The appendices are not considered authoritative, especially those just named, unless the single decretals contained in the last of them have been universally received; and the same principle applies to the *Extravagantes*. The position taken at the councils of Constance and Basel was not affected by the edition of Gregory XIII., whose purpose was not to give them an official character by including them, but merely to establish a correct and authentic text of the documents which had previously been included in widely circulated collections. Acting on the same principle in regard to this edition of Gregory XIII., most modern canonists deny the positive authority of the *Decretum Gratiani* as such, since it was a mere private collection, never officially authorized by the Church or the pope, and regard it only as a valuable collection of documents for the history of canon law. This view was even expressed in a decision of the *Rota Romana*, too long to quote here, and more than once by Benedict XIV But though this may be theoretically the case, yet in practise the *Decretum* has retained a large measure of authority; and Gregory XIII. himself would scarcely have displayed so much zeal in having it edited and completed if he had regarded it as no more than a private compilation, without legal authority. Its contents, however, have in the lapse of time been to a great extent modified or rendered obsolete by later decretals, so that its practical importance is small.

Besides the general principle that a new law supersedes an older one, which has destroyed the validity of so much that is in the *Corpus juris* (not merely in Gratian's part of it), the course of secular legislation since the fourteenth century has had a marked influence in the same direction. The canon law covers not merely the doctrine, worship, sacraments, and discipline of the Church, but a vast mass of other things in which ecclesiastical interests were supposed to be concerned, such as vows, oaths, betrothals, wills, funerals, benefices, church property, tithes, and the like. The reaction against the all-embracing claims of the Church has taken many of these things out of the hands of the ecclesiastical tribunals (see JURISDICTION, ECCLESIASTICAL), while by its proclamation of the principle of the unity of national law and government it has reduced the Church to the position of any other corporation within the limits of the State; and thus a large number of canonical provisions, such as those covering the procedure against heretics, which conflict with the civil constitution, have necessarily become ineffective. In France, Belgium, and Italy it is still regarded as a part of the general body of law. In the German

Empire, after gradual restrictions in many of the component states, it ceased on Jan. 1, 1900, to have any legal validity outside of the internal discipline of the Roman Catholic Church.

(J. F. VON SCHULTE.)

BIBLIOGRAPHY: On the conception and apologetics of church law consult: W. T. Krug, *Das Kirchenrecht nach Grundsätzen der Vernunft und im Lichte des Christentums*, Leipsic, 1826, cf. F. Schirmer, *Kirchengeschichtliche Untersuchungen*, Berlin, 1829; C. Gross, *Zur Begriffsbestimmung und Würdigung des Kirchenrechts*, Graz, 1872.

Collections or digests supplementing those mentioned in the text are: Z. B. van Espen, *Jus ecclesiasticum universale*, 2 vols., Louvain, 1700; A. Reiffenstül, *Jus canonicum universum*, 3 vols., Venice, 1704; J. H. Böhmer, *Jus ecclesiasticum Protestantium*, 5 vols., Halle, 1714; F. Schmalzgrüber, *Jus ecclesiasticum universum*, 5 vols., Ingolstadt, 1726. Other discussions are: J. F. Schulte, *Das katholische Kirchenrecht*, 2 vols., Giessen, 1856–60; D. Craisson, *Manuale totius juris canonici*, 4 vols., Paris, 1863; F. Walter, *Lehrbuch des Kirchenrechts aller christlichen Konfessionen*, 14th ed., Bonn, 1871; F. Thudichum, *Kirchenrecht*, 2 vols., Leipsic, 1877–78; A. L. Richter, *Lehrbuch des katholischen und evangelischen Kirchenrechts*, 8th ed. by W. Kahl, Leipsic, 1877–86; W. Kahl, *Kirchenrecht und Kirchenpolitik*, Freiburg, 1894; E. Geigel, *Reichs- und reichsländisches Kirchen- und Stiftungsrecht*, Strasburg, 1900; E. Friedberg, *Lehrbuch des katholischen und evangelischen Kirchenrechts*, Leipsic, 1903.

Works in Eng. on the general question are: J. Fulton, *Index Canonum, Gk. Text with Translation and Complete Digest of Canon Law of the Universal Church*, New York, 1892; S. B. Smith, *Elements of Ecclesiastical Law, with Reference to the Syllabus, Constitutiones apostolicæ sedis of Pope Pius IX., the Council of the Vatican* , 3 vols., ib. 1893–94. For English church law consult: E. Gibson, *Codex juris ecclesiastici Anglicani: or, the Statutes, Constitutions, Canons, Rubrics, and Articles . Methodically Digested . with a Commentary*, London, 1713, cf. [M. Foster], *An Examination of the Scheme of Church-Power Laid Down in the Codex juris eccl. Anglicani*, ib. 1735; C. H. Davis, *English Church Canons of 1604; with historical Introduction and Notes*, ib. 1869; M. E. C. Walcott, *Constitutions and Canons Eclesiastical of the Church of England Referred to Their Original Sources . . .*, ib. 1874; Sir. W. Phillimore, *Law of the Church of England*, 2 vols., ib. 1895; F. W. Maitland, *Canon Law in England*, ib. 1898; A. T. Wirgman, *Constitutional Authority of the Bishops in the Catholic Church Illustrated by History and Canon Law*, ib. 1899. Consult also E. Taunton, *The Law of the Church. A Cyclopædia of Canon Law for English-speaking Countries*, London, 1906.

For American church law consult: F. Vinton, *Manual Commentary on the General Canon Law of the Protestant Episcopal Church*, New York, 1870; M. Hoffmann, *Ecclesiastical Law in the State of New York*, ib. 1868; idem, *Ritual Law of the Church*, ib. 1872; W. S. Perry, *The General Ecclesiastical Constitution of the American Church*, ib. 1891; *Revised Constitution and Canons of the Protestant Episcopal Church*, ib. 1895; H. J. Desmond, *The Church and the Law, with Special Reference to Ecclesiastical Law in the United States*, Chicago, 1898.

CANON OF SCRIPTURE.

Canon of Scripture is a term that designates the books of the Bible accepted as authoritative. The word "canon" (Gk. *kanōn*) means primarily a straight staff, then a measuring-rod, hence, figuratively, that which is artistically, scientifically, or ethically a guide or a model; so in the earliest Christian use (Gal. vi. 16; Phil. iii. 16; Clement of Rome, i. 7, 41) the canon was a leading thought, a normal principle. The next change of meaning (indicated by Clement of Alexandria, *Strom.*, VII. xvi. 94) was to a type of Christian doctrine, the orthodox as opposed to the heretical. Since 300 the plural form "canons" has been used of ecclesiastical regulations (see CANON). Now, since the Christian doctrines were professedly based upon the Scriptures, the writings themselves were naturally known as the canon; and the test of the canonicity of any particular writing was its reception by the Church. The earliest use of the word in this sense is in the fifty-ninth canon of the Council of Laodicea (363), "No psalms of private authorship can be read in the Church, nor uncanonical books, but only the canonical books of the Old and New Testaments," and contemporaneously in Athanasius (*Epistola festalis*, i. 961, Paris, 1698). A few years later the use was general.

I. The Canon of the Old Testament.—1. History Among the Jews: The theory, which was almost universally received for fifteen hundred years, that Ezra was the author of the Old Testament canon, dates from the first Christian century; for it is found in IV (II) Ezra xiv. 44 that Ezra was inspired to dictate during forty days to five men ninety-four books, of which twenty-four were to be published. These twenty-four quite evidently are the twenty-four books of the Hebrew canon, according to the counting given below; and the seventy are the Jewish Apocrypha alluded to in the *Gospel of Nicodemus* xxviii. (*ANF*, viii. 453). What the

1. Traditional Account of the Rise of the Collection.

Fathers have to say upon this matter is derived in part from IV Ezra, and is equally fabulous.

2. The Theory of the Synagogue.

The theory above mentioned has been supposed to be the one prevalent among the Jews themselves. But this has no other support than that the eminent rabbis David Kimchi (d. 1240) and Elias Levita (1472–1549) remarked on the work of Ezra and the men of the Great Synagogue, in bringing together the twenty-four books in their divisions. The only Talmudic passage which can be quoted directly in its behalf is in *Baba Bathra*; for the other quotations commonly made prove merely the care of Ezra and the men of the Great Synagogue for the law, not for the canon; indeed, mostly for the oral law, and some also for alterations in the text. The passage is in these words: "The order of the prophets is Joshua and Judges, Samuel and Kings, Jeremiah and Ezekiel, Isaiah and the Twelve. Hosea is the first, because it is written, 'The beginning of the word of Jehovah by Hosea' (i. 2). Did God, then, speak to Hosea first? and have there not been many prophets between him and Moses? R. Johanan explained this as meaning that Hosea was the first of the four prophets who prophesied at that time,—Hosea, Isaiah, Amos, and Micah. Why, then, was he not put first? Because his prophesy stands next to that of the latest prophets, Haggai, Zechariah, and Malachi: he is therefore counted with them. So this prophet should have been kept by himself, and inserted before Jeremiah? No: he was so small that he might then easily have been lost. Since Isaiah lived before Jeremiah and Ezekiel, ought he not to have been put before them? [No.] because Kings closes with destruction, Jeremiah is entirely occupied with it, Ezekiel begins with it but ends with consolation, while Isaiah is all consolation; hence we can not connect destruction with destruction, and consolation with consolation. But Job lived in the time of Moses; why should he not come in the first part? No; for it would never do to begin with misfortune. Yet Ruth contains misfortune? True; but it issues in joy. And who wrote them? Moses wrote his book and the Balaam section and Job. Joshua wrote his book and eight verses in the Law (Deut. xxxiv. 5-12). Samuel wrote his book, Judges and Ruth. David wrote Psalms for ten Elders. Jeremiah wrote his book, Kings, and Lamentations. Hezekiah and his company wrote Isaiah, Proverbs, the Song, and Ecclesiastes. The men of the Great Synagogue wrote Ezekiel, The Twelve, Daniel, and Esther. Ezra wrote his book and the genealogies in Chronicles up to his time. That is a support for the saying of Rab; for Rab Jehuda says, in the name of Rab, 'Ezra did not leave Babylon until he had written his own family register.' Who ended it? Nehemiah the son of Hachaliah." The understanding of this passage depends upon observing that the word "wrote" is used in different senses, of actual authorship, of editorship, and of merely collecting and placing together books which had not before been brought into connection. It will be perceived that the passage says nothing about the closing of the canon, but also that it would readily furnish ground for the idea that the canon was closed in the time of Ezra and the Great Synagogue.

3. Criticism of the Two Theories.

Both theories agree in assigning the collection of the Old Testament to Ezra and his companions and successors, and also asserting that the division into the Law, the Prophets, and the Hagiographa (see below) was primitive. But against this, two objections may be urged: (1) Critical investigation assigns the first part of the Book of Daniel, on account of its Greek words, to a time when Greek was understood, and the second part to the Maccabean age (see DANIEL, BOOK OF); (2) The position of some of the historical books, e.g., Ezra and Daniel, among the Hagiographa, is inexplicable if the canon was made at one time. Moses Maimonides, David Kimchi, and Abarbanel explained the fact by a difference in inspiration. But Christ calls Daniel a prophet (Matt. xxiv. 15; Mark xiii. 14).

4. Positive Exposition. a. The Pentateuch— the So-called "First Canon."

The Hebrews, like other ancient peoples, preserved their sacred writings in sacred places. So the law was put by the side of the ark of the covenant (Deut. xxxi. 26), with its additions by Joshua (Josh. xxiv. 26); Samuel laid the law of the kingdom "before the Lord" (I Sam. x. 25); Hilkiah, the high priest under Josiah, found the book of the law "in the house of the Lord" (II Kings xxii. 8). We are, therefore, safe in believing that since the time of Moses documents and intelligence concerning the Mosaic giving of the law, besides the tables of the covenant, and also whatever of law and history Moses had written, were carefully preserved in the sanctuary (Ex. xxiv. 4, 7, xxxiv. 27; Num. xxxiii. 2). The priests also would retain partly oral and partly written information (subsequently combined in the Priest-code) in regard to many similar matters. The existence of an authoritative code is proved (a) by the use of the "Book of the Covenant" in Deut., and (b) in the Priest-code; (c) by Hos. viii. 12; (d) by II Kings xxii. The Books of Kings, finished during the exile, mention by name the "Book of the Law of Moses," by which only Deuteronomy is meant (cf. II Kings xiv. 6; Deut. xxiv. 16; I Kings ii. 3; II Kings xxiii. 25). The mention of the Book of the Law of Moses (Josh. i. 7–8; viii. 31, 34, xxiii. 6) can not be taken without limitation, since it proceeds from the Deuteronomic editor of Joshua. Hag. ii. 11–13 shows the existence of the Priest-code, dealing, as the passage does, with two statutes of that code. The Wellhausen hypothesis, that the Priest-code was the private possession of Ezra till 445 B.C., and that Neh. viii.–x. tells of the introduction of the law, is in incompatible contradiction with that passage. The lowest date for the separation of Joshua [from the Pentateuch] is the time of Nehemiah and the Samaritan schism.

The prophets were the spiritual exhorters and guides of the people, and therefore held in high esteem by the faithful, whose natural desire to have a collection of their writings there is every reason to believe was early gratified. At all events, it is quite evident from the prophetic parallels that the prophets were acquainted with one another's writings.

b. The Historico-prophetic and Distinctively Prophetic Books—the "Second Canon."

The loss of so much sacred literature in the destruction of Jerusalem by the Chaldeans made the collection of the remaining historic as well as prophetic books the more imperative. The success of a collection of historical books was furthered by the fact that Joshua continued the narrative of the Pentateuch. Since Kings continues the history in I and II Sam., and may be placed in the latter half of the exilic period, the close connection with the earlier prophets gave the name to them of "the Former Prophets" and secured a high estimate for them on the return from Babylon.

David and Solomon began the arrangement of the temple praise-service and a collection of Psalms, and later collections and individual Psalms were added.

c. The Hagiographa—the "Third Canon."

The time of Nehemiah was very productive. The division into five books is older than the Chronicler. The first collection of the Proverbs of Solomon (cf. Prov. x. 1–xxii. 16) was so highly valued that Hezekiah ordered a second to be prepared (Prov. xxv. 1). The name of the wise man sufficed to recommend Canticles; its age and contents, the Book of Job. Lamentations appealed directly to every patriotic Jew during the exile, and was accepted as sacred, although Jeremiah was not its author. Ruth, by age, and especially by its genealogy of David, was put in the third canon, and formed an introduction to the Psalter. These early writings were followed gradually by the others, Ezra–Neh., I and II Chron., Eccles., Esther (an explanation of Purim, the festival the Persian Jews brought back with them), and finally Daniel, in the time of the Maccabees. After this time, and down to the destruction of Jerusalem by Titus, 70 A.D., the nation was so affected by Greek customs, and divided by the growing rival parties, the Pharisees and Sadducees, that its religious development was too much hindered for any work to receive universal recognition, and hence canonicity. The reception of Dan. into the canon appears explicable under the circumstances only if a Daniel narrative, the basis of Dan. ii.–vi., already existed (cf. Ezek. xiv. 14, 20; xxviii. 3). Not long after the Maccabees, the second collection or canon received its name, the Prophets, descriptive not only of a portion of its contents, but of their authorship; and thus the three divisions of the Old Testament canon—the Law, Prophets, and Hagiographa—dated from the second century B.C. (cf. the Prologue to Ecclesiasticus). Valentin Loescher (*De causis linguæ Hebrææ*, p. 71, Leipsic, 1706) said rightly: "The canon came not, as they say, by one act of man, but gradually from God."

2. Witnesses for the Second and Third Parts of the Canon: Jesus Sirach (Ecclus. xlvi.–xlix., especially xlix. 10) shows acquaintance only with the Prophets in the wider sense, the "second canon." His grandson testifies to the third division also. The Second Book of Maccabees, dated by Niese (*Kritik der beiden Makkabäerbücher*, Berlin, 1900) 125–124 B.C., in the section i. 10–ii. 18 contains an account of the recovery of the sacred fire, a quotation from the "records" of Jeremiah (a lost apocryphal writing); and then follows ii. 13: "And the same things also were reported in the records, namely, the memoirs of Nehemiah [another apocryphal writing], and how he, founding a library, gathered together the books concerning the kings and prophets, and those of David, and epistles of kings concerning holy gifts." This reference to the "epistles of kings concerning holy gifts" can not denote the Book of Ezra, but only a collection of documents regarding international matters, such as would be of value to a statesman like Nehemiah, and which had connection with the temple and its offerings. It, therefore, bears witness to Nehemiah's collection of the second canon substantially as we have it to-day, in addition to the Psalms and the documents so weighty for the rebuilt city. The next verse, "And in like manner also Judas gathered together all those books that had been scattered by reason of the war we had, and they are with us," applies only to the third canon. Therefore, the last enlargement of the Hebrew canon took place under Judas Maccabæus; although probably most of the books of the third canon had previously been preserved in the temple archives.

Philo had the same canon as ours (cf. C. Siegfried, *Philo*, p. 161, Jena, 1875), and quotes from almost all the books; while from the Apocrypha he makes no excerpts or citation, not giving it the honor he accords to Plato, Hippocrates, and several other Greek writers.* The New Testament contains quotations principally from the Pentateuch, Prophets, and Psalms, as might be conjectured from its scope, but recognizes the threefold division of the canon (Luke xxiv. 44). In this verse "The Psalms" does not stand for the entire Hagiographa; for our Lord meant to emphasize the fact that the Psalms spoke of him. The use of the phrase "the Law and the Prophets" (Matt. v. 17; Acts xxviii. 23) does not imply a division into two parts. The Syrians used the same expression for the whole Old Testament. The absence of quotation in the New Testament of any Old Testament book argues nothing against its canonicity. The use by the New Testament of Apocrypha or Pseudepigrapha has no bearing on the canonical status of the books used or cited. Josephus (*Apion*, i. 8)

* P. C. Lucius, *Die Therapeuten und ihre Stellung in der Askese*, Strasburg, 1880, has proved that the *De vita contemplativa* was not written by Philo, and consequently the classic passage—"In every house there is a sacred shrine, which is called the holy place, and the monastery in which they [the Therapeutics] retire by themselves, and perform all the mysteries of a holy life . . studying in that place the laws and the inspired words through the prophets and hymns and the other [writings], by which knowledge and piety are increased and perfected" (*De vita contempl.*, iii.), which is the only direct reference to the threefold division of the canon found in Philo's works (genuine and pretended)—must be given up. [The passage is translated by C. D. Yonge, *Philo*, in Bohn's Library, iv. 6. F. C. Conybeare, in his edition of *Philo About the Contemplative Life* (Oxford, 1895) defends the Philonian authorship.]

bears the strongest testimony for the canon,* and, as is evident, expresses the national and not his private opinion. And, further, the books mentioned are not mere literature, but a sacred, divine collection. He enumerates twenty-two books; thus, 1. The five books of the Law; 2. The thirteen Prophets, counting the twelve minor Prophets as one book, and Lamentations with Jeremiah; 3. The four Hagiographa—Psalms, Proverbs, Ecclesiastes, and Canticles. But this arrangement is not to be looked upon as either old or correct.

3. Supposed Jewish Dissent from the Canon: This dissent is not real, only apparent; but appeal has been made (a) to the Talmudical controversies about certain books, e.g., Esther; on further examination these "controversies" are perceived to be mere intellectual displays; there is no intention of rejecting any book. (b) The Book of Sirach, it is said, is quoted as Scripture; but there is no proof that it was regarded as Scripture, and the two or three quotations are *memoriter*, and probably made under a misapprehension of their source. (c) A high regard for the Book of Baruch is asserted, but all Jewish literature furnishes no proof. On the other hand, the late origin of the book is against the assumption; it is dependent upon Dan. ix., and was not composed till after the capture of Jerusalem by Titus. (d) The Septuagint is supposed by some to show that the Alexandrian Jews had a different canon from the Palestinian, because books are added to the canonical twenty-four and additions are made to some of the canonical books; but this does not follow. For the Palestinian idea of a canon (namely, the compositions of inspired prophets, a class of men not then existent) was not known in Alexandria, where, on the contrary, the statement of Wisdom (vii. 27), "[Wisdom] from generation to generation entering into holy souls prepares them friends of God and prophets," was fully believed, as by Philo (cf. *De cherubim*, ix.) and Josephus (*War*, I. iii. 5, II. viii. 12, III. viii. 3, 9), who even declared that they themselves had been at times really inspired, and freely accorded the fact unto others. Therefore, to an Alexandrian Jew, there was no impropriety in enlarging the Greek translation of the Old Testament, not only by additions of sections to the canonical books, but of entirely new books. The great respect entertained for the Septuagint was extended to these additions, but without giving the latter any canonical authority. There was no Alexandrian canon; for neither the number nor the order of the books added was fixed.

4. History of the Old Testament Canon Among the Jews: The Triple Division of the Hebrew canon is testified to by the prologue to Sirach and the New Testament (Luke xxiv. 44).

1. The Triple Division.

The Septuagint gave up this division in favor of a different one—the present Christian arrangement of the books in the order, history, poetry, prophecy—and inserted the apocryphal books and sections in appropriate places.

2. Order.

The order of the books in the Hebrew canon is as follows: 1. The *Torah* or "Law"—the five books of Moses; 2. The *Nebhiim* or "Prophets"—(a) the "Former Prophets," Joshua, Judges, I and II Samuel, I and II Kings; (b) the "Latter Prophets," Isaiah, Jeremiah, Ezekiel, the twelve minor Prophets; 3. The *Kethubhim* ("Writings") or *Hagiographa*—Psalms, Proverbs, Job, Canticles, Ruth, Lamentations, Ecclesiastes, Esther, Daniel, Ezra, and Nehemiah, I and II Chronicles, in all, twenty-four books. The view once entertained that Ruth and Lam. once were in the second canon and were transferred to the third when it was formed has no basis in fact. The principle of arrangement of the historico-prophetical books is chronological. The Mishnah arranges the prophetical books proper in order of length: Jer., Ezek., Isa., the Twelve. But with this went probably the recollection that as a whole Isa. was later than Jer. and Ezek. The Masorites put Isa. first. In some MSS. of the third canon the most important book, Ps., introduced by Ruth, is at the head, then Job and the three books connected with Solomon's name, and the four latest books at the close. The Masorites arrange: Chron., Ps., Job, Prov., Ruth, Song of Sol., Eccles., Lam., Esther, Dan., Ezra. Manuscripts differ greatly in the order of these books.

3. Number of the Canonical Books.

Jewish tradition, except when influenced by Alexandria, unanimously gives the number as twenty-four. Nevertheless, it is usual to say that the original reckoning was twenty-two. If, however, the witnesses for the latter number be not counted, but weighed, it is plain that the authority they rest upon is Alexandrian; and this is worthless for getting at the primitive reckoning, because the Alexandrian Jews not only altered the order and division of the books, but added to them others not in the canon. Furthermore, the Alexandrians arrived at the number twenty-two by joining Ruth to Judges, and Lamentations to Jeremiah. Having thus made twenty-two, they were impressed with its numerical agreement with the number of letters in the Hebrew alphabet. This idea was thought significant, part of the divine intention indeed; and so it became fixed in the Jewish mind. The Church Fathers took it up in their uncritical fashion; and so it has come down to our day. Josephus first gives twenty-two; but he makes greater use of the Septuagint than of the Hebrew original. It is noteworthy that Epiphanius and Jerome, who reckon the books twenty-two, mention also twenty-seven; i.e., the Hebrew twenty-two letters, with the five final letters (the letters which have a special form

* This passage in condensed form is as follows: "We have twenty-two books containing the records of all the past times, and justly believed to be inspired. Five of them are Moses'. These contain his laws and the traditions of the origin of mankind till his death. From Moses to Artaxerxes the prophets made the record in thirteen books. The remaining four books contain hymns to God, and precepts for the conduct of human life. The history written since that day, though accurate, is not so much esteemed, because there has not been an exact succession of prophets. No one dares add to, take from, or alter them; but all Jews esteem these books to contain divine doctrines, and are willing to die for them."

when at the end of a word); made by separating the double books, Samuel, Kings, Chronicles, and Ezra. But this double counting was only possible for Jews using the Septuagint, since the original does not divide these books. Further, neither in the Talmud nor in the Midrash is there the least trace of any acquaintance with the number twenty-two; but, on the contrary, twenty-four is always given, not because it corresponds with the twenty-four Greek letters, but simply as the natural result of the gradual rise of the canon. In the present printed Hebrew Bible the number is thirty-nine, similarly counted, though not arranged, with those of Protestant Bibles.

5. The Old Testament Canon in the Christian Church: The Fathers did not impugn the authority of the Old Testament; but, because of the universal use of the Septuagint, they recognized as Scripture what we regard as Apocrypha. Origen, who counts only the books of the Hebrew canon, yet speaks of Jeremiah, Lamentations, and the Epistle as in one [book]. Justin Martyr used the additions to Daniel; Irenæus, Tertullian, Clement of Alexandria, Cyprian, and others used the Apocrypha with the same formula of citation as when they used the Old Testament. From the fourth century the Greek Fathers make less and less use of the Apocrypha; while in the Latin Church conciliar action justified and emphasized their use. Jerome alone speaks out decidedly for the Hebrew canon. During the Middle Ages the Apocrypha were not recognized by the majority of the Greeks; while just the opposite was true of the Latins, although not a few followed Jerome.

1. Patristic and Medieval Writers.

The Book of Esther, because of its contents, was sometimes excluded from the Christian Old Testament canon. Melito of Sardis (170 A.D.) omits it from his list (see Eusebius, *Hist. eccl.*, IV. xxvi.), although perhaps it has rather dropped out after Esdras (Ezra), inasmuch as in other lists it comes next to this name. It is also omitted by Athanasius (*Epistola Festalis*, i. 961, ed. Bened.), Gregory Nazianzen (*Carm.*, xxxiii.), and in the sixth century by Junilius (*De partibus legis divinæ*, i. 3–7). On the other hand, it is included in the canon by Origen, Cyril of Jerusalem, and Epiphanius.

The old Syrian Church did not receive the Apocrypha. They are not in the Peshito, although found in a later Syriac translation. Ephraem Syrus (d. 373) does not give them canonical authority. Aphraates (fourth century) cites from every canonical book, but uses the Apocrypha sparingly and not in such a way that they must be regarded as canonical. A great difference is perceptible in the Peshito translation between Chronicles and the other books. This has started the query whether Chronicles was accepted as canonical by the Syrian Church. The Nestorians certainly rejected it and Esther. The Ethiopic translation follows the Septuagint throughout, and contains not only the canonical but also the apocryphal books, except that for I and II Maccabees it substitutes two books of its own under the same name, and some pseudographs of which the Greek texts do not now exist; for the Ethiopic Church makes even less difference than the Alexandrian between canonical and uncanonical books. (See PSEUDEPIGRAPHA, OLD TESTAMENT.)

2. The Ancient Oriental Versions.

The Roman Catholic Church is committed to the use of the Apocrypha as Scripture by the decision of the Council of Trent at the fourth session. In order to get a normal text for purposes of quotation, a Bible was published in Rome in 1592 under the order and care of the pope. In it is given Jerome's remark, that the additions to Esther and Daniel which are printed are not in the Hebrew text; and in smaller type the candid announcement is prefaced to the Prayer of Manasses and the Third and Fourth Books of Ezra, that, while it is true they are not in the Scripture canon of the Council of Trent, they are still included because they are quoted occasionally by certain of the Fathers, and are found both in printed and manuscript copies of the Latin Bible. The decree of the council was not passed without opposition; and later Roman Catholics, such as Du Pin, *Dissertation préliminaire ou prolégomènes sur la Bible*, Paris, 1699; and B. Lamy, *Apparatus biblicus*, II. v. 333, Lyons, 1723, have endeavored to establish two classes of canonical books—the protocanonical and the deuterocanonical—attributing to the first a dogmatic, and to the second only an ethical authority; but this distinction contravenes the decision of Trent, and has found little support.

3. The Roman Catholic Church.

In early times and in the Middle Ages many distinguished three kinds of writings, the canonical, recognized, and apocryphal. So the "Easter Epistle" of Athanasius. The synods of Constantinople (1638), Jassy (1642), and Jerusalem (1672) expressly reject the view of Cyril Lucar, patriarch of Constantinople, and others, which distinguishes the canonical form from the apocryphal. And the last, which is the most important in the history of the Eastern Church, defined its position in regard to the Apocrypha in the answer to the third question appended to the *Confession of Dositheus*, in which it expressly mentions Wisdom, Judith, Tobit, History of Bel and the Dragon, History of Susannah, the Maccabees (four books), and Ecclesiasticus as canonical. Reuss (*Geschichte der heiligen Schriften*, § 338, Brunswick, 1878) says that the official Moscow edition of the Bible of 1831 has all the Apocrypha, Ezra, in both recensions, with Neh. and I–IV Macc. at the end of the historical books, the Prophets before the seven Poetical or Wisdom books. But the "Longer Catechism" of Philaret (Moscow, 1839), the most authoritative doctrinal standard of the orthodox Greco-Russian Church, expressly leaves out the apocryphal books from its list on the ground that "they do not exist in the Hebrew" (cf. Schaff, *Creeds*, ii. 451). See EASTERN CHURCH, III., § 9.

4. The Greek Church.

The Lutheran symbols do not give any express declaration against the Apocrypha. Nevertheless, they are denied dogmatic value. Luther translated them, not, however, III and IV Ezra, and recommended them for private reading, excepting Baruch and II Macc. In the first complete edition of the Bible (Zurich, 1530) the Apocrypha stood at the end. With this agree the decisions of the other Reformed Protestant churches: the "Gallican Confession," 1559, §§ 3, 4; "Belgic Confession," 1561, §§ 4–6; "Thirty-nine Articles," 1562, § 6 (cf. Schaff, *Creeds of Christendom*, iii.). The Book of Common Prayer contains readings from the Apocrypha and especial recommendation of portions of Wisdom and Sirach. At the Synod of Dort (1618), Gomarus and others raised an animated discussion by demanding the exclusion of the apocryphal Ezra, Tobit, Judith, and Bel and the Dragon from the Bible. This the synod refused to do, although speaking strongly against the Apocrypha. Similarly opposed to them was the Westminster Assembly of Divines, 1647, *Confession of Faith*, i. 3; the Arminians, *Confessio pastorum, qui remonstrantes vocantur*, i. 3, 6; the Socinians (Ostorodt, *Unterrichtung von den vornehmsten Hauptpunckten der christlichen Religion*, Rakau, 1604) and the Mennonites (Johann Ris, *Præcipuorum Christianæ fidei articulorum brevis confessio*, xxix.) agree with the other Protestants. For history of the relation of the Bible societies to the Apocrypha, see BIBLE SOCIETIES. For the Apocrypha in general, see APOCRYPHA.

5. The Protestant Church.

6. The Names of the Old Testament and of Its Chief Divisions: (a) Hebrew. Neh. viii. 8 has the expression *Miḳra*, "Reading," which here must signify the Law. Dan. ix. 2 has *Sepherim*, "the Books"; *Kitebe haḳḳodesh*, "the Holy Writings," is Talmudic. The division into three parts is common in the Talmud, with the names *Torah, Nebhiim*, and *Kethubhim*, "Law, Prophets, and Writings," with the abbreviation *TNK*. Often the whole is embraced in the term *Torah*. The first part is named also "The Five Fifths of the Law." The first part of the prophetical canon is called "the Former Prophets"; the second part "the Latter Prophets." The third part of the canon is known as "the Writings" and "the Sacred Writings." The Song of Sol., Ruth, Lam., Eccles., and Esther are classed together as *Megillot*, "Rolls." The second and third parts are often named together as the *ḳabbalah*. (b) Greek. It may be concluded that by the time of the translator of Ecclus. the words "the Books" were in use, since he speaks of "the other [books]," "the rest [of the books]." In the New Testament they are called "the Scripture," "Holy" or "Sacred Writings"; the Pentateuch is called "the Old Covenant" in II Cor. iii. 14. Among the Greek Fathers the following names are used: "The Books of the Old Covenant," "The Sacred (Holy) Writings of the Old Covenant," the "Old Covenant," "the Twenty-two Books of the Old Covenant," "the Covenant Books," and "Law and Prophets." (c) Latin. *Vetus testamentum* translates Hebr. *berith*, "covenant"; *instrumentum, totum instrumentum utriusque testamenti, vetus scriptura, vetus lex*, and *veteris legis libri* are used. (H. L. STRACK.)

II. The Canon of the New Testament.—1. The Terms Used: Alongside the word canon, expressing the idea of the collection of scriptures, were used the terms "covenant" (derived from the Old Testament, Ex. xxiv. 27), "Scripture" or "Scriptures" with the qualifying words "holy," "sacred," "divine," or "of the Lord," also "Law and Gospel," "Prophets and Apostles." The word *endiathekos*, "contained in the covenant," was opposed to *apokryphos*, "apocryphal," the former word often containing the meaning "used in public service."

2. The New Testament, 170–220: Since there are at command no specific reports concerning the origin of the New Testament, an examination of the facts which may throw light upon the problem must be made in order to discover that origin. A starting-point is found in the period of the contest between the Gnostic sects, particularly the Marcionites and the Valentinians, and the orthodox. The Montanistic movement was under way during this period, though it was concerned not so much with the New Testament as with its own objects. The Church had a New Testament already commonly so called, over against the Montanistic contention of a new period of prophecy already opened which was to lead the way to a wider development. The Church regarded the age of revelation as closed with the death of the last surviving apostle and the canon of the New Testament as completed, though discussion still went on as to the inclusion of some books therein. In opposition to Marcion and Montanus the Church had the feeling that it had an inviolable possession in the two Testaments, and the Montanist himself distinguished them from the body of "new prophecy."

1. The Four Gospels.

Opposed to the gospel which Marcion prepared for his communities, to the *Evangelium veritatis* used by the Valentinians alongside the four Gospels of the Church, to the discarding of the Johannean Gospel by the Alogi, and to the exclusive use of Matthew or Mark by other parties of the Church, is the statement of Irenæus that the spirit which created the world had given to the Church its gospel in fourfold form (*Hær.*, III. xi. 8), to violate which was a sin against God's revelation and spirit. The unity of these is asserted in the designation of them as "the Gospel" (in the singular), and in the titles "the Gospel according to Matthew," etc. Clement of Alexandria in his discussion of the origin of the Gospels dealt only with the four. Recollection was soon lost of the fact that a gospel not among the four had striven to be retained in use in public service, and that one of the four had had to win its place among them. But even the Alogi did not deny that the Fourth Gospel belonged to the age of John and had ever since been in the Church. Tatian's preparation for the Syrians of the "Diatessaron" witnesses by its very title to the fact that for an ecclesiastical book of the Gospels no other sources than the four were conceivable. The very permission given by Serapion of Antioch (c. 200) to certain of his parishioners to read a gospel called that of Peter, which he gave without reading the book and through confidence in them, really speaks for the same set of facts, as does the subsequent annulment of the permission. Origen sums up the practise of that period in the saying:

"The Church values only the four Gospels" (*I Hom. in Lucam*).

2. The Pauline Letters. Generally thirteen epistles of Paul were received. If in the Muratorian Canon the reception of four private letters is justified, it appears to have been caused less by a recollection of a late introduction of them into public service than through a thought-process of the author, equating the seven letters of Paul to the communities in symbolical fashion with the letters to the seven churches of the Apocalypse. No statement can be made regarding any favorable feeling for the letters to the Laodiceans and the Alexandrians there rejected. Great difference of opinion existed as to Hebrews. The Alexandrians regarded it as Pauline, and Origen supposed it substantially Pauline through one of Paul's disciples, a position which was widely adopted in the eastern Church. But the western Church disputed its Paulinity, while holding it in high esteem. This was the case in Lyons, Rome, and Carthage. In the Montanistic and Novatian Churches there was a decided tendency to ascribe it to Barnabas.

3. The Acts of the Apostles. Of the Book of Acts all that need be said is that its name, its general recognition as of Lucan authorship, its position between the Gospels and the Pauline Epistles in the Muratorian Canon, its abundant use by Irenæus, Tertullian, and others, and the condemnation by Tertullian of Marcion for rejecting it speak abundantly for its canonicity.

4. The Apocalypse. The strongest proofs are found of the reception of the Apocalypse by all parts of the Church. It was cited by Theophilus of Antioch about 180, and by the church of Lyons in 177, as "Holy Scripture." Neither Irenæus nor the Muratorian Canon regard any defense of it as necessary. As against the high value attached to it by the Montanists, the Alogi scornfully criticized it as the work of Cerinthus. Caius of Rome assumed this attitude also, and Hippolytus defended it against him. But the general feeling of the catholic Church was that the book was inspired, written about 95 A.D., and properly closed the New Testament.

5. The Catholic Epistles. The position of the Catholic Epistles about 200 was a very varied one, though about 300 they were known as one division of the New Testament. II and III John must have been attached to I John, if their history in the Church and their preservation are understood. Testimony to II John comes from Irenæus and Clement of Alexandria; that III John was not treated by Clement does not really damage the case. The doubt which stood in the way of the unconditional recognition of II and III John was soon banished. It is almost certain that the Muratorian Canon designated the two lesser epistles as recognized. Where it was not known that the Apostle John was by his disciples called "the Elder," there was likelihood of the authorship of those two being questioned on the matter of genuineness. Their brevity was against both frequent citation and frequent use in public and equally against serious question. Jude, as one of the Catholic Epistles, was the subject of comment by Clement of Alexandria. The Muratorian Canon quoted it as received. Tertullian cited it as the convincing writing of an apostle, though Origen remarked that it was not generally received. In the fourth century it was among the *antilegomena* (Eusebius, *Hist. eccl.*, III. xxv. 3). The canonicity which it had in the earlier times was later lost for it in a wide circle of the Church. James, though read in the West in early times and known probably both to Irenæus and to Hippolytus, was until the middle of the fourth century not in the New Testament of the western Church. The Canon Muratori is silent; among the Greeks of the East it was among the generally recognized scriptures. Though Origen placed it among the *antilegomena*, in *Codex Claromontanus* it stands before I John. A noteworthy fact is that Methodius mistakenly ascribed it to Paul. In 325 it was by many considered not genuine and Eusebius put it among the *antilegomena* (*Hist. eccl.*, III. xxv. 3). The general recognition of I Peter about the year 200 is vouched for by Irenæus, the Epistle of Lyons, Clement of Alexandria, Tertullian, and Hippolytus. The silence of the Muratorian Canon would have been inexplicable, and to it must refer the remark that a letter of Peter is received as is the Apocalypse. Against II Peter there were many protests. At Rome it was not unknown, but was not on the same footing as I Peter. It is doubtful whether Irenæus knew it. Origen's personal opinion was favorable, but he recorded a divided opinion in the Church concerning the letter. In the East its position was different from that of I Peter in that there it was not a New Testament book (Eusebius, *Hist. eccl.*, IV. xxv. 8). As late as 380 Didymus pronounced it uncanonical and the Syrians determinedly rejected it. Of the Epistle of Barnabas it may be said that Clement of Alexandria seems to have included it among the Catholic Epistles, and the same is true of Origen. *Codex Claromontanus* puts it after the seven Catholic Epistles and before Revelation. It is pertinent here to remark that the first and second Epistles of Clement are by the *Canones Apostolorum*, lxxxv., put between the Epistle of Barnabas and the Didache. I Clement is elsewhere given as a Catholic Epistle; at Corinth it was used occasionally in public service, a usage which spread to Alexandria and to Syria. It was cited by Clement of Alexandria and by Origen. But its connection with the New Testament was less firm even than that of Barnabas; in the West it was not considered as of the canon, and Irenæus seems to have employed it as belonging to the subapostolic age.

6. Writings Temporarily Regarded as Canonical. The Shepherd of Hermas was used as scripture by Irenæus, Clement of Alexandria, and in Antioch. At the beginning of the third century there was in Catholic and Montanistic circles a loosening of the connection between this book and the canon. Tertullian, contrary to his earlier practise, owing to the laxity of discipline attributed to this book, declared that it should be regarded as apocryphal and even as false. The Muratorian Canon excluded it from the regular and public reading of the Scriptures, though its perusal was permitted and even enjoined. This was the first attempt to form a secondary canon. There are two Latin translations of the book, and an unknown Roman bishop cited it as scripture, while Novatian and Commodian indorsed it, and the Latin liturgies show its influence. Yet by an ecclesiastical decision about 200-210 the Shepherd was set outside the canon. While Clement of Alexandria did not include the Shepherd in his brief commentary, he did treat the Apocalypse of Peter, a little book of about 300 lines. This book closed the canon of *Codex Claromontanus*; but the Armenian List put it among the Apocrypha, and Eusebius (*Hist. eccl.*, III. xxv. 4, cf. iii. 2) declared against its genuineness. Sozomen says that it was used as late as 430 in Palestine at Easter. The Didache was cited and used as scripture by Clement and Origen, and during the next century this was its status in Egypt. Eusebius (*Hist. eccl.*, III. xxv. 4) put it among the *antilegomena* of the second grade. It was known in the neighborhood of Antioch and in the West. The apocryphal Acts of the Apostles were often read in the early Church without question. The Acts of Paul came the nearest to winning canonical authority, and received favorable notice from Clement and Tertullian.

The New Testament of the Greek and Latin Church of 170-220 included as in quite definite authority the four Gospels, thirteen letters of Paul, Revelation, I Peter, I John (to which were attached II and III John), probably also Jude.

7. Summary. Up to 210 the Shepherd was also included. On the other hand, there were questionings about James, Hebrews, II Peter, the Apocalypse of Peter, the Didache, Barnabas, I and II Clement, Acts of Paul, and the Shepherd. The polemic against Marcion, the Gnostics, and the Alogi brought the discussion of the New Testament canon to a focus about the time of Irenæus and Clement of Alexandria. There was yet lacking that definiteness of organization of all the churches which alone could secure uniformity. The New Testament of about 200 was not the result of a revolution occurring 150-170, but of a broad development which was many-sided. The sharply bounded canon of Marcion had pointed the way to a definiteness in canonicity which the Church was soon to follow.

3. The New Testament, 140-170: Valentinus had founded his school which had divided into many sections and spread from the Rhone to the Tigris with a rich literary activity and yet a general consensus of action. Marcion founded his church at Rome after he had separated from the catholic Church probably about 147. Alongside the polemic against these movements, Christian writers were engaged in the apologetic of the Church which was to go before the pagan rulers and populations. The apologetic, however, found far less occasion to deal with the Christian Scriptures than did the writings against the heretics.

Knowledge of Marcion's Bible is due chiefly to Tertullian, who claimed to use as a weapon against the heretic his own New Testament, and so came to traverse the latter from beginning to end. After Tertullian as a source of knowledge comes Epiphanius (*Hær.*, xlii.), and a number of

1. Marcion's Bible. citations from Greeks and Syrians up to the fifth century which enable one to reconstruct quite securely Marcion's canon. Marcion issued not only his New Testament but also his *Antithesis* as a defense of his dogmatic position and of his critical edition of the New Testament, and this became the doctrinal basis of his Church, which was studied by Tertullian, Ephraem Syrus, and others. His Bible consisted of a "Gospel" and an "Apostle," both anonymous. Since Paul seemed to him the one preacher of an unadulterated gospel, his "Apostle" embraced ten epistles of Paul and in the following order: Gal., I and II Cor., Rom., I and II Thess., Laodiceans (i.e., Eph.), Col., Phil., Philem. It is of course evident that this collection must have been received by him from the Church. He sought to show that the letter to the Ephesians was the letter to the Laodiceans mentioned in Col. iv. 16. Galatians he especially prized because of the anti-Judaic polemic it contains. I and II Tim. and Titus he discarded as private letters, Philemon was admitted on the ground that it is a letter to a church in a household, and this alone was left intact and unedited. For the criticism of the writings he received he depended neither upon historic tradition nor on testimonies to historicity; his basis was his own subjective conception of what true Christianity was and what the Pauline Gospel was; from this standpoint proceeded all his text-criticism. That he recognized the Gospel of Luke, the basis of his own, as the work of one of the Pauline school is shown by his elimination of the words "the beloved physician" in Col. iv. 14. His gospel, so far as its text can be made out, proves that he had before him the third Gospel, and this, in consequence of its long association with the first and second Gospels, had received amplifications of its text from them. But no trace of influence due to extracanonical Gospels upon Marcion has ever been shown. It follows from this that the canon of the Gospels of the Church at Rome from about 140 on was our four Gospels. Marcion's canon of the epistles coincides with that of the Muratorian Canon. It is natural that he should place no value upon the letters of Peter, John, or James, the last-named especially in view of Gal. ii. 9, 12. Acts and Rev. he appears to have expressly rejected. In comparison with the ecclesiastical New Testament not only of his times but of the next two centuries with its varying boundaries and its variant text, the Marcion canon is a sharply drawn work of art in miniature, though it was the work of an arbitrary lawgiver.

What Marcion accomplished with knife and eraser the Valentinians sought to do by means of exposition. Since they had not voluntarily separated from the Church, but merely distinguished themselves from the *communes ecclesiastici*, they had no objection to raise to the common edition of the "Prophets and Apostles." They needed no special Bible. They used the Gospels freely, particularly the Fourth. Apart from the prologue to this last, the structure of the series of eons of Valentinus are unintelligible. Heraclion commented on all four of the Gospels. In the different branches of this sect Eph., Col., and I Cor. were especially valued, but Rom., II Cor., Phil., and Gal. were also used. In their criticism of the Gospels they laid stress upon a secret tradition. They used also an *Evangelium veritatis*, a fifth Gospel, which probably contained the sum of apocryphal tradition, derived, according to Serapion, not from the Docetes but from their precursors. The Gospel of Peter may have arisen about 150 from the eastern branch at Antioch as did the *Evangelium veritatis* among the western school of Valentinians. To a branch of the Valentinian school of Asia Minor belonged Leucius, the author of the Acts of Peter and John. They probably used also the Gospel of the Infancy. Leucius wrote also a "Journeyings of John," suggested by the "Letters to the Seven Churches" of Revelation. In short, the foundation of the canon of the most important schools of Gnostics, 140–170, is that of the Church of 200, only that these "men of the spirit" used alongside of the canonical writings a mass of other traditions and poetical and subjective creations which were not employed among the orthodox.

2. The Bible of the Valentinians.

In his short description of the Sunday service as observed by Christians in city and country, Justin names as taking the first place the reading of the "Memorabilia of the Apostles," "which are called Gospels" (I Apology, lxvi.–lxvii., *ANF*, i. 185–186), and the "collection of the Prophets." "Gospel" in the singular is also used by the Jew Trypho and by Justin as a collective. Out of deference for his readers who were not acquainted with the term "gospel," Justin commonly used the term *Apomnemoneumata*, "Memorabilia." While generally such memorabilia took their name from the author, Justin named these from the subject, "The Memorabilia of our Savior." As under the term "prophets" the whole Old Testament is included, the term *memorabilia* in Justin may include the New Testament writings. The answer to the question what gospels are meant has long been, those commonly used about 150 in the places Justin visited or lived in, in Ephesus and Rome, in the public service and known as the product of the Apostles or their disciples. Trypho (*Dialogue*, x.) speaks of the "so-called gospel" as a totality, a unit. They can be no other than what Marcion criticized and Valentinians so fully employed. In one place Justin expressly discriminated between the Apostles and their disciples in a passage which goes back to Luke xxii. 44 (*Dialogue*, ciii.). He named the second Gospel "The Recollections of Peter," a designation which implies the old tradition of the connection of this Gospel with that apostle. What has partly or entirely produced the idea that Justin's "memorabilia" are not the Gospels of the Church is first the looseness and inexactness of quotation, and second the material additions of facts or reports grounds for which are not found in the Gospels. But in Justin's citations exactness is no more to be expected than in Clement's; and much that appears apocryphal to us may have been read in the Gospels of his time. Justin regarded Revelation as the work of the apostle John and as a true testimony of Christian prophecy. Investigation of his writings shows contact of Justin with Rom., I Cor., Gal., Eph., Col., II Thess., Heb., I Pet., Acts and the Didache: more questionably with Phil., Titus, I Tim., and James.

3. The Apostolic Writings in Justin Martyr.

4. The Oldest Traces and the Origin of Collections of Apostolic Writings: From the preceding array of facts it appears that by 140 in the entire circle of the catholic Church the collection comprising the four Gospels and thirteen Epistles of Paul were read alongside of the Old Testament writings, and that in one part or another of the Church other writings such as Acts, Rev., Heb., I Pet., James, and the Epistles of John were held in like honor.

The collection of Pauline letters seems to go back to the first century, judging from I Clement, the Ignatian Epistles, and Polycarp. The bishops of Smyrna and Antioch had a knowledge of Paul which involved acquaintance with his letters, and the way in which they employ them shows that the letters were before them. Polycarp advised the Philippians to read Paul's letters for edification; Ignatius knew Eph. under the title used later by Marcion as part of an ecclesiastical collection. Polycarp included Phil. and Thess. in a group directed to the Macedonians just as Tertullian knew them a century later. Clement seems to make the collection begin with I Cor., an order which the Muratorian Canon supports, closing with Rom. This aggregation, which contained also the order Phil.–Thess. and the title "to the Ephesians," has every claim to originality and to have circulated before 97 That there was an interchange of letters among the churches before this collection was made is clear from Col. iv. 16, but the circulation and use implied in II Pet. iii. 15 involve a collection in one manuscript, perhaps not official but private. The passage last cited implies a Pauline letter to Jewish Christians, and I Cor. v. 9 and Phil. iii. 1 imply other letters of Paul which have not survived. These facts suggest a deliberate selection from the available letters of Paul, made probably in some important center of Christianity, which came into general use and was seen to be available for public service. But the settlement of the order of arrangement implies that the collection was made very early, soon after the death of Paul. Where this was done can not be stated, though the placing of I and II Cor. at the head suggests Corinth. Rome is also to be thought of as explaining the closing of this collection with the Epistle to the Romans.

1. The Collection of Pauline Letters.

The word *euaggelion*, which, 150–200, designated the collection of four Gospels, is frequently found in the earlier literature so used that by it must be meant a written exposition of the words and deeds of Jesus in possession of the churches and generally known to the communities (*Didache*, viii. 2;

II Clem., viii. 5; Ignatius, *Smyrna*, v. 1; *Philadelphia*, viii. 2). That "Gospel" was the authoritative document. The general knowledge of its contents involves its regular use in public service. It was cited with the formula "the Lord says," with or without the addition "in the Gospel," and with the formula (used with Old Testament citations) "it is written." But what was this "Gospel"? A clear understanding of what it was existed between the writers of the period 90–140 and their readers. Papias declared that during the lifetime of John in the vicinity of Ephesus a Gospel of Mark was used, and Cerinthus, a contemporary of John, preferred it to the others (Irenæus, *Hær.*, III. xi. 7, cf. I. xxvi. 1). Papias asserted that the Hebrew Matthew was long used in the province of Asia with the aid of oral interpretation until a Greek version superseded it. Even the Fourth Gospel recalls the very words of Mark and Luke (T. Zahn, *Einleitung*, Leipsic, 1900, pp. 505–506, 520). The spurious passage Mark xvi. 9–20 is derived from Luke, John, and Papias. The earliest Gospels of the Infancy and the Gospels of Peter and Marcion go back to the canonical Gospels. In the literature of 95–140 among a mass of ordinances for ecclesiastical direction only four gospel citations are not traceable to the four Gospels (*II Clem.*, v. 2, 4, viii. 5, xii. 2–6; Ignatius, *Smyrna*, iii. 2). Such uncanonical sayings as these four were circulated orally as well as in writing; Papias about 125 collected many of them. Of the origin of the making of the Gospel canon there is no trustworthy report, nor can it be said where it took form.

2. The "Gospel."

Other writings which are found afterward assigned to the New Testament were not unified in any one collection as were the Gospels and the Pauline Epistles. They appeared first either as indisputable or as debated parts of the New Testament in the stage it then had reached. A very wide use in extended circles of the Church during public service is provable for I Pet., I John, Rev., and the Shepherd, none of which was originally addressed to a single community.

3. Other Writings.

5. Origen and His School: During the third century the New Testament underwent no essential change. The achievement of Origen was the comparison of the content of the traditional possession of various communities. His varied life and travels gave him the opportunity to learn through observation existing variations; his philological training and his decided vocation for learned work in the service of the Church qualified him to pronounce a discreet judgment. Before 217 he was welcomed at Rome as one of the rising stars of the Church; his travels took him to Athens, Antioch, and Cæsarea in Cappadocia, while his later years were spent in Palestine. Students flocked to him both in Alexandria and in Palestine. But Bible student though he was, he was no thoroughgoing critic. He quoted Prov. xxii. 28 in reference to discussion of the canon; tradition spoke for him the last word, though indeed that tradition was to be investigated. Hence he voiced the distinction between the *homologoumena*, the writings universally recognized as scripture, and the *antilegomena*, or those more or less opposed. To the former, according to Origen, belonged the four Gospels, thirteen Pauline Epistles, I Pet., I John, Acts, and Rev., the last the closing book of the New Testament. To the latter belonged Heb., II Pet., II and III John, Jas., Jude, Barnabas, the Shepherd, the Didache, and the Gospel of the Hebrews. Hebrews was frequently cited by him as though Pauline and canonical, especially in his earlier writings; and he defended its Paulinity rather as coming through a member of Paul's school than from Paul himself. II Pet. was also frequently cited by him as scripture, in which his scholar Firmilian followed him. Jas. was also frequently cited both as scripture and as "the apostle James." Jude appears to have been valued by him, though not often appearing in his writings. Barnabas is called a Catholic Epistle and in the *Onomasticon* is put with the other Catholic Epistles. He regarded the Shepherd as an inspired work and useful. He appears also to have cited the Didache as scripture. The Gospel of the Hebrews is not mentioned in his list of the apocryphal gospels; on the other hand, it is often cited with the formula he used when citing from such writings. He sharply discriminated the Jewish-Christian communities, whose one gospel this was, from the heretical Ebionites on the ground that the former held fast the ecclesiastical rule of faith.

The allegorical interpretation by means of which Origen undertook to reconcile the most divergent materials and the most varied writings and to unite them thus in one Bible found opposition. The composition of Nepos, bishop of Arsinoe, "Against the Allegorists" advanced and spread a chiliasm which to Bishop Dionysius of Alexandria about 260 appeared unendurable. To Origen it appeared that Rev. was written by an inspired man of the apostolic age named John, but the difference in style and conception from the Fourth Gospel did not allow its ascription to the apostle. It was especially a book for the application of the allegorical method.

6. The Original New Testament of the Syrians: On the beginnings of the church in Edessa there is a legendary report in Syriac, *The Doctrine of Addai*, ed. Phillips, London, 1876, which contains some significant words about the books introduced there for use in the service. Addai, the founder of the church of Edessa, is made to say expressly that beside the Old Testament no other scriptures shall be read than the Gospel, the Epistles of Paul, and the Acts. And by the Gospel is doubtless meant the Diatessaron of Tatian. On the other hand, Ephraem knew well the four Gospels, and a Syrian canon contained not the Diatessaron but the four Gospels in our order. The Syrian collection of the Pauline letters embraced, about 330–370, according to the commentaries of Aphraates and Ephraem, Heb. and the apocryphal III Cor., but not Philem. The last-named book failed to appear in the otherwise complete commentary of Ephraem. A summary from Sinai gives Philem. at the end and does not contain III Cor.; on the other hand, it has a II Phil., which may be another name for

III Cor. It is now known that this apocryphal writing is but a section out of the *Acts of Paul* which belongs to the period about 170 at the earliest. It could, therefore, not have belonged to the original Syrian Canon. Tatian became a Christian at Rome, and, according to the legend, the canon of the Epistles was received from Rome. Eusebius (*Hist. eccl.*, IV. xxix. 6) heard an obscure report that there was a recension of the Pauline Epistles by Tatian. The oldest Syrian text both of Epistles and of Gospels has a relationship to the Western text. The Sinai summary throws new light on the subject. The order of the Epistles there is Gal., I and II Cor., Rom., Heb., and so on, and just this is the order in which Ephraem commented upon them and it is the order of Marcion, and no one was more likely to follow in the footsteps of Marcion than Tatian. It is very remarkable too that in the Syriac summary II Tim. is mentioned, but I Tim. is omitted. The Syrian Church could not maintain its original individuality. While before the time of Aphraates and in the third century it received Heb. and I Tim., it could not exclude all the Catholic Epistles. The Syriac translation of Eusebius's Church History, which Ephraem had diligently read, acquainted the Syrians with the older history of the New Testament. Intercourse sprang up in the fourth century between Greek and Syrian Christians, and Greeks and Greek Bibles appeared in Edessa; it is, therefore, no wonder that Ephraem was familiar with all the Catholic Epistles. In the Peshito a selection was made of Jas., I Pet., I John, while II Pet., II and III John, Jude, and Rev. were excluded.

7. Lucian and Eusebius: While the New Testament of the early Church in Antioch had its individuality, the canon of Chrysostom was exactly that of the Peshito and carried the exclusion of II and III John back to the decision of the Fathers. This can not be due to the efforts of Eusebius, since he would set aside the Apocalypse, but would recognize the seven Catholic Epistles; to reach the roots of the matter, one must go back to the beginning of the exegetical school, to Lucian. Report says that Lucian was born in Samosata and that he labored in Edessa before he became a priest and the founder of the school in Antioch. It is doubtless true that he extended his text-critical work to the New Testament, and that his recension of that as well as of the Septuagint was diffused as far as Constantinople. So that the Antiochean school's text of about 380–450 probably goes back to Lucian and was a compromise between the Edessan and the Antiochean traditions. Rev. was excluded while Jas., I Pet., and I John of the Catholic Epistles were taken in. This doubtless influenced the Peshito.

In Palestine the Bible-studies of Origen were continued by Pamphilus and Eusebius. But Eusebius was affected both by the Origenistic tradition and by the Antiochean school, with representatives of which he was connected in the debate over the Trinity. In his Church History according to his promise he has diligently given the pronouncements of earlier writers about the *antilegomena* of the New Testament, and also interesting information about both acknowledged and doubtful writings. With Origen, he found two classes, *homologoumena* and *antilegomena*; but the second he divided into two subclasses, the one containing the books he would have acknowledged and the other the *notha* or "spurious." His table then is: (1) *Homologoumena*, the Gospels, Acts, fourteen Pauline Epistles, I Pet., I John, and Rev.; (2) *Antilegomena*, (a) the better sort, Jas., Jude, II and III John, and (b) the *notha*, Acts of Paul, Shepherd, Apocalypse of Peter, Barnabas, and the Didache. But Eusebius's treatment is not always either clear or consistent. He uses a term *endiathekos*, "within-the-New-Testament," as a synonym of *homologoumenos* and appears thereby to exclude from the New Testament the first class of the *antilegomena*. On the other hand, in naming the second subdivision of the *antilegomena* "spurious" he seems to argue the genuineness of the first subdivision. But for him the seven Catholic Epistles are a closed collection. It was about Rev. that Eusebius found it hard to come to a decision. Many times he cites it and adduces the strongest testimony for its ecclesiastical importance (*Hist. eccl.*, IV. xviii. 8, xxiv. 1, xxvi. 2, V. viii. 5, xviii. 14, VI. xxv. 9). But when in III. xxiv. 18 he reports the vacillation of opinion about the book, he calls attention to the influence of the Lucian school. He cites it as "the so-called Apocalypse of John" (III. xviii. 2, cf. xxxix. 6), briefly refers to the vituperation of Caius (III. xxviii.), and notes the more cautious criticism of Dionysius (VII. xxiv. 5). His conjecture that another John wrote it he follows out with diligence, and in the interest of this hypothesis seeks to prove the existence of a presbyter John as distinct from the apostle. He would disrobe the book of its apostolic dress and remove it from the New Testament, though he never expressly utters this decision. On account of its quite universal recognition in the Church he leaves open the choice between placing it among the *homologoumena* or among the *notha*. Apart from this book, however, his New Testament is the same as ours. The making of fifty copies of the New Testament on parchment for Constantine gave him an opportunity to diffuse his opinions, and the result showed that he inclined to the Lucian form of text rather than to the Origenistic, though including therein the lesser Catholic Epistles.

8. Athanasius: According to the Easter Letter of 367, recently recovered through a Coptic translation, in which is given a view of the continuous undiscriminating usage of all kinds of Apocrypha as scripture in the ecclesiastical province where Athanasius was, there was afforded him the opportunity of setting forth a definitely limited canon arranged in order of books and in groups. He was the first to name the twenty-seven books of the New Testament as exclusively canonical. He ignored the opposition to which several of them had so long been subjected, notably II Pet., which Didymus continued to oppose. But not to break completely with the Alexandrian tradition, he placed in sharp distinction from the "canonized" books and equally from the apocryphal ones a class of *anagignoskomena*. The Fathers had designated these as to be placed before the catechumens for their instruction. They included Wisd. of Sol., Ecclus., Esther, Judith, Tobit, the Didache, and the Shepherd. The Didache had great influence upon the liturgy in Egypt, and to the Shepherd Athanasius himself attached high value. The surprising element, however, is the complete silence concerning other writings which at least in Alexandria had equally with the Didache and the Shepherd been reckoned with New Testament writings. Serapion, the friend of Athanasius, had cited Barnabas as "the most honored apostle Barnabas" along with the Romans of Paul, and in *Codex Sinaiticus* it stood between Rev. and the Shepherd. The New Testament of twenty-seven books seemed to be as firmly settled as that of Eusebius's twenty-six had been. And this view came to have the victory in the Church, ruling out finally the shorter canon of Eusebius and the use of a class of books merely for the instruction of catechumens.

9. The Development in the Orient till the Time of Justinian: The peculiar criticism of Theodore of Mopsuestia did not essentially change the situation established by Lucian and Eusebius. The concordant testimony of Theodore's opponent Leontius and of his admirer Jesudad is that Theodore rejected the seven Catholic Epistles. And since as an Antiochean he rejected the Apocalypse, his New Testament was the Syrian one of about 340. In the arrangement of the Pauline Epistles (Rom., I and II Cor., Heb., Eph.) he followed the Syrian usage in respect to Heb., and the Greek in respect to Rom. and Gal. He defended the canonicity of Philemon, but rejected III Cor. It is no wonder that, admired as he was by the Syrian Nestorians, these latter adopted his canon. And the Nestorian Jesudad (ninth century) still regarded the three greater Catholic Epistles as a sort of *antilegomena*. How tenacious the opposition to the Apocalypse was, as also that to the four lesser Catholic Epistles, has been shown above. Nevertheless, by the sixth century the Apocalypse had won all along the line from Jerusalem to Constantinople. If Philoxenus of Mabug, c. 508, had Rev. and the lesser Catholic Epistles translated for the first time into Syriac, this implies that in the contiguous Greek ecclesiastical province, in the patriarchate of Antioch, the Apocalypse was no more ignored as it was c. 400, that on the contrary it was again received. About the year 500 Andrew wrote in Cæsarea his great commentary on the Apocalypse, in which with a certain assiduity by appeal to the older teachers from Papias to Cyril he defended the inspiration of the book, and in a note on Rev. xxii. 18–19 assailed the critics. About 530 Leontius designated, in lectures delivered in the monastery at Jerusalem, the "Apocalypse of the Holy John" as the latest canonical book of the Church.

10. The Assimilation of the West: By the vacillation and the attempts at fixation which the canon underwent in the East the Latin Church was not immediately affected. Until the fourth century the New Testament there excluded Heb., had an incomplete canon of the Catholic Epistles, but included the Apocalypse, which was seriously assailed only by Caius. The events of the fourth century made isolation impossible. The settlement of Pierios, "the new Origen," in Rome was a significant preparation. There followed the councils, the exile of Athanasius in Trier (336–337), in Rome (340–343), and in other parts of the West (till 340); of Hilary of Poitiers in Asia Minor (356–360), of Lucifer of Cagliari, Eusebius of Vercelli, and others; the long sojourn of Jerome and Rufinus in Palestine, Egypt, and Syria, and during this whole period the close connection of Latin Church literature, especially of exegesis, with Greek models. The ecumenical consciousness of the Church overleaped all barriers and affected even the canon. The influence of Athanasius in this respect is not to be underestimated, especially in connection with the production of a recension of the Bible at Rome 340–343.

Hebrews, prized by the Novatians as a production of Barnabas, began after the time of Hilary and Lucifer to be quoted more and more in the West as Pauline and, therefore, canonical. The growth of sentiment in favor of James took place unnoted, as did that of the lesser Catholic Epistles. The African Canon (350–365), published by Mommsen, has a more or less official air; it makes no mention of Heb., Jas., or Jude, but includes I and II Pet., I, II, and III John; but it was corrected by a reviser so as to omit II Pet. and II and III John. In a synod of c. 382 the controlling spirit was Jerome, so that II and III John were received as the presbyter's while the rest of the Catholic Epistles were ascribed to Apostles. Hebrews was reckoned as a fourteenth Pauline letter. The influence of Augustine was dominant in the synods of Hippo (383) and Carthage (397), the pronouncement of which was for thirteen Pauline Epistles, to which Hebrews was added as a sort of stranger.

The history of the canon was closed in the West by the beginning of the fifth century, a hundred years earlier than in the East. (T. ZAHN.)

BIBLIOGRAPHY: On the general topic of the canon for the reader of English possibly the best survey of the results of modern scholarship is W. Sanday, *Inspiration . . Early History and Origin of the Doctrine of Biblical Inspiration*, London, 1896 (fairly advanced on the O. T., conservative on the N. T.); L. Gaussen, *Le Canon des saintes écritures au double point de vue de la science et de la foi*, 2 vols., Geneva, 1860, Eng. transl., London, 1863; E. Reuss, *Histoire du canon des saintes écritures dans l'église chrétienne*, Strasburg, 1864, Eng. transl., Edinburgh, 1891; T. H. Horne, *Introduction to the Critical Study . . of the Holy Scriptures*, 3 vols., London, 1872 (though written a century ago, it contains much that is still valuable); S. Davidson, *The Canon of the Bible*, ib. 1880 (radical, but the work of a scholar); F. Overbeck, *Zur Geschichte des Kanons*, Chemnitz, 1880 (contains an essay on the origin of the canon); J. J. Given, *The Truth of Scripture in Connection with . . the Canon*, Edinburgh, 1881; G. T. Ladd, *The Doctrine of Sacred Scripture*, 2 vols., New York, 1883 (abstract and wordy, but scholarly); C. A. Briggs, *Study of Holy Scripture*, chaps. v.–vi., ib. 1899; W. H. Bennett and W. F. Adeney, *Biblical Introduction*, London, 1899 (brief, but accurate); F. E. C. Gigot, *General Introduction to the Study of the Holy Scriptures*, vol. i., New York, 1901 (an example of the newer Roman Catholic scholarship).

On the canon of the O. T. there are four works of first rank, viz., H. E. Ryle, *Canon of the O. T.*, London, 1892; F. Buhl, *Kanon und Text des A. T.*, Leipsic, 1891, Eng. transl., Edinburgh, 1892 (a short treatise, but lucid and uncumbered with technicalities); G. Wildeboer, *Het onstaan van den Kanon des Ouden Verbonds*, Groningen, 1891, Eng. transl., *Origin of the Canon of the O. T.*, London, 1895 (much like Buhl); E. Kautzsch, *Abriss der Geschichte des alttestamentlichen Schrifttums*, Freiburg, 1897, Eng. transl., London, 1898 (lucid, altogether a model brief discussion). Other works which may be consulted are: J. Fürst, *Der Kanon des A. T.*, Leipsic, 1868; A. Loisy, *Histoire du Canon de l'A. T.*, Paris, 1890 (Roman Catholic and scientific); G. H. Dalman, *Traditio Rabbinorum veterrima de librorum V. T. ordine et origine*, Leipsic, 1891; Smith, *OTJC*; X. Koenig, *Essai sur la formation du Canon de l'A. T.*, Paris, 1894; W. J. Beecher, *The Alleged Triple Canon of the O. T.* in *JBL*, xv. (1896) 118–128; W. H. Green, *General Introduction to the O. T.*, 2 vols., New York, 1898–99 (states the extreme conservative position); Magnier, *Étude sur la canonicité de l'A. T.*, Paris, 1899; F. E. C. Gigot, *General Introduction to the Study of the Holy Scriptures*, vol. i., New York, 1900; J. P. Peters, *The Old Testament and the New Scholarship*, New York, 1901.

On the N. T. canon the best work is by B. F. Westcott, *A General Survey of the Hist. of the Canon of the N. T.*, London, 1889; K. A. Credner, *Geschichte des neutestamentlichen Kanons*, Berlin, 1860 (though an old work, much of the material is still usable); R. F. Grau, *Entwicklungsgeschichte des neutestamentlichen Schriftthums*, 2 vols., Gütersloh, 1871; A. H. Charteris, *Canonicity: a Collection of early Testimonies to the Canonical Books of the N. T.*, London, 1880; idem, *The N. T. Scriptures, their Claims, Hist., and Authority*, ib. 1882 (a popular form of the preceding); T. Zahn, *Forschungen zur Geschichte des neutestamentlichen Kanons*, 5 parts, Erlangen, 1881–93; idem, *Geschichte des neutestamentlichen Kanons*, Erlangen and Leipsic, 1888–92; A. Loisy, *Histoire du Canon du N. T.*, Paris, 1891; H. J. Holtzmann, *Historisch-kritische Einleitung in das N. T.*, Freiburg, 1892; G. Salmon, *Historical Introduction to the Study of the Books of the N. T.*, London, 1894; A. Harnack, *Das N. T um das Jahr 200*, Freiburg, 1889; idem, *Altchristliche Litteratur*, 2 vols., Leipsic, 1897–1904 (exhaustive); B. W Bacon, *Introduction to N. T.*, New York, 1900 (condensed); D. S. Muzzey, *Rise of the N. T.*, ib. 1900; A. Jülicher, *Einleitung in das N. T.*, Tübingen, 1901, Eng. transl., London, 1904; C. R. Gregory, *Canon and Text of the N. T.*, Edinburgh, 1907; J. Leipoldt, *Geschichte des neutestamentlichen Kanons*, vol. i., *Die Entstehung*, Leipsic, 1907.

CANONICAL HOURS: Certain portions of the day set apart according to the rule (*canon*) of the Church for prayer and devotion. It seems likely that the Apostolic Church observed the Jewish custom of praying three times a day (Ps. lv. 17; Acts ii. 15, iii. 1, x. 30), at the third, sixth, and ninth hour. In the fourth century the zeal of the Psalmist ("seven times a day do I praise thee," cxix. 164) was held up for Christian imitation by Ambrose, Augustine, and Hilary, and by the time of Cassian (d. about 435) it had become a general rule of devotion. (See BREVIARY.) In England the term "canonical hours" also refers to the time within which marriage may legally be solemnized in a parish church without a license, which was from eight to twelve in the morning, until a recent Act of Parliament extended it to three in the afternoon.

CANONIZATION: The process of attributing the title of saint to a man or woman already known as "blessed." The word refers to the inclusion of the person's name in the list (*canon*) of the saints and recognizing his right to a fitting veneration, which includes the setting apart of a day in the ecclesiastical calendar for the commemoration of the saint's feast, together with an office in the breviary and a mass for the day in his honor. To promote the veneration of a saint throughout the universal Church, no better method existed than to seek papal confirmation of his claims. This probably happened now and then even in early times, or the popes gave such confirmation of their own motion. We have definite evidence of the formal canonization of Bishop Ulric of Augsburg in 993. But canonization as a right reserved exclusively to the pope appears first under Alexander III. (1159–81). The bishops continued to feel justified in canonizing for their own dioceses, until this was declared unlawful by Urban VIII. in 1625 and 1634. At present a formal and very carefully regulated process is gone through before canonization. The candidate, having died in good repute, is first designated as "of pious memory," and when a regular investigation has been set on foot, as "venerable." If it is conclusively shown that he has lived a holy life and worked miracles, his beatification may be requested, but normally not until fifty years after his death. The process is first conducted by the bishop of his home; a commission of the Congregation of Rites examines whether it is permissible, in which case papal authority to proceed is granted. In order to make the necessary demonstration that the candidate possessed "heroic" virtues and worked miracles, three separate investigations are held—one before the Congregation of Rites, one before the whole college of cardinals, and one before a consistory held under the pope's presidency. When the pope has approved the request, a brief is drawn up which grants the title of *beatus*, and determines the limits of the consequent *cultus*, including commemoration and invocation in public worship, the erection of altars, public exposition of relics, and the like. The solemn publication of the decree of beatification takes place in St. Peter's. After repeated miracles and a similar process of investigation, canonization may follow later, with still more imposing ceremonies, the pope or his representative singing high mass in honor of the new saint. While the veneration of the "blessed" is limited to a certain definite part of the Roman Catholic Church, that of the saints is extended to the entire Church. (N. BONWETSCH.)

BIBLIOGRAPHY: Giusto Fontanini, *Codex constitutionum quas summi pontifices ediderunt in solemni canonizatione, 993–1729*, Rome, 1729; W Hurd, *Religious Rites and Ceremonies*, p. 244, London, 1811; C. Elliott, *Delineation of Roman Catholicism*, book iv., chap. 4, New York, 1842; Boissonnet, *Dictionnaire . des cérémonies . . sacrées*, in Migne, *Encyclopédie théologique*, xv.–xvii.; L. Ferraris, *Prompta bibliotheca canonica*, s.v. "Veneratio Sanctorum," new ed., Rome, 1844–45.

CANSTEIN, cān'stain, **KARL HILDEBRAND, BARON VON:** Founder of the Canstein Bible Institute at Halle; b. at Lindenberg (a village near Fürstenwalde, 21 m. w. of Frankfort) Aug. 4, 1667; d. at Berlin Aug. 19, 1719. After completing his legal studies at the University of Frankfort-on-the-Oder, in 1686, he traveled through Holland, England, France, Italy, and southern Germany, but was called to Berlin by the death of the Elector in 1688. In the following year he was appointed gentleman of the bed-chamber, but resigned after a few years, and enlisted as a volunteer with the Brandenburg troops sent to Flanders. There he fell seriously ill, was converted, and after recovering his health, returned to Berlin, where he lived in retirement, devoting himself to philanthropy. In 1691 he became acquainted with Spener, and thus formed a lifelong friendship with August Hermann Francke (q.v.), whom he aided in all his enterprises.

A literary result of Canstein's unceasing study of the Bible was his *Harmonie und Auslegung der heiligen vier Evangelisten* (Halle, 1718), but his crowning life-work was his establishment of the Canstein Bible Institute. Seeking to make the Scriptures known in the widest circles, he expounded his views in a small pamphlet entitled *Ohnmassgebender Vorschlag, wie Gotteswort den Armen zur Erbauung um einen geringen Preis in die Hände zu bringen sei* (Berlin, 1710), in which he expressed his conviction that the use of stereotype plates would render it possible to sell copies of the New Testament for two groschen, and of the entire Bible for six. His first edition of the New Testament appeared at Halle in 1712, and was followed by the entire Bible in the next year. Before Canstein's death the New Testament had appeared in twenty-eight editions, and the Bible in eight octavo and eight duodecimo editions, making a total of about 100,000 New Testaments and 40,000 Bibles. When the founder died, Francke took charge of the Institute. In 1727 the buildings were enlarged, and in 1734–35 the Cansteinische Buckdruckerei was established. The Bible was printed in Bohemian and Polish in 1722, and in 1868–69 versions in Wendish and Lithuanian appeared. The revised text of Luther's version was also first printed by this Institute (Halle, 1892). See BIBLE SOCIETIES, II., 1.

CANTATA. See MUSIC, SACRED, II., 2, § 5.

CANTERBURY: The ancient metropolitan see of England. The city is of great antiquity, succeeding the British village of Durwhern, the Roman Durovernum, and the Saxon Cantwarabyrig. Augustine, sent from Rome by Gregory the Great in 596 to convert the Anglo-Saxons, made it the headquarters of his missionary activity; but it was not until the episcopate of the great organizer Theodore of Tarsus (668–690) that the claim of the see to metropolitan jurisdiction over the whole of England was acknowledged by the other bishops and confirmed by Pope Vitalian. This authority extended over Ireland as well until the elevation of the see of Armagh (q.v.) to primatial rights. Owing, however, to the important position of York in the north of England, the archbishops of that see for a long time contested the first place with Canterbury, and it was not until the pontificate of Alexander III. (1159–81) that the latter enjoyed an unquestioned primacy. Among the long line of archbishops some distinguished names occur: Dunstan (959–988); Ælfheah martyred by the Danes (1006–12); Lanfranc (1070–89) and Anselm (1093–1109), the great defenders of the rights of the Church and people against the first Norman kings; Thomas Becket (1162–70), murdered in the cathedral itself for his resistance to the king's encroachments; Stephen Langton (1207–28). William Warham (1503–32) was, with the exception of the two years' tenure of the see by Cardinal Pole under Mary (1556–58), the last Roman Catholic archbishop. Thomas Cranmer (1533–56) begins the Anglican succession, followed by Parker, Grindal, and Whitgift under Queen Elizabeth. William Laud (1633–45) kept up the earlier traditions of the see by giving his life for his principles; but in the post-Reformation annals few names of great significance occur—though Archbishops Tait, Benson, and Temple in the latter half of the nineteenth century were men of broad and statesmanlike abilities. The archbishop of Canterbury ranks as the first peer of the realm after the princes of the blood royal, and has the right to crown the sovereign and to other secular prerogatives. The cathedral in its present shape was begun by Lanfranc on the site of St. Augustine's monastery; it contains work extending from his time to that of Prior Goldstone in the fifteenth century, thus exhibiting specimens of all schools of Gothic, and affording the best guide to the study of the development of architecture in England. From the death of Becket until the Reformation, it was a favorite place of pilgrimage. His body, brought from the crypt, was placed in 1220 in a shrine of such magnificence that Erasmus, who visited it in 1512, recorded that "gold was the meanest thing to be seen." In 1538 Henry VIII. destroyed the shrine, as that of a rebel against royal authority, and confiscated its treasures. Among the other interesting ecclesiastical remains in Canterbury are St. Martin's church, said to be the oldest in England and to date in part from the period of the Roman occupation, and the first house of the Dominicans in England. See the biographical notices of Augustine, Theodore, and other archbishops of Canterbury; also the articles ANGLO-SAXONS, CONVERSION OF THE; CELTIC CHURCH IN BRITAIN AND IRELAND; ENGLAND, CHURCH OF.

BIBLIOGRAPHY: The history of the diocese is given by R. C. Jenkins, in *Diocesan Histories, Canterbury*, London, 1880. On the cathedral consult: A. P. Stanley, *Historical Memorials of Canterbury Cathedral*, ib. 1900; J. M. Cowper, *Memorial Inscriptions of the Cathedral Church of Canterbury*, Canterbury, 1897. For the monastery consult: *Literæ Cantuarienses. Letter Books of the Monastery of Christ Church*, 3 vols., ed. by J. B. Sheppard for Rolls Series, London, 1881–89. Consult also: S. R. Gardiner, *Student's Hist. of England*, passim, ib. 1895; W. Bright, *Early English Church Hist.*, Index, Oxford, 1897; W. A. Shaw, *History of the English Church, 1640–1660*, London, 1900 (contains much material); W. W. Capes, *English Church in 14th and 15th Centuries*, ib. 1900; W. R. W. Stephens, *The English Church, 1066–1272*, p. 33, ib. 1901; J. Gairdner, *The English Church in the 16th Century*, pp. 1, 66, 104, et passim, ib. 1903

CANTHARUS: A well, cistern, fountain, or simply a vessel for water, in the center of the atrium just in front of the entrance of the ancient basilica, used by the faithful for the ablution of hands and face before entering the church building. See HOLY WATER.

CANTICLES. See SONG OF SOLOMON.

CANTOR: A name applied in the early Church to those who were specially set apart to conduct the singing. They are mentioned as a special class in the Apostolic Constitutions and in the canons of the Council of Laodicea (365), and were set apart by the clergy with a particular rite. In the later Western Church the name was also applied in cathedrals and collegiate churches to one of the canons who had the oversight of the musical instruction of the younger members and led the musical part of the service; called also precentor. It is sometimes used quite generally for specially designated singers, whether clerical or lay, who intone or begin the psalms, antiphons, and hymns.

CANZ, cänts. **ISRAEL GOTTLIEB.** See WOLFF, CHRISTIAN, AND THE WOLFFIAN SCHOOL.

CAPECELATRO, cā-pê″chê-lā′trō, **ALFONSO:** Cardinal priest; b. at Marseilles Feb. 5, 1824. He entered the oratory of St. Philip Neri, and in 1878 was appointed sublibrarian of the Holy See. Two years later he was consecrated archbishop of Capua, and in 1885 was created cardinal priest of Santi Nereo ed Achilleo. In the following year, however, he chose the church of Santa Maria del Popolo in preference to that of Santi Nereo ed Achilleo. He still retains his archiepiscopal see, and also remains the official librarian of the Holy See. In addition to a number of briefer contributions, he has written: *Storia di Santa Caterina e del papato del suo tempore* (2 vols., Naples, 1856); *Newman e la religione cattolica in Inghilterra* (2 vols., 1859); *La vita di Gesù Cristo* (1862); *Storia di San Pier Damiano e del suo tempore* (Florence, 1862); *Scritti Vari religiosi e socioli* (3d ed., Milan, 1873); *La dottrina cattolica* (3 vols., 2d ed., Sienna, 1879); *Vita di San Filippo Neri* (2 vols., Naples, 1879; Eng. transl., by T. A. Pope, London, 1882); *Prose sacre e morale* (Sienna, 1884); and *Nuove Prose* (2 vols., Milan, 1899). An edition of his works was published in eighteen volumes at Rome in 1886–93.

CAPE COLONY: The most important of the British possessions in South Africa, comprising, in general, that portion of the continent south of the Orange River; area, 277,000 square miles; population (1904), 2,409,804, of whom less than one-fourth (not quite 580,000) are Europeans or whites; the remainder (still predominantly heathen) includes 1,114,100 Kafirs and Bechuanas, 310,720 half-breeds classed as Fingo stock, 91,260 Hottentots, 15,680 Malays, and 298,340 classed as half-breeds and of miscellaneous origin.

The more important religious bodies of the colony are as follows: (1) The *Dutch Reformed Church*, with 390,500 members (1904), of whom 296,800 were white. It is the church of the original European (Dutch) settlers, who spread widely through the land by conquest from 1652 onward. Their Church is governed by a general synod, whose sessions are held every three years. The separate congregation is administered by a church council (*kerkeraad*), and six to twelve congregations constitute a congregational circuit ("ring"), whose chosen representatives become members of the General Synod. A standing committee of the Synod administers the principal affairs of the Church as a whole. The colored congregations are for the most part the result of missionary labor; only a small number of their clergy have a higher education. (2) The *Church of England*, 281,440 members (122,560 white). The diocese of Cape Town was founded in 1847; the incumbent has borne the title of archbishop since 1897 and is metropolitan of the province of South Africa, which comprises nine dioceses besides the metropolitan see, viz.: Bloemfontein (formerly the Orange Free State, formed 1863), Grahamstown (1853), Lebombo (1891), Mashonaland (1891), Natal (formerly Maritzburg, 1853), Pretoria (1878), St. Helena (1859), St. John's, Kaffraria (1873), and Zululand (a missionary bishopric, 1870). (3) The *Wesleyan Methodist Church of South Africa*, 277,300 members (35,900 white). This body very early employed colored teachers and has applied less rigorous tests of conversion than others; in 1891 it had about 1,250 lay helpers. Two other Methodist bodies have an inconsiderable aggregate membership. (4) *Congregationalists*, 112,200 members (5,000 Europeans), for the most part connected with the London Missionary Society. The Congregational Union of South Africa was formed in 1900 from the Union of South Africa (1877) and the Union of Natal and Southeastern Africa (1882). (5) *Presbyterians*, 88,660 members (26,360 of European origin). The Scotch Church began missionary activity in the east of the colony in 1821. (6) *Lutherans*, 37,050 members (13,100 Europeans), mostly of German origin. They are united in the German Evangelical Lutheran Synod of South Africa. (7) The *Rhenish Mission Church* has 20,800 members and (8) the *Moravians* 23,100, nearly all colored. (9) The *African Methodist Episcopal Church* has 12,060 members; (10) the *Baptists* number 14,100, of whom 9,950 are white, their congregations being organized practically on a European basis; (11) the *Church of Christ* has 7,600 members (1,075 Europeans), and (12) the *South African Reformed Church* 6,210, nearly all Europeans. Further, there is a group of mission congregations, of which the largest is Dutch (4,790) and the smallest American (215), and more than forty additional sects or denominations witness the tendency to religious division which manifests itself in English-speaking lands. For further information concerning missionary activity, see AFRICA, II.

The *Roman Catholic Church* has had a vigorous growth in the last ten years, and now counts more than 37,000 members (28,500 of European origin). The organization includes the apostolic vicariates of western and eastern Cape Colony, dating respectively from 1837 and 1847, with residence at Cape Town and Port Elizabeth, and the apostolic prefecture of central Cape Colony (1874), with residence at Cape Town. The Roman Catholic Church is active throughout South Africa and has established vicariates for Natal (1850), the Transvaal (1904), and Orange Free State (1886), and a prefecture of Basutoland (1894).

The *Greek Orthodox Church* reckons 1,050 adherents, almost exclusively European. The *Israelites* have decreased on account of emigration; still 19,500 remain. *Mohammedanism* is represented by 22,630 members (among them 15,100 Malays).

and 2,035 Hindus are enumerated. In spite of the missionary zeal of so many Christian sects, more than half the natives continue in heathenism, the official figures of colored heathen being 1,015,230.

The number of illiterates, after deduction of children under school age, is 1,368,000. The religious bodies are engaged in active rivalry to meet the needs of education and thereby to increase their numbers, and the government has latterly applied itself to the building and equipment of schools on a scale of greatly increased expenditure. Attendance at school was made compulsory in 1905. WILHELM GOETZ.

BIBLIOGRAPHY: For general facts and status, J. Bryce, *Impressions of South Africa*, London, 1899. For statistics, *South African Year Book*, annual, London. For phases of mission and other church work consult: A. T. Wirgman, *History of the English Church in South Africa*, London, 1895; A. G. S. Gibson, *Sketches of Church Work in the Diocese of Capetown*, Cape Town, 1900; *Mission Chronicle of the Scottish Church, with the Kaffrarian Diocesan Quarterly*, Edinburgh; *South African Catholic Magazine*, Cape Town; *Reports of the Wesleyan Missions in the Cape of Good Hope District*, annual, Cape Town; *Almanak voor de gereformeerde Kerk*, annual, Cape Town; *Handelingen der Vergadering van de synode der gereformeerde Kerk*, Cape Town (published subsequent to the meeting of each synod); J. Mackenzie, *Day-Dawn in South Africa*, London, 1884; idem, *London Missionary Society in South Africa*, ib. 1888; A. Brigg, *Missionary Life in the South of the Dark Continent*, ib. 1888; W. S. Walton, *Cape General Mission*, ib. 1889; A. G. S. Gibson, *Eight Years in Kaffraria*, ib. 1891; T. Cook, *My Mission Tour in South Africa*, ib. 1895; Merensky, in *Missionszeitschrift*, 1897–1898; *Basler Missionsmagazin*, 1900.

CAPEN, ELMER HEWITT: Universalist; b. at Stoughton, Mass., Apr. 5, 1838; d. at Medford, Mass., Mar. 22, 1905. He was graduated at Tufts College, 1860; admitted to the bar, 1863; was pastor of the Independent (Universalist) Christian Society of Gloucester, Mass., 1865–69; of the First Universalist Church of Providence, R. I., 1870–75; and after 1875 president of Tufts College, Medford, Mass. He belonged to the school of Universalists who make the final triumph of good over evil a corollary of the nature of God—a result to be wrought out through those moral processes which are seen in operation around us. He was member of the legislature from Stoughton, 1859–60. His publications consisted of sermons, addresses, reports, etc.

CAPERNAUM, ca-per'na-um: The name of a Galilean city, situated near the Sea of Galilee. The form of the word follows the *textus receptus*, though the best manuscripts give *Capharnaum*. It is a compound name meaning "village of Nahum" or "of consolation." Jesus made it the center of his Galilean activities and it was called "his own city" (Matt. iv. 13, ix. 1); his disciples Simon Peter and Andrew had a house there; he taught in the synagogue there, in Peter's house, and on the seashore, and performed a number of wonderful cures. There he obtained his disciples Peter, Andrew, and Levi-Matthew, and near-by James and John (Mark i. 16–17, 19, ii. 14). The city lay on the west shore of the sea, had a customs-office and royal collector and a garrison in command of a captain who was a friend of the Jews and had built them a synagogue. Josephus in describing the plain of Gennesaret (*War*, III. x. 8) speaks of a copious spring watering the plain which was called by the inhabitants Capernaum. There are still near the north of the plain two springs. One of these, the Ain-el-Tine, issues from the rock under the roots of a fig-tree not far from Khan Minyeh. But this can not be the one meant by Josephus, since it lies too low to water the plain. The other lies northwest of the first and outside the boundaries of the plain. This is the most copious spring in Galilee, stronger by far than the Banias source of the Jordan, known now as Ain-el-Tabigah, the waters of which are collected in a hexagonal reservoir of old masonry, showing that the spring was used for irrigation purposes. This is doubtless the spring mentioned by Josephus, and Capernaum must have been in the neighborhood, and, like the spring, not within the limits of the plain. Josephus states (*Life*, lxxii.), that in a skirmish against the troops of Agrippa II. which took place on the banks of the Jordan, he was thrown from his horse and wounded, and had himself carried to the village *Cepharnome* and in the following night to Tarichea. In spite of different textual readings of the name of the place, it is probable that Josephus here meant Capernaum.

Eusebius (*Onomasticon*, 273) discusses "in the borders of Zebulun and Naphtali" of Matt. iv. 13 in connection with Isa. ix. 1. The meaning of the phrase is "in the district of," not "on the boundary of." With Tel-Hum goes well Jerome's statement of two Roman miles as the distance between Chorazin and Capernaum (the "twelve miles" of Eusebius seems a copyist's error). Put alongside the foregoing that Capernaum and Bethsaida were adjacent (Epiphanius, *Hær.*, 1. 15), and early reports are quite exhausted.

Tel-Hum is the one old site in the vicinity of the spring, forty minutes distant in a northwestern direction. E. Robinson in 1838 visited and described the ruins, some quite pretentious buildings, of black basalt and limestone, among which travelers have thought they identified the remains of a synagogue. The name of the fountain, even though forty minutes away, makes for the identification of Tel-Hum with Capernaum. And the form Tel-Hum may be an Arabic variation for Tenhum, abbreviated from the Talmudic *Kaf Tanhumim* ("Village of Consolation").

The Franciscan Quaresmio in 1616–26 identified Khan Minyeh near Ain-el-Tine as the site of Capernaum, and he has been followed by many scholars. On this site appear the traces of the larger streets which a garrison city seems to require. A conclusion has been urged that John vi. 1–21 and Mark vi. 45–53 imply that Capernaum was on the plain of Gennesaret, but this falls after close examination of the passages. Arguments drawn from the element "Minyeh" in the modern name have also no cogency.

The ruins of Tel-Hum belong now to the Franciscans, who have enclosed them with a wall, intending to excavate there in the future.

(H. GUTHE.)

BIBLIOGRAPHY: Authorities and literature favoring Tel-Hum are: J. Wilson, *Lands of the Bible Visited and De-*

scribed, ii. 139–149, London, 1847; A. E. Wilson and W. Warren, *Recovery of Jerusalem*, pp. 375–387, ib. 1871; W. M. Thomson, *Land and the Book*, 3 vols., New York, 1880, i. 352–356 of London ed., 1873; V. Guérin, *Description . . . de la Palestine*, part 3, *Galilée*, i. 227–228, Paris, 1880; F. Buhl, *Geographie des alten Palästina*, pp. 224–225, Freiburg, 1896. Favoring Khan Minyeh are: A. P. Stanley, *Sinai and Palestine*, London, 1866; E. Robinson, *Biblical Researches*, Boston, 1868; T. Keim, *Jesus of Nazara*, 2 vols., London, 1879; C. R. Conder, *Tent Work in Palestine*, ib. 1880; A. Henderson, *Palestine*, Edinburgh, 1885; G. A. Smith, *Historical Geography of the Holy Land*, pp. 456–457, London, 1897; *DB*, i. 350–351; *EB*, i. 696–698.

CAPEROLANI, cā-pê″rō-lā′nî. See Francis, Saint, of Assisi, and the Franciscan Order, III., § 7.

CAPEROLO, cā-pê′rō-lō, PIETRO. See Francis, Saint, of Assisi, and the Franciscan Order.

CAPE VERDE ISLANDS. See Africa, III.

CAPERS, ELLISON: Protestant Episcopal bishop of South Carolina; b. in Charleston, S. C., Oct. 14, 1837; d. at Columbia, S. C., Apr. 22, 1908. He was graduated from the South Carolina Military Academy 1857, was assistant professor there 1858–60. On the outbreak of the Civil War he entered the Confederate Army, in which he attained the rank of brigadier-general. From the close of the war until 1868 he was secretary of the South Carolina Legislature, but in the mean time studied theology, and was ordained to the priesthood in 1867. He was then rector of Christ Church, Greenville, S. C., 1867–87, except for a year (1875–76) as rector of St. Paul's, Selma, Ala., and of Trinity, Columbia, S. C., 1887–93. In 1886 he had been tendered and had declined the bishopric of Easton, but in 1893 he was consecrated bishop of South Carolina.

Bibliography: W. S. Perry, *The Episcopate in America*, p. 355, New York, 1895.

CAPHTOR, caf′tor: A locality provisionally identified with Crete, though the question can not be regarded as settled. According to Amos ix. 7 it was the original home of the Philistines; Jer. xlvii. 4 (Masoretic text) makes of it an island or coast-land; Deut. ii. 23 and Gen. x. 14 use the term "Caphtorim" of the inhabitants. The early tradition is indicated by the fact that the Septuagint, Vulgate, Peshito, and Targums use "Cappadocia" and "Cappadocians" in Amos ix. 7 and Deut. ii. 23; this was based, however, on a misunderstanding. Attempts to find the meaning have been made by investigating the word "Cherethites" (I Sam. xxx. 14–16; Zeph. ii. 5; Ezek. xxv. 16), used of a people in the Philistine region and of Philistine stock. The transliterations of the Hebrew in the Septuagint show that the latter did not understand the meaning. In the prophetical books the form *Krites* is used by the Septuagint, implying immigration from Crete; but how far this rested upon data known to the interpreters is indeterminable.

On Egyptian monuments of the time of Thothmes III. appears mention of a land the name of which takes a form corresponding to "Caphtor" minus the final consonant (*Kefti*). Ebers explained this by "Phenicians," only to have the explanation shown untenable by W. Max Müller. According to G. Steindorff, the Egyptian word connotes "islands of the Ægean"; and the same authority notes among the representations of tribute to Thothmes III. from the *Kefti* vessels of the Mycenæan type of about 1450–1250 B.C. The *Kefti* must have been within the sphere of influence of Mycenæan culture. But Müller connects them with Cilicia. Evans in his investigations in Crete has discovered numerous evidences of the existence there of Mycenæan culture, thus bringing Crete within the sphere of influence of that civilization. Alongside of them are articles of Egyptian workmanship, showing exchange of commodities between Egypt and Crete. Steindorff puts the two facts together, and equates Crete and the Egyptian *Kefti*. But this may prove superfluous provided success is attained in geographically defining the word *kptar* recently found at Ombos, a word which closely corresponds with the Hebrew Caphtor. The equation *Kefti* = *kptar* is not fully proved. (H. Guthe.)

Bibliography: W. M. Müller, *Asien und Europa*, pp. 337 sqq., Leipsic, 1893; idem, in *Mittheilungen der vorderasiatischen Gesellschaft*, i. 1 sqq., 1900 (places Caphtor on the Lycian or Carian coast); G. Ebers, *Aegypten und die Bücher Mosis*, p. 130, Leipsic, 1868; G. A. Smith, *Historical Geography of the Holy Land*, p. 171, London, 1897; *DB*, i. 351–352; *EB*, i. 698–700; *JE*, iii. 553–554.

CAPISTRANO, GIOVANNI DI: Franciscan; b. at Capistrano (22 m. s.e. of Aquila), in the Abruzzi, 1386; d. at Illok (Ujlak, 26 m. w. of Peterwardein), Slavonia, Oct. 23, 1456. He first studied jurisprudence, but joined the Franciscans in 1416 and in the school of Bernardin of Sienna became a theologian and preacher. After 1426 he acted as inquisitor against the Fratricelli and Jews, and by cruel measures attained a moderate success. His main achievement was the defense and extension of the order of the Observantines, of whom he was made vicar-general in Italy in 1446. In 1451 he was sent to Germany against the Hussites. Followed by large crowds, he went to Vienna, and is reported to have performed 320 miracles on the way, while the number of his hearers is said to have increased from 150 to 300,000. He intended now to go to Bohemia to destroy the heresy there; a disputation to which he was invited by the Utraquist bishop Rokyczana he managed to avoid, and finally he did venture to enter the country. Æneas Silvius states that he did, indeed, convert a few Hussites, but, considering the multitude of the heretics, they are hardly worth mentioning. At any rate Bohemia, in spite of his sermons, remained as it was before. By way of Bavaria, Saxony, and Lusatia, he went to Silesia and Poland, and on account of his sermons and miracles was everywhere revered like a saint. After the fall of Constantinople (1453) he tried to induce the princes of Germany at the Diets of Frankfort and Wiener-Neustadt to make war against the Turks, but failed, and was very little successful generally in preaching the cross. He went to Hungary in 1455 and when Mohammed II. advanced against Belgrade (1456) Capistrano, the papal legate Carjaval, and John Hunyadi were almost the only men who bestirred themselves to repel the foe. In spite of his age, Capistrano with a number of crusaders went to Belgrade and by a daring sally gave Hunyadi opportunity to beat the Turks. For this the friends of his order have celebrated him as savior of Europe. He died soon after, exhausted by hardships. Although revered in his lifetime as a saint, he was not canonized until 1690. Prominent contemporaries, among them the subsequent pope Pius II., expressed some doubts as to his miracles and had no favorable opinion of him because of his bragging self-glorification and choleric irritability. E. LEMPP.

BIBLIOGRAPHY: The early *Vitæ* and some of John's letters are in *ASB*, Oct., x. 269-552, with which cf. L. Wadding, *Annales Minorum*, vols. iv.-vi., Leyden, 1648, or ix.-xiii., Rome, 1734 (an excellent source). The most comprehensive biography is by A. Hermann, *Capistranus triumphans*, Cologne, 1700; the first scientific life is by G. Voigt, in Sybel's *Historische Zeitschrift*, x. (1863) 19-96; cf. idem, *Enea Silvio di' Piccolomini*, vol. ii., Berlin, 1860; the latest life is by E. Jacob, *Johannes von Capistrano*, Breslau, 1903. A considerable list of literature is given in Potthast, *Wegweiser*, pp. 1396-97.

CAPITAL PUNISHMENT.

I. The Historical Development of Capital Punishment: It must be borne in mind that the killing of a person guilty of grievous crime does not, in primitive society, belong to the class of deliberate ordinances enacted by the community. It is rather a form of the impulse of revenge, which the primitive institutions of all the older civilized nations first tolerate, and then regulate and uphold or limit (see BLOOD-REVENGE). In primitive conditions revenge has a twofold operation. It is directed in some cases against offenses which affect the individual or the family (such as theft, adultery, and the murder of a freeman); in these cases the injured family proceeds against the offender or his family, and the community takes part only in the interests of public peace, by establishing a penalty on payment of which the offender is to be safe from revenge. Quite a different form of procedure is that against crimes which offend the consciousness of the whole community (sacrilege, unnatural vices, treason in war, etc.). Here the vengeance of the community is provoked, and it acts first by formal delivery of the offender to the will of the members or outlawry, then later by actual execution, in connection with which sacred ceremonies analogous to those of sacrifice are often found. As organized government grows stronger, it takes an official interest in crimes which were originally in the private sphere, withdraws them from individual vengeance, and subjects them to capital punishment. Religion has its influence here; the interference of government in such cases is usually brought about by the conception that the crime, apart from the injury to the immediate victims, defiles the community and must be punished in order to retain peace with the deity. This can be clearly shown in the Greek law of the post-Homeric age, less clearly but still probably in ancient Roman law; and the same course was followed in Hebrew history. In the primitive law (cf. Ex. xxi. 12 sqq.) the murderer is exposed to the pursuit of the avenger of blood, and the elders of the community cooperate only to the extent of driving the fugitive from an asylum and delivering him to the avenger. In the case of the other crimes mentioned in Ex. xxi. the punishment of death is either private vengeance, or at most a sort of tribal vengeance or lynch law. As late as the period of Deut. xix. the blood-vengeance is mentioned; but by the side of it appears the idea that the whole community is affected with blood-guiltiness by a deliberate murder, and must be purified by the death of the offender. The same law began, when priestly influence increasingly dominated all departments of life, to be applied to other offenders (blasphemers, traitors, adulterers, etc.). The formal abandonment to the avenger was replaced by stoning, in which all the men of the community took part.

1. In Primitive Society.

In so far as the religious influence remained a permanent factor in the penal code, the Jewish State stands alone among the Mediterranean communities. In the others, especially the Greek and Roman, punishment became exclusively a matter of secular enactment. In the Roman the principle is continuously applied from the fifth century that the death penalty (whether by decapitation, burning, or throwing down a precipice) is due to all grave crimes (including murder, arson, perjury, treason, etc.); but in practise this was mitigated by the frequent substitution of the "interdiction of fire and water," i.e., banishment from the community, especially after the introduction of the *provocatio ad populum*, an appeal to the whole body of the people against the decision of consuls and other magistrates empowered to pronounce sentence of outlawry. In the last two centuries of the republic capital punishment was seldom applied, to members of the upper classes at least. But it was never abolished, and when the reorganization of the Roman system took place under imperial legislation it was again more frequently employed, even against Roman citizens. Thus at the beginning of the Christian era it was an accepted institution throughout the Roman Empire, though with variations in usage due to local law.

2. In Roman Law.

The teaching of Christ made no substantial alteration in these conditions. Of his own recorded sayings, the only one directly bearing on the subject is Matt. xxvi. 52, which (like Gen. ix. 5) refers rather to the eternal working out of the divine justice in the abstract. But Paul speaks expressly in Rom. xiii. 1 sqq. of the legal death-penalty—although here it is merely designated as reconcilable with the divine law, not required or imposed as a duty upon the State. Accordingly Christian teaching made no change in the Roman law, and, when the Christians became dominant, after having been for two centuries frequent victims to its provisions, they still allowed it to take free course. In fact, it was applied with increasing frequency even to Roman citizens of the higher classes, and from the time of Constantine to a large number of minor offenses.

Although the Church was more firmly and fully organized when it came into contact with the institutions of the new Germanic kingdoms, and assumed the right of extensive interference with their penal legislation on principles resembling those of the Jewish theocracy, its influence in the question of capital punishment was not decisive.

3. Attitude of the Church. Germanic law at first, like all primitive systems, made private vengeance and the mitigation of it by surrender of property on the part of the offender the principal factor in the punishment of crime. The Church undertook to regulate this to the extent of minimizing private vendettas, both by providing and supporting means of reconciliation between the contending parties and by strengthening orderly official justice. But in spite of the "horror of bloodshed" consistently emphasized by the Church, which from the tenth century on created an impressive mechanism against private vendettas in the Truce of God (q.v.), it was obliged to give a general support to the gradual upbuilding of the secular system of corporal, including capital, punishment in the kingdoms of western Europe. When the death-penalty had been finally established as a regular part of settled secular law, the Church in theory took the position of a simple spectator of its exercise. It forbade the clergy to take any part in its administration, laid down the principle *Ecclesia non sitit sanguinem* ("The Church does not thirst for blood"), and admonished ecclesiastical authorities to provide asylums and in other ways to work for mercy to the offender in the hope of his improvement. This position was somewhat modified when the war against heresy began. Even in the eleventh century the State threatened heretics with death in isolated cases in France and Germany; and by the middle of the twelfth century the growth of heresy led to a formal alliance between Church and State, by which Frederick Barbarossa in 1184, and then other sovereigns of southern Europe, pledged the pope the support of the secular arm for the suppression of heresy. The penalties were at first outlawry, infamy, and confiscation of goods; but in 1224 Frederick II. approved of death by fire as the penalty in Lombardy: and this penalty, soon applied throughout Italy, was not only sanctioned but directly called for by Gregory IX. It was not long before the new principle was extended to Germany, France, England, and Spain, and the death-penalty, while theoretically administered by secular officials, was actually the consequence of an ecclesiastical condemnation.

The teaching of the Reformers brought about no essential alteration in the general attitude toward capital punishment; it might seem that the Reformation strengthened the institution, but really this attitude is rather the result of contemporary conditions. The death-penalty had been more frequently employed in all European states since the fifteenth century as a result of violent proletarian risings and the increase of the dangerous unemployed and vagabond population, and the period from 1530 to 1630 is that in which the number of executions reached its high-water mark. When a reaction came about, it was directed primarily against an excessive use of this penalty, and then toward the establishment of penitentiaries (London 1580, Amsterdam 1596, Hamburg 1622, etc.), which brought about a decrease in the number of executions. The movement for the abolition of capital punishment did not proceed from a religious source. While Locke, Voltaire, Montesquieu, and Thomasius had all recognized it as a necessary part of the social system, and Rousseau in the *Contrat social* had left it theoretically free play, it was Cesare Beccaria in 1764 who, as a deduction from Rousseau's general ideas, proclaimed its irreconcilability with abstract justice. In modern times no agreement has been reached on the basis of religious convictions.

II. Place of Religious Ideas in the Question: The historical outline given above shows clearly that the sanction and province of capital punishment in secular law can not be brought directly under religious control. The old philosophical doctrine of the "Christian State" is now no longer recognized. On modern principles, the State's justification for existence lies in its necessity to the unhampered development of human activity; and on this rests its power of punishing, and in particular its right to apply the death-penalty. The essential characteristics of a just and proper punishment will thus have to be determined by a course of empirical historical research.

In the older development of the penal code of all nations, corporal punishment is found concurrently with penalties affecting the property of the offender; but the corporal is finally preferred because it is capable of application alike to all, while money fines have a varying effect according to the wealth of the offender. By degrees the permission of compounding for corporal penalties is abolished, with the gradual building up from the twelfth century of modern principles of government. The death-penalty is increasingly preferred as emphasizing the thought of the equality of all men before the law. It is misused for a time as the easiest way of ridding society of dangerous persons, and then, in the sixteenth and seventeenth centuries, the question is widely discussed how far it ought properly to be applied, and the principle of justice is urged in favor of its restriction to very grave crimes. These arguments, however, produced no great effect until the reaction from the excessive use of it led to the creation of a third form of penalty in a regular system of imprisonment, thoroughly established about 1700. The considerations which moved John Howard and others in the eighteenth century to agitate for prison reform on the ground of humanity led also to the more frequent discussion of the desirability of abolishing capital punishment, and finally to an almost universal recognition of the sole ground on which its maintenance can be defended. It is now admitted that on grounds of humanity the State has no right to annihilate the individual existence, and that so far as these grounds go, the heaviest penalty that may be inflicted is that of penal servitude for life. From the standpoint, however, of abstract justice, it is still possible to defend the death-penalty, not in the interest of terrifying offenders, nor yet on the basis of a *lex talionis*, but on that of a proportion between crime and penalty, which may fairly demand that the severity of the punishment shall correspond in some measure to the importance of the social function injured by the crime. With this is connected the requirement that the penalty shall be impressive—as much so as the crime—in order that the authority of the law shall be upheld, and equal, falling with the same severity on all classes of the community. The validity of this argument will be denied by those who reject the principle of equivalent compensation and, taking their stand exclusively on the principle of humanity, seek as the result of punishment the amelioration of the offender and the deterrence of him from any further crimes. But the fact that many of those who take this theoretical view acquiesce in the retention of capital punishment in practise shows that the traditional verdict of many centuries as to the relation of crime and punishment is still to be reckoned with in any discussion of this question.

(Richard Schmidt.)

III. Capital Punishment in Modern Times: In modern times the maintenance or abolition of the death-penalty has been considered mainly from the standpoint of social utility and social justice. In the history of penology the influence of Christian and humane sentiments has been distinctly felt; but many drastic punishments have been laid aside, not because they were cruel and severe, but because they were ineffective. As mutilation has been practically abandoned in civilized countries, so reliance upon capital punishment as a means of repressing crime has been greatly weakened. A conclusive proof of this is seen in the restriction of the number of offenses to which it is applied. Scarcely more than a century ago 200 offenses were included in the list of capital crime in England. Until 1894 twenty-five offenses were made capital under the military code of the United States, twenty-two under the naval code, and seventeen under the penal code. Under Federal laws the number of capital offenses has now been reduced to three. Many advocates of capital punishment to-day are willing to limit its application wholly to cases of murder.

Publicity was formerly regarded as absolutely necessary for the deterrent effect of executions. Even after death the body of the criminal was exposed for weeks on the gibbet as a warning to malefactors. The practise of gibbeting has now been abandoned, and the practise of public execution is gradually following it. Within recent years seven or eight States of the Union, including New York, Massachusetts, New Mexico, North Dakota, have decided that attendance on executions should be limited to a number of legal or specified witnesses. The governors of Georgia and Kentucky have recommended similar legislation. In several States the electric chair has been substituted for the gallows with a view of mercifully rendering death instantaneous. Other States of the Union have abolished the death-penalty altogether. Michigan abolished it in 1847, Rhode Island in 1852, Wisconsin in 1853. Maine abolished it in 1876, restored it in 1883, and again abolished it in 1887. In 1903 New Hampshire abolished the death-penalty for murder in the first degree unless the jury should have fixed the same to the verdict; otherwise the sentence is for life imprisonment. In Kansas there have been no official executions since 1872, as no governor has exercised his power to order the execution of a prisoner. In 1907 the legislature amended the law by substituting life imprisonment for the death-penalty. The governor of Nebraska in 1903 urged the legislature to abolish capital punishment. Colorado abolished the death-penalty in 1897, but restored it 1901, as a result of a lynching outbreak in 1900.

In its session 1906–07 the subject of the abolition of capital punishment occupied a prominent place in the discussions of the French parliament without final result. Russia, one of the first countries to respond to the appeal of Beccaria, abolished it in 1753, except for political offenses. It was abolished in Portugal in 1867, in Holland in 1870, in Italy in 1890; and it has been abolished in the majority of the Swiss cantons, in Costa Rica, Brazil, Ecuador, Guatemala, Venezuela, and three states of Mexico. Some countries which have not formally abolished it by legislative act have suppressed it in practise. This is true of Belgium, and of some states of Mexico. It remains yet to be proven that an increase in capital crimes has followed the abolition of the death-penalty in any country. On the contrary, the higher development of civilization in these countries, the growth of the humane sentiment, and increased reliance upon educational and preventive measures, instead of upon drastic deterrent laws, have led to a gradual reduction of crimes of violence. Samuel J. Barrows.

Bibliography: G. B. Cheever, *Punishment by Death: its Authority and Expediency*, New York, 1849 (one of the most vigorous defenses of the practise); H. Seeger, *Abhandlungen aus dem Strafrechte*, Tübingen, 1858; C. J. Mittermaier, *Die Todesstrafe nach den Ergebnissen der wissenschaftlichen Forschungen*, Heidelberg, 1862 (the standard work against capital punishment, Eng. condensation by J. M. Moir, *Capital Punishment*, London, 1865); R. E. John, *Ueber die Todesstrafe*, Berlin, 1867; H. Hetzel, *Todesstrafe in ihrer kulturgeschichtlichen Entwickelung*, ib. 1870; F. von Holtzendorff, *Das Verbrechen des Mordes und die Todesstrafe*, ib. 1875; L. von Bar, *Handbuch des deutschen Strafrechts*, vol. i., ib. 1882; H. Romilly, *The Punishment of Death*, London, 1886; A. J. Palm, *The Death Penalty*, New York, 1891; J. MacMaster, *The Divine Purpose of Capital Punishment*, London, 1892; S. R. D. K. Olivecroner, *De la peine de la mort*, Paris, 1893; R. Schmidt, *Aufgaben der Strafrechtspflege*, pp. 178 sqq., 224 sqq., Leipsic, 1895; R. Katzenstein, *Todesstrafe in einem neuen Reichsstrafgesetzbuch*, Berlin, 1902; D. P. D. Fabius, *De doodstraf*, Amsterdam, 1906. For the ancient enactments consult *Jurisprudentiæ anteiustinianæ*, ed. E. Huschke, 5th ed., Leipsic, 1886 (cf. Index under "Capite puniuntur"), and "The Institutes of Justinian," Book IV., title xviii., in Moyle's transl., 4th ed., pp. 205–207, Oxford, 1906; A. H. J. Greenidge, *Infamia; its Place in Roman Public and Private Law*, 1894.

CAPITO, WOLFGANG FABRICIUS: Reformer at Strasburg; b. at Hagenau) 16 m. n. of Strasburg) 1478; d. at Strasburg Nov., 1541. He was the son of a blacksmith named Koepfel, whence the Latin name *Capito*. Having passed the schools at Pforzheim and Ingolstadt, he studied at Freiburg first medicine, then law, and finally theology. In 1512 he became parish priest at Bruchsal and there made the acquaintance of Œcolampadius and Pellican. Called to Basel in 1515 as preacher and professor, he became intimate with the humanists, including Erasmus, and, abandoning scholasticism.

betook himself to the study of the Bible. He published the Psalter in the original (1516), became personally acquainted with Zwingli and from 1518 corresponded with Luther. Contrary to all expectation, he was appointed in 1519 chaplain to Albert, elector and archbishop of Mainz. For a time he tried to mediate with humanistic liberality between the elector and Luther, but in 1522 he was brought over completely to the cause of the Reformation, and resigned his position at Mainz. In May, 1523, he went to Strasburg and as provost of St. Thomas (a position obtained by the favor of Leo X.) preached in accordance with his conviction. In 1524 he married and became pastor of the Jung-St. Petergemeinde. From this time on, he belonged, with Butzer and the burgomaster Jacob Sturm, to the leaders of the Strasburg Reformation. In his *Kinderbericht* (1527 and 1529) he prepared a catechism, which, by its peculiar arrangement and characteristic treatment of the matter, forms a noteworthy pendant to Luther's contemporaneous smaller catechism. With Butzer, Capito prepared the *Confessio Tetrapolitana* (1530). His most important reformatory work is the *Berner Synodus*, the result of the synod held at Bern in 1532, a kind of church-discipline and pastoral instruction, distinguished by apostolic power and unction, great simplicity, and practical wisdom. He took an active part in Butzer's efforts to bring together the Evangelicals of Germany, France, and Switzerland. He also had part in bringing about the Wittenberg Concordia of 1536. Toward the Anabaptists and other sectaries who disturbed the church at Strasburg he was more friendly and confiding than Butzer, and for a time sided with them, thus destroying the good understanding between himself and Butzer. But in 1534 he became convinced of the necessity of stricter measures against the Anabaptists. Characteristic of Capito were not only his mildness and large-heartedness, but also a certain timidity and uncertainty in his theological and ecclesiastical position. However, this was not due to diplomatic opportunism, but to a sincere repugnance to unfruitful theological controversy and a religious individuality which had more regard to the inner possession of the fruits of salvation than to a dogmatic definition of the doctrine of salvation.

He died of the plague after having attended the Diet at Regensburg. PAUL GRÜNBERG.

BIBLIOGRAPHY: J. W. Baum, *Capito und Butzer*, Elberfeld, 1860; *ADB*, iii. 772–775; A. Baum, *Magistrat und Reformation in Strassburg bis 1529*, Strasburg, 1887; C. Gerbert, *Geschichte der Strassburger Sektenbewegung 1524–1534*, ib. 1889; A. Ernst and J. Adam, *Katechetische Geschichte des Elsasses*, pp. 22–36, ib. 1897; S. M. Jackson, *Huldreich Zwingli*, passim, New York, 1903; J. Ficker, *Thesaurus Baumianus*, pp. 52–57, Strasburg, 1905; A. Hulshof, *Geschiedenis van de Doopsgezinden te Straatsburg van 1525 tot 1557*, Amsterdam, 1905.

CAPITULARIES: A term which designates a certain class of royal edicts in the Carolingian period, and which is frequently employed not only for the Carolingian *capitularia* but also for the *edicta*, *præceptiones*, *decreta*, or *decretiones* of the Merovingian kings and the mayors of the palace under Arnulf. They are distinguished from the other class of *diplomata* or *mandata*, not so much by the division into chapters, from which they get their name, or by the general nature of their provisions as by their form and by the absence of any attestation in the way of signatures or seal. This absence is explained by the fact that they were either put into execution by the kings in person or had to pass through the hands of officials. They attained their highest importance under Charlemagne, and were scarcely less used under Louis the Pious; after his death they ceased in the East Frankish kingdom, to be kept up for a while in the West Frankish and in Italy by his sons and grandsons, disappearing here also toward the end of the ninth century. They contain partly instructions for officials, especially the *missi dominici*, and partly supplements or modifications of the old tribal law; but to a still greater extent they are substantive regulations for all departments of both secular and ecclesiastical life. The former include the most diverse matters, of administration, commerce, the army, markets, coinage, tolls, protection against robbers, etc. These substantive regulations go deeply into not merely the external organization of the Church and its relation to the temporal power, but also the monastic system, education, church discipline, and even liturgical matters.

The origin of the capitularies and the basis of their authority have been much discussed. The prevalent view, derived in the first instance from Boretius, distinguishes between *capitularia legibus addenda* and *per se scribenda*, which means practically a class of laws originating (like those specifically known as *leges*) in the assent of the whole people, and another class originating from the king alone, at most with the advice of the nobles assembled in a diet. But there seems to be no sufficient ground for this distinction between popular and royal law; in so far as there is any contrast between *leges* and *capitularia*, it may be fully explained by the special reverence which was felt for the ancient tribal law. In the cases in which the capitularies do not contain merely instructions to officials, they were less legislative enactments than promulgations of a law already existing. This law, so far as we can trace its origin, came into being with the assent of the temporal and spiritual lords, assembled in diets or synods. But the diet must not be conceived of as a representative assembly of the whole people; its decisions were held to be binding upon the individual by virtue of his allegiance to the sovereign, and the period of the capitularies is precisely that in which the oath of allegiance was most punctiliously required from all adults within the empire. The multiplication of capitularies led before long to the need of codification; for the collection made by Ansegis of Fontanella, see ANSEGIS, and for the forged capitularies appended to his collection by Benedictus Levita, see PSEUDO-ISIDORIAN DECRETALS.

(SIEGFRIED RIETSCHEL.)

BIBLIOGRAPHY: Critical editions of the *Capitularia regum Francorum*, ed. G. H. Pertz, are in *MGH*, *Legum*, i., ii., 1835, 1837; and, ed. A. Boretius and V. Krause, ib. *Leg.*, sectio II. i., ii., 1883–97 (cf. A. Boretius, in *GGA*, 1882, pp. 65 sqq., 1884, pp. 713 sqq.). Consult: A. Boretius, *Die Kapitularien im Langobardenreich*, Halle, 1864; idem, *Beiträge zur Kapitularienkritik*, Leipsic, 1874; R. Sohm, *Die fränkische Reichs- und Gerichtsverfassung*, pp. 102 sqq., Weimar, 1871; Fustel de Coulanges, *De la confec-*

tion des lois au temps des Carolingiens, in *Revue historique*, iii. (1878) 3 sqq.; M. Thévenin, *Lex et capitula*, in *Mélanges de l'école des hautes études*, pp. 137 sqq., 1878; H. Brunner, *Deutsche Rechtsgeschichte*, i. 539 sqq., Leipsic, 1906; E. Glasson, *Histoire du droit et des institutions politiques et administratives de la France*, i. 281 sqq., Paris, 1890; G. Seeliger, *Die Kapitularien der Karolinger*, Munich, 1893; R. Schröder, *Lehrbuch der deutschen Rechtsgeschichte*, pp. 253 sqq., Leipsic, 1902.

CAPPADOCIA, cap″pa-dō′shi-a. See ASIA MINOR IN THE APOSTOLIC TIME, XI.

CAPPEL (CAPPELLUS): A French family which produced many noteworthy statesmen and scholars between the fifteenth and seventeenth centuries, as well as three theologians, Louis Cappel the Elder, Jacques Cappel the Third, and Louis Cappel the Younger.

1. Louis Cappel the Elder: Reformed theologian; b. at Paris Jan. 15, 1534; d. at Sédan Jan. 6, 1586. Despite the early death of his father, he received an excellent education, and in his twenty-second year went to Bordeaux to study law, but before long accepted a professorship of Greek. Becoming acquainted with certain of the Reformers, he was converted to their doctrines, and went to study theology at Geneva, where Calvin controlled the Church. Returning to Paris about 1560, he won the confidence of his coreligionists by his zeal for the interests of the Reformed, and was finally ordained pastor. He officiated successively at Meaux, Antwerp, and Clermont, but the constant outbreak of disturbances rendered any continuous activity impossible, and he was repeatedly obliged to retire to Sédan, where he was safe, since it lay in the duchy of Bouillon. In 1575 he was appointed professor of theology at the University of Leyden, but was recalled in the following year to France and made preacher and professor of theology at Sédan, holding these positions until his death.

2. Jacques Cappel the Third: Nephew of the preceding; b. at Rennes Mar., 1570; d. at Sédan Sept. 7, 1624. After completing his theological education at Sédan, he went in 1593 to his ancestral estate le Tilloi, where he preached for several years. In 1599 he accepted a call to Sédan as professor of Hebrew, and eleven years later was appointed professor of theology. His learning, piety, and charity won him high esteem. Among his numerous works special mention may be made of his *Observationes in selecta Pentateuchi loca* (ed. J. Cappel, in his *Commentarii et notæ criticæ in Vetus Testamentum*, Amsterdam, 1689) and his *Historia sacra et exotica ab Adamo usque ad Augusti ortum* (Sédan, 1612).

3. Louis Cappel the Younger: Youngest brother of the preceding; b. at St. Élier (a village near Sédan) Oct. 15, 1585; d. at Saumur June 18, 1658. His father, Jacques Cappel the Younger, who had been a parliamentary counselor at Rennes, had been forced to resign on account of his conversion to the Reformed Church and had been driven by the adherents of the League from his estates of le Tilloi. During his flight to his brother Louis Cappel the Elder at Sédan, his son was born and named for his uncle. After his father's death in 1586, the boy was taken by his mother to le Tilloi, where he was educated by Roman Catholics until his brother Jacques Cappel took him from their charge. He then studied theology in Sédan, and in 1609 received from the church in Bordeaux the means to study four years in England, Belgium, and Germany. On his return he was appointed professor of Hebrew at Saumur, but in 1621 the war forced him to take refuge with his brother at Sédan, where he remained three years. In 1626 he became professor of theology, and through him, together with Moïse Amyraut and Josué de la Place, Saumur attained high fame. Of his five sons two died in early youth, the eldest, Jean, became a convert to the Roman Catholic Church, and the youngest, Jacques the Fourth, when eighteen years of age succeeded his father as professor of Hebrew at Saumur. Louis Cappel was a man of piety, sincerity, courage, energy, and learning. His life-work was devoted to the study of the history of the text of the Old Testament and the refutation of false views concerning it. His first book, *Arcanum punctationis revelatum*, was completed in 1623, and sought to prove that the Hebrew punctuation did not originate with Moses and the other Biblical authors, but had been introduced by Jewish scholars after the completion of the Babylonian Talmud. The novelty of the book is not its assertion, but its logical proof. The work was sent by its author to various scholars for their opinions, but while Buxtorf at Basel counseled caution, Erpenius at Leyden had it printed anonymously on his own responsibility in 1624. The book found a friendly reception in many quarters, but twenty years later Buxtorf's son attacked the author bitterly in his *Tractatus de punctorum origine* (Basel, 1648). Cappel replied with his *Vindiciæ arcani punctationis*, although it first appeared thirty years after his death in the *Commentarii et notæ criticæ in Vetus Testamentum* edited by his son, Jacques Cappel the Fourth (Amsterdam, 1689). His second famous work was the *Critica sacra* (Paris, 1650), based on the theory of the integrity of the text and completed in 1634, although it remained unprinted for many years on account of the opposition of the Protestants in Geneva, Leyden, and Sédan. The work is divided into six books with the following subjects: parallel passages in the Old Testament; citations from the Old Testament in the New; the various readings of the *keri* and *kethibh*, the manuscripts of the Oriental and Occidental Jews, printed Bibles, and the Masoretic and Samaritan texts of the Pentateuch; deviations in the Septuagint from the Masoretic text; variants in other ancient translations, the Talmud, and early Jewish writings; the choice of readings and the restoration of the original text. Cappel was obliged to meet repeated attacks. Even when his work first appeared, it contained a defense against the younger Buxtorf, who had learned the contents of the book before it was printed, and had combated it in the *Tractatus* already mentioned. Certain passages which had been omitted in the original edition against his will were added by Cappel in his *Epistola apologetica* (Saumur, 1651), another work in his own defense. A new edition of the *Critica* *sacra* was prepared by G. J. L. Vogel and J. G. Scharfenberg (3 vols., Halle, 1775–86). His third important writing was the *Diatriba de veris et antiquis Hebræorum literis* (Amsterdam, 1645), in which he proved the priority of the Samaritan script over the square characters and thus refuted the treatise of the younger Buxtorf, *De litterarum Hebraicarum genuina antiquitate* (1643). In these writings Cappel discussed problems which were of the utmost importance to the Protestants in their controversy with the Roman Catholics. Of his opponents the younger Buxtorf was the most important, and had practically all the theologians of Germany and Switzerland on his side, while many prominent scholars of France, England, and Holland defended the views of Cappel. The first sentences of the Helvetic Consensus Formula of 1675 are directed against Cappel, the greater number of the rest being aimed at Amyraut. In later times a fairer and calmer judgment prevailed concerning the investigations of Cappel, and his results are now generally accepted. A list of his printed and unprinted works is given by his son Jacques in the *Commentarii* noted above. Special mention may also be made of his *Templi Hierosolymitani delineatio triplex* and *Chronologia sacra* (both contained in Walton's Polyglot), as well as of his *Historia apostolica illustrata* (Geneva, 1634). [His *Pivot de la foi et religion* (Saumur, 1643) was translated into English by P. Marinel (London, 1660).]

Carl Bertheau.

Bibliography: Nicéron, *Mémoires*, vol. xxii.; *Biographie universelle*, vii. 75–80, Paris, 1813; I. A. Dorner, *Geschichte der protestantischen Theologie*, pp. 450 sqq., Munich, 1867, Eng. transl., Edinburgh, 1880; L. Diestel, *Geschichte des Alten Testaments in der christlichen Kirche*, pp. 336 sqq., 346 sqq., Jena, 1868; G. Schnedermann, *Die Controverse des L. Cappellus mit den Buxtorfen*, Leipsic, 1878; C. A. Briggs, *Study of Holy Scripture*, pp. 222 sqq., New York, 1899.

CAPREOLUS, JOHANNES: The most distinguished Thomist theologian of the fifteenth century; d. 1444. Little is known of his life. According to Quétif, he joined the Dominican order at Rodez. The subscriptions of the four books of his *Defensiones* (first printed in Venice, 1483), where he is described as of Toulouse, tell that he finished the first book in 1409 at Paris, where he was then lecturing, the others at Rodez in 1426, 1428, and 1433. So, at least, Quétif asserts; but an extant copy of the *editio princeps* assigns the composition of the first three books to 1409, and the fourth to 1432, no place given; and the second edition (Venice, 1514–15) gives 1409 for the first two, 1428 and 1432 for the others, all in Paris. The diversity renders all the dates uncertain; nor can we be sure of the date (Apr. 6, 1444) assigned to his death by an inscription on his tomb at Rodez, of evidently later composition. The Dominicans of Toulouse assert that he was for some time at the head of their *studium generale*. (A. Hauck.)

Bibliography: J. Quétif and J. Échard, *Scriptores ordinis prædicatorum*, i. 795 sqq., Paris, 1719; K. Werner, *Der heilige Thomas von Aquino*, iii. 151 sqq., Regensburg, 1859.

CAPTIVITY OF THE JEWS. See Israel, History of, I., § 9.

CAPUCHINS: A branch of the order of Franciscans, founded in the third decade of the sixteenth century by Matteo di Bassi, an Observantine Franciscan. Repeated attempts had been made since the fourteenth century to restore the primitive strength and simplicity of the Franciscan rule, and one of these movements was concerned especially with the habit of the order. In connection with this attempted reform, Matteo was told by a brother monk that the cowl worn by St. Francis differed essentially from that adopted by his order. Matteo thereupon left his monastery of Montefalcone and hastened to Rome, where in 1526 he obtained permission from Clement VII. to wear a pyramidal hood and a beard, to live as a hermit, and to preach wheresoever he wished, on condition that he should report annually to the provincial chapter of the Observantines. Matteo's example was followed by his fellow Observantines Lodovico and Raffaelle di Fossombrone, both of whom received similar privileges from the pope; and the three, soon joined by a fourth, found a home with the Camaldolites and the duke of Camerino. Through the duke's influence, they were received among the Conventuals in 1527, whereupon Lodovico and Raffaelle returned to Rome and obtained from the pope the bull of May 18, 1528, by which they were permitted to preach repentance, have the care of souls, especially of abandoned sinners, and form a congregation with the privileges already granted them. They were freed, moreover, from the Observantines and placed under the control of the Conventuals, since their vicar-general must be confirmed by the general of the Conventuals, while they were to receive visitations from the Conventuals and were obliged in their processions to march under the cross either of the Conventuals or the parish clergy. The members of the new order speedily became conspicuous by their long beards and pointed hoods or capuches, whence they were termed Capuchins in ecclesiastical documents as early as 1536 (*Capucini ordinis fratrum minorum* or *Fratres minores Capucini*). Their first monastery was given them by the duchess of Camerino, but by 1529 they possessed four houses and in the same year their first chapter was convened. At the same time the rules of the order were drawn up, and thenceforth remained essentially unchanged.

Early History.

The Capuchins were required to preserve the primitive service, to refuse all compensation for singing mass, to devote two hours daily to silent prayer, to observe silence throughout the day with the exception of two hours, to practise flagellation, to beg only what was necessary for each day, to provide only for three or at most seven days, and never to touch money. The use of meat and wine in strict moderation was allowed, but the friars were forbidden to beg for meat, eggs, or cheese, although they might accept them when they were offered. The habit was to be poor and coarse, and the brothers, who might ride neither on horseback nor in wagons, were required to go barefoot, sandals being allowed only in special cases. The monasteries, which were to contain at most ten or twelve friars each,

Rule.

were to be fitted in the most meager manner possible. In addition to the general, the Capuchins had provincials, custodians, and guardians, but no procurators or syndics. Elections were held annually, except in the case of the general, who was elected by the chapter triennially.

Since the Reformation.

The first vicar-general was Matteo di Bassi himself, but two months after his election in 1529 he resigned, and in 1537 returned to the Observantines. He was succeeded by Lodovico di Fossombrone, who failed of reelection in 1535 and was expelled for exciting dissatisfaction within the order. The next heads of the Capuchins were Giovanni de Fano and Bernardino Ochino (q.v.). The defection of the latter to Protestantism in 1543 caused Paul III. to contemplate the dissolution of the order, and for a number of years the Capuchins were forbidden to preach. The result of Ochino's act was the transformation of the Capuchins into a rigidly ultramontane order which renounced all independent judgment in matters of faith and doctrine.

After the middle of the sixteenth century the spread of the order was rapid. Originally restricted to Italy, it was established in France at the request of Charles IX. in 1573, and in 1593 entered Germany, after having already been implanted in Switzerland. In 1606 it was in Spain, and thirteen years later was freed from the Conventuals and received its own general, as well as the right to march in processions under its own cross. The Capuchins, who then had 1,500 monasteries and fifty provinces, followed the Spaniards and Portuguese across the sea, and toiled valiantly for the Church in America, Africa, and Asia beside their great rivals, the Jesuits. In the suppression of the monastic orders in France and Germany at the end of the eighteenth century, the Capuchins suffered severely, and had also to endure much south of the Pyrenees. In the nineteenth century, however, they again prospered, and at its close numbered fifty provinces with 534 monasteries and 294 hospices. The twenty-five Italian provinces are officially suppressed, but retain a limited existence. Of the other twenty-five, Germany contains two, Austria and Hungary seven Switzerland two, Belgium and Holland one each, France five, Great Britain three, Russia and Poland two, and the United States two, that of Detroit with sixty-eight fathers and that of Pittsburg with sixty-five.

Capuchin nuns were founded at Naples in the first half of the sixteenth century, although, strictly speaking, they are a branch of the Clares. They now have a number of houses in France, Italy, Spain, and America, and are subject, when the nunnery contains the full number of thirty-three, to the jurisdiction of the general of the Capuchins, and in other cases to the bishop of the diocese in which they live.

Capuchin scholars have been authors of works of edification, practical exegesis, moral theology, and sermons. Among their most famous preachers have been Ochino, John Forbes, St. Laurence of Brindisi, Jacques Bolduc, Conrad of Salzburg, and Martin of Cochem. Father Joseph, the confidant and adviser of Richelieu, and Father Matthew, the noted temperance lecturer, were Capuchins.

(O. ZÖCKLER†.)

BIBLIOGRAPHY: Sources for the history are: Z. Boverius, *Annales ordinis minorum sive Francisci qui Capucini nuncupantur*, vols. i.–ii., Leyden, 1632–39, vol. iii., by Marcellin de Pisa, 1676; Michael a Tugio, *Bullarium ordinis fratrum minorum Capucinorum*, 7 vols., Rome, 1740–52; *Ordinationes et decisiones capitulorum generalium Capucinorum*, ib. 1851; *Analecta Capucinorum*, an annual, ib. 1884 sqq. Consult further: Heimbucher, *Orden und Kongregationen*, i. 279, 315–328, 359, 361–362; L. Wadding, *Annales Minorum*, 2d ed. by J. M. Fonseca, xvi. 207, 24 vols., Rome, 1731–1860; Helyot, *Ordres monastiques*, vii. 164–180; P. Lechner, *Leben der Heiligen der Kapuziner*, 3 vols., Munich, 1863; A. M. Ilg, *Geist des . Franz von Assisi dargestellt in Lebensbildern aus der Geschichte des Kapuziner-Ordens*, Augsburg, 1876; K. Benrath, *B. Ochino*, passim, Leipsic, 1892; Currier, *Religious Orders*, pp. 244–248.

CAPUTIATI, cā-pū'ti-ā"tî ("hooded," "capuched"; also known as *Paciferi* and *Blancs Chaperons*): A society founded in 1183 at Puy-en-Velay (Le Puy, 68 m. s.w. of Lyons) in the Auvergne by a poor artisan called Durand to oppose the fearful devastations caused by the mercenary and predatory bands of the "Brabançons" or "Cotereaux." Durand claimed that the Madonna had authorized him to do this; the members of the society were to wear a white dress with a capuche and a leaden image of the wonder-working Madonna of Puy. Organized after the manner of an ecclesiastical brotherhood, the Caputiati followed the royal troops and took bloody vengeance on the destroyers of peace. The society did not last long. Later reports, but little reliable, make its members rebels against State and Church, who, as is alleged, were routed about 1186 and condemned to do penance. Even in late times, from too implicit reliance on these reports, the Caputiati have been considered a sect opposed to the Church.

HERMAN HAUPT.

BIBLIOGRAPHY: A. Kluckhohn, *Geschichte des Gottesfriedens*, pp. 126 sqq., Leipsic, 1857; E. Sémichon, *La Paix et la trève de Dieu*, pp. 194, 390, Paris, 1857; L. Huberti, *Studien zur Rechtsgeschichte des Gottes- und Landfriedens*, i. 462 sqq., Ansbach, 1892; Legrand d'Aussy, in *Notices et extraits des manuscrits de la Bibliothèque Nationale*, tom. v., anno vii., pp. 290–293, Paris, 1798–99.

CARACCIOLI, cā-rā'chî-ō"lî, **GALEAZZO** (*Marchese di Vico*): Italian Protestant; b. at Naples 1517; d. at Geneva July 5, 1586. He was the most distinguished of the Italians who sought a refuge at Geneva when the reaction came over Italy; his mother was a sister of Pope Paul IV., he was in the royal service, and his wife was a Caraffa. At Naples he became acquainted with Juan de Valdès and Peter Vermigli, who at that time preached there, and was deeply impressed by these reformatory men. The evangelical ideas which he imbibed at Naples and which caused him many struggles in his family and in society, were deepened by a journey to Germany in 1544. He found it impossible to make open profession at Naples; the efforts to introduce the Inquisition after the Spanish pattern were frustrated by the resistance of the people in 1547 bordering on a revolution; but, nevertheless, the vice-regent urged the suppression of every anti-Roman opinion. Caraccioli decided to forsake fatherland, position, and possessions rather than to continue as a hypocrite. Pretending to go to the imperial court at Augsburg, he left Italy, his wife refusing to follow him. He reached Geneva June 8, 1551, and joined the Italian community which was founded there in 1542. All efforts of his people to bring him back, renewed by Paul IV., after his accession in 1555, were in vain. Toward the end of 1555 he became a citizen of Geneva. He kept up correspondence with his wife and his son and in 1558 met them once more in a little isle of the Adriatic Sea and in the paternal castle at Vico; as they refused to follow him, in spite of his entreaties, he left them forever. The consistories of Geneva and other places declared his marriage dissolved, and in 1560 he married again. K. BENRATH.

BIBLIOGRAPHY: His life was written by N. Balbani, *Historia della Vita di G. Caraccioli*, Geneva, 1587, republished, Florence, 1875.

CARAFFA, cā-rāf'fā, **GIOVANNI PIETRO.** See PAUL IV., Pope.

CARCHEMISH, cār'che-mish (modern Jerabis): A city situated on the right bank of the Euphrates in the upper part of its course. In the cuneiform inscriptions the name denotes either a Hittite state or the capital of that state, which long maintained itself against the Assyrians. Its earlier identification with Circesium, at the confluence of the Chebar with the Euphrates, is obsolete. The earliest mention dates from Ammi-zaduga (about 2200 B.C.), which speaks of the weight (measure) of Carchemish, a mention which agrees with a later Assyrian note of the "Mina of Carchemish," and with the city's location on one of the most important routes of commerce. It appears first in Assyrian annals in the accounts of Tiglath-Pileser I. about 1110 B.C. The Hittite power was at that early date already breaking under the pressure of the northern immigrations then going on, and was completed later by the Aramean migrations. King Sangara paid tribute to Asshurnasirpal (about 880 B.C.), was worsted in a conflict with Shalmaneser II., and was compelled again to pay heavy tribute and to send his daughter to the Assyrian's harem. Its last king, Pisiris, was taken prisoner by Sargon II., 717 B.C., and under Sennacherib the region was made an Assyrian province. Near it was fought the battle between Nebuchadrezzar and Necho which decided the fate of western Asia. (A. JEREMIAS.)

BIBLIOGRAPHY: G. Maspéro, *De Carchemis oppidi situ*, Leipsic, 1872; idem, *Struggle of the Nations*, pp. 144-145, London, 1896; J. Menant, *Kar-Kamis, sa position*, an appendix to the Fr. transl. of A. H. Sayce's *Hittites*, Paris, 1891; W. M. Müller, *Asien und Europa nach altägyptischen Denkmälern*, p. 263, Leipsic, 1893; *DB*, i. 353; *EB*, i. 702-703.

CARDALE, JOHN BATE: Apostle of the Catholic Apostolic Church; b. in London Nov. 2, 1802; d. at Albury (26 m. s.w. of London), Surrey, July 18, 1877. After his schooling at Rugby he was admitted to the bar in 1822, became head of a London firm of solicitors, and retired with a competency in 1834. He had already become interested in the religious movement, originating in Scotland, known as the "Catholic Apostolic Church" (q.v.), whose distinguishing feature is its belief in the revival of the ministries and gifts seen in the apostolic age of the Church, especially of the ministries of apostles and prophets. Mr. Cardale was the first called of the twelve "apostles" of the Church, Henry Drummond (q.v.) being the second. This was in 1832, although it was not until July 14, 1835, when the number was completed, that the twelve were formally set apart to their work as an Apostolic College. Mr. Cardale was the author of a number of anonymous religious publications, the most noteworthy of which was *Reagdins upon the Liturgy*, London, vol. i., 1849-51, vol. ii., 1852-78. G. C. Boase, in the *Dictionary of National Biography*, says of him: "His strength of will, calmness and clearness of judgment, and kindness of heart and manner, added to the prestige of his long rule, made him a tower of strength. He was indefatigable in labour, of which he accomplished a vast amount; besides Latin and Greek, he was a good French and German scholar, and late in life learned Danish." SAMUEL J. ANDREWS.

BIBLIOGRAPHY: *DNB*, ix. 36-38.

CARDINAL. See CURIA, § 1.

CAREY, WILLIAM: Baptist missionary and Orientalist; b. at Paulerspury, Northamptonshire, Eng., Aug. 17, 1761; d. at Serampur, India, June 9, 1834. By baptism a member of the Established Church, he was early in life convinced of the Scriptural authority for the Baptist views, and joined this sect, in which he soon became a preacher. His congregations were very poor, and he supported himself and family by shoemaking. But his thirst for knowledge was strong; and he managed, notwithstanding the pressure of poverty, to acquire Latin, Greek, Hebrew, and a goodly amount of other useful learning, especially in natural history and botany. His attention was turned to the heathen, and he saw plainly his duty to go to them. On Oct. 2, 1792, largely through his exertions, the first Baptist missionary society was founded; and on June 13, 1793, he and his family sailed for India, accompanied by John Thomas, who had formerly lived in Bengal. On reaching Bengal early in 1794, Carey and his companion lost all their property in the Hugli; but, having received the charge of an indigo-factory at Malda, he cut off his pecuniary connection with the missionary society, and began in earnest what, instead of regular missionary labor, was to be the work of his life—the study of and translation both from and into the languages of India. In 1799 the factory was closed; and he went with Thomas to Kidderpur, where he had purchased a small indigo-plantation. Here, joined by Marshman and Ward, he started, under bright hopes, a mission, but soon encountered the opposition of the Indian government, which forbade the mission's enlargement, and compelled its removal, at a great pecuniary loss, to Serampur, a Danish settlement (1800), where it took a fresh lease of life. For some time Carey and Thomas had been diligently at work upon a version of the New Testament in Bengali. In 1801 it was published by the press

Carey instituted. About the same time the Marquis of Wellesley appointed him professor of Oriental languages in the Fort William College, which the marquis had founded at Calcutta for the instruction of the younger members of the British Indian civil service. Carey held this position for thirty years, and taught Bengali, Mahrati, and Sanskrit. He wrote articles upon the natural history and botany of India for the Asiatic Society, to which he was elected, 1805, and thus made practical application of acquisitions of former years; but this was only a part, and by far the less valuable part, of his work That which has given him his undying fame was his translation of the Bible, in whole or in part, either alone or with others, into some twenty-six Indian languages. The Serampur press, under his direction, rendered the Bible accessible to more than three hundred million human beings. Besides, he prepared grammars and dictionaries of several tongues; e.g., *Mahratta Grammar*, 1805; *Sanscrit Grammar*, 1806; *Mahratta Dictionary*, 1810; *Bengalee Dictionary*, 1818; and a dictionary of all Sanskrit-derived languages, which unhappily was destroyed by a fire in the printing establishment in 1812. Later students have discovered errors and omissions in these works; but all honor is due to Carey for "breaking the way," and every inhabitant of India is his debtor.

BIBLIOGRAPHY: John Taylor, *Biographical and Literary Notices of William Carey. Bibliographical Notices of Works* , Northampton, 1886; J. C. Marshman, *Life and Times of Carey, Marshman and Ward*, 2 vols., London, 1859; J. Culross, *William Carey*, New York, 1882; George Smith, *Life of William Carey*, London, 1887; H. O. Dwight, H. A. Tupper, and E. M. Bliss, *Encyclopædia of Missions*, pp. 133–134, New York, 1904; *DNB*, ix. 77.

CARGILL, DONALD (or **DANIEL**): One of the leaders of the Scotch Covenanters; b. in the parish of Rattray, Perthshire, 1619; beheaded at Edinburgh July 27, 1681. He was educated at Aberdeen and St. Andrews; and about 1650 he became pastor of the Barony Church, Glasgow. In 1661, when Episcopacy was established in Scotland, he refused to accept his charge from the archbishop, and was banished (1662) beyond the Tay; but he did not go; instead he became one of the "field preachers," who, deprived of their churches, preached in the open air. In 1679 he joined Cameron, Douglas, Hamilton, and others in the rebellion against prelacy, which arose out of the "Rutherglen Declaration" of May 29 of that year, and with his fellow Covenanters endured the defeat of Bothwell Bridge, June 22. He fled to Holland, but soon returned. The next year he and Cameron, with their adherents, drew up the "Sanquhar Declaration," June 22. The government set a price upon the leaders' heads. They were attacked at Ayrsmoss, July 22, and Cameron was slain; but Cargill succeeded to the leadership, and, as if to testify in the most signal manner his abhorrence of the tyrannical persecutors, he publicly excommunicated the king and several of the nobles at a field-preaching held at Torwood in Stirlingshire in September. When the Duke of York, one of the "excommunicated," came to Scotland, the persecution of the followers of Cargill increased. He himself was hunted from place to place; but on July 11, 1681, he was captured between Clydesdale and Lothian, and taken to Edinburgh for trial. He readily confessed that he had done what the council had called treason. The council were equally divided whether to imprison him for life or to execute him; but the vote of the Duke of Argyle decided in favor of the latter—a vote which cost Argyle, later on, the support of the Covenanters, to say nothing of deep remorse. Accordingly Cargill was put to death. See COVENANTERS.

BIBLIOGRAPHY: *Biographia presbyteriana*, vol. ii., Edinburgh, 1827 (life of Cargill); R. Wodrow, *Hist. of the Sufferings of the Church of Scotland*, 2 vols., ib. 1721–22; T. McCrie, *Sketches of Scottish Church Hist.*, ib. 1875; J. Cunningham, *Church Hist. of Scotland*, 2 vols., ib. 1883; *DNB*, ix. 79–80.

CARLILE, WILSON: Church of England; founder of the Church Army (q.v.); b. at Brixton (a suburb s.w. of London) Jan. 14, 1847 He was educated at Highbury College, London, but did not take a degree. He entered commercial life in 1862, but in 1878 matriculated at the London College of Divinity, and was ordered deacon in 1880 and ordained priest in the following year. He was curate of Kensington from 1880 to 1882, when he founded the Church Army in the Westminster slums, and in 1890 established the Social System of Church Army in Marylebone. He was also rector of Netteswell, Essex, in 1890–91, and since the latter year has been rector of St. Mary-at-Hill, Eastcheap, London. He was appointed a prebendary of St. Paul's Cathedral, London, in 1906, and has written: *The Church and Conversion* (London, 1882); *Spiritual Difficulties* (1885), and *The Continental Outcast* (in collaboration with V W. Carlile; 1906).

CARLSTADT, carl'stat (**KARLSTADT, CAROLSTADT**), **ANDREAS RUDOLF BODENSTEIN VON**: Protestant Reformer; b. at Karlstadt (14 m. n.w. of Würzburg), Bavaria, c. 1480; d. at Basel Dec. 24, 1541. The assumption that he pursued his academical studies at foreign universities rests upon a confusion with his later journey to Rome. In the winter term of 1499–1500 he entered the University of Erfurt, where he remained until 1503, and then removed to Cologne. In 1504 he turned to the newly established University of Wittenberg, in which he acquired considerable fame as a teacher of philosophy. He was a zealous adherent of scholasticism, advocating the unconditional authority of Thomas Aquinas. By 1510 he had obtained all the higher academical degrees. In 1508 he received a canonry at the collegiate church in Wittenberg and in 1510 became archdeacon. As such he had to preach and read mass once a week and to lecture at the university. In 1515 he left Wittenberg, without the permission of the university and the elector, and went to Rome, where he studied law and took a degree, hoping to obtain the first prelacy at Wittenberg, for which legal training was necessary. He did not succeed, however, in obtaining the position after his return. His journey to Rome brought about a rupture with scholasticism. The evidence of the worldliness of the papacy which Carlstadt

Training and Life to 1518.

saw in Rome may have been the chief factor in the change of his religious views. His 151 theses of Sept., 1516, contain the fundamental traits of his later theology. He combats the scholastics and Aristotle (theses xxxvii., cxliii.), and even anticipates Luther, on the basis of Augustine, concerning the inability of the human will to attain unto God and in attributing the act of redemption exclusively to the work of divine grace. Thus no direct dependence of Carlstadt upon Luther can be assumed; each influenced the other after 1516, although a bond of personal friendship never united them.

In the spring of 1518 Carlstadt published a comprehensive collection of theses, on the occasion of Eck's attack upon the ninety-five theses of Luther. Here he affirms for the Bible the most absolute authority as a source of religious knowledge and adheres to its literal interpretation. In June and July a disputation took place between Carlstadt and Eck, and although the former was always equal to the dialectic cleverness of his opponent, he became more and more conscious of the impossibility of reconciling his convictions with the ruling doctrine of the Church.

Deviates from Church Teachings.

He emphasized more and more the efficacy of divine grace alone in the redemption of humanity, and wrote polemical treatises against the church doctrine of justification by works and against indulgences. In 1521 he went to Denmark by invitation of King Christian II. and helped in the establishment of ecclesiastical laws, but after a few weeks in Copenhagen he had to give way before the united resistance of nobility and clergy. In June he was again at Wittenberg, where he expressed his views concerning the Lord's Supper in a treatise *Von den Empfahern Zeichen und Zusag des heiligen Sacraments*. In this treatise he still clings to the corporal presence of Christ in the sacrament, but looks upon it only as a sign of divine promise. In another treatise Carlstadt places beside the literal explanation of Scripture a spiritual interpretation which penetrates its deeper sense and rests upon divine interpretation. Here are to be found certain points of contact between the views of Carlstadt and those of the enthusiasts.

The attitude of Carlstadt in the Wittenberg disturbances and his doings there during Luther's stay at the Wartburg have frequently been represented in an erroneous light. When the Augustinians, in Oct., 1521, refused to hold mass and demanded the administration of the Lord's Supper in both kinds, the university appointed a commission of four theologians, among them Carlstadt, to investigate. Against the more decided attitude of Melanchthon, Carlstadt conceded that the abolition of the mass could only be accomplished with the consent of the magistracy. A letter, expressing the same spirit and signed

The Reformation at Wittenberg, 1521–22.

by seven professors, was sent to the elector. As the excitement did not abate, Carlstadt tried to quiet the more strenuous by emphasizing the Gospel as the proper guide in all actions. Nevertheless, the disturbances continued until on Christmas day he administered the Lord's Supper in both kinds. His action was approved by all Evangelicals. From this moment he was silently acknowledged as the leader of the reformatory movement in Wittenberg. He did not stop with the reformation of the Lord's Supper. At the end of 1521 and at the beginning of 1522 auricular confession, the elevation of the host, and the injunctions concerning fasting were abolished. Jan. 19, 1522, Carlstadt married. On being informed of the events in Wittenberg, the so-called Zwickau prophets arrived (see Anabaptists, II., § 1; Zwickau Prophets), but Carlstadt kept aloof; it was only at the end of 1522 that he began to correspond with Thomas Münzer (q.v.). He proceeded in his reforms in entire conformity with the Council of Wittenberg, in which he saw the supreme authority in the ecclesiastical affairs of the city. He soon opened the battle against pictures in the churches, in which he was assisted by the council. Some small excesses occurred, which, however, were severely condemned by both the council and Carlstadt.

These ecclesiastical changes had aroused the displeasure of Frederick the Wise, who was especially offended by the abolition of the mass. Carlstadt and Melanchthon were called to account. Melanchthon immediately showed himself submissive; Carlstadt also promised in Feb., 1522, to renounce further innovations after he had carried through the reforms which he deemed essential. But Frederick desired an entire rehabilitation of the Old Church usages. The course of events made it impossible for Luther to remain at the Wartburg. He did not agree with Carlstadt's radical measures, believing that forbearance ought to be shown toward the weak. After his arrival at Wittenberg, on Mar. 6, he succeeded in shaking the dominating position of Carlstadt and counteracting his reforms. The Lord's Supper *sub una specie* was restored, also the elevation of the host. Carlstadt remained as professor in the university, but lost all his influence. As he was thus deprived of the possibility of being active in a practical way, he devoted himself to speculative theology. His views were somewhat mystical, but, unlike the true mystics, Carlstadt was not satisfied with the contemplative rapture in the union of the soul with God, and set up ethical standards for the practical realization of his new convictions. In his desire to do away with all intermediary agencies in the religious communication between God and man, he denied the indelible character of orders and did not even acknowledge the ministry as a special profession. He called himself after 1523 *"ein neuer Lai,"* put off his clerical robes, and lived for some time as a peasant in Segrena, near Wittenberg, with relatives of his wife.

In 1524 Carlstadt became preacher in Orlamünde, where he carried on the reform of the church service as he had done two years before in

At Orlamünde, 1524.

Wittenberg. He expounded the book of Acts daily to his congregation, and on Sundays and holidays the Gospel of John. In the course of his development Carlstadt arrived at the conviction that baptism and the Lord's Supper are not sacraments.

At the same time he strongly attacked the mass. Against Luther he wrote *Verstand des Worts Pauli Ich begeret ein Verbannter sein.* Without mentioning Luther's name, he shows the dangerous consequences to which the exaggeration of the principle concerning forbearance for the weak might lead. Apart from his controversial writings, Carlstadt emphasized the necessity of personal devotion and sanctification.

Carlstadt did not derive his political or social principles from his theological views. When Münzer's revolutionary measures in Allstädt became threatening, Carlstadt cautioned him, and he induced the people of Orlamünde to separate themselves formally from those of Allstädt. Nevertheless, the points of difference between Wittenberg and Orlamünde were so considerable that the university took active measures against Carlstadt. Luther met Carlstadt at Jena, in Aug., 1524, and thence proceeded to Orlamünde; he was not successful, however, in settling the difficulties. In September Carlstadt with his family, his adherents Martin Reinhard, preacher in Jena, and Gerhard Westerburg, his brother-in-law, were expelled from the territory of the elector. Carlstadt now encountered a time full of hardships and dangers, but he developed an extraordinary activity as a writer.

Hardships of his Later Life.

The assumption of the corporal presence of Christ in the Lord's Supper is, according to him, in contradiction to the fundamental presuppositions of Christian doctrine. He found adherents to these ideas not only among the people, but many even in the clergy. In Oct., 1524, he sojourned at Strasburg, then lived temporarily in Heidelberg, Zurich, Basel, Schweinfurt, Kitzingen, and Nördlingen. He was active for a considerable time in Rothenburg-on-the-Tauber, where his sermons carried away the great majority of the citizens. It was at this time that the Peasants' War broke out in Rothenburg. Carlstadt was sent as envoy to the peasants, thus making himself unpopular among them. After the defeat of the South German peasants and the capture of Rothenburg by Margrave Casimir, Carlstadt escaped from the town with difficulty. The collapse of his hopes broke down his power of resistance. He wrote humbly to Luther to open the way for his return to Saxony. Luther took pity upon him, and Carlstadt returned to Wittenberg after he had recanted to some degree his doctrine concerning the Lord's Supper; but he had to pledge himself not to teach or preach. He lived at first in Segrena, after 1526 in Bergwitz, where he had to earn his living like a peasant. Before the close of the year he was reduced almost to poverty, and he removed to the little town of Kemberg and kept a small store. He soon retracted his former recantation and was compelled to flee. In Mar., 1529, he was with Melchior Hofmann, the Anabaptist, in Holstein. Being expelled hence also, he wandered with Hofmann to East Friesland, where he remained until the beginning of 1530 and gathered a great number of adherents. Thence he went to Switzerland, where he was kindly received by Zwingli, who secured for him a position as assistant preacher in Zurich. In Sept., 1531, he became preacher in Altstätten in the valley of the Rhine, but the unfortunate battle near Kappel (Oct. 11) compelled him after a few months to return to Zurich, where he lived in close union with the Reformers of that city. The preachers of Zurich took Carlstadt's part when Luther renewed his attacks. In 1534 he was called to Basel as preacher and professor in the university. Here he became involved in disputes with Myconius; the people took Carlstadt's part, but he estranged himself from his friends in Zurich. He fulfilled his last public task in 1536, when the government of Basel sent him with Grynæus to Strasburg to negotiate with the theologians of that city concerning a reconciliation with the Wittenberg theologians on the question of the Lord's Supper. He showed a very conciliatory spirit, which was not approved by the Swiss theologians.

Carlstadt's earliest writings, *De intentionibus* (1507), *Distinctiones sive formalitates Thomistæ* (1508), were of a scholastic nature. His journey to Rome occasioned his treatise *Von päpstlicher Heiligkeit* (1520), in which he criticized the abuses of popery. In *De canonicis scripturis* (1520) he laid down the results of his investigations of the Old and the New Testament writings; he shows himself a free and independent critic, but does not shake the authority of the literal sense.

Writings.

In 1521 appeared *Von den Empfahern Zeichen und Zusag des heiligen Sacraments* and *Von Gelübden Unterrichtung;* in the latter treatise he advocated the abolition of monastic vows, especially the vow of celibacy. In Sept., 1521, appeared *De legis litera sive carne et spiritu;* here Carlstadt propounded for the first time an entirely new principle of interpretation which became of much importance in the further development of his theology—the spiritual interpretation of the words of Scripture. Against pictures in churches he wrote in 1522 *Von Abthuung der Bilder.* In 1524 he published *Priestertum und Opfer Christi.* After his expulsion from Saxony in 1524 appeared the most radical of his writings, *Ob man gemach faren soll,* in which he denies the corporeal presence of Christ in the Lord's Supper, and *Anzeig etlicher Hauptartikel christlicher Lehre,* which contains a comprehensive summary of his views. He combats the central position which the conception of sin had assumed in Luther's theology, as he understood it, and emphasizes the necessity that Christian liberty and justice must produce fruits in good works.

(HERMANN BARGE.)

BIBLIOGRAPHY: The authoritative biography is H. Barge, *Andreas Bodenstein von Karlstadt*, 2 vols., Leipsic, 1905. Among the older literature the following may be consulted: Mayer, *Dissertatio de Karolstadio*, Greifswald, 1703; Füsslin, *Lebensgeschichte des A. B. von Karlstadt*, Frankfort, 1776; J. F. Köhler, *Beiträge zur Ergänzung der deutschen Litteratur*, i. 1-162, ii. 239-269, 2 vols., Leipsic, 1792-94; M. Kirchhofer, *Oswald Myconius*, pp. 153, 316-343, Zurich, 1813. More modern treatment will be found in: A. W. Dieckhoff, *De Carolstadio Lutheranæ doctrinæ contra Eckium defensore*, Göttingen, 1850; idem, *Die evangelische Abendmahlslehre im Reformationszeitalter*, ib. 1854; Jäger, *A. B. von Karlstadt*, Stuttgart, 1856; G. P. Fisher, *The Reformation*, pp. 93, 113, New York, 1873; W. Walker, *The Reformation*, passim, ib. 1900; J. Köstlin, *Martin Luther*, passim, 2 vols., Berlin, 1903 (important); *Cambridge Modern History*, vol. ii., *The Reformation*, passim, ib. 1904; Moeller, *Christian Church*, vol. iii. passim, especially pp. 27-35; Schaff, *Christian Church*, vol. vi. passim. Consult also: G. Bauch, in *ZKG*, xi. (1890) 448 sqq. (on Carlstadt's scholasticism); D. Schäfer, ib. xiii. (1892) 311 (on the *De legis litera*).

CARLSTADT, JOHANN. See DRACONITES.

CARLYLE, THOMAS: Historian, biographer, and essayist; b. at Ecclefechan (60 m. s. of Edinburgh), Dumfriesshire, Scotland, Dec. 4, 1795; d. in London Feb. 5, 1881.

Life and Writings.

He was early noted for his extraordinary memory, and for his love of reading. He entered the University of Edinburgh in 1810, and distinguished himself as a mathematician, but declared that he owed nothing to the university but the miscellaneous reading afforded by its library. Having abandoned the study of theology, he taught mathematics in the high school at Annan for two years. In 1816 he was appointed rector of the Burgh School at Kirkcaldy. Here he devoted himself to the study of German, and translated Legendre's *Geometry*, adding an introductory essay on proportion.

Carlyle removed to Edinburgh in 1818, where he supported himself by literary work, pursued a large and varied course of reading, and devoted much time to the study of German. From 1820 to 1823 he contributed a number of articles to the *Edinburgh Encyclopædia* and the *Edinburgh Review*. In 1824 he introduced Goethe to English readers by the translation of *Wilhelm Meister's Lehrjahre*, and in 1825 published the *Life of Schiller*. He married Jane Welsh in 1826, and removed in 1828 to Craigenputtoch, where he wrote his *Critical and Miscellaneous Essays*, and *Sartor Resartus*, a philosophic romance in the form of a treatise on dress, containing his views on the problems of religion and life; it was published during 1833–34, in *Fraser's Magazine*.

In 1834 he removed to London, to the house in Cheyne Row, Chelsea, where he resided until his death. In 1837 appeared *The French Revolution*, the first of his works to which his name was formally attached. In the same year he began lecturing, and, during 1837–43, delivered courses on *German Literature*, *The Periods of European Culture*, *the Revolutions of Modern Europe*, and *Heroes and Hero-Worship*, besides publishing *Chartism*, a political treatise, and *Past and Present*.

One of his most important works, *Oliver Cromwell's Letters and Speeches*, was issued in 1845, and produced a great revolution of sentiment in favor of Cromwell. In 1840 Carlyle inaugurated the movement which resulted in the London Library, of which he was afterward elected president. During 1848–50 he wrote a number of political and social treatises, notably *The Latter Day Pamphlets*, the ultimate and most violent expression of his political creed.

The *Life of John Sterling*, especially valuable as a partial expression of his own religious views, appeared in 1851. His *magnum opus*, *The History of Frederick the Great*, was begun in 1858, and finished in 1865. It is a monument of patient industry and minute research, and contains a complete political history of the eighteenth century. In 1866 Carlyle was chosen rector of the University of Edinburgh, and delivered an inaugural on *The Choice of Books*. Mrs. Carlyle died during his absence on this occasion (Apr. 21). A few newspaper articles, with *Historical Sketches of the Early Kings of Norway*, and *The Portraits of John Knox*, marked the next five years, and completed his literary labors.

Carlyle's life is marked by great unity of purpose and concentration of energy. He lived for literature. With his imaginative genius, his poetic insight, and his opulent diction, he was a poet by constitution; but his lack of the sense of form and proportion, and his impatience of measured expression, made him despise poetry. He is a preacher and a prophet rather than an artist. His keen sense of the grotesque, with the real depth of his nature, made him a humorist at once racy, subtle, and satirical; but this element developed itself disproportionately, and ran into cynicism as he grew older.

Ethics and Philosophy.

Notwithstanding the large admixture of ethics and philosophy in his writings, it is well-nigh impossible to define accurately his position as a philosopher, moralist, or religionist. Veracity is the basis of his ethical conceptions, by which he means the disposition to go behind appearances to facts, and the assertion of reality as against mere symbols and conventionalities. His hatred of shams is intense, and often leads him into needless roughness of speech. His ethical ideal is defective from its identification of physical and moral order, of might and right. It is too subjective, lodging the test of right in each man's moral consciousness. Hence his fundamental fallacy, expounded in *Hero-Worship*, and applied in *Frederick*—the reverence for strength, regardless of moral quality. He is a dangerous guide, therefore, as a historian and political philosopher. His conception of history as only the record of the world's great men is radically false. He has no sense of the popular power in the solution of political problems. The moral teaching of his histories is unsound in blinding the reader to vice through the admiration of greatness. The logical outcome of his political philosophy is slavery and despotism. As a historian he is distinguished by exact and laborious attention to detail. He studies folios and pasquinades alike; and no detail of topography, feature, or costume escapes him. His histories are a series of striking portraits or pictures. He stands committed to no philosophical system. With much talk about the real and practical, his philosophy is intuitional and sentimental, emphasizing feeling above reason.

Religious Views.

Theologically he can not be accurately placed. The *Life of Sterling* throws most light upon his religious views. He may fairly be regarded as a theist. He is mainly silent on the truth of creeds, always reverential toward Christ, and, while agreeing that Christianity is the supreme religion, denies that it embraces all truth. He seems to hold that responsibility to God is the essential truth foreshadowed in all religions, and that the essence of all religion is to keep conscience alive and shining. He believes in retribution as the natural outcome of wrong. He revered genuine piety, and his own moral life was singularly pure. As a critic he has great knowledge and keen discernment, but is too liable to be swayed by his personal prejudices.

His earlier style, as in the essays on Burns and Scott, was natural, simple, dignified, and vigorous. His later style is figurative, abrupt, enigmatical, sometimes turgid and involved, inverted, declamatory, and at times coarse, yet withal often beautiful, rich, and powerful, and always picturesque.

M. R. VINCENT.

BIBLIOGRAPHY: *DNB*, ix. 127 appends to account of Carlyle's life a list of the uncollected writings as well as of his books. R. H. Shepherd has published a *Bibliography of Thomas Carlyle*, London, 1881, and in *Notes and Queries*, 6th series, iv. 145, 201, 226 are lists of articles referring to Carlyle. The authorities for Carlyle's life are his *Reminiscences*, ed. J. A. Froude, London, 1881; J. A. Froude, *Thomas Carlyle, a History of the First Forty Years of his Life*, 2 vols., 1882, and *History of his Life in London*, 2 vols., 1884; *Correspondence of Thomas Carlyle and Ralph Waldo Emerson*, ed. C. E. Norton, Boston, 1883; *Letters and Memorials of Jane Welsh Carlyle, prepared . by Thomas Carlyle and edited by J. A. Froude*, 3 vols., London, 1883.

For accounts of his life and estimates of his writings and activities consult: G. MacCrie, *The Religion of our Literature, Essays upon Thomas Carlyle*, London, 1875; M. D. Conway, *Thomas Carlyle*, ib 1881; E. D. Mead, *The Philosophy of Carlyle*, Boston, 1881; R. H. Shepherd, *Memoirs of the Life and Writings of Thomas Carlyle*, London, 1881; H. James, *Literary Remains, Some Personal Recollections of Carlyle*, Boston, 1884; D. Masson, *Carlyle personally and in his Writings*, London, 1885; A. S. Arnold, *The Story of Thomas Carlyle*, ib. 1888; E. Flügel, *T. Carlyles religiöse und sittliche Entwicklung und Weltanschauung*, Leipsic, 1887, Eng. transl., London, 1891; J. M. Robertson, *Modern Humanists, Sociological Studies of Carlyle*, ib. 1891; David Wilson, *Mr. Froude and Carlyle*, New York, 1898; May Alden Ward, *Prophets of the Nineteenth Century*, Boston, 1900; J. M. Sloan, *The Carlyle Country*, Philadelphia, 1903; H. Paul, *Life of Froude*, London, 1905; *Illustrated Memorial Volume of the Carlyle's House Purchase Fund Committee, with Catalogue of Carlyle's Books, MSS., Pictures, and Furniture*, London, 1897.

CARLYLE, THOMAS: Apostle of the Catholic Apostolic Church (q.v.); b. at King's Grange (90 m. s.w. of Edinburgh), Kirkcudbrightshire, Scotland, July 17, 1803; d. at Albury (26 m. s.w. of London) Jan. 28, 1855. After studying at Edinburgh University he was called to the Scottish bar in 1824. The same year by the death of a relative the dormant title of Baron Carlyle passed over to him. In 1831 he figured as legal counsel of the Rev. John McLeod Campbell (q.v.) in the famous Row heresy case. He believed that the revival in Scotland of the speaking in prophecy and tongues was a true work of the Spirit, and in Apr., 1835, was himself called to the apostolate. Thereupon he gave up his practise at the bar and settled with his wife at Albury, where was the seat of the Apostolic College, and the center of its work. He was much in Germany, and made the acquaintance of many theologians, among them H. W. J. Thiersch (q.v.) and C. J. T. Boehm. In 1845 he published at London *The Moral Phenomena of Germany*, which introduced him to King Frederick William IV. of Prussia. He wrote many pamphlets, among which may be mentioned *Pleadings with my Mother, the Church of Scotland* (1854). A volume of his collected writings was published in 1878.

SAMUEL J. ANDREWS.

CARMEL: The mountain in the west of Palestine which separates the Plain of Acre from the Plain of Sharon. I Kings xviii. 40–46 locates it near the Kishon and between the Mediterranean and Jezreel (q.v.); Joshua xix. 26 and Jer. xlvi. 18 locate it as the southern boundary of Asher and as abutting on the sea. Jabal Karmal is the name it still bears, and it is also called "Mount of the Holy Elijah." In the Hebrew the name has the article, and means "wooded garden," setting forth the contrast between the greenness of Carmel and the bareness of the hills of central Palestine. This fact is often referred to in Scripture, the wooded Bashan, Lebanon, and Carmel being named together, though the bushy rather than forest growth of the last is sometimes noted.

The mountain is wedge-shaped, with the edge toward the sea; the western extension turning toward the south runs approximately parallel to the coast, while the northern cliffs curve gently along the plain of the Kishon. Its stone is a gray limestone, and caves are numerous. It is about thirteen miles in length and eight and a half broad at its eastern end. It is marked off by the Wadi-al-Milh, emptying into the Kishon, and the Wadi-al-Matabin, which flows to the coast plain.

The northern point is occupied by the convent of the Carmelites and a shelter provided for pilgrims. The situation affords an unobstructed view both of the coast to the south and of that to the north as far as Acre. There are at present only two villages on the mountain, both in the southern part and inhabited by Druses. In earlier times the mountain was more densely populated, as is shown by the remains of cisterns and oil- and wine-presses. In 1820 the Druses made seventeen settlements there, but in the Turco-Egyptian war all were destroyed but two.

From its striking characteristics of position, form, and abundance of tree-growth, it is hardly to be wondered at that Carmel was a sacred place. I Kings xviii. connects this fact with the memory of Elijah. The site of the episode related there is given by tradition as El-Mahraka, "the Place of Burning," a terrace, 1,600 feet above the sea, where are a [Druse] chapel and some ruins. Beneath this on the bank of the Kishon is a little mound to which the name "Hill of the Priests" is given, pointed out as the place where the priests of Baal were slain. Tradition locates also the place where Elijah dwelt, in a valley, in which there is a spring known as Ain-al-Sih, about two miles south of the convent. The Mohammedans regard the place as sacred, and point out the site of Elijah's garden, where appear numbers of "Elijah's melons," geodes which characterize the Carmel formation. Near it the first monastery was built about 1200, replaced by a new one somewhat later, which was destroyed by Abdallah Pasha in 1821 that it might not be used as a fort by his enemies. It was reconstructed about 1828, and the church is built over an "Elijah-grotto"; that is, a cave in which Elijah is said to have lived.

The Old Testament does not determine to which of the tribes Carmel belonged, whether to Asher, Zebulun, or Manasseh. At various times it was counted to Galilee and to Phenicia. Tacitus, asserts that "Carmel" was the name of a mountain and a deity, and Vespasian had the oracle there consulted.

The coast at the foot of the mountain is about 100 yards wide, broadening north and south. At the foot of the bay of Akko there was an old city called Sycaminum by Greeks and Romans and Haifa in the Talmud, coins of which are known. The place was destroyed and the material used to build the present Haifa at the mouth of the Kishon, 1760, the growth of which in recent years has been quite rapid. (H. GUTHE.)

BIBLIOGRAPHY: C. R. Conder and H. H. Kitchener, *Survey of Western Palestine, Memoirs*, i. 264 sqq., London, 1881; G. A. Smith, *Historical Geography of the Holy Land*, 337-340, 7th ed., London, 1897; E. Robinson, *Biblical Researches in Palestine*, iii. 189, Boston, 1841; A. Reland, *Palæstina*, 2 vols., Utrecht, 1714; J. de S. Thérèse, *Le Sanctuaire du Mont Carmel depuis son origine jusqu'à nos jours*, Marseilles, 1876; T. Saunders, *Introduction to the Survey of Western Palestine*, London, 1881; *PEF, Quarterly Statements*, particularly for the years 1882-86; G. Ebers and H. Guthe, *Palästina in Bild und Wort*, ii. 106 sqq., 1884; C. R. Conder, *Tent-work in Palestine*, new ed., London, 1889.

CARMELITES.

Carmelites (*Ordo fratrum Beatæ Virginis Mariæ de monte Carmelo*) is the name of a Roman Catholic order founded in the twelfth century by a certain Berthold (d. after 1185) on Mount Carmel, whence the order receives its name. Carmelite tradition traces the origin of the order to a community of hermits on Mount Carmel that succeeded the schools of the prophets in ancient Israel, although there are no certain records of monks on this mountain before the ninth decade of the twelfth century. Berthold, who had gone to Palestine from Calabria either as a pilgrim or as a crusader, chose Mount Carmel as the seat of his community because it was the traditional home of Elijah. It was but natural that this community of Eastern hermits in the Holy Land should gain constant accessions from pilgrims, and in 1209 they received a rule from the patriarch Albert of Jerusalem. This

1. Origin and Early History.

consisted of sixteen articles, which enjoined strict obedience to their prior, residence in individual cells, constancy in prayer, the hearing of mass every morning in the oratory of the community, poverty and toil, daily silence from vespers until terce the next morning, abstinence from all forms of meat except in cases of severe illness, and fasting from Holy Cross Day (Sept. 14) to Easter of the following year. This rule received the approval of Honorius III. in 1226. With the increasing cleavage between the West and the East, however, the Carmelites found it advisable to leave their original home, and in 1238 they settled in Cyprus and Sicily. In 1240 they were in England, and four years later in southern France, while by 1245 they were so numerous that they were able to hold their first general chapter at Aylesford, England, where Simon Stock, then eighty years of age, was chosen general. During his rule of twenty years the order prospered, especially by the establishment of a monastery at Paris by St. Louis in 1259.

The original rule of the order was now changed to conform to that of the mendicant orders on the initiative of Simon Stock and at the command of Innocent IV. Their former habit of a mantle with black and white or brown and white stripes was discarded, and they wore the same habit as the Dominicans, except that the cloak was white. They also borrowed much from the Dominican and Franciscan rules. Their distinctive garment

2. Habit and Scapular.

was a scapular of two strips of gray cloth, worn on the breast and back, and fastened at the shoulders. This, according to the traditions of the order, was given to Simon Stock by the Virgin herself, who descended from heaven and promised that all who wear it in this world, or at least in the hour of death, should be saved, she herself going each Saturday to purgatory to rescue those to whom this might apply. Thus arose a sodality of the scapular, which affiliated a large number of laymen with the Carmelites. The order speedily became infected with arrogance, however, contesting the invention of the rosary with the Dominicans, terming themselves the brothers of the Virgin, and asserting, on the basis of their traditional association with Elijah, that all the prophets of the Old Testament, as well as the Virgin and the Apostles, had been Carmelites. Their second general, Nicholas of Narbonne (1265-70), protested in vain, only to be deposed from his office.

In the fourteenth and fifteenth centuries the Carmelites, like other monastic orders, declined, and reform became imperative. Shortly before 1433 three monasteries in Valais, Tuscany, and Mantua were reformed by the preaching of Thomas Conecte of Rennes and formed the congregation of Mantua, which was declared independent of the order by Eugenius IV. In 1431 or 1432 the same pope sanctioned certain modifications of the Carmelite rule, and in 1459 Pius II. left the regulation of fasts to the discretion of the general. Soreth, who was then general, and had already established the order of Carmelite nuns in 1452,

3. Reforms Within the Order.

accordingly sought to restore the primitive asceticism, but died of poison at Nantes in 1471. In 1476 a bull of Sixtus IV. founded the Carmelites of the Third Order, who received a special rule in 1635, which was amended in 1678. The sixteenth century saw a number of short-lived reforms, but it was not until the second half of the same century that a thorough reformation of the Carmelites was carried out by St. Theresa, who, together with St. John of the Cross, established the Discalced Carmelites. In conscious opposition to Protestantism the order was now inspired with an asceticism and a devotion hitherto unknown to it. In 1593 the Discalced Carmelites had their own general, and by 1600 they were so numerous that it became necessary to divide them into the two congregations of Spain and of Italy, or St. Elias, the latter including all provinces except Spain. Henceforth there were four Carmelite generals: the general of the Observantines, of the independent congregation of Mantua, and of the two congregations of the Discalced Carmelites.

By the middle of the seventeenth century the Carmelites had reached their zenith. At this period, however, they became involved in controversies with other orders, particularly with the Jesuits. The special objects of attack were the traditional origin of the Carmelites and the source of their scapular. The Sorbonne, represented by Jean Launoy, joined the Jesuits in their polemics against the Carmelites. Papebroch, the Bollandist editor of the *Acta Sanctorum*, was answered by the Carmelite Sebastian of St. Paul, who made such serious charges against the orthodoxy of his opponent's writings that the very existence of the Bollandists was threatened. The peril was averted, however, and in 1696 a decree of Rocaberti, archbishop of Valencia and inquisitor-general of the holy office, forbade all further controversies between the Carmelites and Jesuits. Two years later, on Nov. 20, 1698, Innocent XII. issued a brief which definitely ended the controversy on pain of excommunication, and placed all writings in violation of the brief upon the Index.

4. Controversies with Other Orders.

The French Revolution and the sequestration of monasteries in southern Europe were heavy blows to the Carmelites. At the present time there are five provinces of Calced Carmelites (Rome, Malta, Iceland, England, and Galicia) and eight of Discalced (Rome, Genoa, Lombardy, Venice, Tuscany, Piedmont, Aquitaine, and Avignon), in addition to a number of isolated cloisters and priories of both Calced and Discalced Carmelites in various countries. (O. ZÖCKLER†.)

5. Present Status.

BIBLIOGRAPHY: For sources consult: *ASB* for Mar. 6 and 29, and Apr. 8; D. Papebroch, *Responsio ad expositionem errorum per Sebastianum a S. Paulo evulgatum*, 3 vols., Antwerp, 1696–99; *Chroniques de l'ordre des Carmélites de la Réforme de Ste. Thérèse . en France*, 5 vols., Troyes, 1846–65, second series, 4 vols., Poitiers, 1888–89. Consult further: Heimbucher, *Orden und Kongregationen*, ii. 1–32; Helyot, *Ordres monastiques*, i. 282–399; H. E. Manning, *Life of St. Teresa*, London, 1865; H. J. Coleridge, *Life and Letters of St. Teresa*, 3 vols., ib. 1881–88; F. H. Reusch, *Index der verbotenen Bücher*, ii. 267-276, 520–521, 691, Bonn, 1885; H. H. Koch, *Die Karmelitenklöster der niederdeutschen Provinz*, Freiburg, 1889; C. W. Currier, *Carmel in America*, Baltimore, 1890; idem, *Religious Orders*, pp. 284–304; L. A. le Moyne de la Borderie, *Histoire des Carmes en Bretagne*, Rennes, 1896; J. P. Rushe, *Carmel in Ireland: Narrative of the Irish Province of Carmelites*, London. 1897; B. Zimmermann, *Carmel in England. Hist. of the Eng. Mission of the Carmelites, 1615–1849*, London, 1899; *Life of St. John of the Cross*, transl. and ed. by David Lewis, London, 1897.

CARNESECCHI, cär'nê-sêc''chi, **PIETRO**. See ITALY, THE REFORMATION IN.

CAROLINE BOOKS.

"Caroline Books" is the name given to a criticism of the proceedings of the Second Council of Nicæa (787), which appeared under the name of Charlemagne toward the end of the eighth century. The acts of the council had been sent to Charlemagne in a very imperfect Latin version. Already displeased with the attitude of the Byzantine court and the equivocal policy of Pope Adrian I., he took occasion to have the whole question of the iconoclastic controversy and of the validity of the council's action discussed by his theologians, and sent on the report of its proceedings to King Offa in England, with a request for the opinion of his bishops. Alcuin, then in England, drew up their reply, and brought it to Charlemagne. It has been lost, and thus it is not now known in what relation it stands to the work which the emperor caused to be written about the same time (790 or soon after), and promulgated as having the assent of the bishops of his realm, under the title *Opus inlustrissimi et excellentissimi seu spectabilis viri Caroli, nutu Dei regis Francorum contra Synodum, quæ in partibus Græciæ pro adorandis imaginibus stolide et arroganter gesta est*. The work, whose contents and spirit are sufficiently indicated by this title, consists of four books containing 120 chapters. It is preserved in two manuscripts, the *Codex Parisinus* and the *Codex Vaticanus*, the latter somewhat defective and apparently dating from the beginning of the tenth century. Two more were known in the sixteenth century, but have since been lost. One was said then to be extant in Rome, and a chapter from it was quoted by Steuchi, the papal librarian, in a polemical work against Laurentius Valla. The other, then extant in France, was the basis of the *editio princeps* of 1549, printed probably in Paris and edited by Jean du Tillet, later bishop of St. Brieux and of Meaux. This edition, which the subsequent ones followed, was used by the Protestants (Flacius, Calvin, Chemnitz, and others) in their attacks on the Roman Catholic Church, and, therefore, put on the Index by the popes from 1564, which accounts for its rarity. Of the subsequent editions the best is that published by Heumann in 1731, which makes use of all the materials at his command and gives the introductions and notes of previous editors. The less perfect edition of Goldast (1608) is followed in *MPL*, xcviii.

1. Origin of the Caroline Books.

2. Manuscripts and Editions.

The authenticity of the work was denied by many of the older Roman Catholic theologians, such as Surius (who thought it a sixteenth-century forgery), Bellarmine, Suarez, Baronius, and as recently as 1860 by Floss of Bonn, who succeeded in convincing Baur that it was at least doubtful. But these doubts have long since been abandoned by Catholic theologians (the Jesuit Sirmond, Natalis Alexander, Du Pin, Hefele). The oldest external evidence in its favor is the letter of Adrian himself (printed by Mansi, Migne, and Jaffé); the next is that of Hincmar of Reims, who says he has seen the book in the imperial palace, and quotes a chapter (iv. 26) from it. If, however, the origin of the work from Charlemagne's immediate entourage and by his authority is indubitable, the question as to the actual author is still unsolved. This can not, of course, have been Charlemagne himself, though his name is used, but must have been one (if not more than one) of the most prominent theologians of his court. The majority of scholars are inclined to favor Alcuin; but there is some reason to think that it may have been Abbot Angilbert of St. Riquier, who stood in close relations to Charlemagne and was entrusted by him with negotiations at Rome regarding this controversy.

3. Problem of Authorship.

The composition of the work was begun, as appears from the preface to the first book, not earlier than the winter of 789-790 and not later than the summer of 791. When it was completed is not now known, but Charlemagne was not likely to have granted his theologians more time than was necessary, so that it may have been finished in 790 or 791. It was intended to affect public opinion in favor of Charlemagne's rejection of the Nicene decrees. He endeavored to obtain like action from Pope Adrian, and sent Angilbert to Rome for this purpose. Adrian's answer referred to above discusses and controverts eighty-five chapters somewhat fully. The question arises whether Angilbert laid before him the whole work or only these chapters, and whether these eighty-five were the basis for a revised and enlarged edition, or a condensation of the larger work. A supplementary question also arises as to the date of Angilbert's mission, whether it was before or after the Synod of Frankfort in 794. The answer to the first question is determined by Adrian's assertion that he has answered each chapter *seriatim*, and by a similar assertion of the Council of Paris (825). Hincmar was probably in error when he said that the "not small volume" which he saw had been sent to Rome. The second question involves more difficulty. The theory, recently supported by Hampe, that Adrian's answer led to the expansion of the original document into the present Caroline Books is invalidated by the fact that in their present shape they contain no reference to Adrian's answer, and make no attempt to rebut it. It is more likely that the eighty-five chapters consisted of extracts from the larger work. Adrian was asked to condemn certain propositions, not to confirm Charlemagne's official pronouncement. As to the date of this proceeding, it must have been before the Synod of Frankfort, whose decision was taken in the presence of papal legates and its validity never questioned, while the rejection of the eighty-five chapters would have been tantamount to a condemnation of it. Angilbert was in Rome in 792, and the occurrence probably took place then—possibly not till the next year. In consequence Charlemagne laid the matter before the synod.

4. The Work Sent to Pope Adrian.

5. Relation of Original Work to Larger Recension.

We come now to the contents and character of the *Libri Carolini*. Each book has its own preface. That of Book I. begins with a rhetorical eulogy of the Church as the ark of safety, Charlemagne's duty to which leads him to take up this question. Pride and ambition have led the Eastern princes and bishops to introduce innovations into the true doctrine "by notorious and senseless synods." The Council of Constantinople (754) erred in one direction, by abolishing the pictures which had from of old served to adorn the churches and commemorate past events, referring what God had spoken of idols to images. The Nicene Council, on the other hand, three years before the date of writing, had erred not less, by exhorting the people to worship such images. Both perverted the teaching of the fathers, who allowed the possession of images, but forbade the worship of them. We, however, resting on the foundation of the Scriptures, the orthodox fathers, and the six ecumenical councils, reject all innovations, especially those of the Nicene Council, whose acts have reached us. We have undertaken to combat these errors with the assistance of the clergy of our kingdom. Neither of these councils deserves the name of ecumenical; and in contrast with both, the *via media* must be followed, which consists in neither breaking down the images nor worshiping them, but retaining them as ornaments and memorials, adoring God alone and rendering due veneration to the saints. The standpoint being thus set forth in the preface, the polemic of Book I. is directed first against the imperial summons to the Nicene Council, whose phraseology is condemned in four several points. The council itself is accused of erroneous exposition of the Scriptures and erroneous employment of patristic citations. The author thinks it necessary (i. 6) to express his acknowledgment of the authority of the Roman Church, both in faith and in worship, founded not on human ordinances but on divine prescription. The section i. 7 ii. 12 examines the passages of Scripture alleged by the council, and ii. 15–20 the patristic passages, some of which are not authentic and others inconclusive. In ii. 26 the conclusion is drawn that, as the whole of Scripture proclaims in thunder-tones, "God alone is to be worshiped and adored," the "cultus of images" is altogether to be reprobated, as contrary to the Christian religion; whether or not pictures are retained in the churches is a matter of indifference, though, indeed, visible memorials of Christ and the saints are unnecessary.

6. Book I.

7. Book II.

The friends of images (obviously including the pope) are warned not to disturb the peace of the Church and the prosperity of Charles's kingdom by their councils. The apostles never taught the veneration of images by word or example; it is an error to compare them with the ark of the covenant, and an absurdity to place them in the same category with the eucharistic host; nor must they be likened to the cross of Christ, the sacred vessels, or the Scriptures, all of which are venerated in their own way and measure for different reasons.

Book III. begins with a confession of faith, for the purpose of evincing the orthodoxy of the Frankish Church. This is supposed to be taken from Jerome, but is really almost verbally the profession of Pelagius (the *Libellus fidei ad Innocentium* of 417), which throughout the Middle Ages was received as orthodox, under the name of *Symbolum Hieronymi* or *Sermo Augustini*. The author then attacks the patriarch Tarasius on the ground of the irregularity of his consecration and the error of his teaching on the procession of the Holy Ghost. The latter reproach and that of further doctrinal aberrations are brought against the other members of the council, and one chapter attacks the impropriety of the empress Irene's assumption of the teaching office.

8. Book III.

A special onslaught is made on a proposition assumed to have been uttered by one of the bishops which clearly rests upon a gross mistranslation. A distinction is drawn between images and relics; and even if it is true that some of the former have worked miracles, no adoration is therefor due them. Still less can dreams and visions, or absurd apocryphal inventions, be adduced in favor of the "adoration of images." Not this, but the keeping of the divine precepts, is the beginning of the fear of the Lord.

Book IV. continues the attack upon expressions of individual members of the council, and upon its authority as a whole. It can in no wise be compared with the First Nicene Council; that asserted the equality of the Son with the Father, while this places pictures on a level with the Trinity.

9. Book IV.

Apart from all the unseemly, obscure, perverted, absurd, illogical, and untheological expressions to be found in the acts of the latter, it does not deserve the name of ecumenical given to it by the Greeks, because it neither utters the pure Catholic faith nor is recognized by all the churches.

The Caroline Books, then, in their fundamental conceptions, attempt to preserve the golden mean indicated by Gregory the Great in his letter to Serenus of Massilia: "We approve unreservedly because you have forbidden to worship them [images]; but we do not approve of their being broken; if any one wants to make images, at least forbid him; but shun in every way the worshiping of them." But their polemic (apart from its vehement, almost passionate tone)

10. Characterization of the Caroline Books.

does material injustice to the Nicene Fathers by ignoring their distinction between *latreia* [worship] which is due to God alone, and *proskunesis timētikē* [honoring obeisance] which may be given to creatures, and in ascribing to them the blasphemous proposition that the same "servitude of adoration" is due to the images as to the Holy Trinity. This is explained by the imperfection of the version of the acts sent to Charles, which always renders the Greek *proskunēsis* by *adoratio*, and by a particular misunderstanding or wrong reading already referred to.

The work as a whole, however, may be taken as giving a good general view of Frankish and Anglo-Saxon theology in its day, of considerable importance for the dogmatic, exegetical, dialectic, and critical attainments of the age. Of special interest is the attitude assumed toward the great fundamental questions of medieval theology—the relations of Scripture and tradition, authority and reason, the Roman and the universal Church.

11. Importance of the Work.

In spite of all its recognition of the teaching authority of the Church, and particularly of the Roman Church, the work postulates the right of critical examination in a way seldom found in the Middle Ages—though it will not do to interpret this tendency in terms of modern views. The theological standpoint of the book as a whole is that of Gregory the Great, a somewhat weakened Augustinianism which allows the author to accept the profession of Pelagius as "the Confession of the Catholic Faith." He follows Gregory, as in the question of images, so also in the doctrines of original sin, of the replacing of the fallen angels by an equal number of redeemed men, of purgatory and prayers for the dead.

12. Theological Standpoint.

Other patristic authorities cited are especially Augustine and Jerome, and sometimes Ambrose and Sedulius. The author attempts to show his universal culture by all sorts of grammatical, rhetorical, philosophical, historical, and literary remarks; by quotations from Plato and Aristotle, Vergil and Cicero, Macrobius and Apuleius, Cato and Josephus; and by the use of scientific terminology and logical formulas. The work, however, has not the character of a theological treatise written by a private person; it is a state document, an official protest on the part of the Frankish Church against Byzantine and Roman superstition and against the unjustified anathemas pronounced by both the Greek and the Roman Church on all who differed from them as well as on their own purer past.

The effect of this protest can not here be followed out in detail. Adrian was clearly much disturbed by it, and sent his defense to Charlemagne with many conciliatory expressions, declaring that he had not as yet given an answer to the Byzantine emperor, because the latter still persisted in his usurpation of what belonged to the Roman See, but that he must, following the ancient tradition of his predecessors, condemn those who refused to venerate the sacred images. Charles's answer was the Synod of Frankfort, the presence at which of the papal legates betokened Adrian's submission.

13. Later Influence of the Caroline Books.

The pope died on Christmas day, 795, and the question slumbered until it came up once more, under Louis the Pious and Eugenius II., at the Synod of Paris in 825. This synod adhered to the position of the *Libri Carolini* and the Synod of Frankfort, venturing openly to condemn Adrian for encouraging superstition, though unconsciously, in the cultus of images. It was mainly through the influence of the Caroline Books that the Frankish Church excluded this cultus all through the ninth century. Even in the tenth we find the Nicene Council spoken of as "The pseudo-synod falsely called the Seventh," and the principle adopted that pictures are tolerated in the churches "only for the instruction of the ignorant," without any attempt on the part of Rome to enforce its anathema.

Charles and his theologians must thus have the credit of holding back for a time the influx of superstition into the West, while at the same time they asserted the rights of Christian art and its value for ecclesiastical decoration. When in the sixteenth century Tridentine Catholicism reaffirmed the proposition assailed in the Caroline Books, that veneration was paid not to the pictures but to their subjects ("honos refertur ad prototypa"), and on the other hand Swiss Protestantism, in its abhorrence of idolatry, renewed the tumults of iconoclasm, the Lutheran controversialists, especially Flacius and Chemnitz, with cheerful confidence "went back to the moderation of Charlemagne." (A. HAUCK.)

BIBLIOGRAPHY: A luminous discussion is found in Hefele, *Conciliengeschichte*, iii. 695–717. Consult: H. J. Floss, *Commentatio de suspecta librorum Carolinorum fide*, Bonn, 1860; R. Baxmann, *Die Politik der Päpste*, i. 29 sqq., 297–299, Elberfeld, 1868; H. Reuter, *Geschichte der Aufklarung*, i. 11 sqq., Berlin, 1877; F. H. Reusch, *Index der verbotenen Bücher*, i. 255, Bonn, 1883; O. Leist, *Die litterarische Bewegung des Bilderstreits*, vol. i., Magdeburg, 1871; Neander, *Christian Church*, iii. 235–243 (still of great value, though supplementary reading is necessary); Schaff, *Christian Church*, iv. 467–468; Hauck, *KD*, ii. 105, 110, 316 sqq.; *DCB*, i. 405–406; *KL*, vii. 190–196; and the literature on Charlemagne.

CARPENTER, J(OSEPH) ESTLIN: English Unitarian; b. at Ripley (22 m. s.w. of London), Surrey, Oct. 5, 1844. He was educated at University College, London (1860–63), and Manchester New College (1860–66; B.A., University of London, 1863), and was successively minister of Oakfield Road Church, Clifton, Gloucestershire (1866–69), and Mill Hill Chapel, Leeds (1869–75). From 1875 to 1906, he was a lecturer on Hebrew, Old Testament literature, and comparative religion in Manchester New College, first in London, then at Oxford, where he was appointed principal in 1906. He has edited the third, fourth, and fifth volumes of Ewald's *History of Israel* (London, 1871–74), a portion of the *Sumañgala Vilāsini* (1886), and the *Dīgha Nikāya* (2 vols., 1890–1903; both in collaboration with Rhys Davids); and *The Hexateuch According to the Revised Version* (2 vols., 1900; in collaboration with G. Harford-Battersby); and has translated C. P. Tiele's *Geschiedenis van den Godsdienst tot aan de heerschappij der Wereldgodsdiensten* (Amsterdam, 1876) under the title *Outlines of the History of Religion* (London, 1878). His independent works include: *Life and Work of Mary Carpenter* (London, 1879); *Life in Palestine when Jesus Lived* (1889); *The First Three Gospels, Their Origin and Relations* (1890); *Composition of the Hexateuch* (1902); *The Bible in the Nineteenth Century* (1903); *Studies in Theology* (1903; in collaboration with P. H. Wicksteed); *The Place of Christianity Among the Religions of the World* (1904); and *James Martineau, Theologian and Teacher* (1905).

CARPENTER, LANT: English Unitarian; b. at Kidderminster (15 m. s.w. of Birmingham), Worcestershire, Sept. 2, 1780; lost overboard from a steamer between Naples and Leghorn Apr. 5, 1840. He studied at Glasgow College 1798–1801; became a popular and successful school-teacher and preacher; was minister at Exeter 1805–17, and at Bristol 1817–39. He did much to broaden his denomination and to consolidate its scattered congregations; was a leader in philanthropic work; and was one of the most efficient of English schoolmasters. His publications were numerous, the most noteworthy being: *An Introduction to the Geography of the New Testament* (London, 1805); *Unitarianism the Doctrine of the Gospel* (1809; 3d ed., with alterations, Bristol, 1823); *Systematic Education*, in collaboration with William Shepherd and Jeremiah Joyce (2 vols., 1815); *An Examination of the Charges Made Against Unitarians by the Right Rev. Dr. Magee* (Bristol, 1820); *Principles of Education* (London, 1820); *A Harmony of the Gospels* (Bristol, 1835). After his death appeared a volume of *Sermons on Practical Subjects* (Bristol, 1840), edited by his son, Russell Lant Carpenter.

BIBLIOGRAPHY: R. L. Carpenter, *Memoirs of the Life of Rev. Lant Carpenter, with Selections from his Correspondence*, Bristol, 1842; *DNB*, ix. 157–159.

CARPENTER, MARY: Philanthropist; b. at Exeter, England, Apr. 3, 1807; d. at Bristol June 14, 1877. She was the eldest child of Lant Carpenter (q.v.), and received an excellent education in her father's school; she taught for several years; became interested in reformatory movements in India through the visit to Bristol of the Rajah Rammohun Roy in 1833, and also in work for destitute children in England through the instrumentality of Joseph Tuckerman, of Boston. She opened "ragged schools" and developed and set in operation a plan for reformatory schools which was legalized by Parliament in 1854; she was also one of the chief promoters of the Industrial Schools Act passed in 1857. She visited India four times between 1866 and 1876, and came to America in 1873. Prison reform also received her attention, and she was earnest in advocacy of the higher education of women. She wrote much in behalf of her projects, and her reports and memorials to Parliament had no little influence in shaping legislation.

BIBLIOGRAPHY: J. E. Carpenter, *Life and Work of Mary Carpenter*, London, 1879; *DNB*, ix. 159–161.

CARPENTER, WILLIAM BOYD: Church of England bishop of Ripon; b. at Liverpool Mar. 26, 1841. He was educated at St. Catherine's College, Cambridge (B.A., 1864), and was ordered deacon in 1864 and ordained priest in the following year. He was successively curate of All Saints', Maidstone, Kent (1864–66), of St. Paul's, Clapham (1866–67), and of Holy Trinity, Lee (1867–70). He was then vicar of St. James's, Holloway (1870–79), and of Christ Church, Lancaster Gate (1879–84). He was chaplain to the bishop of London from 1879 to 1884 and canon of Windsor from 1882 to 1884, while he was also honorary chaplain to Queen Victoria in 1879–83, and chaplain in ordinary in 1883–84. In 1884 he was consecrated the bishop of Ripon. He was select preacher at Cambridge in 1875 and 1877, and at Oxford in 1883–84, and was also Hulsean Lecturer at Cambridge in 1878, Bampton Lecturer at Oxford in 1887, Pastoral Lecturer on theology at Cambridge in 1895, and Noble Lecturer at Harvard University in 1904. He has been a clerk of the closet since 1903, and is also a knight of the Prussian Order of the Royal Crown. In addition to numerous volumes of sermons, he has written: *Thoughts on Prayer* (London, 1871); *Narcissus, a Tale of Early Christian Times* (1879); *The Witness of the Heart to Christ* (1879; the Hulsean Lectures for 1878); *District Visitor's Companion* (1881); *My Bible* (1884); *Nature and Man* (1888); *Permanent Elements of Religion* (Bampton Lectures for 1887, 1889); *The Burning Bush* (1893); *Twilight Dreams* (1893); *Lectures on Preaching* (1895); *Thoughts on Reunion* (1895); *Religious Spirit in the Poets* (1900); *Popular History of the Church of England* (1900); and *Witness to the Influence of Christ* (Noble Lectures for 1904; 1905). He likewise contributed the notes on Revelation in C. J. Ellicott's *New Testament Commentary* (London, 1879).

CARPOCRATES, cār-pec'ra-tīz, **AND THE CARPOCRATIANS:** An Alexandrian Gnostic of the first half of the second century and the sect which he founded. His teachings rested upon a Platonic basis, and were interspersed with Christian ideas. According to Irenæus (*Hær.*, i. 25), supplemented here and there by Epiphanius (*Hær.*, xxvii.), he taught that in the beginning was the divine primitive source, "the father of all," "the one beginning" (Gk. *archē*). Angels, far removed from this source, have created the world. The world-builders have imprisoned in bodies the fallen souls, who originally worked with God, and now have to go through every form of life and every act to regain their freedom. To accomplish this a long series of transmigrations through the bodies is needed. The words of Jesus in Luke xii. 58 (Matt. v. 25) expressed this thought very clearly in Carpocrates's view; the "adversary" is the devil, who drags the souls to the highest of the world-builders; the latter delivers them to another angel, his messenger, to be incarcerated in bodies until they have paid the last farthing, i.e., have won freedom, and can rise to the highest God. During their transmigrations the souls have retained the power of remembering (Gk. *anamnēsis*), though in different degree. The soul of Jesus, son of Joseph, possessed the power of remembering God in greatest purity. Therefore God bestowed upon him power to escape the world-builders and to despise the Jewish customs in which he was brought up. Whosoever thinks and acts like him obtains the same power; whosoever is still more perfect can reach higher. This is the faith and the love through which we are saved; everything else, essentially indifferent, is good or bad, godless or shameless only according to human conceptions; for by nature nothing is bad. This is the teaching which Jesus himself gave to his disciples, "privately in a mystery," ordering them to disseminate it among the faithful ("the worthy and believing"). The Carpocratians rendered divine honor to Jesus as to the other secular sages (Pythagoras, Plato, Aristotle). They claimed for themselves the power of ruling the world-builders: magic arts, exorcism, philters and love-potions, dreams and cures were at their command, and like other secret societies they had a special mark of recognition, which they burned with a hot iron on the back of the lobe of the right ear.

Later writers follow Irenæus. Clement alone adds new matter in some quotations from a Carpocratian manuscript. He says that Carpocrates had a son, Epiphanes, whose mother was Alexandria of Cephalonia; that this son became an author, died when seventeen years old, and was honored as a god at Same in Cephalonia. This story has been declared mythical (cf. Volkmar, in the *Monatsschrift des wissenschaftlichen Vereins in Zürich*, 1858, pp. 276–277; Lipsius, *Zur Quellenkritik des Epiphanius*, pp. 161–162, Leipsic, 1865), and it is maintained that traits of the moon-god worshiped at Same (Gk. *theos epiphanēs*) were transferred to Epiphanes, the Gnostic. Though this suggestion is striking, there is hardly reason for making a myth of the entire statement of Clement, so much the more as he has filled out his account by a long extract from a work of Epiphanes "On Righteousness." In this work the young idealist advocated community of goods and women without the intention of preaching general immorality. Even Irenæus had written: "I can hardly believe that all the ungodly, unlawful, and forbidden things of which we read in their books are really done among them." One needs only to reflect how inconsistently highly endowed advocates of similar views think and act nowadays, though of course it must be admitted that such conceptions in earlier times might have caused in immature minds the same troubles as they do to-day. At all events, Carpocratianism can not be called Christianity. It is a specifically ethnic phenomenon, easily explicable from the religious syncretism of the second century. G. KRÜGER.

BIBLIOGRAPHY: The sources are accessible in Eng. in *ANF*, i. 350, ii. 382 404, iii. 216, 651, v. 113; *NPNF*, i. 114, 179, 199. Consult also: C. W. F. Walch, *Historie der Ketzereien*, i. 302–335, Leipsic, 1762; A. Neander, *Genetische Entwickelung der vornehmsten gnostischen Systeme*, pp. 355–360, Berlin, 1818; idem, *Christian Church*, i. 292, 399, 449–451, 484; W. Möller, *Geschichte der Kosmologie*, pp. 335–343, Halle, 1860; A. Hilgenfeld, *Ketzergeschichte des Urchristentums*, pp. 397–408, Leipsic, 1884; Harnack, *Litteratur*, i. 161–162.

CARPZOV: A family of German lawyers and theologians, of which the following are the most important members:

1. **Benedikt Carpzov:** Lawyer; b. at Wittenberg May 27, 1595; d. at Leipsic Aug. 30, 1666. He was educated at Wittenberg, Leipsic, and Jena, and after a tour through Italy, France, and England became a member of the court of sheriffs at Leipsic,

where he remained with little interruption for forty years. He was later appointed assessor of the supreme court in Leipsic and counselor of the Dresden court of appeals. In 1645 he was made professor in the faculty of law at Leipsic, and was for eight years a member of the privy council of Dresden, but returned to Leipsic in 1661. Although he had not a creative mind, his diligence, judgment, and system enabled him to become the founder of German jurisprudence, and in his *Practica nova imperialis Saxonica rerum criminalium* (Wittenberg, 1638) he formulated the first system of German criminal law, while his *Jurisprudentia ecclesiastica seu consistorialis* (Leipsic, 1649) formed the earliest complete system of Protestant ecclesiastical law. He distinguished carefully between ecclesiastical and canon law, and was the first to use the ordinances of the Evangelical Church, the rescripts of the sovereigns, and the decisions of the consistories, thus summarizing the legal development of Protestantism since the Reformation.

2. Johann Benedikt Carpzov the Elder: Theologian, brother of the preceding; b. at Rochlitz (16 m. n.n.w. of Chemnitz) June 22, 1607; d. at Leipsic Oct. 22, 1657. He studied at the University of Wittenberg from 1623 to 1627, and then entered the University of Leipsic. In 1632 he was appointed pastor at Meuselwitz and five years later became deacon at the Church of St. Thomas at Leipsic. In ten years he rose to the archdeaconry and received the additional appointments of assessor of the consistory and canon, having become professor of theology at the university in 1641, although his pastoral duties allowed him little time for teaching. He maintained a certain reserve in the syncretistic controversies of the period, and though in harmony with his colleague Hülsemann, he carried on a friendly correspondence with Calixtus and later with his pupil Titius. His most important work, which has won him the title of the father of symbolics, was his *Isagōgē in libros ecclesiarum Lutheranarum symbolicos* (Leipsic, 1665), which was completed after his death by Olearius, general superintendent of Magdeburg. Still more famous, however, is his *Hodegeticum brevibus aphorismis olim pro collegio concionatorio conceptum et nunc revisum* (1656), which gives 100 methods of arranging sermons.

3. Johann Benedikt Carpzov the Younger: Theologian, son of the preceding; b. at Leipsic Apr. 24, 1639; d. there Mar. 23, 1699. He was educated in his native city and at Jena, and was also influenced by Buxtorf in Basel and by Johann Schmid in Strasburg. In 1659 he became privat-docent at Leipsic, and in 1665 was appointed professor of ethics. Three years later he was made licentiate of theology and professor of Oriental languages. In 1684 he became professor of theology, having already been made deacon in 1671, archdeacon in 1674, and pastor of St. Thomas's in 1679. His pastoral duties forbade extensive literary activity, and he therefore restricted himself to editing the works of others, such as the *Jus regium* of Wilhelm Schickhard (Leipsic, 1674), the *In Prophetas Minores commentarius* of Johann Tarnov (1688), the *Horæ Talmudicæ et Hebraicæ* of John Lightfoot (1674), and an enlarged edition of his father's *Hodegeticum* (1689). Through this last-named work an interest was aroused in homiletics which completely overshadowed philosophy and exegesis. There was gradually evolved, therefore, an antagonism between Carpzov and Spener, which increased in bitterness until in 1691 three programs assailed Pietism, and five years later Carpzov attacked Thomasius in his *De jure decidendi controversias theologicas* (1696), vainly attempting to support a failing cause.

4. Samuel Benedikt Carpzov: Theologian, son of Johann Benedikt the Elder; b. at Leipsic Jan. 17, 1647; d. at Dresden Aug. 31, 1707. After studying philosophy and philology at the university of his native city from 1663 to 1668, he went to Wittenberg, where he became a close friend of Calov and Aegidius Strauch. In 1674 he was called to Dresden as court-preacher, and five years later he was transferred to the *Kreuzkirche*, being also appointed superintendent and thus given the right to attend the sessions of the high consistory. He conducted the negotiations for the call of Spener, and proved himself a true friend of the Pietist until his brother at Leipsic became the leader of the opposition and persuaded him to change his attitude. After the retirement of Spener and the death of Green, Carpzov was chosen to succeed them, and he accepted with much hesitation, although he held the position for the remainder of his life.

5. Johann Gottlob Carpzov: Theologian, son of the preceding; b. at Dresden Sept. 26, 1679; d. at Lübeck Apr. 7, 1767. He was educated at Leipsic and Altdorf, and though the most learned theologian of his family, was indoctrinated with reactionary principles by his father and uncle. In 1708 he went from Dresden to Leipsic as deacon. He ranked among the foremost of Old Testament scholars, although in the preface to his *Introductio in libros Veteris Testamenti* (Leipsic, 1721) he declared that only the entire absence of such a work had rendered it possible for him to publish his own. This book, like his *Critica sacra* (1728), is characterized by clear arrangement, deep knowledge, and thorough criticism. Equally valuable was his *Apparatus historico-criticus antiquitatum Veteris Testamenti* (1748). His chief attacks were reserved for R. Simon, Clericus, and Spinoza, as representatives of the new criticism, and his point of view was that of Buxtorf and Hottinger, so that he postulated the verbal inspiration of the text of the Bible, and admitted no error whatsoever. He was, moreover, a consistent opponent of Pietism and the Moravians, and gladly accepted a call as superintendent to the orthodox city of Lübeck in 1730, after having been obliged to decline a similar invitation to go to Danzig. There he continued his polemics against the Moravians, publishing in 1742 one of the sharpest of all attacks on them in his *Religionsuntersuchung der böhmischen und mährischen Brüder von Anbeginn ihrer Gemeinden bis auf gegenwärtige Zeiten*.

6. Johann Benedikt Carpzov: Classical scholar and theologian, grandson of Johann Benedikt the Younger; b. at Leipsic May 20, 1720; d. at Königslutter (9 m. w.n.w. of Helmstädt) Apr. 18, 1803.

He was educated at the university of his native city, where he was appointed associate professor in 1747, but was called in the following year as professor of Greek to Helmstädt, and in 1757 became abbot of Königslutter. Adhering to the orthodoxy of his family, he was commissioned by the duke to save the reputation of the university, endangered by the rationalism of Albrecht Teller, and he accordingly published his *Liber doctrinalis theologiæ purioris* (Brunswick, 1768). His philological learning was shown in his editions of the classics and in his *Sacræ exercitationes in epistolam ad Hebræos ex Philone Alexandrino* (Helmstädt, 1750); *Stricturæ theologicæ in epistolam S. Pauli ad Romanos* (1756); and *Epistolarum catholicarum septenarius* (Halle, 1790). His lectures, which he delivered in Latin, were devoted to classics, the New Testament, patristics, and Dolscius's Greek translation of the Augsburg Confession.

(GEORG MUELLER.)

BIBLIOGRAPHY: On the family consult: *ADB*, iv. 10–26; R. Stintzing, *Geschichte der deutschen Rechtswissenschaft*, i. 723, ii. 56, Munich, 1880. On Benedikt Carpzov consult: K. Rieker, *Die rechtliche Stellung der evangelischen Kirche Deutschlands*, pp. 218–220, Leipsic, 1893. On Johann the Elder consult: A. H. Kreysig, *Album der evangelisch-lutherischen Geistlichen in Sachsen*, pp. 265–267, Dresden, 1883; T. Spizel, *Vetus academia Jesu Christi*, pp. 227–233, Augsburg, 1671. On Johann the Younger consult: H. Pipping, *Sacer decadum septenarius memoriam theologorum . . .*, pp. 763–784, Leipsic, 1705; K. Rieker, ut sup., pp. 220–222; A. H. Kreysig, ut sup., pp. 265, 277. On Samuel Benedikt consult: J. A. Gleich, *Annalium ecclesiasticorum*, ii. 522–550, Dresden, 1730; G. L. Zeissler, *Geschichte der sächsischen Oberhofprediger*, pp. 111–119, Leipsic, 1856. On Johann Gottlob consult: A. H. Kreysig, ut sup., pp. 108, 266; L. Diestel, *Geschichte des Alten Testaments in der christlichen Kirche*, p. 352, Jena, 1869. On Johann Benedikt consult: F. Koldewey, *Geschichte der klassischen Philologie*, pp. 165–168, Brunswick, 1897 (gives further literature).

CARRANZA, cār-rān'thā, **BARTOLOMÉ**: Archbishop of Toledo; b. at Miranda (175 m. n.e. of Madrid), Navarre, 1503; d. at Rome May 2, 1576. He entered the order of the Dominicans and from 1528 lectured on philosophy and scholastic theology at Alcala, afterward at Valladolid. Charles V. offered him the bishopric of Cuzco in Peru, but he declined. At the request of the emperor he took part in the deliberations of the Council of Trent after 1546, and insisted that the bishops should reside in their own dioceses. Strange to say, Carranza came into conflict with the Roman theologians because he asserted that the bishops had their rights *jure divino*, not by papal appointment. When the council was suspended he might have gone to Flanders as confessor of the infante Philip, but he declined this influential position to work in Spain as provincial of his order. He accompanied Philip to England (1554) when the latter was married to Mary Tudor, and shared in the persecution of the Protestants there. For this he was rewarded by Philip in 1557 and made archbishop of Toledo, which proved the culmination of his career. When Charles V was dying (1558), Carranza gave him the sacrament. His opponents circulated the report that the emperor had not died in the faith of the Church and that this was owing to Carranza. The Inquisition had statements made by prisoners, which offered sufficient material to justify intervention, and his enemies, especially the inquisitor-general Valdez and Melchior Cano, called attention to his catechism (*Comentarios del reverendissimo Fray Bartolomé Carranza sobre el Catechismo Christiano*, Antwerp, 1558), which contained anything but Protestant doctrines, but deviated in some expressions from the Roman tradition. Carranza was imprisoned, his papers were confiscated, and some further material for charges was found. The examinations of Protestants in Valladolid which he held in 1558 and 1559 were especially scrutinized, and it was found that on the doctrine of justification and purgatory he had made oral statements which were not Catholic. In spite of his appeal to the pope, the Spanish Inquisition kept him in prison eight years and when he was transferred in 1567 to Rome at the behest of Pius V. he was kept there under examination nine years longer. The Roman process ended with a solemn abjuration of fourteen statements especially taken from his writings and with canonical punishment. He was suspended for five years and died in Rome without returning to Spain. The court of inquisition had overcome in his person the highest episcopal dignitary, but Gregory XIII. allowed a laudatory epitaph to be set up in Santa Maria sopra Minerva.

K. BENRATH.

BIBLIOGRAPHY: Carranza's most noted work, *Summa conciliorum et pontificum* (a church history to Julius III.), was published at Venice, 1546 and often. His life, by H. Laugwitz, *Bartholomeo Carranza, Erzbischof von Toledo*, was published at Kempten, 1870. Consult also: J. Quétif and J. Échard, *Scriptores ordinis prædicatorum*, vol. ii., Paris, 1721; F. H. Reusch, *Der Index der verbotenen Bücher*, i. 254, 398, 588 et passim, Bonn, 1883; Moeller, *Christian Church*, iii. 317; H. C. Lea, *Inquisition in Spain*, ii. 45–87, iv. 15, 486, 502, New York, 1906.

CARRASCO, cār-rās'co, **ANTONIO**: Spanish Protestant; b. in Malaga Jan. 19, 1843; lost with the steamer "Ville du Havre" Nov. 22, 1873, while returning home from the Sixth General Conference of the Evangelical Alliance held in New York Oct., 1873. He was converted at sixteen and joined a band of Bible-readers in Malaga connected with Manuel Matamoros (q.v.); was imprisoned for two years (1860–62), and then condemned to the galleys for a term of nine years, but at the solicitation of the Evangelical Alliance, supported by representations of the Prussian government, the sentence was changed to banishment (1863). He studied theology in Geneva; on the downfall of Queen Isabella in 1868 he returned to Spain and undertook the work of evangelization; at the time of his death he was pastor of the Free Church in Madrid, with a membership of 700, and president of the Protestant Synod of Spain.

BIBLIOGRAPHY: A brief sketch of his life may be found in the *History, etc., of the Sixth General Conference of the Evangelical Alliance*, p. 764, New York, 1874.

CARROLL, HENRY KING: Methodist Episcopalian; b. at Dennisville, N. J., Nov. 15, 1848. He was self-taught, and early entered journalism, being successively editor of the *Havre Republican*, Havre, Md. (1868–69), and assistant editor of *The Methodist*, New York (1869–70), and of the

Hearth and Home, New York (1870–71). From 1876 to 1898 he was religious and political editor of *The Independent*, New York, but resigned in the latter year to accept the appointment of special commissioner of President McKinley to Porto Rico. In 1881 he was a delegate to the Ecumenical Methodist Conference in London, and in 1884 was organizing secretary of the Methodist Centennial Conference, of which he edited the proceedings (New York, 1885), while in 1890 he was special commissioner of the United States census for religious denominations. In 1900 he was elected corresponding secretary of the Methodist Missionary Society, and was reelected four years later. He is a member of the Methodist Historical Society, a manager of the Methodist Sunday School Union and of the American Sabbath Observance Society, and a trustee of the United Society of Christian Endeavor. In theology he is in thorough accord with the doctrinal position of the Methodist Episcopal Church. In addition to a number of minor contributions, he has written: *Religious Forces of the United States* (New York, 1893, 2d and enlarged ed., 1895).

CARROLL, JOHN: First Roman Catholic bishop in the United States; b. at Upper Marlborough, Prince George's County, Md., Jan. 8, 1735; d. in Baltimore Dec. 3, 1815. He studied with the Jesuits at Bohemia, on the east shore of Maryland, and at the College of St. Omer, France; joined the Jesuits in 1753; was ordained priest in 1759; taught at St. Omer, Liége, and Bruges; traveled through Europe as tutor to the son of a Roman Catholic nobleman; returned to America in 1774 and became missionary and priest of his native region with headquarters at his mother's residence at Rock Creek, not far from Washington. Like his kinsman Charles Carroll of Carrollton, he warmly supported the cause of the colonies in the Revolutionary war. When the Roman Catholic Church in the United States was organized as a distinct body, free from the authority of the vicar apostolic of London, he was made prefect apostolic in 1784; in 1789 he was chosen bishop of Baltimore and consecrated in England in 1790; in 1808 he became archbishop. He founded Georgetown College in 1791.

Bibliography: John G. Shea gives *Carroll's Life and Times* in *History of the Catholic Church in the U. S.*, vol. ii., New York, 1888.

CARROLL, JOHN JOSEPH: American Roman Catholic; b. at Enniscrone, County Sligo, Ireland, June 21, 1856. He was educated at St. Michael's College, Toronto (B.A., 1876), and St. Joseph's Provincial Theological Seminary, Troy, N. Y., from which he was graduated in 1879. In the following year he was ordained priest, and was appointed assistant rector of the Cathedral of the Holy Name, Chicago, and since 1887 has been rector of St. Thomas Church in the same city. In 1898 he was elected chairman of Gaelic history in the Gaelic League of America and in 1902 was chosen national librarian of the same organization. He has written: *Notes and Observations on the Aryan Race and Tongue* (Chicago, 1900); *Tale of the Wanderings of the Red Lance* (1902); and *Pre-christian Occupation of Ireland by the Gaelic Aryans* (2 vols., 1903–06).

CARSON, ALEXANDER: Irish Baptist; b. at Annahone, near Stewartstown (30 m. w. of Belfast), County Tyrone, Ireland, 1776; d. at Belfast Aug. 21, 1844. He studied at Glasgow and was ordained a Presbyterian minister at Tobermore, near Coleraine, County Londonderry, 1798. After a few years he left the Presbyterians and published as justification of his action *Reasons for Separating from the General Synod of Ulster* (Edinburgh, 1804); a portion of his congregation followed him, and for ten years he preached in barns or the open air. A stone church was built for him in 1814. In the early part of his independent career, while studying the New Testament in order to confute the Baptists, he became a Baptist himself, and thenceforth advocated their views with the exception of close communion. His *Baptism in Its Mode and Subjects Considered* (Edinburgh, 1831; enlarged ed., 1844) is a Baptist classic. His other writings were numerous and treat topics of Bible interpretation, philosophy, doctrinal and practical theology, and the like. He was a bitter controversialist. His collected works were published in six volumes at Dublin, 1847–64.

Bibliography: G. C. Moore, *Life of Alexander Carson*, New York, 1851; John Douglas, *A Biographical Sketch of A. Carson*, London, 1884; *DNB*, ix. 186.

CARSTARES, WILLIAM: Scotch clergyman and political leader; b. at Cathcart (5 m. w.n.w. of Glasgow) Feb. 11, 1649; d. in Edinburgh Dec. 28, 1715. He studied at Edinburgh (graduated 1667) and at Utrecht, whither he went because of the political troubles at home, in which his father was implicated. Toward the close of 1674 he was arrested in London, being suspected of having a hand in the distribution of a seditious pamphlet and of being the bearer of despatches to the disaffected in Scotland from their sympathizers in Holland; he was kept in confinement till Aug., 1679. When released he entered actively into the plots which were then rife, and appears at different times in Ireland, England, Scotland, and Holland. After the discovery of the Rye House plot (a scheme to assassinate Charles II.) in July, 1683, he was caught in Kent, and was sent to Edinburgh and examined under torture before the Scottish Council, but displayed "great discretion" in the disclosures which he made. In 1686 or 1687 he settled at Leyden, and thenceforth was seldom separated from William of Orange, whom he had known from his student days in Utrecht and who trusted him implicitly and often took his advice, especially on Scotch affairs. After William became king of England, he made Carstares chaplain for Scotland, and the latter rendered valuable services both to his country and his king, especially in reconciling the Scotch Presbyterians to the new régime. His personal influence at court ceased with the death of William, and thenceforth he resided in Edinburgh, where he was made principal of the university in 1703; he also became minister of the Gray Friars' Church, and distinguished himself in both capacities. He retained his position as royal chaplain under Anne, and at the accession of George I. was chosen by the

General Assembly to make the usual congratulatory speech. He was four times moderator of the General Assembly.

Bibliography: *State-Papers and Letters Addressed to William Carstares*, with life by J. M'Cormick, Edinburgh, 1774; R. H. Story, *William Carstares, a character and career of the revolutionary epoch, 1649-1715*, London, 1874; *DNB*, ix. 187-190.

CARTER, JAMES: American Presbyterian; b. in New York Oct. 1, 1853. He graduated at Columbia College in 1882, and at Union Theological Seminary in 1885. He was pastor at Williamsport, Pa., from 1889 till 1905, when he became professor of church history and sociology in Lincoln University, Pa. He has written the biography of his father, Walter Carter (New York, 1901), and two volumes of poems.

CARTER, THOMAS HENRY: United Brethren; b. in Carroll Co., Tenn., Jan. 1, 1851; entered the ministry, 1869; elected bishop, 1905.

CARTESIANISM. See Descartes, René.

CARTHAGE, SYNODS OF.

I. Synods before and under Cyprian.
II. Synods during the Donatist Controversy.
III. Synods in Connection with the Pelagian Controversy.
IV. Concluding Synods.

Carthage, the ancient rival of Rome, preserved a remnant of its former greatness in the commanding position assumed by its bishops, at least from the beginning of the third century, in the North-African Church. By right of their see, they were *ex officio* primates of their province, while this position in Numidia, and later in the other provinces of North Africa, went by seniority. But many bishops of these provinces paid great heed to the counsels of the bishop of the capital, at least in Cyprian's time, and even earlier than that had formed the habit of meeting there for conference. The decisions taken in regard to the controversies agitating the African Church, especially the Donatist and Pelagian, were of permanent and far-reaching importance for the development of theology.

I. Synods before and under Cyprian: (1) That under Bishop Agrippinus (c. 220), to whose decision Cyprian appealed in the controversy about baptism by heretics. (2) That held c. 240 at Lambese in Numidia (or Carthage), which condemned the heretic Privatus. (3) The first under Cyprian after his return to Carthage, just after Easter, 251. After a long debate, it decided that the lapsed, especially those who had offered sacrifice, should be restored only on an extended penance, except in danger of death, while the *libellatici* (see Lapsed) might, provisionally at least, be at once received. It seems to have been customary at this time to hold an annual Easter synod; and at least one (4) is known in 252, to which probably the letter of Cyprian and sixty-six bishops to Fidus (*Epist.*, lxiv.) refers; here Privatus attempted to have his case reopened, but was refused and joined the opposition that set up Fortunatus as a rival bishop. (5) In 253, with reference to the new persecution under Gallus, the procedure in the case of the lapsed was modified, so that, if truly penitent, they might be at once restored (*Epist.*, lvii.). Subsequent synods dealt with baptism by heretics, concerning which the African bishops held strict views: (6) One attended by thirty-one bishops in 255 (*Epist.*, lxx.). (7) A more general one, of seventy-one bishops, from Numidia as well, in the spring of 256 (*Epist.*, lxxiii.). (8) One of eighty-seven bishops, this time including the Mauritanians, in September of the same year. The views expressed in the last-named were controverted by Augustine, *De baptismo contra Donatistas*, vi., vii.

II. Synods during the Donatist Controversy: (1) In 312, composed of seventy bishops, opponents of Cæcilian, who was excommunicated. (2) One of 270 Donatist bishops, about 330, which showed a conciliatory spirit, and sanctioned the admission of traditores to communion. The succeeding synods for some time are all on the Catholic side, and show a more or less severe attitude toward the Donatists according to the position taken at the time by the schismatics. (3) The so-called "First Council of Carthage," between 345 and 348, attended by fifty bishops, at the close of a heavy persecution. This, like 8, 10, 11, 15, and 20, dealt only cursorily with the Donatist question, while 4, 5, 6, 7, 9, and 18, as far as we know, did not touch upon it at all. Under Bishop Genethlius of Carthage, who was much esteemed by the Donatists, took place (4) a synod in the "Prætorium," and a year later, or in 390, (5) the so-called "Second Council of Carthage," attended by sixty bishops. Under his successor, Aurelius, twenty synods are said to have been held, in the most important of which Augustine participated. In a general African council held at Hippo in 393 it was decided that the various provinces should take turns in holding such general gatherings; but this system was difficult of execution, since Mauritania and Tripolis were too distant, and the latter had only five episcopal sees. Among such general councils may be reckoned, besides that of Hippo which began the series, that of Hadrumetum, 394, those numbered here 3, 5, 8, 11, 12, 15, and 20, and that of Mileve, 402. In 407 it was decided to abandon the attempt and call them when and where it seemed expedient, while the provincial synods were to go on as before. (6) and (7) Two synods held respectively on June 26, 394, and June 26, 397, of which little is known.

What is known as the *Breviarium canonum Hipponensium* corresponds substantially with (8) the *Carthaginiense III.* of the Spanish collection, Aug. 28, 397. The canons of 393 and 397, confirmed at Mileve in 402, give a comprehensive view of the church life of the time. The most famous is that containing the list of Scriptural books, and dealing with the reading of the martyrologies. The position of the presbyters in relation to the bishops is restricted, aggressions by bishops on neighboring dioceses reprobated, and the whole conduct of the clergy within the bounds of the Church regulated. In regard to the Donatist matter, a change is made, allowing clerics coming from the schism to exercise their function, under certain conditions, where formerly they had been relegated to lay communion. Legations from the court often appeared, as at (9) a synod of Apr. 27, 399, when the right of asylum in churches was considered. From 401 on more attention is paid to the Donatist controversy, at first in a conciliatory spirit; in that year two synods were held (10) on June 16 and (11) on Sept. 13, both of which occupied themselves also with the removal of the remains of paganism. (12) The general synod of Aug. 25, 403, laid down a formula to be accepted by the Donatists which only increased the bitterness, and the following synod (13) of June 16, 404, appealed to the emperor to repress the schismatics by legal measures. This was done, and the next synod (14), Aug. 23, 405, returned thanks to him. At the general synod (15) of June 13, 407, measures were adopted to facilitate the reception into the Church of entire schismatic communities; and, after the issue of an imperial decree which mitigated the former severity, both on (16) June 16 and (17) Oct. 13, 408, delegations were sent to impress the ecclesiastical view on the emperor. The only extant provision of (18) the provincial synod of June 15, 409, has no direct connection with the burning question; but after the issue of a decree of toleration, the next (19), on June 14, 410, sent another delegation to the emperor, and this time with success. (20) The synod of May 1, 418, is occupied again with the reception of Donatist communities and the duty of the conversion of heretics; while some of its provisions look forward to the next division.

III. Synods in Connection with the Pelagian Controversy. For these see PELAGIUS, PELAGIANISM.

IV. Concluding Synods: At the head of these comes the frequently cited synod of 419, attended by 217 bishops, which held two sessions, May 25 and 30 (designated in the *Hispana* as *Carthaginiense VI.* and *VII.*). It codified and to some extent shortened the preceding legislation. Part of its work dealt with the claims of the Roman See, based improperly on the decrees of the First Council of Nicæa. It drew up also a reply to a letter of Pope Boniface, who had laid four points before it—the question of appeals, the journeys of the African bishops to the imperial court, the right of excommunicated clerics to apply for restoration to neighboring bishops, and the conduct of the bishop of Sicca in deposing a priest who had appealed to Rome. The council temporized on the first and third points, agreed to the restoration of the priest, though not in the same diocese. A still firmer tone was taken toward Rome by the synod which (after 422) wrote to Pope Celestine in connection with the priest above mentioned, which showed that the ancient independence and conciliar spirit of the African Church were still unbroken.

But with the invasion of the Vandals from the west, threatening Carthage in 439, the existence of the Church of North Africa drew to a close. In the face of such dangers as the persecutions of the Arian kings brought upon the Christians of those parts, minor differences disappeared. The conference on religion held in 484 did not give them much relief; but more was accomplished by the synod of Feb. 5, 525, in the reign of Hilderic, attended by sixty bishops from different provinces. After the annexation of North Africa by the Byzantine government, Bishop Reparatus held a synod of 217 bishops in 535; it dealt with Rome about the reception of converted Arians into the service of the Church, regulated the relation of monasteries to the bishops, and sent a deputation to Justinian to ask the restoration of property and privileges. Thenceforth the history of the North-African Church is merged in the general development of the state religion, and has no more separate importance before its final extinction by the Arabs.

(EDGAR HENNECKE.)

BIBLIOGRAPHY: For the canons of the synods consult: W. Beveridge, *Synodikon, sive pandectæ canonum*, Oxford, 1672 (includes the canons of the African synods); G. D. Fuchs, *Bibliothek der Kirchenversammlungen*, iii. 1–476, Leipsic, 1783. On the general question consult: F. Maassen, *Geschichte der Quellen und der Literatur des kanonischen Rechts*, i. 149 sqq., Graz, 1870; J. Lloyd, *The North African Church*, London, 1870; O. Ritschl, *Cyprian von Karthago*, pp. 153 sqq., Göttingen, 1885; Hefele, *Conciliengeschichte*, vols. i., ii. passim, Eng. transl., vols. i., ii. passim; the brothers Ballerini in Appendix to the *Opera* of Leo I., vol. i., chapp. iii., xxi.–xxix., Venice, 1757. Detailed treatment may be found in Neander, *Christian Church*, vols. i., ii. passim, consult *Index* under "Councils and Synods." Short discussions are also in Schaff, *Christian Church*, iii. 793, 798; Moeller, *Christian Church*, i. 263, 267, 332, 447, 452–453, 457; *DCA*, i. 36–39; and literature under DONATISM.

CARTHUSIANS.

The Carthusians are a Roman Catholic order founded by St. Bruno of Cologne at Grande Chartreuse (14 m. n. of Grenoble) in Dauphiné in the latter part of the eleventh century. The period was particularly favorable to the formation of new monastic orders. The monastery of Cluny (q.v.) inspired a tendency to the religious life throughout the surrounding regions, but this cloister, which had adopted the cenobitic monasticism of St. Benedict, gave no impetus to eremitic life. In the course of time, however, the longing for meditation in solitude peopled the wastes of Burgundy and Lorraine, apparently gaining inspiration from Italy by way of Dauphiné. To this period belonged Hugo, bishop of Grenoble (1080–1132), who had barely ascended the episcopal chair when he renounced it to bury himself in the monastery of Chaise-Dieu, whence he was recalled to his high office by the mandate of Gregory VII. In a like spirit two canons of St. Rufus in Dauphiné retired to the north of France, returning after some years with Bruno.

He was born of noble parentage at Cologne before the middle of the eleventh century, and educated at the cathedral school of Reims. Successively canon of St. Cunibert at Cologne and scholastic of the cathedral of Reims, Bruno had held this latter office with distinction for some twenty years and had diligently inculcated the stern principles of Hildebrand and the monks of Cluny. Appointed chancellor of the archbishopric of Reims in 1075, Bruno relaxed his energies as a teacher to assail the simony of his own archbishop, Manasseh of Gourney (1067–80). After a long struggle, in which Bruno was seconded by the best element in his chapter, as well as by the neighboring clergy, Manasseh was deposed. His antagonist, however, had become disheartened with the condition of the Church. In equal despair regarding the theology to which he devoted himself, he resolved to abandon the world and live the life of a hermit. Where he met the two canons who were later to take him to the Chartreuse is uncertain, but at all events he retired with a few friends of like sympathies to Molesme in the diocese of Langres to live the life of an anchorite in the center of French asceticism. He there joined the adherents of Robert, then abbot of Molesme and later founder of the Cistercians, and with his permission established a small community of hermits in the neighboring Sèche-Fontaine. Feeling that this refuge was insufficiently sundered from the world, Bruno left all his followers but six in Sèche-Fontaine, pushed southward, and in 1084 reached Grenoble, where the little company was welcomed by Hugo, who had but recently resumed his episcopal office.

1. The Life of St. Bruno.

Partly through the influence of the abbot of Chaise-Dieu, Bruno and his companions received from Hugo the lofty and almost inaccessible valley of Cartusia as their place of refuge, and on June 24, 1084, they began the construction of the hermitage, originally consisting of three wretched huts, each to be occupied by two anchorites, and a chapel. At first the new community had no special rule, although they seem to have been influenced by the Italian Camaldolites in many respects. They were clad in white, and were bound to perpetual silence, to the observance of the monastic hours, to the most rigorous renunciation and mortification, and to the copying of books of devotion. After directing his little colony of hermits for six years, Bruno was summoned to Rome by Urban II., who had once been his pupil at Reims. Bruno obeyed with reluctance, but went accompanied by some of his monks, while others remained in their hermitage, although for some time they proved restive under the administration of Landuin, whom Bruno had placed at their head. In Rome the hermits found themselves longing for their mountain valley, and Bruno obtained permission for them to return, bearing letters of commendation from the pope to Hugo of Grenoble and Hugo, archbishop of Lyons. Bruno, however, remained in Rome, although he was neither energetic enough nor polemical enough to exercise an influence on Urban's rule of the Church. He declined the proffered archbishopric of Reggio in Calabria, and shortly before the first crusade, apparently in 1091, he retired to the wild region of La Torre near Squillace in Calabria, where he gathered about him a number of hermits and formed a community like that at the Chartreuse. In 1097 Count Roger of Calabria gave him La Torre and Santo Stefano in Bosco, and two years later presented him with San Jacobo de Mentauro, so that he was able to establish two large cloisters for his order. He was buried in Santo Stefano in 1101, but the monastery, which then contained thirty monks, soon passed into the hands of the Cistercians, nor was it until 1137 that the Carthusian cloisters even reached the number of four, all situated in France.

2. Foundation of Chartreuse.

3. Carthusians in Italy.

After the middle of the twelfth century the order steadily increased, and in 1170 the Carthusians were deemed worthy of the special protection of the pope and were officially recognized by Alexander III. In 1258 the monasteries of the order numbered fifty-six, but in 1378 the Carthusians were obliged to contend with a division corresponding to the papal schism and lasting until the Council of Pisa. The entire body of Carthusians recognized Martin V as pope, and the two generals of the order resigned in favor of John of Greiffenberg, the prior of the Carthusian monastery of Paris, who thus became sole general. In 1420 Martin V. granted the order exemption from tithes for all its estates, and in 1508 Julius II. issued a bull enacting that the prior of the mother house should always be the general of the order, and that the annual chapters should be held there. Five years later the Calabrian monastery of Santo Stefano, where the founder of the order was buried, was restored to the Carthusians, and in 1514 Bruno was canonized. At the beginning of the eighteenth century the Carthusian monasteries numbered 170, of which seventy-five were in France. The Revolution struck the order a heavy blow, but it survived and in 1819 the mother house near Grenoble was again occupied. In 1905, in consequence of the legislation enacted in France concerning religious orders, the Grande Chartreuse of Grenoble as well as the other Carthusian monasteries was again vacated, and most of the monks retired to Spain.

4. Growth of the Order.

The Carthusian spirit may be learned from its rule. Until 1130 the order had no special regulations, but in that year Guigo de Castro, the fifth prior of Chartreuse, prepared the *Consuetudines Cartusiæ*. In 1258 the resolutions of the chapters from 1141 were collected by Bernard de la Tour and designated *Statuta antiqua*, while additional collections were made in 1367, 1509, and 1581. The chief aim of them all was the most absolute detachment, not only from the world and all its attractions and interests, but even from the brother monks of the order and the monastery. The lay brothers, who are divided into the three classes of *conversi*, *donati*, and *redditi*, are sharply distinguished from the professed. Each monastery is strictly separated from the surrounding population and from all other orders, while every form of ecclesiastical and secular influence, whether active or passive, is carefully avoided. The faithful adherence of the Carthusians to their rule spared them the necessity of reform felt by many orders in the transition from the Middle Ages to modern times.

5. Organization.

The Carthusians now control twenty-six monasteries, and still retain their absolute retirement from the world. The order likewise includes Carthusian nuns, who are said to have existed as early as the twelfth century, although in the eighteenth only five nunneries were known, all dating from the thirteenth or fourteenth century. Over these convents Carthusian monks presided, who as vicars ranked above the prioresses and lived in separate houses with other professed and lay brothers. The nuns, who were first permitted to become professed by the Council of Trent in the sixteenth century, may eat together and converse more frequently than is allowed to the monks.

6. Scholarship. Although in scholarship the Carthusians can not rival the Benedictines, Dominicans, or Jesuits, they are not without their men of fame. From the pre-Reformation period mention may be made, in addition to the Guigo already noted, of such authors of the fourteenth and fifteenth centuries as Ludolf of Saxony, Hendrik of Coesfeld, Gerhard of Schiedam, and Henry of Kalkar, as well as of Jacob of Jüterbogk and Dionysius of Rickel. Noteworthy names of later date are the hagiographers Lorenz Surius and H. Murer, and such historians of the order as Petræus, Le Vasseur, and Le Couteulx. In recent times, moreover, the order entered upon a revival of literary activity.

(O. Zöckler†.)

Bibliography: Heimbucher, *Orden und Kongregationen*, i. 251-263; Le Vasseur, *Ephemerides ordinis Carthusiensis*, 2 vols., Montreuil, 1892 (a biography arranged by the calendar, goes only to July 31; the author died 1693); Helyot, *Ordres monastiques*, vii. 366-405; *Magna Vita S. Hugonis*, ed. J. F. Dimock for *Rolls Series*, no. 37, London, 1864; F. A. Lefebure, *S. Bruno et l'ordre des Chartreux*, 2 vols., Paris, 1883; idem, *La Chartreuse de Nôtre-Dame-des-Pres à Neuville*, Neuville, 1890; C. Reichenlechner, *Der Karthäuserorden in Deutschland*, Würzburg, 1885. C. le Couteulx, *Annales ordinis Cartusiensis, 1084-1429*, 2 vols., Montreuil, 1887-88; C. Boutrais, *The Monastery of the Grande Chartreuse*, London, 1893; *Vie de S. Bruno*, Montreuil, 1898, H. Löbbel, *Der Stifter des Karthäuserordens*, . *Bruno aus Köln*, Münster, 1899; Currier, *Religious Orders*, pp. 153-161. On the Eng. Carthusians consult: W. H. Brown, *Charterhouse, Past and Present: a Brief History*, London, 1876; W. D. Parish, *List of Carthusians, 1800-1879*, ib. 1880; T. Mozley, *Reminiscences of Towns, Villages, and Schools*, i. 376-436, ib. 1885; D. L. Hendriks, *London Charterhouse, Its Monks and Martyrs*, ib. 1889.

CARTWRIGHT, PETER: American Methodist; b. in Amherst County, Va., Sept. 1, 1785; d. near Pleasant Plains, Sangamon County, Ill., Sept. 25, 1872. His parents removed to Kentucky while he was a child, and there he was "converted" in 1801; he was licensed as an exhorter in 1802, and spent eight years in the old Western conference, four in the Kentucky, eight in the Tennessee, and forty-eight in the Illinois. He is said to have received more than 10,000 members into the Church, baptized more than 12,000 persons, and preached more than 15,000 sermons. He was known as the "backwoods preacher," and it is reported that when moral suasion proved ineffective with the rough characters with whom he had to deal he was able and willing to quiet them by physical force. He was once a member of the Illinois legislature and was defeated for Congress by Abraham Lincoln in 1846.

Bibliography: He wrote several tracts, an *Autobiography*, ed. W. P. Strickland, New York, 1856, and *Fifty Years a Presiding Elder*, ed. W. S. Hooper, Cincinnati, 1872.

CARTWRIGHT, THOMAS.

Leader of the Puritan Party (§ 1).
Controversial Writings (§ 2).
Minister in Antwerp (§ 3).
Again in England (§ 4).
Attitude Toward the Brownists (§ 5).

Thomas Cartwright, English Puritan and Presbyterian, was born in Hertfordshire 1535; d. at Warwick Dec. 27, 1603. He was matriculated as a sizar of Claire Hall, Nov., 1547, and as a scholar at St. John's College, Cambridge, Nov. 5, 1550. Being a Protestant and refusing to return to the Roman Church, he was debarred from the university during Mary's reign (1553-59). In 1560 he became a minor fellow of Trinity College, and on Apr. 6 of the same year a fellow of St. John's College; in Apr., 1562, a major fellow of Trinity College. In 1567 he took his bachelor's degree, and in 1569 was chosen Lady Margaret professor of divinity, and began to lecture on the Acts of the Apostles.

1. Leader of the Puritan Party. His lectures were exceedingly popular, and made a profound impression in favor of his distinctively Puritan views, but created a storm of opposition from the Prelatical party, headed by Dr. Whitgift. This conflict, under these two great champions, continued to grow more and more severe, and was continued by their successors in two great parties in the Church of England—the Presbyterian and the Prelatical. The Puritan platform is well stated in the six propositions which Cartwright delivered under his own hand to the vice-chancellor, the grounds of his persecution by the Prelatists:

1. That the names and functions of archbishops and archdeacons ought to be abolished. 2. That the offices of the lawful ministers of the Church, viz., bishops and deacons, ought to be reduced to their apostolical institution: bishops to preach the word of God, and pray, and deacons to be employed in taking care of the poor. 3. That the government of the Church ought not to be entrusted to bishop's chancellors, or the officials of archdeacons; but every church ought to be governed by its own ministers and presbyters. 4. That ministers ought not to be at large, but every one should have the charge of a particular congregation. 5. That no man ought to solicit, or to stand as a candidate for the ministry. 6. That ministers ought not to be created by the sole authority of the bishop, but to be openly and fairly chosen by the people.

Having been deprived of his professorship Dec. 11, 1570, and of his fellowship at Trinity College in Sept. 1571, Cartwright went to the Continent, and in Geneva conferred with Beza and other chiefs of the Reformed Churches. He was prevailed upon by his friends to return in Nov., 1572.

2. Controversial Writings. *An Admonition to Parliament for the Reformation of Church Discipline* had been issued by his friends John Field and Thomas Wilcox, for which they had been cast into prison. Cartwright espoused their cause, and issued *The Second Admonition, with an Humble Petition to Both Houses of Parliament for Relief Against Subscription*, 1572. Whitgift replied in *An Answere to a Certen Libell, Intituled An Admonition to the Parliament*, 1572. Cartwright rejoined in *A Replye to an Answere Made of M. Doctor Whitegifte Againste the Admonition to the Parliament*, 1573. This was a renewal of the old discussion on a larger scale, going to the roots of difference; Cartwright and the Puritans contending that the church government and the discipline, as well as the doctrine, must be reformed according to the Scriptures. The discussion took a wide range—as to the standard of church government, the choice of ministers, the offices of the Christian Church, clerical habits, bishops, archbishops, the authority of princes in matters ecclesiastical, confirmation, etc. Whitgift replied in *A Defense of the Ecclesiasticall Regiment in Englande Defaced by T. C. in his Replie againste D. Whitgifte*, 1574, and also *The Defense of the Answere to the Admonition, against the Replye of T. C.*, 1574, pp. 812, folio.

An order for Cartwright's apprehension was issued Dec. 11, 1574; but he fled to the Continent, and became minister of the English congregation of merchants at Antwerp and Middelburg. In 1576 he went to the isles of Jersey and Guernsey, aided the Puritans there in settling the discipline of their churches, later returning to Antwerp, where he preached for several years. While abroad, he wrote the *Second Replie of Thomas Cartwright Agaynst Maister Doctor Whitgiftes Second Answer Touching the Churche Discipline*, 1575, and also *The Rest of the Second Replie*, 1577. He, in 1574, prepared also a preface to the Latin work of William Travers, and translated it under the title *A Full and Plaine Declaration of Ecclesiasticall Discipline owt off the Word off God and off the Declininge off the Churche off England from the Same*, 1574, which still more embittered his foes. In 1583, at the solicitation of the Earl of Leicester, and Lord Treasurer Burleigh, and a large number of Puritan friends, he undertook to write a confutation of the Rhemish version of the Scriptures, which took him many years; but he was prevented by the ecclesiastical authorities of England from publishing his work. The year before his death, however, his *Answere to the Preface of the Rhemish Testament*, 1602, was issued; but the work itself, not until 1618, under the title *A Confutation of the Rhemists Translation, Glosses, and Annotations on the New Testament, so farre as they containe Manifest Impieties, Heresies, Idolatries, etc.*, fol., pp. lviii., 761, xviii., Leyden. In 1584 he was invited to the divinity chair in St. Andrews, Scotland, but declined.

3. Minister in Antwerp.

In 1585 Cartwright returned to England without the royal permission, and was apprehended by Bishop Aylmer of London and cast into prison, where he remained from April until June, when he was released through the influence of his powerful friends, and the Earl of Leicester appointed him master of a hospital which he had founded at Warwick. His preaching was opposed by his enemies, but without success, until 1590. During this time he went over a great part of Proverbs and Ecclesiastes. The latter was published in 1604 under the title *Metaphrasis et homiliæ in librum Solomonis, qui inscribitur Ecclesiastes*, 4to; the former in 1617, *Commentarii succincti et dilucidi in Proverbia Solomonis*, 4to. He is said to have been the first preacher in England who practised extempore prayer before sermon, although he usually employed forms of prayer. During this period the ecclesiastical conflicts waxed hotter and hotter. The Puritans had been making rapid progress. The first presbytery was organized at Wandsworth within the Church of England in 1572. Classes were rapidly organized in all parts of England, but secretly. In 1583 a rough draft of a book of discipline was drawn up by Thomas Cartwright and Walter Travers, and at an assembly held either at London or Cambridge it was resolved to put it in practise. It was revised at a national synod in London (1584), and referred to Mr. Travers "to be corrected and ordered by him." It was then passed around the various classes. It was adopted and subscribed by an assembly of all the classes of Warwickshire in 1588, and then by a provincial synod in Cambridge; and by 1590 the Directory had spread all over England, and was subscribed to by as many as 500 ministers. The episcopal party were greatly alarmed, and determined to arrest Cartwright with the other leaders and to destroy as large a number of copies of the *Holy Discipline* as possible. A few copies were, however, preserved, two copies in manuscript, one in the British Museum, another in Lambeth Palace, in Latin, entitled *Disciplina ecclesiæ sacra*. These were discussed and the Lambeth manuscript published by F. Paget in his *Introduction to the Fifth Book of Hooker's Treatise*, London, 1899, pp. 238 sqq. An edition in English with slight modifications was issued in 1644 by authority of the Long Parliament, entitled *A Directory of Church Government anciently contended for, and as farre as the Times would suffer, practised by the first Non-Conformists in the Daies of Queen Elizabeth. Found in the study of the most accomplished Divine, Mr. Thomas Cartwright, after his decease; and reserved to be published for such a time as this.*

4. Again in England.

The discussion between the Presbyterians and the Prelatists was complicated by the Brownist party and the Marprelate tracts (q.v.), which bitterly satirized the bishops. Cartwright took strong ground against the Brownists and their doctrine of separation, and opposed the Marprelate method of controversy; but it was the policy of the Prelatists to make the Puritans bear all the odium of the weaker and more obnoxious party. Manuscripts of Cartwright against the Brownists are preserved and lately published (see BROWNE, ROBERT). In May, 1590, he was summoned before the High Commission, and committed to the Fleet. He and his associates were confronted with thirty-one articles of charges, afterward increased to thirty-four, besides articles of inquiry. He was willing to reply to the charges, but refused to give testimony against his brethren. He was then summoned before the Star Chamber with Edmund Snape and others; but the case never reached an issue. Powerful friends worked in his behalf, and

5. Attitude Toward the Brownists.

he was finally released from prison in 1592, on the promise of quiet and peaceable behavior, in broken health. From 1595 to 1598 he lived on the island of Guernsey, and afterward at Warwick. To a bitter attack, he wrote *A Brief Apologie of Thomas Cartwright against all such slaunderous Accusations as it pleaseth Mr. Sutcliffe in his Severall pamphlets most injuriously to load him with, etc.*, 4to, pp. 28, 1596. In the main, the Presbyterian churches of Great Britain and America still stand by his principles.

Other works besides those mentioned in their historical connections were published after Cartwright's death by his disciples: *A Catechisme*, 1611; *A Treatise of the Christian Religion*, 1611 (anonymous), 2d ed., 4to, 1616, edited by William Bradshaw; *A Commentary on the Epistle to the Colossians*, 1612; *Harmonia Evangelica*, Amsterdam, 4to, 1627; *Commentaria Practica in totam Historiam Evangelicam*, 1630, 3 vols., 4to. See also PURITANS, PURITANISM, § 7

C. A. BRIGGS.

BIBLIOGRAPHY: C. H. and T. Cooper, *Athenæ Cantabrigienses*, ii. 360–366, London, 1861; B. Brook, *Lives of the Puritans*, ii. 136 sqq., 3 vols., ib. 1813; idem, *Memoir of the Life and Writings of Thomas Cartwright*, ib. 1845; F. L. Colvile, *Worthies of Warwickshire*, pp. 92–100, 878, ib. 1870; J. B. Mullinger, *History of the University of Cambridge*, ib. 1888; *DNB*, ix. 226–230.

CARUS, PAUL: Philosopher and student of comparative religion; b. at Ilsenburg (27 m. s.e. of Brunswick), Germany, July 18, 1852. He was educated at the universities of Tübingen, Greifswald, and Strasburg (Ph.D., Tübingen, 1876), and after teaching in two realgymnasia in Dresden and in the Royal Saxon Cadet Corps, he came to America in 1883, and since 1887 has been editor of *The Open Court*, Chicago, also editing *The Monist*, Chicago, since 1890. He has been secretary of the Religious Parliament Extension since its inception, and has shown an active interest in the knowledge and appreciation of ethnic religion by the West. He is also a member of the Leopoldina, Germany, the Press Club, Chicago, the American Oriental Society, and the American Association for the Advancement of Science. In theology he holds that religion is to be purified by scientific criticism and ultimately to be based upon the facts of experience. He has written, in addition to a large number of minor articles and contributions: *Helgi und Sigrun, ein episches Gedicht der nordischen Sage* (Dresden, 1880); *Metaphysik in Wissenschaft, Ethik und Religion* (1881); *Algenor, eine episch-lyrische Dichtung* (1882); *Gedichte* (1882); *Lieder eines Buddhisten* (1882); *Ursache, Grund und Zweck* (1883); *Aus dem Exil* (1884); *Monism and Meliorism* (New York, 1885); *Fundamental Problems* (Chicago, 1889); *The Ethical Problem* (1890); *The Soul of Man* (1891); *Homilies of Science* (1892); *Primer of Philosophy* (1893); *The Religion of Science* (1893); *Truth in Fiction* (1893); *The Gospel of Buddha, According to Old Records* (1894); *De rerum natura, philosophisches Gedicht* (1895); *Religion of Enlightenment* (1896); *Buddhism and its Christian Critics* (1897); *Chinese Philosophy* (1898); *Kant and Spencer: A Study of the Fallacies of Agnosticism* (1899); *Sacred Tunes for the Consecration of Life* (1899); *The Dawn of a New Era, and Other Essays On Religion* (1899); *Whence and Whither: An Inquiry into the Nature of the Soul, Its Origin and Its Destiny* (1900); *The History of the Devil and the Idea of Evil* (1900); *The Surd of Metaphysics* (1903); *Friedrich Schiller* (1905); *Magic Squares* (1906); and *The Rise of Man* (1906). His works of fiction include: *Karma: A Story of Early Buddhism* (Chicago, 1895); *Nirvana: A Story of Buddhist Psychology* (1897); *The Chief's Daughter: A Legend of Niagara* (1901); *The Crown of Thorns: A Story of the Time of Christ* (1901); and *Amitabha* (1906). He has also translated from Latin the *Eros and Psyche* of Apuleius (Chicago, 1900), and from German the *Xenions* of Goethe and Schiller (1896) and Kant's *Prolegomena to any Future Metaphysics* (1902), while he has edited and translated the Chinese texts of Lâo-tse's *Tao-Teh-King* (Chicago, 1898), as well as the *Kan Ying P'ien* (1906) and the *Yin Chih Wen* (1906).

CARY, ALICE: Poet and hymn-writer; b. on a farm 8 m. n. of Cincinnati Apr. 26, 1820; d. in New York Feb. 12, 1871. Her name is inseparably connected with that of her sister, **Phœbe**, b. Sept. 4, 1824; d. at Newport, R. I., July 31, 1871. Both began to write verses early and published jointly a volume of *Poems* in 1850. In 1850–51 they removed to New York, where they supported themselves by literary work and gathered a wide circle of friends. Alice was the more productive writer and published stories and novels as well as poems. *Ballads, Lyrics, and Hymns* (Boston, 1865) is her most important volume of verse. Phœbe published independently *Poems and Parodies* (1854) and *Poems of Faith, Hope, and Love* (1868); with Dr. Charles F. Deems she compiled *Hymns for all Christians* (1869). The poems of both sisters are collected in the "Household Edition" (Boston, 1882) and *Early and Late Poems* (1887). The most familiar of their hymns is Phœbe's "One sweetly solemn thought comes to me o'er and o'er."

BIBLIOGRAPHY: Mary Clemmer Ames, *Memorial of Alice and Phœbe Cary*, New York, 1872; S. W. Duffield, *English Hymns*, pp. 447–449, ib. 1886; Julian, *Hymnology*, p. 214.

CARY, GEORGE LOVELL: Unitarian; b. at Medway, Mass., May 10, 1830. He was educated at Harvard College (B.A., 1852), and was acting professor of Greek in Antioch College, Yellow Springs, O., in 1856–57, being appointed full professor of Greek and Latin in the following year and serving in this capacity until 1862. In the latter year he was made professor of New Testament language and literature in Meadville Theological School, where he remained until 1902, when he became professor emeritus. He was also acting president of the institution in 1890–91 and president in 1891–1902. His theological position is, in general, that of modern Unitarianism. He has written: *An Introduction to the Greek of the New Testament* (Andover, Mass., 1878) and *The Synoptic Gospels, Together with a Chapter on the Text-Criticism of the New Testament* (New York, 1900).

CARY, HENRY FRANCIS: Translator of Dante; b. at Gibraltar Dec. 6, 1772; d. in London Aug. 14, 1844. He studied at Christ Church, Oxford (M.A., 1796), took orders, and became vicar of Abbot's Bromley, Staffordshire. In 1800 he removed to Kingsbury, Warwickshire, and after 1807 lived in London. He was assistant keeper of printed books in the British Museum, 1826–37. His translation of Dante was begun in May, 1800, and finished twelve years later; the *Inferno* was published in 1805 and the completed work in 1814. It attracted little attention at first, but was commended by Coleridge in his lectures in 1818, and Southey afterward pronounced it "one of the most masterly productions in modern times." Four editions were issued during Cary's life, and it still remains the standard translation in English blank verse.

Bibliography: Henry Cary, *Memoir of Rev. H. F. Cary*, 2 vols., London, 1847; *DNB*, ix. 242–244.

CARYL, JOSEPH: English Independent clergyman; b. in London 1602; d. there Mar. 10, 1673. He studied at Exeter College, Oxford, and became preacher at Lincoln's Inn; was appointed minister of St. Magnus' Church near London Bridge, 1645; ejected by the Act of Uniformity, 1662, but gathered a new congregation and continued to preach in the same neighborhood. He was a member of the Westminster Assembly and one of the triers for the approbation of ministers in 1653. He is remembered for his *Exposition with Practical Observations on the Book of Job* (12 vols., 4to, London, 1664–66; 2d ed., 2 vols., folio, 1676–77; abridged ed. by Berrie, Edinburgh, 1836).

CASALI DEL DRAGO, cā-sā'lī del drā'gō, **GIOVANNI,** jō-vān'nī, **BAPTISTA,** bāp-tis'tā: Cardinal; b. at Rome Jan. 30, 1838. He was educated at the Roman Seminary, and was ordained to the priesthood in 1860. Six years later he was appointed chamberlain by Pope Pius IX., and was then canon successively of the Lateran (1867–71) and of St. Peter's (1871–78). In 1878 he became domestic prelate, and in 1895 Leo XIII. created him titular Latin patriarch of Constantinople. He received the cardinal's hat in 1899, being created cardinal priest with the title of Santa Maria della Victoria. Died at Rome Mar. 17, 1908.

CASAÑAS Y PAGÈS, cā-sā'nyās ī pā-нēz', **SALVATORE,** sāl"vā-tō'rē: Cardinal, b. at Barcelona, Spain, Sept. 5, 1834. He was educated in his native city, and in 1879 was consecrated titular bishop of Keramus and seven months later became bishop of Urgel. In 1901 he was translated to Barcelona, and in 1895 created cardinal priest of Santi Quirico e Giulitta. Died Sept. 27, 1908.

CASAS, BARTOLOMÉ DE LAS. See Las Casas.

CASAUBON, ca-sō'bon *or* cā"zō"bōn', **ISAAC:** Scholar; b. in Geneva Feb. 18, 1559; d. in London July 12, 1614. His father was a poor Huguenot preacher, who could give his son little education, nevertheless he came to be considered the most learned man in Europe after Joseph Scaliger. He was professor of Greek at Geneva, 1582–96, at Montpellier, 1596–99; in 1600 he went to Paris, where he might have been professor in the university if he had embraced Roman Catholicism; this, however, he refused to do, although he offended the rigid Calvinists by denying their extreme positions. He was given a pension by Henry IV. (1600), and in 1604 became sublibrarian of the royal library. In 1610 he went to England, where he was well received by King James and the Anglican bishops and was made prebendary of Canterbury and Westminster. His works belong for the most part to the field of classical scholarship, but he edited a Greek New Testament (Geneva, 1587), and published some minor pamphlets of theological interest; his criticism of the *Annales* of Baronius, begun at the request of King James, was left unfinished. His letters (in Latin), with life, were published by D'Almeloveen (Rotterdam, 1709); his diary, *Ephemerides*, ed. Russell, was printed at Oxford, 1850.

Bibliography: Mark Pattison, *Isaac Casaubon*, London, 1875, 2d ed., by Nettleship, 1892.

CASELIUS, cā-sē'li-us, **JOHANNES,** yō-hān'es: German scholar; b. at Göttingen 1533; d. at Helmstadt Apr. 9, 1613. He belonged to the Dutch family of Chessel, which during the Reformation period had emigrated on account of its faith. His father, Matthias Bracht von Chessel, found a refuge at Göttingen and became a teacher there. Johannes studied at Wittenberg under Melanchthon and at Leipsic under Joachim Camerarius. Under their guidance he became one of the most distinguished humanists of Germany; he was made a doctor of law at Pisa in 1566, and was ennobled in 1567 by the emperor Maximilian II. From 1563 to 1589 he labored at Rostock and then accepted a call to Helmstädt. He enjoyed there the favor of his prince, Duke Henry Julius of Brunswick, and the fame of his learning made him a kind of European celebrity. But the orthodox theologians in the university, who opposed Melanchthonianism, soon attacked Caselius. The leader of the orthodox was Professor Daniel Hoffmann (q.v.), who considered all use of reason and philosophy in theology as dangerous, because the revealed truth is injured thereby. In this and similar tendencies Caselius saw the approach of a new barbarism, and he was not far wrong. He had the encouragement of a few bright pupils, including the young Georg Calixtus (q.v.), and comforting messages came to him from friends abroad. But unfortunately his material circumstances became more and more wretched, and for this reason his life ended in discord and darkness. In the barbarism which came over Germany with the Thirty Years' War his numerous writings, distinguished by spirited contents and elegant form, were soon almost forgotten. As far as they are printed, they can only be found in larger libraries. They refer to Greek authors, ancient grammar, hermeneutics, and rhetoric, as well as to pedagogics and political science. Caselius was the first to separate political science from the Roman jurisprudence and raise it to a distinct discipline.

Paul Tschackert.

Bibliography: For the letters consult: J. a Draesfeld, *Opus epistolicum I. Caselii*, Frankfort, 1687; *Commer-*

cium literarum clarorum virorum e museo R. A. Noltenii, Bremen, 1737. See CALIXTUS. Consult: E. L. T. Henke, *Calixtus' Briefwechsel*, Halle, 1833; idem, *G. Calixtus und seine Zeit*, vol. i., Halle, 1850; *ADB*, iv. 40 sqq. F. Koldewey has projected a monograph on Casclius, for which he has access to the best sources.

CASPARI, cās'pā-rî, **CARL PAUL:** Norwegian Lutheran; b. at Dessau Feb. 8, 1814; d. at Christiania Apr. 11, 1892. He was of Jewish parentage and was brought up in the faith of his fathers. From 1834 to 1838 he studied at Leipsic, where he acquired a knowledge of Arabic and Persian under Fleischer. Partly from the influence of fellow students, among whom was Franz Delitzsch, he adopted Christianity and was baptized in 1838. His Jewish training naturally fitted him for work in Old Testament exegesis, and he spent two years at Berlin under Hengstenberg. In 1842 he became doctor of philosophy at Leipsic, and in 1847 he accepted a call to Christiania, where he remained from choice the rest of his life, declining calls to Rostock in 1850, to Dorpat in 1856, and to Erlangen in 1857 and again in 1867. His linguistic ability enabled him speedily to master the Norwegian language, so that he could begin lectures in less than a year. He was made full professor in 1857. In his university work Caspari interpreted various books of the Old and New Testaments and treated Old Testament introduction. His lectures were inspiring, thorough, earnest, and bore evidence of a living Christian faith. In his exegesis and apologetics he followed Hengstenberg, and he remained to the end an opponent of modern critical scholarship. But his work and interest were not confined to the Old Testament field. In 1825 a Danish preacher, Nicolai Frederik Severin Grundtvig (q.v.), propounded peculiar views, viz., that the baptismal formula, the renunciation, the Lord's Prayer, and the words of the Lord's Supper come directly from the Lord, have never been changed, and therefore stand above the Scriptures. The view found adherents in Denmark and Norway, and fear was felt that the formal principle of the Lutheran Church was in danger. Caspari undertook a careful investigation of the questions connected with the baptismal formula and its history and thus was led on to extensive ecclesiastico-patristic studies. He published a long series of articles and books as the result, most of them in the Norwegian language. Under the auspices of the Norwegian Bible Society he assisted in making a new translation of the Old Testament, which was completed for the seventy-fifth anniversary of the Society, May 26, 1891; at the time of his death he was working on the New Testament (see BIBLE VERSIONS, B, XV., § 2). He was a member of the central committee of the Bible Society, president of the Norwegian mission among the Jews, and belonged to numerous learned and honorary societies.

His most important publications were: A commentary on Obadiah (in Delitzsch and Caspari's *Exegetisches Handbuch zu den Propheten des Alten Bundes*, Leipsic, 1842); *Grammatica Arabica* (2 parts, Leipsic, 1844–48; 5th Germ. ed., by August Müller, Halle, 1887; Eng. ed., by W. Wright, London, 1859–62, 1874–75; by W. Robertson Smith and M. J. de Goeje, Cambridge, 1896–98); *Beiträge zur Einleitung in das Buch Jesaia und zur Geschichte der jesaianischen Zeit* (vol. ii. of Delitzsch and Caspari's *Biblisch-theologische und apologetisch-kritische Studien*, Berlin, 1848); *Ueber den syrisch-ephraimitischen Krieg unter Jotham und Ahas* (Christiania, 1849); *Ueber Micha den Morasthiten und seine prophetische Schrift* (2 parts, 1851–52); *Ungedruckte, unbeachtete und wenig beachtete Quellen zur Geschichte des Taufsymbols und der Glaubensregel* (3 vols., 1866–75); *Zur Einführung in das Buch Daniel* (Leipsic, 1869); *Alte und neue Quellen zur Geschichte des Taufsymbols und der Glaubensregel* (Christiania, 1879); an edition of Martin of Bracara's *De correctione rusticorum* (1883); *Kirchenhistorische Anecdota nebst neuen Ausgaben patristischer und kirchlich-mittelalterlicher Schriften* (1883); *Eine Augustin fälschlich beigelegte Homilia de sacrilegiis* (1886); *Briefe, Abhandlungen und Predigten aus den zwei letzten Jahrhunderten des kirchlichen Alterthums und dem Anfang des Mittelalters* (1891); *Das Buch Hiob in Hieronymus's Uebersetzung* (Christiania, 1893). *Der Glaube an der Trinität Gottes in der Kirche des ersten christlichen Jahrhunderts nachgewiesen* (Leipsic, 1894). In Norwegian he published a translation of the Book of Concord (Christiania, 1861); an essay upon the Wandering Jew (1862); a commentary on the first six chapters of Isaiah (1867); a historical essay on the confession of faith at baptism (1871); on Abraham's trial and Jacob's wrestling with God (1871); on Abraham's call and meeting with Melchizedek (1872); a volume of Bible essays (1884); etc. With his friend G. C. Johnson (q.v.) he established in 1857 the *Theologisk Tidskrift for den evangelisk-lutherske Kirke i Norge*, of which a volume appeared annually till shortly before Caspari's death. Most of the articles were written by the editors, and in this and other periodicals a large number of Caspari's writings were originally published.

J. BELSHEIM.

CASPARI, WALTER: German theologian; b. at Sommerhausen (a village of Lower Franconia) June 19, 1847. He was educated at the universities of Munich, Erlangen, and Leipsic from 1864 to 1868, after which he was pastor in Memmingen and Ansbach until 1885. In the last-named year he was appointed associate professor of practical theology, pedagogics, and dogmatics, and university preacher at Erlangen, and became full professor two years later. In addition to contributions to the Hauck-Herzog *RE* and briefer studies, he has written: *Ausgewählte Lesestücke der ausländischen Literatur* (Munich, 1877); *Die epistolischen Perikopen nach der Auswahl von Dr. Thomasius exegetisch-homiletisch erklärt* (Erlangen, 1883); *Die evangelische Konfirmation* (Leipsic, 1890); and *Die geschichtliche Grundlage des gegenwärtigen evangelischen Gemeindelebens* (1894).

CAS-SAN'DER, GEORGIUS: Roman Catholic theologian; b. at Pitthem (15 m. s.e. of Bruges) Aug. 21, 1513; d. in Cologne Feb. 3, 1566. He lectured at Bruges and Ghent on antiquities, theology, and canon law, but retired to Cologne in 1549 and devoted himself to study. The Duke of Cleves employed him in an effort to win back the Anabaptists in Duisburg, and still more important was the charge of the Emperor Ferdinand I., who endeavored to unite the Catholics and Protestants in his territories. Cassander had already published anonymously an irenic writing, *De officio pii ac publicæ tranquillitatis vere amantis viri in hoc religionis dissidio* (Basel, 1561), which elicited a sharp rejoinder from Calvin. Strict Roman Catholics also disliked the work, and it was placed on the Lisbon Index in 1581. At the emperor's request Cassander prepared a *Consultatio de articulis inter Catholicos et Protestantes controversis*, which he presented to Maximilian II. in 1564, Ferdinand having died in the mean time (published at Lyons,

1608; ed. H. Grotius, Amsterdam, 1642). To bring about a union Cassander starts with the "consensus" of the most ancient church, expressed in the Apostles' Creed. Though the Holy Scripture is to be authoritative, he wishes to maintain the importance of tradition, especially of the great Church Fathers (down to Gregory I.); only a difference which concerns the position to Christ himself, not "opiniones" or "ritus," may become a cause of division, but the bond of "caritas" is by no means to be violated. In the doctrine of original sin, the Lord's Supper, and justification, he tries to mediate. He is even inclined to give the cup to the laity, and he will also admit of the marriage of the clergy as a makeshift. In the other controversial questions (worship of saints, monasticism, indulgences, papal power) he tries to soften the difficulties and do away with exaggerations. A recantation before his death has been imputed to him. It is hard to save him for the Roman Catholics, however, and still less can he be claimed by the Protestant side. Seckendorf is correct when he says in the *Commentarius* (Frankfort and Leipsic, 1680, p. 347): "Georgius Cassander, a good theologian, to be sure not a Lutheran, but a lover of truth." K. Benrath.

Bibliography: The *Opera* appeared Paris, 1616. Consult F. H. Reusch, *Index der verbotenen Bücher*, i. 361 sqq., Bonn, 1883.

CASSEL, CONFERENCE OF: A religious colloquy at Cassel, July 1–9, 1661, between certain Reformed theologians from the University of Marburg and Lutheran theologians from the University of Rinteln, arranged by Landgrave William VI. of Hesse. The aim was to bring about agreement or at least mutual toleration. They succeeded in finding some not unessential points, in the doctrines of the Lord's Supper, predestination, the person of Christ, and baptism, on which both parties agreed. It was resolved, moreover, not to revile one another in the future because of the differences still remaining, to free sermons from the burden of confessional polemics, and in any case no longer to attack an opponent personally. But this peaceful agreement did not meet with a kind reception in the rest of Germany. Frederick William, the Great Elector of Brandenburg, was, to be sure, an exception, and the Reformed party in France and Holland were inclined to come halfway; but the Lutherans rejected the arrangement absolutely. The union became the subject of lively literary combats, and the final result was a further intensification of confessional differences. Carl Mirbt.

Bibliography: E. L. T. Henke, *Das Unionskolloquium zu Cassel 1661*, Marburg, 1861; H. Heppe, *Kirchengeschichte beider Hessen*, vol. ii., ib. 1876; H. Landwehr, *Die Kirchenpolitik Friedrich Wilhelms*, Berlin, 1894.

CASSEL, PAULUS STEPHANUS (SELIG): German Protestant theologian; b. at Gross-Glogau (55 m. n.w. of Breslau), Silesia, Feb. 27, 1821; d. at Friedenau, a suburb of Berlin, Dec. 23, 1892. He was of Jewish parentage, studied history at Berlin, and from 1850 to 1856 edited a newspaper at Erfurt. On May 28, 1855, he was baptized at Büssleben near Erfurt, and the next year became librarian of the Royal Library at Erfurt. In 1859 he settled at Berlin, where he acted as tutor and devoted himself to literary work. In 1866–67 he was a member of the Prussian Parliament, then he entered the service of the London Jewish Missionary Society and became its minister at the Christuskirche in Berlin. In 1891 he resigned his position and died shortly afterward. Cassel was a most prolific writer, and his article on the history of the Jews from the destruction of Jerusalem by Titus to the year 1847, written while still a Jew for Ersch and Gruber's *Allgemeine Encyklopädie*, sect. II., vol. xxvii., pp. 1–238, Leipsic, 1850, is still valuable. By public lectures delivered in different cities of Germany, he tried to influence the educated Jews in favor of Christianity, and baptized many. He also combated anti-Semitism. Other works by him include the commentaries on Judges and Ruth in Lange's Commentary; also *Weihnachten, Ursprünge, Bräuche und Aberglauben* (Berlin, 1862); *Altkirchlicher Festkalender nach Ursprüngen und Bräuchen* (1869); *Vom Wege nach Damaskus* (Gotha, 1872); *Die Gerechtigkeit aus dem Glauben* (1874); *Das Buch Esther* (Berlin, 1878); and *Die Symbolik des Blutes* (1882). (H. L. Strack.)

CASSETTA, cās-set'tā, FRANCESCO DI PAOLA: Italian cardinal; b. at Rome Aug. 12, 1841. He was educated at the Roman Seminary and was ordained to the priesthood in 1865. In 1884 he was consecrated titular bishop of Amiata and appointed canon of Santa Maria Maggiore, and three years later became titular archbishop of Nicomedia and grand almoner to Pope Leo XIII. As titular patriarch of Antioch he was nominated vicegerent of Rome, in which capacity he acted as the deputy of the cardinal vicar. He was created cardinal priest of Santi Vito, Modesto e Crescenzia in 1899, and is titular bishop of Sabina, perpetual abbot of Farfa, apostolic visitor of the Hospice of the Catechumens, commissioner for the apostolic visitation of the Italian dioceses, and a member of the Congregations of Bishops and Regulars, the Council, the Index, the Consistory, the Propaganda, the Propaganda for the Oriental Rite, and Indulgences.

CASSIAN: A martyr whose death is described by Prudentius in the ninth hymn of his *Peristephanon*. The poet says that he saw the martyr's grave at Forum Cornelii (Imola), with a picture of him, and that the custodian related that Cassian had been stabbed by his own pupils with their styli and otherwise cruelly handled. Gregory of Tours gives substantially the same account. The *Martyrologium Hieronymianum* names Aug. 11 as the day of his death. The fact of his martyrdom at Forum Cornelii need not be doubted, but the manner related by Prudentius is improbable, and it is impossible to fix the date. (A. Hauck.)

CASSIANUS, cas"si-ā'nus, JOHANNES: Monk of the fifth century and the real founder of Semi-Pelagianism (q.v.); b. probably in Provence c. 360; d. at Marseilles c. 435. He received a thorough education, and then visited the East with an older friend named Germanus. At Bethlehem he entered a cloister, but the desire to know the famous Egyptian hermits led him and Germanus to Egypt, where they remained seven years, after which they revisited Bethlehem, but soon returned to Egypt. Thence Cassianus went to Constantinople, where he became the pupil of John Chrysostom, who ordained him deacon. The exile of Chrysostom in 403, however, obliged Cassianus and Germanus to take refuge with Innocent I. When Cassianus was ordained priest and returned home is unknown, and the fate of Germanus is equally uncertain. At Marseilles Cassianus founded two cloisters, one for monks and the other for nuns, and seems to have died shortly after completing his polemic against Nestorius.

His earliest work, written before 426, was entitled *De institutis cœnobiorum et de octo principalium vitiorum remediis libri duodecim*, and was composed at the request of Castor, bishop of Apta Julia, who wished to introduce the Oriental and especially the Egyptian rules into the monastery which he had founded. His second work was his *Collationes viginti-quattuor*, completed before 429. Both were widely spread throughout the Occident; Benedict of Nursia commanded that they be read to the monks in the refectory; Cassiodorus esteemed them highly, although he warned his monks against the heretical views of the author concerning the freedom of the will; and Gregory of Tours mentions them as used, together with other Oriental rules, in the monastery of St. Yririx. A brief compend was made by the friend of Cassianus, Eucherius, bishop of Lyons, which served as a source for the *Concordia regularum* of Benedict of Aniane.

The thirteenth collation of Cassianus is important in the controversy on Augustine's doctrine of grace. Against his enemies, who were centered in Marseilles, the latter addressed, shortly before his death, his *De prædestinatione sanctorum* and *De dono perseverantiæ*, his chief opponent being Cassianus, who in this collation had enunciated the doctrine called Semi-Pelagianism in the Middle Ages, although it might more properly be termed Semi-Augustinianism, since Cassianus separated himself sharply from Pelagius and branded him as a heretic, while he felt himself in complete harmony with Augustine. His Greek training, however, rendered it impossible for him to accept Augustine's doctrine of unconditional predestination, particular grace, and the absolute denial of the freedom of the will. Cassianus, on the other hand, recognized the necessity of divine grace throughout the process of salvation, while postulating the existence of free will as a necessary condition for the operation of grace, and asserting that God never destroys the freedom of the will, even in such an extraordinary case as the conversion of Paul. He regarded it as a religious axiom, therefore, that salvation through Christ is not restricted to a small number of the elect, but is intended for all. This non-Augustinian concept of the process of salvation conditions Cassianus's view of original sin. He believed that the fall of Adam had brought destruction on the whole human race, although it still retained the power to seek goodness in virtue of its original state of immortality, wisdom, and complete freedom of the will. After the victory of a modified Augustinianism at the Synod of Orange in 529, the doctrines of Cassianus were generally regarded as heterodox, although this did not injure his fame as a monastic author, and in southern Gaul he was officially honored as a saint. See SEMI-PELAGIANISM.

In the latter part of his life Cassianus became involved in the Nestorian controversy, and at the request of the archdeacon Leo (later Pope Leo I.) wrote his *De incarnatione Domini contra Nestorium libri septem*, the date being subsequent to the letters written by Nestorius to Pope Celestine in 430. The work lacks the importance which it would otherwise possess as the only extensive contribution of an Occidental to the Nestorian controversy, through its restriction to personal attacks on the opponent of its author and a complete omission of positive and independent Christological statements. Cassianus sought to prove that the divinity of Christ had existed from eternity and had never been renounced, so that Mary must be called not merely the mother of Christ, as Nestorius taught, but the mother of God. The work is especially valuable as showing the close sympathy of the interests and methods of Nestorianism and Pelagianism, while Cassianus, following the Gallic monk Leporius, who had renounced Pelagianism in 426, held that Christ possessed in a single person the two coexistent substances of God and man.

(G. GRÜTZMACHER.)

BIBLIOGRAPHY: The *Opera*, ed. A. Gazäus, were published at Douai, 1616, reprinted in *MPL*, xlix., l.; best ed. by M. Petschenig, in *CSEL*, 2 vols., 1886–88. An Eng. transl., with a well-written *Life*, is contained in *NPNF*, 2d series, xi. 163 sqq. Consult: G. F. Wiggers, *Pragmatische Darstellung des Augustinismus und Pelagianismus*, ii. 7–153, Berlin, 1833; A. Harnack, *Dogmengeschichte*, iii. 154, Tübingen, 1897, Eng. transl., v. 246 sqq., 253 sqq., Boston, 1899; A. Hoch, *Die Lehre des J. Cassians von Natur und Gnade*, Freiburg, 1895.

CASSIANUS, JULIUS. See DOCETISM; ENCRATITES.

CASSIODORUS, cas"si-o-dō'rus **(CASSIODORIUS), MAGNUS AURELIUS:** Roman historian, statesman, and monk; b. at Scylacium (the modern Squillace, on the gulf of the same name, 40 m. s.s.e. of Cosenza), Calabria, c. 480; d. in the monastery of Vivarium, near Scylacium, c. 570. Owing to the esteem in which his father was held by Theodoric, a public career was early open to him; and he pursued it until he had reached the highest dignities under the Ostrogothic monarchs. He stood in close personal relations with Theodoric, with whose efforts to bring about a fusion between the Germanic and Roman elements among his subjects he thoroughly sympathized. About 540 he retired from public life to the peace and quiet of the monastery founded by him on his own estates at Vivarium. Here he devoted himself to literary work, of which he had already made a beginning amidst his political activity, and pursued it zealously until his ninety-third year. He insisted on the duty of intellectual labor for his monks, helped their studies by every means in his power, of which his own example was not the least, and so contributed largely to the establishment of the tradition which made the monasteries, especially of the Benedictine order, the homes of learning throughout the dark ages.

His literary work, like his life, falls into two periods. To the first belong a consular chronicle written in 519; twelve books of Gothic history, composed in the spirit of the policy of fusion already referred to, known to us only in the recast version of Jordanes, *De origine actibusque Getarum* (the work of Cassiodorus seems to have borne the same title); panegyrics on the kings and queens of the Goths, of which only dubious fragments remain; a collection (made about 538) of rescripts composed by him during his long and varied official life, and formulas of appointment to a great variety of offices, in twelve books, under the title *Variæ;* a small philosophical work, *De anima*, written immediately after the completion of the *Variæ*, at the request of friends, whose questions about the soul he answers, following Claudianus Mamertus and Augustine. The last-named work forms a sort of transition to those of the second period. The most important of these, composed probably in 544, is the *Institutiones divinarum et sæcularium litterarum* (or better *lectionum*). The first book is devoted to spiritual learning, the second to secular; and both together form the first part of a complete course of instruction designed by Cassiodorus for the Western clergy, and especially for his own monks. The first book is only an introduction to the study of theology, explaining the most important preliminary knowledge required and the literary helps at the student's command for his further education; the second gives brief compendiums of various branches of secular learning. To this the last work of Cassiodorus, *De orthographia*, forms a supplement. Another voluminous theological work, begun before the *Institutiones* but finished long after, was a full explanation of the Psalms in their threefold aspect, spiritual, historical, and symbolic. He wrote other exegetical works, of which his *Complexiones in epistolas et acta apostolorum et apocalypsin* is still extant. Of much greater value to posterity is his *Historia ecclesiastica tripartita* in twelve books, composed of extracts from the Greek historians Socrates, Sozomen, and Theodoret, whose works he had translated by Epiphanius. It is in no sense an original work, and is put together in a patchwork fashion; but it filled up a great gap in the general Western knowledge of church history, and, incomplete as it is, was the principal handbook used in the Middle Ages for its period.

(A. Hauck.)

Bibliography: The *Variæ* and *Orationum reliquiæ*, with introduction, are in *MGH, Auct. ant.*, xii. 1–385, 459–484; the *Variæ* are also in *MPL*, lxix. *The Letters of Cassiodorus, a Condensed Transl. of the Variæ*, ed. T. Hodgkin, appeared London, 1886. Consult: A. Olleris, *Cassiodore, conservateur des livres de l'antiquité latine*, Paris, 1841; R. Köpke, *Deutsche Forschungen. Die Anfänge des Königtums*, pp. 78–94, Berlin, 1859; A. Thorbecke, *Cassiodorus Senator*, Heidelberg, 1867; A. Franz, *M. Aurelius Cassiodorius Senator*, Breslau, 1872; H. von Sybel, *Entstehung des deutschen Königtums*, pp. 184–208, Frankfort, 1881; A. Ebert, *Geschichte der Literatur des Mittelalters*, i. 198, 498–514, Leipsic, 1889. For further literature consult Potthast, *Wegweiser*, p. 198.

CASSOCK. See Vestments and Insignia, Ecclesiastical.

CASTELL, EDMUND: English Orientalist; b. at East Hatley (12 m. s.w. of Cambridge), Cambridgeshire, 1606; d. at Higham Gobion (10 m. s.s.e. of Bedford), Bedfordshire, 1685. He studied at Emmanuel and St. John's colleges, Cambridge (B.A., 1625; M.A., 1628; B.D., 1635; D.D., 1661). He assisted Walton on his *Polyglot* (1657), contributing the editions of the Samaritan, Syriac, Arabic, and Ethiopic versions, and other (unacknowledged) portions, and also spent freely of his own fortune for the work. In 1669 he brought out in two volumes, folio, at London, his *Lexicon Heptaglotton, Hebraicum, Chaldaicum, Syriacum, Samaritanum, Æthiopicum, Arabicum, conjunctim; et Persicum separatim*, specially prepared to supplement the *Polyglot*. This work was the result of eighteen years of the most unremitting labor, cost the author £12,000, and left him ruined in fortune and health. His work was enthusiastically received on the Continent, but neglected in England. Late in life he received some favor from the king, was appointed chaplain in ordinary in 1666, prebendary of Canterbury and professor of Arabic at Cambridge 1667, and was successively vicar of Hatfield Peverell, Essex; rector of Wodeham Walter, Essex; and rector of Higham Gobion.

Bibliography: A. à Wood, *Athenæ Oxonienses*, ed. P. Bliss, iii. 883, 4 vols., London, 1813–20; twenty-three of his letters appear in J. Lightfoot, *Whole Works*, ed. J. R. Pitman, 13 vols., London, 1822–25. Consult *DNB*, ix. 271–272.

CASTELLIO(N), SEBASTIANUS (SEBASTIEN CHÂTEILLON): French Reformer; b. at Saint-Martin du Fresne (30 m. w. of Geneva) 1515; d. at Basel Dec. 29, 1563. He pursued his studies under difficult circumstances until he became tutor to three young noblemen. In 1540 he went to Strasburg, lived in Calvin's house, and accompanied him to Geneva, where on Calvin's recommendation he became rector of the high school. But disagreement soon arose between him and the great Reformer, Castellio holding views of his own concerning election and Christ's descent into hell, and regarding the Song of Solomon as an erotic poem which should be excluded from the canon. He left Geneva in 1544 and settled in Basel, where he lived in great poverty till 1552, when he was appointed professor of Greek literature. His first publication was *Dialogi sacri* (Geneva, 1543; Eng. transl., *The History of the Bible, collected into 119 dialogues*, London, 1715; again under the title, *Youth's Scripture Remembrancer*, 1743), much used as a school-book. In 1551 he published in Basel his chief work, an elegant annotated Latin translation of the Bible, which he dedicated to Edward VI. of England (12th ed., Leipsic, 1778). The notes gave offense, as they betrayed skepticism as to the attainability of religious truth, and the dedication, a noble plea for religious toleration, was unacceptable to the age. In 1555 he published at Basel a complete French translation of the Bible, with a dedication to Henry II. of France. He was violently attacked by Calvin and Beza because of his criticism of their conduct in burning Servetus, but defended himself vigorously in his *De hæreticis* (Basel, 1554); and in *Contra libellum Calvini, in quo ostendere conatur hæreticos jure gladii coercendos esse*. Calvin's influence suppressed the latter, and it was not published till 1612.

Bibliography: F. Buisson, *Séb. Castellion, sa vie et son œuvre*, 2 vols., Paris, 1892 (i., p. xvii. gives literature concerning him; ii. 341 sqq. gives list of his writings); C. Jarrin, *Deux oubliés; Séb. Castellion, Léonard Racle*, Paris, 1895.

CASTLE, NICHOLAS: United Brethren; b. at Bristol, Ind., Oct. 4, 1837; entered the ministry, 1857; elected bishop, 1877; emeritus, 1905.

CASTOR, SAINT: According to legend, a companion of St. Maximin of Treves, who had an influential career as a missionary and ascetic on the lower Moselle. His relics are said to have been miraculously discovered under Bishop Weomad (d. 791). They were first placed at Carden on the Moselle; but in 836 a part of them was translated to Coblenz (of which city Castor has since been known as the patron) by Archbishop Hetti of Treves, and preserved in the minster founded there by him. (A. Hauck.)

CASUISTRY: The name of a special form of discipline, or branch of ethics, constituting a somewhat elaborated scheme of doctrine concerning proper moral action in single and concrete instances. The evaluation of this kind of activity evolves itself generally as consequence of a lawful and rightful apprehension of the moral walk, whereby we accentuate external conduct according to definite prescriptive rules. Coordinately with a fundamental moral code for this action, certain ethical norms with legal adjuncts were in practical operation so far back as the Jewish "scribes and Pharisees." Jesus came forward in sharpest contrast with this casuistical doctrine of morals.

Teaching of Jesus and Paul.

As he suffered his disciples to become derivately participant of his integral community with God, he kindled in them a love to God, which was to verify itself in love to men. To this love he brought back the conception of the Law fulfilled; and accordingly he teaches in the place of casuistry a direction of life spontaneously individual. Even where he appears himself to set up casuistical requirements (Matt. v. 21 sqq., vi. 1 sqq., xxii. 17 sqq.; Luke xiv. 3 sqq.) it is always expressly in order to lay emphasis upon the spiritual interpretation of the Law, over against legalizing constructiveness. These thoughts were but dialectically expanded through Paul's epistles, inasmuch as he teaches that faith in God's grace in Christ has its operation in the love which fulfils the requirements of God's will in agreement with the spirit of the Law. Yet he knew that even though faith and love be present, still the certainty is not immediately vouchsafed as to what is right in this or that particular instance (Rom. xii. 2; Phil. i. 9, 10). He, therefore, dwells on a persistently proving examination of God's will, and gives corresponding instructions to his own congregations; which instructions now and then through their touching upon particular conditions have a certain casuistic stamp about them (cf. I Cor. vii. 8, 10); but, in distinction from every form of casuistic legalism by means of morally postulated direction, they seek to develop the proper moral consciousness of the congregations themselves.

But even early in the postapostolic age, the tendency set in, coordinately with a one-sided intellectualizing conception of the faith, to regulate by outward legalism the moral life as thus robbed of its religious mainspring; and the same tendency involved the casuistical treatment of ethics. Still further was this disposition fostered in Western theology through the influence of Stoicism, and in part through the legalizing development of ecclesiastical doctrine. It shows itself even in Augustine, despite his obliteration of ethics, and continued to be characteristic of the entire Western Catholic ethical system. What ministered still more widely to the development of casuistry was the very early and momentously

Development of Casuistry.

elaborated ecclesiastical institution of penance, with the infliction of ecclesiastical penalties for individual sins. The appertaining customary rules of the ancient forms of procedure and the relevantly codified decrees of separate synods were brought together, supplemented, and arranged by the compilers. There thus arose the definite manuals on penance for the use of confessors; among which the best known were those attributed to Archbishop Theodore of Canterbury (d. 690) and the Venerable Bede (d. 735). A still greater amplification of casuistry was promoted by the entire method of the scholastic ethics, with its subtle disputations; by the influence of the canonical repetition; and by the universally obligatory institution of auricular confession (1215). Under such influences there arose a distinctive systematic discipline, which in contradistinction to the philosophic and legal came to be designated as theological casuistry. The scholars who cultivated the same constituted, under the name of casuists or schemists, both in the Middle Ages and at Roman Catholic universities much later still, a special class of teachers, notably so as against the canonists. The writings which embodied this discipline were the so-called "*summæ* of cases of conscience" (*summæ casuum conscientiæ*). Of these the most ancient was compiled in the thirteenth century by Raymond of Peñaforte (printed at Lyons, 1719). There then followed a good many such writings while scholasticism was approaching the term of its decay through the fourteenth and fifteenth centuries. The most renowned of these *summæ*, which are usually designated in brief by the author's name or birthplace, are the following: the *Astesana* (printed 1468, and often); *Pisanella* (written 1338; printed, Paris, 1470); *Pacifica* (written c. 1470; printed, Venice, 1576); *Rosella*; *Angelica*; and lastly the one usually known as *summa summarum*; properly the compilation merely of Sylvester Prierias, which dates from the beginning of the Reformation period.

As the Reformers revived the Pauline idea of a free motive power in faith, casuistry proper was fundamentally set aside, and they even occasionally declared themselves expressly opposed to it (Calvin, "Institutes," IV. x. 1 sqq.; Luther, *Resol. t. concl. Ecc.*, ii.). Existing conditions nevertheless gave rise to a certain evangelical counterpart to the Roman Catholic casuistry. The Reformatory movement introduced a multitude of new problems in morality. So in difficult contingencies people frequently appealed for enlightenment to the Reformers and other persons of esteem, or in turn to the theological faculties. In this way the collected letters of Luther and Calvin, as well as Melanchthon's counsels (*Berathschlagungen*, etc., issued by Petzel, 1601), have furnished copious illustrations at large in the matter of evangelical resolutions of conscience. The systematic collections of faculty decisions (*Thesaurus consiliorum*, etc., by Dedekenn; Gerhard's *In richtigerer Ordnung*, 1676) even early denote the transition to a distinctive evangelical casuistry. The more legalizing spirit of the post-Reformation era became thus practically effective. Even here, however, the various particular moral transactions were not viewed, in their development, as in the Roman Catholic casuistry, but as fruits of faith, of knowledge in part, and of the life according to the spirit of Christ. The Reformed theology took precedence in the elaboration of casuistry. The first treatise of this kind is that of the Cambridge professor William Perkins (d. 1602; see PERKINS, WILLIAM), *A Case of Conscience* (originally in English; Latin by Meyer, 1603), of a strict Puritan tone. A similar book of kindred thought was written by his pupil the Scotchman William Ames (*De conscientia*, Amsterdam, 1630). Somewhat prior to this, the German theologian Alstedt had published a work on casuistry (*Theologia casuum*, Hanover, 1621). But although he represented casuistry as a singularly important science, there were in the Reformed Church only a few English theologians that still espoused casuistry. The first Lutheran work on casuistry grew out of lectures delivered by Professor Baldwin at Wittenberg in opposition to the Roman Catholic casuistry, and with the design of systematically setting forth the import of the faculty's opinions. His manuscript was published after his death by the Wittenberg Theological Faculty (*Tractatus de casibus conscientiæ*, Frankfort, 1659). Of the remaining Lutheran writings of this nature, there should still be noted the works of Dannhauer (1679), Bechmann (1692), and Johannes Olearius (1699). Pietism, although Spener's views on moral questions (*Theologische Bedenken*, 1700; *Letzte theologische Bedenken*, 1711) have a casuistical tone, still contributed not a little to the shelving of casuistry, in that it deepened the understanding with reference to the interdependency of the Christian's total transactions with his religious-moral basic intuitions. After Buddeus in his moral theology had shown casuistry to be superfluous, only isolated works on the subject appeared in the Lutheran Church.

Casuistry in Protestantism.

In the Roman Catholic Church, on the contrary, the ethics of the Jesuits came to be out and out casuistical. And even apart from them, in that quarter, casuistry was cultivated (cf. P. Lambertini, *Casus conscientiæ*, Augsburg, 1763; S. Sobiech, *Compendium theologiæ moralis*, Breslau, 1822).

F. SIEFFERT.

BIBLIOGRAPHY: F. D. Maurice, *The Conscience: Lectures on Casuistry*, London, 1872; K. F. Stäudlin, *Geschichte der christlichen Moral*, Göttingen, 1808; W. M. L. de Wette, *Christliche Sittenlehre*, vol. ii., part 2, Berlin, 1821; S. Pike and S. Hayward, *Religious Cases of Conscience*, new ed., Philadelphia, 1859; C. Beard, *Port Royal*, pp. 262–291, London, 1861; J. Cook, *The Conscience*, Boston, 1879; W. Gass, *Geschichte der christlichen Ethik*, i., ii., parts 1–2, Berlin, 1881–87; W. T. Davison, *The Christian Conscience, a Contribution to Ethics*, London, 1888; C. E. Luthardt, *Geschichte der christlichen Ethik*, 2 vols., Leipsic, 1888–93. Many of the treatises on ethics deal with the subject of casuistry.

CASUS RESERVATI ("Reserved Cases"): In the Roman Catholic Church, cases in which absolution can be given only by a priest specially authorized. The practise of such reservation is defended on the ground that Christ granted the power of absolution only to the apostles and their successors (John xx. 21–23), and that the pope and bishops have thus the right to reserve to themselves as much of this power as in their judgment the good of the Church requires. This view is formally sanctioned by the Council of Trent (Sess. XIV., cap. vii., *de pœnitentia*, 11). The cases in question are "certain graver cases of offense," "certain more atrocious and graver offenses" grave external sins, definitely completed and specifically determined by the legislator, i.e., by the pope or bishop. The details were gradually fixed in practise. Ordinarily speaking, the popes reserved to themselves only sins for which excommunication was the penalty, from which only the apostolic see could release the culprit, though there are some to which this did not apply. The principal instances are those named in the bull *In cœna Domini* (q.v.). Where, in these cases, the sin is not matter of public knowledge, the bishops are allowed to absolve (in person or by deputy) *in foro conscientiæ*; and other cases reserved to the pope are placed in their jurisdiction by their quinquennial faculties (see FACULTIES). The constitution *Apostolicæ sedis* of Pius IX. (1869) gives precise details on the different classes of reserved cases at the present day. The cases reserved to the bishops vary according to the locality; in general, they include a number of the graver sins, certain forms of unchastity, homicide, breach of the seal of confession by priests, etc. Bishops commonly depute their powers over a number of these cases to subordinates, either permanently or for special seasons. In all kinds of reserved cases, however, a penitent may be absolved by any priest in case of urgent necessity, such as approaching death. (E. FRIEDBERG.)

BIBLIOGRAPHY: M. Hausmann, *Geschichte der päpstlichen Reservatfälle*, New York, 1868; H. C. Lea, *History of Auricular Confession and Indulgences in the Latin Church*, i. 312 sqq., Philadelphia, 1896.

CASWALL, EDWARD: Hymn-writer; b. at Yateley (35 m. w.s.w. of London), Hampshire, July

15, 1814; d. at the Oratory, Edgbaston, near Birmingham, Jan. 2, 1878. He studied at Brasenose College, Oxford (B.A., 1836; M.A., 1838); was curate of Stratford-sub-Castle, near Salisbury, 1840–47; in 1850 he joined the Oratory of St. Philip Neri under Newman, to whose influence his conversion to Roman Catholicism was due. He wrote original poems, but is best known for his translations from the Roman breviary and other Latin sources, which are marked by faithfulness to the original and purity of rhythm. They were published in *Lyra Catholica, containing all the breviary and missal hymns* (London, 1849); *The Masque of Mary* (1858); and *A May Pageant* (1865). *Hymns and Prose* (1873) is the three books combined with many of the hymns rewritten or revised.

CATACOMBS. See Cemeteries, I.; II., 3; III., 1.

CATAFALQUE: A structure erected to represent a corpse lying in state, decorated with emblems of mourning (also called *tumba, castrum doloris*). The custom of erecting such structures arose in the Catholic Church when the corpse of the deceased was no longer brought into the church, where, according to the Roman rite, the office of the dead, the requiem-mass, and the *Libera* were to be sung, before the interment. The object of the catafalque was to keep the older custom in mind, and to add greater solemnity to the service The bier is covered with black hangings, and surrounded with lights. The officiating priest sprinkles it with holy water, as a symbol of the purifying blood of Christ and the water of eternal life, and then censes it as a token of honor to the body of the deceased, which has been the temple of the Holy Ghost, and as a symbol of the prayers for the departed soul which are to go up as a sweet savor before the Lord.

CA-TAL'DUS: According to legend, a native of Ireland and bishop there of a place called Rachan, otherwise unknown. He is said to have made a pilgrimage to Jerusalem and to have been directed in a vision to preach the Gospel to the heathen at Tarentum. With signs and wonders he performed his mission, became bishop of Tarentum or even archbishop, and converted the entire region before his death. The historical fact which underlies the legend is probably that a pious Irishman named Cataldus or Cathaldus (= Cathal or Cathald, a real Irish name) preached in Lower Italy. His time can not be earlier than the sixth or seventh century. The veneration of Cataldus begins in the early Middle Ages. His relics were discovered in 1071, and many churches are dedicated to him in Lower Italy, and also in France, where he is honored as St. Carthauld or St. Catas. He is commemorated on Mar. 8, May 8, and May 10, the last being the day of his death according to the *Martyrologium Romanum.*

(O. Zöckler†.)

Bibliography: *ASB*, May, ii. 568–577; J. Colgan, *Acta sanctorum veteris et majoris Scotiæ sive Hiberniæ*, pp. 544–562, Louvain, 1645; Lanigan, *Eccl. Hist.*, iii. 121–128; J. Healy, *Insula Sanctorum*, pp. 457–465, Dublin, 1890.

CATECHESIS, CATECHETICS.

The education which the Christian Church imparts to its immature members through its chosen servants, and the theory of this education, is called catechesis. The Greek word *katēchein* means literally "to sound downward," Hippocrates, connecting it with the accusative of the person, signified by it the oral instruction which the physician imparts to the layman concerning the nature and treatment of disease. Lucian applied the word in a similar sense to the relation of the dramatic poet to his audience. Thus it gradually came to denote the making of an oral communication to another (Acts xxi. 21, 24), or the instruction of another. It is used in the sense of religious instruction in Luke i. 4; Acts xviii. 25; Rom. ii. 18; I Cor. xiv. 19; Gal. vi. 6. In ecclesiastical usage it signified preparation of adults for baptism (see Catechumenate). Here instruction was the principal, but not the only factor; heart, will, and conduct were to be influenced. The word catechesis, therefore, properly covers the whole training given by the Church to its children. It is distinguished from Christian pedagogics in that it furnishes only an elementary knowledge of Christian truth, while pedagogics leads to a detailed and scientific knowledge.

1. Origin and Signification of the Terms.

In the ancient Church ecclesiastical education began as soon as a heathen announced his willingness to be received into the Church. He was then accepted among the catechumens and bore the name of Christian. Nowadays Christian education is concerned no longer primarily with the heathen, but with the children of Christians. They are baptized in infancy, on condition that their parents promise to give them a Christian education. Moreover, the baptized, when they come to years of discretion, must evince a desire for the blessings of the Church, and give promise of Christian conduct.

It is more difficult to define the aim of ecclesiastical education. This can not be intellectual only; for catechesis is to lead to Christian feeling, to a Christian formation of will and conduct. Nor is it merely to inculcate obedience to the teachings and commandments of the Church; for catechesis is intended to lead to personal conviction. Others have considered qualification for the Lord's Supper as its aim, but this definition begs the question; for who is really qualified for the Lord's Supper? Others regard living faith as the aim of Christian education; but children of Christian parents can not be regarded as unbelievers. They come from Christian surroundings and possess already a certain unconscious faith in God and the Savior; ecclesiastical education is rather to confirm this implicit faith and develop it into Christian conviction and conduct.

2. Divergent Views of the Object of Catechesis.

Thus faith is the presupposition of ecclesiastical education, but not its aim. As to what this really is, Scripture does not give a definite answer; the distinction, however, between immature and mature Christians (I Cor. iii. 1; Eph. iv. 13; Heb. v. 12) brings nearer to a solution of the problem. There is a childlike faith in the Lord which is still ignorant and without a firm hold, and there is a faith of the adult who has attained a convinced knowledge of Christian truth and a certain perfection in Christian conduct. Whoever of his own will and upon the basis of his faith seeks communion with Christ in the means of grace and in prayer is mature, and ecclesiastical education exists for the purpose of attaining that maturity. It is evident that no definite age can be laid down for such **3. True Aim of Catechesis.** an attainment, because faith and Christian conduct are based upon moral freedom. Maturity depends altogether upon the individual, and can not be affirmed of any one because the heart can not be read. On that account every person must be considered mature who possesses a sufficient knowledge of Christian truth and who promises to lead a Christian life. Maturity is, therefore, more than a qualification for the reception of the Lord's Supper; a child of ten years may have the faith and knowledge necessary for receiving the sacrament in a becoming manner, but he is not mature. Ecclesiastical education must be continued after the first communion. This further growth may be gradually attained by the continuation of Christian fellowship in the family and in the Church; but since this, under the conditions of modern life, is not always applicable, theologians usually lay down the necessity of special institutions whose educational work shall continue until the attainment of maturity.

Instruction is the principal although not the only means of education. Religious instruction is first and foremost instruction of the heart, intended to lead to a knowledge of God. But this knowledge is based upon inner experiences, and these experiences again have their foundation in observation. God has revealed himself in nature, but more completely in the spiritual life. This, as manifested in Christ, is the perfect revelation of God; and as the record of this life is found in Holy Scripture, the Bible is the principal book of instruction. Owing to the wealth of material contained therein, it has been considered advisable to condense and select certain stories specially adapted for the young without paying particular attention to **4. Methods of Catechesis.** their connection as a whole. From this book of stories the pupil is gradually led to the Bible itself. He is to memorize certain passages and read different portions of it in order to penetrate its spirit and attain practise in its use. The Gospels, some historical sections of the Old Testament, and the Psalms are best adapted for this purpose. Another source of material for religious instruction is found in the Church hymns, which awaken religious sentiment and enable the pupil to participate intelligently in public worship. After the pupil has acquired a number of religious truths from the selections or from the Bible itself, it is possible to present these truths in their most concise form and in their connection. This is necessary in order to give the pupil a clear survey of the Christian truths and to strengthen his conviction. Such an epitome is given in the catechism. The part of it longest in use is the Apostles' Creed; next followed the Lord's Prayer, and in the Middle Ages the decalogue was added as a basis of instruction, to give a proper understanding of sin. These three articles form the main portions of the Evangelical catechism; from the law the pupil learns the greatness of his sin, in the creed he professes his faith in the means of salvation from it, and in the Lord's Prayer he expresses his longing for Christian conduct as a disciple of Christ. Since the immediate aim of religious instruction is participation in the Lord's Supper, the doctrine of the sacrament forms the fourth division of the Catechism. This is the order of the Reformation catechisms; and though objections have been made to it, they may be shown to be unfounded.

As the catechist has not only to communicate knowledge, but to move the heart and will, the instruction must be oral and personal. No book ought to be used in religious instruction, except the Bible at the time fixed for reading it. Biblical stories, hymn-books, and catechisms are only aids to be used at home. As children like to hear stories, the teacher should begin his instruction with telling them. Verses of hymns, texts and answers from the catechism are to be used mainly in illustration of the Biblical story. As the child's attention is attracted only a short time by the talk of the teacher, his interest has to be retained by asking him questions. There is a distinction made between analytical and synthetical instruction. In analytical instruction the material is ready at hand, as in the Biblical story, in Scripture-reading, and hymns, and the religious truth is developed from it. In synthetical instruction only the theme is given, as in the catechism and Bible texts, and the material has to be gathered elsewhere.

Owing to the amount of material, religious instruction must be spread over several years. In the German system it covers eight, during the first four of which the Bible story forms the basis of instruction. In the fifth year hymns are treated in connection with the church year, and Bible-reading and instruction in the catechism are begun. The pupils receive practise in the use of the Bible, and some portions of the historical books are read in connection with the Biblical stories. The decalogue, the creed, and the Lord's Prayer are briefly explained and thus stamped upon the memory. The last two years place Bible-reading and the catechism in the foreground. The instruction should be imparted by both pastor and teacher. It is advisable that the pastor should instruct the pupils at least two years; he should confine himself mainly to the catechism in connection with Bible-reading, and leave the Biblical stories and hymns to the teacher. On any arrangement it is essential that pastor and teacher should work in harmony, each with an eye to the special instruction imparted by the other.

As religious education addresses itself to the heart as well as to the mind, the cultivation of the former is not less the duty of the catechist. Common devotional exercises are held, consisting of the singing of hymns, reading of Scripture, and an extempore prayer by the teacher. Moreover, observance of Sunday and regular attendance on the Church services should be required of the children. As the sermons at those services can not be sufficiently grasped by younger children, special services are to be arranged for them. With the religious practise moral practise must go hand in hand. Order, diligence, modesty obedience, truth, and other virtues must be inculcated.

5. Practical Application of Catechesis.

While the pupil must be taught obedience and respect. the teacher should not be immoderate and unjust in his demands or irascible. If he shows the least partiality or injustice, he weakens his authority. Reproof should come before punishment, and should be made to suffice as long as possible, so that the teacher shall not come too soon to the end of his resources. Older scholars should be won by private exhortation where necessary, and led to self-examination and self-judgment, so that they may find the path of goodness for themselves.

Christianity as a spiritual religion demands a definite religious conviction and moral sentiment. The Christian Church, therefore, receives as members only those who make their confession of faith and promise Christian conduct. In the early Church a profession of faith and a vow were made before baptism, and the first communion followed after it. When infant baptism became general, the need was felt of bringing in this profession and vow later as a preliminary to the first communion. In this way originated the rite of confirmation (q.v.) in the Protestant churches. Confirmation is not a declaration of maturity. The faith of a child may be of such a kind as to admit him or her to the Lord's Supper, but not yet to a life that may dispense with all further religious aid. The profession and the vow must be spontaneous, they must proceed from the candidate's own moral decision; therefore, the child should not be forced to confirmation at a fixed age. The custom of confirming children as a matter of course at the age of fourteen has led to insincerity and hypocrisy, and it is the duty of the Church to check it as much as possible, which can to a certain extent be accomplished by emphasizing the purely voluntary character of the act, and by having an intervening time between the examination in religious knowledge and the profession of faith.

6. Relation of Catechesis to Confirmation.

If the confirmed are still immature in the religious sense, their education must be continued. The influence of the Christian home and of church fellowship are hardly sufficient for this. Our ancestors in both the Lutheran and the Reformed churches demanded that the children should continue to participate, even after their first communion, in the regular catechetical instruction of the Church until their eighteenth year or until their marriage. These customs have disappeared in the last century because confirmed children have been considered mature, but this is a grave mistake, in view of the diminution of wholesome family influence and the observance of Sunday, and the reform of these conditions is an urgent necessity of our modern Church. (E. Sachsse.)

The preceding article is written from the standpoint of a subject of Germany, where Church and State are united and religious instruction is consequently a part of the curriculum of the schools. A treatment of catechetics from a more general point of view is given by implication in Catechisms (q.v.).

Bibliography: The bibliographies under Catechisms and Catechumenate should be consulted; C. I. Nitzsch, *Praktische Theologie*, ii. 133–235, Bonn, 1860; C. Palmer, *Evangelische Katechetik*, Stuttgart, 1875; R. Kübel, *Katechetik*, Barmen, 1877; J. G. Wenham, *The Catechumen*, London, 1881; E. Daniel, *How to Teach the Church Catechism*, ib. 1882; T. Harnack, *Katechetik*, Erlangen, 1882; S. J. Hulme, *Principles of the Catechism of the Church of England*, Stow-on-the-Wold, 1882; N. Haus, *Wie soll der Religionslehrer öffentlich katechisieren?* Regensburg, 1885; E. Bather, *Hints on the Art of Catechising*, London, 1888; K. Buchrucker, *Grundlinien des kirchlichen Katechismus*, Berlin, 1889; J. E. Denison, *Catechising on the Catechism*, London, 1889; F. A. P. Dupanloup, *The Ministry of Catechising*, ib. 1891; P. Schaff, *Theological Propædeutic*, part ii., pp. 500–504, New York, 1893; K. Schultze, *Evangelische Volksschulkunde*, Gotha, 1893; G. R. Crooks and J. F. Hurst, *Theological Encyclopædia*, pp. 514–526, New York, 1894; E. Sachsse, *Die Lehre von der kirchlichen Erziehung*, Berlin, 1897; E. C. Achelis, *Praktische Theologie*, ii. 1 176, Leipsic, 1898; J. Lütkemann, *Anleitung zur Katechismuslehre*, Hermannsburg, 1898; R. Staude, *Der Katechismusunterricht, Präparationen*, 3 vols., Dresden, 1900–01.

CATECHISMS.

Catechisms are written or printed summaries of the principal doctrines of the Christian faith, intended for the instruction of the unlearned and the young. These formal aids to systematic instruction are of comparatively modern growth. For the system of the primitive Church, see Catechumenate.

I. The Middle Ages: The beginnings of modern catechetical instruction, as to the development of which see CATECHESIS, CATECHETICS, are found principally in the Germanic Churches. Here, as in primitive days and for the same reason, it originally addressed itself chiefly to adults. Sometimes whole tribes had been converted to Christianity in which the individuals did not possess the most elementary knowledge of the Christian faith, and it was necessary to impart by further teaching what had been neglected at the time of baptism. The Anglo-Saxon Church, and afterward Charlemagne, under the influence of his Anglo-Saxon adviser Alcuin, decreed that every baptized person should know by heart the Creed and the Lord's Prayer. But the rising generation was not left altogether out of view. There was from the beginning an indefinite feeling among the Teutonic Churches that the Church, by its acceptance of infant baptism, was bound to care for the instruction of the children thus brought into its fold. It was naturally impossible, in view of the widely scattered parishes and the necessity of instruction being almost exclusively oral, to undertake the actual teaching; but the need was to some extent indirectly met by the requirement that no sponsor should present a child for baptism without being able to recite the Creed and the Lord's Prayer, and that sponsors should teach the same articles to their godchildren.

1. Need of Catechetical Instruction.

Another influence that helped to enforce a certain amount of Christian knowledge was the system of regular confession, especially after an annual confession was made obligatory by the Fourth Lateran Council of 1215. With the act of confession was usually connected a recitation of the articles which the sponsors were supposed to have impressed upon their godchildren. The system further led to an enlargement of the scope of regular instruction. As the Creed and the Lord's Prayer hardly formed a suitable basis for the confession of sins, there originated lists of the sins which required ecclesiastical penance; and these, with corresponding lists of virtues, were often ordered to be learned by heart; in this connection the decalogue was redeemed from oblivion. It became a regular practise to preach sermons on the Ten Commandments in Lent, the most usual time for confession; and thus catechetical preaching developed. The reformers of the fourteenth and fifteenth centuries, such as Gerson and Geiler von Kaisersberg, were strong advocates of these sermons on the foundations of Christian doctrine. The Ave Maria was included among the articles to be learned, and came to take equal rank with the Creed and the Lord's Prayer. The tendency was to enlarge the material, though some attempts were made, on the other hand, to condense it; thus Johann Wolf of Frankfort showed that all the articles used in confession could be traced to the decalogue. He also laid special emphasis upon the religious instruction of youth in a period when the councils of the Church paid no particular attention to it as a distinct branch of church work. The beginning of a reformation in this respect was the work of humanists like Jakob Wimpheling and Erasmus. Colet in England drew up a manual of religious instruction under the title of *Catechyzon* for the boys of St. Paul's School, which Erasmus put into Latin hexameters, thereby perhaps giving the impulse to Petrus Tritonius to produce a similar work. Outside, however, of such efforts, which were rather scholastic than ecclesiastical, catechisms in the modern sense, or compilations of the principal articles of faith for children, were practically unknown to the medieval Church.

2. Influence of Confession.

3. Pre-Reformation Catechisms.

There were, indeed, such compilations for the clergy, which with the invention of printing began to circulate widely among the laity. The *Tafel des christlichen Lebens* (c. 1480) is in more ways than one a direct predecessor of Luther's smaller catechism, but a comparison shows the characteristic difference between the medieval and the Evangelical Church. In the Catholic table are found numerous pieces without any explanatory word, sacred formulas that were frequently repeated without comprehension; in Luther's catechism appear the five main articles, with the emphasis laid upon the explanation. Great importance was attached to the religious instruction of youth by the Bohemian Brethren and the Waldenses. The *Interrogacions menors* of the Waldenses date from the end of the fifteenth, or at least from the beginning of the sixteenth, century. The *Kinderfragen* of the Bohemian Brethren are still older, since they served as a model for the *Interrogacions*.

II. The Post-Reformation Period: From the beginning of the Reformation care was taken to provide for the religious instruction of youth. Almost simultaneously the two places where the movement had its origin established institutions which were followed as models; in 1521 Johann Agricola was appointed catechist at Wittenberg, and in 1522 systematic instruction of youth in the Christian faith was established in Zurich in place of the Roman confirmation.

Luther's popular expositions of the Ten Commandments, the Creed, and the Lord's Prayer, especially his *Kurze Form* and his *Betbüchlein*, are not catechisms in the proper sense of the word, but rather prepared the way for them. Several adaptations of the *Kinderfragen* of the Bohemian Brethren, German translations of Melanchthon's *Enchiridion* and *Scholia*, and numerous other compilations of the Christian truth adapted for children show the demand for an Evangelical text-book. Toward the end of 1524 Justus Jonas and Agricola were ordered to write such a book; they did not execute their commission, but toward the end of 1525 there was published the *Büchlein für die Laien und Kinder* (possibly by Bugenhagen), which provisionally at least supplied the want. About the same time Luther urged, in his *Deutsche Messe*, the introduction of religious instruction for children. His appeal called forth numerous expositions of the articles of faith, and in many places systematic teaching was begun. In 1529 Luther published his Smaller Catechism

1. Early Lutheran Catechisms.

(sometimes known as *Enchiridion*), and with it the material of the catechism was firmly established for the future (see LUTHER'S TWO CATECHISMS). In some places, especially under the influence of the Nuremberg *Kinderpredigten* (1533), the power of the keys was added as a sixth article, and is still used as such in some of the churches of Germany.

At first Luther's catechism was merely one among several others, though it was almost universally adopted in both parts of Saxony, in Brandenburg, and in Pomerania. Apart from manuals produced under the influence of the Swiss theology, like those of Leo Jud and Bullinger, there are others which follow Luther's doctrine, among them Kaspar Löwer's *Unterricht des Glaubens* (1529), Johann Brenz's *Fragestücke* (1535), which is still used in Württemberg, Butzer's catechisms for Strasburg (1534 and 1537), and others. It was only by degrees that Luther's work assumed the supremacy over other catechisms of the same tendency, until it finally attained the importance of a standard of doctrine. It was treated as such for the first time in 1561 in the articles of Lüneburg, where it had its place beside the Augsburg Confession, the Apology, and the Schmalkald Articles (see CORPUS DOCTRINÆ). It attained a still stronger position in contradistinction to the Heidelberg Catechism (q.v.). The latter, which from the first was considered in the light of a confession of faith, was compiled in 1563 by Olevianus and Ursinus from the catechisms of Leo Jud and Bullinger, from the Emden catechism of 1554, from Calvin's catechism of 1542 (see below), and from two catechisms used among Low-German emigrant churches of the sixteenth century, and was soon introduced in all countries where the Reformed faith prevailed. In 1580 the Smaller Catechism was included in the Book of Concord, and took rank everywhere as the corresponding standard of Lutheran doctrine. While the Heidelberg Catechism, as the more comprehensive work, retained everywhere its old form, Luther's *Enchiridion* formed frequently only the basis for fuller expositions, in connection, e.g., with Brenz's *Fragestücke* of 1535 and a booklet printed in 1549 at Erfurt under Luther's name, though really compiled by Johann Lang, entitled *Fragestücke fur die, so zum Sacrament gehen wöllen.*

2. Gradual Supremacy of Luther's Smaller Catechism.

No little influence on the development of a traditional form for catechisms was exercised by the Latin ones prepared for the Latin schools. The material of these, based partly upon the *Loci* of Melanchthon, grew to such an extent that they almost formed regular dogmatic works. Among the catechisms which originated from such sources on the basis of Luther's *Encheiridion* the *Kleiner Catechismus D. M. Lutheri* by Nicolaus Herco (1554) shows a fairly definite form already assumed by the development. A wider circulation was attained by the *Fragestücke* of Bartholomæus Rosinus (1580). The first regular catechism with expositions was the *Goldene Kleinod* of Johann Tetelbach (1568); and the first of such to receive official sanction was the Nuremberg *Kinderlehrbüchlein* (1628).

3. Early Catechisms Based on Luther's Work.

During this whole period catechetical instruction consisted of nothing more than the memorizing by the children of the catechisms. Further explanations were left to the catechetical sermons which gradually became more common, modeled after Luther's Larger Catechism and the Nuremberg *Kinderpredigten* of 1533. Frequently it was decided that the children should be questioned on these sermons. On the other hand, efforts were early made to guard children against a mechanical memorizing by making the text intelligible to them. A school edition of the Heidelberg Catechism (1610) gives four rules in this respect; (1) difficult passages are to be explained; (2) a long paragraph is to be condensed by the pupil; (3) the text of the catechism is to be analyzed by the teacher, putting questions which the children have to answer from the text; (4) the catechism is to be confirmed and proved by Bible texts and stories. The method laid down in these rules dominated catechetical instruction until a late time in the eighteenth century. Orthodox and pietistic catechists agreed in the use of the analytical method; but the latter emphasized more strongly the cultivation of the heart, and in formulating the questions and answers of the catechism laid stress upon the practical side of life, as may be seen from Philipp Jakob Spener's *Tabulæ catecheticæ* (Frankfort, 1683). The two principal pietistic catechisms are Spener's *Erklärung der christlichen Lehre* (1677) and the Dresden *Kreuz-Katechismus* (1688). But even Pietism could not hinder the gradual degeneration of catechetical instruction into mere formalism.

4. Orthodox and Pietistic Catechisms.

A fresh impulse was received from the new methods introduced by the rationalist school. Starting from rationalistic premises, Johann Bernhard Basedow (q.v.) demanded in his *Abhandlung vom Unterricht der Jugend in der Religion* (Lübeck, 1764) that children should not be forced to memorize anything but what they already understood, and that they should be left to acquire new knowledge only by their own thinking, with the help of instructive questions. Basedow laid down these views in his catechism for two grades entitled *Grundriss der Religion, welche durch Nachdenken und Bibelforschen erkannt wird* (1764). This, which gradually became known as the Socratic method, was developed further by Karl Friedrich Bahrdt in his *Philanthropinischer Erziehungsplan* (Frankfort, 1776) and confirmed from the philosophy of Kant by Johann Friedrich Christian Graeffe in his *Vollständiges Lehrbuch der allgemeinen Katechetik* (Göttingen, 1799). Its most prominent representatives were Johann Peter Miller, Johann Christian Dolz, and especially Gustav Friedrich Dinter. With these new ideas new manuals appeared which either dropped altogether the old catechisms based on the articles of faith or relegated them to an appendix. Johann Gottfried Herder attempted

5. Rationalistic Catechisms of the Eighteenth Century.

to explain the smaller catechism of Luther according to the new principles (Weimar, 1800). The weak point of the Socratic method is its inseparable connection with rationalist theology. Pestalozzi criticized this method because it tried to elicit from children what is not in them. Schleiermacher pointed out that the Socratic method ignored the revelation of the Christian religion and its history. Marheinecke, Nitzsch, Kraussold, Harms, and Hüffell followed him in opposition to it. The modern method of catechizing has retained from the Socratic method its feature of development; it does not, however, consider human reason and natural religion as the basis of this development, but rather the documents of revelation and the history of the Church.

The catechisms used in the different territories of Germany are too numerous to mention. In the territories of the Evangelical Union as well as among the orthodox Lutherans the Smaller Catechism of Luther forms the basis of instruction. But in accordance with their peculiar doctrines the Unionists have made concessions to the Reformed teachings, so that their manuals represent more or less a compromise between Luther's Smaller Catechism and the Heidelberg Catechism. The chief country of the Union is Prussia, and here the consistories in agreement with their respective provincial synods have selected a number of compendiums to be used in instruction. Manuals of the same sort are found in the other Unionistic territories, Anhalt, Baden, Hesse, Waldeck, Hanau, the Rhenish Palatinate, Nassau, and Birkenfeld.

6. Modern German Lutheran Catechisms.

In the distinctively Lutheran territories Luther's Smaller Catechism is used everywhere, in Hesse in connection with the so-called *Hessische Fragestücke,* in Württemberg with Brenz's catechism. The text is at present formulated after the revision proposed by the Evangelical conference held at Eisenach in 1882. In the selection of aids to be used besides the text a certain freedom exists in Saxe-Coburg, in the Lutheran Church of Alsace-Lorraine, in Hamburg, in the Lutheran Church of the province of Hanover, and in Frankfort-on-the-Main. In certain places besides the text of the Smaller Catechism are mostly *Spruchbücher*, that is, collections of Bible texts and hymns. The use of such books for the explanation of Luther's catechism has been made obligatory in the kingdom of Saxony, in Altenburg, Meiningen, the principalities of Reuss, in Sleswick-Holstein and Eutin, in Oldenburg and Schaumburg-Lippe. Besides the *Spruchbücher*, various expositions of Luther's catechisms have been introduced, the use of which has been made obligatory in Mecklenburg-Schwerin, Lübeck, Mecklenburg-Strelitz, Brunswick, Schwarzburg-Sondershausen, Schwarzburg-Rudolstadt, the former county of Schaumburg, Weimar, Bavaria, and in the Free Lutheran Church of Prussia.

As regards the Reformed territories, the Heidelberg Catechism is used in the Reformed Church of Lippe-Detmold, in the Reformed congregations of East Friesland, in the former county of Bentheim, in the synodal district of Bovenden (near Göttingen), and in the confederation of Reformed Churches in Lower Saxony. In the Reformed territories of the consistorial district of Cassel (Lower Hesse) and in the synodal district of Hamburg the *Hessischer Landeskatechismus*, a Reformed revision of Luther's Smaller Catechism with the *Hessische Fragestücke* inserted, is used. In Bremen and in the Reformed Church of Alsace-Lorraine no special manual for religious instruction is prescribed.

7. Modern German Reformed Catechisms.

In Switzerland there appeared at St. Gallen in 1527 a compilation of the *Kinderfragen* of the Bohemian Brethren. About the same time Œcolampadius published his *Kinderbericht* for Basel. In 1534 Leo Jud published his catechism for Zurich. An epitome of it followed in the next year, which in 1598 was declared obligatory to the exclusion of the catechisms of Heinrich Bullinger (1559) and Burckhardt Leemann (1583), and was introduced also in Grisons and Schaffhausen. In 1536 Kaspar Grossmann (Megander) revised Jud's catechism for Bern; as in the course of time it was made to serve the views of Zwingli, it had to be revised anew, and in this form became known as the Bern Catechism. These old catechisms were either superseded or influenced by the Heidelberg Catechism. The Zurich Catechism of 1609, the work of Marcus Bäumlein, originated in a combination of the Heidelberg Catechism with those used in Zurich. It was introduced in different cantons and used until 1839. Under the influence of rationalism most of the cantons adopted new catechisms between 1830 and 1850. Basel took the lead in 1832, then followed Zurich with a new catechism (1839). In French Switzerland Calvin's *Catechismus Genevensis* (1542) was used at the beginning. In the canton of Vaud it was replaced in 1552 by a translation of the Bern Catechism, which gave way to that of Heidelberg in the eighteenth century. In 1734 there appeared in Geneva the small catechism of Jean Frédéric Osterwald, which, after revision, was also adopted in Vaud. About 1620 Stephen Gabriel, pastor at Ilanz, compiled a catechism for the Romance districts which remained in use even after a translation of Osterwald's catechism had appeared. But entire freedom exists as to the choice of religious manuals in Switzerland. In many cases the individual preachers write their own books of instruction.

8. Switzerland.

Since the edict of toleration of Joseph II., the Lutheran Church in Austria has used Luther's Smaller Catechism and the Reformed Church the Heidelberg Catechism. According to the constitution of the Evangelical Church in Austria, all further guides in religious instruction have to be sanctioned by the Evangelical Supreme Church Council in Vienna, and approved by the ministry of ecclesiastical affairs and public instruction. Some of the approved manuals are, in German, Buchrucker's and Ernesti's editions of Luther's Smaller Catechism, in Bohemian that of Molmar. Among those approved for the Reformed Church

9. Austria-Hungary.

may be mentioned the enlarged German edition of the Heidelberg Catechism by Franz (Vienna, 1858), and the Bohemian by Von Tardy (Prague, 1867), and by Vesely (1885). In Hungary and Transylvania the same conditions exist as in Austria.

In the Baltic provinces of Russia an Esthonian translation of the Smaller Catechism seems to have appeared as early as in 1553. In 1586 a Lettish translation by J. Rivius was printed at Königsberg. It was revised in 1689 by E. Glück and used a long time among the Lettish congregations of Livonia.

10. Slavic Countries. Another by H. Adolphi appeared in 1685 and found a large circulation in Courland. In accordance with a resolution of the Synod of Livonia and Courland in 1898, a new Lettish standard text has been established (Riga, 1898), which has supplanted all earlier translations. An Esthonian exposition of the Smaller Catechism was introduced in Esthonia in 1673 as the official catechism, and used almost exclusively until 1866. The catechism of Martin Körber (1864), modeled after the official catechism of Neustrelitz, has found a considerable circulation. The Germans in the Baltic provinces also produced numerous interpretations of their own; Jodocus Holst, *Einfältige Auslegung des Kleinen Katechismus Luthers* (Riga, 1596); Immanuel von Essen, *Christliche Katechismusübung* (1781); Werbatus, *Dr Martin Luthers Kleiner Katechismus* (1895); and many others. For the Lutheran congregations of Poland there has been recently approved *Maly Katechizm Doktora Marcina Lutra* (Lublin, 1900). It is an exposition of the Smaller Catechism by Alexander Schönaich, preacher at Lublin. An official text of the Smaller Catechism has been published for the Russian-speaking Lutherans (St. Petersburg, 1865).

The first catechetical writings in Sweden were a working-over of Luther's *Betbüchlein*, a translation of the revision of the *Kinderfragen* of the Bohemian Brethren published at Magdeburg in 1524, and a translation of the *Handbüchlein für junge Christen* by Johann Toltz. The Smaller Catechism was translated by Laurentius Petri into Swedish perhaps as early as 1548; the oldest extant copy dates from 1572. In 1595 the Smaller

11. Scandinavian Countries. Catechism was officially introduced, but came into general use only after the Church Order of 1686. An official translation of Luther's Larger Catechism dates from 1746. The exposition of the Smaller by Olaf Swebelius, which had been in use for some time, was revised in 1811 by Archbishop J. Axel Lindblom and introduced as an official catechism. In 1843 a new revision appeared, but in 1878 the *Doktor Mårten Luthers Lilla Katekes med kort utveckling, stadfäst af konungen den 11. Oktober 1878* took its place and is still used. In 1532 the Smaller Catechism was translated into Danish by Jorgen Jensen Sadolin. In 1537 there appeared almost simultaneously two further translations, *Den lille danske Catechismus* by Franz Wormodson and *Luthers lille Katekismus* by Petrus Palladius. The latter was republished in 1538 as *Enchiridion sive Manuale ut vocant* and officially recognized. H. P Petersen edited the Latin text of the Smaller Catechism side by side with a Danish translation for the use of schools (1608). In 1627 he used the Danish text for a manual destined for popular instruction. The text deviates frequently from the original, and these variants have crept into other compilations modeled after it. It retained its authority in Denmark until 1813, in Norway until 1843. The standard work for Norway is at present *Dr. M. Luthers Lille Katekismus* (9th ed., Christiania, 1897), and for Denmark C. F Balslev's *Luthers Katekismus meden kort Forklaring* (Copenhagen, 1899).

In the Dutch Reformed Church absolute freedom exists in the choice of guides to be used in

12. Holland. religious instruction. Besides the Geneva and Heidelberg catechisms, Abraham Hellenbroek's *Vorbeeld der goddelyke Waarheden* has been used.

The Established Church of England uses to-day the catechism from the Book of Common Prayer, with but slight changes from the original form of 1552. An exposition of it by John Palmer (London, 1894) shows the text of the original catechism in prominent type and provides each individual paragraph with an introduction. The Congregationalists have also adopted the catechism of the Established Church, but besides this they use a manual by Samuel Palmer, *A Catechism for Protestant*

13. England. *Dissenters* (London, 1772, 29th ed., 1890), which contains a brief history of non-conformity and treats of the reasons for it. In the Sunday-schools the Congregationalists use a catechism by J. Hilton Stowell revised by A. M. Fairbairn (1892). The Presbyterian Church of England and the Church of Scotland have accepted the Westminster Catechism as the basis of their instruction. It is divided into the doctrines we are to believe and the duties we are to perform (The Moral Law; Faith and Repentance; Sacraments; Prayer). The form of religious instruction chiefly cultivated in England is the Sunday-school, for which the Sunday-school Union furnishes manuals. Dr. Watt's first and second catechisms have also found a large circulation; the former contains a short survey of the doctrines of Christian salvation and especially a catechism on Scriptural names, the latter an interpretation of the decalogue and information on the sacraments and prayers. Before the catechism of the Book of Common Prayer appeared, Luther's Smaller Catechism was used for several years in England; at the instance of Cranmer the Nuremberg *Kinderpredigten* which interpret it was in 1548 translated into English under the title *A Short Introduction into the Christian Religion.*

In the French Reformed Church Calvin's catechism of 1542 was at one time almost universally used, later with Osterwald's smaller catechism, but has now been superseded by Bonnefon's

14. France. *Nouveau catéchisme élémentaire* (14th ed., Alais, 1900) and Decoppet's *Catéchisme populaire* (Paris). Less popular are Babut's *Cours de religion chrétienne* (6th ed., 1897) and Nyegaard's *Catéchisme à l'usage des Églises evangéliques* (13th ed., 1900). The Free Church uses the same catechisms. In the "Église de la Confession d'Augsbourg" Luther's Smaller Catechism has always been in use. The *Petit catéchisme de Luther* (Chateauroux) has added to Luther's text Bible texts and stories and renders the Ten Commandments exactly as they are found in Ex. xx. 1-17, combining the ninth and tenth commandments and treating the prohibition of the worship of images as a separate commandment.

15. Italy. As a result of the Evangelical movement in Italy, there originated about 1535 the "Christian Instruction for Children" by Juan de Valdés, apparently first written in Spanish, but published first in Italian and then translated into various languages (cf. the polyglot edition of E. Böhmer under the title *Instruction cristiana para los niños por Juan de Valdés*, Bonn, 1883). To-day the "Free Church" uses *Il catechismo ossia sunto della dottrina cristiana secondo la parola di Dio*, by G. P. Meille (Florence, 6th ed., 1895). Of a similar nature are the catechisms used by the Waldenses, *Catechismo della Chiesa evangelica Valdese o Manuale d'istruzione cristiana ad uso dei catecumeni di detta Chiesa* (1866) and *Catechismo evangelico ossia sunto della dottrina cristiana* (1895).

16. American Lutheran Catechisms. The Lutherans in the United States use Luther's Smaller Catechism, which exists in many German, English, and German-English editions. In the Synodical Conference the Dresden *Kreuzkatechismus* of 1688 has a large circulation, in the Missouri Synod *Dr. M. Luthers Kleiner Katechismus in Frage und Antwort gründlich ausgelegt* by J. K. Dietrich (St. Louis, Mo.) and a condensed edition of the same are much used; the former also in English. In the Ohio Synod originated *Der Kleine Catechismus Dr. M. Luthers mit erklärenden und beweisenden Bibelstellen*, also in English (Allentown, Pa.). It contains besides the Smaller Catechism the "Order of Salvation," that is, a survey of the whole contents of Christian doctrine, an analysis of the catechism formed like Spener's catechetical tables, and the Württemberg *Konferenz-Examen*, which is an epitome of the *Kinderlehre* introduced in 1682 in Württemberg. Prof. M. Loy, Prof. F. W. Stellhorn, and Rev. C. H. Rohe wrote an exposition of the Smaller Catechism on the basis of Dietrich's, under the title *Dr. M. Luthers Kleiner Katechismus, in Frage und Antwort ausgelegt* (Columbus, O., 1882). On the basis of Caspari's catechetical exposition, W. J. Mann and G. F. Krotel, of the Synod of Pennsylvania, published *Luthers Kleiner Katechismus in Fragen und Antworten zum Gebrauch in Kirche, Schule und Haus* (Allentown, 1863). The General Council uses also a catechism which contains the Württemberg *Konferenz-Examen* as an appendix. It appeared under the title *Dr. M. Luthers Kleiner Katechismus mit Erklärung für die evangelisch-lutherische Kirche in den Vereinigten Staaten*, also in English (New York). A recent addition explains Luther's text by Bible texts and stories—*Luthers Kleiner Katechismus mit Bibelsprüchen* (Philadelphia). The German-Evangelical synod, which is akin to the Evangelical Union in Germany, has published its own official catechism, *Kleiner evangelischer Katechismus*, also an edition with German and English on parallel pages (St. Louis). It is a free revision of the Smaller Catechism, differing from it especially in the doctrine of the sacraments. The German-Reformed Church uses a catechism prepared in 1862 by Philip Schaff and entitled *Christlicher Katechismus: ein Leitfaden zum Religionsunterricht in Schule und Haus* (Philadelphia). These rather comprehensive books are intended for the school and especially for young people to be confirmed. In the numerous Sunday-schools the children are frequently instructed only in Biblical stories. A catechism intended for that purpose is *The Little Lamb's Catechism* by J. R. Lauritzen (Knoxville, Tenn.). The same author wrote another manual which has become very popular—*Dr. M. Luther's Kleiner Katechismus*, also in English (Knoxville, Tenn.). The German-Evangelical Synod possesses an excellent manual for the instruction of Sunday-schools in *Kurze Katechismuslehre* (St. Louis, 1899), which extends its material over three grades and is considered a preparation for the catechism proper.

17. The Moravians and Bohemian Brethren. In the German Moravian congregations the department for churches and schools under the direction of the Unitas Fratrum has reserved to itself the right of selecting manuals to be used in instruction. Luther's Smaller Catechism is chiefly used, in some places also *Hauptinhalt der christlichen Heilslehre zum Gebrauch bei dem Unterricht der Jugend in den evangelischen Brüdergemeinden* (8th ed., Gnadau, 1891), compiled by Samuel Lieberkühn in 1769. Among the Bohemian Brethren the *Katechismus der christlichen Lehre zum Gebrauch bei dem Unterricht der Jugend in den evangelischen Brüdergemeinden* (Dauba) has become the standard. It is based upon a catechism written by L. T. Reichel for the American congregations of Brethren. Among the earlier catechisms which are out of use now may be mentioned Zinzendorf's works—his strange production *Lautere Milch der Lehre von Jesu Christo* (1723) and his *Gewisser Grund christlicher Lehre nach Anleitung des einfachen Catechismi seel. Herrn Dr. Luthers* (1725).

18. Methodist Catechisms. Among the German-speaking Methodists of the United States the only books used are the manuals written at the order of the General Conference in 1868 by Wilhelm Nast in Cincinnati, especially with the aid of Schaff's catechism, *Der grössere [kleinere] Katechismus für die deutschen Gemeinden der Bischöflichen Methodistenkirche* (Cincinnati). The English Methodists use *A Brief Catechism for the Use of Methodists Compiled by Order of the Conference* (London) and *The Catechism of the Wesleyan Methodists* (ib.). The latter work consists really of three catechisms, arranged in gradation for pupils of different ages.

The manuals used among the Baptists in Germany are Rode's *Christlicher Religionsunterricht für die reifere Jugend* (Hamburg, 1882) and Kaiser's *Leitfaden für den Religionsunterricht*, which first appeared in English under the title of *Prize Catechism*. Besides these, Weert's *Katechismus, ein*

Leitfaden für den Religionsunterricht (Cassel, 1899) is used. [Several catechisms were prepared by English Particular Baptists in the seventeenth century: *A Soul Searching Catechism*, by Christopher Blackwood (1653); *Catechism for Children*, by Henry Jessey (1673); *The Child's Instructor: a New and Easy Primer*, by Benjamin Krach (1664). The General Assembly of the Particular Baptists at its session in London in June, 1693, requested William Collins to draw up a catechism "containing the substance of the Christian religion, for the instruction of children and servants." It has been reproduced in authentic form in *Confessions of Faith, and other Documents, edited for the Hanserd Knollys Society, by E. B. Underhill* (London, 1854). Among the Baptists of the United States in the South and Southwest *Question Books* (four series) by A. C. Dayton, and a *Catechism* by J. A. Broadus, have been widely used. A. H. N.]

19. Baptist and Irvingite Catechisms.

The catechism of the Irvingites contains three chapters; the first two represent practically the Prayer-book catechism; the third part treats of the doctrines peculiar to the Irvingites, the doctrine of the Church and its offices.

[For the catechisms used in most Presbyterian communions see Westminster Standards.]

20. Unitarian Catechisms.

The English Unitarians use especially two small manuals—*Ten Lessons in Religion* by Charles Beard (London, 2d ed., 1897) and *A Catechism of Religion* by H. W. Hawkes. While the former contains only an exposition of the Lord's Prayer and instruction on the Bible, the latter treats in fifty-two questions of the most important terms in Christian faith and interprets them in the Unitarian sense. The latter is in some respects dependent on *An Evangelical Free Church Catechism for Use in Home and School* (London), which is used by Unitarians, Methodists, Baptists, Congregationalists, Presbyterians, and some smaller denominations.

21. Roman Catholic and Old Catholic Catechisms.

The Roman Catholic Church learned from the Evangelicals its solicitude for the religious instruction of youth. Numerous manuals appeared as imitations of Evangelical catechisms. The catechism of John Dietenberger, a very popular book, was in some passages copied verbatim from Luther's. But all the catechisms previously published were far surpassed in popularity by the *Summa doctrinæ christianæ, per quæstiones tradita et ad capitum rudiorum accommodata* (1556) by the Jesuit Peter Canisius. It forms an epitome of his *Summa doctrinæ christianæ* of 1555 and was translated into all European languages. It was used even in India and remained for about two centuries the principal catechism of the Roman Catholic Church. In 1559 Canisius enlarged it under the title *Parvus Catechismus catholicorum*, which became the model for numerous expositions of the *Summa*. In 1566 appeared the *Catechismus ex decreto Concilii Tridentini ad Parochos Pii V Pontificis Maximi iussu editus*, intended as a homiletical and catechetical handbook for the clergy; but the influence of the Jesuits was so great that it could not compete with the catechisms of Canisius; and even those of Bellarmin, which appeared in 1598, did not attain equal popularity with them. The Roman Catholic books of instruction, like the Evangelical catechisms, did not escape the influence of rationalism, at first in method and then even to some extent in contents. A return to the stricter teaching of the Church made itself felt in the first decades of the nineteenth century. Since 1847 J. Deharbe's catechisms have been generally recognized as standard works. They include *Katholischer Katechismus für Stadt- und Landschulen* (Regensburg, 1847); and *Kleiner katholischer Katechismus zunächst für solche Landschulen, welche nur während des Sommer- oder Wintersemesters besucht werden* (1847). In the United States the Catholic Church provides manuals of catechetical instruction, such as those edited by W. Faerber in German and English (St. Louis, 1897 and often), and *Catechisms of Catholic Teaching* (New York, n.d.).

The Old Catholic Church has two official catechisms, the *Katholische Katechismus, herausgegeben im Auftrage der altkatholischen Synode* (Bonn) and *Leitfaden für den katholischen Religionsunterricht an höheren Schulen, herausgegeben im Auftrage der altkatholischen Synode* (Bonn, 1877).

22. The Greek Church.

In 1721 the synod of the Russian Orthodox Church decreed that three small manuals for the instruction of youth and the common people should be made, one on the principal doctrines of faith and on the decalogue, a second on the special duties of each class, and a third containing sermons on the principal doctrines, virtues, and vices. On the strength of this order there appeared a book entitled "First Instruction of Youth, Containing a Primer and a Short Exposition of the Decalogue, the Lord's Prayer and the Creed, by order of his Majesty Peter I., emperor of all the Russias," which is probably the first real catechism in the Greek Church. The catechism used at the present time, the "Complete Christian Catechism of the Orthodox Catholic Eastern Church," first published in 1839, originated under the influence of a manual composed by Jeromonach Platon in 1765 for the heir to the throne, the Grand Duke Paul Petrovitch, which is influenced in the arrangement of material by the *Confessio orthodoxa* of Peter Mogilas (1643). Like the latter, it groups its material under the three Christian virtues of faith, hope, and love. After an introduction on revelation, Holy Scripture, and catechetical teaching, it begins with an exposition of the Nicene Creed, followed by the Lord's Prayer and the Beatitudes, the union between faith and love, and an exposition of the Ten Commandments. The book closes with the application of the doctrine of faith and of piety.

(Ferdinand Cohrs.)

Bibliography: The works under Catechesis, Catechetics; Catechumenate; Luther's Two Catechisms; and Heidelberg Catechism should be consulted. Collections of early catechisms are made in *Monumenta Germaniæ pædagogica*, ed. C. Kehrbach, vols. 4, 20–33, 39, Berlin, 1887–1907, and in *Katechetische Handbibliothek*, ed. F. Walk, Kempten, 1891–1905 (containing not only catechisms but works on catechetics). On the catechisms of the Middle Ages consult: G. Langemack, *Historia catechetica*, vol. i., Stralsund, 1729; J. Geffcken, *Der Bilderkatechismus des fünfzehnten Jahrhunderts und die katechetischen Hauptstücke in dieser Zeit bis auf Luther*, vol. i., Leipsic, 1855; H. Brück, *Der religiöse Unterricht . in Deutschland*, Mainz, 1876; P. Göbl, *Geschichte der Katechese im Abendlande vom Verfall des Katechumenats bis zum Ende des Mittelalters*, Kempten, 1880; F. Probst, *Geschichte der katholischen Katechese*, Breslau, 1887; F. Falk, *Der Unterricht des Volks in den katechetischen Hauptstücken am Ende des Mittelalters*, in *Historisch-politische Blätter*, cviii (1891), 553 sqq., 682 sqq., cix (1892) 81 sqq., 721 sqq.; P. Bahlmann, *Deutschlands katholische Katechismen bis zum Ende des sechszehnten Jahrhunderts*, Münster, 1894; Hauck, *KD*, vols. i.–iii.

For collections of catechisms in post-Reformation times in Germany consult, besides the collections of Kehrbach and Walk, ut sup.: J. Hartmann, *Aelteste katechetische Denkmale der evangelischen Kirche*, Stuttgart, 1844; F. W. Bodemann, *Katechetische Denkmale der evangelisch-lutherischen Kirche*, Harburg, 1861; G. Kawerau, *Zwei älteste Katechismen der lutherischen Reformation*, Halle, 1890. For a bibliography of newer literature consult: F. Schneider, *Kritischer Wegweiser durch die Litteratur des Konfirmandenunterrichts und der öffentlichen Christenlehre*, Stuttgart, 1899. The history of catechisms is treated in: G. Langemack, ut sup., vols. ii.–iii., Stralssund, 1730–40; K. J. Löschke, *Die religiöse Bildung der Jugend und der sittliche Zustand der Schulen im 16. Jahrhundert*, Breslau, 1846; F. R. Ehrenfeuchter, *Zur Geschichte des Katechismus*, Göttingen, 1857; K. Neumann, *Der evangelische Religionsunterricht im Zeitalter der Reformation*, Berlin, 1899.

On other than German lands consult: S. Hess, *Geschichte des Zürcher-Katechismus*, Zurich, 1811; *Tercentenary Monument, In Commemoration of the Three Hundredth Anniversary of the Heidelberg Catechism*, Philadelphia, 1863; C. A. Toren, *Der evangelische Religions-Unterricht in Deutschland, Grossbritannien und Dänemark*, Gotha, 1865; H. Bonar, *Catechisms of the Scottish Reformation*, London, 1866; A. T. Mitchell, *Catechisms of the Second Reformation . with Historical Introduction*, London, 1886; A. C. Bang, *Dokumenter og studier vedrörende den lutherske katekismus' historie in Nordens kirker*, 2 vols., Christiania, 1893–99; I. Moschakes, *Catechism of the Orthodox Eastern Church*, London, 1894; J. Poynet, *The Real Reformation Catechism of 1553*, ib. 1894; W Eames, *Early New England Catechisms. A bibliographical Account of some Catechisms published before 1800*, Worcester, 1898.

The literature on Roman Catholic catechisms is very voluminous; the following may be consulted: *The Catechism of John Hamilton*, Oxford, 1844; C. Moufang, *Die Mainzer Katechismen von der Erfindung der Buchdruckerkunst bis zum Ende des achtzehnten Jahrhunderts*, Mainz, 1877; *Commentaire sur le catéchisme des provinces ecclésiastiques de Québec, Montréal, Ottawa*, Montreal, 1897; F. X. Thalhofer, *Entwickelung des katholischen Katechismus in Deutschland von Canisius bis Deharbe*, Freiburg, 1899; F. Spirago, *The Catechism Explained*, New York, 1899; T. E. Cox, *Biblical Treasury of the Catechism*, ib. 1900; T. L. Kinkead, *Explanation of the Baltimore Catechism*, ib. 1902; J. Perry, *Explanation of the Catechism*, St. Louis, 1902.

CATECHUMENATE.

Catechumenate is a term applied to the method of receiving and instructing, in preparation for baptism, those who applied for membership in the early Christian Church. As soon as the apostolic mission had reached the stage of founding a Christian society, it was natural that those who wished to enter it should be required to go through a course of instruction as to the meaning of the hopes which it held out and the demands which it made of its members. Our information as to the method pursued in the earliest period is very scanty. Apparently the gatherings of the disciples were at first freely opened to any one (I Cor. xiv. 24) who desired to know more of their faith and practise; and baptism was probably often administered with but a short delay. As time went on, more care was exercised; the need of it was demonstrated by cases of relapse into heathenism and of the seeking of membership from interested or treacherous motives.

1. Earliest Data.

We find traces of this greater caution as early as the first Apology of Justin (c. 150). A demand is made for some security as to the belief and conduct of the candidate, who is not apparently admitted to the assembly of the faithful until he has been adjudged worthy of the baptism. How this security was obtained is not clear; the preparation seems to have been private, and the one who conducted it probably answered for the candidate, as at once sponsor and catechist. Tertullian portrays a somewhat different system; though catechumens are still excluded from the assembly, the application of this name to them implies that they were already reckoned as in a sense belonging to the Church and under its care. This is still more clearly the case in Origen's account.

2. According to the Church Fathers.

The much discussed passage *Contra Celsum*, iii. 51 shows plainly that there was a definite system of examination and of instruction. It gives also the fact that at this period, besides the class which (as in Justin and Tertullian) is excluded from the assembly, there is another which has advanced far enough to claim the privilege of admission, and is only waiting for the last decisive step of baptism. It is a mistake to attempt to deduce from his words three classes divided by a hard and fast line, or to apply to these classes the names *audientes (Gk. akroōmenoi), genuflectente (gonuklinontes)*, and *competentes (phōtizomenoi)*. The last occurs in the Apostolic Constitutions, and in Cyril of Jerusalem passim, for the candidates approaching baptism, who are definitely distinguished from the catechumens. The name *akroōmenoi* occurs for the first time in the passage of Origen referred to, but without a distinct meaning; its use later in the proclamation of the deacon in the liturgy, summoning those not entitled to be present to depart, relates to a class of penitents not allowed to hear a part of the service to which catechumens were admitted. In like manner the application of *gonuklinontes* to a class of catechumens rests on a misunderstanding of the corrupt Greek text of the fifth canon of the Synod of Neocæsarea (314), which really means that catechumens falling into sin are to be put among the penitents, and expelled altogether if they do not amend.

To sum up, then, what has been said, Origen shows a development of the catechumenate from what Justin gives, while Tertullian exhibits an intermediate stage. We must, however, remember that these witnesses are from different parts of the Church. The development was probably largely influenced by local conditions. In Tertullian's time, Septimius Severus had forbidden conversions to Christianity, and formal arrangements for the preparation of converts would have been direct rebellion. In Origen's day, on the other hand, the Church had enjoyed a long period of peace, and was not afraid to allow trusted catechumens to be present at its services; but the large number of converts made it more probable that some unworthy ones would be among them, and so to the original examination before baptism, a second and earlier one was added. Origen's account of the catechumenate gives all the essential features of the institution, as we meet with it when fully established, after persecution had ceased. Christianity had become the state religion, and it was possible to work out in detail institutions which had been carefully planned in the dark days preceding.

3. First Period of Development.

This second or established period covers roughly the fourth and early fifth centuries. The candidate, accompanied by a sponsor, announces his desire, normally to a deacon, who informs the bishop or presbyter. The grounds of his desire are investigated; people of certain sinful or dubious occupations are *ipso facto* excluded unless they will abandon them. If the candidate is acceptable, he receives a preliminary instruction, and is then set apart by the sign of the cross, laying on of hands, and (in the West) with blessed salt, as a catechumen. For a time he receives no special instruction, sharing that which the whole congregation gets in the *missa catechumenorum*, though departing before the later and more solemn part of the liturgy. After two (or three) years, he may ask for baptism; he enters the class of *competentes*, and his name is inscribed on the church list. The immediate preparation includes special instructions, usually given by the bishop; certain ceremonies, especially of exorcism, which show the influence of the pagan mysteries; and finally the *traditio symboli*, or instruction in the precise words of the baptismal creed, whose general sense has long been known to him. After learning and repeating this, he is taught the words of the Lord's Prayer, which has also been withheld from him until now by the *Arcani disciplina* (q.v.). The recitation of the creed as a solemn act and the final renunciation of paganism accompany the act of baptism, which usually takes place in the night before Easter. During the following week the neophyte receives further instructions, and on the next Sunday, still wearing his white baptismal robe, he takes his place among the congregation as a baptized Christian, and joins in the recitation of the Lord's Prayer, the prayer of the children of God. As to the matter contained in the instructions to the catechumen in this period, fullest information comes from Augustine in the West and Cyril of Jerusalem in the East.

4. Second Period of Development.

The decline of the institution was brought about by the constantly increasing numbers of those who sought admission to the Church. A thorough examination of them all became impossible; the preliminary instruction was gradually dropped, and the catechumenate was reduced to the immediate preparation for baptism. The growing practise of baptizing infants and young children completed the process, since there was no place for instruction in their case. Something still remained, however, of the ancient procedure. On the Monday after the third Sunday in Lent, notice was given to present the children who were to be baptized at Easter. On the following Wednesday their sponsors brought them to the church, where their names were registered. The ceremonies of signing with the cross, laying on of hands, exorcism, giving of salt, and a final prayer made them catechumens. Seven masses were said on succeeding days, five containing similar ceremonies, while the last two were especially solemn. The sixth contained the "opening of the ears," a reminder of the ancient *traditio symboli*; the book of the Gospels was borne in procession to the altar and a short extract from each Gospel read, after which the creed was given to the candidates, and an acolyte brought forward two children, a boy and a girl, and recited the creed for them (the ancient *redditio symboli*); with the subsequent communication of the Lord's Prayer were usually connected short expositions of each clause. The last "scrutiny" took place the day before Easter, and followed much the same order, but more solemnly and formally; and baptism took place at the traditional time.

5. Decline of the Catechumenate.

6. Ritual Survivals.

When the time came that nothing remained of the original institutions of the catechumenate except the outward ceremonies, these were more and more condensed, until they formed but a single rite leading up to the baptism which immediately followed them. In the *Ordo baptismi* of the Roman Ritual the order of the ancient preparations for baptism may still be traced without difficulty, and not a few relics of it remain in the evangelical baptismal ceremonies (see BAPTISM).

(FERDINAND COHRS.)

A very interesting survival of the ancient catechumenate is found in the Armenian work found among the modern Paulicians, translated and edited by F C. Conybeare (*The Key of Truth: A Manual of the Paulician Church of Armenia*, Oxford, 1898) and believed by the editor to have been written not later than the ninth century and to represent an almost primitive form of Oriental Christianity. It is adoptionist in its Christology and drastic in its opposition to infant-baptism. It provides for a solemn consecration of the infant of Christian parents by the minister when it is seven days old, the careful training by parents and church until maturity is reached, the thorough testing of the candidates for baptism in life and in knowledge of Christian doctrine and morals, and the administration of baptism with considerable ceremony to those who have fulfilled all the conditions and have attained to the age at which Christ was baptized. A brief catechism, embracing the points of doctrine in which catechumens must be grounded, is given at the end. A. H. N.

BIBLIOGRAPHY: The sources are to be found in the works of Justin Martyr, Origen's *Contra Celsum*, the "Catechetical Lectures" of Cyril of Jerusalem, Augustine's *De catechizandis rudibus*, and the *Didache*, all of which are accessible in Eng. transl. The history of the institution is traced in: G. von Zezschwitz, *System der christlichen Katechetik*, 2 vols., Leipsic, 1863–72; J. Mayer, *Geschichte des Katechumenats . . in den ersten sechs Jahrhunderten*, Kempten, 1866 (Roman Catholic); A. Weiss, *Die altkirchliche Paedagogik . der ersten sechs Jahrhunderte*, Freiburg, 1869; F. X. Funk, in *Tübinger Theologische Quartalschrift*, 1883, pp. 41–77, 1886, pp. 353 sqq., 1899, pp. 434 sqq.; E. Hatch, *Organization of the Early Churches*, London, 1888; J. Heron, *Church of Sub-Apostolic Age; its Life, Worship, and Organization*, London, 1888; E. Sachsse, *Evangelische Katechetik; die Lehre von der kirchlichen Erziehung*, Berlin, 1897; F. Wiegand, *Die Stellung des apostolischen Symbols im kirchlichen Leben des Mittelalters*, i. *Symbol und Katechumenat*, Leipsic, 1899; Neander, *Christian Church*, vols. i. and ii. contain much valuable matter, consult the Index; Schaff, *Christian Church*, ii. 255–257; Bingham, *Origines*, books x., xi., xiv.; *DCA*, i. 317–319; the literature on the *Didache* (q.v.) usually discusses the catechetics of the early Church.

CATENÆ.

Origin (§ 1).
Meaning of the Term (§ 2).
Sources (§ 3).
Value (§ 4).
Method (§ 5).
Form (§ 6).
Catenæ Previous to the Fourteenth Century (§ 7).
Medieval Catenæ (§ 8).
Post-Reformation Catenæ (§ 9).

The term catena, "a chain" (plural, catenæ), designates a commentary on Holy Scripture made up by piecing together short extracts from the Fathers and older writers. This plan of construction was suggested by the accumulation of exegetical materials made both by Origen and his school and by the theologians of Antioch in the third and fourth centuries.

The principal motive which impelled later scholars to collect and examine the early utterances was a dogmatic one. After the conversion of Constantine, the Church was anxious to put together in a clear and systematic form the results

1. Origin. of previous theological work, and to emphasize the connection of the past with the present. For this purpose in regard to doctrine the decrees of the ecumenical councils answered admirably; but it was not so easy to attain the same result in the exposition of Scripture. The problem was to represent the results arrived at by the recognized commentators in propositions that had a unity of scheme and an admitted authority. The principles of its solution are laid down in the nineteenth canon of the Quinisext (Second Trullan) Council: that Holy Scripture is the standard of truth, that the limits of doctrine already fixed and the traditions of the Fathers are not to be transgressed, and that if any question concerning the Scripture comes up, it is to be expounded in no other way than as the great teachers of the past have given it in their works. The exposition of the Scripture was thus firmly attached to the recognized orthodox doctrine. The second canon of the same council had named some of the "lights and doctors" who were to be followed, and the first canon had given warning against all heretics, not merely against Arius, Macedonius, Apollinaris, and Nestorius, but also against Theodore of Mopsuestia, Origen, Didymus, Evagrius, and Theodoret. It was, however, found impossible to carry out these principles strictly. The writings of the authors suspected of heresy offered material too valuable to be neglected; and it was found impossible to arrive at a unity of results in an anthology of this kind without doing violence to the individuality of the authors and damaging their authority, so that nothing could be done but to put together what was selected.

In this manner arose the collections of extracts which are so characteristic of Byzantine theology, covering all the books of the Bible (especially Genesis, Job, the Psalms, Canticles, Isaiah, Matthew, and John) by extracts from patristic commentators, and setting an example of method which was widely followed in Western and medieval commentaries. These collections are usually known as *Catenæ* (*Seirai*). The origin of the name is obscure, but its meaning is plain. It refers to collections of material put together

2. Meaning of the Term. in a purely external but visible connection, and strung upon the thread of the text. There may have been originally a mystical significance attached to it. As the hermetic chain of the later Neoplatonists symbolized the harmonious conjunction of the bearers of wisdom to the world, hand joined in hand from the earliest to later times, so the line of the Fathers was to hand down the approved expositions of the one true Church.

The first compilers have no fixed phrases to describe their process; but their lengthy titles give an idea of the plan they set before them. They collected their material according to the maxim of Seneca, *Quod verum est, meum est* ("What is true is mine"). The manner in which literary property was handled in the ancient world permitted not only straightforward appropriation of other people's work, but the utmost freedom in adaptation to the borrower's special purpose. The retention of the original authors' names here is an evidence of the weight attached to their testimony as authoritative expositors; where the compiler adds comments of his own, he is usually careful to distinguish his additions. Great variety is found in the manner of reproduction and in the extent of the material included. In the Catena of Possinus on Matthew we have one constructed on the exact lines laid down by the Quinisext Council—a mosaic of verbal citations from

3. Sources. commentaries or other writings of orthodox Fathers. Where the compiler, like Nicetas of Serræ, added reflections of his own, he generally put them at the head of the group of quotations following a fresh section of the text. Where he adapted and condensed, he either kept to the serial order, or worked over all the material he had accumulated without making divisions for the separate authors. This is the manner adopted by Procopius, Œcumenius, and Theophylact, who emphasize at the same time the fact that they are not originators but transmitters. There is no sharp dividing line between this kind of Catena and the Byzantine commentary; for the latter also patristic tradition is the standard, though the sources are not indicated in the margin, as is usually the case in the Catenæ, and the exposition proceeds without a break.

The value of the Catenæ is measured by their judgment in selecting and their skill in combining the material they borrow. The difficulty of choice is increased by the dogmatic limitations, which are sometimes in inevitable conflict with the scholarly interest. Origen, for instance, the first great Christian critic and commentator, was of inestimable value to exegesis; and for the Old Testament Catenæ both Philo, who had been studied by all learned theologians from Origen down, and Josephus were invaluable authorities. A compromise was reached in the principle (still followed by Roman Catholic commentators) of Cyril of Alexandria: "We need not avoid or question everything that heretics have said; for they confess many things which we also confess." Another difficulty was found in the occasionally conflicting expositions; their diversity was explained by Drungarius, with reference to the obscurity of the text, as providential. He contents himself with placing side by side the varying renderings and explanations of Isaiah, leaving the reader to form his own judgment.

4. Value.

The simplest method of making a Catena was to follow one principal authority, to whose exposition shorter scholia are added from other sources. Thus Chrysostom is the main source in the Catena of Possinus on Matthew, as well as in the Gospel commentaries of Euthymius and Theophylact, though all of these differ in the additions they make to what they take from him. Other Catenæ are indiscriminate anthologies, no one authority being preferred. Of this type are those of Procopius and Nicetas, and most of those on the Epistles.

5. Method.

The external form of the Catenæ differed according to their extent. Where they were not too extensive, the text was placed in the middle of the page, surrounded by the exposition, usually in smaller characters, sometimes even in tachygraphy. The names of the authorities are sometimes in the margin, sometimes in the body of the exposition, as a rule abbreviated. Occasionally diacritical marks show the connection between text and commentary. If the Catena is too extensive to allow this arrangement, the sections of the text are followed by the commentary, in separate paragraphs, with the authors' names on the margin, or else written without a break. The manuscripts, of which few date further back than the tenth century, differ much in execution. Some are of admirable workmanship, with illustrations; others are plain copies for students, with the marks of long use upon them, and some seem to have been hastily and carelessly made to supply the demand of the bookselling trade. Besides the commentaries, the Catenæ contain a good deal of introductory or illustrative matter. Thus the Gospels are frequently prefaced by the canons of Eusebius and his epistle to Carpianus, as well as by arguments and biographies of the evangelists; the Pauline epistles have a life of Paul, a list of his journeys, and an account of his martyrdom.

6. Form.

Whether the beginnings of the manufacture of Catenæ can be traced back to the patristic period it is impossible to say with certainty, though it seems not improbable. After Eusebius the work of theologians to a great extent took the direction of codifying and criticizing what had been handed down. But Procopius (d. 528) is the first who can be demonstrated to have made Catenæ. The value of his work, which rests not only upon the Fathers from the third to the fifth century but upon Josephus and Philo and upon some of the teachers before Origen, gave it an epoch-making position. From the manner in which he speaks of his task in the prefaces to Genesis and Isaiah, we may conjecture that he was not an imitator of others but an originator in this line. Other extant Catenæ were compiled by Andreas the presbyter (seventh to tenth century); Johannes Drungarius (tenth century); Michael Psellus, and Nicetas, bishop of Serræ, later metropolitan of Heraclea in Thrace (eleventh century); Nicolaus Muzalon and Neophytus Eucleistus (twelfth century); and Macarius Chrysocephalus (fourteenth century). To these may be added not only the commentaries arranged more or less in catena style, though without names of authorities: Œcumenius, of whose date and personality we know nothing certain, though he was probably a contemporary of Arethas of Cappadocia; and the Gospel commentaries of Theophylact and Euthymius, composed under the Comneni. There is, however, a much larger number of anonymous Catenæ; and this fact is surprising, since Byzantine theologians were not given to hiding their light under a bushel. It may possibly be explained by the theory that these Catenæ were produced not by any one man but by a group of collaborators. Their dates are very hard to determine; the surest way to reach conclusions on this point is by examining their relations to those whose dates we know, which requires a good deal more investigation than has yet been given to them. In fact, what has been done in the way of scientific study of the Catenæ in general has only covered certain specific points; and those which have been printed cover only a small part of the extant material, and that not always selected with judgment.

7. Catenæ Previous to the Fourteenth Century.

The catena form impressed itself as a model upon medieval exegesis in the West, which also imitated the spirit in which the Eastern compilers went about their work. Here too the aim was to preserve the tradition of the Church in a uniform arrangement of Scriptural exposition, "so that the line of prophetic and apostolic interpretation may follow the norm of the ecclesiastical and catholic sense" (Vincent of Lerins). The principal sources were Ambrose, Hilary, Augustine, and Jerome; less often the Greek Fathers, such as Origen, Chrysostom, and Cyril of Alexandria, are cited. The prototypes of the medieval catena commentaries may be seen in the expositions of Cassiodorus and Isidore of Seville. On the Carolingian period the numerous commentaries of Bede exercised a decisive influence. He knew Greek, and shows some feeling for textual criticism; but he was not an exegetical individuality. He col-

8. Medieval Catenæ.

lects his fragments of exposition mainly from Jerome, Ambrose, Augustine, and Gregory, and lays his chief stress on the edifying explanation of the moral and mystical sense. In this tendency he was followed by Alcuin, Rabanus Maurus, Walafried Strabo, Dietrich of Hersfeld, Haimo, and Remigius of Auxerre, all less careful in the reproduction of their sources than Bede, with whom it was a matter of principle to designate clearly the intellectual property of his authorities. Among later commentaries of the catena sort especial influence was exerted by that of Peter Lombard on the Pauline epistles, which made no pretense of indicating sources, and the *Catena Aurea* of Thomas Aquinas on the Gospels, which makes use of some Greek Fathers as well as of Augustine, Jerome, Rabanus, and Remigius. Mention should also be made of the "glosses"—the *Glossa ordinaria* of Walafried Strabo, the *Glossa interlinealis* of Anselm of Laon (1110), and the *Postillæ perpetuæ* of Nicholas of Lyra (1340; see GLOSSES, BIBLICAL AND ECCLESIASTICAL).

These works lead up to the exegetical collections which were made after the Reformation and under its influence. The expository standpoint was different, but the method of compilation remained the same. They either gave the observations of certain selected expositors side by side without change, or they made groups of extracts from as large a number as possible. Instances of the first method are the *Biblia magna* of De la Haye (Paris, 1643), the *Biblia maxima* (ib. 1660), the English *Annotations upon all the Books of the Old and New Testament* (London, 1645), and the *Critici sacri* edited by J. Pearson and others (ib. 1660). The second class is represented by Matthew Pole's *Synopsis criticorum aliorumque scripturæ sacræ interpretum et commentatorum* (London, 1669), which contains the most varied extracts from more than eighty theologians of all ages and beliefs, even including the Jewish. The Roman Catholic expositors, such as Cornelius a Lapide, Estius, and Calmet, followed the lines laid down by the older Catenæ, to which, however, with their uncritical subservience to a tradition presupposed as authoritative, they are far inferior.

9. Post-Reformation Catenæ.

(G. HEINRICI.)

CATHARI. See NEW MANICHEANS, II.

CATHARINE, SAINT, OF ALEXANDRIA. See CATHARINE, SAINT, THE MARTYR.

CATHARINE, SAINT, OF BOLOGNA: Roman Catholic saint; b. at Bologna or, according to other accounts, at Verona Sept. 8, 1413; d. at Bologna Mar. 9, 1463. About 1430 she entered the order of the Poor Clares at Ferrara after having been a lady of honor at the court of Princess Margaret of Este for about two years. She later became abbess of a convent of her order which was founded at Bologna. Her name was included in the Roman martyrology in 1592, and she was canonized by Benedict XIII. in 1724. Later tradition wove many legends about her name, and her body was preserved undecayed in her convent until recent years. To St. Catharine is ascribed a prophetic work entitled *Revelationes, sive de septem armis spiritualibus*, composed about 1438 and first edited probably at Bologna in 1475 and repeatedly since. In art she is represented in the habit of the Poor Clares, carrying the Christ-child, since the Virgin is said to have appeared to her and to have placed in her arms the infant Jesus in his swaddling-clothes.

(O. ZÖCKLER†.)

BIBLIOGRAPHY: The *Vita* which is the earliest source was published at Bologna, 1502, from which a number of biographies were drawn in the next century. Consult: J. Görres, *Die christliche Mystik*, ii. 53 sqq., 158–159, 4 vols., Regensburg, 1836–42.

CATHARINE, SAINT, OF GENOA: Roman Catholic saint; b. at Genoa 1447; d. there Sept. 14, 1510. She was the daughter of Roberto Fieschi, who had been viceroy of Naples under René of Anjou. Despite her desire for a life of religion, she was obliged to marry a nobleman of her native city named Giuliano Adorno, whence she is often called Catharina Flisca Adurna. After a life of extravagance her husband died in 1474, but not before he had been converted by his wife's piety and had become a Franciscan of the third order. For the remainder of her life his widow, as a member of the order of the Annunciation of St. Marcellina, was distinguished both for her care of the sick in the Genoese hospital Pammatone (especially during the plagues of 1497 and 1501) and by her extreme asceticism. For twenty-three years during the seasons of Lent and Advent she is said to have fasted absolutely, taking at most a glass of water with salt and vinegar "to cool the raging flame within." She was formally canonized by Clement XII. in 1737, and the following pope, Benedict XIV., placed her name in the Roman martyrology, appointing her feast for Mar. 22. St. Catharine was one of the numerous mystic and prophetic authors of the latter part of the Middle Ages and wrote *Demonstratio purgatorii* or *Tractatus de purgatorio* (ed. C. Marabotto and E. Vernazza in their biography of St. Catharine, Genoa, 1551; Eng. transl., London, 1858), *Dialogus animam inter et corpus, amorem proprium, spiritum, humanitatem ac Deum*, and a treatise on the Christian life (both contained in the edition already mentioned). Her visions were assailed by Adrian Baillet in his *Vies des saints* (Paris, 1701) from the Gallican point of view, but other Roman Catholic authorities, such as St. Francis of Sales and the modern Jesuit Christian Pesch, have esteemed them highly.

(O. ZÖCKLER†.)

BIBLIOGRAPHY: The anonymous *Vita* with commentary is in *ASB*, Sept., v. 123–176, and was translated into French by the Abbé Piot, Paris, 1840. Consult: P. Lechner, *Leben und Schriften der heiligen Katharina von Genua*, Regensburg, 1859; T. de Bussière, *Vie et œuvres de S. Catherine de Gênes*, Paris, 1873; P. Fliche, *S. Catherine de Gênes*, Paris, 1880; F. von Hügel, in *The Hampstead Annual*, 1898, pp. 70 sqq.

CATHARINE, SAINT, THE MARTYR (SAINT CATHARINE OF ALEXANDRIA): One of the most honored saints both of the Eastern and the Western Church. Many modern hagiographers identify her with a wealthy and noble Christian lady of Alexandria who, according to Eusebius (*Hist. eccl.*, VIII. xiv. 15), resisted the licentious advances of the emperor Maximinus, and was consequently deprived of her estates and banished. This identification, however, does not agree with the statement of Rufinus (*Hist. eccl.*, viii. 17) that this lady was named Dorothea, nor does it harmonize with the legend of St. Catharine as given both by Simeon Metaphrastes and the Roman martyrology. According to these sources, St. Catharine was a maiden of royal birth (the daughter of King Konstos, in the Greek *Officium*), and of extraordinary wisdom and beauty. At the age of eighteen, she engaged in a controversy, at the command either of Maximinus or Maxentius (although the latter never ruled Alexandria), with fifty pagan philosophers, whom she converted so signally that they remained faithful to Christianity even to martyrdom. In prison, a few days before her own execution, she converted the empress, the general Porphyrius, and his 200 soldiers, all of whom suffered death by the sword for their faith. Resisting both the pleadings and the threats of the tyrant, Catharine remained unharmed by torture, even on a machine of sharp-pointed wheels, until she was finally beheaded by the command of Maximinus.

The day of St. Catharine is celebrated either on Nov. 25 or on Mar. 5. Her body is said to have been borne by angels to Mount Sinai, where Justinian I. built a cloister in her honor and where her bones were said to have been discovered by Egyptian Christians in the eighth century, thus giving rise to the feast of the discovery of the body of St. Catharine on May 13 or 26. About 1027 Simeon, a monk from Sinai, is said to have carried a portion of the relics of St. Catharine to Rouen, and her monastery on Mount Sinai now retains only her head and one hand. [These are enclosed in a marble sarcophagus.] Inspired by the tradition of her victory over the philosophers of Alexandria, the philosophical faculty of the University of Paris later chose her as their patron saint. According to Occidental tradition, she is one of the fourteen "helpers in need," the only other feminine members of this band being SS. Barbara and Margaret. See HELPERS IN NEED.

In Christian art, both of the East and the West, St. Catharine is an important figure. Her usual attributes are a sword and a wheel (either entire or broken), through which curved knives are thrust. To these are frequently added a palm of victory, a book in token of her learning, and occasionally a crown, or, more often, a bridal ring which the Christ-child himself is said to have placed on her finger in emblem of betrothal. The oldest Oriental picture of this saint is a mosaic over the apse of the basilica of the Transfiguration in the monastery on Sinai, which represents simply a female head without attributes. In a picture by Simon of Sienna (d. 1344) she bears in her hand a palm and a book. Among the numerous representations of St. Catharine in Western art, special mention may be made of the works of Altichiero da Zevio (c. 1380) in the frescos of the chapel of St. George at Padua, the frescos of Masaccio (c. 1420) in the upper church of St. Clement at Rome, eleven marble bas-reliefs (probably dating from the fourteenth century) in the church of Santa Chiara in Naples, nine pictures of 1385 in the cloister of St. Paul at Leipsic, and the miniatures in the *Vie de Sainte Catherine d'Alexandrie* by Jean Mielot, secretary of Philip the Good, duke of Burgundy (c. 1462). After the middle of the fifteenth century the most noteworthy artists of Italy, Flanders, and Germany, such as Fiesole, Raffael, Carlo Dolce, Jan van Eyck, Hans Memling, and Lukas Cranach, vied with one another in the production of pictures of St. Catharine, and the medieval Christian drama repeatedly represented the legend of the saint in mysteries, the earliest being that of the Norman Geoffrey, abbot of St. Albans, which was played at Dunstable about 1120. (O. ZÖCKLER†.)

BIBLIOGRAPHY: *The Legend of St. Katherine, ed. from a MS. in the Cotton Library by J. Morton for the Abbotsford Club*, London, 1841; *Life and Martyrdom of St. Katherine of Alexandria*, Roxburghe Club publications, no. 99, ib. 1884; *Life of St. Katherine*, ed. E. Einenkel for Early Text Society, ib. 1884; *The Life Metrical*, by J. Capgrave, ed. F. C. Hingeston, in *Rolls Series*, no. 1, pp. 337-354, ib. 1858. Consult: C. Hardwick, *Historical Inquiry Touching St. Catharine of Alexandria*, Cambridge, 1849; H. Knust, *Geschichte der Legenden der heiligen Catharina*, Halle, 1890. On the art side, consult: Mrs. Jameson, *Sacred and Legendary Art*, ii. 74-97, Boston, 1893; J. Wipfli and J. J. von Ah, *Das Leben der heiligen Katharina von Alexandrien*, Einsiedeln, 1898.

CATHARINE DE' RICCI, rît'chî, SAINT: Roman Catholic saint; b. at Florence [Apr. 23] 1522; d. at Prato (11 m. n.w. of Florence) Feb. 2 [1590]. She was educated in a convent at Monticelli and at the wish of her father lived in the world for a short time, after which she took the veil and entered the Dominican nunnery of St. Vincent at Prato. At the age of twenty-five she became prioress, and spiritual counsel was sought from her by bishops, cardinals, and princes. She was also a close friend of St. Philip Neri, with whom she maintained an active correspondence. The intensity of her meditation on the Passion was such that she actually felt the sufferings of Christ and frequently shed blood as if from scourgings and wounds. St. Catharine was canonized by Benedict XIV in 1746 and her feast was appointed for Feb. 13. In art she has the attributes of the crown of thorns and a marriage ring. The elegant style of her letters ranks her as one of the best Italian classics of the second half of the sixteenth century [ed. A. Gherardi, Florence, 1890]. (O. ZÖCKLER†.)

BIBLIOGRAPHY: F. M. Capes, *Life of St. Catherine de' Ricci*, London, 1905, which gives a transl. of a number of her letters.

CATHARINE, SAINT, OF SIENNA: Roman Catholic saint; b. at Sienna [Mar. 25] 1347; d. at Rome Apr. 29, 1380. She was the twenty-third child of a dyer named Jacomo Benincasa. Her early home in the vicinity of a Dominican monastery made a deep impression on the sensitive child, and she believed that St. Dominic himself appeared to her in a dream and urged her to enter his order. Disregarding her mother's wish that she should marry, Catharine, then about twelve years of age, cut off her long blond hair to escape unwelcome attentions. Three years later smallpox destroyed her beauty and she was able to fulfil her heart's desire, to which her mother had consented some time previously, by entering the order of penitents of St. Dominic. She no longer drank wine, while her only food was uncooked herbs, taken as a salad, or with oil, fruit, and bread. She scourged herself thrice daily according to the most rigid Dominican custom, once for herself, once for the living, and once for the dead. Under her habit she wore a shirt of haircloth for which she substituted later an iron chain about her waist. She passed the night in prayer until the bells on the monastery called to matins and then lay down between boards which symbolized her coffin. This asceticism she practised in a tiny room in her father's house which she scarcely left for three years except to attend mass in the neighboring Dominican church. After 1366, however, she appeared more frequently in public and became conspicuous for her deeds of mercy to the poor and sick, especially during the plague of 1374. Through her devotion and her piety she gathered around her a spiritual household of about twenty persons of both sexes, chiefly members of the Dominican order.

Early Life.

The chief cause of St. Catharine's fame was her reputation for visions and for prophecy. Even during the time of her novitiate she believed that Christ often appeared to her and, toward the end of this period of preparation, that he himself betrothed her formally as he had the first St. Catharine (see CATHARINE, SAINT, THE MARTYR), by placing a ring upon her finger. This marriage symbol, she declared, was always visible to her, although no other eyes might see it. Her union with Christ was further sanctified by an interchange of hearts and finally by the divine stigmata, beginning with the print of a nail on her hand and ending with the painful impress of the four other wounds. This stigmatization also, as in the case of her German contemporary, Margareta Ebner (q.v.) of Medingen, always remained invisible, whereas in St. Francis and the majority of the stigmatists, the wounds might be seen of all. She likewise believed that she associated much with the Virgin and with Christ, not only being convinced that she drank the blood from the wounded side of the Lord, and the milk from Mary's breast, but also that she received divine instruction, admonition, and comforts, which she was frequently able to communicate to others in her ecstasies. Many of her letters and writings, especially her "Dialogues," were dictated by her in trances. She once fasted during the forty days from Easter to Ascension, being supported solely by the Eucharist and thus becoming a model for later saints, particularly for the two Catharines of the fifteenth century.

Visions.

Despite her death to the world, St. Catharine was compelled, during the closing years of her life, to take part repeatedly in the political and ecclesiastical affairs of her country. After 1374 she frequently left Sienna for the promotion of peace between the hostile nobles of Tuscany. In 1375 she was in Pisa, where she wrote Queen Joan of Naples to undertake a crusade to free the Holy Land. A year later she went to Avignon to reconcile the republic of Florence with Gregory XI., but was unsuccessful on account of the treachery of the Florentines. Later, however, after she had in great measure been instrumental in securing the return of the pope to Rome, she effected her purpose by a journey to Florence in 1378. The schism between Urban VI. in Italy and Clement VII. in Avignon also engaged her attention. She was a firm partizan of the former, who summoned her to Rome and after listening to her exhortations of peace sent her to the court of Joan together with St. Catharine of Sweden to win the queen from Clement to himself. The mission failed, since Bridget's daughter would not be subordinate to her sister saint, but Catharine of Sienna lived to see the longed-for, though brief, adherence of Naples to her pope. She was recalled to Rome by this turmoil and struggle and there died. She was buried in the Dominican Church of Minerva in Rome, although her skull is said to be in the Dominican Church of her native city. She was canonized by Pius II., in 1461, while Urban VIII. appointed her feast for Apr. 30. She is represented in art as carrying a crucifix with stigmata on her hands, as well as with the bridal ring. Occasionally she carries in her hand a lily or a book.

Political Activity.

The chief writings of St. Catharine of Sienna are 373 letters (best separate edition by N. Tommaseo, *Le Lettere di Santa Caterina da Siena*, 4 vols., Florence, 1860), many of them addressed to popes, cardinals, princes, and nobles, and important for the history of the period. She likewise wrote twenty-six prayers, various short prophetic oracles, and a dialogue between herself and God the Father, dictated in a trance in 1378, under the title *Libro della Divina Dottrina* (Eng. transl., by A. Thorold, *Dialogue of the Seraphic Virgin Catharine of Sienna*, London, 1896), later divided by G. Gigli into four treatises on religious wisdom, prayer, providence, and obedience; an older division is into six treatises under the title *Dialogi de providentia Dei*. Historically, the most interesting of these treatises is the one on prayer, in which St. Catharine emphasizes the value of the prayer of the heart, which needs no words, in contradistinction to mere formalism. In her criticisms she spared neither priests, cardinals, nor pope, sternly reproving them for their derelictions and admonishing them of their high duty. Yet though she proclaimed the necessity of reformation, she desired it to be within the Church and was unswerving in her orthodoxy and in her allegiance to the Roman Catholic faith. Her complete works were first edited by Aldus at Venice in 1500, but the best of the older editions is that of G. Gigli, *L'Opere della Serafica Santa Caterina da Siena* (5 vols., Sienna, 1707–26). (O. ZÖCKLER†.)

Writings.

BIBLIOGRAPHY: The early *Vita* and other documents are collected in *ASB*, April, iii. 853–978. For later lives and criticism consult: A. Capecelatro, *Storia di Caterina da Siena e del Papato del suo tempo*, 4th ed., Sienna, 1878; Augusta T. Drane, *Hist. of St. Catherine of Siena and her Companions*, 2 vols., London, 1887; A. H. Chirat, *S. Catherine de Sienne et l'église au 14. siècle*, Paris, 1888; Josephine E. Butler, *Catharine of Siena*, London, 1895; Comtesse de Flavigny, *S. Catherine de Sienne*, Paris,

1895; Vida D. Scudder, *St. Catherine of Siena as seen in her Letters*, New York, 1905; *St. Catherine of Siena and Her Times*, London, 1906; E. G. Gardner, *St. Catherine of Siena*, London and New York, 1907. Also L. Gazet, *Le Grand Schisme d'Occident*, 2 vols., Florence, 1889.

CATHARINE, SAINT, OF SWEDEN: Roman Catholic saint; b. in Sweden 1331 or 1332; d. at Vadstena (130 m. s.w. of Stockholm) Mar. 24, 1381. She was the second daughter of St. Bridget, the founder of the Brigittines (see BRIDGET, SAINT, OF SWEDEN). At the age of thirteen or fourteen she married a young nobleman of German extraction named Eggart of Kürnen—the marriage was, however, by mutual consent only nominal, and both parties preserved a lifelong virginity. During the lifetime of her husband, Catharine accompanied her mother on the last-named's first journey to Rome, where through a vision of St. Bridget she learned of her husband's death in Sweden. She then made a pilgrimage with her mother to the Holy Land, but was in Rome with her brother Birger when St. Bridget died there in 1373. She was one of those who escorted her mother's bones to Sweden, and she then took up her abode at Vadstena, the mother house of the Brigittines, where she ruled as the successor of St. Bridget. About the time of the return of the popes from Avignon, St. Catharine again resided for some years in Italy and twice secured papal confirmation of the rule of her order, first from Gregory XI. in 1377 and again from Urban VI. two years later. The day appointed for her feast in the Roman martyrology is Mar. 22. In art her attribute is a hind. She wrote a "Consolation of the Soul," which has been lost. According to the preface, it was a compilation from many books and treated of the ten commandments, the seven benedictions, the seven joys of Mary, the seven gifts of the Holy Spirit, and the seven deadly sins. (O. ZÖCKLER†.)

BIBLIOGRAPHY: The early *Vita* with commentary is in *ASB*, March, ii. 503-531, and in E. M. Fant, *Script. rer. Suecicarum*, iii., section 2, pp. 244-275; cf. A. Butler, *Lives of the Fathers, Martyrs, and Other Saints*, Nov. 25th, London, 1860; *KL*, vii. 344-345.

CATHARINUS, AMBROSIUS: The monastic name of Lancelotto Politi, Dominican, bishop of Minori and archbishop of Conza; b. in Sienna 1487; d. in Naples Nov. 8, 1553. In 1517 he entered in Florence the monastery of Savonarola, against whom he wrote a polemic treatise in 1548. Eager in opposing every form of heresy, he appeared against Luther in 1520 with an *Apologia pro veritate catholicæ ac apostolicæ fidei*. Luther replied in 1521 (*Ad librum A. Catharini responsio*), and Catharinus answered. Then he went to France, and wrote in Paris against a member of his own order, Cardinal Cajetan, *Annotationes in commentaria Cajetani*. After returning to his country he wrote against his fellow townsman Bernardino Ochino, who in the mean while had fled from Italy to live according to his own belief (see OCHINO, BERNARDINO). A little later Catharinus issued two treatises against Italian Protestant works; viz., *Trattato utilissimo del benefizio di Gesu Cristo crocifisso* and *Sommario della Sacra Scrittura*. The polemic theologian was present at the Council of Trent. He arrived in 1545 with the legate Del Monte and made a speech at the third session. As a reward for his services Paul III. made him bishop of Minori in 1546. Julius III. made him archbishop of Conza in 1552, and was on the point of naming him cardinal when Catharinus died. The earliest of the works of Catharinus are collected in his *Opuscula* (Leyden, 1542), but there is no complete edition. K. BENRATH.

BIBLIOGRAPHY: The life and writings of Catharinus are discussed in: J. Quétif and J. Échard, *Script. ordinis prædicatorum*, ii. 144 sqq., 332, 885; K. Werner, *Geschichte der apologetischen und polemischen Literatur*, vol. iv. passim, Schaffhausen, 1865; F. H. Reusch, *Der Index der verbotenen Bücher*, vol. i. passim, Bonn, 1883.

CATHCART, WILLIAM: American Baptist; b. at Londonderry, Ireland, Nov. 8, 1826. He was educated at Glasgow University and Horton (now Rawdon) Baptist Theological College, Yorkshire, England, from which he was graduated in 1850. He was minister of a Baptist church at Barnsley, near Sheffield, from 1850 to 1853, when he went to the United States, and accepted a call to Mystic River, Conn., where he remained four years. He was then pastor of the Second Baptist Church, Philadelphia, from 1857 to 1884, and was also president of the American Baptist Historical Society from 1876 to 1884. He has written: *The Papal System, from Its Origin to the Present Time* (Philadelphia, 1872); *The Baptists and the American Revolution* (1876); and *The Baptism of the Ages and of the Nations* (1878), and edited *The Baptist Encyclopædia* (Philadelphia, 1881). Since 1884 he has held no regular charge, his health not permitting him to accept a pastorate, although he has been able to devote part of his time to literary labors.

CATHEDRA: The ancient Latin title for the special seat occupied by the bishop in Christian churches. Even in the catacombs such seats were used, either cut out of the solid rock or portable. In the basilicas the cathedra stood at the back of the semicircular apse, behind the altar, which was on the chord of the arc; but when it became customary to place the altar back against the wall, the bishop's seat was brought down into the choir and placed on the north or gospel side. The early Church preserved with great reverence the seats of its first bishops; thus it is learned from Eusebius (*Hist. eccl.*, VII. xix. 32) that the church of Jerusalem preserved that of James, and the church of Alexandria that of Mark. A very ancient chair traditionally believed to be that of Peter is preserved in St. Peter's at Rome, and was used for many centuries for the enthronement of new popes, until Alexander VII. (1655-67), for its better preservation, had Bernini enclose it in a colossal bronze throne. At the celebration of the eighteenth centenary of the apostle's martyrdom in 1867, Pius IX. had it again exposed to view; an exact description and picture of it may be found in Kraus, *Roma sotterranea*, Freiburg, 1873. The bishop's seat was often used as a symbol of the teaching office of the Church, exercised through him; this is frequently referred to in the mosaics and carving of extant chairs dating from the fifth to the ninth century. Thus in the definition of the doctrine of papal infallibility, the pope is said to speak *ex cathedra* when he proclaims a doctrine "in the exercise of his office as pastor and teacher of all Christians."

CATHEDRAL: In the churches with episcopal organization, the principal church of a diocese, the especial seat of the bishop. It is the normal place for the principal episcopal functions, such as ordination, and is directly under the charge of the bishop, who is assisted in its administration and in the performance of divine service by a body of canons (see CHAPTER), whose head is a dean or provost. In England, from the Reformation until 1840, a distinction was drawn between cathedrals of the old and of the new foundation. The former were those where the chapter had been always composed of secular canons, and whose constitution remained, therefore, unchanged; in the latter, after the suppression of the monasteries by Henry VIII., a new organization was required to replace the earlier monastic chapter. The older cathedrals, from their rank and importance in the history of the Church, offer some of the most splendid and imposing examples of Christian architecture. See ARCHITECTURE, ECCLESIASTICAL.

BIBLIOGRAPHY: M. E. C. Walcott, *Cathedralia: a Constitutional History of Cathedrals of the Western Church*, London, 1865 (authoritative); idem, *Documentary History of English Cathedrals*, London, 1866; J. S. Howson, ed., *Essays on Cathedrals, by various writers*, London, 1872; C. A. Swainson, *Hist. of a Cathedral of the Old Foundation*, London, 1880; P. Schneider, *Die bischöflichen Domkapitel*, Mainz, 1885; *Bell's Cathedral Series*, 35 vols., London, 1896–1903 (deals with history and archeology); J. J. Bourassé, *Les plus belles cathédrales de France*, Paris, 1896; L. Cloquet, *Les Grandes Cathédrales du monde catholique*, Paris, 1897; *The Cathedrals of England and Wales*, New York, The Churchman Company, 1907.

CATHOLIC (Gk. *katholikos*, "general, universal," from *kath' holou*, "on the whole"): The phrase *hē katholikē ekklēsia*, "the catholic church," was first used by Christian writers to distinguish the entire body of believers from individual bodies. It then came naturally to designate the orthodox in distinction from heretics and schismatics. Later it was applied to faith, tradition, and doctrine; it was understood as expressing the universality of the Church ("in Greek that is called 'catholic' which is spread through all the world," Augustine, *Epist.*, lii. 1); it distinguished a cathedral from parish churches, or the latter from oratories or monastic chapels. After the separation between the Greek and Latin churches, the epithet "catholic" was assumed by the latter, as "orthodox" was by the former. At the Reformation it was claimed by the Church of Rome in opposition to the Protestant or Reformed churches; in England the theory was maintained that the national Church was the true catholic Church of the land, and the expression "Roman Catholic" came into use for the sake of distinction. "Anglo-Catholic" was coined by analogy with this at the time of the Tractarian movement. On the Continent the single word "catholic" is the common designation for that branch of the Church in affiliation with Rome. By Protestants the term has generally been interpreted to mean the entire communion of the saved in all time and places. The word "catholic" in the phrase "the holy catholic Church" of the Apostles' Creed is explained by Pearson (*Exposition of the Creed*, art. ix.) as indicating that the Church is to be disseminated through *all* nations, extended to *all* places, and propagated to *all* ages; that it contains in it *all* truths necessary to be known, exacts absolute obedience from *all* men to the commands of Christ, and furnishes us with *all* graces necessary to make our persons acceptable and our actions well-pleasing in the sight of God. The word was not in the earliest form of the Creed.

CATHOLIC APOSTOLIC CHURCH: The outcome of a religious movement which began in Scotland in 1830, but took its full and distinctive form in 1835. Its adherents do not use the term "The Catholic Apostolic Church" as implying that they alone constitute the Church, but as affirming that they are members of it. It embraces all the baptized.

In 1828 about fifty gentlemen, some clergymen and some laymen, but mostly of the Church of England, met at the country seat of Henry Drummond (q.v.) at Albury, West Surrey, for the study of the prophetic Scriptures. The subjects considered were those connected with the return of the Lord and the present office of the Spirit in the Church. In Feb., 1830, some members of a Presbyterian family living near Glasgow began to speak in what were believed to be supernatural utterances. They affirmed that their organs of speech were used by the Spirit of God to express the divine mind and will. It is said by one who had intimate personal knowledge of those speaking that the subject of spiritual gifts had not at all occupied their attention; much less had they any thought or expectation of their revival.

Supernatural Utterances.

These utterances, both from the religious character of those speaking and from their own intrinsic nature, awakened great attention in all the region round; and having come to the knowledge of certain gentlemen in London, some of whom had attended the conferences at Albury, a deputation was sent up to Scotland in July to inquire into them, and ascertain whether the utterances were of the Spirit, or not. They returned fully convinced that the utterances were divine. In May, 1831, like utterances were heard in London, the first in a congregation of the Church of England. This being reported to the bishop, he forbade them in the future as interfering with the service. Their occurrence in several dissenting congregations brought forth similar prohibitions, and this led to the utterances being made chiefly in the church of Edward Irving (q.v.), he being a believer in their divine origin. But they were not confined to London. At Bristol and other places the same spiritual phenomena appeared. Of these utterances one of the earliest was, "Behold the Bridegroom cometh. Go ye out to meet him"; and another often repeated, "The body of Christ."

The meaning of this was for a long time not understood, but it was gradually made plain that the Lord could not return till due spiritual preparation had been made in the Church, and that this could be effected only through the Spirit working in all the ministries and ordinances appointed by God in it. It was also made known that it was his purpose to restore the ministry of apostles; and twelve men were designated as such by the Spirit speaking through prophets. The first was so designated in 1832; but it was not until 1835 that the number was completed, and in a solemn service they were separated to their work as an apostolic college. The names of the apostles were J. B. Cardale, H. Drummond, H. King-Church, S. Perceval, N. Armstrong, F. V. Woodhouse, H. Dalton, J. O. Tudor, T. Carlyle, F. Sitwell, W. Dow, and D. Mackenzie. The following account has been given of their antecedents by one who knew them personally:

Apostles Appointed.

Classed by their religious position, eight of them were members of the Church of England; three of the Church of Scotland; and one of the Independents. Classed by their occupations and social positions, three were clergymen, three were members of the bar, three belonged to the gentry, two of them being members of Parliament; and of the remaining three, one was an artist, one a merchant, and one held the post of Keeper of the Tower. Some of them were of the highest standing socially and politically, some of them of great ability as scholars and theologians; and all of them men of unblemished character, soundness in the faith, and abundant zeal in all Christian labors.

To prepare them for their work two things were necessary—knowledge of the purpose of God in the Church, and of its present actual condition. Their separation was followed by a retirement to Albury that the Scriptures might be read with such light through prophecy as God might please to give. Later they visited the several countries of Christendom, which were divided among them, to seek for all that was good and true in doctrine and ritual. Another step was a work of testimony to the Church in general of the Lord's acts in the restoration of his ministries. In 1836 they delivered an address to the king of England and the privy councilors, and another later to the archbishops and bishops of the United Church of England and Ireland; and in 1837 a testimony addressed to the rulers in Church and State in Christian lands. So far as practicable, these testimonies were delivered by the apostles in person to the patriarchs, archbishops, bishops, emperors, kings, and sovereign princes to whom they were addressed.

In these documents, as well as in the whole course of their apostolic labor, the apostles witnessed to such things as these:—That the Church is the company of the baptized, the body of Christ, and constituted by God in infinite wisdom that the Head in Heaven might manifest himself through it in word and act; that its constitution was permanent, having a fourfold ministry—apostles, prophets, evangelists, pastors; that these ministries were adapted to the mental and spiritual constitutions of man; that all were needful that the Head might carry on his work and perfect his saints; that the Head only could appoint his ministers; that apostles chosen by him were his representatives, the bond of unity, having universal jurisdiction; that prophets speaking through the Holy Ghost were media of light from God to the apostles; that evangelists were to preach to those without the Church, bringing them to baptism, and then to transfer them to the pastor; that the pastoral ministry embraces bishops, priests, and deacons; that the retention by the Church of the pastoral ministry only points to its having departed in measure from the ways of the Lord, and that this departure ultimately leads to the apostasy and the man of sin spoken of by St. Paul. The adherents of this movement point to the apostolic congregations as the true credentials of apostles—their faith in the Scriptures, their order, their obedience, their worship, their calm and patient waiting for the Lord, their catholic spirit.

Doctrines.

The gathering of these congregations was of necessity, not of choice, as otherwise the divine order in ministries and worship could not be manifested. Their relation to the members of the Church in general is thus defined: "We are not separatists nor schismatics. We are not gathered together and distinguished from others in any hostile or aggressive attitude. The Head is not erecting new altars, but rebuilding that which was decayed." The liturgy used was not a mere compilation from existing liturgies, but was based upon the Mosaic ritual, its spiritual antitype and fulfilment. In the worship the three great creeds of the Church, the Apostles', Nicene, and Athanasian, are used. In all congregations sufficiently large, daily worship is appointed at six A.M. and five P.M., the opening and closing hours of the day. The Eucharist is the chief forenoon service on every Lord's day, and at other times as appointed. The ministers of each fully organized local church are a chief pastor, or angel, or bishop, and under him priests and deacons. All members pay tithes of income as of obligation, and, as able, voluntary offerings.

Congregations and Worship.

As no official statistics of the number of congregations have ever been published, it is impossible to say how many there may now be, but congregations are formed in most of the larger cities of Christendom. The death of the apostles made necessary some changes in the administration and worship, but the faith is apparently strong that the Lord will in some supernatural way speedily confirm the work already done, and will complete it.

(SAMUEL J. ANDREWS†.)

This body repudiates the title "Irvingites," by which it is generally known (see IRVING, EDWARD). In the early days of the movement there was no little uncertainty as to the final arrangement of the offices and jealousy between the different ranks. In 1839 Cardale was recalled from his second mission abroad to compose the differences which had arisen on account of the claim of the elders, which was supported by the prophets, to a voice in the government of the church. The apostolate succeeded in suppressing this revolt, and to avoid any recurrence of it the full general council was not again convoked, and only revived in 1877 in the form of a conference of the seven angels of London under the presidency of the apostle. In the same crisis (1840) the principle was laid down that the purity of the prophets' doctrine must be attested by the apostles, and thus the superiority of the apostolic office vindicated. The same year marks the beginning of another important change. The apostles who had been traveling on the Continent had come there into contact with Roman Catholicism, and the result was a definite assimilation to its ways of the "Catholic Apostolic Church," as it was now officially called. All traces of Scotch Presbyterian or English non-conformist traditions were gradually eradicated. Altars were now erected separated from the body of the church by a rail at which the communicants knelt. The people were taught to regard the Eucharist as a sacrifice of praise and thanksgiving in which the elements, changed by the Holy Ghost into the body and blood of Christ, were offered to God in commemoration of his death. The same tendency appeared in the liturgy introduced in 1842 and drawn up mainly by Cardale, which went back to early forms, Eastern as well as Western. The eucharistic vestments were adopted practically as in the Roman Catholic Church; extreme unction was introduced in 1847; from 1850 the consecrated elements were reserved in a tabernacle and every morning and evening (on the analogy of the showbread) exposed, not as objects of adoration but to assure the people of the Lord's presence and abiding intercession. In 1852 the use of candles on the altar and incense was added, and in 1868 holy water. The most original ceremony is the "sealing," which was introduced in 1847 on Cardale's motion; with reference to Rev. vii. 3 sqq. it was taught that those who were to be saved must be sealed in order to escape the great tribulation. This was to be done by the apostles with laying on of hands and unction; candidates must be at least twenty years old.

The result of the discord which followed these innovations, of the defection of the apostle Mackenzie, and of the failure of prophecy to fix the exact date of the Lord's coming, all contributed to keep down the numbers of the body, which in 1851 counted 4,018 members with thirty-two churches, a decline from the days of the first enthusiasm. But the movement had already spread to other countries. In 1835–36 it had gained a foothold in Geneva; in 1841 a propaganda had been undertaken in southern Germany by Caird (husband of Mary Campbell, one of the original claimants of the gift of tongues), and still more zealously in northern Germany by the apostle Thomas Carlyle (q.v.), who established public worship in Berlin in 1848. Outside of Holland, however, little progress was made in other countries. Doubts were awakened by the death of one apostle after another, and in 1860, at a meeting of the apostolic college at Albury the prophet Geyer called for the elevation of the evangelists Böhm and Caird to the apostolic office. These two then, and in 1870 some others, were recognized as coadjutor apostles. Geyer was not satisfied, and in 1861, being in Königsberg with Woodhouse, proclaimed the call of a local evangelist Rogasatzki to the apostolate. The latter soon made his submission, but a schism ensued. In 1863 Geyer himself was called, and ten months later one Schwartz, especially for Holland; on the assumption that there must always be twelve apostles, there were six in Hamburg and three in Amsterdam by 1875. Woodhouse, the last English apostle, died in 1901. In the English body prophecy was allowed less and less importance, and Cardale's treatise *Prophesying and the Ministry of the Prophet in the Christian Church* (1868) practically gave it its death-blow.

The accessible figures give the present number of churches in England as about eighty, and in the United States as ten, with 1,491 communicants. Probably more numerous are the followers of the German and Dutch branch, which has increased in strength, though its separation from the English body has favored a tendency to fanatical extravagance and to the abandonment of the likeness to Roman Catholicism in externals. Apostles, prophets, and other functionaries appear in ordinary dress, and the altar is usually replaced by a common table. The element of adoration in public worship is less and less emphasized, while more stress is laid upon conversion by preaching and prophecy and the assembling of the faithful for the speedy coming of the Lord. The insistence on the number of twelve apostles which was the justification for the schism is now considered merely as the letter, the essential being the permanence of the office, so that in 1900 there were fourteen apostles ministering in this branch. Its principal seats are Brunswick, Hamburg, Berlin, and Königsberg. In recent years it has extended also to North and South America, and claims that with the help of a native missionary no less than 15,000 converts have been "sealed" in the island of Java. Its official organ is the *Wächterstimmen aus Ephraim,* published monthly by the apostle Fr. Krebs at Iserlohn, Westphalia, Prussia, containing reports of the journeys of the apostles and statistics of conversions. (T. Kolde.)

Bibliography: The sources are found in the writings of Edward Irving, and in the following works on his life: W. Jones, *Biographical Sketch of Rev. Edward Irving, with Extracts from his . . . Principal Writings,* London, 1835; W. Wilks, *Edward Irving, an Ecclesiastical and Literary Biography,* ib. 1854; Mrs. O. W. Oliphant, *Life of Edward Irving, Illustrated by his Journals and Correspondence,* 2 vols., ib. 1862, new ed., 1865 (on this consult D. Ker, *Observations on Mrs. Oliphant's Life of Edward Irving,* Edinburgh, 1863); T. Carlyle, in his *Reminiscences,* ed. C. E. Norton, 2 vols., London, 1878; T. Kolde, *Edward Irving,* Leipsic, 1901. For the history and doctrine of the Church consult: J. N. Köhler, *Het Irvingisme,* The Hague, 1876; E. Miller, *History and Doctrines of Irvingism,* 2 vols., London, 1878; H. M. Prior, *My Experience of the Catholic Apostolic Church,* ib. 1880; S. J. Andrews, *God's Revelations of Himself to Men,* New York, 1886; E. A. Rosstauscher, *Der Aufbau der Kirche Christi auf den ursprünglichen Grundlagen,* Basel, 1886; A. S. Dyer, *Sketches of English Nonconformity,* London, 1893.

CATHOLIC EMANCIPATION: The name given to the Act by which Parliament, on Apr. 13, 1829, finally removed the civil disabilities under which the Roman Catholics of England and Ireland had labored ever since the reign of Elizabeth, when those who refused to take the oath of supremacy and conform to the Established Church were excluded from the House of Commons and from all political power. They suffered from a mass of accumulated disabilities, which, if the law had been strictly enforced, would have deprived them of their rights, not only as citizens, but as parents, proprietors, and men. With the growth of toleration, a bill abolishing some of these disabilities was passed in 1778, to be followed by the uprising of the London mob known as the "Gordon Riots." Pitt had intended that the union between England and Ireland should be followed by a measure admitting Catholics to Parliament, with a provision for their clergy and a commutation of tithes. This hope, informally held out, probably helped to win their support for the union; but George III. was inflexibly opposed to this measure of justice, and Pitt resigned in consequence of its failure. In 1821, with Canning for its eloquent champion, a measure of emancipation was carried through the House of Commons, only to be defeated by Lord Eldon in the upper house. But a mighty agitation followed in Ireland, led by Daniel O'Connell and fomented by a great Catholic Association. This body was dissolved when Canning became minister in 1825, but revived when he was replaced by the anti-Catholic ministry of Wellington and Peel, and soon showed such formidable strength that the great Duke, with his political insight, saw that the hour for concession had come. The bill which Peel introduced threw open to Catholics Parliament and all the great offices of state, except those of regent, lord lieutenant of Ireland, and chancellor, the crown remaining limited, by an Act of Settlement to the Protestant Concession, and gave the electoral franchise to English Catholics. As the removal of an unjust anachronism, this measure was inevitable; but it failed to restore tranquillity to Ireland, since the concession had been robbed of its grace by delay and enforcement, and since the chief cause of Irish disaffection was, after all, not the religious disabilities but the tenure of land, as the sequel clearly showed.

Bibliography: Sources: A. Wellesley (Duke of Wellington), *Supplementary Despatches, edited by his son*, 7 July, 1812, London, 1867-80, *Speeches*, 17 May, 1819, 2 vols., ib. 1854; T. S. Larpent, *Private Journal*, i. 95, ii. 20, London, 1853; *Memoir of Sir Robert Peel*, pt. i., *The Roman Catholic Question*, London, 1834; J. F. Stephen, *History of Criminal Law of England*, ii. 476 sqq., London, 1883 (exceedingly valuable); W. J. Amherst, *History of Catholic Emancipation in the British Isles*, 2 vols., London, 1886 (fairly complete).

CATHOLIC EPISTLES: A name given to seven of the epistles of the New Testament; viz., James, I and II Peter, I, II, and III John, and Jude. Different explanations have been given of the significance of the name. (1) It has reference to the *writers*, who were the apostles in general, whereas the other New Testament epistles were believed to be written by Paul. (2) It refers to the *contents*, which do not treat of any particular topic, but are general. (3) It refers to the *recipients*, the letters not being addressed to a particular church, but to the Church universal. (4) It refers to *opinion* concerning these writings and indicates that they were generally accepted as authentic, in distinction from the many writings current and ascribed to apostolic authorship but not everywhere so received. The name was given to the First Epistle of John in the East about the second century, and by the fourth century it included the seven epistles named. In the West they were called "canonical" epistles. Certain non-canonical writings (as the Epistle of Barnabas and the letter from the apostles at Jerusalem in Acts xv. 23-29) are also called "catholic" by early writers. See Canon of Scripture, II., 2, § 5.

Bibliography: The Catholic Epistles are of course dealt with in the principal works on the N. T. Canon, N. T. Introduction, and in the Commentaries. Consult: P. J. Gloag, *Introduction to the Catholic Epistles*, Edinburgh, 1887; W. Sanday, in *Biblical Inspiration*, London, 1896; W. H. Bennett, in the *Century Bible*, ib. 1901; and C. A. Bigg, *Commentary on St. Peter and St. Jude*, Edinburgh, 1902.

CATHOLIC OR UNITED COPTS. See Uniates.

CATHOLICUS: In the time of Constantine, a civil officer established after the organization of dioceses, each diocese having its catholicus, or receiver-general. As an ecclesiastical officer occurring in several Eastern churches, the catholicus occupied a position between the metropolitan and the patriarch. The title is also applied to the head of an independent or schismatic communion, such as the Armenian Church.

CATTLE. See Pastoral Life, Hebrew.

CAVAGNIS, cā"vā"nyīs, FELICE: Roman Catholic cardinal; b. at Bordogna (near Bergamo, 39 m. n.e. of Milan) Jan. 13, 1841; d. at Rome Dec. 29, 1906. He was educated at the Roman Seminary, and was ordained to the priesthood in 1863. Three years later he became a teacher at Celano, and later became a member of the faculty of the Roman Seminary, of which he was rector from 1887 to 1893. Later still he was appointed secretary of the Congregation for Extraordinary Ecclesiastical Affairs, and in 1901 was created cardinal deacon of Santa Maria ad Martyres. In addition to the Congregation for Extraordinary Affairs, he was a member of the Congregations of the Consistory, the Bishops and Regulars, the Council, the Index, and the Sacred Visitation.

CAVALIER, JEAN. See Camisards.

CAVE, ALFRED: English Congregationalist; b. at London Aug. 29, 1847; d. there Dec. 19, 1900. He was educated at New College, London (B.A., London University, 1872), and was Congregational minister successively at Berkhampstead, Herts (1872-76), and Watford, Herts (1876-80). He was appointed professor of Hebrew and church history in Hackney College, London, in 1880, and two years later was chosen principal and professor of apologetic, doctrinal, and pastoral theology in the same institution, retaining both these positions until his death. He was also Congregational Union Lecturer in 1888, vice-president of the London Board of Congregational ministers in 1888 and 1898, and Merchants' Lecturer in 1893-94. He collaborated with J. S. Banks in translating the *System der christlichen Glaubenslehre* of I. A. Dorner (2 vols., Berlin, 1879-81) under the title *System of Christian Doctrine* (4 vols., Edinburgh, 1880-82), and also wrote the independent works: *Scriptural Doctrine of Sacrifice and Atonement* (Edinburgh, 1877); *An Introduction to Theology:*

Its Principles, Its Branches, Its Results, and Its Literature (1886); *The Inspiration of the Old Testament Inductively Considered* (Congregational Union Lectures; London, 1888); *The Battle of the Standards, the Old Testament and the Higher Criticism* (1890); *The Spiritual World, the Last Word of Philosophy and the First Word of Christ* (1894); and *The Story of the Founding of Hackney College* (1899). An enlarged edition of his *Introduction to Theology* appeared in 1896.

CAVE, WILLIAM: Church of England patristic scholar; b. at Pickwell (13 m. e. by n. of Leicester) Dec. 30, 1637; d. at Windsor Aug. 4, 1713. He studied at Cambridge, in St. John's College, and was made M.A. in 1660, D.D. in 1672, in 1681 D.D. by Oxford. He was vicar of Islington, now part of London, 1662–91; rector of All Hallows the Great, Thames Street, London, 1679–80; became chaplain of Charles II. and canon of Windsor in 1681; and in 1690 vicar of Isleworth, London. His reputation rests on his eminent attainments in patristics. His principal works are: (1) *Primitive Christianity* (London, 1672; reprinted, Oxford, 1840, in connection with his *Dissertation Concerning the Government of the Ancient Church by Bishops, Metropolitans, and Patriarchs*, 1683); (2) *Tabulæ ecclesiasticæ*, tables of ecclesiastical writers (1674; improved ed. under the title *Chartophylax ecclesiasticus*, 1685); (3) *Apostolici, or the Lives of the Primitive Fathers for the Three First Ages of the Christian Church* (1677); (4) *Ecclesiastici: or, the Histories of the Lives, Acts, Deaths and Writings of the Most Eminent Fathers of the Church That Flourisht in the Fourth Century* (1683; 3 and 4 were combined and edited by Henry Cary under the title *Lives of the Most Eminent Fathers of the Church That Flourished in the First Four Centuries*, 3 vols., Oxford, 1840); (5) *Scriptorum ecclesiasticorum historia literaria* (1688; in Latin, to the fourteenth century, continued by others to 1617 and reprinted, Oxford, 2 vols., 1740–43).

Bibliography: J. Darling, *Cyclopædia Bibliographica*, pp. 605–607, London, 1854; S. A. Allibone, *Critical Dictionary of English Literature*, i. 356–357, Philadelphia, 1891; *DNB*, ix. 341–343.

CAVICCHIONI, cā-vî'chō"nî, BENJAMIN: Roman Catholic cardinal; b. at Veiano (a village near Viterbo, 42 m. n.n.w. of Rome) Sept. 27, 1836. He was ordained priest in 1859, and, after teaching for several years, went to Rome, where he studied canon law. In 1872 he became a member of the Congregation of the Council, and twelve years later was consecrated titular archbishop of Amida and appointed apostolic delegate to Peru, Bolivia, and Ecuador, where he remained until 1889. In the latter year he was appointed secretary of the council, with the title of archbishop of Nazianzum, and in 1903 was created cardinal priest of Santa Maria in Ara Cœli. He is a member of the Congregations of Bishops and Regulars, the Council, the Propaganda for the Oriental Rite, the Index, and Indulgences.

CAYET, cā"yê' (CAHIER, CAIET, *Cajetanus*), **PIERRE VICTOR PALMA:** Roman Catholic convert; b. at Montrichard (18 m. s.s.w. of Blois), Touraine, 1525; d. in Paris May 10 (or July 22), 1610. He studied at Paris and Geneva, was Protestant pastor at Poitiers and in its neighborhood, and in 1584 became chaplain to Catherine of Bourbon, sister of Henry IV.; in 1595 he embraced Romanism, was made professor of Hebrew in the Sorbonne in 1596, and became priest in 1600. He was accused of scandalous writings and immorality, but claimed that all charges were prompted by ill will because of his change of faith. His most noteworthy writings were *Chronologie septénaire de l'histoire de la paix entre le roi de France et d'Espagne* (Paris, 1605) and *Chronologie novénaire sous le règne de Henri IV* (1608).

CAZALLA, cā-thāl'yā, AUGUSTINO: Spanish Protestant; b. at Valladolid 1510; executed by the Inquisition there May 21, 1559. He was a scholar of Bartholomé Carranza (q.v.) and studied at Valladolid and Alcala. The influence of his father, the chief officer of the royal finances, opened to him a brilliant career in the Church, and his own ability won him the reputation of being one of the foremost preachers in Spain. In 1545 he became chaplain and almoner to Charles V. and accompanied the emperor to Germany on the outbreak of the Schmalkald war. There he undertook to confute the Lutherans, but ended by accepting their doctrines. Returning to Spain in 1552, he was cautious at first in expressing his opinions, but ultimately his mother's house in Valladolid became the meeting-place of the Protestants of the city and Cazalla himself the head of the congregation. In 1558, with his brothers and sisters and about seventy-five others, he was put into prison. On Mar. 4, 1559, when threatened with torture, he acknowledged that he had accepted Luther's teachings, but denied that he had taught them to others except to those already of like mind; further concessions he steadfastly refused to make. The *auto da fé* at which he perished was the first of these sad spectacles. Sixteen persons, including a brother and a sister of Cazalla, brought to judgment at the same time, were condemned to imprisonment for life; two, Cazalla's brother Francisco and Antonio Herezuelo, a lawyer of Toro, were burned alive; and twelve others, including Cazalla, were strangled before being burned. At the place of execution he was persuaded to address his fellow prisoners. (O. Zöckler†.)

Bibliography: T. McCrie, *History of the Progress and Suppression of the Reformation in Spain*, pp. 226–231, 285–289, Edinburgh, 1829; C. A. Wilkens, *Geschichte des spanischen Protestantismus*, pp. 79 sqq., 224 sqq., 234 sqq., Gütersloh, 1888; H. C. Lea, *History of the Inquisition in Spain*, ii. 318, 512, iii. 201, 430, 431, 438, New York, 1906.

CEADDA (CHAD), ST.: Third bishop of Mercia; d. at Lichfield Mar. 2, 672. He was one of Aidan's pupils at Lindisfarne and also spent some years at the monastery of Rathmelsige (Melfont, near Drogheda?) in Ireland. His oldest brother, Cedd (q.v.), chose him to succeed himself as abbot at Lastingham, Northumbria, in 664. After the Synod of Whitby (q.v.) Wilfrid was elected to the Northumbrian bishopric and went to Gaul to be consecrated. As he did not return immediately King Oswy saw fit to appoint Ceadda, and he was consecrated (665?) by Wine of Winchester and two British bishops. Wilfrid acquiesced on going back to England, but when Theodore became archbishop of Canterbury (669) objection was raised to Ceadda's consecration; he expressed his willingness to lay down an office of which he had never deemed himself worthy, retired to his monastery in Northumbria, and Wilfrid was instated in his place. Theodore, however, impressed by Ceadda's humility and worth, reconsecrated him as bishop of the Mercians to succeed Jaruman, and he fixed his residence at Lichfield (Sept., 669). His simplicity, piety, and devotion to duty won the hearts of all, and in later times he was one of the most popular of English saints.

Bibliography: Bede, *Hist. eccl.*, iii. 23, 24, 28; iv. 2, 3; v. 19, 24; *Fasti Eboracenses*, ed. W. H. Dixon and J. Raine, i. 47–55, London, 1863; W. Bright, *Early English Church History*, pp. 243–246, 259–266, Oxford, 1897; *DNB*, ix. 391–393.

CECIL, RICHARD: English "evangelical"; b. in London Nov. 8, 1748; d. at Hampstead (London) Aug. 15, 1810. His early life was profligate, but he was converted about 1772, and in 1773 entered Queen's College, Oxford (B.A., 1777); he was ordained priest 1777 and, after holding various livings, was appointed minister of St. John's Chapel, Bedford Row, London, in 1780. He was the leading "evangelical" clergyman of his time, and exerted a wide influence. He had an original mind, dignified carriage, and impressive delivery. His works were collected and published with memoir by the Rev. J. Pratt (4 vols., London, 1811; new ed., with his letters and memoir by Mrs. Cecil, 1854). Perhaps the most noteworthy of his works is *The Remains of Richard Cecil, with numerous selections from his works*, new ed., with introduction by his daughter and preface by R. Bickersteth (London, 1876), containing reminiscences of his conversations.

CECILIA, SAINT: Roman maiden of noble family, who is said by different versions of the uncertain and contradictory tradition to have suffered martyrdom under Marcus Aurelius and Commodus, under Alexander Severus, and under Diocletian. Her *Acta* relate that on the eve of her marriage she converted her husband, Valerianus, to Christianity. Angels appeared to both Cecilia and Valerianus charging them that her virginity should not be impaired. Tibertius, the brother of Valerianus, was then converted. The two brothers, refusing to sacrifice to the gods at the bidding of the prefect, Almachius, were executed by the sword, and Cecilia was exposed to death in an overheated bath in her own house; when this means failed she too was beheaded. The remains of the three martyrs were placed in the catacombs of St. Calixtus, whence Pope Paschal I., in 821, is said to have removed the relics of Cecilia to a church called after her name (Sta. Cecilia in Trastevere); her coffin of cypress wood was found there in 1599 (Baronius, *Annales*, ad an. 821). De Rossi discovered what is probably the original crypt of Cecilia, adjoining the papal crypt in the cemetery of Calixtus, and has attempted to prove that she belonged to the old patrician family of the Cæcilii; also that the date of her martyrdom was 177 under Marcus Aurelius. Toward the end of the Middle Ages Cecilia begins to be represented in art with musical attributes. The conception of her as patroness of the organ dates probably from Raffael's painting of 1513, now in Bologna, and may be based upon a misunderstanding of certain words of her *Acta* which refer to the (secular) musical instruments at her wedding, but were thought to indicate a particular instrument played by herself. The rôle which she fills among both Roman Catholics and Protestants as patroness of church music in general may be due to the founding of a musical academy at Rome by Gregory XIII. in 1584 under her protection and named after her. (O. Zöckler†.)

Bibliography: *ASB*, April, ii. 203–211; A. Bosio, *Acta S. Cæciliæ*, Rome, 1600 ed. J. Laderchi, with title, *Acta S. Cæciliæ et transtiberina basilica illustrata*, 2 vols., Rome, 1722; J. B. de Rossi, *Roma sotterranea christiana*, ii., pp. xxxii.-xliii., 113–161, Rome, 1867, Eng. transl., i. 315–333, London, 1879; Dom Guéranger, *Ste. Cécile*, Paris, 1874 (richly illustrated, but of little scientific value); C. Martin, *Die heilige Cäcilia*, Mainz, 1878; Bertha E. Lovewell, *The Life of St. Cecilia*, in *Yale Studies in English*, vol. iii., New York, 1898.

CEDD (CEDDA), ST.: Bishop of Essex; d. at Lastingham (25 m. n.n.e. of York), Northumbria, Oct. 26, 664. With his youngest brother Ceadda or Chad (q.v.), he was brought up at Lindisfarne, and was sent in 653 by his abbot, Finan (q.v.), and Oswy, king of Northumbria, as missionary, first to Peada, king of Mercia, and then to Sigbert, king of Essex. He was very successful and was consecrated bishop of the East Saxons by Finan and two Scotch bishops in 654. He founded two monasteries in Essex and the one at Lastingham and governed them strictly, according to the Columban rules. He was present at the Synod of Whitby (q.v.) in 664 and acted as interpreter; he inclined to the British side, but when the Roman prevailed he acquiesced. He died of the plague while on a visit to Northumbria. He has been called the second bishop of London, but Bede, who is the source of all information concerning him (*Hist. eccl.*, iii. 21–23, 25, 26, 28; iv. 3), never speaks of him as such.

CEILLIER, sel"lyé', **REMY:** French bibliographer; b. at Bar-le-duc May 14, 1688; d. at Flavigny, near Nancy, Nov. 17, 1761. He entered the Congregation of St. Vannes (reformed Benedictines) in 1705, and became titular prior of Flavigny. His great work was an *Histoire générale des auteurs sacrés et ecclésiastiques, qui contient leur vie, le catalogue, la critique, le jugement, la chronologie, l'analyse, et le dénombrement des différentes éditions de leurs ouvrages; ce qu'ils renferment de plus intéressant sur le dogme, sur la morale, et sur la discipline de l'église* (23 vols., Paris, 1729–63; *Table générale des matières* by Rondet and Drouet, 2 vols., 1782; new ed., 16 vols., 1858–69). This work is brought down to the middle of the thirteenth century, and is more complete and exact than the similar undertaking of Du Pin (q.v.), but is inferior in respect to style and critical judgment; it is of most value for the first six centuries, for which Ceillier was able to use Tillemont and the Benedictine editions.

BIBLIOGRAPHY: A. Beugnet, *Étude biographique et critique sur Dom Rémi Ceillier*, Bar-le-Duc, 1891.

CELE, JOHANNES: Teacher at Zwolle; b. at Zwolle, about the middle of the fourteenth century; d. there May 9, 1417. He received his early education in his native place, continued his studies in some unknown school, and, returning to Zwolle, in 1374 was entrusted with the school-management there. Having been awakened by the preaching of Gerard Groote, he thought of joining the order of Minorites, but was prevented from doing so by Groote, who advised him to complete his studies at Prague. Whether he went to Prague is not known. Depressed in mind, Cele spent some time in the monastery at Munnikhuizen and in company with Ruysbroeck. Through the influence of Groote, in spite of opposition, Cele was made rector of the school at Zwolle. He received much help from the Brethren of the Common Life and assisted them especially in the difficult task of securing houses at Zwolle for their adherents and those committed to their charge, but he did not join the brotherhood, remaining rector of the ever-growing school, which numbered 1,000 pupils. He taught Latin, grammar, and rhetoric, and expounded the Scriptures, admitting laymen to his lectures against the will of the city ministers. He founded a large library by buying and copying manuscripts. For more than forty years he stood at the head of the institution, highly esteemed for his learning and piety and his lasting influence on his pupils. The lazy and presumptuous were kept under rigid discipline. All wore the simple dress of the brethren. He had no method of his own, but labored in the spirit of his friend Groote, recognizing in a pious personality the source of all morality, and thus he gave to the growing humanism the right direction and true basis in the Christian faith and genuine piety. Many prominent men were his pupils, such as Heinrich von Herxen, Wessel Gansfort, Alexander Hegius, Rudolf Langen, Rudolf Agricola, Ludwig Dringenberg, Moritz von Spiegelberg, and Johannes Busch.

L. SCHULZE.

BIBLIOGRAPHY: Besides the works mentioned in the article COMMON LIFE, BRETHREN OF THE, valuable sources for Cele are the personal reminiscences of Thomas à Kempis in the *Chronicon monasterii S. Agnetis*, ed. H. Rosweyde, p. 171, Antwerp, 1615, and of his scholar, Johannes Busch, in the *Chronicon Windeshemense*, ed. K. Grube, pp. 204-222, Halle, 1887. Consult also *ADB*, iv. 79.

CELESTINE: The name of five popes.

Celestine I.: Pope 422-432. He was a Roman by birth, and only a deacon when, in Sept., 422, he was raised to the episcopate. The main endeavor of his pontificate was to extend the jurisdiction of his see. To this end he made use of a conflict which had been going on for years in the African Church in order to assert the right of the Roman pontiff to receive appeals thence. He restored to communion Apiarius, an African priest who had been deposed by his bishop and had appealed to Rome under Zosimus and Boniface I. The Africans, however, in a synod at Carthage in 424 or 425, denied his right to interfere. Celestine's part in the dogmatic controversies of his time was also influenced by political considerations (see SEMI-PELAGIANISM; NESTORIUS). He died at the end of July, 432. (A. HAUCK.)

BIBLIOGRAPHY: *Liber pontificalis*, ed. Duchesne, i. 230, Paris, 1886; Jaffé, *Regesta*, i. 55; Hefele, *Conciliengeschichte*, ii. 159 sqq., Eng. transl., ii. 476 sqq.; Bower, *Popes*, i. 166-186; Milman, *Latin Christianity*, i. 200-238.

Celestine II. (Guido de Castellis): Pope 1143-1144. He was a Tuscan of noble birth, reputed to be learned and pious. He occupied the papal throne only from Sept. 26 to Mar. 8, not long enough to fulfil the hopes which his elevation had raised. (A. HAUCK.)

BIBLIOGRAPHY: Jaffé, *Regesta*, ii. 1; Bower, *Popes*, ii. 475.

Celestine III. (Jacinto Bobo): Pope 1191-98. After being a cardinal forty-seven years, at eighty-five he was elected, Mar. 30 (?), 1191, the first pope of the house of Orsini. The times were troublous (see CLEMENT III.), and the aged pope, a man of mild temper and inclined to half measures, was no match for his formidable opponent Henry VI., who appeared before Rome and demanded his coronation, which Celestine was obliged to perform on the day after Easter. Henry surrendered Tusculum to him, but later forced him, in compliance with the agreement of May 31, 1188, to give it up to the Romans for destruction. From 1194 he saw the Norman kingdom, with which his predecessors had invested Tancred, in the possession of the hated Hohenstaufen. Henry refused to take the oath of fealty or to pay tribute; he appointed bishops and judged them, and gave the lands of Countess Matilda to his brother Philip in fee. Celestine did not venture to excommunicate him, but did break off relations with him, though he offered reconciliation when Henry took the cross (May 31, 1195). It soon became evident that Henry was a crusader only for political advantage, and the territory and rights of the Church were invaded in various quarters. Humiliations beset the aged pope. He was obliged to release Philip Augustus of France from his unperformed vow to free the Holy Sepulcher; and could not force the recognition of his legate in England, William of Longchamp (the bishop of Ely, Richard Cœur de Lion's chancellor), by Prince John and the barons; nor did Philip Augustus heed his admonitions against the arbitrary dissolution of his marriage with Ingeborg of Denmark and the contracting of a new one. His fear of the emperor prevented him from protesting against Richard's imprisonment; only after the English king had paid his ransom did he excommunicate Leopold of Austria. Celestine survived Henry VI. by only a few months, dying Jan. 8, 1198. (A. HAUCK.)

BIBLIOGRAPHY: Jaffé, *Regesta*, ii. 577; J. M. Watterich, *Pontificum Romanorum vitæ*, ii. 708, Leipsic, 1862; F. Gregorovius, *Geschichte der Stadt Rom*, iv. 591, Stuttgart, 1890, Eng. transl., iv. 626 630, 699, London, 1896; Bower, *Popes*, ii. 531-534; Hauck, *KD*, iv. 663-681.

Celestine IV. (Galfrido di Castiglione): Pope 1241. A Milanese by birth, he was elected pope in a conclave held by permission of Frederick II. on Oct. 25. He was old and feeble, and died, before he could be consecrated, on Nov. 10. (A. HAUCK.)

BIBLIOGRAPHY: Bower, *Popes*, ii. 559-560.

Celestine V. (Pietro di Murrhone): **Pope 1294.** He was born about 1215 in the Abruzzi; d. at Fumone, near Anagni, May 19, 1296. At twenty he entered the Benedictine order, and lived for years in retirement first on the Murrhone, then on the Majella, where numerous followers gathered around him (see CELESTINES). After the death of Nicholas IV (Apr. 4, 1292), dissensions among the cardinals hindered an election, until in March, 1294, Charles II. of Naples, who needed a pope to support his designs on Sicily, took up the matter. Since there was no hope of agreeing on a cardinal, Latinus, the head of the Angevin party in the sacred college, drew his attention to the hermit of the Abruzzi, whose sanctity was universally revered; and Pietro was elected on July 5. His unfitness for high affairs of state was equally well known; the various leaders hoped to rule through him. But the remarkable choice can only be fully explained by a study of the mystical reform movement represented by Joachim of Fiore (q.v.), which had spread so widely among a section of the Franciscan order. Their prominent men favored the election of Pietro enthusiastically, flocked to his coronation, and renewed their old relations with him by a formal embassy. The new pope sanctioned their observance of the rule of the order in its strictest form, and took them under his special protection, allowing them to be known by the name which he had assumed as pope. Meantime Charles was preparing to use his candidate for his own purposes; he surrounded him with Sicilian counselors, and brought him to Aquila, where he had him crowned in the presence of only three cardinals. The king's influence, however, finally induced the others to appear one by one, the last being Benedetto Gaetani, Celestine's successor as Boniface VIII., and the coronation ceremony was repeated. Celestine's whole interest was given to the promotion of monasticism; in other things he was merely a tool in the hands of Charles, who got him to create twelve Angevin cardinals, confirm his treaty with Aragon, and supply large sums of money for the Sicilian war. The strict regulation of Gregory X. for the conclave was reenacted, that Charles might have the next election also securely in his hands, and in October the curia was removed to Naples. Both the cardinals and the pope were discontented with the state of affairs, and the latter began to think of abdication, that he might be able to give himself once more wholly to his ascetic practises. The thing was without precedent, and offered great constitutional difficulties, which, when Celestine's resolve was seen to be fixed, were as far as possible removed by the legal wisdom of Gaetani, and the abdication took place on Dec. 13. While Dante speaks scornfully of the pope "who made the great refusal," others lauded the act highly—Petrarch among them, who regarded it as an example of humility entitling the poor hermit to rank above the apostles and many other saints. Gaetani was later accused of having brought about the abdication by guile in order to secure his own advancement. The charge is not justified, but he undoubtedly had his eye on the tiara in view. After he had attained it, he wished to keep his predecessor with him in Rome, lest he should be used as a tool by the opposition; but the ascetic fled, and was finally taken and imprisoned in the mountain castle of Fumone, where he died the next year. He was canonized by Clement V.

(HANS SCHULZ.)

BIBLIOGRAPHY: The older documents are collected in *ASB*, May, iv. 419-498, cf. Muratori, *Scriptores*, III. i. 613-641. Consult: A. Potthast, *Regesta pontificum Romanorum*, ii. 1915-22, Berlin, 1875; Don Josaphet, *Der heilige Papst Coelestin V.*, Fulda, 1894; F. Gregorovius, *Geschichte der Stadt Rom*, v. 490 sqq., Stuttgart, 1892, Eng. transl., v. 523-534, London, 1898; Bower, *Popes*, iii. 40-43.

CELESTINES: A name borne by two monastic societies which owe their origin to Pope Celestine V. (q.v.). (1) The *Benedictine Celestines*, known also as Moronites and Murrhonites, were originally composed of men who were members of the Benedictine order, but lived as hermits on Monte Majella in the Abruzzi from about 1258, under the guidance of the future pope Celestine, who gave them a severer rule and obtained papal confirmation for the congregation from Urban IV., probably in 1264, though the alleged bull of this year, as well as another of Gregory X. from 1274, is of doubtful genuineness. The early history of the congregation is, in fact, frequently open to critical objection; as, for example, the statement that it already had sixteen houses in 1274, when its founder is said to have gone to the general council at Lyons and attracted great attention as a wonder-worker. After about 1290, the mother house seems to have been at Monte Murrhone near Sulmona. On the founder's elevation to the papacy in 1294, he attempted by rich grants of indulgences and other privileges to give it a commanding position in the Benedictine monastic family; indeed, he aspired to reform the mother house of the whole order at Monte Cassino on the principles of his congregation. But the brevity of his pontificate prevented the execution of his plans. The congregation, however, continued to grow, until in Italy it had at the beginning of the eighteenth century ninety-six houses. Its rule, which in some points, especially as to fasting, surpasses the original Benedictine rule in strictness, was revised by Urban VIII. in 1629. The French province never got beyond twenty-one houses. In Bohemia and Lusatia the congregation had some famous seats, as at Prague, Königstein, and Oybin near Zittau, the last of which was founded by Charles IV. in 1366 and suppressed in the sixteenth century.—(2) The *Franciscan Celestines* (*Poveri eremiti di Celestino*), called also Fraticelli, were a congregation within the Franciscan order, founded in 1294, on an impulse given by Celestine V., by two of the "spiritual" sections of the order, Pietro da Macerato (Liberato) and Pietro da Fossombrone (Angelo Claremo, d. 1337). It existed down to about 1340 in nearly all its original strength as a congregation of the Minorites. See FRANCIS, SAINT, OF ASSISI, AND THE FRANCISCAN ORDER.

(O. ZÖCKLER†.)

BIBLIOGRAPHY: For (1) Helyot, *Ordres monastiques*, v. 51 sqq., vi. 180-191; Heimbucher, *Orden und Kongregationen*, i. 134-136 (gives the later literature); Currier, *Religious Orders*, p. 147; *KL*, iii. 582-584. For (2) Felice Tocco,

I fraticelli o poveri eremiti di Celestino, in the *Bollettino della società storica Abruzzese*, vii. (1895) 117–159.

CELESTIUS. See PELAGIUS, PELAGIANISM.

CELIBACY.

Celibacy, in the Roman Catholic Church, means the permanently unmarried state to which men and women bind themselves either by a vow or by the reception of the major orders which implies personal purity in thought and deed. The Jewish priests and high priests were married, being restricted only in the choice of a wife (Lev. xxi. 7, 8, 14, 15). In preparation for the exercise of their office, they were to abstain from commerce with their wives, which was also required of the whole people before the reception of the Law on Sinai (Ex. xix. 15). The New Testament contains no prohibition of marriage; some of the apostles were married (Matt. viii. 14; I Cor. ix. 5), and Paul recommended marriage to the heads of churches (I Tim. iii. 1), though he considered that under some circumstances it was better not to marry (I Cor. vii. 38). Very early in the history of the Church the idea grew up that the unmarried state was preferable (Hermas, I. ii. 3; Ignatius to Polycarp, v.), and grew into a positive contempt of marriage (Origen, *Hom. vi. in Num.*; Jerome, *Ad Jovinianum*, i. 4).

1. Celibacy in the Early Church.

As early as the second century examples of voluntary vows of virginity are found, and the requirement of continence before the performance of sacred functions. By the fourth century canons began to be passed in that sense (Synod of Neocæsarea, 314 A.D., canon i.; Synod of Ancyra, 314 A.D., canon x.). Unmarried men were preferred for ecclesiastical offices, though marriage was still not forbidden; in act, the clergy were expressly prohibited from deserting a lawfully married wife on religious grounds (Apostolic Canons, v.). The Synod of Gangra (355?) anathematized in its fourth canon, against the Eustathians, those who refused to accept the ministrations of a married priest. The stricter view prevailed so far, however, that the Council of Nicæa could speak of it as an ancient custom that priests and deacons should not marry after ordination, unless, in the case of deacons, they had expressed an intention of marrying at the time of their ordination—though both were allowed to retain wives already married, and a marriage contracted in contravention of this regulation was valid.

2. Marriage of the Clergy Still Permitted.

The standpoint of the Roman Church was different from this. Thus Pope Siricius declared in 385 that priestly marriage had been allowed in the Old Testament because the priests could only be taken from the tribe of Levi; but that with the abandonment of that limitation this permission had lost its force, and that "obscœnæ cupiditates" (i.e., marriage) hindered the proper performance of spiritual functions. Succeeding popes adhered to this view (cf. decretals of Innocent I., 404, 405, and Leo I., 456, 458), and the rest of the Western Church came to it (Synods of Carthage, 390, 401). Candidates for the higher orders were accordingly required to take a vow of celibacy, and from the fifth century those for the subdiaconate also.

3. In the Early Roman Catholic Church.

A breach of this vow entailed degradation from office, but not the nullity of the marriage. Those in minor orders were still permitted to marry, but not a widow or for the second time (Fifth Synod of Carthage, 401; Gregory I., 601). Secular legislation confirmed these regulations in so far as it forbade married men, or men who had children, to be made bishops, and even went further by declaring the marriages of those in major orders void and their children illegitimate. The Eastern Church adhered to the older legislation, with the modifications introduced by the imperial decrees just referred to; prohibited marriages were now declared void, but married men could still be admitted to orders without giving up their wives, except in the case of bishops (Council of Constantinople, 692). This system the modern Roman Catholic Church still allows for the Uniat Greeks, as explained by Benedict XIV. in the constitutions *Etsi pastoralis* (May 26, 1742) and *Eo quamvis tempore* (May 4, 1745). But within its own boundaries the Latin Church has held more and more strictly to the requirement of celibacy, though not without continual opposition on the part of the clergy. The large number of canons on this subject enacted from the eighth century on shows that their enforcement was not easy. After the middle of the eleventh century the new ascetic tendency whose champion was Gregory VII. had a strong influence in this matter. Even before Hildebrand's accession to the papacy, the legislation of Leo IX. (1054), Stephen IX. (1058), Nicholas II. (1059), and Alexander II. (1063) had laid down the principles which as pope he was to carry out.

4. The Medieval Period.

In the synod of 1074 he renewed the definite enactment of 1059 and 1063, according to which both the married priest who said mass and the layman who received communion at his hands were excommunicate. Urban II. decreed in 1089 that the marriage of one in major orders should be punished by the loss of both office and benefice. The Councils of Reims (1119) and of the Lateran (1123) ordered that the parties to such a marriage should be separated and sent to places of penance. The Lateran Council of 1139 confirmed this provision, with the declaration "that such connection was not marriage." These strict principles were not extended to the minor orders. It is true that Alexander III. and Innocent III. prescribed the loss of clerical rank and privileges for even the holders of these in case they married; but Boniface VIII. (1298) and Clement V (1311) reasserted the older law. After the Reformation had done its work, Charles V endeavored by the Interim of 1548 to bring about the abolition of these rules, and with several other princes requested the discussion of the question at the Council of Trent. The council, however, maintained the system as a whole, and the following rules are now in force: (1) through the reception of major orders or the taking of monastic or other solemn vows, celibacy becomes so binding a duty that any subsequent marriage is null and void. (2) Any one in minor orders who marries loses his office and the right to go on to major orders, but the marriage is valid. (3) Persons already married may receive the minor orders if they have the intention of proceeding to the major, and show this by taking a vow of perpetual abstinence; but the promotion to the higher orders can only take place when the wife expresses her willingness to go into a convent and take the veil. The Council of Trent further lays down that the functions of the minor orders may be performed by married men in default of unmarried—though not by those who are living with a second wife. In the nineteenth century attempts were not lacking, even within the Roman Catholic Church, to bring about the abolition of celibacy. They were rather hindered than helped by temporal governments, and always firmly rejected by Rome. Celibacy has been abolished among the Old Catholics; and modern legislation in Germany, France, Belgium, Italy, and Switzerland authorizes the marriage both of priests and of those who have taken a solemn vow of chastity. Austria, Spain, and Portugal still forbid it.

5. The Council of Trent on Celibacy.

The evangelical churches at the very outset released their clergy from the obligation of celibacy, professing to find no validity in the arguments adduced in its favor on the Roman side. The question is carefully discussed and decided against the Roman practise in the Augsburg Confession (xxiii.) and the Apology (vi.). Similar ground is taken in Art. xxxvii. of the first Helvetic Confession and Art. xxix. of the second, as well as in Art. xxxii. of the Thirty-nine Articles. Likewise disapproval is expressed of binding vows of celibacy in the Augsburg Confession (xxvii.) and Apology (xi.). (E. Friedberg.)

6. Protestant Rejection of Celibacy.

Bibliography: The book best worth consulting from the Protestant standpoint is H. C. Lea, *Sacerdotal Celibacy in the Christian Church*, 3d ed., 2 vols., London and New York, 1907; for the Catholic presentation consult Migne, *Encyclopédie Théologique*, vol. xxv., "Célibat," Paris, 1856; *Dictionnaire de Théologie catholique*, "Célibat ecclésiastique," ib. 1905. Other treatises are: J. Schmitt, *Der Priestercölibat*, Münster, 1870; P. M. R. des Pilliers, *Le Célibat ecclésiastique*, Chambéry, 1880; *Clerical Celibacy*, Oxford, 1891; F. Chavard, *Le Célibat, le prêtre et la femme*, Paris, 1894; L. Bocquet, *Le Célibat ecclésiastique jusqu'au concile de Trente*, Paris, 1895; A. Vassal, *Le Célibat ecclésiastique au premier siècle de l'église*, ib. 1896; *Essay on the Law of Celibacy*, Worcester, n.d.; E. Carry, *Le Célibat ecclésiastique devant l'histoire et devant la conscience*, Paris, 1905; E. A. Sperry, *An Outline of the Hist. of Clerical Celibacy in Western Europe to the Council of Trent*, New York, 1906 (contains a bibliography). On the change of status in the Eng. Church consult J. Collier, *Ecclesiastical History*, ii. 262 sqq., London, 1714, and G. Burnet, *History of the Reformation*, ii. 54 sqq., ib. 1715. The subject of celibacy is treated at greater or less length in the church histories, e.g., Neander, *Christian Church*, consult the Index.

CELL: Usually the room or hut in which a monk, nun, hermit, or friar lives, but also a dependency of a large monastery, ruled by a prior, dean, or abbot, who was the virtual choice of the abbot of the mother house. Such "cells" were frequently country houses which with the grounds were bestowed upon the abbey as a source of revenue, as the monks living therein had to pay a certain part of their revenue to the mother house. Sometimes the "cell" was an important building, as Tynemouth Priory near Newcastle, England, which was a "cell" of the Benedictine abbey of St. Alban's (20 m. n. of London); or Bermondsey, which was a "cell" of the Cluniac abbey of La Charité (140 m. s. of Paris). Originally a "cell" was an oratory erected over the grave of a martyr or saint.

CELLARIUS. See Borrhaus, Martin.

CELLITES (CELLITÆ). See Alexians; Beghards, Beguines.

CELSUS: A pagan philosopher and controversialist against Christianity. In the period of peace which the Church enjoyed under the emperor Philip in the year 248, Origen brought to notice, by an exhaustive reply (the *Contra Celsum*), a treatise written about seventy years earlier against Christianity by a highly educated Platonist. The occasion of this reply may have been the celebration in that year of the thousandth anniversary of the founding of Rome, which gave the Christians reason to fear religious excitement on the part of the pagan population. Origen gives the arguments of Celsus sometimes word for word, sometimes in substance; in the latter case there is little abbreviation and not many omissions, so that there is very fair material for an attempt to reconstruct the original text of Celsus. This attempt was first made, not very systematically or successfully, by Jachmann in 1836; in 1873 Keim undertook a restoration of Celsus in a German version which, in spite of its defects, has many merits, and this was partially improved on in the French version of Aubé in 1878. The recent reconstruction by Neumann in the Greek shows that not more than one-tenth of the original has been lost, and that three-fourths of what we have is word-for-word quotation.

Origen's Contra Celsum.

The "True Discourse" of Celsus was composed in the last years of Marcus Aurelius. It notices the rescript of that emperor, issued in 177 (or 176 at the earliest), against popular tumults caused by the introduction of a new religion (viii. 69). In viii. 71 the author speaks of two emperors reigning at the time, which fixes the date in the joint rule of Marcus Aurelius and Commodus, from 177 to 180. He was thus at least a contemporary of the Celsus to whom Lucian dedicated his "Alexander," and some have supposed the two to be identical. Lucian's friend, however, was an Epicurean, while our Celsus, in spite of Origen, stands out clearly as a Platonist; and the books κατὰ μάγων (Lucian, *Alex.*, lxi.; Origen, i. 68, κατὰ μαγείας) do not seem to fit in with the conception and tone of the "True Discourse."

The "True Discourse" of Celsus.

The latter, though usually divided into eight books, seems to have been but one originally; and, according to Origen (viii. 76), Celsus intended to write another, "in which he engaged to supply practical rules of living to those who felt disposed to embrace his opinions." In iv. 36 Origen mentions two more books written by a Celsus whose identity with ours he leaves uncertain; but as he seems to know nothing of these, it is at least possible that he has misunderstood a notice referring to the two already mentioned. Keim, followed by Pélagaud, places the home of Celsus in the West, probably in Rome, where he thinks the "True Discourse" was written—partly on the ground that the Jew depicted by Celsus is a Roman and not an Eastern Jew. The old view, adopted also by Aubé, that the book was composed in the East, probably in Alexandria, rested upon its accurate knowledge of Egypt; and this view might be supported by the contention that as a matter of fact Celsus's Jew is really not the Roman type, but belongs to those Eastern Jewish circles in which the doctrine of the Logos was familiar; thus in Origen, ii. 31, the Jew of Celsus says, "If your Logos is the Son of God, we also give our assent to the same."

Criticism of Celsus.

After the introduction, there follow objections against Christianity from the Jewish standpoint, which should be compared with Justin's dialogue with Trypho. With book iii. begins the direct attack, which is directed not against Christianity alone, but also against Judaism, although a slight preference is shown for the latter. Celsus shows a good knowledge of Genesis and Exodus; Aubé thinks he can prove an acquaintance with the Prophets and with the Psalms, and a reference to Jonah and Daniel is indeed found in vii. 53. His knowledge of Christianity is sufficient to be of some value to the historian of to-day, and Harnack has used it in his *Dogmengeschichte*. The manner in which Celsus employs the New Testament corresponds to the stage of development of the canon which the Acts of the Martyrs of Scili show in 180. He knew and used our Gospels, showing a preference for the synoptic type; his acquaintance with the Acts is disputed, while familiarity with Pauline ideas, though not with the epistles themselves, is generally admitted. Gnosticism he knew well; his relation to Marcion needs further investigation. His whole criticism is not irreligious; it is that of a pious pagan of Platonic tendencies, though his Platonism is that of his age, as we meet with it, for example, in Plutarch. It is the religion of well-to-do, self-confident people, and shows no conception of those crying needs of the time which helped Christianity to spread so rapidly, of the reasons why it was welcomed by the poor and oppressed. Again, he fails to appreciate the significance of the church idea, though he understands the relation of the local communities to the Church at large (v. 59, 61), and knows that all Christians do not belong to the latter (iii. 12). But it presents itself to him rather in its opposition to the Gnostic sects than as a great bond of unity, whose importance he undervalues while seeing in the conflict of sects a sign of weakness. Still, Christianity seems to him important enough to make him desirous of winning back its adherents; and he closes, not, as he began (i. 1), with the accusation of secret and illegal association, but with the hope that an understanding may be reached.

Later History of His Work.

The book had no influence on the attitude of the Roman government, and scarcely a trace of acquaintance with it can be found in classical literature. Such traces have been seen, on the other hand, in Minucius Felix and in the *Apologeticum* of Tertullian; but Origen was the first to call general attention to it. The Neoplatonic controversialists naturally went back to it; certain fundamental thoughts reappear in Porphyry, whom Julian follows, and the *Λόγοι φιλαλήθεις* ("Truth-loving Discourses") of Hierocles point to it in their very title. Meantime, however, the canon of the New Testament had been completed, and it was possible for assaults on Christianity to take the form of assaults on its sacred writings. Later Christian antiquity saw the typical literary attack from the pagan side not in Celsus but in Porphyry; Theodosius II. ordered the books of Porphyry, not those of Celsus or of Julian, to be burned in 448. (K. I. NEUMANN.)

According to the account of Origen, the principal charges brought by Celsus against Christianity were as follows. The Christians were members of illegal secret associations which were necessary to them because they would suffer death if their practises were known. The origins of Christianity were derived from secondary sources, some of these even barbarous, and Moses himself simply borrowed the ordinances which he promulgated. The alleged divinity of Jesus can not be proved from his miracles, since they were the mere tricks of a juggler, while the indications of his life and character are equally against the doctrine. Jewish converts to Christianity were ipso facto renegades, since the new religion was no improvement upon the old. Both the Jewish and the Christian religions were really rebellious against the state. The alleged theophanies were really the appearances of demons, and the Christian eschatology is irrational and incredible.

BIBLIOGRAPHY: The best edition of Origen's *Contra Celsum* is by P. Koetschau, Leipsic, 1899, and the translation is most accessible in *ANF*, iv. 395 sqq. T. Keim, *Celsus' Wahres Wort*, Zurich, 1893, puts together in German the quotations by Origen and so reconstructs the original text. Consult: K. R. Jachmann, *De Celso philosopho*, Königsberg, 1836; B. Aubé, *La Polemique païenne à la fin du deuxième siècle*, Paris, 1878; E. Pelagaud, *Un conservateur au second siècle. Étude sur Celse*, Lyons, 1878; C. Bigg, *Christian Platonists of Alexandria*, pp. 254–268, Oxford, 1886; idem, *Neoplatonism*, pp. 98–118, London, 1895; K. J. Neumann, *Der römische Staat und die allgemeine Kirche*, i. 58–59, 256–273, Leipsic, 1890; J. A. Robinson, *On the Text of Origen contra Celsum*, in *Journal of Philology*, xviii. (1890) 288–296; P. Koetschau, *Die Gliederung des Alethes Logos des Celsus*, in *JPT*, xviii. (1892) 604–632; J. Patrick, *Apology of Origen*, Edinburgh, 1892; F. M. Müller, *Die wahre Geschichte des Celsus*, in *Deutsche Rundschau*, lxxxiv. (1895) 79–97; Harnack, *History of Dogma*, vols. i.–ii., passim, Boston, 1895–97; idem, *Litteratur*, II. i. 314–315; A. C. McGiffert, in his edition of Eusebius, *NPNF*, i. 278–279; Moeller, *Christian Church*, i. 169–170; Neander, *Christian Church*, vol. i., passim; Schaff, *Christian Church*, ii. 89–93; *DCB*, i. 435–436.

CELTIC CHURCH IN BRITAIN AND IRELAND.

By the Celtic Church in Britain and Ireland is meant the Christian Church which existed in parts of Great Britain and Ireland before the mission of Augustine (597), and which for some time thereafter maintained its independence by the side of the new Anglo-Roman Church. It comprises two branches, one in Roman Britain and a continuation of it in Wales, the other in Ireland and Alba (Scotland).

I. Origin and Early History, to c. 500.—1. In Britain: There is no trustworthy account of the introduction of Christianity into Britain. That the British Church of the first half of the sixth century had no knowledge or tradition of the time or manner may be inferred from the silence of Gildas. The Lucius story may be dismissed at once as fabulous (see Eleutherus; Chur, Bishopric of). Foreign writers give no more reliable information than the native sources. The arguments of Warren (pp. 46–62) for the introduction of Christianity into Britain from Greek churches in Lyons and Vienne as a consequence of the persecutions under Marcus Aurelius are not convincing [cf. F. Haverfield, *Early British Christianity*, in *The English Historical Review*, xi. (1896) 418, n. 2]. It is more probable that the Gospel came to the island by ordinary intercourse with other countries, and Gaul and the Lower Rhine lands are those of which it is most natural to think. Had there been organized or individual missionary effort, tradition would have preserved names. That Christianity was widely spread in Britain by the beginning of the third century can hardly be inferred from the notices in Tertullian and Origen (Haddan and Stubbs, i. 3–4), which are too rhetorical to be safe testimonies. It does seem certain, however, that much progress was made during the third century. This rests, not upon the sixth-century tradition of martyrs in Britain during the Diocletian persecution, which probably did not have any noteworthy extension into Britain (cf. Haddan and Stubbs, i. 5–6), but upon the fact that three bishops, a presbyter, and a deacon from York, Lincoln [according to others Colchester or Carleon-on-Usk], and London took part in the Synod of Arles in 316 (Haddan and Stubbs, i. 7). The towns from which they came as well as the localities assigned for the martyrdoms mentioned by Gildas (St. Albans, Carleon-on-Usk) show distinctly that Christianity first took firm foothold in the cities and stations of the Roman highways.

The records are sufficient to show that throughout the fourth century there was a well-organized Church in Britain which stood in constant touch with the rest of the Church, particularly in Gaul, and considered itself an active member of that body (Haddan and Stubbs, i. 7–12). British bishops attended the synod summoned at Ariminum (Rimini) by Constantius in 359 [Haddan and Stubbs, i. 9–10], and their presence shows that their Church was drawn into general doctrinal disputes. Gildas maintains that it was much injured by Arianism (p. 32, ll. 20–25). His testimony is controverted by that of Hilary of Poitiers (c. 358) and Athanasius (363; both in Haddan and Stubbs, i. 7, 9). But it must be admitted that Arian views found acceptance in Britain during the second half of the fourth century, and as the Roman power was waning there from that time on, it is conceivable that such views may have lingered and found expression as late as 600, possibly in the baptismal formula (cf. F. C. Conybeare, *The Character of the Heresy of the Early British Church*, in the *Transactions of the Society of Cymmrodorion*, 1897–98, pp. 84–117). It is noteworthy that a life of Gildas written in the eleventh century, but based upon materials taken from the sixth century, and a life of Patrick of the second half of the seventh century lay stress on their devotion to the Holy Trinity (*Chronica minora*, iii. 95, ll. 8–9; *Tripartite Life*, ii. 273, ll. 12–13; 286, ll. 6–7); and Gregory the Great is said to have suspected Columba of not being quite sound in the doctrine (Bernard and Atkinson, i. 64, ii. 25).

1. Heresies.

It is certain that Pelagianism appeared in Britain during the fifth century (see Agricola). Germanus (q.v.), bishop of Auxerre, was sent thither in 429, and "overthrew the heretics and directed the Britons to the Catholic faith" (Prosper of Aquitaine, *Chronicle*, anno 429). Some years later, on a second mission, he completed the extirpation of Pelagianism in the island (*Vita Germani*, used by Bede, i. 17, 21). Gildas, writing a century later, does not mention the heresy. For a hundred years after the mission of Germanus nothing is heard of the Church in Britain. The land was abandoned by the Romans, and the Anglo-Saxon conquest caused Christianity to disappear completely from the East. With those Britons who kept their independence it found a refuge in the mountains of the West, whence it gradually comes again into view in the sixth century (see below, II., 1).

2. In Ireland: There is native tradition of the introduction of Christianity into Ireland, the two oldest records of which can scarcely be dated earlier than the last quarter of the seventh century.

1. Native Tradition of Origin.

They are (1) the life of Patrick, written by Muirchu Maccu-Machtheni at the wish of Bishop Aed of Sletty (d. 698), and (2) the collections of a certain Tirechan, a pupil of Ultan of Ardbrechan (d. 656), based upon information about Patrick which his teacher had communicated to him personally or had left in his papers. Both records, but with additions and amplifications, are in the Book of Armagh (*Liber Ardmachanus*), the several parts of which were written between 807 and 846. In brief this native tradition is as follows: In 431 Ireland was entirely heathen. In that year Pope Celestine I. sent a certain Palladius to preach to the people, but he turned back and died in Britain. His place was at once (c. 432) taken by a Briton, Patrick, who in his youth had been a prisoner in Ireland. He evangelized the entire land, founded churches everywhere, ordained bishops and presbyters, and died (459) universally revered as the head of the Church, in which he held a sort of metropolitan rank, with his see at Armagh in Ulster.

Everything discredits the authenticity of this tradition. (1) It represents Patrick as a personality comparable to Martin of Tours or Columba, the apostle to the Picts; such men do not fail to find a biographer among their admirers and associates; their fame grows and is spread in the next generation.

2. The Tradition Unreliable.

But the name of Patrick does not appear till the second third of the seventh century, and then it is in the letter of Cummian (q.v.) to the abbot Seghine of Iona, in connection with the introduction of the Dionysian (!) paschal computation, which is ascribed to him. He is not mentioned in the full report of the Synod of Whitby (664), although the arguments were historical and the Irish referred to the traditions of their forefathers and to Columba (Bede, iii. 25). Bede must have been well informed concerning the Church in North Ireland and his interest in the beginnings of Christianity in the British Isles was keen; yet he says nothing about Patrick in his *Historia ecclesiastica.* It seems impossible that there can have existed in the North of Ireland in the seventh century a tradition of a founder of the Irish Church called Patrick. And yet it is in the North (at Armagh) that the tradition (the first reports of which come from the South) represents Patrick as having his see and ending his days. (2) The tradition describes the Irish Church as *episcopal*, dependent on Patrick's see of Armagh. But as a matter of fact the Church of Columba and of Finnian of Clonard, i.e., from the end of the fifth century, is a *monastic church without central organization* and with no traces of such a past as the tradition presupposes. How intensely the Irish cling to the customs of their fathers was shown at Whitby; it took four hundred years to transform this monastic church of the sixth and seventh centuries even after the theoretical acceptance of an episcopal constitution. If, then, the organization was so fundamentally changed within one generation, as it must have been if the tradition be correct, an explanation is needed. And none is forthcoming. (3) There is good reason to believe that Ireland was not entirely heathen in 431. The island is easily accessible from Britain; and active intercourse, particularly between the Southwest of Britain and the Southeast of Ireland, existed as early as the third and fourth centuries (cf. Zimmer, *Nennius vindicatus*, pp. 85–93, Berlin, 1893; Kuno Meyer, *Early Relations Between Gael and Brython*, in the *Transactions of the Society of Cymmrodorion*, 1895–96, pp. 55–86). As has been seen, there was a well-organized British Church in the fourth century. It is natural to assume, then, that Christianity was carried to Ireland from Britain before the time assigned to Patrick. And the assumption is corroborated by certain saints' lives, particularly those of Declan, Ailbe, Ibhar, Ciaran, and Abban (*ASB*, July, v. 590–608; Sept., iv. 26–31; Apr., iii. 173; Mar., i. 389–399; Oct., xii. 270–293; cf. also Ussher, *Antiquitates*, ed. of 1687, pp. 408 sqq.). In all these lives Patrick figures as "Archbishop of Ireland," but this is due to the time of redaction. These same men are not only Patrick's contemporaries, but *older* contemporaries, *independent of him*, and recognized as the apostles of their districts. Their locality is the Southeast, the coast counties of Wicklow, Wexford, and Waterford, and the adjoining inland counties of Kilkenny and Tipperary, where local testimonies to their cult still survive. Further evidence may be found in the fact that the two lives of Patrick, mentioned above, limit his activity to the North. The Patrick legend originated in the South and was forced upon the North from the time of Cummian's letter, the object being to win over the North Irish to conformity with the Roman Church. But this alone does not explain the silence of the lives concerning the South. It must be that, while the Southerners were willing to acknowledge Patrick theoretically as apostle of the North with his see at Armagh, hoping thereby to win over the mainstay of the opposing party, the abbot-bishop of Armagh, the traditions in the South concerning the founders of the monasteries there were too well known to admit of a description of Patrick as the apostle of the South. A third testimony is the fact that Ireland cherished the memory of the heresiarch Pelagius and was well acquainted with his writings (cf. Bede, ii. 19). In the seventh, eighth, and ninth centuries, the Irish Church possessed the original *unmutilated* commentary of Pelagius (when it had disappeared everywhere else in the West) and knew that Pelagius was the author. Pelagius may himself have been an Irishman (cf. Jerome, in *MPL*, xxiv. 682a, 758b). He was a sincere and earnest thinker and did not adopt heretical views until he went to Rome (c. 400). His learning was great and would naturally gratify the pride of his countrymen. If he came from a monastery of southeastern Ireland, it is easy to understand how his books were brought thither and how they came to be preserved. But, whatever may have been the nationality of Pelagius, his celebrity in Ireland is incompatible with the Patrick legend. Pelagianism was annihilated in the Roman State and See by Honorius and Zosimus in 418. In 429 Germanus successfully combated it in Britain. If, then, Ireland was wholly heathen in 431 and Patrick Christianized the land and organized its Church, he must himself have carried Pelagianism thither—which is, of course, absurd. But if the South was already Christian in the first quarter of the fifth century, it is quite comprehensible how Pelagianism found its way to the island. (4) Linguistic facts prove that Christianity came to Ireland from Britain. British and Irish are Celtic tongues, but certain differences of sound had developed by the fourth century. Ecclesiastical and other loan-words, introduced into Irish from Latin with the Christian religion, show forms hard to explain if they came directly from the Latin, but quite comprehensible if they came, through the medium of British (cf. Güterbock, *Lateinische Lehnwörter im Irischen*, pp. 91 sqq. Leipsic, 1882). Patrick himself was a Briton, it is true; but he is said to have studied on the Continent, and his associates are represented as of Romance origin (*Tripartite Life*, ii. 273, 305; Haddan and Stubbs, ii. 292). (5) Among the writings attributed to the supposed apostle of Ireland are two, the so-called "Confession" and the "Epistle Concerning Coroticus," which are undoubtedly authentic. They are the work of a man "unlearned and rustic, not at all such a one as later times extolled with the highest praises" (Schöll, p. 71; cf. p. 68), or one who could have founded in the fifth century the Irish Church—a Church in which from the sixth to the ninth century Christian and classical learning were united as nowhere else in the West. Moreover, the "Confession" is the work of a man looking back upon a long life, complaining bitterly of ingratitude, trying to defend himself from the reproach of having presumed to undertake a calling above his capabilities, and threatening to turn his back on Ireland because he recognizes the failure of his life's work there. And he makes not the slightest mention of ever having consecrated a bishop or established a single church in the island. (6) Finally there is the definite statement of Prosper of Aquitaine (*Chron.*, anno 431) that Pope Celestine "ordained Palladius and sent him as their first bishop to the Irish believers in Christ." Prosper was probably in Rome in 431 and issued the first edition of his "Chronicle," which contains the statement quoted, in 433. Here then is a record, as certain and credible as may be, which confirms the supposition that the Irish, in part at any rate, were Christians in 431. The meaning of Prosper's expression "first bishop" is clear, bearing in mind the organization of the Irish Church. Palladius was the first bishop canonically ordained according to Prosper's view, in distinction from the missionary and monastic bishops of the Irish Church during the fifth century. In his later *Liber contra collatorem* (written probably about 437), in the course of a fulsome eulogy of Celestine, Prosper states that "while he [Celestine] endeavored to keep the Roman island [Britain] Catholic, he made also the barbarous island [Ireland] Christian" (in *MPL*, li. 271b–c). But a rhetorical statement of this sort does not impair the value of the careful entry in the "Chronicle." Moreover, the supposition that Celestine ordained a simple deacon—for such Palladius still was in 431—as bishop of a land considered wholly heathen is in itself untenable. It was not customary to consecrate "bishops" for lands where there were no Christians. Augustine was sent by Gregory to preach to the Angles; but he was not consecrated till he had made converts among them.

Before attempting to reconstruct the early history of Christianity in Ireland, it must be noted that the historical Patrick and Prosper's Palladius are the same. Various reasons may be mentioned: (1) Palladius went from Rome to the Irish Christians in 431; Patrick appeared in Ireland in 432. In view of the difficulties of travel of the time, it is hardly conceivable that two different persons should have been despatched to Ireland within the space of one year. (2) Palladius went as the ordained bishop of the Irish Christians; Patrick (in the first sentence of the "Epistle") calls himself with emphasis the appointed bishop for Ireland. (3) Palladius is first mentioned by Prosper under the year 429 as instigating the mission of Germanus against Pelagianism, from which it may be inferred that Palladius was a Briton and stood in somewhat intimate relations with Germanus. This is true of Patrick according to his own testimony and statements of the lives ("Confession," Haddan and Stubbs, ii. 309, ll. 1–4; *Tripartite Life*, ii. 370, ll. 9–14; lives, ib. ii. 272, ll. 4–5; 302, ll. 19–23). (4) If Palladius was a Briton, his Romanized name, according to the general custom of the time, should be a translation of his native name. Hence the latter should have some such signification as "warlike" or "having to do with war." Patrick's British name was Sucat (Muirchu, *Tripartite Life*, ii. 494, l. 6; Tirechan, ibid. 302, l. 5; Fiacc's Hymn, ibid. 404–405), composed of *su*, "good," and *cat*, "war," a word still in use in modern Welsh in the form *hygad*, signifying "warlike." If, as was but natural, he resumed his native name on reaching Ireland and the name Palladius first became known there from Prosper's work, it is easy to understand how the idea of two persons arose. As for the name Patrick, it is not improbable that Sucat-Palladius assumed it himself. He was especially proud of his alleged aristocratic descent (cf. his words in Haddan and Stubbs, ii. 316, ll. 15–17; 306, ll. 26–27; *Tripartite Life*, ii. 377, ll. 19–22; 368, ll. 1–2), which, however, was not so distinguished as he would make out. In Rome at that time the title *Patricius* was often conferred upon high officials of the empire to indicate rank. The somewhat narrow-minded Sucat, applying Roman conditions to the little British country town of Bannaventa, where his father had been senator or mayor, may have taken to himself the title *Patricius*, and so

3. Prosper's Palladius the Same as Patrick.

figured in Ireland as Sucat Patricius, and in his writings merely as Patricius. If this name entered into the Irish vernacular of the fifth century, according to linguistic laws it should appear in Irish of the seventh century as Cathrige or Cothrige. And it is a fact that a number of sources (Tirechan, Fiacc's Hymn, and others) state that Patrick was also called Cothrige.

As a result of the foregoing argument, the origin and early history of the Celtic Church in Ireland seems to be as follows: Christianity was brought to Ireland from Britain during the fourth century as a natural outcome of the close intercourse between southwest Britain and southeast Ireland. The actual foundation of a Church, extending over large parts of the island, must be regarded as a result of that first great wave of monasticism which swept over Gaul and Britain from the middle of the fourth century and carried a number of half-Romanized Christian Britons to Ireland. Two facts confirm this view: (1) The great repute of Martin of Tours in Ireland, so great that in the ninth century it was thought desirable to bring the new apostle, Patrick, into close relations with Martin, and he was even accounted the latter's nephew. (2) The difference between the organization of the Irish Church and that of the British Church from which it sprang. Just how fast and how far Christianity spread can not be ascertained, but it seems safe to say that the northeast coast was Christian about 400. It is noteworthy that Patrick, in the two passages of the "Confession" where he speaks of his six years' captivity in North Ireland (Haddan and Stubbs, ii. 296, ll. 5 sqq.; 300, ll. 16 sqq.; *Tripartite Life*, ii. 357, ll. 7 sqq.; 361, ll. 19 sqq.), does not intimate by a single word that the Irish with whom he lived were heathen. This is the more remarkable since he dwells with horror on the paganism of the pirates into whose hands he fell when he made his escape (Haddan and Stubbs, ii. 301, l. 16–303, l. 2; *Tripartite Life*, ii. 362, l. 19–363, l. 34). No doubt the Saxons drove a number of Christian Britons into Ireland, as well as to the Armorican coast of Gaul, during the fifth century.

4. True Origin of the Irish Church.

A Briton named Sucat played a prominent part in the Irish Church during the second third of the fifth century. The following outline of his life is based upon his own statements in the "Confession," and the notices of Prosper, interpreted as above. He was born about 386 in the borough of Bannaventa in central Britain, probably near the modern Daventry in Northamptonshire. His family possessed some wealth and had been Christian for generations. He led an easy worldly life until the age of sixteen (402), when plundering Irish carried him off as a slave to North Ireland. For six years (402–408) he was a swineherd. Reflection and changed circumstances made him a new man. He practised austerities, saw visions, and heard voices which counseled him to flee. He reached the coast and fell in there with heathen (doubtless Saxons), who took him to Britain and led him about the country for sixty days. Then he escaped and finally arrived at his home (408 or 409). There he became a deacon. His visions continued, and eventually he came to believe himself called to be the bishop of Ireland. In his native place, where he was looked upon as an enthusiast, narrow-minded, and of defective education, obstacles arose to his consecration. His parents and friends were against it. So he left home at the age of thirty-eight (c. 424), and followed the old road by way of Auxerre (where he stayed some time with Germanus), through the Rhone valley, by way of Arles, along the coast of Provence and the Lerinian islands, through Upper Italy, to Rome. If Ultan may be believed (Tirechan, *Tripartite Life*, ii. 302, ll. 19–23), he spent seven years wandering through Gaul and Italy. His barbarian name was Latinized into Palladius. At Rome he gained influence, probably the more readily since for twenty years Britain had been separated from the empire and the connection between the British Church and Rome had become difficult. Perhaps also he exaggerated his family's position and influence to the leading ecclesiastical circles. In 429 he was instrumental in sending Germanus of Auxerre to Britain, and in 431 he attained his heart's desire and was consecrated *episcopus* for Ireland. He reached Ireland in 432, dropped the Roman translation of his name, and assumed in its stead the title *Patricius*. There are no trustworthy details of his activity in Ireland. But he was never recognized as its "appointed bishop." In the letter on Coroticus he says complainingly "although now I am despised by some," and in the "Confession," written near the end of his life, he characterizes himself as "despised by most." His very limited literary education may well have aroused the scorn and derision of his more cultured associates. How far he extended his missionary efforts in Connaught and the Northwest, where there must still have been opportunity for such work, can hardly be ascertained from the "Confession," the only source of any authority. Its words are those of a monkish ascetic to whom *convertere ad deum* is identical with "to enter a monastery," and definite inferences can not be drawn from its statements.

5. St. Patrick.

There are some indications of the locality where the historical Patrick lived. Muirchu (*Tripartite Life*, ii. 275, l. 13) says that the legendary Patrick landed at a port called *Hostium Dee*, near the present Wicklow. As the tendency of the legend required Patrick to settle in the North as soon as possible, it is probable that an item of true tradition is preserved here. Muirchu was himself from County Wicklow and used the "Confession" and "Epistle" of Sucat as sources of his life. Aed, at whose request Muirchu wrote, was bishop of Sletty in Queen's County, near Carlow. Cummian, who was the first to mention the legendary Patrick, was also a native of the South. Therefore the South of Ireland possessed the material left by the historical Patrick (the *Confessio* and the *Epistola*) as well as notices of his life. Hence it is probable that Patrick settled somewhere in County Wicklow. He died Mar. 17 459, according to the statement in the Luxeuil Calendar and the most trustworthy entries of the Annals. He was soon forgotten.

save in the district of his special activity; and here, in the seventh century, under the influence of a specific tendency, he was resurrected and made the apostle of the Irish, as Augustine was the apostle of the Saxons and Columba of the Picts.

It is not possible to say definitely why Patrick does not mention his consecration by Pope Celestine in the "Confession." But it may be recalled that for three hundred years the Roman Empire was a standing menace to the liberty of the Irish. Without doubt bitter feelings and hatred were still alive in 432, and the Irish were not likely to distinguish carefully between spiritual and temporal Rome. If, therefore, when Patrick arrived in Ireland he tried to impress the Christian Irish with his ordination by Celestine, he must soon have found out his mistake. With his religious feelings and views, Patrick would look upon Celestine merely as the instrument of God, who had himself appeared to him in visions and dreams and appointed him apostle to the Irish. And it was only natural that to the old man on the brink of the grave Celestine's slight and casual intervention in his life should fade away before the image of God Almighty, whose chosen one he was. (For other views concerning St. Patrick, see the article PATRICK, SAINT.)

3. In North Britain (Alba): From statements by Bede (iii. 4) we know that a Briton named Nynia (St. Ninian, q.v.) founded a monastery on the peninsula of Wigtown, in the extreme Southwest of Scotland, about 400, and thence spread Christianity among the Picts south of the Grampians. The germs of the young faith seem to have been destroyed in the confusion which arose in North Britain early in the fifth century. In two passages of his letter concerning Coroticus Patrick with evident anger calls the Picts "apostates" (Haddan and Stubbs, ii. 314, l. 13; 318, l. 5; *Tripartite Life*, ii. 375, l. 26; 379, l. 7). Coroticus was probably a king of the Strathclyde Britons, ruling near the modern Dumbarton between 420 and 450. His subjects were Christians; and as Patrick does not reproach the Irish (*Scotti*), living to the northwest, with paganism, it may be that they also, like their countrymen on the opposite coast of Antrim, were Christians.

II. Development and Full Maturity, 500–800. —1. In Britain: The British Church reappears in Wales in the second third of the sixth century, and is the direct continuation of the Church of the fourth century. That the latter consisted mainly of Roman residents of the towns while the Britons in the country remained heathen, and that the Celtic Church first arose after the withdrawal of the Romans, is an opinion based upon defective knowledge of conditions in Roman and post-Roman Britain and is disproved by the fact that the Christian missionaries to Ireland in the fourth century and the Christians who settled in Armorica in the fifth spoke British, i.e., they were native Britons, not Roman occupants of the country. The external organization of the sixth century, however, is not an uninterrupted development from the fourth. When the Britons fled from the Saxons to the thinly populated hill-regions of the West, they found there no cities to serve as centers of ecclesiastical organization. But monasticism, which had flourished in Britain from the end of the fourth century, soon created new centers. Dioceses were formed, each based on the monastery of a clan and comprising the territory belonging to the clan. In time these were combined into larger organisms, and during the seventh century the ecclesiastical organization of Wales was definitively fixed by the constitution of four bishoprics, corresponding to the four political divisions, viz.: Bangor on Menai Straits in Gwynedd; St. Asaph in the Northeast in Powys; Menevia (St. David's) in the Southwest in Dyfed; and Llandaff in the Southeast in Gwent. They were independent of one another and based on the chief monasteries of the territories named. Abbot and bishop were generally the same. According to the *Annales Cambriæ*, the founders of the four bishoprics died in 584 (Daniel of Bangor), 601 (David of Menevia), and 612 (Dubricius of Llandaff and Kentigern of St. Asaph).

1. The Church in Wales.

The result of Gregory's mission to the Saxons (see ANGLO-SAXONS, CONVERSION OF THE; AUGUSTINE, SAINT, OF CANTERBURY) was to intensify and perpetuate the isolation from which the British Church already suffered. Two conferences were held between its representatives and Augustine (602 or 603), but the Britons rejected the proposals of the Roman missionary and refused to have him for archbishop (Bede, ii. 2; cf. Bright, pp. 80–93). Augustine's unskilful management may have contributed to the result—he is said to have offended the Britons by not rising to meet them—but he offered to overlook all other differences if the Britons on their part would accept the Roman computation for Easter, would remove divergences from Roman practise in the baptismal rite, and would join him in preaching the Gospel to the Saxons. The third requirement was probably the chief obstacle, and union was not effected because the Britons regarded the missionary as the representative of their hated foes. In his disappointment Augustine is said to have threatened the obstinate Celts with death at the hands of the English if they would not preach to them the way of life. Eight, or perhaps twelve, years after Augustine's death Ethelfrid, the heathen king of Northumbria, massacred a large company of British priests and the monks of Bangor at Chester, and the prophecy was thought to be fulfilled.

2. The British Church and Augustine.

When the South Irish Church conformed to Rome, about 630, the Welsh Church was cut off on both sides, and this isolation proved fatal to its spiritual culture. Its most eminent representative in the sixth century is Gildas, and after him there is no one of greater literary merit than Nennius at the end of the eighth century. According to the *Annales Cambriæ*, Elbodug, bishop of Bangor, adopted the Roman Easter computation in 768: the *Chronicle of Welsh Princes* gives the date as 755 and says that South Wales followed in 777 (Haddan and Stubbs, i. 203–204). But opposition did not cease at that time, for the same source says that when Elbodug died in 809 "a great controversy arose because of Easter."

2. In Ireland and North Britain: The earliest native and foreign sources show a flourishing church in Ireland in the sixth century. Its type is that of a mission-church, resting not on the labors of a single man, but growing, without central organization, in a land divided among many clans, through the constant activity of a missionary monkhood. It is the natural development of the seed sown in southeastern Ireland by British missionaries from the middle of the fourth century, springing up and increasing undisturbed by outside influences. This view is quite different from the prevalent one, which assumes, on the one hand, a complete collapse of the Irish Church at the end of the fifth century, and, on the other hand, a revival in the sixth century due to the influence of the Welsh Church, and particularly of such men as Gildas, Cadoc, and David.

1. The Irish Church not Revived from Wales in the Sixth Century.

A collapse about 500 is inexplicable, and is assumed only because necessitated by the Patrick legend and the hypothesis of a revival from Britain in the sixth century. This hypothesis rests upon: (1) statements concerning the activity of Gildas in Ireland, made in his life written at Ruys in Brittany in the eleventh century; (2) the view of the Irish Church of the fifth and sixth centuries found in the eighth century *Catalogus sanctorum Hiberniæ* [1]; and (3) notes of certain saints' lives [such as that of St. Disibod, q.v.], certainly not older than the eleventh or twelfth century (cf. Haddan and Stubbs, i. 115, n.a.). On the other hand, a mere enumeration of dates shows that the Irish Church was in no need of revival. Finnian of Clonard, the father of the "twelve apostles of Ireland," died in 548. Columba founded the monastery of Derry about 546 and Durrow before 560. Ciaran founded Clonmacnoise 541 and died 548. Comgall founded Bangor in Ulster 554 or 558. Brendan founded Clonfert in Longford 552. In 563 Columba went to Iona. The authority of an eleventh-century monk of Ruys is not to be put above such evidence as this. Nor can the statements of ignorant authors of saints' lives, who confuse different centuries, furnish the basis for a historical construction at variance with all fixed dates. There is no evidence of British influence in Ireland apart from the visit of Gildas there in 566 (cf. Mommsen, *Chronica minora*, iii. 6, ll. 3–23). [This visit is considered doubtful by some; see GILDAS.] The Church of Gildas, Cadoc, and David, it may be noted, was *episcopal;* if then these men, and men like them, revived the dying Irish *episcopal* Church, why did they substitute another entirely *monastic* with no trace of an episcopal character? Furthermore, the Church in Britain at this time was in no condition to infuse fresh life into the Irish Church. In the trouble and turmoil of the fifth century it had lost all organization, and Gildas himself draws a gloomy picture of the state of things in Britain before 547. Ireland, however, did not suffer from barbarian attacks, and her Church was able to develop undisturbed. Hence the natural supposition is that at this time the Irish Church was the giver and the British Church the recipient. And we know that from the very beginning of the sixth century Irish clerics went to southwest Britain and to Brittany, giving and spreading knowledge, not receiving it. The foundation of new monasteries in Ireland by Finnian of Clonard and men regarded as his disciples between 520 and 560 can not be considered a restoration or reformation of the Irish Church. There was already a large number of older monasteries, such as Emly in Munster and Armagh in Ulster, which for centuries played a greater rôle in the entire life of the Irish Church than any of these new foundations. Finnian was a sort of Irish Benedict of Nursia; he established his new house at Clonard by the side of the older institutions—rather mission-stations than monasteries—with stricter rules, and through the influence on Comgall and Columba it became the model of the Irish monasteries in North Britain and on the Continent.[2]

[1] This document is the source of the familiar division of Irish saints into three "orders." It states that the first order belonged to the time of Patrick. They were all bishops, 350 in number, founders of churches. They had one head, Christ, and one lord, Patrick; they observed one mass, one celebration, and one tonsure from ear to ear; they kept one Easter, on the fourteenth day of the moon after the vernal equinox; and what was excommunicated by one church all excommunicated. They did not reject the services and society of women, because, founded on the rock of Christ, they feared not the blast of temptation. This order lasted through four reigns, and its members were all bishops, from the Romans, the Franks, the Britons, and the Irish (*Scotti*).

In the second order bishops were few and presbyters many, 300 in number. They had one head, our Lord; they celebrated different masses and had different rules, but their Easter and tonsure were as in the first order. They rejected the services of women, separating them from the monasteries. They lasted through four reigns, and received a mass from Bishop David, and Gildas, and Docus, the Britons.

The members of the third order were holy presbyters and a few bishops, 100 in all. They dwelt in solitary places, and lived on herbs and water and alms, shunning private property. Their rules, masses, tonsure, and Easter were all different, and they lived through four reigns.

The first order was *sanctissimus;* the second, *sanctus sanctorum;* the third, *sanctus.* They were like the sun, the moon, the dawn. These three orders were foreseen by Patrick in a vision from on high. Consult Haddan and Stubbs, ii. 292–294.

[2] Irish monasticism of the sixth century was very different from that of a later period. It has been characterized as the transition from the hermit life to the religious orders of the Middle Ages—a transition that was soon made in the East, but in Ireland proceeded more slowly and lasted till the subjection to Rome. The primitive Irish monasteries were of the same type as those of Egypt and Syria. The nucleus was a church or oratory, always oblong (from ten to forty feet in length, rarely sixty), and without chancel, aisles, or apse. No remains have been found showing any approach to the basilica form or anything of Roman type. Round the church were grouped "beehive" huts or cells, each for a single occupant, and the whole was surrounded by a wall or rampart, with a ditch, and a hedge or palisade on top. There is mention of kitchens and the "great house" (refectory); and there were also guest houses, storehouses and barns, workshops, and the like. The so-called "Round Towers" are always connected with ecclesiastical foundations, and belong for the most part to the ninth and tenth centuries. They probably served as bell-towers, for refuge or defense in case of attack, and as beacons and lighthouses.

2. Learning of the Irish Monks.

The Irish Church of the sixth, seventh, and eighth centuries, then, was the natural development of the Church of the fourth and fifth centuries, without interference from outside. This freedom accounts for the high standard of learning maintained by the Irish monasteries till the ninth century. They kept the knowledge and culture received with Christianity, and cherished it at a time when everywhere else, in Britain, Gaul, and Italy, barbarian hordes came near to stamping it out. The erudition of the Irish monks in the sixth century—surely not derived from a Church whose greatest scholar was Gildas—surpassed on the whole that of Italy. Greek was studied at Bangor when Gregory the Great probably had no knowledge of the language. In the seventh century Aldhelm, writing to a young friend returning home from the Irish schools (*MPL*, lxxxix. 94c–d), reluctantly admits the superiority of Irish scholarship. And in the eighth century Bede speaks with admiration of Irish learning (iii. 7, 27; [cf. Plummer's note to iii. 27, p. 192]).

3. Travels and Missionary Labors.

Besides their zeal for learning, a noteworthy love of wandering characterized the Irish monks. Singly or in groups they went forth from the great monk-colonies—for such the monasteries really were—to seek a form of the anchorite's life. They were content at first with the isles of their own lakes and rivers; then they betook themselves to the many islands of the Irish coast; then to the Hebrides, the Orkneys, and the Shetland Islands, and before 800 they had reached Iceland. At the same time others went to Britain—where many Christian inscriptions of the fifth, sixth, and seventh centuries with Irish names and written in Ogham bear witness to their presence north and south of the Severn estuary—and to Brittany, and then through the land of the Franks to the Alps and across the Alps, so that Bobbio (perhaps Tarentum; see CATALDUS; COLUMBAN) became the southern, as Iceland was the northern, limit of their wanderings. Their primary purpose was not missionary work; but circumstances made them missionaries and teachers of the people among whom they settled to lead the contemplative life.

4. North Britain Christianized.

The greatest achievement of the Irish Church and its monks in the sixth and seventh centuries, the Christianization of North Britain, must be regarded from the same point of view. With twelve companions Columba (q.v.) left Ireland in 563, "wishing to go into exile for Christ" (Adamnan's *Life of Columba*, p. 9). They settled on the little island of Iona (Eo, Io, Hi), belonging to the Irish (Christian) state north of the Clyde, took up missionary work among the heathen Picts of the neighborhood and rapidly extended it, so that when Columba died (597), the mainland north of Glasgow and Edinburgh, as well as the western islands, was studded with monasteries, whose inmates looked after the spiritual welfare of the neighboring population, all of them dependent on the mother monastery at Iona (q.v.). A generation later Oswald, king of Northumbria, who had been converted to Christianity during a seventeen years' exile in Ireland, applied to Columba's successor for missionaries to introduce Christianity in his realm. Aidan (q.v.) was sent (635) and under his lead and that of his successors, Finan (652–661) and Colman (661–664), with the earnest support of Oswald and his brother Oswy, the Gospel made rapid and splendid progress. Monasteries were founded, such as Mailros (Old Melrose) by Aidan, the first nunnery by Heiu at Hartlepool, the double monastery for both men and women at Coldingham by Oswald's half-sister, Ebba, the monastery at Whitby by Hilda, and others. Christianity and the Irish Church reached to the Angles living south of the Humber.

This flourishing state of the Irish Church was disturbed by the Roman mission to the Saxons in 597 Like the British Church, that of Ireland

The whole establishment was called a "city" (*civitas*), and the designation is not inapt for the larger communities, with two or three thousand members, each having his own house, and its complex of public or common buildings. The first step in the foundation was to obtain a site, which was frequently given by the chieftain when he was converted, and sometimes was his fortress. It was often necessarily in the forest, as the extent of cleared land was very limited. The building material was most commonly wood or wattles and clay, but stone sometimes was used; the earliest stone structures are without mortar. As the first building operation was commonly the driving of stakes, "to drive" came to be the usual expression to designate the founding of a monastery. Each monastery had its own rules, followed also by the affiliated houses, which were governed by a local head under the abbot. The abbot was not chosen by the monks, but was appointed by the chieftain, generally from his own family or that of the founder, and hence was known as the *coarb* or heir of the founder. He was seldom a bishop, but there were always one or more bishops in each community, always subject, however, to the abbot. Poverty, chastity, and obedience were considered essential. The rule of St. Columban (q.v.) no doubt represents the life and practise of the Irish monasteries, particularly that at Bangor, of which Columban had been a member. Adamnan also gives many interesting details of the life at Iona in Columba's time, and this monastery, doubtless, did not differ materially from the others. Divine service and private devotion, study, and manual labor occupied the time of the brethren. Sundays and saints' days were marked by celebration of the Eucharist, rest from toil, and an allowance of better food. Easter was the chief festival and during the *Paschales Dies* (from Easter to Whitsunday) there was some relaxation in the severity of discipline. Christmas was the other great festival. Wednesdays and Fridays were fast-days except during the *Paschales Dies*. Lent was strictly kept, and the forty days before Christmas were observed by some in a like manner. Holy Scripture was the chief object of study and the Psalms were learned by heart. Much effort was spent in the copying of books and there are two Irish manuscripts of the Vulgate, known respectively as the *Book of Kells* and the *Book of Durrow* and dating from the seventh century, which are among the finest extant specimens of illuminated work. It is a question where such work was done, as it must have been impossible in the poorly lighted cells; perhaps it was executed in the open air, and we read of the monks writing "on their knees." Besides writing, the production and preparation of food was the chief labor. Strangers were hospitably received and fasts were relaxed in their honor. Consult: Reeves's *Adamnan*, pp. 339–369, Dublin, 1857; J. T. Fowler's *Adamnan*, pp. xxxvii.–1, Oxford, 1891; J. Lanigan, *Ecclesiastical History*, iv. 348 sqq., Dublin, 1829; F. E. Warren, *Liturgy and Ritual*, chap. ii., Oxford, 1881; G. T. Stokes, *Ireland and the Celtic Church*, lectures ix. and xi.; G. Petrie, *Ecclesiastical Architecture of Ireland*, Dublin, 1845; Margaret Stokes, *Early Christian Art in Ireland*, London, 1887; J. Anderson, *Scotland in Early Christian Times*, 2 vols., Edinburgh, 1881; J. Healy, *Insula sanctorum*, pp. 144–159, Dublin, 1890.

differed in some respects from the Roman Church of Gregory's time, the most important divergences being the form of the tonsure and the method of computing Easter [cf. Plummer's *Bede*, ii. 348–354; Bright, pp. 86–93, 224–225]. In 604 Augustine's successor, Laurence, with his fellow bishops, Mellitus and Justus, sent a letter to Ireland exhorting to conformity to Roman usage, but without success (Bede, ii. 4). A party favorable to conformity gradually arose through visits of Irish clerics to Gaul and Rome, and partly perhaps through influence of the Anglo-Roman Church, but in 627 it was still in the minority, for the exhortation of Pope Honorius I. to conform in 628 was again unsuccessful (Bede, ii. 19). Honorius then excommunicated Ireland (Cummian's letter, 977, ll. 5–6) and in 629 the Southeast generally observed the Roman date. Farther west opinions wavered, but in 630 the abbots met in a synod at Mag Lena near Tullamore, and decided to celebrate Easter the next year with the Roman Church. Opposition, however, made another meeting necessary and the Roman party failed to win a decisive victory. They sent an embassy to Rome, which returned in 633. Through the influence of this embassy and the death (636) of Fintan, abbot of Taghmon in County Wexford (see FINTAN, SAINT), leader of the opposition, the Roman party finally prevailed in the South. The North held out stubbornly for sixty years longer. Cummian's letter to Seghine, abbot of Iona (634), and a letter from Pope John IV. (partly preserved by Bede, ii. 19) in 640 to the prominent abbots of the North were ineffectual. The details of the struggle are not known, but it may be assumed that the Patrick legend was not the least important of the expedients resorted to to work upon the North Irish.

5. Relations with Rome.

It was natural for the Irish to seek for an apostle who should be to them what Columba was to the Picts and Augustine to the Saxons. In the neighborhood of Wicklow a certain Patricius was remembered who had called himself the "appointed bishop of Ireland." Is it unreasonable to assume that about 625 it came to be believed in the Southeast that the apostle was found in this man? The scanty history of Patrick was filled out by analogy with that of Columba and Augustine. The Irish were supposed to have been all heathen in 432 as the Picts had been in 563 and the Saxons in 597 Patrick converted the land in a brief time, established a Christian Church, and won the favor of King Laeghaire as Columba had that of King Brude and Augustine that of Ethelbert of Kent. This legend was at once utilized, if not invented, by the Roman party, as is evident from the first mention of it in Cummian's letter. He attributes to Patrick the introduction of the Dionysian cycle in Ireland, although it was not introduced in Rome till the sixth century (col. 975c).

6. The Patrick Legend.

The legend was also useful in winning over the bishop of Armagh. As the presumed successor of St. Patrick he was acknowledged in the South as metropolitan (cf. *Tripartite Life*, ii. 346, ll. 21–24). The claims of Armagh, however, met with violent opposition in the eighth and ninth centuries both in Connaught and Munster. Northumbria conformed to Rome after the Synod of Whitby (q.v.) in 664, whereupon the Irish returned to their native land (see COLMAN, SAINT). Adamnan, ninth abbot of Iona (679–704), was persuaded to yield while visiting the court of Aldfrid in Northumbria in 686 or 687–688, but was unable to control the abbots of the dependent monasteries or his own monks at Iona when he returned home (Bede, v. 15). Then he went to North Ireland and with an Angle, Egbert (see EGBERT, SAINT), took the lead in efforts to win over the Irish party. The bishop of Armagh yielded in 697. The Columban monasteries continued obstinate. In 713 Naiton, king of the Picts, enlisted the services of Ceolfrid (q.v.), the distinguished abbot of Wearmouth and Jarrow; the latter wrote a long letter on the Easter question, which Naiton sent in copy to all clerics in his dominion with an order to obey (Bede, v. 21). Those who continued recalcitrant were expelled from the country in 717. In 716 Egbert persuaded the abbot and monks of Iona to celebrate Easter at the Roman date. Their compliance, however, came too late to save the position of Iona as the center of a great monastic church. It was reduced to a mere parent monastery with a few affiliated houses on the west coast of North Britain and belonging to the Irish state. Armagh, on the other hand, by timely yielding and a skilful use of the Patrick legend had prepared the way for becoming the head of an episcopal church comprising all Ireland.

7. Conforms to Roman Usage.

III. Complete Assimilation to the Roman Church, 800–1200.—1. In Wales: The Church in Wales, having been episcopal from the first, differed from the Roman Church only in subordinate points after it had conformed in respect to Easter and the tonsure. Political conditions hastened its complete assimilation to the Roman-Saxon Church. From the time of Egbert of Wessex (d. 836) the weaker Welsh chieftains sought the protection of the English kings against their more powerful countrymen. The attacks of the Northmen also, which from 853 on were felt more and more severely in Wales, promoted friendly feelings and relations between the two nations. That the culture of its clergy was higher after the isolation of the Welsh Church was ended is evident from the appointment and position of Asser (q.v.), a nephew of Bishop Novis of Menevia, as teacher, counselor, and friend of Alfred. At the end of the tenth and beginning of the eleventh century, consecration of bishops of Llandaff by the archbishop of Canterbury seems to have been the rule, and there is some reason to believe that an earlier bishop, Cyfeiliawc (d. 927), was so consecrated. The Anglo-Norman archbishops Lanfranc (1070–89) and Anselm (1093–1109) repeatedly interfered in Welsh matters as if the Welsh bishops stood legally under the primate of England. Disputes concerning the boundaries of the Welsh dioceses of St. David's and Llandaff and the English diocese of Hereford between 1119 and 1133 were referred to Rome. About this time the bishop of St. David's began to set up the claim to metropolitan rank. After 1187, when Archbishop Baldwin of Canterbury as papal legate held a visitation in parts of Wales and preached the Crusade, the Welsh Church may be regarded as part of the English Church, although as late as 1284 the bishop of St. David's formally protested against the visitation of Archbishop Peckham of Canterbury. [Welsh tradition and the rapidity with which the Lollard movement in the fourteenth century spread among the English-speaking people on the borders of Wales favor the theory that the ancient British form of Christianity persisted in Wales throughout the Middle Ages side by side with the Roman Catholic establishment. The mountainous character of the country and the character of the language, which Englishmen rarely acquired, were favorable to the perpetuation of evangelical dissent. A. H. N.]

2. In Ireland: A systematic sketch of the development of the Irish branch of the Celtic Church in this period is not yet possible owing to the defective character of the special investigations. A factor deserving more attention than it has commonly received is the influence of the incursions and settlements of the Norsemen.

1. Incursions of the Norsemen.

The Viking period—beginning in 795 and lasting more than 150 years—brought indescribable wo to all Britain and particularly to Christian Ireland. Churches and monasteries, as the centers of civilization and the Christian religion, were marked for destruction by the heathen Norwegians and Danes. Certain of the Irish monasteries (such as Iona, Bangor in Ulster, and many others) lay temptingly exposed to seafaring robbers. The rivers gave them easy access to the heart of the land from both the east and the west coast. The wooden structures of the monasteries were an easy prey to the flames, in which both books and monks perished. If any manuscripts escaped burning they were thrown into the water. A heathen Viking state in Armagh between 832 and 845 compelled the abbot-bishop, Forindan, to flee to Munster. At the same time the Norwegian heathen were settling in the interior, but they were either ultimately expelled or absorbed by the native population and became Christian. In 852, however, a Viking kingdom was set up at Dublin, which remained heathen and plundered Ireland and all the coasts of the Irish Sea for more than a century. Under such conditions it is not surprising that the exodus of Irish monks to the Continent continued and increased from 800 on.

2. Irish Monks on the Continent.

In the ninth century they were teachers in the monastic schools everywhere in the land of the Franks, at St. Denis, Pavia, and on the Upper and Lower Rhine, and they spread the repute of Irish learning so that it is almost a truism to say: Whoever knew Greek on the Continent in the days of Charles the Bald was an Irishman or had learned it from an Irishman (cf. H. Zimmer, *Ueber die Bedeutung des irischen Elements für mittelalterliche Kultur*, in *Preussische Jahrbücher*, lix., 1887, pp. 27–59; L. Traube, *O Roma nobilis*, in *Abhandlungen der philosophisch-philologischen Klasse der königlich-bayerischen Akademie*, xix., 1892, pp. 332–363). They took their manuscripts with them in such numbers that no fewer than 117 Irish manuscripts, or fragments of such, older than the eleventh century are still extant in Continental libraries, not counting those in the Vatican or the Bibliothèque Nationale (cf. W. Schultze, *Die Bedeutung der iroschottischen Mönche*, in *Centralblatt für Bibliothekswesen*, 6th year, 1889, pp. 287–298). But if this was the Continent's gain, it was Ireland's loss. King Brian (1002–13) had to send across the sea "to buy books" (J. H. Todd, *The War of the Gaedhil with the Gaill, Rolls Series*, no. 48, p. 138, London, 1867). The standard of education in the monasteries sank with each generation, and the new and inferior priesthood had less power to resist the forces which were substituting for the native monastic church an episcopal church with metropolitan head. The Irish chieftains and princes also, instead of uniting against the common foe, thought the time most fitting to fight out their domestic feuds. The monasteries were involved in these quarrels, not to mention fierce and bloody disputes between monasteries themselves when their interests happened to clash. Thus the old organization was weakened and broken up. Furthermore, the Patrick legend became a sort of dogma during the eighth century; and its view of the Christianization of Ireland and the position of the *episcopus* in church government was an additional force shaking the firmly built edifice of the monastic church of the sixth and seventh centuries. It can be shown from the Annals of Ulster that the abbot-bishop of Armagh,

3. Rise of Armagh.

making free use of his opportunities, between 730 and 850 attained to some extent to that primacy in the Irish Church which was the logical outcome of the Patrick legend. The year 805 was decisive for Meath, 824 for Connaught, and 822, as well as Forindan's stay in Munster from 841 to 845, for South Ireland; thenceforth the see of Armagh had its tax-gatherers for Patrick's pence in all Ireland, excluding of course the Viking state whose ruler resided at Dublin. In 943 this ruler, Amlaib mac Sitricca (Norse, Olafr Sigtriggvasonr), became a Christian in England and was baptized by Wulfhelm, archbishop of Canterbury, Edmund, king of England, standing as his godfather. As Christianity spread among his subjects they naturally looked toward Canterbury and drew their clerics from England. The incumbents of newly established Norse bishoprics of Dublin, Waterford, and Limerick were consecrated at Canterbury. This was not satisfactory to the bishop of Armagh, who desired revenues from the rich Norse settlements in Dublin. He again had recourse to the Patrick legend, utilizing a detail of it which had already become current; namely, that Patrick had converted the Vikings. One of his adherents, writing about 1000, tells how the saint had converted the heathen Norse of Dublin, and consequently asserts that the successor of "Patrick of Armagh with the great revenues" had a right to an ounce of gold "from each nose" in the Dublin Viking state (cf. H. Zimmer, *Keltische Beiträge*, iii., in *Zeitschrift für deutsches Alterthum*, xxxv., 1891, pp. 54–85).

4. The Culdees. Another phenomenon in the inner development of the Irish Church in this period which deserves attention is the appearance of the so-called Culdees (Irish, *céli dé;* Latin, *colidei*). It is difficult to define exactly the origin and position of these men. The Irish name does not furnish a trustworthy clue. It meant originally one who enters God's service and devotes himself to him to death, and could be applied, like *vir dei* in Latin, to monks and anchorites in general. Hector Boece, the Scottish historian of the sixteenth century, started the theory that the *Culdei,* as he calls them, were the direct continuation of Irish monasticism of the sixth, seventh, and eighth centuries, or even of Celtic monasticism in general. But Bishop Reeves has shown that the term as used from the ninth to the twelfth century was applied to members of spiritual associations whose existence can not with certainty be traced earlier than about 800. Hence the associations of the *Colidei* must have been formed in Ireland about this time and an existing term of general application was given a more limited signification to designate their members. Apparently Chrodegang's monastic rule (749), designed originally for Metz, was brought to Ireland in the eighth century, and Irish anchorites, who were not under regular monastic rule, were first associated in accordance with it. The Culdees were never of great importance in Ireland. They are mentioned in nine places, often in connection with monasteries to which the house of the Culdees forms a sort of annex. The care of the sick and the poor was their chief charge, and they also seem to have been entrusted with the choral part of the service. In North Britain, however, whither they went from Ireland, they attained to greater importance. Naiton's expulsion of the refractory monks of Iona in 717 left gaps in the clergy which the new associations of the *Colidei* helped to fill. They appear in Scotland as a mixture of secular clergy and anchorites organized after monastic pattern; at a later time they resemble the regular canons of the Continent. There was a want of connection between different convents due to the lack of a common head and fixed forms. Hence there were wide divergences, and contemporary descriptions and opinions differ greatly. They were ultimately absorbed in the Roman orders, which were introduced in Ireland and Scotland during the twelfth century.

5. Final Subjection to Rome. The full subjection of the Celtic Church of Ireland to that of Rome was accomplished after 1050. Archbishop Lanfranc of Canterbury found opportunity to interfere in Ireland in 1074 and sent a letter to the king, Torlogh O'Brian, through Gilpatrick, the Norse bishop of Dublin. Instigated by both, Gregory VII. sent a letter to Ireland and appointed Gilbert, the Norse bishop of Limerick, papal legate for Ireland. As in the seventh century, so now, the bishop of Armagh resisted. But in the end Gilbert found a man who fell in with his views, when in 1106 Celsus succeeded to the see of Armagh. At the Synod of Rathbreasail in 1120 it was decided to divide Ireland into twenty-four dioceses, all except Dublin subordinate to Armagh. In 1152 a synod was held at Kells, under the presidency of the papal legate, Paparo, and Ireland was divided into four provinces, Armagh was selected as the see of the primate, and the bishops of Dublin, Cashel, and Tuam were promoted to archbishops and received pallia brought from Rome. The complete Romanization of the Irish Church in internal affairs was effected in furtherance of the political interests of the Anglo-Normans at a synod held at Cashel in 1172 by command of Henry II.

3. In North Britain: In 844 Kenneth mac Alpin, ruler of the Irish state in North Britain, mounted the throne of the united North and South Picts, and thereby created a united kingdom of Alba, later known as Scotland. In 850 Kenneth had the bones of Columba removed from Iona (which, because of constant attacks from the Vikings, had fallen into complete decay) and deposited at Dunkeld, in the land of the South Picts, the mainstay of his power. At the same time he established a bishopric at Dunkeld, apparently aiming to form here a center for a national church like Iona in the seventh century, with a different basis, however, the abbot-bishop of Dunkeld being at the head of the church government as bishop and not as abbot. In 865 Kenneth's son, Constantine, removed the see of the bishopric to Abernethy, leaving Dunkeld with an abbot only. In 908 the see of the primate was transferred to St. Andrews and a parliament of the same year exempted the Church from taxation. Margaret, grandniece of Edward the Confessor and queen of Scotland 1069–93, took energetically in hand the reformation of the Scottish Church according to Roman rules and usages. She received efficient support from her confessor, Turgot, abbot of Durham (see TURGOT). Her sons, Edgar (1097–1107), Alexander (1107–24), and David (1124–53) continued and completed their mother's reforms. In 1107 Turgot was appointed to the see of St. Andrews and was consecrated at York. His successor, Eadmer, a Canterbury monk, at the desire of King Alexander was chosen and consecrated by Ralph, archbishop of Canterbury (1115). By 1188 the outward and inward transformation of ecclesiastical Scotland into a Roman province was complete. It was then declared independent of Canterbury and, like the Irish Church, came directly under the sovereignty of Rome through a bull of Clement III. (cf. Haddan and Stubbs, ii. 273–274). The land was divided into nine dioceses with strictly defined boundaries, and Augustinian, Benedictine, and Cistercian monks were introduced and absorbed the remnant of the national Celtic monasticism.

IV. Some General Considerations: Concerning institutions and doctrine, neither tradition nor history offers any support to the view that the Celtic Church in its prime almost reproduced the Church of the Apostolic Age. The British Church of the fourth century was a part of the Catholic Church of the West, just as Britain was a part of the Roman Empire. And the Irish Church was an offshoot of the British Church. The divergences from Rome which both branches of the Celtic Church showed at the beginning of the seventh century are easily explicable. It must not be forgotten that the position of the bishop of Rome in the time of Leo the Great (440–461) was different from that of Pope Gregory the Great (590–604); that the fourth century knew nothing of that rigid uniformity of institutions which at the beginning of the seventh century was looked upon as an essential requirement of the *unitas catholica;* and that innovations domesticated themselves slowly in the more distant members of the Church. About 400 the British branch of the Catholic Church was cut off because political Rome lost its hold on Britain. A series of events of the early fifth century is instructive for the immediate consequences. The popes Innocent, Zosimus, and Boniface (401–422) energetically opposed the teaching of Pelagius, and the emperor, Honorius, supported them by issuing a rescript (Apr. 30, 418) threatening banishment to every Pelagian. The suppression of the heresy in the empire was thus due to the civil power. But the arm of the emperor did not reach to Britain and in 429 Pope Celestine could only send Germanus of Auxerre thither to eradicate the heresy by moral suasion. Later all connection between the Celtic Church and Rome was broken for 150 years by a double and threefold wall of barbarians—Burgundians, Visigoths, Franks, and Saxons. The development of the Western Church during all this time left no impress on the Celtic; and local conditions could not fail to influence the latter. This explains how a Columban of Luxeuil presumes to address the pope in a way which two hundred years earlier would not have been remarkable in a bishop of North Africa or Alexandria. It explains why the Welsh Church of the sixth century knew only of independent bishops without metropolitan; the British Church in 400 knew nothing of this institution. The difference in the date of Easter is due to the fact that in 600 the Celtic Church still used the older *supputatio Romana,* which had been followed by Rome till 343, but was then superseded by the younger *supputatio Romana.* Other changes—the paschal table of Zeitz in 447, the nineteen-year cycle of Victorius in 501, the cycle of Dionysius about 550—were all unknown to the Celtic Church.

1. Reason for the Divergences from Rome.

The representatives of Britain at the Synod of Arles subscribed the canon that when possible seven, and in any case three, bishops should take part in the consecration of a bishop. Yet consecration could be performed by a single bishop in both the British and Irish Churches long after their contact with Rome. This is not as surprising as it has been thought (cf. Warren, pp. 68–69). In the nature of things, particularly in the earlier period, consecration often had to be by one bishop if it took place at all. Gregory the Great recognized the necessity and gave Augustine permission to consecrate alone with the remark, "Since you are the only bishop in the English Church you can not ordain otherwise than without other bishops" (Bede, i. 27). Boniface V. gave the same permission to Justus, Augustine's third successor, "when the occasion made it necessary" (Bede, ii. 8). Custom with the English makes law without specific enactment. Hence it is comprehensible how consecration by a single bishop became first established usage and then law. In respect to the markedly monastic character of the Irish Church and the position of the bishop in it unlike that in the Western Church, it must be noted that in the older monasteries (such as Armagh in the North and Emly in Tipperary) the abbots were also bishops; that is, the heads of the dioceses were abbots and bishops in one person, but their power of church government rested on their position as abbots. This is explained by the political and social conditions of the Celts and the time and manner of their conversion. The first step was the establishment of a monastic missionary station with a clan. A member of the chief's family inevitably became the head of such a station. In some cases the right of succession to the abbacy remained hereditary in the chief's family for centuries. The necessity for some one to perform episcopal functions would not be felt immediately. When it did arise an original lay abbot may have received consecration, but, living as he did far from the sight and influence of an episcopal church, it was only natural that he should continue to perform the duties of church government in the church of the clan by virtue of his position as abbot and member of the chief's family.

2. Consecration by a Single Bishop.

3. Monastic Character of the Irish Church.

It is not advisable to attempt a complete picture of the doctrines and institutions of the Celtic Church in its prime. The material at hand is not sufficient, although it is adequate to support the conclusion that the Celtic Church of the sixth and seventh centuries was a reproduction of the Western Church of the fourth century, modified only in special points. An important difference, however, must be noted. The spirit of the Roman and Celtic Churches when they first came in conflict was not the same. The representatives of the former were intolerant and uncharitable, as Augustine toward the British bishops (Bede, ii. 2), Wilfrid toward Colman (ib. iii. 25), Aldhelm in his letter to Geraint (*MGH, Epist.,* iii. 231–235). The Irish, on the other hand, such as Columban on the Continent and Aidan and the rest in Northumbria, only asked that they be allowed quietly to follow the customs of their fathers. As soon, however, as an Irishman went over to the Roman party a new spirit entered into him. Ronan, an Irishman who had been in Gaul and Italy, began the quarrel in Northumbria with the gentle Finan (Bede, iii. 25). Cummian in his famous letter expresses the pious wish that God would "strike" Fintan (his chief opponent) "as he would" (col. 977b), although four or five years earlier he had himself kept Easter at the Celtic date. Again, the spirit of deliberate falsification to serve church interests does not appear in the Irish Church before its contact with Rome. That it appears immediately thereafter is abundantly shown by the history of the Patrick legend. Lastly, the new spirit which

4. The Celtic and Roman Spirit.

begins to pervade the Irish Church in the seventh century is indicated by the unprecedented extension of the cult of relics. Ireland had no martyrs. There is no reason to believe that relics were known or honored in any part of **5. Relics.** the Irish Church before contact with Rome. In 633 the embassy sent to Rome because of the Easter contest (see above, p. 475) returned laden with books and relics. And the next year Cummian writes to Seghine: "And we have proof that the virtue of God is in the relics of holy martyrs and the writings which they have brought. We have seen with our own eyes a girl totally blind open her eyes before these relics and a paralytic walk and many demons cast out" (col. 978b). Everything here, even to the wording (*reliquiæ*), is Roman, not Irish. Muirchu Maccu-Machtheni's life of Patrick witnesses the progress of the cult of relics in South Ireland during the seventh century. Speaking for his own time (before 697), the author mentions with emphasis that in three different places in the Roman-Irish territory relics are worshiped and he even makes Patrick prophesy such worship (*Tripartite Life*, ii. 281, ll. 1–2; 283, ll. 3–5; 497, ll. 14–19). To Adamnan, writing his life of Columba in North Ireland at the same time and before he had joined the Roman party, relics are utterly unknown. But no sooner did Roman influence find entrance in the North through the yielding of Armagh (697) and Iona (716) on the Easter question than the same change of attitude took place which had occurred seventy years earlier in the South. The Annals of Ulster give much information on the history of the Church, but in the sixth and seventh centuries they contain not a single entry respecting relics. In 726, however, occurs the first of a long series of entries recording the transference or enshrining of relics, and a little later Armagh exhibited at the great fairs of Ireland the relics of Patrick, supposed to have been found at Downpatrick in 733, and took them to Connaught and Munster.

Enough has been said to show that the spirit which animated the Celtic Church about 600 was quite different from that which the emissaries of the Roman Church brought to the British Isles. Both had the same dogmas. But on the one side was a striving after individual freedom and personal Christianity, on the other side a bigoted zeal for rigid uniformity and systematizing. The Celt emphasized a Christianity manifesting itself in word and deed, the Roman Catholic valued a formal Christianity above all else. As has been said, there is no reason to believe that the Celtic Church greatly resembled the Apostolic Church in institutions or doctrines. But the practical results of its teaching as seen in the life of such men as Aidan and Finan (cf. Bede, iii. 17) unquestionably come nearer the popular conception of the Apostolic Age than does the spirit manifested by the representatives of Rome.

(H. Zimmer.)

Bibliography: A. W. Haddan and W. Stubbs, *Councils and Ecclesiastical Documents Relating to Great Britain and Ireland*, a convenient collection of the sources with valuable notes, vol. i., Oxford, 1869, dealing with the British Church in Roman times and the period of Anglo-Saxon conquest, the Church in Wales and Cornwall; vol. ii., part i., 1873, with the Church in Cumbria or Strathclyde, branches of the British Church in Armorica and Gallicia, the Church of Scotland till declared independent of York; vol. ii., part ii., 1878, with the Church in Ireland and the memorials of Patrick; vol. iii., 1871, with the English Church during the Anglo-Saxon period. Adamnan's *Life of St. Columba*, ed. W. Reeves, Dublin, 1857, Edinburgh, 1874 (see Adamnan). Bede, *Historia ecclesiastica gentis Anglorum*, ed. A. Holder, Freiburg, 1890, ed. C. Plummer, 2 vols., Oxford, 1896. Cummian's letter to Seghine, abbot of Iona, in *MPL*, lxxxvii. 969–978. Gildas and Nennius, *Historia Britonum*, ed. T. Mommsen, in *MGH*, *Auct. ant.*, xiii., *Chronica minora sæculorum iv. vii.*, iii., 1898. Prosper of Aquitaine, *Chronicon*, ed. idem, ib. i. *Auct. ant.*, ix., 1892. The *Tripartite Life of Patrick with Other Documents Relating to That Saint*, ed. Whitley Stokes, in *Rolls Series*, no. 89, 2 vols., 1887 (see Patrick, Saint). The *Lives of the Cambro-British Saints of the Fifth and Immediate Succeeding Centuries*. ed. W. J. Rees, Llandovery, 1853, dating from the eleventh and twelfth centuries, which is also true in part of the material in the so-called *Liber Landavensis* ("Book of Llandaff," ed. W. J. Rees, Llandovery, 1840; ed. J. G. Evans, Oxford, 1893). The *Acta sanctorum Hiberniæ ex codice Salmanticensi*, ed. C. de Smedt and J. de Backer, Edinburgh, 1888, and *Lives of Saints from the Book of Lismore*, ed. Whitley Stokes, in *Anecdota Oxoniensia*, 1890, also present only relatively late material. The various annalistic works give important data for ecclesiastical history, viz.: for the British and Welsh Church, the *Annales Cambriæ*, ed. J. W. ab Ithel, in *Rolls Series*, no. 20, 1860; the oldest part also in *Y Cymmrodor*, ix., 1888; for the Irish-Scotch branch, the *Annals of Tigernach*, ed. Whitley Stokes, in *Revue Celtique*, xvi.–xviii., 1895–97; the *Annals of Ulster*, ed. W. M. Hennessy and B. MacCarthy, 4 vols., Dublin, 1887–1901; the *Chronicon Scotorum*, ed. W. M. Hennessy, in *Rolls Series*, no. 46, 1866; *Annals of Ireland, Three Fragments*, ed. J. O'Donovan, Dublin, 1860; *Annals of the Kingdom of Ireland by the Four Masters*, ed. idem, 7 vols., 1848–51; *Annals of Clonmacnoise*, ed. D. Murphy, Dublin, 1896; *Chronicles of the Picts and Scots*, ed. W. F. Skene, Edinburgh, 1867. The oldest of the Irish collections is that of Tigernach (d. 1088). Since the sources upon which they are based are all lost, and the sources themselves appear in part to have been compilations of the eighth, ninth, and tenth centuries from older monastic annals, it is clear that statements concerning Irish church history of the fifth century have no decisive value when they coincide with the views concerning the earlier period current after 750. In using the collections of Welsh and of Irish laws (*Ancient Laws and Institutes of Wales*, London, 1841; *Ancient Laws of Ireland*, 6 vols., Dublin, 1865–1902) it must be remembered that the former dates from the tenth century and the latter can not be much older. Other sources are: the *Stowe Missal*, ed. F. E. Warren, in *The Liturgy and Ritual of the Celtic Church*, pp. 198–268, Oxford, 1881; the *Antiphonary of Bangor*, ed. idem, and the *Irish Liber Hymnorum*, ed. J. H. Bernard and R. Atkinson for Henry Bradshaw Society, iv., x. and xiii., xiv., 1893–98; F. W. H. Wasserschleben, *Die Bussordnungen der abendländischen Kirche*, Halle, 1851; idem, *Die irische Kanonensammlung*, Leipsic, 1885; the *Félire of Oengus*, ed. Whitley Stokes, Dublin, 1881; the *Martyrology of Tallagh*, ed. M. Kelly, Dublin, 1857; the *Martyrology of Donegal*, ed. J. H. Todd and W. Reeves, Dublin, 1864; the *Martyrology of Gorman*, ed. Whitley Stokes, for Henry Bradshaw Society, ix., 1895.

The father of Celtic church history was Archbishop Ussher, whose work, *Britannicarum ecclesiarum antiquitates*, Dublin, 1639; 2d ed., enlarged, London, 1687, however, has now only historic interest. The monograph of C. Schöll, *De ecclesiasticæ Britonum Scotorumque historiæ fontibus*, Berlin and London, 1851, and the introduction and notes of Reeves's *Adamnan*, u.s., were pioneer work in the critical investigation and appreciation of the sources; it is to be regretted that not all their successors have continued in the same spirit. The legends of the Celtic Church are briefly but fully told in Cardinal Newman's *Life of St. Augustine*, chaps. i.–v., London, 1845. Works dealing with the Celtic Church in both Britain and Ireland are: J. H. A. Ebrard, *Die iroschottische Missionskirche des sechsten, siebenten und achten Jahrhunderts*, Gütersloh,

1873; F. E. Warren, *Liturgy and Ritual*, u.s.; F. Loofs, *Antiquæ Britonum Scotorumque ecclesiæ quales fuerunt mores*, Leipsic and London, 1882; W. Cathcart, *The Ancient British and Irish Churches*, Philadelphia, 1894 (adverse to Roman Catholic claims); H. Zimmer, *The Celtic Church in Britain and Ireland*, London, 1902. For the British branch noteworthy works are: R. Rees, *An Essay on the Welsh Saints*, London, 1836; J. H. Overton, *The Church in England*, i., *The National Churches*, 2 vols., London, 1891; H. Williams, *Some Aspects of the Christian Church in Wales during the Fifth and Sixth Centuries* (London, 1895, reprinted from the *Transactions of the Society of Cymmrodorion*, 1893–94, pp. 55–132); E. J. Newell, *A History of the Welsh Church to the Dissolution of the Monasteries*, London, 1895; J. W. W. Bund, *The Celtic Church of Wales*, ib. 1897; W. Bright, *Chapters of Early English Church History*, Oxford, 1897; J. W. W. Bund, *The Celtic Church of Wales*, London, 1897; W. E. Collins, *The Beginnings of English Christianity, with special Reference to the Coming of St. Augustine*, London, 1898; W. Hunt, *The English Church from Its Foundation to the Norman Conquest*, London, 1899. For Ireland: J. Lanigan, *An Ecclesiastical History of Ireland to the Thirteenth Century*, 4 vols., Dublin, 1829; R. King, *A Primer of the History of the Holy Catholic Church in Ireland to the Formation of the Modern Branch of the Church of Rome*, 2 vols. and supplement, Dublin, 1851; idem, *A Memoir Introductory to the Early History of the Primacy of Armagh*, Armagh, 1854; C. J. Greith, *Geschichte der altirischen Kirche*, Freiburg, 1867; W. D. Killen, *The Ecclesiastical History of Ireland*, 2 vols., London, 1875; G. T. Stokes, *Ireland and the Celtic Church*, 6th ed., London, 1907; idem, *Some Worthies of the Irish Church*, ib. 1900; J. Healy, *Insula sanctorum et doctorum or Ireland's Ancient Schools and Scholars*, Dublin, 1890; A. Bellesheim, *Geschichte der katholischen Kirche in Irland*, 3 vols., Mainz, 1890–91; T. Olden, *The Church of Ireland*, in *The National Churches*, London, 1892; J. Heron, *The Celtic Church in Ireland*, London, 1898; Eleanor Hall, *Early Christian Ireland*, Dublin, 1905. For Scotland: W. F. Skene, *Celtic Scotland*, ii., *Church and Culture*, 3 vols., Edinburgh, 1887; A. Bellesheim, *Geschichte der katholischen Kirche in Schottland*, 2 vols., Mainz, 1883, Eng. transl., with additions and notes, by D. O. H. Blair, 4 vols., Edinburgh, 1887–1890; H. M. Luckock, *The Church in Scotland*, in *The National Churches*, London, 1893; J. Dowden, *The Celtic Church in Scotland*, London, 1894; W Stephen, *History of the Scottish Church*, 2 vols., Edinburgh, 1894–96; Dom Columba Evans, *The Early Scottish Church*, London, 1906 (claims original Roman supremacy). For the Culdees: W. Reeves, *The Culdees of the British Islands as They Appear in History*, Dublin, 1864; Skene, u.s., pp. 226–277; J. von Pflugk-Hartung, *Die Kuldeer*, in *ZKG*, xiv. (1894) 169–192. Fuller bibliographies may be found in Warren, u.s., pp. xiii.–xix.; Bellesheim, *Irland*, pp. xix.–xxii.; *Schottland*, pp. vii.–xv.; and Olden, pp. 430–432.

CEMETERIES.

Cemeteries is a term used to designate the burial-places of the early Christians, including the subterranean burying-grounds commonly known as catacombs.

I. Names Used in Early Times: Among the various titles by which the Christians of the first few centuries designated the burial-places of their dead, the most frequent and probably the oldest is the Greek *koimētērion* or the equivalent Latin *cœmeterium*. It is not found in the Septuagint or in the New Testament, but the verb *koimasthai*, "to lie down to rest," "to sleep," occurs in both the literal and the metaphorical sense, usually the latter in the New Testament (metaphorical: Matt. xxvii. 52; Acts vii. 60, xiii. 36; I Cor. vii. 39, xv. 6, 18, 20, 51; I Thess. iv. 13; II Peter iii. 4; literal: Matt. xxviii. 13; Luke xxii. 45; Acts xii. 6). While the word *koimētērion* is of rare occurrence in classical Greek (it was applied by the Cretans, according to Athenæus, to a room for the entertainment of guests), it was constantly used by both Christians and Jews for single and family graves and for larger burying-grounds, whether above ground or under ground. On the other hand, there is only one doubtful case of its use in a heathen inscription for a burial-place (*CIL*, viii. 7543), against thousands in which other terms are used. That the expression was recognized as a distinctly Christian and Jewish term is evident from the way in which it is used as an unfamiliar term in the edicts of the Roman emperors (Eusebius, *Hist. eccl.*, VII. xi. 13). Latin-speaking Christians also occasionally employed the term *accubitorium*, which originally meant (from the Roman habit of reclining at table) a dining-room. These words show their connection with the Christian hope, which saw in death only a sleep. Besides these specifically Christian expressions, the inscriptions give a number of others, of a more general nature. Besides some of minor importance, there is, for example, *hypogæum* (or in one place Gk. *katagaion*) to designate small underground burial-places among both Christians and pagans. Modern scholars frequently employ this term to designate underground burial-places, no matter what their size or arrangements. The word *area* is also found among the Latin-speaking races, especially in North Africa, and it has become customary, following De Rossi, to use it for all surface burying-grounds of the primitive Church. The name "catacomb" is more recent than any of the above-named, but has come into more general use to designate not only the subterranean burial-places of the primitive Christians but frequently also those of the Jews and other races. It is first met with in connection with the circus of Maxentius near the Appian Way outside of Rome, in an inscription which has the phrase *fecit et circum in catecumbas*. As relating to a Christian burial-place, it is not demonstrable before the year 354, when it appears as a specific designation of the cemetery of St. Sebastian on the Appian Way, to which it was limited for centuries. Johannes Diaconus is the earliest evidence for its application to other Christian cemeteries, outside of Rome as well as within. Familiar as the word now is, however, there is no certainty as to its original signification. The most probable theory is that of De Waal, followed by Schultze, that the circus of Maxentius and the cemetery of St. Sebastian were called *in catacumbas* (Gk. *kata kumbas*, "in the ravine") because of the sudden dip which the land, including the Appian Way, takes at that point into a deep hollow.

II. Christian Burial and Burial-Places in General.—1. Fundamental Ideas: The burial of Christ in the garden was taken as the model for that of his disciples. The fact that never in the oldest Christian literature (including the New Testament) and not often later is a prohibition of cremation found, and the absence of traces of cremation, cinerary urns, and the like, demonstrate that burial in the earth was the unwritten law. Based originally upon the example of Christ, it was supported later by reasoning which connected the resurrection of the body more or less with its burial. Minucius Felix, however, prefers burial to cremation merely as "the older and better custom" (*Octavius*, xxxiv. 11). Augustine (*De civitate Dei*, i. 22; *De cura pro mortuis*, iii., etc.) takes burial for granted, and so does Origen in the East (*Contra Celsum*, v. 23, viii. 49; *De principiis*, ii. 10). It is impossible to decide how far Christians of the Apostolic Age were buried in Jewish and pagan graveyards; but later a strict line of demarcation was drawn, at least as early as Tertullian. The Christian graves were not required to be at a great distance, but there was to be a distinct interval between them and the heathen, and the burial of individual Christians in heathen graveyards was strictly forbidden, and vice versa. Primitive Christianity was thus as exclusive in death as in its worship during life.

2. Predecessors of the Cemeteries: While Christian antiquity agreed in condemning cremation, it made no attempt at enforcing uniformity in the manner of burial. Both of the earlier methods of sepulture, under and above the ground, were employed. The choice between the two was determined partly by the geological conformation of the place, though perhaps not as largely as has been usually assumed. Other prevailing reasons are to be sought in the customs of pre-Christian times in regard to the disposal of corpses. That the early Christians should have undertaken, in the absence of any definite prescription, to strike out wholly new lines for themselves in this matter is unlikely, especially since they did not attempt this in the analogous matter of the construction of their houses and churches. Naturally, therefore, they adopted in each place the prevailing local custom—the Hebrew Christians of Palestine following the Jewish mode, and the Gentile Christians of Sicily that of their pagan neighbors. The fuller our knowledge grows of both ancient Christian and ancient pagan burial-places, the more clearly is this theory demonstrated, not only in regard to the choice mentioned above, but equally in regard to the shape, decoration, and equipment of the sepulchers. Thus it may be remarked, without anticipating too much what will be said later, that private vaults, holding but a small number of bodies, are characteristic of the earliest period of Christian burial. As far as inscriptions and other indications go, these were restricted to the members of one family, its friends, etc., with, it is true, the addition (as in the *familia* of the imperial period) of Christian freedmen and their Christian offspring. It is not yet certain whether so early as this (on the analogy of the older Roman and later Christian custom) individuals joined together in associations for the purpose of providing a common burial-place. In a word, it is safe to say that the primitive Christians followed Jewish models in Palestine and pagan elsewhere, almost without exception.

3. Development of Cemeteries and Their Types: As in other things, so here Christianity proved itself a religion of development; and, once more following the general rule, this development was more rapid in the West than in the East. To take but a single important point, the development from the family vault to the general cemetery, the East never went beyond a few experiments, and burying-grounds for the whole of a local church remained exceptional, even at a much later period. The West, on the other hand, while it began with the family vault, and examples of this form persist through the whole of Christian antiquity, was not long in adopting the large common cemetery. The development was not everywhere equally rapid; Sicily was least affected by it, and Rome most. By the third century the common cemetery was the rule here.

The Roman catacombs mark the highest point reached in the development of ancient Christian burial, the greatest and most speedy advance upon its pre-Christian prototypes and upon its own beginnings. The most striking feature of this is not the immense extent attained by the wonderful underground city, but the motive power which created it—the spirit of brotherly love and *esprit de corps*. As nearly as the obscure beginnings can be traced, this, rather than practical considerations or needs, was responsible for the vast extension of the system. Before the advent of Christianity, it was not uncommon for philanthropists to provide either individuals or whole classes, principally among the poor, with burial-places, and there was nothing in itself remarkable about Christians

1. Origin of the General Cemetery.

being inspired with the same benevolent idea. But the earlier instances were the product of mere kindness of heart, while the motive of the Christian benefactions was distinctly the spirit of brotherhood. The most famous among those who thus endowed the oldest Roman church was a member of the imperial family, Flavia Domitilla, who possessed an estate on the Via Ardeatina, of which she allowed portions to be used for burial. The largest common cemetery of Rome, the catacomb which bears her name, was constructed on this spot, and some of her own relations buried in it. Other Christians followed her example, and the Church as a whole, so renowned for its spirit of charity, can not have been idle in this good work.

These beginnings date from the second century; the third is the great epoch of subterranean burial in Rome; and the new development ceased there first, as it had begun there. It is true that new catacombs were established in the fourth century, such as that of St. Felix on the Via Aurelia, but their number and extent were comparatively insignificant. Burial on the surface, previously rare, increased in frequency with the cessation of persecution, and by the beginning of the fifth century became the rule. The dated inscriptions give an accurate view of the change: if their proportion may be taken, one-third of the burials between 338 and 360, half between 364 and 369, two-thirds between 373 and 400, and after 450 all those who died were buried outside the catacombs. This striking change is not sufficiently explained by the recognition of Christianity; the decisive change does not coincide with the date of the Edict of Milan (313), and both in Sicily and in Palestine burial continued to be as before—in the former on the surface, in the latter underground. It may perhaps be better taken as merely an expression of the general consciousness of the change in the Church's position during the century, corresponding to the change which has been noticed in the ideal portrait of Christ in the same period (see JESUS CHRIST, PICTURES AND IMAGES OF).

2. Period of the Catacombs.

After the Roman catacombs ceased to be burial-places, they were by no means deserted, but remained the destination of pious pilgrimages. The veneration of the martyrs and their relics received a great extension in the fourth century, and the use of the ancient burial-places in this way was furthered by the restoration of the passages and chambers and the opening of new approaches by Pope Damasus. A number of fifth and sixth-century popes followed his example. The old chambers were enlarged into chapels, or regular basilicas were established in the catacombs (Sant' Agnete, San Lorenzo fuori le Mura, Santi Nereo ed Achilleo).

While burial either in catacombs or in the open ground was the common practise of primitive Christianity, it sometimes took place in mausoleums or churches. The construction of churches to mark the sepulchers of the martyrs and render them accessible to large numbers of the faithful began soon after the recognition of Christianity. In churches of this kind burial was practised, either by graves dug in the earth or by sarcophagi. The principal churches used in this way in Rome were those of St. Peter and St. Paul, St. Laurence and St. Agnes without the Walls, and St. Pancreas, in and around which large numbers of Christians were buried until late in the sixth century.

3. Burial in Mausoleums and Churches.

If in the first three centuries the Christians had respected the civil ordinance which required burial outside the walls of cities, the fourth witnessed a tendency to break down these restrictions. In Constantinople this took place about 381; in the mean while the relics of martyrs had been translated to the churches within the city, and promoted the desire of others to be buried in their neighborhood, so that an imperial edict was required which strictly prohibited such intramural burial. Chrysostom, however, who had sanctioned this restriction, was himself buried in a church in Constantinople in 438, and near him a number of persons of prominence. The increasing prevalence of the practise gradually broke through the law; in Rome there were intramural burial-places in the sixth century—a cemetery on the Esquiline and a number of places in and around the churches of the city, though the solemn translation of the relics of martyrs from the cemeteries outside to the city churches did not begin till the eighth and ninth centuries.

4. Establishment and Administration of Cemeteries: The same spirit of love which watched over not only the poor and the sick but also the dead in the primitive Church must have had before it the problem of the setting apart of definite officers for the care of this part of its work. It seems probable that as early as Cyprian's day special persons were officially charged with the care of funerals. Where vaults were hewn out of the rock or built up in masonry, special grave-diggers were not required; but the laying out of the larger catacombs required the services of technical knowledge. Thus it happens that next to nothing is heard about the organizers of cemeteries before the reign of Constantine, and in and after that reign more in the East than in the West. The Roman Church had no special officials in the middle of the second century, but at Cirta in North Africa as early as the beginning of the persecution of Diocletian *fossores* appear as the lowest of the clerical orders (see FOSSARIANS).

1. Fossores.

Accordingly they came to be reckoned among the clerics between 250 and 350. Outside of Africa the *fossores* are sometimes named before the *ostiarii*. Their function was to dig the graves and act as custodians of the cemeteries. In the catacombs there are a number of pictures which show them at their work; here they are evidently of a higher class than mere laborers. In view of the complicated nature of their task, they are rather to be compared with architects. They seem to have been supported at first, like other church officials, from the free-will offerings of the faithful; but a number of fourth and fifth-century inscriptions imply that they received considerable sums from the sale of graves. This sort of traffic probably led to abuses, and so ultimately to the decline of the order as an order. It seems to have been definitely suppressed in Rome in the first half of the fifth century. Constantinople also had its official grave-diggers, though here they were not reckoned among the clergy. As a class established by Constantine and added to by Anastasius, they attended to burials without charge, but received immunity from taxation and other privileges, so that their position was a desirable one, and coveted even by well-to-do tradesmen. It is learned from Ambrose (*MPL*, xvii. 745) that in the church of Milan the whole charge of burials was in the hands of the clergy, but he gives no details.

2. Administrative Officials. Earlier and fuller information is extant in regard to the officials who had the administration of the cemeteries. With the development from private vaults to burial-grounds for the whole local church, this naturally came within the bishop's sphere of influence. He would of course deputize some of his clergy to assist him, and in Rome from the third century the names of such clerics appear as administrators of the common burying-ground; the first who can be positively identified was in deacon's orders. The *Liber pontificalis*, in its account of Pope Dionysius (259–268), implies that each of the titular or parish churches of Rome had one cemetery specially assigned to it, and that the priest of each church had the oversight of the corresponding cemetery. At the beginning of the fourth century, the growth of the local church required an enlargement of the number, and a redistribution was made (again according to the *Liber pontificalis*) by Pope Marcellus (308–309). Assistants of the parish priest in this matter were those called from the end of the fifth century *præpositi*, who had charge of the more important cemeteries, and the *mansionarii*, who had charge of the less important burial-places. The *præpositi* of the catacomb of St. Calixtus, which was not classed with the others, and of St. Peter's, St. Paul's, and St. Laurence's, were subject not to parish priests but directly to the pope.

5. Acquisition, Use, and Protection of Graves: In Christian antiquity graves were acquired and prepared as in pre-Christian times, either by purchase or gift, and in the lifetime of the destined occupant or at death. People provided their relatives, friends, and servants with graves by their wills or by deed of gift. The only innovation is that which has been already remarked, that local churches provided burial-places for the poor out of the common funds. Both single graves and family vaults were frequently purchased, and the

1. Purchase of Graves. records of the transaction sometimes occupy more space than the funeral inscription proper, giving the names of buyer, seller, and witnesses, the price and location of the grave. In some of the Roman inscriptions, probably relating only to particular churches, the permission of the pope is mentioned. In cases where the purchase-price is mentioned, though it may have included the cost of construction, it seems in some instances to be excessive, and the *fossores* are likely to have driven a good bargain, especially for places near the tombs of the martyrs, for which there was an increasing demand. Gregory the Great set his face against the selling of graves, but after his death the system seems to have revived. Though the question can not be positively decided, it seems that in Christian antiquity the practise of providing a burial-place during life was more common in the East than in the West, and during the period after Constantine than that before.

A passage in Tertullian (*De anima*, li.) and the decrees of certain councils against the crowding of bodies on top of one another or close together has led many archeologists to believe that in the primitive Church each Christian had a grave to himself. But this view is untenable, as is shown especially by the excavations of Paolo Orsi in the cemeteries of Sicily, where he frequently found more than one body in a grave, and in one case as many as eighteen.

2. The Same Grave Used for Several Bodies. Even in Rome, where more respect was paid to the dead, the inscriptions not seldom show that an old grave was used again for fresh interments, the original tablet being reversed and made to bear the name of the new tenant. The practise seems to have originated and to have been carried on with the least scruple in the East, where as early as the third century measures had to be taken against the violators of graves, not merely those who opened them for the purpose of interring more corpses, but some even who did not shrink from robbing them.

The custom of putting an inscription on a tomb to guard it from profanation is very old, and on the other hand was common in the Middle Ages. The Christian inscriptions of this kind warn those who read them most frequently and expressly against the use of the grave for burial by unauthorized persons; but the writings of fourth-century Fathers and the edicts of Christian emperors in the same period show that this was not the only danger feared. Gregory Nazianzen has left more than eighty epigrams directed against grave-robbers, and John Chrysostom was obliged to

3. Violation of Graves. scourge this abuse again and again in his sermons. A startling fact is that the Christian inscriptions affixed to graves as a protection seem to be addressed mainly to Christians, if one may judge from their appeals to God and the last judgment. In all the principal sections of the ancient Church numerous inscriptions are found which threaten violators of tombs either with secular or with divine penalties, or with both; but they are nowhere so numerous as in Phrygia and the adjoining provinces of Asia Minor. This frequency may be explained partly by the open and comparatively unprotected nature of the cemeteries there, although such inscriptions are found also in the Roman and Sicilian catacombs; but it is probably due more largely to the pre-Christian tradition in Asia Minor, where pagan inscriptions of the kind were very numerous—while in Rome, on the other hand, they are equally rare among pagans and Christians. Secular rulers imposed heavy penalties upon violators of graves; they were excluded from profiting by the usual Easter indulgences, and their wives were allowed to get a divorce from them.

Nor was the Church behindhand in warning and punishing offenders. But the evil was so deeply rooted that in spite of all these measures it lasted much longer than Christian antiquity.

6. Commemoration of the Dead in the Cemeteries: Besides the solemnities of interment, the primitive Church had a number of arrangements for the subsequent commemoration of the dead. The earliest recorded is the annual commemoration at the grave of Polycarp on the day of his martyrdom (*Martyrium Polycarpi*, xviii.). In the time of Tertullian it was customary in Africa to celebrate the anniversary of the death of other Christians (*De corona*, iii.; *De monogamia*, x.; cf. also *Apostolic Constitutions*, viii. 42; Cyprian, *Epist.*, xxxix. 3). Other commemorations took place on the third, seventh, ninth, thirtieth, and fortieth days after death or burial. As has been seen in regard to the mode of burial, so here also these variations may be referred to the influence of pre-Christian local customs, whether Jewish or pagan. Thus Ambrose (*De obitu Theodosii*, iii.) ascribes the celebration of the thirtieth day to the example of Deut. xxxiv. 8 and of the fortieth to Gen. l. 3; and Augustine (*Quæstiones in Heptateuchum*, i. 172) shows the pagan origin of the ninth by objecting to it as reminding people of the Roman *novendial* and being without Biblical precedent.

1. Various Commemorations.

The place of these commemorations is not always mentioned in the early authorities. Those described in the *Martyrium Polycarpi* and the early Gnostic *Acta Joannis* took place at the sepulcher. What may be inferred from the latter to have been the practise of the Christians of Asia Minor is shown by Tertullian and Cyprian to have prevailed also in Africa—the celebration of the Eucharist in connection with these observances. By this sacred feast, which consolingly united the living with those who had gone before, the memorial ceremonies acquired a specifically Christian character. Later it came to be surrounded by a number of other ceremonies. Of these the first to come up was a meal, not the ancient *agape* but one partaken of in the ordinary way as simple nourishment. These feasts on the anniversaries of the saints led to abuses and excesses which are frequently rebuked by the Fathers, especially in Africa, but also at Milan and in Rome. Offenses not merely against temperance but against morality seem to have taken place on these occasions in the East, according to Chrysostom, and also at the beginning of the fourth century in Spain, where a council legislates against them. In fact, the influence of the pagan *dies parentales* and *femoralia* continued to be felt, as was clearly the view of Ambrose and Augustine when they endeavored to regulate such customs, and especially to abolish anything which could seem like the heathen custom of offering food and drink to the dead (Augustine, *De moribus ecclesiæ catholicæ*, i. 34; *Confessiones*, vi. 2; and a canon of the Second Synod of Tours, 567). These authorities, however, do not raise any objection to other survivals of pre-Christian customs, such as the offering of balsam and other sweet-smelling spices, which were frequently poured into the grave in liquid form, through specially prepared openings such as are still to be seen in one of Orsi's discoveries in the catacombs of Syracuse, and at San Paolo fuori le Mura in Rome. Incense was also used. It was a common practise to deck the graves with flowers, and lights were sometimes burned, though this was forbidden by the Synod of Elvira on the singular ground that "the spirits of the saints are not to be disturbed." This custom is evidenced by the large numbers of small lamps found in the catacombs, either placed in niches or fastened to the walls, which can hardly have been intended merely for lighting the dark passages.

2. Ceremonies of Commemoration.

III. Arrangement, Structure, and Grave-Formation of the Cemeteries: In the consideration of these points, the geographical division is evidently the right one; but lack of space will allow it to be carried out only in the description of the subterranean burial-places, while a generic classification will have to be adopted for those above ground.

1. Subterranean Burial-Places.—a. The Oriental Group (Asia Minor, the Crimea, Lower Egypt, and Cyrenaica): Palestine is rich in tombs hollowed out of the rock, more or less reminding the beholder of the sepulcher of Abraham (Gen. xxiii., xxv. 9). There has not been sufficient scientific investigation into their origin and age to enable an accurate distinction to be drawn between Jewish and Christian tombs in the individual instances. Either naturally perpendicular or artificially filled-out walls of rock were dug into horizontally, or, where such were difficult of attainment, an excavation was made downward in suitable rocky ground, into which a flight of steps or a ladder led down. Places for single or family graves were excavated horizontally, with a low and narrow door to each, closed with a stone, often cylindrical in form. In the single graves a sort of niche, or sometimes two, were chiseled out, at the base of which, on the semblance of a couch, the corpse was laid, wrapped in cloths without a coffin. A variant or development of this was the hollowed-out grave, corresponding to the *arcosolium* of the Roman catacombs, allowing the body to be laid in an excavation resembling a coffin. The best-known single graves in Palestine are those called the tombs of Absalom and of Zechariah at Jerusalem and a number of tombs on the south side of the Valley of Hinnom. The family tombs present the same forms, and later frequent instances are found of another kind, in which the excavation in the walls is shaped so as to allow the body to be pushed in head or feet foremost; of these a large number have been found in Palestine. This latter class may be taken to be exclusively Jewish in origin, and, where they are found in connection with indisputably Christian graves, it is commonly assumed that the Christians merely appropriated them. There is no doubt that the Jewish Christians also used the hollowed-out and the vertically sunk graves. An interesting burial-place with the latter type of grave is that on the Mount of Olives, which in more than one particular differs from the normal arrangement in Palestine, and probably belongs to a comparatively late period of Christian antiquity.

1. Palestine.

Elsewhere in the country, even down to the fifth and sixth centuries, the original character of both single and family tombs was preserved.

2. Syria.

Syria offers a considerable number both of ancient church buildings and of ancient cemeteries, both above and below ground, and a type which is a combination of the two, at once hollowed out in the rock and built over above. The openings to the subterranean burial-places are either vertical or horizontal. In the former case they are covered by a stone like the lid of a sarcophagus, or sometimes by a roof with columns or a complete chamber; in the latter, a door leads directly into them by a flight of steps, or one passes first through a portico or anteroom. The inner space, usually rectangular, has in most cases two or three hollowed-out and vaulted graves, each along one wall; six is the largest number cited by De Vogüé. The coffin-shaped place for the body is generally covered, not by a slab, but by a heavy stone shaped like the arched sarcophagus-lids. The principal difference between the known Christian burial-places of Syria (mostly fifth century, to judge from the inscriptions) and their pagan prototypes is the almost universal choice of the *arcosolium* form among those used in pre-Christian times.

3. Mesopotamia.

The cemeteries of Mesopotamia seem to correspond in their main features to those of central Syria, including structures wholly or partially above ground and excavations in the rock. An important necropolis is that outside the walls of Constantina in northern Mesopotamia, above ground, containing nearly 2,000 graves. The subterranean burial-places seem to have been mostly connected with ancient stone-quarries, and some of them are more extensive than the similar ones in Syria, though numerous smaller ones have been found.

4. Asia Minor.

The best-known early Christian cemeteries in Asia Minor are in the extreme southeastern provinces of Isauria and Cilicia, of which the former had the good fortune to be explored by L. Duchesne. Near the ancient Seleucia (now Selefkeh) are numerous rectangular chambers at irregular distances from each other, excavated in soft limestone and entered by doors. They contain from three to ten graves apiece, somewhat like *arcosolia*, but standing out further from the walls. Rock-chambers and isolated *arcosolia* are also found near the village of Libas, and many isolated coffins were scattered around three basilicas at Mout, the ancient Claudiopolis, as well as graves dug straight down and covered with stone slabs. Anazarbe in Cilicia has a large necropolis dating from a late period of Christian antiquity, in which both rock-chambers and rock-coffins are found, as also at Elæussa. A still larger cemetery was probably that of Corykos (now Ghorigos), where chambers are excavated in the rock, sometimes in several lines one above another. These seem to have been all for families or small groups. All about the neighboring hills are large isolated sarcophagi with saddle-back covers. In Pisidia, at Termessos, there are burial-chambers which the crosses show to have been Christian. Since Armenia has Christian rock-tombs at Arabissos (now Yarpuz), it is not unlikely that the intervening province of Cappadocia will yet furnish some examples. It is possible that the lack of interest hitherto shown in the Christian cemeteries of Asia Minor is due to the close resemblance between them and the pagan burial-places; and evidence is not lacking to support the theory that a considerable number which have heretofore been classed as pagan will, upon further investigation, be proved to be Christian.

5. Egypt.

Accurate modern scientific investigation of the Christian sepulchral remains of Egypt has borne no proportion to the importance of the northern part of that country in the early Church, and the question must be here discussed principally from the evidences to be found in Alexandria. Among the catacombs to which access was gained in the nineteenth century the best known is that discovered in 1858, lying near the Serapeum in the southwestern part of the ancient city. A flight of steps leads down into a square anteroom, with a semicircular niche adjoining it on the west side, and two burial-chambers extending out from it. One of these is long and narrow, vaulted above, and containing thirty-two tombs of the kind into which the body is pushed head or feet first. The other, smaller and square, has three hollowed-out graves, one on each side, and another sunk in the floor. That these were used by Christians is demonstrated by paintings and inscriptions, though more recent in date than the construction. Néroutsos, the most thorough student of the Alexandrian catacombs, mentions another, discovered in 1876, which he believes to be Christian. In this the anteroom resembles a Greek or Roman *ædicula*, though the capitals of the columns are decorated with lotus-flowers instead of acanthus-leaves. The oblong burial-chamber leading out of this has on three sides rows of graves of the kind described, at right angles with the wall, one above another, to the number of fifty-four. These cemeteries were probably family burial-places, serving for more than one generation. The pagans and Jews of Alexandria undoubtedly began with this system, but there is reason to believe that the Christians did not always adhere to it.

6. Cyrenaica.

Cyrenaica contains a great number of burial-places hollowed out in the rock, both pagan and Christian, especially in the old capital city; but they have not been explored with sufficient completeness and accuracy to allow the formation of definite conclusions. As far as can be determined, most of the burial-places of Cyrene are excavated in the side of perpendicular cliffs near the city. Only a few of them give positive evidence of Christian use, though there is reason to think that these are not all. A great variety of methods appears, including movable and immovable stone sarcophagi, *arcosolia*, *loculi*, graves sunk in the floor, and long, narrow holes in the cliff in which the dead were laid one above another, separated by horizontal slabs.

The *arcosolia* show considerable artistic feeling, and where the vaulted roof occurs it resembles not a little the vaulting of the apse in early churches, like which, again, it is often painted. In these catacombs several chambers are sometimes united to form a larger whole, evidently serving for more than one family, and in one case it is possible to conclude with certainty that it was a common burial-place for the Christian community. In this particular alone the Christians of Cyrenaica developed beyond their predecessors, whom they followed only in the variety of shapes used for the graves.

b. The Western Group: Even if the assumption frequently made that there were no subterranean cemeteries in North Africa is abandoned, it is true, at least, that they have but little significance compared with the large number in the open air or in and near buildings above ground. There seem really to be but two subterranean burial-places to consider. One at Tipasa has ten adjoining chambers dug out of the rock of the foothills. The chamber, trapezoid in form, approximately ten feet by nine, has an *arcosolium* on each of three sides and three graves dug in the floor, apparently covered with flat slabs. Gavault, its discoverer, compares it with some chambers in the Roman catacombs, but it is more analogous to the Oriental and Sicilian. The other cemetery, discovered in 1885, is at Arch-Zara. The accessible portion is elliptical in shape, terminating in a sort of apse. Four parallel passages, the longest about eighty-eight yards, crossed by others at right angles, are found in it. In the walls of these galleries are placed *loculi*, closed by slabs of brick. It is quite possible that the place extends further in, or even that there is a second level below the one which has been excavated.

1. North Africa.

The cemeteries of Sicily surpass in number those of any other province of the Roman Empire, and show more varied forms than even Rome itself can offer. Each of the races which successively ruled the island brought its own customs with it, while none was strong enough to enforce them to the exclusion of the old. In dealing with the problem of sepulture, Christianity had a number of methods, both aboriginal and mixed, to choose from, and needed only to adopt or adapt. Nor was it limited to Sicilian types; the many ties which connected the island, even in Christian times, with Asia Minor, Syria, Egypt, North Africa, and Rome rendered it possible for still other architectural types to find an entrance. The geological formation of the island favored the excavation of subterranean burial-places. Limestone and tufa abound, the latter usually of firmer substance than the *tufa granulare* of the neighborhood of Rome.

2. Sicily.

The first stage in the development is formed by the family vaults, of which the simplest show a square, oblong, or trapezoid form with graves in the walls, usually of the *arcosolium* or *loculus* type. Next, the small vault developed into a hall, from which recesses ran off on each side, usually shaped like a bell or a flower-pot, though sometimes square, with an opening at the top for light and air. Structures based upon older cisterns are confined to the vicinity of Girgenti, and tombs with a baldachin covering, to eastern Sicily and Malta. Some of these stand free from the walls with the covering supported by pillars on all sides, like the ciborium of an altar; others are supported from one side on pillars, and from the other connect with the wall. In the eastern part are some with decorative façades in front either of a single grave or of a group, furnished with doors and windows.

The main differences in structure depend upon the size of the cemetery. The galleries of the larger catacombs were laid out with one or more main alleys and a number of smaller ones running across or parallel to them. The passages are as a rule comparatively wide, much wider than in Rome. Occupying an intermediate position between passages and chambers are the recesses, as wide as or wider than the corridors, but shorter. These are met with frequently in Sicily, and often contain (besides other types of graves) sarcophagi, sometimes arranged in terraces. Where chambers occur in the large catacombs, they are connected with the galleries, and are in shape square, oblong, trapezoid, or circular, the last being especially preferred in the principal catacombs of Syracuse. The rectangular ones have either a flat or a vaulted roof, the circular are often covered with a cupola, with an opening in the top for light and air. Where the size was sufficiently great to admit the possibility of a fall of the roof, this was guarded against by the construction of pillars out of the solid rock or by the erection of columns. The corridors and chambers are sometimes all on one level, sometimes in different stories.

The variety of grave-forms is even greater than that of the general structure. In most places the commonest type is the *arcosolium*, sometimes double, one above another. Single graves are found relatively seldom; usually several occur in a row (up to fifteen or even more) under the same vaulted roof. In Sicily *loculi* are much less common than *arcosolia*, and where they are numerous certain corridors contain them almost exclusively for children. The "table-tomb" and the grave at right angles with the wall are rare. Sarcophagi, on the other hand, were common, either cut out of the natural stone, built up with masonwork, or made of better material, such as marble; and so were graves sunk in the floor of chambers, recesses, and galleries, to the extent of forming a characteristic of the Sicilian cemeteries. The most important of all the Sicilian catacombs was that of San Giovanni near Syracuse, which in extent and skilful laying out surpasses even the Roman.

In Malta most of the ancient cemeteries lie near the capital, in the neighborhood of Carthaginian burial-places. Where the sides of rocky cliffs were accessible, the excavations were horizontal, vertical in the flat country. Some of these have nothing but galleries, others nothing but chambers. As a rule, the galleries are few and short, their height that of a man. Among the grave-forms is one which so far has not been found outside of Malta, known for convenience as the "oven-grave." This is an opening in the wall at a greater or less distance from the floor, with the bottom and sides straight, and the top in the shape of either an arch or a shell, or sometimes straight. These external parts are carefully constructed and decorated, often with pilasters in the front; at the back is a rectangular opening which gives access to the length of a grave usually for two, less often for one or three bodies. These graves are generally arranged in a row; in the catacomb of Tal-Liebru **3. Malta.** there are two rows, one above the other. This peculiar form can hardly be of Christian origin, but is rather, as Mayr has shown, the development of a type used by the Phenician population of the island. In a number of burial-places it is the only form used, in others it appears concurrently with the more usual types, among which the *arcosolium* is the most frequent. Both in the oven-graves and in the others a head-rest with a semicircular depression is common. The Maltese cemeteries, most of which date from the fourth and fifth centuries, are as a rule small, and must have served for families or other small groups. Only a single catacomb is known on the neighboring island of Gozzo.

Near the village of Trypiti in Melos, surrounded by pagan tombs, is a Christian necropolis unquestionably used as early as the fourth century, composed originally of five separate catacombs, four of which were afterward connected; and it is probable that others still lie concealed in the vicinity. The oldest, that in the middle, consists of a broad main gallery and several side corri- **4. Melos.** dors. The width of the galleries varies from 3 ft. 3 in. to 16 ft. 4 in., the height from 4 ft. 7 in. to 7 ft. 6 in. The walls contain *arcosolia* with semicircular arches and a few *loculi*, and there are graves sunk in the floor of all the passages, usually in pairs. The three undoubtedly Christian catacombs have no chambers, but the other two, which are probably Christian, have them. Bayet counted 150 *arcosolia* and sixty-six sunk graves in the whole five.

Far as Melos and Apulia are from each other, it would be difficult to find a closer affinity between types of catacombs than exists between these just described and those of Venosa, of which the one most fully studied is apparently of Jewish origin. Here again one finds the same unusual breadth of galleries, in spite of the friable nature of the tufa, the *arcosolium* is the predominant **5. Apulia.** form, at least in the main galleries, and the floor is full of sunk graves, while chambers are once more lacking. The principal difference is in the form of the *arcosolia*, which in Melos are of only one kind, in Venosa of several, answering to the Sicilian variety; and in fact the Jewish catacomb of Venosa offers to a certain extent the intermediate step between Melos on one side and Sicily and southern Italy on the other.

The catacombs of Naples are the most important among those of Campania; and of these the largest and oldest are those of San Gennaro dei Poveri, whose beginnings apparently go back to the first century. Four are enumerated nowadays; but there is reason to suppose that there were originally more. The oldest is trapezoid in ground-plan, with a maximum width of thirty-three feet and length somewhat more. Other smaller rooms open from it to left and right, the latter of which was later remodeled into a church. At the back of the large hall are the entrances to **6. Naples.** two parallel galleries nearly 100 yards long, connected by numerous transverse passages. From the outer side of each of these stretch out other chambers and galleries, which in their turn ramify still further, though to a much less extent than in the Roman catacombs. The second catacomb is less important, and the other two still less. They exhibit three types of graves—*arcosolia*, *loculi*, and sunk graves. The first are the most numerous in the halls and chambers, as well as in the oldest and most important galleries; unlike the Roman, but like those of Melos and Sicily, they are sometimes in two rows, one above the other. From the irregular disposition of the *loculi*, which look as if they had been crowded in, it is safe to attribute a later date to them. They form, however, an actual majority of the total number of graves.

At Castellamare there is a later but not uninteresting catacomb, named after St. Blasius. Besides a nearly square entrance-hall, it contains a main gallery nearly twenty-two yards long, with an average breadth of 9 ft. 10 in., lined with *arcosolia*. On the left of it three side galleries **7. Castellamare.** branch out, and at its further end is a chamber from which further galleries continue. The weight of evidence is in favor of a Christian origin. The arrangement of the graves in the chambers at Castellamare and Sorrento is peculiar; they are placed in rows one above another so as to resemble a honeycomb, a form which is lacking in the older catacombs, though it is impossible to say whether it originated with the Christians of these places.

The history of the immense and widely known catacombs of Rome begins, as is the case elsewhere, with the family plot. In the first two centuries, and even later, individual Christians picked out places for the interment of themselves and their families, including in some cases their freedmen. The arrangement of the first **8. Rome.** cemeteries is not demonstrably derived from pagan models, since there were many Jews in Rome and in the primitive Church there, and these also buried their dead in subterranean cemeteries. But there is reason to believe that, while it would be too much to say that Jewish traditions had no influence on the early development, the first beginnings of the Christian burial system in Rome were derived rather from pagan prototypes.

With the extension of the family plot into the common cemetery for the faithful, underground Rome became apparently a labyrinth, though really its plan is more simple and intelligible than that of some of the larger catacombs outside of Rome. Since the ground was either flat or slightly rolling, the excavation was begun by digging down at an angle into the earth, the descent being furnished with steps, usually covered with brick or marble. After it had reached the required depth (averaging about twenty feet), the excavation continued horizontally in a main gallery and others roughly parallel with it, connected by cross passages into a regular network. The dead were interred usually in the walls, less often in the floor of the passages. Here and there, at the side, end, or intersection of passages, doors were cut which led to one or more chambers (*cubicula*). The shape of these was as a rule nearly rectangular, less often polygonal, semicircular, or circular; the roof nearly or quite flat or cross-vaulted in the rectangular ones, and of the nature of a cupola in the polygonal or circular. The later catacombs usually have smaller chambers, sometimes not more than about four square yards in extent.

As to the form of the tombs, the *loculus* here is the most frequent, larger than necessary in the oldest cases, but later closely following the shape of the body. Sometimes they were dug in deep enough to afford room for several bodies. Above the *arcosolia* there was usually a nearly or quite semicircular arch. If two bodies were to be buried together in these, a *loculus* was cut at the back of the hollowed-out space, or sometimes the arch was carried further back and two spaces hollowed out side by side; or again *loculi* were cut, especially for children, in the lunette of the arch. A combination of the *loculus* and the *arcosolium* is the so-called *loculus a mensa* or "table-tomb." The grave dug in the floor is found less often than in southern Italy and Sicily, and most of those which exist probably date from a time when the walls were already full. Sarcophagi were also used, made of marble in most cases; these were placed mostly in the *cubicula* and galleries, but sometimes on the side of the stairs. When the wall-space of a catacomb was filled, the *fossores* gained more room by digging the floor of the passages deeper. When this had gone so far as to threaten the stability of the walls, a second shaft or gallery was begun at a downward angle from the first, and the whole process repeated. Thus in the catacombs of St. Calixtus and St. Domitilla five different levels are found, the lowest more than eighty feet beneath the surface. An approximate conception of the vast extent of the Roman catacombs may be gained from the calculations of Michele Stefano de Rossi and of Marchi. The former estimated the total length of the passages at 550 miles, the latter at 750. The number of bodies buried there is variously given as from three and a half to six millions.

The catacombs of the towns around Rome and in Etruria resemble the Roman, it is true, more than the Sicilian; but there are striking differences, as in the typical ones of Bolsena, Chiusi, and Soriano, which, when examined in detail, lead to the conclusion that the influence of the ancient Etruscan burial-customs had much to do with them. It extended, in fact, very nearly to the gates of Rome, and some of its characteristics are found in the catacombs of Rignano and at the twentieth milestone on the Via Flaminia.

2. Cemeteries Above Ground.—a. Plan and Construction: The simplest form of cemeteries in the open air is found in Upper Egypt, where, in order to save the soil available for agriculture and at the same time to protect the graves from inundation, the Christians laid their dead to rest on the border of the desert, in large cemeteries used by a considerable district. They seldom used wooden coffins, but tied the corpse, mummified with asphalt or natron, to a sycamore board, then wrapped cloths around it and buried it in an ordinary grave.

1. In the Open Air.

The discovery in 1873 of a cemetery dating from the fourth and fifth centuries at Portogruaro, the ancient Julia Concordia, gives an accurate idea of other vanished burying-grounds, especially in northern Italy. Several hundred sarcophagi of Istrian limestone rest either directly on the ground or on large square bases. They are carved out of a single block of stone, usually without anything on their sides except inscriptions, and covered with heavy roof-shaped covers. The cemeteries of Arles, Vienne, and Treves were similarly laid out. At Arles five layers of graves ultimately existed, one above another, separated only by a layer of earth—the lowest heathen, the upper ones Christian. Much the same was the arrangement at Vienne and at Treves, except that in the latter there are both sarcophagi and graves lined with masonry or brick and covered with slabs of brick, limestone, or sandstone. Here again the lowest layer contains a number of pagan inscriptions and sarcophagi, the most probable inference being that the Christians in Gaul and the Rhine country occupied former pagan burial-places. The *areæ* of northern Africa attained a certain celebrity even during the epoch of persecution, and were carefully investigated by French scholars during the nineteenth century. One at Lambèse, about sixty-five by fifty-three yards in extent, was surrounded by a slight wall, and apparently contained nothing but ordinary graves. Elsewhere, in addition to these, small vaulted structures were erected over the bodies, as at Cæsarea (modern Cherchel) in Mauretania. Two important open-air cemeteries existed at Tipasa; in the center of one was a basilica erected over the body of the martyr Salsa.

The word "mausoleum," now usually restricted to large and imposing monuments, was used in ancient times for less important tombs, and *memoria* is also frequently employed. These small memorial buildings have mostly disappeared. They must have been particularly numerous in regions where the small family burial-place was the rule, and where the custom of erecting them had been prevalent in pre-Christian times. Syria and Mesopotamia have supplied a considerable proportion of them, and Asia Minor probably had as many; but they existed also in countries where the common burying-ground was the rule. Some stood among graves in the open air, as above the Catacomb of St. Calixtus in Rome; others near or attached to churches, as at Tipasa and two that adjoined the old St. Peter's in Rome; others, again, were isolated, like the tomb of Galla Placidia and that of Theodoric at Ravenna.

2. Memorial Buildings.

The frequency of nearly or quite rectangular

grave-chambers in the underground cemeteries would lead to the expectation of finding the same structure above ground; and as a matter of fact it is the rule in Syria and Mesopotamia, while the early existence of numerous examples of this class may be inferred from paintings and sculptures representing the raising of Lazarus, which nearly always depict an oblong tomb like a house or temple. Actual examples from the West are one built like a tower above the Catacomb of St. Calixtus in Rome, another vaulted one at Tropea, two adjoining ones by the side of a basilica at Morsott, and another at Tipasa in North Africa. Occasionally to the rectangular ground-plan was added a semicircular termination at the rear, as in the group of tombs in the cemetery of Manastirine near Salona, of the fourth century or earlier, and other examples at Tipasa and Ancona. The rotunda shape, however, was also of frequent occurrence from the earliest times. Two large mausoleums of this shape, Santa Petronilla and Santa Maria della Febbre, stand near St. Peter's in Rome, and the church of St. George at Salonica was probably sepulchral in origin. The tomb of Theodoric at Ravenna is externally a decagon, on the ground floor within a Greek cross, and circular above. After semicircular additions to an original rectangular plan became common, suggesting the form of a cross, the idea received further development at the hands of Christians. The most prominent representative of this was the mausoleum of the first Christian emperors, the church of the Apostles at Constantinople, of whose sumptuous structure, unhappily, little more is known now than that it had the shape of a Greek cross. The tomb of Galla Placidia at Ravenna also deserves study from this point of view. Probably earlier than the time of Constantine is the original construction of the two mausoleums above the catacombs of St. Calixtus, which later received the names of St. Sixtus and St. Soter.

3. Ground-Plan and Form.

When, after the cessation of persecution, the erection of churches over or near the graves of the saints was carried out on a large scale, the development of cemeteries in connection with them followed as a consequence of the desire of Christians to be buried near the resting-place of the martyrs. In spite of the ancient law forbidding burial within the walls of the city, such burials continued after the relics of the martyrs were brought in to the principal churches of various places (see CHURCHYARD). Burial within the church itself was not everywhere approved. In Spain and Gaul, particularly, it was even a subject of adverse conciliar legislation, although this barrier did not suffice to keep back the flowing tide of popular piety. Both literary and monumental evidence attests the existence in the most widely separated portions of the primitive Church of buildings used both for worship and for interment. A large number of them arose outside the walls of Rome. Unfortunately many smaller buildings of this class sank into decay or oblivion during and after the Middle Ages, while the larger ones were so transformed in course of time that to-day they have scarcely a trace of their original use. It is thus easier to examine the extant ruins in order to form an idea of the construction adopted in the first instance. Of these undoubtedly the most significant is that discovered and explored by Delattre at Damous-el-Karita near Carthage. Here, in the church proper and *atrium* as well as in the immediate neighborhood, more than 14,000 inscriptions or fragments of inscriptions were brought to light. The dead were buried in ordinary sunk graves, lined and covered with slabs, though some were constructed of masonry, frequently covered with stone slabs, and a number of sarcophagi were found, these latter sunk flush with the floor. Of the great burial-churches in Rome, the best example was until recently furnished by that of Santi Nereo ed Achilleo, the floor of which was literally crowded with graves and sarcophagi. The church of St. Paul without the Walls, also at Rome, which from the fourth century was a favorite burial-place, was surrounded by a space intended especially for interment, covered by a roof supported on columns, and adorned with paintings; and that of St. Balbina, also outside the city, had a *teglata* under which the dead were buried.

4. Cemeteries Connected with Churches.

b. Types of Graves: In the primitive age, the simple grave dug in the earth was the commonest form for cemeteries above ground. It was ordinarily not so deep as the graves of to-day, and was frequently lined with slabs of stone, with brick, or with masonry. This custom led to the enlargement of the simple grave into a vault capable of holding several bodies. Of these vaults none have been so thoroughly investigated as were those of the upper cemetery of St. Calixtus and the churches of St. Laurence and St. Paul without the Walls by De Rossi. In the first-named large holes were dug, and then divided off by partitions into spaces each large enough for one body. The materials used in construction were tufa, brick, marble, and thick layers of mortar. In these compartments the corpses were placed one above another, a slab covering the one first buried and serving as a support for the next. The place of the slab was occasionally taken by an arched covering of brick or by a layer of masonry. In this particular cemetery the excavation was carried deep enough to contain ten or even more bodies thus superimposed; the average is between eight and nine. The same system is found at Ostia, Porto, and Tropea in Calabria, as well as in North Africa and at Athens. In other cases, as in the same cemetery of St. Calixtus, the corpses were laid side by side and separated by an upright slab. While the usual shape of all these graves was rectangular, some occur in North Africa which correspond roughly to the shape of the body, and are rounded off at the head and foot. They were frequently also wider at the head than at the foot, giving a bell-shaped type which corresponds to examples found in the Sicilian catacombs. In both cases this type is a survival of native pre-Christian usage.

1. The Ordinary Grave.

The closing of the graves, whichever of these

forms they took, was done in various ways. In Upper Egypt commonly, but elsewhere as well, the earth removed in excavation was heaped over the grave. In other cases slabs were laid either flat on the ground or on the top of the sides where an artificial lining was placed in the grave. These slabs were frequently decorated in the fifth century with mosaic, including an inscription and various pictorial representations, sometimes the portrait of the deceased or symbolic designs. Instead of slabs, large heavy stones cut into a rough shape were used in some places, especially in the East, and in North Africa, where it was an inheritance from Carthaginian custom.

2. The Covering of the Grave.

The term sarcophagus was originally used by the ancients in connection with a kind of stone found near Assos in Asia Minor, which was supposed to have the property of consuming the flesh of the corpse in a short time (Pliny, *Hist. nat.*, XXXVI. xvii. 27), but it was often employed for receptacles made out of other stone. The early Christians, taking over both name and things, used the stone they found at hand. For relief decorations, however, the porous and often flawed limestone was ill adapted, and marble was generally selected where these were desired. The most usual form was that of a parallelepiped, hollowed out to receive the body. The shape of the body was sometimes partially reproduced on the outside, especially in North Africa, or at least the head was semicircular; while at Rome the head and foot were alike. Sarcophagi for children seldom occur, because they were usually buried with their parents in the larger ones. When more than one body was to be placed in the same sarcophagus, stone partitions were sometimes placed in the interior. Christian sarcophagi were frequently adorned with more or less elaborate decorations, usually in relief, though the taste of the North African Christians for mosaic led them to employ it in some cases.

3. Sarcophagi.

Wooden coffins were also used, either enclosed in the sarcophagi or buried in the earth; but on account of their perishable material they have almost disappeared. A coffin of cypress was found in the marble sarcophagus of St. Cecilia, and Gsell found others of oak and pine in sarcophagi at Tipasa. A plain rectangular chest of cedar, but richly decorated with plates of gold and silver, received the remains of St. Paulinus at Treves, and was afterward enclosed in a large sandstone sarcophagus. Coffins of lead were also known; but the most peculiar receptacles were those in the shape of an amphora or large water-vessel. These easily held the corpses of little children; when they were used for full-grown persons, they were sometimes taken apart and lengthened by the addition of cylindrical pieces taken from other amphoræ, and then cemented together.

4. Other Receptacles.

IV. Equipment and Decoration of Tombs: Corresponding to the great variety of arrangement and structure noticed above is a still greater wealth of objects pertaining to the equipment and decoration of the resting-places of the dead. Many of these objects seem natural and intelligible to-day, but others appear peculiar, especially the provision of household utensils. The furnishing of tombs with inscriptions and with painted or carved images is but an inheritance of the traditions of earlier civilized peoples, especially the Greeks and Romans; and it seems on the face of it not unlikely that the provision of these various other objects was similarly a following of ancient custom. It is indisputable that these pre-Christian peoples regarded the grave as a house, and gave it corresponding arrangements and decorations. Roman tombs sometimes accurately resemble dwelling-houses, with *atrium*, *triclinia*, and the like. Numerous pagan inscriptions designate either a burial-vault or a single grave as a house, the eternal house, etc. These same designations and an analogous form of construction are not uncommon in early Christian usage, as might be shown, did space permit, from monuments, inscriptions, and the writings of the Fathers. This conception of the grave as a house offers the only satisfactory explanation of what would otherwise be so mysterious, the character of the objects in the tombs as gifts to the dead. In themselves unnecessary if not senseless additions, they merely demonstrate the power of long custom, from which even medieval Christianity was not able wholly to emancipate itself.

1. The Grave Itself.—a. The Interior: Proper clothing for the corpse was universal, no matter what form of grave was used. Even those who died of the plague in Alexandria had their seemly vesture (Eusebius, *Hist. eccl.*, vii. 22). Linen seems to have been the usual material, and white the color, though costly stuffs, such as silk and purple and gold brocade were sometimes used. Ambrose, Chrysostom, and Jerome protested against the use of gold-embroidered garments, and the first and last also against silk. At a later period synods even found it necessary to legislate against luxury in grave-clothes, e.g., that of Auxerre in 578. In the same century Gregory of Tours relates that a kinswoman of King Childebert was buried "with great ornaments and much gold," which, however, were soon stolen. The indications thus given in the literature of the period are confirmed by numerous discoveries, the largest number of which have been in Upper Egypt. Here the garments are mostly of linen, less often of pure wool or silk. As to mere ornaments, though Gregory of Nyassa says that the body of his sister Macrina was stripped before burial of rings and necklaces, the discoveries show that this was not the common practise. On the contrary, the number of such objects found leads to the conclusion that many bodies were more richly adorned in death than in life. Among them are rings, ear-rings, bracelets and anklets, necklaces, combs and hairpins, fibulæ, etc., made of various materials and frequently bearing Christian emblems, such as the monogram of Christ, the Good Shepherd, the dove, fish, and cross. With these ornaments it is easy to confuse the amulets sometimes found,

1. Objects Pertaining to the Corpse.

since many of them were made in the shape of rings, bracelets, or pendants for the neck (see AMULET).

Where the grave-diggers of the catacombs, or the stone-cutters who made sarcophagi, designed the space for the corpse, as was often the case, so that its head was higher than its feet, there was no need for any support for the head. But in other cases such supports were placed in the tomb, the most primitive sort being of one or more stones. In Upper Egypt rich leather cushions stuffed with tow have been found, so sumptuously decorated as to deserve the name of works of art. Vessels of clay served the same purpose in North Africa. Sometimes supports were provided for the whole body—in North Africa a layer of beton, here and elsewhere simple arrangements of flat bricks, in Catania perforated brick supports on low feet, like benches. On sanitary grounds the grave was often lined with unslacked lime, which was also sprinkled over the corpse. Traces of this custom have been found in the Roman catacombs and elsewhere, as in North Africa. The dead were also laid in some places on a bed of laurel leaves.

2. Disposition of the Corpse.

While the Christians of the primitive age usually contemned the use of perfumed oils and waters, they used such things for the dead in considerable quantities. The dead were anointed before they were dressed for burial, and then sprinkled with perfumes or regularly embalmed with spices, though this latter practise seems to have been comparatively rare in Rome. Anything like mummifying was still more uncommon, outside of Egypt. Usually cloths wet with perfumes were laid upon the body, especially the face, and vessels of the most diverse shapes filled with perfumery were set near it. It is practically certain that some of the vessels known as *Ampullæ* (q.v.) contained these perfumes, and others wine. As food and drink were set out for the martyrs and other saints at the commemorative feasts, it is safe to say that this took place also at burials. There is also the often-discussed possibility that such vessels contained the elements of the Eucharist, or at least the consecrated wine, in connection with the practise condemned at the Third Council of Carthage and often later, of making the dead partakers in the communion.

3. Gifts to the Dead.

Another class is formed by the large number of domestic utensils of every sort which have been found in the graves. These comprise vessels of all kinds, mostly of clay but sometimes of glass or more costly materials, knives, forks, spoons, writing-tablets, styluses, ink-stands, hammers, nails, spinning-wheels, chisels, and tools of many different kinds. Other objects of daily use pertain less to mere utility than to luxury and adornment. A varied collection of articles such as served the women of those days for the toilet have been discovered in and near the tombs of the catacombs, made of metal, mosaic, ivory, glass, enamel, and mother-of-pearl. The grave being conceived, in a certain sense, as the house or chamber of the departed, there is nothing surprising in the discovery that parents, for example, placed near the bodies of the children they had lost even the trifles which had been dear to them in life—dolls, small figures of men and animals, small lamps, spoons, etc., savings-banks, and ivory letters of the kind used in the schools. Even things relating to the amusements of grown-up people—boards for games, dice, and the like—are occasionally found. Pieces of money are of frequent occurrence. Since there is evidence that the old pagan custom of providing the dead with money to pay Charon for the ferriage persisted among Christians in Greece and elsewhere, there is no doubt that at least some of these coins were placed there from that point of view.

b. The Exterior: After the burial was finished, it was a common practise to fix in the still wet mortar with which the *loculi* and *arcosolia* of the subterranean cemeteries were closed small vessels, usually of glass, sometimes shells, for the same purpose as the vessels inside the grave. A repeated renewal of these is evidenced by the tomb of one Peregrina (d. 452) in the Catacomb of San Giovanni at Syracuse; several glasses must have been broken and replaced, and there was also a clay censer still containing coals and some grains of incense. The lamps similarly affixed to the outside of the graves were intended to be lighted at the funeral and on memorial days. Semicircular niches were made in the adjacent walls to hold them. From the reign of Constantine the lamps burning at the graves of the martyrs were kept up with special reverence; the oil from them was credited with miraculous power, and pilgrims often took a small quantity of it home with them.

1. Vessels for Lights and Incense.

Many of the objects mentioned above (a, § 3) are found embedded in the mortar outside the graves, sometimes as gifts, but in other cases undoubtedly as means of identification among the thousands of graves in the large catacombs, the majority of which had no inscriptions, possibly owing to the poverty of the survivors. Some of these substitutes for the regular incised blocks of marble or other stone are letters, numbers, etc., embedded or scratched in or above the place where the tomb is closed; others are small objects of great variety, rings, buttons, glasses, bits of mosaic, animals' teeth, shells, coins, stones of fruit and leaves of plants, fixed in the mortar before it dried.

2. Marks of Identification.

In their use of sepulchral inscriptions the early Christians merely continued the tradition of still older civilizations. Outside of the family vaults, on or over the door of which the name of the occupants or owners appeared, the inscriptions were placed on or at least near the graves. The most peculiar exception to the general usage is formed by those which have the inscriptions inside the graves, where they can not have been visible to passers-by. Karl Schmidt discovered a number of inscribed gravestones in the necropolis of Antinoe in Egypt which seemed to have been laid originally well down in the graves,

3. Inscriptions and Paintings.

at the foot, with the writing underneath. The inscriptions were either cut with a chisel or other sharp tool, scratched with a sharp point, painted with a brush, or composed in mosaic. These inscriptions offer most trustworthy and striking evidence of the mode of thought, faith, and hope of the primitive Christians, especially in regard to death, the grave, and the resurrection (see INSCRIPTIONS; PAINTING).

2. The Chambers and Passages: In these the presence has already been noted of tables, benches, and chairs for the observance of the commemorations of the dead. The dimensions of such tables as have been discovered imply that the number of participants was small. While such furniture is practically absent from the Roman Catacombs, where wood must accordingly have been used, several tables of more durable material have been found in North African burial-places. The galleries and chambers of the catacombs also contained receptacles for the materials used in mixing mortar for closing up the tombs. Those which have been preserved, made usually of clay, with incrustations of mortar and lime still upon them, may have been used either for this purpose or on sanitary grounds, to counteract the effluvia of the place. Lighting arrangements are found here too, although the galleries must have been in comparative darkness, to judge from the way in which Jerome quotes Ps. lv. 15 and Vergil, *Æneid*, ii. 755 in connection with the memory of his visit to the Roman Catacombs. As the *arcosolia* were frequently ornamented with paintings in their vaults and lunettes, and the *loculi* on their exterior side, so also the chambers and less frequently the galleries of the catacombs were decorated in the same way. No doubt the structures above ground connected with the cemeteries were painted in much more numerous cases than the scanty remains extant at the present day would lead one to suppose.

(NIKOLAUS MÜLLER.)

BIBLIOGRAPHY: J. Townshend, *Catalogue of Books Relating to the Disposal of Bodies*, New York, 1887. On the general question consult: F. Piper, *Einleitung in die monumentale Theologie*, Gotha, 1867; J. Wilpert, *Principienfragen der christlichen Archäologie*, Freiburg, 1889; F. X. Kraus, *Ueber Begriff, Umfang und Geschichte der christlichen Archäologie*, Freiburg, 1879; idem, *Real-Encyklopädie der christlichen Alterthümer*, 2 vols., ib. 1880–86; V. Schultze, *Archäologische Studien*, Vienna, 1880; *Die Katakomben, die altchristlichen Grabstätten*, Leipsic, 1882; R. Grousset, *Étude sur l'histoire des sarcophages chrétiens*, Athens, 1885; L. Wagner, *Manners, Customs and Observances*, London, 1885; A. Hasenclever, *Der altchristliche Gräberschmuck*, Brunswick, 1886; H. Marucchi, *Éléments d'archéologie chrétienne*, Paris, 1900; Neander, *Christian Church*, vols. i.–iv., consult Index, s.v. "Burial"; Schaff, *Christian Church*, ii. 286–310, 380–385; Moeller, *Christian Church*, i. 279–283.

For burial in Palestine consult: T. Tobler, *Golgatha*, pp. 201 sqq., et passim, St. Gall, 1851; idem, *Zwei Bücher Topographie von Jerusalem*, ii. 227 sqq., Berlin, 1854; J. N. Sepp, *Jerusalem und das heilige Land*, i. 273 sqq., Schaffhausen, 1873; *Survey of Western Palestine*, London, 1881 sqq.; *Mittheilungen und Nachrichten des deutschen Palästina-Vereins*, Leipsic, 1895 sqq.; *Palestine Exploration Fund Quarterly Statement*, passim; C. Mommert, *Golgotha und das heilige Grab zu Jerusalem*, Leipsic, 1900. For Syrian burial consult: F. E. C. Dietrich, *Zwei sidonische Inschriften*, pp. 11 sqq., Marburg, 1855; C. J. M. de Vogüé, *Notice archéologique sur les monuments encore existants en Terre Sainte*, Paris, 1870; idem, *Syrie centrale*, Paris, 1865–77.

For North Africa consult: A. L. Delattre, *Inscriptions chrétiennes provenant de la basilique de Damous-el-Karita à Carthage*, Constantine, 1863; idem, *Les Tombeaux puniques de Carthage*, Lyons, 1890; idem, *Antiquités chrétiennes*, Paris, 1900; R. M. Smith and E. A. Porcher, *History of the Recent Discoveries at Cyrene*, London, 1864; Néroutsos-Bey, *Notice sur les fouilles récentes* . . pp. 26 sqq., 48, Alexandria, 1875; idem, *L'Ancienne Alexandrie*, pp. 38 sqq., 53–54, 61, Paris, 1888; Pierre Gavault, in *Bibliothèque d'archéologie Africaine*, part 2, 1897; S. Gsell, *Recherches archéologiques en Algérie*, Paris, 1893; idem, *Les Monuments antiques de l'Algérie*, ib. 1899; M. de Bock, *Matériaux pour servir à l'archéologie de l'Égypte chrétienne*, St. Petersburg, 1901.

For Asia Minor consult: J. T. Wood, *Discoveries at Ephesus*, pp. 12 sqq., London, 1877; F. Cumont, *Mélanges d'archéologie et d'histoire*, xv. (1895) 245 sqq.; W. M. Ramsay, *Cities and Bishoprics of Phrygia*, vol. i., parts 1, 2, Oxford, 1895–97; idem, in *Journal of Hellenic Studies*, passim.

On the Greek Islands consult: L. Ross, *Reisen auf den griechischen Inseln*, iii. 145–151, Stuttgart, 1845; L. P. di Cesnola, *Cyprus*, New York, 1877; C. Bayet, in *Bulletin de correspondance Hellénique*, ii. 347–359, Paris, 1878.

On the catacombs at Rome the literature is enormous. The following is a selection: G. B. de Rossi, *Roma sotterranea*, 3 vols., Rome, 1864–77 (the one great book, largely reproduced in English in J. S. Northcote and W. R. Brownlow, *Roma sotterranea*, 2 vols., London, 1879, an authorized summary); with De Rossi's monumental work should be mentioned the periodical edited by him, *Bollettino di archeologia cristiana*, Rome, 1863 sqq. (the repository of reports of discovery and decipherment); F. X. Kraus, *Roma Sotterranea*, Freiburg, 1879 (based on De Rossi and Northcote and Brownlow); S. d'Agincourt, *Histoire de l'art par les monuments*, 6 vols., Paris, 1809–23; W. Röstell, in E. Z. Platner et al., *Beschreibung der Stadt Rom*, i. 355–416, Stuttgart, 1830; G. Marti, *Architettura della Roma sotterranea cristiana*, Rome, 1844; C. Maitland, *Church in the Catacombs*, London, 1847; L. Perret, *Les Catacombes de Rome*, 6 vols., Paris, 1851–55 (plates are valuable, the text is superseded); W. I. Kip, *Catacombs of Rome*, New York, 1854; D. de Richemont, *Les Catacombes de Rome*, Paris, 1870; P. Allard, *Rome souterraine*, Paris, 1874; J. H. Parker, *Archæology of Rome*, parts ix., x., xii., London, 1877 (a standard work); T. Roller, *Les Catacombes de Rome*, Paris, 1881; W. R. Brownlow, *Cemetery of St. Priscilla and Recent Discoveries*, London, 1892; M. Armellini, *Le Catacombe romane*, Rome, 1880; idem, *Gli antichi cimiteri cristiani di Roma e d'Italia*, ib. 1893; R. Lanciani, *Ruins and Excavations of Ancient Rome*, Index "cemeteries," Boston, 1897; A. Weber, *Die römischen Katakomben*, Regensburg, 1900.

For cemeteries in Italy outside Rome consult: G. B. Pasquini, *Un antico cimitero*, Sienna, 1831; idem, *Relazione di un antico cimitero* , Montipulciano, 1833; C. F. Bellermann, *Die ältesten christlichen Begräbnisstätten*, Hamburg, 1839 (at Naples); G. Scherillo, *Le Catacombe Napolitane*, Naples, 1870; F. Liverani, *Le Catacombe* . di *Chiusi*, Sienna, 1872; T. Roller, *Die Katakomben von San Gennaro* , in *Neapel*, Jena, 1877; V. Schultze, *Die Katakomben von San Gennaro*, ib. 1877; F. Colonna, *Scoperto di antichità in Napoli, 1876–1897*, Naples, 1898.

For Sicily, Malta, and Sardinia consult: G. P. Badger, *Description of Malta and Sardinia*, pp. 255–260, Malta, 1838; A. A. Caruana, *Recent Discoveries at Notabile*, Malta, 1881; idem, *A Hypogeum* . , ib. 1884; B. Lupus, *Die Stadt Syracus im Alterthum*, pp. 271, 275, 323–327, Strasburg, 1887; V. Strazzulla, in *Archivio storico Siciliano*, xxi. 104–188, Palermo, 1896; J. Führer, in *AM.A*, 1 Klasse, xx. (1897), part 3; idem, *Forschungen zur Sicilia sotterranea*, Munich, 1897 (a work of the first importance).

For England: Caroline B. Southey, *Chapters on Churchyards*, London, 1870; E. E. Jarrett, *Lessons on the Churchyard*, ib. 1880; Mrs. B. Holmes, *London Burial Grounds*, ib. 1896.

Consult also: J. B. D. Cochet, *La Normandie souterraine ou Notices sur des cimetières romains et des cimetières francs*, Dieppe, 1855; idem, *Sépultures gauloises, romaines, franques et normandes*, 2 vols., ib. 1857.

The original article by Müller, in Hauck-Herzog, *RE*, x. 794–877f. is a learned treatise and should be consulted by advanced students.

CENSER OR THURIBLE: The vessel in which incense is burned during divine service in the Eastern, Roman Catholic, and of late years many Anglican churches. The usual shape is that of a small metal bowl, with a base on which to stand it when not in use, and fitting over it a high conical cover in which are perforations to let the smoke out. The whole is carried by three chains, on which the cover slides up and down, when it is raised to allow incense to be thrown upon the live coals contained in the lower part. In connection with the censer another smaller vessel, called the incense-boat, is used to carry the supply of incense; as its name implies, it is shaped like a small boat, but with a lid and a base on which to stand it.

CENSORSHIP AND PROHIBITION OF BOOKS: By censorship is meant the provision that no publication shall be issued without preliminary examination and permission by the authorities, either ecclesiastical or secular. The prohibition of books as dangerous to religion, to morals, or to the State dates back to an early period. Thus all works on magic were ordered to be destroyed by the later Roman Empire. **Early Instances.** Constantine issued an edict that the works of Arius should be burned, and numerous like edicts against books of other heretics followed. Those who used or possessed such books were threatened with death. The Church forbade, on its own account, the reading of pagan and heretical books (*Apostolic Constitutions*, i. 6, vi. 16; canon xvi. of the Council of Carthage, 398). During the Middle Ages, both Church and State adhered firmly to the same principles; a salient instance is the decree of the Council of Constance against the writings of John Huss and its execution.

After the printing-press was invented and used to advance the cause of the Reformation, measures for its regulation were introduced by the Church, which first established a formal censorship of books. In a letter addressed to the archbishops of Cologne, Mainz, Treves, and Magdeburg, Alexander VI. ordered (1501) that no book should be printed without special authorization. The Lateran Council of 1515 sanctioned the constitution of Leo X., which provided that no book should be printed without having been examined in Rome by **Censorship by the Church.** the papal vicar and the master of the sacred palace, in other countries by the bishop of the diocese or his deputy and the inquisitor of heresies. Further and more detailed legislation followed, and the Council of Trent decreed (session iv.): "It shall not be lawful to print, or cause to be printed, any books relating to religion without the name of the author; neither shall any one hereafter sell any such books, or even retain them in his possession, unless they have been first examined and approved by the ordinary, on pain of anathema and the pecuniary fine imposed by the canon of the recent Lateran Council." On these regulations are based a number of enactments in different dioceses which are still in force. The Council decreed also that no theological book should be printed without first receiving the approbation of the bishop of the diocese; and this rule is extended in the monastic orders so far as to require the permission of superiors for the publication of a book on any subject.

The Council of Trent left the further provision concerning the whole subject to a special commission, which was to report to the pope. In accordance with its findings, Pius IV. promulgated the rule submitted to him and a list of prohibited books in the constitution *Dominici gregis custodiæ* of Mar. 24, 1564. Extensions and expositions of this ruling were issued by Clement VIII., Sixtus V., Alexander VII., and other popes. **Present Practise.** The present practise is based upon the constitution *Sollicita ac provida* of Benedict XIV. (July 10, 1753). The maintenance and extension of the *Index librorum prohibitorum* was entrusted to a special standing committee of cardinals, the Congregation of the Index (see CURIA), which from time to time publishes new editions (the latest, Turin, 1895). There is also an *Index librorum expurgatorum*, containing books which are tolerated after the excision of certain passages, and another *librorum expurgandorum*, of those which are still in need of such partial expurgation. The prohibition to read or possess books thus forbidden is binding upon all Roman Catholics, though in special cases dispensations from it may be obtained. The most recent regulation of the whole matter was made by the bull *Officiorum ac munerum* of Leo XIII., Jan. 25, 1897.

The State in many cases for its own purposes approved the principle of censorship until comparatively recent times. In Germany it was abolished only in 1848. In England after the Reformation the licensing power was in the hands of the archbishop of Canterbury; after Milton's famous onslaught upon it in the *Areopagitica* (1643), it came to an end by the refusal of the House of Commons in 1695 to renew the Licensing Act. The Reformed Church of Germany maintained similar regulations in some places, where the synodal form of organization prevailed. Among the Lutherans, the matter was as a rule left in the hands of the State.

(E. FRIEDBERG.)

BIBLIOGRAPHY: E. G. Peignot, *Dictionnaire . . . des principaux livres condamnés au feu*, Paris, 1806; H. Arndt, *De libris prohibitis*, Regensburg, 1855; J. Fessler, *Das kirchliche Bücherverbot*, Vienna, 1859; F. Sachse, *Die Anfänge der Bücherzensur in Deutschland*, Leipsic, 1870; *Suppressed and Censured Books*, in *Edinburgh Review*, vol. cxxxiv., July, 1871; T. Wiedemann, *Die kirchliche Bücherzensur in der Erzdiöcese Wien*, Vienna, 1873; F. H. Reusch, *Der Index der verbotenen Bücher*, Bonn, 1883 sqq.; G. H. Putnam, *Censorship of the Church and its Influence upon . . . Literature*, 2 vols., 1906; *JE*, iii. 642–652.

CENSUS.

Census is a term used to designate an enumeration of the people, generally for purposes of taxation or for service in the army.

[I. **In the Old Testament:** Of censuses of the whole population there are recorded in the Old Testament ten cases: (1–2) under Moses (Ex. xxxviii. 26, cf. Num. i.; Num. xxvi.); (3) under David (II Sam. xxiv. 1–9: see DAVID); (4) under Solomon (II Chron. ii. 17–18); (5) under Rehoboam (I Kings xii. 21); (6) under Jehoshaphat (II Chron. xvii. 14–19); (7) under Amaziah (II Chron. xxv. 5–6); (8) under Uzziah (II Chron. xxvi. 12–13); (9–10) under Zerubbabel (?) and Ezra (Ezra ii. 64, viii. 1–14). There are other enumerations given, but they concern merely the strength of the army, as in II Chron. xiii. 3.

II. **In the New Testament:** The subject here is of interest principally in its relation to the census mentioned Luke ii. 2 and Acts v. 37, and in connection with the birth of Jesus.]

1. The Roman Census of Citizens.

Originally the Romans made a census of Roman citizens only, the primary object being the adjustment of their quota in the taxes for the costs of war. This census was intended to exhibit not only the pecuniary but the total effective utility of the individual toward the State. So it included attestation of personal circumstances, capacity for service, civil and military, and the moral worthiness of those enumerated. Gradually this census of Roman citizens lost significance. While in earlier times it was repeated every five years in connection with a religious festivity (*lustrum*), during the civil wars it lapsed. Augustus, it is true, consistently with his general policy of bringing about an ostensible restoration of the republican order (T. Mommsen, *Römisches Staatsrecht*, ii. 337, Leipsic, 1893), adopted the census anew. He put on record that he had thrice held a complete census of citizens, viz., in the years 29 B.C., 8 B.C., and 14 A.D. A census of this kind was made for the last time under the Emperor Vespasian.

2. Provincial Census to Regulate Tribute.

The census of the Roman provinces, introduced much later, was quite distinct from this census of citizens, the difference corresponding to that between the Roman people as conqueror and the provinces as conquered. Since in this light the provincial census was designed to regulate not the rights but the obligations of those enumerated, it served only to define military service and tribute. The forms of the latter in the various provinces showed great diversity. There was doubtless everywhere some sort of ground tax (*tributum soli*), usually in the form of a definite tribute, partly in money, partly in natural products, which could also be levied as communal tithes, except that if in case of a defective harvest the amount of the requisite tribute was not realized, the tithes were made good through other taxes. The real-estate tax was everywhere supplemented by a personal tax (*tributum capitis*), which might be levied as a uniform capitation tax for all, or (as in Egypt) as a graduated poll-tax; or as property or income tax. In all forms, however, it was let by contract to tax farmers. These taxes, which in the main came down from the republican era, were in the earlier period regulated partly by means of a census. But only from the time of the government of Augustus were they organized on a more extensive basis. Especially in the provinces incorporated by Cæsar and the emperors into the Roman Empire were the fiscal relations thus regulated.

3. Cases and Methods of Roman Census.

According to literary records well known, this was done three times in Gaul under Augustus, then under Nero and Domitian; in Syria, Judea, and Spain under Augustus; among the Clitæ under Tiberius; in Britain under Claudius; in Dacia under Trajan. Besides these provinces, the following are named in inscriptions as subjected to a census in imperial times: Aquitania, Belgium, Lugdunensis, Lower Germany, Macedonia, Thrace, Paphlagonia, Africa, and Mauritania. In the republican era the administration of these provincial censuses had been combined with the office of provincial governor; but in imperial times it was transferred to the emperor. Augustus personally executed this office in Gaul, in other cases the emperor was represented by men of the highest rank; for entire provinces, as a rule, persons of senatorial station were appointed; for smaller districts, knights. At the outset in the imperial provinces, the census was delegated only occasionally (Mommsen, ut sup., ii. 410, a, 4) to the provincial governor. The essential uniformity of organization of taxes and assessments throughout the empire, such as is proved for the later imperial times by the classic legal sources, although no traces are apparent of a sudden reorganization in relation to the provinces under the earlier period, was early anticipated by the census regulations of Augustus. As to the detailed constitution of this provincial census, which later became universal, there is still some debate; it is fairly certain, however, that it regulated a real-estate tax for proprietors and a personal tax for the landless; that it included the taxpayers' personal assessment; that its organization was not communal but provincial; and that the formal declaration took place in the principal centers of the fiscal districts. Of the interval between censuses there is certain knowledge only in relation to Egypt, through the new discoveries of Egyptian papyri (U. Wilcken, *Griechische Ostraka*, in *Archiv für Papyrusforschung*, vol. i., 1899), according to which in that country two kinds of assessments (*apographai*) were executed at stated times: a popular enumeration every fourteen years, and a declaration of movable property annually.

4. Palestinian Census of 6 A.D. Quirinius.

In Palestine, at all events, a census quite in the Roman manner was executed in the year 6 A.D., though only in the southern part of the country, which in that year came under immediate Roman jurisdiction. The Syrian legate Quirinius was at that time entrusted with the extraordinary imperial commission of undertaking a census not only in the newly annexed country but also throughout Syria (cf. also *CIL*, iii., supplement, no. 6687). The vehement opposition which the regulation provoked among the Jewish population and especially with a faction whose leader was Judas of Galilee (q.v.) shows that in that form it was new to the region. This census, as the mention of Judas of Galilee implies, is referred to in the words of Acts v. 37, "in the days of the enrolment."

More difficult of solution is the other New Testament passage, in which mention is made of a census decreed from Rome (Luke ii. 2). It is here distinctly stated that this census, commanded by Cæsar Augustus for the whole Roman Empire, was the first which took place in Palestine (as decreed by Augustus) when Quirinius was governor of Syria; and that by it Joseph was obligated to go with Mary to Bethlehem, his place of enrolment, where the birth of Jesus came to pass.

5. Luke ii. 2 in Error. Jesus not Born Under Quirinius. From the starting-point of Acts v. 37, it were most plausible to bring the birth of Christ, according to Luke ii., down to the time of the census of the year 6 A.D. This is antagonized by the chronology of Luke iii. 23, also by the fact that both Matthew and Luke presuppose the birth of Jesus during the reign of Herod the Great, who died in the year 4 B.C. of the Dionysian era (see HEROD AND HIS FAMILY); that is, the birth of Christ would have occurred in the last preceding years. But in those years Quirinius could not have been governor of Syria, because Sentius Saturninus was governor in the years 8–6 B.C. (Josephus, *Ant.*, XVI. ix. 1), and from 6 B.C. until after Herod's death the governor was Quintilius Varus (Josephus, *Ant.*, XVII. v. 2, x. 1). It has been therefore proposed on exegetical grounds to set aside the synchronism between the governorship of Quirinius and the birth of Jesus. But these attempts are impossible artifices. It has also been affirmed on the strength of the later governorship of Quirinius in the year 6 A.D., that he served an earlier preceding term (T. Mommsen, *Res gestæ divi Augusti*, Berlin, 1865). But the evidences of this are quite uncertain. And since in no case can an earlier term of Quirinius as governor coincide with the reign of Herod the Great, it would not elucidate Luke ii. 2. If it be assumed that the census of the year of Christ's birth was begun by Saturninus, continued by Varus, and completed by Quirinius (Zumpt), against this in Luke ii. 2, the governorship of Quirinius is evidently intended to indicate the time when the event recorded there took place; and a census by a Roman officer in Judea before the annexation of that country is improbable. Accordingly Zahn assumes that only one Roman census took place in Palestine, namely, under Quirinius, which is meant both in Luke ii. and in Acts v.; save that this occurred not in the year 6 A.D., but in the year 4 B.C., several months after the death of Herod. But the particularity of the data in Josephus contradicts this hypothesis, which at all events does not clear the Gospel of Luke of error. On this account it is to be assumed that the governorship of Quirinius, Luke ii. 2, has been erroneously transposed from the census of the year 6 to the year of Christ's birth.

Still again, the report in Luke ii. of a general Roman imperial census is not historically warrantable according to the literal text. Disregarding later untrustworthy accounts, there are no literary or epigraphic traces of an imperial census in the time of Augustus, and such an event could not have occurred without leaving some traces.

6. No General Census Under Augustus. And from the monument of Ancyra it is evident that Augustus did not hold a census of Roman citizens in the period from 8 B.C. to 14 A.D. Only in the emperor's financial reform projects with reference to the whole empire, and in the assessments held by him in many parts of the empire, appears a certain nucleus of truth for that statement in Luke ii.

If then in the light of Luke ii. the governorship of Quirinius and the Roman imperial census can not be verified, this report is not to be rejected as unhistorical in all other respects. That Herod at that time received orders from Augustus to undertake a census in his country is not an impossibility. Highly as Herod was esteemed even by the emperor, he nevertheless remained the emperor's subject. This is manifest from the words of Augustus, that he would henceforth

7. Solution, a Census by Herod. treat him not as his friend but as his subject (Josephus, *Ant.*, XVI. ix. 3); as likewise from his rating in the number of the Syrian procurators (*Ant.*, XV. x. 3). Consequently, since the Jews of Palestine from Pompey's time forth had been obliged to pay tribute in various forms to the Romans, Herod was also bound to the payment of tribute promptly after his appointment as king (Appian, *Bella civilia*, v. 75). It is, therefore, arbitrary to doubt (Schürer) that he also paid such dues continually (cf. Wieseler, *TSK*, 1875, pp. 541 sqq.). Nevertheless he was not deprived of the right of imposing and increasing taxes in his own name (cf. Josephus, *Ant.*, XV. x. 4; XVII. ii. 1, xi. 2). It is accordingly to be assumed that he had to furnish tribute to a prescribed amount at Rome the collection of which was generally left to him out of Jewish revenues. Where, however, the Roman interest required it, the emperor, as a matter of course, could intervene for raising the necessary taxes to make up the tribute. This is apparent from a similar case, wherein Augustus commanded Archelaus to remit one-fourth of the Samaritans' taxes (Josephus, *Ant.*, XVII. xi. 4). It is then conceivable that he commanded Herod to regulate the taxes necessary for the Roman tribute by means of a census by virtue of the forms already in vogue. For that Augustus did not at that time order a specifically Roman census in Palestine, but adhered to the Jewish practises, is borne out by other analogies in Roman procedure (Tacitus, *Annales*, iv. 72), by the operations of the Roman census of the year 6 A.D., and by indications afforded by the Gospel of Luke, according to which the census in question was decreed conformably to Jewish tribal enrolments. [For reply to above see QUIRINIUS.] F. SIEFFERT.

BIBLIOGRAPHY: The older literature on II. is given in *TSK*, 1852, pp. 663 sqq. P. E. Huschke, *Ueber den zur Zeit der Geburt Christi gehaltenen Census*, Breslau, 1840; idem, *Ueber den Census und die Steuerverfassung der . . Kaiserzeit*, ib. 1847; C. Wieseler, *Chronologische Synopse der* vier Evangelien, Hamburg, 1843; idem, *Beiträge zur richtigen Würdigung der Evangelien*, Gotha, 1869; idem, in *TSK*, 1873, pp. 435 sqq.; J. von Gumpach, in *TSK*, 1852, pp. 663 sqq.; A. W. Zumpt, *Commentationes epigraphicæ*, ii. 73–74, Berlin, 1854; idem, *Das Geburtsjahr Christi*, pp. 20 sqq., Leipsic, 1869; Aberle, in *TQ*, 1865, pp. 103 sqq., 1868, pp. 29 sqq.; A. Hilgenfeld, in *ZWT*, 1865, pp. 408 sqq., 1870, pp. 151 sqq.; H. Gerlach, *Die römischen Statthalter in Syrien und Judäa*, pp. 23 sqq., Berlin, 1865; T. Lewin, *Fasti Sacri*, London, 1865; H. Lutteroth, *Le Recensement de Quirinius en Judée*, Paris, 1865; C. E. Caspari, *Chronologisch-geographische Einleitung in das Leben Christi*, Hamburg, 1869; J. Marquardt, *Römische Staatsverwaltung*, vol. i., ii. 204 sqq., Leipsic, 1881–84; P. Schegg, *Das Todesjahr des Herodes und das Geburtsjahr Christi*, pp. 37 sqq., Munich, 1882; F. Riess, *Nochmals das Geburtsjahr Christi*, Freiburg, 1883; T. Zahn, in *NKZ*, 1893, pp. 633 sqq.; W. M. Ramsay, in *Expositor*, 1897, pp. 274 sqq., 425 sqq.; idem, *Was Christ Born at Bethlehem*, London, 1898; Schürer, *Geschichte*, i. 508 sqq., Eng. transl., I. i. 357, ii. 80, 105–143; Haverfield, in *Classical Review*, July, 1900, pp. 309 sqq.; *DB*, iv. 183; *EB*, iv. 3994–96; also the commentaries on the passages in Luke and Acts, and the works on the Life of Christ.

CENTRAL AMERICA: The extreme southern portion of the continent of North America, including seven independent states, as follows, enumerated in geographical order from north to south:

	Area. Square miles.	Population.
Colony of British Honduras....	7,562	40,000
Republic of Guatemala.......	46,774	1,800,000
Republic of Honduras...	42,658	775,000
Republic of Salvador..........	8,130	1,000,000
Republic of Nicaragua.........	51,560	400,000
Republic of Costa Rica.......	23,000	331,000
Republic of Panama.	31,890	330,000

The population is overwhelmingly Indian, negro, and mixed. In British Honduras in 1891 there were only 400 whites. In Guatemala 60 per cent of the people are Indians and 28 per cent mixed. About one-twentieth of the population of Salvador and one-fifth of that of Nicaragua are classed as white. In Costa Rica there are 8,000 Indians, and the remainder is almost entirely creole. The Indians in many localities retain their native language and live in almost primitive conditions; where classed as Roman Catholic converts their relation to the Church is often little more than nominal. But few of the colored population still persist in heathenism.

The republic of Panama was formed by revolution from Colombia in 1903. Religious statistics for this state are not available, but it may be said, in general, that conditions are the same as in the rest of Central America and the mother country (see COLOMBIA). The five older Central American republics, after the disruption from Spain, formed from 1821 to 1839 the "United States of Central America." Their present independent status was attained gradually, often after internal dissension and warfare. During the revolutionary and formative period the Church suffered much. Its property was confiscated, monasteries were abolished, monks were banished, and the secular clergy were persecuted. Poverty has also been a heavy burden to the Church. Ecclesiastical affairs were regulated by a series of concordats with Pope Pius IX. between 1852 and 1863 (see CONCORDATS AND DELIMITING BULLS, VI., 5).

The religion is everywhere Roman Catholic, but toleration is now legally assured in all states. The diocese of Guatemala was founded in 1534 and raised to archiepiscopal rank in 1743. The suffragan bishoprics are Nicaragua (1534), Comayagua (for Honduras, 1561), San Salvador (1842), and San José of Costa Rica (1850). A vicar apostolic has resided at Belize in British Honduras since 1893.

An Anglican diocese of Honduras and Central America was founded in 1883. The bishop resides at Belize. Guatemala has approximately 4,500 Protestants representing English and American churches and including a congregation of about 1,000 Germans resident in the capital. Protestants in Honduras number about 1,000 and in Costa Rica 3,200. They are barely represented in Salvador. In Nicaragua are fifteen "stations" of the Moravians.

All the states have public schools, colleges, and universities, and progress is being made in both elementary and the higher education. As might be expected, however, the majority of the population is illiterate. Attendance at the elementary schools is compulsory in Costa Rica, Guatemala, and Honduras. WILHELM GOETZ.

BIBLIOGRAPHY: In general: T. Child, *Spanish American Republics*, London, 1892; *Etnologia Centro-Americana*, Madrid, 1893; C. Sapper, *Das nordliche Mittel Amerika*, Brunswick, 1897; idem, *Mittelamerika, Reisen und Studien*, ib. 1902; C. Haebler, *Die Religion des Mittleren Amerika*, Münster, 1899. On British Honduras: A. R. Gibbs, *British Honduras*, London, 1883; *British Honduras Almanac*, annual, Belize. On Guatemala: O. Stoll, *Reisen und Schilderungen von Guatemala*, 1886; T. Brigham, *Guatemala*, New York, 1887; A. C. Maudsley, *A Glimpse at Guatemala*, London, 1899; *Missionary Review of the World*, xiv. (1901) 168 sqq.

CEOLFRID, chōl'frid, **SAINT:** Abbot of Wearmouth and Jarrow; b. of noble parents in Northumbria c. 642; d. at Langres, France, while on his way to Rome, Sept. 24, 716. He became a monk at the age of eighteen, and was made prior by Benedict Biscop (q.v.) of his new abbey of St. Peter at Wearmouth, which was begun in 674; accompanied Biscop to Rome in 678; became abbot of his second monastery founded at Jarrow in 681 or 682 (where he had Bede among his pupils), and in 688 abbot of both Wearmouth and Jarrow. He was a good manager and increased and enriched his monasteries, at the same time making them centers of learning and industry. He took special pains to learn the Roman methods of reading and singing the services and influenced the Irish in Scotland to adopt the Roman date for Easter.

BIBLIOGRAPHY: Bede, *Historia abbatum;* also *Hist. eccl.*, iv. 18, v. 21 (where Ceolfrid's letter to Naiton [Nechtan], king of the Picts, on the Easter question, is given), v. 24; also the anonymous *Historia abbatum*, by a monk of Wearmouth, contemporary with Ceolfrid, in Plummer's *Bede*, i. 388–404; W. Bright, *Early English Church History*, pp. 308–309, Oxford, 1897.

CERDO (CERDON): A Syrian Gnostic, who, according to Irenæus (I. xxvii. 1, III. iv. 3) and Eusebius (*Chron.*, ed. Schoene, i. 168), lived in Rome in the time of the bishop Hyginus (c. 136–140). Epiphanius (xli. 1) connects him with Saturninus. He is of importance chiefly as having been the teacher of Marcion (q.v.). G. KRÜGER.

CERINTHUS: Gnostic teacher of Asia Minor, about 100 A.D. According to Irenæus (I. xxvi. 1), he taught that the world was not created by the first God, but by a subordinate power. Jesus was a son of Joseph and Mary, but was wiser and more righteous than other men. After his baptism the spirit of the all-sublime power of God descended upon him in the form of a dove. From now on he preached the unknown Father and performed miracles. Finally the "Christ" forsook him, but "Jesus" suffered and rose again, whereas the spiritual Christ did not suffer. John directed his Gospel especially against Cerinthus (III. xi. 1), and in proof of the aversion which the apostle felt toward this heretic Irenæus (III. iii. 4) tells a story from Polycarp that the two met once in the baths at Ephesus, whereupon the apostle fled, "lest even the bath-house fall down because Cerinthus is inside." In the main the story is credible, but the later story (cf. Epiphanius, *Hær.*, xxviii. and others) of the Judaism of Cerinthus is an invention. The assertion of the Roman Caius that Cerinthus is the author of the Apocalypse is certainly erroneous. G. Krüger.

Bibliography: R. A. Lipsius, *Zur Quellenkritik des Epiphanius*, pp. 115 122, Vienna, 1865; A. Hilgenfeld, *Ketzergeschichte des Urchristentums*, pp. 411–421, Leipsic, 1884; A. Harnack, *Dogmengeschichte*, i. 234–235, Freiburg, 1894, Eng. transl., iii. 14–19, Boston, 1897; T. Zahn, *Geschichte des neutestamentlichen Kanons*, 2 vols., Erlangen, 1888–92; Krüger, *History*, p. 68 and literature given there.

CESARINI, chē"sū-rī'nī, **GIULIANO (JULIAN CESARINI)**: Cardinal. He belonged to a distinguished family of Rome and attracted the attention of the curia as a humanist and teacher of law at Padua. Pope Martin V. made him cardinal (1426) and Eugenius IV. promoted him to cardinal bishop of Frascati. His knowledge of law and ability as a diplomatist fitted him for delicate missions. The Hussite question was entrusted to him and he entered Bohemia with a crusading army, but the army was defeated and the cardinal fled ignominiously (1431). From 1431 to 1438 he presided at the Council of Basel with marked ability.* In 1438 and 1439 he was active in Ferrara and Florence, and shortly after went to Hungary to incite King Vladislav to war against the Turks. He succeeded, and war broke out in 1443, but Vladislav was defeated and slain at Varna, Nov. 10, 1444, and Cesarini also perished while trying to escape; he was probably assassinated and robbed while endeavoring to cross the Danube.

Paul Tschackert.

Bibliography: The older accounts are in A. Chacon, *Vitæ . pontificum et . . . cardinalium*, ii. 861 sqq., 4 vols., Rome, 1677; and E. Baluze, *Miscellanea*, vol. iii., 4 vols., Lucca, 1761–64. Consult also: F. von Bezold, *König Sigmund und die Reichskriege gegen die Husiten*, 3 parts, Munich, 1872–77; Creighton, *Papacy*, ii. 163–165, 194 sqq.; Hefele, *Conciliengeschichte*, vol. vii. passim; *KL*, iii. 26–28.

CHAD, SAINT. See Ceadda, Saint.

CHADERTON, LAURENCE: Puritan; b. near Oldham (8 m. n.e. of Manchester), Lancashire, Sept. 14, 1536 or 1538; d. at Cambridge Nov. 13, 1640. He studied at Christ's College, Cambridge (B.A., 1567; B.D., 1578; D.D., 1613), and there embraced the Protestant religion, for which his father threatened to disinherit him. He became fellow, dean, tutor, and lecturer of his college, and as afternoon lecturer of St. Clement's Church, Cambridge, for nearly fifty years acquired fame as a preacher and exerted a far-reaching influence. When Sir Walter Mildmay founded Emmanuel College in 1584 he insisted on Chaderton's becoming master, and the latter filled the office with much ability and success till 1622, when he resigned. From 1598 to 1640 he was prebendary of Lincoln. Though a Puritan he was moderate in views and conciliatory in manners. He was a member of the Hampton Court Conference (q.v.), and was one of the Cambridge committee of Bible translators. He appears to have published nothing except an anonymous tract, *De justificatione*, and a single sermon.

Bibliography: W. Dillingham, *Vita Chadertoni*, ed. J. Dillingham, Cambridge, 1700, Eng. transl. by E. S. Schuckburgh, ib. 1884; *DNB*, ix. 430–432.

CHADWICK, JOHN WHITE: American Unitarian; b. at Marblehead, Mass., Oct. 19, 1840; d. in Brooklyn Dec. 11, 1904. His father was a seafaring man, and he was apprenticed to a shoemaker. But in 1857 he entered the State Normal School at Bridgewater, Mass., and while there determined to become a minister. From the Normal School he passed to Phillips Exeter Academy and the Divinity School of Harvard University, from which latter institution he was graduated in 1864. He was immediately asked to supply for three months the pulpit of the Second Unitarian Church of Brooklyn, N. Y., but made so favorable an impression that his relation became a permanent one and he was its pastor at the time of his death. Besides being well known as a preacher and lecturer and highly esteemed as a man, he won distinction as an author both in prose and poetry. He described himself as a "radical Unitarian," but he was heard with respect by those who most differed from him. Besides many other contributions to the press, he published: *Life of Nathaniel Alexander Staples* (Boston, 1870); *A Book of Poems* (1876, now in its 10th ed.); *The Bible of To-day* (New York, 1878); *The Faith of Reason, a Series of Discourses on Leading Topics of Religion* (Boston, 1879, 2d ed., 1880); *Some Aspects of Religion* (New York, 1879); *Belief and Life* (1881); *The Man Jesus* (Boston, 1881, 2d ed., 1882); *Origin and Destiny* (1883); *In Nazareth Town: a Christmas Fantasy, and Other Poems* (1883); *A Daring Faith* (1885); *The Good Voices*, poems (Troy, N. Y., 1885); *Charles Robert Darwin* (Boston, 1889); *Evolution and Social Reform* (1890); *Evolution of Architecture* (New York, 1891); *Evolution as Related to Citizenship* (1892); *George William Curtis: an Address* (1893); *The Old and the New Unitarian Belief* (Boston, 1894); *Theodore Parker* (1900); *William Ellery Channing* (1903); and *Later Poems* (1905).

CHAITANYA, chai"tū-nī'a: Brahman formulator of the doctrine of *Bhakti*. See India, I., 3, § 3.

CHALCEDON, kal'se-don: A city of Bithynia, on the Bosporus, near Constantinople, the scene of the Fourth General Council (451), at which

* At the Council of Basel Cesarini's attitude toward the Hussites was highly conciliatory; and he urged a thorough reformation of ecclesiastical abuses as the only safeguard against further schisms.—A. H. N.

Eutychianism was condemned and the so-called Creed of Chalcedon adopted. See CHRISTOLOGY, IV; EUTYCHIANISM.

CHALDEA. See BABYLONIA, VI, 7.

CHALDEAN CHRISTIANS. See NESTORIANS.

CHALICE. See VESSELS, SACRED, § 1.

CHALLONER, RICHARD: English Roman Catholic prelate; b. at Lewes (50 m. s. of London), Sussex, Sept. 29, 1691; d. in London Jan. 12, 1781. His father was a Protestant, but died soon after his son's birth, and the latter was brought up by Roman Catholics and embraced their religion at about the age of thirteen. In 1704 he was sent to Douai and remained there as student, professor, and vice-president for twenty-six years (B.D., 1719; D.D., 1727; ordained priest 1716). In 1730 he joined the London mission, and in 1741 was consecrated coadjutor to Dr. Benjamin Petre, vicar apostolic of the London district; he became vicar apostolic on Dr. Petre's death in 1758. He was a learned and pious man, and performed his duties with faithfulness and ability, in the midst of persecution from the penal laws and the fanaticism of the English populace. He wrote upward of forty different works, controversial, devotional, historical, etc. His *Memoirs of Missionary Priests and of other Catholics that have suffered death in England on religious accounts from the year 1577 to 1684* (2 vols., London, 1741–42; many later eds.) is the Roman Catholic "Book of Martyrs"; *The Garden of the Soul* (1740) is still the most popular prayer-book with English Roman Catholics; and *The Rheims New Testament and the Douay Bible, with annotations* (5 vols., London, 1749–50; 3d ed., revised, 1752), prepared by Challoner and under his direction, is the best-known version of the Douai Bible. His *Life* was written by J. Barnard (London, 1784), and by Dr. John Milner (in the 5th ed. of his *Grounds of the Old Religion*, 1798).

BIBLIOGRAPHY: J. Barnard, *Life of R. Challoner*, London, 1784; John Milner, *Brief Account of the Life of Richard Challoner*, prefixed to the 5th ed. of Challoner's *Grounds of the Old Religion*, ib. 1798; J. Gillow, *Bibliographical Dictionary of English Catholics*, i. 447–457, London (1885); *DNB*, ix. 440–443.

CHALMERS, JAMES: London Missionary Society missionary; b. at Ardrishaig, Argyleshire, Scotland (45 m. w. by n. from Glasgow), Aug. 4, 1841; d. at Risk Point, Goaribari Island, Gulf of Papua, New Guinea, April 8, 1901. Converted at the age of fourteen, he was soon after called to the foreign mission field and after study at Cheshunt College and at Highgate, an institution conducted by the London Missionary Society, he was sent by that Society to Raratonga, one of the group of Cook Islands in the Southern Pacific, where he arrived in 1867. The island had been partially Christianized, but he did a good work in education and evangelization. In 1877 he removed to New Guinea, where he encountered cannibals and did a memorable work at the constant risk of life. It was on one of these many journeys that he was killed. He takes his place beside Williams and Patterson as a missionary hero in the South Seas.

BIBLIOGRAPHY: Consult his own *Pioneer Life and Work in New Guinea, 1877–1894*, London 1895; and the biographies by W. Robson, ib. 1901; C. Lennox, ib. 1902; and R. Lovett, ib. 1902 (the last-named containing Chalmers's *Autobiography and Letters*).

CHALMERS, THOMAS: The leader of the Free Church of Scotland; b. in East Anstruther, Fifeshire, Mar. 17, 1780; d. in Edinburgh May 30, 1847. The family to which he belonged was composed of middle-class people of the strictest type of Calvinism; and hence in his opening years, he received thorough indoctrination. He entered St. Andrews University when only eleven years old, and confined his attention almost exclusively to mathematics, but did not give up his original intention of becoming a preacher, and accordingly was licensed by the presbytery of St. Andrews Jan., 1799. His character early developed into maturity. Instead of beginning his professional work, he continued the study of mathematics and natural science; and during the winter of 1802–03 he acted as assistant to the professor of mathematics at St. Andrews. He showed an extraordinary power to awaken enthusiasm in almost any topic he took up; although it was this very fact which at that time cost him his place, the authorities disliking the novelty of his methods. He settled as minister of Kilmeny, nine miles from St. Andrews, May, 1803, and in the following winter, while preaching regularly, opened voluntary and independent classes in mathematics at the university, which were largely attended, although vigorously discouraged by the authorities. He was a faithful pastor at Kilmeny, and his preaching attracted wide attention, but his heart was not in his work. He was trammeled by the prevailing moderatism, which put culture above piety, and state support above independence. In 1808 evidence of the trend of his thinking appeared in his *Inquiry into the Extent and Stability of National Resources.* The supply of man's physical and social needs was uppermost in his mind. In the midst of such work he was visited with severe domestic afflictions, and a serious illness brought him to death's door; but he recovered after a year. David Brewster asked him to contribute to his Edinburgh Encyclopedia. He at first chose "Trigonometry," but at length took "Christianity" (separately published, 1813). And as he examined the doctrines of this religion, and went deeper into its mysteries, he realized its importance, and by studying about Christianity he became a Christian. The parishioners quickly became aware that he had really not so much resumed his work among them as begun it. His whole soul was on fire, and his culture was now used to make the saving truth of saving power. He cut loose from the moorings of moderatism, and became a decided Evangelical. His eloquence was expended in new channels, and with great results.

Ministry at Kilmeny.

In July, 1815, he was formally admitted as minister of the Tron Church, Glasgow. In 1816 he delivered on week-days the famous series of seven *Discourses on the Christian Revelation, Viewed in Connection with Modern Astronomy.* In Sept., 1819, he removed from the Tron parish to that of

St. John's, in order that he might, in a newly constituted parish, have an opportunity of testing the practicability in a large city of the old Scottish scheme of providing for the poor. In the parish there were two thousand families. These he distributed into twenty-five divisions; and over each such district he put an elder and a deacon—the former to attend to their spiritual, the latter to their temporal needs. Two commodious school-houses were built; four competent teachers were employed, and by school-fees of two and three shillings each a quarter, seven hundred children were educated; while on Sunday the forty or fifty local schools supplied religious instruction. Dr. Chalmers not only presided over all this system of work, but made himself familiar with all the details, even visiting personally every two years each family of the parish, and holding evening meetings. He also assumed complete charge of the poor; and by thorough system, and consequent weeding-out of unworthy cases, he reduced the cost of maintaining them from fourteen hundred to two hundred and eighty pounds per annum. This efficient system, however, in 1837 was given up; and the "English" plan of compulsory assessments, which requires much less trouble, and probably does much less good, was substituted. In Nov., 1823, Dr. Chalmers became professor of moral philosophy in St. Andrews University, and in Nov., 1828, professor of theology in Edinburgh. In 1833 he issued his Bridgewater Treatise, *On the Adaptation of External Nature to the Moral and Intellectual Constitution of Man.* This work made a great sensation; and his biographer, Rev. William Hanna, says that, in consequence, he received "literary honors such as were never united previously in the person of any Scottish ecclesiastic." In 1834 he was elected fellow of the Royal Society of Edinburgh, and soon after one of its vice-presidents, in the same year a corresponding member of the Institute of France; and in 1835 the University of Oxford conferred on him the degree of D.C.L.

In Glasgow.

Up to this time he had taken little part in church government; from then on he was destined to have more to do with it than any other man of the century. The friction between Church and State in Scotland was rapidly producing trouble. The attempt to settle ministers who were obnoxious to the congregations was the commonest complaint.* The historic case is that of Marnoch. Here only one person in the parish signed the call; and yet the presbytery of Strathbogie decided, by a vote of seven to three, to proceed with the ordination, and did, although these seven were suspended. In so doing they were upheld by the civil authority, which annulled their suspension. But this case was only an aggravation of a common ill. Matters became so serious in all parts of Scotland that a convocation was held in Nov., 1842, to consider the matter; and a large number of ministers resolved that, if relief was not afforded, they would withdraw from the Establishment. No help came; and accordingly, on May 18, 1843, four hundred and seventy clergymen withdrew from the General Assembly, and constituted themselves into the Free Church of Scotland, electing Dr. Chalmers as their first moderator. He had foreseen the separation, and drawn up a scheme for the support of the outgoing ministers. But, after he had safely piloted the new church through the stormy waters, he gave himself up more exclusively to professional work, especially in connection with the New College, Edinburgh, of which he was principal, and to the composition of his *Institutes of Theology.* He died suddenly.

The Organization of the Free Church.

Dr. Chalmers is to-day a molding influence. All the churches of Scotland unite to do him reverence. He was a greater worker than writer, and a greater man than either. It was surely enough honor for one life to inspire spiritual life throughout an entire land; and as the tireless and practical reformer, as the Christian philanthropist, and, above all, as the founder of the Free Church of Scotland, he will live.

* The point at issue was lay patronage, British law having conferred upon landowners the right to nominate to pastorates in their possessions.—A. H. N.

Bibliography: The principal Life is by his son-in-law, W. Hanna, *Memoirs of the Life and Writings of Thomas Chalmers*, 4 vols., Edinburgh, 1849–52. Consult also: A. J. S[ymington], *Thomas Chalmers, the Man, his Times, and his Work*, Ardrossan, 1878; D. Fraser, *Thomas Chalmers*, London, 1881; J. L. Watson, *The Life of Thomas Chalmers*, Edinburgh, 1881; J. Dodds, *Thomas Chalmers*, ib. 1892; W. G. Blaikie, *Thomas Chalmers*, ib. 1896 (in *Famous Scots Series*); Mrs. Oliphant, *Thomas Chalmers, Preacher, Philosopher, and Statesman*, London, 1896; *DNB*, ix. 449–454.

CHAMBERLAIN, JACOB: Reformed (Dutch) missionary; b. at Sharon, Conn., Apr. 13, 1835; d. at Madanapalli, Madras, India, March 2, 1908. He was educated at Western Reserve College, O. (B.A., 1856), the Reformed Theological Seminary, New Brunswick, N. J., and the College of Physicians and Surgeons, New York. In 1859 he went as a medical missionary to the Arcot Mission, Madras, and was stationed successively at Palmaner, Madras (1860–1863), and at Madanapalli, Madras (1863–1901). From 1891 he was lector in Biblical languages and prophecy and acting principal of the Theological Seminary in the Arcot Mission, Palmaner. He was chairman of a committee for the translation of the Bible into Telugu, 1873–94; member of the Telugu Revision Committee of the Madras Tract Society in 1873–80, and in 1878 was elected vice-president of the American Tract Society for India. In 1901 he was first moderator of the South India United Church Synod, and since engaged in literary work in Tamil and Telugu. He translated the liturgy of the Reformed Dutch Church into Telugu (Madras, 1873), and also prepared a Telugu version of the *Hymns for Public and Social Worship* (1884), as well as other devotional works in the same language. His English works include: *The Bible Tested* (New York, 1878); *Native Churches and Foreign Missionary Societies* (Madras, 1879); *The Religions of the Orient* (Clifton Springs, N. Y., 1896); *In the Tiger Jungle* (Chicago, 1896); *The Cobra's Den, and Other Stories of Missionary Work Among the Telugus of India* (1900); and *The Kingdom in India*, with introductory biographical sketch by Henry N. Cobb (1908).

Zeitfracht Medien GmbH
Ferdinand-Jühlke-Straße 7
99095 Erfurt, Deutschland
produktsicherheit@kolibri360.de